Guide to Gale Literary Criticism Series

For criticism on	Consult these Gale series
Authors now living or who died after December 31, 1959	*CONTEMPORARY LITERARY CRITICISM (CLC)*
Authors who died between 1900 and 1959	*TWENTIETH-CENTURY LITERARY CRITICISM (TCLC)*
Authors who died between 1800 and 1899	*NINETEENTH-CENTURY LITERATURE CRITICISM (NCLC)*
Authors who died between 1400 and 1799	*LITERATURE CRITICISM FROM 1400 TO 1800 (LC)* *SHAKESPEAREAN CRITICISM (SC)*
Authors who died before 1400	*CLASSICAL AND MEDIEVAL LITERATURE CRITICISM (CMLC)*
Black writers of the past two hundred years	*BLACK LITERATURE CRITICISM (BLC)*
Authors of books for children and young adults	*CHILDREN'S LITERATURE REVIEW (CLR)*
Dramatists	*DRAMA CRITICISM (DC)*
Hispanic writers of the late nineteenth and twentieth centuries	*HISPANIC LITERATURE CRITICISM (HLC)*
Native North American writers and orators of the eighteenth, nineteenth, and twentieth centuries	*NATIVE NORTH AMERICAN LITERATURE (NNAL)*
Poets	*POETRY CRITICISM (PC)*
Short story writers	*SHORT STORY CRITICISM (SSC)*
Major authors from the Renaissance to the present	*WORLD LITERATURE CRITICISM, 1500 TO THE PRESENT (WLC)*

Contemporary
Literary Criticism

ISSN 0091-3421

Volume 90

Contemporary Literary Criticism

Excerpts from Criticism of the Works
of Today's Novelists, Poets, Playwrights,
Short Story Writers, Scriptwriters, and
Other Creative Writers

Jeff Chapman
Christopher Giroux
Brigham Narins
EDITORS, *CLC*

Pamela S. Dear
John D. Jorgenson
Deborah A. Stanley
Aarti S. Stephens
Polly A. Vedder
Thomas Wiloch
Kathleen Wilson
Janet Witalec
ASSOCIATE EDITORS

GALE

an International Thomson Publishing company I**T**P®

Library of Congress Catalog Card Number 76-38938
ISBN 0-8103-9268-2
ISSN 0091-3421

Printed in the United States of America

10 9 8 7 6 5 4 3 2 1

I(T)P™   Gale Research, an ITP Information/Reference Group Company.
ITP logo is a trademark under license.

Contents

Preface vii

Acknowledgments xi

Preface

A Comprehensive Information Source
on Contemporary Literature

Named "one of the twenty-five most distinguished reference titles published during the past twenty-five years" by *Reference Quarterly*, the *Contemporary Literary Criticism (CLC)* series provides readers with critical commentary and general information on more than 2,000 authors now living or who died after December 31, 1959. Previous to the publication of the first volume of *CLC* in 1973, there was no ongoing digest monitoring scholarly and popular sources of critical opinion and explication of modern literature. *CLC*, therefore, has fulfilled an essential need, particularly since the complexity and variety of contemporary literature makes the function of criticism especially important to today's reader.

Scope of the Series

CLC presents significant passages from published criticism of works by creative writers. Since many of the authors covered by *CLC* inspire continual critical commentary, writers are often represented in more than one volume. There is, of course, no duplication of reprinted criticism.

Authors are selected for inclusion for a variety of reasons, among them the publication or dramatic production of a critically acclaimed new work, the reception of a major literary award, revival of interest in past writings, or the adaptation of a literary work to film or television.

Attention is also given to several other groups of writers—authors of considerable public interest—about whose work criticism is often difficult to locate. These include mystery and science fiction writers, literary and social critics, foreign writers, and authors who represent particular ethnic groups within the United States.

Format of the Book

Each *CLC* volume contains about 500 individual excerpts taken from hundreds of book review periodicals, general magazines, scholarly journals, monographs, and books. Entries include critical evaluations spanning from the beginning of an author's career to the most current commentary. Interviews, feature articles, and other published writings that offer insight into the author's works are also presented. Students, teachers, librarians, and researchers will find that the generous excerpts and supplementary material in *CLC* provide them with vital information required to write a term paper, analyze a poem, or lead a book discussion group. In addition, complete bibliographical citations note the original source and all of the information necessary for a term paper footnote or bibliography.

Features

A *CLC* author entry consists of the following elements:

- The **Author Heading** cites the author's name in the form under which the author has most commonly published, followed by birth date, and death date when applicable. Uncertainty as to a birth or death date is indicated by a question mark.

- A **Portrait** of the author is included when available.

- A brief **Biographical and Critical Introduction** to the author and his or her work precedes the excerpted criticism. The first line of the introduction provides the author's full name, pseudonyms (if applicable), nationality, and a listing of genres in which the author has written. To provide users with easier access to information, the biographical and critical essay included in each author entry is divided into four categories: "Introduction," "Biographical Information," "Major Works," and "Critical Reception." The introductions to single-work entries—entries that focus on well-known and frequently studied books, short stories, and poems—are similarly organized to quickly provide readers with information on the plot and major characters of the work being discussed, its major themes, and its critical reception. Previous volumes of *CLC* in which the author has been featured are also listed in the introduction.

- A list of **Principal Works** notes the most important writings by the author. When foreign-language works have been translated into English, the English-language version of the title follows in brackets.

- The **Excerpted Criticism** represents various kinds of critical writing, ranging in form from the brief review to the scholarly exegesis. Essays are selected by the editors to reflect the spectrum of opinion about a specific work or about an author's literary career in general. The excerpts are presented chronologically, adding a useful perspective to the entry. All titles by the author featured in the entry are printed in boldface type, which enables the reader to easily identify the works being discussed. Publication information (such as publisher names and book prices) and parenthetical numerical references (such as footnotes or page and line references to specific editions of a work) have been deleted at the editor's discretion to provide smoother reading of the text.

- Critical essays are prefaced by **Explanatory Notes** as an additional aid to readers. These notes may provide several types of valuable information, including: the reputation of the critic, the importance of the work of criticism, the commentator's approach to the author's work, the purpose of the criticism, and changes in critical trends regarding the author.

- A complete **Bibliographical Citation** designed to help the user find the original essay or book precedes each excerpt.

- Whenever possible, a recent, previously unpublished **Author Interview** accompanies each entry.

- A concise **Further Reading** section appears at the end of entries on authors for whom a significant amount of criticism exists in addition to the pieces reprinted in *CLC*. Each citation in this section is accompanied by a descriptive annotation describing the content of that article. Materials included in this section are grouped under various headings (e.g., Biography, Bibliography, Criticism, and Interviews) to aid users in their search for additional information. Cross-references to other useful sources published by Gale Research in which the author has appeared are also included: *Authors in the News, Black Writers, Children's Literature Review, Contemporary Authors, Dictionary of Literary Biography, DISCovering Authors, Drama Criticism, Hispanic Literature Criticism, Hispanic Writers, Native North American Literature, Poetry Criticism, Something about the Author, Short Story Criticism, Contemporary Authors Autobiography Series,* and *Something about the Author Autobiography Series.*

Other Features

CLC also includes the following features:

- An **Acknowledgments** section lists the copyright holders who have granted permission to reprint material in this volume of *CLC*. It does not, however, list every book or periodical reprinted or consulted during the preparation of the volume.

- Each new volume of *CLC* includes a **Cumulative Topic Index,** which lists all literary topics treated in *CLC, NCLC, TCLC,* and *LC 1400-1800.*

- A **Cumulative Author Index** lists all the authors who have appeared in the various literary criticism series published by Gale Research, with cross-references to Gale's biographical and autobiographical series. A full listing of the series referenced there appears on the first page of the indexes of this volume. Readers will welcome this cumulated author index as a useful tool for locating an author within the various series. The index, which lists birth and death dates when available, will be particularly valuable for those authors who are identified with a certain period but whose death dates cause them to be placed in another, or for those authors whose careers span two periods. For example, Ernest Hemingway is found in *CLC,* yet F. Scott Fitzgerald, a writer often associated with him, is found in *Twentieth-Century Literary Criticism.*

- A **Cumulative Nationality Index** alphabetically lists all authors featured in *CLC* by nationality, followed by numbers corresponding to the volumes in which the authors appear.

- An alphabetical **Title Index** accompanies each volume of *CLC*. Listings are followed by the author's name and the corresponding page numbers where the titles are discussed. English translations of foreign titles and variations of titles are cross-referenced to the title under which a work was originally published. Titles of novels, novellas, dramas, films, record albums, and poetry, short story, and essay collections are printed in italics, while all individual poems, short stories, essays, and songs are printed in roman type within quotation marks; when published separately (e.g., T. S. Eliot's poem *The Waste Land*), the titles of long poems are printed in italics.

- In response to numerous suggestions from librarians, Gale has also produced a **Special Paperbound Edition** of the *CLC* title index. This annual cumulation, which alphabetically lists all titles reviewed in the series, is available to all customers and is typically published with every fifth volume of *CLC*. Additional copies of the index are available upon request. Librarians and patrons will welcome this separate index: it saves shelf space, is easy to use, and is recyclable upon receipt of the next edition.

Citing *Contemporary Literary Criticism*

When writing papers, students who quote directly from any volume in the Literary Criticism Series may use the following general forms to footnote reprinted criticism. The first example pertains to material drawn from periodicals, the second to material reprinted in books:

[1]Alfred Cismaru, "Making the Best of It," *The New Republic,* 207, No. 24, (December 7, 1992), 30, 32; excerpted and reprinted in *Contemporary Literary Criticism,* Vol. 85, ed. Christopher Giroux (Detroit: Gale Research, 1995), pp. 73-4.

[2]Yvor Winters, *The Post-Symbolist Methods* (Allan Swallow, 1967); excerpted and reprinted in *Contemporary Literary Criticism,* Vol. 85, ed. Christopher Giroux (Detroit: Gale Research, 1995), pp. 223-26.

Suggestions Are Welcome

The editor hopes that readers will find *CLC* a useful reference tool and welcomes comments about the work. Send comments and suggestions to: Editor, *Contemporary Literary Criticism,* Gale Research, Penobscot Building, Detroit, MI 48226-4094.

Acknowledgments

The editors wish to thank the copyright holders of the excerpted criticism included in this volume and the permissions managers of many book and magazine publishing companies for assisting us in securing reprint rights. We are also grateful to the staffs of the Detroit Public Library, the Library of Congress, the University of Detroit-Mercy Library, the Wayne State University Purdy/Kresge Library Complex, and the University of Michigan Libraries for making their resources available to us. Following is a list of the copyright holders who have granted us permission to reprint material in this volume of *CLC*. Every effort has been made to trace copyright, but if omissions have been made, please let us know.

COPYRIGHTED EXCERPTS IN *CLC*, VOLUME 90, WERE REPRINTED FROM THE FOLLOWING PERIODICALS:

America, v. 120, April 12, 1969. © 1969. All rights reserved. Reprinted with permission of America Press, Inc., 106 West 56th Street, New York, NY 10019.—*The American Book Review,* v. 10, May-June, 1988; v. 15, August-September, 1993. © 1988, 1993 by The American Book Review. Both reprinted by permission of the publisher.—*The American Poetry Review,* v. 15, November-December, 1986 for "'Homeward Ho!': Silicon Valley Pushkin" by Marjorie Perloff. Copyright © 1986 by World Poetry, Inc. Reprinted by permission of the author.—*American Studies in Scandinavia,* v. 7, 1975. Reprinted by permission of the publisher.—*American Theatre,* v. 6, October, 1989. Copyright © 1989, Theatre Communications Group. All rights reserved. Reprinted by permission of the publisher.—*The Atlantic Monthly,* v. 224, September, 1969 for a review of "As I Walked Out One Midsummer Morning" by Edward Weeks. Copyright 1969 by The Atlantic Monthly Company, Boston, MA. Reprinted by permission of the author.—*Belles Lettres: A Review of Books by Women,* v. 9, Fall, 1993. Reprinted by permission of the publisher.—*The Bloomsbury Review,* v. 8, July-August, 1988 for "Voices of Sadness & Science" by Gary Soto; v. 9, November-December, 1989 for "Lost in the Funhouse" by David Ulin; v. 10, May-June, 1990 for a review of "The Whirlpool" by Bin Ramke. Copyright © by Owaissa Communications Company, Inc. 1988, 1989, 1990. All reprinted by permission of the respective authors.—*Book Week—Chicago Sunday Times,* June 5, 1966. © News Group Chicago, Inc., 1995. Reprinted with permission of the *Chicago Sun-Times.*—*Booklist,* v. 86, June 1, 1990; v. 90, February 15, 1994. Copyright © 1990, 1994 by the American Library Association. Both reprinted by permission of the publisher.—*Books,* London, v. 5, September-October, 1991. © Gradegate Ltd., 1991. Reprinted by permission of the publisher.—*Books and Bookmen,* n. 335, August, 1983 for a review of *Selected Poems* by Derek Stanford. © copyright 1983 by Derek Stanford. Reprinted by permission of the author.—*Books in Canada,* v. 16, June-July, 1987 for "Through the Looking Glass" by Timothy Findley; v. IXX, April, 1990 for "Stormy Weather" by Janice Kulyk Keefer; v. XXII, October, 1993 for "Magically Real" by Janet McNaughton; v. XXIV, May, 1995 for an interview with Jane Urquhart by Elaine Kalman Naves. Reprinted by permission of the respective authors.—*Caliban XIII,* n.s. v. XII, January, 1976. Reprinted by permission of Université de Toulouse-Le Mirail.—*The Canadian Fiction Magazine,* n. 55, 1986 for an interview with Jane Urquhart by Geoff Hancock. Copyright © 1986 by The Canadian Fiction Magazine. Reprinted by permission of the publisher.—*Canadian Literature,* n. 104, Spring, 1985 for "Museum & World" by Lola Lemire-Tostevin; n. 106, Fall, 1985 for "Sleight of Tongue" by Ian Sowton; n. 110, Fall, 1986 for "Blue Streaks" by Gerald Lynch; n. 132, Spring, 1992 for "Held Hostage" by Hallvard Dahlie; n. 132, Spring, 1992 for "Train & Balloon" by Susan MacFarlane. All reprinted by permission of the respective authors.—*Chicago Tribune—Books,* May 26, 1991. © copyright 1991, Chicago Tribune Company. All rights reserved. Used with permission.—*Choice,* v. 12, January, 1976. Copyright © 1976 by American Library Association. Reprinted by permission of the publisher.—*The Christian Science Monitor,* April 6, 1976; December 15, 1987; November 21, 1990. © 1976, 1987, 1990. The Christian Science Publishing Society. All rights reserved. All reprinted by permission from *The Christian Science Monitor.*—*CLA Journal,* v. XXIX, December, 1985; v. 32, September, 1988. Copyright, 1985, 1988 by The College Language Association. Both used by permission of The College Language Association.—*College Literature,* v. XI, 1984. Copyright © 1984 by West Chester University. Reprinted

reprinted by permission of the Editor of *Poetry* and the respective authors./ v. LXXXIX, December, 1956 for "Five Young English Poets" by Samuel French Morse. © 1956, renewed 1984 by the Modern Poetry Association. Reprinted by permission of the Editor of *Poetry* and the author.—***Poets & Writers Magazine,*** v. 18, January-February, 1990. Reprinted by permission of the publisher.—***Publishers Weekly,*** v. 239, March 30, 1992; v. 240, May 10, 1993; v. 241, March 14, 1994; v. 242, August 21, 1995. Copyright 1992, 1993, 1994, 1995 by Reed Publishing USA. All reprinted from *Publishers Weekly,* published by the Bowker Magazine Group of Cahners Publishing Co., a division of Reed Publishing USA.—***Quill and Quire,*** v. 50, May, 1984 for a review of "The Little Flowers of Madame de Montespan" by Rhea Tregebov; v. 52, November, 1986 for a review of "The Whirlpool" by Brent Ledger; v. 53, July, 1987 for "Jane Urquhart's Short Stories in the Landscape of the Poet" by Patricia Bradbury; v. 59, August, 1993 for a review of "Away" by Nancy Wigston. All reprinted by permission of the respective authors.—***San Francisco Review of Books,*** Spring, 1984. Copyright © by the San Francisco Review of Books 1984. Reprinted by permission of the publisher.—***Saturday Night,*** v. 105, March, 1990 for "Inside Stories" by Katherine Ashenburg. Copyright © 1990 by Saturday Night. Reprinted by permission of the author.—***The Saturday Review,*** New York, v. XLIX, May 21, 1966. © 1966 Saturday Review magazine. Reprinted by permission of the publisher.—***The Saturday Review of Literature,*** v. XXX, September 6, 1947. Copyright 1947, renewed 1975 Saturday Review magazine. Reprinted by permission of the publisher.—***The Sewanee Review,*** v. XCIV, Summer, 1986 for "A Satirical Neoformalist" by Bruce King. © 1986 by The University of the South. Reprinted with the permission of the editor of *The Sewanee Review* and the author.—***The Southern Humanities Review,*** v. XXII, Winter, 1988. Copyright 1988 by Auburn University. Reprinted by permission of the publisher.—***The Southern Literary Journal,*** v. XXVII, Spring, 1995. Copyright 1995 by the Department of English, University of North Carolina at Chapel Hill. Reprinted by permission of the publisher.—***The Southern Review,*** Louisiana State University, v. 19, Spring, 1983 for an interview with Barry Hannah by R. Vanarsdall. Copyright 1983, by the authors. Reprinted by permission of Barry Hannah.—***The Spectator,*** v. 194, June 17, 1955; v. 267, October 26, 1991; v. 267, December 21, 1991; v. 272, January 22, 1994. © 1955, 1991, 1994 by *The Spectator.* All reprinted by permission of *The Spectator.*—***Studies in Short Fiction,*** v. 14, Fall, 1977; v. 19, Fall, 1982. Copyright © 1977, 1982 by Newberry College. Both reprinted by permission of the publisher.—***Theatre Journal,*** v. 42, March, 1990. © 1990, University and College Theatre Association of the American Theatre Association. Reprinted by permission of the Johns Hopkins University Press.—***The Times Literary Supplement,*** n. 3528, October 9, 1969; n. 3855, January 30, 1976; n. 4066, March 6, 1981; v. 4344, July 4, 1986; October 2-8, 1987; v. 4564, September 21, 1990; March 22, 1991; n. 4620, October 18, 1991; v. 4694, March 19, 1993; n. 4672, October 16, 1994. © The Times Supplements Limited 1969, 1976, 1981, 1986, 1987, 1990, 1991, 1993, 1994. All reproduced from *The Times Literary Supplement* by permission./ n. 2783, July 1, 1955. © The Times Supplements Limited 1955, renewed 1982. Reproduced from *The Times Literary Supplement* by permission.—***The University of Mississippi Studies in English,*** v. 9, 1991. Copyright 1991 by The University of Mississippi. Reprinted by permission of the publisher.—***The Village Voice,*** v. XXVII, February 23, 1982 for a review of "A Bigamist's Daughter" by Stephen Harvey; v. XXVIII, December 27, 1983 for "'Tis the Reason ..." by Erika Munk; v. 34, August 1, 1989 for "Boy's Life" by Pagan Kennedy. Copyright © News Group Publications, Inc., 1982, 1983, 1989. All reprinted by permission of *The Village Voice* and the respective authors.—***Vogue,*** v. 179, March, 1989. Copyright © 1989 The Condé Nast Publications Inc. Courtesy *Vogue.*—***The Wall Street Journal,*** February 7, 1984. © 1995 Dow Jones & Company, Inc. All rights reserved Worldwide. Reprinted with permission of *The Wall Street Journal.*—***West Coast Review of Books,*** v. 8, April, 1982; v. 15, November-December, 1990; v. 16, January, 1991. Copyright 1982, 1990, 1991 by Rapport Publishing Co., Inc. All reprinted by permission of the publisher.—***Western American Literature,*** v. XXIII, May, 1988. Copyright, 1988, by the Western Literature Association. Reprinted by permission of the publisher.—***Western Humanities Review,*** v. XXXIII, Spring, 1982. Copyright, 1982, University of Utah. Reprinted by permission of the publisher.—***Women's Studies: An Interdisciplinary Journal,*** v. 15, 1988. © Gordon and Breach Science Publishers. Reprinted by permission of the publisher.—***World Literature Today,*** v. 53, Winter, 1979; v. 65, Summer, 1991; v. 67, Spring, 1993; v. 69, Winter, 1995. Copyright 1979, 1991, 1993, 1995 by the University of Oklahoma Press. All reprinted by permission of the publisher.—***The Yale Review,*** v. 82, October, 1994. Copyright 1994, by Yale University. Reprinted by permission of the editors.

COPYRIGHTED EXCERPTS IN *CLC*, VOLUME 90, WERE REPRINTED FROM THE FOLLOWING BOOKS:

Baldwin, James. From *Going to Meet the Man.* Dial Press, 1965. Copyright © 1948, 1951, 1957, 1958, 1960, 1965, renewed 1993 by James Baldwin. Used by permission of Doubleday, a division of Bantam Doubleday Dell Publising Group, Inc.—Betsko, Kathleen and Rachel Koenig. From an interview in *Interviews with Contemporary Women Playwrights.* Beech Tree Books, 1987. Copyright © 1987 by Kathleen Betsko and Rachel Koenig. All rights reserved. Reprinted by permission of Beech Tree Books, a division of William Morrow and Company, Inc.—Charney, Mark J. From *Barry Hannah.* Twayne, 1992. Copyright © 1992 by Twayne Publishers. All rights reserved. Reprinted with permission of Twayne Publishers, an imprint of Macmillan Publishing Company.—Dahlie, Hallvard. From *Medieval and Modern Ireland.* Edited by Richard Wall. Colin Smythe, 1988. Copyright © 1988 Hallvard Dahlie. All rights reserved. Reprinted by permission of the publisher.—Finney, Brian. From *The Inner I: British Literary Autobiography of the Twentieth Century.* Oxford University Press, 1985. Copyright © 1985 by Brian Finney. All rights reserved. Reprinted by permission of Peters Fraser & Dunlop Group Ltd. In the U.S. by Oxford University Press—Gould, Jean. From *Modern American Women Poets.* Dodd, Mead & Company, 1984. Copyright © 1984 by Jean Gould. All rights reserved.—Kael, Pauline. From "Childhood of the Dead," in *Taking it All In.* Holt, Rinehart, and Winston, 1984. © 1980, 1981, 1982, 1983, 1984 by Pauline Kael. Reprinted by permission of Curtis Brown Ltd. In North America by Henry Holt and Co., Inc.—Lee, Laurie. From *A Moment of War.* Penguin Books Ltd., 1991. Copyright © Laurie Lee, 1991. All rights reserved.—Lee, Laurie. From *As I Walked Out One Midsummer Morning.* Atheneum Publishers, Inc., 1969. Copyright © 1969 by Laurie Lee. All rights reserved.—Lee, Laurie. From *Cider With Rosie.* The Hogarth Press, 1960. © Laurie Lee 1959, renewed 1987. Reprinted by permission of Chatto & Windus.—Lee, Laurie. From *I Can't Stay Long.* Atheneum, 1976. Copyright © 1975 by Laurie Lee. All rights reserved.—Maxwell, William. From *The Outermost Dream.* Knopf, 1989. Copyright © 1989 by William Maxwell. Reprinted by permission of Alfred A. Knopf Inc. In the British Commonwealth by Wylie, Aitken & Stone, Inc.—McDermott, Alice. From *A Bigamist's Daughter.* Random House, 1982. Copyright © 1982 by Alice McDermott. All rights reserved.—McDermott, Alice. From *At Wedding and Wakes.* Farrar, Straus and Giroux, 1992. Copyright © 1992 by Alice McDermott. All rights reserved.—McDermott, Alice. From *That Night.* Farrar, Straus, and Giroux, 1987. Copyright © 1987 by Alice McDermontt. All rights reserved.—Meyer, Bruce and Brian O'Riodran. From "In Celebration of the Commonplace" in an interview with Brian Moore, in *Their Words: Interviews with Fourteen Canadian Writers.* Anansi, 1984. Copyright © 1984, Bruce Meyer and Brian O'Riordan. All rights reserved. Reprinted by permission of Stoddart Publishing Co. Limited, Don Mills, Ontario.—Moore, Brian. From *Black Robe.* E. P. Dutton, 1985. Copyright © 1985 by Brian Moore. All rights reserved. Reprinted by permission of Curtis Brown Ltd. In Canada by McClelland & Stewart. In the British Commonwealth by Jonathan Cape.—Moore, Brian. From *Lies of Silence.* Copyright © 1990 by Brian Moore. Reprinted by permission of the author.—Moore, Brian. From *No Other Life.* Doubleday, 1993. Copyright © 1993 by Trancas Enterprises, Inc. All rights reserved.—Pratt, Louis H. From *James Baldwin.* Twayne, 1978. Copyright © 1978 by G. K. Hall & Co. All rights reserved. Reprinted with permission of Twayne Publishers, an imprint of Macmillan Publishing Company.—Salinas, Luis Omar. From *Partial Autobiographies: Interviews with Twenty Chicano Poets.* Edited by Wolfgang Binder. Palm & Enke, 1985. Reprinted by permission of the editor.—Savery, Pancho. From "Baldwin, Bebop, and 'Sonny's Blues'" in *Understanding Others: Cultural and Cross-Cultural Studies and the Teaching of Literature.* Edited by Joseph Timmer and Tilly Warnock. National Council of Teachers of English, 1992. © 1992 by the National Council of Teachers of English. All rights reserved. Reprinted by permission of the publisher and the author.—Telotte, J. P. From "'Westworld', 'Futureworld', and the World's Obscenity" in *State of the Fantastic: Studies in the Theory and Practice of Fantastic Literature and Film.* Edited by Nicholas Ruddick. Greenwood Press, 1992. Copyright © 1992 by Nicholas Ruddick. All rights reserved. Reprinted by permission of Greenwood Publishing Group, Inc., Westport, CT.—Tolley, A. T. From *The Poetry of the Thirties.* St. Martin's Press, 1975. © St. Martin's Press, Inc., 1975. Reprinted by permission of the author.—Urquhart, Jane. From *Away.* Viking Penguin, 1994. Copyright © Jane Urquhart, 1993. All rights reserved.—Urquhart, Jane. From *Changing Heaven.* David R. Godine, Publishers, 1993. Copyright © 1993 by Jane Urquhart. All rights reserved. Reprinted by permission of Jane Urquhart. In the U.S. by David R. Godine, Publishers, Inc.—Wasserstein, Wendy. From *Bachelor Girls.* Alfred A. Knopf, Inc., 1990. Copyright © 1984,

PHOTOGRAPHS AND ILLUSTRATIONS APPEARING IN *CLC*, VOLUME 90, WERE RECEIVED FROM THE FOLLOWING SOURCES:

"Sonny's Blues"

James Baldwin

The following entry presents criticism on Baldwin's short story "Sonny's Blues" (1957). For further information on his life and works, see *CLC,* Volumes 1, 2, 3, 4, 5, 8, 13, 15, 17, 42, 50, and 67.

INTRODUCTION

The short story "Sonny's Blues" is Baldwin's most highly acclaimed treatment of his signature themes: the nature of identity, race relations in the United States, human suffering, and the function of art. Set in the early 1950s in New York City, the story is narrated by an unnamed man who relates his attempts to come to terms with his long estranged brother, Sonny, a jazz musician. John M. Reilly, noting that an "outstanding quality of the Black literary tradition in America is its attention to the interdependence of personal and social experience," has concluded that "Sonny's Blues" both depicts and manifests the belief that the "artful expression of personal yet typical experience is one way to freedom."

Plot and Major Characters

After reading in a newspaper of Sonny's arrest for the possession and sale of heroin, the narrator—a high school algebra teacher aspiring to middle-class values, tastes, and security—recoils from the idea of getting involved in his brother's life. As he ponders the meaning of Sonny's situation and of his own fraternal obligations, the narrator recalls scenes and impressions from his childhood. He remembers in particular the story his mother told him about the murder of his uncle, a blues musician, the effect this had on his father, and his mother's subsequent entreaty to the narrator to always look after Sonny. After his relatively brief time in jail, Sonny comes to live with the narrator and his wife. The awkward, tentative conversations that ensue result in Sonny inviting his brother to hear him play at a Greenwich Village bar. Accepting the offer as an attempt at reconciliation, the narrator experiences—through the nuances of the music and the subtle interplay of the musicians—a sublime understanding of his brother and of the importance of music as a release from existential suffering.

Major Themes

Like much of Baldwin's writing, fiction as well as nonfiction, "Sonny's Blues" addresses specific racial issues and themes regarding the human condition. Displaying the influence of Jean-Paul Sartre and Albert Camus, whose works were largely responsible for articulating the philosophy of Existentialism, Baldwin depicts a world in which suffering characterizes man's basic state. The story's principal characters, however, not only struggle through an

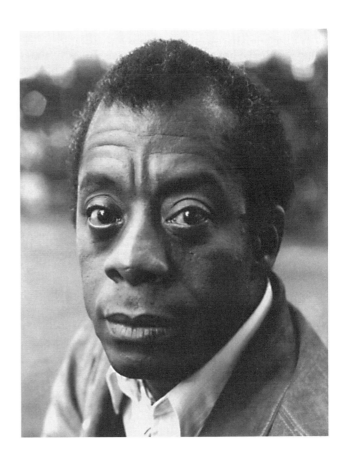

absurd world devoid of inherent meaning, but must also persevere in a society that tolerates racism. Baldwin thus sees black Americans suffering doubly: from the existential angst of the human condition, and from the humiliation, poverty, and violence imposed on them by a prejudiced society. In "Sonny's Blues" Baldwin addresses these issues by employing metaphors of darkness and anxiety, incorporating images of confinement, and offering portraits of life in contemporary Harlem and, through the narrator's recollection of his childhood and family, the American South. Another of the story's major themes concerns music, specifically jazz and blues. Baldwin uses these forms, which are African American in origin, for various purposes. Music is associated with particular eras and places–blues with the South's past and jazz, specifically bebop, with the modern urban setting. Also, Baldwin characterizes the narrator, in part, by his lack of musical knowledge; critics note that the emotional distance between the brothers is symbolized by the narrator's unfamiliarity with bebop and his ignorance of the great saxophone player Charlie "Bird" Parker. Moreover, commentators note that the narrator's epiphanic experience at the end of the story, when he hears Sonny's playing, instantiates the theme of the redemptive powers of music and signals the rebirth of the brothers' relationship.

Critical Reception

"Sonny's Blues" is generally considered one of Baldwin's finest works. Many commentators have discussed the story in relation to the author's role as a civil-rights leader. John M. Reilly has noted that "Sonny's Blues" "states dramatically the motive for Baldwin's famous polemics in the cause of Black freedom." A minority of critics have commented negatively that the social and political messages in "Sonny's Blues" are presented in a heavy-handed manner. Joseph Featherstone, for example, remarked that at various points in the story one hears "not the voice of Sonny or his brother, [but] the intrusive voice of Baldwin the boy preacher." Most critics, however, agree with John Rees Moore, who stated that "Sonny's Blues" is "unequivocally successful."

PRINCIPAL WORKS

Autobiographical Notes (autobiography) 1953
Go Tell It on the Mountain (novel) 1953
The Amen Corner (drama) 1955
Notes of a Native Son (essays) 1955
Giovanni's Room (novel) 1956
*Giovanni's Room (drama) 1957
"Sonny's Blues" (short story) 1957; published in the journal *Partisan Review*
Nobody Knows My Name: More Notes of a Native Son (essays) 1961
Another Country (novel) 1962
The Fire Next Time (essays) 1963
Blues for Mister Charlie (drama) 1964
†Going to Meet the Man (short stories) 1965
This Morning, This Evening, So Soon (novella) 1967
Tell Me How Long the Train's Been Gone (novel) 1968
A Rap on Race [with Margaret Mead] (conversations) 1971
No Name in the Street (essays) 1972
One Day, When I Was Lost: A Scenario Based on "The Autobiography of Malcolm X" [adaptor; from *The Autobiography of Malcolm X* by Alex Haley] (drama) 1972
A Dialogue [with Nikki Giovanni] (dialogue) 1973
A Deed from the King of Spain (drama) 1974
If Beale Street Could Talk (novel) 1974
The Devil Finds Work (essays) 1976
Little Man, Little Man: A Story of Childhood [with Yoran Cazac] (juvenilia) 1976
Just above My Head (novel) 1979
Jimmy's Blues: Selected Poems (poetry) 1983
The Evidence of Things Not Seen (nonfiction) 1985
The Price of the Ticket: Collected Nonfiction, 1948-1985 (nonfiction) 1985
Harlem Quartet (novel) 1987

*This is an adaptation of the novel.

†This collection includes "Sonny's Blues."

CRITICISM

John M. Reilly   (essay date July 1970)

SOURCE: " 'Sonny's Blues': James Baldwin's Image of Black Community," in *Negro American Literature Forum*, Vol. 4, No. 2, July, 1970, pp. 56-68.

[*A respected American critic and educator, Reilly has published many book-length studies on such major African-American authors as Richard Wright and Ralph Ellison. In the following essay, considered one of the most influential treatments of "Sonny's Blues," he examines Baldwin's handling of the themes of individuality and community.*]

A critical commonplace holds that James Baldwin writes better essays than he does fiction or drama; nevertheless, his leading theme—the discovery of identity—is nowhere presented more successfully than in the short story **"Sonny's Blues."** Originally published in *Partisan Review* in 1957 and reprinted in the collection of stories ***Going to Meet the Man*** in 1965, **"Sonny's Blues"** not only states dramatically the motive for Baldwin's famous polemics in the cause of Black freedom, but it also provides an esthetic linking his work, in all literary genres, with the cultures of the Black ghetto.

The fundamental movement of **"Sonny's Blues"** represents the slow accommodation of a first-person narrator's consciousness to the meaning of his younger brother's way of life. The process leads Baldwin's readers to a sympathetic engagement with the young man by providing a knowledge of the human motives of the youths whose lives normally are reported to others only by their inclusion in statistics of school dropout rates, drug usage, and unemployment.

The basis of the story, however, and its relationship to the purpose of Baldwin's writing generally, lies in his use of the Blues as a key metaphor. The unique quality of the Blues is its combination of personal and social significance in a lyric encounter with history. [According to Janheinz Jahn in his *Neo-African Literature*, 1968], "The Blues-singer describes first-person experiences, but only such as are typical of the community and such as each individual in the community might have. The singer never sets himself against the community or raises himself above it." Thus, in the story of Sonny and his brother an intuition of the meaning of the Blues repairs the relationship between the two men who have chosen different ways to cope with the menacing ghetto environment, and their reconciliation through the medium of this Afro-American musical form extends the meaning of the individual's Blues until it becomes a metaphor of Black community.

Sonny's life explodes into his older brother's awareness when the story of his arrest for peddling and using heroin is reported in the newspaper. Significantly the mass medium of the newspaper with the impersonal story in it of a police bust is the only way the brothers have of communicating at the opening of the story. While the narrator says that because of the newspaper report Sonny "became real to me again," their relationship is only vestigially personal, for he "couldn't find any room" for the news "anywhere inside. . . ."

While he had his suspicions about how Sonny was spending his life, the narrator had put them aside with rationalizations about how Sonny was, after all, a good kid. Nothing to worry about. In short, the storyteller reveals that along with his respectable job as an algebra teacher he had assumed a conventional way of thinking as a defense against recognizing that his own brother ran the risk of "coming to nothing." Provoked by the facts of Sonny's arrest to observe his students, since they are the same age as Sonny must have been when he first had heroin, he notices for the first time that their laughter is disenchanted rather than good-humored. In it he hears his brother, and perhaps himself. At this point in the story his opinion is evidently that Sonny and many of the young students are beaten and he, fortunately, is not.

The conventionality of the narrator's attitude becomes clearer when he encounters a nameless friend of Sonny's, a boy from the block who fears he may have touted Sonny onto heroin by telling him, truthfully, how great it made him feel to be high. This man who "still spent hours on the street corner . . . high and raggy" explains what will happen to Sonny because of his arrest. After they send him someplace and try to cure him, they'll let Sonny loose, that's all. Trying to grasp the implication the narrator asks: "You mean he'll never kick the habit. Is that what you mean?" He feels there should be some kind of renewal, some hope. A man should be able to bring himself up by his will, convention says. Convention also says that behavior like Sonny's is deliberately self-destructive. "Tell me," he asks the friend, "why does he want to die?" Wrong again. "Don't nobody want to die," says the friend, "ever."

Agitated though he is about Sonny's fate the narrator doesn't want to feel himself involved. His own position on the middle-class ladder of success is not secure, and the supporting patterns of thought in his mind are actually rather weak. Listening to the nameless friend explain about Sonny while they stand together in front of a bar blasting "black and bouncy" music from its door, he senses something that frightens him. "All this was carrying me some place I didn't want to go. I certainly didn't want to know how it felt. It filled everything, the people, the houses, the music, the dark, quicksilver barmaid, with menace; and this menace was their reality."

Eventually a great personal pain—the loss of a young daughter—breaks through the narrator's defenses and makes him seek out his brother, more for his own comfort than for Sonny's. "My trouble made his real," he says. In that remark is a prefiguring of the meaning the Blues will develop.

It is only a prefiguring, however, for [by] the time Sonny is released from the state institution where he had been confined, the narrator's immediate need for comfort has passed. When he meets Sonny he is in control of himself, but very shortly he is flooded with complex feelings that make him feel again the menace of the 110th Street bar where he had stood with Sonny's friend. There is no escaping a feeling of icy dread, so he must try to understand.

As the narrator casts his mind back over his and Sonny's past, he gradually identifies sources of his feelings. First he recalls their parents, especially concentrating on an image of his family on a typical Sunday. The scene is one of security amidst portentousness. The adults sit without talking, "but every face looks darkening, like the sky outside." The children sit about, maybe one half asleep and another being stroked on the head by an adult. The darkness frightens a child and he hopes "that the hand which strokes his forehead will never stop." The child knows, however, that it will end, and now grown-up he recalls one of the meanings of the darkness is in the story his mother told him of the death of his uncle, run over on a dark country road by a car full of drunken white men. Never had his companion, the boy's father, "seen anything as dark as that road after the lights of the car had gone away." The narrator's mother had attempted to apply her tale of his father's grief at the death of his own brother to the needs of their sons. They can't protect each other, she knows, "but," she says to the narrator about Sonny, "you got to let him know you's *there*."

Thus, guilt for not fulfilling their mother's request and a sense of shared loneliness partially explain the older brother's feeling toward Sonny. Once again, however, Baldwin stresses the place of the conventional set of the narrator's mind in the complex of feelings as he has him recall scenes from the time when Sonny had started to become a jazz musician. The possibility of Sonny's being a jazz rather than a classical musician had "seemed—beneath him, somehow." Trying to understand the ambition, the narrator had asked if Sonny meant to play like Louis Armstrong, only to be told that Charlie Parker was the model. Hard as it is to believe, he had never heard of Bird until Sonny mentioned him. This ignorance reveals more than a gap between fraternal generations. It represents a cultural chasm. The narrator's inability to understand Sonny's choice of a musical leader shows his alienation from the mood of the post-war bebop sub-culture. In its hip style of dress, its repudiation of middle-brow norms, and its celebration of esoteric manner the bebop sub-culture made overtly evident its underlying significance as an assertion of Black identity. Building upon a restatement of Afro-American music, bebop became an expression of a new self-awareness in the ghettos by a strategy of elaborate non-conformity. In committing himself to the bebop sub-culture Sonny attempted to make a virtue of the necessity of the isolation imposed upon him by his color. In contrast, the narrator's failure to understand what Sonny was doing indicates that his response to the conditions imposed upon him by racial status was to try to assimilate himself as well as he could into the mainstream American culture. For the one, heroin addiction sealed his membership in the exclusive group; for the other, adoption of individualistic attitudes marked his allegiance to the historically familiar ideal of transcending caste distinctions by entering into the middle class.

Following his way Sonny became wrapped in the vision that rose from his piano, stopped attending school, and hung around with a group of musicians in Greenwich Village. His musical friends became Sonny's family, replacing the brother who had felt that Sonny's choice of his style of life was the same thing as dying, and for all practical purposes the brothers were dead to each other in the extended separation before Sonny's arrest on narcotics charges.

The thoughts revealing the brother's family history and locating the sources of the narrator's complex feelings about Sonny all occur in the period after Sonny is released from the state institution. Though he has ceased to evade thoughts of their relationship, as he had done in the years when they were separated and had partially continued to do after Sonny's arrest, the narrator has a way to go before he can become reconciled to Sonny. His recollections of the past only provide his consciousness with raw feeling.

The next development—perception—begins with a scene of a revival meeting conducted on the sidewalk of Seventh Avenue, beneath the narrator's window. Everyone on the street has been watching such meetings all his life, but the narrator from his window, passerby on the street, and Sonny from the edge of the crowd all watch again. It isn't because they expect something different this time. Rather it is a familiar moment of communion for them. In basic humanity one of the sanctified sisters resembles the down-and-outer watching her, "a cigarette between her heavy, chapped lips, her hair a cuckoo's nest, her face scarred and swollen from many beatings. . . ."

"Perhaps," the narrator thinks, "they both knew this, which was why, when, as rarely, they addressed each other, they addressed each other as Sister." The point impresses both the narrator and Sonny, men who should call one another "Brother," for the music of the revivalists seems to "soothe a poison" out of them.

The perception of this moment extends nearly to conception in the conversation between the narrator and Sonny that follows it. It isn't a comfortable discussion. The narrator still is inclined to voice moral judgments of the experiences and people Sonny tries to talk about, but he is making an honest effort to relate to his brother now and reminds himself to be quiet and listen. What he hears is that Sonny equates the feeling of hearing the revivalist sister sing with the sensation of heroin in the veins. "It makes you feel—in control. Sometimes you got to have that feeling." It isn't primarily drugs that Sonny is talking about, though, and when the narrator curbs his tongue to let him go on, Sonny explains the real subject of his thoughts.

Again, the facts of Sonny's experience contradict the opinion of "respectable" people. He did not use drugs to escape from suffering, he says. He knows as well as anyone that there's no way to avoid suffering, but what you can do is "try all kinds of ways to keep from drowning in it, to keep on top of it, and to make it seem . . . like *you*." That is, Sonny explains, you can earn your suffering, make it seem "like you did something . . . and now you're suffering for it."

The idea of meriting your suffering is a staggering one. In the face of it the narrator's inclination to talk about "will power and how life could be—well, beautiful," is blunted, because he senses that by directly confronting degradation Sonny has asserted what degree of will was possible to him, and perhaps that kept him alive.

At this point in the story it is clear that there are two themes emerging. The first is the theme of the individualistic narrator's gradual discovery of the significance of his brother's life. This theme moves to a climax in the final scene of the story when Sonny's music impresses the narrator with a sense of the profound feeling it contains. From the perspective of that final scene, however, the significance of the Blues itself becomes a powerful theme.

The insight into suffering that Sonny displays establishes his priority in knowledge. Thus, he reverses the original relationship between the brothers, assumes the role of the elder, and proceeds to lead his brother, by means of the Blues, to a discovery of self in community.

As the brothers enter the jazz club where Sonny is to play, he becomes special. Everyone has been waiting for him, and each greets him familiarly. Equally special is the setting—dark except for a spotlight which the musicians approach as if it were a circle of flame. This is a sanctified spot where Sonny is to testify to the power of souls to commune in the Blues.

Baldwin explicates the formula of the Blues by tracing the narrator's thoughts while Sonny plays. Many people, he thinks, don't really hear music being played except so far as they invest it with "personal, private, vanishing evocations." He might be thinking of himself, referring to his having come to think of Sonny through the suffering of his own personal loss. The man who makes the music engages in a spiritual creation, and when he succeeds, the creation belongs to all present, "his triumph, when he triumphs, is ours."

In the first set Sonny doesn't triumph, but in the second, appropriately begun by "Am I Blue," he takes the lead and begins to form a musical creation. He becomes, in the narrator's words, "part of the family again." What family? First of all that of his fellow musicians. Then, of course, the narrator means to say that their fraternal relationship is at last fulfilled as their mother hoped it to be. But there is yet a broader meaning too. Like the sisters at the Seventh Avenue revival meeting Sonny and the band are not saying anything new. Still they are keeping the Blues alive by expanding it beyond the personal lyric into a statement of the glorious capacity of human beings to take the worst and give it a form of their own choosing.

At this point the narrator synthesizes feelings and perception into a conception of the Blues. He realizes Sonny's Blues can help everyone who listens be free, in his own case free of the conventions that had alienated him from Sonny and that dimension of Black culture represented in Sonny's style of living. Yet at the same time he knows the world outside of the Blues moment remains hostile.

The implicit statement of the esthetics of the Blues in this story throws light upon much of Baldwin's writing. The first proposition of the esthetics that we can infer from

"Sonny's Blues" is that suffering is the prior necessity. Integrity of expression comes from "paying your dues." This is a point Baldwin previously made in *Giovanni's Room* (1956) and which he elaborated in the novel *Another Country* (1962).

The second implicit proposition of the Blues esthetics is that while the form is what it's all about, the form is transitory. The Blues is an art in process and in that respect alien from any conception of fixed and ideal forms. This will not justify weaknesses in an artist's work, but insofar as Baldwin identifies his writing with the art of the singers of Blues it suggests why he is devoted to representation, in whatever genre, of successive moments of expressive feeling and comparatively less concerned with achieving a consistent overall structure.

The final proposition of the esthetics in the story **"Sonny's Blues"** is that the Blues functions as an art of communion. It is popular rather than elite, worldly rather than otherwise. The Blues is expression in which one uses the skill he has achieved by practice and experience in order to reach toward others. It is this proposition that gives the Blues its metaphoric significance. The fraternal reconciliation brought about through Sonny's music is emblematic of a group's coming together, because the narrator learns to love his brother freely while he discovers the value of a characteristically Afro-American assertion of life-force. Taking Sonny on his own terms he must also abandon the ways of thought identified with middle-class position which historically has signified for Black people the adoption of "white" ways.

An outstanding quality of the Black literary tradition in America is its attention to the interdependence of personal and social experience. Obviously necessity has fostered this virtue. Black authors cannot luxuriate in the assumption that there is such a thing as a purely private life. James Baldwin significantly adds to this aspect of the tradition in **"Sonny's Blues"** by showing that artful expression of personal yet typical experience is one way to freedom.

Elaine R. Ognibene (essay date January 1971)

SOURCE: "Black Literature Revisited: 'Sonny's Blues'," in *English Journal,* Vol. 60, No. 1, January, 1971, pp. 36-7.

[*In the essay below, Ognibene examines the main themes in "Sonny's Blues."*]

Barbara Dodds Stanford (*English Journal,* March 1969) calls black literature "a godsend to the teacher who wants his class to deal with genuine communication problems. . . ." Citing among others, two Baldwin classics: *Notes of a Native Son* and *Go Tell It on the Mountain,* she mentions that in such works "it is a relief to recognize our own struggle to find ourselves," and she further intimates that students can relate to "young people struggling to assert their own independence and identity. . . ." A work which she fails to list, a story which is often lost among Baldwin's writings, is **"Sonny's Blues."** This work is particularly relevant, not only because it concerns itself with problems facing many in this era of disintegrating family bonds and uncertain norms, but also because it af-

fords an opportunity to elicit the type of "affective" response which Mrs. Stanford justly considers important. In it Baldwin deals with the question of prejudice and stereotypes; with an attempt to bridge a modern cliché—the generation gap; with an ascent from drugs to something more real and more lasting; and with a search for self-identity that is every man's. [Presented with] such pertinent content, one needs to take a more careful look.

Close perusal of **"Sonny's Blues"** reveals that while it is ostensibly about Sonny—his descent to the underworld through drugs and his resurrection through jazz—Baldwin's deeper concern is with the narrator, the respectable schoolteacher, the "white" Negro, Sonny's big brother. The author shows that the nameless "I" of his story, though older, is not wiser, and he uses both Sonny and his music as tools to help the narrator reconcile himself to his racial heritage.

Reading the newspaper account about his brother, the narrator says that he is "scared" for Sonny, but his next words belie his statement. "I couldn't believe it. . . . I couldn't find any room for it anywhere inside me." It is not Sonny but he himself he fears for, for, if he reestablishes contact with Sonny, he is faced with a condition of dissonance: his carefully ordered middle class existence cannot acknowledge a drug addict brother, yet somehow he feels vaguely "responsible." Baldwin mentions that this deliberation was carrying the narrator "someplace he didn't want to go," and he intimates that the "someplace" is a past which Sonny's brother has rejected and tried to escape by leaving Harlem and accepting the bourgeois values of the white community. But when Sonny returns and they ride together through the park, the past that the narrator has exiled to the periphery of his consciousness intrudes upon him in the person of the young boys that he sees playing, and he finds himself "seeking . . . that part of himself which had been left behind."

Baldwin uses suffering as a bond and as an impetus to communication.

—Elaine R. Ognibene

Returning to the house, he again senses the impending danger that self knowledge brings, and Baldwin has him reiterate his avowed purpose: "I was trying to find something out about my brother." What the author leaves unsaid is that he is also searching for a lost part of himself. When Sonny's brother loses himself in reminiscence, Baldwin, in a classic dialog of non-communication, reveals the true relationship that exists between the brothers.

Upon being questioned, Sonny admits that he wants to be a musician, but the narrator feels that it's not right for his brother; he feels that it is beneath him, perhaps because it is too close to the white stereotype of the Rhythm 'n Blues Blackman. He dismisses Sonny's ambition as a stage that "kids go through," and when things don't go exactly his way he gives up. But Sonny, although young, is mature enough to realize that "things take time," and he sees the distinction between a job done for money and a chosen vocation. He can make a living elsewhere, but being a musician is "the only thing" he wants to do. And when his brother pleads for him to "be reasonable," Baldwin hints that what he really means is: See things my way or not at all. Sonny justly accuses him, "I hear you. But you never hear anything I say," and his accusation holds, for the narrator, in closing himself to the sights and sounds of the ghetto, has even deafened himself to his brother's voice.

When Sonny returns from the army, his brother yet is "unwilling to see that he is a man," and, still clinging to his middle class standards, he treats Sonny's music as only "an excuse for the life he led." It is not until his own personal suffering that he can begin to understand his brother's anguish or experience. Baldwin uses suffering as a bond and as an impetus to communication. He has the narrator make his first honest attempt to listen when Sonny explains his use of drugs: "Something inside me told me that I should hold my tongue." The author shows that at last he is beginning to realize the proportions of the barrier that he has erected: "I had held silence—so long!—when he had needed human speech to help him." But he is still struggling; he finds it difficult to accept even suffering that is not done on his own terms. "You're just hung up on the way some people try—it's not *your* way!" Sonny calls his bluff as he had done as a teenager, and his brother reluctantly agrees to meet him on his own ground.

At the nightclub, in Sonny's world, the narrator states that the music "hit something in me." It evokes an image of his collective past, and he sees that the tale of a people's joys and sorrows "must always be heard," for "it's the only light we've got in all this darkness." If he rejects the past of his race, there is nothing to sustain him. He hears Sonny's blues and senses that freedom that comes in acknowledging one's origins: "I understood . . . he could help us be free if we would listen." He does listen and the music evokes memories; it gives him back a personal history that no longer needs to be repressed, a history that now could "live forever."

Though he is realistic enough to see it as "only a moment," though the world outside is still threatening, nevertheless, the music has penetrated his cultural deafness. Through contact with Sonny and his music Baldwin has brought the narrator to a gradual enlightenment and shown that in accepting Sonny's blues he has made them, in part at least, his own.

Sherley Anne Williams (essay date 1972)

SOURCE: "The Black Musician: The Black Hero as Light Bearer," in *Give Birth to Brightness,* Dial Press, 1972, pp. 135-66.

[*Williams is an American novelist, poet, critic, and author of children's books whose most highly acclaimed work is the novel* Dessa Rose *(1986). In the following excerpt, a portion of which appeared in CLC-3, she examines the significance of music and the musician in "Sonny's Blues."*]

The musician in the works of James Baldwin is more than a metaphor; he is the embodiment of alienation and estrangement, which the figure of the artist becomes in much of twentieth century literature. Most of his characters have at the center of their portrayal an isolation from the society, the culture, even each other. They are also commentaries upon the brutal, emasculating, feared—and fearing—land from which they are so estranged. The musician is also for Baldwin an archetypal figure whose referent is Black lives, Black experiences and Black deaths. He is the hope of making it in America and the bitter mockery of never making it well enough to escape the danger of being Black, the living symbol of alienation from the past and hence from self and the rhythmical link with the mysterious ancestral past. That past and its pain and the transcendence of pain is always an implicit part of the musician's characterization in Baldwin. Music is the medium through which the musician achieves enough understanding and strength to deal with the past and present hurt.

The short story, **"Sonny's Blues,"** sketches this kind of relationship between the individual and his personal and group history. Sonny is a jazz pianist who has recently returned from a drug cure. The story is set in New York, Harlem, and seems at first glance merely another well-written story about a young Black man trying to become himself, to attain his majority and retain his humanity amid all the traps which have been set to prevent just that. But the simplicity of the tale is only surface deep; in a rising crescendo of thematic complexity, the present struggle is refracted through the age-old pain, the age-old life force. The story is narrated by Sonny's older brother who has found it difficult to understand what music means to Sonny. Sonny's desire to be a jazz musician, which his brother associates with the "good-time" life, has created a schism between himself and his more orthodox brother. And because the brother cannot understand what lies between himself and Sonny, he cannot forgive Sonny for Sonny's own pain, which he, for all his seniority, is powerless to ease, or for the pain which their ruptured relationship has caused him. The closing pages of the story are a description of the brother's reaction as he listens to Sonny play for the first time.

> All I know about music is that not many people ever really hear it. And even then, on the rare occasions when something opens within, and the music enters, what we mainly hear, or hear corroborated, are personal, private, vanishing evocations. But the man who creates the music is hearing something else, is dealing with the roar rising from the void and imposing order on it as it hits the air. What is evoked in him, then, is of another order, more terrible because it has no words, and triumphant, too, for that same reason. And his triumph, when he triumphs, is ours. I just watched Sonny's face. His face was troubled, he was working hard, but he wasn't with it.

The attempt to once again make it through music brings no instant transformation. Sonny is approaching the center of his life and he cannot know what he will find there. But he understands that if he is to live, he must deal with that dread, that terror, chance the terrifying in order to triumph.

> And I had the feeling that, in a way, everyone on the bandstand was waiting for him, both waiting for him and pushing him along. But as I began to watch Creole, I realized that it was Creole who held them all back. He had them on a short rein. Up there, keeping the beat with his whole body, wailing on the fiddle, with his eyes half closed, he was listening to everything, but he was listening to Sonny. He was having a dialogue with Sonny. He wanted Sonny to leave the shoreline and strike out for the deep water. He was Sonny's witness that deep water and drowning were not the same thing—he had been there, and he knew. And he wanted Sonny to know. He was waiting for Sonny to do the things on the keys which would let Creole know that Sonny was in the water.

The musical group, Ellison's "marvel of social organization" [Ralph Ellison, "Living with Music"], is the catalyst which makes it possible for Sonny to begin to see himself through the music, to play out his own pain through the expression of it.

> And Sonny hadn't been near a piano for over a year. And he wasn't on much better terms with his life, not the life that stretched before him now. . . . And the face I saw on Sonny I'd never seen before. Everything had been burned out of it, and, at the same time, things usually hidden were being burned in, by the fire and fury of the battle which was occurring in him up there.

> Yet, watching Creole's face as they neared the end of the first set, I had the feeling that something had happened, something I hadn't heard. . . . Creole started into something else, it was almost sardonic, it was *Am I Blue*. And, as though he commanded, Sonny began to play. Something began to happen. And Creole let out the reins. The dry, low, black man said something awful on the drums. Creole answered, and the drums talked back. Then the horn insisted, sweet and high, slightly detached perhaps, and Creole listened, commenting now and then, dry, and driving, beautiful and calm and old. Then they all came together again, and Sonny was part of the family again. I could tell this from his face. He seemed to have found, right there beneath his fingers, a damn brand-new piano. It seemed that he couldn't get over it. Then, for awhile, just being happy with Sonny, they seemed to be agreeing with him that brand-new pianos certainly were a gas.

Sonny's music and his life become one and he is fused with the musical group in a relationship which sustains one because it sustains all. And finally, through the music, Sonny's brother begins to understand not so much Sonny, as himself, *his* past, *his* history, *his* traditions and that part of himself which he has in common with Sonny and the long line of people who have gone before them.

> Then Creole stepped forward to remind them that what they were playing was the blues. He

hit something in all of them, he hit something in me, myself, and the music tightened and deepened, apprehension began to beat the air. Creole began to tell us what the blues were all about. They were not about anything very new. He and his boys up there were keeping it new, at the risk of ruin, destruction, madness, and death, in order to find new ways to make us listen. For, while the tale of how we suffer, and how we are delighted, and how we may triumph is never new, it always must be heard. There isn't any other tale to tell, it's the only light we've got in all this darkness.

> And this tale, according to that face, that body, those strong hands on those strings, has another aspect in every country, and a new depth in every generation. Listen, Creole seemed to be saying, listen. Now these arc Sonny's blues. He made the little black man on the drums know it, and the bright, brown man on the horn. Creole wasn't trying any longer to get Sonny in the water. He was wishing him Godspeed. Then he stepped back, very slowly, filling the air with the immense suggestion that Sonny speak for himself.

> Then they all gathered around Sonny, and Sonny played. Every now and again one of them seemed to say, amen. Sonny's fingers filled the air with life, his life. But that life contained so many others. And Sonny went all the way back, he really began with the spare, flat statement of the opening phrase of the song. Then he began to make it his. It was very beautiful because it wasn't hurried and it was no longer a lament. I seemed to hear with what burning he had made it his, with what burning we had yet to make it ours, how we could cease lamenting. Freedom lurked around us and I understood, at last, that he could help us to be free if we would listen, that he would never be free until we did. Yet, there was no battle in his face now. I heard what he had gone through, and would continue to go through until he came to rest in earth. He had made it his: that long line, of which we knew only Mama and Daddy. And he was giving it back, as everything must be given back, so that, passing through death, it can live forever.

It is this then, this intense, almost excruciating, but always sustaining relationship among musicians and between them and their audiences which the musician is meant to evoke. The emphasis is gradually transformed from pain to survival to life. All are linked together by invisible webs, indestructible bonds of tradition and history, and this heritage, once revealed, becomes the necessary regenerative power which makes life possible.

Suzy Bernstein Goldman   (essay date Fall 1974)

SOURCE: "James Baldwin's 'Sonny's Blues': A Message in Music," in *Negro American Literature Forum*, Vol. 8, No. 3, Fall, 1974, pp. 231-33.

[*In the following essay, Goldman discusses the main themes in "Sonny's Blues."*]

In **"Sonny's Blues"** theme, form, and image blend into perfect harmony and rise to a thundering crescendo. The story, written in 1957 but carrying a vital social message for us today, tells of two black brothers' struggle to understand one another. The older brother, a straight-laced Harlem algebra teacher, is the unnamed narrator who represents, in his anonymity, everyman's brother; the younger man is Sonny, a jazz pianist who, when the story opens, has just been arrested for peddling and using heroin. As in so much of Baldwin's fiction, chronological time is upset. Instead the subject creates its own form. In this story of a musician, four time sequences mark four movements while the leitmotifs of this symphonic lesson in communication are provided by the images of sound. Musical terms along with words like "hear" and "listen" give the title a double meaning. This story about communication between people then reaches its climax when the narrator finally hears his brother's sorrow in his music, hears, that is, Sonny's blues.

The story begins when the narrator learns of Sonny's arrest in a most impersonal manner—by reading the newspaper. Yet this rude discovery sounds the initial note in these two brothers' growing closeness. The shock of recognition forces the narrator to confront his past refusal to accept the miserable truths around him. For too long, he admits, he had been "talking about algebra to a lot of boys who might, every one of them . . . be popping off needles every time they went to the head." He completes his own first lesson in understanding and takes his first step towards Sonny when he begins to hear his own students:

> I listened to the boys outside. . . . Their laughter struck me for perhaps the first time. It was not the joyous laughter which . . . one associates with children. It was mocking and insular, its intent to denigrate. It was disenchanted, and in this, also, lay the authority of their curses. Perhaps I was listening to them because I was thinking about my brother and in them I heard my brother. And myself.

> One boy was whistling a tune, at once very complicated and very simple, it seemed to be pouring out of him as though he were a bird, and it sounded very cool and moving through that harsh, bright air, only just holding its own through all those other sounds.

This last boy particularly suggests Sonny, the young man who makes himself heard and transcends the disenchantment, the darkness, with his song. Then immediately the narrator encounters another surrogate brother in Sonny's old friend who has come to the school to bring the news. Conversation between the two is guarded and hostile until the narrator, although he has never liked his brother's friend, begins to hear the boy and to feel guilty for never having heard him before, "for never having supposed that the poor bastard had a story of his own, much less a sad one." Standing together outside a bar while a juke box sounds from within, the friend confesses that he first described to Sonny the effects of heroin. Again the narrator psychologically retreats. Fearful of learning about heroin and too anxious himself to help Sonny, he timidly asks what the arrest means. The friend's reply is telling. "Lis-

ten," he shouts. "They'll let him out and then it'll just start all over again. That's what I mean." The two part after the friend, pretending to have left all his money home, plays upon the narrator's guilt and basic kindness to the tune of five dollars. Thus the first movement ends.

The second movement opens with the narrator's first letter to Sonny. Sonny's answer, equating drug addiction with prison and both with Harlem, shows his need to reach his brother. Finally the two men have begun to communicate with one another. The letters continue until Sonny's return to New York when the narrator, who has started at last "to wonder about Sonny, about the life that Sonny lived inside," takes him home. The narrator is awkward here, wanting only to hear that Sonny is safe and refusing to accept the fact that he might not be. He is still unwilling to see Sonny on Sonny's terms; like an overly anxious parent he must make Sonny conform to his own concepts of respectability.

The word "safe" is the note that takes us into the third movement, to time past when Sonny's father claimed there was "no place safe." In the flashbacks the narrator recalls events that fuse past, present, and future. Parallels are drawn between the father and Sonny, between the Harlem of one generation and the Harlem of the other. Images of darkness mingle with those of sound. For each generation, however, the tragedy is new, for the older people are reluctant to inform the young ones of the condition of the Black race. The old folks who sit in the dark quit talking, because if the child "knows too much about what's happened to *them,* he'll know too much too soon about what's going to happen to him." Thus even in the past, silence was preferable to expression.

We learn also of another pair of brothers, Sonny's father and uncle. The uncle, like Sonny, was a musician, but he got killed one night when some drunk white men ran him over in their car. The narrator's mother tells her older son this story to make him look after his brother, but her death, occurring shortly after this conversation, only shows the immeasurable gulf between the two boys. The narrator, recently married, thinks he is taking care of Sonny by forcing him to live with his wife's family, but Sonny, already on drugs though unable to admit it, could not want anything less. Their failure to communicate is at its peak. When Sonny announces his ambition "to play jazz," the appalled narrator is totally unresponsive. The most he can promise is to buy Charlie Parker's records, although Sonny insists he doesn't care what his brother listens to. Certainly he doesn't listen to Sonny, urging him only to be respectable and stay in school:

> "You only got another year. . . . Just try to put up with it till I come back. Will you please do that? For me?"

> He didn't answer and he wouldn't look at me.

> "Sonny, you hear me?"

> He pulled away. "I hear you. But you never hear anything *I* say."

The narrator, though he didn't know what to say to that, reminds Sonny of the piano at his in-laws, and Sonny gives in. Later we learn of Sonny's obsession with the piano. Because he has no one to communicate with, the piano becomes his only source of expression:

> As soon as he came in . . . , until suppertime. And, after supper, he went back to that piano and stayed there until everybody went to bed. He was at the piano all day Saturday and all day Sunday. . . .
>
> Isabel finally confessed that it wasn't like living with a person at all, it was like living with sound. And the sound didn't make any sense to her, didn't make any sense to any of them—naturally. . . . He moved in an atmosphere which wasn't like theirs at all. . . . There wasn't any way to reach him. . . .
>
> They dimly sensed, as I sensed, . . . that Sonny was at that piano playing for his life.

They succeed in reaching him, however, when they discover he has not been in school but in a white girl's Greenwich Village apartment playing music. After that Sonny enlists. When he returns, a man, although the narrator "wasn't willing to see it," the brothers fight, for to the narrator Sonny's "music seemed to be merely an excuse for the life he led. It sounded just that weird and disordered."

At this point they cut off all contact.

The fourth movement begins by recapitulating and developing the first. "I read about Sonny's troubles in the spring. Little Grace died in the fall." We move through time easily now, perceiving the connection between the narrator's first letter to Sonny and his daughter's death: "My trouble made his real." He has begun, finally, to sympathize, to understand.

The last movement then begins its own theme, the new relationship between the brothers. A subtly presented but major change in this relationship occurs when they watch a street revival meeting:

> The revival was being carried on by three sisters in black, and a brother. All they had were their voices and their Bibles and a tambourine. . . .
>
> *"Tis the old ship of Zion,"* they sang. . . . Not a soul under the sound of their voices was hearing this song for the first time, not one of them had been rescued. . . . The woman with the tambourine, whose voice dominated the air, whose face was bright with joy, was divided by very little from the woman who stood watching her, a cigarette between her heavy, chapped lips, her hair a cuckoo's nest, her face scarred and swollen from many beatings, and her black eyes glittering like coal. Perhaps they both knew this, which was why, when, as rarely, they addressed each other, they addressed each other as Sister.

There is a greater brotherhood among people than mere kinship. Moreover, the narrator realizes that their music saves them, for it "seemed to soothe a poison out of them." The narrator's simultaneous recognition of the meaning of brotherhood and the power of music leads directly to Sonny's invitation. He asks his brother to listen, that night, to his own music. That street song is thus a prelude

to the brothers' first honest talk and carries us to the finale when Sonny plays for the narrator.

Sonny now tells his brother that the woman's voice reminded him "of what heroin feels like." This equation of music and drugs, recalling the narrator's discussion with Sonny's friend outside a bar, explains why the one could be a positive alternative to the other. We better understand Sonny's desperate commitment to the piano. Sonny is "doing his best to talk," and the narrator knows that he should "listen." He realizes the profundity of Sonny's suffering now and sees also his own part in it: "There stood between us, forever, beyond the power of time or forgiveness, the fact that I had held silence—so long! —when he had needed human speech to help him."

The narrator's epiphany allows Sonny to continue, and he makes explicit now the connection between music and his own need to be heard:

> There's not really a living ass to talk to, . . . and there's no way of getting it out—that storm inside. You can't talk it and you can't make love with it, and when you finally try to get with it and play it, you realize *nobody's* listening. So *you've* got to listen. You got to find a way to listen.

Playing his own song, Sonny finds a way to listen, though he confesses that heroin sometimes helped him release the storm. Now he wants his brother to hear the storm too.

And he finally does. When Sonny, his voice barely audible, says of heroin "It can come again," the brother replies, "All right . . . so it can come again. All right." For that first true acceptance of himself, Sonny tells the narrator, "You're my brother."

The finale brings our two themes of interpersonal communication and music together. Baldwin arranges a discussion between the musicians and their instruments using the language of ordinary conversation. Creole, the leader of the group, is guiding Sonny as they begin to play. "He was listening to Sonny. He was having a dialogue with Sonny." Then they work towards the climax:

> The dry, low, black man said something awful on the drums, Creole answered, and the drums talked back. Then the horn insisted, . . . and Creole listened, commenting now and then. . . . Then they all came together again, and Sonny was part of the family again. . . .
>
> Creole began to tell us what the blues were all about. . . . He and his boys up there were keeping it new, at the risk of ruin, destruction, madness, and death, in order to find new ways to make us listen. For, while the tale of how we suffer, and how we are delighted, and how we may triumph is never new, it always must be heard. There isn't any other tale to tell, it's the only light we've got in all this darkness.

Finally Creole steps back to let Sonny speak for himself:

> Listen, Creole seemed to be saying, listen. Now these are Sonny's blues. . . .
>
> Sonny's fingers filled the air with life, his

life. . . . Sonny . . . really began with the spare, flat statement of the opening phrase of the song. . . . I understood, at last, that he could help us to be free if we would listen, that he would never be free until we did.

Sonny's music stirs special memories in the brothers' lives, but these blues belong to all of us, for they symbolize the darkness which surrounds all those who fail to listen to and remain unheard by their fellow men.

Sigmund Ro   (essay date 1975)

SOURCE: "The Black Musician as Literary Hero: Baldwin's 'Sonny's Blues' and Kelley's 'Cry for Me'," in *American Studies in Scandinavia,* Vol. 7, No. 1, 1975, pp. 17-48.

[*In the following excerpt, Ro discusses the intellectual and philosophical influences on Baldwin at the time he wrote "Sonny's Blues," examining in particular the ways in which the story reflects the existential philosophies of Jean-Paul Sartre and Albert Camus. Ro also situates this and other examples of Baldwin's work in the larger context of African-American literature in the pre- and post-Civil Rights eras, suggesting that Baldwin's strategy for writing about the human condition by emphasizing, or universalizing, his characters' existential predicaments was rejected by later generations of black writers.*]

This essay presents two case studies of the intellectual and ideological sources of the black hero in Afro-American fiction. The two stories by James Baldwin and William Melvin Kelley ['**Sonny's Blues**' and 'Cry for Me'] have been selected because they are representative of their times and provide convenient mirrors of intellectual and ideological continuities and discontinuities in black American writing in the post-war era.

Art and culture intersect. To look at fictional heroes is at the same time to be looking at refracted images of cultural realities beyond the internal verbal structures of the literary artifact. In the words of Edmund Fuller, 'every man's novel may not have a *thesis,* but it must have a *premise*—whether declared or tacit, whether conscious or unconscious [*Man in Modern Fiction,* 1958]. That premise, without which no work of literature can be coherent or even intelligible, must ultimately be located in the extra-literary and extra-linguistic reality of the writer's culture. Character is perhaps the formal component most immediately dependent on such non-literary premises.

Black fiction in the post-war period illustrates this interdependence between society and art with particular clarity. In the first decade, the spirit of the black intellectual community was characterized by integrationist views and a wish to join the mainstream of American literary life. This tendency was exemplified by the use of white characters, milieus, and authorial postures in Ann Petry's and Willard Motley's fiction, and further buttressed by an emerging black critical establishment in the 1940's and '50's, trained in Northern graduate schools and rigorously applying the literary standards of white critics. Saunders Redding, Nick Aaron Ford, Nathan Scott, and Hugh

Gloster were all agreed in urging black artists to emancipate themselves from 'the fetters of racial chauvinism' and to deal with universal human experience. [see Hugh M. Gloster, 'Race and the Negro Writer,' in *Black Expression,* Addison Gayle, Jr., ed., 1969; essay was originally published in 1950.]

In retrospect, it is not hard to discern the broader cultural context of this trend in black literary expression and criticism. In the overall effort of the black minority to achieve a position of equality in society, the strategy was understandably to emphasize the common humanity of black and white at the expense of the ethnocentricity and nationalism of the inter-war period. The same tendency prevailed in the Jewish-American community. In literary terms, this meant insistence on the writer's freedom to deal with his material in a non-racialist and universal spirit. Specifically, it meant literary characters created or interpreted in terms of archetypes or generalized human identity quests. In accordance with this mood, John Grimes of *Go Tell It on the Mountain* and Ellison's unnamed hero as well as Bellow's and Malamud's Jews were read as symbols of Youth, the Artist, or the human condition.

In this light, Baldwin's best known short story, '**Sonny's Blues**' (1957), merits reconsideration in terms of the modern Euro-American intellectual stance underlying it which appears to have escaped critical notice. Reflected in Baldwin's portrait of a black blues artist is, for all his discovery of racial community noted by commentators, the whole integration ethos of the first post-war decade, stated in the familiar existentialist categories of the Left Bank coteries in which Baldwin moved between 1948 and 1958. Though not actively seeking admission to the white world, Sonny is conceived in the image of Kierkegaard-Sartre-Camus and provided with an authentic black exterior. Behind Sonny there looms the non-racial esthetic of the Baldwin who proclaimed in 1955 that he merely wanted to be 'an honest man and a good writer' [*Notes of a Native Son*].

With the radicalization of the civil rights movement, the new militant nationalism, and the impact of African liberation, the literary situation for the black writer changed, spelling the end of the esthetic upon which Baldwin's Sonny was predicted. *Négritude* or *soul* gradually became a focal point of black cultural activity, involving separatist notions of artistic creation and the role of the artist.

The dimension of *Négritude* which has informed so much recent black writing is less the political implications of Pan-Africanism than the highly effective mystique of blackness as a special moral and spiritual sensibility which has evolved out of the writings of such theoreticians as Aimé Césaire, Alioune Diop, and Léopold Senghor. Here *Négritude* is thought of as a distinct ethos; that is, a body of traits, habits, and values crystallized into a peculiar life style and producing a psychology common not only to black Africans, but to blacks living in the American diaspora as well. It involves a sense of self and community which derives from an exclusive group identity forged by a unique historical experience or even, as intimated by Senghor, having its origin in biological-genetic facts. It is a condition as well as a fate, preceding and transcending the vicissitudes of economics, politics, and history. Thus, at the 1956 Conference of Negro African Writers and Artists in Paris, Senghor could appeal to American blacks to reinterpret their literature in terms of their common heritage of *Négritude,* taking himself the first step by discussing Richard Wright's poetry and *Black Boy* as African works.

In America, the corresponding concept of *soul,* if not the word itself, existed well before the historical *Négritude* movement. Although not interchangeable concepts, they share a vision of a 'Soul Force,' a unique source of moral and spiritual energy, peculiar to blacks everywhere. The real boost of the *soul* ethos and its ideologization for political and literary uses, however, occurred with the coinciding emergence of the latest phase of the civil rights movement in the U.S. and the African liberation from European colonialism in the late 1950's. The impact of *soul* was soon felt in black writing, especially as LeRoi Jones's seminal influence made itself felt after 1964, and led, in its extreme form, to a de-emphasizing of the mimetic principle of the Western conception of art and its traditional distinction between 'art' and 'life,' stressing instead the oral, utilitarian, and communal nature of African art as an ideal for black Americans to emulate. . . .

Together, Baldwin's and Kelley's two stories provide interesting case studies of what happens to fiction when it is subjected to the pressures of ideological change.

The two stories lend themselves particularly well to a comparative analysis of the black literary hero because the external formal frameworks are so similar. The geographical settings overlap almost completely. Except for short excursions into the Bronx neighborhood of Carlyle's family [in 'Cry for Me'], both stories move within a world circumscribed, physically as well as symbolically, by Harlem and Greenwich Village. In both, Village cabarets play central roles as scenes of epiphanic illuminations in the lives of the two narrators. To each story the urban setting is indispensable either as the source of the peculiar strains and frustrations of the characters or as a foil to the unadulterated pre-urban black 'soul.' The characters operate within the same structural pattern. In each case, the story hinges on the opposition of two characters, related by blood, but opposed in every other respect. One is a bourgeois Negro and the narrator of the story, the other is a 'soul' character with no desire to join the middle-class Establishment to which his relative belongs or to which he aspires. Sonny's brother is already firmly ensconced in the black bourgeoisie, while Carlyle appears to be bent on making it in the white world into which his family have moved since their beginnings in Harlem. In both cases, the development of the characters lends itself to description in terms of the 'initiation' pattern. Carlyle and Sonny's brother both grow from either a state of ignorance or guilty innocence to higher levels of consciousness through contact with their soulful relatives. This pattern is also the principle governing the two plots. In either case, a narrator whose presumed superiority makes him adopt the role of teacher and authority, receives a relative who is seen as ignorant, innocent, or immature. Ironically, both plots proceed to overturn this relationship by reversing their relative positions. By the end of the stories, the visitors have become the teachers and authorities by virtue of their charisma and insight while the narrators have been relegated to the position of humble apprentices and recipients of their mentors' messages. Thus the narrative structures are made to serve the educational process in the two characters initiated into the mysteries communicated by the black heroes whose medium of expression is, in both cases, music. Finally, the realism of the two stories is modified by the same set of symbols and images. Sonny and Uncle Wallace both become high priests and their concerts ceremonial occasions re-enacting semi-religious dramas of sacrifice and redemption.

This formal resemblance makes the differences in the larger implications of the two musician-heroes stand out all the more clearly. It would seem, however, from the criticism elicited by 'Sonny's Blues,' that this aspect has not been given the attention it deserves. Commentators appear unanimous in their emphasis on the racial element as it appears in the hero's individual identity quest within the boundaries of black culture. Both Marcus Klein and Shirley Anne Williams agree that the thrust of Sonny's message is the expression of his black identity. He is, in Klein's words, 'full of unspecified Negroness,' his problem is the 'burden of his racial identity' to be expressed through his music. Ultimately, the story undertakes to reveal 'the Negro motives that may issue in the blues' [see Marcus Klein, *After Alienation,* 1992]. Shirley Williams is willing to see Sonny as the typical alienated artist of so much twentieth-century literature, but she insists that his main 'referent is Black lives, Black experiences and Black deaths.' His estrangement is primarily an estrangement from his 'ancestral past' [see Sherley Anne Williams, *Give Birth to Brightness,* 1972]. The cure can only be effected through a restoration of the relationship between his personal history and that of his racial group. This delicate, but healing balance between private and group selves Sonny is finally able to achieve in his solo performance within the context of Creole's jazz band. On the other hand, Edward Margolies sees Sonny's music as a means of self-expression reflecting Baldwin's Christian-Protestant heritage. Even so, however, he sees Sonny's outbursts of 'the grief and terror that rage within his soul' as patterned on the testimony of the redeemed saint in the presence of witnesses, presumably to be equated with the audience, thus ultimately relating the story to the black religious tradition of the storefront church as the context of the protagonist's identity quest [see Edward Margolies, *Native Sons,* 1968].

It cannot of course be denied that Sonny's art is conditioned by racial factors. His despair is the despair of the sensitive black ghetto youngster feeling the stifling effect of his environment. His need to escape is easily attributable to fear of victimization by the same forces that turn his brother's students into drug addicts or naturally sensuous women into the frenziedly pious church sisters testifying in the street. The music has a direct therapeutic function, permitting him to contain his pent-up frustration and even enabling him to temporarily transcend his circumstances. Sonny needs his music to master his potentially self-destructive anger at being trapped in a black slum. He must play not to smash somebody's skull, his music is a form of mental hygiene. In this respect, the psychology involved is essentially the same as that of other musician- or artist-heroes in Baldwin's work or of Clay Williams in *Dutchman*.

As Sonny realizes the deeper implications of what he is playing, his music acquires the significance it has in **Go Tell It on the Mountain** and in Baldwin's essays: that of putting himself and his audience in touch with their common ancestral past. In the final scene, it evokes in his brother's mind the reality of family, forefathers, and community in black life. Memories are stirred of childhood scenes of Sunday afternoon reunions of relatives and 'church folks' huddled together against the darkness of the outside world. In an attempt to impress upon him the necessity of protecting Sonny, their mother tells him of the murder of his uncle by white men and the traumatic effect of this experience on her husband. At the piano, Sonny becomes a high priest invoking the collective and accumulated experience of 'that long line, of which we know only Mama and Daddy'—one of the central images in the first novel—and mediating with the authority of a shaman between the living and the dead members of the tribe. Throughout this ever expanding perspective from present into past, from personal experience into family history and the history of 'that long line,' this telescoped racial history, captured and re-enacted by Baldwin's musician-hero, is evoked literarily in the story in images of light and darkness. There is a consistent—and ironic—association of light with black community feeling and togetherness and of darkness with a racist and oppressive white world. Thus Sonny's music has an unmistakable racial core. It functions as a means of escape from the ghetto and as a psychological buffer to his bruised black ego by enabling him to identify with and draw strength from the past and the present group experience of his race.

This concern with his racial heritage is a prominent feature in Baldwin's other early work as well. Originally intending to escape the burden of race through a self-imposed exile, he gradually discovered the futility of such an endeavor. Cast in the form of the personal myth writers often create of their artistic coming of age, his account in **'Stranger in the Village'** tells the story of how he immured himself in a Swiss village armed only with a typewriter and Bessie Smith records in order to put himself through the painful process of overcoming his feelings of shame and self-hatred through unconditional self-acceptance. Out of this experience was born his first novel. The problem of self-acceptance continued to haunt him, however, until he returned to make peace with his native land and go South in search of his ancestral roots in the late 1950's. Written in 1956-57, **'Sonny's Blues'** can be directly related to the author's concern during the first post-war decade with coming to terms with the fact and meaning of being black in a racist white world which imposes upon its racial minorities its own notions of superiority and inferiority. The resulting syndromes of self-destructive flight into 'white' values and behavior patterns and the opposite impulse of revolt generated by this imposition are demonstrated by the narrator and Sonny respectively. In fact, one might view this antithetical grouping of the two main characters as a reflection of the latent tension in Baldwin's own imagination between his ambivalently alternating identifications with the black masses and the world of the black and white middle-class in a way which is strongly reminiscent of Langston Hughes's self-confessed projection of similar conflicting impulses in himself into the folk character Jesse B. Simple and the genteel, intellectual narrator in his war-time sketches in the *Chicago Defender*.

In Baldwin's story this tension is resolved in favor of Sonny's identification with his racial past and his brother's 'conversion' to a similar position, symbolized by the ritual of sharing a sacramental drink in the final scene. This racial self-acceptance is, however, a more complex matter than has hitherto been recognized. While certainly genuine and valid in racial terms, the identity achieved ultimately transcends race to become a statement on the human condition in the modern world in a universal sense. Furthermore, it can be demonstrated in considerable detail that the story's universalizing formula derives from the concepts and, occasionally, the explicit vocabulary of contemporary existentialist thought.

As already pointed out, Baldwin's story in this respect parallels the familiar pattern in post-war literature and criticism of employing racial heroes as archetypes of the modern human predicament. Characteristically, Jean-Paul Sartre's interest in Richard Wright's work is based on the supposed susceptibility of the alienated outsider-victim to interpretation in general existentialist terms. Black critic Esther Merle Jackson's essay, 'The American Negro and the Image of the Absurd' [*Phylon*, Vol. 23, 1962], rests on the assumption that there is an essential likeness between Bigger Thomas, Ellison's invisible man, and Faulkner's Joe Christmas and, on the other hand, the heroes of Dostoevsky, Proust, Gide, Malraux, Mann, and Sartre. Indeed, in the case of *Native Son* and *The Outsider*, it has become almost a critical commonplace to regard their black protagonists as symbols of suffering, alienated, rebelling mankind. In the same critical tradition, the theologian-critic Nathan A. Scott has pointed to the kinship of Wright's writings with what he calls 'a main tradition in the spiritual history of the modern world' ['Search For Beliefs: Fiction of Richard Wright,' *University of Kansas City Review*, Vol. 23, 1966]. Scott's specific reference is to the French-inspired existentialist mode of thought, notably in Camus's version, and the grounds for the alleged sameness of the black and the existentialist experience is the analogy of the Negro's historical familiarity with anxiety, violence, rejection, nihilism, and revolt with similar phenomena in Europe as a result of the ravages of global war and totalitarian politics. The reality of the concentration camp—whether in Germany or in Mississippi—is the common ground on which the black American and the modern European meet.

Indeed, the basis for such a parallelism between the black experience and the condition of modern man was prepared by Wright himself in his threefold conception of Bigger as simultaneously a 'bad nigger,' proletarian class hero, and a symbol of uprooted modern man in an industrial and technological civilization [Richard Wright, 'How Bigger

Was Born,' originally published in *Saturday Review of Literature,* Vol. 22, June 1, 1940]. This was further emphasized and elaborated in *White Man, Listen!* (1957), where he reminded his European audience that the Negro, brutally uprooted from his tribal origins in Africa and transplanted to a Western world already in the throes of the industrial revolution, epitomizes the fate of the Westerners themselves in the modern world: 'So, in historical outline, the lives of American Negroes closely resemble your own. . . . The history of the Negro in America is the history of America written in vivid and bloody terms; it is the history of Western Man writ small. It is the history of man who tried to adjust themselves to a world whose laws, customs, and instruments of force were leveled against them. The Negro is America's metaphor.' In his own fiction, Wright dramatized this universal perspective not only in the character of Bigger Thomas, but even more explicitly in Fred Daniels in 'The Man Who Lived Underground' (1944) and in Cross Damon.

The same tendency to see the Negro in universal and symbolic terms is present in Baldwin's work in the 1950's, prompted by the same desire after the War to play down racial differences in favor of a global vision of mankind and environmental explanations of racial characteristics. After his disappointing encounter with black Africans in Paris, he discovered the close resemblance of his own experience with that of white Americans: 'In white Americans [the American Negro] finds reflected—repeated, as it were, in a higher key—his tensions, his terror, his tenderness' [*Notes of a Native Son*]. The experience is the same as Wright's, except that, interestingly, for Baldwin it seems to be the other way round: It is the white man's condition which epitomizes his own.

Thus Baldwin and his musician-hero can be seen as placed squarely within the mainstream of both black and white racial thought in the first post-war decade. Intellectually, they are akin to the ontology and idiom constituting the framework of black writing before the racial revolution of the 1960's, reflecting the prevailing ideology of a black intelligentsia striving to de-emphasize the stigma of race through integration and universalizing formulas. Through the twist he gives to Wright's metaphor Baldwin reveals the ideological perspective of his first post-war position. Somewhat unkindly put, the implicit strategy is to plead for the Negro's equal worth by stressing that the same 'tensions,' 'terror,' and 'tenderness' that move the white man also move him. The closeness of this argument to the white liberal position is neatly revealed by comparing it to the premise of Kenneth Stampp's study of slavery from 1956: '. . . innately Negroes *are,* after all, only white men with black skins, nothing more, nothing less' [*The Peculiar Institution*].

It is within this larger context that Sonny yields up meanings beyond his narrowly racial significance which critics so far have tended to stress. In the effort to make him a modern man fully as human as his white brother, Baldwin turned to the concepts and vocabulary of existentialism flowing into Europe and America from the Paris in which he was living. On this background, Sonny acquires a definable 'intellectual physiognomy' and his ideological impli-

cations can be more clearly perceived. [In an endnote, Ro adds that the "term is used by Georg Lukács in his essay 'The Intellectual Physiognomy of Literary Characters,' *Radical Perspectives in Art,* ed. Lee Baxandall, 1972. Originally published in 1936."] It is significant that the straining toward integrated and universalizing statements on man's existential condition has a special urgency in the case of black heroes. In the 1950's, it was imperative to assert the universal humanity of the racial hero in order to overcome the tragic legacy of racism in Western culture.

This is not to say that Sonny is an intellectual or a simple embodiment of clear-cut ideological aims. As Georg Lukács points out, a literary character does not have to operate consciously on a high level of abstraction and verbal articulateness in order to have an intellectual physiognomy. Nor is there any need for authorial analysis and comment. Intellectual assumptions and attitudes are, and indeed should be, embedded in the whole range of responses to the pressures to which he is subjected. In Baldwin's story, instead of conceptualizing and articulating his hard-won insight verbally to his brother, Sonny prefers to expose him directly to its musical expression. Similarly, his brother's 'conversion' to Sonny's message is not presented in terms of intellectual discovery, but as a direct revelation and a ritualized initiation suggested by his symbolic non-verbal gesture of buying a sacramental 'Scotch and milk' for Sonny as a token of their communal sharing of a new wisdom. Sonny's intellectual profile and ideological significance emerge from the totality of his story, not from self-conscious philosophical contemplation or crude propaganda statements.

The existentialist concept most immediately visible in Baldwin's story is the Sartrean distinction between authentic and inauthentic living. Central to Sartre's distinction is the idea of self-delusion. Having defined man's situation as 'one of free choice, without excuse and without help,' he argues that 'any man who takes refuge behind the excuse of passion,' or by inventing some deterministic doctrine, is a self-deceiver.' The inauthentic life is that which 'seek[s] to hide from itself the wholly voluntary nature of existence and its complete freedom.' Conversely, the authentic person is he who actively wills freedom, 'that man . . . whose existence precedes his essence . . . who cannot, in any circumstances but will his freedom,' and who therefore cannot but will the freedom of others [see Sartre, *Existentialism and Humanism,* 1946].

The character in the story who most obviously reflects the concept of inauthenticity is Sonny's brother. His whole life is an elaborate structure of false props, based on exclusion of large hunks of reality, and erected in panicky pursuit of that bourgeois chimera: 'safety.' Incapable of facing the terror of Sonny's life, he says: 'I was dying to hear him tell me he was safe.' Constantly, he dodges reality. He does not want to believe that Sonny is being destroyed, or to know how he must feel: 'I didn't want to believe . . . ,' 'I certainly didn't want to know,' 'I guess it's none of my business.' Whenever the dark forces with which Sonny is involved threaten his carefully constructed illusion of safety, he panics. A fear that feels like 'a great block of ice' settles in his belly. The idea of Sonny preferring the bohemian life style of the artist to a respectable career, or jazz and the blues to classical music, arouses in him vehement reactions of fear and anger that clearly betray anxieties beyond brotherly love and solicitude. In his puritan and middle-class mind, black music is associated with intimate knowledge of the realities of existential chaos and absurdity.

Ultimately, what the narrator's anger conceals, is his guilty failure to stop deceiving himself and to heed his mother's words that 'Safe, hell! Ain't no place safe for kids, nor nobody.' It is hardly accidental that he is forever watching life through windows: subway windows, classroom windows, cab windows, and living-room windows. His is a life of non-involvement and detachment behind a fragile glass structure liable to crack or break at any moment. The only advice he is able to offer his brother is derived from the clichés he has adopted from the bourgeoisie he is aping: 'I wanted to talk about will power and how life could be—well beautiful.' In short, self-reliance and the sure reward of virtuous living. The algebra he teaches is an accurate symbol of the kind of orderly and predictable world he attempts to establish for himself. Seeking refuge in a 'safe' profession, a conventional marriage—the safety of which is ironically negated by the sudden death of his daughter—and conventional ideas, Baldwin's narrator consistently avoids facing 'the voluntary nature' of existence, thereby denying freedom not only to himself but to Sonny as well. He commits what in Sartre's terms is the ultimate sin, the very hallmark of inauthenticity: willed self deception.

On the other hand, Baldwin's black musician-hero lends himself to description in positive existentialist terms. This is not to say that Sonny is reducible to a simple set of philosophical abstractions. In the same way that his brother's evasions are in part responses to his need to escape suffering and degradation, Sonny's acts stem from his need to break the drug habit and avoid self-destruction. Knowing the precariousness of human life in the ghetto, they are involved in real, down-to-earth problems of survival which are part of the story's fictionally established social illusion.

Within this framework of racial and social realism, however, Sonny is endowed with a peculiar charisma and insight into the nature of human existence. A clear indication that Sonny is meant to carry philosophical-ideological meaning is the repeated emphasis on the mythic dimension of his character. Isabel confesses that having Sonny in the house 'wasn't like living with a person at all.' He is not so much a flesh-and-blood human person as 'god . . . a monster.' It is as though he is 'all wrapped up in some cloud, some fire, some vision all his own.' He is beyond reach, a mystical 'presence' or force. The nightclub is his 'kingdom' where 'his veins bore royal blood.' From the beginning, his peculiar 'privacy' is insisted upon. He moves in a world all his own, a solitude in which he is supremely alone with his 'visions.' While he is performing, his fellow players are seen gathering around him on the stage as if offering up prayers to him: 'Every now and then one of them seemed to say, amen.' No doubt, Baldwin is at pains to establish Sonny as a vehicle express-

ing a vision of human life, a type embodying truth beyond the literal and specific problems in which he is involved. In several important respects, Sonny comes as close to Absured Man as any American literary hero of the 1950's. Such concepts as Dread (Angst), nausea, alienation, and absurd freedom sum up his isolated stance as outsider-hero with considerable accuracy.

His disenchantment with America and its discredited Christian cosmology has begun at an early age. At 14, 'he'd been all hipped on the idea of going to India.' He is attracted to Oriental mysticism and the true spirituality of 'people sitting on rocks, naked, in all kinds of weather . . . and walking barefoot through hot coals and arriving at wisdom.' The Western myths of rationalism and automatic evolutionary progress are rejected in favor of subjective quests for personal truths and static or cyclic concepts of time. In a letter he writes his brother, he states explicitly his religious apostasy: 'I wish I could be like Mama and say the Lord's will be done, but I don't know it seems to me that trouble is the one thing that never does get stopped and I don't know what good it does to blame it on the Lord.' The educational system has nothing to offer. Nothing in it corresponds with his perception of reality: 'I ain't learnt nothing in school. . . Even when I go.' Eventually he drops out.

But his disillusionment goes deeper than any specific grievances he may have against society. The meaninglessness he feels at the sight of the big city jungle that surrounds him has its roots in an awareness that human existence itself is dislocated. The 'vision all his own' which he has had in his solitude is a vision of the irreconcilable divorce between man and his world. In prison, he has experienced the palpable reality of Nothingness: 'I feel like a man who's been trying to climb up out of some deep and funky hole.' He has discovered the ludicrous indecency of human suffering. Watching the revival meeting in the street, he experiences anew the nihilist's revulsion for the universe: '. . . listening to that woman sing, it struck me all of a sudden how much suffering she must have had to go through . . . It's repulsive to think that you have to suffer that much.' He has encountered 'the roar rising from the void,' and he has felt that nauseous 'storm inside.' Playing the blues means facing it again and again as he 'leave[s] the shoreline and strike[s] out for deep water,' every time running the risk of 'drowning in it.' This experience generates in him a feeling of the unreality of reality: 'it was that they weren't real,' accompanied by a feeling of utter estrangement from it all, including his own self: 'I can't forget—where I've been. I don't mean just the physical place I've been, I mean where I've *been*. And *what* I've been . . . I can't really talk about it. Not to you, not to anybody . . . I was all by myself at the bottom of something, stinking and sweating and crying and shaking, and I smelled it, you know? *my stink.* . . .'

What Sonny is haltingly, stumblingly trying to convey in words and imagery of chaos, disorder, and nothingness is ultimately Kierkegaard's 'sickness unto death,' Sartre/Roquentin's 'nausea,' and Camus/Meursault's experience of absurdity and unreality. In the final analysis, Sonny is the ego recoiling passionately from the human condition, opposed to it by his whole consciousness and instinctual urge toward order and familiarity. It is not fear that he experiences, but Angst—that self-generating, abysmal dread when confronting *le grand néant*. He has become Absurd Man doomed to living, in Camus's phrase, 'without appeal.' He has discovered the truth about the 'wholly voluntary nature of existence,' life as total possibility, total freedom, total responsibility. Indeed, he has realized that 'existence precedes essence,' that there is no preordained human nature, that identity is created by the self through its choices and acts. In Camus's terminology, he is a 'metaphysical rebel' whose insurrection is ultimately bound to dispute 'the ends of man and creation' [see *The Rebel,* 1951]. The human condition is perceived as fundamentally unintelligible, which explains his words that it is the instinct of any man who has looked into the naked terror of an absurd universe to resort to any means to repress the truth 'in order to keep from shaking to pieces.'

It is significant that at no time does Sonny feel guilty about his absurdist vision: 'I'm not talking about it now because I feel *guilty* or anything like that—maybe it would be better if I did, I don't know.' Sonny's words here are a near-verbatim echo of Camus: '[Absurd Man] does not understand the notion of sin . . . An attempt is made to get him to admit his guilt. He feels innocent. To tell the truth that is all he feels—his irreparable innocence' [*The Myth of Sisyphus,* 1943]. To Sonny's brother there is something almost obscene and immoral about such a view of life. To him life is a rational and anti-tragic affair in which prudence, will power, and hard work will remove all obstacles to that 'beautiful' world of progress, success, and safety which he is chasing. According to his smug vision, Sonny's ideas are the result of his perverse pride. Therefore he attempts to impose upon Sonny a feeling of guilt by pointing out how perversely 'unreasonable' he is. For Sonny to pursue his vision is labelled as a 'sin' against Isabel's desire to live respectably, a 'sin' against himself trying to make it in society, and even a sacrilegeous crime against the memory of their dead mother. These charges fall completely outside Sonny's frame of reference, however. Sonny's 'irreparable innocence' cannot conceive of any such notion of sinfulness and criminality.

It gradually dawns on the narrator that Sonny's music grows out of a valid existential experience. Being told by Isabel's relatives about the fanaticism with which Sonny practices, he realizes that the music is 'life or death' to him. His 'education' is completed in the Greenwich Village nightclub when he discovers that Sonny's 'tale' is not just his own personal story, or the story of his race's trials and tribulations, but that 'this tale . . . has another aspect in every country, and a new depth in every generation.' The blues revive memories not only of the troubles of 'that long line,' but also of the non-racial death of his little daughter from polio. Sonny's message expands into the timeless tale of human suffering, of the irrationality and sheer contingency of existence, and of the 'freedom that lurked about us.' Describing the impact of the music on the audience and on himself, he feels that it hits something in him, and he senses the growing mood of 'apprehension' as Sonny and Creole begin to 'tell us what the blues were

all about.' Thus what the music does is to create in the presumably interracial audience an experience of existential anguish and a heightened awareness of life as total freedom: 'Freedom lurked around us and I understood, at last, that he could help us be free, if we would listen, that he would never be free until we did.' For Sonny, as for Camus's metaphysical rebel, the reason for his inner freedom is the knowledge that there is no future. Like Sisyphus endlessly pushing the boulder back up to the top of the hill, he is doomed to playing the blues. His life must be a life in the present, an indefinite succession of blues acts paradoxically bestowing upon him the same modicum of freedom that Sisyphus enjoys. Sonny's freedom lies in his awareness of the nature of existence, and it is this awareness which liberates him to live to the maximum here and now. The meaning of his life is in the struggle itself. As with Sisyphus, one must imagine Sonny happy.

Defining the blues in terms close to the existentialist sensibility, Ralph Ellison states:

> The blues is an impulse to keep the painful details and episodes of a brutal experience alive in one's aching consciousness, to finger its jagged grain, and to transcend it, not by the consolation of philosophy but by squeezing from it a near-tragic, near-comic lyricism. As a form, the blues is an autobiographical chronicle of personal disaster expressed lyrically. . . . Their attraction lies in this, that they at once express both the agony of life and the possibility of conquering it through sheer toughness of spirit. They fall short of tragedy only in that they provide no solution, offer no scapegoat but the self. [*Shadow and Act,* 1964]

This description fits Baldwin's Sonny to a remarkable degree. His music is nothing if not 'an autobiographical chronicle of personal disaster expressed lyrically' and thereby made representative of the lot of all men. The extent to which it is a self-transcending endeavor is suggested by the elaborate ritualization surrounding the concert from the solemnly 'ceremonious' appearance of the players on the bandstand to the subtle interaction between the soloist, the group, and the audience. The performance is metaphorically represented as a progressive movement away from the safe shoreline out into deep water, punctured only by voices whispering 'amen' as new mysteries are revealed. They all gather around Sonny as their priest-shaman, vicariously facing the void through him and his music, and partaking of the freedom he is able to wrestle from it by 'imposing order on it.' The last stage of the narrator's development, especially his final act of sharing a sacramental drink with his brother, is modelled on the pattern of baptism, Holy Communion, and initiation. The effect of this ritualization is to make Sonny's art a public act and a communal experience to be shared. In the final scene, Sonny becomes the bard and the truthsaver of all mortals. Acting as their voice and mediator, he is assigned the public function of officiating at a communal ritual of exorcism. Darkness is momentarily pushed back, the forces of destruction appeased. Riding on the waves of Sonny's artistically ordered sound, they enjoy a common triumph, however short-lived, over chaos. Ultimately, then, Baldwin's black musician has transcended both his private destiny and his role as a racial voice to become the modern existentialist Isolato speaking, [in Ellison's words from *Invisible Man,* 1952] 'on the lower frequencies,' for all human beings. Before the fact of absurdity, all racial and personal distinctions fade away, and the blues become the tragic song of all men.

This is the trans-racial Sonny the story has been straining toward all along, and the underlying ideological requirements motivating Baldwin's character portrayal have already been hinted at. That such an interpretation is not wholly arbitrary is demonstrated by a recent short story by Sam Greenlee which is an explicit rebuttal of 'Sonny's Blues' on ideological grounds.

Coming out of the new mood of blackness and celebration of racial solidarity among the post-Wright-Ellison-Baldwin generation, 'Sonny's Not Blue' [collected in *Black Short Story Anthology,* edited by Woodie King, 1972] is designed to counteract what the author sees as the spirit of 'white' individualism, integrationism, and defeatist resignation in Baldwin's story. Greenlee's Sonny is firmly anchored in the community and his actions subject to scrutiny by the group. Faced with the necessity of doing better in school, he does not, like his namesake of 15 years before, drop out, but receives the full support of his racial group who actively encourage him to improve himself so that his achievement will reflect favourably on the whole group. All the blacks in Sonny's housing project feel and act as one family. Whenever the welfare checks arrive late, the principle of group cooperation and solidarity starts operating. There are communal celebrations every time someone stops conking their hair and starts wearing a ''Fro.' They all stick together in manipulating the welfare agency. The 'white' Standard English insisted upon by the school system is rejected in favor of Black English. Healthy, unpolluted soul food is eaten. Sonny's mother is no meek praying woman scrubbing the white folks' floors, but a proud, resourceful person who takes Sonny to concerts at the Afro-Arts Theatre. The milk he drinks is 'Joe Louis milk,' and when he dreams of buying his mother a color television set, it is for the purpose of enabling her to watch the black color of Aretha Franklin's skin.

The spirit of the story is in deliberate contrast to 'Sonny's Blues.' The virtues of blackness are extolled. The social life of the group seems patterned on African-style village communism in which the individual has no life apart from the tribal family and where individual ambition finds its fulfillment within the context of the group. In contrast to the defensively struggling loner in Baldwin's story, Greenlee's black characters realize themselves through racial solidarity and collective action. His Sonny is emphatically *not* 'blue.' Reclaimed by his Afro-American tribe, he is not tained by the spirit of resignation and decadent despair in which Baldwin's 'whitewashed' Sonny, cut off from his tribal roots, permits himself to indulge. Seen from Greenlee's ideological standpoint, Baldwin's existentialist hero is anathema to the needs of the black cause in the 1960's and '70's. Even in his most assertive moments he appears curiously defensive. His triumphs are temporary. Although he is provided with the privilege of a usable racial past and a sense of community, the value of these resources is heavily restricted. The usable part of his past is limited to the black urban experience, the Southern folk culture being dismissed by Sonny as 'that old-time, down-home crap.' For all his discovery of a racial community, he remains the solitary individual going it alone. History are recognized as resources, but they can only be of help in enduring the paralyzing feeling of absurdity which is a symptom of white decadence in the first place. From the point of view of the *engagé* black literature of recent years, Baldwin's vision is too pessimistic, individualistic, and white-oriented to be acceptable.

Thus, ironically, the very qualities which were meant to prove Sonny's universal humanity and modernity, and hence his equality with the white man, were what made him most offensive in the eyes of the next generation of black writers. What Sonny proved to Greenlee and Kelley in the 1960's was not his equality with whites in a commonly shared humanity, but his author's submission to the allegedly decadent values of a decaying Western civilization. The ideological situation confronting the black community and the black writer in the post-civil-rights era was to require an esthetic and a conception of literary character very different from those that produced Baldwin's musician-hero.

Donald C. Murray   (essay date Fall 1977)

SOURCE: "James Baldwin's 'Sonny's Blues': Complicated and Simple," in *Studies in Short Fiction,* Vol. 14, No. 4, Fall, 1977, pp. 353-57.

[*In the following essay, portions of which appeared in* CLC-13, *Murray explores themes of identity, loss, and transcendence in* "Sonny's Blues," *linking them with the story's key metaphors of light, dark, and water.*]

> One boy was whistling a tune, at once very complicated and very simple, it seemed to be pouring out of him as though he were a bird, and it sounded very cool and moving through all that harsh, bright air, only just holding its own through all those other sounds.

In the world of **"Sonny's Blues,"** the short story by James Baldwin, the author deals with man's need to find his identity in a hostile society and, in a social situation which invites fatalistic compliance, his ability to understand himself through artistic creation which is both individual and communal. **"Sonny's Blues"** is the story of a boy's growth to adulthood at a place, the Harlem ghetto, where it's easier to remain a "cunning child," and at a time when black is not beautiful because it's simpler to submerge oneself in middle-class conformity, the modish antics of the hipster set, or else, at the most dismal level, the limbo of drug addiction, rather than to truly find oneself. Sonny's brother, the narrator of the story, opts for the comforts of a respectable profession and his specialty, the teaching of algebra, suggests his desire for standard procedures and elegant, clear-cut solutions. On the other hand, Sonny at first traffics with the hipster world; yet not without imposing "his own halfbeat" on "the way the Harlem hipsters walk." Eventually, however, as if no longer able to hold his own through all those other sounds of enticement and derision, Sonny is sentenced to a government institution due to his selling and using heroin.

With his brother in a penal establishment and himself a member of the educational establishment, it's fitting that the narrator would learn of Sonny's imprisonment while reading the newspaper, probably an establishment press, and while riding in a subway, an appropriate vehicle for someone who hasn't risen above his origins so far as he hopes. The subway world of roaring darkness is both the outside world of hostile forces and the inner heart of darkness which we encounter at our peril, yet encounter we must. The narrator at first cannot believe that Sonny has gone "down" ("I had kept it outside me for a long time."), but he is forced to realize that it has happened, and, thinking of heroin, he suspects that perhaps "it did more for [Black boys like Sonny] than algebra could." Playing upon the homonym of Sonny, Baldwin writes that, for the narrator's brother, "all the light in [Sonny's] face" had gone out.

Images of light and darkness are used by Baldwin to illustrate his theme of man's painful quest for an identity. Light can represent the harsh glare of reality, the bitter conditions of ghetto existence which harden and brutalize the young. Early in the story the narrator comes upon a boy in the shadow of a doorway, a psychologically stunted creature "looking just like Sonny," "partly like a dog, partly like a cunning child." Shortly thereafter he watches a barmaid in a dingy pub and notes that, "When she smiled one saw the little girl, one sensed the doomed, still-struggling woman beneath the battered face of the semi-whore." Both figures will appear again, in other forms, during the revival meeting later in the story. At this point, however, the narrator turns away and goes on "down the steps" into the subway. He retreats from the light, however dim.

Another kind of light is that of the movie theater, the light which casts celluloid illusions on the screen. It is this light, shrouded in darkness, which allows the ghetto-dwellers' temporary relief from their condition. "All they really knew were two darknesses," Baldwin writes, "the darkness of their lives, which was now closing in on them, and the darkness of the movies, which had blinded them to that other darkness." This image of the movie theater neatly represents the state of people who are at once together and alone, seated side-by-side yet without communication. Baldwin deftly fuses the theater and subway images: "They were growing up with a rush and their heads bumped abruptly against the low ceiling of their actual possibilities." The realities are far different from the idealistic dreams of the cinema; as outside the subway window, so behind the cinema screen there is nothing but roaring darkness.

There is no escape from the darkness for Sonny and his family. Dreams and aspirations are always dispelled, the narrator comments, because someone will always "get up and turn on the light." "And when light fills the room," he continues, "the child is filled with darkness." Grieved by the death of his child, fortuitously named Grace, and aware of the age difference between himself and Sonny, the narrator seems unconsciously to seek out the childlike

qualities of everyone he meets. He is not quite the self-satisfied conformist which some critics have made him out to be. He looks back toward a period in the lives of others when they presumably were not tormented by the need to choose between modes of living and to assert themselves. To the extent that he is given to this psychological penchant, the narrator is close in age to Sonny and **"Sonny's Blues"** is the story of the narrator's dawning self-awareness. The revelation of his father's brother's murder and the fact of Grace's death make Sonny's troubles real for the narrator and prompt the latter's growth in awareness.

To be aware of oneself, Baldwin believes, is to feel a sense of loss, to know where we are and what we've left behind. Sonny's presence forces the narrator to examine his own past; that is, the past which he left behind in the ghetto ("the vivid, killing streets of our childhood") and, before that, in the South. "Some escaped the trap," the narrator notes, "most didn't." "Those who got out always left something of themselves behind," he continues, "as some animals amputate a leg and leave it in the trap." The image is violent and is in keeping with the narrator's tendency to see people "encircled by disaster." The violence reminds us of the fate of the narrator's uncle, a kind of black Orpheus who, carrying his guitar, was deliberately run-down by a group of drunken whites. The narrator's father, we are told, was permanently disturbed by the slaughter of his brother. The age difference between the narrator and Sonny, like that between the narrator and his uncle and that between Sonny and his fellow musician Creole, all suggest that the fates of the generations are similar, linked by influences and effects. "The same things happen," the narrator reflects, "[our children will] have the same things to remember."

So, too, the story is cyclical. We begin in the present, move into the immediate past, then into the more remote past of the narrator's family, then forward to the time of the narrator's marriage and his early conversations with Sonny about his proposed career as a musician, thereafter to Sonny's release from prison and his most recent discussion of music ("It makes you feel—in control"), and finally to the night club episode in the immediate present. Similarities in characters and events link the various sections of the story. The barmaid in the opening section, who was "still keeping time to the music," and the boy whose bird-like whistling just holds its own amid the noise, are linked to the revivalists, whose "singing filled the air," and to Sonny, whose culture hero is "Bird" Parker and whose role is to create music rather than merely keep time. The revivalists are singing near the housing project whose "beat-looking grass lying around isn't enough to make [the inhabitants'] lives green." Looking like one of the narrator's schoolboys, Sonny watches the three sisters and brother in black and carries a notebook "with a green cover," emblematic of the creative life he hopes to lead. Unlike his brother's forced payment to the indigent, child-like man, Sonny drops change into the revivalists' tambourine and the instrument, with this gratuitous gift, turns into a "collection plate." The group has been playing "*If I could only hear my mother play again!*" and Sonny, after "faintly smiling," returns to this brother's home, as if in response to the latter's promise to their mother that he will safeguard Sonny. Recognizing Sonny as both a creative individual and a brother, the narrator is "both relieved and apprehensive."

The narrator's apprehension is justified in that he is about to witness Sonny's torturous rebirth as a creative artist. " 'But I can't forget—where I've been,' " Sonny remarks to his brother and then adds: " 'I don't mean just the physical place I've been, I mean where I've *been*. And *what* I've been.' " In terms which might recall Gerard Manley Hopkins' anguished sonnet "I wake and feel the fell of darkness," Sonny goes on to describe his own dark night of the soul: " 'I was all by myself at the bottom of something, stinking and sweating and crying and shaking, and I smelled it, you know? *my* stink, and I thought I'd die.' " Because of the enormous energy and dedication involved in his role as Blues musician, Sonny is virtually described as a sacrificial victim as well as an initiate into the mysteries of creativity. Somewhat like the Christ of *noli me tangere,* Sonny's smile is "sorrowful" and he finds it hard to describe his own terrible anguish because he knows that it can come again and he almost wonders whether it's worth it. Yet his anguish is not only personal but representative, for as he looks down from the window of his brother's apartment he sees " 'all that hatred and misery and love,' " and he notes that, " 'It's a wonder it doesn't blow the avenue apart.' " As the pressure mounts within Sonny, the author sets the scene for the final episode of the story.

Befitting the special evening which ends **"Sonny's Blues,"** the locale shifts to the "only night club" on a dark downtown street. Sonny and the narrator pass through the narrow bar and enter a large, womblike room where Sonny is greeted with " 'Hello, boy' " by a voice which "erupted out of all that atmospheric lighting." Indeed the atmosphere is almost grandly operatic in its stage quality. The booming voice belongs to the quasi-midwife, Creole, who slaps Sonny "lightly, affectionately," as if performing the birth rite. Creole is assisted by a "coal-black" demiurge, "built close to the ground," with laughter "coming up out of him like the beginning of an earthquake." As if to underscore the portentousness of this evening in Sonny's "kingdom," the narrator thinks that, "Here it was not even a question that [Sonny's] veins bore royal blood." The imagery of light now blends with that of water as the narrator, describing the light which "spilled" from the bandstand and the way in which Sonny seems to be "riding" the waves of applause, relates how Sonny and the other musicians prepare to play. It is as if Sonny were about to undergo another stage in his initiation into mature musicianship, this time a trial by fire. "I had the feeling that they, nevertheless, were being most careful not to step into that circle of light too suddenly," the narrator continues, "that if they moved into the light too suddenly, without thinking, they would perish in flame." Next the imagery suggests that Sonny is embarking upon a sacred and perilous voyage, an approach to the wholly other in the biblical sense of the phrase; for the man who creates music, the narrator observes, is "hearing something else, is dealing with the roar rising from the void and imposing order on it as it hits the air." The roaring darkness of the subway is transformed into something luminous. Appro-

priately, the lighting turns to indigo and Sonny is transfigured.

Now the focus again shifts to Creole, who seems to hold the musicians on a "short rein": "He wanted Sonny to leave the shore line and strike out for the deep water. He was Sonny's witness that deep water and drowning were not the same thing—he had been there, and he knew." Creole now takes on the dimensions of the traditional father-figure. He is a better teacher than the narrator because he has been in the deep water of life; he is a better witness than Sonny's father because he has not been "burned out" by his experiences in life. Creole's function in the story, to put it prosaically, is to show that only through determination and perseverance, through the taking of a risk, can one find a proper role in life. To fail does not mean to be lost irretrievably, for one can always start again. To go forward, as Sonny did when Creole "let out the reins," is to escape the cycle which, in the ghetto of the mind, stifles so many lives, resulting in mean expectations and stunted aspirations. The narrator makes the point that the essence of Sonny's blues is not new; rather, it's the age-old story of triumph, suffering, and failure. But there is no other tale to tell, he adds, "it's the only light we've got in all this darkness."

Baldwin is no facile optimist. The meaning of **"Sonny's Blues"** is not, to use the glib phrase, the transcendence of the human condition through art. Baldwin is talking about love and joy, tears of joy because of love. As the narrator listens to his brother's blues, he recalls his mother, the moonlit road on which his uncle died, his wife Isabel's tears, and he again sees the face of his dead child, Grace. Love is what life should be about, he realizes; love which is all the more poignant because involved with pain, separation, and death. Nor is the meaning of **"Sonny's Blues"** the belief that music touches the heart without words; or at least the meaning of the story is not just that. His brother responds deeply to Sonny's music because he knows that he is with his black brothers and is watching his own brother, grinning and "soaking wet." This last physiological detail is important, not just imagistically, because Baldwin is not sentimentalizing his case in **"Sonny's Blues."** The narrator is well aware, for example, that his profound response to the blues is a matter of "only a moment, that the world waited outside, as hungry as tiger"—a great cat ready to destroy the birdlike whistling—"and that trouble stretched above us, longer than the sky." The final point of the story is that the narrator, through his own suffering and the example of Sonny, is at last able to find himself in the brotherhood of man. Such an identification is an act of communion and **"Sonny's Blues"** ends, significantly, with the image of the homely Scotch-and-milk glass transformed into "the very cup of trembling," the Grail, the goal of the quest and the emblem of initiation.

Louis H. Pratt (essay date 1978)

SOURCE: "The Fear and the Fury," in *James Baldwin,* Twayne Publishers, 1978, pp. 31-49.

[*In the following excerpt, Pratt discusses the ways in which*

Sonny is portrayed as the older and wiser of the brothers in "Sonny's Blues."]

The life of the black man in America today is replete with crucial crises on a day-to-day basis. His very existence is threatened by the inner conflict between the satisfaction of his basic needs and the nameless, paralyzing, and insurmountable fears—conscious and unconscious—which grow out of the experience of being black in a white-oriented society. These fears result in the imploding of the personality and render him incapable of coping effectively with the situations of life. In turn, the implosion gives rise to explosion, the sudden release of black fury from which white society has sought to cushion itself through the most brutal and savage means possible. It is this fear and this fury that Baldwin explores in *Going to Meet the Man*.

In **"Sonny's Blues,"** for example, we encounter the first-person narrator, Sonny's brother, who is comfortably surrounded by the trappings of middle-class success. He has escaped "the vivid, killing streets" of Harlem, obtained a college education and a high school teaching job, and he has become firmly entrenched in middle-class traditions. Yet there is a sense of uneasiness as he stares at the newspaper announcing Sonny's arrest and observes ". . . my own face, trapped in the darkness which roared outside." He has yet to become aware of the enslaving darkness within himself.

Unaware of his origin and destiny—his identity—the narrator has fabricated an image of himself, and he has tried desperately to fashion his life in accordance with that image. He now lives with his family in a rundown apartment house and attempts to maintain the facade of middle-class respectability. He is now a "collaborator," an "accomplice" of his oppressors because, as Baldwin points out [in *A Dialogue,* with Nikki Giovanni], "they think it's important to be white, and you think it's important to be white; they think it's a shame to be black and you think it's a shame to be black. And you have no corroboration around you of any other sense of life. All the corroboration around you is in terms of the white majority standards. . . ."

In a state of complacency, the narrator manages to sustain the charade until the news of Sonny's arrest begins to intrude upon his delusions. Although he had been "suspicious" about his brother's possible involvement with drugs, he could not reach out to help the boy. There was no way to reconcile Sonny's drug addiction with the white image which he had accepted for himself: "I couldn't find any room for it anywhere inside me. I had kept it outside me for a long time. I hadn't wanted to know . . ." Similarly, the narrator's adherence to white standards rendered him unable to understand Sonny's preference for jazz over classical music: "I simply couldn't see why on earth he'd want to spend his time hanging around nightclubs, clowning around on bandstands, while people pushed each other around on a dance floor. It seemed—beneath him, somehow . . ."

In spite of these efforts, the narrator is unable to repress an inner anxiety resulting from the compulsive urge to discover his identity. He is deeply affected by the reminiscences of Sonny, the conversation with the talkative boy, and the encounter with the barmaid dancing to a "black and bouncy" tune. All of this begins to impinge upon his fabricated reality, and he discovers a powerful impulse to avoid the confrontation and to preserve his cherished illusion. Yet, in spite of himself, he begins to realize the need for "seeking . . . that part of ourselves which had been left behind."

For the older brother, Sonny becomes a living embodiment of his identity and heritage, and it dawns upon the narrator's consciousness that he must find a way to open a line of communication with that past. But in the Baldwin canon, this channel can be opened only through personal suffering. Thus, the untimely death of the narrator's little girl Grace serves as a bridge to Sonny's anguish and experience and reunites the brothers.

At this point, Sonny's remarkable insight into the nature of suffering as an unavoidable aspect of daily life becomes apparent: "There's no way of getting it out—that storm inside. You can't talk it and you can't make love with it, and when you finally try to get with it and play it, you realize *nobody's* listening. So *you've* got to listen. You got to find a way to listen." It is this perception, this sense of frustration, that characterizes the younger brother's superior wisdom. As the older brother listens to "Am I Blue?" he grows in the knowledge that the story of human suffering, which is as old as recorded time, must continue to be sung and listened to, because it alone can shed a ray of light on the massive darkness in our lives. It was here, in Sonny's "world," in Sonny's "kingdom," that a full awareness dawned: "I understood, at last that he could help us to be free if we would listen, that he would never be free until we did." Thus, Sonny's brother has become liberated from the enslaving image of himself projected by white society. He has recovered a personal history and an ethnic pride, excavated from the ruins of his warped personality. He is now free to discover his own destiny. Sonny the teacher, by virtue of his experiences, becomes Sonny the elder, by virtue of his wisdom. Once the narrator draws near to listen, the blues becomes the means by which Sonny is able to lead his brother, through a confrontation with the meaning of life, into a discovery of self.

Edward Lobb   (essay date Summer 1979)

SOURCE: "James Baldwin's Blues and the Function of Art," in *The International Fiction Review,* Vol. 6, No. 2, Summer, 1979, pp. 143-51.

[*In the following essay, Lobb discusses Baldwin's characterization of the nature and purpose of art in "Sonny's Blues," arguing that he juxtaposes key images and metaphors at a symbolic level distinct from that of the narrated events.*]

James Baldwin's short story **"Sonny's Blues,"** first published in 1957, has been anthologized several times since its inclusion in Baldwin's *Going to Meet the Man* (1965). It is a fine and immediately appealing story, but it has never received critical treatment adequate to its complexity. The best analysis—an essay by John M. Reilly [" 'Sonny's Blues': James Baldwin's Image of Black Community," *Negro American Literature Forum,* Vol. 4, No.

2, July, 1970]—rightly asserts the centrality of the blues in the story as a means of personal and social communication. In the last scene, Reilly sees the reconciliation of the narrator and his brother (which certainly does occur) and an affirmation of the blues as "a metaphor of Black community." But the meaning of the blues is, as I hope to show, rather wider than Reilly seems to think, and is part of a larger theme which is conveyed almost wholly through the story's images. **"Sonny's Blues"** is Baldwin's most concise and suggestive statement about the nature and function of art, and is doubly artful in making that statement through life situations.

Throughout most of the story, the narrator is unable to understand his younger brother Sonny, who is a jazz pianist. He feels guilt at not having looked after Sonny, but is really incapable of understanding what has driven Sonny to heroin. Sonny himself is not too articulate on the subject when he writes to his brother from prison: he says "I guess I was afraid of something or I was trying to escape from something and you know I have never been very strong in the head (smile)." This "something" is never precisely defined, but it is always associated with darkness. Sonny writes that he feels "like a man who's been trying to climb up out of some deep, real deep and funky hole and just saw the sun up there, outside," and the temptation is to suppose that the bleak life of Harlem is "the danger he had almost died trying to escape." In part it is: Sonny says that he has to get out of Harlem, and he escapes first to the navy, then to Greenwich Village. The narrator realizes that Harlem is a place without a future; he sees his students' heads bump "against the low ceiling of their actual possibilities" and thinks that "all they really knew were two darknesses, the darkness of their lives, which was now closing in on them, and the darkness of the movies, which had blinded them to that other darkness, and in which they now, vindictively, dreamed, at once more together than they were at any other time, and more alone." But if the danger were simply the grim facts of life in Harlem—the poverty, the lack of a future, the dope, the seemingly impenetrable wall of white racism—surely the narrator, and Sonny, could be more precise about them.

The fact that they are not is an indication that these things are simply aspects of the larger terror of existence in a universe devoid of meaning. The narrator imagines (and remembers) a child's first awareness of this terror, again employing the metaphor of darkness; ironically, the child's awareness comes after the reassurances of church and a Sunday dinner.

> And the living room would be full of church folks and relatives. There they sit, in chairs all around the living room, and the night is creeping up outside, but nobody knows it yet. You can see the darkness growing against the windowpanes and you hear the street noises every now and again, or maybe the jangling beat of a tambourine from one of the churches close by, but it's real quiet in the room. For a moment nobody's talking, but every face looks darkening, like the sky outside. . . . Everyone is looking at something a child can't see. For a minute they've forgotten the children. . . . Maybe there's a kid, quiet and big-eyed, curled up in a big chair in the

corner. The silence, the darkness coming, and the darkness in the faces frighten the child obscurely. He hopes that the hand which strokes his forehead will never stop—will never die. He hopes that there will never come a time when the old folks won't be sitting around the living room, talking about where they've come from, and what they've seen, and what's happened to them and their kinfolk.

> But something deep and watchful in the child knows that this is bound to end, is already ending.

This first sense of the world's darkness—its menace—is soon borne out by experience. The narrator's mother tells him about his uncle's death and its effect on his father: "Your Daddy was like a crazy man that night and for many a night thereafter. He says he never in his life seen anything as dark as that road after the lights of that car had gone away." The "hole" that Sonny is in, then, is a metaphysical one, the result of his sense that the world is a place of meaningless pain. He writes from prison, "I wish I could be like Mama and say the Lord's will be done, but I don't know it seems to me that trouble is the one thing that never does get stopped and I don't know what good it does to blame it on the Lord. But maybe it does some good if you believe it."

There is, of course, no escape from this darkness. The only things that can make it tolerable are human companionship and perhaps some kind of awareness of the truth of our situation. The latter is traditionally associated with light, and it seems natural that light in this story should be the means of saving the characters from the menace of darkness. We know from Sonny's prison letter that he has seen "the sun up there, outside"; but most of the references to light suggest that it is even worse than the darkness. The headlights of the car that kills the narrator's uncle, for example, simply intensify the blackness they leave behind, and the children in the darkening living room are made more apprehensive when the light is turned on.

> In a moment someone will get up and turn on the light. Then the old folks will remember the children and they won't talk any more that day. And when light fills the room, the child is filled with darkness. He knows that every time this happens he's moved just a little closer to that darkness outside. The darkness outside is what the old folks have been talking about. It's what they've come from. It's what they endure. The child knows that they won't talk any more because if he knows too much about what's happened to *them,* he'll know too much too soon, about what's going to happen to *him.*

Sonny for one has learned too much too soon, and has fled to heroin as a result.

The dialectic of the story so far is uncompromisingly bleak. The only thing worse than the pain of existence is full consciousness of that pain; knowledge is presumably desirable but unquestionably dangerous, and there seems to be no way of acquiring it without being annihilated, mentally or physically, by its blinding white light. Even in the last scene of the story the musicians avoid the spotlight, knowing what it means. The narrator describes them as being "most careful not to step into that circle of light too suddenly: . . . if they moved into the light too suddenly, without thinking, they would perish in flame." The resolution of the difficulty is beautifully simple and thematically apt. The lights on the bandstand turn "to a kind of indigo" and in this muted light—a mixture of light and darkness—the musicians begin to play, at first hesitantly, then with growing confidence. "Without an instant's warning, Creole started into something else, it was almost sardonic, it was 'Am I Blue.' And, as though he commanded, Sonny began to play. Something began to happen. And Creole let out the reins." Playing the blues in a blue light, they achieve an equipoise. The darkness of the human situation is there in the light and the music, as is the light of our awareness; but the annihilating power of each is controlled and shaped by art. "Creole began to tell us what the blues were all about. They were not about anything very new. He and his boys up there were keeping it new, at the risk of ruin, destruction, madness, and death, in order to find new ways to make us listen. For, while the tale of how we suffer, and how we are delighted, and how we may triumph is never new, it must always be heard. There isn't any other tale to tell, it's the only light we've got in all this darkness."

In that complex experience comes comfort—the knowledge that others have suffered and endured. The narrator remembers his uncle's death and his daughter's, but is gladdened: "It [Sonny's performance] was very beautiful because it wasn't hurried and it was no longer a lament. I seemed to hear with what burning he had made it his, with what burning we had yet to make it ours, how we could cease lamenting." What the narrator discovers is the paradox of the blues and of tragedy generally—that melancholy subject matter can be beautifully rendered, without essential distortion, and produce a kind of joy. The experience is not prettified, any more than the white light of knowledge is extinguished by the blue filter; but the *form* of the vision makes it tolerable and saves us from its destructive energy. Nothingness itself assumes a shape; "the man who creates the music is hearing something else, is dealing with the roar rising from the void and imposing order on it as it hits the air. What is evoked in him, then, is of another order, more terrible because it has no words, and triumphant, too, for that same reason. And his triumph, when he triumphs, is ours." In this scene, as Reilly rightly points out, the narrator comes to understand his brother and his own place in the community; the community he acknowledges, however, is not the black community alone but the whole human community of suffering.

The opposed images of darkness and light, and their paradoxical reconciliation in the blue spotlight, outline the essential thematic movement of **"Sonny's Blues,"** the very title of which can now be seen as a punning oxymoron. The theme is reinforced by another pair of images which deserve discussion—those of sound and silence.

Music is traditionally associated with order of one kind or another (the music of the spheres, etc.), and in the last scene of the story music communicates a tragic sense of life. Listening, then, is an attempt to understand the nature of things. Sonny says, "And other times—well, I needed a fix, I needed to find a place to lean, I needed to clear a space to *listen*." The problem comes when one listens and hears nothing. Silence, like darkness, is a form of absence, a something *not* there, a quality of the void; and when Sonny listens he apparently hears only what Pascal called the terrifying silence of the interstellar spaces. Certainly the narrator has reason to associate silence and horror: the first sign of his daughter's polio is her silence after a fall. "When you have a lot of children you don't always start running when one of them falls, unless they start screaming or something. And, this time, Grace was quiet. Yet, Isabel says that when she heard that *thump* and then that silence, something happened in her to make her afraid. And she ran to the living room and there was little Grace on the floor, all twisted up, and the reason she hadn't screamed was that she couldn't get her breath." And, we recall, the children in the living room are frightened by the adults' silence as well as by the encroaching darkness. It is, then, no mere metaphor when the narrator says that Sonny in his teens "was at that piano playing for his life."

On the metaphysical level, silence is parallel to darkness; on the human level, it is indicative of a surrender to the coldness of the universe, a kind of moral death. Sonny expresses his rage by means of silence. When Isabel's family complains of the noise he makes at the piano, he stops playing, and his brother writes that "the silence of the next few days must have been louder than the sound of all the music ever played since time began." The narrator acknowledges his guilt about Sonny in similar terms: ". . . there stood between us, forever, beyond the power of time or forgiveness, the fact that I had held silence—so long!—when he had needed human speech to help him." After Sonny's release from prison the brothers do talk, but not with any real ease. "I wanted to say more, but I couldn't." It is only in the nightclub that any real communication occurs, and then in wordless ways. Sonny's music breaks the silence that has existed between the brothers, and breaks down the wall of reserve that has removed the narrator, for all practical purposes, from the human community. He teaches algebra—an abstract subject—and lives *above* Harlem in a housing project which "looks like a parody of the good, clean, faceless life." Himself almost faceless, he never reveals his name and says nothing about the effect his daughter's death had upon him: it is only as he listens to Sonny in the nightclub that he remembers the family's troubles and feels his tears begin to rise.

The moment of his redemption is no easy triumph of art, however. He remains aware "that this was only a moment, that the world waited outside, as hungry as a tiger, and that trouble stretched above us, longer than the sky." The music is, as poetry was for Robert Frost, a momentary stay against confusion, not an alternative to the real world. Lest the point be missed, Baldwin has included a guitar in the scene of the uncle's death: no Orphean lyre, it is destroyed along with its owner.

We have established, then, that Baldwin's ideas about the nature and function of art are conveyed more by the images of the story than by its narrative. Even in the last paragraph of **"Sonny's Blues,"** new images appear to deepen the argument. The narrator sends a round of drinks to the band: "There was a long pause, while they talked up there in the indigo light and after a while I saw the girl put a Scotch and milk on top of the piano for Sonny. He didn't seem to notice it, but just before they started playing again, he sipped from it and looked toward me, and nodded. Then he put it back on top of the piano. For me, then, as they began to play again, it glowed and shook above my brother's head like the very cup of trembling." Like many of Baldwin's images, this contains several levels of meaning. The drink is both a Damoclean sword and the cup of the brothers' communion of understanding; Donald Murray sees it as "the Grail, the goal of the quest and the emblem of initiation." It is also "the cup of trembling" referred to in Isaiah (51, 17-23). The passage alluded to suggests, in the context of the story, both despair ("There is none to guide her") and the universality of suffering—a suffering which is momentarily in abeyance, but which can return, like "the trouble stretched above us," at any moment.

Having said that, we have perhaps said enough; but a rereading of the story suggests other and deeper meanings in the image. There are repeated references in the story to trembling and shaking, usually as an appropriately fearful response to the silence and darkness of the world. At the beginning of the story, after reading of Sonny's arrest, the narrator encounters one of Sonny's old high school friends who is coming down from a "high," reentering the world, and "shaking as though he were going to fall apart." Later, when Sonny explains why some jazzmen use heroin, he says "It's not so much to *play*. It's to *stand* it, to be able to make it at all. On any level. . . . In order to keep from shaking to pieces." His own experience has shown him the necessity of facing the abyss: "I can never tell you. I was all by myself at the bottom of something, stinking and sweating and crying and shaking, and I smelled it, you know? *my* stink, and I thought I'd die if I couldn't get away from it and yet, all the same, I knew that everything I was doing was just locking me in with it. . . . I didn't know, I still *don't* know, something kept telling me that maybe it was good to smell your own stink, but I didn't think that *that* was what I'd been trying to do—and—who can stand it?" What Sonny has learned is part of the lesson all tragic heroes learn in their extremity: when Gloucester says to Lear "O, let me kiss that hand," Lear answers, "Let me wipe it first; it smells of mortality."

The wrong way of coping with the trembling is to retreat into illusion, as one does with heroin; the right way is to face the abyss in the manageable form that art gives it. The trembling of the drink is the authentic human trembling in the face of the empty immensity of the universe, but it is controlled by art—by the form of the glass and by the piano which causes the trembling. Once again, we are presented with an image of potentially destructive energy controlled and contained, as the white light is controlled and contained by the blue filter. It would not be going too far, I think, to see in the drink itself another emblem, the Scotch representing the harshness of reality and the milk the smoothness of art.

"Sonny's Blues" is so complete a treatment of the art-theme that it includes bad art as well as good, and suggests its effects. Bad art, like heroin, is merely a refuge from the real world. Early in the story, in a passage cited earlier, the narrator mentions the boys who spend their time in "the darkness of the movies, which had blinded them to that other darkness." Like the blue spotlight, the movie screen is a modulated light; unlike the spotlight, it illuminates nothing, providing only sterile fantasies which feed the boys' rage. The narrator says that they are "at once more together than they were at any other time, and more alone." Their fellowship is as delusory as the version of reality on the screen, for they are united only in frustration and anger; each of them dreams alone, "vindictively." The blues, on the other hand, provide a real sense of community, as does the music of the street revival: ". . . the music seemed to soothe a poison out of them; and time seemed, nearly, to fall away from the sullen, belligerent, battered faces, as though they were fleeing back to their first condition, while dreaming of their last." The singers address each other as "Sister," anticipating the narrator's recognition of brotherhood (literal and figurative) in the last scene.

The other form of false art in the story, though it is mentioned only once, is television, and here again an image is paired with its opposite. At various points in the story the narrator finds himself by a window, and his looking out is obviously analogous in meaning to the act of listening. Sonny, more of a seeker than his brother, is drawn to the window "as though it were the lodestone rock." Most of the inhabitants of the housing project, on the other hand, "don't bother with the windows, they watch the TV screen instead."

Beyond the narrative events of **"Sonny's Blues,"** then, is a level of symbolic discourse on the relation of art and life. Art is distinguished from fantasy by contrast with heroin and the cheap satisfactions of film and television; it is associated with light, sound, and form, and stands against darkness, silence, and "fear and trembling." But if it is to be good art and provide a true picture of experience, it must include the elements it fights against—hence the paradoxical nature of Baldwin's emblems of art: the union of darkness and light, of form and the trembling which shakes things apart, of the roar from the void and the order of music. These and the other pairs of opposites I have mentioned (sound and silence, window and television, tragic matter and joyous form) suggest that the whole story, including the characterization of the brothers, is based on the idea of contrast or paradox—a suspicion borne out by even the most casual details in the story. The narrator, for example, hears a boy whistling a tune which is, like the story itself, "at once very complicated and very simple."

But we should be loath to describe any story as though it were an essay, however fine. Critical paraphrase tends to reduce narrative to a structure of symbols and ideas, and what makes **"Sonny's Blues"** a compelling story is its rendering of life, not its comments on art. It is similar to Baldwin's other fiction in its insistence that people must understand their past if they are to have any future. The

An excerpt from "Sonny's Blues"

Then he bought a record player and started playing records. He'd play one record over and over again, all day long sometimes, and he'd improvise along with it on the piano. Or he'd play one section of the record, one chord, one change, one progression, then he'd do it on the piano. Then back to the record. Then back to the piano.

Well, I really don't know how they stood it. Isabel finally confessed that it wasn't like living with a person at all, it was like living with sound. And the sound didn't make any sense to her, didn't make any sense to any of them—naturally. They began, in a way, to be afflicted by this presence that was living in their home. It was as though Sonny were some sort of god, or monster. He moved in an atmosphere which wasn't like theirs at all. They fed him and he ate, he washed himself, he walked in and out of their door; he certainly wasn't nasty or unpleasant or rude, Sonny isn't any of those things; but it was as though he were all wrapped up in some cloud, some fire, some vision all his own; and there wasn't any way to reach him.

At the same time, he wasn't really a man yet, he was still a child, and they had to watch out for him in all kinds of ways. They certainly couldn't throw him out. Neither did they dare to make a great scene about that piano because even they dimly sensed, as I sensed, from so many thousands of miles away, that Sonny was at that piano playing for his life.

But he hadn't been going to school. One day a letter came from the school board and Isabel's mother got it—there had, apparently, been other letters but Sonny had torn them up. This day, when Sonny came in, Isabel's mother showed him the letter and asked where he'd been spending his time. And she finally got it out of him that he'd been down in Greenwich Village, with musicians and other characters, in a white girl's apartment. And this scared her and she started to scream at him and what came up, once she began—though she denies it to this day—was what sacrifices they were making to give Sonny a decent home and how little he appreciated it.

Sonny didn't play the piano that day. By evening, Isabel's mother had calmed down but then there was the old man to deal with, and Isabel herself. Isabel says she did her best to be calm but she broke down and started crying. She says she just watched Sonny's face. She could tell, by watching him, what was happening with him. And what was happening was that they penetrated his cloud, they had reached him. Even if their fingers had been a thousand times more gentle than human fingers ever are, he could hardly help feeling that they had stripped him naked and were spitting on that nakedness. For he also had to see that his presence, that music, which was life or death to him, had been torture for them and that they had endured it, not at all for his sake, but only for mine. And Sonny couldn't take that. He can take it a little better today than he could then but he's still not very good at it and, frankly, I don't know anybody who is.

James Baldwin, "Sonny's Blues," in his Going to Meet the Man, *Dial Press, 1965.*

narrator must work through his and Sonny's past—as well as his father's and uncle's—if he is to move forward. In the nightclub, with his memories of hard times, he thinks that Sonny "could help us to be free if we would listen, that he would never be free until we did." This theme informs Baldwin's social criticism as well: America, too, must face the reality of its past and clear a space in which to listen. In **"Sonny's Blues,"** the themes of art and life converge, for the chief obstacle to our obtaining a clear view of the past, individually or as a people, is simply our preference for bad art, for the pleasant lies which the media peddle and we in our sadness desire.

Keith E. Byerman (essay date Fall 1982)

SOURCE: "Words and Music: Narrative Ambiguity in 'Sonny's Blues'," in *Studies in Short Fiction,* Vol. 19, No. 4, Fall, 1982, pp. 367-72.

[*In the following essay, Byerman analyzes the narrator's discourse in "Sonny's Blues," arguing that his use of language necessarily contains and blunts the impact of his experiences. Byerman further states that Baldwin's body of work stands in ironic contradiction to the notion that language is insufficient to convey reality.*]

"Sonny's Blues" has generally been accorded status as the best of James Baldwin's short stories. It tells of the developing relationship between Sonny, a musician and drug addict, and the narrator, his brother, who feels a conflict between the security of his middle-class life and the emotional risks of brotherhood with Sonny. The critics, who differ on whether the story is primarily Sonny's or the narrator's, generally agree that it resolves its central conflict. If, however, resolution is not assumed but taken as problematical, then new thematic and structural possibilities are revealed. The story becomes a study of the nature and relationship of art and language. The commentary on the story has centered on the moral issue; the purpose of this essay is to focus on the underlying aesthetic question.

According to Jonathan Culler, resolution can be accomplished in a story when a message is received or a code deciphered [*Structuralist Poetics: Structuralism, Linguistics, and the Study of Literature,* Cornell University Press, 1975]. In most cases the message is withheld in some manner—through deception, innocence, or ignorance—until a key moment in the narrative. In the case of **"Sonny's Blues,"** however, the message is apparent from the beginning and is repeatedly made available to the narrator. The story, in part, is about his misreadings; more importantly, it is about his inability to read properly. The source of this inability is his reliance on a language that is at once rationalistic and metaphoric. His sentences are always complete and balanced, and his figurative language puts on display his literary intelligence. Even in the description of his own emotional states, the verbal pattern overshadows the experience. Whenever the message is delivered, he evades it through language; he creates and then reads substitute texts, such as the messenger, or distorts the sense of the message by changing it to fit his preconceived ideas.

The message is first presented in the simplest, most straightforward manner, as a newspaper story: "I read about it in the paper, in the subway, on my way to work. I read it, and I couldn't believe it, and I read it again. Then perhaps I just stared at it, at the newsprint spelling out his name, spelling out the story." The information is clearly there, "spelled out," a text that cannot be ignored. But the narrator's immediate action is to refract his emotions through metaphor: "I stared at it in the swinging lights of the subway car, and in the faces and bodies of the people, and in my own face, trapped in the darkness which roared outside." This oblique allusion to the underground man is followed in the next paragraph by a reference to the ice at the center of his emotional Inferno. What is noteworthy is that these images call attention to themselves as images and not simply as natural expressions of emotional intensity. His response has built into it a strong sense of the need for proper verbal expression. This deflection from emotion to art is accompanied by repeated statements on the impossibility of believing the message.

The second scene dramatizes and verifies the information presented by the newspaper story. The narrator encounters an addict who had been a friend of Sonny's. In fact, "I saw this boy standing in the shadow of a doorway, looking just like Sonny." Again there is a darkness and an explicit identification with Sonny. Again there is distancing through figurative language: "But now, abruptly, I hated him. I couldn't stand the way he looked at me, partly like a dog, partly like a cunning child." Such language prepares us for, while guaranteeing, the failed communication of this episode. The narrator is offered knowledge, but he chooses to interpret the messenger rather than the message. He expresses a desire to know, and remorse when he does not listen, but he also repeats his unwillingness to understand.

A further complication occurs when, in the midst of this encounter, the narrator turns his attention from the addict to the music being played in a bar. The mark of his refusal to know is in his act of interpreting those associated with the music. "The juke box was blasting away with something black and bouncy and I half watched the barmaid as she danced her way from the juke box to her place behind the bar. And I watched her face as she laughingly responded to something someone said to her, still keeping time to the music. When she smiled one saw the little girl, one sensed the doomed, still-struggling woman beneath the face of the semi-whore." Rather than listen to the conversation he is directly involved in, the narrator observes one he cannot possibly hear. In the process, he can distance himself by labeling the woman he sees. He is thereby at once protected from and superior to the situation. The music, a motif repeated in subsequent scenes, here is part of what the narrator refuses to know; he substitutes his words for the non-verbal communication that music offers. In telling the incident, he suggests that he is listening to the music to avoid the addict-messenger; in fact, their

messages are identical, and he avoids both by imposing his verbal pattern.

A similar evasion occurs in the next major scene, which is a flashback within a flashback. The narrator's mother, after hearing her son reassure her that nothing will happen to Sonny, tells him the story of his father and uncle, a story that parallels the one occurring in the present time of the narration. Her story, of the uncle's death and the father's inability to prevent it, is a parable of proper brotherly relationships. After telling the tale, she indicates its relevance: " 'I ain't telling you all this,' she said, 'to make you scared or bitter or to make you hate nobody. I'm telling you this because you got a brother. And the world ain't changed.' " The narrator immediately offers his interpretation: " 'Don't you worry, I won't forget. I won't let nothing happen to Sonny.' " His mother corrects his impression: " 'You may not be able to stop nothing from happening. But you got to let him know you's *there*.' "

No ambiguity can be found here. The message is clearly delivered, in transparent, non-metaphoric language. What prevents it from being received can only be the substitutions in the pattern. The musically-talented uncle is Sonny's double and the helpless father is the narrator's. This parallel structure makes the point obvious to the reader, but the fact that it is *only* parallel justifies the continuation of the narrative. In his positivistic way, the narrator will not believe what does not occur to his immediate experience or what cannot be contained within his linguistic net. His mother's fatalistic message cannot be so contained. Thus, the story must continue until he has both evidence and the means of controlling it.

The final scene of the story, instead of validating the meaning, only deepens the ambiguity. The bar where Sonny plays and the people in it are presented as alien to the narrator's experience. The room is dark and narrow, suggestive not only of a birth passage, but also of the subway where the narrator first felt troubled by Sonny. The musicians tend to fit stereotypes of blacks: Creole, the band leader is "an enormous black man" and the drummer, "a coal-black, cheerful-looking man, built close to the ground . . . his teeth gleaming like a lighthouse and his laugh coming up out of him like the beginning of an earthquake." The language grows more serious when the music itself begins:

> All I know about music is that not many people ever really hear it. And even when on the rare occasion when something opens within, and the music enters, what we mainly hear, or hear corroborated, are personal, private, vanishing evocations. But the man who created the music is hearing something else, is dealing with the roar rising from the void and imposing order on it as it hits the air. What is evoked in him, then, is of another order, more terrible because it has no words, and triumphant, too, for that same reason.

Little preparation has been made for such a reaction to the music. The act of the musician seems a creative response to the impinging chaos described in the opening subway scene. But this perception springs full-bodied from the brow of a man who has repeatedly indicated his antagonism to such music. One resolution of this apparent contradiction might be found in his comment about the terrible wordlessness of what he is hearing. A man committed to language, he finds himself confronted with a form whose power seems precisely its ability to create order without language.

In this context, it is highly significant that he immediately undertakes to explain the music through the metaphor of conversation. "The dry, low, black man said something awful on the drums, Creole answered, and the drums talked back. Then the horn insisted, sweet and high, slightly detached perhaps, and Creole listened, commenting now and then, dry, and driving, beautiful and calm and old." If the terror of the music is its lack of words, then to explain it *as* language is to neutralize its power. By creating the metaphor, the narrator can control his experience and limit its effect. He can make the music fit the patterns that he chooses.

This is not readily apparent in what he calls the "tale" of Sonny's music. "For, while the tale of how we suffer, and how we are delighted, and how we may triumph is never new, it always must be heard. There isn't any other tale to tell, it's the only light we've got in all this darkness." While music is changed to language, with the attendant change in meaning, and while the obsession is still with bringing light and thus reason, the narrator is opening up the meaning with reference to "we" and to the emotional conditions of suffering and delight. His language seems less logical and self-consciously artistic than before.

The specifics of the tale strengthen its emotional impact. The music frees the narrator and perhaps Sonny: "Freedom lurked around us and I understood, at last, that he could help us to be free if we would listen, that he would never be free until we did." The narrator's freedom comes through his recapturing and acceptance of the past; the music conjures up his mother's face, his uncle's death, Grace's death accompanied by Isabel's tears "and I felt my own tears begin to rise." Yet for all the emotional content, the form remains very logically, artistically structured. Sentences are very carefully balanced and arranged, the emotion is carried on such verbs as "saw" and "felt," and finally "we," after a series of generalizations, quickly becomes "I" again. This scene only has to be compared to the prologue of *Invisible Man* to demonstrate the extent of control. Both scenes deal with the emotional impact of the blues, but whereas Ellison's is surrealistic and high paradoxical, with its narrator barely living through the history of the vision, Baldwin's narrator remains firmly planted in the bar and firmly in control of the emotion he describes.

The story's underlying ambiguity has its richest expression in the final metaphor, a cocktail that the narrator sends to Sonny. As a symbolic representation of the message of the narrative, the scotch and milk transformed into the cup of trembling suggests the relief from suffering that YHWH promised the children of Israel. Thus, Sonny's suffering will be made easier by the narrator's willingness to be involved in his life. But, as in earlier cases, this is not the only possible reading. First, the drink itself, scotch and milk, is an emblem of simultaneous destruction and nurture to the system; it cannot be reduced to one or the other. Sonny's acceptance of it indicates that his life will continue on the edge between the poison of his addiction and the nourishment of his music.

The narrator's reading of the drink as the cup of trembling offers a second ambiguity, which is not consistent with the first, for it implies clear alternatives. The cup of trembling was taken from Israel when YHWH chose to forgive the people for their transgressions. But it was YHWH who had given the cup of suffering to them in the first place [see Isaiah 51:17-23]. Thus, it becomes important to the meaning of the story which verse is being alluded to in the metaphor. If the cup is given, then Sonny will continue to suffer and feel guilt; if the cup is taken away, then Sonny returns to a state of grace. There is no Biblical reference to the cup merely remaining.

The choice of image indicates the continuation of the narrator's practice of reading events through the vehicle of his own language. But the very limits of language itself raise problems as to the meaning of the narrative. The need to turn an act into a metaphor and thereby "enrich" the meaning depends upon limitation in the use of language. The words, though, carry traces of meaning not intended. The result, as in this case, can be that the meaning can carry with it its very opposite. In such a situation, intended meaning is lost in the very richness of meaning.

"Sonny's Blues," then, is a story of a narrator caught in the "prison-house of language" [Byerman points out in a footnote that this phrase comes from the title of a book by Frederic Jameson, *The Prison-House of Language: A Critical Account of Structuralism and Russian Formalism*, 1972]. Both in describing experiences and explaining them, he is locked into a linguistic pattern that restricts his understanding. With the presentation of such a character, Baldwin offers an insight into the limits of language and the narrative art. In the very act of telling his story, the narrator falsifies (as do all story-tellers) because he must use words to express what is beyond words. The irony is that much of Baldwin's own writing—essays, novels, stories—is premised on the transparency and sufficiency of language rather than on its duplicity.

Clearly a dialectic is at work. **"Sonny's Blues"** moves within the tension between its openly stated message of order and a community of understanding and its covert questioning, through form, allusion, and ambiguity, of the relationship between life and art. With the latter, the story suggests that literary art contributes to deceit and perhaps anarchy rather than understanding and order. What makes this tension dialectical is that the artifice of narration is necessary for the existence of the story and its overt message. The measure of Baldwin's success is his ability to keep this tension so well hidden, not his ability to resolve the conflict. What finally makes **"Sonny's Blues"** such a good story is its author's skill at concealing the fact that he must lie in order to tell the truth.

Richard N. Albert   (essay date 1984)

SOURCE: "The Jazz-Blues Motif in James Baldwin's

'Sonny's Blues'," in *College Literature,* Vol. XI, No. 2, 1984, pp. 178-85.

[*In the following essay, Albert discusses the meaning of Baldwin's references to blues and jazz in "Sonny's Blues," suggesting that what appear on first inspection to be inconsistencies that betray Baldwin's incomplete knowledge of the music, may in fact be deliberate "contraries" designed to enhance the inclusive, humanistic closing theme.*]

James Baldwin's **"Sonny's Blues,"** a popular selection among editors of anthologies used in introductory college literature courses, is one of his most enduring stories because it is less polemical than many of his latter efforts and because it offers several common literary themes: individualism, alienation, and "Am I my brother's keeper?" The story has also generated some perceptive critical views, some of which emphasize Baldwin's metaphorical use of the blues. However, none of the criticism bothers to look more closely at the significance of the jazz and blues images and allusions in relation to the commonly-agreed-upon basic themes of individualism and alienation.

A closer examination of Baldwin's use of jazz and blues forms and of Louis Armstrong, Charlie Parker, the character Creole, and the song, "Am I Blue?" reveals some solid support for the basic themes, as well as some possible important thematic and structural flaws that might cause some readers to question whether Baldwin really understood the nature of the jazz/blues motif that he used. On the other hand, he may have intentionally injected "contraries" that imply an interpretation which emphasizes a coming together in harmony of *all* people—not just Sonny's brother and his people and culture.

The blues, both as a state of being and as music, are basic to the structure of the story. [In his *Stomping the Blues,* 1976] Albert Murray says, "The blues as such are synonymous with low spirits," and both the narrator and his brother Sonny have had their share. The narrator's major source of discontent has been his selfish desire to assimilate and lead a "respectable," safe life as a high-school algebra teacher. When he learns of Sonny's troubles with drugs and the law, he feels threatened. Sonny, on the other hand, has a stormy relationship with his father. He is unhappy in Harlem and hates school. He becomes alienated from his brother because of his jazz-oriented life style and his continued attraction to Greenwich Village. Finally, Sonny's using and selling heroin leads to a jail sentence.

The blues as music, as opposed to "the blues as such," take into account both form and content. In this story, content (message) is all important. As music, the blues are considered by many blacks to be a reflection of and a release from the suffering they endured through and since the days of slavery. [In *The Jazz Book,* 1975] Joachim Berendt says, "Everything of importance in the life of the blues singer is contained in these [blues] lyrics: Love and racial discrimination; prison and the law; floods and railroad trains and the fortune told by the gypsy; the evening sun and the hospital . . . Life itself flows into the lyrics of the blues. . . ." When Sonny plays the blues at the end of the story, it is the black heritage reflected in the blues that im-

presses itself upon Sonny's brother and brings him back into the community of his black brothers and sisters.

Beyond this basic use of the blues motif as background for the unhappiness of the narrator and Sonny and their resultant alienation from one another, Baldwin uses the jazz motif to emphasize the theme of individualism. Sonny is clearly Thoreau's "different drummer." He is a piano player who plays jazz, a kind of music noted for individuality because it depends on each musician's ability to improvise his or her own ideas while keeping in harmony with the progression of chords of some tune (often well-known). It has often been described as being able to take one's instrument, maintain an awareness of one's fellow players in the group, and in this context spontaneously "compose a new tune" with perhaps only a hint of the original remaining, except at the beginning and end of the number. [In his *Shadow and Act,* 1964] Ralph Ellison refers to this as the jazz musician's "achieving that subtle identification between his instrument and his deepest drives which will allow him to express his own unique ideas and his own unique voice. He must achieve, in short, his self-determined identity."

One of the greatest jazz improvisers of all time was Charlie Parker, Baldwin's choice as the jazz musician that Sonny idolizes. No better choice could have been made. Parker was one of a group of young musicians in the late 1940s and early 1950s who played what was called bebop, or bop. They developed new and difficult forms—faster tempos, altered chords, and harmonies that involved greater ranges of notes which were frequently played at blistering speeds. Parker was more inventive and proficient than any of the others. His records are widely collected today, especially by young, aspiring jazz musicians, and he remains an inspiration to many. An individualist beyond compare not only in his music, but also in his life style, he died in 1955 at the age of 34, the victim of over-indulgence in drink, drugs, and sex.

That Sonny should have Parker, whose well-known nickname was "Bird," as an idol is important. Parker flew freely and soared to the heights in all aspects of his life. He was one of a kind and he became a legend ("Bird Lives" is a popular slogan in jazz circles even today). Sonny's life begins to parallel Parker's early. [In his *The Jazz Book*] Joachim Berendt says of Parker: "He lived a dreary, joyless life and became acquainted with narcotics almost simultaneously with music. It is believed that Parker had become a victim of 'the habit' by the time he was 15." So also, it seems, had Sonny. A further reference to Parker is made when the narrator thinks of Sonny when he hears a group of boys outside his classroom window: "One boy was whistling a tune, at once very complicated and very simple, it seemed to be pouring out of him as though he were a bird, and it sounded very cool and moving through all that harsh, bright air, only just holding its own through all those other sounds." The key words in this passage are "complicated," "bird," and "holding its own through all those other sounds," all of which evoke the image of Bird Parker blowing his cool and complicated improvisations over the accompaniment of the other members of a jazz combo.

When Sonny tells his brother that he is interested in playing *jazz*, the essential difference of the two brothers becomes evident. Sonny expresses his admiration for Charlie Parker, whom the older brother had never heard of. For the narrator, jazz means Louis Armstrong. Armstrong certainly was a highly-regarded, popular jazz musician—probably the best known in the world, having become known as Ambassador Satch because of his frequent trips abroad—but among bop musicians he represented the older, more traditional form of jazz.

Baldwin's equating Sonny with Parker and his brother with Armstrong is important because it emphasizes the difference between the two brothers with reference to both individualism and knowing oneself. Sonny refers to Armstrong as "old-time" and "down home." There is a strong Uncle Tom implication in this and it is true that Armstrong was viewed this way by many of the young black musicians in the 1940s and 1950s. Had Armstrong become "the white man's nigger"? Had Sonny's brother? Probably so. He had tried, as best he could, to reject his black self through becoming a respectable math teacher and dissociating himself from black culture as much as possible. He was careful not to do those things that he felt whites expected blacks to do. Baldwin understood this attitude, acknowledging that only when he went to Europe could he feel comfortable listening to Bessie Smith, the well-known black blues singer of the 1920s and early 1930s. However, in fairness to Sonny's brother, it must be noted that after World War II bop musicians and their music were the subject of considerable controversy. [In their *Jazz: A History of the New York Scene*, 1962] Samuel Charters and Leonard Kunstadt observe: "The pathetic attempts of Moslem identification, the open hostility, the use of narcotics—everything was blamed on bop. It was the subject of vicious attacks in the press, the worst since the days of 'Unspeakable Jazz Must Go,' and the musicians were openly ridiculed." It is in this context that we must consider the narrator's concern about Sonny and the life style that he seems to be adopting.

Up to the final section of the story, Baldwin uses jazz references well, but then some surprising "contraries" begin to appear. As Sonny begins to play his blues in the last scene, he struggles with the music, which is indicative of how he struggles with his life: "He and the piano stammered, started one way, got scared, stopped; started another way, panicked, marked time, started again; then seemed to have found a direction, panicked again, got stuck." As Sonny flounders about, Baldwin brings into play two key references that lead and inspire Sonny to finally find himself through his music: The character of Creole and the playing of the song "Am I Blue?" Baldwin's use of these two elements is, to say the least, unusual.

The use of Creole as the leader of the group Sonny plays with in this last and all-important section of the story is paradoxical. Baldwin seems to be emphasizing Sonny's bringing his brother back to a realization of the importance of his roots as epitomized in Sonny's playing of the blues. Why did Baldwin choose a leader who is not strictly representative of the black heritage that can be traced back through the years of slavery to West Africa with its concomitant blues tradition that includes work songs, field hollers, and "African-influenced spirituals"? [According to James Collier in *The Making of Jazz*, 1979] Creoles were generally regarded as descendants of French and Spanish settlers in Louisiana. Over the years, many Creole men took as mistresses light-skinned girls and produced that class referred to as black Creoles, many of whom passed for white and set themselves above the Negroes. From the early 1800s they were generally well-educated and cultured, some even having gone to Europe to attend school. Music was also an important part of life among the Creoles. According to James Collier (and this is very important for the point I am making),

> . . . The black Creole was what was called a "legitimate" musician. He could read music; he did not improvise; and he was familiar with the standard repertory of arias, popular songs, and marches that would have been contained in any white musician's song bag. The point is important: The Creole musician was entirely European in tradition, generally scornful of the blacks from across the tracks who could not read music and who played those "low-down" blues.

After the Civil War, the advent of Jim Crow laws deeply affected the status of black Creoles. In particular, the passage of Louisiana Legislative Code III was devastating in that it declared that any person "with any black ancestry, however remote, would be considered black." Many Creoles with musical training were hard hit and sought work as musicians. The competition with Negroes was keen and unpleasant, but eventually, Leroy Ostransky notes [in his *Jazz City*, 1978], both groups "discovered each other's strengths and the resulting synthesis helped bring about the first authentic jazz style, what came to be called the New Orleans style."

Though Creoles did contribute to the development of jazz as it is played in Baldwin's story, it must be remembered that the story seems to emphasize the importance of the strictly black experience and tradition, which for most people means the heritage that includes not only post-Emancipation Jim Crow laws, but also the indignities of slavery, the horrors of the middle-passage, and the cruelties of capture and separation from families in West Africa. The black Creoles were not distinctly a part of that culture.

The second confusing element in the last section of the story is Baldwin's use of the song "Am I Blue?" It is certainly not an example of the classic 12-bar, 3-lined blues form. However, it might be pointed out that in the context of this story it would not have to be, because Sonny is part of a jazz movement that is characterized by new ideas. Nevertheless, we must not forget the main thrust of the last scene: The narrator's rebirth and acceptance of *his* heritage. Certainly most musicologists would agree that blues music has a complexity that includes contributions from many sources, but the choice of song is questionable for other reasons.

It would have seemed appropriate for Baldwin to have chosen some song that had been done by one of his favorite blues singers, Bessie Smith. In *Nobody Knows My Name* he says: "It was Bessie Smith, through her tone and her cadence, who helped me dig back to the way I myself must have spoken when I was a pickaninny, and to remember the things I had heard and seen and felt. I had buried them very deep." In relation to the idea of the narrator's rebirth through his experience of hearing Sonny play the blues, choosing a song made famous by Bessie Smith would have been fitting and would have reflected Baldwin's personal experiences. But this is not the case.

Why did Baldwin choose "Am I Blue?" a song far-removed from the black experience? It was written in 1929 by composer Harry Akst and lyricist Grant Clarke, who were both white, as far as I can determine. Akst was born on New York's East Side, the son of a classical musician who played violin in various symphony orchestras and wished Harry to become a classical pianist. However, Harry became a composer of popular music and eventually worked with well-known show business personalities like Irving Berlin and Fred Astaire. One of his best-known songs is "Baby Face." Grant Clarke was born in Akron, Ohio, and worked as an actor before going to work for a music publisher. In 1912, his "Ragtime Cowboy Joe" became a hit.

Akst and Clarke wrote "Am I Blue?" specifically for Ethel Waters, an extremely popular black singer who had paid her dues and sung her share of the blues through the years, but who had by 1929 achieved fame on the stage and in films. The song was written for the film musical "On With the Show." Ethel Waters received a four-week guarantee in the making of the film at $1,250 per week. Bessie Smith never achieved a comparable fame among general audiences. Ethel Waters seems to have been more in a class with Louis Armstrong in terms of general entertainment value and popularity. The bop musician's point of view was antithetical to the Uncle Tom image they had of Armstrong. Ralph Ellison observes: "The thrust toward respectability exhibited by the Negro jazzmen of Parker's generation drew much of its immediate fire from their understandable rejection of the traditional entertainer's role—a heritage from the minstrel tradition—exemplified by such an outstanding creative musician as Louis Armstrong [*Shadow and Act*]. Why would Baldwin choose a song made popular by Ethel Waters, rather than one by his favorite, Bessie Smith?

All of this is not to say that "Am I Blue?" is not in the blues tradition in terms of message. The lyric expresses the sadness of a lonely woman whose man has left her, not unusual content for all forms of blues songs through the years. But it is what Paul Oliver refers to [in *The Meaning of the Blues,* 1963] as one of those "synthetic 'blue' compositions of the Broadway show and the commercial confections of 52nd Street that purport to be blues by the inclusion of the word in the titles." Therefore, in view of the song's origin, Baldwin's fondness for Bessie Smith, and the possible intent of Sonny's playing the blues to bring the narrator back to an acknowledgment and affirmation of his roots, the choice of this particular song seems inappropriate.

And yet Baldwin may have known what he was doing. Is it possible that in **"Sonny's Blues"** he is indicating that tradition is very important, but that change is also important (and probably inevitable) and that it bluids on tradition, which is never fully erased but continues to be an integral part of the whole? Ellison is again relevant here: "Perhaps in the swift change of American society in which the meaning of one's origins are so quickly lost, one of the chief values of living with music lies in its power to give us an orientation in time. In doing so, it gives significance to all those indefinable aspects of experience which nevertheless help to make us what we are." Both Ellison and Baldwin seem to be saying that we are an amalgam of many ingredients that have become fused over the centuries. We cannot separate ourselves, *all* people, from one another. Having Sonny, inspired by Creole, playing "Am I Blue?" for what we must assume is a racially mixed audience in a Greenwich Village club gives credence to these ideas and helps to explain what might otherwise appear to be some inexplicable incongruities.

Michael C. Clark   (essay date December 1985)

SOURCE: "James Baldwin's 'Sonny's Blues': Childhood, Light, and Art," in *CLA Journal,* Vol. XXIX, No. 2, December, 1985, pp. 197-205.

[*In the following essay, Clark examines the ways in which Baldwin uses images of light and darkness in "Sonny's Blues."*]

"Sonny's Blues" by James Baldwin is a sensitive story about the reconciliation of two brothers, but it is much more than that. It is, in addition, an examination of the importance of the black heritage and of the central importance of music in that heritage. Finally, the story probes the central role that art must play in human existence. To examine all of these facets of human existence is a rather formidable undertaking in a short story, even in a longish short story such as this one. Baldwin not only undertakes this task, but he does it superbly. One of the central ways that Baldwin fuses all of these complex elements is by using a metaphor of childhood, which is supported by ancillary images of light and darkness. He does the job so well that the story is a *tour de force,* a penetrating study of American culture.

One of the most important passages in this story is the description of Harlem's stultifying environment, a place where children are "smothered": "Some escaped the trap, most didn't. Those who got out always left something of themselves behind, as some animals amputate a leg and leave it in the trap." The implicit assumption here is that childhood is a holistic state, whereas the process of growing older maims the individual. Indeed, there is frequent evidence throughout the story that Baldwin sees childhood as a touchstone by which to judge the shortcomings of adulthood.

One of the more explicit statements of this same theme occurs in flashback when the narrator remembers his own childhood home. There seems to be some autobiographical recollection here by Baldwin since he distances this material even from the fictitious narrator: in the course of this passage the boy narrator is transmuted into an autonomous and anonymous "child":

> And the living room would be full of church folks and relatives. There they sit, in chairs all around the living room, and the night is creeping up outside, but nobody knows it yet. You can see the darkness growing against the windowpanes and you hear the street noises every now and again, or maybe the jangling beat of a tambourine from one of the churches close by, but it's real quiet in the room. For a moment nobody's talking, but every face looks darkening, like the sky outside. And my mother rocks a little from the waist, and my father's eyes are closed. Everyone is looking at something a child can't see. For a minute they've forgotten the children. Maybe a kid is lying on the rug, half asleep. Maybe somebody's got a kid in his lap and is absentmindedly stroking the kid's head. Maybe there's a kid, quiet and big-eyed, curled up in a big chair in the corner. The silence, the darkness coming, and the darkness in the faces frightens the child obscurely. He hopes that the hand which strokes his forehead will never stop—will never die. He hopes that there will never come a time when the old folks won't be sitting around the living room, talking about where they've come from, and what they've seen, and what's happened to them and their kinfolk.
>
> But something deep and watchful in the child knows that this is bound to end, is already ending. In a moment someone will get up and turn on the light. Then the old folks will remember the children and they won't talk any more that day. And when the light fills the room, the child is filled with darkness. He knows that everytime this happens he is moved just a little closer to that darkness outside. The darkness outside is what the old folks have been talking about. It's what they've come from. It's what they endure. The child knows that they won't talk any more because if he knows too much about what's happened to *them,* he'll know too much too soon, about what's going to happen to *him.*

This passage has much of the same idea—and imagery—of Wordsworth's "Ode: Intimations of Immortality": growing up is an initiation into the trouble of this world. Wordsworth characterizes youth as a time of "light"; adulthood, on the other hand, embraces us like the doors of a prison closing around us, darkening our lives. The imagery that Baldwin uses replicates Wordsworth's, as does in part his theme. In childhood man is in a holistic state, closer to a heavenly condition.

If growing up in general entails the losing of an envied state, then growing up in the ghetto is even worse. The high school kids that the narrator must teach show every evidence—even in their youth—of having already "matured":

> I listened to the boys outside, downstairs, shouting and cursing and laughing. Their laughter struck me for perhaps the first time. It was not the joyous laughter which—God knows why—one associates with children. It was mocking and insular, its intent to denigrate. It was disen-

chanted, and in this, also, lay the authority of their curses.

These children are not children. Already, the seeds of their destruction are sown. These children are "growing up with a rush and their heads bumped abruptly against the low ceiling of their actual possibilities. They were filled with rage."

It is interesting to note that in the midst of this despair, the narrator's attention is grabbed by a solitary "voice" in the schoolyard: "One boy was whistling a tune, at once very complicated and very simple, it seemed to be pouring out of him as though he were a bird, and it sounded very cool and moving through all that harsh, bright air, only just holding its own through all those other sounds." As Suzy Goldman has astutely observed [in "James Baldwin's 'Sonny's Blues': A Message in Music," *Negro Americans Literature Forum,* Vol. 8, No. 3, Fall, 1974], this passage foreshadows the concern of the story, for Sonny will be the "one" child who stands out in the otherwise bleak landscape; he is the "singer" in the midst of all the other sounds. And he is the one person through all his hardships who has managed to maintain an unalloyed vision—as vital as a child's—in the midst of complication. For in this story, childhood is the measure of the man.

Baldwin makes good use of the childhood imagery throughout the story. When Sonny's junkie friend comes to tell the narrator of the fate of Sonny, the reader is confronted with a picture of a grotesque child, a person who "though he was a grown-up man, he still hung around that block, still spent hours on the street corners." When he grins, "it made him repulsive and it also brought to mind what he'd looked like as a kid." Here, then, is the adult who has never accepted adult responsibility, a mature man whose "childlike" qualities emphasize his adult deformity. Childhood here serves as the measure of adult shortcomings. And it is not the last time that the image is used in this story.

When the junkie and the narrator are walking towards the subway station, they pass a bar and the narrator spies a barmaid inside: "When she smiled one saw the little girl, one sensed the doomed, still-struggling woman beneath the battered face of the semi-whore." She is just one more example of the trapped animal who has become deformed in order to survive. The "little girl" deserves much better.

It is in the context of such examples as this that the core of this story achieves meaning. This is, after all, a story about a "baby brother." But in order to understand Sonny's position in the world, we might first look at the illustrative example of his father. This story is told by the mother to the narrator. It is meant to be a parallel to the main action.

When the father and his brother (the narrator's uncle) were youths, they were happy-go-lucky spirits. The uncle loved music, as is evidenced by his guitar. One bright, moonlit night, the father and uncle were walking down a hill and the uncle was struck by a car driven by some white men, who did not stop. The "accident" is a blatant example of racism; the people in the vehicle are drunk and "aim the car straight at him." This anecdote, or symbolic tableau, is meant to provide a thematic backdrop to the narrator's own situation. He, too, has a brother that is musically oriented. The mother tells the story so that the narrator might be more diligent in looking after Sonny. The design of this anecdote, however, is further illuminating. This incident in the father's life is parallel to the narrator's description of what took place in the living room of his youth: it is a maturing experience, after which the father's life is never the same. It marks the critical moment when youth gives way to adulthood and responsibility. And this scene partakes of the same imagery that controls the living-room scene, as well as the rest of the story. Before the accident, it was "bright like day," while after the terrible accident, the father "says he never in his life seen anything as dark as that road after the lights of that car had gone away." This accident marks the transmutation of the father's life from youth to adulthood. In addition, the hand of the author is manifest in the controlling imagery, in the change from light to darkness.

So far this essay has shown that the light and dark imagery is pervasive in **"Sonny's Blues"** and that this imagery can be roughly equated with the respective conditions of childhood and adulthood. The question still remains as to how exactly this information can lead us to a better appreciation of Sonny's character. To begin, it might be useful to contrast the narrator and Sonny. There is some evidence for seeing Sonny as a *doppelganger* for the narrator. At least, such lines as the following are susceptible to this interpretation: when the narrator discovers that Sonny has been arrested for heroin possession and use, he notes that "I couldn't believe it: but what I mean by that is that I couldn't find any room for it anywhere inside me. I had kept it outside me for a long time. I hadn't wanted to know." The *lawlessness* of Sonny is something that is excluded from the highly controlled rationality of the narrator, the very kind of split that we find in such classic stories of the "double" as Poe's "William Wilson." Let it suffice for our argument, however, to note only that the narrator possesses qualities that are ambiguous. He is certainly a "success"—he has a college degree and a conventional job teaching high school. He represents middle-class values. But more can be said. He teaches algebra, which suggests his devotion to the scientific and formulaic. When Sonny talks to him about music, he shows no empathy for jazz, especially not for the avant-garde music of players like Charlie "Bird" Parker.

Though the narrator has escaped the most terrible consequences of growing up in the ghetto, then, he still is maimed in some way—and he knows it. When he and Sonny are in a cab on the way to the narrator's apartment, he notes that "it came to me that what we both were seeking through our separate cab windows was that part of ourselves which had been left behind." Both of these characters have been damaged by life. It is significant, then, that the story opens with the narrator looking at a newspaper, reading about Sonny's arrest and then staring at the story "in the faces and bodies of the people, and in my own face, trapped in the darkness which roared outside." The narrator, indeed, is trapped in the darkness. Only the events of the story will show him how to escape.

Sonny's quest is best described by himself when he writes to the narrator: "I feel like a man who's been trying to climb up out of some deep, real deep and funky hole and just saw the sun up there, outside. I got to get outside." Sonny is a person who finds his life a living hell, but he knows enough to strive for the "light." As it is chronicled in this story, his quest is for regaining something from the past—from his own childhood and from the pasts of all who have come before him. The means for doing this is his music, which is consistently portrayed in terms of light imagery. When Sonny has a discussion with the narrator about the future, the narrator describes Sonny's face as a mixture of concern and hope: "[T]he worry, the thoughtfulness, played on it still, the way shadows play on a face which is staring into the fire." This fire image is reinforced shortly afterward when the narrator describes Sonny's aspirations once more in terms of light: "[I]t was as though he were all wrapped up in some cloud, some fire, some vision all his own." To the narrator and to Isabel's family, the music that Sonny plays is simply "weird and disordered," but to Sonny, the music is seen in starkly positive terms: his failure to master the music will mean "death," while success will mean "life."

The light and dark imagery culminates in the final scene, where the narrator, apparently for the first time, listens to Sonny play the piano. The location is a Greenwich Village club. Appropriately enough, the narrator is seated "in a dark corner." In contrast, the stage is dominated by light, which Baldwin reiterates with a succession of images: "light . . . circle of light . . . light . . . flame . . . light." Although Sonny has a false start, he gradually settles into his playing and ends the first set with some intensity: "Everything had been burned out of [Sonny's face], and at the same time, things usually hidden were being burned in, by the fire and fury of the battle which was occurring in him up there."

The culmination of the set occurs when Creole, the leader of the players, begins to play "Am I Blue." At this point, "something began to happen." Apparently, the narrator at this time realizes that this music *is* important. The music is central to the experience of the black experience, and it is described in terms of light imagery:

> Creole began to tell us what the blues were all about. They were not about anything very new. He and his boys up there were keeping it new, at the risk of ruin, destruction, madness, and death, in order to find new ways to make us listen. For, while the tale of how we suffer, and how we are delighted, and how we may triumph is never new, it always must be heard. There isn't any other tale to tell, it's the only light we've got in all this darkness.

James Baldwin has written [in *A Rap on Race,* 1971] that "[h]istory is the present . . . You and I are history. We carry our history. We act our history." Sonny's "blues" becomes an apt symbol in this story because Sonny has managed to look back at and *use* his own personal life of grief. But from the narrator's perspective, Sonny has looked back even further than that. Undoubtedly, he has looked back to his childhood, to that time before the "amputations" that formed his adult consciousness. This explains what the narrator means when he says that he "seemed to hear with what burning he had made it his." In the context of much of the other light imagery of the story (i.e., the time associated with the light of childhood), this image signifies in practical terms that music taps the very roots of existence, that it puts the artist in touch with the fluid emotions that he has known in perfection only as a child. But Sonny looks back not only to his own past, but also back to *all* the experience that makes up his history—which is the history of his race. Contained in the music that Sonny is playing is the culmination of all the suffering that Sonny and his race have suffered. Consequently, sorrow is transformed into a pure emotion that is not solitary but communal. The music becomes an expression of history: "He had made it his: that long line, of which we knew only Mama and Daddy. And he was giving it back, as everything must be given back, so that, passing through death, it can live forever."

The implication of this story is that art—whether it be the music that Sonny plays or the fiction that Baldwin writes—can give us some temporary relief from brutal reality. The narrator sees Sonny's music as giving him a "moment" though "the world waited outside, as hungry as a tiger, and . . . trouble stretched above us, longer than the sky." Clearly, the moment is worth the effort.

Sonny has succeeded in making his life whole once again. Though he is an adult who has suffered much, who has suffered metaphoric "amputations," he has also through his music managed to recapture the holism that we usually associate with childhood. Baldwin emphasizes this when he has the narrator buy Sonny a drink at the close of the story: "a Scotch and milk." As Sonny began to play again, this drink sat atop the piano and "glowed." It is an apt symbol for the value of Sonny's success: milk, childhood, and light all suggest that this manchild has achieved a reconciliation with reality that is far superior to the narrator's conventional lifestyle.

Ronald Bieganowski (essay date September 1988)

SOURCE: "James Baldwin's Vision of Otherness in 'Sonny's Blues' and *Giovanni's Room*," in *CLA Journal*, Vol. 32, No. 1, September, 1988, pp. 69-80.

[*In the following excerpt, Bieganowski discusses the ways in which the characters in "Sonny's Blues" acquire self-knowledge and the implications such knowledge has for their relationships with others.*]

For several decades now, James Baldwin has maintained his position of importance among black writers through his novels, stories, essays, and interviews, generating continued scholarly interest. In her recent book on Baldwin [*James Baldwin*, 1980], Carolyn Sylvander points to the "nuclear ideas and beliefs" around which Baldwin's works have developed and grown over the years. For many readers, Baldwin establishes as the basis of his fiction "the quest for identity," for "true, fundamental being" and the dislocations of the modern world. For instance, Shirley Ann Williams summarizes the core of Baldwin's fiction: "Most of his characters have at the center of their portrayal an isolation from the society, the culture, even each

other" [Shirley Anne Williams, "The Black Musician: The Black Hero as Light Bearer," *James Baldwin: A Collection of Critical Essays*, ed. Keneth Kinnamon, 1974]. While Baldwin's characters do show deep alienation from the world about them and certainly from other people, most significantly Baldwin's major characters show a profound alienation from themselves. That tension directs the energies of his stories.

One of the most recurrent but least defined of Baldwin's nuclear ideas is his equation: "To encounter oneself is to encounter the other" [*The Devil Finds Work*]. For several of his important characters, reconciliation with society and with each other can occur only after they have made peace with themselves. Two focal works, **"Sonny's Blues"** and *Giovanni's Room*, together define the full range of this equation between the *self* and *other* as well as reveal a recurrent process in his writings. As John Reilly suggests, Baldwin's "leading theme—the discovery of identity—is nowhere presented more successfully than in the short story 'Sonny's Blues.'" *Giovanni's Room*, often overlooked because it appears to be Baldwin's weakest novel, represents, in Robert Bone's judgment, "a key position in Baldwin's spiritual development" ["The Novels of James Baldwin," *Tri-Quarterly*, Winter, 1965]. Brother in **"Sonny's Blues"** and David in *Giovanni's Room* clearly focus Baldwin's vision of otherness requiring a profound sense of one's *self*.

For Baldwin, a fully human understanding of another person depends upon truthful self-knowledge: "One can only face in others what one can face in oneself" [*Nobody Knows My Name*]. This interdependence between a vision of otherness and one's sense of self operates vividly in Baldwin's fiction. Such mutual knowledge operates at significant levels in *Go Tell It on the Mountain, Another Country, Tell Me How Long the Train's Been Gone, If Beale Street Could Talk*, and *Just Above My Head*. Specifically, Baldwin's masterfully fashioned **"Sonny's Blues"** can alert us to some brilliant facets of the larger, more roughly drawn, *Giovanni's Room*: Brother's understanding of himself allows him to recognize Sonny's pain as well as Sonny's own self-understanding; because David never comes fully to accept himself, he never truly loves Giovanni. Among Baldwin's writings, the two stories share a common narrative structure; they echo with comparable imagery, reflecting windows and mirror; most importantly, they address, with their central energies, this human truth based on the reciprocal knowledge of *self* and *other*. And finally, together these stories reveal Baldwin's larger devotion as artist to the freedom and fulfillment of the human person.

In each story, the narrator confronts his own self-image as he struggles with understanding, with love of the important other person in his life. Though Sonny's brother's preoccupation with himself makes him intolerant of Sonny's troubles, the pain and mystery of his daughter's death waken him to his wife's wound and to Sonny's need. Brother (Baldwin gives him no proper name) achieves his identity as Brother in his listening to Sonny. David, in *Giovanni's Room*, cannot turn his gaze fully away from himself toward Giovanni. David remains isolated in the egotism of his sympathies. As Robert Bone has pointed out, both Sonny and Giovanni share priestly roles as journeymen in suffering ["The Novels of James Baldwin"]. More significantly, however, the narrators—Brother and David—contain the dynamic tension in each story. **"Sonny's Blues"** begins with Brother staring at his own reflection in a subway window and closes with his watching Sonny play; *Giovanni's Room* begins with David watching his reflection in the "darkening gleam of the window pane" and ends with his image trapped in the bedroom's mirror. Each story gains its vitality from the intimacy each narrator gains with himself through feeling compassion for Sonny and Giovanni.

"Sonny's Blues" shows the narrator's (Brother's) growth from apparent self-reflection, really self-absorption, to authentic self-knowledge gained through honestly listening to Sonny himself. The story opens with Brother's shock at the news of Sonny's arrest for using and selling heroin. The first paragraph records Brother's astonishment at this news: "I read about it in the paper, in the subway, on my way to work. . . . I stared at it in the swinging lights of the subway car, and in the faces and bodies of the people, and in my own face, trapped in the darkness which roared outside." Transfixed by Sonny's arrest, Brother identifies the dread reflected back to him in the subway window as finally dread not for Sonny but for himself: "I couldn't believe it: but what I mean by that is that I couldn't find any room for it anywhere inside me." Through Brother's further self-reflections, the story probes his feeling of being "trapped in the darkness which roared outside." Darkness outside reveals his own inner darkness.

Brother's reflection in the subway's window occurs simply because the train tunnel is darker than the lighted subway car. The outer darkness provides the background against which he can see himself. In an important reminiscence of his childhood, Brother describes the role outer darkness played at his family's Sunday night dinners. He remembers his mother along with older church folks and relatives on Sunday afternoon, talking after the big dinner:

> There they sit, in chairs all around the living room and the night is creeping up outside, but nobody knows it yet. You can see the darkness growing against the windowpanes and you hear the street noises every now and again, or maybe the jangling beat of a tambourine from one of the churches close by, but it's real quiet in the room. For a moment nobody's talking, but every face looks darkening, like the sky outside.

Brother's memory is from a child's perspective as he recalls that "everyone's looking at something a child can't see." An adult's stroking the child's forehead eases the fear caused by the coming night's blackness.

When the lights are turned on, the children are filled with inner darkness, confusion, insecurity. The children do not understand because they have not yet lived through outer darkness. In reminiscence, Brother recognizes what the adults then were seeing and talking about because now, as an adult, he understands that there exists outside a good deal of darkness. Brother's memory of those Sunday dinners ends with this recognition.

> The darkness outside is what the old folks have been talking about. It's what they've come from. It's what they endure. The child knows that they won't talk anymore because if he knows too much about what's happened to *them,* he'll know too much too soon, about what's going to happen to him.

Pain or suffering or death constitutes the bleak substance of experience from which these people fashion themselves. The adults, telling their stories, achieve a moment of authority over their experience and testify to the success, though perhaps minimal, with which, for the present, they have met the outer darkness. Because of the outer night, they have had to find inner light to live. In their talking, they bear witness as individuals and as a religious family to the presence of that inner light. After a painful argument, Brother leaves Sonny's room in the Village. With tears in his eyes, Brother whistles to himself, *"You going to need me, baby, one of these cold, rainy days."* At that moment, Brother believes that he is addressing Sonny. Later, in the midst of his own outer darkness, Brother realizes that he needs Sonny. Only when Brother admits that he lives in the nightmare of his child's death can he then understand what the adults were talking about after dinner and what Sonny plays in his music. The day of his daughter's funeral, Brother can write Sonny in jail, recognizing, "My trouble made his real."

Sonny, of course, knows dim streets as well as heroin's blankness. For him music, the blues, instead of talking, helps tame the terror of the roaring night. Sonny, in telling his own blues, gains some sense of who he is. Talking, telling, and playing the blues require a reciprocal understanding that starts with one's own sense of self. Trying to explain to Brother why he must play, Sonny describes the self-knowledge, the self-possession, necessary for authentic blues, for meaningful talk.

> You walk these streets, black and funky and cold, and there's not really a living ass to talk to, and there's nothing shaking, and there's no way of getting it out—that storm inside. You can't talk it and you can't make love with it, and when you finally try to get with it and play it, you realize *nobody's* listening. So *you've* got to listen. You got to find a way to listen.

The loneliness of Sonny's own storm tempers his spirit so that he gains some momentary hold on himself. Though precarious, incomplete, and temporary, that sense of himself allows him to speak through his music. (Ida Scott, in *Another Country,* sings movingly not because of her vocal power but because she sings out of a profound sense of self.) As Sonny achieves a sense of identity through suffering his private pain, so analogously does Brother deepen his sense of self when he finds room inside for Sonny and his trouble.

While listening to a gospel singer in the street, Sonny recognizes in her song a parallel to his own trial: "Listening to that woman sing, it struck me all of a sudden how much she must have had to go through—to sing like that. It's *repulsive* to think you have to suffer that much." When Sonny tells through music his tale of suffering, Brother hears corroborated his own pain: his daughter's death and his temporary rejection of Sonny. In that moment of recip-rocal understanding, Brother knows that "the man who creates the music is hearing something else, is dealing with the roar rising from the void and imposing order on it as it hits the air." For Brother, the musician, the artist ad-dresses the darkness outside:

> For, while the tale of how we suffer, and how we are delighted, and how we may triumph is never new, it always must be heard. There isn't any other tale to tell, it's the only light we've got in all this darkness.

For Brother, Sonny's blues replaces the family's talk after Sunday dinner. Sonny, in the night club's center light, of-fers hope to those in the circles of darkness outside. As John Reilly concludes, Sonny, with his insight into suffer-ing, can lead Brother to a discovery of self in community [see " 'Sonny's Blues': James Baldwin's Image of Black Community," in *Negro American Literature Forum*, Vol. 4, No. 2, July 1970]. Brother recognizes Sonny with his own "cup of trembling." He finally listens to Sonny telling how he suffers; in that listening Brother hears his own storm inside. Now he can fully acknowledge Sonny as "my brother." In affirming that relationship, Brother takes possession of his own identity. He who had no proper name throughout the story has learned who he is from Sonny. Brother, in saying "my brother" of Sonny, neces-sarily says "brother" of himself.

. . . . .

In **"Sonny's Blues,"** this reciprocal vision of otherness is also described in the imagery of music. At the nightclub where Sonny plays his blues, Brother says:

> All I know about music is that not many people ever really hear it. And even then, on the rare oc-casions when something opens within, and the music enters, what we mainly hear, or hear cor-roborated, are personal, private, vanishing evo-cations.

Brother, of course, finally has that something open within and he can really hear Sonny's blues. David appears never to really hear Giovanni, fearing corroboration from Gio-vanni of the needs deep within David himself. Other Baldwin characters also struggle to gain their own self-understanding as they come to know another more deeply; certainly Leo Proudhammer of *Tell Me How Long* and Hall Montana of *Just Above My Head* do so.

Brother goes on with his consideration of music as he de-scribes the musician. The artist hears something other than person, private, vanishing evocations. The musician addresses the roar rising from the void and imposes order on it. Sonny's playing provides a moment of revelation for Brother and for the reader. Sonny leads Brother to under-standing himself and others through listening to the blues. In his vision of otherness, James Baldwin, through Broth-er's and David's telling their tales, leads his reader to human truth.

Some years before publishing these stories, Baldwin of-fered a description of the truth he believes fiction must ap-proach. He writes in **"Everybody's Protest Novel"**:

> Let us say, then, that truth, as used here, is meant to imply a devotion to the human being, his freedom and fulfillment.

Baldwin distinguishes this devotion to the human being from devotion to humanity, wanting to avoid devotion to a cause or to a cultural invention. He specifies this truth necessary to fiction by identifying what a human being is. The human person is

> . . . something resolutely indefinable, unpre-dictable. In overlooking, denying, evading his complexity—which is nothing more than the disquieting complexity of ourselves—we are di-minished and we perish; only within this web of ambiguity, paradox, this hunger, danger, dark-ness, can we find at once ourselves and the power that will free us from ourselves. It is this power of revelation which is the business of the novel-ist, this journey toward a more vast reality which must take precedence over all other claims.

The reciprocal understanding necessary for Brother and Sonny and for David and Giovanni defines the reciprocal vision necessary to seeing the truth in Baldwin's fiction. One can only face in Baldwin's writing what one can face in oneself. For Baldwin, "our humanity is our burden, our life; we need not battle for it; we need only to do what is infinitely more difficult—that is accept it."

Patricia R. Robertson   (essay date 1991)

SOURCE: "Baldwin's 'Sonny's Blues': The Scapegoat Metaphor," in *The University of Mississippi Studies in En-glish*, n.s., Vol. 9, 1991, pp. 189-98.

[*In the following essay, Robertson investigates the "scape-goat" theme in "Sonny's Blues," illuminating its signifi-cance by citing relevant passages from the Bible.*]

In James Baldwin's only book of short stories, ***Going to Meet the Man,*** **"Sonny's Blues"** stands out as the best, most memorable. This story is both realistic and symbolic, part autobiography and part fiction. So memorable is **"Sonny's Blues"** that a student once put it at the top of a list of thirty stories read for a course in fiction. She com-mented, "The story haunts you; its beauty continues in your mind long after the original reading and discussion." The story's haunting beauty comes from our participation in the scapegoat metaphor that creates the intricate trac-ery which holds the story together, forming a graceful spi-ral, a pattern of correspondences which informs and en-tices as it helps us to be free.

The scapegoat metaphor is developed through several im-ages, the most important of which is music, with its links to suffering and brotherhood. But we are only dimly aware of this scapegoat pattern until we see the final, startling biblical image of the scotch and milk drink, "the very cup of trembling," which follows Sonny's playing of the blues and which clarifies the story's meaning. This "cup of trem-bling", then, is at once the Old Testament cup of justice and the New Testament cup of Gethsemane, or mercy. The Old Testament allusion to the "cup of trembling" leads directly to the scapegoat metaphor and the idea of pain and suffering of a people. [In an endnote, Robertson cites several relevant passages from the Bible: "See Leviticus 16:15-16; 20-22: 'Then he shall kill the goat of the sin offering, that is for the people and bring his blood within the veil, and do with that blood as he did with the blood of the bullock, and sprinkle it upon the mercy seat, and before the mercy seat: And he shall make an atonement for the holy place, because of the uncleanness of the children of Israel, and because of their transgressions in all their sins: and so shall he do for the tabernacle of the congregation, that remaineth among them in the midst of their uncleanness. . . . And when he hath made an end of reconciling the holy place and the tabernacle of the congregation, and the altar, he shall bring the live goat: And Aaron shall lay both his hands upon the head of the live goat, and confess over him all the iniquities of the children of Israel, and all their transgressions in all their sins, putting them upon the head of the goat, and shall send him away by the hand of a fit man into the wildemess: And the goat shall bear upon him all their iniquities unto a land not inhabited: and he shall let go the goat in the wilderness.' See also Zechariah 12:2: 'Behold, I will make Jerusalem a cup of trembling (or slumber, or poison) unto all the people round about when they shall be in the siege both against Judah and against Jerusalem.' And see also Isaiah 51:17; 22: 'Awake, awake, stand up, O Jerusalem, which hast drunk at the hand of the Lord the cup of his fury; thou hast drunken the dregs of the cup of trembling, and wrung them out. . . . Thus saith thy Lord the Lord, and thy God that pleadeth the cause of his people, Behold, I have taken out of thine hand the cup of trembling, even the dregs of the cup of my fury; thou shalt no more drink it again.' "] The New Testament story of hope is carried in Sonny's name which suggests Christ symbolism and leads to the New Testament message of the 'cup of trembling' as the cup of Gethsemane which Christ drank, symbolizing the removal of sins for all who believe and hope for eternal life through belief in him. [In an endnote, Robertson cites further relevant Biblical passages: "See Matthew 27:34: 'They gave him vinegar to drink mixed with gall: and when he had tasted thereof, he would not drink.' However, in his death he symbolically drank the cup of trembling, the cup of God's wrath. See Matthew 26:39: 'And he went a little farther, and fell on his face, and prayed, saying, "O my father, if it be possible, let this cup pass from me: nevertheless not as I will, but as thou wilt." ' See also Matthew 20:22-23: ' "Are ye able to drink of the cup that I shall drink of, and to be baptized with the baptism that I am baptized with?" "Ye shall drink indeed of my cup, and be baptized with the baptism that I am baptized with." ' See also Mark 14:36: ' "Abba, Father, all things are possible unto thee; take away this cup from me; nevertheless not what I will, but what thou wilt." ' Also consider Isaiah 53:6: 'All we like sheep have gone astray; we have turned every man to his own way; and the LORD hath laid on him the iniquity of us all.' "] Sonny's name echoes this special relationship. Sonny, the scapegoat, is the hope of his particular world.

The power of guilt and suffering is revealed in Sonny's tenuous relationship with his own brother and in his immediate empathy with the revivalists; it has been foreshadowed in the anguish of the young friend who still feels a connection with Sonny. Through these people's responses we come to understand that brothers—literal or metaphorical—rescue, redeem, bring righteous anger, and act as scapegoats to open up the world of suffering; the friend begins this for Sonny's brother, the revivalists for Sonny, and Sonny for his brother and for us.

Further, the scapegoat metaphor is strengthened and enriched by the metaphor of shared suffering carried through music—either by a young boy's whistle, by the revivalist's hymns, or finally and most significantly by Sonny's hot piano on which he plays the blues. The blues metaphor also involves suffering and the sharing of suffering that supercedes race and time and cements us all together within our shared humanity. Sonny's music—the blues—has power to transform both his and our pain; through his sharing, Sonny becomes the ultimate scapegoat.

The term 'scapegoat' means 'sharing of pain'; it implies a true understanding of another's suffering. According to *Webster's New World Dictionary,* the scapegoat, the *caper emissarius,* or azazel, was originally "a goat over the heads of which the high priest of the ancient Jews confessed the sins of the people on the Day of Atonement, after which it was allowed to escape." More secularly and popularly, the scapegoat is "a person, group, or thing upon whom the blame for the mistakes or crimes of others is thrust."

Baldwin, himself, defines for us the scapegoat metaphor when he asserts "That all mankind is united by virtue of their humanity" [quoted by Louis H. Pratt in his *James Baldwin,* 1978]. He writes elsewhere, " 'It is a terrible, an inexorable, law that one cannot deny the humanity of another without diminishing one's own: in the face of one's victim, one sees oneself ' " [**Nobody Knows My Name**]. In another context, Jack Matthews, in *Archetypal Themes in the Modern Story,* asks "When is a person not himself ?" He answers, "When he reminds you of someone else and you can't see the living presence because of the remembered image. Or when, through accident or muddled design, he begins to embody our own secret fears. In psychology, this is termed projection; in a story or folktale, it is a celebration of the Scapegoat theme." Thus the literary scapegoat, through his own personal suffering or by his metaphorical sharing of his own sorrow, may allow us to see into life and into ourselves and thus vicariously transfer our guilt and pain through him and his suffering.

In this story music is the thread that accompanies and develops the brotherhood/scapegoat metaphor. For in his music Sonny reveals both his suffering and his understanding of others' pain. His music becomes a mystical, spiritual medium, an open-ended metaphor simultaneously comforting the player and the listener and releasing their guilt and pain. No words *could* have expressed so well what Sonny's music conveyed effortlessly. For, according to Cirlot, "Music represents an intermediate zone between the differentiated or material world and the undifferentiated realm of the 'pure will' of Schopenhauer" [J. E. Cirlot, *A Dictionary of Symbols,* 1962]. The power of this emotional transfer is seen in the brother's response. For through Sonny's music his brother comes to understand his own life, his parents' experience, his daughter's death, and his wife's grief. The brother recapitulates his own, Sonny's, and the family's suffering here at the end of the story. But as Kirkegaard says, in *Repetition,* "repetition" replaces "the more traditional Platonic term anamnesis or recollection." This is "not the simple repeating of an experience, but the recreating of it which redeems or awakens it to life, the end of the process . . . being the apocalyptic promise: 'Behold, I make all things new' " [These lines summarizing Kierkegaard were written by Northrop Frye, see his "Tentative Conclusion" in *Anatomy of Criticism,* 1957]. Sonny's awakening is done through his blues, and its effect is revealed through the brother's sudden understanding, conveyed in the final image of the Scotch and milk drink, "the very cup of trembling." This central biblical image reverberates with life and reinforces the scapegoat metaphor. This recreation of life is also what the blues are all about. We come full circle.

The scapegoat metaphor is first presented very quietly when Sonny's childhood friend offers to become a scapegoat, insisting upon his symbolic action when he tells Sonny's brother, "Funny thing, . . . when I saw the papers this morning, the first thing I asked myself was if I had anything to do with [Sonny's arrest for using and selling heroin]. I felt sort of responsible." The young man offers to take the blame for Sonny's fall, but his hesitant plea is offensive to the brother who, like us, does not understand the symbolic significance of the act. For, instead of accepting and sharing the man's guilt, the brother becomes angry at the friend's panhandling. He feels superior to him and rejects his offer and his sympathy.

Just prior to this meeting with the old friend a boy's whistle echoes through the school yard. The whistle is "at once very complicated and very simple; it seemed to be pouring out of him as though he were a bird, and it sounded very cool and moving through all that harsh, bright air, only just holding its own through all those other sounds." But this music creates a central abstract image, a tone poem carrying the sadness and guilt of the brother, a simple yet complicated sounding of pain.

This first subtle pairing of music with guilt and pain sets the tone for the story. This young man, this emotional 'brother,' cannot comfort Sonny's brother, but paradoxically his sincere concern increases the brother's understanding of Sonny's problems. Further, this sad young man illustrates the community's desperate need for a savior as well as setting up the scapegoat metaphor. For the brother sees in the friend as in a mirror the great sadness and courage of Sonny. He says "All at once something inside gave and threatened to come pouring out of me. I didn't hate him [the friend] any more. I felt that in another moment I'd start crying like a child." This emotional release is the first step toward understanding and the first presentation of the Old Testament scapegoat motif so delicately interwoven in this story.

The scapegoat metaphor is next presented and perfectly symbolized by the street revival. The street people are a paradigm of life, a kind of representative cross-section of humanity. All sorts of people watch and listen to the street revivalists—working people, children, older folks, street women, Sonny, and Sonny's brother who watches from above at the window. At this "old fashioned revival meet-ing" there are "three sisters in black, and a brother. All they [have are] their voices and their Bibles and a tambourine." These people sing "Tis the old ship of Zion . . . it has rescued many a thousand!"

The listeners hear nothing new, only the old pain and suffering and the offer of relief from three sisters and a brother, mortals like themselves; yet these four make suffering real. Their music acts as a mirror for the watchers whose response illustrates the scapegoat metaphor in action: "As the singing filled the air the watching, listening faces underwent a change, the eyes focusing on something within; the music seemed to soothe a poison out of them; and time seemed, nearly, to fall away from the sullen, belligerent, battered faces, as though they were fleeing back to their first condition, while dreaming of their last." These spirituals are an amalgam of joy and the blues, touching everyone who listens and helping them share the guilt and pain of the human condition.

The revival, central to the brother's awareness since it incorporates music, religion, and suffering, helps Sonny to articulate the relationship between suffering and human understanding. Also, for Sonny, the woman revivalist serves as a scapegoat; she helps him to understand his own suffering just as she had helped those who listened and contributed to her cause. For Sonny, this insight into the woman's suffering makes his own pain bearable, makes it possible to reach out to his brother. For Sonny understands this scene. Touched by their pain, he alone articulates its universal meaning—suffering. New Testament echoes of brother and savior are palpable in his response: "It's *repulsive* to think you have to suffer that much." But ironically, the biblical scapegoat metaphor suggests group suffering as well as individual suffering.

Sonny's own pain has been personal and private. He had tried to tell his brother about his suffering in the letter from prison, but he was almost inarticulate. His suffering went beyond words. Now, after the brothers have experienced the revival, Sonny tries again to communicate with his brother by explaining his relationship with music: "you finally try to get with it and play it, [and] you realize *nobody's* listening. So *you've* got to listen. You got to find a way to listen," to distance the pain, to look at despair and deal with guilt in order to live. To play this way requires brutal honesty and empathy with the suffering of others. Sonny says, I "can't forget—where I've been. I don't mean just the physical place I've been, I mean where I've *been.* And *what* I've been. . . . I've been something I didn't recognize, didn't know I could be. Didn't know anybody could be." But the painful rendition of the revivalists shows him musically that others have been there too.

Significantly, Sonny invites his brother to hear him play right after the street revival when they talk for almost the first time. Sonny understands his own need and his brother's suffering because someone else's suffering mirrors his own, effectively causing his confession and his sharing of his own pain through his music, mirror of man's soul. Music is able to heal wounds, for when Sonny is in perfect harmony with himself and with his environment, when he understands, he plays the piano effortlessly. Now Sonny's confession of failure also prepares for the final scene where

Sonny plays the blues, an appropriate musical form based on folk music and characterized by minor harmonies, slow tempo, and melancholy words. The blues, like the tuneless whistle and the melancholy spirituals sung by the revivalists, reinforce the idea of human suffering carried by the scapegoat metaphor. For the blues, sad and melancholy jazz, are a mood, a feeling, a means of escape and entertainment; the blues, especially, are a way of sharing suffering, a way of strengthening the idea of community. The blues, the tune without the words in this instance, help the inarticulate young pianist to communicate with his brother and with the world. Thus he enriches the central metaphor for the story. For according to C. W. Sylvander, "Art can be a means for release from the 'previous condition' when it is heard, listened to, understood" [Carolyn Wedin Sylvander, *James Baldwin,* 1980].

The linkage between the scapegoat motif and the music is clearly revealed when Creole has the group play the blues and signifies that this particular rendition is 'Sonny's blues.' L. H. Pratt notes that "Once the narrator draws near to listen, the blues becomes the means by which Sonny is able to lead his brother, through a confrontation with the meaning of life, into a discovery of self." Through the blues the brothers can communicate. The blues become the last and greatest reinforcer of the scapegoat metaphor. For through the music something magical happens.

The narrator comes to understand that "not many people ever hear [music]. [But] . . . When something opens within, and the music enters, what we mainly hear, or hear corroborated, are personal, private, vanishing evocations." The same thing is true of our suffering and our alienation from others. Until we understand another's pain, we cannot understand our own. We must be transformed as the musician is. The musician, a kind of scapegoat, removes the pain of existence and helps us understand our suffering.

Sonny—the name echoes his strong New Testament scapegoat position—takes the pain away for all those who listen when he plays the blues. But as Baldwin says, Sonny cannot be free unless we listen and we will not be free either until he removes our pain—or until we believe in his ability to remove that suffering; Sonny thus serves to free those who listen as the cup of Gethsemane serves to free those who believe. Sonny's name echoes this special relationship and speaks of him as the ultimate scapegoat.

The brother, then, represents us also as he vividly illustrates our human response to the scapegoat offer. We accept, as understanding and insight come through the music; we change, for the function of the scapegoat is vicarious death. The ancient scapegoat was presented *alive* and allowed to escape; but metaphorically he represented the death of sin and pain for those covered by his action. Metaphysically what happens when we hear, as Sonny knows, is a death of our old understanding or the old ways and a recreation of a new way of being. So finally, at the end, in the image of the Scotch and milk drink, an image so unprepared for as to be startling, we see Sonny's symbolic value as the scapegoat. The transformation occurs as the music plays, because for the musician "What is

evoked . . . is of another order, more terrible because it has no words, and triumphant, too, for that same reason. And his triumph, when he triumphs, is ours."

Only in music can Sonny truly tell all and fulfill his function as a scapegoat. Only in music can he reach our hearts and minds. Thus the last and clearest presentation of the scapegoat metaphor comes at the end of the story. Here "Sonny's fingers filled the air with life, his life. But that life contained so many others. . . . It was no longer a lament." This is a clear expression of the scapegoat metaphor. For Sonny's sharing through music transforms the pain. As the narrator says, "Freedom lurked around us and I understood at last that he could help us be free if we would listen, that he would never be free until we did." This freedom is the Black's escape, the reader's escape, Sonny's escape. It is the scapegoat metaphor in action, a release for Sonny's brother and for us too. For Sonny "was giving it back, as everything must be given back, so that, passing through death, it can live forever."

The reversal of the situation at the end is important. The blues which Creole guides Sonny to play are central. For to play the blues one must first have suffered; then one creates the form to hold the pain, a fluid changing style where, according to John Reilly, "One uses the skill one has achieved by practice and experience in order to reach toward others" [John M. Reilly, " 'Sonny's Blues': James Baldwin's Image of Black Community," *Negro American Literature Forum,* Vol. 4, No. 2, July 1970]. The narrator expresses it best: "For, while the tale of how we suffer, and how we are delighted, and how we may triumph is never new, it always must be heard. There isn't any other tale to tell, it's the only light we've got in all this darkness."

Sonny's brother indicates that he both understands and symbolically shares Sonny's pain and guilt by sending the Scotch and milk drink. He affirms the religious connection with his comment, "For me, then, as they began to play again [the cup of Scotch and milk] glowed and shook above my brother's head like the very cup of trembling." The drink of Scotch and milk develops the image of Sonny as sinner and savior, the God/man, the scapegoat, the unlikely mixture which saves. This image conveys Sonny's complex purpose and suggests, on an earthly level, that Sonny's pain will continue, but his pain is shared and understood by his brother. On the second level it suggests that as God took away the pain for Israel, and as Christ takes away the pain and sin of the world for the believer, so does Sonny, the scapegoat, take away pain and guilt for his brother, for the listeners, and for us. As Keith Byerman said, "The drink itself, Scotch and milk, is an emblem of simultaneous destruction and nurture to the system; it cannot be reduced to one or the other. Sonny's acceptance of it indicates that his life will continue on the edge between the poison of his addiction and the nourishment of his music" [Keith E. Byerman, "Words and Music: Narrative Ambiguity in 'Sonny's Blues,' " *Studies in Short Fiction,* Vol. 19, No. 4, Fall 1982]. But Sonny *has* drunk the cup of pain before; now the brother joins in, empathizes, understands. Sonny drinks the Scotch and milk and continues to suffer, but part of his suffering is removed by his brother's understanding. For the brother, the action itself suggests increased understanding and a sharing of Sonny's pain.

The brother's final comment about the 'cup of trembling' emphasizes the narrator's understanding and reinterprets the image, making Sonny a true scapegoat for the reader and enlarging our vision as well. Only with the last image do we reflect on the biblical imagery, seeing Sonny's linkage to Aaron and to Christ. Then we concentrate on Sonny's name; he is transformed before our very eyes and we see in his ceremonial acceptance of the drink his function as a scapegoat, a substitute for all.

Pancho Savery   (essay date 1992)

SOURCE: "Baldwin, Bebop, and 'Sonny's Blues'," in *Understanding Others: Cultural and Cross-Cultural Studies and the Teaching of Literature,* edited by Joesph Trimmer and Tilly Warnock, National Council of Teachers of English, 1992, pp. 165-76.

[*Savery is an American critic and educator who has written extensively on African-American literature. In the following excerpt, he discusses the historical and musical contexts relevant to "Sonny's Blues," noting in particular the social, political, and aesthetic significance of the form of jazz known as Bebop.*]

Although there have been interesting analyses of **"Sonny's Blues,"** none of them has gotten to the specificities of the music and the wider cultural implications. Music is not simply the bridge the narrator crosses to get closer to Sonny, nor is it sufficient to point out that the music in the climactic scene is labeled as blues. What kind and form of these particular blues make all the difference.

An interesting way to begin thinking about **"Sonny's Blues"** is to think about when the story is supposed to be taking place. We know from the acknowledgments that it was first published in the summer of 1957, but can we be more precise? Part of the story takes place during "the war," but which one is it, Korea or World War II, and does it matter?

Baldwin tells us that Sonny's father "died suddenly, during a drunken weekend in the middle of the war, when Sonny was fifteen." "[J]ust after Daddy died," Sonny's brother, whom we know is seven years older, is "home on leave from the army," and has his final conversation with his mother. In the passage, which begins with that wonderful evocation of the coming of the darkness on Sunday afternoon with the old and young together in the living room, "Mama" admonishes her older son to watch out for Sonny "and don't let him fall, no matter what it looks like is happening to him and no matter how evil you gets with him." But the narrator tells us that he did not listen, got married, and went back to war. The next time he comes home is "on a special furlough" for his mother's funeral. The war is still going on. The narrator reminds Sonny that Sonny must "finish school," "And you only got another year." The school that Sonny must finish is obviously high school. Thus, no more than a year or so has passed since the death of the father, who died "in the middle of the war." The United States was in World War II from De-

cember of 1941 until August of 1945. "The middle of the war" would have been approximately 1943, or 1942 if you start from the beginning of the war in Europe. Thus, the crucial conversation between Sonny and his brother, in which Sonny first says he wants to be a jazz musician, takes place about 1944. If, on the other hand, the war being fought is the Korean War (June 1950 to July 1953), the conversation takes place about 1952.

When Sonny reveals to his brother that first he wants to be a musician, and then a jazz musician, and then not a jazz musician like Louis Armstrong but one like Charlie Parker, the brother, after asking "Who's this Parker character," says, "I'll go out and buy all the cat's records right away, all right?" From 1942 to 1944, there was a ban on recordings, at least in part due to a scarcity of materials because of the war. In 1944, Sonny's brother would not have been able to go out and buy new material by Bird (Parker) because there wasn't any. Bird's seminal recordings were made between 1945 and 1948. It is, thus, reasonable to conclude that the war is the Korean.

By 1952, Bird had already revolutionized music. And so when Sonny's brother asks Sonny to name a musician he admires and Sonny says "Bird" and his brother says "Who?," Sonny is justified with his, "Bird! Charlie Parker! Don't they teach you nothing in the goddamn army?" Sonny's brother, at age twenty-four in 1952, can certainly be expected to have heard of Bird. After all, he has heard of Louis Armstrong.

But it is in Sonny's response to Armstrong that one of the keys to the story lies. Sonny's brother admits that, to him, the term "jazz musician" is synonymous with "hanging around nightclubs, clowning around on bandstands," and is, thus, "beneath him, somehow." When, from this perspective, jazz musicians are "in a class with . . . 'good-time people'," his mentioning of Louis Armstrong needs to be looked at.

From one perspective, Louis Armstrong is one of the true titans of jazz. On the other hand, to many of the Bebop era, Armstrong was considered part of the old guard who needed to be swept out with the new musical revolution, and Armstrong himself was not positively disposed towards Bop. One turning point came in February of 1949 when Armstrong was chosen King of the Zulus for the Mardi Gras parade in New Orleans. To many, he seemed to be donning the minstrel mask of acceptability to the larger white world, and this seemed confirmed when, the same week, he appeared on the cover of *Time* (February 21, 1949). It would be "natural" that Sonny's brother, the future algebra teacher, would have heard of Armstrong, here the symbol of the old conservative, but not of Parker, not only the new and the revolutionary, but the "had been a revolutionary" for seven years. Sonny's response to Armstrong makes this clear:

> I suggested, helpfully: "You mean—like Louis Armstrong?" His face closed as though I'd struck him. "No. I'm not talking about none of that old-time, down home crap."

But the differences between Armstrong and Parker represent something much larger. Throughout history, African

Americans have been engaged in intramural debate about the nature of identity. Du Bois, of course, put it best when he defined "double-consciousness" in *The Souls of Black Folk* and concluded:

> One ever feels his twoness,—an American, a Negro; two souls, two thoughts, two unreconciled strivings; two warring ideals in one dark body, whose dogged strength alone keeps it from being torn asunder.

Du Bois's battles with Booker T. Washington and later with Marcus Garvey are one of the major moments in African American history when this debate was articulated. But there have also been many others; for example, Frederick Douglass and Martin Delany debating whether Africa or America was the place for blacks, and King and Malcolm on the issue of integration. But in order to look at African American culture fully, we cannot limit ourselves to the study of politics and history. As numerous commentators have pointed out, music is the key to much of the African American dispute over this issue of culture; and, therefore, knowledge of it is essential. For example:

> The complexities of the collective Black experience have always had their most valid and moving expression in Black music; music is the chief artifact created out of that experience. [Sherley Anne Williams, *Give Birth to Brightness*, 1972]

> To reiterate, the key to where the black people have to go is in the music. Our music has always been the most dominant manifestation of what we are and feel. . . . The best of it has always operated at the core of our lives, forcing itself upon us as in a ritual. It has always, somehow, represented the collective psyche. ["And Shine Swam On," in *Visions of a Liberated Future: Black Arts Movement Writings*, edited by Michael Schwartz, 1989]

> I think it is not fantastic to say that only in music has there been any significant Negro contribution to a *formal* American culture. [Amiri Baraka, *Blues People*, 1963]

> The tenor is a rhythm instrument, and the best statements Negroes have made, of what their soul is, have been on tenor saxophone. [Ornette Coleman, quoted in A.B. Spellman's *Black Music: Four Lives (Four Lives in the Bebop Business)*, 1970]

> There has never been an equivalent to Duke Ellington or Louis Armstrong in Negro writing, and even the best of contemporary literature written by Negroes cannot yet be compared to the fantastic beauty of the music of Charlie Parker. [Baraka, "The Myth of a 'Negro Literature,'" in his *Home: Social Essays*, 1966]

Houston Baker has gone as far as suggesting that there is a "blues matrix" at the center of African American culture and that "a vernacular theory" of African American literature can be developed from this idea.

What I am arguing in general is that music is the cornerstone of African American culture; and that, further, Bebop was an absolute key moment. In African American

culture, Bebop is as significant as the Harlem Renaissance, and Armstrong and Parker's roles somewhat resemble those of Washington and Du Bois, and Du Bois and Garvey. Armstrong, Washington, and Du Bois (to Garvey) represented the known, the old, and the traditional whose accomplishments were noted but who were considered somewhat passé by the younger, more radical Parker, Du Bois (to Washington), and Garvey.

Musically, Bebop was to a large extent a revolt against swing and the way African American music had been taken over, and diluted, by whites. Perhaps no more emblematic of this is that the aptly named Paul Whiteman and Benny Goodman were dubbed respectively "The King of Jazz" and "The King of Swing." As Gary Giddins succinctly puts it [in his *Celebrating Bird: The Triumph of Charlie Parker*, 1987]:

> Jazz in the Swing Era was so frequently compromised by chuckleheaded bandleaders, most of them white, who diluted and undermined the triumphs of serious musicians that a new virtuosity was essential. The modernists brandished it like a weapon. They confronted social and musical complacency in a spirit of arrogant romanticism.

Ortiz Walton [in *Music: Black, White, & Blue: A Sociological Survey of the Use and Misuse of Afro-American Music*, 1972] describes the musical revolution as "a major challenge to European standards of musical excellence and the beginning of a conscious black aesthetic in music" because of Bebop's challenge to the European aesthetic emphasis on vibrato. This emphasis produced music that was easily imitable, and thus open to commercialization and co-optation. By revolting against this direction the music had taken and reclaiming it, "Afro-American musicians gained a measure of control over their product, a situation that had not existed since the expansion of the music industry in the Twenties."

Another aspect of this Bop reclamation was a renewed emphasis on the blues. Although some people seem to think there is a dispute over this issue, it is clear from listening to Parker's first session as a leader that "Billie's Bounce" and "Now's the Time" are blues pieces. In his autobiography, Dizzy Gillespie asserts:

> Beboppers couldn't destroy the blues without seriously injuring themselves. The modern jazz musicians always remained very close to the blues musician. That was a characteristic of the bopper. [*To Be or Not . . . To BOP: Memoirs*, 1979]

To this we could add the following from Baraka:

> Bebop also re-established blues as the most important Afro-American form in Negro music by its astonishingly comtemporary restatement of the basic blues impulse. The boppers returned to this basic form, reacting against the all but stifling advance artificial melody had made into jazz during the swing era. [*Blues People*]

We could also look at Bebop in terms of the movement from the diatonic to the chromatic, from a more closed to an open form, a movement in the direction of a greater concern with structure, the beginning of jazz postmodernism that would reach its zenith in the work of Ornette Coleman. In "The Poetics of Jazz," Ajay Heble concludes, "Whereas diatonic jazz attempts to posit musical language as a way of thinking about things in the real world, chromaticism begins to foreground *form* rather than *substance*" [see *Textual Practice,* Vol. 2, 1988].

What becomes clear in most of the above is that Bebop must be viewed from two perspectives, the sociopolitical as well as the musical. In Gary Giddins's words, "The Second World War severely altered the texture and tempo of American life, and jazz reflected those changes with greater acuteness by far than the other arts." When Bebop began in the 1940s, America was in a similar position to what it had been in the 1920s. A war had been fought to free the world (again) for democracy; and once again, African Americans had participated and had assumed that this "loyal" participation would result in new rights and new levels of respect. When, once again, this did not appear to be happening, a new militancy developed in the African American community. Bebop was part of this new attitude. The militancy in the African American community that manifested itself in the 1941 strike of black Ford workers and the 1943 Harlem riot also manifested itself in Bebop. As Eric Lott notes:

> Brilliantly outside, bebop was intimately if indirectly related to the militancy of its moment. Militancy and music were undergirded by the same social facts; the music attempted to resolve at the level of style what the militancy combatted in the streets. ["Double V, Double-Time: Bebop's Politics of Style," *Callaloo,* Vol. 11, 1988]

Of course, this made Bebop dangerous and threatening to some, who saw it as (or potentially as) "too militant," and perhaps even un-American. And in response to this, Dizzy Gillespie retorts:

> Damn right! We refused to accept racism, poverty, or economic exploitation, nor would we live out uncreative humdrum lives merely for the sake of survival. But there was nothing unpatriotic about it. If America wouldn't honor its Constitution and respect us as men, we couldn't give a shit about the American way. And they made it damn near un-American to appreciate our music.

The threat represented by Bebop was not only felt by the white world, but by the assimilationist black middle class as well. Baraka offers these perspectives:

> When the moderns, the beboppers, showed up to restore jazz, in some sense, to its original separateness, to drag it outside the mainstream of American culture again, most middle-class Negroes (as most Americans) were stuck; they had passed, for the most part, completely into the Platonic citizenship. The willfully harsh, *antiassimilationist* sound of bebop fell on deaf or horrified ears, just as it did in white America. [*Blues People*]

> Bebop rebelled against the absorption into garbage, monopoly music; it also signified a rebel-lion by the people who played the music, because it was not just the music that rebelled, as if the music had fallen out of the sky! But even more, dig it, it signified a rebellion rising out of the masses themselves, since that is the source of social movement—the people themselves! ["War/Philly Blues/Deeper Bop," in *Selected Plays and Prose of Amiri Baraka/LeRoi Jones,* 1979]

> What made bop strong is that no matter its pretensions, it was hooked up solidly and directly to the Afro-American blues tradition, and therefore was largely based in the experience and struggle of the black sector of the working class. ["War/"]

In light of this historical context, Sonny's brother's never having heard of Bird is not just a rejection of the music of Bebop; it is also a rejection of the new political direction Bebop was representative of in the African American community.

When the story picks up several years later, some things have changed. Sonny has dropped out of high school, illegally enlisted in the navy and been shipped to Greece, returned to America, and moved to Greenwich Village. Other things have not changed: his brother has become an algebra teacher and a respected member of the black bourgeoisie. After Sonny has been released from prison, he invites his brother to watch him sit in "in a joint in the Village."

What is usually discussed concerning this final scene is that the brother enters Sonny's world, recognizes that he is only a visitor to that world tolerated because of Sonny, that here Sonny is respected and taken care of, and that here is Sonny's true family:

> I was introduced to all of them and they were all very polite to me. Yet, it was clear that, for them, I was only Sonny's brother. Here, I was in Sonny's world. Or, rather: his kingdom. Here, it was not even a question that his veins bore royal blood.

When the music Sonny plays is discussed, it is usually done either abstractly, music as the bridge that allows Sonny and his brother to become reunited and Sonny to find his identity, or simply in terms of the blues. It is, of course, totally legitimate to discuss the music in either of these ways. After all, music does function as a bridge between Sonny and his brother; and twice we are reminded in the same page that "what they were playing was the blues," and "Now these are Sonny's blues."

At the climactic moment of the story, when Sonny finally feels so comfortable that his "fingers filled the air with life," he is playing "Am I Blue." It is the first song of the second set, after a tentative performance by Sonny in the first set. Baldwin presents the moment of transition between sets by simply noting, "Then they finished, there was scattered applause, and then, without an instant's warning, Creole started into something else, it was almost sardonic, it was *Am I Blue*."

The word "sardonic," it seems to me, is key here. One of

the characteristics of Bebop is taking an old standard and making it new. As Leonard Feather explains:

> In recent years it has been an increasingly common practice to take some definite chord sequence of a well-known song (usually a standard old favorite) and build a new melody around it. Since there is no copyright on a chord sequence, the musician is entitled to use this method to create an original composition and copyright it in his own name, regardless of who wrote the first composition that used the same chord pattern. [*Inside Jazz*, 1949]

This practice results in a song with a completely different title. Thus, "Back Home Again in Indiana" becomes Parker's "Donna Lee"; "Honeysuckle Rose" becomes "Scrapple from the Apple"; "I Got Rhythm" becomes "Dexterity," "Confirmation," and "Thriving on a Riff"; "How High the Moon" becomes "Bird Lore"; "Lover Come Back to Me" becomes "Bird Gets the Worm"; and "Cherokee" becomes "Warming Up a Riff" and "Ko-Ko." But it is also characteristic of Bebop to take the entire song, not simply a chord sequence, and play it in an entirely different way. Thus, for example, Bird's catalogue is filled with versions of tunes like "White Christmas," "Slow Boat to China," "East of the Sun and West of the Moon," "April in Paris," and "Embraceable You." As Baraka notes:

> Bebop was a much more open rebellion in the sense that the musicians openly talked of the square, hopeless, corny rubbish put forth by the bourgeoisie. They made fun of it, refused to play it except in a mocking fashion. ["War/"]

Baldwin's use of the word "sardonic," therefore, is clearly intended to tell us that something more is going on than simply playing a standard tune or playing the blues. "Am I Blue" is exactly the type of song that by itself wouldn't do much for anyone, but which could become rich and meaningful after being heated in the crucible of Bebop.

The point of all this is that, through his playing, Sonny becomes "part of the family again," his family with the other musicians; likewise, Sonny's brother also becomes part of the family again, his family with Sonny. But in both cases, Baldwin wants us to view the idea of family through the musical and social revolution of Bebop. Note the brother's language as Sonny plays:

> Then he began to make it his. It was very beautiful because it wasn't hurried and it was no longer a lament. I seemed to hear with what burning we had yet to make it ours, how we could cease lamenting. Freedom lurked around us and I understood, at last, that he could help us to be free if we would listen, that he would never be free until we did.

In the mid to late 1950s, the word "freedom" is obviously a highly charged one. Not only does it speak to the politics of the Civil Rights Movement, but it also points forward to the "Free Jazz" movement of the late 1950s and 1960s, the music of Ornette Coleman, Cecil Taylor, Albert Ayler, and Eric Dolphy. Baldwin's concept of family is, therefore, a highly political one, and one that has cultural implications.

In *Black Talk* [1971], Ben Sidran concludes about Bebop:

> The importance of the bop musician was that he had achieved this confrontation—in terms of aesthetics and value structures as well as social action—well before organized legal or political action. Further, unlike the arguments of the NAACP, his music and his hip ethic were not subject to the kind of rationalization and verbal qualification that had all too often compromised out of existence all middle-class Negro gains.

In **"Sonny's Blues,"** Baldwin makes clear that, contrary to many opinions, he is in fact a major fiction writer; and that, Larry Neal notwithstanding, he *has* used to its fullest extent "traditional aspects of Afro-American culture" [See Neal, "The Black Writer's Role, III: James Baldwin," in *Visions of a Liberated Future*]. The implications are clear. Not only does Baldwin's fiction need to be looked at again, but when we are looking at it, writing about it, and teaching it, we need to be conversant with the specific cultural context he is writing in and from. And when we are, new things are there to be seen and heard.

FURTHER READING

Criticism

Jones, Harry L. "Style, Form, and Content in the Short Fiction of James Baldwin." In *James Baldwin: A Critical Evaluation,* edited by Therman B. O'Daniel, pp. 143-50. Washington, D.C.: Howard University Press, 1977.

> Considers "Sonny's Blues" to be "the most perfectly realized story" in *Going to Meet the Man*.

Levensohn, Alan. "The Artist Must Outwit the Celebrity." *The Christian Science Monitor* 57, No. 301 (18 November 1965): 15.

> Positive assessment of *Going to Meet the Man,* with particular emphasis on "Sonny's Blues."

Mosher, Marlene. "Baldwin's 'Sonny's Blues.'" *Explicator* 40, No. 4 (Summer 1982): 59.

> Notes religious allusions in "Sonny's Blues."

———. "James Baldwin's Blues." *CLA Journal* XXVI, No. 1 (1982): 112-24.

> Explores Baldwin's use of the blues as a metaphor in "Sonny's Blues," *The Amen Corner, Another Country,* and *If Beale Street Could Talk*.

Additional coverage of Baldwin's life and career is contained in the following sources published by Gale Research: *Authors and Artists for Young Adults,* Vol. 4; *Black Literature Criticism; Black Writers,* Vol. 1; *Concise Dictionary of American Literary Biography, 1941-1968; Contemporary Authors,* Vols. 1-4 (rev. ed.), 124; *Contemporary Authors Bibliographical Series,* Vol. 1; *Contemporary Authors New Revision Series,* Vols. 3, 24; *Contemporary Literary Criticism,* Vols. 1, 2, 3, 4, 5, 8, 13, 15, 17, 42, 50, 67; *DISCovering Authors; Drama Criticism,* Vol. 1; *Dictionary of Literary Biography,* Vols. 2, 7, 33; *Dictionary of Literary Biography Yearbook,* 1987; *Major 20th-Century Writers; Something about the Author,* Vols. 9, 54; *Short Story Criticism,* Vol. 10; and *World Literature Criticism.*

T. Coraghessan Boyle

1948-

(Born Thomas John Boyle) American short story writer and novelist.

The following entry provides criticism on Boyle's works through 1995. For further information on his life and works, see *CLC*, Volumes 36 and 55.

INTRODUCTION

An author of irreverent comic fiction, Boyle is often likened to such absurdist writers as John Barth, Robert Coover, and Thomas Pynchon for his bleak vision and black humor, and for exuberantly stylized prose which blends the archaic with the contemporary and the erudite with the colloquial. Boyle has explained that he is fascinated by history as a means of understanding the present, and he has satirized diverse historical epochs as well as contemporary America. His fictional treatments of both past and present are praised for their intricate plots and their detailed evocations of the spirit of the times. However, Boyle is most widely acclaimed for the manic energy of his prose, variously described as anarchic, bawdy, and lyrical. As Charles Dickinson has written, "No one writing fiction today has his touch with the language, the inspired word, the sense of humor, the playfulness, the sheer weight of talent."

Biographical Information

Born in Peekskill, New York, a town located on the Hudson River, Boyle grew up in a working-class, Catholic family. Although he claims that he did not read fiction until he was eighteen, he recalls being intrigued by the newspaper stories his mother read to him. Boyle, a self-proclaimed hellion who cut classes and abused drugs throughout his youth, enrolled at the State University of New York at Potsdam intending to major in music, but "didn't have the discipline to do the practicing." He began writing as a junior at Potsdam, when he enrolled in a creative writing course. Following his graduation from college, Boyle taught high school English in Peekskill to avoid serving in Vietnam. During this interval he published his first short story, "The OD & Hepatitis RR or Bust," in *The North American Review,* and this piece won him admission to the University of Iowa Writers' Workshop. Once enrolled in the Workshop, Boyle became eligible to take classes in the English department and began work on a Ph.D. in literature. "The minute I got there," he has written, "I grew up. Instead of cutting classes, I sat in the front row and took notes." Although his declared specialty was the Victorian period, Boyle received his doctorate in 1977 for a collection of short fiction published two years later as *Descent of Man, and Other Stories.* He currently teaches English and creative writing at the University of Southern California, Los Angeles.

Major Works

Following his 1979 debut, Boyle published several collections of short stories, and many of the motifs introduced in *Descent of Man* recur throughout his short fiction. One of these themes is his conviction that, beneath the technological innovations and ostensible sophistication of modern life, humans remain primitive beings who fall into one of two categories–predator or prey. Boyle traces the struggle between these two groups in *Greasy Lake, & Other Stories* (1985), *If the River Was Whiskey* (1989), *The Collected Stories* (1993), and *Without a Hero, and Other Stories* (1994). Other themes in his short fiction include the tension between reason and instinct, the self-indulgent materialism that he considers endemic to consumer society, and the jaded complacency that results, in his view, from media excesses. Boyle has explained that his first novel, *Water Music* (1981), "comes out of having done a Ph.D. in nineteenth-century British literature," citing the essays of John Ruskin and the novels of Charles Dickens as particular influences. Set in Africa at the beginning of the nineteenth century and replete with the historical and philosophical disquisitions that characterize much nineteenth-century fiction, *Water Music*—which took Boyle three and a half years to write—interweaves two plot strands, one involving the historical Scottish surgeon Mungo Park's quest for the source of the Niger River and the second concerning Ned Rise, a fictive criminal from the London slums who takes part in one of Park's expeditions. For his second novel, *Budding Prospects* (1984), Boyle chose a more contemporary subject that required less laborious research. Set in Northern California, the novel concerns the experiences of a group of marijuana farmers and satirizes the American myth that hard work guarantees success. In terms of both critical and popular reception, *World's End* (1987) represented a watershed for Boyle. Recounting the tangled histories of three families living in the Hudson River valley, the narrative alternates between scenes featuring the seventeenth-century members of these clans and depictions of their descendants in the 1960s; the more recent passages also feature flashbacks to the 1920s and '30s. *World's End,* which won a prestigious PEN/Faulkner Award in 1988, drew many new readers to Boyle's work. His fourth novel, *East Is East* (1990), first alternates between and then conjoins the stories of Ruth Dershowitz, an ambitious but untalented writer staying at a South Carolina artists' colony, and Hiro Tanaka, a young Japanese sailor who considers himself a samurai warrior and who goes AWOL to search for his American father. In *The Road to Wellville* (1993), Boyle mocks the excesses related to the American infatuation with health food in a plot that entwines the stories of several characters with varying relationships to a turn-of-the-century sanitarium in Battle Creek, Michigan. Set in southern California, *The Tortilla Curtain* (1995) contrasts the struggles of Cándido Rincón and his wife América, a pair of illegal aliens from Mexico, with the privileged lifestyle of Delaney and Kyra Mossbacher, a pair of yuppies.

Critical Reception

Admiring the creative discipline that enabled Boyle to publish ten volumes between 1979 and 1994, critics have particularly appreciated the substantial cultural and historical research evident in *Water Music, East Is East,* and *The Road to Wellville.* Many also have commended the inventiveness of Boyle's plotting, although some have charged that the structure of *World's End* remains too byzantine to follow. Others have contended that Boyle's enthusiasm for style further burdens the already cumbersome plots of his novels, and many have maintained that the narrative pacing of *World's End, East Is East,* and *The Road to Wellville* becomes especially tedious. Commentators have also noted that the influence of such English comedic novelists as Henry Fielding and Charles Dickens is evident in Boyle's reliance on ensemble casts; many, however, have charged that the predictable interaction of such casts reveals the latent determinism and reductiveness found in Boyle's application of ecological predator-prey models to human social dynamics. Moreover, critics often have maintained that Boyle utilizes ensemble casts because this broader focus facilitates his interest in mocking his characters' behaviors rather than exploring—or empathizing with—their motives. As Lorrie Moore has written, "Boyle is not psychological. He's all demography and zeitgeist." "[Boyle] can write," Bill Seligman has argued,

"and he can imagine, with more energy than any of his contemporaries. But energy isn't enough; there's only so far you can go on sheer technique. And until he goes further, he'll remain a satirist cut off from the oxygen of morality." Nevertheless, Boyle, whom Bill Marx has described as "the self-styled wildman of American letters," is almost universally praised for consistently producing a humor unsurpassed in contemporary fiction, despite occasional lapses into adolescent crudity. Most critics have additionally praised Boyle's prose style, which they laud as supple enough to evoke a far broader range of emotions.

PRINCIPAL WORKS

Descent of Man, and Other Stories   (short stories)   1979
Water Music   (novel)   1981
Budding Prospects: A Pastoral   (novel)   1984
Greasy Lake, & Other Stories   (short stories)   1985
World's End   (novel)   1987
If the River Was Whiskey   (short stories)   1989
East Is East   (novel)   1990
The Collected Stories   (short stories)   1993
The Road to Wellville   (novel)   1993
Without a Hero, and Other Stories   (short stories)   1994
The Tortilla Curtain   (novel)   1995

CRITICISM

Geoff Dyer   (review date 26 August 1988)

SOURCE: "A Collision with History," in *New Statesman & Society,* Vol. 1, No. 12, August 26, 1988, p. 36.

[*Dyer is an English critic. In the following review of* World's End, *he maintains that complex time shifts and elaborate familial relationships exacerbate the novel's slow pace.*]

In his last two books—the novel ***Budding Prospects*** and ***Greasy Lake,*** a collection of stories—Coraghessan Boyle took off in the opening paragraphs like a sprinter exploding from the blocks. For the first 150 pages of [***World's End***], by contrast, you are left flicking back to the list of characters trying to grapple with dozens of almost identical names: remember all those Aurelianos and Arcadios in *One Hundred Years of Solitude?* By then, by the time the narrative stagger unwinds and a tangled genealogy is emerging, the general shape of the novel is becoming clear.

Essentially the book chronicles the interlocked destinies of three families in the Hudson valley of New York. In the 17th century, when the area was still under Dutch rule, the Van Warts were wealthy landowners, the Van Brunts were tenant farmers and the Mohonks indigenous Indians whose claim to the land had been brutally shoved aside. In successive episodes we switch from the conflict between these families to that of their 20th century descendants.

By 1949 Depeyster Van Wart is a powerful manufacturer; Truman Van Brunt is part of a group of left-wing activists whose attempts to organise a peaceful festival end up in a night of wild anti-communist rioting by redneck patriots loosely controlled by Depeyster. Amid rumours that he betrayed his comrades to Van Wart, Truman abandons his child, Walter, and disappears in the aftermath of the riot.

Twenty years later, stoned and drunk, Walter crashes his motorbike and suffers "a collision with history" that leaves him haunted by ghosts from the past. His increasingly delirious search for the truth about his father—what really happened on the night of the riot?—eventually leads him to realise that he is re-enacting a pattern of events set in motion over two centuries earlier.

Word for word Boyle has never been a cost-effective writer. Like a fast car he gets through a lot of fuel, *guzzling* up words in an amphetamine rush of similes. *World's End* is uneconomic in a very different way. Here he has embarked on such a long haul with such a freight of material that there is no point in hurrying. He dawdles *en route* through the centuries, taking in unexpected diversions here, admiring the perspective there, as attentive to the view unfolding in the rear-view mirror as he is to the uncertain road ahead. The impression is of weight rather than speed and by the halfway stage the novel's momentum is actually generated by the bulk which initially impeded it.

Yet those early frustrations re-surface as unsatisfied rumblings soon after finishing the book. *World's End* stays with us for such a short time after turning the last page that we remember it less as a complex saga of temporal engineering than as a narrative elaborately compounded for its own sake.

Boyle on the inspiration for *World's End:*

The inspiration [for *World's End*] is a story I've told many times. Just an awareness that history precedes us, and that we're walking on dirt that's been walked on before. And to try to remind the public about that. There's a chapter called "The Finger" where Tom Crane goes to a concert at Vassar, and the narrator of the book talks about the hippies and how they were dimly aware that history had preceded them. They knew about Adolf Hitler and Jack Kennedy and the Depression, because their parents wouldn't let them forget it. But they believed that they'd invented sex and rock music and so on. And that the world began and lived and ended with them. That's the way everybody feels at a certain age. But it ain't necessarily true.

> *T. Coraghessan Boyle, in "An Interview with T. Coraghessan Boyle," by Elizabeth Adams, in* Chicago Review, *1991.*

Michiko Kakutani (review date 2 May 1989)

SOURCE: "Stories In Which the Unusual Is the Usual," in *The New York Times,* May 2, 1989, p. C18.

[*In the following review of* If the River Was Whiskey, *Kakutani contends that Boyle, now depicting yuppies rather than hippies, has here used his "disparate talents" to produce "showy, but shallow effects."*]

The America of T. Coraghessan Boyle is a wild and crazy place, where anything can happen. In his most recent novel (*World's End*), a garrulous epic that chronicled the fortunes of several generations of a single family, "the barbaric new world" of America spawned ghosts and demons, not to mention every imaginable variety of human eccentricity and prejudice. His collections of short stories (*Greasy Lake and Other Stories, Descent of Man*) have also tended to pivot around the strange and the surreal: neighboring survivalists, holed up in the wilderness to await the apocalypse, come to blows; a group of hippies watches television and smokes marijuana as the skies begin to rain blood; a rowdy gang of teen-agers discovers a bloated corpse in the neighborhood lake.

Similarly disturbing events surface in his latest collection of stories, *If the River Was Whiskey*: a couple receive a death threat from their adopted son, who suffers from the delusion that he's a killer bee (**"King Bee"**); a Hungarian circus performer achieves fame and fortune by scaling a skyscraper and by tying himself to the wing of an airplane (**"The Human Fly"**); a retired primatologist tries to settle down to a normal life in Connecticut with one of her chimpanzees (**"The Ape Lady in Retirement"**).

On the surface at least, it appears as though Mr. Boyle has changed narrative terrain, trading the 60's backdrop of communes and crash pads that figured so prominently in his earlier fiction for a new yuppified world of suburban houses and upscale restaurants. His characters pay less attention now to the quality of their dope and stereo systems than to the brand names of their clothing (Fila sweats, Nikes, hand-knit hat-and-scarf sets imported from Scandinavia) and the purity of their designer food (forest mushrooms, sun-dried tomatoes, fennel sausage). One woman is so obsessed with cleanliness and health that she makes her lover wear "a full-body condom." Another couple, who have quit their tenured teaching jobs to start a fly-by-night adoption agency, vote for Ronald Reagan, though they won't admit it to their friends.

Indeed the acquisitive, image-obsessed values of the 80's permeate these stories. In **"Hard Sell,"** a press agent attempts to upgrade public perception of the Ayatollah. "Tell him," he says to an intermediary, "beards went out with Jim Morrison—and the bathrobe business is kinda kinky, and we can play to that if he wants, but wouldn't he feel more comfortable in a nice Italian knit?" In **"The Devil and Irv Cherniske,"** a bond trader makes a pact with Satan, and goes on to become one of the wealthiest men in New York. And in **"Peace of Mind,"** a fast-talking young woman preys on her wealthy clients' worst fears in order to sell them elaborate burglar-alarm systems.

Of course, neither they—nor the young woman, as it turns

out—can buy real "peace of mind," for in Mr. Boyle's America, one's worst paranoid worries have a terrible way of coming true. A prospective client turns out to be a psychopathic con man. A suburban neighbor turns out to be a madwoman, intent on flooding herself out of her house by turning on every available faucet. A man in a black BMW turns out to be the Devil.

It's no wonder that Mr. Boyle's characters continually feel menaced. As he writes of one man, who has just seen a stranger in his backyard:

> Though he wasn't nearly the bruiser he'd been when he started as nose tackle for Fox Lane High, he was used to wielding his paunch like a weapon and blustering his way through practically anything, from a potential mugging right on down to putting a snooty maitre d' in his place. For all that, though, when he saw the size of the man, when he factored in his complexion and considered the oddness of the circumstances, he felt uncertain of himself. Felt as if the parameters of the world as he knew it had suddenly shifted. Felt, unaccountably, that he was in deep trouble.

As his previous fiction has amply demonstrated, Mr. Boyle is richly endowed with an old-fashioned storyteller's gifts (a hyperactive imagination, an exuberant way with language, a penchant for exaggeration), combined with the self-consciousness of a good, card-carrying postmodernist. In his strongest work, these talents come together to create a compelling—and often very funny—tale that's both a portrait of contemporary reality and comment upon earlier fictional forms. Some of the stories in *Greasy Lake* and *Descent of Man* stand as small satirical marvels; and for all its windy effusions, *World's End* evinces an admirable ambition—a desire to take apart and reassemble the clockwork of the American dream.

In Mr. Boyle's weaker efforts—which this volume, unfortunately, seems to feature—his disparate talents are used, singly, for showy, but shallow effects. **"Me Cago en la Leche (Robert Jordan in Nicaragua),"** for instance, is a cynical parody of "For Whom the Bell Tolls," transporting Hemingway's hero, Robert Jordan, from the Spanish Civil War to Central America, where he's supposedly engaged in fighting the contras. **"Sorry Fugu"** is a cutesy diatribe against critics, staged as a battle between an earnest chef and a stupid restaurant reviewer. And **"The Devil and Irv Cherniske"** is nothing but a tired retelling of the Faust legend, gussied up with contemporary references to insider trading, real estate and Krugerrands.

Curiously enough, two of the more persuasive stories in this collection eschew Mr. Boyle's trademark pyrotechnics. The title story, **"If the River Was Whiskey,"** is a dark portrait of a family in disrepair; **"Thawing Out,"** a similarly somber examination of a romance gone awry. In the past, the author's efforts in this naturalistic territory have always seemed somewhat insincere and forced, but the deeply felt emotion in these two tales points to a new direction in the career of this gifted and highly versatile young writer.

Elizabeth Benedict   (review date 14 May 1989)

SOURCE: "Having a Good Time with Our Worst Fears," in *The New York Times Book Review,* May 14, 1989, pp. 1, 33.

[*Benedict is an American novelist, short story writer, and critic. In the following review of* If the River Was Whiskey, *she praises Boyle's humorous, satiric treatment of contemporary society as entertaining but finds his somber stories more rewarding.*]

Half a dozen shysters, a talking three-foot-tall statue of the Virgin Mary, a mendacious adoption counselor, a Los Angeles public-relations man hired to "upgrade" Ayatollah Ruhollah Khomeini's image, a woman who makes her lover wear a "full-body condom" when he goes to bed with her—even the Devil himself—make appearances in T. Coraghessan Boyle's daring, irreverent and sometimes deeply moving new collection of stories, *If the River Was Whiskey.*

With the linguistic acrobatics and hip, erudite audacity we've come to expect from his two other story collections and three novels, Mr. Boyle here lampoons our most terrible fears—that our homes are not safe and our lovers are riddled with communicable diseases—and ridicules our cupidity, racism and cultural insensitivity. In his universe, those who live by the deal—the Ivan Boeskys, the snake-oil salesmen—always get their comeuppance. But before the marshals arrive, the nice guys among us, saps and all, have been snookered out of our life savings. Only in the title story ["**If the River Was Whiskey**"] and "**Thawing Out**" does Mr. Boyle completely drop his comic persona and insistent cynicism and tell straightforward stories about human frailty, love and loss.

"Humor resides in exaggeration, and humor is a quick cover for alarm and bewilderment," a character says in **"Two Ships,"** a story in Mr. Boyle's second collection, *Greasy Lake.* The sentiment still holds. In his choice here of conceits, characters and figures of speech, Mr. Boyle remains a four-star general of hyperbole. A woman gives a man "a look that would have corroded metal." An explosives expert "waited till the flame was gone from his throat and the familiar glow lit his insides so that they felt radioactive." A character's wife "clung to his arm like some inescapable force of nature, like the tar in the La Brea pits or the undertow at Rockaway Beach." Mr. Boyle's plot lines are no less outrageous. A crazed Hungarian daredevil rides the axle of a truck from Maine to Los Angeles. A stock trader meets up with the Devil in his backyard.

Many of Mr. Boyle's characters, in their immensity and their colorful, inflated gestures, loom like Mighty Mouse in the Macy's Thanksgiving Day Parade. He's so huge that we have to pay attention, even marvel at how he was put together—and how he stays up there—but for all the space he takes up and the impression he makes, he doesn't leave us much in the way of depth to remember him by.

Sometimes Mr. Boyle's parade is fun, sometimes it's hilariously funny, and often his imaginative leaps and midair somersaults are breathtaking. He is fluent in any number of slick American dialects: the hip patois of the vanishing

1960's counterculture, the sleazy patter of Hollywood agents and P.R. men and the lingua franca of those who speak *haute nouvelle cuisine.* And though he sneers at an inordinate number of his characters, putting them down with easy shots—corrupt businessmen who wear gold chains have become Mr. Boyle's Jewish-mother joke—he clearly feels a playful affection for others. He's fond of them not because they're lifelike—often they're not—but because they represent impulses more akin to his own than bilking people, and fears closer to his heart than, say, the threat of nuclear attack, which he exploited brilliantly in **"On for the Long Haul"** in *Greasy Lake.*

I know of no other story by Mr. Boyle that is nearly as powerful or poignant as "If the River Was Whiskey." It's the last story in the collection, and so different from the others in texture and tone that it is startling to come upon.

—*Elizabeth Benedict*

Call them impulses and fears writers can relate to. Albert, the chef in **"Sorry Fugu,"** believes himself to be "potentially one of the great culinary artists of his time." When he's visited by the hard-nosed food writer Willa Frank, he's determined to win her over, to get a great review from the toughest critic out there. He distracts her lunkish boyfriend with burned steak and boiled peas—"shanty Irish" food, the chef calls it, like the fellow's mother used to make—and lures Willa into his kitchen for a supreme culinary seduction. She tumbles to his taglierini alla pizzaiola and admits that her negative reviews reflect her boyfriend's tastes. Why not her own? "To like something," she says, "to really like it and come out and say so, is taking a terrible risk. I mean, what if I'm wrong? What if it's really no good?"

Zoltan Mindszenty (a. k. a. the Human Fly) couldn't care less about critical acclaim. Wearing tights, a cape, swimming goggles and a red bathing cap, he marches into the closet-size office of a Hollywood agent and announces, "I want to be famous." In a series of wacky, death-defying stunts—including an attempt to ride on the wing of a jet—the Human Fly gets his wish. And his agent, who now and then feels ambivalent about watching "a man die for ten percent of the action," gets his: a bigger office.

In **"Thawing Out"** and the title story, Mr. Boyle reveals the naked "alarm and bewilderment" he usually cloaks in humor. **"Thawing Out"** is a somber, eloquent love story about the redemptive powers of water, and of love. A cocky young man abandons his girlfriend, Naina, and then returns. Naina and her mother belong to the Polar Bear Club; in the dead of winter, they swim the Hudson River. They are made, he comes to realize, of tougher stuff than he is.

I know of no other story by Mr. Boyle that is nearly as powerful or poignant as **"If the River Was Whiskey."** It's the last story in the collection, and so different from the others in texture and tone that it is startling to come upon. A young boy, Tiller, spends a summer month at a lakeside cabin with his parents, fishing and trying to become closer to his troubled alcoholic father, who has recently lost his job. After two weeks in the cabin, Tiller's father still hasn't "done one damn thing" with him. "You haven't even been down to the lake," scolds his wife. "What kind of father are you?"

As the story unfolds in vivid, tightly written vignettes told in alternating points of view—Tiller's and his father's—it becomes clear that the answer is "not much of one." His attempts at being a better parent are occasions for heartbreak. After his wife's scolding, he vows not to drink and goes fishing with Tiller, who, with "the novelty of his father rowing, pale arms and a dead cigarette clenched between his teeth, the boat rocking, and the birds whispering . . . closed his eyes a minute, just to keep from going dizzy with the joy of it." Mr. Boyle evokes their shared pain with a sure hand.

I have no way of knowing whether the story is autobiographical, but it has the ring of something deeply felt. Its placement at the end of the book was a shrewd move, for if we wonder, as we read nearly all of the previous 15 stories, what makes Mr. Boyle run, what psychic forces drive his hyperactive prose, what childhood losses have inspired his cynicism, we can look on the title story as an analyst's gold mine. If we choose not to read it as autobiography, but simply as a departure onto the rocky terrain of emotional candor, we nevertheless come to the last page feeling a more profound respect for Mr. Boyle than many of his satiric stories inspire.

Humor and exaggeration have served Mr. Boyle well. He is a consummate entertainer, a verbal showman, an explosively gifted satirist. If he uses humor to provide "quick cover" for his "alarm and bewilderment," and for other more powerful feelings, it's refreshing now and then—it's almost a relief—when he ditches his cover, as he does in the last story, and allows us a peek at his heart.

Richard Eder   (review date 21 May 1989)

SOURCE: "Short-Story Canvas Small for a Large-Scale Brush," in *Los Angeles Times Book Review,* May 21, 1989, p. 3.

[*An American critic and journalist, Eder received the Pulitzer Prize for criticism in 1987. In the following review, he contends that the stories in* If the River Was Whiskey *are flawed by Boyle's awkward plotting and maintains that novels provide a better vehicle for Boyle's talents.*]

The stories in *If the River Was Whiskey* are for the most part short tales, many of them ironic or satiric, and with a touch of contemporary fable to them.

T. Coraghessan Boyle, who wrote *Budding Prospects,* a fresh and funny novel about a hippie turned cash-crop farmer, and *World's End,* an ambitious entwining of historic legend and present-day lives, has prefaced his collection with an epigraph from the late Italo Calvino.

There is, in fact, an occasional suggestion of one of Calvino's tiny myths going off suddenly in the pocket, like a defective exploding cigar. A banal detail is turned upside down so its false teeth pop out.

Boyle will take a contemporary fad or practice and inflate it to a parodic extreme. He will, upon occasion, try for a moment of charged sadness or radiance, of the kind that Calvino would introduce by surprise into his elegant allegories.

Unfortunately, Boyle's sensibility is not really suited to such a thing. His odd plots and characters are oddities without connection; they suggest no strangeness outside of themselves. And even in the better tales, a good parodic contrivance will go wrong, as if it had lost its sense of direction.

"Sorry Fugu," the first story of the collection, starts off with a promising spin. A much-feared restaurant critic is going to get her come-uppance, but before she does, Boyle skewers food-critic language as many of us, no doubt, have longed to see it skewered. Here is a specimen:

"Limp radicchio . . . Sorry Fugu . . . A blasphemy of baby lamb's lettuce, frisee, endive . . . A coulibiac made in hell . . . For all its rather testy piquancy, the orange sauce might just as well have been citron preserved in pickling brine."

As he recounts the efforts of Albert, a restaurateur, to tame the formidable Wilma Frank, who has never been known to praise a meal, Boyle comes up with a lovely notion or two. Albert discovers that Frank is scared of food, so she invariably brings along a friend to tell her what to think.

Since the friend's taste runs to overdone steak and boiled peas, his verdicts are consistently negative; so, accordingly, are hers. And as she confesses to Albert, once he gets her in his power through a stratagem, it's really safer for a critic to pan than to praise.

It is a nice thought. After all, a bad review, since it keeps people away, will have fewer detractors than a good one, which will bring the potential second-guessers flocking in.

The trouble is that Boyle has a frustratingly uncertain command of his plot. The stratagem by which Frank is unmasked is fuzzed up by a series of peculiar deflections.

The same is true for **"Modern Love,"** a satirical piece about the current fear of contamination.

"There was no exchange of body fluids on the first date, and that suited both of us just fine," it begins. It goes on to tell of a woman so fastidious that when she finally agrees to have sex with her boyfriend, it is on condition that both encase themselves entirely in plastic. Before she will agree to marry, her fiance must undergo a thorough physical examination. The notion is amusing, if not brilliant, but here again, the author fogs up the ending.

A different contemporary worry—security—is parodied in **"Peace of Mind,"** which tells of a high-powered burglar-alarm sales-woman who sells $5,000 systems by telling householders of the terrible things that have happened just down the street. She manages to push one deranged potential client over the edge; he goes on a rampage that claims as victims two of the saleswoman's own clients. She then uses *their* story, of course, to make still more sales.

Again, the concept is promising and Boyle gets in some funny lines. One client is obsessed with the notion that a burglar will tie her up and gag her with her underwear; "Can you imagine that, I mean, the taste of it—your own underwear?" But the story is told awkwardly and with uncertain effect.

Several of the pieces are little more than gimmicks. There is a routine about a Hollywood PR type trying to convince the Ayatollah Khomeini to brighten up his image; a story about a stunt man, obsessed with making it big, who rides from Maine to California suspended under the axle of a trailer truck; another about a child with criminal tendencies who terrorizes his adoptive parents up to a final grisly denouement.

There are a couple of strained literary parodies, one of Hemingway, the other of the film, *The Big Chill*. There is a different kind of strain in a story of a woman scientist who prefers apes to people, and who dies with her pet chimpanzee in a kind of airborne Liebestod. You feel the author is trying to suggest a wider mystery; he does not get beyond an individual peculiarity.

A more successful connection between the askew and the universally askew is made in the story of an old widow who declares her loneliness by opening every water outlet in her house and flooding the neighborhood. And there is a lighter but quite perfect bit of satire in **"Zapatos,"** the story of a Latin American shopkeeper who outwits his country's corrupt authorities by an ingenious scheme that involves the separate importing of 30,000 left-foot and 30,000 right-foot shoes, each lot through a different customs zone.

For the most part, though, Boyle's talents do not seem to fit the form he uses in this collection. His brush is large; it does not work with miniatures.

David L. Ulin   (review date November-December 1989)

SOURCE: "Lost in the Funhouse," in *The Bloomsbury Review*, Vol. 9, No. 6, November-December, 1989, p. 5.

[Below, Ulin favorably reviews If the River Was Whiskey.*]*

T. Coraghessan Boyle has never been one to shy away from the challenges of his own imagination. Throughout the course of his career, he has written with astonishing energy and originality about a carnival of characters and situations; his work—and particularly his short work—is based on a willingness to be outrageous, to take risks, to tap into the essential absurdity of the universe and let it run its course. It's no surprise, therefore, that like his previous story collections, ***If the River Was Whiskey*** is a literary funhouse, its stories a set of crazy mirrors reflecting the odd mixture of the ridiculous and the sublime that has become Boyle's trademark.

What *is* surprising, though, is the topicality of this book, its sense of relation to the world outside its pages. Boyle has always been interested in history, but even the most outlandish of these new stories—and there are quite a few—are rooted with a directness that is startling. **"Modern Love,"** for instance, begins "There was no exchange of body fluids on the first date," and goes on to chronicle ultimate "safe sex" in the "Age of Disease," but the fears it reports are very real indeed. **"Hard Sell,"** a monologue by a Hollywood PR executive sent to Iran to work on the Ayatollah's image, is so assured in its tone and in its nightly news immediacy that, in many ways, its excesses do not seem so unlikely, nor very far from the truth. By keeping his exaggerations sharp and controlled, Boyle lets them work as both entertainment and commentary, an effort that establishes a broad context for the book as a whole, and deepens the resonance of each of the individual stories.

That resonance is very important, because *If the River Was Whiskey* is not just a book of comic routines. Some of the strongest work here, in fact—the title piece, **"King Bee," "Thawing Out"**—is that in which the author moves his eye from the broad spectrum of social satire and focuses instead on smaller, more personal movements. Although even the most naturalistic of those stories is refracted through the lens of Boyle's absurdist vision, the topicality of the book frames and heightens them all. Thus, when **"Sinking House"** reveals a young housewife slowly awakening to the ennui and regret that inevitably await her, the revelation carries with it a sense of the woman's place in the world that makes her somehow real, a person as well as a literary creation. And when a security-conscious family gets more than they bargained for in **"Peace of Mind,"** the action hits home with the authority of a gut punch. Even in the funhouse, after all, we must sometimes see ourselves as we really are.

Which, in the end, seems to be the point. In these stories—as in life—people worry about diseases, or they worry about the paths their lives are taking. They try to make decisions, try to live with the decisions they have already made. And if it sometimes gets crazy, then so be it. For these are exaggerated times we live in, and, absurd or naturalistic, there is very little in *If the River Was Whiskey* that isn't real.

David Stanton (essay date January-February 1990)

SOURCE: "An Interview with T. Coraghessan Boyle," in *Poets & Writers Magazine*, Vol. 18, No. 1, January-February, 1990, pp. 29-34.

[*In the following excerpt from an essay based on an interview with Boyle, Stanton discusses Boyle's education and provides an overview of his career up to the publication of* East Is East.]

"A large part of what motivates a writer is a need to express oneself," Boyle says, "but you don't want to express yourself in a closet. You want to let the world know that you are alive in this time and age, and that you have something to say about it. And so the next largest part of what motivates you is to get [your work] out to the public and to have your ego stroked and to be gratified by that."

Boyle left his first publisher, Atlantic/Little, Brown, after two books because he felt the company was not putting enough promotional muscle behind him. (In retrospect, however, he says that he may have had unrealistic expectations—a recurring problem with Boyle.) He apparently had the same feeling about . . . Viking/Penguin for several years, but is now pleased with their work on his behalf. "It takes a hell of a struggle sometimes to let publishers know that they should invest the time and money and effort in you," he says. "But I think a combination of luck, persistence, and talent may win out.

"I have never been deterred from what I want to do by any amount of pessimism or nay-saying. From the very beginning, when I even had the first thought of being a writer, people would say, 'Don't be ridiculous, you can't make a living at that.' I said, 'Maybe one person can, and I don't care about the rest—it'll be me.' "

Boyle's interest in fiction was sparked by an undergraduate writing course at the State University of New York at Potsdam, where he started out as a music major but ended up in English and history. His writing career began in earnest in 1972, when the *North American Review* published his story **"The OD & Hepatitis RR or Bust."** On the strength of this piece, he was accepted into the Iowa Writers' Workshop, where his teachers included John Cheever and John Irving.

"It was really marvelous for me," Boyle says of the Iowa program. "The workshop gave me time to write and the opportunity to get into a Ph.D. program, something I could never have gotten into on my record."

Despite his fond memories of Iowa, and despite the fact that he himself is now a professor of creative writing, Boyle has reservations about writing programs. "A writer immediately out of undergraduate school may be thrust into a writing program where many of the writers are ten, fifteen years older," Boyle observes, "and this can be difficult. The older writer, even though he may not be better or more talented, seems to speak with more authority and may damage the younger writer's ego.

"I think a young writer also may go into a writers' program starry-eyed, thinking, 'I will go here, and I will be taught how to write, and I will emerge a writer who can write.' If you think you're going to be put in somebody's hands and transformed, I think you'll be disappointed."

Boyle's first short-story collection, *Descent of Man and Other Stories* (1979), won the St. Lawrence Award for Short Fiction. The book modulates between the farcical and the surreal; the title story, for example, tells of a husband who discovers that his anthropologist wife is having an affair with a gifted laboratory chimp. In reviewing the book, Katherine Kearns of the *Carolina Quarterly* wrote, "There is a gargantuan irreverence about *Descent of Man* that refuses to acknowledge the profound complications of living and being human; and that irreverence is Boyle's weakness and his strength." Kearns's statement could be applied, in fact, to nearly all of Boyle's work, and it deftly summarizes the opinions of both his supporters and detractors.

At Iowa, Boyle believed that he would be content to write only short fiction, but in fact that plan died quickly. His second book, *Water Music* (1981), is a 437-page burlesque novel based on the adventures of eighteenth-century Scottish explorer Mungo Park, the first white man to see the Niger River. "I think every American writer thinks he or she should write a novel at some point," Boyle says now. "Some do and some don't. I just tried it and it seemed to fit."

The novel format is an amenable one for Boyle; it allows his expansive prose to wrap itself around an intricate plot. Novels also give Boyle access to the many readers who hesitate to buy short-story collections—a situation made evident by the *New York Times* bestseller lists, where books of stories make infrequent appearances.

Boyle finds that writing novels has changed his approach to short stories. "When you write a novel that goes on for 550 pages," he says, "you have to learn something about inventing character, and I think that enriched my stories. Now I'm more concerned with a balance of elements and making a story that is seamless—that isn't as self-conscious and doesn't call attention to itself as a story as much as my earlier work did."

After *Water Music,* Boyle completed a second novel, *Building Prospects* (1984), the story of a restless thirty-one-year-old divorcee who becomes a professional marijuana grower. In 1985 came a second collection of short fiction, the highly praised *Greasy Lake and Other Stories*; and, three years later, *World's End,* a 456-page saga that alternates between the seventeenth and twentieth centuries and takes place in Boyle's native Westchester County. The book, his third novel, won not only awards but also praise from critics for its "seriousness," a quality they had perceived as lacking in his previous work.

Boyle does not think that his fiction is, as critics have suggested, socially and politically disengaged. "I think of my stories—and all stories, in fact—not as serious and comic, but as comic and noncomic. Satire, which much of [*East Is East*] is, can be corrective. It can hold up certain attitudes as being fraudulent, and in doing that suggest that the opposite might be an appropriate way to behave. And I hope that if my work is socially redemptive, it is in that way."

At times, Boyle does seem to rely on television-style stereotypes in his portrayals of women and minorities. . . . *East Is East,* which has been excerpted in *Rolling Stone,* is about a Japanese man who washes ashore in Georgia, and one gets the feeling it will poke fun at both Japanese and Southern culture—and at writers' colonies, one of which serves as the backdrop for part of the book.

"As you know," Boyle deadpans, "I'm working my way through all the ethnic groups of the world and making fun of each one so that I'll finally be covered." And in fact, nearly all of Boyle's comic characters—regardless of sex or nationality—are skewed versions of familiar character types.

Some of Boyle's most "noncomic" work to date appears in. . . . *If the River Was Whiskey*. "Thawing Out" is the story of a detached young man alternately seeking and resisting a serious relationship with a stable woman. And the title story, which closes the book, deals with a boy attempting to enjoy a lakeside vacation in spite of his parents' constant drinking and bickering. Neither story seeks to be funny, and the latter is based in part on Boyle's own troubled childhood.

"It came pretty easily," Boyle says of *"If the River Was Whiskey."* "I was living in Ireland at the time and the distance helped me, I think. It's a story I'd been trying to write and had thought about in various incarnations for probably a decade, and it just happened to click at that moment."

Boyle's father, a school bus driver, and his mother, a high school administrator, were both alcoholics and died before Boyle was thirty. His father was raised in an orphanage and fought in World War II, "an experience that changed him, made him morose and silent," Boyle told *Publishers Weekly* in 1987. "Life had beaten him down in a way that I couldn't understand, and I was probably too young to care. Later, in my early twenties, when I was able to appreciate him, he was dead." The search for this "absent" father in part fueled the creation of *World's End,* in which ignorance of one's past becomes a tragic flaw.

Now Boyle has a family of his own. He and his wife, Karen Kvashay, have three children, a red BMW and a red Jeep, and a house in the San Fernando Valley. In addition to writing fiction, Boyle teaches creative writing at the University of Southern California, where he is a tenured professor. He is, as he told one reporter, "if not a pillar of society, then a flying buttress."

At times, however, one gets the feeling that Boyle invents and mythicizes his own life as much as he does his characters'. His middle name, for example, is John, not Coraghessan, though the latter is reportedly a part of his family tree. (The "T" stands for Thomas, and though his students call him Tom, his oldest friends know him as just T.) He has also said that he read few or no books before he was eighteen. Given his penchant for exaggeration, one can't help but wonder where the truth might leave off in such claims.

"Everything that [people] perceive about me is true," Boyle says, "but they could also paint another picture of me that's equally true. On the one hand they could say, yes, I came from poor beginnings, nihilistic roots, shot dope, etcetera. That is true. But they could also say, yes, but his parents pampered him and gave him everything they could and sent him to college, and it's a natural result of a bourgeois environment that he is what he is. I think fans tend to believe the first because it's more fun, it makes a better story. The press loves it. And it is true."

One apparent difference between the reckless Boyle of the past and the semi-bourgeois version of the present is discipline—his ability to focus on his work and be consistently productive. In fact, it is difficult to imagine Boyle—who so enjoys companionship and adulation—practicing the supremely lonely art of writing. (One of the benefits of his teaching, Boyle says, is that it keeps him in touch with the outside world.) But . . . since *Descent of Man* was published, he has written three long novels and two books of short stories, as well as . . . *East Is East,* which he turned in two months ahead of schedule. How did a degenerate youth become a megawatt generator of fiction?

"I think it's a process of maturing," Boyle says. "You find your direction and you pursue it, that's all. It's totally single-minded—[writing is] the one thing I want to do, the one thing I've wanted to do for many, many years. It has nothing to do with earning a living or money, either, although happily those are concomitants of what I do. Everything has just narrowed down to an obsession with fiction.

"I could easily go the other way," he says, "into drug addiction, alcoholism, or both—squared—but I have something else to do. A lot of people romanticize the writer's life, and my life in particular, and think I'm burning the candle at both ends, that I'm out at clubs every night with groovy so-and-so, but the fact is that you can't do that if you're committed to your work."

Yet Boyle also recognizes that it helps to add a little spice when promoting reputedly "dry" stuff like literature. With his new-wave clothes, "bad boy" image, and outrageous statements—all backed up by literary awards and solid reviews—Boyle is that happy anomaly, the respectable iconoclast.

"The work has to stand on its own," Boyle says. "No amount of hype, no amount of personality is going to sell books unless the books are good. However, I do think the culture is dominated by a certain amount of flash and sex in selling things, and I don't think it's necessarily bad for a writer to attract attention. If your personality accords with that, then why not ride with it? I think you need to wake the public up and alert them to the fact that it's actually hip to touch this book—and hey, read a paragraph!"

What's most unsettling [about *World's End*] is that Boyle's gift for word play, his ability to make even the bleakest themes dazzling in their expression, is sabotaged by his grimly insistent plotting. By the close of his tale, three centuries of ships (and how many wounded lives?) lie scuttled in a water graveyard called World's End—and so, alas, do most of his readers' sympathies.

—Alida Becker, in "Imperfect Pasts," in Chicago Tribune—Books, *October 11, 1987.*

Gail Godwin   (review date 9 September 1990)

SOURCE: "Samurai on the Run," in *The New York Times Book Review,* September 9, 1990, p. 13.

[*Godwin is an American novelist, short story writer, and*

critic. In the following review, she praises Boyle's "virtuoso language" and "cross-cultural insights" in East Is East.]

This irresistible novel is T. Coraghessan Boyle's finest yet. It has the vital language and inventiveness of plot that we have come to expect from him, but this time there is a keener focus of intention, a more profound level of empathy than were evident in his previous novels—even the ambitious and highly imaginative *World's End,* which won the 1988 PEN/Faulkner Award for Fiction.

A simple plot description of *East Is East* makes the novel sound like the mere high jinks of a clever writer: a young Japanese seaman jumps ship off the coast of Georgia and, through a series of mishaps and cultural misunderstandings, finds himself hiding out in an artists' colony from the police and immigration officials. And in the merely clever writer's hands, the book might have been only an entertaining romp with an international twist, a satirical putdown of the foibles and pretensions of artists, both real and *manqué,* when they "colonize" self-consciously under one roof.

But Mr. Boyle, with his consummate artistry, has shaped this story into an absorbing tragedy. That we find ourselves laughing all the way to the increasingly inevitable catastrophe does not in any way blur the book's impact, for ours is the laughter of recognition and revelation, rueful and cleansing. All of us who have ever weighed the desperate desire to belong against the coexisting need for self-respect will recognize ourselves in Mr. Boyle's lowly Japanese sailor as well as in his counterprotagonist, the frantically ambitious young writer Ruth Dershowitz, who becomes Hiro Tanaka's protector and, ultimately, his nemesis. That Hiro—the hero—at last does the honorable, albeit doomed, thing, according to his code, and that Ruth, in marked contrast, joyfully sells out after a brief pang of conscience, results in a double catharsis. When it comes to an ending, the reader gets to have it both ways.

Hiro, who plunges from his freighter, the Tokachi-maru, as it heads north for Savannah with its cargo of recorders, tractor parts and microwave ovens, and who floats on his life ring toward the shores of his fantasied America, has been shunned his entire life (he's 20) by his Japanese peers because he is "a half-breed, a *happa,* a high-nose and butter-stinker—and an orphan to boot—forever a foreigner in his own society." Shortly after he was born, his American hippie father (known only by his nickname, Doggo) deserted his Japanese mother, a bar hostess who then "sank into a shame worse than miscegenation" and eventually drowned herself. "She did what she had to do" is Hiro's Japanese grandfather's stoic comment to the boy regarding his mother's suicide.

As Hiro struggles to the Georgia shore, "a pale certificate of flesh" clinging to his cork ring, he carries with him an explosive mix of expectations and values. The America he envisions is composed of impressions from films, books and popular music. Yet encased in layers of Ziploc bags and taped to his chest, along with some American bills and a faded photograph of his father, is his bible, *The Way of the Samurai.* Hiro has memorized its arcane advice along with its grimmer maxims. ("One should take important considerations lightly. . . . Small matters should be taken seriously"; "In a fifty-fifty life or death crisis, simply settle it by choosing immediate death.")

When he's in doubt in America—where he dreams of blending into the polyglot "Beantown or the City of Brotherly Love," and where he even dares to hope that he may discover his father "in some gleaming, spacious ranch house and sit down to cheeseburgers with him"—Hiro will seek his direction from *Hagakure,* the ancient monk Jocho Yamamoto's code of samurai ethics as interpreted by the 20th-century novelist Yukio Mishima. Jocho and Mishima have been Hiro's magical allies back in Japan, lifting him above the despair caused by the insults and beatings inflicted by his schoolmates and helping him to draw a sharp critical bead on modern Japanese society:

> Where was the glory in being a nation of salary-men in white shirts and western suits making VCRs for the rest of the world like a tribe of trained monkeys? Hiro . . . saw it clearly: [his classmates] and all the rest of them, they were nothing, eunuchs, wimps, gutless and shameless, and they would grow up to chase after yen and dollars like all the other fools who made fun of him, who singled *him* out as the pariah. But he wasn't the pariah, they were. To live by the code of *Hagakure* made him more Japanese than they. . . . He'd been made to feel inferior all his life, and here was a way to conquer it. . . . He would fight back . . . with the oldest weapon in the Japanese arsenal. He would become a modern samurai.

The modern samurai doesn't even get to shore before he collides with the boat in which Ruth Dershowitz is making love with her boyfriend, Saxby Lights, whose mother, Septima, owns and runs an artists' colony, Thanatopsis House, on remote Tupelo Island. (In remembrance of her husband's choice of demise, Septima has named all the studio-cottages after famous artists who have committed suicide.)

Ruth, who is staying in the lowliest of these cottages, named Hart Crane, is 34, has published only four "intense and gloomy" stories in little magazines and owes her presence at the colony largely to her romance with the patron's son. But even when she is entwined with Saxby, she is consumed by her mania for fame ("and its unfortunate concomitant, work") and fueled by the specter of her enemy, the phony, scheming young writer Jane Shine, with her "extraterrestrial eyes" and "iridescent flamenco-dancer's hair," who has published in *The Atlantic* and *The New Yorker* and has a collection of stories out now. Worse still, "her picture was everywhere."

Besides the hated Jane Shine (whose stagy arrival scene is hilarious), Ruth's fellow guests at Thanatopsis House include Irving Thalamus, that one-man institution of Jewish-American letters; the haunted, hollow-cheeked Laura Grobian, doyenne of WASP novelists, who sits in a corner with her sherry and a notebook and worries aloud in a voice of "exotic ruination" about the mass suicides at Masada and Jonestown and Saipan; and the austere, Serious Writer Peter Anserine, who reads European books ("never in translation") at the silent table during meals.

There is also a walleyed composer whose music sounds like "slow death in the metronome factory" and a celebrated "punk sculptress." Mr. Boyle has fun here, yet the members of his gallery of artists are never just cartoon figures. The renowned Irving Thalamus, for instance, whose patronage Ruth desires, is nursing two crushing personal defeats behind his confident exterior, and even the glossy Jane Shine has her breaking point in extremis.

The point of view of the novel alternates mainly between Ruth, struggling for her share of the limelight among the luminaries at Thanatopsis House, and the truant Hiro as he flees into darker and deeper terrain, his unintended crimes compounding. He is pursued by an immigration official with his own outcast complex (his skin has been mottled from birth), assisted by a tough and bigoted part-time agent who specializes in "Nips" (and who, amazingly, might possibly be Hiro's father).

Before our hero's flight ends, he faces 34 criminal charges, including arson and manslaughter (these being the result of two encounters with the same elderly, superstitious black man and arising out of language deficiencies and woeful cultural ignorance on the part of each). Hiro's hideouts (and his one brief incarceration by the local rednecks' posse) will have included the swamps on Tupelo Island; Ruth Dershowitz' one-room cabin (it is Ruth's exploitation of giving shelter to this momentarily newsworthy figure that will provide her, in a debased way, with her breakthrough as a writer); the palatial home of a dotty, symphony-loving dowager who confuses Hiro with Seiji Ozawa; an old slaveholding cell; and, ultimately, the swamp of swamps ("bastion of cottonmouth, rattlesnake and leech, mother of vegetation, father of mosquito, soul of silt"), the Okefenokee.

Hiro's Okefenokee nightmare frames Ruth's twin hells: Jane Shine's triumphal public reading of her work to the guests at Thanatopsis House and Ruth's own disastrous reading the following evening. These ordeals, taking place in such vastly different terrains, are shown by Mr. Boyle to be equally funny and terrible.

At last comes the moment of truth for each of the fatefully intertwined characters: Hiro's resultant act is swift and poignant, but somehow not a surprise to us, knowing him as we now do. Ruth's sellout is strangely more shocking, but, we realize upon reflection, thoroughly in keeping with what she has most valued all along.

As he lays out the fates of these characters, Mr. Boyle gives us an absolutely stunning work, full of brilliant cross-cultural insights, his usual virtuoso language and one marvelous scene after another. ***East Is East*** is a novel about the way we appear to others, the way others appear to us and the lengths to which some of us will go to be accepted by others—or to become acceptable to ourselves.

Oliver Conant   (review date 12-26 November 1990)

SOURCE: "Nothing to Laugh About," in *The New Leader,* Vol. LXXIII, No. 15, November 12-26, 1990, pp. 22-3.

[*In the following review, Conant disparages* East Is East's *plotting, characterization, and prose as superficial.*]

A young sailor in the Japanese Merchant Marine, Hiro Tanaka, jumps ship off the coast of Georgia, swims ashore and tries to survive on his own as an illegal alien. Such is the unlikely premise of T. Coraghessan Boyle's farcical, often crude and, on occasion, mordantly funny new novel [*East Is East*]. Despite its heavy dose of unreality, the account of Hiro's brief, disastrous sojourn in the New World is at times strangely compelling.

The author of many short stories and three previous novels, most recently the highly regarded *World's End*, Boyle is fond of the narrative of strenuous physical adventure. Although his latest work casts a somewhat wider satirical net, at base it simply continues to mine that imaginative vein. *East Is East* details Hiro's trials from his initial escape, vividly described in the novel's opening—"He was swimming, rotating from front to back, thrashing his arms and legs and puffing out his cheeks, and it seemed as if he'd been swimming forever. He did the crawl, the breast-stroke, the Yokohama kick . . ."—to his last desperate bid for freedom, toward the end of the book, in the Okefenokee swamp. "Was it all a swamp, the whole hopeless country?" Hiro exclaims miserably as he finds himself slogging through its vast expanse, "Where were the shopping malls, the condos, the tattoo parlors and supermarkets?"

Hiro, whose name is a sort of literary joke (hero), functions chiefly as a device; as a character he has almost no reality. In only one respect does the invention betray some actuality: The author carefully supplies his protagonist with a body that suffers horribly, and (in Boyle's hands) comically, from the indignities of life on the run in the utter wilderness we forget our country still contains.

As a literary convenience, Hiro serves his creator well. He allows Boyle an odd vantage point from which to make fun of Southerners, caricature American attitudes toward Japanese and vice versa, and above all spoof the Immigration and Naturalization Service INS—an agency whose officials in recent years have certainly made every effort to behave as if their sole mission was to provide material for comic novelists. But "Hiro Tanaka" is so far from being a developed persona that for the most part he strikes us as a piece of research, a tissue of guidebook phrases and ethnographic shorthand about contemporary Japanese mannerisms and mores.

As it happens Hiro is only half-Japanese. He is the unfortunate by-blow of an American father, a hippie on a visit to Japan during the '60s, who abandoned him soon after he was born, and a Tokyo bargirl, who in her shame committed suicide when he was six. Abused all his life for his mixed parentage, he develops an idealized view of America, nourished by pop music, movies and TV. He expects to find in the United States a kind of paradise of miscege-nation, a land of "glorious, polyglot cities" where "you could be one part Negro, two parts Serbo-Croatian and three parts Eskimo and walk down the street with your head held high." What he discovers instead is that nearly everyone he encounters is as xenophobic and racially intolerant as any of the taunters he left behind, and that, at least in the noisome bogs where he makes his landing, there is hardly a street to be seen.

The grotesque disparity between Hiro's expectations and the unpleasant realities that confront him in the swampy back country of the American South is the source of much of the comedy in *East Is East*. It is not humor that appeals to the reader's kindlier feelings, however; it is closer to the cruel amusement aroused in a native by the discomfiture of a hapless foreigner.

Hiro is more than discomfited, of course—he is literally dragged through the mud. That the result should be as killingly funny as it sometimes is testifies to Boyle's professional skill, but it leaves one uneasy about his intentions. The book is filled with the emotions and vocabulary of ethnic antagonism—words like *gaijin* (apparently Japanese slang for non-Japanese), and the more familiar American epithets for Tanaka's countrymen are thick on the page. The thought that a segment of the novel-reading public is eager to be given permission to laugh at a series of torments undergone by an impoverished illegal immigrant is a bit disturbing; the idea that an established writer might wish to capitalize on the opportunity more disturbing still.

> At its best, *East Is East* is an exuberant combination of proficient adventure writing and burlesque. It is a tall tale—or, more accurately, a spoof of a tall tale.
>
> —*Oliver Conant*

I should say that, on the evidence of this book, it is entirely unclear whether Boyle has a thought in his head concerning his themes and purposes. Nor can one determine how much he really aspires to satire, an honorific reviewers regularly bestow on his writing. If anything, there are stylistic tendencies that betray an ambition to write a more thoughtless kind of popular fiction: lots of one sentence paragraphs, one word sentences, and a tedious, sudsy subplot involving the loves and careerist maneuverings of a struggling female writer from California who harbors Hiro at a preposterous artists' colony.

Ruth Dershowitz is a monster of selfishness; she uses Hiro repeatedly, beds him when her boyfriend pays undue attention to a rival, and attempts to exploit him, first for fictional material and then as a springboard to a career in journalism. Her fellow residents, supposedly famous avant-garde literary celebrities, are all pretentious fools, and the treatment of their goings-on is labored and gratuitous.

At its best, *East is East* is an exuberant combination of proficient adventure writing and burlesque. It is a tall tale—or, more accurately, a spoof of a tall tale. Boyle has great fun parodying Hemingway, Faulkner and even Melville (along the way there's some malarkey about an albino INS man and a hunt for a rare type of white pygmy sunfish).

Significantly, the author appears to have the most fun of

all writing about the savage, predatory, nonhuman life of the swamps: He concocts horrific descriptions of the Oke-fenokee: "Vast and primeval, unfathomable, unconquer-able, bastion of cottonmouth, rattlesnake and leech, moth-er of vegetation, father of mosquito, soul of silt, the Okefenokee . . ." etc. And he remarks on the hideous cries of the birds swooping across "the cremated sky": "Somewhere a bird began to cry out, hard and urgent, as if some unseen hand were plucking it alive."

The minor characters in this novel have names like Detlef Abecorn, Irving Thalamus, Septima Light, Mignonette Teitelbaum, and Orlando Seezers. From this one is en-couraged to conclude nothing more than the fact that a Dickensian flair for creating names does not guarantee Dickens' substance, satirical intelligence or appeal to readers' sympathies.

Boyle commands a quirky, ferociously energetic prose that seems to owe nothing to anyone writing today, with the possible exception of Tom Wolfe. He should do more with his considerable gifts than squander them on cynical conceits like *East is East*.

Tom Hymes   (review date November-December 1990)

SOURCE: A review of *East Is East*, in *West Coast Review of Books*, Vol. 15, No. 6, November-December, 1990, p. 23.

[*In the following review of* East Is East, *Hymes asserts that Boyle's characterization and plotting serve short stories bet-ter than novels but notes that his wit prevents the book from becoming tiresome.*]

T. Coraghessan Boyle is a writer who's hot, relatively new in town, and very good. He has a glib wit and a superb at-tention to detail. He is his best, though, when his talents are geared toward his short stories. His novels can have the feel of elongation and a certain weightlessness, as though they have been stretched a little too thin and then fattened with hot air, like French pastry or rhetoric. His fourth novel, *East Is East,* has that feel.

The story concerns Hiro Tanaka, a Japanese seaman who has had to jump ship off the coast of Georgia and swim for it. He winds up on a small island, on which there is a writer's colony of some apparent repute. Hiro's father was an American hippie who deserted the family, so Hiro can easily be said to be running from a nightmare toward a dream.

He lands right in the middle of hell, a hell that is circus-like and mostly populated by freakish characters who are hardly recognizable as human by either Hiro or the read-er. They include Ruth, a young writer at the colony who is plagued by uncertainty about a talent she apparently does not posses; Saxby, who makes love to Ruth and searches for a new species of fish (and whose part would be considered thankless if this were a movie); and a whole slew of other caricatures who are meant to resemble real people but don't.

Only Hiro achieves depth and pathos, and those in only the last few pages. On the very last page he obtains even

a sort of martyrdom, while every American encountered is remembered as petty and self-centered. The point is ob-viously to elaborate on an insidious spiritual bankruptcy of which even our artists are ignorant, but it would be more powerfully made with characters who are not so vac-uous.

Otherwise, *East is East* is very well written and, though too long, not boring. Boyle employs a neat technique in overlapping characters' accounts of events, thus achieving a Rashomon effect in seeing the same thing different ways. It works at first and then becomes a little tiresome, though, provoking the thought that maybe he just didn't have much for these people to do. In short, Boyle should stay short, even in novel form.

Robert Towers   (review date 17 January 1991)

SOURCE: "Enigma Variations," in *The New York Review of Books,* Vol. XXXVIII, Nos. 1 & 2, January 17, 1991, pp. 31-3.

[*Towers is an American educator, novelist, and critic. In the following excerpt, he observes that, although Boyle's satire is "more farcical than witty," *East Is East* is a funny book, particularly in its portrayal of the protagonist, Hiro Tanaka.*]

T. Coraghessan Boyle's third novel, *World's End,* won the PEN/Faulkner Award for Fiction in 1988. It is a long, complex work, a kind of mock history of a Hudson River community that jumps backward and forward from the 1660s to the 1960s. Often satirical, full of grotesque and comically horrendous incidents, *World's End* is reminis-cent in tone of John Barth's densely written historical pas-tiche, *The Sot-Weed Factor,* though Boyle's prose is far more readable. His new novel, *East Is East,* is shorter than *World's End* and more topical, dealing as it does with the cross-cultural blind spots afflicting a hapless Japanese and his American protector-persecutors. It is also, I think, funnier.

The victim is Hiro (hero?) Tanaka, the overweight, food-obsessed, red-haired offspring of a Japanese mother and a hippie American father who was "so dirty and hairy . . . that he could have grown turnips behind his ears." Hiro, whose father disappeared before his birth and whose mother died six months after, has had a miserable child-hood in Kyoto, taunted by his schoolmates as "a half-breed, a *happa,* a high-nose and butter-stinker—and an or-phan to boot—forever a foreigner in his own society." To compensate for his feelings of inferiority, he becomes a devotee of the heroic and rigorous seventeenth century Samurai code of Jocho Yamamoto and its latter-day inter-preter, Yukio Mishima, who committed hari kari in pro-test against contemporary degeneracy. But Hiro also yearns to see America, to "see the cowboys and hookers and wild Indians, maybe even discover his father in some gleaming, spacious ranch house and sit down to cheese-burgers with him":

> If the Japanese were a pure race, intolerant of
> miscegenation to the point of fanaticism, the
> Americans, he knew, were a polyglot tribe,

mutts and mulattoes and worse—or better, depending on your point of view. In America you could be one part Negro, two parts Serbo-Croatian and three parts Eskimo and walk down the street with your head held high.

Such is the poor naif who signs on to a Japanese freighter and then jumps ship off the coast of Georgia.

Tupelo Island, where Hiro comes ashore, is swampy, insect- and reptile-infested, and inhabited by rednecks, Gullah-speaking blacks, and a community of well-to-do retirees. More important, Tupelo is the seat of Thanatopsis House, an artist's colony very much like Yaddo, which has been established by a patrician Southerner, Septima Lights, on her late husband's ancestral estate. The catastrophic relations between Hiro, the inhabitants of the island, and especially one of the artist guests at Thanatopsis House produce the baleful comedy of *East Is East*. Misunderstanding is piled upon misunderstanding, and the luckless Hiro, who longs only for a square meal and some way to reach the mainland, finds himself a fugitive from justice, accused, among other things, of arson and murder, and hounded by idiotic immigration inspectors and brutal southern sheriffs. Finally Hiro is allowed to escape from the swamps of Tupelo (in the trunk of Septima's Mercedes) only to find himself deposited in the greatest swamp of them all, the Okefenokee. Can this really be, he wonders, the "mainrand" of America?

As important to the novel as Hiro himself is a writer at Thanatopsis named Ruth Dershowitz. Thirty-four but admitting to twenty-nine, Ruth has put in time at the creative writing programs of Iowa and Irvine, has spent a summer at Bread Loaf, and has published four "intense and gloomy" stories in the quarterlies. La Dershowitz, as she is called, is consumed with envy and ambition; she is only too aware that she owes her presence at Thanatopsis not to her literary achievements but to the fact that she is the lover of Septima's son. It is through this striving, insecure woman that we meet the other residents of Thanatopsis in their little world of status-seeking, sexual manipulations, and one-upmanship. And it is to her woodland studio (called Hart Crane—all the studios at Thanatopsis are named after famous suicides) that the hunted, starving, filthy, insect-lacerated Hiro makes his way, thereby joining the novel's two centers of interest and providing one of its major misunderstandings.

Boyle's approach to literary satire is clearly broad rather than subtle, more farcical than witty. Boyle obviously has a good time setting up and knocking down the resident artists of Thanatopsis. One of the things La Dershowitz most eagerly pursues is the approval of Irving Thalamus, "whose trade-in-stock" is "urban Jewish angst," and what she most dreads is the arrival of her rival, Jane Shine, whose flamboyant good looks and sex-dripping fiction have led her to a series of triumphs both literary and romantic. Another resident is Laura Grobian, described as "the doyenne of the dark-eyed, semi-mysterious upper-middle-class former-bohemian school of WASP novelists, famous for a bloodless 209 page trilogy set in 1967 San Francisco." Unfortunately artists' colonies, like academic communities, have lately been the butt of so much heavy-handed ridicule that one shrinks from yet another account of the petty-mindedness and sexual sloppiness of supposedly gifted people. Eventually, the series of humiliations to which La Dershowitz is subjected comes to seem more mean-spirited than amusing.

The strength of *East Is East* lies in the story of Hiro, where Boyle's previously demonstrated talent for comic-grotesque invention comes into play. One of the funniest episodes occurs when a rich, garrulous, Japanophile old woman, Ambly Wooster, takes Hiro into her beach house under the impression that he is Seiji Ozawa. The cultural confusions multiply, as do the vigorously narrated mishaps that befall Hiro in his desperate attempts to leave the island and reach the City of Brotherly Love. While there is a considerable degree of Waugh-like cruelty in the fate Boyle metes out to his antihero, who follows the example of Mishima to its bloody conclusion, Hiro himself is engaging enough to provide a pathos at the end that in no way clashes with the comedy that precedes it. This is an exuberant reworking of the innocents-abroad theme that goes back at least as far as Voltaire's *L'Ingénu*.

Andrew Rosenheim (review date 22 March 1991)

SOURCE: "A Crusoe in Georgia," in *The Times Literary Supplement,* No. 4590, March 22, 1991, p. 19.

[*Rosenheim is an American novelist and critic. In the following review of* East Is East, *he praises Boyle's vivid, humorous style.*]

T. Coraghessan Boyle writes a rich and masterful prose which enhances his visceral attachment to the story he tells. In *East Is East,* Hiro Tanaka is half Japanese, half American, bastard product of a hippie guitarist's union with a Tokyo bar hostess. Embittered by a Japanese childhood spent being ostracized as a half-breed, Hiro heads West, lured by the promise implicit in America's composition: "polyglot tribe, mutts and mulattoes . . . you could be one part Negro, two parts Serbo-Croatian and three parts Eskimo and walk down the street with your head held high".

This is not the America he finds. Jumping ship—"a sixty-eight-foot drop from the bridge to the water"—Hiro swims to a Georgia island where he is spotted and chased by an ignorant citizenry who provide a latter-day parody of the "Yellow Peril" scares in America after Pearl Harbor. This invader is a modern-day, voluntary Crusoe, equipped only with the Spartan philosophy of his hero, Yukio Mishima; the island he lands on, however, is not as suitably pristine. It holds the usual Faulknerian mix of slave descendants, white crackers and plantation folk, but here the local aristocrat, Septima Hollister Lights, has endowed a local artists' community in honour of her suicide husband.

Thanatopsis House is Yaddo-like in the preciousness of its arrangement, with working cabins for each artist named after notable suicides—Hart Crane and Diane Arbus among them. One of the residents, Ruth Dershowitz, a tyro ambitious writer and the lover of Mrs. Lights's amateur marine biologist son, discovers the half-starving Hiro and furtively befriends him. The patronage takes the form of yuppie ambrosia gone South: sneaked provisions of "pâté, crab salad, sandwiches of smoked turkey or provolone with roasted peppers, homegrown tomatoes, fruit, a Thermos of iced tea, réal silver and a linen napkin". These jaunty, hip, satirical notes, reminiscent of the early novels of Thomas McGuane, disguise the tragic potential of the scenario; such is the frantic fertility of Boyle's comedy, any pathos is slow to emerge.

The multiple viewpoints from which **East Is East** is told preserve a certain distance between Boyle's characters and the reader, but this slightly troubling lack of engagement is compensated for by the striking, sometimes preposterous comedy at play. Mistaken by an elderly dowager for Seiji Ozawa, Hiro is forced to sing, or rather conduct, for his supper—"as best he could and with the sweeping muscular movements of the long-distance swimmer". An evening recital at Thanatopsis House by an avant-garde composer is summarized then skewered:

> *Bang! Bang!* she slammed at the keyboard with the ball of her fist. And then: nothing. For three full agonizing minutes she sat rigid. . . . Finally the alarm went off—ding-ding-ding—and *Bang!* she hit the keyboard. The piece was called *Parfait in Chrome,* and it went on for forty-five minutes.

Boyle's style is as lively as his imagination, a mix of the demotic and the elegant. His diction is at times vivid and poetic ("he woke to a parliament of birds and the trembling watery light of dawn"), at others aptly colloquial— "the day was terrifically hot, a real slap-in-the-face, dog-under-the-house sort of day." Each sentence seems precisely wrought, yet energized, and as the plot accelerates with Hiro's capture, escape, then re-capture, the frenzied blend of elements threatens to unhinge the novel. What saves this book from self-combustion or entropy, other than the manifest skilfulness of its author, is the progressive reduction of distance between characters and reader. Ruth Dershowitz or La Dershowitz as this Jewish-American Princess (and thus caricature "Jap") styles herself, is not, it seems, much of a writer after all. Her hatred of a more successful rival is merely envy, and her reading of her work to a night-time convocation of Thanatopsis colleagues is a disaster:

> Halfway through . . . Orlando Seezers began to snore . . . His snores were soft, almost polite, but audible for all that—and everyone was aware of them.

Journalism, unsurprisingly, proves the next port of call for her ambition, with her experiences as Hiro's putative saviour the springboard to commercial success.

Hiro himself senses the corruption he is suffering from in his pursuit of a non-existent American dream: "This lying business wasn't so hard really. It was the American way, he saw that now." What he sees he cannot adapt to, and it is to a Japanese model (Mishima's suicide) that he reverts for his own resolution. His is an immigrant's dream turned nightmare, an Ellis Island saying no.

Jane Smiley   (review date 25 April 1993)

SOURCE: "Snap, Crackle, Pop in Battle Creek," in *The New York Times Book Review,* April 25, 1993, pp. 1, 28.

[*Smiley is an American educator, novelist, short story writer, nonfiction writer, and critic. In the review below, she discusses* The Road to Wellville, *focusing on Boyle's characterization as she compares the novel to Boyle's previous works.*]

Throughout his career, T. Coraghessan Boyle has shown a special affinity for dirt and a special relish for depicting the feckless self-absorption of the post-war generation. In his early story **"Bloodfall,"** seven commune dwellers who wear only white are subjected to a rain of blood, then feces, but their response is to nestle more closely together and go back to sleep. In his last novel, **East Is East,** the members of the Jeffcoat family, as replete with naivete as they are with all the most modern camping conveniences, set out for a week in the Okefenokee Swamp and never begin to comprehend the perils they escape. In these works—and many of those in between—Mr. Boyle has excelled at holding up a mirror in which our own faces grin foolishly against the very dark background of a world we don't comprehend, and don't even try to comprehend.

The experience of reading Mr. Boyle is thus an uncomfortable one. His precise and often delicious comic style and his exuberant wordplay promise pleasure, yet the justly deserved fates of his narcissistic and sometimes cruel characters withhold a final portion of pleasurable satisfaction. His works are easy to savor but hard to embrace; they have, I think, aroused much admiration, but not so much love.

In his new novel, **The Road to Wellville,** Mr. Boyle seems to have abjured baby boomers—and, for a little while, dirt. The subject, indeed, is health. It is 1907 and the reader is invited to contemplate the inventor of cornflakes, Dr. John Harvey Kellogg of Battle Creek, Mich., a paragon of clean living who prescribes for the patients in his sanitarium not one but five enemas every single day, as well as a diet featuring nut butter, grapes, milk, a mysterious substance called Protose and a drink called kumyss (which, according to one reluctant diner, "smelled like a wet dog"). The patients at the Battle Creek Sanitarium (known to devotees simply as the San) include the usual gaggle of the wealthy and influential: "On the horizon were visits by Henry Ford, Harvey Firestone, Thomas Edison, Admiral Richard E. Byrd and the voluminous William Howard Taft." It does not escape the doctor that his fortune and power owe much to their faith in him. But Dr. Kellogg is a man of convictions, too, and part of Mr. Boyle's purpose is to explore the workings of such deeply held beliefs.

Every religion needs a skeptic, and for the religion of "biologic living," the author provides Will Lightbody, a wealthy young man from Peterskill, N.Y., who follows his wife, Eleanor, to Battle Creek, partly to protect his marriage and partly to seek relief from his own affliction, a gut that sings with pain every time he takes a bite. Will is a victim of earlier misguided home medication: in an attempt to wean him from drink, Eleanor has been surreptitiously dosing him with Sears' White Star Liquor Cure, which turns out to be tincture of opium. To break himself of his narcotic habit, he goes back to Old Crow. By the time he arrives at the San, Will is "just one more sick man in a wheelchair," watching his wife flirt with her doctor. Kellogg diagnoses Will's problem as "autointoxication" and prescribes a regimen of fasting, exercise, enemas and "sinusoidal" baths (wherein an electric current is passed through the patient's body while his hands and feet are immersed in water).

John Harvey Kellogg's real antagonist, though, is his adopted son, George, a 19-year-old ne'er-do-well for whose ultimate benefit and in whose ultimate interest the doctor is certain he has always acted. George is a vision of physical corruption ("teeth rotted to stubs, breath stinking like a dead thing, the miasma of his catastrophic odor enveloping him"). And this despite the efforts of Dr. Kellogg, who has raised the boy along with an ever-changing collection of adoptive siblings according to the sort of institutionalized, rigorous discipline common to the era. Dr. Kellogg has a weakness for George that springs not from affection but from a goading sense of failure; George's very existence undermines the doctor's convictions by demonstrating how emphatically his methods can backfire. George, though, is not simply a misunderstood victim. He really does stink, really commits crimes, really seeks to destroy Dr. Kellogg and the sanitarium for purely vengeful reasons.

In a Boyle novel, there are major characters but no true heroes or heroines. Instead, Mr. Boyle invariably complicates and muddies the conventional play of good against evil. Even in *East Is East,* in which such a protagonist does seem to appear in the form of Hiro, the Japanese sailor who only wants to find an America where he can melt into the pot, the reader's identification with this figure seems to be prohibited by his enigmatic and dogged inability to understand what is happening to him. The author himself appears far more interested in Ruth Dershowitz, an ambitious but untalented novelist who finally scores a big publishing contract to tell Hiro's story—even though the reader knows perfectly well that she doesn't understand that story at all.

In *The Road to Wellville,* as in his previous works, Mr. Boyle evokes the world of the senses with remarkable skill. As always, his prose is a marvel, enjoyable from beginning to end, alive with astute observations, sharp intelligence and subtle musicality.

—*Jane Smiley*

At first, it seems as though the hero of *The Road to Wellville* might be Charlie Ossining, an acquaintance of Will's and a future business partner of George's. Charlie is a well-meaning young entrepreneur, also from Peterskill, whose plan is to get rich with Per-Fo, a flaked cereal with a celery additive. It is soon clear that Charlie's sufferings for the sake of his fortune are to be significant. But just as George Kellogg is repellent, his father wrongheaded, Will Lightbody weak and Eleanor unfaithful, Charlie lies, cheats and steals in his effort to climb aboard the gravy train.

But even as Mr. Boyle is resisting casting these characters as heroes, he seems to have mellowed in his depiction of the world they live in. Images abound of ordered, moderate well-being—represented, for example, by the presence of Dick, the Lightbodys' wire fox terrier, in the house on Parsonage Lane that Will Lightbody longs to return to. The natural world around Battle Creek is not as fallen as the landscape of *Greasy Lake & Other Stories,* the Florida and Georgia swampland of *East Is East* or the early Hudson Valley of the novel *World's End.* And while the "primitive" is present (Charlie boards at Mrs. Eyvindsdottir's rooming house, where the daily fare usually includes stews made of various small mammals trapped by the proprietor's beau, Bjork Bjorksson), it is on the fringes of the more inviting wholesomeness of this early-20th century America, where, as Will notices on a rare excursion outside the grounds of the San, "the lake gave back the sunlight in rolling flashes and sudden incendiary sparks, pushing at the shore as if testing its limits."

In *The Road to Wellville,* as in his previous works, Mr. Boyle evokes the world of the senses with remarkable skill. As always, his prose is a marvel, enjoyable from beginning to end, alive with astute observations, sharp intelligence and subtle musicality. Possibly as an effect of his highly developed style, Mr. Boyle's vision has been one of the most distinctive and original of his generation. "I've always written about man as an animal species among other animals, competing for limited resources," he once observed, then added, with characteristically mordant humor, "When there are too many rabbits, they all get tularemia and die off, and that's the way we're heading."

In *The Road to Wellville,* Mr. Boyle suggests that such a view is all the more appropriate to those, like John Harvey Kellogg, who presume to transcend, through spurious cleanliness and the false claims of science, both the painful and the pleasurable realities of the human-animal body. Kellogg's principal false promise is that of self-improvement, of willed change through reason. But animals don't change, and, in Mr. Boyle's view, neither does Dr. Kellogg, Will, Charlie, George or Eleanor. The most they can do, when pressed by circumstances, is reveal their eternal natures.

The Road to Wellville is T. Coraghessan Boyle's lightest, least fierce novel. But in the end, as a reassurance to those of us who have savored the sharpness, complexity and bitterness of his previous works, the animals still bite, the fecal matter still flies and foolishness is still on ample display.

Robert Cohen (review date 30 May 1993)

SOURCE: "Flakes, Nuts and Capitalists," in *Los Angeles Times Book Review,* May 30, 1993, pp. 2, 11.

[*Cohen is an American educator, novelist, and short story writer. In the following review, he maintains that, despite Boyle's prodigious comedic gifts,* The Road to Wellville *proves too shallow and crude to sustain interest.*]

One of the more endearing and exasperating facets of the American appetite is its hunger for self-improvement. Think of Bill Moyers and his attentive, homespun, secular romanticism; he roams from coast to coast like a political candidate—our candidate—on an eternal campaign for betterness, for a philosophy or paradigm that will lend coherence to our lives on this messy, bloated continent. If the old religions fail to serve us, we invent new ones—or recycle slightly used ones. If nothing else, it keeps us busy.

It keeps our satirists busy, too, of course. And none more prolifically or acutely so than T. Coraghessan Boyle, who thrives on our aspirational mania in all its forms. Since his breakthrough with *World's End* (1987), Boyle, a prodigiously gifted, high-octane prose writer, has been on something of a creative roll, culminating in his last and funniest novel, *East Is East*. With each new book it becomes harder to resist the confidence and exuberance of his style, the boldness of his reach.

In *The Road to Wellville* (from a slogan of C. W. Post's), he gives us turn-of-the-century Battle Creek, Mich., with its gold-rush ambience of cereal manufacturers, health food enthusiasts and scam artists, and its god-like presiding genius: the estimable John Harvey Kellogg, inventor of the corn flake, peanut butter and countless other nutritional icons, and director of the renowned (and nonfictional) Battle Creek Sanitarium, "the single healthiest spot on the planet." A gleaming and prosperous spa, the "San" operates on a strict regimen of dietary restraint, exercise and inspirational invective. Guests include such luminaries as Henry Ford, Upton Sinclair, Thomas Edison and a generous assortment of rich neurotics such as Eleanor Lightbody and her husband, the dyspeptic and befuddled Will, who has followed her to the San in hopes of saving his marriage and his stomach both.

Also in town, on a very different mission, is the young wanna-be entrepreneur Charlie Ossining (Boyle shows, as always, a wondrous touch with names), who means to parlay a small borrowed investment into a brand new cereal company called Per-Fo. The arc of Charlie's descent into the capitalist black hole of Battle Creek parallels that of Will Lightbody as he stumbles through the tortuous, hygienic corridors of the San ("a purgatory of the unwise and the unwell"), so that in time we begin to see each as a kind of shadow or double of the other—two small men of limited vision in this land of entrepreneurial giants. Their struggle to gain control over their respective fates propels the plot forward. Taken together with Dr. Kellogg, who strives to maintain his immaculate fiefdom, and his adopted son George, a poor man's Frankenstein monster, the castoff demi-urge of a Promethean obsession, these earnest bumblers and lunatic pedagogues appear to be the perfect vessels for Boyle's comic talents.

And yet the novel that results is something of a disappointment. For one thing, Dr. Kellogg's head turns out to be an only fitfully rewarding place to spend time:

> The Doctor had triumphed, as usual, but at what cost? His stomach was sour, his joints ached, his eyes were tired. There were just too many troubles, too many things pressing on him, too many hands reaching into his pockets. Despite the rigors of the physiological life and the fortitude of mind and body it inspired, he was depressed. Tired. Overworked.

With his triplicate syntax, his impresario's cynicism and his dogged, humorless pedantry, the doctor is a tough nut to crack—and like George, he does not inspire much intimacy or affection from his creator. Or from us. For all his messianic fervor he comes across as a distant and hypocritical sadist; as when, to demonstrate to his patients the evils of meat, he tosses a steak to a hungry wolf: "What he didn't mention was that she had been trained, through negative reinforcement, to view meat as the prelude to a beating . . . or that her vegetarian diet had so weakened her, she wouldn't have had the strength to chew it in any case."

Then too, neither Charlie nor Will nor Eleanor—all victims of their own weak constitutions and the predatory designs of others—are, to put it mildly, terribly quick on the uptake. Because of this the story, untypically for Boyle, moves slowly, with every turn signaled well in advance. The pace may be in part a function of the setting, the dull uneventfulness of sanitarium life. Out of similar materials, of course, Thomas Mann built a towering philosophical novel, but Boyle has a very different set of intentions, and his trademark wit and inventiveness, his referential quickness, all seem oddly smothered here, as if they too have fallen victim, like Will Lightbody, to the San's endless, static routine: "Another meal . . . but was it life, life as it was meant to be lived, raw and untamed and exhilarating, or just some glassed-under simulacrum? Will lifted the fork to his mouth, inserted a tasteless lump of roughage and sighed."

Because the answer to Will's question is never in doubt, there is not much in the way of thematic tension to sustain the reader's intrigue. We are left with the considerable research Boyle has done into the period, which proves fascinating (I particularly enjoyed learning the alcohol content of the era's various "tonics") though not always dramatic. And after several hundred pages of colonic enemas, stool samples, meals of hash, nut bread and macaroni cutlets, and the good doctor's hellfire sermons on nutrition and vegetarianism, the satiric edge gets a little blunt. There is an ambitious, pull-out-the stops climax, and an extended coda that manages to be both deft and moving, but there are also times when the book reads like a Marx Brothers farce ("A Day at the Races," say) minus Groucho, Chico and Harpo.

The Road to Wellville is craftily paved, but it is also somewhat longer and straighter than you'd expect. Boyle, who has delivered plenty of giddy rides in the past, seems to be relying this time on cruise control.

My interest is to use history to explore
how I feel about things and to
communicate that to others—hopefully in
an entertaining and edifying and
satisfactory way. Where the facts stand in
the way of what I'm trying to accomplish,
well, the facts will have to be altered.

—*T. Coraghessan Boyle, as quoted by
Tobin Harshaw in his "The Uses of
History," in* The New York Times Book
Review, *25 April 1993.*

Craig Seligman   (review date 4 October 1993)

SOURCE: "Survival of the Cruelest," in *The New Republic,* Vol. 209, No. 14, October 4, 1993, pp. 43-5.

[*In the following review of* The Road to Wellville, *Seligman surveys Boyle's career, contending that the novelist's "pyrotechnical exhibitionism" fails to conceal the "black-hearted fatalism" that ultimately renders all his works simplistic.*]

A sanitarium is a funny place to set a novel if you don't believe in cures. But the Battle Creek Sanitarium, temple to healthy vegetarian living and stomping ground of Dr. John Harvey Kellogg (1852-1943), apostle of colonic hygiene and inventor of the cornflake, is where T. Coraghessan Boyle, a pessimist if there ever was one, has set *The Road to Wellville,* in the years 1907 and 1908. Boyle's pitiless and brilliant first novel, *Water Music* (1981), unfolds around the British exploration of the Niger circa 1800; *World's End* (1987) shifts back and forth between a Hudson River community in the seventeenth and twentieth centuries; and he has riffed on Carry Nation and Robert Johnson and characters from Hemingway and Gogol, among others. He has a gift for animating bygone eras, partly because his somewhat fusty, slightly hyperbolic language—probably learned at Mailer's knee—is so offhand in its mixture of the antiquated and the up-to-date. The anachronism soothes, directs your attention away from the verbal structures and toward the plot. And everything, in Boyle, is a handmaiden to the plot.

More happens in one of Boyle's short stories than in most post-Victorian novels. He plots his characters onto the page with a minimum of fuss and off they run, the action filling in their contours. What interests him is behavior, not motive, and even behavior only to the extent that it oils the Rube Goldberg contraptions of his plots. His preferred way of structuring a book, and frequently even a story, is to intertwine two or more barely related strands. Thus *Water Music* darts back and forth between the historical figure of Mungo Park, the explorer, and Ned Rise, a fictional London lowlife. *World's End* offers parallel tales in different centuries, the modern characters helplessly perpetrating the same betrayals and blunders that sank their ancestors. In *East Is East* (1990), a comedy

about backbiting writers in an artists' colony alternates with the trials of a Japanese sailor who has jumped ship and is hiding out in the nearby swamp.

The strands in *The Road to Wellville*—that is, the principal characters—are three: Dr. Kellogg, master in his marble-walled domain and an insufferable quack; Will Lightbody, a patient at the San (as it's informally known) with his wife, Eleanor; and Charlie Ossining, confidence man and would-be entrepreneur. This time the parts are even less bound up with one another than in the past, but the novel hardly suffers for their diffuseness. Boyle has always known how to edit so that his jump cuts are pleasurably violent. Often he'll end a chapter on a cliffhanger, and the escape from the maximum-tension situation comes as a relief. He'll return two or three chapters later, after the crisis has been resolved, then back up and tell you what happened. There's a small drawback to this approach in that once you know the outcome, the flashback account, no matter how harrowing, loses some of its force. Which is fine, because Boyle harrows like a professional sadist.

Boyle only pretends to be a comic novelist, though from the standpoint of funny he's pretty convincing. His worldview—set forth now in five novels and three collections of stories—is a black-hearted fatalism: you are who you are, you poor schmuck, and there's not a damn thing you can do about it, because something in the cosmos (he never gets around to discussing what, exactly) has stacked the cards against you and in somebody else's favor. Staging tragic ordeals as slapstick lightens the load on the reader's emotions, though it also robs his heroes of the dignity that is classically their due. But it doesn't rob them of their pluck. "He clung there, a man with a purpose, a man who would fight and scratch, manipulate and maneuver—a man who would survive." (Ned Rise in *Water Music.*) "He was down, but not defeated. No, never defeated." (Jeremias Van Brunt in *World's End.*) And it's the same with Charlie Ossining in *The Road to Wellville*:

> Somehow, when he rose up off that bench and stepped into the surging crowd, he found the strength to fight down the fear and loathing than ran through his veins like an infection. . . . He felt the smile leap to his face, tasted the sweet syrup of the lies gathering on his tongue, saw the world come into focus as if for the first time.

I'm not down yet, these Sisyphuses keep muttering as they get up—slowly, painfully—and dust themselves off. But Boyle never lets them stay up for long; he keeps a finger pressed maliciously against their rock. The novels are treadmills—no one makes it from point A to point B. Their only real progress is from resolve to resignation (if not despair) as it dawns on them that they'll never make it: once a chump, always a chump.

Boyle paints the world as a jungle (often literally, as in *Water Music* and *East is East*), a Nietzschean bad dream of the strong eating the weak and the wealthy cheating the poor. "I've always written about man as an animal species among other animals, competing for limited resources," he has explained. For him society splits into swindlers and suckers, and he sees nothing particularly admirable about being a sucker.

In *The Road to Wellville,* Charlie Ossining is the sucker trying to ascend to the status of swindler, this book's Ned Rise (whose name was no coincidence). That makes him the character Boyle has the most fun visiting disaster on. Charlie meets Will and Eleanor on a train to Battle Creek early in the book. They are bound for the San; he's on his way to make his fortune (he thinks) in breakfast foods—the Kellogg Company, an outgrowth of the doctor's nutritional researches, and its main rival, Post, having by this time put the town on the business map.

Charlie isn't the first of Boyle's characters to be stitched together from contradictions, but he's the one on whom the needlework is most exposed. In one chapter he's a shark out to flimflam every moneybags he can into making an investment in Per-Fo (for "perfect food"). The next time we see him he's an honest entrepreneur-in-embryo, with dreams of life as a breakfast-food magnate. The two sides never gel. Instead we get two characters, one sweet, one sleazy, one ingenuous and one canny, together in a single body, if not on a single page.

Good or bad, poor Charlie faces one crippling setback after another. The stars start fading from his eyes as soon as he steps off the train and learns that he is one among a legion of get-rich-quick schemers who have descended on Battle Creek envisioning a cereal bonanza. In Boyle's familiar pattern, he is overworked, humiliated, defrauded, pummeled and punished. He plays the fool over and over and over, because that's his nature: he *is* a fool.

John Kellogg is nobody's fool. Boyle's Kellogg is a man devoted to health fads, without any real concern for his wealthy patients and none at all for the seriously ill (who are too likely to die and become "the very worst sort of advertisement"). By the end he is demonstrably no better than a murderer—a "beast of the jungle," Boyle calls him, though of course that tag implies a certain admiration, too. He couldn't care less about the doctor's place in nutritional history, but then Boyle doesn't view history as a continuum: the past, as he contemptuously presents it, isn't the foundation of the present, it's the discarded husk. His Georgian London and Dutch New York are sewers of the most appalling injustice and inequity and moral ignorance. Kellogg, with his cracked faith in colonic irrigation and biologic living and, above all, strict sexual abstinence, is a mascot for the benightedness of times gone by. (There is no mascot for progress.)

The central character, Will Lightbody, is harder to place in Boyle's schema. Alcoholism and addiction have done their damage, and now he can't even eat a hamburger without giving himself fits of pain. He has lost control of his life, and of his wife, a neurasthenic harpy who has fallen for the biologic-living craze and would be happy to settle into permanent hypochondria at the San. But Will, who is genuinely ill, hates the place.

In the Kellogg program to restore his health, Will suffers under a barrage of hair-raising treatments, beginning with a nauseating all-milk diet. But Boyle focuses so single-mindedly on the doctor's mania for control that the efficacy of his strategies never really comes under debate. Will isn't faced with much of a choice. If he goes off the diet,

stalks into town and gorges himself on hamburgers and whiskey, he winds up doubled over in pain and close to death. But to submit to the odious regimen, or even embrace it like the other zombies at the San, is spiritual suicide—which, in Boyle's hairy-fisted scheme, means loss of manhood.

And Will's manhood is already being severely challenged by his wife. Sex is strictly forbidden at the San, which is fine with Eleanor. Again, Boyle doesn't show much interest in the psychology of repression. He just wants to demonstrate that it's a lousy idea, and typically, he loads the dice. He sends Eleanor off to an even bigger quack than Kellogg, a Teutonic therapist who "manipulates her womb" to orgasm (which is to say, you get what you need).

In her husband's case he moves onto more taboo (and more novel) terrain. Once Will is deprived of sex and palatable food and placed on the Kellogg regimen of five enemas a day, his anus becomes his only source of pleasure. Boyle makes the connection explicit the first time Will receives an enema from his pretty nurse:

> Her hands. The warm bulb of the apparatus. What was he doing? What was going on? "Eleanor," he blurted. "My wife. Where's Eleanor?"
>
> "Hush," Irene whispered. "She's fine. She's on the second floor, room two-twelve, no doubt undergoing this very same procedure . . . to flush her system, relax her."
>
> Will was stunned. "Then she, she won't be staying here, with me?"
>
> The nurse's voice caressed his ear, soothing, soft, as much a part of him as the secret voice that spoke inside his head. "Oh, no. The Chief keeps couples separate here. For therapeutic reasons, of course. Our patients need quiet, rest—any sort of sexual stimulation could be fatal."
>
> *Sexual stimulation.* Why did those two words suddenly sound so momentous?
>
> "Relax," she whispered, and all at once Will felt the hot fluid surprise of it, his insides flooding as if a dam had burst, as if all the tropical rivers of the world were suddenly flowing through him, irrigating him, flushing, cleansing, churning away at his deepest nooks and recesses in a tumultuous cathartic rush. It was the most mortifying and exquisite moment of his life.

But this notion of enema-as-sex shows up just once more, nearly 300 pages later. (" 'And now'—and the soft soothing whisper of the words made him tingle as if it were seltzer water and not blood percolating through his veins—'are you ready for your irrigation?' ") Boyle doesn't examine what it might suggest about the doctor's own sexuality—as far as we can see, he doesn't have any—or explore it any more deeply in Will. Instead he just drops it. Maybe the suggestion of inversion in a character who is fighting for his manhood is too explicit, or too troubling. Or maybe Victorianism is not as dead as Boyle, who has a field day mocking the doctor's square ideals, would like to think. Because in the end he frames the case in startlingly Victorian terms: to recover his manhood, Will has to banish the influence of Kellogg, vanquish the womb manipulator, and reestablish his dominance over his wife. Boyle has never sounded like a troglodyte before—in fact *World's End,* his most overtly political book, suggests Tom Robbins in his hippy-dippy phase. But this novel will make ideal reading matter for Republican bedsides.

Boyle's pyrotechnical exhibitionism recalls Tom Wolfe and Hunter S. Thompson and, of course, Mailer—like them, he makes a virtue of excess—but the author who comes through is, for all the bleakness of his vision, a sweeter, less troubled man. The darkness that besets his work is cosmic; personally, he seems lighthearted and, on the whole, free of anguish. In temperament, the novelist he evokes isn't his hero, Dickens, but Fielding: his interest in neurotic states goes only as deep as their comic possibilities.

Picaresque is the natural form for a writer like that: riots of plot without a lot of ink wasted on psychological analysis. (Sociological analysis is something else; the brief descriptions of Japanese society in *East is East* are the most brilliant parts of the book.) Boyle loves a mess. He loves chaos. He loves marshes and jungles, and he loves the jungle of language: luxuriant sentences overgrown with lianas of lists, sesquipedalian words hanging down like rare fruits. For all its exoticism, though, his prose is lucid to the point of transparency. It doesn't require much deeper concentration than a good newspaper (though it does require a dictionary).

It would help if he made bigger demands on his readers. For all the surface messiness of his fiction, Boyle's fatalism is reductive (you're born to screw or born to get screwed), and as a result his comedy tends not merely toward the pop but toward the lite. You may read compulsively to find out what happens, but when you finish, the elaborate edifices can seem as lightweight as jokes. (This is especially true of the stories.) You come away feeling that very little is at stake. Yes, he takes risks—big risks—but they're technical risks; he throws himself into spots that demand writerly bravado, but he seldom puts anything more than his technique on the line. His artistry always surprises, always amuses, always impresses. And yet there is something strangely impersonal, something inexplicably bland about his sentences. His voice isn't one of those that make you love a writer for saying things in a way that nobody else would ever put them. All the lavish wordplay, the go-for-broke imagery and the wild, dumb jokes don't make a style—they're a substitute for a style.

East is East is the closest Boyle has come to an aesthetic manifesto. He uses the artists' colony setting to jeer at his recondite contemporaries (writers who "frowned ascetically over their incomprehensible texts"), and he sums up his opinion of their work in this description of an evening musicale:

> After dinner, there was a recital by Patsy Arena, a squat, broad-faced woman of Cuban extraction who looked as if she'd stepped out of a Botero painting. She was new to the colony, having come just that week at the invitation of Clara Kleinschmidt, and she played the old Steinway in the front parlor as if she were tenderizing meat. . . .
>
> *Bang!* Patsy Arena hit the piano like a boxer. Silence. *One and two, one and two,* she whispered, bobbing her frizzy head. *Bang! Bang!* she slammed at the keyboard with the ball of her fist. And then: nothing. For three full agonizing minutes she sat rigid, staring at the cheap plastic alarm clock perched atop the gleaming ebony surface before her. Finally the alarm went off—*ding-ding-ding*—and *Bang!* she hit the keyboard. The piece was called *Parfait in Chrome,* and it went on for forty-five minutes.

Boyle is no philistine, but he's suspicious of an avant-garde that doesn't aspire to popularity. His own allusions, which are plentiful and scholarly, are never snotty or obscure; he wants you to enjoy his exhibitionism. And there's certainly nothing compromising about going after a large audience—in theory, anyway. There is a note of compromise in the new book, though. The viciously funny narrative, a long progress of failures and mortifications, ends with a jarringly ebullient, optimistic coda. The last ten pages feel about as genuine as a happy ending tacked on to a Hollywood movie to sell it. (And guess what: *The Road to Wellville* has already been sold to the movies.)

Asked in an interview once to name his greatest source of joy in life, Boyle shot back, "Knocking my enemies dead flat and triumphing over them." You hear the same sanguinary note when he talks about sales. "Each book I put out, I think, 'Goodbye, Updike and Mailer, forget it'. . . . I joke at Viking that I'm going to make them forget the name of Stephen King forever, I'm going to sell so many copies."

If there's no mock modesty, though, it has to do with more than arrogance. Boyle considers modesty an error—an aesthetic error. In *East is East,* Ruth Dershowitz, the writer who, as a matter of integrity, avoids theatrics and lets her work speak for itself, puts her audience to sleep when she gives a reading. It's her nemesis, Jane Shine—who goes in for stark lighting and a dramatic costume and a diva's hairdo—who holds them spellbound. And you only have to study Boyle's jacket portraits, with his goatee and his ear clip and his dark, Byronic gaze, to know which one of them he identifies with. He says it himself: "I believe writers are people who should attract attention, and I dress accordingly." He's a ham right down to his splendid middle name. Coraghessan isn't his given name—he was born plain Thomas John Boyle—but a family name that he took when he was 17: "I suppose it's an affectation, of a sort, but what the hell. There are 5 billion of us on the planet all screaming for attention."

The picture of cutthroat competition in *East is East* is a rotten thing for a writer to carry around in his heart, though. Henry James's celebrated remark that the three important things in life are to be kind, to be kind and to be kind is alien to any quality you can find in Boyle's work, which sends off its most brilliant sparks when it gets darkest—at the end of *Water Music,* and in the dry-eyed, unsparing story **"Greasy Lake."** Observing the struggle to dominate without recoiling from its cruelty takes Boyle close to greatness. Buying into it is what coarsens him. He wants to dominate. His motives aren't pure. Are any-body's? Maybe not, but he relishes their impurity. He rec-ognizes his own pugnacious macho streak, and he loves it, and it vitiates his work, not so much because it's ugly as because it's juvenile. He can write, and he can imagine, with more energy than any of his contemporaries. But en-ergy isn't enough; there's only so far you can go on sheer technique. And until he goes further, he'll remain a satirist cut off from the oxygen of morality, a superb, hilarious novelist but, when you get down to it, an inessential one—an evil clown who slips from your memory as soon as the show is over.

Malcolm Bull (review date 6 January 1994)

SOURCE: "Corn," in *London Review of Books,* Vol. 16, No. 1, January 6, 1994, pp. 19-20.

[*In the excerpt below, Bull comments on Boyle's* The Col-lected Stories, *noting the opposition between body and rea-son and the prominence of such motifs as water and alco-hol.*]

If Haile Selassie, whom some remember as a bit of a biker from his days of exile in the West of England, had been stretched to 6'3" and given a part in *Easy Rider,* he would have looked rather like Tom Coraghessan Boyle as he ap-pears on the front of the **Collected Stories**—an improba-ble confection of soulful eyes, hollow cheeks, frizzy facial hair and black leather. But although the impression that Boyle is a low-life lion of the interstates is strenuously maintained by his publishers—who report that he was a child of the Sixties, 'a maniacal crazy-driver' who ate any-thing he could lay his hands on, bought heroin for £5 a bag and listened to music with Linda Lovelace—his writing suggests an altogether less exotic and more wholesome mi-lieu. Boyle studied at the Iowa Writers' Workshop and teaches at the University of Southern California, and his fiction often relies on the kind of farmboy irony that may come naturally to Ross Perot, but which appears to have been institutionalised in some American creative writing programmes. In such stories, the setting is the affluent sub-urbs: the Mercedes is in the garage, the *National Geo-graphic* is on the table, and the jokes are about new-fangled technologies that don't work or have unexpected consequences—security alarms, genetic engineering, re-search on primate intelligence. The implication is always that back on the farm, no one would have been fooled in the first place. . . .

[If] government causes political problems, psychiatrists madness, and doctors illness, how do the people live? How is it possible to survive in a society where being part of the solution automatically makes you part of the problem?

One answer to this question is given in a story called **'Modern Love'.** Having eaten a . . . meal of 'cold cream-of-tofu-carrot soup and little lentil-paste sandwiches for an appetiser and a garlic soufflé with biologically con-trolled vegetables for an entrée', two lovers watch *The Boy in the Bubble,* a film about the germ-free adolescence of a child without an immune system, and then put on full-body condoms for sex. But their promising, if intactile, re-lationship ends when, for wholly trivial reasons, the man

fails an exhaustive medical examination taken at the insis-tence of the hypochondriacal woman. . . . [It] is the doc-tor who invents the diseases that keep the sexes apart; the suggestion is that anyone who conforms to the divisive morality of public health will eventually find themselves sealed into a private bubble and deprived of the reassuring intimacy of human contact.

The contrast between the isolated world of modernity and the tactile 'way of the centuries' is, in part, the usual comic juxtaposition of the body against reason, common sense against professional expertise, the familiar past against the uncertain present. But in Boyle's writing, these dichoto-mies are given an almost obscurantist degree of polarisa-tion, with the result that the proffered alternative to the isolation created by dysfunctional expert systems is not ra-tional communication, but primitive communion. As the abstract of his PhD (a collection of short stories, not, as the publishers claim, a study of Victorian literature) puts it: there is an 'opposition between the primitive (irrational) and the civilised (rational) poles of man's nature', and in 'a universe in which certainty is both essential and impos-sible, superstition is no less viable than rationality.'

This is a philosophy with a long history. In the 20th centu-ry it might almost be called the unofficial social theory of the novel. But Boyle's version is particularly unsatisfacto-ry because he gives little evidence of being able to imagine what the superstitious intimacy of human relationships might actually be like. He appears to have no feeling for the primitive values he espouses. On the contrary, the characters he realises most successfully are self-absorbed egomaniacs. . . .

When Boyle's characters do manage to connect, interac-tion is usually lubricated by water or alcohol. In **'Greasy Lake'**, one of his best stories, three teenagers have to drive to the shores of the lake in order to find the drunken ex-citement for which they have been searching unsuccessful-ly all evening. . . . This parallel between water and alco-hol (and the dangers inherent in both) is made explicit in **'If the River Was Whiskey'**, the story of a family splitting up as the result of the man's alcoholism. Father and son talk only when sharing a beer or fishing on the lake, but when the father dreams of being separated from his son, he sees him drowning.

There are many such drownings in Boyle's fiction; . . . his lakes are littered with floating corpses, in case we forget that water and alcohol can dissolve individuality as well as lubricate sociability. The starkest of these stories is **'Drowning'**, in which a girl sunbathing at the edge of the water is repeatedly raped while, five hundred yards along the beach, the one person who might have saved her swims out to sea and drowns unobserved. It is a chilling but un-satisfactory tale, and it raises the question of whether the author could have written a convincing story in which the victim and her potential saviour were not just well-greased monads moving in synchronisation, but individuals able to intervene in one another's lives. No doctor sealed the bathers into separate bubbles, but Boyle gives them no more chance of meeting than the lovers in **'Modern Love'**.

John Mort   (review date 15 February 1994)

SOURCE: A review of *Without a Hero,* in *Booklist,* Vol. 90, No. 12, February 15, 1994, p. 1035.

[*In the following excerpt, Mort comments favorably on* Without a Hero, *and Other Stories.*]

If he wants to, Boyle can summon the angst for your standard realistic novel. In this collection's title story ["**Without a Hero**"], for example, he tells of a newly divorced fellow who inadvertently becomes the host of a young Russian woman who is awestruck by the bounty of America; our distinctly unheroic narrator won't marry her and thus forces her into prostitution. Boyle draws from this premise an indictment of capitalism as well as two engaging character studies. His mockery is at the center of things elsewhere, however, in stories that are less psychological studies than satirical conceits, such as "**Big Game.**" Set on a hunting preserve near Bakersfield, it's send-up of *Green Hills of Africa,* complete with Boyle's deadpan gun lore and a decrepit but still deadly charging elephant, "**Hopes Rise**" features two frazzled, precious, altogether contemporary characters, or caricatures. The story seems to lament the universal death of frogs and impending ecological disaster but, in the end, comments instead on the separation from nature that urban lifestyles entail. Perhaps Boyle's most arch effort is the slight "**Filthy with Things,**" about people so inundated with possessions they must enter a recovery program. Boyle's fabulist tendencies are much restrained here; not every story is remarkable, but at his best he reminds you of Evelyn Waugh.

Publishers Weekly (review date 14 March 1994)

SOURCE: A review of *Without a Hero,* in *Publishers Weekly,* Vol. 241, No. 11, March 14, 1994, p. 68.

[*Below, the critic presents a favorable review of* Without a Hero, *and Other Stories.*]

Most effective of the 16 technically ingenious and rudely funny, satirical stories in Boyle's fourth collection [*Without a Hero*] are the sketches of disaffected individuals who take refuge in hermetic surroundings, self-help programs, political causes and conspicuous consumption to hold at bay the banal world of convention and compromise. In "**Big Game,**" Bernard Puff, impresario of Puff's African Game Ranch in Bakersfield, Calif., peddles a simulacrum of the African bush. His carefully nurtured fantasy world is punctured by the arrival of a cynical young real estate mogul who detects "every crack in the plaster," and whose rapacious hunting leads to a grisly twist of fate when the animals revolt on the veldt. In "**Filthy with Things,**" a pathological couple whose home is sinking under the weight of their "collectibles" enlists the services of an evangelical professional organizer who banishes them to a "nonacquisitive environment" while she takes inventory of their astounding clutter ("three hundred and nine bookends, forty-seven rocking chairs [and] over two thousand plates, cups and saucers"). Other poignant tales tell of an ephemeral romance between a Russian and an American, the introduction of anti-drug rhetoric in a suburban grade school and the experience of growing up in postwar suburbia, a world Boyle regards with anxiety, nostalgia and a properly grim sense of humor.

Lorrie Moore   (review date 8 May 1994)

SOURCE: "No One's Willing to Die for Love," in *The New York Times Book Review,* May 8, 1994, p. 9.

[*Moore is an American short story writer, novelist, educator, and critic. In the review below, she remarks favorably on the stories in* Without a Hero *but laments Boyle's inability to go beyond sarcasm.*]

Readers of T. Coraghessan Boyle's amazing stories are probably most familiar with the salacious Lassie in "Heart of a Champion," the Bruce Springsteen song run amok in "**Greasy Lake**" or the updated Gogol of "**Overcoat II.**" Mr. Boyle situates his fictional ideas at the center of an available culture and then bursts forth with strange, engaging narratives that neither deconstruct nor reconstruct but perhaps, skeptically and inventively, *dis*construct. His dreamed-up reconfigurations seem nocturnal, pouched, alternatively formed and conceived—like animal life in Australia or a half-mad cousin from Dubuque.

In *Without a Hero,* Mr. Boyle's fourth collection of stories, once more there is nothing casual or tired; the literary performances here retain Mr. Boyle's astonishing and characteristic verve, his unaverted gaze, his fascination with everything lunatic and queasy. His stories are artifacts of psychic aberrance, lampoons fashioned in shadow and void, and they fill a reader (as they are intended to do) with the giddy nausea of our cultural and theological confusions.

In "**Big Game,**" a Hemingwayesque story impossibly reset in Bakersfield, Calif., a man runs a "safari" hunting range filled with decrepit elephants and lions from downsized zoos and circuses. For large sums, he allows rich people to shoot the poor beasts, though, in a rare pang of conscience, he still regrets "the time he'd let the kid from the heavy-metal band pot one of the giraffes." Nonetheless, he reminisces, "he'd taken a cool twelve thousand dollars to the bank on that one."

In "**Filthy With Things**" the protagonist—a man who wants to "go up to the mountains and let the meteor showers wash him clean, but he can't"—hires a "professional organizer" to help him make neatness and sense of his myriad possessions. The organizer, a chic, black-garbed woman (dressed much like the figure of Death in Jean Cocteau's film *Orpheus*), treats her clients as addicts and their spouses as co-dependents. She catalogues and removes the man's belongings. He may have one thing back each day for 60 days, but he has to ask for them specifically, one by one.

"You'd be surprised how many couples never recall a thing," she says, "not a single item." Stripped of his material clutter, he is left with nothing of substance to take its place—except, perhaps, litigation. "When he shuts his eyes he sees only the sterile deeps of space, the remotest regions beyond even the reach of light. And he knows this: it is cold out there, inhospitable, alien. There's nothing there, nothing contained in nothing. Nothing at all."

In **"Hopes Rise"** a young man, after a lecture by an eminent biologist, becomes obsessed with the dying frogs of the world. But when at last, searching for some, the young man finds a pond full of them, they function merely as an aphrodisiac for him and his increasingly exasperated girlfriend. In their attempt to outwit the bad news of the world, the couple enact and express what seems to be even more bad news: a false rapture, a road-show holiness.

Indeed, it is hard to think of writers to compare him with. In his sheer energy and mercilessness, his exuberantly jaundiced view, he resembles perhaps a middlebrow Donald Barthelme, or Don DeLillo crossed with Dr. Seuss, or Flannery O'Connor with a television and no church.

—*Lorrie Moore*

In the title story [**"Without a Hero"**], one of the book's best, a divorced man tells the story of his "passionate Russian experience" with a Soviet émigré lover named Irina: "Slovenly, indolent, nearly inert, she was the end product of three generations of the workers' paradise, that vast dark crumbling empire in which ambition and initiative counted for nothing. Do I sound bitter? I am bitter." Irina consumes large quantities of sushi and Grand Marnier; she quizzes her lover about mutual funds. She bemoans a world in which no one is willing to die for love. "I am the one who can die for love," she says finally to the narrator.

"Then die for it," he says, and the reader feels the intended violence of the moment so purely, strongly and sadly that it is a surprise: such moments are rare in the brash, wacky world of Mr. Boyle's fiction.

The reason, of course, is that Mr. Boyle is not typically that kind of writer. He is not psychological. He's all demography and *Zeitgeist*, a nerdy wizard of literary what-ifs (given the what-ares). He is fairly bored, it seems, with the nuances of the ordinary human heart; he does not linger there for long, or without tap shoes and sparklers.

Indeed, it is hard to think of writers to compare him with. In his sheer energy and mercilessness, his exuberantly jaundiced view, he resembles perhaps a middlebrow Donald Barthelme, or Don DeLillo crossed with Dr. Seuss, or Flannery O'Connor with a television and no church. The emotional complexity that could secure his characters at a safe distance from caricature confines him, slows him down. In his few stabs at poignancy or earnestness, as in one story here, **"Acts of God,"** he cannot shake the mean and theatrical habits of irony, the repudiating hiccup of sarcasm: "The house was gone, but he'd lost houses before—mainly to wives, which were a sort of natural disaster anyway; that he could live with—and he'd lost wives, too, but never like this. It hit him then, a wave of grief that started in his hips and crested in his throat: Muriel."

Part P. T. Barnum, part F. Lee Bailey, Mr. Boyle here is the dying Mercutio, unable convincingly to leave the stage. He is the biologist from his own tale, pulling dead frogs from his pockets and crying, "We're doomed, can't you see that?" while "the audience sat riveted in their seats." There are writers who intend to satirize a thing but then forget. They tip their hands. They reveal too much affection for and participation in the very object of their satire and their literary performance falters. Mr. Boyle is the opposite of such a writer. His prolific pen is, perhaps, in satirical overdrive. He may try to smile warmly, wisely, sadly, but his Cheshire grin won't go away.

One of the most successful exceptions here is the story **"The Fog Man,"** an evocative first-person narrative of one suburban boy's brief foray into racism. It is a beautifully narrated story of the misty demarcations in a child's knowledge and innocence, in a neighborhood's poison and magic, and the telling seems almost to overflow the form. It seems to want, as novels do, to re-create exhaustingly a time and world within our own, rather than make quick reference to the one we already inhabit—a necessary aspect of stories. One can imagine a whole novel spilling forth from this tale; it constitutes a strange and lovely fusion, a collision with another book entirely, and it is evidence of the author's true range. Elsewhere in this collection, Mr. Boyle's impulses—his penchant for the sardonic, for the put-on, for the manic unanswerable question—are perfectly suited to and accommodated by the short story's brevity and force.

God knows, Mr. Boyle can write like an angel, if at times a caustic, gum-chewing one. And in this strong, varied collection maybe we have what we'd hope to find in heaven itself (by the time we begged our way there): no lessening of brilliance, plus a couple of laughs to mitigate all that high and distant sighing over what goes on below.

Francine Fialkoff (review date 15 June 1995)

SOURCE: A review of *The Tortilla Curtain*, in *Library Journal*, Vol. 120, No. 11, June 15, 1995, p. 92.

[*In the review below, Fialkoff remarks favorably on* The Tortilla Curtain.]

Appearing after the wackiness of ***The Road to Wellville***, Boyle's sixth novel [***The Tortilla Curtain***] is a dash of cold reality. The lives of two couples living in Topanga Canyon (Los Angeles) intersect when Delaney Mossbacher slams his car into Cándido Rincón. But the couples couldn't be more disparate: Delaney is a nature writer ("Pilgrim at Topanga Canyon") whose wife, Kyra, is a successful realtor; the Rincóns are illegal aliens camping out, looking for any work at all, and América pregnant. From that impact on, Boyle explores the aliens in "our" midst, the progressive, growing fear of "them" by even the liberal Mossbacher, whose column about coyotes sounds suspiciously like his wife's reaction to Mexicans: "[They] keep coming, breeding up to fill in the gaps, moving in where the living is easy. They are cunning . . . unstoppable." Boyle builds gut-roiling tension with not one but many conflagrations (including an actual one), and the ending is no release but a test of people's endurance. Though the novel has perhaps too many one-dimensional characters, and Kyra seems unrealized (or perhaps just unsympathetic), this is a brutally powerful, frightening commentary on contemporary America.

Scott Spencer   (review date 3 September 1995)

SOURCE: "The Pilgrim of Topanga Creek," in *The New York Times Book Review,* September 3, 1995, p. 3.

[*In the following review, Spencer faults Boyle's presentation of the two story lines in* The Tortilla Curtain *as uneven.*]

Viking has somehow got the idea it has another *Grapes of Wrath* on its hands. Then again, T. Coraghessan Boyle may have contributed to the delusion by using a few lines from Steinbeck's novel as the epigraph to his own meditation on the dispossessed and the American dream, California style. But while Steinbeck's tale of the Joad family was the very apotheosis of the proletarian novel, with its almost surreal emotional clarity and passages of nearly overpowering pathos, *The Tortilla Curtain* is, as the dust jacket would have it, about "the Okies of the 1990's." This apparently means that the narrative contains no real heroes or villains, and that the suddenly old-fashioned hopefulness of Steinbeck's book is nowhere to be found.

In *The Tortilla Curtain,* Mr. Boyle deftly portrays Los Angeles's Topanga Canyon, catching both its privileged society and its underlying geological and ecological instability. But while the book has heft, its story is slight, and not unfamiliar: An undocumented Mexican couple struggle for survival in the interstices of society and in the canyon itself, even as an affluent Anglo couple live their fearful, selfish existence behind the dubious protection of a walled development called Arroyo Blanco Estates.

We first meet Cándido Rincón when he is hit by a car driven by the male half of the novel's Anglo couple, a self-styled Annie Dillard disciple named Delaney Mossbacher. Cándido is in California with his young pregnant wife, América, having recently braved another crossing of the border. Cándido and América are part of California's unacknowledged work force, cogs in the vast human machine that does the state's brute labor and without whom (Proposition 187 to the contrary) the state could probably not survive.

Mr. Boyle is first-rate in capturing the terror of looking for work in an alien society, as in this passage describing Cándido's experience at a parking-lot labor exchange:

> The contractors began to arrive, the white men with their big bleached faces and soulless eyes, enthroned in their trucks. They wanted two men or three, they wanted four or five, no questions asked, no wage stipulated, no conditions or terms of employment. A man could be pouring concrete one day, spraying pesticide the next— or swabbing out urinals, spreading manure, painting, weeding, hauling, laying brick or setting tile. You didn't ask questions. You got in the back of the truck and you went where they took you.

Mr. Boyle is convincing, and even stirring, in his telling

of Cándido and América's story, bringing to it an agitprop artist's perspective on both society's injustices and the cold implacability of the privileged classes, as well as a Brechtian vision of how those cast to the bottom of society blindly victimize one another. Indeed, the journey of the Rincóns—from their desolate Mexican village to the terrors of exploitation on the undocumented edge of American society and finally into the whirling, pyrotechnically presented catastrophe toward which the story builds— more than confirms Mr. Boyle's reputation as a novelist of exuberance and invention, gained with such pop extravaganzas as *World's End* and *The Road to Wellville.* It also adds to his fictional range an openhearted compassion for those whom society fears and reviles.

But Mr. Boyle was clearly not interested in merely writing a novel about illegal aliens scrabbling for a living. For he has divided his considerable narrative and stylistic gifts between the Rincóns' story and that of Delaney and Kyra Mossbacher, the rather contemptible yuppie couple whose deeply unremarkable experiences are set in opposition to the Rincóns'. It is here, alas, that Mr. Boyle undoes himself.

Delaney is described on the very first page as "a liberal humanist with an unblemished driving record and a freshly waxed Japanese car with personalized plates." It is a mode of portrayal that is characteristic of much of Mr. Boyle's earlier work, a kind of comedy that finds its roots in sarcasm. In Mr. Boyle's case, this sarcasm is often taken for buoyancy and even daring, but in *The Tortilla Curtain* it rings hollow. When a character is described in terms of his driving record and his vanity plates, the reader can only hope that character is a minor one, a walk-on. But when you realize that you are being asked to read on and on about someone the author obviously doesn't care deeply about (and has, in fact, just trashed with the flick of an easy laugh), your heart begins to sink. Even when the novel's plot begins to activate Delaney and sour his usually beatific goofy world view, our reaction to the transformation is interrupted by the necessity of coping with Mr. Boyle's persistent elbow in our ribs: "He was in a rage, and he tried to calm himself. It seemed he was always in a rage lately—he, Delaney Mossbacher, the Pilgrim of Topanga Creek—he who led the least stressful existence of anybody on earth besides maybe a handful of Tibetan lamas."

Like her nature-writer husband, Kyra Mossbacher is cut up and offered to us on a Lazy Susan of rude remarks. "Real estate was her life," the omnipotent narrator would have us believe, the moment Kyra appears on the scene. A bit later, we learn the following:

> For Kyra, sex was therapeutic, a release from sorrow, tension, worry, and she plunged into it in moments of emotional distress as others might have sunk themselves in alcohol or drugs—and who was Delaney to argue? She'd been especially passionate around the time her mother was hospitalized for her gall bladder operation.

Mr. Boyle's fictional strategy is puzzling. Why are we being asked to follow the fates of characters for whom he clearly feels such contempt? Not surprisingly, this is ultimately off-putting. Perhaps Mr. Boyle has received too much praise for his zany sense of humor; in this book, that wit often seems merely a maddening volley of cheap shots. It's like living next door to a gun nut who spends all day and half the night shooting at beer bottles.

The great risk of a novel with a dual structure is that the reader will fasten on one of the stories at the expense of the other. In *The Tortilla Curtain,* the drama, feeling and stylistic bravado, the emotional reach that Mr. Boyle brings to the story of the Rincóns so profoundly exceed what he brings to the Mossbachers that the book itself ends up feeling as disunited as the society Mr. Boyle is attempting to portray. And that's a pity, because there is life here and moments of very fine writing. ("The fire sat low on the horizon, like a gas burner glowing under the great black pot of the sky.")

A few months ago, Mr. Boyle was asked in an interview how he voted on Proposition 187. Perhaps anticipating being asked the same question over and over on his upcoming book tour, he replied, "I don't want to reveal that. I'm not running for office." It's hard to imagine John Steinbeck being quite so coy about the rights of migrant workers or the importance of unions, but, as they say on television, "Hey, it's the 90's!"

The Tortilla Curtain is a political novel for an age that has come to distrust not only politicians but political solutions, a modernist muckraking novel by an author who sees the muck not only in class structure and prejudice but in the souls of human beings. Yet where the socially engaged novel once offered critique, Mr. Boyle provides contempt—even poor Cándido, whose plight has been engaging our sympathies throughout this novel, is eventually seen "weaving his way through the scrub, drawn like an insect to the promise of distant lights." Contempt is a dangerous emotion, luring us into believing that we understand more than we do. Contempt causes us to jeer rather than speak, to poke at rather than touch. Despite his celebrated gifts, T. Coraghessan Boyle may be the most contemptuous of our well-known novelists.

FURTHER READING

Criticism

Bell, Pearl K. "Fiction Chronicle." *Partisan Review* LVIII, No. 3 (1991): 482-92.
> Admires Boyle's imaginative resourcefulness, stylistic exuberance, and detailed research in *East is East,* but criticizes the novel as shallow and cruel.

Birnbaum, Jane. "To Live and Discriminate in L.A." *Los Angeles Times Book Review* (24 September 1995): 4.
> Mixed review of *The Tortilla Curtain.*

Blaise, Clark. "Down the Natural Path." *Chicago Tribune Books* (9 May 1993): 1, 9.
> Praises the historical verisimilitude and contemporary relevance of *The Road to Wellville.*

Champlin, Charles. "The Great American Short Story Rides

Again." *Los Angeles Times Book Review* (30 June 1985): 1, 7.
> Asserts that the stories in *Greasy Lake, and Other Stories* "have a sort of undergraduate exuberance, though it is carried off with a postgraduate control. . . ."

Cotts, Cynthia. Review of *World's End,* by T. Coraghessan Boyle. *VLS* No. 60 (November 1987): 3.
> Commends the erudition and humor evident in *World's End* but asserts that Boyle's satire proves more effective in the novel's twentieth-century passages than in its seventeenth-century segments.

Delbanco, Nicholas. "Tongue in Cheek." *Chicago Tribune Books* (21 May 1989): 6-7.
> Praises the range of Boyle's reference and humor in *If the River Was Whiskey* but laments that the stories' endings seem contrived.

Dickinson, Charles. "Joking Across Cultures." *Chicago Tribune Books* (9 September 1990): 5.
> Maintains that the characters and plot in *East Is East* do not equal the novel's superlative wordplay.

Eckhoff, Sally. S. "Where the Wild Things Are(n't)." *Village Voice* XXXIIII, No. 36 (5 September 1989): 59.
> Observes that the plots and characters in *If the River Was Whiskey* are so tightly controlled that, despite Boyle's evocative prose, the stories will not stir his readers' imagination.

Eder, Richard. "Man Overboard; Woman Underhanded." *Los Angeles Times Book Review* (23 September 1990): 3.
> Asserts that Boyle handles humor more successfully than serious cultural comparison in *East Is East.*

Gamerman, Amy. "Japanese Sailor's Fall from Grace in America." *The Wall Street Journal* (7 September 1990): A13.
> Remarks unfavorably on *East Is East,* pronouncing the novel's scope too narrow to accommodate Boyle's historical imagination.

Kakutani, Michiko. "A Samurai in the South and a Joke on America." *The New York Times* (7 September 1990): C25.
> Praises *East Is East,* particularly admiring Boyle's "keen sociological eye and his ability to parody cultural preconceptions through manic exaggeration."

Loose, Julian. "Torn in the U.S." *New Statesman and Society* 4, No. 144 (29 March 1991): 31.
> Admires Boyle's satirical treatment of the South Carolina artists' colony in *East Is East* but maintains that the novel "fails as an allegory of cultural misunderstanding."

Review of *East Is East. Publishers Weekly* (29 June 1990): 87.
> Lauds the novel as both satirical and tragic.

Rifkind, Donna. "When Worlds Collide." *Washington Post–Book World* XXV, No. 34 (20 August 1995): 3, 8.
> Mixed review of *The Tortilla Curtain.*

Taylor, Douglas Allen. "A Bunch of Flakes." *San Francisco Review of Books* 18, Nos. 4-5 (August-October 1993): 42-3.
> Praises Boyle's research and "deadpan delivery" in *The Road to Wellville* but criticizes the novel's ending and Boyle's use of an unrealistic character, which Taylor considers inappropriate for historical fiction.

Interviews

Adams, Elizabeth. "An Interview with T. Coraghessan Boyle." *Chicago Review* 37, Nos. 2-3 (1991): 51-63.

Discusses Boyle's education, the influences on his writing, and his responses to critics.

Friend, Tad. "Rolling Boyle." *Rolling Stone* (9 December 1990): 50, 64-6, 68.

Provides a comprehensive analysis of Boyle's career, offering the observations of his friends, family, critics, and publishers, and of Boyle himself, who remarks on his past intentions and future ambitions.

Peabody, Richard. "Wisecracking with T. Coraghessan Boyle." *Gargoyle* Nos. 17-18 (1981): 36-9.

Queries Boyle about shifting from the short fiction of *Descent of Man, and Other Stories* to his first novel, *Water Music,* and discusses the role of comedy and music in his fiction.

Additional coverage of Boyle's life and career is contained in the following sources published by Gale Research: *Bestsellers 1990,* **No. 4;** *Contemporary Authors,* **Vol. 120;** *Contemporary Authors New Revision Series,* **Vol 44;** *Contemporary Literary Criticism,* **Vols. 36, 55;** *Dictionary of Literary Biography Yearbook: 1986;* **and** *Short Story Criticism,* **Vol. 16.**

Michael Crichton

1942-

(Full name John Michael Crichton; has also written under the pseudonyms Jeffrey Hudson and John Lange, and with Douglas Crichton under joint pseudonym Michael Douglas) American novelist, nonfiction writer, screenwriter, film director, and autobiographer.

The following entry focuses on Crichton's career from 1981 to 1995. For further information about his life and work, see *CLC*, Volumes 2, 6, and 54.

INTRODUCTION

Crichton is best known as a novelist of popular fiction whose stories explore the limitations of a humanistic worldview in the age of advanced technology. *Jurassic Park* (1990), his best-selling novel about re-creating living dinosaurs from preserved DNA fragments, examines the dangers of exploiting and coming to rely on highly sophisticated scientific breakthroughs, like computers and biogenetic engineering, whose "inherent unpredictability" ultimately mocks humankind's belief that it can control its world. Although a number of critics fault Crichton for stereotypical characterizations and trite plotlines, many have praised his taut, suspenseful, and fast-paced stories, his entertaining narrative style, and his ability to convey technical information in a readable, exciting manner.

Biographical Information

Crichton was born in Chicago, Illinois, and raised on Long Island, New York. When he was fourteen, he wrote and sold travel articles to the *New York Times*. In 1964 he earned a B. A. in anthropology from Harvard University. Returning to Harvard in 1965 to pursue a career in medicine, Crichton began writing novels under the pseudonym John Lange in order to support his studies. While doing postdoctoral work at the Salk Institute for Biological Studies in La Jolla, California, Crichton published *The Andromeda Strain* (1969), a popular thriller, and soon began a full-time writing career. Crichton is also a respected figure in the motion picture and entertainment industries. In 1972 he adapted his novel *Binary* (1971) for television and then began writing and directing his own films, including *Westworld* (1973), *The Great Train Robbery* (1979), *Looker* (1981) and *Runaway* (1984). He is also the creator of the critically acclaimed television drama *E.R.*

Major Works

Crichton has written on a variety of subjects and in a variety of genres: *The Great Train Robbery,* for example, recalls the history of an actual train robbery in Victorian England; the 1976 novel *Eaters of the Dead* explores the myths of tenth-century Vikings; the nonfiction work *Electronic Life* (1983) focuses on the practical applications of

computers; and *Travels* (1988) is an autobiographical account of Crichton's life. He first established himself, however, as the author of *Odds On* (1966) and *A Case of Need* (1968), detective novels written under the pseudonyms John Lange and Jeffrey Hudson, respectively, while he was in medical school. Crichton is best known, though, for his work in the science fiction genre. Writing under his own name, he published *The Andromeda Strain* in 1969, a novel about a seemingly unstoppable plague brought to Earth from outer space; he has said that this story was influenced by Len Deighton's *The Ipcress File* (1962) and H. G. Wells's *The War of the Worlds* (1898). In his film *Westworld,* he depicted modern Americans as jaded individuals who depend on technology as a means of escaping reality. At the Delos theme park, guests live out their fantasies in various "worlds" populated by androids. Westworld guests, for example, stay in an "Old West" town where they win all their gunfights and brawls because the androids are programmed to lose. Computer programming problems occur, however, and the robotic cowboys begin to threaten and harm the guests. *Congo* (1980) similarly explores the dangers of technology, greed, and power. Likened to H. Rider Haggard's adventure novel *King Solomon's Mines* (1885), *Congo* tells the story of a behavioral scientist who attempts to return a gorilla capable of linguistic communication to the jungle. In the process they must overcome the ruthless activities of a group of corporate-sponsored explorers who are searching for the Lost City of Zinj, where a band of hostile apes guards a cache of rare diamonds. An encounter with alien life and technology is the central focus of *Sphere* (1987). Scientists investigating an alien spacecraft that landed in the ocean three centuries earlier get trapped inside the extraterrestrials' ship during a raging storm and are set upon by aliens. In 1990 Crichton published his best-seller *Jurassic Park*, which tells of greed and technological experimentation gone awry. Set in a wild animal preserve called Jurassic Park, the novel relates how a wealthy entrepreneur and his scientists lose control of the living dinosaurs they have recreated from preserved DNA fragments. Steven Spielberg's 1994 Academy Award-winning film of *Jurassic Park*—for which Crichton helped write the screenplay—ensured the worldwide popularity of the novel. In more recent works, Crichton turned away from such fantastic tales. Focusing on contemporary Japanese-American relations, *Rising Sun* (1992) begins with the murder of a young woman and explores the seemingly exploitative and unprincipled actions of Japanese businessmen. *Disclosure* (1994), which is also set in the business world, examines the issue of sexual harassment. Reversing the traditional tale of a patriarchal abuse of power, Crichton's novel concerns a female executive who accuses a subordinate male employee—with whom she was once romantically involved—of sexual harassment when he spurns her advances. The story focuses on the employee's fight to save his job and reveal the truth. In *The Lost World* (1995), a sequel to *Jurassic Park*, Crichton returns to such science fiction themes as genetic engineering and the misuse of technological capabilities. This work focuses on scientists and entrepreneurs investigating an island thought to be inhabited by dinosaurs.

Critical Reception

Crichton's works have received mixed reviews. Initially praised for his detective stories—he received the Edgar Allan Poe Award of the Mystery Writers of America in 1968—he is recognized by most critics for his ability to make technological information understandable and engaging. Some, however, have argued that his plotlines—such as the battle-of-the-sexes scenario in *Disclosure* and the well-worn story line of *Jurassic Park*, which exploits the fear of scientific advancement—are hackneyed and predictable. While some critics have favorably commented on Crichton's well-organized narratives and use of clear and simple prose, they also lament his use of stock characters. For instance, the unprincipled entrepreneur John Hammond and the greedy computer genius Nedry of *Jurassic Park* are seen as caricatures, while the female antagonist of *Disclosure* is seen as a predictable *femme fatale*. As Robert L. Sims has asserted, most of "Crichton's characters are one-dimensional figures whose psychological makeups are determined by the particular drama in which they are involved." A few commentators have also remarked on Crichton's ability to identify and successfully capitalize on current public issues and concerns. For ex-

ample, *Disclosure* examines the issue of sexual harassment in the business world, and *Rising Sun* focuses on the fear associated with Japan's growing presence in American business. These two novels, however, have also generated criticism. *Disclosure* has been compared to the film *Fatal Attraction* (1987) for its sexist depiction of predatory women and weak men, and *Rising Sun* was deemed racist for its presentation of the Japanese as ruthlessly bent on destroying the American economy. Nevertheless, Crichton's concise prose style, tightly organized plots, and examination of contemporary concerns continue to make his works popular.

---

*PRINCIPAL WORKS

Odds On [as John Lange] (novel) 1966
Scratch One [as John Lange] (novel) 1967
A Case of Need [as Jeffrey Hudson] (novel) 1968
Easy Go [as John Lange] (novel) 1968; also published as *The Last Tomb*, 1974
The Andromeda Strain (novel) 1969
The Venom Business [as John Lange] (novel) 1969
Zero Cool [as John Lange] (novel) 1969
Drug of Choice [as John Lange] (novel) 1970
Five Patients: The Hospital Explained (nonfiction) 1970
Grave Descend [as John Lange] (novel) 1970
Binary [as John Lange] (novel) 1971
Dealing; or, The Berkeley-to-Boston Forty-Brick Lost-Bag Blues [with Douglas Crichton, under joint pseudonym Michael Douglas] (novel) 1971
The Terminal Man (novel) 1972
Extreme Close-up (screenplay) 1973
Westworld (film) 1973
The Great Train Robbery (novel) 1975
Eaters of the Dead (novel) 1976
Coma [adaptor; from the novel *Coma* by Robin Cook] (film) 1977
Jasper Johns (nonfiction) 1977
The Great Train Robbery (film) 1979
Congo (novel) 1980
Looker (film) 1981
Electronic Life: How to Think about Computers (nonfiction) 1983
Runaway (film) 1984
Sphere (novel) 1987
Travels (autobiography) 1988
Jurassic Park (novel) 1990
Rising Sun (novel) 1992
Jurassic Park [with David Koepp] (screenplay) 1993
Rising Sun [with Michael Backes and Philip Kaufman] (screenplay) 1993
Disclosure (novel) 1994
The Lost World (novel) 1995
Volcano (novel) 1995

---

*Many of Crichton's novels have served as the bases for movies. *A Case of Need* inspired the 1972 film *The Carey Treatment*, directed by Blake Edwards and written by James P. Bonner. The 1971 film version of *The Andromeda Strain* was directed by Robert Wise and written by Nelson Gidding. Crichton wrote and directed the 1972 television film *Pursuit*, which was based on his novel *Binary*. The 1974 film version of *The Terminal Man* was written and directed by Mike Hedges. Crichton's screenplay *Extreme Close-up* was directed by Jeannot Szwarc. The films *Westworld, Coma, The Great Train Robbery, Looker*, and *Runaway* were written and directed by Crichton. *Congo* was adapted for the screen in 1995 by director Frank Marshall and screenwriter John Patrick Shanley. The 1993 film version of *Jurassic Park* was directed by Steven Spielberg. Philip Kaufman directed the 1993 film based on *Rising Sun*, and *Disclosure* was adapted for the screen in 1994 by director Barry Levinson and screenwriter Paul Attanasio.

CRITICISM

Pauline Kael   (review date 9 November 1981)

SOURCE: "Childhood of the Dead," in *The New Yorker*, Vol. LVII, No. 38, November 9, 1981, pp. 170-84.

[*Kael was a widely-read and respected film critic for* The New Yorker *until her retirement in 1991. In the following excerpt, she unfavorably reviews* Looker, *focusing on Crichton's "cold" direction, the lack of character development, and the weakness of the film's plot.*]

Michael Crichton directs like a technocrat. This ties in with a small problem he has with his scripts: he can't write people. His new film, **Looker** (it's his fourth), gives the impression of having never been touched by human hands; it's a shiny, cold job of engineering that manages to turn even Dorian Harewood, as a Los Angeles police lieutenant, into a piece of furniture. The plot is pseudo-scientific piffle about the machinations of the head of a conglomerate, played by the now completely white-haired James Coburn in the desiccated-amoral-old-bastard manner of John Huston. This old rascal's laboratories at Digital Matrix are developing computer-generated images to make hypnotic TV commercials for political as well as economic use. To the rescue of civilization as we know it comes Albert Finney, like a lame tortoise. Finney gives what looks to be the laziest performance by a star ever recorded on film. Boredom seems to have seeped into his muscles and cells; he's sinking under the weight of it, and the only part of him still alert is his wiry hair. He plays an eminent plastic surgeon who has "perfected" several women models according to mathematically exact specifications supplied by Coburn's lab; his highest point of animation comes when he selects Vivaldi for the day's accompaniment to his tiny incisions. (There can't be much choice: he could hardly use "Kitten on the Keys" or Terry Riley's "In C.") He's the target of a murderous thug who is so characterless that if he didn't wear a thick-brush mustache we'd have no way of recognizing him from one scene to the next. With no people around, **Looker** is as empty as Crichton's **Coma** would have been without Geneviève Bujold.

The picture begins promisingly, with a couple of the models who have been worked on by the doc coming to mystifying violent ends. But Crichton's iciness is effective only when he's ingenious; he isn't, here. The plot explanations seem to be babble. It isn't clear why Coburn's evil scheme requires models to be surgically perfected in order to be the basis for computer images, especially since the hypnotic effect of the images is achieved only with the models' eyes. And we never learn why the girls are then marked for destruction. For that matter, we don't find out in what way Coburn's elaborate technology is more effective than simple subliminal messages. Thinking about this movie could give you frostbite of the brain. Susan Dey is the pertly pretty heroine, who poses another riddle. We're told that she, like the others, has been physically perfected, down to the shadow of a millimetre, but she has a highly visible individual feature—a friendly little wart on her belly that should set off alarm systems or topple the towers at Digital Matrix.

At the end, it comes as quite a surprise that Doc Finney is meant to have a sexual interest in this charmingly blemished beauty. So *that's* why he was trudging around trying to keep his eyes open. (He'd need electric shock to consummate the union.) When the man with the mustache shoots hypnotic flashes at Finney that are meant to numb him, you think, What a waste of special effects. Couldn't Crichton, with his medical background, invent an excuse for the doc's thick torpor—make him a sufferer from narcolepsy, at the least? This is the film that should have been called **Coma**. What's worst about it may be the exact, knowing readings that the actors give their computer-generated (or close to it) dialogue. So much care has gone into this dumb, hollow thing, and all it does is sell a few impressively constructed semi-nude models. In the big climax, people stalk each other amid computer-generated images just like the men and humanoids stalking each other in Crichton's **Westworld**; it's a little early in his career for a recap. He tries to tone up the purpose of **Looker** by providing a cautionary statistic and then having a disembodied voice repeat it at the end. It sinks in, all right: one and a half years of an average American's time is spent watching commercials. But there is no qualitative difference between this affectless, impersonal film and a commercial. There was no reason for Finney to rouse himself. One and a half years plus ninety-three minutes.

David Denby   (review date 16 November 1981)

SOURCE: "The Wizards of ID," in *New York* Magazine, Vol. 14, No. 45, November 16, 1981, p. 118.

[*In the following excerpt, Denby unfavorably reviews* Looker.]

Will Michael Crichton ever make a really good movie? Crichton, the author of **The Andromeda Strain** and other scientific-medical thrillers and the director of **Westworld, Coma,** and **The Great Train Robbery,** is a clever fellow with a talent for conventional suspense and a fondness for slightly bizarre stories about technology run amok. **The Great Train Robbery,** his most assured work as a director, was overpadded and smug, but at least it had some big-movie sweep and detail, and its Victorian setting took Crichton away from his machinery fetish—the computer screens and dials, the research-lab corridors. But now, in **Looker,** Crichton is back in the corridor: Half the movie consists of people stalking up and down holding black ray guns out in front of them.

Looker is a TV movie with skin. Albert Finney, formerly an attractive and accomplished human being and now a zombie, brings his dead voice, his baggy eyes and heavy gut (which he tries to hold in with a look of pained boredom) to the role of a successful Beverly Hills plastic surgeon who performs tiny adjustments on the features of girls acting in TV commercials. It seems that a large corporation uses these paragons as models in commercials made with computer-animation techniques. Once the girl is copied by the computer, the corporation has her killed off. (Why, I wonder? But never mind.) Since these commercials are the type that manipulate the audience subliminally, Crichton probably intends some sort of attack on the sinister effect of television, but what we actually see is yet another offering in the endless stream of movies about gorgeous girls—models or actresses or coeds or nurses—being stalked or raped or terrorized or flung about and killed. The dominant image here is of a nude blonde falling out of her apartment in slow motion. The beautiful-girl-in-danger has become the schlock-moviemaking obsession of our day. Only Brian De Palma has raised it to the level of art, and I wish to God he'd make some other kind of movie.

Gary Jennings   (review date 11 November 1990)

SOURCE: "Pterrified by Pterodactyls," in *The New York Times Book Review,* November 11, 1990, pp. 4, 15.

[*Jennings is an American novelist, nonfiction writer, author of children's literature, and critic; his novels include* Aztec *(1980) and* Spangle *(1987). In the following review of* Jurassic Park, *he applauds Crichton's ability to make scientific information understandable and interesting but laments the predictability of the plot and characters.*]

With his 1969 novel, *The Andromeda Strain,* Michael Crichton invented the "techno-thriller" fully two decades before that term became the fad description for every book by Tom Clancy, Dean R. Koontz and W. E. B. Griffin. However, whereas those writers deal mainly with arcane military hardware, Dr. Crichton dares to contrive even more craftily credible plots by writing about the basic, infinitesimal building blocks of life and the universe.

Since the title of this new novel pretty well indicates what is inside it, I am not giving anything away by saying that *Jurassic Park* tells of a modern-day scientist bringing to life a horde of prehistoric animals. The notion is hardly original; check any video rental store. But here it transcends armchair escapism or B-movie camp. Without the usual mad scientists or mutations caused by radiation accidents, Dr. Crichton's tale is grounded in the very latest advances in human knowledge. It may sound daunting to say that a reader will encounter recombinant DNA technology, chaos theory, fractal geometry, nonlinear dynamics and even sonic tomography, but Dr. Crichton is adept at making every one of those ingredients comprehensible, often beguiling, frequently exciting.

The introduction alone is worth the price of the book.

What it recounts is true, and frightening: how science has of late become almost wholly the handmaiden of big business. The decipherment of the DNA molecule, Dr. Crichton tells us, promises "the greatest revolution in human history." Nonetheless, he says, biotechnology (that is, genetic tinkering) is being taken over by commercial companies, and the researchers have become those companies' employees, working to develop every sort of thing from marketable new drugs to cubical tomatoes that are easier for McDonald's to slice. Nowadays, many epochal discoveries in the field are shrouded by protective patents. Nowhere is there a governing body competent to control the experimentation. Hence, says Dr. Crichton ominously, "it is done in secret, and in haste, and for profit." His novel makes his point.

The first 80 pages of *Jurassic Park* are full of suspense: Why is an eccentric tycoon buying up all the amber in the world? Why are children getting gnawed by what appear to be innocuous little lizards? Why are so many powerful supercomputers being shipped to a remote Costa Rican island? But less than a quarter of the way into the book we are told why. As it happens, the tycoon heads a scientific research company that has found a way (and this is the most ingenious touch in the whole story) to recover the DNA of dinosaurs that have been extinct for eons, and thereby to clone them in quantity. The company comes up with a host of tyrannosaurs, pterodactyls, stegosaurs and the like.

Since this is a company not of mad scientists but of merely *money*-mad scientists, their intention is to construct and ballyhoo a vast island park containing their creations. There, the expected throngs of tourists will pay for admission, pay for guided tours and thrill rides, pay for voluptuous accommodations, even pay for miniaturized (but real) pet dinosaurs their kids can take home. In sum, the plan is for a sort of Dino-Disneyland. If this seems a trifle silly—such a mountain of effort, genius and investment bringing forth such a Mickeyish mouse—well, as a wise man recently observed, "All the great themes have been turned into theme parks." And, come right down to it, what else *would* you do with a herd of assorted dinosaurs?

> The introduction to *Jurassic Park* alone is worth the price of the book. What it recounts is true, and frightening: how science has of late become almost wholly the handmaiden of big business.
>
> —*Gary Jennings*

Anyhow, from the page when the scientists' plot is revealed, the author's puppet strings begin to dangle in plain view. The best-laid plans go predictably awry, the power plants fail, the computers go haywire, the dinosaurs get loose and wreak havoc, and coincidences abound. The attempts at suspense are all contrived and strained. Most of the rest of the book is just a working script for the special-effects boys in Hollywood.

Still, there are some good bits. As paleontology has shown in recent years, dinosaurs were not all lumbering, feeble-minded, overgrown lizards. Actually, many were more akin to birds, and birds of a fairly high order of intelligence. *Jurassic Park* does a splendid job of giving us this revised and improved rendition of them. Indeed, some of the critters—even the most savage—are likable, and in one lovely scene (which I won't give away), some evoke genuine pity.

They all are certainly more interesting than the human characters. As in every techno-thriller, the humans exist only to push buttons, to explain to one another why they're pushing the buttons they're pushing and then to suffer the consequences of having pushed those buttons. The cast here is about standard. Besides the money-hungry tycoon, there is a paleontologist hero, a botanist heroine, a dedicated mathematician, a sleazy industrial spy, a cowardly lawyer, the (almost inevitable) 11-year-old computer whiz kid who eventually tidies up everything the adults have screwed up. And lots of other folks. They don't matter. When they're not expatiating on their various specialties, they're scuttling frantically and futilely about, exactly as they used to scurry to avoid the trampling feet of King Kong and Dr. Cyclops and Godzilla. As one after another gets mauled by the dinosaurs, the reader is inclined to root for the maulers.

All in all, *Jurassic Park* is a great place to visit, but 400 pages is rather too long a trip.

Ronald Preston   (review date 21 November 1990)

SOURCE: "Terrible T. Rex and Other Dinosaur Daydreams," in *The Christian Science Monitor,* November 21, 1990, p. 12.

[*In the following review of* Jurassic Park, *Preston praises Crichton's ability to present technical material clearly and provocatively but faults his poorly developed characters and trite plot.*]

"Soon to be a major motion picture," brays the cover of Michael Crichton's *Jurassic Park.* Dr. Crichton's books have become films before. *The Great Train Robbery* and *The Andromeda Strain* come to mind. But this time the book anticipates the production. This is a screenplay frilled for publication.

Master-of-the-universe financier bamboozles Japanese into underwriting a zoo for dinosaurs on a remote, be-clouded isle (shades of King Kong). Biotechnologists conjure up the beasts by splicing dinosaur genes gotten from blood sucked by prehistoric gnats and preserved in amber. Multinational corporation divides island into dinosaur habitats with massive works of concrete, steel, and fail-safe automation run from a fortified command center (shades of James Bond). Escape is impossible. Dinosaurs get out anyhow. Scientists come to investigate. Carnivores lunge relentlessly (shades of Aliens).

One can envision the movie, a two-star sci-fi adventure.

The characters are movie types: the quiet manly scientist, the leggy blonde in cut-offs (also a scientist), the precocious kid, the garrulous philosopher, the decrepit financier, the nerdy computer hack (named Nedry!), the smarmy public-relations man, the lawyer.

There is action. The unattractive people get gored. The attractive people narrowly escape. Dinosaurs star—improved through *Star Wars* special effects and advances in paleontology.

Although formulaic, the book may be better than the movie. The book is an educational romp. Crichton is a master at splicing scientific explanation into his plots, asides that will be hard to capture on film. His prologue summarizes a new science, biotechnology. He describes the manipulation of genetic material to create new life. Crichton's twist is his protagonists' use of biotechnology to recreate old life forms, dinosaurs.

Crichton conveys the gist of how biology combines with computer science to break genetic codes. Once the dinosaurs appear, he introduces the new paleontology, a revisionist view of dinosaurs as warm-blooded, active, intelligent, and birdlike. Amazingly, one finds oneself imbibing science with pap, page by page. The dose is insufficient for understanding, but enough to burnish one's cultural literacy. Even more astonishingly, Crichton's science is the spice that keeps the tale interesting. People and plot are trite. One turns the pages anticipating dinosaur developments.

The obligatory evocation is the weakest. What's a dinosaur saga without Tyrannosaurus Rex? Here Crichton goes through Godzilla motions. T. Rex roars in the rain, his head haloed in lightning. T. Rex mashes a car. T. Rex snaps at the children who are just out of reach.

More interesting are Crichton's speculative creations. One dinosaur hoots like an owl and spits snake venom to nail prey at 50 paces. A diminutive dinosaur travels in packs that scavenge like jackals crossed with dung beetles. Some herbivores resemble Titanic cows; others rhinos. Most vicious is the velociraptor, a lizardized ostrich: fast, cunning, deadly, and only marginally larger than man.

The velociraptors are the antagonists, Mother Nature's revenge for human hubris. Their sightings bring on the investigation that is the story. After dallying with T. Rex, Crichton musters the velociraptors for the inevitable showdown. The people win, but the raptors escape into the jungle for the sequel.

This book disappoints most in its failure to develop the personality and philosophy of its dinosaur people, the velociraptors. The real people don't matter much in this story. The dinosaurs do. OK, they're birdlike, but a dearth of bird profundity ultimately turns the contest between people and raptors into *Aliens,* the movie, revisited. When the contest ends, lots of raptors remain but the plot peters out, in large part because the raptors get California dreamy—which, even given our short acquaintance, seems uncharacteristic.

However lightly, *Jurassic Park* touches on hoary themes: Pride goes before a fall; humans cannot control events; science is fraught with potential for evil. Crichton faintly recalls Frankenstein, and other works of modern remonstration.

In comparing dinosaurs and people, he diminishes the distinction between them and us. Collectively, people are mighty, but individually, they can be as specialized and therefore as unadaptable as dinosaurs. The tycoon, the computer whiz, and the genius biotechnician are "thintelligent" and therefore become puny when nudged beyond their purviews. Not surprisingly, these gents become extinct.

Jurassic Park is more daydream than nightmare. It is lurid and improbable. But it is also alluring, setting the reader to musing on wondrous beasts and scientific possibilities.

J. P. Telotte   (essay date 1990)

SOURCE: "*Westworld, Futureworld,* and the World's Obscenity," in *State of the Fantastic: Studies in the Theory and Practice of Fantastic Literature and Film,* edited by Nicholas Ruddick, Greenwood Press, 1990, pp. 179-88.

[*Telotte is an American critic and educator who frequently writes about film and film history; his works include* Dreams of Darkness: Fantasy and the Films of Val Lewton *(1985) and* Voices in the Dark: The Narrative Patterns of Film Noir *(1989). In the following essay, he utilizes key concepts from French philosopher and sociologist Jean Baudrillard in an examination of how* Westworld *and its sequel,* Futureworld, *portray the dangers of living in a technological society where the boundaries between reality and fantasy break down.*]

> The schizo is bereft of every scene, open to everything in spite of himself, living in the greatest confusion. He is himself obscene, the obscene prey of the world's obscenity. What characterizes him is less the loss of the real, the light years of estrangement from the real, the pathos of distance and radical separation, as is commonly said: but . . . the absolute proximity, the total instantaneity of things, the feeling of no defense, no retreat. It is the end of interiority and intimacy, the overexposure and transparence of the world which traverses him without obstacle. He can no longer produce the limits of his own being. [Jean Baudrillard, "The Ecstasy of Communication," translated by John Johnston, in *The Anti-Aesthetic: Essays on Postmodern Culture,* edited by Hal Foster, 1983.]

In the modern world, Jean Baudrillard suggests, we seem to be in the process of redefining our relationship to reality. We no longer inhabit a world of objects separate and distinct from the Self, one of objective spectacle; rather, thanks to what he terms the "ecstasy of communication" that has evaporated many traditional boundaries, we seem to move, much like a culture of schizophrenics, in a world of blurred distinctions—in fact, in a world where the real seems practically to have vanished. The result, he feels, is a kind of "obscenity" characterizing modern life, a forced and intimate mingling of the Self and the world, a confusion that can be at the same time frightening and exhila-

rating, and one with which we are finding it difficult to come to terms.

We can find this shift from distance to intimacy, from detachment to obscenity, precisely measured in a series of films that take as their very focus what Baudrillard calls "the loss of the real." Michael Crichton's *Westworld* (1973) and its sequel *Futureworld* (1976) depict a near future in which man's technological ability to reshape reality, even to tailor his own versions of the real, becomes yoked to the gratification of his innermost desires. The experiences that result from the loss of distance in these films suggest a kind of threatening obscenity that may lurk even in what may conventionally seem the least "obscene" of contexts: a cold, rational, thoroughly technologized modern world. As Baudrillard might put it, these films obscenely sketch the difficulty of being human—or at least of being something other than a schizophrenic human—in a technological age.

But let me clarify first what Baudrillard means by the "world's obscenity." The truly obscene, he says in "The Ecstasy of Communication" (1983) rests not in any display or abuse of the body, but in the very *displayability* of all things in the modern world, in their immediate openness and vulnerability. Literally, it denotes a standing in front of the scene of life, without any secure boundaries or borders for protection, with the Self left open and defenseless. In this humanly shaped, technologically defined, media-suffused environment, all distinctions between public and private space seem to disappear, as private life and public spectacle collapse together, so that everything "becomes transparence and immediate visibility" in an excessive way reminiscent of a "sexual close-up in a porno film." While the distinction we once enjoyed between public and private served a salutary function—a "symbolic benefit"—of constituting an Other for the Self (so affirming "that the Other exists"), its contemporary collapse and attendant "forced extroversion of all interiority" leave us unsure of our limits, uncertain in what the Self consists, lost in a veritable culture of schizophrenics.

Westworld and *Futureworld* address just such a turn of circumstance, as if reflecting a growing awareness of how much our sense of Self has collapsed, disappeared, been swallowed up by an "obscene" modern world. What these films describe is a process at work in our technologized environment—a tendency of the Self to disappear that is directly proportional to its growing ability to rework this world. Both films take place in a kind of Disneyland for adults, a place devoted to translating private "scenes" into public space. The first begins in the future with a television commercial touting a new theme park, Delos, which offers visitors three venues for their amusement: Romanworld, Medievalworld, and Westworld. The second film starts with a similar televised introduction to the theme park but emphasizes that this is a reopening of a redesigned world, pointedly different, safer yet more exciting than its predecessor, and with more venues from which to choose. In effect, it is a reconstruction of a world dedicated to reconstruction and thus a place where the very notion of limits or differentiation seems practically irrelevant.

What both films have in common—and what seems to

constitute their main attraction—is not simply the quaintly different *experiences* they describe in these public arenas; rather, it is the *human dimension* they give to those experiences. As a commercial advertising Delos notes at the start of *Westworld,* these vacation venues are peopled with "robots scientifically programmed to look, act, talk, and even bleed just like humans do," and they "are there to serve you and to give you the most unique vacation experience of your life." In *Futureworld* that impulse goes a step farther, as a vacationland peopled with even more lifelike robots and partly designed by robots begins producing a next generation of genetically engineered, programed beings, completely indistinguishable from their human models and intent on taking their places in the outside world. In fact, since the original robots were already nearly indistinguishable from the guests, it might be argued that this process is already well advanced. By linking the appeal of this human similitude to the ultimate threat that every double invariably poses—namely, that it might replace the Self—these films suggest a sense of self that is rapidly collapsing, becoming schizophrenic in the face of this world's "obscenity."

At the outset, both films reassuringly suggest a context of distance, a public space quite separate from the private one about which we are often so protective. As their very titles imply, they seem to designate other worlds and other times than our own. Like Disney World, these venues simply offer visitors re-creations or spectacles for their amusement. Indeed the space they describe can only be reached by hovercraft in *Westworld* and by jumbo jet in *Futureworld,* and the trips to this isolated locale are infrequent. Delos is, in effect, portrayed as the ultimate "getaway" from the real world.

However, the real—and the nearness to which we can approach it—is the true lure of this resort. The various vacation worlds, guests are assured, are "precise to the smallest detail." In testimony to this precision, a returning vacationer gushes, "It's the realest thing I've ever done; I mean that!" Of course, this remark hints at a general impoverishment of human experience, at a common inability of the people in this world to gain meaningful access to reality in their normal lives, as if the everyday was already little more than a public space, a realm of simulacra, an unreal world inhabited by people who are increasingly unsure of their own reality. While the Delos experience is presented as a resort or vacation from the pressures of the real world, then, it seems designed as a kind of insulation against a universal "loss of the real." By offering guests a wealth of simulacra, an almost obscene surfeit of what they are encouraged to take for the real, it disguises that condition of loss and effectively re-presents itself as more real than the real.

This strange mixture of distance and intimacy, of a desire to get away from the world and a need to gain some new contact with it, says much about the project of both films. On one level, these theme parks by their very nature thrive on obliterating distance, on inviting guests to cast off—along with their normal inhibitions—any sense that what they are experiencing is different from the real. The cowboys who get shot in Westworld look like, fall like, and bleed like the real thing. The maidens who are pursued and bedded by the "knights" visiting Medievalworld feel and respond like the real thing. The slaves who are used and abused in Romanworld's orgies and circuses appear genuinely human. They seem intended to put us back in touch with ourselves, to help us regain a lost private Self. Yet on another level, these worlds encourage a kind of retreat from whatever reality they seem to represent—a retreat from pain, responsibility, human caring, ultimately from the world we inhabit.

They are, in a sense, realms that cater to—and effectively reinforce—the general schizophrenia of modern life. Delos is designed to encourage visitors to immerse themselves completely in these ersatz environments, to take on and, for a short time, live to the hilt whatever roles they might desire. As one vacationer, John, tells his partner Pete in *Westworld,* "You got to get into the feel of things." Yet even on the simplest level that "feel" turns out to be rather discomforting. As Pete quickly notes about the "West of the 1880s" with its scratchy clothes, dirty streets, and poor accommodations, "At least they could have made it more comfortable." Even in the antiseptic conditions of simulated spaceflight in *Futureworld,* the response is similar; as one anxious guest puts it to another, "There's nothing to worry about; it's all play-like. We're not really going anywhere—I think."

Of course, visitors like John and Pete are made comfortable in other ways—for instance, by the willing companionship of robot "saloon girls." Moreover, the gunslingers are programed to lose every gunfight, while at night cleanup crews remove the "bodies" and restock the venues with more "authentic" characters and future victims. Yet for all this, one can only really enjoy these worlds by becoming a kind of schizophrenic. Violence and even murder become exciting acts but only insofar as the guest puts aside his normal Self and acts freely in the knowledge that ultimately no one is truly hurt. A successful encounter with a gunslinger makes the pulse race and strokes the ego but only because the encounter is rigged from the start. As one character explains, the guns "won't fire at anything with a high body temperature, only something cold like a machine," so the guest always wins. In effect, every encounter, including a sexual dalliance with a saloon girl or Roman slave, requires that the human involved adopt two personalities at the same time: that of the participant, fully committed to this "real" experience; and that of the observer, who stands safely outside this reality, beyond the implications of his involvement, able to relish his seemingly irresistible or invulnerable self.

What *Westworld* proceeds to explore is the danger that accompanies this schizophrenia. As is almost invariably the case in narratives that begin by describing an achieved technological perfection, something goes wrong. Robots begin acting contrary to their programing. In a kind of technological reworking of original sin, the logic circuits on a snake fail to respond, a medieval queen programed for infidelity refuses a guest's seduction, another guest is stabbed at a duel, and the robot gunslinger starts winning his showdowns by shooting the guests. The controls go awry, leaving the technicians locked in their airtight control rooms, where eventually they all suffocate. In such circumstances the observing and participating Selves suddenly and disturbingly collapse together, and in that collapse any sense of irresistibility or invulnerability quickly vanishes.

The ultimate getaway that *Westworld* describes thus simply models the sort of schizophrenia toward which much of modern life seems heading. It is, after a fashion, a getaway of the Self from the Self, a splitting of the Self that, the film warns, can only end in a collapse of those identities in upon the Other—a collapse imaged in the figure of Pete, who slumps down exhausted and terrified at film's end, as he waits for the next onslaught of the seemingly implacable, infinitely renewable robot gunslinger who has been stalking him. Like the technicians who earlier asserted that they were in full control of their robotic paradise, only to end up trapped and suffocated, Pete and the other guests at Delos are left with precisely the "feeling of no defense, no retreat" Baudrillard describes; or, as one of the dying technicians simply puts it, "You haven't got a chance." To yield to that modern schizophrenia—the ultimate vacation—the film suggests, leaves one with no private space to which to retreat, and thus unable to offer any resistance, totally vulnerable to the "world's obscenity."

If *Futureworld* makes that schizophrenic menace more explicit, it also seems to accept it as almost a given of modern life. During the credit sequence, the camera tracks in to a close-up of a human eye, in the iris of which we see reflected an image of a man. We move closer and closer to that reflected image until all we see is his eye, the iris of which eventually matches, even replaces, that of the original eye into which we had been looking. So when the camera tracks back out to the face with which the scene began—a face identical to that of the reflected image—we can no longer tell whose eye or face we see. It is a disturbing scene that sets the tone for the ensuing narrative; it is an image in which all sense of distance blurs, in which man comes face to face with his own image, and in which an eye not only matches but eventually replaces its model. What that image quickly points to is not only a potential for alternate versions of the Self, but also the menace implicit in all duplication tales—in the blurring of distinctions between versions of the Self, coincident with a distortion of the space the Self occupies. With its opening focus on the eye, implying a threat to the very way in which we see, *Futureworld* challenges viewers to see clearly and confront squarely the challenge of the simulacrum.

The opening pattern of duplication and replacement is again linked to the effort to turn the private into the public. This film too focuses on the "dream resort" Delos, which has improved and expanded its operation—indeed, it even promises to expand into the ultimate private space, the world of our dreams. The main emphasis of this film, though, is on how Delos operates. As newspaper reporter Chuck Browning and television personality Tracy Ballard tour the reopened resort, what comes into focus is less its Disney World allure than its curious inner workings, less the spectacles it offers than the impulses that drive it and the way it tries to reshape *everything,* including its visitors, as spectacle. Everything here seems to be appropriated

and publicized: every action is displayed on television screens, every robotic function produces a host of sensor readings, every interaction with a visitor is carefully monitored. Delos's latest innovation takes this universal monitoring to its logical end: it is a machine that lets one look directly into the mind, a dream chamber that can "convert thought waves back into the images the mind creates," and thereby turn one's dreams into a spectacle for all to see, even record them for later playback. So all that we normally internalize, repress, keep to the Self can be turned outward and monitored, or be replayed for others as a kind of ultimate home movie. The result is that within this ultimate vacation resort there simply is no private space.

This monitoring is only a sort of panoptic model for the larger transformation of the private into the public that, as Chuck and Tracy discover, is the final aim of the new Delos. Impelled by a sense of what a "very unstable, irrational, violent animal" mankind is, Dr. Schneider, the genius behind the resort, has devised a plan to avert what he sees as man's inevitable destruction of the planet. In it, the key leaders and opinion makers of the world will gradually be replaced by duplicates so precise that "even those of us who create them can't tell the original from the duplicate"; and all are programed to advance one fundamental agenda, namely the interests of Delos. What the plan implies is a general supervision designed to render everyone and everything transparent. The plan aims, in effect, to invert the world itself, for as all life becomes monitored and supervised, the resort itself replaces the Self as the one private, privileged secret space at the heart of life because as the embodiment of one unquestioned principle behind all supervision it is the only place free from supervision.

In its extrapolation of *Westworld*'s original conception, *Futureworld* presents an even more disturbing vision than its predecessor. While *Westworld,* through its robots and robotic resort, forces us to look directly at the sort of physical obscenities in which we too easily take pleasure— killing, bondage, gluttony, and so on—the later film explores the impulses at work beneath these simple, personal obscenities: the widespread impulses to objectify, oversee, and dominate all things, urges typically associated with an increasingly technologized world. These impulses, implicit in the first film, explicit in the second, work to turn the world inside out, make it transparent, a public spectacle, and in the process render reality itself ever more elusive and evanescent.

Thus we might see a kind of evolution at work in these two films. In many ways, Baudrillard suggests, the violence to which we are so prone—the violence so coldly detailed in *Westworld*—is actually less transgressive, less dangerous than the spread of simulacra that *Futureworld* envisions. For violence is waged over the real; to Baudrillard in *Simulations* (1976-78), it is simply another way in which that common human activity of contention surfaces. But simulation, by contrast, "is infinitely more dangerous . . . since it always suggests, over and above its object, that *law and order themselves might really be nothing more than a simulation*"—even that the *only* order might be that of simulation. Surely that is the prospect a film like *Future-*

world sketches: a world governed by simulacra, all of them produced and monitored by other simulacra, and put in place precisely to extend the general order of simulacra. It is a world in which there can no longer be anything but public space, and consequently one in which there can only be schizophrenic beings, figures like those created deep within Delos. They are beings driven by their implanted "natural" memories and genetic traits—much like the replicants of a later film, *Blade Runner* (1982)—and they are beyond all conscious reason the psychic slaves of Delos.

It seems fitting that *Futureworld* balances this prospect against a more personal confrontation, that between Chuck and Tracy. He is an old-fashioned investigative reporter who plays hunches while looking for the real story behind the glamorous world around him. She is a failed reporter—Chuck had in fact fired her, despite a brief romantic fling, because she was "not a very good reporter" and did not like digging up "dirt and bad news," as she puts it. Since then, though, Tracy has become a major television newscaster who speaks to an audience of "fifty-five million worldwide," while gloating that Chuck's readership is just "a couple of thousand old prunes in the library." The human dynamic played out here, then, is that between one who suspects a hidden reality behind Delos, a privacy despite the great show of openness, and one who accepts it as it appears, as simply an enthralling and thoroughly satisfying spectacle, another extension of the mass-mediated environment in which she moves so comfortably.

To win her help in his investigation, Chuck appeals to Tracy's earlier journalistic training. In essence, he tries to reactivate another, private side of herself that she has, in a kind of schizophrenia, denied under the influence of that electronic "ecstasy" Baudrillard described. While the world of simulacra that Dr. Schneider unveils seems to have a seductive influence on Tracy—tellingly, the dream she visualizes shows her being pursued and then seduced by *Westworld*'s robotic gunslinger—Chuck revives his earlier affection for her, in effect to challenge the electronic with a human ecstasy. In a climactic scene that recalls the science fiction classic *Invasion of the Body Snatchers* (1956), Chuck kisses Tracy—in order to determine whether she is real or a robotic replacement—and then notes with some satisfaction, "There are some things you just can't fake."

Clearly, both of these films oppose the "fake," the simulacrum, the robotic, with the "real," the genuine, the human. They did so in the context of a culture wherein boundaries of all sorts were increasingly being eroded and even vanishing. Both appeared in the mid-1970s, the era of Watergate and the Patty Hearst affair, the period that also saw the production of the first functional synthetic genes. It was an era when the line between lawful and criminal activity indeed seemed to be disappearing, when the rapid spread of photocopying machines and the introduction of the videocassette recorder were blurring the distinctions between originals and copies, when the unprecedented pervasiveness of the mass media was making it nearly impossible to distinguish personal desires from those conjured up for us by commercials, and when a flourishing pornography industry was defying efforts to distinguish between obscenity and the exercise of free speech.

Both these films, however, express their concern with the simulacrum in terms of the robot and robotic technology, so we should consider this specific motif in the context of the broader cultural context. In fact, these films are finally not just about the confrontation between the human and the copy or double, a theme explored in such earlier films as *It Came from Outer Space* (1953), *Invasion of the Body Snatchers,* and even *Forbidden Planet* (1956). The robot always poses an ontological threat, one that Gary K. Wolfe summarizes well when he asks, "Once a simple function of human beings has been replaced, where will it stop?" [*The Known and the Unknown: The Iconography of Science Fiction,* 1979]. Because of advances in robotics and computers, this threat was clearly coming back into focus in this period, which saw a spate of robot/android films including *The Terminal Man* (1974), and *The Questor Tapes* (1974), *The Stepford Wives* (1975), and *The Demon Seed* (1977). But in *Westworld* and *Futureworld,* at least, we might interpret the robot not so much as threat as symptom. Through their roboticized environments, these films bring into focus the kind of "obscenity" Baudrillard describes, one that threatens to become a pervasive modern characteristic. By placing their characters in a world where the difference between human and robot, real world and artificial one, private desire and public spectacle simply vanishes, these films delineate a common vulnerability while also suggesting a strategy of resistance to these conditions.

Of course, it might be argued that such resistance is pointless for it merely represents an ideological denial of an extant situation. Baudrillard at various points implies that the transformation (which these films locate in the future) has already occurred, that we already inhabit an obscene world where there is no possibility of privacy, where schizophrenia is the common condition, and where reality itself has become "hyperreal" through the dizzying proliferation of simulacra. Thus in *Simulations* he describes Disneyland in a way that recalls the future according to *Futureworld,* as a place that is "presented as imaginary in order to make us believe that the rest is real, when in fact all . . . surrounding it are no longer real, but of the order of the hyperreal and of simulation." However, the absence of such resistance is also difficult to imagine, even for Baudrillard. For the result of this transformation of the real, finally, is the loss of all private space, perhaps even of all distinct identity, the individual having to live "with no halo of private protection, not even his own body, to protect him anymore" ("Ecstasy of Communication")

Moreover, we need to read this notion of resistance in light of the preexisting sense of schizophrenia in science fiction. For on the one hand, science fiction, especially as film, bases its appeal on what is public: on the spectacle of technology and scientific development, on the changes it foresees, and on the material accomplishments our culture so readily applauds. On the other hand, it has an abiding stake in the private or personal which, as Susan Sontag notes [in "The Imagination of Disaster," in *Against Interpretation, and Other Essays,* 1966], results in a constant anxiety over conditions that produce "impersonality and dehumanization." While it recognizes and exploits the lure of the public, then, science fiction also invariably questions those transformations and accomplishments, often qualifying its support for them as if such changes were fundamentally opposed to what is human. Ultimately, science fiction tries to mediate between these two positions, to take its own schizophrenia in hand.

Westworld and *Futureworld* do this by examining the seductive powers of the simulacrum. They admit to a world in which the real is already slipping away, note a certain lure in that disappearance, and then explore how we might deal with the situation, perhaps even come to live with it, like the technician Harry Cross in *Futureworld,* who lives deep in the bowels of Delos with an old robot named Clark. After many years, he explains, he has developed "a taste for the iron," namely a fondness for this battered mechanism. These robot-populated, robot-monitored and even robot-controlled worlds promise to make this taste easily acquired by fulfilling our age-old dream of linking the private with the public, permitting us to live out our dreams and private fantasies. Through these devices, we can create a fictional Self, craft a narrative for it, and have it act out that role in a public space. However, in creating this transcendent Self, one free to order up its own reality, we risk turning the self inside out, leaving it open and vulnerable in the public space usually occupied by our technology.

What these films suggest is that it is not so much the robot or android that we fear as a loss of the private, a loss of that place of refuge and security to which we can retreat when the challenge of the public world becomes too great. They sketch this situation by describing how we have begun to link and even to collapse the private and the public. Transcendence has a price, as marked by the robots in *Westworld* who refuse to play their allotted roles, and by those in *Futureworld* who threaten to displace humanity from the narrative that is life itself. Similarly, transforming the real into a theme park comes at a cost—that of the theme park becoming our only reality. Yet because the lure of the simulacrum is a powerful, perhaps inescapable one, we find ourselves in a double bind. Certainly, it is becoming ever harder to determine just what we "can't fake." But perhaps it is only in that almost automatic resistance, only in that stubborn belief in the possibility of the fake, only in that reflexive recoil before what O. B. Hardison, Jr. terms "a horizon of invisibility [that] cuts across the geography of modern culture," that we do, briefly, find a kind of private space for the Self [Hardison, *Disappearing through the Skylight: Culture and Technology in the Twentieth Century,* 1989]. It is simply our human way of coping with our vulnerability, our seeming schizophrenia, the obscenity of the modern world.

Robert Nathan   (review date 9 February 1992)

SOURCE: "Is Japan Really Out to Get Us?," in *The New York Times Book Review,* February 9, 1992, pp. 1, 22-3.

[*Nathan is an American novelist, dramatist, and critic. In the following favorable review of* Rising Sun, *he contends that Crichton's presentation of Japanese-American economic relations raises important questions "about America's condition at the end of the American century."*]

Every so often, a work of popular fiction vaults over its humble origins as entertainment, grasps the American imagination and stirs up the volcanic subtexts of our daily life. *Uncle Tom's Cabin* was that kind of book; so was Laura Z. Hobson's *Gentleman's Agreement.* Michael Crichton's eighth novel, ***Rising Sun,*** a thriller set against the background of current American-Japanese tensions, is likely to be another. Unlike the clear evils of slavery and anti-Semitism, however, the issues Mr. Crichton seeks to address succumb less easily to simplification. A shocking and ominous polemic, ***Rising Sun*** is at heart a rallying cry: the American economy is being invaded, cries Mr. Crichton, and the guards are asleep at the gates.

The story begins routinely enough. A beautiful young woman named Cheryl Austin, a paid escort to the wealthy and well connected, is found, raped and apparently strangled to death, on a conference table in the executive offices of Nakamoto Industries' new American headquarters in Los Angeles. On the floor below, at the time of her murder, political and show business royalty had been making merry in celebration of the building's grand opening.

An enthralling premise for a story? Not particularly, but it soon becomes clear that Mr. Crichton's performance— and a bravura performance it is—only superficially concerns the death of an expensive call girl. Early on, for example, a recorded Japanese voice makes announcements in an elevator in the Nakamoto Tower. "If an elevator's going to talk," says one police detective, "it should be English. This is still America." Another detective replies, "Just barely."

With dialogue like that rushing at you from almost the first page, it takes no great intelligence to realize that *Rising Sun* is no ordinary murder mystery.

Among those summoned to deal with the crime is a police detective called Peter Smith—with his common name, surely meant to be our Everyman. As a new member of Special Services, the police department's diplomatic section that often acts as a liaison to the Japanese community, Smith has the task of smoothing the ruffled feathers of Nakamoto's Japanese executives, who understandably prefer that a murder not mar their evening's festivities, and who are finding Tom Graham, the detective in charge of the investigation, racist and otherwise offensive.

On his way to the crime scene, Smith picks up John Connor, a retired police detective who has lived in Japan, speaks the language and now acts as a consultant for the police on difficult cases. As Connor and Smith run their own investigation, parallel to the official one, Mr. Crichton cleverly delivers the requisite plot elements—kinky sex (or allusions to it, anyway), powerful interests that don't want the case solved, a body burned beyond recognition in a car crash. Far more dazzling (in a kind of sequel to the 1981 ***Looker,*** one of Mr. Crichton's seven ventures as a movie director) are several chapters describing videotapes of the crime taken by Nakamoto's security cameras, tapes whose images have been electronically altered. Mr. Crichton's relentless narrative energy transforms lessons in video technology into the stuff of high tension; this kind of fiction rarely gets much better.

Eventually Connor and Smith tie the call girl's death to a Japanese corporation's imminent purchase of an American high-technology company, a twist that grafts an invented murder mystery onto a business deal that recalls the real-life turmoil surrounding a Japanese company's attempt in the mid-1980's to buy Fairchild Semiconductor. With the clock set ticking in a subplot involving Smith's former wife, who is a lawyer in the district attorney's office; with witnesses being intimidated, bought off and refusing to talk; with a United States senator and the future of the American standard of living thrown into the equation, the story lifts off into full-blooded conspiracy.

But if the plot makes *Rising Sun* as well built a thrill machine as a suspense novel can be, that's not enough: Mr. Crichton aims to tap into larger and more important fears. Peter Smith and John Connor have barely walked onto the stage before the reader catches on to their roles. Connor, the cynical and knowledgeable Japanophile, is the author's voice. Smith, the innocent, the supplicant, stands in for us, the readers—asking Connor questions, building a moral calculus to puzzle out the ambiguities of our relations with the Japanese. "If they bow to you, don't bow back," Connor tells Smith, "just give a little head nod. A foreigner will never master the etiquette of bowing." Similarly, "When you start to deal with the Japanese, remember that they don't like to negotiate. They find it too confrontational. . . . Control your gestures. Keep your hands at your sides. The Japanese find big arm movements threatening." Connor describes the Japanese as so foreign, their differences so unconquerable, that they sometimes seem not simply another race but another species.

**That Mr. Crichton effortlessly weaves a mesmerizing mystery comes as no surprise. That he should now write so passionately and engagingly on matters of Japanese culture and the survival of a free and productive America—that is the surprise of *Rising Sun.*

—Robert Nathan**

Figures in a Greek chorus, Connor and Smith sing their refrains on the gap between the Americans and the Japanese. Scenes open and close with discussions of the murder case, but they often veer off into disquisitions on economics and sociology. Listening to rich Americans joke about Japanese economic power, Connor is pointedly amused. "In no other country in the world," he says, "would you hear people calmly discussing the fact that their cities and states were sold to foreigners." Peter Smith counters that

the bankers and brokers, the ones doing the discussing, are also the sellers. "Yes. Americans are eager to sell," Connor admits. "It amazes the Japanese. They think we're committing economic suicide. And of course they're right." As further evidence of Mr. Crichton's gifts, these discourses never obscure Smith and Connor's investigation, not least because every aspect of the murder mystery echoes the larger mystery of Japan and its relationship with the United States.

Early in the novel, Mr. Crichton's characters, though often dyspeptic about the success of Japanese industry, are in many ways sympathetic to the Japanese as individuals. Connor's observations, while trenchant, are generally benign. The Japanese may practice a different social code, adhere to different business values, but it is arrogant of us, Connor suggests, to expect them to change. When Smith expresses outrage that a Japanese executive has lied to the police, Connor explains that in the executive's view lying is an inappropriate description of his behavior. "Americans believe there is some core of individuality that doesn't change from one moment to the next," says Connor. "And the Japanese believe context rules everything." When Smith remarks that this sounds like an excuse, Connor replies: "Our problem in this country is that we don't deal with the Japanese the way they really are."

As *Rising Sun* progresses, however, the benign gives way to the caustic. Almost imperceptibly, Connor's and other characters' attitudes toward the Japanese seem to shift, with the heat level escalating. Characters meant to be intellectually astute, believable and of unquestioned integrity repeatedly assault Japan's motives and behavior, until the death of Cheryl Austin begins to seem a metaphor for the death of America.

"The Japanese think everybody who is not Japanese is a barbarian," Connor says. "They mean it, literally: *barbarian.* Stinking, vulgar, stupid barbarian." Later he says, "The Japanese are the most racist people on earth" and "the most racist people on the planet." A half-black, half-Japanese woman, an outcast in Japan, quotes a joke attributed to the former Japanese Prime Minister Noboru Takeshita: "He said America is now so poor, the Navy boys cannot afford to come ashore to enjoy Japan. Everything is too expensive for them. He said they could only remain on their ship and give each other AIDS. Big joke in Japan."

As for the failure of American industry to penetrate Japanese markets, Connor says, "Overall, foreign investment in Japan has declined by half in the last ten years. One company after another finds the Japanese market just too tough. They get tired of . . . the collusion, the rigged markets . . . the secret agreements to keep them out. . . . And eventually they give up. . . . Because no matter what they tell you, Japan is closed."

Here is Connor on the subject of American cars: "Japan is always telling us that their markets are open. Well, in the old days, if a Japanese bought an American car, he got audited by the government. So pretty soon, nobody bought an American car. . . . The obstructions are endless."

Strong stuff? Maybe, but well mannered and mild compared to what follows. An American financial reporter matter-of-factly explains Japan's campaign to dismantle and ultimately destroy American industry. Citing one example after another of what he characterizes as Japan's protectionist and corrupt trade policies, he responds to charges that incompetent American management accounts for our economic drubbing by the Japanese. "That's the standard line. . . . As promoted by the Japanese and their American spokesmen. It's only with a few episodes that people ever glimpsed how outrageous the Japanese really were. Like the Houdaille case. You know that one? Houdaille was a machine-tool company that claimed its patents and licenses were being violated by companies in Japan. A federal judge sent Houdaille's lawyer to Japan to gather evidence. But the Japanese refused to issue him a visa."

A university physics professor, shut out of his makeshift computer laboratory when he tries to help Connor and Smith, sadly observes that the Japanese are buying control of American education by endowing professorships and financing research. A newspaper reporter who does Smith a favor denounces the Japanese for spending "half a billion" dollars a year in a successful lobbying effort to influence the American Government and media.

Is *Rising Sun* merely a mystery novel? Hardly. Which raises the question of why Mr. Crichton felt the need to deliver his polemic in this form. The answer, obviously, is that the American people will find his view of the world easier to assimilate as entertainment; fiction, after all, can often operate on the psyche with a more visceral power than nonfiction. (Witness the conspiracy theories of the Kennedy assassination; despite endless reportage, the story had essentially faded from public attention before it was excavated in Oliver Stone's recent film *J.F.K.*) Briefly, the frightening argument of *Rising Sun* runs like this: The Japanese have declared full-scale economic war on all nations, but with particular vigor on the United States. By refusing to recognize this war and by refusing to fight back on Japan's terms—with tariffs, subsidies to our own industries and a coordinated, long-term economic plan—the United States dooms itself to a permanently declining standard of living and, probably, to the loss of its traditional freedoms.

The Japanese are different, says Mr. Crichton. They think differently and act differently. They move through the world with assumptions about human society very different from ours.

Such talk makes us uneasy. What do we make of recent news that a public outcry in Los Angeles forced officials to reconsider a mass-transit contract awarded to a Japanese supplier? How do we respond to a bid for the Seattle Mariners baseball team that would have kept it in Washington, but with partial Japanese ownership? How do we cope with accusations by a Japanese politician that American workers are lazy and illiterate, or react to his suggestion that the United States is becoming nothing more than "Japan's subcontractor"? When we think back to Pearl Harbor, to President Franklin D. Roosevelt's Executive Order 9066, which led to the internment of 120,000 Japanese-Americans, do we see a connection between the old war and the new? Will economic warfare, as one character in *Rising Sun* suggests, turn inevitably and horribly into a war of guns and bombs? Implicitly and overtly, these are among the questions raised by *Rising Sun.*

That Mr. Crichton effortlessly weaves a mesmerizing mystery comes as no surprise. Witty and erudite, a film maker and over the past 20 years author of one best seller after another, he can already lay claim to one of America's heavyweight titles: Most Serious Suspense Novelist. That he should now write so passionately and engagingly on matters of Japanese culture and the survival of a free and productive America—that is the surprise of *Rising Sun.*

For that, indeed, is what he has done. More compellingly than the work of most scholars, politicians or journalists, including those whom he credits in his bibliography, Mr. Crichton's novel has launched into the public arena an argument bound to disturb his readers. Economists may tell us that Mr. Crichton has stacked the deck, even that he has marked the cards. Nonetheless, *Rising Sun* exposes the raw nerves of a country in profound economic distress, of a people with declining faith in themselves, their leaders and their past, a people very uneasy about their future. Despite the book's provocative tone, Mr. Crichton is no xenophobe, no fool, no ranting bigot. The questions he poses are of great consequence in the debate about America's condition at the end of the American century. What more could one ask of popular fiction?

Ian Buruma   (review date 23 April 1992)

SOURCE: "It Can't Happen Here," in *The New York Review of Books,* Vol. XXXIX, No. 8, April 23, 1992, pp. 3-4.

[*Buruma is a Dutch-born American critic and editor who has written extensively about Japan and Japanese culture. In the following review of* Rising Sun, *he compares Crichton's negative portrayal of the Japanese to the German anti-Semitic film* Jew Süss (1940) *and to a contemporary Japanese anti-Semitic book,* The Day the Dollar Becomes Paper.]

Once in a while—in America perhaps more than once in a while—a book comes along whose interest is chiefly in the hype attending it. *Rising Sun* is such a book. The text of the publicity handout announced that this "explosive new thriller [was] rushed to publication one month earlier than previously announced because of its extraordinary timeliness with regard to US-Japan relations."

This is unusual: thrillers are not generally rushed out to match political events. Odder still is the sheaf of newspaper clippings about the decline of American industries and the predatory methods of Japanese corporations stapled onto the advance reader's edition. Singular, too, is the bibliography at the end of the book, listing mostly academic works on Japan, but also, for example, Donald Richie's study of Kurosawa's movies. Strangest of all, however, is Crichton's afterword, which ends with a homily: "The Japanese are not our saviors. They are our competitors. We should not forget it."

With such a buildup, the literary press could not be left

behind. On the front page of *The New York Times Book Review* the thriller was compared to *Uncle Tom's Cabin,* for stirring up "the volcanic subtexts of our daily life." *Kirkus Reviews* promised the return of the "Yellow Menace," only now "he wears a three-piece suit and aims to dominate America through force of finance, not arms."

Volcanic subtexts, Yellow Menace, Main Selection of the Book-of-the-Month club, first printing 225,000 copies, top of the best-seller lists, a Hollywood picture in the works—what exactly is going on here?

Michael Crichton clearly wanted to do more than entertain with a murder mystery. He wrote his book, so he told *The New York Times,* "to make America wake up." Now, on the whole, people who go around trying to wake us up, as though we were all asleep, oblivious to some apocalyptic Truth, tend to be boring, or mad—like those melancholy figures who wander about with signs announcing the end of the world.

Crichton's book isn't boring. He is good at snappy dialogue—though his copious use of Japanese is often incongruous and sometimes wrong—and he is a deft manipulator of suspense. And he takes great pains to avoid giving the impression that he is mad. Indeed, the whole idea of the newspaper clippings, the bibliography, the afterword, and so on, is to make sure we get the serious message buried in the "explosive new thriller." He dislikes the term "Japan-bashing," he says, because it threatens to move the US-Japan debate into "an area of unreasonableness." The thriller, by implication, is reasonable.

Well, I wonder. But before going on, perhaps I should mention the story, the vessel, as it were, for Crichton's awakening message to the American nation. In brief, it is this: a large Japanese corporation called Nakamoto is celebrating the opening of its new US headquarters, the Nakamoto Tower in downtown LA. A beautiful young American woman—Caucasian, naturally—is murdered during the party. Investigations follow. The Japanese obstruct, the American police humble, the Japanese corrupt, the Americans are corrupted, and only through the brilliance of a semi-retired detective called Connor, who speaks Japanese and knows the Japanese mind—who can see "behind the mask," so to speak—is the case more or less solved. Along the way, we have some kinky sex—the Japanese, unlike us, have no guilt, you see—and a couple of spectacular suicides: a US senator, framed for the murder of the girl, shoots himself through the mouth, and a Japanese gets himself a concrete suit by jumping into wet cement from a considerable height.

Sex and violence aside, the story has two leitmotifs that are bound to appeal: the decline of America, our way of life, etc., and a clearly identifiable enemy. The first is constantly alluded to by characters in the story, as well as by the author himself. "Shit: we're *giving* this country away," says a crude cop. "They already own Los Angeles," says a woman at a party ("laughing"). "Our country's going to hell," says a television journalist. "They *own* the government," says the crude cop. "The end of America, buddy . . ."

"They" is of course the enemy, Japan. There is a great deal of talk about "they" in the book. The enemy is identified all right, but it has no face. It is present everywhere, manipulating us, corrupting us, in our offices, our newspapers, our government, our universities, and, who knows, perhaps soon on our beaches and our landing grounds. "They" have a mind, a mentality, but no characters, no ideas. The pervasive, manipulative, inscrutable, mysterious mind is never expressed openly or directly. It is masked by subterfuge. Nakamoto Corporation, we are told, "presents an impenetrable mask to the rest of the world." One of the few Japanese with a name, though without much in the way of human personality, Mr. Ishigura, has a face, but: "His face was a mask."

Masked minds and inscrutable cultures need to be decoded, hence the stock character in many colonial and tropical fantasies: the expert, the man who has the lingo and knows the native mind, the white hero dancing dangerously on the edge of going native himself. This role is performed by Connor, who knows his way around sushi bars and knows when to be polite and when to be firm. Firmness in his case means breaking into the rough language of Japanese gangster movies. But in a good mood, he will hold forth on the finer points of Japanese manners, why "they" behave as they do, and so on. Connor likes Japan, but never forgets that we are at war.

The other stock figure in war propaganda is the good enemy, who has crossed over to the side of the angels. In Japanese wartime movies this role was often played by the Japanese actress Li Ko Ran, later known, during her brief Hollywood career, as Shirley Yamaguchi. She was the Chinese beauty who invariably fell in love with the dashing and sincere Japanese soldier; a love that symbolized the glorious future in Asia under Japanese tutelage. In nineteenth-century anti-Semitic fiction it is the "good Jew," such as the beautiful Miriam in Felix Dahn's *Fight for Rome* (1876), who identifies wholly with the German tribe and hates the rootless and treacherous Jews.

In **Rising Sun** we have the beautiful Theresa Asakuma. Theresa works in a high-tech research lab, one of the last not to fall into Japanese hands, hence, I suppose, its dilapidated state. Theresa is happy to help Connor and his wholesome American sidekick, Lieutenant Pete Smith, the narrator who plays Doctor Watson to Connor's Holmes. She is happy to help because she hates the Japanese.

The beautiful Theresa is a useful character, because she represents the perfect target for Japanese bigotry. Her father was a black GI, and she has a crippled arm. She grew up in a small Japanese town, where the tolerance for blacks and cripples was low. Her story offers an opportunity to expound a little on Japanese racism—even the notorious treatment of polluted outcasts, the *burakumin,* many of whom work in the leather trade, gets an airing. Not that any of this is implausible or wrong. Outsiders do have a hard time in Japan. But it functions as yet another stake driven through the heart of "they." It is a bit like European or Japanese descriptions of America, in which every American is either a gangster, a redneck, or a poor black.

Uncle Tom's Cabin is actually the last book I would have thought of comparing to **Rising Sun**. I can think of two anti-Semitic works that are much closer in tone and imagery. One is *Jew Süss,* the German film, directed by Veit Harlan in 1940. The other is a Japanese pop best seller by Uno Masami about the Jewish conspiracy to dominate the world. It is entitled *The Day the Dollar Becomes Paper: Why We Must Learn From Jewish Knowledge Now.*

Harlan's version of *Jew Süss* (there were many versions) shows how peaceful, prosperous eighteenth-century Württemberg is almost destroyed by letting the Jews in. The vain and gullible Duke of Württemberg has virtually exhausted the state budget by indulging his taste for pomp and dancing girls. The Jew Süss-Oppenheimer contrives, by oily flattery and promises of bottomless riches, to persuade the Duke to let him take care of his finances. He also presses the Duke to allow the Jews to settle in his city. Soon they control everything through their evil manipulation. As a symbol of German humiliation the Jew has his wicked way with the county sheriff's daughter. She commits suicide, the good people of Württemberg at last rise up against the Duke and his Jews, Oppenheimer is hanged, and the Jews are driven out of town. The message at the end of the film is that the burghers of Württemberg woke up to the danger in their midst and banished the Jews by law. This law should be upheld, not only for the sake of our generation, but for our children, our grandchildren, and so on forever and ever.

Uno Masami's book is a collection of more or less mad conspiracy theories. Among the more *outré* ones is the notion that Roosevelt, scion of the well-known Dutch Jewish family, tricked Japan into going to war, so that the US, as a front for world Jewish interests, could save the Jews from Hitler. The basic premise of the book is a simple one: Jews control world public opinion by controlling the media. Jews have convinced the decent and gullible Japanese that Japan should be internationalist instead of looking after its national interests. Thus American Jews wrote the post-war Japanese constitution to make Japan impotent. Thus the Jewish-controlled press made the Japanese feel guilty about the war. Thus decent Japanese companies such as Mitsubishi or Fujitsu cannot compete with IBM, because IBM is controlled by Jewish interests which are out to dominate the world. One salient point about this lunacy is that, to the likes of Uno, Jewish and American interests are more or less interchangeable.

Michael Crichton's thriller is not quite as zany as Uno's tract, or quite as odious as Harlan's *Jew Süss*. And to call his book racist is perhaps to miss the point. After all, as he told *The New York Times,* he likes Japan very much. He may have painted a picture of the Japanese as liars and cheats, but as Connor, the expert on the native mind, points out, that is only from our point of view, not theirs. No, the problem with Crichton is that, like Uno and the makers of *Jew Süss,* he has conceived a paranoid world, in which sincere, decent folks are being manipulated by sinister forces. These forces need not be from a different race. In a different era, they might have been Communist.

Paranoia can be based on half-truths. To say that the craziest red-baiters were paranoid is not to say that commu-

nism bore no threat. Just so, undeniable problems with Japan do not alter the fact that some of the wildest alarmists are a trifle unhinged. Crichton describes, again in Connor's words, how the Japanese in America are part of a "shadow world. . . . Most of the time you're never aware of it. We live in our regular American world, walking on our American streets, and we never notice that right alongside our world is a second world." Couple this to the refrain that "they own" our city, our government, our country, and one is not so very far removed from Veit Harlan's Württemberg.

The metaphors are remarkably similar. Masks are a key image in **Rising Sun** and in *Jew Süss*. The idea in *Jew Süss* is to contrast an organic, decent, even somewhat slow-witted German community, rooted in its native clay, and the artificial, devious, clever floating world of the rootless Jews. The Duke of Württemberg is warned by one of his courtiers that the Jew is always masked. In both Crichton and Harlan, the enemy is pictured as omnipresent, omnipotent, and certainly more sophisticated. "The Jews are always so intelligent," says an exasperated Württemberger. "Not intelligent, just shrewd," answers another. As Richard Wagner liked to say, the Jew can only imitate, not create.

Connor, only a little ironically, calls America "an underdeveloped peasant country." Compared to the Japanese, he says, we are incompetent. But on the other hand, of course, "they" have bought our universities, because, as an American scientist tells Connor, "they know—after all the bullshit stops—that they can't innovate as well as we can." Not intelligent, just shrewd.

In *Jew Süss* and in **Rising Sun,** we are shown how native institutions are slowly taken over by alien forces. Veit Harlan suggests this by using dissolves and music: the German motto on the Württemberg shield of arms dissolves into Hebrew; a Bach chorale gradually melts into the song of a cantor. In **Rising Sun,** as in Uno's book, our press is infiltrated; one of "their" people is "planted" at the *LA Times,* no less. Another *LA Times* reporter, one of "ours," explains the situation: "The American press reports the prevailing opinion. The prevailing opinion is the opinion of the group in power. The Japanese are now in power."

At the beginning of **Rising Sun,** Connor rides an elevator in the Nakamoto Tower with some American cops. An electronic voice anounces the floors in Japanese. "Fuck," says the cop, "if an elevator is going to talk, it should be English. This is still America." "Just barely," says Connor.

This kind of paranoia is more complex than mere xenophobia. It suggests a deep frustration. Again, Harlan's film is instructive: the fiancé of the girl who falls prey to the wicked Jew's designs is shown as an impotent man—handsome in a blond, romantic, German sort of way, but incapable. In the beginning of the film, the girl makes advances to him, but he fails to respond. The Jew succeeds, albeit violently, where the decent German fails. The enemy as a potent stud: this is how an American floozy in Crichton's book describes her Japanese patrons: " 'A lot of them, they are so polite, so correct, but then they get turned on, they have this . . . this *way* . . .' She broke off, shaking her head. 'They're strange people.' "

There runs a streak of masochism through all this. And, to be sure, it wouldn't be the first time that American self-flagellation has sold many books. But there is also a hint of awe for the enemy, as though we would like to be more like "them." In 1942, Hitler quoted "the British Jew Lord Disraeli" as the source of the idea that the racial problem was the key to world history. The anti-Semitic jurist Carl Schmitt had a picture of Disraeli above his desk. Uno Masami wants the Japanese to learn from the Jews, to learn how they maintained the purity, the virility, and the independence of their race.

It is striking how often the fiercest Western critics of Japan are the ones who most want to emulate Japanese ways: protectionism, industrial policies, order, discipline. Crichton, or, rather, Connor speaks about being at war with Japan, and at the same time repeats with admiration all the clichés of Japanese cultural chauvinists: how the Japanese people are "members of the same family, and they can communicate without words," or how good the Japanese police are, because "for major crimes, convictions run ninety-nine percent." Connor forgets, perhaps, that confessions are enough to convict in Japan, and that the Japanese police are rather good at getting confessions.

Could it be, then, that some Americans are feeling frustrated with the messiness of American democracy, with its many competing interests and its lack of strong central power; that people are getting tired of freewheeling individualism and the hurly-burly marketplace; that they despair of all the immigrants, who barely speak English yet occupy American cities in their expanding shadow worlds; that, in other words, many Americans would secretly like to feel part of one family, with order imposed from above? If so, it would be a sad thing. For America, thus awakened, would stop being the country to which millions came to escape from just such tribal orders. And those millions included quite a few Japanese.

Karl Taro Greenfeld (review date 11 May 1992)

SOURCE: "Return of the Yellow Peril," in *The Nation,* New York, Vol. 254, No. 18, May 11, 1992, pp. 636-38.

[*In the following review of* Rising Sun, *Greenfeld faults the book for its stereotyping of the Japanese people and suggests that the novel's popularity may render legitimate criticism of Japan and Japanese society suspect.*]

Michael Crichton's **Rising Sun,** judging from its enormous sales (first on *The New York Times*'s best-seller list for three weeks and still second as of April 19), could be the only book about Japan many Americans will ever read. If this is true, its portrayal of the Japanese as inscrutable, technologically proficient, predatory aliens who communicate through telepathy, subsist on unpalatable foods, manipulate *everything* and *everyone* and enjoy kinky, violent sex with white women will be more influential in shaping opinions about Japan and the Japanese than

any of the more thoughtful and insightful books recently published.

Rising Sun is a thriller revolving around the postcoital murder of Cheryl Austin, a Texas blonde, on a conference table at the Nakamoto Tower in downtown L.A., the U.S. headquarters of the fictitious Nakamoto *keiretsu* (holding company). As detectives Peter Smith and John Connor unravel the mystery, every character they encounter puts in his two yen about Japan-U.S. relations. And each speaks in improbable paragraphs of exposition familiar to readers of revisionist Japan experts Chalmers Johnson, Clyde Prestowitz, James Fallows or Pat Choate.

There has been for some time a demand for perfidious, post-cold war villains, and Crichton's Japanese are the supply.

> **The Japanese in *Rising Sun* are portrayed as aliens, as perfidious and threatening as the virus from outer space in Crichton's *The Andromeda Strain*.**
>
> **—Karl Taro Greenfeld**

Crichton has brought to the surface an idea that has been lurking for some years in America's collective pop-culture unconscious: The Japanese are evil. The Japanese have been accused of bearing the responsibility for any or all of the following: unemployment, budget deficits, the declining industrial base, trade imbalances, low savings rates, unfair trading, high real estate prices and, now, low real estate prices. And to all this Crichton adds the final indignity. In **Rising Sun,** Japanese men have sex exclusively with white women, whom they force to live in subjugation in secret locales. ("We demand reciprocity," a Lee Iacocca might insist.) By making the leap into the realm of hysteria—an appropriate cover for the paperback might be a caricature of World War II-era Prime Minister Tojo skulking off into Rockefeller Center with Doris Day over one shoulder and an eighteen-inch dildo sheathed where his samurai sword would have been—Crichton has changed the context in which I, and I suspect others, will perceive what is written about Japan and the Japanese.

Suddenly, revisionist Japan experts like Prestowitz or Johnson, who have been criticized by some as Japan-bashers, seem moderate and reasonable—as George Bush appears reasonable when compared with Pat Buchanan. Prior to **Rising Sun,** those Americans who bothered to think about tensions in Japan-U.S. relations focused on economic matters: opening rice markets, for example, or accusations of semiconductor dumping. At worst, there were the racist insults clumsily blurted out by Japanese politicians who sometimes forget they have become actors on the international media stage. (I suspect some American politicians harbor reciprocal xenophobic views on the Japanese but are far too media-savvy to voice them.)

But Crichton's novel suggests that if the Japanese finally buy up enough of America they will not only have their way with our cultural treasures (Columbia's or MCA's debatable status as treasures notwithstanding), they will also have their way with our women—which means, of course, blonde women. The threat sounds familiar—it is a time-worn and chillingly effective cry that rallies white men to string innocent men of color from trees. Savor this quote from **Rising Sun** spoken by Julia Young, a "beautiful" girl with a Southern accent who lives in a *bettaku,* a "love residence" kept by Japanese executives in Westwood, California:

> "These guys come over from Tokyo, and even if they have a *shokai,* an introduction, you still have to be careful. They think nothing of dropping ten or twenty thousand in a night. It's like a tip for them. Leave it on the dresser. But then, what they want to do—at least some of them. . . . their wishes, their desires, it's just as natural as leaving the tip. It's completely natural to them. I mean, I don't mind a little golden shower or whatever, handcuffs, you know. Maybe a little spanking if I like the guy. But I won't let anyone cut me. I don't care how much money. None of those things with knives or swords. . . . A lot of them, they are so polite, so correct, but when they get turned on, they have this . . . *way.* . . . They're strange people."

The Japanese in **Rising Sun** are portrayed as aliens, as perfidious and threatening as the virus from outer space in Crichton's **The Andromeda Strain**. If African-Americans or Jewish-Americans were portrayed in a similarly negative caricature, there would be storms of protest. Unfortunately, **Rising Sun** received a positive front-page review in *The New York Times Book Review*. Recessionary America's need for a scapegoat has created an atmosphere of fear of Japan. "We are definitely at war with Japan," says fictional character John Connor.

In this climate, thoughtful books about Japan, like *In the Realm of a Dying Emperor,* by Norma Field, or *The Outnation,* by Jonathan Rauch, can be too easily overlooked. Field, an associate professor of East Asian languages and civilizations at the University of Chicago, was born to an American father and Japanese mother in occupied Japan. *In the Realm of a Dying Emperor* is a skillful rendering of her feelings about returning to the land of her birth—a nation that was, in many ways, exclusionary and cruel to outsiders like herself. It is also a tale about three Japanese: a flag burner, a widow and Nagasaki's outspoken Mayor Hitoshi Motoshima, who in their own ways fought the rigid conformity that envelops too much of Japanese life. Field's description of flag burner Chibana Shoichi's home of Okinawa, an island still struggling to come to terms with its World War II history as a battle site where 250,000 people died, is vivid and moving. She thought-provokingly juxtaposes scenes of Okinawa's unique status as a formerly independent nation, now "occupied" (small o) by the Japanese while previously having been "Occupied" (big O) by the Americans, with Emperor Hirohito's (the dying emperor of the title) endless blood transfusions and rectal bleeding, and with the posture of "self-restraint" that settled over Japan during his prolonged decline. It was considered bad taste to celebrate lavishly or show exuberant joy during the Emperor's illness. (I was in Japan at the time and recall one curious example of "self-restraint." Mitsukoshi department store found itself in a quandary over its Christmas wrapping paper, which had the unrestrained word "Merry" printed before "Christmas." Disseminating the word "Merry," even in English, would be in very bad taste during a season of self-restraint. The solution was to print new wrapping paper with the more restrained adjective "Holy" preceding "Christmas.")

That Field's book is an intelligent, if critical, look at Japan should come as a relief. But could the Japanese, even in her account, be seen as congenitally creepy? "The sophisticated cynics do not see that they cannot disengage by choice," she writes at one point. "In their submission to an education that robbed them of their childhood, that holds their own children hostage through secret records passed from school to school, reinforcing an ever more tyrannical regimen of competition, in their surrender to a crushing routine of work and commute, they are participants in a compulsory game."

Before reading **Rising Sun** I would not have been struck by a passage like that. Now I must pause. Crichton's sensationalism has made me wary of even legitimate criticism of Japan. Have I become the Anti-Crichton? Now I worry that Americans will detect evidence of Japanese dastardliness in every subtle observation of their differentness—in the way they bow instead of shake hands, in the way they eat raw fish, and so on.

The Outnation is an interesting book of aphorisms gleaned from Jonathan Rauch's six-month stay in Japan. But why, in the course of an otherwise acute and perceptive discussion, does Rauch feel compelled to explain that the Japanese aren't clones and that "this is immediately evident even if you are unused to looking at Asians and still haven't noticed that the hair comes in infinite fine gradations of blackness: black-black, brown-black, dark brown, even reddish brown." Is Rauch making a valid point? Or has **Rising Sun** made me excessively sensitive?

It seems to me that an honorable writer like Rauch, who clearly wants to understand, should not explain to Americans that the Japanese are not clones. A few years ago I would have said that we had outgrown stereotypes and fear. But the climate has apparently changed, thanks to the likes of Iacocca and now to Crichton.

Rauch eloquently expresses the same sentiment: "There was no dark secret. The Japanese are precisely as mysterious and unique as my aunt in Hackensack. I came to Japan wanting to know how I ought to feel about the place. I left knowing only how not to feel. Frightened: that is how not to feel."

Julian Loose   (review date 22 October 1992)

SOURCE: "Number One Passport," in *London Review of Books,* Vol. 14, No. 20, October 22, 1992, pp. 26-7.

[*In the following excerpt, Loose faults Crichton's negative and unbalanced view of Japanese economic power and influence in* Rising Sun.]

For all its awesome success in the world market, Japan remains somehow stubbornly Other. Yet few can afford to ignore its looming presence. Certainly not in America, where the annual trade imbalance stands at 50 billion dollars in Japan's favour, where nearly a third of the budget deficit is shouldered by Japanese investors, and where many now recognise Japan as employer, banker and landlord. When Sony bought up Columbia Pictures in 1989, a *Newsweek* cartoon replaced the Statue of Liberty in the Columbia logo with a geisha; other icons now under Japanese management include the Rockefeller Center, Universal Studios and Michael Jackson. Such high-profile acquisitions are seized upon by opportunistic commentators, all too keen to foster suspicions of Japanese duplicity, racism and greed. Writing about Japan, its society and its foreign affairs has to an overwhelming degree become the preserve of alarmist political economists. Yet who is served by the perpetuation of the simplistic image of Japan Inc? We turn from such commentators to other voices and different genres, in the hope of moving beyond such stereotypes.

Crichton gives full scope to a rather paranoid sense of Japanese control over American institutions in *Rising Sun*.

—Julian Loose

The American novelist Michael Crichton, whose best-selling thrillers are usually based on less divisive topics—great train robberies, genetically re-animated dinosaurs, messages from other planets—has in *Rising Sun* chosen to dramatise the troubled relationship between Japan and the United States. According to Crichton, Japanese influence now extends to all spheres of American life, and anyone who attempts to speak out against it is ruthlessly suppressed. Presumably Crichton had a hard time explaining to himself how it is that his own book has seen the light of day—why his publishers have not yet been bought up by Japanese money, or Crichton himself discredited in some fabricated scandal.

Crichton's insipid hero, Detective Peter Smith, is an officer in the diplomatic section of the Los Angeles Police Department. His task is to investigate a murder committed during the glitzy opening party for the American headquarters of the Nakamoto Corporation. The narrative proceeds on a twin track: as Smith unravels the events which culminate in the murder (a tale involving computer chips, video trickery and blackmail), so he also receives an education in the predatory methods of the dastardly Japanese.

Everyone Smith meets has things to say on the Nippon question, and we soon realise that this is less a novel than yet another remorseless tract. Arriving at the scene of the crime, he overhears real estate agents discussing how the

Japanese own at least 70 per cent of downtown Los Angeles; a press secretary at the Jet Propulsion Laboratory complains that the Japanese are hiring the best American researchers; two farmers discuss selling a sizeable chunk of rural Montana to the Japanese, raising the enticing prospect of Japanese cowboys out on the range; and a cable news producer reflects that the Japanese cleaned up during Reagan's Presidency ('In the name of free trade, he spread our legs real wide'). This unnerving barrage continues even on the freeway, as Smith surveys enormous billboards advertising the likes of Canon (AMERICA'S COPY LEADER) and Honda (NUMBER ONE RATED CAR IN AMERICA!).

Smith's senior partner on this case is John Connor, the most knowledgeable of Special Services officers on matters Japanese. Some of his fellow policemen suspect that Connor went native during his years in Japan. His apartment is decorated in Japanese style, with tatami mats and shoji screens, he converses through silences and indirection, and his method of investigation relies heavily on *dai rokkan,* or intuition. In Connor's view, Americans compare unfavourably to the Japanese in almost every respect: in Japan (as in Mussolini's Italy), 'trains are on time. Bags are not lost. Connections are not missed. Deadlines are met.' In Japan you can safely walk in the parks at night, companies are more interested in fixing the problem than the blame and at times of trouble, executives are the first to take a pay cut.

But in spite of his respect for Japanese efficiency, Connor remains a true blue patriot who 'always keeps his balance'. If he dismisses the conventional 'prejudices and media fantasies' which lead people to dislike the Japanese, it is only to outline the real reasons for fearing them: 'Our problem in this country is that we don't deal with the Japanese the way they really are.' And so he sets about explaining to Smith (and the reader) how the Japanese retain their edge: get a bribe in ahead of time, to ensure good will when it is needed; create a scandal to eliminate powerful business or political opponents; above all, always remember that, as the saying goes, 'business is war'.

During the course of the novel Crichton delivers a few critical swipes at America, whose terminal decline is best illustrated, as one typically well-informed character explains, by the fact that it now has 4 per cent of the world population, but 50 per cent of its lawyers. America must wake up to the true danger of allowing foreign investment in its high technology. But Crichton's central proposition is that 'Japan doesn't and won't do things our way': the Japanese have invented a new kind of trade, 'adversarial trade, trade like war, trade intended to wipe out the competition'. As his extensive bibliography and note of thanks to the likes of Karel van Wolferen and Senator Albert Gore make clear, Crichton follows 'a well-established body of expert opinion'. Like most of his fellow Japan-bashers, he singularly fails to recognise that nominating Japan as America's bogeyman is symptomatic of America's problem, and has little to do with its solution.

Crichton gives full scope to a rather paranoid sense of Japanese control over American institutions. A police officer, whose uncle happens to have been killed during the war in 'terminal medical experiments in Japan', declares that a number of his fellow citizens are siding with the enemy: 'Just like in World War Two, some people were paid by Germany to promote Nazi propaganda.' Detective Smith is sceptical, until he realises that he, too, has been bought, the extra stipend of several thousand dollars he receives from 'the Japan-America Amity Foundation' being patently designed to ensure his good will. Crichton develops this theme to a ludicrous pitch: but no one can deny that Japanese manna rains down on the academic world, particularly on university technical departments. Noting that Japanese companies now endow 25 professorships at MIT, Crichton pithily identifies the academic experts who deliver the Japanese propaganda line as 'the Chrysanthemum Kissers': trapped by the need for access to Japan, they know that if they start to sound critical, 'their contacts in Japan dry up. Doors are closed to them . . . Anybody who criticises Japan is a racist.'

Stephen Jay Gould   (review date 12 August 1993)

SOURCE: "Dinomania," in *The New York Review of Books,* Vol. XL, No. 14, August 12, 1993, pp. 51-6.

[*Gould is an American paleontologist, educator, critic, and prizewinning essayist. In the following excerpt, he discusses the novel and film versions of* Jurassic Park, *comparing their presentations of characters and science.*]

Contemporary culture presents no more powerful symbol, or palpable product, of pervasive, coordinated commercialization than the annual release of "blockbuster" films for the summer viewing season. The movies themselves are sufficiently awesome, but when you consider the accompanying publicity machines, and the flood of commercial tie-ins from lunch pails to coffee mugs to T-shirts, the effort looks more like a military blitzkrieg than an offer of entertainment. Therefore every American who is not mired in some Paleozoic pit surely knows that dinomania has reached its apogee with the release of Steven Spielberg's film version of Michael Crichton's novel *Jurassic Park*. As a paleontologist, I could not possibly feel more ambivalent about the result—marveling and cursing, laughing and moaning. One can hardly pay greater tribute to the importance of an event than to proclaim the impossibility of neutrality before it.

John Hammond (an entrepreneur with more than a touch of evil in the book [*Jurassic Park*], but kindly and merely overenthusiastic in the film) has built the ultimate theme park (for greedy profits in the book, for mixed but largely honorable motives in the film) by remaking living dinosaurs out of DNA extracted from dinosaur blood preserved within mosquitoes and other biting insects entombed in fossil Mesozoic amber. Crichton deserves high praise for developing the most clever and realistic of all scenarios for such an impossible event, for such plausibility is the essence of science fiction at its best. (The idea, as Crichton acknowledged, had been kicking around paleontological labs for quite some time.)

Until a few months ago, the record for oldest extracted DNA belonged to a twenty-million-year-old magnolia leaf from Idaho. A group of my colleagues managed to recover nearly the entire sequence—1320 of 1431 base pairs—of a chloroplast gene prominently involved in photosynthesis. (Most DNA lies in chromosomes of the nucleus, but mitochondria—energy factories—and chloroplasts—sites of photosynthesis in plants—also contain small DNA programs.)

But amber has also been yielding results during the past year. In the September 25, 1991, issue of *Science* a group of colleagues reported the successful extraction of several DNA fragments (fewer than two hundred base pairs each) from a 25-30-million-year-old termite encased in amber. Then, in a publishing event tied to the opening of *Jurassic Park,* the June 10, 1993, issue of the leading British journal *Nature*—same week as the film's premiere—reported results of another group of colleagues on the extraction of two slightly larger fragments (315 and 226 base pairs) from a fossil weevil. The amber enclosing this insect is 120-135 million years old—not quite as ancient as Jurassic, but from the next geological period, called Cretaceous, when dinosaurs were also dominant creatures of the land (most of the *Jurassic Park* dinosaurs are Cretaceous in any case). [In a footnote, Gould continues: "Pardon some trivial professional carping, but only two of the dinosaurs featured in the film version of *Jurassic Park* actually lived during the Jurassic period—the giant sauropod *Brachiosaurus,* and the small *Dilophosaurus*. All the others come from the subsequent Cretaceous period—a perfectly acceptable mixing given the film's premise that amber of any appropriate age might be scanned for dinosaur blood. Still, the majority might rule in matters of naming, though I suppose that Cretaceous Park just doesn't have the same ring. When I met Michael Crichton (long before the film's completion), I had to ask him the small-minded professional's question: 'Why did you place a Cretaceous dinosaur on the cover of *Jurassic Park*?' (for the book's dust jacket—and now the film's logo—features a Cretaceous *Tyrannosaurus rex*). I was delighted with his genuine response: 'Oh, my God, I never thought of that. We were just fooling around with different cover designs, and this one looked best.' Fair enough; he took the issue seriously, and I would ask no more."]

The nearly complete blurring of pop and professional domains represents one of the most interesting byproducts—a basically positive one in my view—of the *Jurassic Park* phenomenon. When a staid and distinguished British journal uses the premiere of an American film to set the sequencing of its own articles, then we have reached an ultimate integration. Museum shops sell the most revolting dinosaur kitsch. Movies employ the best paleontologists as advisers to heighten the realism of their creatures. Orwell's pigs have become human surrogates walking on two legs—and "already it was impossible to say which was which" (nor do I know anymore who was the pig, and who the person, at the outset—that is, if either category be appropriate).

If all this welcome scientific activity gives people the idea that dinosaurs might actually be re-created by Crichton's narrative, I hasten (with regret) to pour frigid water upon this greatest reverie of any aficionado of past life. Aristotle wisely taught us that one swallow doesn't make a summer—nor, his modern acolytes might add, does one gene (or just a fragment thereof) make an organism. Only the most prominent, easily extracted, or multiply copied bits of fossil DNA have sequenced—and we have no reason to believe that anything approaching the complete genetic program of an organism has been preserved in such ancient rocks. (The magnolia study, for example, found no nuclear DNA at all, while the recovered chloroplast gene occurs in numerous copies per cell, with a correspondingly better chance of preservation. More than 90 percent of the attempts yielded no DNA at all. The amber DNA is nuclear, but represents fragments of coding for the so-called 16S and 18S ribosomal RNA genes—among the most commonly and easily recovered segments of the genetic program.)

DNA is not a geological stable compound. We may recover fragments, or even a whole gene, here and there, but no wizardry can make an organism from just a few percent of its codes. *Jurassic Park* honorably acknowledged this limitation by having their genetic engineers use modern frog DNA to fill in the missing spaces in their dinosaur programs. But in so doing, they commit their worst scientific blunder—the only one that merits censure as a deep philosophical error, rather than a studied superficial mistake consciously permitted to bolster the drama of science fiction.

An amalgamated code of, say, 50 percent dinosaur DNA and 50 percent frog DNA would never foster the embryological development of a functioning organism. This form of reductionism is simply silly. An animal is an integrated entity, not the summation of its genes, one by one. Fifty percent of your genetic code doesn't make a perfectly good half of you; it makes no functioning organism at all. Genetic engineers might get by with a missing dab or two, but large holes cannot be plugged with DNA from a different zoological class (frogs are amphibians, dinosaurs are reptiles, and their lines diverged in the Carboniferous Period, more than 100 million years before the origin of dinosaurs). The embryological decoding of a DNA program into an organism represents nature's most complex orchestration. You need all the proper instruments and conductors of an evolutionarily unique symphony. You cannot throw in half a rock band playing its own tunes by its own rules and hope for harmony.

When a scientist soberly states that something cannot be done, the public has every right to express doubts based on numerous historical precedents for results proclaimed impossible, but later both achieved and far surpassed. But the implausibility of reconstructing dinosaurs by the amber scenario resides in a different category of stronger argument.

Most proclamations of impossibility only illustrate a scientist's lack of imagination about future discovery—impossible to see the moon's backside because you can't fly there, impossible to see an atom because light microscopy cannot resolve such dimensions. The object was always there: atoms and the moon's far side. We only lacked a technology that was possible in principle to attain, but unimagined in practice.

But when we say that a particular historical item—like a dinosaur species—can't be recovered, we are invoking a different and truly ineluctable brand of impossibility. If all information about a historical event has been lost, then it just isn't there anymore and the event cannot be reconstructed. We are not lacking a technology to see something that actually exists; rather, we have lost all information about the thing itself, and no technology can recover an item from the void. Suppose I want to know the name of every soldier who fought in the Battle of Marathon. The records, I suspect, simply don't exist—never, nowhere, and nohow. No future technology, no matter how sophisticated, can recover events with crucially missing information. So it is, I fear, with dinosaur DNA. We may make gene machines more powerful by orders of magnitude than anything we can now even conceive. But if full programs of dinosaur DNA exist nowhere—and we can find only the scrap of a gene here and there—then we have permanently lost these particular items of history.

Crichton deserves high praise for developing the most clever and realistic of all scenarios for such an impossible event as bringing dinosaurs back to life, for such plausibility is the essence of science fiction at its best.

—Stephen Jay Gould

I liked the book version of *Jurassic Park*. In addition to using the best possible scenario for making dinosaurs, Crichton based the book's plot upon an interesting invocation of currently fashionable chaos theory. To allay the fears of his creditors, John Hammond brings a set of experts to Jurassic Park, hoping to win their endorsement. His blue ribbon panel includes two paleontologists and a preachy iconoclast of a mathematician named Ian Malcolm—the novel's intellectual and philosophical center. Malcolm urges—often, colorfully, and at length—a single devastating critique based on his knowledge of chaos and fractals: the park's safety system must collapse because it is too precariously complex in its coordination of so many, and so intricate, fail-safe devices. Moreover, the park must fail both unpredictably and spectacularly—and does it ever! Malcolm explains,

It's chaos theory. But I notice nobody is willing to listen to the consequences of the mathematics. Because they imply very large consequences for human life. Much larger than Heisenberg's principle or Godel's theorem, which everybody rattles on about. . . . But chaos theory concerns everyday life. . . . I gave all this information to Hammond long before he broke ground on this place. You're going to engineer a bunch of prehistoric animals and set them on an island? Fine. A lovely dream. Charming. But it won't go as planned. It is inherently unpredictable.

We have soothed ourselves into imagining sudden change as something that happens outside the normal order of things. An accident, like a car crash. Or beyond our control, like a fatal illness. We do not conceive a sudden, radical, irrational change as built into the very fabric of existence. Yet it is. And chaos theory teaches us. . . .

Moreover, Malcolm uses this argument—not the usual and romantic pap about "man treading where God never intended" (to invoke the old language as well as the old cliché)—to urge our self-restraint before such scientific power:

> And now chaos theory proves that unpredictability is built into our daily lives. It is as mundane as the rainstorm we cannot predict. And so the grand vision of science, hundreds of years old—the dream of total control—had died, in our century.

This reliance on chaos as a central theme did, however, throw the book's entire story line into a theoretically fatal inconsistency—one that, to my surprise, no reviewer seemed to catch at the time. The book's second half is, basically, a grand old, rip-roaring chase novel, with survivors managing (and with nary a scratch to boot) to prevail through a long sequence of independent and excruciatingly dangerous encounters with dinosaurs. By the same argument that complex sequences cannot proceed as planned—that is, in this case, toward the novelistic necessity of at least some characters surviving—not a human soul in the park should have stood a chance of proceeding harmless through such a sequence. Malcolm even says so: "Do you have any idea how unlikely it is that you, or any of us, will get off this island alive?" But I'm willing to accept the literary convention for bending nature's laws in this case.

I expected to like the film even more. The boy dinosaur nut still dwells within me, and I have seen them all, from *King Kong* to *One Million Years B.C.,* to *Godzilla.* The combination of a better story line, with such vast improvement in monster-making technology, and all done by the most masterly hands in the world, seemed to guarantee success at a spectacular new level of achievement. I did not feel that I wasted my two hours or my seven bucks (plus another two for the indigestible "raptor bites" candy tie-in), but I was deeply disappointed by much about the movie.

The dinosaurs themselves certainly delivered. As a practicing paleontologist, I confess to wry amusement at the roman-à-cleffery embedded in the reconstructions. I could recognize nearly every provocative or *outré* idea of my colleagues, every social tie-in now exploited by dinosaurs in their commanding role as cultural icons. The herbivores are so sweet and idyllic. The giant brachiosaurs low to each other like cattle in the peaceable kingdom. They rear up on their hind legs to find the juiciest leaves. The smaller species care for and help each other—down to such subtle details as experienced elders keeping young *Gallimimus* in the safer center of the fleeing herd.

Even the carnivores are postmodernists of another type.

The big old fearsome standard, *Tyrannosaurus rex,* presides over Jurassic Park in all her glory (and in her currently fashionable posture, with head down, tail up, and vertebral column nearly parallel to the ground). But the mantle of carnivorous heroism has clearly passed to the much smaller *Velociraptor,* Henry Fairfield Osborn's Mongolian jewel. Downsizing and diversity are in; constrained hugeness has become a tragic flaw. *Velociraptor* is everything that modern corporate life values in a tough competitor—mean, lean, lithe, and intelligent. They hunt in packs, using a fine military technique of feinting by one beast in front, followed by attack from the side by a co-conspirator. In the film's best moment of wry parody of its own inventions, the wonderfully stereotyped stiff-upper-lip-British-hunter Muldoon gets the center beast in his gun's sight, only to realize too late that the side-hunting companion is a few inches from his head. He looks at the side beast, says "Clever girl" in a tone of true admiration (all of Jurassic Park's dinosaurs are engineered to be female in another ultimately failed attempt to control their reproduction), and then gets gobbled to death.

Even so, Spielberg didn't choose to challenge pop culture's canonical dinosaurs in all details of accuracy and professional speculation; blockbusters must, to some extent, play upon familiarity. Ironically, he found the true size of *Velociraptor*—some six feet in length—too small for the scary effects desired, and enlarged them to nearly ten feet, thus moving partway back toward the old stereotype, otherwise so effectively challenged. He experimented, in early plans and models, with bright colors favored by some of my colleagues on the argument that bird-like behavior (and closeness to bird ancestry) might imply avian styles of coloration for the smaller dinosaurs (the original *Velociraptor* models were tiger striped). But he eventually opted for conventional reptilian dullness ("Your same old, ordinary, dinosaur shit-green," lamented one of my graduate students).

But let me not carp. The dinosaur scenes are spectacular. Intellectuals too often either pay no attention to such technical wizardry or, even worse, actually disdain special effects with such dismissive epithets as "merely mechanical." I find such small-minded parochialism outrageous. Nothing can be more complex than a living organism, with all the fractal geometry of its form and behavior (compared with the almost childishly simple lines of our buildings, and of almost anything else in the realm of human construction). The use of technology to render accurate and believable animals therefore becomes one of the greatest all-time challenges to human ingenuity.

The field has a long and honorable history of continually improving techniques—and who would dare deny this story a place in the annals of human intellectual achievement. An old debate among historians of science asks whether most key technological inventions arise from practical need (more often in war than in any other activity), or from opportunities to fool around during periods of maximal freedom from practical pressures. My friend Cyril Smith, the wisest scientist-humanist I ever knew, strongly advocated the centrality of "play domains" as the major field for innovations with immense practical utility down the road. (He argued that block-and-tackle was invented, or at least substantially improved, in order to lift animals from underground storage pits to the game floor of the Roman Colosseum.) Yes, *Jurassic Park* is "just" a movie—but for this very reason, it had freedom (and money) to develop techniques of reconstruction, particularly computer generation or CG, to new heights of astonishing realism. And yes, it matters—for immediately aesthetic reasons, and for all manner of practical possibilities in the future.

Spielberg originally felt that computer generation had not yet progressed far enough, and that he would have to do all his dinosaur scenes with the fascinating array of modeling techniques long used, but constantly improving, in Hollywood—stop-motion with small models, people dressed in dinosaur suits, puppetry of various sorts, robotics with hydraulic apparatus moved by people sitting at consoles. (All this is described clearly, if uncritically, in *The Making of Jurassic Park*, the formula-book by Don Shay and Jody Duncan—just one of the innumerable commercial tie-ins generated by all blockbusters, but a worthy effort in this case.)

But computer generation improved spectacularly during the two-year gestation of *Jurassic Park* and dinosaurs are entirely machine-constructed in some of the most spectacular scenes—meaning, of course, that performers interacted with empty space during the actual shooting. (Cartoons have been computer-generated for many years, but remember the entirely different problem that Spielberg faced. Roger Rabbit was supposed to be a "toon"; the computer-generated dinosaurs of *Jurassic Park* must be indistinguishable from real beasts.) I learned, after watching the film, that my two favorite dinosaur scenes—the fleeing herd of *Gallimimus*, and the final attack of *Tyrannosaurus* upon the last two *Velociraptors*—were entirely computer-generated.

The effect does not always work. The very first dinosaur scene—when paleontologist Grant hops out of his vehicle to encounter a computer-generated *Brachiosaurus*—is the film's worst flop. Grant is clearly not in the same space as the dinosaur, and I could only think of Victor Mature, similarly out of synch with his beasts, in *One Million Years B.C.*

The dinosaurs are wonderful, but they aren't on the set enough of the time (yes, I know how much more they cost than human actors). Unfortunately, the plot line for the human actors reduces to pap and romantic drivel of the worst kind, the very antithesis of the book's grappling with serious themes. It is so ironic, but I fear that mammon and the perception (false I hope) of the need to dumb-down for mass audiences have brought us to this impasse of utter inconsistency. How cruel, how perverse, that we invest the most awesome expertise (and millions of bucks) in the dinosaurs, sparing no knowledge or expense to render every detail, every possible nuance, in the most accurate and realistic way. I have nothing but praise for the thought and care, the months and years that went into each dinosaur model, the pushing of computer generation to a new world of utility, the concern for rendering every detail with consummate care, even the tiny bits that few

will see and the little sounds that fewer will hear. I think of medieval sculptors who lavished all their skills upon invisible statues on the parapets, for God's view is best (internal satisfaction based on personal excellence in modern translation). How perverse that we permit a movie to do all this so superbly well, and then throw away the story because we think that the public will reject, or fail to comprehend, any complexity beyond a Neanderthal "duh" or a brontosaurian bellow. I just don't believe it.

We feel this loss most in the reconstruction of the mathematician Ian Malcolm as the antithesis of his character in the book. He still presents himself as a devotee of chaos theory ("a chaotician"), but he no longer uses its argument (as previously documented in this article) to formulate his criticism of the park. Instead, he is given the oldest diatribe, the most hackneyed and predictable staple of every Hollywood monster film since *Frankenstein:* man (again I prefer the old gender-biased term for such an archaic line) must not disturb the proper and given course of nature; man must not tinker in God's realm. What dullness and disappointment (and Malcolm, in the film, is a frightful and tendentious bore, obviously so recognized by Spielberg, for he effectively puts Malcolm out of action with a broken log about halfway through).

Not only have we heard this silly argument a hundred times before (can Spielberg really believe that his public could comprehend no other reason for criticizing a dinosaur park?), but its formulation by Malcolm utterly negates his proclaimed persona as a theoretician of chaos. In the film's irony of ironies, Malcolm's argument becomes the precise antithesis of chaos and also relies on whopping inconsistency to boot. Consider these two flubs that make the story line completely incoherent:

1. As Malcolm rails against genetic reconstruction of lost organisms, Hammond asks him if he would really hesitate to bring the California condor back to life (from preserved DNA) should the last actual bird die. Malcolm answers that he would not object, and would view such an act as benevolent, because the condor's death would have been an accident based on human malfeasance, not an expression of nature's proper course. But we must not bring back dinosaurs because they disappeared along a natural and intended route: "Dinosaurs," he says, "had their shot, and nature selected them for extinction." But such an implied scenario of groups emerging, flourishing, and dying, one after the other in an intended and predictable course, is the antithesis of chaos theory and its crucial emphasis on the great accumulating effect of apparently insignificant perturbations, and on the basic unpredictability of long historical sequences. How can a chaotician talk about nature's proper course at all?

2. If "nature selected them for extinction," and if later mammals therefore represent such an improvement, why can the dinosaurs of Jurassic Park beat any mammal in the place, including the most arrogant primate of them all. You can't have it both ways. If you take dinosaur revisionism seriously, and portray them as smart and capable creatures able to hold their own with mammals, then you can't argue against reviving them by claiming that their extinc-

tion was both predictable and appointed as life ratcheted onward to greater complexity.

Since Malcolm actually preaches the opposite of chaos theory, but presents himself as a chaotician and must therefore talk about it, the film's material on chaos is reduced to an irrelevant caricature in the most embarrassing of all scenes—Malcolm's half-hearted courting of the female paleontologist (before he learns of her partnership with the male paleontologist), by grasping her hand, dripping water on the top and using chaos theory to explain why we can't tell which side the drop will run down! How are the mighty fallen.

Christopher Lehmann-Haupt   (review date 6 January 1994)

SOURCE: "Sex, Power and a Workplace Reversal," in *The New York Times,* January 6, 1994, p. C12.

[*Lehmann-Haupt is a Scottish-born American critic and chief book reviewer for the* New York Times. *In the following mixed review of* Disclosure, *he maintains that the plot—despite its contemporary, "high-tech" appearance which masks various implausibilities—is a traditional and exciting "battle of the sexes" story.*]

If you think Japan got a bashing in Michael Crichton's *Rising Sun,* just wait till you see what happens to the cause of equal opportunity in his clever new novel, *Disclosure,* about a sexual-harassment suit.

The story opens with its protagonist, Tom Sanders, looking forward to the acquisition of the Seattle-based company he works for, Digital Communications, by a New York publishing conglomerate. This merger stands to bring Tom a promotion as well as lucrative stock options when the division he works for goes public.

But when Tom arrives late at the office, because he has helped feed the children, he learns that Meredith Johnson, a flame from 10 years earlier, has been given the promotion instead, by a boss who apparently wants to enhance the role of women in the company.

Swallowing his rancor, Tom accepts his new boss's invitation to a day's-end briefing in her locked office with a bottle of wine. When Meredith tries to reignite their sexual past, Tom eventually protests. Furious at the rejection, Meredith vows to make him pay.

The next day, Tom learns from the company lawyer that while Meredith's complaint of sexual harassment will not be made public, Tom will have to accept transfer to a division of the company he secretly knows is about to be sold off. Rather than capitulate, he decides to hire a lawyer and sue.

Now, Meredith Johnson, as Mr. Crichton paints her, happens to be the embodiment of all those antiquated, chauvinistic stereotypes of the power-hungry woman: she is two-faced, underhanded, manipulative, mendacious, underqualified for her position and delighted to wield sex as a weapon. You quickly grow to loathe her. Yet for a reader to admit this is to risk making common cause with the

Neanderthal characters in the story who cry out, "We told you so!," or ridicule Tom for effetely failing to service the boss and keep the peace.

Meanwhile, Mr. Crichton seems to remain above such flinging around of raw meat. He is too busy lecturing on the true meaning of his subject. "Sexual harassment is about power," says the lawyer whom Tom hires, Louise Fernandez, "and so is the company's resistance to dealing with it. Power protects power. And once a woman gets up in the power structure, she'll be protected by the structure, the same as a man."

The author wants us to know that while only 5 percent of sexual harassment suits are brought by men against women, only 5 percent of corporate supervisors are women. As Ms. Fernandez concludes: "So the figures suggest that women executives harass men in the same proportion as men harass women. And as more women get corporate jobs, the percentage of claims by men is going up. Because the fact is, harassment is a power issue. And power is neither male nor female."

Finally, Mr. Crichton offers an afterword in which he solemnly intones: "The advantage of a role-reversal story is that it may enable us to examine aspects concealed by traditional responses and conventional rhetoric. However readers respond to this story, it is important to recognize that the behavior of the two antagonists mirrors each other, like a Rorschach inkblot. The value of a Rorschach test lies in what it tells us about ourselves."

> **Mr. Crichton's only real concern is to keep his pot boiling. In fact *Disclosure* reads as if a fourth of it were dedicated to answering some editor querying its potential implausibilities.**
>
> **—*Christopher Lehmann-Haupt***

Can you flunk a Rorschach test? Why, you almost feel ashamed for getting so worked up over *Disclosure,* and for cheering on Tom Sanders, the poor innocent, and hissing at Meredith Johnson, the vile scheming wretch!

Still, you do get involved, to the point where you worry more about the story than the issues. So along with rooting for Tom Sanders, you wonder about certain technical flaws in the book's elaborate narrative.

Why, for example, can the story switch away from Tom's point of view when it serves to heighten the tension, but not when it might satisfy the reader's curiosity? Why does so much depend on Tom's errant memory when a major attack in the book is leveled against therapists who rely too credulously on children's errant memories?

Why are there more scenes of unlikely eavesdropping than in an early Shakespeare comedy? And why is Tom's marriage so cold that his wife goes away with his children when his troubles begin and never once even telephones until the story is resolved?

Actually, I know the answer to these questions. Mr. Crichton's only real concern is to keep his pot boiling. In fact, *Disclosure* reads as if a fourth of it were dedicated to answering some editor querying its potential implausibilities.

Still, the results keep your blood boiling, too. *Disclosure* is an elaborate provocation of rage in which a thousand fragments of revenge finally fall into place, like acid rain on wildfire. Meanwhile, Mr. Crichton also irrelevantly entertains us with a complex vision of the digital future, complete with cellular phones the size of credit cards, CD-ROM players that can store 600 books and database environments you can virtually walk around in with the guidance of a helpful angel who cracks wise.

That this vision is so much fun and so easy to follow seems pleasantly flattering. It partly makes up for the discomfort of enjoying in *Disclosure* what is deep down an old-fashioned battle of the sexes.

John Schulian   (review date 16 January 1994)

SOURCE: "From Dinophobia to Gynephobia: He Said . . . ," in *Los Angeles Times Book Review,* January 16, 1994, pp. 1, 9.

[*Schulian is an American journalist and critic. In the following negative review of* Disclosure, *he examines what he argues are stereotyped characters in "a polemic masquerading as a novel."*]

The decline of American manhood can be traced from a daffy heavyweight champion named Leon Spinks, who snuggled up with a lady of the night and awoke the next morning to discover that she had stolen his false teeth. Since then, of course, things far dearer to men than dentures have become targets in the war between the sexes. (Take a bow, John Wayne Bobbitt.) But not until the publication of Michael Crichton's *Disclosure* has it been so obvious that the women's movement possesses the power to turn an admirable male mind to guacamole.

Because Crichton has apparently convinced himself that testosterone is out of fashion, his latest bid for the best-seller list is filled to overflowing with men who are whining, conniving, backpedaling paranoids. Even his hero is a coward and a hypocrite, a self-deluded lunkhead who thinks he is standing on principle when he is really just protecting an investment. So forget the propaganda about *Disclosure* being the big-issue novel that proves sexual harassment cuts both ways. In truth, it is nothing more than Crichton's unwitting confession that the modern woman plays too rough for him.

You get the message as soon as you meet Tom Sanders, the empty vessel in whom Crichton places his fear and anxiety. Tom's wife has the day off from her law practice, but she still wants him to feed their two children breakfast even though he's running late. She pouts, she flashes a little skin, she gets her way. Their 4-year-old daughter is just as willfully bitchy, goosing poor dad when he should be

headed for the Seattle-based computer company where he's counting on being named a vice-president.

And there is no relief for Tom when he finally escapes the harpies at home for the relative calm of takeovers and corporate treachery. From his company's plant in Texas comes a report that the women on the clean-up crew are demanding that the pin-ups in the men's locker room to be taken down. But that is nothing compared to the news from the plant in Malaysia, where the line foreman has gone into hiding because his cousin's sister put a curse on him.

Once Crichton has established women as the root of all evil—no subtlety for him—he drops the big one: The ever-suffering Tom gets passed over for the vice presidency in favor of Meredith Johnson, a scheming blond vixen who was his girlfriend a decade ago. Meredith inspires the only good line in a book written with all the style and grace of a how-to manual. "I mean face it," the company's head of programming says, "she's got an outstanding molded case, with superior fit and finish."

Bless her hard heart, Meredith also has a libido in overdrive, albeit one she is using to advance her own devious cause. But Tom doesn't realize that until after she tries to rape him in a scene that would be howlingly funny if it didn't trivialize the ugliest crime there is short of murder. Meredith remembers Tom's preference for cold Chardonnay, she admires his "nice hard tush," she hints at hanky-panky on business trips, and she works them both into a sexual lather—all before finishing her first day on the job. But Tom backs off because she coughs, and in his book, a cough in the heat of passion suggests a lack of sincerity. Fussy, fussy.

After Tom has gone from hot and bothered to cold and bewildered, he cries sexual harassment. He still finds himself in the company of strange females, though. The kindest adjective applied to his attorney is *brisk,* the mediator for his harassment case is an old bat in the making, one of his supporters at work is an intense geek and the other is a withdrawn geek. Damn, what kind of women has Michael Crichton been hanging around?

Whoever they are, they convinced him to check his brains at the door while writing *Disclosure,* the brains that got him through Harvard Medical School and made him a big-name author with The *Andromeda Strain* and *Jurassic Park.* There isn't a guy worth his hormones who doesn't know the type that must have driven Crichton around the bend. You say gingerbread man and they say it's gingerbread *cookie,* as if their nit-picking could possibly do anything but move you closer to that nincompoop Rush Limbaugh. Then you meet a woman who appreciates the joke when the eminent country philosopher Kinky Friedman sings "Get Your Biscuits in the Oven (And Your Buns in the Bed)," and your world is back in balance.

Not that anyone should expect balance in a polemic masquerading as a novel, but you do expect Crichton to be smart. He isn't. Case in point: his bemoaning that long gone era when all you had to be to get promoted was good. He never pauses to note that men almost always got the promotions back then because other men were in charge. Even a guy who would think all kinds of politically incorrect thoughts if a woman got a job he wanted can figure that out. What he can't figure out is why so many women, after seeing how the business world can turn men into such prize asses, still want to be just like them.

Patt Morrison   (review date 16 January 1994)

SOURCE: "From Dinophobia to Gynephobia: She Said . . . ," in *Los Angeles Times Book Review,* January 16, 1994, pp. 1, 9.

[*In the following review of* Disclosure, *Morrison applauds Crichton's role-reversing plot about sexual harassment but faults the cartoon-like characterizations and the use of "preposterous devices" to maintain the plot.*]

At last, at last it's been published, a dead-bang bestseller that puts the explosive social issue of sexual harassment between bestselling hardcovers, not in some incoherent government report destined for the recycling bin.

Here is the predatory, omnipotent, salacious boss, and here is the prey, the dependent employee afraid to say no or even yes to the boss's advances, for fear of losing job and family and reputation.

Oh, wait, sorry. I skipped something. There's this asterisk. The gimmick. The switcheroo.

The predatory, omnipotent, salacious boss is Meredith Johnson, a woman with all the usual longs—legs, hair, eyelashes—and a few shorts, like temper and judgment.

And the employee is Tom Sanders, husband, father, corporate good guy at a computer firm, who, for several months many years ago, shared a bed and broke bread with Meredith, or in their case broke a bed and shared bread.

This is **Disclosure,** Michael Crichton's *gotcha* novel, his sucker punch, his dodgem computer game of modern sex roles.

Even with its novel role-reversing, **Disclosure** lays out some classic elements of abuse of power. Realign the gender roles—male boss, female employee—and it's a textbook sexual harassment case. Problem is, no one reads textbooks—they read novels, novels with engaging devices like this one. And no one pays $3.5 million to make a textbook into a movie.

Crichton says his case is based in truth. I have no doubt of it. Yet, as I would tell my journalism students when they were gloating over finding out, say, what make of car a public official drove . . . just because it's true doesn't make it significant.

Sexual harassment is wrong and illegal, women *or* men. Making the female predator *the* sexual harassment story—as this one is bound to for a time, because Crichton is a powerhouse storyteller whose books make movies that make money—is to elevate the simply true to the significant, the way the old man-bites-dog story of the journal-

ism trade can obscure the 99% of the time that dogs bite men.

At worst, this book makes Crichton a kind of an emotional profiteer, cutting in a line that women have been waiting in for a very long time. (Think of native Americans' anger at New Agers co-opting their religious rituals, and charging fancy prices for them.)

It put me in mind of "Good Morning, Merry Sunshine," columnist Bob Greene's 1984 diary of new fatherhood, extolling its sentimental wonders. He waxed lyrical over his child's tiny garments even as he disdained the chores of diapers and spit-up that he marvels that women have performed for eons—and without the rewards of a bestseller congratulating themselves on it, his critics noted acidly.

Crichton bulletproofs himself against that. He opens **Disclosure** quoting the Civil Rights Act and publisher Katharine Graham—"Power is neither male nor female"—and ends with a disclaimer that **Disclosure** is "not intended to deny the fact that the great majority of harassment claims are brought by women against men . . . the advantage of a role-reversal story is that it may enable us to examine aspects concealed by traditional responses and conventional rhetoric."

In other words, he has his beefcake/cheesecake and eats it too.

That doesn't immunize him from preposterous devices. My favorite was when Meredith comes to work in high heels and suit but no stockings, because, she explains to Tom, it's "so much cooler on a hot day." In *Seattle?* I've read nothing so silly since a scene in a screenplay described a woman frying bacon naked.

Disclosure is populated with a large cast of cartoons: Tom's wife, the lawyer with a housekeeper who complains until Tom says she is "about as oppressed as Leona Helmsley," and she, cartoonishly, responds, "This is because a woman got your job, isn't it?" Everyone will enjoy loathing the hellbent-for-Pulitzer femi-columnist and the smarmy PC male lawyer whose finger is "chapped from wetting it and holding it to the wind."

Crichton is no slouch himself when it comes to reading the breezes. In **Rising Sun,** he jacked up a murder novel into a debate on the flaws of American business and the venal triumphs of the Japanese. **Disclosure** takes a high-tech computer company merger-massacre and ornaments it like a Christmas tree with hot-button sexual politics.

The cheat is that yes, Meredith is a nympho-braniac and a serial harasser, but her semi-rape of Tom is also a calculated squeeze play to cut him from the DigiCom herd and out of a multimillion-dollar windfall. No one has such grand designs in mind when he feels up a $7-an-hour typist.

The "men are people too" stuff is laid on a tad thick. Tom orders the foreman at one plant to get the girlie pinups out of the men's locker room, even if the women have photo hunks in *their* locker room. And, after his awful encounter, he echoes the female rape victim's concern "that it was all his fault, that he had misled [her] in some important way."

God knows we need to talk about these matters, from acquaintance rape and the plaint that "pale males eat it again" to corporate genetics; when Tom whines about Meredith's unfair advantage in having plastic surgery to look like the boss's dead daughter (another absurd moment), he is reminded that he, too, performed to please the boss, from playing golf to guzzling beer.

Disclosure is a thin forum for such heavy debate, but apart from Oprahvision, in this country, movie-fiction is, dismally, all we've got.

All the more reason for Crichton to play it straight. The test is, will *Disclosure* be celebrated for its admonitions and its questions, or for its sensational Rush Limbaugh fodder? Do I really think I need to answer that question?

Julie Burchill   (review date 22 January 1994)

SOURCE: "Sometime After Dinosaurs, God Created Woman," in *The Spectator,* Vol. 272, No. 8637, January 22, 1994, pp. 25, 27.

[*Burchill is an English novelist, screenwriter, and nonfiction writer. In the following unfavorable review of* Disclosure, *she contends that Crichton's writing is poor, that the story maligns women, and that it fails to deal with the issue of sexual harassment seriously.*]

Novelization—of a film, or of a popular television serial—has always been a moderately quick way to earn a moderately good sum of money. (Often, people educated far beyond their intelligence are drawn to this way of life; I once owned an *EastEnders* novelisation prefaced by three quotes from Nietzsche.) But Michael Crichton—author of *Jurassic Park* and *Rising Sun,* as well as a bunch of earlier books no one's ever heard of (*Eaters of the Dead,* anyone?)—has happened upon a brilliantly clever way of making huge amounts of money out of a novel twist on novelisation. That is, he doesn't bring the novel out after the film, but before; they are basically screenplays, very flash and cinematic, but with all the 'he saids' and 'she saids' (though more often 'he saids').

The books sell moderately well on publication—and then, of course, Hollywood buys the rights for a handsome sum. The film comes out, like *Jurassic Park,* millions see it, a still from the film is pasted over the old cover of the novel and hey presto!—sales of Michael Crichton books have reached 30 million in the US alone. Since 1992. What Crichton is doing, in essence, is getting film studios to pay millions of dollars for the privilege of advertising his novels on the big screen. The difference is that unlike other cinema commercials, for Nintendo or Opal Fruits, these adverts last up to two and a half hours.

Disclosure (bad title—sounds like substandard Dick Francis) is the latest lob in the tide of woman-hating which is currently engulfing the United States. *Fatal Attraction,* Camille Paglia, *Oleanna,* Iron John; they are the theory, the serial rapist and murderer is the practice. And like most of the theory, it comes with a mealy-mouthed

denial of its loathing for more than half the human race. In a press release so graceless that Crichton himself might have managed it on a good day, we are told that *Disclosure* supports feminism and equality, acknowledging the right of women to take power, but at the same time revealing their capacity to abuse it. Phew! That's all right, then; we feminists can now sleep safely in our beds (having checked first that we have our ice picks to hand under them), knowing that Dr Crichton is on our side.

The book also comes with a page of statistics about sexual harassment which tells us that 'it is proven that the number of allegations by man of harassment is roughly proportionate to the number of corporate women'. Oh yeah? And all harassing the same man, too—he must be one hot item. If publishers are going to pay through the nose for these books, can't they send out a press release that wasn't written for peanuts by a monkey?

But on with the show—sorry, book. Within three pages, three major irritants kick in. It starts with the communiqué—in the old days this would have been a letter and now it's a fax, but the purpose and effect are the same—to set up the story without having to slog away at those boring old speech marks. This communiqué tells us that the hero, Thomas Sanders, believes he is about to be promoted at his high-tech workplace, Digicom. Ho ho ho.

Secondly, it's set in Seattle. Seattle is the new fave American location in which to set books and films—and it's done for such a pitifully transparent reason, which is to show that these are books/films about Real Folks—not LA airheads or New York neurotics. And thirdly, Crichton has the sheer gall to make the first scene—sorry, chapter—the Mirror Bit, where we get the hero described to us through the extremely naturalistic device of having him eyeball himself while shaving (when male writers do the Mirror Bit on female characters, they hold the shaving and have them nude, after a bath, shyly dropping the towel). Looking into the mirror with Thomas, we discover that he's dead dishy, getting on and all man. He's even got a bruise, from playing football. (Touch football, the faggot.)

Enter his wife, Susan. In woman-hating narratives, wives always have sweet girlish names like Susan or Beth; single women sterile, asexual names like Alex, or here Meredith. Susan has the kind of fresh beauty that requires no makeup but I bet old Meredith slaps it on with a trowel.

But however fresh, Susan is far from being the perfect wife. A woman with a good job, she expects Thomas to help her with the kids. She has to flash her naked body at him to persuade him to pour them a few bowls of cereal, and even then the lazy so-and-so won't do it until she yells at them. Then he does it, o.k. It's a creepy first chapter; what women want, women bloody well make sure they get. (Not like men, eh?)

Remember that fax? Well, a fax comes before a fall and the Digicom lawyer soon informs Thomas that he hasn't been promoted after all. I've noticed in recent years that writers who don't like women also loathe lawyers; perhaps they see lawyers as token women, because they work with their brains and believe in keeping the law and stuff. Anyway, this one's a really bad guy—and, on the side, it's rubbed in how 'decent' Thomas is—because he wants to insist on the sexes being integrated at work at Digicom's Malaysian plant.

> Sanders kept telling him, 'It's a Muslim country, Phil.'
>
> 'I don't give a damn,' Phil said. 'Digicom stands for equality.'
>
> 'Phil, it's their country. They're Muslim.'
>
> 'So what? It's our factory.'

I liked Phil the more after this exchange and Tom the less, even though it was meant not to be so. But I feel I have noticed, over the past two decades, that men who are anti-women are often antiracist, too. Why is this? Because they admire the way the Third World keeps its women down? Because they wish things were like that here? So who got the promotion? Yes, Tom's old girlfriend! Does she try to screw him? You bet, in both senses. Does Michael Crichton like women? Not a lot—even Tom's beautiful, loving wife, when she's good enough to make a pass at him, provokes a burst of sudden anger. What was the matter with her? She never had any sense about these things. She was always coming on to him at inappropriate times and places.

Disclosure is a bad book; bad as in not well written, but bad as in malign, too. Crichton's last two books were about evil dinosaurs and evil Japanese; in evil women he seems to have found a hothouse hybrid of the two—brutal, sly, with enormous appetites and smelling of sushi.

—*Julie Burchill*

As a conversation piece, this book isn't even juicy and vile; so much of it is about Tom's job at Digicom that I often felt as though I had picked up my computer manual by mistake. When not being high-tech, Crichton is being too low-brow for words; he actually makes Jeffrey Archer read like Oscar Wilde trying particularly hard to impress Daniel Day-Lewis over a late, light supper at English's.

This is a bad book; bad as in not well written, but bad as in malign, too. Crichton's last two books were about evil dinosaurs and evil Japanese; in evil women he seems to have found a hothouse hybrid of the two—brutal, sly, with enormous appetites and smelling of sushi.

But what is really offensive about this book is that while pretending to deal with the issue of sexual harassment, Crichton completely ignores the source of it—male aggression. Yes, men are bringing more harassment suits than they used to—but 96 per cent of them are against other men. Now that would have been a great story; a rabidly heterosexual but incandescently ambitious young man, hit on by a powerful homosexual. Real sexy—and realistic, too.

But who cares? When all's said and done, Michael Crichton merely wanted to give us the same old Hell Hath No Fury shtick one more time. But actually, Hell does have a fury greater than a woman scorned; and that's the fury of a dominant group who've just discovered that you can't kiss the girls and make them cry, anymore.

Unless it's all the way to the Equal Opportunities Commission, that is.

Geraldine Brennan (review date 30 January 1994)

SOURCE: "Tears Before Bed," in *The Observer*, January 30, 1994, p. 19.

[*In the following unfavorable review of* Disclosure, *Brennan contends that the novel's plot is contrived and its sexual harassment theme contains misogynistic sentiments.*]

Sexual harassment suits are about more than reputations: the scent of big money is in the air, making corporate America twitchy. Crichton has put his finger on the latest anxiety; if women and men are equal in the workplace, does a male subordinate's claim of sexual harassment by a woman employer carry the same weight as a woman employee's claim against a man?

One difference is that the harassed man's predicament qualifies as thriller material: Tom Sanders, a middle-manager in a computer company, has his trousers removed over a bottle of Chardonnay in the boss's suite. If she had groped him every day for three years behind the photocopier, it would have been a dull read. Sexual harassment often boils down to an accumulation of many unglamorous, humiliating incidents, trivial to everyone except the person being harassed.

No time for accumulation in *Disclosure*: within 24 hours of being promoted, Sanders's ex-lover Meredith Johnson tries to seduce him, then claims that he sexually harassed her; he insists that the harassment was on her part and is greeted with the ridicule and disbelief familiar to women in his situation.

Crichton condenses the conflict into a five-day week by taking Sanders and Johnson through an instant mediation hearing—real cases can take three years to come to court. His introduction of two other agendas—some executive-level dirty tricks and Sanders and Johnson's former relationship—detracts from the central issue. Employers don't need a clever narrative structure to sexually harass their staff: they do it because they can.

Sanders's values have a solid, nitty-gritty male flavour—he understands production lines, but he's not ashamed to mop up his children's cereal. Johnson is straight out of Backlash Central casting: all mouth and MBA in the boardroom and also sexy, single and therefore, it is implied, a screwball and a threat to family values—a rabbit stew short of *Fatal Attraction*. In the seduction scene, the Chardonnay is laced with Crichton's contempt for her.

The novel deftly plays with true and false appearances,

giving Sanders's employers' new toy—a virtual reality database—a key role. Techno-jargon in general is prominent. Closet misogynists who are having trouble with their compact disc drives will love this. But telling it like it is? Get real.

Douglas Kennedy   (review date 4 February 1994)

SOURCE: "A Soft Touch," in *New Statesman & Society,* Vol. 7, No. 288, February 4, 1994, p. 49.

[*In the following unfavorable review, Kennedy contends that* Disclosure *is formulaic and timid in its handling of the sexual harassment issue.*]

On a recent flight to Hong Kong, I took a stroll down the aisles of the jumbo jet, looking at what my fellow passengers were reading. Yes, I did see one earnest-looking speedreader who risked excess baggage charges with *A Suitable Boy*. But most people were engrossed in easy-to-digest commercial fiction.

And of the 300 or so passengers, around a quarter appeared to be in possession of a novel by Michael Crichton. The 52-year-old Harvard-trained doctor has—in between directing Hollywood movies and hanging out with Laotian monks—also become the most bankable commercial novelist of the moment, thanks to *Jurassic Park* and *Rising Sun*. Unlike schlock merchants of the Jeffrey Archer ilk, he is also promoted as that oddity: a *serious* popular writer.

In fact, his alleged *gravitas* is one of the principle reasons why he is so absurdly successful. He has a canny eye for the big contemporary issue and—like any good clinician—he is a research junkie who adores *technospeak*. Cleverly woven into one of his no-nonsense narratives, this lends his fiction a voice of authoritative knowledge.

Given his preoccupations with the matter of the hour and "cutting edge" technology, it's not at all surprising that *Disclosure* is a story of sexual harassment set in a Seattle software company. Yet the greatest strength of this contrived novel is not its supposedly "electrifying" examination of one of "the most burning issues of today" or its impressive hi-tech scholarship, but its acidic glimpse into the nasty gamesmanship of US corporate life.

Thomas Sanders is a 41-year-old corporate man—yet he's not a team player, let alone adept at internecine company warfare. Still, he is hugely respected by his immediate colleagues for his excellent work as a division manager at DigiCom, where he's involved in the development of CD-Roms and electronic data bases. But when he's passed over for an all-but guaranteed promotion and the job goes to a 35-year-old corporate *femme fatale* named Meredith Johnson, Sanders is worried. Because his new boss is a former lover, with whom he once lived a decade ago.

Johnson has a ferocious sexual appetite: on her first day in the job, she invites Johnson up to her office for a little after-work wine and chat. And before you can say "Wanna look at my microchips?", she's fellating him on her office floor. But being that rare species—a married guy with a conscience—Sanders breaks loose from her oral embrace and hightails it to the lift, with Meredith screaming after him, "I'll fucking kill you for this!"

Which, of course, she metaphorically tries to do. Sanders arrives at work the next morning to learn that Meredith has accused him of sexual harassment. The company wants to hush everything up and offers him a nowhere transfer to Austin, Texas, but Sanders realises that would be professional death. So, retaining the services of a Cuban-American woman lawyer, *he* threatens to sue for sexual harassment—on the grounds that she as his superior demanded sexual favours and menaced him when they weren't forthcoming.

Can a man be sexually harassed? Has the entire issue of harassment become a weapon in corporate warfare? And why has the US become so obsessed with victim-culture, the belief that there is always someone else to blame for the woes of your life? Crichton toys with these big questions, but never really grapples with them. Sexual harrassment becomes a minor consideration in a narrative more preoccupied by the wonders of virtual reality and the vicious corporate battlefield.

Add to this Crichton's workmanlike prose and his obvious characters (the honest executive, the yuppie bitch from hell whose knickers are always wet, the wily old patriarch, the scheming company counsel, the tough-as-nails woman attorney) and you can begin to see why there is a strong whiff of the formulaic emanating from *Disclosure*.

More tellingly, the novel eventually becomes a corporate conspiracy yarn. It lacks the energy of a good thriller, let alone the passionate anger of Crichton's anti-Japanese homily, *Rising Sun*. You end up begging for some of the provocative misanthropy that so distinguished David Mamet's attack on PC, *Oleanna*. When it comes to the issue of sexual harassment, it's much more interesting if the writer comes out of his or her corner swinging hard. *Disclosure* is ultimately a timid exercise in shadow boxing.

Michael Coren   (review date 21 February 1994)

SOURCE: "Office Romance," in *National Review,* New York, Vol. XLVI, No. 3, February 21, 1994, p. 63.

[*In the following mixed review of* Disclosure, *Coren applauds Crichton's handling of the sexual harassment theme but faults the unbalanced portrayal of good and evil in the characterizations.*]

One really has to admire the masters and mistresses of the middle-brow, those novelists who swoop down upon an issue that is capturing headlines and sound-bites and make it the theme of a bestselling novel. Are they vultures or are they eagles? The answer will vary from reader to reader. But for me Michael Crichton's wing-span, his grace in flight, and the clarity of his vision place him firmly in the eagle's nest.

We experienced some of this author's gifts when he dealt with Japanese-American relations in *Rising Sun,* genetic engineering in *Jurassic Park,* and the future of the rainforest in *Congo*. At his most astute and poignant Mr.

Crichton popularizes and, in the best sense of the word, simplifies highly complex ideas and controversies and presents them in the form of novels for mass consumption. Because of the nature of the subjects that he has already tackled, it seemed only a matter of time before Mr. Crichton took on that contemporary chimera, sexual harassment. I use the term "chimera" because, although workplace harassment does obviously exist, and although it is vulgar and unjust, it is clearly not as ubiquitous and one-sided as some would have us believe. As with the well-publicized figures on rape, child abuse, and homosexuality, subjective experience must now take precedence over tendentious and fraudulent research. There are no longer lies, damned lies, and statistics; there are now statistics, damned statistics, and lies.

But [in *Disclosure*] Mr. Crichton has done more than question the conventional wisdom about sexual harassment: he has turned that wisdom completely on its head. "The advantage of a role-reversal story is that it may enable us to examine aspects concealed by traditional responses and conventional rhetoric," he writes in his brief afterword. This is provocative stuff, for to question the racial or gender exclusivity of self-awarded victim status is to kick at the very foundations of modern liberalism.

The plot of the book is relatively straightforward. Tom Sanders is a married, happy, deliberately average, and thus altogether believable executive at a Seattle high-tech company who is expecting a promotion to vice president. The prize is taken from him, however, by a rival. She is Meredith Johnson, an attractive and intelligent woman with whom he had conducted an affair some ten years earlier. One evening she invites him into her office for a private, after-work meeting and tries to seduce him. She is partly successful, but his conscience extinguishes his lust and he runs out of the room with his lascivious colleague's wine glass just inches behind his head.

And then the fun begins. Female boss claims that male underling harassed her. The suitably repugnant and insidious company lawyer, a man known as PC Phil, gleefully takes up the case and informs the innocent Sanders that he is to be exiled to a branch plant where he will have effectively no chance of future promotion. The "contemporary climate" is such that men were assumed to be guilty of "anything they were accused of," as Mr. Crichton puts it. "Don't smile at a child on the street, unless you're with your wife," is the book's lugubrious but wise advice. "Don't ever touch a strange child. Don't ever be alone with someone else's child. . . . This was a world of regulations and penalties entirely unknown to women." Nonetheless, Tom Sanders decides to fight back.

With the help of a woman lawyer who is renowned, ironically, for her prosecution of men charged with sexual harassment, Sanders digs a trench, a gaping wound, into the premise upon which this sexual power-play has been built, and in so doing also exposes corruption and hypocrisy within his own company. The PC notion that all men are potential harassers and abusers is shown to be a proposition so weak it ought to be attached to a life-support system. In some quarters Michael Crichton has made himself a very unpopular man indeed.

The flaw in the book is its lack of balance. The divide between good and evil is seldom as obvious and crisp as it appears here, and Mr. Crichton might do well to recall Hilaire Belloc's comment that "the bad are at their most bad when they appear at their least bad." There is also the troubling absence of any major female voice, an omission that tilts the book and occasionally gives it an unsavory and unsatisfying flavor. But in the final analysis this doesn't matter very much and is probably best observed as a form of redressment. Mr. Crichton, or anybody else who wrote a similar book and argued a similar thesis, would be accused of rampant misogyny no matter how sensitive and empathetic he attempted to be.

Disclosure is a refreshingly uncluttered and sinewy entertainment free of pretension and eminently readable.

—*Michael Coren*

The author has dragged a steaming and obfuscated problem before the eyes of millions of people. It is not an issue that will be dismissed, nor indeed is it an issue that *should* be dismissed. And it is because of its very importance that the definition and judgment of sexual harassment and the concomitant wrongs of rape and domestic violence ought to be, must be, taken out of the hands of the neurotic, the needy, and the nasty and given to objective, moderate men and women.

On one level *Disclosure* is a literary pebble tossed into a political pond, and the ripples just might dampen some of the strident howls and emotional spasms that currently dominate discussion of the issue. On another it is a refreshingly uncluttered and sinewy entertainment, free of pretension and eminently readable. I wonder if Meredith Johnson will be played by a real actress or by one of Stephen Spielberg's mechanical monsters in the inevitable movie. Just a thought—and, God forgive me, a terribly sexist one at that.

Francine Prose   (review date October 1994)

SOURCE: A review of *Disclosure*, in *The Yale Review*, Vol. 82, No. 4, October, 1994, pp. 121-32.

[*Prose is an American novelist, short story writer, critic, and educator. In the following review of* Disclosure, *she faults Crichton's facile manipulation of deep-seated anxieties about women and his poorly developed sexual harassment theme.*]

Some years ago I had the misfortune to read a magazine essay by a writer and academic colleague in which he bravely charted his dogged struggle to see women as human beings. One measure of the psychic distance he had traveled was his ability to admit that he had once belonged to a college fraternity in which a ritual of initiation or bonding (I forget the exact purpose) required that a fraternity brother go out on the street, select a woman at random, and bite her on the buttocks.

One would need to have spent the last decade on another planet in order not to know how essential confession is for the "recovery process": indeed, it's often the first sign of recovery. But alas, too little attention is paid to the effect of our confessions on the unfortunate person or persons to whom we elect to confess. Surely I am not the only woman who, ever since reading that essay, has found it difficult to have a simple chat with the recovering biter and not notice that, on leaving the room, I am backing toward the door.

One of the pleasures of great fiction is that it frees us not only from the strictures of time, the narrow circumscriptions of our individual lives, but also from the limits imposed by biology. Reading Chekhov or William Trevor, we are at once old and young, male and female. Reading *Anna Karenina,* we're not only Anna and Vronsky, but Karenin, Levin, Dolly, even Frou-Frou, Vronsky's hapless horse. Under the spell of a first-rate writer, we become Raskolnikov, Humbert Humbert, Molloy, gleefully bashing landladies, chasing nymphets, sucking stones. Nothing human is foreign to us. It suddenly all makes sense.

Bad writing—particularly bad writing about sex—has quite the opposite effect. Perusing some of this season's new fiction, we may feel that sex is more of an insoluble mystery than we ever suspected, and that the limits and solipsisms of gender are steadily closing in on us like the advancing prison walls in Poe's "The Pit and the Pendulum." We are not so much transported to some new height of understanding as left enmired on the front lines of gender war. . . .

[The] hero of Michael Crichton's *Disclosure* imagines that he likes women—or at least doesn't realize how deeply they appall him. We recognize Tom Sanders as a good guy when, at the novel's beginning, he remarks that his wife looks beautiful *even without her makeup* and patiently endures a temper tantrum from his small daughter that would drive most members of the Nurturant Sex straight up the nearest wall. "We don't kick Daddy there," is how Tom fields a well-aimed little foot to the groin, a cautionary reminder that might have served him just as well during the long and humiliating day ahead of him at the office.

Tom's a rising star at Digicom, a high-tech computer communications company on the brink of a major corporate merger or takeover, or whatever. But the promotion Tom is expecting goes (thanks to a boss committed to affirmative action at its most criminally mediocratizing) to Meredith Johnson, who is not only a woman—but Tom's former girlfriend! And though Tom is adept at diagnosing the glitches in disk drives and production lines, he somehow fails to read the signals when Meredith invites him to an intimate after-hours meeting and orders out for white wine and condoms.

> **Crichton is a genius at the sort of meretricious fiction that seems to have been written with one hand on the computer and the other on the pulse of our basest and most unenlightened prejudices and fears.**
>
> *—Francine Prose*

It's worth suppressing our fastidious shivers of distaste and accepting Crichton's invitation to be flies on the wall at this scene of seduction, rejection, and betrayal. For what happens is particularly revealing of what's really at issue here: not the legal and moral implications of turnabout sexual harassment (it's Tom whose job is at risk unless he accedes to Meredith's grabby advances) but a much more primitive, instinctive, and, as it were, knee-jerk misogyny. Despite Tom's reservations, he finds himself responding to Meredith's embraces until she makes a critical mistake: "And then she turned her head aside and coughed. . . . Something snapped in him. He sat back coldly."

Given *Disclosure*'s long reign at the top of best-seller lists, sales of over-the-counter cough suppressants may skyrocket as women get the message that men are repulsed by their unwilled, unbidden, all-too-human reflexes. Later in the novel, Tom convinces his (female) lawyer that Meredith's cough was a sign of chilly, passionless distance and calculation ("But at the moment, right in the intense moment, I'm telling you—nobody coughs.") Lovers with pesky throat tickles may want to remember this and be warned, unless they are fortunate enough to have found partners who will love them and not despise them for inhabiting their cumbersome, unruly, reflex-ridden bodies.

As always, Crichton is a genius at the sort of meretricious fiction that seems to have been written with one hand on the computer and the other on the pulse of our basest and most unenlightened prejudices and fears. His earlier novels have skillfully exploited the popular distrust of scientists, of research, of technology, our xenophobic angst about competition from the Japanese. *Disclosure* digs even deeper, down to men's primal fear of women. To hear Tom Sanders and his pals complain, men really have a raw deal—and it's getting worse. "Sometimes women scare the hell out of me," says one of Tom's buddies, and several hundred pages later, Tom comes to the realization that we are living in a "climate where men were assumed to be guilty of anything they were accused of. . . . There were new rules now, and every man knew them."

Are there actually thousands of readers silently shaking their heads in agreement? Do they really imagine that the modern world is run by ruthless, powerful, castrating women who have somehow managed to bend the legal and political systems to do their vile bidding? Sadly, I'm reminded of the writing student who assured me that his violent pornographic novel would probably never see the light of day because of the international conspiracy of women controlling the publishing industry.

Publishers Weekly (review date 21 August 1995)

SOURCE: A review of *The Lost World,* in *Publishers Weekly,* Vol. 242, No. 34, August 21, 1995, p. 48.

[*In the following review of* The Lost World, *the critic applauds Crichton's grasp of science but faults the characterizations and the originality of the story.*]

One fact about [*The Lost World,* which is the] sequel to *Jurassic Park* stands out above all: it follows a book that, with spinoffs, including the movie, proved to be the most profitable literary venture ever. So where does the author of a near billion-dollar novel sit? Squarely on the shoulders of his own past work—and Arthur Conan Doyle's. Crichton has borrowed from Conan Doyle before—*Rising Sun* was Holmes and Watson in Japan—but never so brazenly. The title itself here, the same as that of Conan Doyle's yarn about an equatorial plateau rife with dinos, acknowledges the debt. More enervating are Crichton's self-borrowings: the plot line of this novel reads like an outtake from *JP*. Instead of bringing his dinos to a city, for instance, Crichton keeps them in the Costa Rican jungle, on an offshore island that was the secret breeding ground for the beasts. Only chaos theoretician Ian Malcolm, among the earlier principals, returns to explore this Lost World, six years after the events of *JP;* but once again, there's a dynamic paleontologist, a pretty female scientist and two cute kids, boy and girl—the latter even saves the day through clever hacking, just as in *JP*. Despite stiff prose and brittle characters, Crichton can still conjure unparalleled dino terror, although the wonder is gone and the attacks are predictable, the pacing perfunctory. But his heart now seems to be not so much in the storytelling as in pedagogy: from start to finish, the novel aims to illustrate Crichton's ideas about extinction—basically, that it occurs because of behavioral rather than environmental changes—and reads like a scientific fable, with pages of theory balancing the hectic action. As science writing, it's a lucid, provocative undertaking; but as an adventure and original entertainment, even though it will sell through the roof, it seems that Crichton has laid a big dinosaur egg.

Mark Annichiarico   (review date 15 September 1995)

SOURCE: A review of *The Lost World,* in *Library Journal,* Vol. 120, No. 15, September 15, 1995, p. 91.

[*In the following review, Annichiarico compares* The Lost World *to* Jurassic Park.]

When strange animal carcasses begin to wash up on the shores of Costa Rica, an eccentric paleontologist suspects that dinosaurs may exist somewhere in the area. [*The Lost World,* the much-anticipated sequel to the megahit *Jurassic Park* (1990),] reads more like a movie novelization: so bereft of plot and characterization in deference to action that it is closer in spirit to Steven Spielberg's movie version (1993) than to the entertaining and educational novel that

preceded it. Reprising their roles from *Jurassic Park* are Ian Malcolm, who bought the farm courtesy of a T-rex in *JP* but whom Crichton seemingly couldn't resist resurrecting, and Lew Dodgson, the evil scientist who makes a living stealing ideas from his fellow researchers. Malcolm and Dodgson, leading separate parties, converge on a small Costa Rican island where the resident raptors, tyrannosaurs, and other carnivores make their field trip distinctly unpleasant. Despite its flaws, however, there will undoubtedly be huge demand in public libraries for Crichton's latest.

Mim Udovitch   (review date 1 October 1995)

SOURCE: "Leapin' Lizards!" in *The New York Times Book Review,* October 1, 1995, pp. 9-10.

[*In the following excerpt, Udovitch favorably assesses* The Lost World *as a thriller but ridicules Crichton for his allusions to what she terms contemporary "hot-button" issues.*]

The director James Cameron once observed that criticizing *Jurassic Park* (the movie, not the book) is like criticizing a roller coaster for not being Proust. Fans of Mr. Cameron's deft touch in such works as *Aliens* and both *Terminator* movies will recognize the grace with which he sidesteps the issue of a direct comparison between *Jurassic Park* (in this instance and hereafter, primarily the book, but the movie too) and *À la Recherche du Temps Perdu.* He is no doubt aware of the superficial similarities between the two. Both Michael Crichton and Proust take on the inherently problematic emotional imperative to recover elements of lost time. Both make liberal use of long, discursive passages of philosophical explication during which the narrative action—characteristically at once minimal and lengthy—grinds to a halt. (In Mr. Crichton's case, this is usually a screeching one, quite literally.) However, with his fine eye for a true lie, Mr. Cameron also probably realizes that such a comparison leads up a blind alley. While Proust is concerned with the uncertainties of the past, Mr. Crichton in his fiction balances the theoretical unpredictability of the future against the sure bet that in real life his efforts will yield buckets of money.

The Lost World is Mr. Crichton's sequel to the enormously successful *Jurassic Park,* and despite the contention of Ian Malcolm, the fictional mathematician and chaos theorist who barely survives both books, that "sequelae are inherently unpredictable," it is a sure bet. The wily velociraptors are back. So are the poultry-sized procompsognathids (*à la recherche* du Frank Perdue). There is a group of good-guy researchers (with the exception of Malcolm, different ones from those in *Jurassic Park,* but, given the rather cursory nature of Mr. Crichton's portrayals of personality, for all intents and purposes the same). There are also two kids, and a villain who is equally devoid of ruth and clue. The plot is slower to start this time around, but it can afford to be, since, the mask of inherent predictability notwithstanding, we know what's coming. It is, however, substantially similar, and since its pleasures are those of a thriller, for review purposes let that suffice.

The most interesting difference between those otherwise twin heavyweights (*Jurassic Park* and *The Lost World,* not Proust and Mr. Crichton) is the development of the raptors as characters. Owing to the fact that in the strictest scientific sense virtually nothing is known for certain about dinosaurs other than that they had skeletons and were very, very thin on one end, thicker in the middle, and then very, very thin again on the other end, they are unusually adaptive fictional symbols, whatever their success in Darwinian terms. (In *The Dechronization of Sam Magruder*, the forthcoming posthumous novel by the preeminent paleontologist George Gaylord Simpson, for example, they are unregeneratively cold-blooded and dull-witted.) And as the reverse sexual harassment theme in **Disclosure** and the enthusiastic if imperfectly absorbed assimilation of chaos theory in both dino-fictions attest, Mr. Crichton is not one to let shame avert him from mining a hot-button trend. (This is not to say that Mr. Crichton may not feel some ambivalence. It is interesting to note that in **The Lost World** the villain, Lewis Dodgson, makes his living taking over the completed, successful intellectual property of others and customizing it slightly to make a profit, much as Mr. Crichton does. I should emphasize that I actually enjoy Mr. Crichton's work very much, and not just his books; I think that **E.R.,** which he also created, is the best show on television.)

In any event, the hot-button trend slot in **Jurassic Park** was shared by the conceit that dinosaurs were warm-blooded, quick and intelligent and by the implications of chaos theory for the human endeavor. This is, incidentally, a subject that, forget Proust, is handled similarly in Tom Stoppard's play *Arcadia,* only without dinosaurs and with exquisite rather than late-capitalist economy. **The Lost World,** while retaining these themes, also addresses the implications for social structure of chosen as opposed to determined behaviors; this is by extension a motif in *Arcadia* as well. (Paging James Cameron; Mr. Cameron, please go to the white comparative literature telephone. Actually, given the predominant attributes of Mr. Stoppard and Mr. Crichton, I like to imagine one laughing, and the other on the way to the bank.) And if the implications for social structure of chosen rather than determined behavior does not sound like a hot-button trend to you, think of welfare reform and family values as you read the following explanation of raptors in **The Lost World.** Bear in mind that the book has already made clear that there are high levels of raptor-on-raptor violence, and that a raptor has attempted a carjacking.

> In a sense, among higher animals adaptive fitness was no longer transmitted to the next generation by DNA at all. It was now carried by teaching. . . . Such actions implied at least the rudiments of a culture, a structured social life. But animals raised in isolation, without parents,

without guidance, were not fully functional. . . . These newly created raptors came into the world with no older animals to guide them, to show them proper raptor behavior. They were on their own, and that was just how they behaved—in a society without structure, without rules, without cooperation. They lived in an uncontrolled, every-creature-for-himself world where the meanest and nastiest survived, and all the others died.

As Mr. Cameron might point out, while the 18th-century poet Christopher Smart considered his cat Jeoffry and saw the servant of the Living God, duly and daily serving Him, Michael Crichton considers raptors and sees the urban underclass. Never mind that Mr. Crichton, in conjuring *un monde* rather than *les temps perdu,* is evoking by his title both Arthur Conan Doyle and the films of Wallace Beery and Jill St. John, making his novel, as it says on the lava lamp box, simultaneously prehistoric and postmodern. This passage from **The Lost World,** among others, implies that the end result of such animal behavior would be unilateral extinction of the species. In this context, it is not a pretty picture. I also take exception to the part Mr. Crichton, while decrying the Internet, lays the blame for global proliferation of Benetton, McDonald's and the Gap at the door of the mass media. (As a member of the mass media, I am willing to accept responsibility for the attrition of regional dialects, but Benetton? Even so culturally nostalgic a writer as Neil Postman doesn't go that far.)

FURTHER READING

Biography

Jaynes, Gregory; Ressner, Jeffrey; and Sachs, Andrea. "Meet Mister Wizard." *Time* 146, No. 3 (25 September 1995): 60-7.
Overview of Crichton's life and literary career.

Criticism

Kakutani, Michiko. "Back in the Land of Dinosaur Cloning." *The New York Times* (10 October 1995): B4.
Faults *The Lost World* as a "predictable and unimaginative" retelling of *Jurassic Park.*

Lemonick, Michael D. "How Good Is His Science?" *Time* 146, No. 13 (25 September 1995): 65.
Focuses on Crichton's technical knowledge of dinosaurs in *The Lost World.*

Additional coverage of Crichton's life and career is contained in the following sources published by Gale Research: *Authors and Artists for Young Adults,* **Vol. 10;** *Authors in the News,* **Vol. 2;** *Contemporary Authors,* **Vols. 25-28 rev. ed.;** *Contemporary Authors New Revision Series,* **Vols. 13, 40;** *Contemporary Literary Criticism,* **Vols. 2, 6, 54;** *Dictionary of Literary Biography Yearbook 1981;* *DISCovering Authors Modules; Junior DISCovering Authors; Major 20th-Century Writers;* **and** *Something about the Author,* **Vol. 9.**

Saul Friedländer

1932-

(Born Pavel Friedländer) Czechoslovakian-born Israeli historian, nonfiction writer, essayist, biographer, and autobiographer.

The following entry provides an overview of Friedländer's career through 1994.

INTRODUCTION

Friedländer is known for historical works on Germany, Nazism, and the Holocaust as well as his examinations of the moral, political, and historiographical ramifications of the Nazis' attempt at genocide during World War II. Gaining initial notoriety for his books *Pie XII et le IIIe Reich* (1964; *Pius XII and the Third Reich*), which documents the Pope's refusal to speak out against the Holocaust, and *Hitler et les États-Unis, 1939-1941* (1967; *Prelude to Downfall*), which examines Hitler's policies toward the United States prior to its entry into World War II, Friedländer is also recognized for his biography of the Nazi who attempted to inform the world about the death camps, *Kurt Gerstein ou l'ambiguité du bien* (1967; *Kurt Gerstein*), his memoir, *Quand vient le souvenir* (1978; *When Memory Comes*), and his book-length essay on contemporary fascination with Nazism, *Reflets du nazisme* (1982; *Reflections of Nazism*).

Biographical Information

Born in Prague, Czechoslovakia—the present-day Czech Republic—just prior to the political rise of Adolf Hitler, Friedländer was upper-middle-class and Jewish, but his family's cultural assimilation was such that they no longer observed the practices of Judaism. Culminating a series of attempts by his parents to protect their son and avoid capture by the Nazis, Friedländer was sent to a Catholic school in France where, under the name Paul-Henri Ferland, he was raised as a Catholic. His parents fled to Switzerland but were turned over to the Nazis by Swiss border guards; the Swiss policy, tragically, was to admit only those Jews accompanied by children, and his parents were eventually killed at Auschwitz. In 1946, during an interview preceding his planned entry into a Jesuit seminary, Friedländer learned of the death camps and of his parents' fate. This knowledge initiated the reclamation of his Jewish heritage. While living in Paris with a family of Russian Jewish immigrants, he became fascinated with Zionism, which at that time entailed both support for the establishment of the state of Israel and a rejection of what many young intellectuals considered the bourgeois values embodied by older generations of western European Jews. In 1947, at the age of fifteen, he left Paris aboard the *Altalena,* a ship carrying arms for the Irgun, Menachem Begin's militant band of Zionists in Palestine; in a move to convince the neighboring governments that Israel's in-

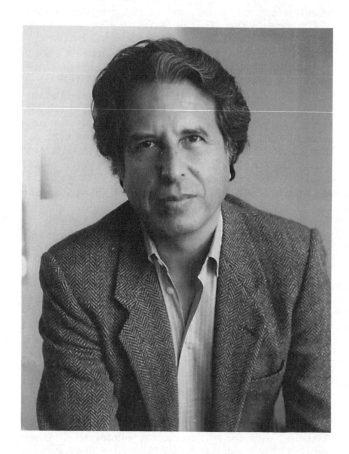

tentions were peaceful, the ship was attacked by the army of the newly-formed Israeli government led by David Ben-Gurion. After living on a kibbutz—a communal farm—in Israel for a number of years, Friedländer eventually grew disillusioned with Zionism. Returning to Paris, he graduated from the Institut d'Études Politiques in 1955 and, in 1957, spent a year working in Sweden at an institution for mentally-ill children; during this time he studied the works of Jewish philosopher and theologian Martin Buber, whose writings on the presence of God in everyday activities and on the stories and legends of the Hasidim of eastern Europe influenced him profoundly. In 1963 he earned his Ph.D. in history from the Graduate Institute of International Studies in Geneva. Friedländer has since taught contemporary history at the Graduate Institute, the Hebrew University in Jerusalem, and the University of Tel Aviv.

Major Works

Prelude to Downfall, a revised and updated version of Friedländer's dissertation, *Le rôle du facteur américain dans la politique étrangère et militaire de l'Allemagne, septembre 1939-décembre 1941* (1963), examines German attempts to maintain and bolster the isolationist policies of the United States in the early years of World War II. In *Pius XII and the Third Reich* Friedländer presents Nazi diplomatic records and other documents that describe the Pope's relationship with Germany and his silence in the face of mounting evidence of the Holocaust. Friedländer argues that it was the combination of Pius XII's fear of Bolshevism, his deep-seated admiration for Germany, and an overestimation of his diplomatic power that accounted for his refusal to condemn the Nazi's genocidal actions. *Kurt Gerstein* documents the life of an SS officer who, though he was responsible for procuring and delivering Zyklon-B, the chemical used in the gas chambers, nonetheless tried to sabotage his own work and disseminate knowledge about the death camps. In *Arabes et israéliens* (1974; *Arabs and Israelis*), Friedländer and two Egyptian Arabs—Bahgat Elnadi and Adel Rifaat, jointly referred to as Mahmoud Hussein—analyze contemporary problems in the Middle East; the debate is moderated by French journalist Jean Lacouture. Friedländer's memoir, *When Memory Comes,* relates his struggle to come to terms with the Holocaust and with his Jewish identity, depicting events from his birth in Czechoslovakia prior to World War II as well as his life in Paris and contemporary Israel. *Reflections of Nazism* presents Friedländer's analysis of Nazi aesthetics and "the new discourse on Nazism." Examining such diverse works as Albert Speer's memoir *Inside the Third Reich* (1970), George Steiner's novel *The Portage to San Cristóbal of A. H.* (1979), and Hans-Jürgen Syberberg's film *Hitler: A Film from Germany* (1978), he argues that many contemporary works of art and history concerned with Hitler and Nazism transform—in the very vividness of their language and images, and irrespective of authorial intention—the abject reality of murder and death into the seductive spectacle the Nazis valorized. The aestheticizing impulse of modern discourses on Nazism, Friedländer believes, diminishes the stark reality of the Holocaust and largely accounts for the continued fascination with Hitler and the Third Reich. Similarly, *Probing the Limits of Representation* (1992) collects essays by numerous thinkers, historians, and scholars on the difficulties of adequately and ethically representing the Holocaust in language and images. Growing out of a conference Friedländer organized at the University of California at Los Angeles in the spring of 1990, the volume includes work by Friedländer, Hayden White, Dominick LaCapra, Geoffrey Hartman, Anton Kaes, and many others.

Critical Reception

Friedländer's work has generally been well received. His historical works are frequently praised for their scholarship and insightful use of primary sources. *Pius XII and the Third Reich* and *Prelude to Downfall,* for example, are considered seminal works in their fields. Some reviewers, however, argued that his selection of documents in the former was biased, although Friedländer himself pointed out the need for material from the Vatican to balance the perspective he presents. Remarking on *Prelude to Downfall,* some historians described Friedländer's claim that he was the first to rigorously examine Hitler's policies toward the United States as disingenuous. Reviewers of *Kurt Gerstein*

frequently praise the book as an insightful examination of a complex individual. However, a minority of commentators argue that Friedländer lapses into moralizing when he extends his discussion of "the ambiguity of good" to account for all of German society during the Nazi era. Friedländer's other works and edited volumes are also highly regarded, and he is considered a leading thinker on Nazism, the Holocaust, Israel, and Arab-Israeli relations. Noted for its focus on the problem of personal identity, *When Memory Comes* is frequently cited with Elie Wiesel's *Night* (1958) and Samuel Pisar's *Of Blood and Hope* (1979) and *La ressource humaine* (1983) as one of the most thoughtful and informative of the Holocaust memoirs. Critics note, in this and all of his works, his rancorless, carefully unbiased point of view in dealing with Nazi Germany and with the rights of Arabs living in Israel. On this latter point, Leon Wieseltier notes that "Throughout his life, Saul Friedländer has seen one nation's triumphant convictions quickly become another nation's oppressive facts. This often happened to the Jews, and it has happened to the Palestinians. Friedländer, who escaped the Nazis and fought the Arabs, has the courage to say so."

PRINCIPAL WORKS

Pie XII et le IIIᵉ Reich; documents [*Pius XII and the Third Reich: A Documentation*] (history) 1964

**Hitler et les États-Unis (1939-1941)* [*Prelude to Downfall: Hitler and the United States, 1939-1941*] (history) 1967

Kurt Gerstein ou l'ambiguité du bien [*Kurt Gerstein: The Ambiguity of Good*] (history) 1967; published in England as *Counterfeit Nazi: The Ambiguity of Good*

Réflexions sur l'avenir d'Israël (nonfiction) 1969

L'antisémitisme nazi: Histoire d'une psychose collective (nonfiction) 1971

Arabes et israéliens: Un premier dialogue [with Mahmoud Hussein and Jean Lacouture] [*Arabs and Israelis: A Dialogue*] (nonfiction) 1974

Histoire et psychanalyse: Essai sur les possibilités et les limites de la psychohistoire [*History and Psychoanalysis: An Inquiry into the Possibilities and Limits of Psychohistory*] (nonfiction) 1975

Some Aspects of the Historical Significance of the Holocaust (nonfiction) 1977

Quand vient le souvenir [*When Memory Comes*] (autobiography) 1978

Reflets du nazisme [*Reflections of Nazism: An Essay on Kitsch and Death;* translated and revised edition, 1984] (nonfiction) 1982

Visions of Apocalypse: End or Rebirth? [editor, with Gerald Holton, Leo Marx, Eugene Skolnikoff] (essays) 1985

A Conflict of Memories?: The New German Debates about the "Final Solution" (nonfiction) 1987

Die Juden in der europaischen Geschichte [*The Jews in European History: Seven Lectures*] (lectures) 1992

Probing the Limits of Representation: Nazism and the

Final Solution [editor and contributor]   (nonfiction) 1992

Memory, History, and the Extermination of the Jews of Europe   (history)   1993

*This work is a revised and updated version of Friedländer's thesis, *Le rôle du facteur américain dans la politique étrangère et militaire de l'Allembre, septembre 1939-décembre 1941,* originally published in Geneva in 1963.

CRITICISM

Guenter Lewy   (review date 21 May 1966)

SOURCE: "Was Silence the Only Solution?" in *The Saturday Review,* New York, Vol. XLIX, No. 21, May 21, 1966, pp. 26-7.

[*Lewy is a German-born American historian, educator, and nonfiction writer. In the following excerpt, he discusses* Pius XII and the Third Reich *and the reasons for the Pope's decision not to speak out against Germany when presented with evidence of the Nazi's "Final Solution," the attempt to exterminate European Jewry.*]

The attitude of Pope Pius XII toward Nazi Germany and the reasons for his silence in the face of the murder of six million Jews have been the subject of extensive and often acrimonious debate ever since the young German playwright Rolf Hochhuth chose this problem as the theme for *The Deputy.*

In Saul Friedländer's **Pius XII and the Third Reich** we now have a source of valuable information that generates light rather than heat. The author is associate professor of contemporary history at the Graduate Institute of International Studies in Geneva, Switzerland. His study consists of documents with brief accompanying notes which provide the historical setting and contribute to the readability of the book. A large proportion of the documents included come from the files of the Nazi Ministry of Foreign Affairs: others are taken from British and American diplomatic papers and from the Zionist Archives in Jerusalem. Most of them have been known to specialists in the field, but many are now published for the first time.

The author admits frankly that a study of the Holy See's policy toward Nazi Germany based in the main on German diplomatic papers cannot but be biased. These German documents give us only one dimension of the problem; moreover, diplomatic reports, especially under a totalitarian régime, are often influenced by a desire of the writers to tell what their governments want to hear. And yet, despite a very real need for caution, the Nazi documents contribute to a better understanding of these tragic events. Much of what they contain is corroborated by accounts of American, British, and Polish diplomats. The documents just released from the Vatican archives, which were not available to Professor Friedländer, further confirm some of his main interpretive findings.

Without claiming to state definitive conclusions Friedländer notes that the documents presented by him reveal impressive agreement on two points. First, Pope Pius XII, who had spent many years in Germany as papal nuncio, had a predilection for that nation which was not substantially diminished by the nature of the Nazi régime. Second, the Pontiff feared a Bolshevization of Europe and therefore was anxious not to weaken Germany by criticizing its wartime policies. The documentary support for the first of these conclusions is extensive; the second finding is based on more circumstantial evidence, though the considerable number of documents quoted serves to enhance the plausibility of this interpretation. The Pope's failure to protest the "final solution," argues Friedländer, is thus in part accounted for by Pius's love for Germany and by his fear of undermining German resistance in the East. Other factors were his desire not to make a bad situation worse and to avoid greater evils—for the Jews as well as for the German Catholics, on whom Hitler might have sought vengeance. The Pontiff's wish to pursue a policy of neutrality also receives mention.

In the years immediately following World War II some Catholic writers attributed the silence of the Pope (and of the German bishops) on Nazi atrocities to lack of knowledge to these deeds. The Pope and the bishops, wrote a high German church dignitary in 1946, did not protest against many Nazi horrors because they did not know of them. This explanation, the documents now available show clearly, is untenable. The Holy See received detailed information about the mass killings of Poles and Jews from a variety of sources. After much prodding by Allied diplomats, Pius XII in his Christmas message of 1942 finally expressed his concern for the "hundreds of thousands of people who, through no fault of their own and solely because of their nation or their race, have been condemned to death or progressive extinction." Beyond this cautious comment the Pope was not prepared to go.

Less than ten days after this Christmas message, Wladislaw Raczkiewicz, President of the Polish government in exile, implored the Pontiff to issue an unequivocal denunciation of Nazi violence in order to strengthen the willingness of the Poles to resist the Germans and to help the Jews. His people, wrote Raczkiewicz on January 2, 1943, "do not ask so much for material or diplomatic help, because they know that the possibilities of their receiving such help are slim, but they implore that a voice be raised to show clearly and plainly where the evil lies and to condemn those in the service of evil. If these people can be reinforced in their conviction that divine law knows no compromise and that it stands above any human considerations of the moment, they will, I am sure, find the strength to resist."

Similarly, on September 5, 1944, after more than half a million Hungarian Jews had been sent to their death at Auschwitz, the Chief Rabbi of Palestine, Isaac Herzog, urged through the Papal Delegate to Egypt and Palestine that "the Pope make a public appeal to the Hungarian people and call upon them to place obstacles in the way of the deportation; that he declare in public that any person obstructing the deportation will receive the blessing of the Church, whereas any person aiding the Germans will be denounced." Whether any sizable number of Polish or Hungarian Catholics would have been influenced by such a papal appeal for the Jews we will never know. Both interventions failed; the Supreme Pontiff maintained his silence.

At the end of his book Friedländer expresses the hope that the documents of the Vatican archives will soon be published "so that the events and personages can be brought into proper perspective."

Walter Laqueur   (review date 22 May 1966)

SOURCE: "Diplomatic Decisions," in *The New York Times Book Review,* May 22, 1966, p. 6.

[*Laqueur is a German-born American historian and novelist who is widely considered an expert on modern German and Israeli history. In the following review of* Pius XII and the Third Reich, *he describes Pius XII's diplomacy toward the Nazis as "masterly inactivity," judging it "tragically inapplicable in an extreme situation."*]

The policy of the Pope and the Roman Catholic Church during World War II has during the last few years been the subject of several historical studies, of plays, polemical essays and theological disputations in various countries. Needless to say, there was in the Catholic Church no uniform reaction to Hitler and Nazism; if the great majority of German bishops collaborated, quite a few of the lower clergy resisted and were incarcerated. In France, especially after the Occupation, the clergy took on the whole a patriotic stand.

Cardinal Tisserant wrote from the Vatican as early as June, 1940, that "Our governments . . . persist in imagining this is a war like the wars of times gone by." He had grasped that Hitlerism had transformed the conscience of the young, and made them willing to commit any crime for any purpose ordered by their leader: "Instead of dying on the battlefield, Frenchmen will be obliged to die by inches—men separated from their wives, and children spared perhaps to serve their conquerors as slaves." Even at the beginning of the war Tisserant was deeply critical of the policy of Pope Pius XII: "I fear history may have reason to reproach the Holy See with having pursued a policy of convenience to itself and very little else." Later on, similar sentiments were expressed by Catholics in the United States and elsewhere.

Saul Friedlander, a young historian now resident in Switzerland, tries to answer the question whether the Pope knew what was happening and whether he should have been silent. His book [*Pius XII and the Third Reich*], is not a polemical work; he lets the documents speak for themselves and provides only a minimum of running commentary. Yet underlying the dispassionate discussion is a feeling of passionate involvement; the author, we learn, was born in Prague in 1932. The family was forced to flee to France, where in 1942 his parents were taken by the Nazis, deported to Auschwitz and killed. The child was hidden in a monastery until the end of the war.

The Pope's position was not an easy one, for Catholics were fighting on both sides. There were 30 million Catholics in Germany and Pius XII wanted to avoid any statement that would lead them away from Rome. As the Osservatore Romano put it after the Nazi conquest of Norway: "There are only 2,000 Catholics in Norway; that being so, the Holy See, though severely condemning the moral aspect of the matter, must take a practical view and bear in mind the 30 million German Catholics."

The "practical view" was no doubt of the greatest importance, but it should not have been the only criterion; considerations of expediency have their limits, and Pius XII apparently never realized when they were exceeded. He was not lacking in courage, but his political and moral assessment of the situation was found wanting. His ambition to enter history as *Pastor Angelicus,* a great maker of peace, led him to persist in appeasement long after such a position had become morally untenable. His many years in Germany made him view world affairs (especially where Russia was involved) through German eyes; as an Italian patriot he sympathized too often with Mussolini's foreign policy.

Polish Catholicism had been traditionally the most faithful daughter of the church. What happened to Poland after the Nazi conquest is well known and was eloquently expressed in a message to the Holy Father by the then President of the Polish Government-in-exile: divine laws trampled underfoot, human dignity degraded, hundreds of thousands of men murdered without trial, churches profaned and closed. He implored the Holy Father to break his silence "that a voice be raised to show clearly and plainly where the evil lies and to condemn those in the service of evil."

Yet the Holy Father with great sorrow refused to break his silence and never budged from his position that a forthright denunciation of Nazi atrocities would only result in the violent death of many more people.

From time to time additional not very convincing reasons were given to justify his silence; if he denounced German atrocities (it was once explained) the Germans in the bitterness of defeat would later reproach him, if only indirectly, for that defeat—just as they had accused Benedict XV after World War I. The Pope apparently subordinated all other political considerations to the importance of victorious resistance to Bolshevism in the East. He failed to understand that Hitler's aggression had made the Sovietization of Eastern Europe inevitable.

If the Pope refused to speak out in defense of the church in Poland, it was unrealistic to expect him to do so on behalf of the Jews. The Holy See knew of the Nazi policy of mass extermination by late 1942; three attempts are known to have been made to alleviate the lot of individual Jews in the Reich. Orsenigo, the Papal Nuncio in Berlin, intervened on one occasion on behalf of a 74-year-old Jewish woman in Amsterdam; on another he expressed ("casually," the files say) concern about rumors of the impending ordinance on the dissolution of mixed marriages. On the third occasion ("somewhat embarrassed and without pressing the point") he simply asked what had become of certain French Jews who had been made to leave their previous place of residence.

There may have been other unofficial approaches of which there is no record. In Pius's secret address to the Sacred College of Cardinals in June, 1943, he said: "Every word We address to the competent authority on this subject, and all Our public utterances, have to be carefully weighed and measured by Us in the interests of the victims themselves, lest, contrary to Our intentions, We make their situation worse and harder to bear . . . The Vicar of Christ, who asked no more than pity and a sincere return to elementary standards of justice and humanity, then found himself facing a door that no key could open." The image of the door that no key could open reappeared several times in his addresses later in the war, but we do not know what the Pope meant, for in the German files on which this book is based there is no reference to any further intervention by the Vatican.

The Pope's belief that his silence prevented worse evil was profoundly mistaken. Pius XII has entered history not as *Pastor Angelicus,* but at best as a very controversial Pope. It would be naive to assume that had he taken a forthright stand the Nazis would have desisted from their crimes. Bishop Galen of Munster's denunciation caused the Nazis to discontinue their euthanasia program, but the "final solution" was a different proposition, and there is no certainty that they would have shut down Auschwitz and Maidenek simply because the Pope had condemned genocide. At best it might have served to delay matters, and so saved thousands of lives; most Catholics would no doubt agree now that the Pope should have broken his silence even had there been no chance at all.

Eugenio Pacelli had been a diplomat for too long before he became Pope Pius XII. He continued to behave like a diplomat, measuring every word, dropping hints, taking half measures, trusting in masterly inactivity at a time when the world was on fire. This traditional policy had on previous occasions proved quite successful. It was tragically inapplicable in an extreme situation that called for character, steadfastness and spiritual leadership rather than traditional diplomacy.

Arno J. Mayer   (review date 5 June 1966)

SOURCE: "The Vatican in WW II," in *Book Week—Chicago Sunday Sun-Times,* June 5, 1966, p. 7.

[*Mayer is a Luxembourgian-born American historian. In the following review of* Pius XII and the Third Reich, *he focuses on Pius XII's "hostility to Bolshevism" as a determinant of Vatican policy during World War II.*]

Anyone who does not literally interpret the claim that the Pope is God's Vicar will not be overly shocked by Pius XII's policies during the Second World War. After all, the man who was Pope never ceased to be a good Italian, a confirmed Germanophile, a punctilious elitist, an impassioned anti-Bolshevik, and a shrewd chief executive of one of the world's vastest institutional structures.

In this untendentious documentary history, [***Pius XII and the Third Reich***], Saul Friedländer, a professor of contemporary history at the Graduate Institute of International Studies at Geneva, quite properly suggests that as an Italian, Pacelli was not about to wish for Italy's defeat. Besides, the concordat with Mussolini worked rather smoothly, the Holy See's autonomy was being respected, and any political alternative to Fascism in Italy threatened to be too left-wing for Pacelli's very conservative predilections.

Of course, Pius XII realized that the fortunes of Italy were tied to those of Germany, whose language and culture he had assimilated while Papal Nuncio in Munich and Berlin from 1917 to 1929. When called upon to carry forward Benedict XV's peace proposal in 1917, Pacelli first discovered his own diplomatic skills, in which he subsequently trusted ever so blindly. More important, in the first half of 1919 he observed first-hand not only the establishment of the Bavarian "Soviet" but also its overthrow with the help of some forerunners of Nazism, whose brutal methods he never publicly questioned. Hereafter Pacelli was captivated by Hitler's anti-Bolshevik rhetoric, as were even those few European bishops who eventually, unlike himself, *explicitly* condemned the anti-Semitic and eugenic atrocities of the Nazis. Admittedly, as Friedländer shows, the Pope kept his remonstrances against what Eugen Kogon so aptly called the *Theory and Practice of Hell* deliberately vague and general. He did so because reports about atrocities struck him, as so many others, as being exaggerated; because he did not want to alienate the German hierarchy and rank and file, whose ultra-nationalism firmly tied them to Hitler's Reich; and because he was afraid that his protests might goad the Nazis into still greater savagery.

Friedländer presents these conventional explanations, if not apologies, for the Pope's inordinate caution in the broader context of the international civil war of this century. Many of his documents from the archives of the German Foreign Ministry suggest that Pacelli's policy toward the Third Reich was at all times influenced, possibly even determined, by his hostility to Bolshevism and his zeal to keep Soviet Russia out of the East European rimland, which was so heavily Catholic. The same documents provide credible indications that the Pontiff continued to favor appeasement after Munich; that once France had fallen he advocated an Anglo-Nazi accommodation designed to free Hitler to turn his full wrath against Stalin; and that following the invasion of Russia he cooled towards the Anglo-Saxon Powers because these went into a defensive partnership with the Soviets. In August 1941 the Secretary of the Congregation for the Propagation of the Faith declared that "just as yesterday on Spanish soil, so today in Bolshevik Russia itself . . . brave soldiers of our own fatherland, along with others, are fighting the greatest battle of all . . . [and] are defending the ideal of our freedom against Red barbarism." Though it is not clear whether such statements had the Pope's explicit imprimatur, undoubtedly they reflected the opinion of high Vatican officials.

Certainly as soon as the battle turned against the Axis at Stalingrad, the westward advance of Bolshevism and Soviet Russia became the Holy See's chief preoccupation, the more so because, simultaneously, the Communists were surfacing in the Italian Resistance. Friedländer concludes that judging by these German documents, especially by the fall of 1943, the Pope "feared a Bolshevization of Europe more than anything else and hoped, it seems, that Hitler's Germany, if it were eventually reconciled with the Western Allies, would become the essential rampart against any advance by the Soviet Union toward the West."

Whereas in 1917 Benedict XV had pressed for a negotiated settlement between *all* the belligerents, in 1943-44 Pius XII appears to have sought a separate peace between the Western Allies and the Axis as a prelude to a joint crusade against Bolshevism. It is to be hoped that some day the Vatican archives will tell us whether Pacelli actually considered giving his blessings to a diplomatic deal which would have prolonged the life of Hitler's extermination system, or whether he considered the overthrow of the Nazi regime as an essential precondition for such a realignment—an overthrow which really was never in the cards. Meanwhile Friedländer's documentation, which is based almost exclusively on the archives of the German foreign ministry, calls attention to the counter-revolutionary impulses which informed the secular policies of the Pope, the Vatican, and the Church before, during, and after the War.

E. H. Wall   (review date 23 August 1966)

SOURCE: "Tragic Dilemma," in *National Review,* New York, Vol. XVIII, August 23, 1966, pp. 843-44.

[*In the following excerpt, Wall faults Friedländer for his possibly biased selection of documents in* Pius XII and the Third Reich *and for "rushing" to publish an admittedly incomplete account of the Vatican's policies toward Nazi Germany.*]

Friedlander's [*Pius XII and the Third Reich*], despite its title, is not the story of Pius XII and the Third Reich. It is a collection of quotations from documents and other books, interspersed with the author's comments and conjectures. What is particularly valuable about the work is that some of the material reproduced is hitherto unpublished diplomatic correspondence between Nazi ambassadors at the Vatican and the Wilhelmstrasse Foreign Office in Berlin during the period 1939-1944. The documents that survive from those ruined archives are interesting in themselves. They are, however, incomplete and the reader is placed in the position of reading Browning's "My Last Duchess" with lines and perhaps even whole sections omitted.

Presumably to remedy the obvious deficiencies of the Nazi documents, and to try to live up to the ambitious title that he has set on his book, the author also throws in quotations from other documents (e.g. from the Zionist Archives in Jerusalem) and from other books (e.g. Jacques Nobecourt's *Le Vicaire et l'Histoire*). It is in doing this that he gets into trouble. Obviously he cannot reproduce all the documents, all the facts, all the data relevant to his announced subject. He has to make selections. But the act of selection is, conversely, the act of exclusion. To select

one thing is *ipso facto* to exclude the others one does not select. Thus Friedlander has already come under attack from the Jesuit historian Robert Graham for having omitted important documents. Inevitably, it must appear that he is not engaged in an objective scholarly inquiry so much as in grinding an ax. The impression is reinforced by his assertions that he is but commenting "on the documents," while he quite glides over the fact that he has antecedently selected the document upon which he is now going to comment.

Although the author speaks of Pius XII and the Third Reich, it is apparent that his main concern is with the question of why Pius did not speak out as brazenly as the massed bells of all the cathedrals of Christendom after the Nazis began the systematic extermination of the Jews in 1942. At least the reviewer can find no other reason for his devoting several pages of quotation to the impressions of a Vichy French diplomat on the theological position of the Catholic Church (including the position of St. Thomas Aquinas) *vis-à-vis* the Jews. The author (for reasons utterly unknown) thinks that this is important enough to devote space to, but oddly reduces to a footnote . . . the report of Angelo Roncalli (later John XXIII) that his numerous activities to help the Jews were made at "the instance of the Pope," at the instance of Pius XII. Other examples of "selectivity" can be cited.

It is not surprising that in concluding his book the author writes: "At the end of this study, which claims to be nothing more than an analysis of documents, I cannot make any definite answer to the questions raised by the wartime policies of the Holy See toward the Third Reich because I have only incomplete documents at my disposal." Why did he bother writing the book? Why did he not wait until he *had* more material and could venture *definite* answers, rather than rush into print now with nothing more than conjectures and insinuations? Scholarship has all of time in which to reach its conclusions, even if Friedlander does not.

Edwin Tetlow   (review date 15 December 1967)

SOURCE: "Of Diplomatic Thrust and Counterthrust," in *The Christian Science Monitor,* December 15, 1967, p. 13.

[*Tetlow is an English journalist and nonfiction writer. In the following highly positive review of* Prelude to Downfall, *he praises the "self-effacing zeal" with which Friedländer writes and relates some of the dramatic political machinations that preceded American entry into World War II.*]

Looking back a quarter of a century, one sees now that it should have been apparent to all concerned that, once Hitler had turned away from an undefeated England and decided instead to take on the sprawling colossus of the Soviet Union, he had lost his war. He had staked everything on a quick kill, and even by the end of 1940 the gamble had obviously failed. But the moment had long ago passed when he could evade paying forfeit. He, and everybody else, had to play to the end the tragedy he had provoked.

How and why did Hitler fail? There were two factors which above all others brought him down. One was the instinctive refusal of the English to give up, and the other was an implacably determined Franklin Roosevelt, who had resolved on behalf of the United States to prove the English right.

The resulting duel between Hitler and Roosevelt, fought while the two countries they led were not yet at war with each other, is the engrossing theme of Saul Friedländer's book [*Prelude To Downfall: Hitler and the United States, 1939-1941*]. This is no tale, then, of blood-and-thunder heroics on the field of battle, but one of diplomatic and political thrust and counterthrust. Men's minds, not their bodies, were at odds here. The weapons they used were ideas and words, not guns, and the ammunition was a mass of documents—official archives, ambassadorial telegrams, speeches, everything that a thorough and painstaking author can now fit together. The story is told, ingeniously and illuminatingly, from the German corner.

Professor Friedländer shows that Hitler's bedrock purpose was to keep the United States out of the war until he had finished off England and the others who stood barring his path to invincibility. Conversely, Roosevelt's was to keep a battered and staggering England in the ring until he guided his country, step by step and guilefully toward the war which he knew it must face.

The two men had one characteristic in common. It was dedication to their purpose. Thus, until war was inevitable after bombs had started falling on Pearl Harbor, Hitler refused the increasingly despairing appeals of his sailors to let them answer one galling provocation after another by attacking and sinking United States ships. Roosevelt was never deterred by powerful sentiments of isolationism in and out of Congress and, with astonishing dexterity, still kept up his offensive against Hitler while fighting another battle at home to get himself reelected.

> In *Prelude to Downfall* Friedländer, for the most part, practices the self-effacing zeal of the scholar in letting the facts and the documents speak mightily for themselves, and as a result we are treated to a brightly lit picture of Hitler's dealings.
>
> —*Edwin Tetlow*

Hitler's henchmen in Washington served him with dogged efficiency during the weird period of prolonged and deepening twilight. They were up to every trick to foster opposition to Roosevelt, "the Jewish faker." Strange indeed is it to read now that Hans Thomsen, the German charge d'affaires, could plan for 50 Republican congressmen to be invited, at a cost of $3,000, to spend three days at the party convention in 1940 to influence delegates toward an isolationist foreign policy; and to arrange behind the scenes for publication of anti-interventionist books by well-known

American authors without their knowing where the money had come from.

Strange also is it to read, in view of what happened between 1941 and 1945 and thereafter, that Roosevelt was reelected by only a small margin in 1940 and that Congress repealed the main provisions of the Neutrality Act, less than a month before Japan attacked, by the smallest majorities obtained for any foreign policy act since the beginning of the war. Professor Friedländer even offers the view that the America First Committee and other isolationists might have succeeded in keeping the United States from intervening in the conflict had it not been for the bombing of Pearl Harbor.

This is one of the few personal views hazarded by the author in his most effective work, and it is a dubious one. For the most part he practices the self-effacing zeal of the scholar in letting the facts and the documents speak mightily for themselves, and as a result we are treated to a brightly lit picture of Hitler's dealings not only with Roosevelt and the United States but with a slippery Franco, a touchy and difficult Vichy, and a double-dealing Japan. All is related carefully and dispassionately. Perhaps the most eloquent tribute one can pay to the author is that unless the reader were told, he would never guess from the book that Saul Friedländer's father and mother were caught by the Nazis in 1942 and killed in Auschwitz.

Francis Loewenheim   (review date 4 February 1968)

SOURCE: "Die Amerikaner," in *The New York Times Book Review,* February 4, 1968, pp. 10, 12.

[*In the following review, Loewenheim states that Friedländer's* Prelude to Downfall, *though its arguments are not original, adequately presents Hitler's perceptions of and policies toward the United States before its entry into the Second World War.*]

It seems clear that many Americans—and especially critics of United States policy in Vietnam—would prefer to hear as little as possible about the history and meaning of American foreign policy in the 1930's. This may help to account for the disturbing fact that neither William L. Langer's and S. Everett Gleason's *The Challenge to Isolation; The World Crisis of 1937-1940* (1952) and *The Undeclared War, 1940-1941* (1953), one of the great works of modern scholarship, nor the impressive chapters on international affairs in James MacGregor Burns's *Roosevelt: The Lion and the Fox* (1956) and William E. Leuchtenburg's *Franklin D. Roosevelt and the New Deal, 1932-1940* (1963), or the important recent work of Manfred Jonas, *Isolationism in America, 1935-1941* (1966), have achieved anything like their deserved impact or general influence.

Saul Friedländer, who teaches contemporary history at the Graduate Institute of International Studies at Geneva, and a year ago published a widely praised study of *Pius XII and the Third Reich,* has not sought to re-examine the whole course of American foreign policy before Pearl Harbor [in *Prelude To Downfall*]. He has set himself the more limited, but no less important, task of examining the role the United States played in German foreign policy in the two years immediately preceding the outbreak of war between the two countries in December, 1941.

"How," he asks, for instance, "did the leadership in Berlin regard the role of the United States in the struggle for world power? How much was Hitler influenced in his strategic deliberations by the probability that this colossus would enter the war? Had it occurred to the German leaders that the fate of the Third Reich might be decided, much as that of the Second had been, by intervention from America?"

Unfortunately, Friedländer's work promises rather more than it actually delivers. He begins with the assertion that "it is astonishing that no systematic treatment has yet appeared of so pivotal a factor as the relation of the Third Reich to the United States"—an astonishing claim that not only ignores the interesting books of James V. Compton, *The Swastika and the Eagle—Hitler, the United States, and the Origins of World War II,* and Alton Frye's *Nazi Germany and the Western Hemisphere, 1933-1941,* published last year (which his publishers ought certainly to have told him about), but also H. L. Trefousse's still valuable pioneer study *Germany and American Neutrality, 1939-1941* (published in 1951 and in fact listed in his bibliography!). Friedländer's work is based, for the most part, on a detailed, but by no means exhaustive, study of the German diplomatic documents that fell into Western hands at the end of World War II.

Since Messrs. Compton and Frye (and Trefousse too) had gone over somewhat the same materials, the result, not surprisingly, is a certain amount of duplication as well as—and this is of course by no means undesirable—considerable agreement on many of the key issues.

Thus Friedländer shows once more, at some length, that while Hitler generally misjudged—that is to say, underrated—American power, prospective and extant, he much preferred to keep the United States out of the war as long as possible, and went to some length to discourage incendiary incidents that might have led to a formal rupture of diplomatic relations or the actual outbreak of hostilities.

Hitler, Friedländer points out, was not "so blinded by his hatred of the United States as not to fear its intervention. On the contrary, the whole of Hitler's policy points to his full awareness of the importance of the American factor in the event of a long war. Did he, nevertheless, think that with Japanese help the Axis powers could stand up victoriously to the formidable coalition that they were going to have to face? The numerous utterances quoted in this book suggest that he did."

In this quite understandable desire to keep the United States out of war as long as possible, Hitler had considerable support on this side of the Atantic, and some of the most intriguing and suggestive (but again by no means definitive) pages of Friedländer's book are devoted to a straightforward account of it. There was a strange collection of professional pacifists, political opportunists, philosophical isolationists, narrow-minded legalists, thinly veiled pro-Nazis, self-appointed peacemakers, glamorous military experts, totalitarian apologists, idealist social reformers, passionate President-haters, thoughtless academics and university students (Yale being a special hotbed of isolationism), devout Quakers and reverend clergy, unprincipled journalists and washed-up novelists—all of them ready, for one reason or another, including in some instances hard cash, to do the Führer's work.

Finally, as Trefousse, Compton and Frye before him, Friedländer has turned up no concrete evidence to the effect that Hitler planned to attack the United States or the Western Hemisphere, once he had achieved effective mastery over the Old World. Does that mean that President Roosevelt was mistaken when, in 1940-1941, he all too belatedly aligned the United States on the side of the Western democracies, or what still remained of them, and certain other powers resisting the spread of Nazi aggression? It will be interesting to hear from the New Left historians on this point—once they have finished rewriting the origins and history of the cold war.

Norbert Muhlen   (review date 12 April 1969)

SOURCE: A review of *Kurt Gerstein: The Ambiguity of Good,* in *America,* Vol. 120, No. 15, April 12, 1969, pp. 454-55.

[*Muhlen was a German-born American journalist and historian. In the following mixed review of* Kurt Gerstein: The Ambiguity of Good, *he faults Friedländer for his facile psychoanalysis of his subject and for the moralistic tone of his conclusions.*]

The hero of this historical study [*Kurt Gerstein: The Ambiguity of Good*] is one of the most enigmatic figures of the Nazi years. In an era characterized by tragedy on a mass basis, his tragedy was unique. A devoutly Lutheran Christian, the son of an old-fashioned Prussian middle-class family, a promising 27-year-old mining engineer when Hitler came to power, Kurt Gerstein joined the Nazi party. Though he had not broken with it, he soon was banned from his occupation and briefly sent to a concentration camp because he tried to defend the integrity of the Protestant youth movement against totalitarian claims. He became a total enemy of the Nazi regime only after he suspected that a sister-in-law of his, together with many other patients of German mental hospitals, had been secretly murdered at the beginning of World War II. His suspicion turned out to be right, as he discovered in an almost incredible, yet fully documented, search for the truth.

It led Gerstein, the passionate Nazi-hater, to join the most fanatically faithful Nazi organization, the S.S., some of whose members were in charge of the mass murder actions. Due to his professional abilities, he was promoted to a position which brought him into personal contact with the Jewish extermination camps. In contrast to the mental hospitals, they were located outside the German borders, and therefore the crimes committed within their walls could be kept a much closer secret of tiny Nazi gangs. Gerstein himself was assigned to procuring some of the lethal gases used to "solve the Jewish problem" in a mass destruction process, and he seemed to do his job.

As he made clear to friends and even to chance acquaintances, he wanted to be a personal witness, and probably the only hostile witness, to the Nazi crimes when the day of their prosecution would arrive. He also wanted to be in a position immediately to warn the world, and to beg it to interfere, for which purpose he related his horrible knowledge, with facts and figures, to some neutral diplomats including the papal nuncio in Berlin, and to a few Protestant churchmen. The Secret State Police never found out about his warnings, which, of course, would have brought his death sentence. Nor was it discovered that this apparent and often actual assistant of the murderers himself tried to counteract the murder plans by sabotaging deliveries of *Zyklon B*, the lethal gas; in a few instances he succeeded. When the Allies invaded Germany, Gerstein gave himself up at the earliest moment, but French authorities imprisoned him as a war criminal. He took his life in a Paris jail cell.

In *Kurt Gerstein: The Ambiguity of Good*, Mr. Friedländer supplies merely an outline of the great tragedy of Kurt Gerstein, a man of good will under an evil dictatorship.

—Norbert Muhlen

If Saul Friedländer, an Israeli historian, had solely related the course of Gerstein's life, he would have contributed an important chapter to the history of the Third Reich. Unfortunately, however, Mr. Friedländer also attempts to set himself up as a supreme moral judge of the large majority of the German people as well as of Gerstein himself. Given his hostile personal bias and his superficial treatment of moral as well as factual questions, which he often answers by cut-rate psychoanalysis and by comic-strip-styled oversimplifications (like the playwright Hochhuth, who depicted Gerstein in *The Deputy*), he appears poorly equipped for such a final judgment. His ambiguous verdict on the "ambiguity of good" remains as meaningless as its fashionable model and companion piece, Hannah Arendt's banal charge against the "banality of evil."

As it is, Mr. Friedländer supplies merely an outline of the great tragedy of Kurt Gerstein, a man of good will under an evil dictatorship.

Arthur A. Cohen   (review date 13 April 1969)

SOURCE: A review of *Kurt Gerstein: The Ambiguity of Good*, in *The New York Times Book Review*, April 13, 1969, p. 10.

[*Cohen was an American historian, novelist, nonfiction writer, and theologian. In the following review, he examines some of the moral complexities Friedländer explores in* Kurt Gerstein: The Ambiguity of Good.]

The enigma of Kurt Gerstein, a lieutenant in the Waffen-SS responsible for securing shipments of Zyklon B, the le-

thal gas used in the crematoria of Auschwitz, first came to the attention of the American public through Rolf Hochhuth's celebrated play, *The Deputy*. There, Hochhuth represents Gerstein as having sought to bring word of the extermination camps to the attention of the Papal Nuncio in Berlin.

However Hochhuth has interpreted the case of Gerstein, the case remains open, and it is to the incredible moral complexities of his case that Saul Friedländer, author of ***Pius XII and the Third Reich,*** (1966) has directed his fascinating, exhaustive and brutally deadpan historical essay, ***Kurt Gerstein: The Ambiguity of Good.***

Kurt Gerstein was a familiar and unexceptional "good German," born in 1905 into a tradition of civil service, educated in middle-class rectitude, trained to all commonplace values, including that of anti-Semitism. (Among notable Protestants only Dietrich Bonhoeffer and Karl Barth—and not Martin Niemoller and Bishop Dibelius—were free of and outspokenly opposed to anti-Semitism.)

The original conflict for Kurt Gerstein was between membership in the Nazi party and his total moral involvement in the defense of the Confessional Churches that were under severe attack by the Nazis. Gerstein agitated, distributed contraband pamphlets, lectured to Bible groups on the moral resistance which Christian faith required. Although his opposition in those prewar years was confused and uncertain, it was enough to earn him expulsion from the party and two brief imprisonments.

The turning point in his life came when he learned that his sister-in-law had been one among the 70,273 mental patients murdered between January, 1940, and August, 1941. It was then that Gerstein set himself the unique task that was to consume the four years remaining to him to join the SS, to dissemble as a dedicated instrument of Hitler's Final Solution, while at the same time impeding its effectuation and bringing news of its horrors to the German people and the outside world.

The ambiguity of fact is that Gerstein did and didn't: he effected the transport of more tons of liquid prussic acid (the essential ingredient of Zyklon B) than he was able to destroy; he tried to tell church authorities, neutrals and underground contacts of the exterminations he had witnessed, but his warnings were ignored. He was left finally spreading the word to any and all, risking his life daily to communicate the horror to casual passersby and strangers. The task became an obsession and the obsession occasioned the deterioration of his use to the cause, to himself. In 1945, imprisoned by the French after his surrender to Allied forces, he ostensibly committed suicide.

The ambiguity of moral judgment is that the denazification proceedings against him conducted posthumously in Tubingen in 1950, having acknowledged that, at considerable risk to his life, he had opposed the Nazi regime from within and sought to bring word of its monstrosities to the outside world, condemned him as suffering "taint" because his actions—given the privileged knowledge which he possessed—were too ineffectual. (He was rehabilitated in 1965 by Kurt Kiesinger then Premier of Baden-Wurttemberg). He was condemned originally, as Friedländer says, *"for the uselessness of his efforts"* (author's italics). It would have been preferable, Friedländer expatiates, in the eyes of the German court, if Gerstein had behaved as millions of "good" and "silent" Germans had, who, with ample suspicion, if not knowledge (as Friedländer demonstrates convincingly that they had), of what was transpiring in the East sat by and watched as passive spectators.

The ambiguity of the good in a totalitarian state is that it is never able to be effectual, particularly if the good is pursued as a solitary, lonely and personal destiny. Had those other Germans—those good, silent, Germans who had come from the same backgrounds as Gerstein, who had the same bourgeois values, the same loyalty and love of *das Volk,* the same tincture of anti-Semitism, and the same Christian conscience—decided to impede and obstruct as Gerstein did, the extermination machinery would have still continued to work, but, as Friedländer concludes, "hundreds of thousands of victims would have been saved."

Guenter Lewy   (review date July 1969)

SOURCE: "A Question of Conscience," in *Commentary,* Vol. 48, No. 1, July, 1969, pp. 71-2, 74.

[*In the following review, Lewy discusses the ethical dilemmas Friedländer explores in* Kurt Gerstein: The Ambiguity of Good, *examining at length the moral untenability of both blind obedience to the law and complete reliance on conscience.*]

The story of Kurt Gerstein involves one of the most bizarre episodes of the Nazi era, a period of human history not lacking in the fantastic. Gerstein was an *SS Obersturmführer,* in charge of supplying the deadly Zyklon B gas to Hitler's murder factories. At the same time, he was a member of the Confessing Church, an opponent of Nazism, and a man who repeatedly risked his life in attempts to alert the Western world and the Vatican to what was happening in the Nazi death camps. At the end of the war Gerstein surrendered to the French; then, in July 1945, he was found dead in a prison cell in Paris, an apparent case of suicide.

This, in very broad outline, is the story of Kurt Gerstein, a story that was popularized and brought to the attention of a wide audience by Rolph Hochhuth's play *The Deputy,* of which Gerstein is one of the heroes. As is so often the case, however, reality is more intricate than a playwright's interpretation. Saul Friedländer, a professor of contemporary history at the Graduate Institute of International Studies in Geneva, and best known for his work of documentation, ***Pius XII and the Third Reich,*** through painstaking research has been able to reconstruct the actual drama of Kurt Gerstein. Beyond telling the life story of one rather unique man, Friedländer attempts [in ***Kurt Gerstein: The Ambiguity of Good***] to come to grips with the moral dilemmas of an entire society. As I shall try to show later, the ramifications of these dilemmas reach into our own lives today.

The early years of Kurt Gerstein do not reveal any very unusual traits: Friedländer calls him "a German like so many others." Born at Münster in 1905, he grew up in a Protestant Prussian middle-class family; his father was an ardent nationalist and later a convinced Nazi. Young Gerstein, too, shared the intense nationalism of so many members of his generation; as a student at the University of Marburg he joined one of the most chauvinistic fraternities in Germany. But he was also a deeply religious person, preoccupied with feelings of guilt and a longing for purity. He became actively involved in the Evangelical Youth Movement, and when the Nazis, in late 1933, insisted on merging this organization into the Hitler Youth, Gerstein protested. Not that he was opposed to Hitler's political aims—Gerstein had joined the Nazi party in May 1933, and for a long time he continued to insist on his loyalty to the Führer. However, he was seriously disturbed by the Nazis' neo-paganism, and he felt duty bound to insist that a nation without God was "a dangerous thing."

During the following years, Gerstein wrote and distributed pamphlets setting forth this view. He was twice arrested and in October 1936 he was expelled from the Nazi party. In a letter which he wrote in 1938 and which he mailed to his uncle in America, he spoke of tragedies arising "from loss of intellectual freedom, religious freedom, and justice." But after the outbreak of the war and Hitler's impressive early victories, Gerstein's attitude to the Nazi regime changed again. He agreed to write for the Hitler Youth and in August 1940 he sought reinstatement in the party. A few months later, or perhaps even earlier, he applied for service in the Waffen-SS and in March 1941 he joined the military branch of the Nazi elite guard.

The motives for this decision are not altogether clear. At war's end Gerstein said that he had wanted to find out for himself about the Nazis' compulsory euthanasia program for the insane and mentally retarded (his sister-in-law had been one of its victims). Then, after seeing clearly into this dreadful mechanism, he wanted to "cry it aloud to the whole nation." But Friedländer thinks that Gerstein's motives were more complex. There is evidence that Gerstein talked about joining the Waffen-SS as early as the end of 1939, well before the first rumors about the killing of the feeble-minded had begun to circulate. Furthermore, the question of how a person twice arrested by the Gestapo could be accepted into the Waffen-SS—at that time still an elite force—remains an enigma.

After basic military training, Gerstein, on account of his technical proficiency, was assigned to the office of the Hygienic Chief of the Waffen-SS. Here he distinguished himself in constructing disinfection and water-purifying equipment, and in January 1942 became head of disinfection services, with the rank of *Obersturmführer.* It was this office that soon thereafter was given charge of supplying the lethal gas for the death camps, and in August 1942 Gerstein personally witnessed mass gassings at Belzec and Treblinka. The experience proved so shattering that from that time on, and in a perfectly reckless manner, he began to reveal the details of the machinery of the Final Solution to a large number of influential people. Contrary to the dramatic account in *The Deputy,* he failed to gain admittance to the Papal nuncio in Berlin, but he did succeed in telling his horrifying tale to several neutral diplomats, German churchmen, and many others.

To Gerstein's utter dismay and distress, nothing happened as the result of his revelations that mass murder was being committed on an unprecedented scale. The Pope and the German churchmen maintained a discreet silence; the Western Allies, while denouncing the crimes, rejected proposals to bomb the gas chambers or the transportation system leading to the death camps. The machinery of destruction continued to function smoothly—with the increasingly distraught Gerstein as the chief purchasing agent of the deadly Zyklon B gas. Here begins the element of high tragedy. After the war Gerstein asserted that he had been able to divert and destroy several shipments of gas, but a German Denazification Court in 1950, while accepting the truth of this assertion—for which substantiating testimony is available—nevertheless refused to exonerate Gerstein: "After his experiences in the Belzec camp, he might have been expected to resist, with all the strength at his command, being made the tool of an organized mass murder." This he did not do. In fact, he became a cog in the machinery of the Final Solution. Despite the fact that Gerstein had destroyed trifling quantities of the gas supplied by him, said the court, and had made courageous attempts to inform the world of the murder of the Jews, he could not be freed of a share of responsibility for the crimes which his actions had facilitated.

In January 1965, Gerstein was rehabilitated in West Germany. Kurt Kiesinger, then prime minister of Baden-Würtemberg, based his decision on the fact that "Gerstein resisted National Socialist despotism with all his strength and suffered consequent disadvantage." Friedländer welcomes this rehabilitation, but finds that the reasons given do not sufficiently come to grips with the earlier condemnation. He argues that unlike most "good" Germans who remained quiet while millions of Jews died, Gerstein accommodated himself to the crime in order to resist it—risking his life in the process. Under a totalitarian regime resistance can be carried out only from within the system. The resister, therefore, often seems indistinguishable from the executioner. Had there been in Germany thousands or even hundreds of Gersteins to divert shipments of gas or cause files to go astray or instigate delays in the construction of the gas chambers or even to warn Jews, then hundreds of thousands of victims would have been saved by these "accomplices" of the regime. Much of Gerstein's tragedy, Friedländer concludes, lay in the loneliness of his action: "his appeals having brought no response and his dedication having proved a solitary commitment, his sacrifice appeared 'useless' and became 'guilt.' "

Friedländer's reasoning is unexceptionable but it does not fully clarify the moral issue posed by the so-called "inner emigration" of officials who stayed at their jobs in order to ameliorate the disastrous results of the system they continued to serve. How does one balance the good such men did against the horrible crimes which resulted from the continued fulfillment of their official duties? Is it not true that the machinery of extermination was able to grind away mercilessly precisely because the Globkes, Weizsäckers, and Gersteins remained at their posts, all the while consoling themselves that their inner opposition plus an occasional act of necessarily minor sabotage left them with clean hands?

If the answers to such questions are difficult to find, it is equally hard to draw the proper lessons to be learned from these tragic events—a task not undertaken by Friedländer but relevant to the moral vocabulary of our time. In a letter written in March 1944, the elder Gerstein reassured his son Kurt on the subject of the latter's guilt feelings: "The person who bears the responsibility is the man who gives the orders, not the one who carries them out. There can be no question of disobedience. You must do what you are ordered to do. As an old official and a former Prussian officer, that is the way I learned things." When the orders in question involve deeds that outrage all accepted canons of morality, it is not difficult to reject this kind of insistence on unquestioning obedience; thus, the Nuremberg courts repudiated the plea of obedience to superior orders by declaring that "individuals have international duties which transcend the national obligations of obedience imposed by the individual State." But the problem becomes more complicated when the immorality or injustice of the actions one is ordered to perform is less clear.

Ever since the revelation of the hideous crimes committed by the Nazis—crimes whose perpetrators often defended themselves by pleading that they were merely following orders—it has become fashionable to celebrate the primacy of the individual's conscience over the commands of the state. Now, the tradition of subjecting legality to the scrutiny and judgment of morality is an old and honorable one, and in some cases disobedience to law can clearly become a moral duty. But are we today perhaps in danger of going to the opposite extreme from that of the Nazi officials who faithfully carried out Hitler's monstrous orders? Is the only lesson to be learned from the Nazi experience that we should distrust all legality, presume it to be in the wrong unless proved otherwise, and follow the commands of our private judgments without regard to the social consequences of our actions?

Unthinking obedience to law just because it is law can lead to gross immorality, but absolute reliance on conscience rather than on law can bring about an equally undesirable state of affairs. In such a situation, the racist, following his conscience, will push around the defender of minority causes, militant Rightists will break up meetings of their opponents on the Left with the justification that they are following the dictates of their own moral convictions. In short, the absolute reliance on conscience leads to an absolute reliance on raw force, with the outcome of disagreements determined by the criterion of strength and ruthlessness. One need hardly add that a Hitler or a Himmler would undoubtedly pass with flying colors the test of strong personal convictions and sincerity.

In this country, the conflict between legality and morality was revived in the days of Martin Luther King's nonviolent civil-rights movement and lives on in the crisis of confidence in democratic government engendered by the war in Vietnam. But uncritical praise of civil disobedience and resistance to a law branded as unjust or immoral has by now itself become an important factor in the spread of hate and violence, and has seriously weakened the social fabric of America. Has the time not come to call a moratorium on the cult of conscience? I do not wish to belabor a point that has been forcefully and eloquently argued in these pages by Nathan Glazer and others, but I do wish to register the opinion that it is possible to criticize American policy and the conduct of the war in Vietnam, on political as well as moral grounds, without speaking of genocide; and that this odious comparison in fact constitutes a veritable act of blasphemy toward the memory of the six million dead, to say nothing of the gross historical obtuseness it reveals.

The moral problem faced by Kurt Gerstein was at once easier and more difficult than the dilemmas we face today. The evil Gerstein confronted was overwhelming and obvious, but the price exacted for his fidelity to conscience was infinitely higher than that which anyone is expected to pay today. The lessons to be learned from Gerstein's predicament are complex and cannot be deduced by crude analogies. But as little as blind and unqualified subservience to law will the apotheosis of conscience help us to act in conformity with our political and moral heritage.

Rose G. Lewis (review date January 1976)

SOURCE: "Shadowboxing," in *Commentary,* Vol. 61, No. 1, January, 1976, pp. 89-92, 94.

[*In the following review of* Arabs and Israelis, *Lewis criticizes Friedländer for inadequately defending Judaism and Israel against the arguments of Marxist Arabs.*]

It was in 1939, I think, that the Arabs for the first time officially refused to talk with the Jewish Palestinians. Their intransigence began, at any rate, years before there were Arab refugees, or occupied territories, or even an independent Israel. What did exist at that time was the claim of Jewish entitlement to basic rights in Palestine and a Jewish demand for self-determination, equality, and freedom from Arab rule. These were ideas so unexpected and so shocking to the Arab mind that, apparently, no compromise with them could be imagined and no discussion was thought possible.

Since then, the Arab policy of non-communication has become fixed in the public awareness and any conversation between an Arab and an Israeli can be viewed as something of a happening in and of itself. So it is that, concerning this recent conversation, [*Arabs and Israelis: A Dialogue*], (which has already been published in France and in Israel and is now translated into English), primary significance is seen in the fact that a "genuine dialogue" took place at all. "For the first time *they* have agreed to meet, to speak together," exclaims France's *Le Figaro* about the book. "In the course of its pages myths crumble, preconceptions fall apart." Strictly speaking, neither of these statements happens to be true. Nonetheless, *Le Figaro's* sentiment does reflect the air of the book. That a few men sat and talked together for three days is presented as such an earthshaking event that, at the very least, something somewhere must surely have crumbled and fallen apart.

The characters in this drama are not easily identifiable as

spokesmen for their governments or for specific political groups. They are only, in a general sort of way, held to be representative of certain sensibilities and points of view. The Israeli, Saul Friedlander, is described as a "liberal in the Anglo-Saxon tradition" and representative of the "liberal current of thought of Israel's politico-intellectual class." He is "in favor of more active attempts to achieve a form of peace that combines justice with security." Friedlander, then, is what is now known as a dove. He was born in Prague in 1932 and is a professor of history at the Hebrew University in Jerusalem and the Graduate Institute of International Relations in Geneva.

Mahmoud Hussein is harder to bring into focus. The name, it turns out, is a pseudonym for not one but *two* Arabs whom, however, we hear speaking in only a single undifferentiated voice throughout the book. Their real names are Bahgat Elnadi and Adel Rifaat. They are Egyptians, recently turned thirty, and Communists since adolescence, who have "divided their lives among militant activism, prison (in Egypt), and exile." They are settled in Paris. Rifaat, while claiming to be a dedicated Marxist, is a Jewish convert to Islam, though the book does not mention it. Mahmoud Hussein's voice, we are told, is the voice of the Arab avant-garde and "an echo of the popular voice . . . typical of the style of reasoning" heard in Cairo and Damascus.

The man who brought the three together around the tape recorder, and who serves as moderator, is Jean Lacouture, who has been a Cairo correspondent for *France-Soir* and a foreign correspondent for *Le Monde.* He had long wished to set up a meeting of this sort, Lacouture writes, and he hoped "more than anything else to show that a lively exchange of views is more fertile than a fight to the death."

Despite this hope, Lacouture expected that he would be called upon often to "cool off the atmosphere or even to stop fights." That such intervention turned out to be unnecessary pleased him very much. The argument, indeed, does not appear to have been very heated, let alone bloody. And it ended, also, not with a bang. There was a last, lengthy statement from Hussein. Then Friedlander, asked for his concluding remarks, responded simply that he had nothing more to add. At this point Lacouture brings the curtain down with a flourish. "How can I convey the significance of that silence?" he asks. It "proved to us all that our meeting had not been in vain." But Friedlander, in an afterword, goes on to interpret his own silence. What he had really meant, he says, was that there seemed no further point in repeating arguments which had already been gone over several times and he was in fact expressing disappointment at the failure to establish a genuine dialogue or to achieve real understanding.

It would appear, then, that the "fertility" of the meeting was finally questionable, and it is difficult in the reading to uncover any promising seeds of fruitfulness. There is in fact little movement, first to last, and the speakers exit pretty much as they entered. They leave behind no hint of a mutually acceptable accommodation, nor have they added much to the prevailing public knowledge. What the book does do, however, is to present a view of the ideological battlefield and of the arguments lined up on either side by these particular types of protagonists. From this standpoint, the debate is worth examination.

We find, at the outset, that the discussion proceeds from some significant assumptions which appear to be held on both sides. One of these assumptions is that there was no important conflict between Arabs and Jews—indeed, no pertinent Arab-Jewish history at all—before modern Zionism. The opening remarks on "The Past," therefore, go back to a point roughly around 1945. That young Maoists can date the world from the day they were born is not surprising. What is odd is that a history professor should let them get away with it. In any event, ignoring the last two thousand years of the history of the Jewish people in the Middle East and in Palestine gives Hussein the freedom to launch the customary assault upon Israel as a foreign body in an Arab world and a country without "authenticity." To all this, Friedlander responds only with some gentle probing. Were Arab perceptions, perhaps, not quite as Hussein described them? Might something more be said about Egyptian attitudes? Just a few small corrections of fact.

In *Arabs and Israelis* Friedlander, outnumbered and out-talked, is tolerant, didactic, defensive, and finally weary. He has no appetite for ideological battle.

—*Rose G. Lewis*

Friedlander makes no attempt to stand up to these first hard-hitting charges against Israel, though they are of course the heart of the matter. Certainly he does nothing so shrill as to suggest that the "original sin" may have been the thirteen centuries of Arab oppression of the Jewish people within as well as outside its homeland. Insofar as silence denotes acquiescence, Friedlander concedes the intruder status in the Middle East into which Hussein has cast Israel and the Israelis. It is a vital point, and round one obviously goes to the Arabs.

A second underlying assumption of the debate is that the only significant imperialism in the Middle East has been European. One of Hussein's major contentions, from which several others flow, is that Arab problems stem uniquely from European imperialism and that the Arabs' primary need therefore is to cast out all Western influence. This tells only a small part of the story, of course. For all but one century or so of the past twelve or thirteen centuries, the prevailing empires in the Middle East have been Arab, Egyptian, and Turkish. Under these Muslim imperialisms, the Jews also were a subject people, they also were exploited, and in addition they suffered from the extra burdens and humiliations of official religious discrimination and local fanaticism.

Nor were the Jews in the Muslim countries, and the Jews similarly afflicted in Christian countries, able except in

meager numbers to take refuge in their own homeland. Muslim imperialist policies had consigned Palestine to a backwater of empire, badly protected, left to raiding nomads and avaricious administrators and economic and physical decay. For their own imperialist reasons, for example, the Mamluk rulers of the 14th-century Egyptian empire deliberately destroyed the harbors and the fertile coastal plains of Palestine and made that area the desert that it remained until the 20th century.

On the subject of imperialism, incidentally, Lacouture adds an interesting comment. "Personally," he says at one point, "my argument for the legitimacy of the State of Israel is largely based on this resistance to a colonial force. It is this struggle for liberation, rather than the struggle of Judah Maccabee, that justifies Israel's existence in my mind." Lacouture's words hang somewhat in midair, and it seems that he is referring to the struggle against the English. What is significant, however, is that for him, as for so many others today, a national-liberation movement requires an oppressive imperialism nearby to give it legitimacy. The many centuries of Arab, Egyptian, and Ottoman imperialism and the accompanying oppression of the Jewish people in and out of Palestine would therefore seem to have some usefulness as an argument in support of Israel's claims. Friedlander gives no attention to this history, nor does he challenge the most sweeping Arab implications about European imperialism and its impact upon the various peoples in the Middle East. It is another major strategic advance for Hussein, and one from which he is able to mount attack after attack upon Israel as merely the servant and symbol of the West in the oppression of the Arab.

Finally, both Friedlander and Hussein ignore altogether the many hundreds of thousands of Jewish refugees who since 1940 have fled from Arab countries. These indigenous Middle Eastern peoples, who can with full semantic propriety be called Jewish Arabs, today make up a majority of the Jewish Israelis. To all our speakers, they are invisible.

It is therefore possible for Friedlander to assert that "for the Israeli man in the street the Arabs . . . were somewhat mythical figures before the 1967 war." It is therefore possible for Lacouture to say that in the last few years the Arabs have "accepted the permanent presence of the Jewish people in the Middle East. In some sense, this was a step forward. . . ." It is therefore possible for Hussein to talk about a "fresh and progressive attitude" among Arabs which gives the Jews "a place in Palestine as a distinct community for the first time." And later Hussein is able to advance as "new" and "innovative" the idea of a Palestine made up of "a Jewish community, a Muslim community, and even a distinct Christian community."

Hussein is in fact describing the organization of the old Muslim empires. Within them, and in Palestine, the Jews were always recognized as distinct communities with some limited degrees of autonomy. Indeed, from the point of view of Middle Eastern history, Israel can be viewed as a coming together of these historic Jewish communities into one self-governing whole. However, it must be remembered that these *millets,* as they were called, suffered consistently from the exploitation and discrimination and threats of an assertive Arab majority. Hussein's new and innovative idea, therefore, is in reality merely a return to the old Arab imperialism. The Arabs will agree, he offers, to recognize the Israelis as a *millet* if the Israelis will submit once again to the political limitations and the economic restrictions and even to the "cultural adaptations" which an Arab majority will see fit to impose. "Our starting point," states Hussein imperiously, "is not what is acceptable to Israel, but what is required by the Arabs." This may be questionable Marxism—but it is certainly orthodox Islam. Has Hussein never heard of the Covenants of Omar? What is even more to the point, has Friedlander never heard of the Covenants of Omar? *He* doesn't mention them, either.

Friedlander's defense of Israel comes from other quarters. He asks, first of all, for understanding of "the constant, living bond between the Jewish people and the land of Israel." He speaks of the Jewish religion, and Jewish prayers, and "an aspiration that is literally almost two thousand years old."

It would be interesting to know why Friedlander thought that these two young Arabs—either as Marxists or as Muslims—could be expected to be responsive to Jewish religious sensibilities. One would think that the record would lead to quite the opposite conclusion. Marxism and Islam, as religions, and each in its own way, have asserted a dogmatic and historic precedence over Judaism and, in fact, a moral imperative to triumph over it. Since Friedlander makes plain that he had hoped to establish some common base of understanding with the Arabs, one must wonder why he chose this approach. It failed, of course.

Friedlander also strives for recognition by Hussein of the problems of Israeli security and the preservation of Israeli independence. To this he can get no response which is not ultimately negative. Hussein will only discuss *rights,* and these only, he says again and again, in the context of the Middle East and its traditions. In this context he clearly does not believe that Israel has a right to independence. He insists upon "the need to replace the old language with a new one, to speak of natural and inalienable rights instead of the balance of power and systems of security. . . . The Arab peoples reason in terms of fundamental rights," he repeats.

Therefore, if Friedlander has not vigorously and effectively defended the fundamental, natural, inalienable, and historic rights of the Jewish people in the Middle East, if he has not forcefully attacked the Arabs for their historic as well as more recent denial of those rights, upon what ground does he stand in demanding Arab recognition of the security of the State? Yet he rests his case simply, at the end as in the beginning, upon a brief statement of the religious bond alone.

For the rest, the book contains much dispute about such matters as who did what in 1967, and who thought what in 1973, and who said what in 1920. There is much lengthy discourse about politicians and people, terrorism and borders, Zionism, Jerusalem, and plans for peace. Only in some lesser sense can one call the book a dialogue; the contacts of perception and purpose are tangential at best.

The two young Arabs are altogether self-righteous and arrogant, given to torrents of numbing radical rhetoric and such a passion of theory and dogma that the real world fades into abstraction and all compromise becomes heresy. They speak in the name of an Arab people whom they paint larger than life with humiliations, agitations, frustrations, and a feverish intensity of needs and demands and revolutionary visions. All other peoples are blocked from view, and the Israelis become shadows and symbols, virtually without a reality of their own.

Friedlander, outnumbered and out-talked, is tolerant, didactic, defensive, and finally weary. He has no appetite for ideological battle. His goal is to achieve some degree of pragmatic understanding, but without really digging into the root assumptions of Arab theory and mythology. Above all, he does not wish to present the Arabs with a bill from the Jewish past. Apparently he does not wish to make them feel guilty. Thus, for example, he discusses the Holocaust, but makes no mention of any Arab massacres or persecutions of the Jewish people. In particular, he says nothing about the sad centuries of Jewish poverty and impotence and exploitation under Arab domination in Palestine. He is apologetic, and therefore defenseless, and in this he demonstrates all too well the ideological weakness of that "liberal current of thought" which he represents.

Amos Elon   (review date 15 July 1979)

SOURCE: "Alone in the World," in *The New York Times Book Review,* July 15, 1979, pp. 1, 27.

[*Elon is an Austrian-born Israeli journalist, historian, and novelist. In the following positive review of* When Memory Comes, *he discusses Friedländer's struggle with identity.*]

Saul Friedländer was born "in Prague at the worst possible moment, four months before Hitler came to power." In this harrowing, deeply moving memoir [**When Memory Comes**]—one part the Gothic tale of a Jewish orphan alone in Nazi-occupied France preparing to become a Catholic priest, the other part the diary he kept many years later in Jerusalem—he undertakes an evocative voyage into his past that is likely to leave many a reader shaken. This is not really a holocaust tale. Saul Friedländer knew nothing of the holocaust until afterward. He knew only a childhood whose calm was continually being shattered, the pieces falling away, picked up and arbitrarily reassembled into new patterns. He tells his tale in wonder, then awe—at how it all happened, that in 10 years he changed his identity four times, his religion twice, his name five times.

He was born to an "assimilated family" that knew little of its Jewishness. His Czechoslovak nanny Vlasta took him to "a great many churches"; only later, as an adult, did he learn of Prague's synagogues. As a young man after the war he became an ardent, militant believer in the Zionist remedy to Jewish insecurity; that Zionism was not necessarily a remedy he also discovered only at a much later date. All this, coupled with the fact that when his parents perished he perceived only vaguely what was happening to them and to him, could not have made this voyage into the past any easier.

"When knowledge comes, memory comes too, little by little," he says. "Knowledge and memory are one and the same thing." Friedländer has spent most of his adult life as a historian and political scientist. His books include *Pius XII and the Third Reich, Prelude to Downfall: Hitler and the United States, 1939-1941, History and Psychoanalysis* and *Kurt Gerstein: The Ambiguity of Good.* Among the many articles he has written are those dealing with psychohistory and the analysis of the Nazi mind. Perhaps with his increasing intellectual forays into the world of Nazism and the world that collapsed before he knew it has come the need and the ability to look into his own experience as well.

He was born Pavel Friedländer in 1932. The first rumblings of upheaval sounded before he was six, when he was shunted into an English-language school in Prague where he remained for a short time before the family fled to France in the wake of Hitler's march into Czechoslovakia. In Paris he became Paul Friedländer, and while his parents struggled to find a new livelihood, he was placed in a boarding "home" at Montmorency, his first encounter with a "traditional" Jewish atmosphere. He was terrorized, tied to a tree and beaten by the earlocked and yarmulked Yiddish-speaking children who had fled Eastern Europe and thought him a "goy," because he was different.

When the Germans marched into France, the family fled southward to Néris-les Bains, near Orleans. The next two years gave the boy "the impression of being a happy period . . . all three of us were together again. Better still, we were crowded together in the intimacy of a tiny dwelling." The boy went to a French school in nearby Montluçon.

In July 1942 the roundup of foreign Jews begins. Panicking, his parents place him in a nearby Jewish boarding school, a move that he cannot fathom even today. The inevitable happens. The children over 10 were the first to be taken away by the gendarmes of Vichy. The younger ones ran into the forest before the gendarmes returned the following day. "I didn't sleep. I had not the feeling of danger, quite the contrary: the warm breeze, the rustling of the trees, the wispy clouds that from time to time drifted across the stars filled me with a sense of well-being."

A friend of his parents returns him to Néris, where, only a few days later, his final memory of family life takes place. He is placed in the hands of Madame M. de L., a local patrician who has befriended the family and responds to his mother's plea. "In my despair I am turning to you," Friedländer's mother wrote to Madame de L., "We have succeeded for the moment . . . in saving our boy. . . . I beg you, dear madame, to look after our child and assure him your protection. . . . I have complete confidence in your goodness and understanding. . . . [Our] fate . . . is now in God's hands. . . . If we must disappear, we will at least have the happiness of knowing that our beloved child has been saved. . . . We can no longer exist legally. . . ."

His parents make a futile attempt to cross into Switzerland, are turned over by the Swiss to the French gendarmerie, who send them off on a train bound for Auschwitz. The 9-year-old Paul Friedländer is turned over (at the urging of Madame M. de L.) to the strictest of French Catholic disciplines, the school of Saint-Béranger, where he becomes Paul-Henri Ferland and embraces another self.

"As I entered the portals of Saint-Béranger, the boarding school of the Sodality where I was to live from now on, I became . . . Paul-Henri Ferland, an unequivocally Catholic name to which Marie was added at my baptism, so as to make it even more authentic, or perhaps because it was an invocation of the protection of the Virgin, the heavenly mother safe from torment, less vulnerable than the earthly mother who at this very moment the whirlwind was already sweeping away . . . I passed over to Catholicism body and soul."

> **When knowledge comes, memory comes too, little by little. Knowledge and memory are one and the same thing.**
>
> —*Saul Friedländer*

Today, looking back, as he tries to picture the world of the Sodality, it is unreal, nothing remains, it has turned to dust, and yet, "perhaps I . . . now preserve, in the very depths of myself, certain disparate, incompatible fragments of existence . . . like those shards of steel that survivors of great battles sometimes carry about inside their bodies." His embrace of Catholicism was apparently total. But in 1946, as the result of an interview with Father L., as the 14-year-old was about to enter the Jesuit seminary at Saint-Etienne to prepare for the Catholic priesthood, Paul Friedländer reemerges. Father L. asks, "didn't your parents die at Auschwitz?" and, discovering the boy's ignorance, explains what has happened and what anti-Semitism has wrought.

He now becomes the ward of a Jewish family in Paris, where he enters a lycée, discovers Communism but embraces Zionism, not by way of a "renewal by contact with buried emotional levels," but rather "as a result of logical argument, of a simple line of reasoning . . . the essential pieces of a puzzle that heretofore had made no sense were falling into place. For the first time, I felt myself to be Jewish—no longer despite myself or secretly, but through a sensation of absolute loyalty . . . something had changed. A tie had been re-established, an identity was emerging."

"People often told me I looked sad. I was not really sad, but I would sometimes fall into a sort of depression, and even though my plans for the future were apparently clear cut . . . I was all alone in the world." A few weeks before he is to complete his baccalaureate, the boy runs away from his foster home and from France on an illegal immigrant ship bound for Palestine. He is fired by a dream of "communion and community." This, too, was to fail; as he sets out to meet his new fate he changes his name again, from Paul to the Hebrew Shaul, and then again to Saul.

"It is impossible to know which name I am," he writes today, "and that, in the final analysis, seems to me sufficient expression of a real and profound confusion." The confusion, and its pain, is the main theme of this voyage. One wonders at the courage that made him embark upon it. He cannot be searching for roots. He knows that any he might have had were effectively destroyed when he was 6 years old; those that he might have found in Israel, one gathers, seem to have eluded him to this day. His complicated and contradictory relationship with Israel, albeit that he is now the father of three Israeli children and divides his year between his home in Jerusalem and his posts as professor of history at the universities of Tel Aviv and Geneva, becomes clear as he travels back and forth in time and place, juxtaposing the past against a discordant present.

In Israel, the feeling of being an outsider was in him from the beginning: "I was as full of *admiration* of my seventeen-year-old friends, those 'born in Israel,' as Tonio Kröger (in Thomas Mann's novella) was of blond Hans Hansen or blonde Inge Holm—and for the same reasons. . . ." And yet, after the first flush had worn off, "the enthusiasm of my early days in Israel began to dwindle, certainly, giving way, little by little, to a contradictory vision. . . . What lay behind this growing contradiction between a basic faith and the more and more problematic aspects of daily life? . . . What is the point, the invisible line beyond which the imperfections of everyday life come to undermine the very meaning of the undertaking?"

It was to a spiritual home that the young man finally came to rest. He spent a year "outside of time" in Sweden, in 1957, with an uncle who had become director of an institution for mentally-ill children. In an encounter with two of them—perhaps the most forceful scene in the book—their powerlessness became, confusedly at first, then clearly, an obsessive symbol, a provocation that opened doors for him that would never close. In his uncle's library he discovered the works of Martin Buber—*On Judaism, Tales of the Hassidim* and *The Legend of the Baal-Shem.* He

> read and reread them several times, and as the result of being in a foreign country, and of a certain solitude too, I felt . . . the hidden grace of this secret world of Hassidism. But, more than this, for the first time I began to feel a clear difference between my identification with Israel, which for a time at least seemed to me to be superficial and almost empty of meaning, and a feeling of my Jewishness, certain aspects of which appeared to me in this unusual setting to be suddenly endowed with a new, mysterious, powerful, magnificent dimension.

This is not the story of parts merging into a whole. The parts remain Pavel, Paul, Paul-Henri-Marie, Shaul—each a separate entity carrying its own meaning. The sum of these parts that became Saul somehow still eludes the author, but these fragments will haunt the reader.

Leon Wieseltier (review date 25 October 1979)

SOURCE: "Between Paris and Jerusalem," in *The New York Review of Books,* Vol. XXVI, No. 16, October 25, 1979, pp. 3-4.

[*An American journalist and critic, Wieseltier is the literary editor of* The New Republic. *In the following review of* When Memory Comes, *he examines the ramifications for contemporary Jews and Israelis of the struggle for Jewish survival since World War II.*]

On June 11, 1942, Heinrich Himmler demanded 100,000 Jews of France, for Auschwitz. Pierre Laval agreed in July to turn over 10,000. This would "cleanse France of its foreign Jewry": the deportations, Laval insisted, would take only Jews from Germany and Central Europe who had sought refuge in the Unoccupied Zone. The roundups began at once. Switzerland sealed its frontiers. "We cannot turn our country into a sponge for Europe," the Swiss Minister of Justice announced. Jews who stole across were promptly returned to their fate. Among these were Jan and Elli Friedländer of Prague. They later perished, as planned, at Auschwitz. In Britain Herbert Morrison, the Home Secretary, entertained a proposal to admit at least the children of Vichy's doomed Jews. The Foreign Office, however, balked. Sir Alexander Cadogan, Under-Secretary at the Foreign Office, observed that "it seems to me wrong to support bringing children to this country at present." Among these children was Jan and Elli's ten-year-old son, Pavel.

Pavel Friedländer survived the war. He had been baptized, becoming Paul-Henri Marie Ferland, and was harbored in the doctrinal gloom of a Catholic seminary in the Indre, where he gladly quit the storm outside for the church, and for its calming certainties. Paul-Henri Ferland was no longer a victim:

> The simple unquestioning faith drummed into us was . . . the one I needed. . . . I had passed over to Catholicism, body and soul. . . . I felt at ease within a community of those who had nothing but scorn for Jews. . . . I had the feeling . . . of having passed over to the compact, invincible majority, of no longer belonging to the camp of the persecuted, but, potentially at least, to that of the persecutors.

The boy who had been fascinated by the tales of the Maccabees his father told on Hanukkah now adored the Virgin and Pétain, the Savior of France. In time France was delivered from its savior. The war ended, but no family returned for Paul-Henri. The seminarist was preparing for his novitiate when a charitable priest, pausing beside the church altar, told him about Auschwitz.

> And so, in front of this obscure Christ, I listened: Auschwitz, the trains, the gas chambers, the crematory ovens, the millions of dead. . . . For the first time I felt myself to be Jewish—no longer despite myself or secretly, but through a sensation of absolute loyalty. It is true that I knew nothing of Judaism and was still a Catholic. But something had changed. A tie had been reestablished, an identity was emerging, a confused one certainly . . . but from that day forward . . .

there could be no doubt: in some manner or
other I was Jewish. . . .

He was Pavel again, the impersonation was ended, but he
did not know who Pavel was.

Pavel had been born in 1932 into the assimilated Jewish
bourgeoisie of Prague. Jan Friedländer's book plates displayed a score by Chopin set within a Star of David, an
emblem of an honorable delusion. "Judaism as a religion
had completely disappeared" from Pavel's family, Friedländer writes, and the filaments of tradition that had ran-
domly come down to him could not make up the Jewishness for which he was renouncing his ecclesiastical haven.
"Had I been born of a 'really' Jewish family I would at
least have had coherent memories. . . ." The troubled orphan moved to Paris, where he lived with Russian Jews,
and among them found

> instead of reserve and carefully controlled emo-
> tions, and the apparent coldness [of my back-
> ground], a noisy exuberance, very soon carried
> to extremes; instead of the almost total absence
> of a Jewish tradition, an atmosphere saturated
> with Jewish emotions, allusions, customs, man-
> nerisms.

From his guardian Pavel first learned, in 1946, of Eretz Israel.

The restitution of Pavel Friedländer's Jewishness eventually took the form of Zionism. For Pavel, as for many of
Europe's other surviving Jews, Zionism was now "a simple line of reasoning": a state was required. From the autumn of 1947 Pavel made of Zionism "the most important
thing in my life." When his Socialist Zionist group refused
to arrange his passage to Palestine, Pavel joined Betar, the
militant youth movement of Menahem Begin's Irgun, and
ran away to Marseille, to board a ship carrying arms to
Begin's underground. The ship was the *Altalena.*

Sailing from Port-de-Bouc on June 11, 1948, the *Altalena*
was still at sea when the first Arab-Israeli truce went into
effect. The Irgun command refused to turn over the ship's
ammunition; David Ben-Gurion correctly recognized a
threat to his young government, and ordered the vessel attacked. Israeli forces on the coast opened fire, the ship
burst into flame, twenty people died. On June 21 the *Altalena* docked in Tel Aviv. What remained of the Irgun
was disbanded. Menahem Begin went into opposition, and
the humiliation of this defeat still rankles. Pavel went to
Nira, a farming village near Natanya, and became Shaul.

In the bright early days of the state, Shaul studied Hebrew, danced *horas,* and tried to do his part. But still,

> Should I confess that since the beginning I had
> nonetheless had vague, confused, intermittent
> feelings that something was missing?

He would wander to the sea to read Fromentin—"I
thought I was thus affirming, for myself alone, the permanence of a culture that remained the only one that mattered to me." In the army he worked on "my secret masterpiece," a map of the Paris *métro,* reconstructed from
memory in Jaffa. "I was a person divided," an aesthete
beached in the cruel Levant. Nor was that all. "I was be-

coming more and more aware of the future dilemmas, almost impossible to grasp, of this first period [of Israel's
history]." There appeared social, political, cultural contradictions. The dream began to disappoint. Shaul understood that dreams often do; but still there remained a
question:

> What is the point, the invisible line, beyond
> which the imperfections of everyday life come to
> undermine the very meaning of the undertaking?

Shaul Friedländer became a distinguished historian at Hebrew University, an authority on the near-Final Solution.
He joined with members of left-wing groups who tried to
save the Jewish state from the more ruinous consequences
of nationalism, and sought out Arabs who would talk
about peace. He buried students killed in the wars. He returned to teach in Europe. But all this he did as Saul, his
last and most appropriate name. Saul: midway between
Pavel and Shaul, between Paris and Jerusalem, between
the burned-over world to which he fell heir and the slowly
dimming society he chose to serve.

The most remarkable feature of *When Memory Comes* is
its composure, an elegance that is unnerving. Friedländer
describes his experiences in lean, graceful sentences; his
language seems armored (even more formidably so in the
French) against the dissolution it describes. Yet dissolution triumphs. The pieces of memory do not cohere: *When
Memory Comes* is a significant work partly because of this
failure. Friedländer's life remains disrupted, despoiled of
its dreams; not least because of the honesty with which he
has attempted to discover what the death of the Jews
might mean.

For understanding Auschwitz, grand patterns of historical explanation have been proposed. Auschwitz has been
attributed to the evolution of European societies, econo-
mies, and political systems; to the contest between culture
and instinct, and the development of the demonic as a
force in the modern world; to the psychological consequences of unprecedented dislocations; to the contradictions of Jewish life in the Diaspora; and to the inevitable
eruption of the anti-Semitism that had polluted Europe for
centuries. It has even been ascribed to the resentment of
the West at the introduction of conscience by the Jews—
this is George Steiner's cranky contribution. The speculations continue to proliferate. Friedländer knows them, but
it is not as a historian that he has produced this book. He
has put aside the conventional logic of historical explanation, and does not even tell his own story in sequence. He
inserts pages from his Israeli journal into the account of
his childhood, and these seem abrupt and intrusive. Even
the structure of his memoir thus seems disconsolate; he refuses to impose narrative order upon his account of the catastrophes, because their victims cannot believe in their
necessity. They may be given causes but never reasons.

The author of *When Memory Comes* knows that memory
is not history. Memory's objects and gestures are not quite
past, and they are not yet interpreted. Memory is the accurate record of the partial, private, passive character of experience. Thus what is gained from memory is incomplete,
and it is all the more illuminating, because memory is the
consciousness of things and events that have not yet disap-

peared completely into knowledge—the panic in the eyes, the halt in the whisper, the flavor of the slop, the stench of the smoke. Such are the memories with which Friedländer has tried to heal the terrifying gaps in his life. Memory makes parting impossible.

Friedländer's book is, I think, a major document of Jewish bitterness in this century. American Jews can learn something from its bitterness, for they tend to be much too enthusiastic in their sorrow. When one considers the states of spiritual exaltation into which some American Jews are cast by "the Holocaust," it almost seems necessary to remind them that the disaster might better not have occurred. Six million dead are no occasion for pride, only for rage, and that rage is missing. The extermination of Europe's Jews has become a "growth experience" for too many Americans.

And the struggle in Israel as well. About this, too, American Jews take too much pride too soon. How many are aware that the Israel which fires their imaginations is dying, and not at the hands of Arabs? Friedländer writes on this matter with rare candor. For the melancholy argument of his book is that, if things did not work out for the Jews in Europe, they are not exactly working out for them in Israel either: "The peace initiatives are going to bring to light the hidden contradictions of our society," Friedländer wrote after Sadat's visit to Jerusalem:

> the will to reach a settlement, certainly, but also territorial ambitions; the will to compromise, but also the belief in a particular and decisive right to the land of Eretz Israel; the will to return to normal, but perhaps also an inability to accept what is normal.

He faithfully reports the gathering uncertainties of Israeli society, and soberly concludes:

> I have done my best in these pages to avoid any sort of strictly political reflections. It is nonetheless true that political decisions now dominate our lives and will determine the future of all of us. If we must one day take up arms again, not to defend what must be defended at all costs, but because we will not have been able to accept compromise at the proper moment, what today is only a temporary situation will have then become the very essence of the gravest of dilemmas, the very essence of tragedy.

Throughout his life, Saul Friedländer has seen one nation's triumphant convictions quickly become another nation's oppressive facts. This often happened to the Jews, and it has happened to the Palestinians. Friedländer, who escaped the Nazis and fought the Arabs, has the courage to say so. Instead of offering hoarse and unthinking support, which serves mainly General Sharon and his army of chiliasts, American Jews committed to Israel would do well to consider, as Friedländer has, the reality of the Palestinians. "The permanence of the Jewish world," he writes, "but the permanence of the Arab world too."

Friedländer is without illusions (unlike many other doves). He recalls an exchange in Geneva with an impassioned young Palestinian from Ramallah. To Friedländer this seemed "a beginning of possible contact, a first step toward brotherhood." Two years later the same Palestinian masterminded the massacre at the Munich Olympics. There are Palestinians who must be met only on the battlefield. But Friedländer believes there are others as well, and that—when they finally come forward—Israelis must be prepared to honor their national needs. There are 750,000 Palestinians on the West Bank who wish to govern themselves, and for Israel's sake they had better.

Tamar Jacoby   (review date 4 July 1980)

SOURCE: "Selfhood and Resistance," in *Commonweal,* Vol. CVII, No. 13, July 4, 1980, pp. 406-08.

[*In the following excerpt, Jacoby offers a review of* When Memory Comes, *outlining the many changes in Friedländer's life and perceptions of himself, the past, and Israel.*]

In 1942 Pavel Friedlander's parents began to sense that the circle was closing in, and that as foreign Jewish refugees living in Vichy France, they could be certain of nothing in the future. They arranged for their son to be put in the care of the nuns of the Catholic Sodality. Rechristened Paul-Henri—an unmistakably French and Catholic name—the Czech boy passed the war years at Sodality boarding schools, unaware that his parents were deported and eventually killed at Auschwitz. In writing **When Memory Comes,** an elliptical, meditative account of his childhood and his decision to go to Palestine in 1947, Friedlander is trying to come to terms with his feeling that he lived "on the edges of catastrophe . . . not so much a victim as—a spectator."

But even in the safe and ordered world of the nuns, the boy was troubled by a strange "melancholy apathy." He sleepwalked and was unable to make friends. He became feverish and, deciding to let himself die, waded into an icy stream. When he recovered, his memory of his parents had faded. He buried himself in his studies, a seamless school routine, the certainties of the Catholic faith. When the resistance fighters arrived in August 1944, the nuns and their charges mourned the passing of Marshal Pétain; Paul-Henri stayed on at the school, studying to become a Jesuit priest. But then his unexplained moodiness returned—a growing, paralyzing fear of death that isolated him from friends and prevented him from working. He had never heard of Auschwitz and seemed to have forgotten that he was a Jew; he vaguely assumed that his parents had been delayed, perhaps by illness or quarantine, in coming to find him at the school. It was some months later, after a conversation with a Jesuit who might have become his teacher, that he realized they were dead: "For the first time, I felt myself to be Jewish." By 1947, when he left France for Israel, he was prepared to fight for the Zionist cause.

Looking back during the summer of 1977, Friedlander returns again and again to the "necessary defenses" that protect us from our own suffering. He writes of "the extraordinary mechanism of memory" and its power to conceal "the unbearable." He mentions a study done by a friend of children's perceptions of death: when young Israelis were shown a picture of animals fleeing gigantic flames—an image that terrified Swiss children—many of them saw only animals playing together. And he himself says very little about the Nazis: there is a single rapid glimpse of Treblinka, a description of another friend's film. It is a single bright flare of the horror that remains hidden in the rest of the book. But even as he recalls the film, he is struck by the incongruous "soft spring sky, in Rome" where one survivor talks of Auschwitz. Friedlander has no fascination with horror. His experience has made him reticent, and he knows the danger of self-pity and of taking pride in one's own suffering.

But he also knows that he cannot deny his memories, not even the unthinkable ones that seem "buried once and for all." He looks back over the interrupted pattern of his life—a series of abrupt and thoroughgoing shifts of identity, as he moved from Prague to Vichy France in 1939, then in 1946 from the Sodality school to the Jewish quarter of Paris, and less than two years later to Israel. And yet for all the changes, he is struck above all by the "imperious resurgence of the past" that he first recognized as a child unable to sleep in a convent dormitory and then again when he decided to go to Israel with a group of Betar, the youth movement associated with the Irgun guerrillas.

He was determined not to become a passive victim—not to repeat the mistake of his parents who died, he suggests bitterly, for a Jewish identity they had denied in trying to live as if they were French or Czech. He also had a personal score to settle: now, some three years after leaving the Sodality school, he would "prove" that he was Jewish by fighting "alongside all the Jews who are dying in Palestine." He left for Israel "to answer violence with force . . . Only within the framework of the state could we answer violence with force."

But if the "logic" that led him to embrace Zionism as a high school student in 1947—"Didn't we have to abandon our role as victims?"—seemed coherent enough, it was in part because Friedlander did not yet know what Zionism would mean for Palestine. He and the other young Betar sailing from Marseilles to Tel Aviv on the cargo ship *Altalena* had been prepared to fight for no less than "both banks of the Jordan," even if that meant subverting the 1947 UN Partition Plan and the official policy of David Ben Gurion's government.

Thirty years later, Friedlander is concerned with the sacrifice of lives and the expulsion of the Arabs who had been living in Palestine. He recognizes "the permanence of the Jewish world, but also the permanence of the Arab world too—now face to face." More disturbing though are the fundamental contradictions in the Zionist project and what he sees as the character of the people who have been drawn to it. Long troubled by the inflexibility of official Israeli policies, it is in 1973 that he first understood that "our intransigence was based on principle."

He circles back again and again to the troubling Israeli habit of unquestioning loyalty to the nation and its ideals. He recalls the Jews that he met in Paris: "they move forward with passion, but also blindly," drawn by a "vision of the group." Many Israelis too, he finds, are guided by a traditional sense of identity: "Since the beginning of its history, this people has seen itself as alone and surrounded by enemies." They are unable to "believe in peace."

Writing at the time of Sadat's first visit to Jerusalem in December 1977, Friedlander is more uneasy than jubilant: more than ever, this was a time to ask why the pursuit of security had led again and again to war. "The peace initiatives are going to bring to light the hidden contradictions in our society."

Finally it is the contradictions in his own feelings about Zionism that seem most vivid, and most unsettling in *When Memory Comes.* He doesn't deny the need he once felt to take up arms. More than anything, though, Friedlander would like to believe in peace—and unlike many Israelis he is prepared to make the necessary compromises.

David Pryce-Jones   (review date 6 March 1981)

SOURCE: "Separation and Survival," in *The Times Literary Supplement*, No. 4066, March 6, 1981, p. 250.

[*Pryce-Jones is an Austrian-born English novelist, biographer, and historian. In the following review of* When Memory Comes, *he addresses the lasting effects on Friedländer of having lost his parents to the Nazis.*]

Forty years have passed since the events described in Saul Friedländer's infinitely sad and haunting memoir [*When Memory Comes*]. His parents separated themselves from him in Hitler's Europe; they died, he lived. The fear of being abandoned still rises in him. What experience, or history itself, has taught him is this fear, fear in its pure state, more terrifying than successive encounters with death. Forty years on, he has become a well-known professor of history in a university in Israel and can look back on what happened with a scholar's knowledge of causes and effects, weighing evidence and motive, using all the resources of language. None the less past and present are one: the professor who mentions his wife and three children and who now and again reflects on contemporary Israel and its predicament, is also the child who reaches out to parents lost to him for reasons never ultimately understandable. Here perhaps is some generalized metaphor for human loneliness, and it is also a concrete and very moving expression of what it is to be Jewish.

Friedländer begins with the words, "I was born in Prague at the worst possible moment, four months before Hitler came to power". His father Jan was vice-president of a large German insurance company in Czechoslovakia, and a man whose timidity or reserve made him repress his deeper passions and turn to books and music. "I will always regret not having had enough naturalness and spontaneity as a child to take the initiative, leap up onto my father's lap, and throw my arms around his neck." Saul's mother Elli came from a family who owned a textile factory at Rochlitz, in the Sudetenland. Winter images of Rochlitz remain; its pine forests and snows—"my mother turns around, a pair of skis on her shoulder, slender and beautiful, with a radiant smile and a face glistening with cold".

The Czech nurse Vlasta took him on Sundays to hear the

military band at the castle, and on to church. Judaism meant nothing to the Friedländers, who were assimilated; bourgeois aesthetes in a civilized city with no inkling of the future. A holiday visit to Palestine in 1937 did not influence Elli to emigrate while it was still possible, and after the journey her younger brother even turned away from Zionism to anthroposophy.

Their first flight was in March 1939, to Brno, where they ran into the invading German army and were redirected back to Prague. Their second flight soon followed, across the Reich to Paris. "We have little money and are not earning any at all. That does not mean that I am sitting around waiting for death, not ours at any event. We must manage to survive"—so Jan wrote to a friend a month before the war. The six-year-old Saul, then called Paul, otherwise Pavel in Czech, was sent for six months to a Jewish school. Orthodox children bullied him and made him a Jewish outcast among Jews; they were avenging themselves upon him for what the gentiles had done to them. In June 1940, as Paris and the north of France were occupied, the family left on a third flight, to the tiny spa of Néris-les-Bains in the Allier, in the Vichy zone.

"Often my father foundered in a sort of wordless sadness". He tried to learn cheese-making but he was ill, tortured by a stomach ulcer. "What could my father have done? Nothing depended on him now. A safer hiding place depended on the good will of others, as did fleeing the country. Rebellion had no meaning for the few scattered Jews who saw the vice closing. Whom could they attack? The Néris gendarmes?" Several local people were kind, even heroically kind, and among them was Madame L. de M. who consented to act as a godmother.

By the summer of 1942 the Vichy government was concluding arrangements with the Germans for the deportation of the Jews from France in accordance with the Final Solution. Requested to remit his sovereignty over French citizens who were also Jewish, the Vichy government prevaricated before reaching the compromise that foreign-born Jews would be deported first, from occupied and unoccupied zones alike. Children were not to be spared. Under German direction, the French bureaucracy and police forces would carry out the operation. Panic-stricken, the Friedländers placed their son in a Jewish children's home near La Souterraine in the Creuse. The very next morning, the gendarmes arrived with trucks to take away all children over the age of ten. "A woman entered, looked at all those youngsters about to depart, raised her hand to her face, and suddenly collapsed." After a night spent out in the local forest with all the other children under ten, Saul was fetched back to Néris.

Distraught, the parents agreed to a plan of Madame L. de M.'s, that the boy should be hidden in the nearby town of Montluçon, in a strictly Catholic boarding-school which in the book is called Saint-Bérenger. He was given the assumed name of Paul-Henri Ferland, and he had to be converted. Some sixth sense warned him that if he was separated from his parents, he would never see them again. He ran away, finding them in a Montluçon hospital where they were temporarily seeking refuge. "Could I be dragged away from them a second time? I clung to the bars of the bed. How did my parents ever find the courage to make me loosen my hold, without bursting into sobs in front of me?" —the image remains of a child walking away in the soft autumn light between two nuns dressed in black.

The parents' last flight was into Switzerland, but they were caught there. A notorious sergeant by the name of Arretaz handed them back across the French border, and so to the Germans. A final letter from Elli to Madame L. de M. said that they had been misinformed: parents with children were allowed into Switzerland; the presence of their son might therefore have saved their lives. What condemned them to die as Jews was perhaps the very outlook which enabled them without qualms to let their son become a Catholic. The *milice* came looking for the boy in Néris, but Madame L. de M. threw them off the scent; she was herself Jewish, had they known.

Saint-Bérenger specialized in forming potential Jesuits, and it was Pétainist and antisemitic. Paul-Henri Ferland willed himself to die, but he could not: he became a server at mass, he made his solemn communion, eventually he supposed he had a vocation. The war was over before he was informed of the essential facts. A Jesuit was to give him special instruction, and led him into a candle-lit church where, out of justice, and charity perhaps, he spoke at length. "I listened: Auschwitz, the trains, the gas chambers, the crematory ovens, the millions of dead. . . . For the first time, I felt myself to be Jewish—no longer despite myself or secretly, but through a sensation of absolute loyalty." (Incidentally the newly appointed Archbishop of Paris, Monseigneur Jean-Marie Lustiger, had also as a boy been placed for the sake of survival in a Catholic school, where he carried through to the priesthood. His mother too was deported and killed.)

Paul-Henri Ferland, that apparition of despair, vanished, but Pavel was beyond recalling, and there was to be more delay and distress before the real Saul Friedländer could emerge. Adopted by a Jewish guardian in Paris, he attended the Lycée Henri IV and was in contact with Zionist organizations. The state of Israel came into existence, and he took his chance to emigrate, absconding from the Lycée. Even then, the ship he sailed on was the *Altalena,* which was beached off Tel Aviv with its cargo of arms for the underground Irgun, and where it was seized, with loss of life, by the official army of the new state.

"What blindness led them from mistake to mistake to the very end?" The question can be asked of the parents but no answer is expected. They were as vulnerable as everyone else to the encompassing madness and violence. No blame or blindness specially attaches to them, and after all their son was kept alive by the expedient they adopted. The details of the horror which engulfed them were singular, but their form of death was common to so many— Jews, Saul Friedländer writes, "obey the call of some mysterious destiny".

Fifteen years old, an orphan, he believed that it would be possible to find hope, heroism, a natural ending. In this mysterious destiny in its new shape, Israel. Discovering the Bible and his teachers, sitting on a village bench watching open-air films, talking to Herr Cohen and Herr

Nehap, survivors from Czechoslovakia, he saw himself as part of a miracle, even if at first he used to creep away alone to read Fromentin's *Dominique* on the sands.

A year caring for mentally ill children in Sweden showed him that suffering is one and indivisible. Friends and students die in the wars. The only Palestinian prepared to debate with him publicly proves to be one of the organizers of the massacre of Israeli athletes at the Munich Olympics. His research as a historian takes him to Germany, where Grand Admiral Doenitz gives him his word of honour that he never knew about the extermination of the Jews—so much for the word of a German Grand Admiral. Vlasta, his old nurse, writes him a letter when he publishes his well-known book *Pius XII and the Third Reich;* they meet and he learns that she had spent the war in Prague bringing up the children of a German general. Look where he may, he is confirmed in his view that his destiny as man and Jew will be no different simply because it happens in Israel—there is hope, there is heroism, and there is also the fear of being abandoned.

Christopher Lehmann-Haupt   (review date 28 May 1984)

SOURCE: "Nazism and Yearning," in *The New York Times,* May 28, 1984, p. 37.

[*Lehmann-Haupt is a Scottish-born American critic and novelist whose reviews frequently appear in* The New York Times. *In the following favorable review of* Reflections of Nazism, *he briefly summarizes Friedländer's arguments supporting his main contention that Nazism remains a dangerously fascinating phenomenon.*]

"Gentlemen, in a hundred years still another color film will portray the terrible days we are undergoing now," said Joseph Goebbels, the Nazi Propaganda Minister, apropos of a film he was discussing in 1945. "I can assure you that it will be a tremendous film, exciting and beautiful, and worth holding steady for. Don't give up!"

It is Saul Friedländer's contention in *Reflections of Nazism: An Essay on Kitsch and Death* that the film Goebbels foresaw is, figuratively speaking, already playing, only four decades after his prediction. It is playing in the form of cinema like Hans-Jürgen Syberberg's *Hitler, a Film From Germany* and Rainer Werner Fassbinder's *Lili Marleen*; in novels like Michel Tournier's *Ogre* and George Steiner's *Portage to San Cristóbal of A. H.* and in nonfiction works like Albert Speer's two volumes of memoirs and Joachim C. Fest's biography *Hitler.* He doesn't have to mention hundreds of other popular works, such as the Broadway musical *Cabaret* or the television mini-series *Holocaust,* or the fascination with Nazi artifacts available in mail-order catalogues.

"Nazism has disappeared," Mr. Friedländer writes, "but the obsession it represents for the contemporary imagination—as well as the birth of a new discourse that ceaselessly elaborates and reinterprets it—necessarily confronts us with this ultimate question: Is such attention fixed on the past only a gratuitous reverie, the attraction of spectacle, exorcism, or the result of a need to understand; or is it,

again and still, an expression of profound fears and, on the part of some, mute yearnings as well?" Mr. Friedländer—who teaches history in Tel Aviv and Geneva and is the author of *Pius XII and the Third Reich, Kurt Gerstein: The Ambiguity of Good,* and a memoir, *When Memory Comes,* among other books—suspects the latter to be the case: that the continuing fascination with Nazism represents an unconscious yearning.

The times may not be ripe for a revival of Nazism; in Mr. Friedländer's view, neither the socioeconomic nor the political conditions exist for such an occurrence. But "the psychological dimension" is another matter, and that dimension he sees latently present everywhere. The creators of works imbued with that psychology need not even approve any aspect of Nazism; in fact, they invariably condemn it. But the psychology of yearning is present nonetheless, and Mr. Friedländer means to anatomize it.

What exactly is this psychology? If I may distill: It is the resolution of certain extreme contradictions—being and nonbeing, death and sentimentality, genocide and esthetics, to name but a few that Mr. Friedländer confronts in his dense but endlessly provocative essay. Nazism reconciled these opposites in a variety of now familiar ways—through its use of spectacle and language, for instance—but most of all through the persona of Adolf Hitler, whom Mr. Friedländer characterizes as a Mr. Everyman, a bourgeois gentleman (of the four major World War II leaders the one we have come to know most intimately) marching us off into the void.

This psychology is now being revived wherever Mr. Friedländer looks, even in works that ostensibly seek to condemn or exorcise the experience of Nazism. Joachim C. Fest ponders Hitler's greatness, albeit in the form of a rhetorical question he answers negatively. Hans-Jürgen Syberberg seeks to purge through self-examination in *Hitler, a Film From Germany,* but in the process he subtly shifts the issue from a moral to an esthetic one.

Revisionists on both the right and the left seek to remove the goal of genocide from the heart of the Nazi program, almost as if the intention, although an unconscious one, were to free the figure of the Jew to play a less time-specific role as the villain in the drama of capitalism. "Modern society and the bourgeois order are perceived both as an accomplishment and as an unbearable yoke," Mr. Friedländer writes. "Hence this constant coming and going between the need for submission and the reveries of total destruction, between love of harmony and the phantasms of apocalypse, between the enchantment of Good Friday and the twilight of the Gods.

"Submission nourishes fury," he continues. "Fury clears its conscience in the submission. To these opposing needs, Nazism—in the constant duality of its representations—offers an outlet; in fact, Nazism found itself to be the expression of these opposing needs. Today these aspirations are still there, and their reflections in the imaginary as well."

It is a much-needed thought-provoking thesis that Mr. Friedländer has offered in these pages, however sketchily

I may have summarized it here, and however obscure the author's illustrations may seem to an American audience. It is worth the effort to grasp in all its subtlety what Mr. Friedländer is trying to say. For, as he concludes, "We know that the dream of total power is always present, though dammed up, repressed by the Law, even at the risk of destruction. With this difference—which perhaps tempers, or on the contrary exacerbates, the apocalyptic dreams: This time, to reach for total power is to assure oneself, and all of mankind as well, of being engulfed in total and irremediable destruction."

Alan Mintz   (review date 1 October 1984)

SOURCE: "Under Hitler's Spell," in *The New Republic*, Vol. 191, No. 3637, October 1, 1984, pp. 40-1.

[*Mintz is an American nonfiction writer and educator who has written extensively on Hebrew literature. In the following positive review of* Reflections of Nazism, *he examines Friedländer's thesis that the "fusion of kitsch and death" is constitutive of both the original and contemporary fascination with Nazism.*]

Since World War II a fascination with the prurient details of Nazism has been a staple of American adolescence. In the "adult" world of pornographic pictures and films, the sadistic possibilities of Nazism have long provided the raw material for a hard-core industry of major proportions. But not until recently has Nazism surfaced into the mainstream of contemporary culture, not just as a subject for middlebrow entertainment but as high art. The phenomenon is not to be confused with Holocaust literature. In Hans Jürgen Syberberg's *Hitler, a Film from Germany*, George Steiner's novel *The Portage to San Cristobal of A.H.*, and in films and books by Michel Tournier, Luchino Visconti, Joachim Fest, Rainer Werner Fassbinder, and Albert Speer, the murder of the Jews and others is entirely eclipsed by a fascination with the spectacle of Nazism and, specifically, the personality of Hitler.

This phenomenon is the subject of this tightly argued essay in cultural analysis by Saul Friedländer [*Reflections of Nazism: An Essay on Kitsch and Death*]. He is not up to a vulgar intellectual form of Nazi hunting, nor does he see in recent American and European culture a crypto-fascism waiting in the wings. The phenomenon is more paradoxical. The declared aim of these films and books is to unmask and exorcise the evil of Nazism by probing its sordid corruptions. Yet despite these ideological intentions, Friedländer argues, the aesthetic effects are quite otherwise. The spectacle of Nazism constitutes so lush and compelling a field of images that fascination edges over into absorption. It is in these charged images and associative emotions—"an activity of the imagination that cannot be reduced to the usual distinctions between right and left"—that Friedländer sees the formation of a new "discourse of Nazism." By speaking of discourse as the French speak of it, as the latent message of the language of a work rather than its declared intentions, Friedländer proposes to get beneath politics and ideas to a psychological dimension which constituted the secret of the attraction of Nazism in its own time, and which—this is the point of Fried-

länder's critique—is the same attraction that can be felt working at the heart of recent books and films about Nazism.

The attraction of Nazism, Friedländer argues, was based on an unprecedented fusion of kitsch and death. Kitsch, which you know when you see it but is notoriously difficult to define, is the effect created by the presence of good taste in the absence of taste, the presence of art in ugliness. In kitsch, art is adapted to the majority's ideals of harmony and order, and extreme situations are neutralized and turned into a sentimental idyll. The seduction of Nazism lay in its applying kitsch to death. In contrast to Marxism, which looked to a future of golden tomorrows, the Nazis' debased romanticism harbored a nostalgia for the pre-modern past, an age in which purity is achieved by fire and the hero remains faithful unto death. Nazi leaders never felt more exalted than when they solemnized the death of their heroes in elaborate funeral spectacles, complete with torches, pyres, and flaming wheels. But the death the Nazis were in love with was not real death but kitsch death, "not death in its everyday horror and tragic banality, but a ritualized, stylized, and aesthetic death, a death that wills itself the carrier of horror, decrepitude, and monstrosity, but which ultimately and definitively appears as a poisonous apotheosis."

The figure of Hitler himself represents the distillation of this phenomenon. On the one hand, Hitler's persona was enveloped in kitsch: a petty bourgeois Everyman, living in domestic serenity with Eva Braun and his dog Blondi, and joking with his comrades-in-arms. On the other hand, he was a man transfixed by the possibilities of mass death and by the spectacle of destruction and apocalyptic conflagration. He appeared as both the sentimental human being and the blind force launched into nothingness. For Friedländer, it is the "coexistence of these two aspects, . . . their simultaneous and alternating presence" that indicates the true source of Hitler's spell.

Friedländer senses the return of this spell today. The ostensible aim of the recent reflections of Nazism in the arts is a kind of exorcism: the belief that the evil will be purged by vividly evoking its full demonic force. Hans Jürgen Syberberg claims that his *Hitler, a Film from Germany*

> is precisely about this Hitler within us. . . . In the name of our future, we have to overcome and conquer him and thereby ourselves, and it is only here can a new identity be found through recognizing and separating, sublimating and working on our tragic past.

Friedländer sees in this enthusiastic confrontation a more dangerous evasion: a neutralization of this past and a concealment, voluntary or not, of what in this past has become unbearable. This artistic commitment to total representation involves re-evoking the phenomenon in all its compelling perversion—in a sense, re-experiencing the spell. Once the attraction has been reconstituted, the original ideological impulse makes little difference. What remains active is not the awareness of horror, but the fascination.

The endless and indiscriminate piling up of stunning images in Syberberg's film, for example, is a sign that the filmmaker has himself been engulfed by the phantasm he sought to exorcise. The reader of Steiner's novel experiences a similar unease when the Hitler figure is exploited to do some fancy probing of the cosmic symbiosis between good and evil and given a mischievous monologue of gripping virtuosity. Although Visconti's film *The Damned* proposes to expose decadence, the gorgeousness of its two big scenes, the SA massacre and the marriage-suicide of Sophie and Freidrich, serve instead to savor the orgiastic paroxysm and ecstatic terror. In each case, Nazism is allowed to become an aesthetic field whose rich opportunities for arresting images and entrancing rhetoric cannot be passed up. The result is "indiscriminate word and image overload on topics that call for so much restraint, hesitation, groping." And the phenomenon becomes so engrossing that it leads as well to a revisionist distortion of the facts: Truffaut's *The Last Metro* and Fassbinder's *Lili Marleen* give the impression that there was almost general opposition to Nazism and collaboration, inside the Third Reich and in France. The murder of the Jews as a central activity of Nazism is also moved to the periphery of dramatic focus.

There is a bit of dazzle in Friedländer's own writing. Friedländer's voice speaks with so much persuasive force in this well-translated volume that one can lose sight of the fact that it remains an essay, not a study based on demonstrated arguments, but a brief, allusive attempt to put forward a thesis. Moreover, Friedländer's assertion that the appeal of Nazism derives from the fusion of kitsch and death, as brilliant as it may be, remains largely unsusceptible to proof. The thesis is embroiled in the problems of the nature of literary and artistic perception, in the difficulties of reconstructing the psychological response of people living in an earlier period. Friedländer attempts to get around this obstacle by positing a correlation between how we—in truth, how he—responds to representations of Nazism in films and novels in our own time, and how the actual followers of Nazism responded in theirs. This is a useful technique but it remains a speculative one.

When Friedländer digresses from the arts, he has some perceptive things to say about the evasions of social science. The economic explanations of the rise of Nazism by Marxist historians are oblivious to the fact that the destruction of the Jews was against the economic self-interest of the Reich. The theory of totalitarianism, the key proposed by liberal social scientists, similarly spirits away the essential relationship of Nazism to anti-Judaism; even in the kind of scholarship you would imagine to be unimpeachable, a documentary account of an extermination presented by a researcher from the Yad Vashem Memorial in Jerusalem, Friedländer finds a detached use of bureaucratic language which effects a neutralization of the horror. Now Friedländer admits, as a practicing historian and political scientist himself, that in dealing with Nazism some form of evasion, given the unspeakable nature of the subject, is inevitable. Aside from exposing the more self-deluding forms of exorcism, all he can propose to men of good will is an interpretive vigilance, a self-awareness that continually inquires into motives and effects.

Friedländer's impasse has something to do with his severing the question of Nazism from the question of the Holocaust. Nazism connotes the world of the victimizers; and the Holocaust, the world of the victims. About the Holocaust there are a number, in fact a growing number, of accomplished works of the literary imagination in several languages. Their artistic achievement depends precisely upon their avoiding the world of the Nazis, with its pull of pornographic fascination, in favor of the inner spiritual world of the victims. The Hebrew writer Aharon Appelfeld, perhaps the most impressive talent now addressing the Holocaust, goes so far as to make the exclusion of the enemy the ground principle of his fictional enterprise. Friedländer knows this literature, and the perceptive criticism of it; and in a brief book there is a usefulness in making separations. Still, in the contrast between the successes of Holocaust literature and the failures of the artistic reflections of Nazism, there is a message to be read. It is a message not only about which story deserves to be told, but which story, in the end, can be told.

Bryan Cheyette   (review date 16 October 1992)

SOURCE: "The Horror and the Words," in *The Times Literary Supplement,* No. 4672, October 16, 1992, p. 10.

[*Cheyette is an English literary critic, nonfiction writer, and educator who has written extensively on racism— particularly anti-Semitism—in literature. In the following review of* Probing the Limits of Representation, *he discusses some of the major issues confronting historians and other writers who seek to account for Nazism and the Holocaust.*]

In recent trials of neo-Nazi publishers who "deny" the existence of the Holocaust, the historical record was dismissed by their defence lawyers as "mere opinion" and their denial was claimed as no less legitimate than other accounts of the Final Solution. *Probing the Limits of Representation*—which began life in 1990 as a conference at the University of California, Los Angeles—examines the implications of a historical relativism which reduces history to opinion and rejects the testimony even of those who witnessed Nazi atrocities. The initial focus of this work is on the influential theorist, Hayden White, who for the past two decades has postulated what he calls an "inexpungeable relativity" when selecting a particular "historical narrative" to represent the past. The implications of this relativism for our understanding of Nazism and the Final Solution are explored by White in his essay, which in turn is opened up to scrutiny in the early chapters of this volume. Should there, White asks, be restraints on the kinds of "stories" used to represent the horrors of Nazism and, if so, how should these narrative limits be conceived? Do we need a critical language which privileges one type of historical or literary "truth" over another? As many of the other essays make clear, these are not just academic issues, but they are important for the "historians' debate" or *Historikerstreit* in Germany and, in general, for popular and literary accounts of the Holocaust.

Not that this volume addresses particularly new areas of interest. Its editor, Saul Friedlander, has long been concerned with the creation of an authentic historical memory as opposed to the baleful mythologizing of the Final So-lution which he, along with many others, has written against. Friedlander has also intervened effectively in the German "historians' debate" in the 1980s and has fre-quently warned against the absorption of the Holocaust into conventional modernizing historiography as well as Hayden White's supposed post-modern relativism. In a deliberately tendentious introduction to this volume, he argues that it is the "reality" of modern catastrophes—and not the self-conscious application of *post hoc* narra-tives—that generates the search for a "new voice" through which the Holocaust can be better understood. But Fried-lander's reclamation of an "allusive or distanced reality" as an "adequate" representation of the Final Solution is less than persuasive. One might equally want to argue that the overwhelming sense of uncertainty and inadequacy in many survivor memoirs undermines the belief in a truth-producing "reality". Friedlander is well aware of this but, in the end, relies on a sense of the gulf between aestheticiz-ing fictions and historical facts.

Probing the Limits of Representation is at its best, howev-er, when these issues are not discussed in the abstract but are applied to particular historical or cultural contexts. Christopher Browning's essay on "perpetuator history", which opens the volume, is a model of its kind. Browning starts with an account of the German Reserve Police Bat-talion 101 which massacred thousands of Polish Jews in the summer of 1942. His painstaking reconstruction of one such atrocity on July 13 highlights the dangers in pos-tulating an unbridgeable distinction between self-evident facts and subjective assumptions. By taking the reader through the choices that he had to make as a historian—in relying on eye-witness accounts of those who committed the massacre—Browning demonstrates convincingly that virtually every "fact" that he deduced was "an act of inter-pretation". His nuanced article qualifies both an extreme relativism and the fear that any history written from the viewpoint of the oppressor simply "normalizes" the un-speakable. And yet, by the end, such nuances are disap-pointingly subsumed into a rather crude vocabulary which sums up as "all too human" the murderousness of Battal-ion 101 and the evasive disposition of some of the reserve policemen.

It is a pity that social and political theorists of the range and quality of Perry Anderson, Martin Jay and Dominic LaCapra are, in this work, reduced to writing close textual commentary. The unnecessarily high level of self-referentiality and repetition in *Probing the Limits of Rep-resentation* seems to be an unforeseen consequence of in-cluding those who are "not the usual interlocutors in dis-cussions of the Holocaust". The focus for discussion tends to be either other essays in the volume or an already well-documented group of German quasi-revisionist historians such as Andreas Hillgruber and Ernst Nolte. It is particu-larly frustrating that none of the four essays which refers to Hayden White discusses James Young's *Writing and Rewriting the Holocaust* (1988), the only full-length appli-cation of White's theories to a variety of Holocaust texts. Much less forgivable is the extraordinary omission of Zyg-munt Bauman's seminal *Modernity and the Holocaust*

(1989) in the five essays that examine the relationship of "modernity" to the Final Solution.

Friedlander is, to say the least, rightly suspicious of turn-ing the Final Solution into an unproblematic object of aca-demic study. He emphasizes the inexplicable nature of "the horror behind the words" and, above all, the impossi-bility of accommodating Auschwitz within, say, the mod-ernizing theories of Jürgen Habermas or the post-modernism of Jean-François Lyotard. The last group of essays, which deal with the question of "aestheticizing" the Holocaust, are particularly strong in that regard. John Felstiner and Sidra Dekoven Ezrahi give an account of the domestication of Paul Celan's poetry in post-war Germa-ny which, they argue, reflects in miniature the need to as-similate that which Celan shows is unassimilable. Anton Kaes's discussion of Hans-Jürgen Syberberg's controver-sial *Hitler—A Film from Germany* (1978), similarly throws into unfortunate relief the more abstract discus-sions of *post-histoire* that precede this chapter. And Geof-frey Hartman's final, humane meditation on his imagined Borgesian "Book of Destruction" points to a new kind of writing about the Holocaust that, for the most part, this volume is only able to postulate.

James E. Young   (review date Fall 1994)

SOURCE: "The Uses of the Holocaust," in *Partisan Re-view*, Vol. LXI, No. 4, Fall, 1994, pp. 700-04.

[*In the following excerpt, Young discusses some of the ways Friedländer and the other contributors to* Probing the Lim-its of Representation *address the difficulties of writing about the Holocaust.*]

"The history of the Holocaust sits uneasily amidst other events of its time," Michael Marrus wrote in *The Holo-caust and the Historians.* "How do we write Holocaust his-tory? Since by writing it, we automatically locate it within some tradition, some epoch, how do we choose one? Is it only Jewish history? Or German? Is it European or more generally Western?" To which we might add, is it part of World War Two history, or in the words of another histo-rian, Lucy Dawidowicz, a separate "war against the Jews"? Do we tell it from the perspective of the perpetra-tors, the victims, or the bystanders? As becomes so very clear . . . every telling creates a variant Holocaust. Only together do they begin to constitute a total history of events. . . .

Friedlander has has been widely revered for his powerful and self-revelatory memoir, **When Memory Comes** (1978); now he has assembled the proceedings of a mam-moth conference he organized at UCLA into a weighty volume [*Probing the Limits of Representation: Nazism and the Final Solution*], devoted to the theoretical limits and possibilities of Holocaust representation. Dozens of distinguished speakers gathered from around the world, most of them in Friedlander's words "not the usual inter-locutors in discussions of the Holocaust."

Though painfully aware of the potential unseemliness in turning the Holocaust into so much grist for theoretical mills, however inadvertently, Friedlander also writes that he could not ignore the essential conundrum at the heart of any historian's enterprise: the need to establish a stable truth of events in a decidedly unstable literary medium. He takes as his starting point the debate between Hayden White and Carlo Ginzburg. White has argued long and persuasively that insofar as historical texts are subject to the vagaries and indeterminacy of narrative, literary metaphor and the conventions of emplotment, they cannot establish perfectly objective, universally true history. Ginzburg vehemently rejects this view of history, arguing passionately against the kind of historical relativism it breeds, especially if it fails to distinguish between "true interpretation and lies." White rejoins that he is not arguing for a history that blurs the distinction between real events and imaginary ones, or that allows one to deny that events have taken place at all. Rather, he believes that "when it comes to apprehending the historical record, there are no grounds to be found in the historical record itself for preferring one way of construing its meaning over another." Ginzburg answers (in Friedlander's paraphrase) "that even the voice of one single witness gives us some access to the domain of historical reality, allows us to get nearer to some historical truth." Carlo Ginzburg first seeks to taint White's argument with what he regards as fascist theoretical antecedents, and he tries to sustain his attack through a series of neological leaps, as unlikely as they are breathtaking. A putative *coup de grace* comes with his conclusion that if taken to its logical extension, White's argument would finally have to regard even the narrative of Holocaust negationist Robert Faurisson as true. As deftly written and rhetorically persuasive as it is, Ginzburg's essay is not a pretty thing to behold.

Throughout his own illuminating essay, it becomes apparent that Friedlander himself is torn between what he knows as an academic historian, as a critic of historical narrative, and what he feels must be made explicitly clear: the absolute facticity of these events. He is torn between the necessary breach dividing history as it happened and history as it is told. Finally, he is also torn between his scholarly obligations to the rigorously scientific, occasionally ponderous working-through of these issues and his own strong impulse to de-mystify the Holocaust through lucid and accessible narratives like **When Memory Comes.**

While most essays that follow tend toward the ponderous side of this equation, several of these are also elegantly written and conceived. The contributions by Christopher Browning, John Felstiner, and Geoffrey Hartman offer themselves as models of lucidity and brilliant insight, intellectual rigor and accessibility. After introducing his essay with a chilling description of events from the German Reserve Police Battalion 101's bloody part in the Final Solution, Browning proceeds to examine how and why he has told history this way, what consequences for understanding this kind of history holds for us. To this end, he examines both the necessity and repulsiveness of "perpetrator history," what it means to descend into the psychologies and everyday lives of the killers—not as a singular alternative to the victims' history, but as a complement to it, all toward a fuller history of events.

Likewise, the meditations by Felstiner and Hartman lay

out in clear-eyed prose the daunting difficulties, the multiple ambiguities and complexities of Felstiner's translation of Paul Celan's masterpiece, "Todesfuge," and Hartman's attempt to add to the "Book of Destruction." By walking us through the myriad choices a translator faces, each one an interpretive act, Felstiner offers an eloquent model of critical self-reflexivity, even as he makes and stands by his own choices. Hartman's own essay on "The Book of Destruction" closes the volume with an erudite and sparkling reflection on the very possibility of such writing, its place (or placelessness) in postmodern culture. "We want to say," Hartman writes, " 'It is inconceivable,' yet we know it was conceived and acted upon systematically. We continue to harbor, therefore, a sense of improbability, not because there is any doubt whatsoever about the Shoah as fact but because what we lived through, or what we have learned about, cannot be part of us: the mind rejects it, casts it out—or it casts out the mind."

This kind of history-telling has both immense rewards and risks. By returning these horrible events to the human times and places in which they occurred, such history becomes humanly, if not divinely, accountable. At the same time, this kind of writing suggests that we, and no one else, are also accountable for both the histories we write and the conclusions we draw from them.

FURTHER READING

Biography

Mitgang, Herbert. "Friedländer's Odyssey." *The New York Times Book Review* (15 July 1979): 35.
    Brief profile of Friedländer on the publication of *When Memory Comes.*

Criticism

Birley, Robert. "Not Guilty." *Spectator* 223, No. 7367 (6 September 1969): 305-06.
    Generally positive review of *Kurt Gerstein: The Ambiguity of Good* (here called *Counterfeit Nazi: The Ambiguity of Good*) in which Birley questions the validity of some of Friedländer's conclusions.

Review of *History and Psychoanalysis: An Inquiry into the Possibilities and Limits of Psychohistory,* by Saul Friedländer. *Choice* 16, No. 1 (March 1979): 128.
    Brief positive review.

Gilman, Sander. Review of *Probing the Limits of Representation: Nazism and the Final Solution,* by Saul Friedländer. *American Historical Review* 98, No. 2 (April 1993): 521-22.
    Positive review lauding the work's wide range of opinions and historiographical approaches. Gilman commends the book as an important contribution to contemporary scholarship.

Jacobson, Peter. " 'God's Spy' in the SS." *The Washington Post Book World* 111, No. 7 (27 April 1969): 7.
    Review of *Kurt Gerstein: The Ambiguity of Good.* After surveying events in Gerstein's life, Jacobson argues that

the book has a "powerful impact" despite appearing "hastily put together."

Kent, George O. Review of *Pius XII and the Third Reich,* by Saul Friedländer. *American Historical Review* LXXII, No. 1 (October 1966): 172-73.

Generally positive assessment that recognizes the value as well as the limitations of the documents Friedländer presents and emphasizes the difficulty of drawing firm conclusions from them.

Lewy, Guenter. Review of *Pius XII and the Third Reich,* by Saul Friedländer. *Political Science Quarterly* LXXXI, No. 4 (December 1966): 680-82.

Positive review and brief summary of the book's major theses.

Monroe, Elizabeth. "Arabs and Israelis." *Book Forum* II, No. 1 (1976): 79-83.

Overview of the participants and the points of view they express in *Arabs and Israelis: A Dialogue.*

Review of *When Memory Comes,* by Saul Friedländer. *The New Republic* 181, Nos. 3 and 4 (21-28 July 1979): 38-9.

Brief positive review in which the critic describes the book as "a tender elegy which moves from the Israeli present to the European past, from fear to memory, in a mosaic of Proustian images."

Schleunes, Karl A. Review of *Probing the Limits of Representation: Nazism and the Final Solution,* by Saul Friedländer. *Central European History* 25, No. 3 (1992): 366-69.

Positive review that summarizes some of the arguments put forth by the book's contributors.

Schmitt, Hans A. "Hitler: Obsession without End." *The Sewanee Review* XCVI, No. 1 (Winter 1988): 158-68.

Reviews a number of books on Hitler and Nazism including *Reflections of Nazism: An Essay on Kitsch and Death.* Schmitt claims that "Friedländer never goes beyond eloquent speculation."

Secher, H. P. Review of *Prelude to Downfall,* by Saul Friedländer; *The German Army and the Nazi Party,* by Robert O'Neill; and *Charisma and Factionalism in the Nazi Party,* by Joseph Nyomarkay. *The American Political Science Review* LXII, No. 2 (June 1968): 590-93.

Generally positive review in which Secher points out that Friedländer's exposition does not necessarily support the conclusion he draws regarding the inevitability of Hitler's declaring war on the United States.

Shandley, Robert R. Review of *Probing the Limits of Representation: Nazism and the Final Solution,* by Saul Friedländer, and *Die Einstellung ist die Einstellung; Visuelle Kon-*

struktionen des Judentums, by Gertrud Koch. *The Germanic Quarterly* 68, No. 1 (Winter 1995): 87-9.

Positive, comparative review that summarizes the arguments of both books.

Sungolowsky, Joseph. "Holocaust and Autobiography: Wiesel, Friedländer, Pisar." In *Reflections of the Holocaust in Art and Literature,* edited by Randolph L. Braham, pp. 131-46. New York: Columbia University Press, 1990.

Examines the nature of Holocaust autobiography, focusing on Friedländer's *When Memory Comes,* Elie Wiesel's *Night,* and Samuel Pisar's *Of Blood and Hope* and *La ressource humaine.*

Review of *Pius XII and the Third Reich,* by Saul Friedländer. *The Times Literary Supplement,* No. 3379 (1 December 1966): 1109.

Argues that Friedländer was biased in his selection of documents.

"Hitler and the United States." *The Times Literary Supplement,* No. 3457 (30 May 1968): 550.

Reviews *Prelude to Downfall* and James V. Compton's *The Swastika and the Eagle.* The critic states that "Dr. Compton and Dr. Friedländer have brought together Hitler's Atlantic and Pacific policies towards the United States and thereby have closed an important gap in our overall picture of Nazi diplomacy."

"The Jews and Their Jews." *The Times Literary Supplement,* No. 3503 (17 April 1969): 415.

Reviews *Réflexions sur l'avenir d'Israël,* Jacob M. Landau's *The Arabs in Israel,* and Marc Hillel's *Israël en danger de paix,* in a discussion dealing with problems involving the Arab population within the borders of Israel.

"A Saboteur in the SS," *The Times Literary Supplement,* No. 3538 (18 December 1969): 1442.

Generally positive review of *Kurt Gerstein: The Ambiguity of Good* (here called *Counterfeit Nazi: The Ambiguity of Good*) that praises Friedländer's scholarship but nonetheless laments the absence of all "the obscure features making up the portrait of this counterfeit Nazi."

Trefousse, Hans L. Review of *Prelude to Downfall,* by Saul Friedländer. *American Historical Review* LXXIII, No. 1 (October 1967): 1107-08.

Argues that while Friedländer closely follows previous accounts of American-Axis relations, he "has added . . . the minute documentation that was unavailable before."

Additional coverage of Friedländer's life and career is contained in the following sources published by Gale Research: *Contemporary Authors,* Vols. 117 and 130.

Barry Hannah

1942-

American novelist, short story writer, and scriptwriter.

The following entry presents criticism on Hannah's works through 1995. For further information on his life and works, see *CLC,* Volumes 23 and 38.

INTRODUCTION

Hannah is among the most prominent American Southern writers of the post-World War II period. His fiction, usually set in the contemporary South, contains unusual narrative twists, elements of absurd humor, surrealistic violence, and a thematic concern with sexuality. Hannah's use of the South as a microcosm for the human condition has invited comparisons to William Faulkner, and his creation of eccentric characters enmeshed in violence has reminded critics of the work of Eudora Welty and Flannery O'Connor. Most commentators, however, have continued to assert that Hannah possesses an original and distinctive comic voice.

Biographical Information

Born and raised in Mississippi, Hannah graduated from Mississippi College in 1964 and received an M.A. and an M.F.A. from the University of Arkansas in 1966 and 1967 respectively. From 1967 to 1973 he taught literature and fiction writing at Clemson University, and it was during his tenure there that he published his first two novels—*Geronimo Rex* (1972), which was nominated for a National Book Award, and *Nightwatchmen* (1973). He has since taught or been writer-in-residence at several universities, including the University of Alabama and the University of Iowa. His first collection of short stories, *Airships* (1978), received the Arnold Gingrich Award for short fiction from *Esquire*; Hannah has also been honored with a special award from the American Academy of Arts and Letters.

Major Works

Much of Hannah's work is distinguished by its Southern setting; its focus on male protagonists, particularly war veterans; its exploration of masculinity; and its emphasis on black humor, sex, and violence. In Hannah's first novel—*Geronimo Rex,* a ribald initiation tale centering on Harry Monroe, a Louisiana youth in search of meaning in his life—the protagonist's personal traumas are set against scenes of social upheaval in the South. Monroe also appears as a secondary character in *Nightwatchmen,* a farcical murder mystery centering on Thorpe Trove, a wealthy eccentric who, with the help of a seventy-year-old detective named Howard Hunter and various graduate students, attempts to solve a series of murders at a fictional Mississippi university. The twenty stories collected in *Air-*

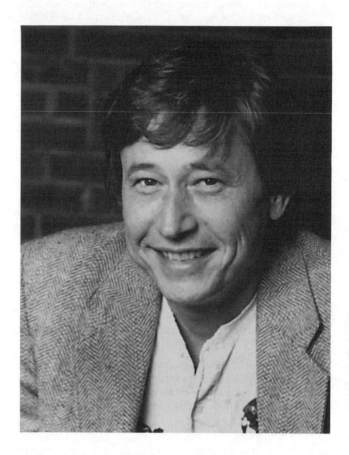

ships represent Hannah's experiments with narrative structure and his wide range of subject matter. For example, "Knowing He Was Not My Kind Yet I Followed" concerns a homosexual soldier's obsessive love for the Confederate general Jeb Stuart, while the cannibalistic story "Eating Wife and Friends" imagines the horrors of an American apocalypse. Hannah's next novel, *Ray* (1980), details the hallucinatory recollections and musings of an alcoholic Alabama doctor who was a pilot during the Vietnam War and often daydreams about the Civil War era. Through the novel's fragmented narrative, Hannah examines the tragedy of war with pathos and humor. *The Tennis Handsome* (1983) is a reworking of two unrelated stories from *Airships*: one about the exploits of a handsome tennis player and his demented coach, and the other about the return of a Vietnam War veteran to his hometown. Commentators note that in *The Tennis Handsome,* as in his previous works, Hannah depicts violence comically. Some of the stories in *Captain Maximus* (1985) eschew black humor and evince a more subdued approach for Hannah. "Getting Ready," for example, is a Hemingwayesque tale about a fisherman's attempt to catch a big fish; "Idaho" is a tribute to the late poet Richard Hugo. Set in a Mississippi university town, the novel *Hey Jack!*

(1987) concerns several characters whose histories are narrated by Homer, a Korean War veteran and writer in his mid-fifties. The stories cumulatively reveal events from Homer's own life and touch on such themes as infidelity, vengeance, weakness, sexuality, and despair. *Boomerang* (1989) is an autobiographical novel in which the narrator ruminates about his life in a series of episodes that are connected by three boomerang-throwing sessions. *Never Die* (1991) is a western set in the frontier town of Nitburg, Texas, in 1910. Like many of Hannah's other works, the novel features several scenes of violence and revolves around the theme of revenge—the protagonist, a gunfighter whose kneecaps were broken at the behest of Judge Nitburg, has vowed to burn the town to the ground. In the collection *Bats out of Hell* (1993), which includes both realistic and surrealistic stories, Hannah examines themes of nihilism, violence, and war. For instance, "That Was Close, Ma" questions the validity of the Persian Gulf War, and "Hey, Have You Got a Cig, the Time, the News, My Face?" presents a successful biographer who, on an impulse, goes to a military school and shoots at the students with an air rifle.

Critical Reception

Critics have noted Hannah's recurrent focus on violence, heroism, masculinity, war, and his penchant for black humor. Commentators have also consistently admired his imaginative use of language and flair for satirical characterization. George Stade commented in a review of *Captain Maximus*: "Of the many American short-story writers who have recently won acclaim, Mr. Hannah is the most invigorating: he does not write in the prevailing style of scrupulous meanness, and the desperation of his characters is anything but quiet." Reaction to some of Hannah's more recent works, however, has been less enthusiastic. *Hey Jack!*, for instance, was criticized for reworking material and characters introduced in Hannah's earlier works, while *Never Die* was faulted for lacking fully developed characters and a compelling plot. Moreover, Hannah has been consistently attacked by critics for what they perceive as his sexist view of women. Nevertheless, commentators have continued to cite and praise the distinctiveness of Hannah's fiction. Charles Israel has stated: "Much of Hannah's fiction is experimental and belongs in the category of dark comedy. All of it composes a highly original portrait of American life, both past and present, particularly American life in the South. It is a fiction that is consistently poetic, with a language and style both dazzling and believable."

PRINCIPAL WORKS

Geronimo Rex　(novel)　1972
Nightwatchmen　(novel)　1973
Airships　(short stories)　1978
Ray　(novel)　1980
The Tennis Handsome　(novel)　1983
Captain Maximus　(short stories)　1985
Hey Jack!　(novel)　1987
Boomerang　(novel)　1989
Never Die　(novel)　1991
Bats out of Hell　(short stories)　1993

CRITICISM

Barry Hannah with R. Vanarsdall　(interview date 27 April 1982)

SOURCE: An interview in *The Southern Review,* Louisiana State University, Vol. 19, No. 2, Spring, 1983, pp. 317-41.

[*In the following interview, which was conducted on April 27, 1982, Hannah discusses his literary influences, his characters, and aspects of his personal life.*]

[*Vanarsdall*]: *To start off, who do you count as influences? You said Walker Percy meant a lot to you.*

[Hannah]: Yeah, the one book *Moviegoer*. That was the one I read when I was reading into everything. I've read what you should have, Hemingway, Faulkner, and Joyce, but the *Moviegoer* was just an honest account by a fellow trying to be decent with a bit of glory and wasn't so drenched in rhetoric. It was possible to think and write without having all this either poetic or pulpit rhetoric around you all the time; it's very refreshing. In that way I think Hemingway was more influential on me than Faulkner, although I love them both.

There was a lot of that compression.

Yeah. I don't think there is anything wrong with a good plain statement. I am not against either of them, but the abstruse in Faulkner that attracts so many scholars and that's not all good. It's the *mysterious* one wants, as in *As I Lay Dying,* not the abstruse. I don't think there will ever be a book like *As I Lay Dying.* It's really marvelous. I live in the backyard of that place he wrote about in [*Sound and the Fury*], all these modernesque houses.

This is the first time I've been up to Oxford.

Well, all kinds of tacky brick stuff is in the backyard of the house that I think they call the Thompson's, only he called it the Compson's. I like his spirit; I like Faulkner's being close and all, but I like it in my own measure. And Faulkner has become a kind of factory up here, you know, the Faulkner interests. It is something that I think he would have resented, although he probably would have had a good time for a while.

He spent half his life here being ignored.

That's right. Well, in the South they like you dead or away. It's wonderful. I mean if Percy expected support from his fellow Louisianians, it'd break his heart. Same thing with Mississippians.

You mentioned you were friends with Jimmy Buffet. He's

in with Thomas McGuane, Richard Brautigan, and that bunch living out in Montana. Are you all friends?

McGuane is a good buddy of mine, and Jimmy Buffet's sister married McGuane. The Buffets' mama and daddy have been awfully nice and I saw them in Biloxi a couple of weeks ago. We are just friends and he dedicated a song to me on his last album named from a story in *Airships,* **"Midnight and I'm Not Famous Yet."** This was a thrill; it got me more points at Ole Miss than winning the Nobel Prize. These people in their tennis shoes and impenetrable Delta dreams, whatever the hell motivates these kids up here. I think they were impressed. I enjoyed the devil out of that. I'll bet Walker Percy's never had a rock-and-roll tune dedicated to him, so tell Walker to take that. Buffet bought the movie option to *Airships* and he's coming up next month and hopefully I can script these Jeb Stuart stories out of *Airships* for some kind of movie.

Are you going to do it yourself?

Yeah. I'd like to.

The road is paved with failures.

I wrote for Altman out in Hollywood; I have a little experience but not enough to get my heart broken. I'm a novelist, short story writer, and whatever happens is gravy on that side.

What were you working on for Altman out there?

I wrote a piece called **"Power and Light"** about four lady hard-hat workers in Seattle. It's a beautiful assignment because I know nothing about women or hard-hat workers. Some of the best writing comes out of sheer lies. Altman is doing one-act plays now and when he comes back to being interested in movies again maybe he'll pick it up.

I just had a good time in Hollywood. I got healthy out there; I quit drinking. It's not going to be the street of broken dreams for me.

Well, it's not necessarily the broken dreams. I just think about all the people who have gone out and made a script attempt, and it went into the house somewhere and came out all churned up and garbaged out by somebody. All of Hemingway's work and Faulkner's work; every writer puts out a denial that he wants his name associated with the final product.

Right. I think the only good thing that came out of Faulkner's work, and he was a terrific overwriter, was [the screen play for] *To Have and Have Not.* That one piece, and that's not a lot for all the work he did.

You go out there to make money and sleep with movie stars. That's very cynical, but then I was living in Tuscaloosa and some poets over there warned me about how you lose your soul in Hollywood, and that's just a myth. People get swallowed up because they want to be. Sure, people lose their souls. I bet they go out there with their souls for sale. I don't believe in people who are worth anything being swallowed up by anything they are totally inimical to.

I could have written a great deal more for a lot more

money, but I just didn't want to. Nobody says you have to.

Sometimes the rent says you have to.

The rent says you have to. In this new book of mine the guy's doing a little for the rent, some high grade pornography, which is an interesting new arrival for me.

I really enjoyed the letters of Lepoyster [in **Geronimo***].*

I'm capable of some of that.

Great florid pornography.

Baroque pornography. Those came from some real letters that we discovered around an old house in Rodney, Mississippi, apparently from an inmate at Whitfield to his love. They were very poignant. I didn't have the letters at hand when I wrote those, but the spirit was there. Very European, baroque, and pornographic.

Lepoyster comes off that way; you sense that sort of old world beyond the bigotry.

In a way it needs that. It's what this guy in my new book says. What the modern hacks forget is elegance in pornography if you're gonna do it. I think *Fanny Hill* is still the best one I ever read. It's got this kind of—she's innocent and there's this elegance.

Have you read Delta of Venus *[by Anais Nin]? It's sort of an opium dream.*

Right. It should be an opium dream. It should have allegory to it, I think. I hate allegory, but pornography needs allegory. You need all the red herrings you can dig up. Something mysterious. It's not like some junior college dropout near Hollywood I met; what she found out from having attended school is that, and this is a real California attitude, "I can just be anything I want to be." Here she's got this bikini with a butterfly on her butt, tattooed. I just felt the chances of her being anything else were remote. And here she was in an ersatz Hell's Angel's bar—I guess she gets three beers in her and she feels like she can do anything.

And there are a lot of people who tell her she can, too.

That's right, and she'll get that enforced if she attends some therapy. And she'll keep being anything she wants to be until she's a toothless hag, cursing the light.

I'm writing about Hendrix and this new book may be of interest. It's called **Maximum Ned.** I'm a real fan of Jimi Hendrix; I take him very seriously. I don't think there's been anybody like him since. The sixties did perpetrate a myth, though, whether they borrowed from existentialism or just from some kind of stoned flower-thinking, that you can get through life with about five phrases.

Far out.

For sure.

Really.

But it's just the same kind of sickness you get from these fraternity boys here at Ole Miss who know five phrases and Nike tennis shoes. Hell, they're being everything they can be, too, and I'm sure that everytime they open a new keg, it's heaven. It's all they do, apparently.

I always place myself more with the beatniks in spirit, for what it matters—hell, I'm not doing an autobiography but they actually did things: Kerouac did write books and Ginsberg did write poems. They were terrific fatalists and pessimists, but they acted on it, and I kind of always admired people who did things.

From what I've read the beats were very insular as personalities as opposed to the people in the sixties. You think of Kesey and, well, I don't know McGuane, but from what I hear of him there is this sort of extended family concept that they both have. That didn't so much happen with the beats; there was more of an individual struggle.

Well, McGuane has a lot of money and a ranch, but his work doesn't come out of the "extended family." I don't know Kesey; I guess McGuane does. You know, whatever makes happiness, but somebody's got to make some bread sometime, unfortunately. I do have three children, you know, some of us incur these things over time, and you have to pay your debts. If you pay no debts at all—and I'm not much of a moralist—but I believe something goes out from you if you constantly pay no debts and avoid it. I think it actually makes you chicken. For one thing, I've always worked better under pressure; it didn't ever hurt me. God knows what I would do if I could be a layabout or had my way paid.

I'm a real fan of Jimi Hendrix; I take him very seriously. I don't think there's been anybody like him since. The sixties did perpetrate a myth, though, whether they borrowed from existentialism or just from some kind of stoned flower-thinking, that you can get through life with about five phrases.

—Barry Hannah

There is a lot to be said for deadlines.

Yeah. I was just with Terry MacDonald up in Pittsburgh, the editor of *Rolling Stone,* and I like Terry a lot. I think he's done a good deal on the magazine. He had a hell of a time recently; of all things, after what I've done for the booze and whiskey companies, I wrote an article about alcoholism and he caught all kinds of fire from concern about the whiskey accounts. That's a good deal of their advertising. I guess the crowd of *Rolling Stone* is stoned a lot. It celebrates early death, as a matter of fact, and every time they do an obit there's a little glory attached. It's an American dream to be like Charlie Parker at the latest, what? Thirty-seven, that's kind of pushing it. Somebody has to fight for the article which I believe Terry did. Somebody's got to put the magazine together. You'd really be hard put to have anything appear from the kind of laissez-

faire stuff the hippies put out in the sixties of their own. Hendrix's music represents untold hours of practice. The guy was always at his instrument.

Apparently a lot of guitarists say that some of his studio stuff just can't be duplicated.

Jimi got high like they did, but he brought something back. Those are the kind of people I respect. I think Walker Percy is a beatnik, too, for that matter. He does think civilization has just beaten the heart out of us. The architecture is shitty. He is just appalled by the New South visions. I am, too. I really think the South is turning chicken.

How so chicken?

I don't think there are as many interesting personalities, say, on the campus, as there used to be. There's something going on right now: students are taking fewer risks. I used to teach at Iowa, and although they will deny it to the wall, the fact is that the students are taking fewer risks in their writing; there were fewer individuals.

When you are in a writing school you expect some really raving visionaries and people who are in the dungeon of art, etc. Well, actually they are quite straight people. The best ones had developed a voice and the rest of them are writing supersubtle stories about ". . . maybe Ned was a queer. We didn't know."

Dr. Simpson said, dealing with the problems of getting stories published, that writing schools in the country have made it harder because there are a lot of good writers out there who come out of writing schools but they don't have anything to say. Taken that they are very good, but there is nothing behind it.

Well, I agree with Dr. Simpson in that. It's hard to find what is important to say. That's why my last book **Ray** was so terribly short. It came out of a period of agony and drunken angst, and it was better to make it short and sweet than just babble or tell some cranked up southern story again. For God's sake, I hope I never get caught doing that.

Do you find that you enjoy writing short stories more than novels? Do you find it harder to write a short story? Your first two books were novels, even though **Geronimo** *came out of that* Intro *short story [*"The Crowd Punk Season Drew"*].*

Physically and emotionally it's more satisfying to write a short story because I can do one in a week usually. You get this instant gratification; it's a complete thing you can look at. I really enjoy that, and you can also make a lot of money if you start selling them.

You are one of the few people who can say that, unfortunately.

I told that to that guy in the picture there, Bob Shacochis, a good buddy of mine in Iowa. He sold about three stories—to *Playboy,* one to *Esquire,* and to *Paris Review*—while I was there. That's the best record I have ever seen from a student. He's thirty, and he's not just a student. I didn't have a lot to do about that except offer encouragement. It happens. There's no point in not thinking that good writing won't get published. There's just no point in your going around with any attitude at all before you write a story. You're dooming yourself. A lot of people do that.

What do you want to call it, luck, or people who wanted my stuff, but they didn't want every damn thing. I mean, *Nightwatchmen* came out and I got blasted in the *New York Times* and my stock I think was very low. I wrote a book about a tennis player that wasn't wanted by anyone, but I pulled it out the other day and a friend of mine read it and he said, "Well hell, this is good." So I sent it up to Gordon Lish, my editor at Knopf, and he said, "Indeed, it is good." I was very down about that book being passed over, and I'm sure with the success that *Ray*'s had and with *Airships* helps. We can put the book in some kind of shape; nobody even wanted to work with me to put it into some kind of shape. This is the book about the tennis player—he emanated from LSU, by the way. There's a lot of Covington and Metairie stuff in there.

But I wasn't defeated. You just don't get defeated. I went ahead and started writing the short stories and selling them to *Esquire.* For about four or five years there I didn't write anything else. This gloom about the American publishing scene and all those doomsayers that go around campus and talk about how impossible it is to get good literature published—I just don't believe it, for one thing. I think it's a myth that somebody is just wonderful and nobody will touch him.

That's probably true, but the standard thing is that you have to get past the Vassar reader who is sitting at the Knopf desk taking the first reading before it gets in.

Well, it could be a good Vassar reader. I think my editor at Viking went to Vassar, and she pulled *Geronimo* out and got the biggest advance they'd given for a first novel in a long, long time.

Of course, she was vindicated on that.

Maybe I'm speaking from a condition of luck or something, but I think that there are plenty of good people in New York, and, by the way, they are not all northeastern, Jewish, or whatever latest paranoia inflicts the writer. They are really alive to good writing and I see them every year. I get good books in the mail and galleys.

Geronimo came out and then Nightwatchmen, which wasn't received very well, and then you switched publishers. What happened?

My editor quit there, and I wrote what was supposed to be a non-fiction tennis book for Lippincott, and my tennis player, Bob Lutz, broke his leg on the tour, so . . . I also found out that tennis players are dull, and I didn't want to write a non-fiction book.

Is that why the tennis player in Airships is brain damaged?

No, this novel of mine coming out next year is about that guy. Further adventures. So I came home and invented my own tennis player. There aren't any top notch southern tennis players that have really shown it at Wimbledon lately. I thought it was high time that there would be a good one, so I invented him, named French Edward.

I wrote that book and then Lippencott didn't want it. So then I wrote Gordon Lish, the editor at *Esquire,* and he bought a lot of the stories, and then Lish went over to Knopf and the stories won the Arnold Gingrich Award for short fiction. Then he wanted *Ray.* So that's how I met Knopf.

I was just wondering how the transition went, whether Viking had given you an option on the strength of Geromino and decided not to renew after Nightwatchmen.

They were probably discouraged with the sales of *Nightwatchmen.* I think it went nowhere; it didn't even get a paperback.

It was under ten thousand copies. There were a couple of scenes in the book that I still can't get out of my mind. There's the scene of Trove as a young boy about to be pulled off the pier when he hooks a shark. This old man saves him and then takes a pack of razor blades and flips them out into the ocean and watches the sharks and barracudas hit them. I can't get that out of my mind to save my life . . . got these little silver razor blades flying out.

Yeah. I heard that story from someone, but I've never witnessed it. There is some good stuff in *Nightwatchmen.* I don't know how good the book is. I haven't gone back and read it in a long time.

Anyway, you just don't give up. Faulkner is very inspirational for that. I got as much out of, when I was in graduate school, reading the biographies of writers as I did their actual work. Very inspirational. Like Conrad, who didn't do anything or publish anything until he was fifty.

And had to learn English first.

Right. And that beautiful, wonderful Henry Miller who had no luck at all until damn near forty and kept pounding away.

Who didn't even start anything until his early thirties.

Right. Of course, for every Henry Miller there's a hundred guys who risk all and go to Paris and maybe publish one poem.

Buffet has a song about that called "He Went to Paris" on his first album.

Miller's a great spirit that just had to win through, and I believe the spirits will win through.

I've always wondered about that. I love Henry Miller's writing at times. About two years ago I read a biography of him called Always Merry and Bright.

I didn't read it.

It's a good biography. You think that Miller's writing is sort of the way he is, and then you find out that he's been through four wives.

Mailer made a point that he always had hemorrhoids. He was always in a little pain.

Mailer's introductions all through Genius and Lust were wonderful.

Miller said he didn't understand one word of that book.

Accused Mailer of having verbal diarrhea: "He's a charming man, but I have no idea what he's talking about." That's just like Miller. He's a great study; Faulkner is another one. I mean *Sound and the Fury* was passed over by about twenty-five people.

The thing is that I have read enough and have been a teacher on and off for about fifteen years, so I see some of us who are belligerent and really feel the angst about our work but just aren't tough enough. That's where teaching or any encouragement is crucial.

You've been teaching at residencies since about 1975; do you find this a satisfying way to work or not? Again, Max Steele up at Chapel Hill said that a lot of people come in for residencies and are sort of truncated in their own work because they are having to read other people and talk to student writers and it slows them down.

Yeah, if you don't watch it, it will. But you've got to pay the rent on your soul, too. I've only been able to write with complete freedom for a year and a half or two years of my adult working life. *Airships* and *Ray* and the movies did that. The schools have been nice to me and it pays the house rent. I don't know if a book of mine is ever gonna hit and free me up, but I do enjoy. . . .

Does it not make any difference?

Yeah, it makes a difference. That's the only reason you go to Hollywood is to make enough to do what you want. Sure it makes a difference. There's something about me that needs pressure, and my classes here don't bother me at all. I've got two classes here, for God's sake; I mean all this whining from writers about no time I think is a false issue. You can write a book if you want to. I wrote a hell of a lot at Clemson; I was teaching twelve hours. In a way it even stimulated me. I find sometimes the more you take on the more you do. You simply do more when you take on more.

I think from what Max was saying was that one of the things that slows you down is having to read other peoples' writing and having to think critically as opposed to sitting down and writing. It's not so much the teaching load and the things you are having to do as a faculty member, but it takes you out of one mode and shifts you into another.

That's right. That's why I don't do book reviews, not for anybody. Unless, you know, I'm just absolutely broke.

The students at Iowa were very good and it took a lot of mental effort for changing modes. Because the critical mode is just diametrically opposed to the creative. You don't want to be a critic when you write. That's death. You want to be willing to be a fool every time you write. You have to be, and to take a lot of risk.

The kind of books I write, I've given away a great deal. I just don't care about plot that much, so I have got to have a voice or tone that's going to carry the thing. Sometimes you read somebody else and it'll bust it for you for a whole week. The kind of tone I want is sometimes just a kind of confluence of music. I keep my music box here, put on some Hendrix or something, you know how music will evoke a whole . . . months of some year that has passed . . . will bring back things very visually.

I deliberately play the music loud to knock out everything. I used to do this with booze; it worked beautifully until my health went. You have to have the clinical, the tunnel vision of a clinical idiot to write, if you are me. It's not being comprehensive at all to me. It's shedding almost everything except what's right in front of you and going straight ahead. Terrific concentration.

In **Airships** *and* **Ray** *there's not much physical geography. It's mostly speech and a little bit of action drawn in to bring you to the point where two people are facing off. That would fit in with the tunnel vision.*

I found it difficult to write out in Hollywood because I was learning as much as I could about California. I had never been out there, and I was really digging it and just kind of eating up the city all the time. It wasn't a loss because I liked what I learned out there.

This new book is full of California. But I was sober and I actually knew too much to write . . . learning new things everyday, and it was tough to write sober; it really was. In fact, I had to get some dexedrine to get back and do something. My best experience out there was regaining my confidence. The *Ray* thing was pretty true as far as the emotions go and after the book came out, at that point in my life, I had just about lost confidence.

John Cheever said that he can smell alcohol on the page when the author has taken a drink.

Absolutely. Sure. It was written in the hottest summer that we've ever had. I was separated and divorced and the air conditioners were freezing over. Remember that summer?

Good summer for gin.

Gin and everything. Deep angst, trying to cope, and everything in writing was true emotionally. The events didn't all happen, but in the psyche they did. So it does come to an end and I wanted hope, and I got back close to my children and got healthy in California. I'll always love California because I got healthy there.

Did you just stop or did you have to go into a hospital?

No, I went into a hospital. You really don't have any choice, if you were in my condition, of stopping. People who don't know say, why doesn't he just quit? Jesus, I wanted to.

Some people apparently do, or do like Faulkner, who drank when he wasn't working.

But he drank when he was working, too. But that's him. Everybody has his own system. Apparently he could shut it off for months and be quite clean and then go back. There's a problem with the whole thing and it's a shame. Right now, being a survivor, I'm not going to come down on booze because it's done a great deal for me, frankly. That's anti-alcoholics anonymous talk, but it's done a great deal for me and I don't want to—it's like scolding an old friend now that you don't need him.

I get this vision of a guy sitting on a curb with a bottle saying, "This has got me where I am today."

Right, that's what they got. But I punched my ticket on alcohol. It was just another experience. The thing is that alcohol will eventually make you bored and sick of everything. It will close down your receivers entirely.

Most of the people I know who are in their mid-thirties and went through the whole drug thing are not opposed to doing a few hallucinogens for special occasions, but as a rule we've all gone back to bourbon and beer, and not even that in real excess.

Oh God, I love it. If I could, I would, I guess. I just played out the odds. There is a bit of a scientist in it, in wanting to push it as far as you can, to get art and vision.

There's a whole history in all of that.

You've got all your idols intact, and my idols were all drunks. Joyce, Faulkner, Hemingway. It was very prescient. I thought that I probably should drink, and at one point in my life maybe I should have.

But that stage is gone?

Right. One thing that I am not so sure happens as beautifully as depicted is a guy dying for his art. These people who get off on Sylvia Plath and all that school, who are really just like southerners, they like you dead.

When you take someone like Berryman, a kindred spirit, I know exactly why the *Dream Songs* are like they are. Some nice editor at Random House compared **Ray** to *Dream Songs*. I know exactly that juncture of thinking, that skipping, illogical skipping. Sometimes when it hits it's beautiful; it's a new logic.

When **Ray** is good I think it hits a new kind of logic I'm still working on in this other book. But as it concerns your life, I just like life too much to rip myself up for the dream songs or anything.

It would be nice if it were a state that you could turn on and off.

Yeah, I can't believe that nobody in my generation, the brilliant generation that has gone to the moon, has not come up with harmless whiskey and cigarettes. When I was in the drying-out clinic, they said it was the wrong attitude to have.

I am still very much interested in people who burn themselves out, and I guess it is sometimes for art. Jimi Hendrix was at a great impasse and apparently was going nowhere, and perhaps he had been everywhere he could go. He seems to have died by a terrible accident: booze, pills, and choking.

I remember all those amazing stories about Hendrix that were folklore in the sixties, about his taking vast quantities of LSD and going to sleep.

Maybe so. During different times he seemed to be a big user of speed and acid. But you get used to the ordinary. I mean, I went bass fishing and roaming around, even hearing rock and roll, it's just not enough. You just do

want to get to the other world. I sympathize entirely with the motives.

In **Airships** *you go backwards and forwards in time. You go back to the Jeb Stuart stories and forward to somewhere beyond World War III.*

Well, I would just like to say this: it would be hateful to lose just the instinct of saying something and letting it go. I like to write. A lot of people don't like to write. One of the things that I like about it is that it is instinctual, almost like sex, and I don't like to lose that by over-discussing it or by nailing down these critical parameters or any of that stuff. It's still something that just happens.

That is something that McGuane says when he's asked about all the pain and effort and everything else it takes to get up in the morning and face the blank page. He says that it's no effort at all. He'd rather do that than do anything else.

When it goes well it's no effort at all. I find when I'm writing poorly usually it's a real strain and a headache. It's still a great joy.

Your corpus is not all that much. Do you find that you do a whole lot of rewriting? This is something that David Madden brings up: the Intro short story **"The Crowd Punk Season Drew"***, that grew into* **Geronimo***, was originally all in the third person, then in the novel got switched into first, which is a pretty major change. Do you do a whole lot of editing and revising like that?*

No. I have a good editor; Gordon Lish is wonderful. He'll never change anything I don't want changed. He sure is good to see shape and tell me the news. It's always been mainly what I want. I've never been smacked around by an editor.

It just takes me a hell of a lot of living to write, mainly because I work so close to my own life. I can write better about the things I've been rather close to and feel. There are others who are not like me who are wonderful, who can do better with other people's stories, but I can only do that a little bit.

In the Jeb Stuart stories you certainly weren't close to any of the events.

Right. I'm close to the emotions. There's something in me that is Jeb Stuart or something like that. I mean I'm not writing about a foreigner at all. He's a glorious fool.

The story **"Dragged Fighting from His Tomb,"** *where the soldier ends up shooting Stuart and finally is at the old soldiers' convention—was that an effort to kill off Stuart?*

No. I really tried to enter the character of Captain Howard. I mean Stuart's attitude about animals throws him over into a homicidal state where he becomes a theoretical assassin.

I wasn't trying to get rid of Jeb Stuart and he didn't go that way, of course. He was shot at Yellow Tavern. I was trying to stay consistent with the character of young Captain Howard to old Captain Howard. You know, he's wondered all his life about the big questions. Darwin had just come out and not many people in America had read him;

if Howard had read him you know that he would have thought deeply about it. In Howard's time the book had been out only about three years, since 1859, and Gettysburg was 1863, and that during the war, and no Confederates read much anyway. So he's a real student and he wants these answers, and I like that in him. He can never find out why Stuart is blasé about horses. When he sees an old man out in the field who can't give him any wisdom, he doesn't see that the race is really progressing any more than rabbits, and he's damn sure that the war isn't making him better, finally. So he becomes a moral assassin. So I was more concerned with Howard than I was with Stuart. Stuart is just a foil who flames around.

I was wondering that because you said that you were attracted to Stuart, and a lot of writers will kill off a character literally as a way of getting them out of their minds—that's the last you will ever hear from Jeb Stuart, is when I kill him off—and that sort of thing.

No. I didn't kill off Jeb Stuart. He's still glorious. I was always attracted to Stuart because he was so much unlike me. He's pretty straight Presbyterian, didn't smoke or drink, and had elegant phrases for his sweetheart and wife. It's an old style that has just about perished.

Allen Tate once worked on a biography of Lee and then later gave it up. Penn Warren asked him how on earth he could be writing a biography of Lee when the man had no sin, which was apparently true.

I gave that book to my daddy, the one about Lee's last five years [*Lee's Final Years*, W. Flood, 1981], and he is pretty damn blameless. It's hard to get material on the guy.

Stuart was better because he liked music and he was capable of being a fool. He failed gravely at Gettysburg; he wasn't in the right place. He didn't tell Lee anything about the disposition of the Union troops. He was up there riding for glory, probably around another army like he did McClellan's. That's the kind of asshole soldier I would be, I fear. There's that weakness in Stuart that makes him more likely for fiction.

Ray's middle name is Forrest. Was that from Bedford Forrest or did that come from somewhere else?

I don't know. I can't remember how that occurred. Forrest's another famous cavalry general, illiterate man from Mississippi. I didn't know much about Forrest until I read Shelby Foote when I came here, as a matter of fact. The whole thing about cavalry's very glorious; the movies are still in love with horses.

The Civil War was the last war that really used cavalry. The trains began to take them out.

Right, and trench warfare. Longstreet advocated trench warfare around Petersburg. The whole thing just became mechanized and all that glory, which was pompous and phony anyway, just disappeared. It's a natural. I grew up near Vicksburg and I was just imbued with this stuff. I knew stuff I didn't know I knew until I started writing.

You might know this from Ole Miss, but do you think that's still happening in students today? I can remember going

through a stage when I got my parents to take me to the battlefields. I can remember crying at Shiloh.

I've never been there, but I understand it will make you cry if you're into it. The only reaction that I've had to that was on a plane with this writer who knew my work named Frederick Busch. I was going from Syracuse back over to Iowa City, and he had taught this *Airships* book, and he had some student who came up to him and said, "What is this with Jeb Stuart? I just don't get it. What the hell has Hannah got on his mind? I mean there are three separate stories and you hear about Jeb Stuart. Who cares about Jeb Stuart?" I mean he was really disturbed. Then I've had other people write me and state that they really enjoyed the whole book, but especially the Stuart stuff. These are young people. Stuart has a western flavor; if they don't like the Civil War, everybody likes a good western.

I think there's another thing: the Stuart stories have that flavor of immediacy. The scene where Captain Howard comes up and points this gun at the old man and says, "Tell me something true." It all happens in that chivalric mode, a knight coming down.

Right. A chivalric mode and he's been wounded. I think that people who have been wounded tend to ask questions like that.

You know you will get it out of them.

If you had a neck wound.

Well, let me oppose it. The first story in the book where the old guys are standing around lying and this one fellow tells the awful story of finding his daughter in the woods, which is the true truth, and everyone is just appalled. It seems like styles of the same technique, except that Captain Howard is approaching it head-on whereas the other people are circumventing.

Right, with all these legends about the lake. I didn't think about it that way. You grow up with the legends and, you're younger than I am, but I grew up with a very whitewashed view of almost everything. These old southern tales of ghosts on the lake that you hear when you're a boy scout and all that . . . and then the reality of this old guy he meets there and his daughter: it's really kind of a growing-up thing, and this is really what happens. You don't meet the ghost of Yazoo out there; it's your own daughter getting fucked by some guy with a mustache that you don't even know.

I really wanted that to be eerie, you know, the sounds of lovemaking coming over the lake. It's another kind of hideous thing, more so than a horror show or any of this crap you learn when you're a boy scout. It's the real shocker. The young man's dealing with it in his wife's story, too.

And the old guy, he's probably heard sounds like that, but from the distance of six inches. It's much different from being out on the lake, and he knows the legends of the ghost on the lake and everything else, so in that context all he's thinking about is the ghost.

Right. It's really a ghostly thing, but it's not just very real. Not many fathers—it is the absolute horror dream of these fathers who send their young daughters to Ole Miss, or to Belhaven, or one of those sanctuaries. Nothing could be worse to the guy and he'll never get over it.

Do you have daughters?

Yes, I have a daughter, and I'm sure that I'm bound to be just a classic dad of the middle class who has had a lot of free life and knows about those bastards waiting for her out there who are no good. You have to face that when you have a daughter. I'm very paternal, very conservative.

I guess being a father I'm kind of on the same level as Mc-Guane. He's got a new little daughter, little Annie. I think McGuane's about forty or forty-one, and on the *Today* show he was talking about place, family, and writing his books. And it's quite true: you just can't do massive cocaine forever. You don't want to be conservative, but the things that really touch you or are close to you are very conservative. You get honest. It's not turning into a Reaganite; it's really a shoring in of what was always solid. Figuring out what is solid, what was good and wasn't, isn't going to go away, and making that your base. When you start pushing forty or so it's hard to be a space pilot with people depending on you, children and all. And although you want to be a pioneer, you don't want to lose yourself.

That was the worst thing with my great experiment with booze—for those that were close to me—it scared the hell out of them. It busted up a second marriage. It's really not worth it to make other people go through that agony. If it was just you, that's the great myth: it's just you. It's my life, damn it. But that's hardly ever the case.

In a lot of alcohol counseling they say it takes two people to make an alcoholic. It's the situation you're in as well, which is the reason they go in for a lot family therapy for couples who are still together.

The fact is that I kind of hold a straight scientific view on that: that genetically if you're going to be an alcoholic, you're going to be an alcoholic. There are plenty of drinking fathers who go through tense situations without being alcoholic.

There are a lot of alcoholics who say that they knew from the first beer that that was it.

Right. I like the fatalism of that, anyway. It gets you off the hook.

And it does give you something to hang it all on. You can say: it's in my chromosomes.

That's true. Although you can get rid of the guilt to a certain extent, you remember that of all diseases, it is the one that you constantly give yourself. Nobody forces that stuff down your throat. Nobody wakes you up and puts that needle in your arm. I don't think you can shake that, I mean, your conscience just really won't shake that. But they try to in therapy.

There are all kinds of drunks, too. There are productive drunks, there are nasty drunks, there are very friendly and kind drunks. I always wanted to be, even when I considered myself a drunk, friendly. And then I started losing that. I was not friendly; I was very down on everything.

I didn't feel good enough to be up about anything. I was letting down people, scaring my children. So I'd become the kind that I hated, belligerent in bars, arguing over meaningless stuff. When you become what you've hated, you sound queer.

A lot of people are kind of curious with what you do to yourself. They just never understand. Living through modern chemistry has never been so available. I think that Leary really did burn himself out. He does deny this, but to me he is testimony to the fact that you can go too far.

But the final thing is to put your body on the line. That's an instinct that seems to have come in the sixties: putting your body on the line.

Yeah. For good, hopefully. My friend Quisenberry, whom I wrote about in **Ray** and in that story **"Testimony of Pilot,"** was over in Vietnam doing his thing. I remember writing him letters and pleading with him. He had the choice to be an astronaut or a fighter pilot. I wanted him to be an astronaut; and I got up and read anti-war poetry at Clemson and all that, and was very moral about it. I'm glad I did; it was a lousy, stupid war. But it is better to believe in something and do it.

What I could count for in that way was getting drunk and blowing a mouse off the back of a sofa with a 30/30. I did that once. That kind of stuff isn't really doing anybody any good.

Hunter Thompson is legendary for that kind of stuff.

Yeah. What I'm saying is that I like people to put their body on the line somewhere to be effective, because one thing I have learned growing older is that attitudes are awfully damned cheap. I really get impatient with people who line up with their attitudes, and their actions speak a whole lot more.

I have a buddy, contemporary of mine, who was always for the Black Panthers, but he didn't ever do anything. He was just a good liberal. It didn't make one damn bit of difference to a hungry black child that he was for the Black Panthers. It would have been better for him to have been Jim Eastland and given some guy a buck on the corner.

Eastland and my old man were roommates up here. They are very much unalike, but it's an interesting fact. It's what you do. . . .

Was Quisenberry the source of most of your information on Vietnam?

Right. He enjoys my writing about that. He had a degree in literature out at Occidental, and I think he wanted to write at one time and pulled back and became a lawyer. I asked him once if he resented my borrowing or kind of living his life, and he said no, not at all. He really enjoyed it.

Sometimes I get cut down for wanting violence, having violence, by some critics who think that I just feed on that, and actually I do. I like violence, but I have wound up living almost the whole damn sad stories in my book. I'd kind of like to explain that. I like the kind of violence that provokes the conversation that Howard had with that

Union old man, that when your body gets threatened, your mind tightens up. You lie less when things are against the wall, and things that are really meaningful come forth. Sometimes I force the action by using violence for that reason, but I also enjoy the spectacle of it. I like the *Wild Bunch* very much, something very cathartic about it.

Lee Marvin said that once. He really appreciated the Wild Bunch *because he said he had been in westerns for so many years where you slug some guy in a bar and you never saw the guy's teeth falling out, and the guy who slugged him, his hand completely ruined. And it was not in any way real. He said that if we are going to have these things, let's show them what it's really like.*

That's what Peckinpah is all about. Although I don't go out looking for fistfights, there's something inside every male body, and I think it's just granted, that you want to run, hit, do something with this great amount of muscle frame you're given.

Hunter and gatherer.

Yeah. Hunter and gatherer. I mean you're not supposed to sit around looking at a Smith-Corona, typing. A motorcycle does that for me. I like the feel of motorcycles. I like the possibility of danger, the fact that you have to protect yourself on it without being foolish about it.

If you go back to Hendrix, and I keep bringing him up because the book's about what he was, and about possibly the art of, what they call, the sixties. But when he released all those sounds you forget that Hendrix was a paratrooper and was close to these airplane noises and sounds of war. He wrote about machine guns; he did a version of "Hey Joe, where you going with that gun in your hand?"

But he used these sounds. You hear that Hendrix guitar, very wrenching and it's got this violence, and that was part of his vision. Then you hear that gentle voice come across. It's quite something; it's a beautiful artistic mix. So I think that Hendrix was that interested in the age. He was no flower child; no flower child could have unleashed those sounds. There's a great bit of fury in all of that. It has to get out some way, hopefully, in the way that Hendrix did it. He was, as far as I know, pretty apolitical and hardly ever talked about the race question.

In the biography they said that Hendrix was really frustrated about the fact that he never achieved any popularity with blacks. His records sold like crazy to whites, but he never achieved any measure of success with blacks, and he couldn't understand it.

He liked Bob Dylan so much he began writing like that "On A Watchtower" ["All Along the Watchtower"]. I guess he kind of left that basic blues place. He did play with some real boogie artists early.

I think he played with Little Richard?

He did play with Little Richard, and they had a conflict of stars trauma. Nobody could be the star around Little Richard. "Scream like a white woman," he said; "that's the secret of success." Hendrix found his own voice and

it didn't happen to be this popular black voice; it wasn't Aretha Franklin.

With his British reputation he became really big. This sheer virtuoso stuff has never been that admired in the black community. BB King is awfully good, but he's not admired for fast playing or weird licks. But you're right, he never did have a big black audience. It's people like Frank Zappa and Eric Clapton and me who worship him, white people more than blacks. I've never heard black musicians extoll him that much, come to think of it.

But anyway, the subject of Hendrix is interesting to me not just because of the sixties, which I think can be really overplayed, but it's the guy who made just a hell of a lot of music out of a kind of down experience. I mean nobody wants to go with the paratroopers when they're eighteen in Seattle; that's a nowhere town for blues. He really kind of came out of nowhere. I like that very much about him; I find it appealing. It harks back to the natural genius theory that they say is discredited, but in this case is very stirring.

I saw Hendrix's grave when I was in Seattle. It was very moving, like one of these Civil War things you were talking about. Let me read this part that I wrote about Hendrix. The reason I'm kind of full about them all over again is because I finally got down some things that I was going to say. See if it sounds right to you.

You might wonder how you could be interested in the Civil War and Jeb Stuart and all that, and gee, it's just right on the point. Maybe I've made this come around:

> Truth is that the drunk has seen everyday a miracle. He's after the miracle. Angels and drunks, they say. He has all the feeling and not quite the substance of a miracle. It is too good, this closeness, and you want to go across the river and into the trees with Stonewall Jackson, who refused liquor because he liked it too much. In the big battle he sucked a lemon all day. Suck, suck, while his foot cavalry hit and hit again.

> And that is what you want, Ned, the bite of yearning a lemon gets you. The mighty thing is at hand and will come down for you.

> Some day, some moment, the army in you will strike on something so good you will not have to lie about it.

> You can bring a few pieces of it back, like our smoking dead Jimi.

> I saw his grave near the little firs in Seattle. That morning it was deep gray and steam was coming out of the ground, ground breathing out fog as if Hendrix had just crashed from the high whining drug altitude of the sixties. It was good to be sober, weeping just a little. Finally hello and never goodbye to the young paratrooper who found a music of his time, bombs away. Played upside down with his left hand, they still don't know just how. You cannot forget the gentle voice behind all the bending thunder he twisted out of his instrument. What weather he evoked: speed, lush, acid, ulcers, and finally lost. The man who just ate too much Jesus.

Adieu and see you in the next one, Jimi. Don't
be late.

*It's as though all we've been talking about has led up to this
point. . . .*

*How much do you think the reviewing process has to do with
a book's final acceptance?*

There are a number of reviews that I skip, but I always
liked the ones that just take me head-on personally. Some
guy in West Virginia said that *Geronimo* was three hundred or whatever pages of raving incoherence. I like that.
In this last, somebody in Columbia, South Carolina, said
that *Ray* proved that I had sold out to the New York establishment and should no longer be considered in near
company with Faulkner.

*That was probably a reply to the successful reviews that
came out from Christopher Lehmann-Haupt and Benjamin DeMott in the* Times *and* Village Voice.

Right. You sold out to the establishment if you get good
reviews. Plastic, too, he mentioned.

*That goes back to something we were talking about at
lunch. It's better to be pure and somehow a literary success
and remain untainted by good reviews.*

There's a type of southern reviewer who is the most pathetic, envious, spiteful, usually dilettantish figure out
there in the United States. It was kind of a shock to me
in *Geronimo* with so many of your southern brothers giving it to you in the back. For one thing, most of the reviewers can't stand literature. But I feel some of these notes in
the columns. This has nothing to do with an honest review
by a guy who despises Ray and all he stands for. So I got
good New York reviews. . . .

Do you keep up with your reviews?

I read a lot of them.

Does it mean anything to you?

No, not much. I write what I can and I don't intend to
write bad books. It's all out there on the line. I mean, I'm
risking being a fool but that's the best I can do, ladies and
gentlemen, and I have no further apology or explanation.
I probably am still about the same cynical rock-and-roller
that Harry Monroe was in *Geronimo Rex;* he's been
through a great deal since.

You wrote a little quib in the Thomas Wolfe Newsletter *a
long time back. It was an appreciation of Wolfe's* Look
Homeward, Angel *["Tom Wolfe was a giant in all ways.
He had the language, the vision, and the huge soul.* Look
Homeward, Angel *is and will remain a miraculous original
of our time, and only impatient midgets—that our time and
the literary profession breeds—would ever cut down the big
old good boy from Asheville."] One of the same criticisms
that the literary establishment aimed at Wolfe was that
Wolfe never grew. It was still the same sort of* Look Homeward, Angel, Lost Boy, You Can't Go Home Again.

You mean grew into a professorship at Chapel Hill or
something. He was only thirty-eight when he died; I mean,
give the guy a break, that's very young.

And, of course he was very prolific.

He wrote too much, but he was on the way there and there
are passages in Wolfe that will still knock you out. If he
wasn't growing he would have got there if he hadn't
burned himself out, although I don't want to read anymore about Asheville and the way he writes about it. Once
is enough.

There's a kind of ambitious grandness to Wolfe and Henry
Miller and Faulkner that the contemporary mind simply
does not want to face. I don't write like they do, but I sure
appreciate what they were trying to do. That is: to get it
all in.

Faulkner said, I think in the Paris Review, *after being
asked to evaluate his contemporaries, that he put Wolfe first
because he thought that Wolfe took the most risks, that he
was willing to abandon everything to vision.*

The people who say that Wolfe starts a terrible strain of
autobiographical confession in American letters are forgetting always who it is that is confessing. It is true that
some people, it's not worth hearing their confessions. But
with Wolfe it was. He's not my favorite writer but he was
a grand soul that I find very inspiring. I think it was Flannery O'Connor, who was also a wonderful writer, who
said the nastiest thing about him, that the schools of writing were good even if they discouraged one Thomas Wolfe
per decade. Well, that's very nasty and witty like she is.

The people I like are looser and fuller like Miller and
Wolfe. The only place I differ with them is that not all
things are interesting to me as they are to them. They remain obsessed by autobiography, but I use it as a mode to
get to the real stuff which is almost always lying.

I like the way that Wolfe moved us into a kind of modernity where you really just forget the definitions, novel, book,
or what the hell it is. I like that. I like to finish a book and
have all those questions precluded. It was just a hell of a
something and I'm glad I went through it.

That was one of the questions the critics brought up about
Ray. *It was so short, and when the chapters, chapters speaking loosely, but when the fragments become smaller and
smaller down towards the end, I think that passed over a
lot of people.*

I guess that would indicate that Ray is getting more frantic. His concentration is going . . . becoming more
desparate . . . it's difficult for him to even speak.

*And as they get smaller and shorter they become more crys-
talline.*

Hopefully, right. I wanted to write about a man who is capable of great banality and also exquisite art. He's a doctor, not a writer, really. I want to keep that in mind. He's
lumbering between banality and some gripping thought,
and he's trying. But he doesn't probably have the natural
thing. He keeps at it, though, which is important.

Then there's Sister's father.

Yeah. Mr. Hooch, who just blows him out of the water.

There are some wonderful passages in there. I guess Ray's

just shot Mr. Hooch up with morphine and you can see the morphine coming into his veins because the language just shifts gears right in the middle of the paragraph. It's wonderful.

It's an experience.

Back at the question again about compression. You said you don't do a lot of rewriting, but it takes a lot of rewriting to come up with a paragraph like that, doesn't it?

When I say that, look, I got about five of these things for this book [Hannah holds up an art sketch book about twelve by sixteen inches.] This writing goes back about a year and a half for this book. I'm doing that. When you start selecting and grabbing around you're rewriting all the time before it ever gets to the typewriter. I consider the typewriter the last version. I've written some of these scenes four or five times in different ways in handwriting. I've also lived and thought them out. I never write the first thing that comes to my mind, hardly ever. So by the time I get to this book I have done a hell of a lot of editing.

Sometimes you get lucky and you'll write four or five pages and you won't change that much at all. It was just an emotional book, **Ray,** that I hit in places like that. It didn't seem like I wanted to change anything. But you are usually changing a great deal, to be honest. You're always re-sorting things in your mind.

You gave your editor a lot of credit. When your editor gets to it, does he provide shape more than anything, or does he . . . ? By this time you're beyond substantive editing.

That's right. Sometimes I write too much and it's just that stroke. Gordon Lish's best stroke is crossing some things because the best thing is to suggest and not explicate. Because I try to remember that you should be a poet, that's the strongest kind of information you can impart.

Let it occur in the reader's mind.

I mean, I treat my readers better than a lot of writers do. I expect a hip, wise reader, and I don't have to tell that boy or girl everything. I expect some complicity with it. I hope I can get this. We're in this together and I'm writing the best I can, but, my God, we know too much anyway and I don't feel provoked into extended nature writing because nature is very personal. Some of the weakest writing I read is where some guy is trying to grab you and hold you up to a telescope: this is nature my way, look at that. I try not to invade the reader's privacy in that way. I don't think a good nature writer really does that. They suggest, too. You'll get a Hemingway landscape that will really move you some way, and you go back and look through it; it's not a photograph.

Very few adjectives, just nouns to hang on.

Right. It's a subjective thing, a spirit. Where was he? How's he feel? Was he fishing? Or what was the mood? It's something to fish for trout when you're wishing you could get laid and you've been shot or injured, and to fish for trout without that feeling.

Trying to extinguish feeling. Trying to just fish.

Right. Beware of the dark swampy part.

You can always fish that tomorrow. Do you write for an audience? Or who do you see your audience as being?

No. It varies. Different times I might. I think mainly just pleasing myself. I think of guys, friends, my girlfriends occasionally, when I write a passage. To see that it would please them.

The main thing is that I love the English language very much. That's the one thing I picked up from all the literary study. I just adore it. My kind of affair with the language has gone through a lot of changes. I'm always trying to get as much as I can out of words. That kind of takes over. You're faithful to experience and you try that with words, you really don't have a lot of time to think about an audience. Just a kind of wise person who might be enjoying some of the experience with you.

Richard Eder   (review date 6 September 1987)

SOURCE: "A War Memorial in the Mind," in *Los Angeles Times Book Review,* September 6, 1987, pp. 3, 12.

[*An American critic and journalist, Eder received a Pulitzer Prize for criticism in 1987. In the following review, he remarks favorably on* Hey Jack!]

In the white hell of winter warfare in Korea, Homer, the narrator of **Hey Jack!** thought of going back to the Mississippi heat, girls and tennis games. But war is a universal condition, and once you have seen it, you recognize it anywhere, any time.

The recognition drives the narration of Barry Hannah's compelling novella. Years after the dreadful fighting around the Chosen Reservoir, the musty smell of an old book at an antiquary's shop brought the deaths back to Homer and sent him into a brief breakdown.

Now, still later, a writer in a Mississippi college town, successful and well-off, in love with a vital and lovely woman whom he is about to marry, Homer's nostrils flare for the odor that seeps up everywhere.

Hey Jack! is a casting-about among the stories and lives that Homer knows in his town. He is like a man on a dark night, who wheels under the stars to find his bearings; only to realize that stars are not the calm beacons of anthropocentric tradition, but churning infernos. Nobody is safe, and love decays.

Hey Jack! is a lethal kaleidoscope. Homer starts right off with the grotesques, whose extravagant extremes are squarely in the Southern tradition of William Faulkner and Flannery O'Connor.

There is the dentist, an assertive racist whose certainty of being on top never recovers from the sudden departure of the two black hired hands on his farm. Before they go, they turn the hogs loose to devour the potato crop and, right afterwards, to founder from overeating. Shaken, the dentist goes to a distant town to consult the psychiatrist, only to find that the real demon tormenting him is a shadow of homosexual inclination.

There is a failed professor, who sets his house and books

on fire. There is the professor's daughter, ravaged by drugs. There is Ronnie Foot, a local boy who becomes a rock star and returns home to house his slovenly and half-mad family in a new-built mansion. The grandfather spends the day pushing chickens out of a top-story window and shooting them on the ground with a .22 rifle.

There is a truck driver who turns to art and, eventually, to junk art. He is overwhelmed and maddened; there is no limit to the junk he finds on the American roadside, his task is infinite. Another artist, also a Korean-War veteran, sends death threats to painters who are more successful than he is.

Homer obsessively collects and recounts these stories. With equal and suspicious vehemence, he lays out his own store of prowess and contentment. There is his recognition as a writer, a fishing expedition, a hell-for-leather motorcycle trip to the Gulf and back.

Most of all, there is the woman he lives with and later marries. She is blond, spunky, sensible and sexy, with "active and helpful legs." He tells of his uxorious contentment with a frightening insistence. He never names her; he hardly even sees her. Happiness, for the man who has never recovered from war, is something you clasp without reaching.

It is with Jack, in fact, that Homer's hopes for reconciliation rest. Jack is quiet and dignified. He has been in the war—World War II—and he has been a sheriff. He has lived with violence and apparently has overcome it. He has taught at college, studied French and German, operated a farm. Now he runs a coffee shop. It is a haven, frequented by college students and townspeople, and it exudes the kind of reassurance that a man of character can impart to a bar or a restaurant.

Jack is an old Southern ideal: warrior, farmer, scholar, a man of measure and justice. Homer finds peace in his company.

But peace is an illusion. Jack's daughter, Alice, a restless 40-year-old teacher, fed up with her husband's middle-age spread and outlook, goes to live with the rock singer, Ronnie. Jack is consumed by blind hatred for the man he knows to be an empty-headed destroyer.

What happens is seemingly farce. Homer preempts Jack's .38 caliber revolver. When he scouts out the rock singer's house, he encounters a fusillade of small-bore shots; the grandfather is peppering his chickens. Homer shoots out a window, scaring the old man out of his one or two wits. Later, Homer and Jack go to a nearby golf course and bombard the house with golf balls. "Old Gramps thought it was some eggs come back for revenge," Alice reports afterwards.

Revenge is accomplished, apparently harmlessly. But Hannah invests the comedy with a murderous quality. The infection of war is as real as if real killing had taken place. Jack, the measured man, is as vulnerable to it as any of the grotesques.

There is a blood-letting, in fact, but it is almost incidental. Later, when Homer encounters Jack, bereaved and sud-

denly aged, on the golf course, the older man is like a disembodied monument to a war nobody can escape. "They gave me and you a certain hell, Homer," he says. "They made us know everything."

Hannah's writing is dappled; sometimes terse and sometimes expansive. Homer's wandering cogitations, his tales, his pleasures and his anguish all ramble to a purpose. They test and reveal the tensile strength of a cord that is never really loosed; that binds him to his deadly memories, that binds his Southern community and perhaps all communities to their own.

Thomas R. Edwards   (review date 1 November 1987)

SOURCE: "Stolen Loves, Manly Vengeance," in *The New York Times Book Review,* November 1, 1987, p. 26.

[*Edwards is an American educator and critic. In the following review, he asserts that* Hey Jack! *pales in comparison to Hannah's earlier works.*]

Since his first novel, *Geronimo Rex,* won the William Faulkner Prize and a National Book Award nomination in the early 1970's, Barry Hannah has been a leading contender for Southern novelist of his generation. Every generation seems to want a Southern novelist of its own; there was Faulkner himself, and then Eudora Welty and Flannery O'Connor and Walker Percy and various other successors and claimants. But now there are not a lot of Southern novelists left. Regional writers are supposed to stay put, more or less, and over the last two or three decades Southern-born talent has tended to leave home, to search in Europe or New York or elsewhere for broader social and imaginative affiliations.

To his credit, Mr. Hannah has stayed put, and his later books, especially *Airships* and *Ray,* have added to his reputation. But in his new novella, *Hey Jack!,* geography, local culture, and a sense of his precursors—especially Faulkner—seem to be interfering with his performance.

Hey Jack! is set in Mississippi, in a small university town rather like Faulkner's Oxford, where Mr. Hannah now lives and works. Its governing subject, pursued through playful narrative indirections, is the isolation and erosion of intelligence and sensitivity by cultural barbarism, in the modern South and of course elsewhere too. The narrator's name is withheld until the last page, but it turns out to be Homer, and his "tales of our little town," centering on stolen loves and manly vengeance, do have modest epic possibilities.

Homer is in his mid-50's, a bookish writer manque, divorced and childless, devoted to the body—he's a drinker, a smoker, a tennis player—but psychically scarred by combat in Korea and a later episode of madness. The figures of his tales are various: a trashy local family that has spawned Ronnie Foot, a repellent rock star; a morose professor who set his books and records on fire and in the excitement perished when his car rolled back over him; a racist, McCarthyite dentist who, having lost his wife, his sons and his money, suffered a fatal heart attack when a malicious young black man tapped on his window in the night; Jack Lipsey, once a sheriff, a poet and a professor of criminal justice, who in his old age runs a coffee shop and worries about his daughter's carryings on with Ronnie Foot.

All these tales weave, gradually, into Homer's own story, but they also gravitate toward each other rather too neatly. There is a running association of intellect, sexual weakness or confusion, and despair. The professor and the dentist were both what Jack Lipsey sardonically calls "hermitsexuals," lonely, epicene men whose investment in knowledge fails to compensate for betrayal by life. (Homer is careful to report that the professor's head exploded when his car crushed him.) The tireless Ronnie Foot corrupts both the professor's daughter, a psychiatric counselor, and Jack Lipsey's daughter, a school teacher. And around the story's edges, creative mind is sinking fast, in the persons of another Korea veteran who's an unsuccessful painter, lives with his mother, advertises frantically for a wife, and spends much time in mental wards, and one of the dentist's effeminate sons, a failed sculptor who is last observed slashing the tires of the bread truck he's been reduced to driving.

Outside these enclaves of hopeless sensitivity, life has turned into a Burt Reynolds movie, an ambiance of truck stops, motorcycles and hot cars, guns and blood sports, boozing, sexual brutality and the Nashville Sound. Homer himself has a thoroughly mixed involvement in all this; his disdain for redneck machismo in others is clear ("people like young Harmon would better serve each other by going back up in the hills and committing incest man on man. Or having saw fights"), yet he himself is an alcohol and nicotine and Ritalin man, a biker and (in Korea) a killer, a moralist who can't resist sexual opportunity. And I would judge that Mr. Hannah shares in this ambivalence—a world of mindlessly aggressive pleasure is both mocked and in an odd way embraced by writing that seems determined never to be shocked into full sobriety by the horrors it keeps conjuring up.

The real enemies of the intelligent life, however, appear to be aging and death, the mere accumulation of experiences that comes with living in time. After a death-ridden denouement, Jack Lipsey exhaustedly remarks: "They gave you and me a certain hell, Homer. . . . They made us know everything," and Jack himself is the measure of what has gone wrong. He is a civil, neat, clean old man, temperate in his pleasures, hard to know but tolerant of human difference, quietly intelligent and feeling, with a physical grace—he's a fine golfer—that age hasn't ruined. Thrice divorced from wives he remained friendly with, he is, like Faulkner's aristocrats, vulnerable only to the insistences of honor and affection.

The South itself looks pretty bad in *Hey Jack!* Mr. Hannah's theory of the causes of the Civil War, for example, is not what you find in history books: "The Civil War was not started by Harriet Beecher Stowe, as Lincoln said, or Sir Walter Scott, as Mark Twain said, or by economics, as somebody said. It was started by about a thousand towns like this, bored out of their minds." Or, as he makes a young psychiatrist say, "In this state . . . I find there are exactly five subjects: money, Negroes, women, religion, and Elvis Presley."

But like Faulkner, who almost persuades us that Quentin Compson doesn't hate the South, Mr. Hannah almost convinces us that he doesn't hate it either. For Homer, place is metaphor, the means of discovering "the hungry dark beneath our bright and serene veneers." The trouble is not that this epiphany sounds too much like Faulkner, though it does, but that it doesn't comfortably mesh with Mr. Hannah's own way of doing things, his fondness for verbal and perspectival teases, his delight (with which I have no quarrel) in the raunchy hilarities he affects to deplore in his native scene, his "just kidding, folks" disclaimers of a moral seriousness he yet can't keep his hands off. His material and the present cast of his imagination seem increasingly at odds; it might be time for him to move, at least for a while.

Allen G. Shepherd, III   (essay date 1987)

SOURCE: "The Latest Whiz-Bang: Barry Hannah's *Captain Maximus*," in *Notes on Mississippi Writers,* Vol. XIX, No. 1, 1987, pp. 29-33.

[*In the following essay, Shepherd argues that* Captain Maximus *is a disappointing work that lacks the focus and freshness of* Airships, *Hannah's first collection.*]

Perhaps exculpatory jacket copy on Barry Hannah's second collection of stories, *Captain Maximus* (1985), refers to the autobiographical derivation of a number of these thin and generally very short fictions. Slices from the author's life average only eight pages each and forty of the volume's ninety-eight pages are given over to an unused "idea" for a Robert Altman movie. To one familiar with the author's earlier work, particularly his first collection, *Airships* (1978), *Captain Maximus* is a puzzling and altogether disappointing performance. What has happened—gone wrong—and perhaps why will be the focus of this essay.

The subject matter—oblique reflections on apocalyptic moments—has not changed substantially, nor has the favored narrator, one of the walking wounded, but the writing has turned exceedingly cryptic, abrupt and jokey. It is occasionally entertaining but no longer stunning. The third story, **"I Am Shaking to Death,"** all of four pages long, offers a generic Hannah title, but the kind of belligerently anything-goes sensibility that inspirited the hyperbolic prose and loopy humor of earlier work, of *The Tennis Handsome* (1983) for instance, appears now to be exhausted or quiescent.

Admirers of earlier volumes, particularly of *Ray* (1980), proclaimed their newness, originality, uniqueness, but the first two stories in *Captain Maximus* seem to be lightweight variations on themes drawn (distantly) from Hemingway, while the third offers a slender study in regional contrasts reminiscent (distantly) of Fitzgerald.

"He was forty-eight, a fisherman, and he had never caught a significant fish." is the opening sentence of **"Getting Ready,"** a.k.a. **"The Middle-Aged Man and the Gulf,"** in which one Roger Laird saves his soul as he preserves his catch, a sand shark four feet long and weighing fifteen pounds, from the axe of an insensitive and apparently hungry fellow fisherman. Laird throws it back into the Gulf and he and his wife live happily in Texas ever after. The story ends with a patented bit of Hannah freakiness as Laird walks a Dallas waterway on twelve-foot stilts yelling obscenities at the rich and famous in their opulent three-riggers.

"Idaho," the second shot of Hemingwayana, was written originally for *Esquire's* "Why I Live Where I Live" series and delivers disjointed, exclamatory reflection on guns, drinking, suicide, male bonding and women, with some rather fulsome remarks on Thomas McGuane. These are the two stories George Stade concluded [in *The New York Times Book Review* (June 9, 1985)] "might have been written by a fiercer and more elliptical Hemingway." I would nominate another, semi-classical antecedent: Jack Kerouac, in his lifelong song of himself.

"I Am Shaking to Death" is a fractured tale of the narrator's loving and losing a Minneapolis matron who "leaned down from something near porcine" on a fat farm outside Yocona, Mississippi, where the women were attached to a jeep and towed naked through hot, buggy pastures and swamps, they having "agreed that they were ugly enough for things to happen to them and they would not be released until they were thin and better." The narrator, who once agreed that he had it made, what with his art on the walls and Scandinavian furniture and a Jaguar at the curb, finds—when he drives her all the way home—that he (the weaker vessel) can't survive in "Ice Palace" country. It is a theme familiar from *Airships,* the male's desolating discovery that there is no keeping up with women, leaned down or not—but here without its earlier resonance.

In less than three pages, in **"Even Greenland,"** Hannah makes accessible, coherent sense of the "damned triumph" of John, a now deceased jet pilot who, in mastering "last-minute things" reclaimed lost good times as he refused to eject from his burning F-14. The story's narrator, who has ingloriously survived to be a lieutenant commander in the reserve, is last seen "absorbed . . . and paralyzed" gazing at the burn in the sand which is the dead man's only visible memorial. **"Even Greenland,"** like snow in Mississippi, the story's central image, doesn't last long but delivers an epiphany.

Among the conditions obtained in a number of these stories are drunkenness, exhaustion, remorse and dramatic weather. Guns are fired, speeches made, heroism contemplated and women won and lost. There is little in the way of conventional plot, settings run to the extreme and hallucinatory; and characterization is generally sketchy, all of which leaves us dependent on voice, style, manic language. Thus, overheard in a bar, from **"Ride, Fly, Penetrate, Loiter"**:

> My children are low-hearted fascists! Their eyebrows meet! The oldest boy's in San Diego, but he's a pig! We're naught but dying animals. Eve and then Jesus and us, clerks!

It's hard to say what would constitute a really adequate response to such an outburst, but Hannah copes: "The owner jams his teeth together, and they crack. He pushes his tongue out, evicting a rude air sound. The other

knocks over a barrel of staves." One can see here, I think, what Christopher Lehmann-Haupt had in mind as he asserted [in a review that appeared in *The New York Times* (April 18, 1983)] that "the appeal of Barry Hannah . . . is that he seems to have chewed up and swallowed the entire rhetorical tradition of the American South. . . ." Even in short takes, however, such language eventually palls as we cease being stunned by zaniness.

Hannah has been praised in some quarters for eschewing the scrupulous meanness and quiet desperation of a number of his more celebrated minimalist contemporaries. Certainly **"Ride, Fly, Penetrate, Loiter"** is neither scrupulous nor quiet, though the narrator might well be charged with meanness and is assuredly desperate.

Stabbed in the eye by a fake Indian but possessed by consequence of second sight into the dark heart of things, Maximum Ned—fleeing dwarves and academics and Dallas and seeking a Dalmatian and Buds and, apparently, Celeste, who has survived from **"Even Greenland"**—Ned is last observed after a prolonged detour through the Waste Land. It is Easy Rider he's become, "in almost any city of the South, the Far West, or the Northwest. I am on the black and chrome Triumph, riding right into your face." Sitting behind him, wearing heavy-duty glasses, might be the shade of T. S. Eliot, whose "long long, bloated epicene tract . . . the slide show of some snug librarian on the rag" is throughout this story prodded, parodied and jumped upon.

"It Spoke of Exactly the Things" is Hannah's California Suite, in which our hero achieves a gratifying victory at sea as from a desperately tacking wind-surfer he overhauls a younger rival and from under water blasts him with a sawed-off gun, both barrels, loaded with whaleshit. "California," the narrator says, "is an excellent place for polishing your hatreds." Best polished is the rival of the moment, grown up and excessively possessive son of the narrator's lady love, who has between her breasts a tiny black tattooed butterfly which epitomizes her rare attraction and which gave the story its original title. As earlier with his leaned down Minneapolis matron in **"I Am Shaking to Death,"** so with the California sweet of this story—she is loved and later lost in some way left unclear.

Most conventional of the narratives collected in *Captain Maximus* is the last story (the final piece being **"An Idea For Film"**). The premise of **"Fans"** is conventionally outrageous—a masochist's hero worship of his lifelong torturer, who has achieved private and public sanctification as a born again star in the Ole Miss defensive secondary, and who has therefore a perfect right, as the story concludes, "to kill them" all. **"Fans"** develops in effective incremental fashion. First, Wright the worshipper is provided with a setting, a bar in Oxford, and an audience—Milton, blind but a rabid fan; Loomis Orange, a dwarf who is one of the team's managers; and Wright, Sr., a hack sportswriter and shill for the team. Then begins the chronicle of outrages performed by J. Edward Toole, a.k.a. Jet, beginning years before with the instigation of group air rifle attacks and proceeding through such intermediate practices as covert flatulation and pornographic revision of young Wright's poetry to near fatal clotheslining and shark incitement to the climactic horror, "the further beautiful thing": "He [Jet] put his arm on my shoulder and said to me, 'Wright. I'm sorry.' "

Several who might be thought to know something of film writing have called **"Power and Light,"** a forty-page screen treatment, the most ambitious narrative in the book, yet despite being five times the average length of pieces in *Captain Maximus,* it reads like preparatory notes rather than finished fiction, or finished anything. Its inclusion in the volume and its engrossing four tenths of it suggests, I should think, a shortage of material, while the presence of **"Idaho,"** from the "Where I live Series," reinforces the impression that *Captain Maximus* is more a miscellany than a collection of stories. It is a thin book with much loose flesh, unhappily unlike *Airships,* with its firmly packed narratives. Finally, whether in *Captain Maximus* we witness a narrowing of authorial ambition or a short vacation or a radical alienation from his own activity, we have good reason to wait in hope for Hannah's next.

Joanne Kennedy   (review date 14 May 1989)

SOURCE: "The Underview," in *The New York Times Book Review,* May 14, 1989, p. 19.

[*In the following review, Kennedy remarks favorably on* Boomerang.]

Though middle age has chastened Barry Hannah a bit, the Mississippi macho-romantic is still a tremendous lover of the lustiness of life in his brief, minor but brilliant autobiographical novel. He has drawn on his own experience with insistent honesty in *Geronimo Rex, Airships* and six other novels and story collections, so there is little of a personal nature in *Boomerang* to surprise, except possibly his obsession with his childhood smallness and a certain wistfulness when he mentions other writers' compliments on his work.

"A lot of people sit back in life and have their overview," he writes. "Compared to my underview, where I scout, under the bleachers, for what life has dropped." Random vivid episodes are held together by three boomerang-throwing sessions, which give a remarkably complete impression of his nearly 50 years. A Southern boyhood as a "tiny sincere guy" was spent surrounded by uncles, fishing, shooting snakes, playing in the band, writing poetry and being randy. Randiness and concern with family carry over to his present life in Oxford, Miss, where he ruminates on his rocky marriages, misses his kids, mourns warm friends and gallant dogs, sneers at organized religion and the middle-aged women who immerse themselves in it and works for the Humane Society. The magazine editor Willie Morris and the country singer Jimmy Buffett are friends, the film director Robert Altman a former associate. "The old guys are me now, is the horror. I'll wander up and get registered and vote."

Mixed in with autobiographical episodes are those from the life of Yelverston, the self-made, older friend who is the one focus of the author's trademark fictional violence, which is somewhat muted here. Through such events as

the death of his son and the maiming of his daughter-in-law, Yelverston becomes Christ-like in forbearance, tragic but noble in defeat. What cannot be missed, however, is that nobility in Mr. Hannah's work is assigned only to the men and animals he dotes on; women, though lovely and oh so painfully necessary, are a cut below.

Mr. Hannah mentions a short stay in "Bryce, state home for the nuts. Because of drinking and shooting," and remarks, "I could not participate in reality anymore. Could not." The word crazy is often used to describe Mr. Hannah's characters. Two striking images, the thrown boomerang and caroming BB's shot almost point-blank at a wall, come richocheting back to damage the child Barry and the adult Yelverston; they convey perfectly the out-of-control quality of the novel, a nearly foolish vulnerability.

No new ground is broken in *Boomerang;* what we get from Mr. Hannah is instinct and impact over plot, as always. And in clean, spare prose and a distinctive raconteur's voice that could only be Southern, there is originality, power, pain and deadpan humor ("I hate my wife, but she still keeps coming back"). And no surrender.

Pagan Kennedy   (review date 1 August 1989)

SOURCE: "Boy's Life," in *The Village Voice,* Vol. 34, No. 31, August 1, 1989, pp. 58-9.

[*In the following review, Kennedy praises Hannah's style in* Boomerang *but finds it difficult to empathize with the author's persona.*]

We must forgive Barry Hannah his inability to mention a woman without leering; we must forgive him his swaggering and name-dropping; we must forgive him because of his sentences.

In his latest, *Boomerang,* Hannah writes as sublimely and tersely as ever. He distills into hard little aphorisms the profound sound and fury of Southern oratory, the sensuous sermonizing of an entire people who've had a few slugs of whiskey and now want to hear their own voices saying scandalous truths about dying and fornicating and The War of Northern Aggression.

Who would think a Southerner could be so short-winded? "Pappy is like the Confederate Army. So awesome in his rudeness." "I was embarrassed by her, but we had a baby." "He had great muscles in his arms and in his legs that you only get in a penitentiary."

Hannah first grabbed wide attention 20 years ago on the pages of *Esquire.* Though his first novel, *Geronimo Rex,* won a PEN prize, perhaps most impressive is his novella *Ray,* about a doctor who disdains the Hippocratic oath and loans out his nurse for certain unorthodox cures. What gives this book its power is not just Hannah's bullet-like sentences, but also his frightening, funny portrayal of the brutal doctor who is fighting a civil war with his own soul.

Boomerang is similar in structure to *Ray*—the language is chopped into short chapters, like journal entries. What's different is that while *Ray* merely pretends to be a journal,

Boomerang is Hannah's account of what it's like to be himself—a "tender weaving of novel and autobiography" according to the publisher. The book's intended scope is his entire life. He whizzes through his childhood, then jumps into the head of an uncle who presumably represents Hannah in old age. But mostly he gushes about his current glamorous doings; sometimes the book seems to be no more than a *Lifestyles of the Rich and Famous* with literary pretensions.

When Hannah employs his powerful fictional techniques, he's as fine as ever. For instance, he uses the central image as a reprise: The boomerang, or something like it, shows up at intervals to remind us what the book's about. Ostensibly, the boomerang is karma, what goes around and then comes around: "If you throw it well, . . . [it] almost comes back into your palm. Every good deed and every good word sails out into the hedges and over the grass and comes to sit in your front yard." At other times, Hannah uses the image to talk about the nature of self-destruction. He explains that when he was a kid, "there was a place where I could go with my own war. I would line up plastic soldiers against the door and shut it and then shoot my Daisy beebee gun against the door. The ricochets, coming right toward my face, were the enemy firing back."

However, in the more overtly autobiographical chapters, Hannah fails to show his life as a series of startling images or to send ***Boomerang*** soaring up on language; instead, he uses it as a blunt instrument to hammer us over the head with what a cool dude he is. Why, he's dear friends with Jimmy Buffet (*I* would keep that secret), Bob Altman, Jack Nicholson. He rides a motorcycle, packs a gun. And "Capote when he was really drunk called me the maddest writer in the USA."

He knows a lot of nobodies too and wants us to understand just how fiercely he loves them all. At times the book seems no more than a string of dedications, or a family Christmas card. "All my nephews and nieces are a blessing to me endlessly." "I owe thanks to my sister."

But for all his love, Hannah lacks compassion, which in autobiography comes off as tactlessness. One can tolerate almost any nonsense from a fictional character— boorishness reads as authorial irony. In ***Ray,*** when Hannah's good ol' boy doctor says, "I don't feel that good about women anyway, nor gooks, nor sand-niggers, nor doctors, nor anything human that moves," it hardly seems like the position of the author. But in ***Boomerang,*** when Hannah says as himself (or as a caricature of himself) that a limo parked in front of his house "makes the darkies at the ice house stretch their necks" or when he gloats, "I have had so much young nooky on my arm telling them about what a famous writer I am," the reader can only get embarrassed for him; darkie and nooky readers may often be tempted to throw the book across the room.

I've always thought that authors should be like good party guests: charming, but not too loquacious. If Hannah were at your party, he'd try desperately to get laid, bore everyone with his bragging, and drink himself into a coma. But even so, you'd grudgingly invite him back because, before passing out in the bathtub, he'd say something like,

The both of us have come back to this pretty and humane town to practice secular humanism as hard as we can. That is when we're just staring out of windows trying to see even the rough face of God in the clouds or in the vapor over the oil spots in the parking lot of the Jitney Jungle.

Joseph Coates   (review date 26 May 1991)

SOURCE: "Barry Hannah's Wild West Gunman Seeks a Place Where a Boy Can Roam," in *Chicago Tribune— Books,* May 26, 1991, p. 3.

[*In the review below, Coates remarks on* Never Die.]

There are all kinds of ways to write good fiction. Barry Hannah's way is to kick capital-L Literature in the crotch and make it wail, a lively tradition that dates back at least to Mark Twain. Hannah's real medium is not prose but a kind of hillbilly haiku that proceeds one sentence at a time, sometimes with no apparent connection between them, and adds up to music—heavy on the brass but with a plaintive obligatto of fiddle, banjo and Jew's harp.

Novelist Richard Stern once called Hannah's work "literary jazz," and if we qualify it further as Dixieland, that's probably as close as anyone is going to get. It's no accident that his first book, ***Geronimo Rex*** (1971), opens with its boy hero eavesdropping on the Dream of Pines Colored High School band, which makes its white counterpart sound like a truckload of scrap metal being driven over a ploughed field. Hannah's been mining those magical riffs ever since, with varying success.

His protagonists are white Southern males trying to live up to reputations they don't quite understand or deserve. In ***Never Die,*** the hero is called Fernando Mure, a 1910 gunfighter with an inflated reputation, an alcohol/morphine habit, a shortage of ammunition and the mission to burn down the corrupt town of Nitburg just to "watch the scum run." More existentially, his "task at hand" is "a race through nullity and mere style" after rejecting the alternative of suicide via "an extended debauch of fine wines until his speech slurred and he died in a fury of drums and small-caliber gossip."

Things, he finds, are not as simple as he is. At 38, he's too young for suicide and too high-minded to recognize the enemy. After his kneecaps are broken by a dwarf goon named Edwin Smoot at the behest of the local landlord, Judge Nitburg, he sees his mistake: "I thought Evil was big but it's really a mighty, mighty . . . small thing."

He's too romantic to have enemies like these. Fernando did his time in prison after robbing a Wells Fargo coach and being caught while "he wept over the letters to loved ones he'd deflected, all those pages around him in a dry blowing wind under a trestle. Little brook under it about the amount of his tears. Collected exactly twenty-three dollars out of one hundred letters."

His polar anti-hero is the ex-pool shark and hermit Nermer, who squanders his meditation time on a mountaintop gazing at "the miserable anthill [of the town] itself. It was not so much the sin but the paltry times there that disgusted him," all the "skinny coyotes of the spirit."

There are also some lively ladies, all of whom end up dead—Nandina, the judge's daughter, who admits to being "something of an alleycat"; Stella, a tubercular whore who is Mure's mistress; and a heroic lesbian prostitute who's more effective than most of the men against the crew of hired gunmen led by the truly bad Luther Nix.

It sounds like pure burlesque scored for ukulele, but Hannah's work here as elsewhere ends up being surprisingly (and depressingly) realistic—so much so that it denies his obvious intention to make this the book in which the American hero finally grows up. Rebuking a mythmaking Eastern photographer, Mure renounces his own legend and says he's "studying up how I can make the next years fine ones, by my little Stella." But Stella's already dead, and Mure makes this speech while off fishing "with Hsu, the Chinaman." Once again, boy loses girl, boy gets boy and stays boyish, full of promise.

The boys are still lighting out for the territory, crowded though it may be with aspiring writers. And there's no end in sight.

Janet Kaye   (review date 7 July 1991)

SOURCE: "Is Nitburg Burning?" in *The New York Times Book Review,* July 7, 1991, p. 18.

[*In following review of* Never Die, *Kaye faults Hannah for not fully developing his characters.*]

Barry Hannah can succinctly and with great good humor evoke the profound bewilderment of the human condition.

Consider, for example, the husband-narrator of the short story **"Love Too Long,"** from Mr. Hannah's 1978 collection, *Airships*: " 'You great bastard!' I yelled up there. 'I believed in You on and off all my life!' "

This element is still present in Mr. Hannah's ninth book, *Never Die*: "The Lord giveth and the Lord taketh away. Rotten Indian-giver, eh?" one character says.

But Mr. Hannah's sly wit is squandered here. The characters in this novel are undeveloped, and Mr. Hannah's fine, wry insight is wasted when applied to caricatures.

The plot, too, lacks conviction. Set in 1910, it involves a university-educated gunfighter's decision (inspired by boredom and distaste) to burn down his frontier hometown of Nitburg, accurately described by the local chronicler as "a frozen headache of a town where nobody couldn't get no grip on heroism nor even a cause." There is no lack of violence, though—everything from broken kneecaps to decapitation.

Violent imagery, prevalent and disturbing in Mr. Hannah's previous works, is unsettling here, too, but for all the wrong reasons. The perpetrators are presented as if they were the Marx Brothers doing a combination western parody and slasher film.

"I thought Evil was big but it's really a mighty, mighty . . . small thing," Fernando, the gunfighter, says near the start of *Never Die*. Mr. Hannah may have been trying to illustrate the point, but he has instead created a confused mishmash of a book that itself seems meanspirited.

"I roam in the past for my best mind," he wrote in his 1980 novel, *Ray.* Here's hoping he can find it again. Because when, as in *Never Die,* bad things happen to bad caricatures, who is to care?

The New Yorker (review date 15 July 1991)

SOURCE: A review of *Never Die,* in *The New Yorker,* Vol. LXVII, No. 21, July 15, 1991, p. 79.

[*In the excerpt below, the critic comments briefly on* Never Die.]

After the uncharacteristic mildness of his last book, *Boomerang,* this Mississippi author has returned to form—and gone West—in a stylish and absurdist chronicle of revenge, misery, and mayhem. [*Never Die*] is set in a corrupt little South Texas frontier town, circa 1910, and it concerns the crippling of a caballero named Fernando Muré and his vow to burn down the iniquitous town. (A subtheme is the promise of escape offered by newly invented forms of transportation: automobiles, motorcycles, and airplanes.) The other characters, almost all of them wicked, have names like Nitburg, Smoot, Fingo, and Nix, and as they wreak and suffer various forms of Jacobean havoc their crazed and swerving thoughts and dreams are conveyed in sentences that are lithe, surprising, and hilariously laconic. The spirit of Sam Peckinpah lurks in the elegiac violence and fatalism of this fabulist Western, but the silver-tongued prose is all Hannah.

Ruth D. Weston   (essay date Fall 1991)

SOURCE: " 'The Whole Lying Opera of It': Dreams, Lies, and Confessions in the Fiction of Barry Hannah," in *The Mississippi Quarterly,* Vol. XLIV, No. 4, Fall, 1991, pp. 411-28.

[*In the following essay, Weston focuses on issues of identity and self-worth in Hannah's male protagonists.*]

In an interview for a 1984 volume of *Contemporary Authors* [Volume 110], Jan Gretlund asked Barry Hannah about the extent of his religious beliefs; and Hannah replied, "If I said that I believed in God, what would it mean? I proceed from the fact that there has been a great lie to me, from the word go. Somebody stands in the pulpit and says, 'I've just talked to God.' You get a little lonely when you realize that's not right, at about sixteen. There's something too frantic about the present religious fervor, especially on TV . . ." This oblique response to Gretlund's question, with its jump-cut to the idea of a "great lie" that Hannah takes personally, suggests one of the pervasive themes in a fiction that, Hannah says, is concerned with "finding and asking the big questions." Many of Hannah's characters are liars who, like Hannah himself, suffer from the perception of some "great lie" that has been perpetrated against them. Thus, they seem to be caught in a double bind of causes and effects that, when aggravated by the specifically gender-based, culturally predicated, dreams and burdens of contemporary men, often lead to grotesque attempts to live meaningful existences in such a bind. The dreams of Hannah's male characters taunt them, often inciting them to a violence that requires expiation; but there is no *religious* expiation for these men, who are "lonely," as is the author. And lacking a religious means of confession, Hannah's protagonists indulge in secular rituals of confession that alternate with dreams and lies in a vicious circle that provides coherent narrative structure to a fiction which appears on its surface to be the epitome of postmodern fragmentation.

According to Joyce Carol Oates [in *The Edge of Impossibility,* 1972], American literature from the beginning reflects the fact that Americans "seeks the absolute dream." Indeed, American authors continue to create tensions between that search and some reality that opposes the dream; in Oates's own fiction it is often materialism. In Barry Hannah the counterforce is what we might call "the great lie," but it is more than the particular "great lie" about religion of which Hannah complained to Gretlund. Rather, it includes all the lies our culture has told us, and that we have told, and continue to tell about ourselves and to ourselves, especially about the reality of the sexual natures of men and women. Even a child like the young Barry Hannah character in the autobiographical fantasy *Boomerang* lies as he tries to rationalize his violence against the poor "preacher's kids." They were, he says, "horrible skinny people with bad complexions," a childish wish he immediately counters with, "That's not true. That's a hideous statement. They were good and swift, and they were mean . . . and they had nothing to eat and we were glad." And the same kind of wish-fulfillment discourse obtains at the end of the novel, when the autobiographical character, now an adult, says, "After three years of trying my wife and I have a new baby coming . . . ," and then says, "What a lie. We have nothing coming."

Hannah's characters experience lies in many ways, which, as G. F. Waller has said of Oates's stories [in *Dreaming America,* 1979], all point to "the tragic gaps between word and act, ideal and reality—not in a trivial everyday sense but almost as a metaphysical principle, felt the more strongly just because we are seekers of meaning, not merely of contentment." Barry Hannah's fiction is played out in those gaps; and the actions of his characters are all in some sense like that of the adolescent trumpet player in *Boomerang,* whose music is an attempt to "make something happen in vacant air [that is] a sweet revenge on reality." This need to "make something happen" is the desire that propels a narrative; as Peter Brooks says [in *Reading for the Plot: Design and Intention in Narrative,* 1984], it "drives the protagonist forward . . . [in such a way that] the ambitious hero thus stands as a figure of the reader's efforts to construct meanings. . . ."

Although brief note has been made of the "poetic" quality of Hannah's prose, I wish to distinguish between the paradigmatic exigencies of lyric modes, which depend upon "an ideal of simultaneity of meaning," and what I perceive in Hannah's fiction as a more syntagmatic dependence upon narrative acts that take shape in time, with "meanings delayed, partially filled in, stretched out" [Peter Brooks]. In these stories delayed meanings depend upon

the dream (which is itself a lie), which begets outrageous behavior, which begets more lies, which beget confessions (which may also be lies). Because, in Barry Hannah's fiction, these actions usually involve sex, violence, and humor, commentators often place his work in some relation to the Southern Gothic, especially to the fiction of Flannery O'Connor. But such attributions of influence are misleadingly simplistic; for, whereas O'Connor's fiction points an orthodox Christian moral, Hannah's is concerned with the more secular aspect of the nature of the human self and with the aesthetic question of how best to—indeed, whether one can—write that self.

Although Hannah's connection with the gothic tradition of the comic grotesque is undeniable, O'Connor, even through mostly female view-points, writes of a non-gendered spiritual illness, whereas Hannah describes symptoms of a contemporary and a particularly masculine disease. His relation to the gothic is more aptly to the gothic sense that Oates describes [in *Time* (October 10, 1969)], in her own use of it, as "a fairly realistic assessment of modern life." It speaks a sense of being as lost in the world as in the labyrinth of a gothic castle, for his characters are searching for the key to the puzzle of themselves. They, like Oates's protagonists, are "haunted" by contemporary versions of the original American dream, which persists as an absolute dream of fulfillment, of significance, of meaning. For, as Oates says, "the crudity of our desire [is not only] for an absolute dream [but also for] an absolute key"; and she discusses the universal need for the "curve of devastation and elevation" that comes to the tragic hero in literature, a vicarious experience, she says, that provides us with the hope that meaning exists. Oates explains our appropriation of such hope in this way:

> The hero dies into our imaginations as we, helplessly, live out lives that are never works of art—even the helpless lives of "artists"!—and are never understood. Suffering is articulated in tragic literature, and so this literature is irresistible, a therapy of the soul. We witness in art the reversal of our commonplace loss of passion, our steady loss of consciousness that is never beautiful but only biological. [*The Edge of Impossibility*]

Hannah's characters, too, are caught in a no-man's land somewhere between tragic stature and the helplessness of "lives that are never works of art"; obsessed with the absolute dream of a wished-for TRUTH, they are thwarted at every turn by lies. Indeed, the most profound reason for the seeming helplessness of his characters is their suspicion that the dream itself is a lie, because they, the dreamers, are great liars. Again, the similarity to Oates's thematic structure is remarkable, for her characters too are obsessed by dreams which contain the seeds of self-betrayals, and thus which turn dreams into nightmares. Hannah's concern is not primarily with the rampant materialism that defeats many of Oates's protagonists, but rather with a more personal agony, a psychological counterpart of the biological loss that makes Grandma Wendall, in Oates's *Them,* for example, "baffled at the failure of her body to keep up with her assessment of herself." In addition, they inhabit a moral void that is the secular version of what

O'Connor depicts as "the absence of sacramental vision in modern consciousness" [Robert H. Brinkmeyer, Jr., *The Art and Vision of Flannery O'Connor*, 1989]. But Hannah creates no fatuous Hulgas or Mrs. Turpins who require divine epiphanies of violence; likewise, there are none like Eudora Welty's Laurel, in *The Optimist's Daughter*, who must be jolted into awareness of her bondage to the past. Hannah's characters already know something is wrong, and their eagerness to confess their culpability modifies the comic grotesque, and thus further complicates the task of assigning genre to works already problematized by their mixtures of real and fictional characters and events.

Both historical and fictional characters suffer absurdly, often comically, in Hannah's writing, because of the tragic gap not only between word and deed but also between the dreams and the realities of their lives. But it is not material things they seek; it is meaning. Whatever else Hannah's protagonists are, they are seekers after the absolute dream of meaning. Thus the more profound link between Hannah and O'Connor is the same as that between Hannah and Oates: a common yearning after an absolute. Hannah creates mostly male protagonists, and the dream of which he writes is the particular dream of the "macho" male in American culture. It is a dream not only of achievement but of heroism, not only of love but of sexual dominance. Yet the critical tensions in the fiction come not so much from any other human or environmental antagonist as from the protagonist's own psyche. One reason for this self-antagonism is that Hannah's adult male characters live in an age that is conscious of feminist politics. They are sensitive but ambivalent idealists who would like to live out an absolute dream that, when they will admit it to themselves, they know is amoral, often immoral, and unfailingly sexist. Indeed, their own consciences tell them that their dream is based on cultural falsehoods which they have internalized. This dual theme of dreams and lies emerges from a fiction that never allows the reader to forget the author's presence, not only because of the intimacy of its narrative voices but also because of tacit authorial statements of literary aesthetics and thematics. Two of the most significant statements are these from **"Testimony of Pilot"**: "It was talent to keep the metronome ticking amidst any given chaos of sound" and "Memory, the whole lying opera of it, is killing me now." Hannah writes about the American male's individual, and lonely, search for an absolute dream of manly behavior among cultural memories that continually betray him. His characters' preoccupation with the dream, the cultural lie, and with their own obsessive need to confess their complicity in the process, then, acts as a "metronome ticking" throughout "the whole lying opera" of Hannah's narratives.

When John Updike [writing in *The New Yorker* (September 9, 1972)] identified the adolescent protagonist of Hannah's first novel, *Geronimo Rex*, as a new "whining" Holden Caulfield, he was correct, of course; but, given Hannah's development in subsequent fiction of what is essentially this same character, that evaluation now seems too simplistic. For the existentially disillusioned Harry Monroe of *Geronimo Rex* can now be seen as the prototype of other Hannah protagonists: of Ned Maximus, for

> **Both historical and fictional characters suffer absurdly, often comically, in Hannah's writing, because of the tragic gap not only between word and deed but also between the dreams and the realities of their lives.**
>
> **—Ruth D. Weston**

example, who not only sees life's fraudulence in "Dallas, city of the fur helicopters" but knows that he himself is a fraud and a liar. His complicity extends even to self-betrayal in **"I Am Shaking to Death,"** when he is so cold he spits soup over the beautiful woman who represents one of his dreams, and who is perhaps emblematic of the absolute dream. Ned's own body, like that of Oates's Mrs. Wendall, has thus conspired against him, in a comic betrayal of this dream that leads to the anguished cry that provides the story's title: "Anything. Help. I am shaking to death." But the more significant component of the dream, and thus the more significant loss in this episode, is Ned's dream of control. For if Ned cannot control himself, he cannot aspire to the "great sullen manliness controlling her" (**Boomerang**) that is a primary fantasy of Hannah's protagonists.

The specifically sexual component of the "great lie" is codified memorably in the first story of **Airships** and played out as a leitmotif throughout the subsequent fiction. In a vodka-generated truth-telling exchange with his wife, the narrator of **"Water Liars"** learns that his and her sexual adventures before marriage were "exactly equal," a fact which incites him to "an impotent homicidal urge" (**Airships**). When he visits the "old liars" on the pier at Farte Cove to take his mind off his anguish over the fact of his wife's sexual nature, the old men's conversation only reminds him of it by confirming the double standard they have all lived by. Women one married were "supposed to be virgins" and supposed to "have a blurred nostalgia" about male sexual promiscuity, as the normal "course of things": although some women were (conveniently) sexual creatures, one's *wife* should be different somehow. His learning that she is not so different necessitates a revision of his memory: thus, every new topic directs his thoughts to his own adolescent sexual misdeeds. The tension peaks when one of the "liars" tells a true story of finding his daughter making love to "an older guy I didn't even know with a mustache." The narrator-protagonist of the frame story recognizes the old liar as a kindred spirit: just as they have both been nurtured on the lie, they have both been "crucified by the truth"; and the young liar who narrates has "never recovered." Thus his dream of a perfect male-female relationship, based as it is on the lie of male sexual license complemented by female chastity and "a blurred nostalgia" as the natural order of things, is revealed as false, ironically, by the one *true* tale told by the "water liars." Also ironic is the fact that his forced recognition of his wife's over sexuality reduces him to "an impotent homicidal urge" as well as to the apparent recognition of his own "blurred nostalgia." And the relation between the young and old liars receives further development when the protagonist in **Boomerang** admits that "the old guys are me now, is the horror."

The situation in **"Love Too Long"** recalls that in Bobbie Ann Mason's "Shiloh," in which a male first-person narrator has been laid off from his job, while his wife is not only working but also taking courses in a "masculine" endeavor (piloting an airplane), while she dreams of a better house. The husband in **"Love Too Long"** is jealous, especially, as in **"Water Liars,"** of a man with a mustache. And, as in **"Water Liars,"** the narrator identifies with the martyred Jesus. However, he also rages *against* Jesus, as if not only all belief but all reason is belied by the fact of Jane's flying "over my house upside down every afternoon" (**Airships**). Jane's flight is of course symbolic of her having "flown" without him and beyond him; and the impotence he feels in the face of this "upside down" state of affairs provokes in him a self-contradictory rage against his wife: he wants to "rip her arm off [but at the same time to] sleep in her uterus with my foot hanging out." Repeatedly, Hannah's male characters take their frustrations out on their women, while they frankly admit their self-destructive, infantile behavior. One of Hannah's alter-ego characters, for example, is well understood by his wife, Westy, who tells him, "There is something about you, Ray, that wants to set yourself deliberately in peril and in trash. One of these days you won't come back alive. You are drinking again. You've had three vodka tonics." Although much of [**Ray**] has been devoted to Ray's adoration of Westy, he orders a fourth drink, confessing, "Some old hideous baby in me wanted to see Westy pissed."

This kind of self-contradiction evinces a contemporary dilemma that is elsewhere apparent in Hannah's anxious protagonists, who describe themselves in alternately macho-heroic and self-deprecatory, often adolescent, terms that suggest the debilitating consequences of gendered expectations for both men and women that have long been the subject of social science research. In 1963, the problem for males was described this way [by Erving Goffman in *Stigma: Notes on the Management of Spoiled Identity,* 1963]:

> In an important sense there is only one complete unblushing male in America: a young, married, white, urban, northern, heterosexual Protestant father of college education, fully employed, of good complexion, weight, and height, and a recent record in sports. Every American male tends to look out upon the world from this perspective, this constituting one sense in which one can speak of a common value system in America. Any male who fails to qualify in any one of these ways is likely to view himself—during moments at least—as unworthy, incomplete, and inferior.

To the extent that Hannah's fiction depicts characters who measure themselves by this limiting value system, who describe themselves as "tiny . . . but . . . sincere" (**Boomerang**) or "swift fodder for the others" (**Captain Maximus**), it confirms the idea that "the birthright of every American

male is a chronic sense of personal inadequacy" [Robert L. Woolfolk and Frank C. Richardson, *Sanity, Stress, and Survival,* 1978]. It is confirmed for the young protagonist of **Boomerang** when he mistakenly thinks he has found a hero in an eighty-four-year-old homeless black man who "looks like a man floating on serene thoughts after his immense history of thinking and deciding." The child wants to "take him some food and offer my respects"; but his illusion that he has found a hero-mentor is destroyed when he hears that the old man carries a gun: "He's just as scared as the rest of us," the child realizes. To be sure, the archetypes that have shaped the American male's understanding of heroism are those characterized not by "thinking and deciding," but by the aggressive means of overcoming fear and taking power that are signified by the weapon. Thus, he understands that adults too are likely to resort to the violent expressions of power that David Madden [writing in *The Southern Review* (Spring 1983)] perceives are Harry Monroe's "adolescent techniques for mental survival" in **Geronimo Rex.**

Because it points up the contrast between intellectual power and violence, the consternation of the child in **Boomerang** who misinterprets an old man's fear for serenity perhaps hints at a more general confusion between traditional and modern male role-expectations. Under traditional conventions, masculinity is validated by "individual physical strength and aggression" and by invulnerability, especially to emotions, while modern males are validated by "economic achievement and organizational or bureaucratic power." And although moderns may value emotional sensitivity, many still think it should occur "only with women" [Joseph H. Pleck, *The Myth of Masculinity,* 1981]. In a recent reevaluation of what heroism should entail [*A Choice of Heroes: The Changing Faces of American Manhood,* 1982], Mark Gerzon lists the frontiersman, the soldier, the breadwinner, the expert, and the lord as symbols of manhood which were "once useful . . . [because] they promised survival and well-being." Gerzon believes that, although men have been well able to adjust to contemporary technological changes, somehow they have not been able to accommodate themselves to the lack of need for those traits which once were considered heroic against a life-threatening enemy, whether human or environmental. Further, as Gerzon argues, not only have traditional images become problematic or, like that of John Wayne, invalid, but the entire issue has been complicated by the women's movement. It may be most complicated for the man who clings in spite of himself to those outdated ideas of what is heroic or manly, and yet who has no peace because he knows these images are now non-productive. The resulting dilemma is enough to account for the savagely dysfunctional nature of Hannah's characters. Hannah himself [in an interview in *The Southern Review* (Spring 1983)] points to "something inside of the male body [that makes him] want to run, hit, do something with this great amount of muscle frame you're given [that makes men continue to act as] hunter and gatherer . . . [because] you're not supposed to sit around looking at a Smith-Corona typing."

The most articulate recent expression of this masculine dis-ease is that of the poet Robert Bly, who conducts seminars and retreats for men to facilitate their search for a for-gotten heritage of generative male power. Bly's theory rests on the psychological truth he finds in the Grimm brothers' tale of "Iron John," a wild, hairy man at the bottom of a pond, who represents the *"nourishing* dark" part of the male psyche, which a young boy must have the courage to claim for his own before he can achieve individuation. Bly hastens to add that the "wild man" is not to be confused with the "savage man," whose mode "does great damage to soul, earth, and humankind." Rather, Bly seems to be advocating a male version of feminism. In the introduction to *Iron John,* Bly identifies the problem this way:

> The grief of men has been increasing steadily since the start of the Industrial Revolution and the grief has reached a depth now that cannot be ignored.
>
> The dark side of men is clear. Their mad exploitation of earth resources, devaluation and humiliation of women, and obsession with tribal warfare are undeniable. Genetic inheritance contributes to their obsessions, but also culture and environment. We have defective mythologies that ignore masculine depth of feeling, assign men a place in the sky instead of earth, teach obedience to the wrong powers, work to keep men boys, and entangle both men and women in systems of industrial domination that exclude both matriarchy and patriarchy.

What Bly does not say is that men have contributed to their "defective mythologies" by assigning women also an unrealistic "place in the sky" or else at some opposite extreme, in keeping with the angel/whore myth that dates at least from the Victorian age.

This kind of thinking allows the narrator of *Boomerang* to say, "Three months ago I heard the rumor that women have feelings too." And it is this myth at work when Yelverston, in the same novel, claims that "women invent the special lovely things of the world," and then implies that his own sexual demands on his wife are incompatible with a woman's nature:

> He knew he was a monster but he had to take her in the mouth this time and then come on her big generous breasts with the nipples dripping. Why do men need this? Yelverston asked himself. To make an elegant woman like her with her dreams of deer submit to this and degrade her?

Had the passage ended at this point, the lament would have revealed merely the stale Victorian dichotomy in Yelverston's psyche. But the scene continues with the wife's positive response to the sexual experience: "He thanked her. No, she said, thank you, darling. I've never done this for any other man, she said." And, following this, actual closure is achieved when Yelverston "was so amazed that he slept." This remarkable exchange problematizes the preceding passage in two ways. Yelverston's account of his wife's answer may be read as a lie: as wishful thinking in the adolescent mode reminiscent of Harry Monroe in *Geronimo Rex.* Or it may be taken at face value, in which case the evidence of equal male and female

sexual desire elicits the male's amazement, as in **"Water Liars,"** and his consequent withdrawal in sleep.

It is the sensitive man of "grief " in the 1980s and 1990s, as Bly describes him, who is compelled to tell again and again the story of such sexual dis-ease and its concomitant guilt feelings. Two such tellers are the dual protagonists of *Hey Jack!*: Homer, the narrator, and Jack, the coffeshop owner "who sits with the old fellows around the courthouse, those ancient mariners in this landlocked and soily town." Homer in particular is afflicted with an existential dilemma related to the psychological agony which has inspired religious confessionals from St. Augustine to Thomas Merton to the modern secular confessional novel of Saul Bellow. A casual reader of Barry Hannah might smile at the mention of the religious confessional, yet reviewers have linked his name with that of Bellow. None, however, has explored Hannah's connection with the diarists and novelists who were conducting what Peter M. Axthelm calls [in *The Modern Confessional Novel,* 1967] a search of their own lives and thoughts for "some form of perception," who were, as Axthelm says of Bellow's Herzog, "groping for meaning." Such men may suffer from the same syndrome which Gerzon would remedy by what he defines, in contemporary society, as "true heroism: the courage to explore oneself deeply and to act with self-awareness."

When Hannah's narrator in **"Love Too Long"** rages at Jesus: "You great bastard! . . . I believed in You on and off all my life!" (*Airships*), he voices a frustration (at what he perceives as Jesus's failure to set his world right) that recalls Augustine's prayer: "I was tossed and spilled, floundering in the broiling sea of my fornication, and you said no word." As a confessional medium, however, these stories fit less well in the religious than in the secular tradition of Rousseau, because they speak, instead of a need for absolution, a fear of shame; and thus they produce, in Hannah as in Rousseau, "both lies and confessions" (Brooks). As fear of judgment by the outside world seemed to "motivate both bad behavior and the confessions that such behavior necessitates" for Rousseau (Brooks), so it does with the characters of Barry Hannah, who well know that "shame happens" (*Boomerang*). In his analysis of Book Two of Rousseau's *Confessions,* Peter Brooks employs the method he calls "reading for the plot": perceiving in the movement of the plot itself a means whereby author, hero, and reader seek "some simulacrum of understanding of how meaning can be construed over and through time" (Brooks); and such a method works well with the stories of Barry Hannah, which are structured around a lie/confession trope.

Often the confessional nature of a story becomes clear through the application of a reader-response technique based on discourse analysis. In **"Coming Close to Donna,"** for example, by comparing the possible points in the plot at which Hannah could have ended the story with the point of true closure, one can intuit not only the story's meaning but even its genre. In the story, Donna has been sexually aroused by the bloody fight in a cemetery that has resulted in the deaths of two of her suitors. When the teenaged protagonist, who has also witnessed the carnage, is seduced on the spot by the naked Donna, he admits that he gamely "flung in and tried" (*Airships*). Had the narrative concluded at that point, the story would have been a modern example of the comic gothic grotesque. If a reader perceives a possible preclosure at that point, he or she may see the slapstick value of the story, and will perhaps then misapprehend the significance of the remaining narrative. But current narrative theory suggests that such a response will perhaps say more about the reader's reading experience than about the text. When the "macrostructure" of the text, however, reveals a story pattern, or textual grammar, of comic grotesque incident followed by narrative deflation, then the perceived preclosure point of comedy only serves to signal the true closure of confessional pathos that follows. Thus, when the narrator of **"Coming Close to Donna"** thinks, "If I were a father, I couldn't conceive of this from my daughter," he (like the disillusioned "water liars" in *Airships*) deflates and upstages the comic grotesque as he voices something of the same anguish one hears in [Thomas Merton's] *The Seven Storey Mountain,* when Thomas the Trappist monk says,

> . . . I was . . . the prisoner of my own violence and my own selfishness, in the image of the world into which I was born. That world was a picture of Hell, full of men like myself . . . living in fear and hopeless self-contradictory hungers.

Further, had the incident been an isolated one, it would not have the tropic force it assumes for a reader who also knows the profusion of such textual grammars in Hannah's fiction.

An extended use of the lie/confession trope is found in the story of Alice Lipsey, the beloved daughter of the title character in *Hey Jack!,* whose tawdry affair with rock star Ronnie Foot causes Jack such patriarchal pain. Jack's wish for the innocence of his forty-year-old daughter has been flouted by Foot, who, Jack insists on thinking, "had her." Homer promises to talk to Alice, but finds, instead of an undone spinster, a highly sexed woman with "merciless bright eyes" who rides a Harley motorcycle "with no helmet, hair streaming." When he also finds her a complex woman—"concerned . . . about Jack's being concerned" but also sexually "voracious," he cannot resist her. Jack eagerly believes the lie of omission in Homer's report on Alice: "She is in no way cheap or cheapened . . . She's still a queen, your daughter. A very strong woman. I like her laugh. She could . . . eat up all the tawdry measures of Foot without tasting a damned thing." Homer's "wife-to-be," on the other hand, seems instantly aware of his unfaithfulness with Alice, as if he were "a blank sheet of paper on which is written *fornication*" (Hannah's emphasis). The fact that Homer expounds at length about his culpability underscores the fact that Hannah's narrator speaks a central concern of the fiction:

> The heartfelt moans of hypocrisy shook me. What an inadvertent lecher I was, what a dog; I could not bear my transparency and my red lying face . . . I could not breathe the kind air I used to breathe. I felt to be a new alien to my town, and my sin ran around my legs like a dog dyed red.

The language of the passage places the speaker, and the reader, in the gap between religious confession and comedy, because of the ludicrous image of sin as a red dog running around one's legs; thus, we rightly think that Homer protests too much. Nevertheless, his self-contradictory effusions recur periodically until true closure is achieved in a tone far removed from the comic grotesque of any number of possible preclosure points in the story. When, at the end of the novel, Ronnie Foot has shot Alice, and Homer has come to console Jack, the passage of military history Homer reads is not incidental; it is the story of two unequal forces, the U.S. Eighth Army and the Chinese in North Korea, one of which "hadn't read the tragedy that would soon be enacted, [while] the other had written it." MacArthur is of course victorious, yet Homer remembers his own experience of the war as "the agony of meeting each incoming little group of survivors and learning who wouldn't be coming back . . . [and of] beating the frozen ground with a stick . . . and wanting to cry for Rex Gunnell and not being able to. . . ." In the midst of this collage of memories about what a "real" man can do, Homer bears witness to the violence of the unequal forces in his own psyche, and to the crisis of meaning he suffers, when he says all that he can say to mourn Alice:

> I live to say this. Jack lives.
>
> Alice doesn't.
>
> Oh, Alice. Hubba hubba, girl. After making it back from the Chinese and with my Silver Star all dogged away behind me, after having that night of you, and then yourself, a ghost talking to me, and then the last phone call, and then you dead.
>
> Killed by a simple stupid millionaire rock star.
>
> I was pulling my trigger finger in the air again.

Homer lacks the emotional resources to mourn properly, as ironically he, a Silver Star recipient, has lacked the courage to be truthful about his and Alice's sexual encounter. Even the combined power of his true feelings and his innate moral sense is unequal to the forces of latent and unfocused violence in his culture-conditioned psyche that lead him to conflate sex and war, and to complete an exuberance-to-deflation curve that inverts, and thus parodies, the move from devastation to elevation that Joyce Carol Oates has identified in classic tragedy (*Edge*). And although Homer would be hard put to explain this disjunction, he instinctively knows that his response to Alice's death and to Jack's grief is as insufficient as was his reaction to the tragedy of Vietnam.

Whereas Augustine and Thomas Merton find religious answers to their existential plight, Hannah's narrators do not: thus the dilemma that provides motivation for story after story in which a male protagonist agonizes over the very lusts and violent behaviors in which he engages with such energy and bleak hilarity. But although the fragmented surfaces of Hannah's narratives mirror a world in which meaning has disintegrated into Merton's "picture of Hell, full of men . . . living in fear and hopeless self-contradictory hungers," the fact that these narratives exist—that the protagonists keep on talking—may be a hopeful sign, one which Axthelm has described in Bellow as "a means of rebuilding that world around a clearly perceived sense of the self."

In high school, the only building blocks of that self perceived by the young protagonist of *Boomerang* are "the horn and my aloofness from the others"; for he essentially grows up without an enabling male mentor. Robert Bly laments the debilitating results of the adolescent male's having to achieve selfhood without initiation by an entire community of older male mentors; for this custom, long in use in many societies, has been discarded in the United States. Bly argues that the lack of ritual masculine initiation inflicts wounds which contemporary males find almost impossible to heal, a theory which Barry Hannah's fiction seems to bear out in its depiction of young males who suffer from hero-worship: who look for larger-than-life mentors, especially for those who model the culture's prevailing mythos of the military hero.

In fact, Barry Hannah's most extensive use of the heroic is seen in his references to war, particularly in (often conflated) fantasies on the Civil War and Vietnam. They are fantasies not only because, as Terrence Rafferty [writing in *The Nation* (June 1, 1985)] has said of *Airships,* they are the result of "an almost mystical belief in [the] manipulation of language—as if the exact combination of words and images will induce visions, like a prayer," but because Hannah is not a war veteran. His ancient-mariner-like compulsion to tell of heroic exploits results in the several voices that tell tales based on the Vietnam experiences of his real-life friend John Quisenberry. But Hannah is not simply performing a journalistic service for any actual veteran. His stories are about what it is to be a hero, or rather about how far a man will go to satisfy the fantasy of his culture about manly behavior. Social psychologists affirm that, in the United States, just as "a *real* boy climbs trees, disdains girls, dirties his knees, [and] plays with soldiers . . . , [he] matures into a 'man's man' who plays poker, goes hunting, drinks brandy, and dies in the war" [Roger William Brown, *Social Psychology,* 1965]. Hannah's stories show the gap between the fantasy and the reality of the hero, as they do that of the lover, and explore the plight of the American male who must come to what maturity he can in this existential abyss.

Thus, when reviewers complain about Hannah's "burying little references, like land mines, beneath the surface of the story, [so that] we don't trust the terrain enough to see it whole" (Rafferty), perhaps they have not perceived that Hannah's fiction is about all the lies that are "like land mines, beneath the surface" of all the dreams young men have grown up with in this country. For example, in **"Idaho,"** the protagonist's lies about having been in Idaho, while having only "bought an Idaho patch for my jacket" (*Captain Maximus*), and about having "not a gun [but] only a pencil" in his hand, taken together with otherwise oblique references to Hemingway and poet Richard Hugo, point to the underlying theme of the lie that connects these literary heroes of Hannah's, who are themselves ambiguously identified with both poetry and violence. Hannah, it seems to me, is attempting to deal with a truth that is not only illusive but too harsh to look at di-

rectly: the truth that one lives by lies, including the poetic indirections or "sheer lies" of fiction that project the illusion of confronting it direct.

Evidence of Hannah's preoccupation with the human propensity for lying is found not only in titles like **"Water Liars"** but also in his comments outside the fiction. His use of violence in the fiction, for example, whether on the tennis court, football field, or in war, he attributes to a fictional necessity to deal with the lie. Violence, he says, "puts your back up against the wall. People tend to lie less in conditions of violent behavior; . . . there is something direct and honest about [such violence]" [Larry McCaffery and Sinda Gregory, *Alive and Writing: Interviews with American Authors of the 1980s,* 1987]. Thus, Hannah's fiction is more than a *tour de force* of language, as some have called it; it is, rather, part confessional ode and part celebration of his attempt to put a lying culture's "back up against the wall," to "make something happen in vacant air [that is] a sweet revenge" on "the whole lying opera" of cultural memory that constitutes the American dream. And although, as Allen Shepherd has pointed out, Hannah's plots are not conventional, they constitute a significant postmodern "chaos" of mini-plots designed to appeal to the narrative desires of writer, hero, and reader to find meaning in the gaps between dreams, lies, and confessions.

Kenneth Seib   (essay date Winter 1991-92)

SOURCE: " 'Sabers, Gentlemen, Sabers': The J. E. B. Stuart Stories of Barry Hannah," in *The Mississippi Quarterly,* Vol. XLV, No. 1, Winter, 1991-92, pp. 41-52.

[In the excerpt below, Seib focuses on several of the stories in Airships *and analyzes Hannah's mythic treatment of J. E. B. Stuart, a prominent general in the Confederate army during the American Civil War.]*

The Confederacy's greatest cavalry officer, J. E. B. Stuart, has long been celebrated in Southern verse and story. John R. Thompson's elegy to the "radiant form" of Stuart, written on the day of the General's death in 1864, was the first of many poems to romanticize and mythologize the warrior-cavalier. In fiction, Stuart appears in the novels of John Esten Cooke (*Surry of Eagle's Nest,* 1866) and Thomas Dixon (*The Man in Gray,* 1922), while William Faulkner, in *Sartoris* (1929), has fictional Colonel Bayard Sartoris shot to death while riding with Stuart's gallant and doomed rebels.

In recent years, Barry Hannah is the Southern writer most fascinated by Stuart. Hannah, who teaches creative writing at the University of Mississippi, has written six novels and two collections of short stories, and while many of them contain allusions to the Civil War, there are three stories in the collection *Airships* (1978) that are specifically about Stuart (and a fourth that refers to him). This Jeb Stuart Trilogy comprises Hannah's attempt to connect past and present, debunk the romantic myth of Stuart as a dashing knight errant, and protest the folly of war, not just the Civil War but the Vietnam War that had been grinding down during the late sixties and early seventies when Hannah was writing these stories. There is even a lot of Hannah himself in his portrait of Stuart, as Hannah admitted in [an April 1983] interview in the *Southern Review*. Like himself, he says, Stuart was "capable of being a fool" and "was up there riding for glory. . . . That's the kind of asshole soldier I would be, I fear."

Because his fiction is often set in the South and is characterized by violence and Gothic humor, Barry Hannah has most often been compared to William Faulkner, Tennessee Williams, and other Southern writers who have explored violent and eccentric human behavior in Southern settings. . . .

In order to see Hannah's stories clearly, one must know something about Virginia-born James Ewell Brown Stuart. Only thirty-one when he was killed at a place called Yellow Tavern, just a few miles from Richmond, Stuart was the Confederacy's most charismatic and manly young officer. Nicknamed "Beauty" by his fellow cadets at West Point (though the term was probably intentionally ironic), Stuart graduated thirteenth in his class of forty-six, and tenth in cavalry tactics. Photographs show him at twenty-one as a dark-haired, large-framed young man with high cheekbones, dark brooding eyes, and a classic nose fit for the bust of a Roman senator. Later he was to grow a mustache and large dark beard, which made him look not unlike a bandit peering from behind a bushy mask.

Beginning as a lieutenant under Colonel Edwin Sumner, Stuart was himself a colonel at the opening of the Civil War and rose quickly to brigadier general, commanding a brigade of six cavalry regiments—more than 1,500 horsemen. His daring military raids into Maryland and Pennsylvania, and his cavalry support of Lee's Army of Northern Virginia, made Stuart one of the Confederacy's most celebrated heroes, and by 1863 he was in command of almost 10,000 men. A prominent figure in some of the South's most important battles—the First and Second Battle of Bull Run at Manassas, Chancellorsville, Fredericksburg, The Wilderness—Stuart was depicted by the Southern press as the very embodiment not only of the fortitude and determination of the Confederate fighting man, but of the ideal of Southern manhood. A Christian, a teetotaler, and a devoted family man, Stuart became the Confederate exemplar of Chaucer's "verray, parfit, gentil knight," self-effacing in victory, brave and fearless in the face of certain defeat, and gallant and courtly to women. In fact, after receiving from one of his female admirers a pair of golden spurs, Stuart henceforth signed some of his personal letters "The Knight of the Golden Spurs."

Moreover, Stuart embodied the Hemingway code of grace under pressure; he was the warrior who, like the matador Pedro Ramirez in *The Sun Also Rises,* held a "purity of line through the maximum of exposure," a man whose actions were always "straight and pure and natural." Nowhere was this purity exhibited more than in Stuart's death at Yellow Tavern. Leading a charge of the First Virginia Cavalry and significantly outnumbered by Federal troops, Stuart was hit in the chest by a .44-caliber bullet. Taken to Richmond and suffering intense pain from internal hemorrhaging, Stuart spent the following day giving instructions regarding his military papers and possessions—two horses, his spurs, and his sword—and singing his favorite hymn, "Rock of Ages." He died peacefully on the evening of May 12, 1864, having, as he said, "fulfilled my destiny and done my duty" [Emory M. Thomas, *Bold Dragoon: The Life of J. E. B. Stuart,* 1986].

What Barry Hannah does with the Stuart mythos is evident in three principal stories: **"Dragged Fighting From His Tomb," "Knowing He Was Not My Kind Yet I Followed,"** and **"Behold the Husband in His Perfect Agony."** All three appear in his first collection of short stories, *Airships* (1978), though one of them, **"Knowing He Was Not My Kind Yet I Followed,"** appeared earlier in the *Black Warrior Review.* Two of the stories directly involve Stuart, while the third, **"Behold the Husband in His Perfect Agony,"** recounts an incident shortly after Stuart's death. Further, Stuart and the Confederacy appear fragmentarily in **"Midnight and I'm Not Famous Yet,"** another story in *Airships* (and later incorporated into the novel *The Tennis Handsome*), and in the novel *Ray* (1980).

The first story, **"Dragged Fighting From His Tomb,"** is narrated by a Captain Howard, whom Hannah sees as the assassin of Jeb Stuart (although the actual name of the Federal soldier who shot Stuart is unknown). Dying of emphysema in a Miami hotel "from a twenty-five year routine of cigars and whiskey," Howard narrates the tale thirty-seven years after Stuart's death. At the beginning of the story, Howard is a Confederate cavalry officer who rides with Stuart on raids and ambushes into Pennsylvania. He remembers Stuart as "a profound laugher" whose personal black minstrel "could make a ballad instantly after an ambush." Stuart is a Robin Hood, leading his merry men against loungers, pickets, and "people of negligent spine," even offering the enemy first shot before routing them.

The central focus of the story is upon an incident at Two Roads Junction in Pennsylvania when Howard and his raiders are repulsed by awaiting Federals with repeating rifles. Howard is shot in the neck, a minor wound that causes him to pass out while astride his horse Mount Auburn, and he awakens to find himself being prodded by a flagstaff held by an elderly Yankee. The flagstaff, a symbol of war and blind patriotism, awakens Howard to higher truths. Holding a pistol to the old man's chest, Howard demands that the man immediately say "wise things" or die. The Yankee has no wisdom to impart, only beliefs, banalities, and bathos. The old man's religious beliefs are a composite of a blind faith ("I believe in Jehovah, the Lord; in Jesus Christ, his son; and in the Holy Ghost") and Sunday-school homilies ("To be square with your neighbor"). If religion gives no "exquisite truths," perhaps science does, for Howard has read Darwin. But Darwin has given him only the concept of the survival of the fittest. Finally his education has given him no truth; he feels "overbrained and overemotioned." Howard, in fact, remembers his professor at the University of Virginia who taught him Jonathan Swift's *Gulliver's Travels.* Recalling Swift's final section on the Houyhnhnms, Howard concludes that man is a Yahoo, "a dizzy and smelly farce."

Howard has been awakened into a new life and into new perceptions, where neither life nor death has any meaning—neither his own nor that of others like the old man—and when the elderly Yankee runs, Howard fearlessly follows him on horseback into the Yankee camp and into the staff house. Astride Mount Auburn, Howard thinks of other noble animals that have served in the war, especially a horse named Black Answer that was killed beneath him by a cannon ball. It is this death, Howard recalls, that "raised my anger against war," and he remembers the animal's "deliberate and pure expression" as he tried to comfort it. With Swift, Howard has come down on the side of the Houyhnhnms. But there is nothing deliberate and pure about the events in the staff house. All is choas: Howard shoots a Union officer before he can draw his gun; "overmurders" another soldier who enters the room shooting wildly, hitting Mount Auburn, and watches the old man and a woman, seemingly a prostitute who has been with the captain, copulate in terror as the staff house is bombarded by cannon fire. A killing machine, Howard dresses Mount Auburn's wound and rides the great steed out of the staff house, firing a pistol in each hand. He has routed the enemy by the time Jeb Stuart arrives to note the number of "dead Christians on the ground."

However, Howard's perception of Stuart has changed along with his perception of war. No longer the laughing Robin Hood of Howard's earlier recollection, Stuart is now described as a shy man who "has the great beard to hide his weak chin and his basic ugliness." Stuart's weakness and ugliness is seen in his exchange with Howard. Recalling one of the general's homilies ("Use your weeping on people, not on animals"), Howard has come to see Stuart as concerned about neither. To Howard's angry question as to what they are doing killing people in Pennsylvania, Stuart answers coldly, "Showing them that we can, Captain Howard." Stuart is a vainglorious egoist ("Damned if I don't think he was jealous," Howard recalls), war is indeed hell, and like the old man who has no wisdom to impart, there is nothing to be learned from the butchery of others. One can even see in Howard's decision to let the old man and the prostitute go free after the staff-house battle the 1970s slogan "Make love, not war."

As many did in the Vietnam War, Howard opposes the cause he once embraced and repudiates the patriotism of his homeland. Now wearing a blue uniform ("I did not care if it was violet"), Howard tracks down Stuart—"I knew how Stuart moved. We were equal Virginia boys"— and shoots him "in the brow, so that not another thought would pass about me or about himself or about the South, before death." Returned to civilian life, Howard is considered a traitorous assassin by Confederate veterans, and lives out his life alone and unrewarded, believing to the end that "we must eradicate all the old soldiers and all their assemblies." Again, the parallels with many Vietnam veterans are unmistakable.

As the story's title suggests, Howard has been dragged fighting from his tomb, brought back from his (probable) death in 1901 to speak to us once again, to fight once again for the same truths about war that Americans learn and forget over and over throughout their history. While Jeb Stuart is the South's mythologized hero, and still part of its pantheon, Howard is the true hero, the true fighter for a noble cause. As Hannah admitted in his *Southern Review*

interview, "I was more concerned with Howard than I was with Stuart. Stuart is just a foil who flames around."

At the end of the story, a dying Howard, dressed in gray, mounts Mount Auburn's grandchild ("It was an exquisitely shouldered red horse, the good look in its eye") for a ride along the lonely beaches of Miami. Although he has never named the horse, he knows that "Christ is his name, this muscle and heart striding under me." Just as the dying Howard is upheld by the power of the horse, so is the South sustained by suffering and redemption, and by Christian precepts of faith and salvation, not by cheap homilies from mythical Jeb Stuarts. The horse is an emblem of the turn-of-the-century South—earlier Howard equated Mount Auburn with the Confederacy—a South that must accurately and honestly remember its dead and its suffering, not mythologize it. The South, too, must be dragged fighting from its tomb.

The second Jeb Stuart story, **"Knowing He Was Not My Kind Yet I Followed,"** is the narrative of Corporal Deed Ainsworth, a homosexual who follows Stuart out of love, not patriotic duty. Ainsworth is a divided man who loves Stuart, even his terrific body odor that "rather draws than repels, like the musk of a woman." "Oh, the zany purposeful eyes, the haggard gleam, the feet of his lean horse high in the air, his rotting flannel shirt under the old soiled grays, and his heroic body odor! He makes one want to be a Christian." At the same time, Ainsworth hates killing, not only because of the waste of all the handsome young males, but because the carnage has ceased to have patriotic significance for him. "We are not defending our beloved Dixie anymore," Ainsworth reflects. "We're just bandits and maniacal." As in the first story, this awareness comes to the narrator during a raid into Pennsylvania, a military action that involves needless killing, not the heroic defense of homeland.

Further, in contrast to Stuart, whom everyone venerates ("There is nobody who does not believe in Jeb Stuart"), Ainsworth is an outsider, a non-Christian, a reluctant warrior, and a gay who is scorned as a "sissy" and a "nancy" by his comrades. He even steals into Stuart's tent one evening to declare his love for the general, but Stuart rejects him, at the same time embracing George, his Negro minstrel, in the manner of Ainsworth's dreams of how Stuart might embrace him. Ainsworth even suffers the minstrel's insults, and in spite of his military bravery, is treated as less than the lowest black slave. Even his horse, appropriately named Pardon Me, is fitting for a man whose very existence is a continual insult and apology.

Ainsworth's internal conflicts emerge when, during a Stuart raid of killing and looting, a wounded Yankee staggers up to Ainsworth armed with nothing but a kitchen fork. When Stuart rides up, his saber drawn, to dispatch this "poor Christian," Ainsworth points his gun at Stuart and threatens to kill him. "You kill him, I kill you, General." The horror of war is an even stronger emotion than Ainsworth's carnal love of Stuart, and like Howard in the earlier story, he writes of the events later on, this time from a Yankee prison cell. What Ainsworth has rejected is the supposed masculine image represented by Stuart, the warrior whose manhood is founded upon swagger, violence, senseless killing, and sexuality with women. Just as much a man, Ainsworth has quiet strength, deplores violence and killing, and is emotionally drawn to his own sex. Imprisoned at the end of the story in actuality just as he has been confined and isolated metaphorically throughout his life, Ainsworth is informed that Stuart has died in Virginia. Still attached to Stuart emotionally, Ainsworth feels little "reservoir of self" left in him, and concludes that the earth will never see Stuart's kind again.

Hannah's ending seems ironic, for the earth sees Stuart's kind in every outbreak of war—the charismatic figure whom others follow, love, and venerate, the warrior whose men crazily follow him to hell. If love is a stronger bond than war in **"Dragged Fighting From His Tomb,"** love proves destructive in this story, for it is Ainsworth's love for Stuart that causes him to kill against his better instincts. Only when he breaks that bond of love—is, in fact, even willing to kill Stuart to escape his emotional tie to the man—does Ainsworth become true to his "self." But the cost is imprisonment and isolation, and his self partly remains bound to the manly figure of Stuart. When Stuart dies, Ainsworth's "reservoir of self" is depleted as well.

The relationship seems a perfect metaphor for the South. The South retains its sense of "self" through ironic figures like Stuart, Hannah tells us, and those like Ainsworth who repudiate this self-image are not considered "real" men at all, and are doomed to isolation and loneliness. As suggested by the title, **"Knowing He Was Not My Kind Yet I Followed,"** Stuart is not Ainsworth's kind—neither sexually nor morally. The general, with ostrich plumes in his hat, is a theatrical figure, a warrior for whom slaughter is entertainment ("Our raids still entertain you?" Ainsworth asks him at one point). Stuart even has his own minstrel, who plays tunes like "All Hail the Power" to bolster his self-image. The South has retained this theatrical view of itself—gallant, masculine, muscularly Christian—to its own detriment and, like Ainsworth, cannot quite repudiate it. The South is, after all, the history of men like Stuart: "The earth will never see his kind again."

The third story, **"Behold the Husband in His Perfect Agony,"** is in some ways a continuation of the first two, although Stuart is only mentioned in the narrative. At the end of Ainsworth's narrative, the colonel hears of Stuart's death while in prison. At the beginning of this story, the news of Stuart's death has reached Richmond. In addition, in **"Knowing He Was Not My Kind Yet I Followed,"** the black minstrel George was ordered to deliver messages to Richmond through Yankee lines. In this third story, the Negro spy Edison is charged with getting a message out of Richmond through Rebel territory. While the first two stories reveal a living Stuart through first-person narratives, this third story is told in objective third-person after his death, as though we are given a privileged glimpse of the repercussions of that death.

The husband of **"Behold the Husband in His Perfect Agony"** is a one-eyed Huron Indian named Isaacs False Corn, who looks "mostly Caucasian" and has a wife and infant son in Baltimore. False Corn, a Northern spy in the Confederate stronghold of Richmond, is trying to get word of Jeb Stuart's death out of Richmond by way of a

Negro contact named Edison, a "black forgettable fool" who feigns lunacy during the day to maintain his cover, but at night puts arsenic into the bourbon of Confederate officers, an activity that False Corn finds "unmanly and entirely heinous." Edison does not even know who Jeb Stuart is ("Their best horse general," False Corn tells him), but he is willing to risk his life for the Northern cause and for President Lincoln ("I do anything for Abe"). He does not get very far, however, for a message, signed by a "Mrs. O'Neal," is delivered to False Corn soon after Edison leaves: "Not only is Gen. Stuart dead. The nigger is dead too."

Fearing the worst, False Corn finds it back in his hotel room in the form of a thin bearded man in oversized clothes who is brandishing a pistol that False Corn left in the room. False Corn, however, has a trick or two up his sleeve—almost literally. He dons a tattered robe that has a small stick of dynamic hidden in its collar, lights the fuse under the pretext of lighting a cigar, hurls the robe on the bearded man, and dives for the hallway. The explosion splinters the doorway, from which emerges a naked and blackened "thing," its breasts scorched black and its hair burned away. It is False Corn's wife, Tess, who tells him with her last breath, "I was your wife, Isaacs, but I was Southern."

This melodramatic tale, the weakest of the three, asks us to believe that False Corn could live with a Southern spy and have a child by her without knowing that she hates him, repudiates the cause for which he fights, and fails to share his politics and commitments. It is possible, perhaps, but highly improbable, and this improbability severely weakens the story. On another level, however, the story successfully depicts the tragic divisions of the Civil War: North and South, black and white, husband and wife. False Corn's one eye suggests his limited vision, even of his own wife, while his name indicates his propensity to hide his true self: he is "False Corn" not True, and while he is an Indian, his Caucasian features and Hebraic first name hide his heritage. He chastises Edison for poisoning the enemy, yet killing the enemy is what the war is all about (something that both the Negro and False Corn's wife clearly understand). False Corn is supposedly fighting in support of blacks, yet he thinks Edison a "fool." The explosion that blackens his wife and singes her hair turns her into a horrible parody of the blacks for whom he fights, and whom he perhaps subconsciously wishes to see destroyed.

Barry Hannah's trilogy of Jeb Stuart stories comprises a coherent commentary on the romanticized South and the mythicizing of historical figures.

—Kenneth Seib

Hannah poses in this story some unsettling questions.

Who are the biggest racists, the Southerners who fought to retain slavery or the Northerners who, under the guise of fighting for black freedom, had scarcely concealed contempt for blacks? What is the meaning of "victory" in a war that destroys normal human relationships like that of husband and wife? When both North and South are disguised from one another, hiding their true selves, how can there be one Union? If, indeed, the "union" of False Corn and Tess is meant to stand for the national union of North and South, the message seems clear: one will destroy the other. In the context of the story, the North destroys the South, just as it did in the Civil War.

While Jeb Stuart is only mentioned in this story, he is in many ways central to it. Stuart's death marks the end of the Southern chivalric myth of a gallant South going romantically to its death. Richmond is depicted not as a glorious Southern capital ravaged by war—the image of Atlanta in *Gone With the Wind,* for instance—but a place of "sighs and derisions and the slide of dice in the brick dust." It is a place where lunatic Negroes dance unnoticed in the streets, where Confederate officers drink themselves to sleep at night, and where even the dogs in the street fail "earnestly to mate." When False Corn chastises Edison for poisoning Confederate bourbon, telling the Negro that his crimes will land him "in a place beyond hell," Edison replies, "Ain't I already been there?" Stuart is dead, along with all the Southern myth attributed to him, and in a few short months the entire South will be a blackened and scorched "thing" just like False Corn's wife.

Barry Hannah's trilogy of Jeb Stuart stories comprises a coherent commentary on the romanticized South and the mythicizing of historical figures like Stuart. Not the dashing Knight of the Golden Spurs, Stuart was a professional military man who killed not only for glory and in defense of homeland, but for self-aggrandizement and, as Hannah puts it, to show the enemy that he could. Military officers are trained to kill, and Stuart was a killer, whose personal charisma, like that of Robert E. Lee and Thomas "Stonewall" Jackson, led a generation of young Southern manhood to destruction. With Jackson's death came the death of the Confederacy, leaving a scorched and blackened South with nothing but romantic memories and myth, fantasies about the glory of war in the face of the tragic reality of defeat.

That this schizophrenia still exists, in Hannah's opinion, is evidenced by other references to Stuart and the Civil War throughout his fiction. The story **"Midnight and I'm Not Famous Yet,"** published in Esquire and later included in *Airships* and as a part of the novel *The Tennis Handsome* (1983), recounts the Vietnam experience of Bobby Smith, a Southern veteran haunted by his past. Smith captures Li Dap, a North Vietnamese general, and after witnessing the death of his friend Tubby Wooten, wipes out the assaulting NVA force with a phosphorus gun, killing Li Dap and some of his own men as well. Sickened by war and killing—"In another three months I'd be zapping orphanages"—Smith returns to Vicksburg to piece his life back together.

In this story, Hannah clearly draws parallels between Vietnam and the Civil War. Li Dap, the captured Viet-

namese general, has studied the strategies of Robert E. Lee and Jeb Stuart, we are told, and sees the battle between North and South Vietnam in terms of the American Civil War. The North will win the war, Li Dap tells Smith, because "It is our country. . . . It's relative to your war in the nineteenth century. The South had slavery. The North must purge it so that it is a healthy region of our country." Bravely leading a tank assault as an example to his men, Li Dap is a modern Jeb Stuart: "All this hero needed was a plumed hat," Smith concludes. Once again the romantic ideals of gallantry, courage, and homeland have culminated in a savage war, and Li Dap is the charismatic hero, the Jeb Stuart, about whom myths are made.

But Li Dap dies unheroically, incinerated by a phosphorus gun, just one more casualty in a meaningless war, and Smith returns to Vicksburg, where Confederate General Pemberton surrendered to General Lee in 1863. Like the Confederacy, Smith has surrendered his romantic ideals at Vicksburg, and has learned to see life realistically, with both its victories and defeats. Watching at the end of the story a tennis match in which the hometown favorite loses, Smith thinks of the despondent crowd: "Fools! Fools! I thought. Love it! Love the loss as well as the gain. . . . We saw victory and defeat, and they were both wonderful." To be alive is to suffer both gain and loss, victory and defeat. And to be alive is better than to be dead.

Perhaps Hannah's final comment on the Civil War comes in his third novel, *Ray* (1980). The narrator, Ray, is an Alabama doctor and an ex-Vietnam pilot whose fantasies of the Civil War, in which heat-seekers and phosphorus bombs, are pitted against sabers and horsemen, equate one war with another. An alcoholic, Ray administers drugs to addicted patients and practices selective euthanasia on the hurtful and depraved. The victim of life's suffering—"I am infected with every disease I ever tried to cure," he says—Ray survives war, the poverty-ridden South, the loss of friends and lovers, and his own self-pity to become the hero of, if nothing more, at least his own life. By the end of the novel, he is plunging forward, saber raised like the Confederate officers of his Civil War fantasies. If Jeb Stuart, the South, and the Confederacy of the nineteenth century are in any way metaphors, Hannah suggests, let them be metaphors of the heroic struggle of all of us against the vicissitudes of life itself, not some metaphor that magnifies men like Stuart into mythic figures of romance and fantasy. Each of us is a Confederate soldier going forth to do battle against overwhelming odds, and ours should be Ray's battlecry at the end of his narrative as we face the deadly enemies of our daily lives: "Sabers, gentlemen, sabers!"

Mark J. Charney   (essay date 1992)

SOURCE: "The Autobiographical and the Violent: *Geronimo Rex* and *Nightwatchmen*," in *Barry Hannah,* Twayne Publishers, 1992, pp. 1-20.

[*In the following excerpt, Charney analyzes* Geronimo Rex *and* Nightwatchmen, *focusing on structure, character, and such themes as violence and identity.*]

In an interview with R. Vanarsdall for the *Southern Re-*

view [Spring 1983], Hannah cited his innovative and controversial use of autobiography as a primary factor distinguishing his work from that of other Southern writers: "They remain obsessed by autobiography, but I use it as a mode to get to the real stuff which is almost always lying." Although often compared to William Faulkner and Eudora Welty on the basis on his Southern heritage, Hannah admires those writers who reinvent autobiographical information in creative fictional form: "The people I like are looser and fuller like [Henry] Miller and [Thomas] Wolfe." In his first two novels, *Geronimo Rex* (1970) and *Nightwatchmen* (1973), Hannah uses autobiographical incident as a catalyst to encourage an imaginative response rather than as a means to convey or relive personal history. Believing that good writing stems naturally from experience, he uses elements of his own life during and after the writing of one novel directly to inspire the focus of his next: "The main part of my stories always comes out of life. I'm terribly affected by something, obsessed with it, or find it a situation I can't forget, and then the rest is imagination. But the emotional part is always something I've been through" [Jan Gretland, "Interview with Barry Hannah," *Contemporary Authors,* Volume 110, 1984]. From his experience, Hannah draws the emotional honesty that drives his characters to act; from his imagination, he discovers the most appropriate framework to express the motivation and inspiration for these actions. . . .

Hannah places *Geronimo Rex* (1970) within the tradition of such writers as Faulkner, Welty, O'Connor, and Wolfe by emphasizing the influence of the South upon a series of grotesque, eccentric, and violent characters. He also attempts to record the struggle of the individual to assert his independence in a community that fosters violence by resisting any change that breaks from tradition and the past. But the originality of his vision lies in his reinterpretation of autobiography to suit his own paradoxical purposes: Hannah begins with the truth, as he judges it from personal experience, to uncover the violent implications of lying.

A bildungsroman, similar in structure to such novels as *The Catcher in the Rye, Geronimo Rex* traces its protagonist, Harriman Monroe, from age 8 in Dream of Pines, Louisiana, to age 23 when he is newly married and enrolled in the graduate English program at the University of Arkansas. Hannah divides the novel into three sections: the first follows Harry through his senior year in high school, the second explores Harry's adventures at the fictional Hedermansever College in Mississippi, and the third spans the period from his senior year at college to the beginning of his graduate program at Arkansas. . . .

[Although] Hannah relies on a traditional narrator to describe his adventures, the structure he chooses purposely lacks the conventional, chronological continuity of most bildungsroman novels. Hannah achieves continuity, for example, not by leading the reader logically or smoothly from one event to another, but by introducing an array of minor characters who serve as foils to define Harry at various stages of his emotional and intellectual growth. Although many of the characters reappear throughout the book, Hannah describes most in terms of specific and dis-

crete episodes. Rather than illustrate his progress toward maturity through a succession of didactic "lessons," Hannah indicates changes in Harry's perspective by describing achronologically his shifting behavior during each segment and his unpredictable reactions to other characters in the novel.

The primary foil in book 1, for example, is Harley Butte, the Sousa-living, mulatto bandsman who works at Harry's father's mattress factory in Dream of Pines, where he even hears music in the making of bedsprings: "The Mulatto really had nothing against making mattress frames. . . . Harley liked to hear the music of hammers and springs, and he liked to see the mattresses take shape through the glass where the women were working with sewing machines alongside his area." In book 1 Harry's reaction to Butte progresses from jealous amusement to respect and admiration. As Butte continues to reappear throughout the novel, Harry's respect for him becomes violent and defensive; it is almost as if Harry must defend Butte against the prejudice of others to exorcise him from his (Harry's) own.

Violence eventually become Harry's preferred method of challenging anyone whom he believes wrongs Butte. In " 'Fight Fight! Nigger and a White!' " (chapter 7 of book 2), for example, Harry receives an invitation to see Butte's Beta Camina High School (Colored) Marching and Concert Band perform on Capitol Street in Jackson, Mississippi. He decides to bring a pistol to the parade after reading an incendiary letter in the Jackson newspaper written by his nemesis Peter Lepoyster. "Whitfield Peter," so-called after his sojourn in Whitfield Asylum, castigates the voodoo sewage, cooties, lice, and "fleamales" supposedly resulting from the "Afracoon" band's appearance in Mississippi. When Peter reaches for a handkerchief during the Beta Camina Band concert at the parade, Harry wants to assume that Peter plans to assassinate Butte: "I knew he was going for a gun; it did not occur to me that he could be reaching for anything but a gun, my forehead was hot with knowing this. . . . I already had mine out and was already to the middle of the street since I knew I could hit nothing from the distance I was from the sidewalk." When the opportunity for violence fails to materialize, Harry is actually disappointed. At this point in his life, Harry romantically sees himself as a twentieth-century warrior, ready to defend Butte's honor even if the musician would prefer *not* to be defended. Butte himself carries little significance in the scene as a character or even as a plot device; his two other reappearances in the novel signal and encourage the violence within Harry stemming from his own inability to eliminate totally the in-bred Southern prejudice within himself.

Other characters in *Geronimo Rex* illustrate Hannah's method of defining Harry. In college, Robert (Bobby) Dove Fleece, Harry's college roommate and a self-proclaimed genius, and Peter Lepoyster become the central foils for illustrating aspects of Harry's progression toward manhood. An initial meeting with Fleece prompts Harry to call him a "flit" and halfheartedly consider physical abuse: "I really didn't want to crush the boy. Right now I could see my fist go into his head as into a cantaloupe, and there was no victory in it." In spite of his effem-inacy and genteel background, Fleece ultimately becomes Harry's friend, accomplice, and even romantic mentor. Fleece's baroque prose and persuasive rhetoric influence Harry to perceive the music and eloquence of the written and spoken word. Although it is Fleece's initial prodding that convinces Harry to attend medical school, his love of language and romantic vision of the world ironically influ-ence Harry to pursue a career in liberal arts.

Harry, in turn, serves as a mentor for Fleece as well; he teaches Fleece the benefits of violence, especially in sexual relationships. Imitating Harry's behavior, Fleece shoots one of his roommates, Silas, when Silas begins dating Fleece's girl, Bet. As the two become better friends, Fleece becomes more like Harry: his relationships with women grow increasingly unbalanced and he is attracted to vio-lence.

Unlike Harley Butte, however, Fleece also serves as a strong plot device. He introduces Harry to "Whitfield" Peter Lepoyster, for whom Harry conceives such a hatred that he is driven to his most obsessive, violent, and roman-tic behavior. On a high school trip to Madison County, Fleece locates and steals pornographic letters that Peter had written to his wife Catherine before her untimely death during their honeymoon. The letters reveal Peter's impassioned and compulsive love for Catherine and his hatred for anyone who is not white, Christian, and south-ern: "They [the Jews] will raise up the nigger and teach him power and pride of position, and somehow too they will have to deal with that barbarous voodoo 'christianity,' and they will fail. . . . I am pointed to action: TO TREAT EVERY NIGGER AS IF HE WERE A JEW AND EVERY JEW AS IF HE WERE A NIGGER." Al-though Harry externally detests Peter's narrow-minded distrust of all that is unfamiliar, he envies in Peter his com-pulsive and all-consuming love for his wife and his niece. Hannah uses the episodes with Peter to illustrate Harry's inability to dedicate himself to any one goal or relation-ship. Harry, much like Hannah himself, wavers in his ca-reer ambitions, from medical to pharmaceutical to musi-cal to academic vocations, as often as he shifts from one woman to the next. He does not understand what drives the single-minded Peter to act; so, ironically, he reacts to Peter much like Peter would like to react to blacks and Jews: with violence.

Although David Madden [writing in *The Southern Review* (Spring 1983)] believes that "Peter is Hannah's most mag-nificent creation, more a product of his imagination, one hopes, than any of his other characters," Hannah based the character on familiar Mississippi types he had encoun-tered in his youth. In his interview with Jan Gretland, he stated that "anybody in Mississippi who's my age or older will tell you that such a character is hardly an invention. I grew up reading letters in the paper down in Jackson that weren't too far off from the letters I wrote for *Geronimo Rex*." And to R. Vanarsdall Hannah admitted that Peter's letters "came from some real letters that we discovered around an old house in Rodney, Mississippi, apparently from an inmate at Whitfield to his love." Although he did not have the letters in front of him while he wrote, he re-

membered their "European, baroque, and pornographic" content and style when he composed Peter's correspon-dence.

But Harry's fear of Peter and his hatred for the prejudice exhibited in his letters do not prevent him from subcon-sciously admiring Peter as a romantic Southern icon. Peter influences Harry as much as Fleece does, especially in relation to women. Before he meets Fleece and Peter, Harry reacts to women on a desperate sexual and emotion-al level. His first high school dreamgirl, Ann Mick, for ex-ample, illustrates Harry's youth and sexual inexperience. A girl with a shady reputation (she is rumored to have given birth to a basketball player's child), Ann represents Harry's infatuation with the idea of being in love. Main-taining a dream relationship with her is ultimately more important and desirable than establishing a realistic rela-tionship: "I tried hard to dream about her again and get her to give me some message in the dream, but I couldn't. The memory of her in the dream was waning, and I got in a desperate funk." Not until he realizes that his own fa-ther holds a similar infatuation for Ann does he abandon dreams of transforming the girl's life through the power of love and money. And, of course, after the infatuation dies, Harry thinks primarily of her violent and fiery de-mise: "and Ann tangled up with her current lover in the back seat of a car parked in her front yard, Ann on fire like a building, with her ribs broiling in my X-ray view, and the guy she was with screeching as his crotch turned to embers and flames took his head."

Harry's relationships with women before he attends col-lege build his ego and further his limited sexual experi-ence. While attending a summer music institute in New York, he has an affair with Sylvia Wyche, a "technical vir-gin" from North Carolina who seduces Harry, but wants to protect her hymen for her fiancé, Charles. In Dream of Pines, he takes Tonnie Ray Reese to the prom, where she vomits on him during his attempt at seduction. A senior who imagines that Harry holds the secret to maintaining her popularity and sense of importance even after gradua-tion, Tonnie Ray never holds real interest for Harry. He dates her primarily to improve his high school reputation and to alleviate rumors of his homosexuality. Meanwhile, he longs for Lala Sink, daughter of Dream of Pines's wealthiest family. In college, he has a brief affair with Bon-nie, a girl from Holly Springs with polio in one leg, "a reg-ular witch at murdering love" who seduces an array of men involved in serious relationships.

But after reading Peter's pornographic letter to his wife and seeing the man's obsessive, almost incestuous love for his white-trash niece renamed Catherine (after Peter's de-ceased wife), Harry modifies his view of relationships, and, in turn, his idea of love. Although he still falls occasionally into liaisons purely for selfish and sexual gratification, such as the one-higher stand with Patsy, the flute player in the Jackson symphony who is attracted to the ugliness of the male torso, he begins to ask out Peter's niece Cath-erine to fulfill his newly formed image of romantic com-mitment. For two years he pursues Catherine, attracted more by her lovely appearance and her enigmatic associa-tion with her deceased aunt than to her inferior mind and lack of grammatical ability, without once attempting to further their relationship physically: "It caused me no special anguish to resist. I heard Peter's voice in my mind while I was with her, but that isn't why I was so chaste." Ultimately, Harry realizes that he easily maintains a chaste relationship with Catherine because his love for her is inspired more by imitation of Peter's depth of feeling and Fleece's romantic ideal of love than his own. The romance, therefore, is inevitably a false one: "she was just a roach, after all. I knew the breed better than any. . . . My dozen nights with her never approached romance, never approached *anything*. It would've been the same if I'd picked her up on the street. I had never met a roach that I couldn't get a good bit of my marvelous self across to." Ironically, it is during his final afternoon with Catherine that he experiences a "butterfly of sentiment," an affection for her naive vulnerability that he cannot shake. But true to Harry's nature, since he does not understand this strange interlude or his feelings for Catherine, he strives to forget his affection before he is defeated by it: "I was absorbed for days in trying to forget the afternoon. . . . I knew if I thought of it too much more, it would fall around my neck like a noose and hang me." Harry longs to share the depth of Peter's and Fleece's emotional commitment, but he continues to run from feelings not easily accessible within his patterns of behavior.

Fleece and Peter also help to inspire in Harry a romanticized view of violence. Harry has always been attracted to violence, but with Fleece and Peter he begins to justify it as a means to achieve morality. His friendship with Fleece and his rivalry with Peter encourage Harry to idealize his own quest for love and righteousness. The associations he affects between himself and the Indian Geronimo (who gives the novel its title) illustrate this shift in Harry's view of violence. At Hedermansever's library, he discover the exploits of Geronimo and begins to parallel the personality of the Indian with what he views as his own true nature: "What I especially liked about Geronimo then was that he had cheated, lied, stolen, mutinied, usurped, killed, burned, raped, pillaged, razed, trapped, ripped, mashed, bowshot, stomped, herded, exploded, cut, stoned, revenged, prevenged, avenged, and was his own man.". . . .

Harry believes that because the world is already a dangerous place, characters must act offensively to ward off immediate and potential evil; therefore, he carries a gun, assuming that violence is inevitable, and waits for the anger in others to surface. Geronimo serves as Harry's symbol of the violence that is not only realistic, but also necessary for survival.

Geronimo appears to Harry's imagination as a genie, giving advice about dress, carriage, and behavior, and Harry begins to justify his own violent nature by comparing his exploits and fantasies to those of the Indian. Geronimo eventually even becomes the voice of Harry's moral conscience, distinguishing the necessary from the unnecessary, the significant from the petty. Ashamed by the manner in which he ends his relationship with Catherine, for example, Harry hears the betrayed voice of Geronimo threatening to leave him because of the pettiness of his behavior; ultimately, the threat of Geronimo's desertion encourages him to see Catherine again and to treat her more honorably.

Geronimo is a suitable choice of symbol for Harry because the immature Mississippian sees himself as a noble savage pursuing an often indefinable quest. Harry admires the idea of Geronimo's reputed six wives, his battles with the Mexicans who murdered his first wife and three children, his legendary rides across the Rio Grande and Arizona border, even "that the name Geronimo translated as 'one who belches' or 'one who yawns' or both at the same time." He admits to himself, "I would like to go into that line of work. I would like to leave behind me a gnashing horde of bastards." But the figure of Geronimo also illustrates the inequities in Harry's comparison between himself and the Indian. A Southerner who finds his traditions threatened, Harry may see himself as the wronged and noble survivor of a similarly ill-treated people, but because his real-life actions do not preserve this broken tradition, readers judge him much less sympathetically. . . .

Harry's actions certainly tend to alienate readers who expect a conventional, sympathetic protagonist with whom they can identify. In one of the first images of second grader Harriman Monroe, Hannah graphically describes the gratuitous murder of a neighbor's peacock: "The old boy was roosting about four feet off the ground this time and jumped on me at head level, making a loud racket in the cane as he launched himself. This terrified me, but I stood still and swung on the peacock with both arms. I caught him in the head and his beak swerved like plastic. He dropped on the bricks like a club, his fantail all folded in. I toed him. He was dead, with an eye wiped away." Throughout the novel, Hannah makes it clear that the slaughtered peacock (featured on the cover of paperback editions of *Geronimo Rex*) is a more appropriate symbol for Harry than the Indian he adapts as his cohort and mentor. In fact, recurrent, vividly described scenes of violence, inspired if not enacted by Harry, consistently remind readers of the true nature of the protagonist. . . .

What redeems Harry and illustrates at least a potential for sensitivity and thoughtfulness is his affection for his father, his sense of self-absurdity, and his depth of thought. He constantly compares his father, Ode Elann Monroe, to Humphrey Bogart and Jack Paar, and he labels him a "puller of the trigger when the chips were down." Genuinely bewildered when an off-color joke he hears at Hedermansever College alienates him from his dad, Harry regretfully admits, "Since then, very little has passed between us except money." He often worries about his father's opinion of him, and, although they disagree, Harry takes his father's advice seriously.

Harry finds humor not only in others' eccentricities, but especially in his own, from the ugliness of his torso to the reputation he earns of being a "desperate queer" in high school. . . . Hannah counters the reader's distaste for Harry's love of violence by heightening elements of the novel that describe the depth of his soul and the complexity of his insight; many incidents in the novel illustrate that Harry cares for more than just himself.

Most indicative of this depth and ability to transcend concern with the self is the music that begins and ends the novel. Although he immaturely celebrates the beauty and benefit of violence, through music Harry exhibits a love for art and an understanding of the soul. The novel begins with the eight-year-old Harry admiring the perfection of the Dream of Pines's "spade" band, in which Harley Butte plays the French horn. The music taps an enigmatic chord in the young southerner, one that he ironically associates with what he knows best—violence: "The way it was affecting me, I guess I was already a musician at the time and didn't know it. This band was the best music I'd ever heard, bar none. They made you want to pick up a rifle and just get killed somewhere. What drums, and what a wide brassy volume; and the woodwinds were playing tempestuously shrill. The trombones and tubas went deeper than what my heart had room for." This emotional and spiritual reaction to music influences Harry to learn the trumpet and to strive for the perfection of the Dream of Pines High School Band. But although Harry excels at the trumpet, because he is unable to capture either the beauty or the magic of Butte's band, he denies himself the pleasure of the instrument. In college, for example, Harry successfully forms a band that eventually becomes good enough to open for the popular Mean Men from Memphis. Although his band is well received by the audience, Harry imagines himself in front of Harley Butte's faultless Beta Camina Band playing perfect Sousa music: "I did not want to get sappy about this, did not want to *think,* aw God, but I felt shoddy, unrehearsed. . . . I knew I had been at the peak of what I wanted, I might still be on the peak, but I couldn't, *couldn't.*" Harry realizes during this musical stint that his best actual music performance will never equal the spiritual one inspired by Butte, so he abandons the profession he admires most.

Geronimo Rex ends with Harry inexplicably married to 17-year-old Prissy Lombarde from Pascagoula, Mississippi, and enrolled in the graduate program in English at the University of Arkansas. But it is once again music, not marriage or career, that inspires within Harry the desire to reach, understand, and achieve perfection. In the last scene of the novel Harry takes Dr. Lariat, the professor who witnesses the shooting of Peter Lepoyster, to hear Harley Butte's Beta Camina Marching Band. Like Harry, Lariat is overwhelmed by the band's sound and appearance: "Would you listen to that. . . . They are superb. That is the best." Instead of playing the traditional Sousa marches, however, the band is playing Butte's own music: driven by the perfection he recognizes in Sousa, Harley is finally able to compose music.

This act of creation inspires Lariat in the last speech of the novel to tell Harry, "That *was* it. Good, good heavens. We're in the wrong field. Music!" Harry realizes at the end of *Geronimo Rex* that it is Harley Butte, and not himself, who understands the power and influence of true creativity. Harry realizes through music and the efforts of Harley Butte to achieve a level of perfection that violence is ultimately an unsuccessful means to an end. Hannah redeems Harry by making it clear that he will dedicate his life to constructive, not destructive, behavior; although he cannot create music as beautiful as Butte's, Harry commits himself to discovering the musical potential within lan-

guage. The beauty of Harley's music exorcises the violence of Harry's actions against Peter and grants him the opportunity for a fresh beginning.

Harriman and Prissy Monroe also appear in Hannah's second novel, *Nightwatchmen* (1973), but the primary character is a dissatisfied, effeminate Southern loner named Thorpe Trove who spends his substantial inheritance on a 14-room estate near the fictional Southwestern Mississippi University in Pass Christian. Whereas *Geronimo Rex* explores Harry's progression toward manhood through events that indicate a maturity of thought and an ability to overcome interest in the self, *Nightwatchmen* traces Trove's circular movement from self-imposed exile to humanitarian to exile again. In *Rex,* Harry's interior monologue and his series of discrete, episodic adventures tie the disparate incidents of the novel together; his random, violent thoughts and actions drive the narrative toward a unity derived more from the consistency of the protagonist's thoughts than the complexity of plot. *Nightwatchmen,* on the other hand, achieves unity through its adherence to plot elements designed to resemble and satirize clues from a murder mystery. The reader is driven to finish the novel, not only because of interest in the future of the protagonist, but just as importantly, to discover the identity of the killer who is decapitating the nightwatchmen in Old Main, the English building on the Southwestern Mississippi University campus.

Hannah told Jan Gretland that *Nightwatchmen* is his "most deliberately Gothic book," and he believes much of its failure stems from his overreliance on a complicated narrative: "The more contrived a book I try to write, the more plot I put in, the worse I become as a writer." And, indeed, much of the novel advances through a series of broadly comic and unlikely plot devices, from mistaken identities to sentimental criminals, from all-destructive hurricanes to mass infatuations. . . .

The central character in the novel is Thorpe Trove, whose parents were slain on their second honeymoon in 1944. After his guardian aunt dies, he buys a house with his inheritance and, to circumvent his increasing loneliness and reliance on alcohol, decides to take in boarders. Most are from the English department at Old Main. Harriman Monroe and his wife Prissy come first, followed by an assortment of eccentrics and academics: the pretentious Englishman Anthony Weymouth, the black Magee, and the nondescript Bob Hill, Hallman Bryant, and Charles Israel. When a mysterious stranger humorously called the "knocker" begins striking academic "bores" on the back of the head at the university and knocking them out (much to everyone's delight), Trove starts to compile taped transcriptions to discover the assailant's identity. But after two nightwatchmen are brutally slaughtered (one by decapitation), Trove suspects that the case is more complicated than he originally assumed: the "knocker" and the "killer" may not be the same person.

Hannah divides *Nightwatchmen* into 15 chapters, 9 recounting the taped transcripts of interviews conducted by Trove. Each subject taped by Trove advances the murder plot while describing the relationships that graduate students and professors at Southwestern Mississippi share with the boarders in Pass Christian. This structure enables Hannah to emphasize the irony implicit in multiperspectivism—each character offers a different version of the "truth" and each version reveals much about the characters being interviewed. Conducted in 1969, each of the first four interviews—"William Tell," "Lawrence Head," "Harriman Monroe," and "Didi Sweet"—reveals information garnered from Trove's taping sessions by recounting the same tale. Not until readers explore all four perspectives do they discover all of the facts beneath the layers of self-deception. So although Hannah abandons his use of characters as foils to define a single protagonist in *Nightwatchmen,* he still relies on a variety of perspectives to narrate the "truth."

Such a structure allows Hannah to replay incidents almost cinematically to provide four very different scenarios of one evening. Tell, for example, frightens fellow graduate student Didi Sweet in order to make sexual advances, while Head, jealous of Tell's apparent success with Didi, terrifies the two hoping to abort their potential lovemaking. Harry, who prefers Didi to his own wife Prissy, forms an alliance with Head to disrupt the ensuing relationship between Didi and Tell, and Didi, in her taped transcript, explains in detail her relationship with all three men. Ultimately, the reader is left to determine the truth from the collective stories.

Between the nine chapters of taped transcripts running from 1969 to 1971, Hannah inserts six chapters entitled "Thorpe Trove" (or "T.T."). Written in first-person narration, these chapters smooth the transitions between transcripts and focus the novel on Trove's eventual escape (albeit temporary and incomplete) from his self-imposed exile. The "transcribed" chapters loosely resemble the variety of perspectives explored in William Faulkner's *As I Lay Dying,* and represent Hannah's attempt to break from the traditional structure of the mystery, not only to satirize its form, but also to heighten the mystery that lies within subjective response. . . .

But Hannah is not striving for individuality through multiperspectivism. He is primarily interested in discovering the humor and irony implicit in perspectives whose similarity depends on sharing the language and identity of professions; in other words, rather than create a plethora of individual voices like Faulkner in *As I Lay Dying,* Hannah originates three distinct categories of voices in *Nightwatchmen,* each influenced by job and social status and each defined by a specific type of violent action.

The first group represents the abstruse and pretentious academic perspective, characterized by circular argument, dense logic, and abstract thought, probably parodying the academic life of which Hannah was then a part. Paralyzed by an overzealous emphasis on critical analysis, academics such as William Tell, Lawrence Head, and Harriman Monroe rely more heavily on abstract thought than on direct action. When Tell, for example, frightens himself in Old Main, he praises the depth of thought that allows him the freedom to daydream: "I congratulated myself on the degree of abstraction I had flung myself into. The fiend might have come in the door, and here I would have been, the statue of an absorbed scholar—my eyes and heart, my

body and mind with Calypso and the sorrowfully fornicating Odysseus." For Head, even urinating inspires a level of personal fantasy and imagination: "I was propulsed by my own water to the surface of another planet, where I saw women petting tigers on the steps of an old temple overgrown with creepers and overhung with leaves of the banana plant." And Harriman Monroe, still obsessed with violence, reacts more slowly than he did in *Geronimo Rex* because of an academically imposed need to analyze a situation before acting upon it: "I had come to some plateau of decisions, a broiling plain, but at least it was a plain, over which hung two dominant clouds wherein there was a directive; on the right: kick Ned's face; on the left: suffer all men, your brothers—."

The nature of violence in *Nightwatchmen,* therefore, differs from that in *Geronimo Rex,* especially with the group of academics. Like Harriman Monroe of *Rex,* they still resort to violent action for self-gratification, but their actions are less spontaneous, more calculated. Hannah contrasts their petty, violent machinations to earn sexual and academic favors with the more desperate violence of the second group, the blue-collar workers.

Two characters in *Nightwatchmen,* Frank Theron Knockre, a security guard and plumber, and Douglas David Lotrieux, a projectionist who eventually reveals himself as the "knocker," illustrate Hannah's experimentation with language to contrast the academic perspective with that of the bluecollar worker. Unlike Tell, Head, or Monroe, Knockre and Lotrieux not only act spontaneously without the deterrent of abstract thought, but also resent the academics for their inability to transmute the conclusions they reach into some form of physical action. . . . Because neither Knockre nor Lotrieux knows how to communicate with the graduate students, the back of the head is literally the closest either comes to sharing thoughts or discussing ideas.

Both Knockre and Lotrieux use concrete images and specific, clear language to inform Trove of their inability to communicate with graduate students. Knockre and Lotrieux's men's club, arranged not around any particular common interest or mutual respect, meets in a projection booth Monday through Thursday nights simply to discuss with other nonacademics confusing current events or to confess embarrassing personal failures. Although their reliance on violence is more base and natural than the forced violence of the academics, the nightwatchmen still find the threat of real danger abhorrent and frightening. When two members of this group, Conrad and Spell, are brutally killed in Old Main, their friends in the men's club long for vengeance but lack the strength to pursue the killer. Hannah strongly suggests that a member of this group is responsible for the deaths in Old Main, but, ultimately, Knockre and Lotrieux only discover information that will lead Trove and detective Howard Hunter to discover the real murderer, Ralph White.

The first-person perspectives of Thorpe Trove and Didi Sweet and the third-person narration of Howard Hunter form the third triumvirate in *Nightwatchmen.* These characters represent the possibility of balancing abstract thought with practical action. Whereas the academics often think themselves out of acting and the nightwatchmen act without thought, Trove, Sweet, and Hunter sense inadequacies in their lives and act thoughtfully, emotionally, and sometimes illogically to overcome them. Trove becomes a landlord to prevent what seems an inevitable drive toward total isolation; Sweet embraces Southern romanticism to find a worthy companion; and Hunter pursues the accidental death of the man assumed to be the killer more to form friendships than to solve the crime itself. Although none of the three successfully reaches his or her goal, each comes closer to finding personal satisfaction than anyone else in the novel.

Ironically, it is through their union that the three profit most. Trove's boarders temporarily alleviate his loneliness, but when Hurricane Camille decimates his house and leaves him nearly destitute, he buys a trailer in the hope of retaining some sense of the community he has fostered. After he is ultimately used and deserted by graduate students such as Harry Monroe, he finds solace and satisfaction in Didi's arms: "All I say is bless God for the man-woman relationship. Bless Didi for being so full of sighs and laughter during the night. Thank God for the enduring strength of Nature that I was no disappointment in our orgy." And although their relationship ultimately fails, Didi still looks to Trove years later for answers to her question of loneliness: "Will you tell me why I can only love in pieces? I can never get my head, my heart, and my body into it all together? I want one long evening on the beach alone with you." The object of affection of every male in Pass Christian and at Southwestern Mississippi University, Didi chooses Trove, not the academics, to fulfill her mission of finding a Southern gentleman, "some man who had etiquette right from the heart and the time to love without anything immediately to gain. Hold you without almost touching you till you had time to fill up with love like a peach ready to bust. Take you out in a grove with a picnic basket his mother fixed for you." Trove fulfills for Didi, at least temporarily, this image of the genteel Southern gentleman while she builds for him his self-esteem. Theirs is a mutually beneficial relationship, and although Didi leaves Trove after he proposes marriage and children, neither is happy without the other.

Nightwatchmen is ultimately, like Geronimo Rex, a novel about the miracle of communication. Whereas Rex ends with Monroe and his professor realizing the communicative power of music, Nightwatchmen concludes with a simple act of humanity every bit as powerful and beautiful as the music that Harley Butte creates.

—Mark J. Charney

After Didi's desertion, Howard Hunter helps to give Trove's life meaning again. The detective who points out

that Trove and the graduate students, in their overzealous search for Ralph White, have shot the wrong man, reinterests Trove first in the murder case and then in life. Financially distressed, Trove takes a job at K-Mart selling shoes and catches mononucleosis. Although they are not yet friends, Hunter takes care of Trove. . . .

Hunter senses the inadequacies in the academics' penchant for discussion rather than action; Hunter's friendship, in which giving is just as significant as taking and concrete action is more important than abstract philosophizing, actually redeems Trove at the end of the novel by making him realize that a simple gesture of kindness is superior to a vague discussion of virtue.

Within this third group, then, both Sweet and Hunter contribute to Trove's eventual return to mankind by encouraging within him an understanding of true humanity and the need for action to accompany philosophy. By the end of the novel Trove has developed into a more satisfied, less ostentatious version of Harriman Monroe in *Geronimo Rex,* one who finds pleasure in a simple game of cards or a conversation with a friend.

The violence Hannah associates with Trove is less destructive than Monroe's in *Geronimo Rex;* in fact, Sweet, Trove, and Hunter are all associated more with the unnecessary violence in the novel, not the grotesque and exaggerated violence of the young Harry or the disturbed Peter Lepoyster. [Donald R. Noble, writing in *The Southern Literary Journal,* Vol. 15, No. 1 (1982)] points out that "*Nightwatchmen* ends in chaos, natural and man-made, with Hurricane Camille roaring through to kill off some of the participants and level the terrain entirely, bringing everyone out into the open physically and emotionally." Hannah parallels the violence of Hurricane Camille with the discoveries of Trove, Sweet, and Hunter; each understands that change is achieved only when the layers of self-deception are stripped away not only by the hurricane, but also by their eventual dissatisfaction with their lifestyles and the inactivity of those around them. Didi threatens to leave her husband when he worships her too completely; she understands finally that obsessive love is less fulfilling than finding a balanced affection derived from mutual respect rather than desperate need. Hunter and Trove find themselves together at the end of *Nightwatchmen.* Hunter nourishes the sick Trove with soup and games of cards, and Trove realizes his strong affection for the "rampant and smug" Hunter:

> I broke out of my death state a few nights later when I was dealt three kings, including my favorite fellow. I woke up betting. There seemed to be everything to live for.
>
> "What you got?" asked Howard.
>
> His spectacles were on fire with hope for me and him.

Trove finds personal salvation in *Nightwatchmen,* not by solving a mystery, capturing the essence of people on taped transcripts, or resorting to violence; rather, he discovers hope for the future through friendship and company, reminiscent of Harry and Lariat's mutual appreciation for music at the end of *Geronimo Rex.*

Nightwatchmen is ultimately, like *Rex,* a novel about the miracle of communication. Whereas *Rex* ends with Monroe and his professor realizing the communicative power of music, *Nightwatchmen* concludes with a simple act of humanity every bit as powerful and beautiful as the music that Harley Butte creates. Although Hannah's experimentation with perspective in *Nightwatchmen* lacks the strength and humor of his language in *Rex,* he does explore with finesse and insight the irony implicit in the lack of communication that often accompanies a higher education. In spite of their disparate backgrounds, the academics, the blue-collar workers, and the humanitarians share a need similar to Whitfield Peter's, Harley Butte's, and Harriman Monroe's in *Geronimo Rex*: the need for compassion and a common basis for communication, be it music, conversation, or a game of cards.

Donald R. Noble points out that much of the significance of *Nightwatchmen* lies in its title: "Hannah seems to be saying, we are all nightwatchmen. We all stand lonely watches and are hungry for communication and friends." The lonely vigils experienced by the security guards in the Old Main are shared by almost everyone in the novel: Didi Sweet, who waits patiently for a man who will treat her with respect; Lawrence Head, who looks for a companion with whom to share ideas; David Lotrieux, who knocks people over the head rather than risk alienation; and Harriman Monroe, who realizes that his heart "is a piece of false junk." Violence toward others brings only a temporary solution to the problems of the characters in *Geronimo Rex* and *Nightwatchmen.* Ultimately, Hannah's characters violently reexamine the self to discover that the true possibility of salvation lies within man's latent and untapped ability to create new avenues for communication.

Shelby Hearon on *Bats out of Hell*:

This is by no means Kmart fiction. Mr. Hannah's people are not ignorant, although they may be innocent; they are not consumers, although they are often collectors. Rather, this is fiction rich in the handed-down language of the Bible, of the Latin and Greek taught at state cow colleges and of a long line of progenitors whose mouths slip easily around such words as enfilade, ophicleide, entropic, prestidigitation.

Shelby Hearon, in "To Be Drunk and Not Young Is Terrible," in The New York Times Book Review, *March 7, 1993.*

Alex Raksin   (review date 28 February 1993)

SOURCE: A review of *Bats out of Hell,* in *Los Angeles Times Book Review,* February 28, 1993, p. 6.

[*In the following review, Raksin distinguishes the representation of violence in Hannah's works from that of such authors as Bret Easton Ellis.*]

There's a scene in Barry Hannah's 1989 autobiographical novel *Boomerang* when Hannah, writing a screenplay at the Malibu mansion of director Robert Altman, realizes that he's working in a beautiful tower of Plexiglas with sea gulls flying overhead and the Pacific rolling in below. Squirming in discomfort at this "white man's dream of peace," Hannah quickly defiles it by turning on the radio: "I needed the music, the tinny loud music, to remind me of all the trouble in the world. . . . I could not accept Paradise. I had to drag in the bad music and the cigarettes."

Hannah arguably does much the same in [*Bats out of Hell*], beginning each tale with humorous, colorfully painted character sketches, but then staining the landscape with pitch-black turns of plot. In **"Hey, Have You Got a Cig, the Time, the News, My Face?,"** a successful biographer who seems wryly amused that he has become "glib to the point of hackery," impulsively drives to a military school, withdraws a Daisy air rifle, and begins "popping some young boys singly, aiming for the back of their necks and, if lucky, an ear." In **"A Christmas Thought,"** a wandering Jew and Methodist, "deliberately feeling alien to the Yule season," taunt "an old tattered half-Chinese Negro" they see near a Laundromat until the man exacts gruesome revenge.

Whether contemporary American fiction needs yet another set of stories to remind us of "all the trouble in the world" is debatable. But important distinctions must be drawn between Hannah's violence and the kind seen in trendy novels like Bret Easton Ellis' *American Psycho.* While Ellis' Jekyll-and-Hyde protagonist inexplicably switches between blithe discussions of Ermenegildo Zegna fashions and zealous disemboweling of people, Hannah does something far more difficult: He shows why his characters have come to need their nihilistic anger—whether expressed in the angry gibes of the old fishermen in **"High-Water Railers"** or in the violence of metal-worshiping punks in **"Allons Mes Enfants"**—in order to survive.

Will Blythe   (review date March 1993)

SOURCE: "Hannah and His Sentences," in *Esquire,* Vol. 119, No. 3, March, 1993, p. 55.

[*In the following excerpt from a review of* Bats out of Hell, *Blythe remarks on Hannah's characters and admiration for Jimi Hendrix.*]

It's altogether fitting that Jimi Hendrix is one of Barry Hannah's idols and literary influences. Not only is there something sweet and otherworldly about both men that complicates their well-deserved reputations for wildness, there is also a parallel in their artistry. What Hendrix did with the guitar, Hannah does with prose: invent a whole new American music, viciously electric, of squawks and cries, of soul rhythms and extraterrestrial riffs. When Hannah plays his typewriter up against the speakers, as it were, the result is strangely angelic feedback about the national psyche, about how tumultuous inner lives finally spill out onto the pavement in gaudy pools of blood.

"I still miss Jimi," Hannah says a bit plaintively about the musician he venerates but never knew. "He was a shy man who didn't trust his voice. And a black man from Seattle, from *Seattle,* for God's sake. I like the alien quality to his story."

Indeed, aliens dominate Hannah's superb and typically bizarre new story collection, ***Bats Out of Hell.*** . . . In some ways it's a collection not simply of stories but of ten thousand strange and marvelous sentences. The book's characters are ruled by awkwardness and longing, never quite feeling at ease on this earth, whether they inhabit the collegiate environs of Oxford, Mississippi, as Hannah himself does, or the grunge pit of Manhattan, the haunt in one tale of a William Burroughs-like writer who loves drugs, boys, and cats, but becomes obsessed with an ancient surgeon who turns into a dog.

In Hannah's view, the new stories are more "tender and meditative" than the ones that appeared in his 1979 classic, ***Airships.*** In fact, their occasional venom is tinged with a fierce acceptance of human idiosyncrasy, perhaps the consequence of the author's third marriage ("I had to stop dating when I got married," he says), his nearly three years of sobriety, and his father's death in 1991. "You get to appreciating every day of life. I saw I was going to die. My father had shown me how."

Marianne Wiggins   (review date 7 June 1993)

SOURCE: " 'Ride, Fly, Penetrate, Loiter', " in *The Nation,* New York, Vol. 256, No. 22, June 7, 1993, pp. 804-06.

[*In the following review of* Bats out of Hell, *Wiggins comments on the major themes of Hannah's fiction and his insights into the male psyche.*]

> Who is he?
> A railroad track toward hell?
> —Anne Sexton, "Despair"

In the story **"Rat-Faced Auntie,"** one of the twenty-three new Barry Hannah tales in ***Bats Out of Hell,*** someone gives a character named Edgar "books by Kerouac, Bukowski, Brautigan, Hemingway and Burroughs; also the poetry of Anne Sexton." Edgar is a horn player in a motley band and he was "coming on strongly to the bassplaying woman, Snooky, and barely knew that he was capturing her with his new vocabulary stolen from Ms. Sexton."

Now, this points to a widely known but little discussed bonus in reading authors of a different stripe than your own. Hannah himself—through his six novels, three volumes of stories and one semiautobiography—goes out of his way to lead us to believe he is a hard-writing, hard-drinking, hard-balling man. His male friends (he never mentions female friends) are all hard-living Southern coots and snards, most of whom played football in their younger days, loved a good prank and loved nooky, especially if both could be purchased through someone else's pain. My own experience is that writers do not run in packs (despite what glossy magazines suggest), but often writers swim in a common current until they need to break for shore, or until one of them drowns. For Hannah, this swim team includes Tom McGuane, Jim Harrison and Willie Morris, about whom he writes with great affection in his novel-stroke-autobiography ***Boomerang.*** What is

particular about the sort of friendship that Hannah has with these other writers is not that it is male but that it is so active—these guys are always fishing and drinking, or grilling meat and drinking, or cutting horses, shooting clay things out of the sky, hopping on Harleys, cruising through our big two-hearted playground in giant cars, Caddies, Bonnevilles, LeBarons with the top down and their testosterone up. Now the point I want to make is this: Not all male fiction writers act this way (and not every female poet ends in suicide). *French* male novelists do not hurl themselves in clusters with abandon into risky ventures, no. And the English—christ, the English: Some of them are known to test the laws of nature periodically in a frenzied game of snooker. Perhaps it is the product of their public schooling, but the English (not the Scottish, not the Irish, not the Welsh), the English males love to show off in front of one another in a form of recitation—not a debate, actually, more a game of talk, like poker, that includes the function of an ante to be upped, a kitty to be won. And when they're really having fun with one another, the English boys will do all this in rippingly hilarious (to them) *Fa-rench* accents. So give me a home where the buffalo roam.

There are a thousand discoveries at hand in any book by Barry Hannah, not the least of which are the noble and amazing tricks he can perform with language. He has snatched himself many times, he tells us, from the hairy jaws of self-destruction; but the truth is, even in sobriety and the bosom of a third marriage, Hannah's writing consistently displays the edginess of one who risks his peace of mind, day in, day out. I (delicate creature of the opposite stripe) approach each new work of his with a degree of horror and trust—horror at the unrelenting violence; and trust in him to push through it, somehow, in a way that is clear, exhilarating, funny. There are people in this country, Hannah's message is, who are big and strong or small and nasty, strung out, fucked up and enraged. Hannah's worst cases are usually male, but hey. Like his character Edgar reading Ms. Sexton so he can court the other sex, one of the reasons I read Barry Hannah is to try to learn how to live with those other creatures from Eden, the snakes and the men.

Hannah's first novel, ***Geronimo Rex,*** was published in 1972 and is, gratefully, still in print. It won the William Faulkner Prize, which, for a Southern writer, means they put your face on local minted money. I am only a half-breed Southerner myself, but the heroic significance of worthless currency is still imprinted on my genes. ***Geronimo Rex*** prefigures many of Hannah's recurring themes (sex, Elvis, war, liquor, drugs), but in the succeeding years Hannah has greatly pared down his style, leaving this first novel, perhaps not so surprisingly, his densest and longest work. A second novel, ***Nightwatchman,*** appeared (and disappeared) before Hannah jolted everybody awake with the publication in 1979 of ***Airships,*** very simply one of the best short-story collections around written by anyone. Ever. Male or otherwise. Even those French guys, who perfected the form.

Between and among ***Airships*** and ***Captain Maximus,*** his second collection of stories, and the new one, ***Bats Out of***

Hell, there is a lot of phantom imaging going on, a lot of shadow hiding, or what the moon people call "coherent backscatter." Characters and places from the stories in *Airships* reapper in *Captain Maximus* and *Bats Out of Hell,* and one of the loveliest threads in current literature runs from **"Water Liars"** in *Airships* to **"High-Water Railers"** in the new collection. Both are fishing tales of profound sweetness and despair, featuring a crew of ancients fishing off a rail on a pier in Farte (pronounced "Far-tay") Cove, off the Yazoo River.

"Water Liars" is the first story in *Airships,* and **"High-Water Railers"** is the opening tale in *Bats Out of Hell;* and for any fan of the former, it's a tender reunion to open this new volume and on the first page find old joy reflected. (Clever, too, is Hannah's reflected use of the words "liar" and "rail" in each story: One word is the other spelled backward.)

On the rail in **"High-Water Railers"** are four old men, "hovered together into one set of eyes three hundred and twenty-three years old." Wren, "a chronic prevaricator whose lies were so gaudy and wrapped around they might have been a medieval tapestry of what almost or never happened"; Ulrich, who "was in the process of 'studying' blue herons, loons and accipiters in flight and for some nagging reason was interested in the precise *weight* of everybody he met"; Lewis; and Sidney Farte:

> Sidney had endured lately a sorry, sorry thing, and all of them knew it. A male grandchild of his had won a scholarship to a mighty eastern university, Yale, and was the object of a four-year gloat by Sidney, who had no college. The young man upon graduation had come over to visit his grandfather for a week, at the end of which he pronounced Sidney "a poisonous, evil old man who ought to be ashamed of yourself." This statement simply whacked Sidney flat to the ground.

But Hannah lifts these men off their individual points of desperation through (of all things) the intercession of a woman, and the promise of that other one of man's best friends, a dog.

In fact, as many dogs run through this new collection as run through old Disney movies. In **"Two Things, Dimly, Were Going At Each Other,"** the unfortunate Harry Latouche suffers from "the grofft," a disease that turns a man into a canine. And in **"Upstairs, Mona Bayed for Dong"** (yes, folks, we could sit here all day and talk about Barry Hannah's titles, like the one on this review—he even claims Jimmy Buffett paid him $7,500 for a title for a song, but **"Mona"** is credited to Tom McGuane) a man who practices snapping cigarettes from the lips of his pregnant wife with a bullwhip ruminates upon the attractions of women by stating, "I know what most men want is the quality of Old Shep, waiting at a Montana train station twelve years for his master who's been taken off dead in a coffin to the East, but there are other qualitites of marriage, rather strangely enjoyed."

As Hannah writes in *Boomerang,* the love between a man and a woman is not especially his strong point. Men and fishing, yes. Men and F-14s. Men and dogs. Men and sons

(a new and pregnant lode). But men and women? "My life," he writes, "is bountiful. It is like the Garden of Eden with a woman who is so goodlooking I took a Polaroid picture of her lying in a bed in Biloxi with her breasts showing and showed it to my close friends. Sharing her beauty, although I hate her often. She challenges the thing: the *thing.* The thing itself."

Possibly the closest he has come to writing about the *love* thing is in the comic novel *Ray*—second in its sidesplitting delights only to *Airships.* But who needs love, anyway, in a nation of what he calls "compulsive videoers"? "Best a man like me can hope for from now on is just to blur out and have a few good days," a phantom cowboy tells a lad whose mother he has just killed in **"Ride Westerly for Pusalina."** "We'll just do some long blurring together."

Long blurring out is not a new perspective in men's writing, but try though he has, Hannah can't quite manage it. There are several wildly surrealist apocalyptic and postapocalyptic tales in *Bats Out of Hell,* and again and again, through all his work, he addresses the horrors of war, all wars—Civil, Nam and Desert Storm—in language that makes it clear that he's opposed to them. **"That Was Close, Ma"** in this new collection is one of the first antiwar stories to come to print since Bush drew his vanishing line in the sand.

Hannah distrusts everything he sees—except, possibly, death—but he refuses to make a hackneyed tragedy out of it by blinding both his eyes (although he writes a lot about men who are blind in one or both eyes). Nope—behind those aviator shades of his he channels all the vicious goop that is this great society into the language of intelligible madness. Much of the crazed certainty that was the hallmark of the stories in *Airships,* though, is gone from these new stories. Each story in *Airships* ended on a note of resolution—in fact, we could string together a sort of manifesto from the last lines of these stories, lines like "Changes like that never bothered my heart" and "We saw victory and defeat, and they were both wonderful."

Uncertainty—or, well, the wisdom of age that nothing is ever for sure carved-in-stone certain—inhabits the stories in *Bats Out of Hell.* Everything, every*thing,* Hannah seems to suggest, has its double, its doubt, its own mirror image. A son (who is a poet) tells his father (who is a biographer) in **"Hey, Have You Got a Cig, the Time, the News, My Face?"** that in the South, "the men who change the world mostly go fishing. . . . They want *out* of this goddamned place."

But of course they stay, these guys, they hang around, waiting to berth out on some modern Pequod of their own. "That's it, lads," the father in **"Hey, Have You Got a Cig . . . ?"** addresses a bunch of punks he has just shot to hell with an air rifle. "Start asking some big questions like me, you little nits. You haven't even started yet." These new stories announce the prospect of a long afternoon for Hannah, fishing, staring into that bright soup, raging, pulling up bones at the end of his lines in search of a new definition, a white whale, perhaps, a lasting name:

Is your name by any chance Rumpelstiltskin?
He cried: The devil told you that!
He stamped his right foot into the ground
and sank in up to his waist.
Then he tore himself in two.
Somewhat like a split broiler,
He laid his two sides down on the floor,
one part soft as a woman,
one part a barbed hook,
one part papa,

one part Doppelgänger.

Anne Sexton wrote that. And she hadn't even laid her eyes on Barry Hannah.

Ruth D. Weston   (essay date Spring 1995)

SOURCE: "Debunking the Unitary Self and Story in the War Stories of Barry Hannah," in *The Southern Literary Journal,* Vol. XXVII, No. 2, Spring, 1995, pp. 96-106.

[*In the following essay, which was first presented in an abbreviated form at the South Central Modern Language Association conference in October 1994, Weston examines themes of war, heroism, honor, and shame in Hannah's short stories about the American Civil War and the Vietnam War.*]

In a new book on storytellers of the Vietnam generation. [*Out of the Sixties: Storytelling and the Vietnam Generation,* 1993], David Wyatt argues that literary generations are defined by, among other things, "the impact of a traumatic historical incident or episode . . . [which] creates the sense of a rupture in time and gathers those who confront it into a shared sense of ordeal." Whether they, their friends, or someone in their families were the actual combatants, the writers born between 1940 and 1950 are those most directly influenced by the Vietnam period: from commitment of troops to Vietnam in 1965 to troop withdrawal in 1972. Recalling the comments of individual writers about their frustration with impersonal accounts of the history of the Vietnam era, Wyatt focuses on the idea of story as a formal structure that mediates between the public history and the intensely personal individual responses to the chaos of this "rupture in time." Historically, the concept of story is as more than mediator; it has been understood as a force for coherence, a form imposed upon the chaos of experience. Philip D. Beidler points out that the best writers about Vietnam are not only committed to the concrete reporting of experience as "at once a thing of the senses, of the emotions, of the intellect, of the spirit"; they are also involved in "a primary process of sensemaking, of discovering the peculiar ways in which the experience of the war can now be made to signify within the larger evolution of culture as a whole," contributing to "the process of cultural myth-making" and to experiences common to all people. Wyatt believes that the so-called Vietnam generation desperately desires its stories to be this kind of formative force. Comparing it with Eliotic "fragments shored against ruins," he argues that story, as that formative force, is the means by which those who write about Vietnam "resist the dominant and violently inarticulare contemporary discourse." But many tellers of war stories do not seem to think of their narratives as "formative" forces but rather as extreme versions of that discourse's violence and inarticulateness. Pointing out that "a true war story" does not "generalize," Tim O'Brien suggests [in *The Things They Carried,* 1990] that such stories fail to cohere in the kind of formal unity that lends itself to the establishing of a theme that can be recognized either by author or reader. "Often," O'Brien says, "there is not even a point." Moreover, he argues:

> you can tell a true war story by the way it never
> seems to end. Not then, not ever. . . . All you
> can do is tell it one more time, patiently, adding
> and subtracting, making up a few things to get
> at the real truth. . . . And in the end, of course,
> a true war story is never about war. . . . It's
> about love and memory. It's about sorrow. It's
> about sisters who never write back and people
> who never listen.

Central to Barry Hannah's narrative structures (especially in *Airships* and **"Bats out of Hell Division"**) is the chaos of war, both *as war* and as metaphor for the more general violence and inarticulateness of his generation. His fiction is intensely concerned with the kind of shattered individual psyches that a Vietnam war correspondent recognized by battle-fatigued soldiers' "eyes that poured out a steady charge of wasted horror" [Michael Herr, *Dispatches,* 1977]. As such, Hannah's stories show how the habit of violence is both cause and consequence of the divided self, for the fragmented narrative of a Hannah war story accurately reflects the lives of its characters. Mark Charney's new critical biography of Hannah [*Barry Hannah,* 1992] asserts that these stories satirize the characters' "inability to make sense out of life"; yet, for Hannah as well as for his fictional narrators, each story constitutes a sensemaking attempt such as that [Philip D. Beidler, author of *American Literature and the Experience of Vietnam,* 1982] finds in other Vietnam literature.

In contrast to many writers on the topic, Hannah does not depict Vietnam as a unique experience, as does Philip Caputo [author of *A Rumor of War,* 1977], who calls it "the only . . . [war] we have ever lost." Rather, in Hannah's fiction, Vietnam is presented in the context of the history of the South and its lost cause: as a modern manifestation of Southern traditions of violence, honor, and dishonor. His approach is appreciated by Owen Gilman, Jr., who shows the extent to which, in many Southern writers, and in the Southern imagination in general, Vietnam was "prefigured in the history of the South" [*Vietnam and the Southern Imagination,* 1992]. To Hannah's characters it is one of two "unfinished" wars, in the sense of unresolved issues that continue to exert force over their lives.

Hannah's unstable male narrators refight the same wars by retelling the same stories, as if the next telling might provide meaning, perhaps vindication, or at least closure. They long for the good fight, even the good death, which is necessary to a culturally enforced idea of honor but which is continually undermined by the perverse human inability to avoid dishonorable acts. His fragmented, often surreal, narratives are at once postmodern and squarely in the mainstream of the American short story tradition that includes both the epiphanic story of innocence, experience, and integration, and its complement, described by Thomas Leitch [in "The Debunking Rhythm of the American Short Story," *Short Story Theory at a Crossroads,* edited by Susan Lohafer and Jo Ellyn Clarey, 1989] as "a means to the author's unmaking, and the audience's unknowing." Hannah most often writes the latter, the kind of story that exhibits what Leitch calls a "debunking rhythm" in which antithesis is unresolved, epiphany is not achieved. Such a narrative rhythm, Leitch says, is integral to the thematic debunking of "the concept of a public identity, a self that acts in such a knowable, deliberate way as to assert a stable, discrete identity . . . that was only an illusion to begin with." Vietnam is a topic made for such a technique, since that experience forced the entire nation to rethink the contradictory nature of its self-concept and its public identity. It is also a topic that embodies the paradox of story fragments that try but always fail to shore up the ragged holes in individual psyches as well as in the culture's heroic myth.

Barry Hannah, born in Clinton, Mississippi, in 1942, did not serve in Vietnam, but in his published interviews, novels and short stories, he bears witness to the fact that he is of the Vietnam generation. His interest in military history, Vietnam, and war in general is no doubt complemented by his admiration for the fiction of two other famous American noncombatants, Ernest Hemingway and William Faulkner, with whom his work has been compared. And since Hannah is a Southerner, for him the concept of war is always colored by the peculiar traditions of violence and the codes of honor, military and otherwise, that coexist in the Southern mind.

Central to Barry Hannah's narrative structures (especially in *Airships* and "Bats out of Hell Division") is the chaos of war, both *as war* and as metaphor for the more general violence and inarticulateness of his generation.

—*Ruth D. Weston*

If Hannah's fiction is not the direct response of a veteran, it is, nevertheless, a response that resonates with the knowledge of wars and other national traumas. Asked about Vietnam, Hannah recalled, "You woke up every day with that war on your TV. . . . You were watching 'The Three Stooges' or whatever, and the next thing on was bloody corpses and body counts [and] the copters always." Asked about a locus of violence closer to home, the Civil Rights Movement in Mississippi, Hannah replied, "You could get a pistol pulled on you for wearing tennis shoes at one point . . . [because it] meant 'hippies' [or] 'Freedom Riders.' "

The other war that most directly informs Hannah's fiction, the Civil War, does so in part by his having grown up surrounded by memorials of the South's honored dead. Allen Tate, in "Ode to the Confederate Dead," asks what is to be done with such memories:

> What shall we say who have knowledge
> Carried to the heart? Shall we take the act
> To the grave? Shall we, more hopeful, set up the grave
> In the house? The ravenous grave?

Historically, that is exactly what Southerners have done. In Barry Hannah's words, "Growing up here, you can almost feel Vicksburg if you're alive. . . . You grow up in that park with those gloomy old busts and those cannons. It's easy to be full of history. . . . You know things just by growing up, like [the fact that] Jackson was Chimneyville." Moreover, if Hannah lacks first-hand knowledge of battle, he has the Southerner's comprehension of the qualities basic to life in general and war in particular: honor, and its mirror image, shame. According to historian Bertram Wyatt-Brown [in *Honor and Violence in the Old South,* 1986], honor and shame "cannot be understood apart from . . . [each] other. [A Southerner] was expected to have a healthy sense of shame, that is, a sense of his own honor. Shamelessness signified a disregard for both honor and disgrace. When shame was imposed by others, honor was stripped away."

Hannah's protagonists are driven by inherited ideas about honor, shame, and vengeance—from ancient Indo-European tribal concepts to Old Testament imperatives—and by the American, especially Southern, translation of these ideas into a personal code that assumes the public nature of private acts. The South has understood the primal honor code as one

> designed to give structure to life and meaning to valor, hierarchy, and family protection. But its almost childlike clarity, its seeming innocence, contained inner contradictions. Within the ethic, there was a conflict never wholly mastered, a point at which the resolutions and the alternations of the system broke down . . . [because of] the discrepancy between honor as obedience to superior rank and the contrary duty to achieve place for oneself and family.

Although meant to "prevent unjustified violence, unpredictability, and anarchy," the honor code could lead to "that very nightmare."

In Hannah's fiction, the individual continues to do battle with the code by aspiring to its mythic, heroic ideal; and conflicts between the exigencies of that public ideal and those of the private self are at the heart of the psychic ruptures in his characters. In their search for honor, love, and power, they tell lies, act reprehensibly, and are in general at the mercy of their own self-defeating behavior. All the heroes of Hannah's stories imagine "high and valiant stuff," as does Horace in **"Scandal d'Estime,"** a story from his most recent volume, *Bats Out of Hell;* but when they cannot live up to such ideals, they resort to "dreams, lies, and confessions" about them [see Ruth D. Weston, "'The Whole Lying Opera of It': Dreams, Lies, and Confessions in the Fiction of Barry Hannah," *Mississippi Quarterly* (1991)]. Reflecting this disjunction, the stories themselves are ruptured by unsettling shifts, gaps, and disavowals of their own truth. Describing such disunities in Vietnam literature, Beidler notes that "everything from official euphemism to battlefied slang seem[s] the product of some insane genius for making reality and unreality—and thus, by implication, sense and nonsense—as indistinguishable as possible."

The trauma of war erupts in Hannah's stories, even in the midst of peacetime settings, through words, thoughts, and acts of his characters, one of whom is modeled on a close friend who flew F-4s in Vietnam. In **"Midnight And I'm Not Famous Yet,"** a story from *Airships,* Hannah illustrates the dilemma of honor betrayed into shame. It is the story of two young soldiers from Mississippi who have the apparent good luck to capture the Vietnamese general Li Dap and his gunner, the two occupants of a tank that had foundered in a pond. The general has been educated at the Sorbonne and is a history buff. The narrator, Captain Bobby Smith, learns from his prisoner that Li Dap's downfall is due to his fascination with "Robert Lee and the strategy of Jeb Stuart, whose daring circles around an immense army captured his mind." As Bobby tells the story, "Li Dap had tried to circle left with twenty thousand and got the hell kicked out of him by idle Navy guns sitting outside Gon. He just wasn't very bright. He had half his army climbing around these bluffs, no artillery or air force with them, and it was New Year's Eve for our side" (*Airships*). Because Li Dap is captured while personally leading this insanely daring attack "as an example to [his] men," Bobby recognizes and honors the heroic ideal the enemy officer represents. In the mind of the young Southern captain, the wars and cultures merge; to him, "all this hero needed was a plumed hat" to be seen as an officer of the Confederate States of America.

Tubby Wooten, the other American soldier in the story, is a photographer who enjoys a brief reverie of the fame that will surely accrue to him when his prize-winning photographs of the captured general are published in *Time* or *Newsweek*. Almost immediately after Li Dap's capture, however, their own unit is attacked by the North Vietnamese Army. Tubby is killed and, when a Vietnamese soldier is about to bayonet the American soldier guarding Li Dap, Bobby "burned them all up" with a phosphorus shotgun. For killing "a captured general" and allowing "twenty gooks to come upon us like that," he is demoted to lieutenant and sent home, his own dream of honor reversed to shame. "That's all right," he rationalizes. "I've got four hundred and two boys out there—the ones that got back— who love me and know the truth, who love me *because* they know the truth." But the picture of Li Dap haunts him; in Tubby's photograph, the NVA general "looked wonderful—strained, abused and wild, his hair flying over his eyes while he's making a statement full of conviction." Thus, through the ironic contrast of a Vietnamese general who dies Hemingway's "good death" and a Southern soldier who dreams of an honor that he turns into shame by his own firepower, Hannah evokes the psychological chaos of war and its literature.

"Midnight and I'm Not Famous Yet" is perhaps not even "about war . . . [but] about love and memory," as Tim O'Brien says of all "true war stories." There is no moral here, no epiphany, and no resolution. Rather, there is a debunking of the heroic ideal, and a concomitant debunking structural rhythm that results from Bobby's inability to resolve his shame at his demotion, especially in comparison with the heroism of the captive enemy he has killed. He is even more alienated in the larger civilian society to which he returns, now that he has failed to measure up to the myth of the hero that American culture continues to validate. The myth reveals itself even in peacetime, in society's worship of the fittest, as Bobby recognizes in the gallery's despair over a favorite golfer who loses a match. "Fools! Fools!" [he thinks]. "Love it! Love the loss as well as the gain. Go home and dig it. Nobody was killed. We saw victory and defeat, and they were both wonderful" (*Airships*). Yet Bobby's fine-sounding rationale is hollow, since it is belied by his inability to countenance his own loss of stature. His fragile sense of self is apparent in his confession that, back home, he "crawled in bed with almost anything that would have [him]."

Bats Out of Hell takes its title partly from the story **"Bats Out of Hell Division."** The narrator is a Civil War soldier whose story reflects the realism of the Confederate defeat—of honor turned to shame for an entire region, and of a betrayal of the soldiers' self-image that involves a falling away of everything they had depended upon. On the level of military action, as the unnamed narrator tells us, "the charge, our old bread and butter, has withered into the final horror of the field, democracy." In other words, the division has lost its coherent structure. Moreover, the beleaguered soldiers, constantly tortured by the smells of the Union camp's cooking food, are betrayed by their starved and failing bodies, so "gaunt . . . [and] almost not there" that the enemy bullets haven't much of a target. They are also betrayed by their minds; even the general is "criminally insane just like the rest of them."

On the level of language, the theme of betrayal is implicit in the many self-contradictions in the narrative, as in the beginning sentence of the story: "We, in a ragged bold line across their eyes, come on." Here is Hannah's version of many an actual battle in the South's lost cause, wherein honor and glory were earned only by continuing to advance when hope of victory was as ragged as the Confederate soldiers' uniforms. In this war story, ironic reversal is seen in the backward waving of the Confederate colors, which continue to advance, while bearer after bearer is shot out from under them. "Shreds of the flag leap back from the pole held by Billy, then Ira," we are told; but, fearing shame more than death, the soldiers go forward, while the tattered shreds of flag seem to point to the rear. "We . . . are not getting on too well," admits the chronicler of the Bats Out of Hell Division. "They have shot hell out of us. More properly we are merely the Bats by now. Our cause is leaking, the fragments of it left around those great burned holes, as if their general put his cigar into the document a few times." The story presents a paradigm of the Hannah hero, whose cause is always "leaking" and whose personality, like the character of the CSA division nicknamed "Bats Out of Hell," is defined by "fragments" and "great burned holes," which betray the truth that its "hellfire," or spirit, has been devastated.

The prospect, and thus the story, would be unbearable were it not for the bleak hilarity and the desperate energy of these would-be heroes. "But we're still out there," the narrator tells us; "We gain by inches, then lose by yards. . . . By now you must know that half our guns are no good, either. Estes—as I spy around—gets on without buttocks, just hewn off one sorry cowardly night. . . . I have become the scribe—not voluntarily, but because all limbs are gone except my writing arm." Note that it is not Estes but rather, in Hannah's rhetorical use of sentence grammar, it is "one sorry . . . night" that is branded as "cowardly." He will not shame his comrade by use of the word *coward*.

The illusion of the heroic also causes the narrator to cling to a shred of vanity about his own personal appearance; for he sees himself in the image of a Southern figural hero, as described by Michael Kreyling: a nearly perfect physical specimen and one who can "instantly render the provisional nature of any situation into a part of a consecrated pattern." The exemplar was General Robert E. Lee, Commander of the Confederate forces, whose personal appearance, according to a fellow cadet at West Point, "surpassed in manly beauty any cadet in the corps," but another was J. E. B. Stuart, who appears in several Hannah stories. Stuart was also a handsome West Pointer who was said to represent "the ideal of Southern manhood" [Kenneth Seid, "Sabers, Gentlemen, Sabers': The J. E. B. Stuart Stories of Barry Hannah," *Mississippi Quarterly* (1991-92)]. Perhaps aspiring to this model, Hannah's narrator in **"Bats Out of Hell Division"** says that his comrades and Captain think him "not unsightly" and that the unit's "benign crone of a nurse" says he is a "man of some charm."

In a passage that ponders the role of this front line nurse, the narrator thinks, "Maybe they use her to make us fight for home"; but he immediately contradicts himself: "Better to think she's part of no plan at all. The best things in life, or whatever you call *this,* happen like that. . . . This marks the very thing, most momentous, I am writing about." In that statement, the narrator suggests that chaos—"no plan at all"—is inherent not only in war but in life, and perhaps in the story too. Moreover, in his analogy of war's death-in-life situation with "the best things in life," with Candide-like humor and a best-of-all-possible-worlds manner, the narrator articulates the ironic truth that war holds a fierce attraction for soldiers. In fact, he interrupts his own story to tell of a soldier killed in the previous Mexican War who "returned out of the very earth once he heard another cracking good one was on. At last, at last! The World War of his dreams." In this fantastic story-within-a-story, the dead-undead soldier rhapsodizes, "There *is* a God, and God is love! . . . Brother against brother! In my lifetime! In my lifetime! Can Providence be this good?" The irony in Hannah's treatment of the romantic mythology of war is heightened by the counterpoint that occurs when his narrator admits, "I have license to exaggerate, as I have just done," and then qualifies that revision by continuing, without even a pause, "but many would be horrified to know how little." Such constant self-revision, which is typical of many fictional and autobiographical war stories, contributes to the debunking

narrative rhythm that Leitch calls "the author's unmaking and the audience's unknowing."

Throughout **"Bats Out of Hell Division,"** the narrative shifts between the grimly real and the surreal, sometimes approaching the operatic. The term "operatic," originally denoting the implausible, artificial, or histrionic nature of operas, can be extended to describe the exaggerated or heightened nature of dreams or, in Hannah's fiction, of memories. In **"Testimony of Pilot,"** for example, the narrator laments, "Memory, the whole lying opera of it, is killing me now." This pattern of incongruities in Hannah's version of the literature of memory conforms to a pattern Beidler has described in many Vietnam narratives in which Vietnam itself is at the same time and "in a single moment, dreadful, funny, nightmarish, ecstatic." In the midst of this bizarre foreign place, "innocent, bloodied eighteen-year-olds tossed off smooth, ugly, epigrammatic zingers," Beidler writes, in a passage that could aptly describe some of Barry Hannah's characters. "Americans in Vietnam looked for something, anything, to sustain the flow of psychic energy that finally had to substitute for even the most remote sense of purpose," Beidler says; thus, some of the unreal reality of the Vietnam experience is the result of soldiers who were "stoned out of their skulls, weighed down with their totems, their talismanic nicknames and buddy-love, their freaky bravado, Jim Morrison and Janis Joplin and Jimi Hendrix and the Stones blasting away in their ears."

In Hannah's story, the soldiers of the Bats Out of Hell Division, so skinny that the Union bullets cannot hit them, advance through the smoke with "happy bayonets high," when they realize they "are running in sudden silence . . . [because the Union troops] are not firing anymore." Here Hannah debunks the idea of war as glorious when his narrator describes the effect of the doomed Confederates' alleged "happy bayonets" on the Union general, who agonizes over the carnage. Through the haze the Southern troops are astonished to see General Kosciusky screaming first at his own troops and then at the Confederates: "Stop it! Stop it! I can't take it anymore. The lost cause! Look at you! My holy God, gray brothers, behold yourself! Cease fire! Cease it all!" [In a footnote, Weston adds: "The name [Kosciusky] bears a close resemblance to that of General Thaddeus Kosciusko, the Polish officer and engineer who designed and built the fortifications at West Point during the Revolutionary War. He also served in the Continental Army as commander of the Engineering Corps. A statue of Kosciusko on the grounds of the U.S. Military Academy, West Point, N.Y., commemorates his service to this country. His sword, part of the West Point museum's collection, is inscribed: 'Draw me not without reason, Sheathe me not without honor.' "] Then Kosciusky surrenders, shouting, "The music. The Tchaikovsky! You wretched specters coming on! It's too much. Too much." At the climax of this fantastic opera, the "stunned" Confederate general takes Kosciusky's sword, and the narrator undercuts his own story by admitting its improbability: "Nothing in history led us to believe we had not simply crossed over to paradise itself and were dead just minutes ago." As historian of the Bats Out of Hell Division, the scribe can tell the story any way he wishes, and so he gives the "Bats" the victory and, by extension, implies a dream self that fits the South's ideal of the victorious warrior. [In a footnote, Weston continues: "Kenneth Seib argues that Hannah's narrators search for meaning in stories that not only demythicize legendary Confederate hero J. E. B. Stuart but also reject the macho warrior image with which Southern men have historically identified."] Yet, the story ends with a mundane anticlimax about what to name this battle, evincing a narrative technique that counters the operatic climax with the matter-of-fact voice of the scribe, who has continually countered his own "license to exaggerate." Each successive narrative act undercuts the previous act; and thus the story's structure, instead of providing a more traditional formal coherence, reflects, by its surface incoherence, a narrative consciousness shattered by violent internal and external conflicts.

Coherence is found, however, in the dialogue—even in the disagreements—both within the story and between the story and its background of cultural myths, including the emerging mythology of Vietnam. It is a coherence based on the play of mind and memory instead of the development of plot and character. And it is of a piece with the Vietnam literature that, in Beidler's words, is set in "a place with no real points of reference, then or now. As once in experiential fact, so now in memory." Hannah creates a landscape like that described in the fiction of other Vietnam writers, one "that never was, . . . a landscape of consciousness where it might be possible to accommodate experience remembered evoking a new kind of imaginative cartography endowing it with large configurings of value and signification." Although their plot curve and setting may at first seem obscure, Barry Hannah's stories, nevertheless, also signify because they are a coherent part of American literary traditions, both of content and structure. He writes, as do most Southern writers, a literature of place; unlike most Southern literature, however, the "place" is often not a tangible locale. Rather, a primary component of the content in Hannah's fiction is that of intellectualized landscapes similar to those Beidler recalls in the journals of early American colonists such as Cotton Mather and in the fiction of J. Fenimore Cooper and Nathaniel Hawthorne.

Mather, Cooper, and Hawthorne found, in the New World, a "beckoning path of discovery and sacrifice amid bloodshed and terror . . . [in the] dark woods, the swamps, the mountains, the rivers, the 'howling wilderness' " (Beidler). Hannah, like others who write war into literature, finds just such a "beckoning path" in the emotional and intellectual consequences of both the American

Civil War and the Vietnam conflict; and his stories explore possible meanings along this path. They exhibit neither the unity afforded by a climactic plot structure nor a clear epiphany, yet each of his war stories challenges thoughtful readers in several ways: by deglamorizing the mythology of war and the myth of the warrior, even while exhibiting Americans' fascination with both, and by dispelling the illusion that even the most devoutly held, most pervasive and seductive cultural ideals and models can engender in any individual aspirant a truly unified self based on them. Perhaps the reader's greatest challenge is to understand that Hannah's war stories cohere around the antiphonal, often cacaphonic, debunking rhythms that contribute to the debunking of the unitary self and story.

FURTHER READING

Criticism

Burgin, Richard. "Burnt-Out Cases." *Washington Post Book World* XXIII, No. 11 (14 March 1993): 8.
> Reviews *Bats out of Hell,* noting the savagery of Hannah's characters and the blackness of his humor.

Edwards, Thomas R. "Sad Young Men." *The New York Review of Books* XXXVI, No. 13 (17 August 1989): 52-3.
> Review of *Boomerang,* Dennis Cooper's *Closer,* and Paul Auster's *Moon Palace.*

Krulish, Robert R. Review of *Never Die,* by Barry Hannah. *West Coast Review of Books* 16, No. 2 (1991): 46.
> Highly unfavorable assessment of *Never Die.*

Rafferty, Terrence. "Gunsmoke and Voodoo." *The Nation* 240, No. 21 (1 June 1985): 677-79.
> Examines the short stories in *Captain Maximus.*

Raksin, Alex. Review of *Boomerang,* by Barry Hannah. *The Los Angeles Times Book Review* (7 May 1989): 6.
> Favorable review of *Boomerang.*

Spikes, Michael P. "What's in a Name? A Reading of Barry Hannah's *Ray.*" *The Mississippi Quarterly* XLII, No. 1 (Winter 1988-1989): 69-82.
> In-depth examination of the title character of Hannah's third novel.

Stade, George. "Lives of Noisy Desperation." *The New York Times Book Review* LXXXX, No. 23 (9 June 1985): 14.
> Review of *Captain Maximus.*

Additional coverage of Hannah's life and career is contained in the following sources published by Gale Research: *Contemporary Authors,* Vols. 108, 110; *Contemporary Authors New Revision Series,* Vol. 43; *Contemporary Literary Criticism,* Vols. 23, 38; *Dictionary of Literary Biography,* Vol. 6; and *Major 20th-Century Writers.*

Sébastien Japrisot

1931-

(Born Jean Baptiste Rossi) French novelist, screenwriter, and translator.

The following entry presents an overview of Japrisot's career through 1991.

INTRODUCTION

Japrisot is recognized as a master of the mystery novel. His stories feature likable protagonists caught up in increasingly complicated predicaments that are often resolved in strikingly simple ways. Acclaimed for their literary style and thematic richness, several of Japrisot's novels have also been adapted for the screen.

Biographical Information

Born Jean Baptiste Rossi, Japrisot achieved literary acclaim in France with his French translation of J. D. Salinger's *Nine Stories* (1953). Writing *Les mal partis* (1950; *Awakening*) and all of his subsequent novels under the pseudonym Sébastien Japrisot—an anagrammatic rendering of his given name—he eventually adapted several of his novels for the screen and wrote screenplays for such noted directors as Constantin Costa-Gavras, René Clement, and Anatole Litvak. Winner of the Grand Prix de la Littérature Policière for *Piège pour Cendrillon* (1962; *Trap for Cinderella*) and the 1966 Prix d'Honneur for *La dame dans l'auto avec des lunettes et un fusil* (1966; *The Lady in a Car with Glasses and a Gun*), Japrisot continues to live and write in France.

Major Works

Japrisot's novels often use complex plots to create intrigue and suspense. In *Trap for Cinderella,* for example, two young women are burned in a fire. One of them survives but has amnesia and is disfigured beyond recognition. The woman's identity becomes the novel's main mystery: she is either a flamboyant heiress or the heiress's sister, the murderess who set the fire. Beginning with the murder of a young woman in a train, *Compartiment tueurs* (1963; *The 10:30 from Marseilles*) reveals, through a series of flashbacks, information about the lives of the main characters as the police attempt to solve the crime. After various suspects are killed off, a small child accidentally stumbles upon the solution to the murders. *The Lady in the Car with Glasses and a Gun* also focuses on a young woman. Borrowing her employer's car for a trip to the seashore, the protagonist picks up a hitchhiker who injures her hand. From then on—though she is in an area she has never visited before—she encounters people who recognize her as a murderess. *L'été meurtrier* (1980; *One Deadly Summer*) is narrated by four characters and concerns the murder of an Austrian woman by her French neighbors.

Hated for unclear reasons, the Austrian woman is derisively nicknamed "Eva Braun"—the name of Adolf Hitler's mistress—and eventually beaten and raped. Before dying from her injuries, she gives birth to a daughter who, years later, avenges her mother's murder. *La passion des femmes* (1986; *The Passion of Women*), considered more erotic and less suspenseful than Japrisot's previous novels, concerns five women and a mysterious young man who, as the story begins, lies dying from a gunshot wound. The young man loved and abandoned each woman, using a different name with each one. As the women narrate the stories of their relationships with him, they eventually reveal why he was shot and who did the shooting. Early twentieth-century France is the setting for *Un long dimanche de fiançailles* (1991; *A Very Long Engagement*), a story about a young woman investigating the death of a soldier to whom she was engaged. Unlike Japrisot's other novels, *A Very Long Engagement* is based on an actual historical event, in which a young soldier and four comrades wounded themselves to avoid combat in World War I. Convicted by their commanding officer of treason, they were thrown into the no-man's-land between French and German lines where, presumably, they would be killed in the ensuing battle. In Japrisot's version of events the soldier's bride-to-be travels throughout France after the war, interviewing people who can provide information about her betrothed's death.

Critical Reception

Most critics have applauded Japrisot's clear, concise language; his well-constructed, complex plots; and his ability to make the conventions of the mystery genre plausible. They have also praised his skill at creating realistic, likable characters while evoking and maintaining an aura of suspense. Critics have noted that Japrisot's use of multiple narrators—in *The Passion of Women* and *One Deadly Summer*—is unusual in the mystery genre. His often intensely erotic portrayal of human relationships adds, most critics agree, another unique aspect to his oeuvre. As Howard Junker has stated: "Japrisot is obviously a great talent, whom students of the popular novel and of the narrative form in general will want to analyze."

PRINCIPAL WORKS

Les mal partis [*Awakening*] (novel) 1950

Piège pour Cendrillon [*Trap for Cinderella*] (novel) 1962

Compartiment tueurs [*The 10:30 from Marseilles*] (novel) 1963; also published as *The Sleeping-Car Murders,* 1978

**Compartiment tueurs* [with Constantin Costa-Gavras] [*The Sleeping Car Murders*] (screenplay) 1966

†*La dame dans l'auto avec des lunettes et un fusil* [*The Lady in the Car with Glasses and a Gun*] (novel) 1966

‡*Adieu l'ami* [*Goodbye, Friend*] (screenplay) 1968

§*Le passager de la pluie* [with Lorenzo Ventavoli] [*Rider on the Rain*] (screenplay) 1970

§*La course du lièvre à travers les champs* [*And Hope to Die*] (screenplay) 1972

L'été meurtrier [*One Deadly Summer*] (novel) 1980

***L'été meurtrier* [with Jean Becker] [*One Deadly Summer*] (screenplay) 1984

La passion des femmes [*The Passion of Women*] (novel) 1986; also published as *Women in Evidence,* 1990

Un long dimanche de fiançailles [*A Very Long Engagement*] (novel) 1991

---

*This film was also directed by Costa-Gavras.

†This work served as the basis for the 1970 film *The Lady in the Car with Glasses and a Gun,* directed by Anatole Litvak and written by Richard Harris and Eleanor Perry.

‡This film was directed by Jean Herman.

§These films were directed by René Clément.

**This film was also directed by Becker.

CRITICISM

Anthony Boucher (review date 17 November 1963)

SOURCE: A review of *The 10:30 from Marseilles,* in *The New York Times Book Review,* November 17, 1963, p. 58.

[*Anthony Boucher was a pseudonym used by William Anthony Parker White, who was a mystery writer and critic. In the following excerpt, he favorably assesses* The 10:30 from Marseilles.]

Sebastien Japrisot, one of France's distinguished translators (he was, for instance, the first French translator of J. D. Salinger), recently won the Grand Prix de Littérature Policière, the major French crime-novel award, for his second novel, ***Piège Pour Cendrillon (A Trap for Cinderella)***—of which one of the jurors exclaimed, "*C'est le Marienbad du roman policier!*" His first novel, ***Compartiment Tueurs,*** which some French critics have preferred to the prizewinner, now appears here, in a highly readable translation by Francis Price, as ***The 10:30 from Marseilles.*** It clearly reveals the most welcome new talent in the detective story to reach us from France since . . . well, probably since the early Simenons almost three decades ago.

This is largely a straight police-procedural starring the likable and believable Inspector Grazziano of the Police Judiciaire; but is also a puzzle-novel in the classic mold, with a fine setup of murder in a train compartment sleeping six, with the remaining five (suspects or witnesses?) being steadily eliminated by death as the Inspector investigates them. There are excellent flashbacks into the lives and characters of the compartment sleepers and admirable use of that rare device, the Least Suspected Detective. In all, a highly satisfactory import that makes one hungry for more.

Anthony Boucher (review date 5 July 1964)

SOURCE: A review of *Trap for Cinderella,* in *The New York Times Book Review,* July 5, 1964, pp. 14-15.

[*In the following excerpt, Boucher offers a favorable review of* Trap for Cinderella, *contending that the novel is "a beautifully intricate essay in novel-writing and mystery-making."*]

Sebastien Japrisot, the French translator (of J. D. Salinger among others), achieved a good deal of recognition here last year with his first novel, ***Compartiment Tueurs,*** translated as ***The 10:30 From Marseilles***—a book which most reviewers, including me, welcomed as the most interesting French import in the crime field since the debut of Simenon. Meanwhile his second novel, ***Piège Pour Cendrillon,*** went on to win the Grand Prix de la Littérature Policière, the most prestigious of France's many crime-novel awards. It has now been ably translated by Helen Weaver, as ***Trap for Cinderella.***

This is a beautifully intricate essay in novel-writing and mystery-making, in which the narrator, having almost been burned to death, finds herself with a mind wiped blank and a body reconstructed by plastic surgery—so that she has no notion whether she is the madcap heiress people tell her she must be. If she is, who tried to kill her? If she is not, may she herself be a murderess? The uncertainties and ambivalence are sustained with great skill. I still find *The 10:30* even more impressive, both in plot and in writing; but *Trap* certainly maintains Japrisot's reputation as a highly original and professional writer of murder-suspense.

Howard Junker   (review date 18 December 1967)

SOURCE: "On the Road," in *Newsweek,* Vol. LXX, No. 25, December 18, 1967, pp. 110-110A.

[*In the following review, Junker praises* The Lady in the Car with Glasses and a Gun.]

Whodunit? Who is responsible for keeping this magnificent thriller hidden? Why haven't critics heaped praise upon it? Why haven't readers fought to buy it? Unlike most novels published this year, *The Lady in the Car* can be—and must be—read in one sitting. It cannot be put down, and that, mystery-lovers, is the ultimate test. Last year in France, *Lady* spent months on the best-seller list—an achievement few suspense novels ever match. And it also won the coveted Prix d'Honneur. In 1963, Sebastien Japrisot's second novel, *Trap for Cinderella,* won the Grand Prix de la Littérature Policière. And his first novel was made into the brilliant film *The Sleeping Car Murders,* with Yves Montand, which had a big success in the U.S.

Japrisot is obviously a great talent, whom students of the popular novel and of the narrative form in general will want to analyze. For suspense seekers, *Lady* is the first-person adventure of a near-sighted blonde, an advertising secretary who wouldn't ordinarily take a joy ride in her boss's Thunderbird but, on a rare impulse, does just that. This first time is almost her last.

It is, of course, the classic situation, the damsel in super-distress, while various sinister types plot her downfall. But assisted by well-remembered advice from "Mama Supe," the head of the orphanage where she grew up, and helped by the kindly attention of a prepossessing hitchhiker (who should be played by Belmondo) and by a kindly truck driver (obviously Jean Gabin), the nearsighted heroine... well, to find out what she does and what is done to her, you must read the book. It is a chilling, baffling psychological fooler that sparkles with all the juicy terrors that can attack the heart and body.

J. Walt   (review date Winter 1979)

SOURCE: A review of *L'été meurtrier,* in *World Literature Today,* Vol. 53, No. 1, Winter, 1979, p. 77.

[*In the following favorable review of* One Deadly Summer, *Walt notes Japrisot's use of multiple narrators.*]

Rebecca West, covering a trial of Southerners indicted in the wake of a "lynching bee," found a partial explanation for the townspeople's violence: the brutal heat that was a sovereign fact of life before the advent of air conditioning. Japrisot's characters (despite his title) are violent in season and out and throw morality to the winds, whether they blow from North Africa or the Alps.

Indeed, the event that sets off a train of horrors in *L'été meurtrier* [*One Deadly Summer*] occurs on a winter day when three men beat and rape an Austrian woman nicknamed "Eva Braun" by hostile French neighbors. The child she bears eight months later was supposedly fathered by one of the rapists. Eva marries a man whom she despises because he seems too cowardly to avenge the crime. It is her daughter—grown, beautiful, ungovernable but devoted to Eva and hyped up by the heat of an abnormal summer—who sets out to explore every possible means of vengeance. To say that the results are unforeseen is only to affirm that Japrisot is a master of sensationalism.

The story is told by four characters, each offering circumstantial detail that illuminates the mores of a town ineffably bored and struggling to escape its shadow through sports, drinking, addiction to movies and television, unending promiscuity. While he probably owes something to Poe and Dumas, Japrisot would hoot at the romanticism of Dumas and the Cinderella motif that turns a common sailor into the Count of Monte Cristo. Yet who will say that contemporary cynicism is less of a posture than yesterday's romanticism?

Jean Strouse   (review date 30 June 1980)

SOURCE: A review of *One Deadly Summer,* in *Newsweek,* Vol. XCV, No. 26, June 30, 1980, p. 68.

[*Strouse is an author and editor, whose books include* Alice James: A Biography *(1980). In the following review, she comments on the way Japrisot constructs characters and plot in* One Deadly Summer.]

This compelling new tale by the author of *The Sleeping-Car Murders* is set in a tiny village, population 143, near the Combes Pass in the south of France. Told in the four voices of its central characters, it takes place in the summer of 1976 but reaches back 21 years, to the winter of 1955, for the key to its mystery.

The main narrator [in *One Deadly Summer*] is Fiorimondo Montecciari, commonly known as "Ping-Pong," the son of a southern Italian emigrant who came to France on foot pulling a player piano behind him. Ping-Pong works in a garage and lusts after "Elle" (short for Eliane and, of course, French for "she"), who has recently moved to the village with her German mother and crippled father. Elle had been elected the previous year's "Miss Camping-Caravaning" in a beauty contest and likes to sashay around the village exciting all the men. She also likes Marilyn Monroe—not her movies but her life: "How wonderful it was that Marilyn died like that, swallowing things, with all those photographs the next day, that she was Marilyn Monroe to the end." Elle doesn't make sense to Ping-Pong or his brothers, one of whom warns that "you couldn't trust people who had such a limited vocabulary—they were often the most complicated people."

Sure enough, she turns out to be the most complicated person around. Fragments of her disturbing story come slowly together like the pieces in a psychological jigsaw puzzle—rape, murder, incest, revenge, split personality. Japrisot slices into these small-town European lives with all the precision of a fine surgeon. He gets each voice just right, in Alan Sheridan's deft translation, and Elle's bizarre behavior gradually begins to make sense. By the end, you feel more sympathy than horror at the ghastly truth.

Charles Mackey   (review date May 1988)

SOURCE: A review of *La Passion des femmes,* in *The French Review,* Vol. LXI, No. 6, May, 1988, pp. 991-92.

[*In the following review of* La Passion des femmes, *Mackey suggests that while much of the novel is captivating, it is, finally, not entirely satisfying.*]

The novelist Jean-Baptiste Rossi, whose anagrammatic *nom de plume,* Sébastien Japrisot, is more widely known, published his eighth novel in 1986, which found its way immediately onto the best-seller lists in France. With the renown of *L'Eté meurtrier* and the hugely successful film, a certain following has apparently been sustained by the commercial reclame of *La Passion des femmes*.

> Japrisot's women speak with a voice and a diction that carefully evokes their milieus, but at bottom there is an exasperating dissonance in their conception, a jarring shallowness in their 'passions.'
>
> —*Charles Mackey*

It is a love story, a work of suspense and pursuit, a collection of often erotic encounters that examine the biases of our perceptions, a surreal glimpse into the question of ultimate reality. It easily ensnares the reader into its strange fiction where different mirrors cast differing versions along a very long road indeed. A young man rises from a sandy beach, his shirt stained by a wound as reddening as the setting sun on this later summer afternoon. One by one images of various young women seem to appear, each taking a turn on a teetertotter from nowhere. Why this wound? Why these apparitions?

Facets of the young man's story (or stories) are revealed through the recollections of seven disparate women, who in turn relate their stories and how their lives have been touched by the appearance of the mysterious stranger. On the eve of World War II a man, perhaps unjustly condemned for murder, escapes from a military prison in the South of France. His first encounter is with Emma, whom he kidnaps on her bridal night, leaving her with a much softer memory than had she spent it with her middle-aged lecher husband. Belinda and Zozo follow, *filles de joie* whose hearts may not always be of gold, yet they love and are beguiled by the macho vulnerability of this odd young person in their midst. Next is Caroline, the young widow

whose repressed sexuality is waiting to be ignited by the intrepid *bagnard* and to whom is revealed the reasons for his judgment and for the pursuit, Javert-like, by the ignoble Captain Malignaud, his accuser and jailor. Months pass, the war has begun and Frou-Frou, a vapid if passionate starlet of the Hollywood B movies *Lips* and *Legs,* secretly harbors the renegade on her director's yacht, *Pandora,* as it sails into the war-torn seas of Southeast Asia. New adventures there await him on an alien island in the avid embraces of Yoko, the Chilean-Japanese survivor of Pacific battles, and thence to Burma and to the less sexually demanding and more pliable American nurse who hails, eponymously, from Toledo.

These recollections have all been assembled by Marie-Martine, the young man's first lover, who has become a lawyer during his peregrinations, and who has now gathered these testimonies, and her own, for his defense. But something else is working here. Why does each woman recall a different name for the man? Vincent, Tony, Francis, Edouard . . . ? Why do several encounters end with a gunshot and a return to an image resembling that of the opening pages? Given the ending that raises still more questions and which is meant to be woven into the opening chapter, one wonders (and hopes) that there are deeper intentions at issue in these prolix confessions.

Japrisot has examined the chiaroscuro of these relationships, the masks men and women wear, the ambiguities of reality and truth. His women speak with a voice and diction that carefully evoke their milieus, but at bottom there is an exasperating dissonance in their conception, a jarring shallowness in their "passions" and in the elusive truths that each of our mirrors tries to capture.

Kirkus Reviews (review date 1 August 1990)

SOURCE: A review of *The Passion of Women,* in *Kirkus Reviews,* Vol. LVIII, No. 15, August 1, 1990, pp. 1029-30.

[*In the following review, the critic contends that* The Passion of Women *is an erotic but slight mystery adventure.*]

Japrisot, who has long specialized in languorous, eroticized suspense (*The Sleeping-Car Murders, One Deadly Summer,* etc.), offers [in *The Passion of Women*] more erotic languor and less suspense than usual in this eight-dimensional portrait of a mysterious convict on the run.

As the novel begins, its hero falls to earth, dying from a gunshot wound. In a series of flashbacks featuring eight successive women he has encountered in his escape—a flight that has taken him from the coast of France to a Pacific island during wartime—the hero shows different faces, or at least different names, to each of his loves. Whether they know him as Vincent, Beau Masque, Tony, Francis, Edouard, Frédéric, Maurice, or Christophe, each woman—from Emma, the young bride he kidnaps on her wedding night, to Marie-Martine, his youthful love who returns as his lawyer when he's finally recaptured by his nemesis Sgt. Malignaud—begins as his victim, gets him into her power, then falls in love with him (even though more than one confesses to shooting him). The chapters are by turns steamy and touching, but they don't generate much momentum, because although the novel comes on like *Rashomon,* the heroines' narratives fit together smoothly except for the contradictions between the accounts of Belinda and Zozo, two Parisian whores; certainly the hero, whatever his name is, is always himself. The solution to the mystery of who shot the hero is a letdown, but Japrisot's neatest puzzle—why are all these desirable women dreaming of romance in terms of such a narcissistic male fantasy? —is resolved by an ending that (though a bit of a cheat) is perfectly in keeping with the texture of the hero's insouciant adventures.

Japrisot's lightest soufflé to date—a sexual odyssey whose few pretensions to depth he handles with more grace and wit than Erica Jong.

Christine Watson   (review date January 1991)

SOURCE: A review of *The Passion of Women,* in *West Coast Review of Books,* Vol. 16, No. 1, January, 1991, pp. 31-2.

[*In the following review of* The Passion of Women, *Watson focuses on how multiple narrators and a clear prose style effectively contribute to the mystery and suspense of the story.*]

The main character in this witty, provocative novel [*The Passion of Women*] is a man who appears only briefly onstage. The story of his life is told to us indirectly, by the eight women who loved and were left by this man, and by the end of the book we feel we know him as well as any of them.

Which is to say, we probably don't really know him at all.

We first see this mysterious figure through the eyes of Emma, a young woman kidnapped on her wedding night by an escaped convict named Vincent. He's described next by Belinda, a prostitute who hides and falls in love with Tony, a man on the run who tells her he was shot by a bride he'd kidnapped. Still later, he appears as Frédéric, the lover of Frou-Frou, a starlet whose acting is outclassed by her skill as a manicurist.

In these, and in his five other appearances, several things about this mystery man appear constant. He is on the run from the law; he has been convicted of a crime he claims never to have committed; and he is, first and foremost, a dreamer and a lover of women. As a boy, he fantasized that he had gone back through time, searching for a way to save Joan of Arc. As a man, he seems to live out his fantasies, running from one woman to the next and recreating himself with every one. And dogging his heels wherever he goes is General Malignaud, who knows the truth about his conviction and will stop at nothing to track him down.

This novel is a kaleidoscope, always shifting, always drawing the reader into a new view. There is love here (in a wide assortment of guises) but there is also hate, fear, amusement, passion and virtually every other sort of emotion. Just as we think we have a grip on who this man is and what is going on, Japrisot deftly changes focus again, and we realize we are no closer to understanding than we

were at the beginning. With his smooth prose and his careful construction, he draws us into his story as surely as his mystery man draws these women into his life. Read *The Passion of Women,* and experience its seductive charms yourself.

Anita Brookner   (review date 21-28 December 1991)

SOURCE: A review of *Un Long Dimanche de Fiançailles* in *The Spectator,* Vol. 267, No. 8528, December 21-28, 1991, p. 80.

[*Brookner is an English novelist, nonfiction writer, critic, and art historian whose books include* Jacques-Louis David *(1981) and the prizewinning novel* Hotel du lac *(1984). In the following excerpt, she focuses on the "clever" plot and the clear "narrative tone" of* Un Long Dimanche de Fiançailles.]

Japrisot is the author of those two classic mysteries, *L'Eté Meurtrier* and *La Dame dans l'auto avec des Lunettes et un Fusil.* Here [in *Un Long Dimanche de Fiançailles*] he tackles more dangerous subject matter. In January 1917 five French soldiers, drafted to the front line, shot themselves in the hand in order to escape the fighting. They were arrested, roped together, marched a certain distance, and then released into no man's land, where they would presumably be shot by the enemy. And so they were, or so it seemed. All were known by nicknames, some may have exchanged their identity numbers, one had stolen a pair of German boots. Back in France a crippled girl called Mathilde Donnay awaits the return of her fiancé, one of the five, whom she knows by another, local name. One day she receives a letter from a nun working in a hospital near Dax, which informs her that a dying man wishes to see her. This man commanded the prisoners' escort, but in fact can tell her very little, only that all five are dead. Mathilde then sets up her own enquiry: she is rich, she is patient, and she is very scrupulous.

Un Long Dimanche de Fiançailles is diabolically clever, and Japrisot has the wit to keep his narrative tone simple, or as simple as his plot will allow.

—Anita Brookner

Her researches lead her up various blind alleys. Gradually she amasses a dossier, makes contact with the wives and mistresses of the deceased. All have reasons of their own for telling or not telling the truth. But in the course of her enquiries she discovers that not one but two of the five survived, and that one of them, if found, will reveal the whereabouts of the other. It is entirely possible that in order to re-enter civilian life the two surviving prisoners have changed their names. One of them, a foundling who had been given an entirely notional name to start with, is tracked down to a farm near Rozay-en-Brie. He tells

Mathilde that her fiancé is alive, but of course has a different name. The expectant reader will be relieved to know that he is eventually found: how will not be revealed here.

This is diabolically clever, and Japrisot has the wit to keep his narrative tone simple, or as simple as his plot will allow. The reader is alternately impressed, beguiled, frightened, bewildered, and finally impatient, for the solution is withheld until endurance is almost exhausted. Japrisot is at all times master of his effects, as he has proved himself to be in previous novels. A considerable achievement.

Richard Eder   (review date 8 August 1993)

SOURCE: "High Above the Trenches," in *Los Angeles Times Book Review,* August 8, 1993, pp. 3, 6.

[*An American critic and journalist, Eder received the Pulitzer Prize for criticism in 1987. In the following highly favorable review of* A Very Long Engagement, *he argues that the novel is thematically richer than most mystery fiction, describing it as "a hybrid of the detective story and the classical quest."*]

Procrastination is the heart of writing, and by that measure, this review starts off with a lot of heart. You can struggle for days, not to say what you want but to resist saying what you don't want. It has been a battle to avoid writing of Sébastien Japrisot's novel [*A Very Long Engagement*] about World War I as a kind of latter-day *War and Peace*. I lost. It is a kind of *War and Peace*.

This is not to call it an epic—though in 300 compressed pages it has something of the spaciousness—or to fit it with the Great Novel collar. I think it could wear one, but a daily reviewer should probably leave the collar to time, and meanwhile regard the neck. The Tolstoy reference is specific. *A Very Long Engagement* finds a chilling and humane way to evoke the trench-fought war of 1914-18, whose self-corrupting stasis was only an extreme variation of what lodges in many other wars. And while telling of France's war, it wanders around telling beautifully of France's peace.

Mathilde, a chestnut-haired, green-eyed young woman whose independent mind is in no way curbed, quite the contrary, by the fact that she is crippled, and who is fortified by her position as the indulged daughter of a wealthy family, learns in 1917 that her lover has been killed in action. He was a fisherman's son in the Landes, where Mathilde's family goes every summer. After some resistance he had been acknowledged as virtually her fiance.

It would have been ordinary fading grief; or perhaps not, since, as we come thrillingly to see, there is nothing in the least ordinary about Mathilde. But in 1919, a letter comes from a sergeant in a nearby veterans' hospital; he is dying and wants to see her. What he has to tell launches a book that is many things: a war story, a story of official corruption, an idyll of young summer love, and a rich and most original panorama of French men and women living in peace and robbed of it. Finally, giving it all an intent energy, it is a hybrid of the detective story and the classical quest.

To explain the quest and the intuitive and stubborn detecting that propel Mathilde and her wheelchair into literary splendor, there is the scrap of history out of which Japrisot has fashioned his novel. In 1915, after a year of mud and massacre in stinking trenches, French soldiers were shooting themselves in the hands or feet to get invalided out. General Henri Petain, the hero of Verdun and, in 1940, of the Vichyites, wanted to shoot 25 of them. Changing his mind, he ordered something less absolute, perhaps, but more ghastly. The order was kept secret and only confirmed, 50 years later, with the publication of a fellow-general's memoirs:

> He orders them bound and tossed over the top of the trenches closest to the enemy. This is to be done under cover of night. He didn't say if they'll be left to starve to death. Character, energy! Where does character end and ferocious savagery begin. . . .

Manech, whom Mathilde thinks of as "her little fisherman"—the other soldiers called him Cornflower—was one of five prisoners whom the sergeant had escorted, bound, to the front; and then through the trenches to a rampart named Bingo Crepuscule, where they were forced over the wire at night into no-man's-land. There were German flares, a little machine-gun fire. Several of the five were heard digging: some hours later, the Bingo company attacked the German lines and most were killed including the captain. Presumably the five prisoners perished, though a company survivor whom the sergent later saw was not absolutely sure.

Mathilde listens to his account in silent shock. All she can think of is to tell the ill, slovenly sergeant to button "his repulsive fly." Later she weeps; and her mission begins to grow in her. She travels, with the stalwart help of the family chauffeur, to various parts of France. She hunts down widows, lovers and relatives of the other four prisoners. She writes their friends, landlords and parish priests.

She enlists the family lawyer in Paris, with his mysterious Army connections and, as it turns out, his mysterious evasions and vague threats. She advertises in newspapers and receives dozens of answers, one or two useful. She employs a rickety but unstoppable private detective who has fallen hopelessly in love, not with her, but with the splashy flower paintings that her father's influence enables her to show in a Paris gallery. She makes her way through lies, half-lies, misapprehensions. She tires, comes to stalemates, starts over again. Finally she will find out what happened to her little fisherman and the four others.

It doesn't come with the force of revelation but with quite another force; that of life, of history and of Japrisot's art. It is impossible to describe all the different things the author succeeds in doing without making this into a list; still less is it possible to convey how he does it. His close-ups and panoramic views are not only equally intense and compelling, but they merge. There is hardly a detail that does not tell far more than itself.

**A Very Long Engagement finds a chilling
and humane way to evoke the trench-
fought war of 1914-18.**

—Richard Eder

Each of the five prisoners—Eskimo, the bluff and life-loving carpenter who is the hero of his Paris bar-set; Ange, the pimp from the Marseilles milieu; Six-Sous, the eloquent working-class Socialist; That Man (for lack of a nickname), the silent and redoubtable peasant; and Manech himself, youthful and frail—are five chapters of France. Other chapters are embodied by Ange's prostitute lover, whose search, parallel to Mathilde's and fatally successful, is for revenge rather than knowledge; by Mathilde's father, a bourgeois out of the Enlightenment not Balzac, and by the captain who has to execute the dreadful order. He is a schoolteacher and stamp-collector—the detail will provide an early clue in Mathilde's search—and he does more than curse his assignment. His fatal charge of the German lines is a suicidal attempt at rescue.

Japrisot, lucidly translated by Linda Coverdale, gives us not only the story but its characters in a series of successive passes, each of which uncovers a new layer of color and configuration. If the five prisoners are a colorful assortment of French types, they deepen into individuals whose declarative vividness gives way to something more complex and mysterious. As for Mathilde, her evolution and revelation is both similar and different.

She begins with immense charm, but with elements of snobbery, willfulness and sentimentality. She becomes a genuine heroine—not of courage and persistence, merely, but of sheer brainy energy—yet the other qualities remain. We do not so much change as grow, Japrisot suggests, and nothing is lost. There is a brilliant light on her from beginning to end, and her only mystery is that of a life lived so completely as to entirely fulfill itself.

Rachel Billington   (review date 12 September 1993)

SOURCE: "No Man's Land," in *The New York Times Book Review,* September 12, 1993, p. 24.

[Daughter of the seventh earl of Longford, Lady Rachel Mary Billington is an English novelist, nonfiction writer, author of children's literature, dramatist, and critic. In the following favorable review of A Very Long Engagement, *she contends that the story is a morality tale about war.]*

World War I has always inspired writers, as if art (in particular poetry) could do something to overcome the dominance of death. The war's notorious trenches introduced a new form of horror that killed, maddened and deformed. Afterward, Europe was filled with widows, mothers without sons, sorrowing sweethearts. It is not surprising, then, that the French writer Sébastian Japrisot, whose prose uses the poetry of the visual, has taken one wartime tragedy and turned it into a tale about morality, a novel in which a few strands of goodness and heroism gleam among so much suffering and degradation.

The protagonist of *A Very Long Engagement* is Mathilde, a young woman whose fiancé, known as Cornflower because of his blue eyes, is reported killed in action in 1917. The story tells of her efforts to discover how he died.

This might seem simple enough—almost a cliché, you would think. But before introducing Mathilde, Mr. Japrisot gives us a terrible curtain raiser: in a series of horrifying scenes, five French soldiers, including Cornflower, are taken, hands bound, and thrown into no man's land at a place called Bingo Crépuscule, where the French and German lines are so close that "muffled noises, snatches of harmonica music" can be heard from the other side. All five men have been convicted of self-mutilation to avoid further service in the war; their macabre and cruel punishment seems to be a way of breaking a stalemate that has fallen on this part of the battlefield.

According to the official records, all five soldiers simply die in the line of duty. But the unofficial stories of just how they die have a nightmarish quality. It is January, and one, smiling insanely, builds a snowman; another brings down an airplane with a grenade he has found. Five bodies are buried by soldiers from Newfoundland who replace the demoralized French forces. But are these the bodies of the five men who were condemned to death? Is it possible that at least one of them has survived?

Not for nothing have all seven of Mr. Japrisot's previous novels been made into films. In *A Very Long Engagement,* the unfolding detective story runs side by side with evocative views of Mathilde and the lives that surround her. Although the reader is ahead of her at the beginning, Mathilde soon catches up. From now on, we must struggle, as she does, to sort out the pieces of the puzzle. Why did one of the five men, a peasant farmer from the Dordogne, fill most of what he knew would be his last, brief letter to his beloved wife with instructions about the manure for his fields? And what was the relationship between two of the condemned, a relationship that involved a woman in Paris and certainly had an effect on who, if anyone, might have eluded the crossfire?

**War is Mr. Japrisot's main theme, its
legacy his main strength; and as the novel
moves onward, he makes it all seem
outlandishly real.**

—Rachel Billington

As the novel progresses, Mathilde's determined probing fills in the background behind the horrors of Bingo Crépuscule. In the process, what at first seemed straightforward becomes extremely complicated. To explain further would spoil the reader's enjoyment of the book.

The author's style, in an exceedingly good translation by Linda Coverdale, is also deceptive, apparently without flourishes but rich in imagery and daringly abbreviated rhythms. If the novel is not perfect, its flaws are created consciously, one feels, for dramatic purpose. Consider, for example, Mathilde's own strange circumstances: at the age of 3, she climbed to the top of a stepladder and tried to fly; although her injuries seemed relatively minor, she has been unable to walk ever since. There are other occasions when Mr. Japrisot's puppeteer's hand moves his characters or plot in ways that fail to convince.

But war is Mr. Japrisot's main theme, its legacy his main strength; and, as the novel moves onward, he makes it all seem outlandishly real. On finishing this book, I was irresistibly drawn to the work of that great British poet Wilfred Owen, whose parents heard of his death as the Armistice bells rang out in 1918. His poem "The Send-Off," written five months earlier, describes soldiers departing for the front. Its final lines echo the revelations that emerge from Mr. Japrisot's fine novel:

> Shall they return to beatings of great bells
>   In wild train-loads?
> A few, a few, too few for drums
>   and yells,
> May creep back, silent, to still
>   village wells
> Up half-known roads.

Michiko Kakutani   (review date 21 September 1993)

SOURCE: "Seeking Fiancé's Fate, and Finding Bigger Issues," in *The New York Times,* September 21, 1993, p. C17.

[*In the following review, Kakutani praises the clear language and philosophical themes of Japrisot's historical wartime thriller* A Very Long Engagement.]

The event is horrific: in World War I, five wounded French soldiers, their arms tied behind their backs, are marched by their own troops through the trenches to the edge of no man's land. There they are abandoned in the snow to die in the crossfire with German troops. All five have been court-martialed and condemned to death for self-inflicted wounds.

This chilling story, which forms the core of Sébastien Japrisot's riveting new novel, is reminiscent of Stanley Kubrick's 1957 movie *Paths of Glory* (in which three French soldiers are tried and executed for cowardice in the line of duty), and *A Very Long Engagement* shares that film's concern with the brutalities of military justice. Mr. Japrisot, however, uses a wider-angle lens than Mr. Kubrick did. His view of people is ultimately more optimistic, more forgiving than the film maker's, and his novel consequently leaves the reader with not only an understanding of the horrors of war but also an appreciation of the kindness and bravery possible amid all the death and pain.

Regarded as a master of psychological suspense in his native France, Mr. Japrisot, whose real name is Jean Bapt-

iste Rossi, has written several crime novels, and *A Very Long Engagement* attests to his easy command of the suspense form. In fact the novel is structured like a kind of detective story: the detective, in this case, is a young woman named Mathilde, who was engaged to one of the condemned men; her search is not for the killers of her beloved Manech but for the truth of what happened to him and his confreres that cold winter day in 1917 on the front near Picardy.

Manech, we learn, was a young, innocent soldier of 19, who had been genuinely fearless until he saw another soldier blown to bits in front of his eyes. Since then, Manech has been afraid of everything: "afraid of his own side's artillery, afraid of his own gun, afraid of the whine of aerial torpedoes, afraid of mines that explode and engulf a whole section of infantry, afraid of the flooding that drowns you in the dugout, afraid of the earth that buries you alive." Many of his fellow soldiers are convinced that Manech has lost his mind.

After days of being berated by his sergeant, after days of rain in a filthy trench near the front, Manech lights a cigarette—he does not smoke—and holds it over the parapet until a German soldier fires and hits his hand. Instead of being sent home wounded, he is court-martialed and sentenced to die. He is to be made an example, a warning to other soldiers of the perils of cowardice and fear.

The other four "examples" who have been court-martialed with Manech are a decidedly motley lot: a former carpenter nicknamed the Eskimo, who has wounded himself accidentally; a robust corporal called Six Sous, who is proud of his Socialist politics and proud of having deliberately shot himself in the hand; a onetime farmer known only as That Man, who has earned a reputation for his taciturn ways; and lastly, Common Law, an ex-convict who has worked as a pimp in Marseilles.

Writing in clean, occasionally lyrical language, Mr. Japrisot does a beautiful job of orchestrating Mathilde's detective work, building suspense even as he multiplies the ambiguities in *A Very Long Engagement.*

—*Michiko Kakutani*

Mathilde has reason to believe that at least one of these men survived the ordeal in no man's land, and she vows to ferret out the truth, hoping against hope that Manech is still alive. A former sergeant in the territorial army, who is tortured by his memories of that night on the front lines, has given her a broad outline of what happened to Manech and the others, and she decides to try to fill in the details of that outline by interviewing other survivors of the war.

Although a childhood accident has left Mathilde confined to a wheelchair—one of the few details in this novel that feels forced and gratuitously sentimental—she soon proves that she is a relentless and highly efficient detective. By placing ads in newspapers and employing a private investigator, she is eventually able to track down other witnesses, as well as the wives and girlfriends of the other condemned men. All these people offer her and the reader highly subjective accounts of what they know. Not surprisingly, their accounts are filled with lies, elisions and misunderstandings; and when Mathilde tries to put them together, like a jigsaw puzzle, all sorts of contradictions and incongruities emerge.

Were orders lifting the death sentence on the five men really received by the officers at the front, and if so, why weren't they obeyed? Was one of the five men misidentified when he was buried in a local cemetery or is this merely a rumor seized upon by one of the men's widows as a sign of hope? Do the letters written by the condemned men to their families contain coded messages that might reveal their fates?

As Mathilde works to unravel these tangled clues, the reader becomes immersed in her search, a search that soon becomes much more than a search for Manech, a search that evolves into a kind of existential quest for a truth that might transcend the myopia of individual memory and reconcile the distortions of time.

Writing in clean, occasionally lyrical language, Mr. Japrisot does a beautiful job of orchestrating Mathilde's detective work, building suspense even as he multiplies the ambiguities of his story. He has written a fierce, elliptical novel that's both a gripping philosophical thriller and a highly moving meditation on the emotional consequences of war.

Laurie Lee

1914-

English memoirist, poet, nonfiction and travel writer, essayist, and dramatist.

The following entry provides an overview of Lee's career through 1994.

INTRODUCTION

Lee is highly regarded for autobiographical works depicting his childhood in the English countryside, his travels in Spain, and his involvement in the Spanish Civil War. Having garnered critical acclaim for his vibrant portraits of village life in the English Midlands and his descriptive characterizations of the chaotic and destabilizing environment of war, he is considered among England's foremost writers of the post-World War II era.

Biographical Information

Born into a large, rural English working-class family in Stroud, Gloucestershire, Lee was a small child when his father abandoned the family. Financially strapped, Lee's mother raised him and his siblings with little economic means, and she has been described in his writings as a resourceful, fun-loving—if at times impractical—woman and a major influence on his life. At the age of nineteen, Lee left the English countryside on foot for London, where, to support himself, he worked a variety of jobs and played the fiddle. He eventually traveled throughout continental Europe, spending much of his time in Spain. In the late 1930s, Lee joined the International Brigade and fought in the Spanish Civil War on the side of the Republicans, or Loyalists, in their struggle to overthrow the fascist regime of Francisco Franco. During World War II he worked in a variety of government ministries in England, eventually undertaking scriptwriting duties with a number of their film units. After publishing several volumes of poetry and a well-received narrative of his leisurely travels in Andalusia, *A Rose for Winter* (1955), Lee turned to autobiographical writing and has since continued primarily in this genre.

Major Works

Lee's best-known work details his childhood and his experiences in Spain. Set in a village in the Cotswolds, *Cider with Rosie* (1959) celebrates nature, boyhood, and rural traditions. Recounting the passing of a pastoral way of life in unsentimental terms, the collection provides an affectionate account of Lee's childhood, family, and friends. *As I Walked Out One Midsummer Morning* (1969) begins with Lee's departure from his childhood home in the 1930s, chronicles his peripatetic wanderings throughout Europe, and ends with Lee—having been evacuated from Spain by a British ship—returning to Europe, crossing the

Pyrenees, and joining the Republican forces of the Spanish Civil War. In *A Moment of War* (1991), Lee examines the effects of the war on a personal level, discussing his own horrors and follies. For example, he details his initial fascination with aerial bombings as well as how, on several different occasions, he was captured and sentenced to death only to be miraculously rescued at the last moment. Although not as well known as *Cider with Rosie, As I Walked Out One Midsummer Morning,* and *A Moment of War,* Lee's *A Rose for Winter,* a memoir recounting his travels through the Iberian peninsula, provides a sensuous picture of the land, its inhabitants, and their customs. His other major works include several volumes of poetry—including *The Sun My Monument* (1944), *The Bloom of Candles* (1947), and *My Many-Coated Man* (1955)—and the essay collection, *I Can't Stay Long* (1975).

Critical Reception

Many critics have praised Lee's skilled use of figurative language and the sharpness of his descriptions. *Cider with Rosie,* perhaps Lee's best known work, was warmly received by both critics and popular audiences. When it was published in the United States as *The Edge of Day,* T. S.

Matthews noted that "once in a blue moon, a book appears that deserves its success. This time the moon is blue, and *The Edge of Day* is the book." Likewise, *As I Walked Out One Midsummer Morning* and *A Moment of War* have both received accolades from many reviewers. Writing about the former, Charles Causley found its romantic style to be "as juicily ripe as an autumn pear" and possessing a "charm in the writing that genuinely makes it difficult to put the book down." In discussing more serious aspects of Lee's work, Albert Hoxie recommended *A Moment of War* "[for] anyone who wants to understand what war is actually like, when it is not being dramatized, hyped, heroized or propagandized." Overall, critics have found Lee's stories both accessible and expressive. As one commentator noted in *The New Yorker,* "Mr. Lee's writing—almost precious, almost naive—has a tone and intensity that are truly entirely his own, and are inimitably pleasing."

PRINCIPAL WORKS

The Sun My Monument   (poetry)   1944
Land at War   (prose)   1945
The Bloom of Candles: Verse from a Poet's Year   (poetry)
     1947
The Voyage of Magellan: A Dramatic Chronicle for Radio
     (drama)   1948
My Many-Coated Man   (poetry)   1955
A Rose for Winter: Travels in Andalusia   (travel essay)
     1955
Cider with Rosie   (memoir)   1959; also published as *The*
     Edge of Day: A Boyhood in the West of England, 1960
As I Walked Out One Midsummer Morning   (memoir)
     1969
I Can't Stay Long   (essays)   1975
Two Women: A Book of Words and Photographs   (remi-
     niscences)   1983
*A Moment of War   (memoir)   1991
†Red Sky at Sunrise   (memoirs)   1992

*This work has also been published as *A Moment of War: A Memoir of the Spanish Civil War.*

†This work contains *Cider with Rosie, As I Walked Out One Midsummer Morning,* and *A Moment of War.*

CRITICISM

Gerard Previn Meyer   (review date 6 September 1947)

SOURCE: "Washed in Happy Air," in *The Saturday Review of Literature,* Vol. XXX, No. 36, September 6, 1947, pp. 23, 30.

[*In the following review, Meyer notes Lee's focus on pastoral life and love in* The Sun My Monument, *as well as the volume's focus on metaphysical concerns.*]

The war years saw in Britain (as they did in some of the Dominions, notably Australia) the rise of a number of "little magazines," among which Cyril Connolly's *Horizon* and John Lehmann's *Penguin New Writing* are best known on this side of the Atlantic. Laurie Lee has published poems in both these periodicals, as well as in the BBC magazine, *The Listener,* and in at least two anthologies of the newer verse; but **The Sun My Monument** is his first book publication. Mr. Lee is to be congratulated on the ready acceptance of his first book on these shores; and the American public for poetry now has another measure by which to appraise the new post-Auden generation of English poets.

Is there a greater freshness in the English air than here? At least, Mr. Lee dares to produce poetry that, by one of the standards now revered in local poetic circles, should be clearly "old hat." For example, he boldly packs his work with country, rather than urban, images. Is it that "England's green and pleasant land" provides greater justification for pastoral poetry than the less embraceable American countryside? Though, indeed, he has left his native Cotswolds:

> O the wild trees of my home,
> forests of blue dividing the pink
>   moon,
> the iron blue of those ancient
>   branches
> with their berries of vermilion stars,

With their fields ("that place of steep meadows"), he never really leaves them:

> But here I have lost
> the dialect of your hills,
> my tongue has gone blind
> far from their limestone roots.

When he writes of war, too, does he write more easily because his British audience, knowing the impact of war first hand, does not require the conscious strain of the poet's imagination to make the described experience its own?

> Fruit is falling in the city
> blowing a woman's eyes and fingers
> across the street among the bones
> of boys who could not speak their
>   love.

Both the pastoral note and the ruined city assume an immediacy in the poems of this British writer that they can hardly possess for the self-conscious American poet.

He is an unashamed romantic, too. What poet of genuine talent in this country today would dare to write a line like "A boy is shot with England in his brain"? The sentiment of this is dangerously close to sentimentality. But, again, sentiment no less than romanticism is an old and honored part of the English literary scene. So we may accept this as a true report of an English war mood, even though we remember that between Rupert Brooke and Laurie Lee there was a Wilfred Owen.

In England, too—and this is a more universal note—death and war are still challenged by their eternal unconquerable enemy, love: love not only for the Wolds, not only for England, but love for a woman:

> Let me with vaporizing breath
> speak to my woman, while the frost
> makes up a grim metallic bed
> for me and summer's broken head.

There is hardly a poem in *The Sun My Monument* from which love is wholly absent.

Withal, the style is of our time—for Laurie Lee has not "snorted in the seven sleepers' den" while modern poetry has been aborning. His association with advance-guard publications is one warrant of that. Another is his constant use of the metaphysical image. Now the metaphysical image, so popular today, is not simply a fashionable trick—though it can be, and has been, employed as such. The metaphysical image, which by violent shocking linking together of disparate objects makes us see resemblances and harmonies "that never were on sea or land," is *direct statement by metaphor:* that is, the metaphor is organic, structural—it more than advances the thought, it *embodies* the thought. By metaphor things are said which could not be said otherwise; and the emotion supplies the fusing force that brings far-fetched things together to make the new harmony.

The fact that Laurie Lee, who in another age might have been simply a pleasant pastoral poet, is writing metaphysical poetry, need not be charged to fashion. The background for metaphysical poetry is conflict, and we are certainly living in an age of many conflicts. The supreme metaphysical poet is supremely aware of the world about him—and within. Let it be said that Mr. Lee seems to be fully conscious of the world's disharmony, and the necessity to resolve the disorder. His weakness, *as* a poet, crops up in the impulse to find a resolution for these conflicts outside of poetry; a laudable impulse, but alien to the muse. Human love, and even love of humanity (as in **"The Long War,"** where he writes:

> But as our twisted arms embrace
> the desert where our cities stood
> death's family likeness in each face
> must show, at last, our brotherhood)

may stimulate, animate poetry, but provide no resolution within the poem. Paradoxically—and this is a conclusion which the poet may protest—there is greater promise of poetic health in the unpleasant but metaphorically more intense and satisfying "see how the sun rubs ulcers in the sky" in the Baudelairean second stanza of **"Black Edge,"** his gloomiest poem, than in the more affirmative and lyrical, but weaker conclusion to the same poem:

> Wash me in happy air,
> restore me with the odor of rivers;
>   then feed o feed my sight
>   with your normal love.

Fleming MacLiesh   (review date 21 December 1947)

SOURCE: "Palsied Apples Fall," in *The New York Times Book Review,* December 21, 1947, p. 8.

[*In the mixed review of* The Sun My Monument *below, MacLiesh faults the uneven lyrical quality of the collection.*]

Poe refused to publish somebody's poem on the ground that the disparity between the good lines and the bad was so incredible that the good must have been stolen. By that criterion a fair amount of his own poetry would have been suspect. If Mr. Lee is certainly not open to the charge, nevertheless the mixture of the excellent and of the perfectly terrible in his verse is equally baffling; so thoroughly are they mingled that there is scarcely a poem in [*The Sun My Monument*] which can be dismissed altogether and scarcely one which succeeds as a whole or represents any kind of sustained achievement.

Both virtues and faults have their source in his employment of images. In this connection, readers should at least applaud his willingness to gamble for an idiom which is original, rich and strange, even at the risk of falling over into the absurd and his refusal to play it safe by harboring up in a safe pedestrianism to which even the most preciously acidulous critics cannot take particular exception. It is unfortunate, however, that he seems as yet unable to perform a simple labor of excision on lines and whole stanzas and so raise to a fairly impressive standard the poems they now ruin.

His images, in the first place, are sensuous to such an extent that in the lyrical celebration of passion they sometimes give the effect of an obsession with the physical. There is little intellectual tension and not much attempt to achieve an unwavering clarity through the use of the exact word or phrase. He proceeds, rather, through a violent juxtaposition of unlike elements and associations to achieve effects which, when successful, are striking, unexpected and memorable. In the over-all sense, his lines may be compared to those isotopes which emerge from the Oak Ridge Pile, where common elements whose atomic nuclei have been subjected to neutron bombardment become radioactive and unstable. Different isotopes, in addition to emitting different kinds of radiation, have, as must be common knowledge now, different rates of radioactive decay, or "half-life." Where Mr. Lee's verse is at its best, his elements are not only radioactive, they are endowed with a considerable half-life. Far too often, however, the image is so forced that it will not hold together at all; it simply explodes, or, like the isotope of Boron, has a half-life of 1/200 of a second.

Examples of this almost instantaneous disintegration may be picked at random: "Your lips are turreted with guns, / and bullets crack across your kiss. . . ." "Wet sunlight on the powder of my eye . . ." ". . . slow from the wild crab's bearded breast / the palsied apples fall." "I want your lips of wet roses / laid over my eyes." Perhaps for this last the figure will have to be altered, since, while there are isotopes which are particularly deadly, it would be difficult to say of any that it is just repulsive.

In those lines where Mr. Lee is at his best there is an effect of lyrical effortlessness and inevitability which leaves considerably in the background a lot of contemporary verse that has been, and will be, better acclaimed. If he knew where to cut or when to stop, he might be one of the more important poets writing today. As this is early work, his first book, he may be yet; he has an open field.

Kingsley Amis (review date 17 June 1955)

SOURCE: "Is the Travel-Book Dead?" in *The Spectator*, Vol. 194, No. 6625, June 17, 1955, pp. 774-75.

[*Amis was an English educator, short story writer, critic, and essayist. In the following negative review, he characterizes* A Rose for Winter *as "vulgar and sensational."*]

The vogue for the highbrow travel-book shows no immediate signs of abating. . . . The usual characteristics of such books are, first, a leaning towards the more elaborate and unfashionable graces of prose—rightly unfashionable they seem to me, if I may show my hand thus early—and, secondly, a desire to get away from the exhausted sterilities of Western civilisation so feelingly alluded to from time to time by Mr. Priestley. In themselves, these two things may be all very well, though I judge it unlikely; in practice, however, the stylistic graces degenerate briskly into an empty and indecent poeticism, apparently based on a desire to get into the next edition of *The Oxford Book of English Prose*, while the escape-motive is only with difficulty to be distinguished from the feeling that the other fellow's grass is greener, that the really good time, or good life, is going on somewhere else. The two tendencies, in these degraded forms, find remarkably unalloyed expression in Mr. Laurie Lee's volume [*A Rose for Winter*].

The experienced reader will know what to do with a book whose blurb announces, as if in recommendation, its author's claim to 'the enchanted eye . . . of a true poet,' but the reviewer must act differently. His part is to soldier grimly on, trying not to mind too much the absence of a verb in the opening sentence, the incessant din of adjective and poeticality ('the scarred and crumpled valleys,' 'the oil-blue waters'), the full close of the first paragraph, mannered as any Ciceronian *esse videatur*:

> And from a steep hillside rose a column of smoke, cool as marble, pungent as pine, which hung like a signal over the landscape, obscure, imperative and motionless.

(The effect is a little marred through having been anticipated, three sentences earlier, by a cadential 'raw, sleeping and savage.') Another item on the list of things to try not to mind too much is the prevalence of lists—cf. Mr. Auden's *Spain*, which Mr. Lee has perhaps been cf.-ing too—like 'the bright facades . . . the beggars . . . the vivid shapely girls . . . the tiny, delicate-stepping donkeys,' and so on; and yet another one is the 'striking' image—'fragrant as water'—which at first sight seems to mean almost nothing, and upon reflection and reconsideration is seen to mean almost nothing. One way of summing up this book would be to call it a string of failed poems—failed not-very-good poems too, for whoever said that bad poetry is much more like poetry than good poetry is, was in the right of it there.

This kind of objection, however, though compulsory for the reader of almost any highbrow travel-book, is here

purely trifling. The really telling strictures emerge from a mulling-over of what Mr. Lee actually reveals to us about Andalusia. The figure of the narrator himself, having terrific fun with a drum in a wedding procession, carrying *two* guitars 'everywhere,' carefully recording every pass made at his wife, drinking like mad at a party in a telephone exchange while the switchboard lights 'twinkled unheeded' (not too good for people who wanted to ring the doctor)—can safely be left on one side. One might even haul to the other side the bullfighting question, although the author's taste for 'the sharp mystery of blood' will remain unshared in some quarters, where, in addition, the use of the phrase 'the moment of truth' will appear a little worse than *naif,* and to upbraid a bull for having no grace or honour or 'vocation for martyrdom' will appear a lot worse; if we enjoined these duties upon a bull, he would not understand us. But the least attractive part of Mr. Lee's portrayal of Spain is his portrayal of Spaniards, so far as this can be debarnacled from rhetoric, generalisation and rhapsody. The effect is not what he evidently intends; where he seeks to show us gaiety, mere instability or hooliganism emerges, unselfconsciousness is detectable as coxcombry or self-pity, while the gift attributed to Andalusians of greeting others' misfortune with a shrug or a grin is neither mature nor admirable. I am sure these people are not as bad as all that, just as I am sure that they are not in touch with the 'pure sources of feeling' and the 'real flavours' of life, whatever these entities may be; Coleridge put Wordsworth right on peasants a long time ago. Perhaps too many people in England do watch television, or do they watch it too much of the time? Anyway, *nostalgie de la boue* is not the answer; it is silly to sleep on straw in the inn yard if you can get hold of a bed; and while it is no doubt better to be gay and have sores than to be ungay and not have sores, it is better still to be fairly gay and not have sores.

Linda M. Shires on Lee as a poet:

Reacting against the poetry of slightly older contemporaries from the Auden generation, who insisted that a poet's main concerns must include social protest or social reportage, Lee is part of a general redirection of poetry in the early 1940s toward reinstating the validity of personal vision. Essentially a lyric poet, Lee was often moved by the countryside around him and by memories of his childhood in the Midlands. This emotional intensity resulted in a slender, but always sensuously arresting, poetic output.

Linda M. Shires, in her "Laurie Lee," in Dictionary of Literary Biography, *Vol. 27, Gale Research Inc., 1984.*

Geoffrey Brereton (review date 18 June 1955)

SOURCE: "South for Sensation," in *The New Statesman & Nation*, Vol. XLIX, No. 1267, June 18, 1955, pp. 852-53.

[*An English educator, editor, journalist, and translator,*

Brereton frequently writes about French literature. In the following, he provides a laudatory assessment of A Rose for Winter.]

As the toad under the stone, beneath the adjectives of the blurb, lurks the potential reader, though the shrewdest publisher's estimate is occasionally wrong. So, ignoring for the moment the mysterious and exotic, the colourful and romantic, the vivid and intimate, one is fatally lured by the bait of Mr. Laurie Lee's publisher, promising "the multitudinous flavour of Spain—acid, sugary, intoxicating, sickening, but above all, real." And the copywriter is right! After ten pages [of *A Rose for Winter*] one concedes him all his adjectives and as many more as he likes to borrow from his author, whose command of them is masterly.

Out of a winter in southern Spain, Mr. Lee has spun a magnificent book, outstanding even in a field where the competition is oppressively brilliant. His itinerary included Algeciras, Seville, Ecija and Granada, but the route hardly matters, except for the responses which it touched off in the author. Given the mood, he could, one feels, have found equally rich material in the Bolton-Leeds-Grimsby triangle. The Andalusians fed from his hand, as he often fed liberally from theirs, all payment refused. Modestly, he ascribes this ease of contact to the attractiveness of his wife and to his own habit of going about with two guitars slung over his shoulders. Seeing these, no Spaniard would believe that they were either English, or proper tourists, and confident, rich relationships were established at once. This, of course, is a mere sop to the armchair traveller. We all have beautiful wives and could take guitar lessons, but we should need as well excellent Spanish, untiring human sympathy and constant freshness of observation.

Like all triumphant travellers, Mr. Lee commanded luck. The set occasions—the carol-singing in Seville, the Christmas carnival in Granada—can be planned in advance. But over and above that, it is the chance encounters which make a journey and a book. They are the bonus given to the good traveller, like a second moon to the good drunkard. So it happened that at a feast given in his honour in a provincial telephone exchange, he met a young Spaniard, otherwise normally voiced, who spoke English in a high-pitched, tinny whine. "This mystified me at first, until I discovered that he had learnt his English from an antique pre-1920 gramophone and could only be said to be suffering from too good an ear." The same outrageous fortune threw up shifty British yachtsman-smugglers, poetic waiters and philosophic child-beggars, an ex-Republican officer doomed to a lifetime on the run, and a woman sleeping out on a hillside on a brass bedstead, while underground her legless husband tunnelled out the cave which was to be their new home. Above all, it brought him an illness in Granada, the evening after a visit to the cemetery. Perhaps it was only severe 'flu, but Mr. Laurie's account of his delirium reads like a page from De Quincey, while in the background is the grimly humorous motif of the twenty medical students who ate at the same inn and were now waiting with pathetic eagerness for his wife to become a widow.

One believes Mr. Lee. The quality of his writing compels it. Just as for the expert marksman there is no hiatus between trigger-finger and target, here there is an absolute compatibility between experience and the expression of it:

> The park was formal yet flouncy, like the dress of an Edwardian beauty. The air was soft and springlike. Children in large hats and long white pinafores bowled their grave hoops among the rose-trees. Black-stockinged girls bent over pools, poking at goldfish with the stems of lilies. And opulent mammas, ripe in black satin, drowsed at their ease on the blue-tiled benches. It was a landscape by Renoir or Steer, an end-of-the-century dream; and as we clopped our way along, smelling the oranges and roses and passing the lacy girls posed like old postcards among the flower-beds, I felt an unnatural sense of distinction, almost as though I had invented the horse.

The Times Literary Supplement (review date 1 July 1955)

SOURCE: "A Winter in Andalusia," in *The Times Literary Supplement,* No. 2783, July 1, 1955, p. 366.

[*In the following commendable review, the critic characterizes* A Rose for Winter *as "poetic" and unlike other travel books.*]

Although its sub-title is "Travels in Andalusia," [*A Rose for Winter*] is no ordinary travel book. It is an account of a return visit to southernmost Spain, in mid-winter, after a break of fifteen years or more. The story begins and ends at Algeciras—"a handsome and lordly city," as Miss Rose Macaulay has described it. From here the author and his wife make visits to Seville, to Granada, where they spend Christmas, to Ecija, at other seasons accounted the hottest place in Spain, and to an unnamed fishing village east of Malaga where Mr. Lee was living at the outbreak of the Civil War. Thence back to Algeciras—"after three months among the great white cities of Andalusia we had returned to our starting point . . . to us the darling of them all."

Another traveller has recently said of the port of Algeciras, "noisy, smells vilely of fish and harbour mud, and has little to offer," and retreat is recommended to a luxurious hotel outside the town. Not so Mr. Lee:

> The evening harbour smelt sweetly of remembered shell-fish, sherry and smuggled tobacco. Porters, touts, boot-blacks and *contrabandistas,* addressing us by name, bore our bags and guitars into the "Queen of the Sea." A dozen girls from the attics descended upon Kati with cries and embraces. Ramón and Manolo advanced to wring my hand, eyes damped politely, compliments flew, and we were given our old room overlooking the bay.

This is one of the closing scenes in a series vividly described in this attractive book.

There is little of ordinary travel talk in it—one or two long drives by autobus through sierras and winter storms, a walk to Tarifa, the most southerly town in Europe, "almost mystically oriental," where "the women wore veils of silence and the men walked cloaked in shadow and the sun," a few comings and goings to and from rather unusual hotels and cafés, an out-of-season bull-fight for amateurs and novices, the dancing of the *Seises* in Seville Cathedral, the Alhambra in winter "like a rose preserved in snow": and there is nearly always a surprise in store. "The Hotel Comercio," for instance, "was about as commercial as the cave of Ali Baba. Around the vast shadowy patio shepherds in fleece-lined coats sat eating and drinking, boot-blacks on their knees seized and polished the boots of anyone who stood for a moment near them, two farmers were tasting each other's crop of olives . . . and a magnificent gypsy wandered among the throng selling silver Virgins and cures for love." At the bull-fight, an eleven-year-old boy leaps over the barrier brandishing a red shirt, evades the attendants, engages the bull, gets trampled under foot, and ends up, not in hospital, but in gaol.

The author's burning curiosity leads him, and indeed transports his readers, to many other diverting scenes—to

---

An excerpt from *A Rose for Winter: Travels in Andalusia*

Granada is probably the most beautiful and haunting of all Spanish cities; an African paradise set under the Sierras like a rose preserved in snow. Here the art of the nomad Arab, bred in the raw heat of deserts, reached a cool and miraculous perfection. For here, on the scented hills above the green gorge of the Darro, he found at last those phantoms of desire long sought for in mirage and wilderness—snow, water, trees and nightingales. So on these slopes he carved his places, shaping them like tents on slender marble poles and hanging the ceilings with decorations like icicles and the walls with mosaics rich as Bokhara rugs. And here, among the closed courts of orange trees and fountains, steeped in the languors of poetry and intrigue, he achieved for a while a short sweet heaven before the austere swords of the Catholic Kings drove him back to Africa and to oblivion.

But Granada never recovered from this flight of the Moors, nor saw again such glory. When the cross-bearing Spaniards returned to their mountain city they found it transformed by alien graces and stained by a delicate voluptuousness which they could neither understand nor forgive. So they purged the contaminated inhabitants by massacre and persecution; and in the courts of the palaces they stabled their mules and horses. But the inheritors of Granada, even today, are not at home in the city; it is still dominated by the spirit of Islam. Fascinated and repelled by it, they cannot destroy it, but remain to inhabit an atmosphere which fills them with a kind of sad astonishment, a mixture of jealousy and pride. The people of Granada, in fact, are known throughout Andalusia as a people apart, cursed with moods which reduce them at times to almost murderous melancholy.

Laurie Lee, in his A Rose for Winter: Travels in Andalusia, *William Morrow & Company, Inc., 1955.*

---

a wedding party at night with a band of serenaders, to a barbecuan feast in a telephone exchange "with dancing, dressing-up, and singing down the telephones," to an evening *paseo* up the Sacro Monte above Granada in company with a dancing, laughing crowd of girl lace-makers. There is indeed a great store of gaiety and friendliness in this book, though it is not without its sombre side. At Ecija, a Spanish *heliopolis,* the bull-ring (which, by the way, was "new and magnificent" in Richard Ford's day) is now almost abandoned. It is built on the site of a Roman amphitheatre. "Big, empty, harsh and haunted, for two thousand years this saucer of stone and sand, dedicated to one purpose . . . still exuded a sharp mystery of blood. . . . We walked across the silent arena now overgrown with grass. All was decay and desertion." If many of Mr. Lee's scenes are strange, still more are some of the characters which figure in them, for whom he and his wife appeared to possess some magnetic attraction. There is a poetry-writing waiter who served him with a new poem every morning, an epicure taverner who insisted on their "approving" a glass of wine from every barrel in his stock, a youthful dentist who courted his fiancée in the dentist's chair, and a melancholy guitar professor who, after a lesson, would play to him "lost in a dream of melody and invention. And faced with the beauty of his technique, the complex harmonies, the ease and grace, the supreme mastery of tone and feeling, I would feel like one of the lesser apes who suddenly catches sight of *homo sapiens.*" There are many more such figures in this poetic book, and if here and there a little strain is put upon our credulity, we cannot complain.

V. S. Pritchett   (review date 8 April 1956)

SOURCE: "In Spain It's Like That," in *The New York Times Book Review,* April 8, 1956, p. 6.

[*The former president of PEN International, Pritchett is an English journalist, educator, critic, nonfiction writer, short story writer, novelist, and scriptwriter. Also known for his work as a memoirist, biographer, autobiographer, journalist, and editor, he additionally wrote a book review column for* New Statesman. *In the favorable review of* A Rose for Winter *below, Pritchett considers Lee's book to be idiosyncratic, "delicate and strong."*]

Laurie Lee is a lyrical poet and he has written [*A Rose for Winter,*] a poet's book about Andalusia. He is also a droll and a wit. His impression is a fantastic one but it bites more deeply than impression usually does and catches exactly the Andalusian flavor, something "acid, sugary, intoxicating, sickening" and pungent. He uses none of the romantic clichés which are dished out regularly by the tourist booklets or the conventional travelers. He sets down all that our senses remember of Spain and his light pages have more of the South than many a more solemn and explanatory volume.

He writes under private enchantment. It is bizarre but that, for Andalusia, is right. One watches him cunningly cadging acquaintance with his guitar. His beautiful wife immediately collected a court of candid and dedicated suitors who traipsed along or sat around, glum or vocal with admiration or desire and hopelessly longing for her early widowhood. From the taverns and smugglers' holes of Algeciras, the couple went off to Granada or Seville, seeing bullfights, serenaded, drinking wine in great quantities, surrounded by friends. The best company in Spain is low company or that of people whose profession is to sit in the sun while there is any: bootblacks, waiters, gypsies, crones, poets by métier or provocation. Smugglers, cooks, barmen, melancholics and chambermaids buzzed about like summer flies, wept, laughed, told beautiful lies or worked out piercing epigrams.

If Mr. Lee is fantastic, that is a proper response to a civilization which pours out fantasy all day in word or action:

"Suddenly we heard screams of laughter in the passage and plump Rosario came staggering in. She threw herself on the bed, tore off a boot and began to fan herself with it. For a while she was unable to speak."

Her Uncle Pedro, the fisherman, had gone out three miles to sea in the night and had anchored there; but, being drunk, he had thought he was alongside the quay and had stepped out into the water and was drowned. The town and Rosario could not stop laughing. That is, beyond question, the classical Andalusian story. It contains delight in personal catastrophe. Mr. Lee himself nearly died of some sort of fever in Granada, a city he likes a good deal more than I do. He had half the neighborhood in a warm state of emotion and expectation at his bedside, offering him sinister remedies. Students turned up, anxious to give slapwork injections and telling him dispassionately he need not worry about his wife if he died. There were plenty of eligible men in the town. This was indeed a queue.

Mr. Lee lived in Spain years ago and knows the people exceedingly well. "We used to swim by night in the bay, and fill sandwiches with sea-urchins and stuff them into the pockets of sleeping policemen. Each night we would pool our money, buy fish and wine, and then go off and serenade the nuns. After that we all slept side by side among the mules." Under the freakish lies a fine, direct knowledge.

Especially in the South, people live out their lives and their passing emotions in public, leave nothing corroding in their hearts. They devote themselves seriously to their sensibility as to a major task. They have the courage of their gestures. They maltreat the modern world as if a machine were no more than an old mule. Not surprising to find a party of pork, butter cakes and cognac spread out among the telephone instruments at the exchange and to hear the aunt of the superintendent singing down the telephones to entranced subscribers. Or of a dentist captivating his girl and soothing her temper by giving her a cast of her teeth. Not surprising to find a young man who had caused offense to a lady, purging his shame on the spot by demanding that he should be publicly forgiven before all his friends; and that everyone there shouts Viva! as honor is restored. The Spanish therapy goes straight to the ego. There is no need of psychiatry in Spain.

Mr. Lee, who has the poet's half naive and half sophisticated quickness of acquaintance, has an excellent eye for these storytelling people. He has an original descriptive

power, a feeling for what is also hard and stone-faced in the people, for the nakedness, rawness and sourness of Spanish things, as well as for what is ornate, sweet, ribald and grave.

> He says: Spain but Spain, and belongs nowhere but where it is. It is neither Catholic nor European but a structure of its own, forged from an African-Iberian past which exists in its own austere reality and rejects all short-cuts to a smoother life. Let the dollars come, the atom-bomb air bases blast their way through the white-walled towns, the people, I feel, will remain unawed, their lips unstained by chemical juices, their girls unslacked, and their music unswung. For they possess a natural resistance to civilization's more superficial seductions, based partly on the power of their own poetry, and partly on their incorruptible sense of humor and dignity.

A large number of books on Spain are machine made and say nothing; Mr. Lee's book, spun out of his own idiosyncrasy and long knowledge, is delicate and strong.

At the end, he takes leave of Spain in these words: "We drew away from the harbor and from the town to the waiting ship, to the smell of brewed tea, to the shuffle of bridge-cards and the snows of London. And Spain slid back from our eyes into the mist, leaving us lost and footless on a naked sea."

Samuel French Morse   (review date December 1956)

SOURCE: "Five Young English Poets," in *Poetry*, Vol. LXXXIX, No. 3, December, 1956, pp. 193-200.

[*Morse is an American educator, poet, critic, and author of children's books. In the excerpt below, he offers praise for* My Many-Coated Man.]

[Laurie Lee's] *My Many-coated Man,* published in 1955, was a choice of the Poetry Book Society and won the William Foyle Poetry Prize. An extremely slim book indeed, it contains fifteen poems Selected from those "written since the war." The austerity of Lee's selection works ultimately to the great advantage of the poems, each of which has a page to itself, without the competition of print on the verso of the preceding leaf.

Read through at a single sitting, which is temptingly easy, *My Many-coated Man* reveals a deceptively narrow range. Metaphors and images recur with unusual frequency; the poems give an immediate impression of being versions of the same poem. A second reading reveals a subtle variety of inflection that amounts to style. The words take on the colors of their context very naturally, and enrich the separate occasions at which they occur. Any poet has to achieve his style within limits: his vocabulary, after all, is simply part of his equipment as poet, like his rhythms and his subject-matter; and it is on his exploitation of the chosen *materia poetica* that his character as a poet largely depends. Lee has achieved his style. What is more, the limits he has imposed upon his work seem to have given him a kind of certitude that not only sustains but also enriches the recent poems. *My Many-coated Man* is therefore a book of greater impact than *The Sun My Monument* or

The Bloom of Candles, in which Lee's fine-grained elegance shows up less well.

A book so coherently planned as *My Many-coated Man* provides an occasion for the observation of a good many details. One notes, for example, the play of light in these poems. In **"Sunken Evening"** it is submarine:

> The green light floods the city square—
> A sea of fowl and feathered fish,
> Where squalls of rainbirds dive and splash
> And gusty sparrows chop the air.
>
> Submerged, the prawn-blue pigeons feed
> In sandy grottoes round the Mall,
> And crusted lobster-buses crawl
> Among the fountains' silver weed.
>
> There, like a wreck, with mast and bell,
> The torn church settles by the bow,
> While phosphorescent starlings stow
> Their mussel shells along the hull. . . .

It is submarine, too, in **"Song by the Sea,"** but with that difference of inflection noted earlier:

> Girl of green waters, liquid as lies,
> Cool as the calloused snow,
> From my attic brain and prisoned eyes
> Draw me and drown me now.
>
> O suck me down to your weeds and fates,
> Green horizontal girl,
> And in your salt-bright body breed
> My death's dream centred pearl.

But in **"Bombay Arrival"** the light beats blind and naked upon the eyes, in all its deceptiveness and power:

> Slow-hooved across the carrion sea,
> Smeared by the betel-spitting sun,
> Like cows the Bombay islands come
> Dragging the mainland into view.
>
> The loose flank loops the rocky bone,
> The light beats thin on horn and hill;
> Still breeds the flesh for hawks and still
> The Hindu heart drips on a stone.

Each of these excerpts furnishes a text for study; each reveals an aspect of subject and style; each makes its special configuration in the larger pattern of Lee's work.

Michael Ramsbotham   (review date 7 November 1959)

SOURCE: "A Gloucestershire Lad," in *New Statesman,* Vol. LVIII, No. 1495, November 7, 1959, pp. 634-35.

[*In the following review, Ramsbotham offers a highly laudatory account of* Cider with Rosie.]

A few years before the first World War a grocer's assistant in Stroud inserted the following advertisement in a local paper: 'Widower (4 children) Seeks Housekeeper'. It was seen by Annie Light, a romantic countrywoman of thirty, who had spent her youth either toiling for her father and five brothers or slaving below-stairs in the manors of the gentry. She took the post, fell in love with her employer, married him, and gave him four more children—one girl

(who died) and three boys. Laurie Lee was the youngest child but one.

The father of these two families, a handsome and prudent go-getter ('a natural fixer,' says his son), had always dreamed of a tidy life in the Civil Service, and when the war started he saw his chance and set off for Greenwich ('in a bullet-proof vest') to join the Army Pay Corps. Eventually demobilised with a pension ('for nervous rash, I believe'), he realised his youthful ambition, settled permanently in London, and remitted home a thin supply of money. His wife, meanwhile, had moved with his seven children to a damp old house in a secluded village some miles from Stroud, where she devoted herself, in her muddled and heroic way, to bringing them up; she never stopped loving her husband and never believed, until he died some thirty years later ('cranking a car in a Morden suburb') that he would not one day come back to her. *Cider with Rosie* is Mr Lee's celebration of his childhood in this Cotswold village. The book is written in prose—a luscious, evocative, poetic prose, with overtones from Wales. There is comedy as well as pathos. Some quiet drawings by John Ward illustrate the story.

In the Twenties an ancient rural culture was disintegrating: cars, buses, and charabancs were beginning to join the villages to the towns. But Mr Lee was born just early enough to have known the arduous, unsophisticated, self-sufficient, and sometimes dotty life of a community still dominated by the squire, the parson, and the horse. He conjures up this past, his own and the village's, in a number of beautifully composed pieces, some of which have already appeared in magazines. 'Grannies in the Wainscot,' for instance, a chapter about two witchlike nonagenarian neighbours, is a perfect short story.

> **Cider with Rosie is Mr Lee's celebration of his childhood in this Cotswold village. The book is written in prose—a luscious, evocative, poetic prose, with overtones from Wales. There is comedy as well as pathos.**
>
> **—Michael Ramsbotham**

Mr Lee can look back on many pastoral pleasures. Some were innocent, some illicit; some were both, like the fiasco of the collective rape of Lizzie Berkeley, a simple girl who liked to chalk texts and 'Jesus Loves Me Now' on the beech trees in Brith Wood. When he recalls his worst exploits, Mr Lee gives thanks that he did not have to contend with the law and morality of today; otherwise, he believes, he and his friends might have been 'shoved into reform school'. This is an amiable delusion, and one shared by many other ex-juveniles whose crimes were not found out—or if found out, never by the wrong people. It is supposed that in these present antiseptic times scarcely any delinquent act by the young can escape punishment. Such a belief underestimates the resourcefulness of children as absurdly as it flatters the eyesight of Authority. Town boys and country boys still manage to lose their innocence without seeing the inside of Juvenile Courts; and young girls, as forward as the cider-drinking Rosie of the title, are still at liberty to be their educators and victims—even in Morden.

T. S. Matthews   (review date 27 March 1960)

SOURCE: "An Acceptance of Life That Is Also an Embrace," in *The New York Times Book Review,* March 27, 1960, p. 4.

[*Matthews is an American-born editor, essayist, poet, autobiographer, and biographer. In the following review, he praises* Cider with Rosie, *also published as* The Edge of Day, *as "funny, unsentimental and beautiful."*]

Suicide, said Camus, is the one really serious philosophical problem. The only simple answer to the questionable human condition is the act that ends all problems. Any other answer ignores the question or shelves the problem. And yet there is another sort of response, oblique as morning sunlight, irrational as joy, absurd as a human being—an acceptance of life that is also a welcoming and an embrace. Perhaps this response is less rare than we suppose, but only a poet can put it into words.

Laurie Lee has done it. Blessed be his name. These recollections of his country boyhood in the West of England are a testament to the wonder, joy, and painful absurdity of being alive, a letter of thanks whose address is plain to be seen: to life, with love. *The Edge of Day* is funny, unsentimental and beautiful. Huck Finn would have given it his complete approval.

The book begins with Lee's earliest memories: of the day when his large fatherless family (his father was an absentee) moved into a cottage in a Gloucestershire valley. Three-year-old Laurie, set down in a field where the June grass was taller than he was, felt abandoned and lost. "High overhead ran frenzied larks, screaming, as though the sky were tearing apart. . . . I put back my head and howled, and the sun hit me smartly on the face, like a bully."

Soon he was wriggling and darting around his new world like a tadpole in a pond. In the old cottage's scullery he

> discovered water—a very different element from the green crawling scum that stank in the garden tub. You could pump it in pure blue gulps out of the ground; you could swing on the pump handle and it came out sparkling like liquid sky. And it broke and ran and shone on the tiled floor, or quivered in a jug, or weighted your clothes with cold. You could drink it, draw with it, froth it with soap, swim beetles across it, or fly it in bubbles in the air. You could put your head in it, and open your eyes, and see the sides of the bucket buckle, and hear your caught breath roar, and work your mouth like a fish, and smell the lime from the ground.

Here is the morning of his first day of school:

> My sisters surrounded me, wrapped me in scarves, tied up my boot laces, thrust a cap on my head, and stuffed a baked potato in my pocket.

"What's this?" I said.

"You're starting school today."

"I ain't. I'm stopping 'ome."

"Now, come on, Loll. You're a big boy now."

"I ain't."

"You are."

"Boo-hoo."

They picked me up bodily, kicking and bawling, and carried me up the road.

"Boys who don't go to school get put into boxes and turn into rabbits, and get chopped up on Sundays."

I felt this was overdoing it rather, but said no more after that.

> I arrived at school just three feet tall and fatly wrapped in my scarves. The playground roared like a rodeo. . . . The rabble closed in; I was encircled; grit flew in my face like shrapnel. Tall girls with frizzled hair, and huge boys with sharp elbows, began to prod me with hideous interest. They plucked at my scarves, spun me around like a top, screwed my nose, and stole my potato.

With a family of eight, life in the small cottage was crowded but also "as separate as notes in a scale." The kitchen was their common-room, the presiding genius their mother,

> a country girl: disordered, hysterical, loving. She was muddled and mischievous as a chimney jackdaw, she made her nest of rags and jewels, was happy in the sunlight, squawked loudly at danger, pried and was insatiably curious, forget when to eat or ate all day, and sang when sunsets were red.

> She lived by the easy law of the hedgerow, loved the world and made no plans, had a quick holy eye for natural wonders and couldn't have kept a neat house for her life. . . . I can still seem to hear her blundering about the kitchen: shrieks and howls of alarm, an occasional oath, a gasp of wonder, a sharp command to things to stay still. A falling coal would set her hair on end, a loud knock make her leap and yell; her world was a maze of small traps and snares acknowledged always by cries of dismay.

At the same time "she fed our oafish wits with steady, imperceptible shocks of beauty . . . by the unconscious revelation of her loves, an interpretation of man and the natural world so unpretentious and easy that we never recognized it then, yet so true that we never forgot it."

Laurie Lee's recollections of his country boyhood in the West of England in *The Edge of Day* are a testament to the wonder, joy and painful absurdity of being alive, a letter of thanks whose address is plain to be seen: to life, with love.

—*T. S. Matthews*

The village life was crowded too: it contained murder, suicide, incest, rape, "an acceptance of violence as a kind of ritual which no one accused or pardoned," and more innocent oddities of festivals, outings, gossip, first love, the freezing hardships and sweaty delights of winter and summer.

Here is the compact record of a visit to relations:

> We sit down and eat, and the cousins kick us under the table, from excitement rather than spite. Then we play with their ferrets, spit down their well, have a fight, and break down a wall. Later we are called for and given a beating, then we climb up the tree by the earth closet. Edie climbs highest, till we bite her legs, then she hangs upside down and screams. It has been a full, far-flung, and satisfactory day; dusk falls, and we say good-bye.

Laurie Lee is a poet, not yet so well known in America as he is in England: a poet of the old tradition, at home with all sorts. Though he looks younger than his forty-five years, he has not had an easy life. At 20 he left home to make his own way in London, and has earned his living, sometimes slim pickings, as an independent writer. His travels about Europe (he has never been to America) have taken him often to Spain, where he has lived off the land by playing the violin in streets and cafes.

He has published several books of poems, a verse play and a travel book on Spain, *A Rose for Winter.* He and his lovely wife, Cathy, live in London's Chelsea, a favorite district of artists and writers.

The Edge of Day has already won an extraordinary wide public: it was a best seller in England (under its original title of *Cider With Rosie*). Parts of it appeared in magazines; excerpts were serialized for two weeks in a popular daily newspaper in London; passages were broadcast over the B.B.C. It is now an April dual Book-of-the-Month choice in America.

Good books don't always sell; the best-seller lists are usually swamped by the second- and third-rate. But now and then, once in a blue moon, a book appears that deserves its success. This time the moon is blue, and *The Edge of Day* is the book.

Max Cosman   (review date 1 April 1960)

SOURCE: "The Gift of Unabashed Recall," in *The Commonweal*, Vol. LXXII, No. 1, April 1, 1960, pp. 22-3.

[*In the following review, Cosman praises the subject matter and stylistic aspects of* The Edge of Day.]

Discussing a book by a lady of whom it might be said she walked with genius throughout her life, the editor of *The Golden Horizon* tells us that though he retains a very clear impression of the complicated characters who were her familiars, to wit, Mahler, Werfel and Kokoschka, he still remains baffled by the author herself. One thing, however, he does claim to understand: her ability to get over everything.

If, by this, Cyril Connolly means a containment of experience as much a forgetting as a remembering, then the animadversion does not apply to Laurie Lee, for the present book proves that he is one who has gotten over nothing in his past.

The Edge of Day, originally called *Cider with Rosie,* is an evocative and vibrant reproduction of that period in his life which extended from the age of three, when he was put down before his home in a Cotswold valley, to the point when his identity as a human being discovered he began "to make up poems from intense abstraction, hour after unmarked hour, imagination scarcely faltering once, rhythm hardly skipping a beat. . . ." Of a period, then, to take it out of the realm of ecstasy and place it in history, that started in the final year of the First World War and continued for a decade or so thereafter.

The setting for Mr. Lee's coming of teenage was the little village of the time: twenty or thirty houses on a southeast slope, a population scaling down from squire to deaf-mute beggar, rank personalities like Cabbage-Stump Charlie, Uncle Sid, or Grannies Trill and Wallon feuding to the very grave, a tiny schoolhouse packed to the brim by "universal education and unusual fertility," and, of course, an assortment of sports, observances, superstitions, acts of violence—the whole kit and caboodle of "the end of a thousand years' life," that is, of the end of a society centering about manor, church, and unfragmented home.

But because Mr. Lee, like his archetype Rousseau, has the gift of unabashed recall, *The Edge of Day* is much more than a sociologist's exhibit. In every sense it is a projection of a primary human being, with nothing that concerns him considered too secret to point a moral or adorn a tale.

It refers to his father, who deserted the family, as "a knowing, brisk, evasive man." It builds up a portrait of a Griselda-like mother which, though a loving memorial, nevertheless goes in for expressions like "buffoon" and "scatter-brained." No less anti-heroic about the autobiographer himself, it gives such details as his tykish running of the nose, his childish weaning from the maternal bed, and, *in extenso,* his boyish induction into sex.

Yet actually frank as all this is, it is never wayward or wanton. Mr. Lee, in contradistinction to something Rebecca West has observed about Kafka, is no sadist disguising himself as a hurt child and getting even now. He may be glorifying crass casualty, but he is also a poet, a consistent one, setting down his wonder at existence with the same precision that he set it down in a book of verse like *My Many-coated Man* or in that former prose achievement of his, *A Rose for Winter*.

This precision implies a superb use of imagery. It is tempting to say that Mr. Lee cannot write a page without waylaying the reader with language richly fashioned and apposite. Does he want to figure a child's frightened reaction to something above him? "High overhead ran frenzied

---

An excerpt from *Cider with Rosie*

With our Mother, then, we made eight in that cottage and disposed of its three large floors. There was the huge white attic which ran the length of the house, where the girls slept on fat striped mattresses; an ancient, plaster-crumbling room whose sloping ceilings bulged like tent-cloths. The roof was so thin that rain and bats filtered through, and you could hear a bird land on the tiles. Mother and Tony shared a bedroom below; Jack, Harold and I the other. But the house, since its building, had been so patched and parcelled that it was now almost impossible to get to one's room without first passing through someone else's. So each night saw a procession of pallid ghosts, sleepily seeking their beds, till the candle-snuffed darkness laid us out in rows, filed away in our allotted sheets, while snores and whistles shook the old house like a roundabout getting up steam.

But our waking life, and our growing years, were for the most part spent in the kitchen, and until we married, or ran away, it was the common room we shared. Here we lived and fed in a family fug, not minding the little space, trod on each other like birds in a hole, elbowed our ways without spite, all talking at once or all silent at once, or crying against each other, but never I think feeling overcrowded, being as separate as notes in a scale.

That kitchen, worn by our boots and lives, was scruffy, warm and low, whose fuss of furniture seemed never the same but was shuffled around each day. A black grate crackled with coal and beech-twigs; towels toasted on the guard; the mantel was littered with fine old china, horse brasses and freak potatoes. On the floor were strips of muddy matting, the windows were choked with plants, the walls supported stopped clocks and calendars, and smoky fungus ran over the ceilings. There were also six tables of different sizes, some armchairs gapingly stuffed, boxes, stools and unravelling baskets, books and papers on every chair, a sofa for cats, a harmonium for coats, and a piano for dust and photographs. These were the shapes of our kitchen landscape, the rocks of our submarine life, each object worn smooth by our constant nuzzling, or encrusted by lively barnacles, relics of birthdays and dead relations, wrecks of furniture long since foundered, all silted deep by mother's newspapers which the years piled round on the floor.

Laurie Lee, in his Cider with Rosie, *The Hogarth Press, 1960.*

---

larks, screaming, as though the sky were tearing apart." Is the enmity of two old women, incapable of living together or away from each other, to be conveyed? "Like cold twin stars, linked but divided," he writes, "they survived by a mutual balance."

Informed with such notation, idyllic in thought and action, *The Edge of Day* adds up to an old-fashioned pastoral but one not untouched, as is to be expected, by contemporary understanding and irony.

William Maxwell   (review date 16 April 1960)

SOURCE: "Bright as a Windblown Lark," in *The New Yorker*, Vol. XXXVI, No. 9, April 16, 1960, pp. 172, 174, 177-78.

[*In the review below, Maxwell lauds Lee's portrait of family, neighbors, and village life in* The Edge of Day.]

The common reader will put up with absolutely anything, but how like getting a stock split or finding a four-leaf clover it is to read a book by a writer who has managed to separate the material that is his from everybody else's, whose style is an approximation of his own manner of speaking, and who with some courage lays his cards on the table. *The Edge of Day,* by Laurie Lee, meets all three of these requirements, and is beautiful besides, as one would expect the autobiography of a poet to be—beautiful, rich, full of stories, full of the humor that fountains from unsuppressed human beings, full of intelligence and point, full of damn near everything.

I have a fondness for first sentences, and the first sentences of this book are "I was set down from the carrier's cart at the age of three; and there with a sense of bewilderment and terror my life in the village began. The June grass, amongst which I stood, was taller than I was, and I wept. I had never been so close to grass before."

He was rescued by his three big sisters, who came scrambling and calling up the steep, rough bank and, parting the long grass, found him. "There, there, it's all right, don't you wail anymore," they said. "Come down 'ome and we'll stuff you with currants." It was the summer of the last year of the First World War, and 'ome turned out to be "a cottage that stood in a half-acre of garden on a steep bank above a lake; a cottage with three floors and a cellar and a treasure in the walls, with a pump and apple trees, syringa and strawberries, rooks in the chimneys, frogs in the cellar, mushrooms on the ceiling, and all for three and sixpence a week."

Shortly before this, his father, "a knowing, brisk, evasive man, the son and the grandson of sailors," had decamped, leaving his mother to bring up their four young children and four more by his first marriage—on what it would be an exaggeration to call a shoestring. But at least he didn't abandon them entirely; he sent them a few pounds a year, and though they were always hungry, they never quite starved, for the simple reason that they had neighbors. "See if Granny Trill's got a screw of tea—only ask her nicely, mind," his mother would say. Or "Run up to Miss Turk and try and borrow half-crown; I didn't know I'd got so low." And the child spoken to would say, "Ask our

Jack, our Mother! I borrowed the bacon. It's blummin'-well his turn now."

"Our Mother" is larger than life-size. She was descended from a long line of Cotswold farmers, and the village schoolmaster, finding that she had a good mind, lent her books and took considerable pains with her, until her mother fell sick and she was needed at home and her father put a stop to her education. At seventeen, wearing her best straw hat and carrying a rope-tied box, she went into domestic service and worked as a scullery maid, household maid, nursemaid, and parlormaid in the houses of the gentry—an experience that haunted her, because she saw luxuries and refinements she could never forget and to which, her son says, she in some ways naturally belonged. "Real gentry wouldn't hear of it," she would tell the children. "The gentry always do it like this"—with the result that they, too, were haunted by what she passed down to them. She had been more than pretty, and she was still a strong, healthy, vivid, impulsive woman. She was also extravagant and a dreadful manager.

> The rent . . . was only three shillings sixpence a week but we were often six months behind. There would be no meat at all from Monday to Saturday, then on Sunday a fabulous goose; no coal or new clothes for the whole of the winter, then she'd take us all to the theatre; Jack, with no boots, would be expensively photographed; a new bedroom suite would arrive; then we'd all be insured for thousands of pounds and the policies would lapse in a month. Suddenly the iron-frost of destitution would clamp down on the house, to be thawed only by another orgy of borrowing, while harsh things were said by our more sensible neighbours and people ran when they saw us coming.

Add to a love of finery unmade beds; add to her anger, which did not last, her gaiety, which was indestructible. To the old newspapers that were knee-deep all over the house add—in bottles, teapots, dishes, and jugs—all manner of leaves and flowers: roses, beach boughs, parsley, garlic, cornstalks. Add to her detailed knowledge of the family trees of all the Royal Houses of Europe her genuinely kind, genuinely compassionate heart. The bus driver is honking his horn and all the passengers are leaning out of the windows and shaking their umbrellas crossly, and a voice, sweet and gay, calls from down the bank, "I'm coming—yo-hoo! Just mislaid my gloves. Wait a second! I'm coming, my dears." She drove her children half crazy; she infected them with the wonder of life.

Here she is getting supper:

> Indoors, our Mother was cooking pancakes, her face aglow from the fire. There was a smell of sharp lemon and salty batter, and a burning hiss of oil. The kitchen was dark and convulsive with shadows, no lights had yet been lit. Flames leapt, subsided, corners woke and died, fires burned in a thousand brasses. "Poke round for the matches, dear boy," said Mother. "Damn me if I know where they got to."

Here she is with a sick child:

Then Mother would come carolling upstairs with my breakfast, bright as a wind-blown lark. "I've boiled you an egg, and made you a nice cup of cocoa. And cut you some lovely thin bread and butter."

And here she is in bed:

> My Mother, freed from her noisy day, would sleep like a happy child, humped in her night-dress, breathing innocently, and making soft drinking sounds in the pillow. In her flights of dream she held me close, like a parachute, to her back; or rolled and enclosed me with her great tired body so that I was snug as a mouse in a hayrick.

Though she bestrides the book, her largeness is not of the kind that results in somebody else's having to be small. The author says that there was no male authority in the house and that he and his brothers were dominated entirely by their mother and sisters, and yet he and the three other boys and every other man he writes about are thoroughly masculine. Somewhere, somehow, it all came out right.

They were not isolated. The stone house they lived in had once been a small manor house and was now divided into three cottages, in two of which lived two immensely old women who referred to each other spitefully as "Er-Down-Under" and "Er-Up-Atop" and lived only to outlive each other. One spent all her time making wine out of almost everything you can name, including parsnips. The other sat taking snuff and "biding still," and, if pressed, would take down the almanac and read about disasters to come, or tell the children about her father, who was a woodcutter and so strong he could lift a horse and wagon.

Gradually, little by little, the reader gets to know the people in other houses round about. The beautiful English landscape had a sufficient number of figures in it, and under the author's hand, one after another, they come to life. But not statically, not as set pieces or portraits, but as people who are being swept along in the current that flows only one way. Old people give up and die, children are picked up bodily, kicking and bawling, and carried off to school. The boys that were roaming the fields are lured under the hayrick and marry, all in good time, as trees come into leaf or shed their foliage, as plants come into flower. But not all of them, of course. For example, in the author's family there was another sister, who slipped away without warning when she was four years old, and every day of his mother's life she continued to grieve for and talk about that dead daughter, whose name is included, most touchingly, in the dedication of the book, among the living sisters and brothers.

The word I have been avoiding using all this time is "love." It is conveyed on virtually every page of this book. All kinds of love. And also, as might be expected of any place where love is amply present, murder and mayhem, fornication, incest, perversion, rape, suicide, grief, and madness. All of which the village managed in its own private way. Outsiders were not called in to punish or adjudicate, and when they came of their own accord, their questions were met by stares, and the information they sought after was given to every man, woman, and child of the village, in detail, so that they would know what it was they were to hide.

On the brighter side, here is the Parochial Church Tea and Annual Entertainment:

> The stage curtains parted to reveal the Squire, wearing a cloak and a deer-stalking hat. He cast his dim, wet eyes round the crowded room, then sighed and turned to go. Somebody whispered from behind the curtain. "Bless me!" said the Squire and came back.
>
> "The Parochial Church Tea!" he began, then paused. "Is with us again . . . I suggest. And Entertainment. Another year! Another year comes round! . . . When I see you all gathered together here—once more—when I see—when I think . . . And here you all are! When I see you here—as I'm sure you all are—once again . . . It comes to me, friends!—how time—how you—how all of us here—as it were . . ." His mustache was quivering, tears ran down his face, he groped for the curtains and left.
>
> His place was taken by the snow-haired vicar, who beamed weakly upon us all.
>
> "What is the smallest room in the world?" he asked.
>
> "A mushroom!" we bawled, without hesitation.
>
> "And the largest, may I ask?"
>
> "ROOM FOR IMPROVEMENT!"
>
> "You know it," he muttered crossly. Recovering himself, he folded his hands: "And now O bountiful Father . . ."

The motorcar brought all this to an end. The last days of the author's childhood were also the last days of the village, the end of a thousand years' life, in that remote valley:

> Myself, my family, my generation [Mr. Lee says] were born in a world of silence; a world of hard work and necessary patience, of backs bent to the ground, hands massaging crops, of waiting on weather and growth; of villages like ships in the empty landscapes and the long walking distances between them; of white narrow roads, rutted by hooves and cart wheels, innocent of oil or petrol, down which people passed rarely, and almost never for pleasure, and the horse was the fastest thing moving. Man and the horse were all the power we had—abetted by levers and pulleys. But the horse was king, and almost everything grew round him: fodder, smithies, stables, paddocks, distances and the rhythm of our days. . . .

Granted that one has to live in one's own Age or give up all contact with life; nevertheless, one puts this book aside not with nostalgia but with a kind of horror at what has happened. There was perhaps no stopping it, one thinks, and at the same time as one thinks that, one thinks that it should never have been allowed to happen, that our grandparents would not have put up with it—with the terrible, heartbreaking impoverishment that is not confined to a single village in a remote valley of the Cotswolds, or to any one country. It is all but general, and very few of us know, at first hand, anything else. Like a fatal disease, it has now got into the blood stream.

Peter Green   (review date 23 April 1960)

SOURCE: A review of *The Edge of Day,* in *The Saturday Review,* New York, Vol. XLIII, No. 17, April 23, 1960, pp. 45-6.

[*In the following review, Green characterizes* The Edge of Day *as a "memorable and heartwarming autobiography," briefly noting the volume's focus on village life and similarities to the work of Dylan Thomas.*]

Laurie Lee's *The Edge of Day* is a creamy Double Gloucester of an autobiography, "tasting of Flora and the country green," flavored with wit and poetry and Cotswold nostalgia. The author, who has played guitars in Andalusia in his time, here turns Pied Piper and leads us an enchanting dance up something that strongly resembles Dylan Thomas's *Fern Hill.* There's a lot of Thomas's verbal magic here, too, the same pristine delight in springtime passions and colorful rural eccentricity. Other parallels that at once spring to mind are Gerald Durrell's *My Family and Other Animals* (Mrs. Lee and her brood are even more idiosyncratic, if you can imagine such a thing) and John Moore's immortal trilogy about the same area, of which *Portrait of Elmbury* most resembles Mr. Lee's autobiography.

The Edge of Day is set in a village near Stroud, during and after the First World War. Somehow the steamroller of industrial development had spared the place long enough for young Laurie to catch an authentic whiff of the fast-dying past: "It was something we just had time to inherit, to inherit and dimly know—the blood and beliefs of generations who had been in this valley since the Stone Age." But by the end of the book, as the author's childish ego is unfolding in the trembling excitements of adolescence, the Stone Age has already given way to the Jazz Age. Feudalism is dying with the old squire, charabancs and motorbikes roar through the secluded valley. *The Edge of Day* shows us, with heartbreaking clarity, the price of progress.

There are the eccentrics with the wonderful Milk-Woodish names: Cabbage-Stump Charlie, Albert the Devil, Tusker Tom, and Emmanuel Twinning, who "made his own suits out of hospital blankets, and lived nearby with a horse." There are the grannies in the Wainscot: 'Er-Up-Atop and 'Er Down-under, who feuded all their lives and died within a fortnight of each other. There is the pre-Raphaelite Miss Fluck, who was a shade cracked and landed up in the village pond. Above all, there are the Lees themselves, six of them plus Mum (but Dad had levanted) all packed into a cottage "with three floors and a cellar and a treasure in the walls, with a pump and apple trees, syringa and strawberries, rooks in the chimneys, fogs in the cellar, mushrooms on the ceiling, and all for three and sixpence a week."

Still, all is by no means Mummerset bliss, with church outings offset by cider-and-sex under hay-wains. The village is tough and independent, meting out private justice, not above a little incest and murder, but at least (as Mr. Lee points out) sparing its teen-agers the cold horrors of police-court justice. All the same, there was a price to pay for Merrie England: in cold weather old people simply "curled up like salted snails" and died. Yet so magical is Mr. Lee's prose, so bursting with the raw stuff of life, that he almost convinces the reader it was worth it.

The Edge of Day itself would alone justify half a dozen certified cases of rural rape, murder, or what-have-you; it is the most memorable and heartwarming autobiography I have read in years.

Edward Weeks   (review date September 1969)

SOURCE: A review of *As I Walked Out One Midsummer Morning,* in *The Atlantic Monthly,* Vol. 224, No. 3, September, 1969, pp. 117-18.

[*Weeks is an American editor, memoirist, and nonfiction writer long associated with* The Atlantic Monthly. *In the following mixed review, he relates the events recorded in* As I Walked Out One Midsummer Morning.]

Laurie Lee was nineteen when on a June morning in 1935 after a hearty breakfast and a pat on the back from his mother, he walked away from his country home in the Cotswolds. He was propelled by the traditional forces that have sent so many younger sons out into the world, and the Depression had doubtless strengthened his resistance to the local girls, whispering "Marry and settle down." For his journey he carried a small rolled-up tent, a violin wrapped in a blanket, a change of clothes, a tin of treacle biscuits, and a hazel stick in hand. He planned to walk to London by way of Southampton so as to have his first look at the sea, and for sustenance he would fiddle his way through any hospitable town, his hat at his feet, with a couple of coppers in it *pour encourager les autres.* After London he would take ship for Spain, drawn there by boyhood fancies of Seville. He had already published some of his early pastoral poems and hoped to compose and sell others along the way. But the violin was to be his mainstay, and a bystander warned him not to play too long at any spot lest he lose his audience and the collection.

Mr. Lee's adventures compose a lighthearted, resourceful travel book, *As I Walked Out One Midsummer Morning,* and the hardihood with which he endured the heat, and when in the mountains, the cold, is a part of the picture. When in town he frequented the disreputable inns—or brothels—where he rarely paid more than a sixpence for a night's lodgings, and when in the open he slept in the fields, bathed in the nearest stream, and as the sun dried him, made a breakfast of goat cheese and berries. Walking, fiddling, or talking in the taverns, all of his senses were employed, including his sense of smell, and his figures of speech are sharp and delightful, as when he speaks of "tea so strong you could trot a mouse on it." The girls were generous to him; so was a professional beggar like Alf, who was "a tramp to his bones"; and a tavern keeper hearing his gay tunes kept Laurie playing for as long as he

chose to stay. In London he supported himself by working for a contractor, pushing "barrows of wet cement till my muscles stretched and burned." After he had got toughened up to the job and could use his evenings for something other than sleep, he found friends in the pubs, won a poetry contest, and in the early summer bought a one-way ticket to Vigo, with a handful of shillings to see him safely in Spain.

Laurie was to walk from one end of Spain to the other—"I'd accepted this country without question, as though visiting a half-mad family"—and his impressions are as fresh now as when they first hit him. Here is his first: "I landed in a town submerged by wet green sunlight and smelling of the waste of the sea. People lay sleeping in doorways, or sprawled on the ground, like bodies washed up by the tide." The medievalism, the garish colors, the sudden hospitality of the peasants and the equally sudden cruelty—he reacts to each in his disarming way. Valladolid, with its beggars, conscripts, and priests, he found a heartless place, and he has few good words for Segovia, with its Roman aqueduct and its blood-stained Cliff of Crows. But his spirits rose as he crossed the Sierra Guadarrama at a point almost two miles high ("Gulping the fine dry air and sniffing the pitch-pine mountain, I was perhaps never so alive and so alone again"). Madrid he enjoyed for its cool and succulent taverns; in Toledo he was befriended by Roy Campbell, the South African poet, and they spent hours together in El Greco's house; Cadiz he calls "a diseased hulk on the edge of a tropic sea"; and in Valdepeñas, where the wine was genial, he was happily at ease.

Lee holed up for the winter in an Andalusian village, where he became half of a two-piece orchestra in a seaside hotel. Here as an outsider he shared in the innocent hope and the fumbling beginning of the Spanish war. But it is never quite clear why he was so insistent on rejoining the Republican forces once he had been picked up and escorted to safety by a British destroyer. His year in Spain had fired his imagination, but his attachment to the people was less than skin-deep, nor had he a mistress to call him back. Why then did he return and what happened after his re-entry?

Charles Causley   (review date 26 September 1969)

SOURCE: "On the Fiddle," in *New Statesman,* Vol. 78, No. 2011, September 26, 1969, pp. 428-29.

[*An English educator, poet, translator, editor, dramatist, short story writer, and author of children's books, Causley has served as the vice-president of the Poetry Society of Great Britain. In the review below, he offers a mixed assessment of* As I Walked Out One Midsummer Morning.]

One evening at his house in the high sierras of Kensington, Roy Campbell told me of an encounter he and his wife once had with a street-musician in Toledo. The fiddler turned out to be not a German, as they'd supposed, but a young man from Gloucestershire walking across Spain with a knapsack and a violin wrapped in a blanket. The Campbells asked him how he was getting on. Fine, he replied with surprising alacrity. Except for the wild dogs that occasionally woke him, sniffing and howling round at night. 'He thought they were dogs!' roared Campbell, delightedly. Then, *pianissimo:* 'They were wolves, man.'

Whether they were or not is irrelevant. In any case, Laurie Lee in his *As I Walked Out One Midsummer Morning* doesn't mention the wolves in connection with Campbell, but merely says 'they may have been'. To Campbell, always extravagantly and imaginatively generous, they had to be: for the same reason that he proudly introduced young Lee to his Toledan friends as: 'A champion, this boy. Walked all the way from Vigo. He walks a thousand miles a week. It's true, by God . . . The funny thing is—he's English.'

Laurie Lee's portrait of the good, gentle, fundamentally shy and uncertain Campbell—a poet shamefully neglected at the moment—is one of the best things in this new volume of autobiography. The encounter between the two poets—one established, the other to be—was unplanned, casual: like Lee's journey from Slad to London and the Mediterranean.

As I Walked Out One Midsummer Morning is a recreation, after a gap of 30 years, of the sensations of late adolescence and early manhood. It's admittedly romantic, and the style is as juicily ripe as an autumn pear. There's a formidable, instant charm in the writing that genuinely makes it difficult to put the book down. (Conversely, some might find it difficult to pick up for a second reading in case the magic had flown.) Now and then one's conscious of a slightly overblown, Renoir-ish bloom on the text, an air of the extended set-piece, that comes dangerously close to choking the senses. But if there is a lot of sweetness, it's pure cane; not a trace of saccharin.

The book has the intensity, as well as the title, of a ballad. There's an undertone of menace as the story moves to the bloody climax of a community and a country exploding into Civil War. Mr Lee begins his journey as a political innocent; he ends it involved inextricably with a beautiful and sinister land, 'so backward and so long ignored . . . [where] . . . the nations of Europe were quietly gathering'.

As a self-portrait, it's a little muzzy: though perhaps this was the intention. Like many a clever peasant before him, Mr Lee doesn't give much of himself away; he remains peering from behind screens of glittering prose. Was he really the innocent he appears? One feels cheated, certainly, when our hero—crossing mountain and plain, hammered by hangovers and sunstroke, but never (apparently) diarrhoea or constipation—suddenly disappears into a post-office to see if there's any mail. Or, just as one gets used to him in an hotel attic, working as fiddler and odd-job man, he appears in the next chapter living in a room in the house of an unnamed expatriate English novelist. Sometimes, too, the observation seems slightly off-target. The characteristic smell of Gibraltar isn't, I'd say, that of provincial groceries. Cigar smoke, surely. And as an ex-Naafi busker myself, I've never heard of a song called 'Wales! Wales!' The title is 'The Land of My Fathers': a tune that Mr Lee rightly remarks will always call up its

supporters from a crowd. So, I hope, will this lollipop of an autobiography.

An excerpt from *As I Walked Out One Midsummer Morning*

Ever since childhood I'd imagined myself walking down a white dusty road through groves of orange trees to a city called Seville. This fantasy may have been induced by the Cotswold damp, or by something my mother had told me, but it was one of several such clichés which had brought me to Spain, and now as I approached the city on this autumn morning, it was as though I was simply following some old direction.

In fact there was no white road, not even a gold-clustered lemon tree, but Seville itself was dazzling—a creamy crustation of flower-banked houses fanning out from each bank of the river. The Moorish occupation had bequeathed the affection for water around which so many of even the poorest dwellings were built—a thousand miniature patios set with inexhaustible fountains which fell trickling upon ferns and leaves, each a nest of green repeated in endless variations around this theme of domestic oasis. Here the rippling of water replaced the coal fire of the north as a symbol of home and comfort, while its whispering presence, seen through grills and doorways, gave an impression of perpetual afternoon, each house turning its back on the blazing street outside to lie coiled around its moss-cool centre.

Seville was no paradise, even so. There was the customary squalor behind it—children and beggars sleeping out in the gutters under a coating of disease and filth. By day their condition seemed somewhat less intolerable, and they presented a jaunty face to the world. All were part of the city—the adored Seville—to which even the beggars claimed pride of belonging, and where ragged little girls would raise their thin brown arms and dance rapturously at the least excuse. It was a city of traditional *alegría,* where gaiety was almost a civic duty, something which rich and poor wore with arrogant finesse simply because the rest of Spain expected it. Like the Viennese, the Sevillanas lived under this burden of legend, and were forced into carefree excesses, compelled to flounce and swagger as the embodiment of Andalusia in spite of frequent attacks of liverish exhaustion. . . .

Seville in the morning was white and gold, the gold-lit river reflecting the Toro del Oro, with flashes of sun striking the Giralda Tower and the spires of the prostrate cathedral. The interior of the cathedral was a bronze half-light, a huge cavern of private penance, with an occasional old woman hobbling about on her knees, mumbling a string of prayers, or some transfixed girl standing in a posture of agony, arms stretched before the bleeding Christ.

Laurie Lee, in his As I Walked Out One Midsummer Morning, *Atheneum, 1969.*

The Times Literary Supplement **(review date 9 October 1969)**

SOURCE: "Fiddler's Eye View," in *The Times Literary Supplement,* No. 3528, October, 9, 1969, p. 1155.

[*In the following review, the critic favorably assesses* As I Walked Out One Midsummer Morning.]

Laurie Lee writes with such apparent ease that [*As I Walked Out One Midsummer Morning,* this] autobiographical sequel to *Cider with Rosie* may be discounted, by readers who think only those books good which are tough going, as merely a charming picaresque trifle. But it is a work of art the finer for appearing artless.

The nineteen-year-old Laurie Lee leaves his home in Stroud, Gloucestershire, to walk to London: a folk-hero like Dick Whittington, except that instead of a cat he has his fiddle, and he does not want to make his fortune, merely his mark as a poet. And on his journey a straight line is not the shortest distance between his point of departure and his goal. The journey is more important than the landfall. He takes weeks to wander to London, going first to Southampton to see the sea and try out his theory that a young man with a fiddle can play his way wheresoever he will.

That fact established, he knows that, provided he remains fancy free, he can see the world even in the mid-1930s when millions are unemployed and most of the footloose characters on the road with him are men who are desperately seeking work or resigned to never finding it. Gifted with youth, oodles of charm and an ability to live and sleep rough, he is invulnerable. At the time when J. B. Priestley was making his *English Journey,* that challenging report on the nation, Laurie Lee's journey to London was merely a poet's first term in the university of life. He landed in the metropolis with almost nu'ppence, but with an American sixteen-year-old girl-friend called Cleo, living with her parents, radical bums, in half a Victorian mansion on a building site on Putney Heath. Love found a way. Invited to stay with them, Laurie climbed up a ladder into Cleo's bedroom.

> As I slipped into her bed she rolled drowsily into my arms, then woke, and her body froze. "If Daddy knew about this, he'd murder you", she said. It was no idle figure of speech.
>
> Scrambling down the ladder in the dawn's early light, I realized that blood could be thicker than theory. Later, that day, Cleo's father got me a job with the builders, and gave me the address of some Putney lodgings. I don't know what she had told him, but he'd acted swiftly. It seemed a reasonable compromise between New Thought and the horsewhip.

Lee worked for a year as a builder's labourer building three blocks of hideous flats on Putney Heath, living part of the time in a brothel-café, part with an odd Irish landlady, always wide-eyed, wide-open to experience and getting good value for his adaptable charm. And then, the flats finished, he sailed for Vigo, with rucksack, blanket and fiddle to explore like George Borrow the strangeness of Spain, but without the burden of Bibles.

Spain is the main subject of this volume, a fiddler's eye view of the peninsula in that twilit period before the election of the Popular Front government, the Spain of glaring contrasts between the starving masses and the rich few, the desperation of beggary and the pride of wealth. Lee was not the first young English writer of the 1930s to walk through Spain; the author of *Marching Spain,* V. S. Pritchett, had preceded him. But Lee's picaresque counterpart was the Wandervögel, footloose young Germans wandering abroad now [that] Hitler was making youth march in step.

Topographically, young Lee moves zig-zaggedly south: Zamora, Toro, Valladolid, Segovia, Madrid, Toledo, Cadiz, Gibraltar, Malaga to Castillo. Spiritually it is a journey towards maturity and, as he finds at last, commitment. The victim by day of thirst and sunstroke, by night of *pulgas* and *chinches,* often as poor as the poorest, but not shackled to land and family, he is blown like tumbleweed by the winds of circumstance across the arid peninsula to the edge of the Middle Sea. And wherever he goes, his poet's eye catches what is vivid in man or nature. Stoically he endures his many downs, hedonistically he enjoys his ups. For a week he is a guest of Roy and Mary Campbell at Toledo, as delighted by the mytho-manic braggadocio of the boozy, blustering, gentle poet as by the Catholic evangelism of his beautiful wife.

The Campbells were all for *Cristo el Rey* and *Abajo el Socialismo!* But Laurie Lee, holed up for the winter as part-time help and hand in a struggling Swiss hotel in Castillo, found himself drawn irresistibly to the people whose only hope was that the *Frente Popular* government meant justice and freedom at last. He took a message up to Vallegas, a farmer in the mountains, that "potatoes" (handgrenades) would soon be coming.

> . . . although he'd made everything, he owned nothing here—40 years working the land for others. Tomorrow might be different, he said, squinting out of the window. Tomorrow, when the "potatoes" came.

The Civil War came and with it the senseless killing. Castillo, loyal to the Republic, was shelled by a Loyalist warship mistaking it for Altofaro, the Rebel-held village ten miles away. The first attack on Altofaro by the men of Castillo failed, because they forgot to take any ammunition, the second because they were not trained to fight.

When a British destroyer appeared to rescue British residents, Laurie Lee went aboard her and soon found himself back in Stroud, where a rich young lady was only too ready to abandon her husband and two children to marry him. But Laurie Lee was too embroiled with Spain to entangle himself with a woman and he was soon back, trying to volunteer for the International Brigade. Failing that, he walked over the Pyrenees, to a little farmhouse and knocked on the door.

> It was opened by a young man with a rifle who held up a lantern to my face. I noticed he was wearing the Republican armband.
>
> "I've come to join you", I said.

"Pase usted", he answered.

I was back in Spain, with a winter of war before me.

And there Mr. Lee leaves us, clamouring for more.

Julian Mitchell   (review date 12 October 1969)

SOURCE: "To Spain with a Violin and a Tin of Treacle Biscuits," in *The New York Times Book Review,* October 12, 1969, pp. 4-5.

[*Mitchell is an English novelist. In the following review, he expresses ambivalence for* As I Walked Out One Midsummer Morning.]

Readers of **The Edge of Day,** Laurie Lee's enchanting memoir of an English west-country childhood, may remember that it ends with the adolescent Laurie sitting on his bed, making up poems. Just about a generation later, an adolescent myself, I thought he was one of the great poets of our time. Lines like:

> Blown bubble-film of blue, the sky
>   wraps round
> Weeds of warm light whose every
>   root and rod
> Splutters with soapy green, and
>   all the world
> Sweats with the bead of summer in
>   its bud

made me dizzy with delight. The physical world seemed dew-bright on the page. Growing up only a village or two away from Lee, along the valley I liked to think inspired the poem, I could identify "Weeds of warm light" with real weeds in the real river Frome.

Brightness, alas, falls from the page, and though I still feel dizzy when I read **"April Rise,"** age has made me suspicious of dizziness, and I've even had doubts about my admiration for **The Edge of Day**—surely I'm biased by the pleasure of recognizing a childhood whose grasses and sky were the same as my own? Youth to that childhood, **As I Walked Out One Midsummer Morning** takes Laurie Lee to people and places quite unknown to me, but I still find it hard to come to a distanced, literary judgment about him. In fact, the book only confirms both my admiration and my doubts.

It's the story, at first, of a young man setting out from his Cotswold village in the mid-1930's, with nothing more than a violin and a tin of treacle biscuits. He wanders round England for a couple of chapters, then heads, on a whim, for Spain. There he scrapes his living, gets sunstruck and drunk, and meets other beggars and eccentrics—including the fiercely anglophobe South African poet Roy Campbell, who was kindness itself.

Much of this is very charming, though unrevealing, the violinist hiding himself behind dazzling cadenzas of similes and metaphors—"an impression of curried moonlight," a face the "color of crumpled pewter," "the patio wore an air of low-lit ennui." You can't open the book without finding at least one genuinely fine phrase, and there are

whole paragraphs of brilliance. He's superb on places—this is Madrid:

> It had a lion's breath, too; something fetid and spicy, mixed with straw and the decayed juices of meat. The Gran Via itself had a lion's roar, though inflated, like a circus animal's—wide, self-conscious and somewhat seedy, and lined with buildings like broken teeth.

No one, I think, will call that "the whimsical rot of the Thirties," to use another of his own fine phrases.

The doubts begin with his descriptions of people. He tells as little about others as he does about himself, and the characters are too often "characters." The dazzling prose sometimes positively obstructs insight, the arresting phrase stops one baffled in one's tracks. Roy Campbell, for instance, "had a long scorched face and the eyes of a burnt-out eagle." Since this was Toledo in summer, few male faces can have been unscorched for miles around; and what can "eyes like a burnt-out eagle" mean? He's usually so good at birds, too—there's nothing so vividly human as this is avian: "Kites and vultures turning slowly overhead, square-winged, like electric fans."

Of course one would happily settle for a young poet's finely written travel book, especially as the young poet is Laurie Lee, but it suddenly becomes something much more impressive. Lee has been carrying his marvelous descriptive gift about just like this violin—playing it merrily, watching the bright coins fall into his literary cap, but not getting down to any serious music. Then, with no warning, the Spanish Civil War is upon him, and the last 50 pages of the book contain a vivid and felt description of the hopes, fears, chaos and disasters of one small Spanish town as the war approaches, then dreadfully breaks. It all makes the notebook felicities of the poet, carefully honing his style, seem rather trivial.

He had holed up for the winter at Castillo, near Malaga, on what is now a thriving tourist coast, but which could then barely attract enough sardines to prevent the population's starving. There was, however, a Swiss hotel, where Lee formed an adaptable violin and accordion combo with the resident tout-gigolo, a Jewish boy from Cologne. The bar-man, less frivolously, was a revolutionary leader. The rain poured down, guests were few, and the Millennium was established over crude brandy.

Then the church and casino were burned. The empty villas of the rich were scrawled with hopeful signs: "Here Will Be the Nursery School," "Workers, Respect This House for Agricultural Science." But the town was divided against itself, a friendly destroyer shelled it by mistake, and an expedition to attack the neighboring town returned ignominiously—the troops had forgotten their ammunition. With the surreal clarity of a dream, Laurie Lee woke up one day to find himself being rescued by a British destroyer. "Shame to break up your holiday like this," said an officer.

All this is extremely well done, even if the intrusion of social and political reality into the aimless wanderings of a beggar-poet does upset the balance of the book—as well as save it from being merely brilliant. The similes and metaphors no longer dazzle, they illuminate; they can't be taken out of context and savored for their own sake like the earlier ones. The book ends with Lee's description of climbing the Pyrenees in midwinter on his way back into Spain to join the Civil War. The midsummer morning seems immeasurably far away. The boy has become a man. The phrase-maker has found something to write about.

Ronald Blythe (review date 20 November 1975)

SOURCE: "All the Best Countrymen," in *The Listener,* Vol. 94, November 20, 1975, p. 680.

[*Blythe is an English novelist, short story writer, and editor. In the following excerpt, he discusses* I Can't Stay Long.]

When Laurie Lee was 17, he strolled out of his Cotswold village and tramped to Spain. The village for him was first base, a privately marked spot he could return to without feelings of betrayal. *I Can't Stay Long* is a group of essays, some about the marked spot but most about his restless forays from it.

On the whole, he takes wide-eyed journeys to touristy places, yet manages to avoid the results of their easy accessibility. 'Tourism is just creating a third world, one that is neither at home nor abroad.' For a natural wanderer like Mr Lee, this middle road is purgatory, and much of his best writing in this unusual collection is inspired by his determination to bring back the old sense of foreigness and distance to such goals as Beirut, Cannes, Dublin, the Caribbean, Warsaw and the remote Spain of his teens.

Laurie Lee reveals an acceptance of the underlying, built-in solitude which accompanies him on these trips. He is friendly, but not involved, and is just looking around. Having the feeling that it hasn't happened if it hasn't been recorded, he notes all he can, writing the average traveloguer under the table in the process. He has a sharp country ear for catching the revelatory chance remark and, like all the best countrymen when far from home, he retains a passion for seeing the sights, whether they be in Gloucestershire or Tzintzuntzan.

Where he goes becomes part of him: 'In common with other writers I have written little that was not for the most part autobiographical. The fear for me is the fear of evaporation—erosion, amnesia, if you like—the fear that a whole decade may drift gently away and leave nothing but a salt-caked mud-flat.' Hence, then, this warm rich texture dyed in the old romance of roving. Even in his chapter on Paradise, which he hopes will incorporate a perfect urban-rural landscape in which city and village look into each other, Mr Lee asks for 'one exclusive indulgence—the power to take off as one does in dreams. . . .'

His urges to taste exile must now relate to the middle-aged compulsion to resavour youth. What prompted these take-offs in the first place?

> Young men don't leave a lush, creamy village life like mine solely for economic reasons. They do it to confound their elders, to show off, to prove their free will, and to win honours of the outside world—and they do it with the image al-

ways in their minds of returning one day, in the cool of the evening, to lay their trophies at the villagers' feet, and watch the old boys gasp.

Laurie Lee (essay date 1975)

SOURCE: "Writing Autobiography," in *I Can't Stay Long,* Atheneum, 1976, pp. 49-53.

[*In the essay below, originally written in 1975, Lee discusses the writing process particularly as it applies to autobiography.*]

Autobiography can be the laying to rest of ghosts as well as an ordering of the mind. But for me it is also a celebration of living and an attempt to hoard its sensations.

In common with other writers I have written little that was not for the most part autobiographical. The spur for me is the fear of evaporation—erosion, amnesia, if you like—the fear that a whole decade may drift gently away and leave nothing but a salt-caked mud-flat.

A wasting memory is not only a destroyer; it can deny one's very existence. A day unremembered is like a soul unborn, worse than if it had never been. What indeed was that summer if it is not recalled? That journey? That act of love? To whom did it happen if it has left you with nothing? Certainly not to you. So any bits of warm life preserved by the pen are trophies snatched from the dark, are branches of leaves fished out of the flood, are tiny arrests of mortality.

The urge to write may also be the fear of death—particularly with autobiography—the need to leave messages for those who come after, saying, 'I was here; I saw it too'. Then there are the other uses of autobiography, some less poignant than these assurances—exposure, confession, apologia, revenge, or even staking one's claim to a godhead. In writing my first volume of autobiography, *Cider with Rosie* (1959), I was moved by several of these needs, but the chief one was celebration: to praise the life I'd had and so preserve it, and to live again both the good and the bad.

My book was a recollection of early years set against the village background of my Cotswold upbringing. The end of my childhood also coincided by chance with the end of a rural tradition—a semi-feudal way of life which had endured for nine centuries, until war and the motor-car put an end to it. Technically the book was not so simple. It took two years, and was written three times. In remembering my life, even those first few years of it, I found the territory a maze of paths.

I was less interested, anyway, in giving a portrait of myself, than in recording the details of that small local world—a world whose last days I had seen fresh as a child and which no child may ever see again. It seemed to me that my own story would keep, whereas the story of the village would not, for its words, even as I listened, were being sung for the last time and were passing into perpetual silence.

The village was small, set in a half mile of valley, but the details of its life seemed enormous. The problem of compression was like dressing one tree with leaves chosen from all over the forest. As I sat down to write, in a small room in London, opening my mind to that time-distant place, I saw at first a great landscape darkly fogged by the years and thickly matted by rumour and legend. It was only gradually that memory began to stir, setting off flash-points like summer lightning, which illuminated for a moment some field or landmark, some ancient totem or neighbour's face.

Seizing these flares and flashes became a way of writing, episodic and momentarily revealing, to be used as small beacons to mark the peaks of the story and to accentuate the darkness of what was left out. So I began my tale where this light sparked brightest, close-up, at the age of three, when I was no taller than grass, and was an intimate of insects and knew the details of stones and chair-legs.

This part of the book was of course easiest. I had lived so near to it, with the world no larger than my legs could carry me and no more complex than my understanding. I ruled as king these early chapters. Then the book moved away from me—taking in first my family, then our house and the village, and finally the whole of the valley. I became at this stage less a character than a presence, a listening shadow, a moving finger, recording the flavours of the days, the ghosts of neighbours, the bits of winter, gossip, death.

If a book is to stand, one must first choose its shape—the house that the tale will inhabit. One lays out the rooms for the necessary chapters, then starts wondering about the furniture. The moment before writing is perhaps the most harrowing of all, pacing the empty rooms, knowing that what goes in there can belong nowhere else, yet not at all sure where to find it. There are roofless books in all of us, books without walls and books full of lumber. I realized quite soon, when writing my own, that I had enough furniture to fill a town.

The pains of selection became a daily concern, and progress was marked by what was left out. The flowing chatter of my sisters, for twelve years unstaunched, had to be distilled to a few dozen phrases—phrases, perhaps, which they had never quite uttered, but bearing the accents of all that they had. A chapter about life in my village school also required this type of compression. Here five thousand hours had to be reduced to fifteen minutes—in terms of reading time—and those fifteen minutes, without wearying the reader, must seem like five thousand hours. In another chapter, about our life at home, I describe a day that never happened. Perhaps a thousand days of that life each yielded a moment for the book—a posture, a movement, a tone—all singly true and belonging to each other, though never having been joined before.

> **The moment before writing is perhaps the most harrowing of all, pacing the empty rooms, knowing that what goes in there can belong nowhere else, yet not at all sure where to find it. There are roofless books in all of us, books without walls and books full of lumber. I realized quite soon, when writing my own, that I had enough furniture to fill a town.**
>
> **—Laurie Lee**

Which brings me to the question of truth, of fact, often raised about autobiography. If dates are wrong, can the book still be true? If facts err, can feelings be false? One would prefer to have truth both in fact and feeling (if either could ever be proved). And yet. . . . I remember recording some opinions held by my mother which she had announced during a family wedding. 'You got your mother all wrong,' complained an aunt. 'That wasn't at Edie's wedding, it was Ethel's.'

Ours is a period of writing particularly devoted to facts, to a fondness for data rather than divination, as though to possess the exact measurements of the Taj Mahal is somehow to possess its spirit. I read in a magazine recently a profile of Chicago whose every line was a froth of statistics. It gave me a vivid picture, not so much of the city, but of the author cramped in the archives.

In writing autobiography, especially one that looks back at childhood, the only truth is what you remember. No one else who was there can agree with you because he has his own version of what he saw. He also holds to a personal truth of himself, based on an indefatigable self-regard. One neighbour's reaction, after reading my book, sums up this double vision: 'You hit off old Tom to the life,' he said. 'But why d'you tell all those lies about me?'

Seven brothers and sisters shared my early years, and we lived on top of each other. If they all had written of those days, each account would have been different, and each one true. We saw the same events at different heights, at different levels of mood and hunger—one suppressing an incident as too much to bear, another building it large around him, each reflecting one world according to the temper of his day, his age, the chance heat of his blood. Recalling it differently, as we were bound to do, what was it, in fact, we saw? Which one among us has the truth of it now? And which one shall be the judge? The truth is, of course, that there is no pure truth, only the moody accounts of witnesses.

But perhaps the widest pitfall in autobiography is the writer's censorship of self. Unconscious or deliberate, it often releases an image of one who could never have lived. Flat, shadowy, prim and bloodless, it is a leaf pressed dry on the page, the surrogate chosen for public office so that the author might survive in secret.

With a few exceptions, the first person singular is one of the recurrent shams of literature—the faceless 'I', opaque and neuter, fruit of some failure between honesty and nerve. To be fair, one should not confine this failing to literature. One finds it in painting, too, whose centuries of self-portraits, deprecating and tense, are often as alike as brothers. This cipher no doubt is the 'I' of all of us, the only self that our skills can see.

For the writer, after all, it may be a necessary one, the one that works best on the page. An ego that takes up too much of a book can often wither the rest of it. Charles Dickens's narrators were often dry as wafers, but they compèred Gargantuan worlds. The autobiographer's self can be a transmitter of life that is larger than his own—though it is best that he should be shown taking part in that life and involved in its dirt and splendours. The dead stick 'I', like the staff of the maypole, can be the centre of the turning world, or it can be the electric needle that picks up and relays the thronging choirs of life around it.

A. T. Tolley   (essay date 1975)

SOURCE: "Newer Signatures," in his *The Poetry of the Thirties,* St. Martin's Press, 1975, pp. 356-73.

[*Tolley is an English educator, editor, and critic. In the following essay, he briefly assesses Lee's poetry.*]

Not every poet of the thirties had a book published during that decade or even appeared extensively in periodicals. Laurie Lee seems to have been writing poems for ten years before the publication of his first book, **The Sun My Monument,** in 1944. He was one of the poets—among them Dylan Thomas, David Gascoyne and Ruthven Todd—who appeared in the *Sunday Referee* poetry column around 1934. He spent some time in Spain before the Civil War, wandering from place to place and supporting himself by playing his violin.

> **The telling use of clear, sharp but slightly over-realised metaphor is the most noticeable characteristic of Lee's better poetry. Lee was, indeed, most effective as a poet of sensation. When he explored feelings that are intense or complex, his poetry tended to be conventionally rhetorical and emotionally somewhat strained.**
>
> **—A. T. Tolley**

While in Spain, he got to know the poetry of Lorca, whose influence seems to have been a congenial and enduring one in Lee's poetry. It shows in the use of traditional images that are simple and clear, almost to the point of quaintness:

Now I am still and spent

and lie in a whited sepulchre
breathing dead

but there will be
no lifting of the damp swathes
no return of blood
no rolling away the stone

till the cocks carve sharp
gold scars in the morning
and carry the stirring sun
and the early dust to my ears.

("Words Asleep", Andalucia, 1936)

The telling use of clear, sharp but slightly over-realised metaphor is the most noticeable characteristic of Lee's better poetry. Lee was, indeed, most effective as a poet of sensation. When he explored feelings that are intense or complex, his poetry tended to be conventionally rhetorical and emotionally somewhat strained.

Though Lee has published only a small amount of poetry in his whole career as a writer, he has remained throughout that career a poet of decided and engaging individuality. In addition, he is one of the few poets of the thirties of working-class background. He grew up in a cottage in the Cotswolds; and, after leaving home in the middle of the decade, supported himself by playing the violin in the streets and as a builder's labourer. Apart from having a poem published in the *Sunday Referee,* his sole contact with the literary world during this period was meeting Philip O'Connor. Reading Lee's poetry, one would hardly suspect his origins, and he certainly does not fit the role of the worker poet. Yet he is the only poet of any talent in the thirties to have had nothing but elementary education or to have come from a working-class home.

Laurie Lee with Nicole and Françoise Cavalerie (interview date January 1976)

SOURCE: An interview in *Caliban XIII,* n.s., Vol. XII, No. 1, January, 1976, pp. 149-60.

[*In the excerpted interview below, Lee discusses various topics, including life in the Cotswolds, his childhood, modern life, and the concept of literary style.*]

[*Nicole and Françoise Cavalerie*]: The Cotswolds.

[Lee]: My Mother's family have lived in the Cotswolds for six or seven hundred years. They were farmers and lived by the river Severn. Then they moved up into the hills. Some of my uncles were foresters, others horse-dealers, some coachmen. My Grandfather is my only authentic, physical link with the past (all the other stories I have heard derive from rumour or custom). He was a coachman at Berkeley Castle but at the end of his life was running a public house in Sheepscombe called "The Plough" which still stands there. He was a great man of the old tradition, with huge moustaches; all his sons were masters in their relationship to the countryside—and particularly to horses.

My forebears on my father's side came from a very small area of Dorset—the Thomas Hardy country. They were seamen and farmers, so my family had a double tradition of farming, but both sides came from counties in the West. If I could have chosen an environment to be born in or to spring from it would have been one of these two counties. But I am a mixture of these two incomparable areas: Gloucestershire and Dorsetshire, so I am very happy about it.

Slad.

I was born in Stroud and came to the village of Slad when I was three, staying here until I was nineteen. I had a feeling that this landscape was as the whole world was, because it was all I knew. I had not switched on electric light 'till I was sixteen; I had not spoken on the telephone till I was eighteen—both terrifying experiences. In my work I want to show how primitive life was: I spent so much of it collecting wood for the fire, trimming the wicks of lamps, making candles. So much of my life, instead of watching television, was spent in these elemental jobs every day just keeping life alive; but it was satisfying. To make light is satisfying, but just to switch on light is not.

When I was nineteen I left home to see the world but I came back all the time. I love travelling, but I always have to come back. There are only two places that I write about and they are similar: Spain and here.

Who is living in the village now?

People living in many parts of the Cotswolds are retired people, or people having a job somewhere else, in town. But where we live it is still a farming community. The country is still alive because it is centred round three or four farms.

They are big farms, aren't they?

Yes, they are quite big—they are all the same as in my childhood. Very much the same situation exists, the difference being that the people who used to work for the Squire now work in shops in Stroud.

The Squire used to have six gardeners—now he has to work for himself. When I was a child the bell used to ring every midday, which meant that the village stopped for its midday meal—the Squire, the men in the field stopped working. So we were a working community depending on the "Big House" and the farms. Now the village is broken up into little bourgeois units having quite good jobs in towns. But the farmers are still a reality, the land is still alive.

The whole of this valley is directed towards the village. You can watch the year's life, the primeval life of the farmers, being acted out from Winter to Summer.

Many of the beautiful villages which, in my youth, were occupied by carpenters, cobblers, grave-diggers, farm-labourers, are now occupied by retired people from town: but the land itself is alive. It is not industrialised, not over-mechanised. Every night in the pub up here, there are chaps who are still working on the land: they have the flush, brown faces which belong to the land. They use some tractors but there is no large-scale farming as in some other parts of England, where all the hedges are de-

> **London is the place where I can work because there is nothing to look at but car parks and supermarkets and traffic meters, so I stay in my room quite happily. London hasn't any mystery for me.**
>
> *—Laurie Lee*

stroyed and huge acreages are run like a factory. Here, the valley makes it too difficult, so we are lucky.

The Cotswolds themselves contain a variety of sceneries. This ridge is like a cliff of another county and the Severn is like a sea. It's strange to us, when we come down to Cheltenham; we feel we are going to another element, because up here we are in the hills. Not only is the landscape different, but the climate is different. I can imagine Cheltenham people once shivering with fear: "Who are they who live up on the hills; who are these dark, secret people?"

What about London?

I like being there, but it does not stimulate my imagination.

Can you write when you are there?

I can write there about somewhere else. London is the place where I can work because there is nothing to look at but car parks and supermarkets and traffic meters, so I stay in my room quite happily. London hasn't any mystery for me. Some people write about cities, great cities; they mean more to them: they are their background and what they consider to be civilisation. I can only write when I am thinking about the vast spaces of Spain, the villages, the peasants and this very pastoral life here. I am a pastoral; shall I say throw-back? I am old-fashioned; I do not accept cities. I find them monstrous but necessary. I am not even appalled by them to the extent of attacking them. They just don't move me; I use them like an apartment, a hotel-room. However, I do realise that 90% of literature today is written about the City.

Like Camus, who wrote the book called The Plague *that's placed in Oran.* [Cider with Rosie] *couldn't exist without the background of the city. It couldn't exist in a rural surrounding or a pastoral surrounding.*

Maybe this is why I am so out of step.

You said you were dissatisfied with the film. [The critics add in a footnote: "The shots of Cider with Rosie *were taken in the village in the autumn of 1970, as the film was to be shown on the television towards Christmas of the same year.] Do they not try to reproduce life as it was?*

I don't think they understand what the reality was. They are all city folk: very good at interpreting modern life, industrial areas. But when faced with the country they go into a kind of fantasy world; they have an idealised or theatrical idea of country life.

When they came to make the film there were five hundred people in the village, dressed up in what they thought were the clothes of the twenties—in fact, they were the clothes of the eighties or nineties. They were supposed to be village people, yet their clothes were spotless. We were peasants; some families were very poor and others were far more respectable, but we were a ragged lot. During the filming the girls wore pinafores: white, spotless; and the boys, new suits. To me this was a big mistake. I would prefer a little more reality. The film was meant to be the portrait of a village but it showed a lack of understanding of what our village was like.

Do you think they try to hide the truth?

I don't think they do; they are merely looking for something charming and sentimental. They think that country life was beautiful, wild, savage. Indeed, I experienced moments of euphoria and romantic happiness because I was young; but life was also quite cruel, with disease, poverty and hunger—just as it is recalled in **Cider with Rosie,** people dying, people committing suicide . . .

It was like any country society, life was not all pretty, but we had a sense of community.

I remember when my book came out; it was written from quite recent memories of mine and of my contemporaries, my brothers and sisters and my neighbours. All these people were shocked and cried: "Oh! you said we were ragged; that we were poor and we had dirty knees and we had fleas. Oh! we were respectable, we were not like that at all." But we were, because the school was closed three times because of the fleas. But they have forgotten, or they thought it was shameful to remember or to have it written down. My brother doesn't want to say we were poor because he has a car now. Well, we were poor since there were eight of us and we only had a pound a week to keep us. There was a cake once a week, and half a sausage (my brother had a half and I had another) on Sundays. Now children have cornflakes, grapefruit, egg, bacon, instant coffee and all that. But people don't want to remember the poor times.

The film makers got the idea that the country is charming, that I am a beautiful figure, and write about beautiful flowers and lovely landscapes. I am not a protester. I don't say how horrible everything is, and that it should be different. But this is how life is: sometimes it is marvellous and sometimes it is black and evil; I just accept it, since I know life is short. My sense of reality imposes on me the necessity of believing that this is all that I should ever have of this world which I love. . . .

Is it your philosophy of life: to enjoy every moment?

"Enjoy" if possible, but at least to appreciate intensively because life is passing all the time and it can never be recovered. If you have any desire to be immortal, the only possible way you can achieve it (if you are lucky) is to leave something behind you; not only children—they have their own lives, their own identity—but also contact with your mates so that they will remember you. For so long as they remember you, you are alive. If you have written something or painted something, people will remember you have lived.

Are you pleased with your success because it gives you an opportunity to be remembered? Is this the main reason?

Well, I don't believe anything is success. It is possible that I have communicated with some people, in **Cider with Rosie** for example, but, honestly, this is not why I did it. When I wrote it, it was in order to preserve a moment in time. I think my instinct, or my main motive, for writing was an attempt to catch something which I knew would pass for ever unless I caught it.

What is the part played by your friends?

I need them. I've always travelled alone and I realise that people are of supreme importance because I live through them. If you make friends you create something. If you lose friends you destroy something, I think to destroy a relationship is a crime. I do not believe in divorce because I think it is destructive. It destroys children, it destroys people's best memories. Every marriage has had good memories; divorce breaks them and everything that has happened before becomes polluted. So you have to preserve the best of life.

Imagination is the thing I would like to see preserved. In a way education destroys it. I don't think we should stay illiterate, but I know there is a certain sterile stage between complete illiteracy and a really cultivated mind. This middle region is a desert, because innocence has disappeared and you are just being given a non-education to destroy yourself.

—Laurie Lee

Are you faithful to your moral background?

I am faithful because I cannot imagine living anywhere else. This is the place—this valley. It is my birth-place and my death-place. This is where I belong.

Do you think people were happier when you were young?

Happiness is a kind of high peak of living which occurs but rarely.

When I was a boy there was no wireless, no television; the people used to come to their garden gates and talk to each other. And now on a bright, golden, summer evening the village is empty. There is nobody in the gardens, in the street, in the pub; they are all inside watching television—the television serial which, quite often, can be about country life.

People used to have more personal satisfactions. I think their sense of harmony with each other and with their environment, their community harmony, was deeper. Happiness is mere luck. You think you are happy, but it is not a constant state—it is just something you pass through, temporarily. When you say: "I am happy", you should say "I was happy".

People enjoyed satisfaction because they were living a kind of balanced life. They suffered, they were ill, children died very easily of no very important disease. But what we did have in those days was a community life. We did things together. What we don't have today is that feeling of shared experience, because like everyone else we seal ourselves off by entertainments, inside the house watching television; or if we go out we seal ourselves in isolation in motorcars. We drive in isolation to the sea, we look at the sea, and we drive back.

People have no contact, either with each other or with the land; I think this is one of the great losses we suffer.

Do you think it is possible to have this state of communion in our modern world?

Do you feel an outcast, or can you manage to be both?

I think the way technology is developing is isolating the members of the family one from the other. In the old days the family was a very closed community—its members were interdependent. It had to be or it was wrecked. Also the family was dependent on its neighbours very often—in time of trouble, and also of punishment, social punishment which had nothing to do with the police. If anyone committed a crime the community considered it a private matter. They punished him by ridicule, by physical punishment or by rejection. But the police would never, never be brought in, because they were not part of the community. They were authority—a kind of neutral authority which had no business to inquire into people's lives. There was a murder here when I was a child. The man who was murdered had broken a taboo; he deserved what he got. Many of the villagers did not really approve of the extreme punishment he received—he was not meant to be killed, but he died because of his injuries. Everybody knew who was responsible for his death, and yet, despite the fact that the police came and came again for ten years, nobody ever betrayed the true facts to them.

But today, if this happened, people would immediately telephone the police . . . We don't belong to each other any more. Technology and, I suppose, education are means to get away from each other, to seal ourselves off from each other. This is partly a result of the population explosion—there are more people but less communication.

Do you think it is a sign of decay?

I think anything which tends to fragment what was once unity is bound to be a sign of decay. The only things we can look to with optimism are forces which tend to unite us and to make a community feeling stronger. And that includes not only this valley and its neighbours but also the country and its neighbours, one continent and another continent.

I am depressed because of the return of petty nationalisms, which is a sign of fragmentation. This has grown up since the war. Once, we lived in small communities which did not understand each other's dialects because physically we were separated. Now, subconsciously, we are separating ourselves. The Welsh say: "We must have more difference; we must have our Welsh language; we don't accept being British". The Scots say the same. But you can preserve the uniqueness and also share a common good. I think that this separation is symptomatic of the social decay of a world which has all the possibilities of becoming unified.

As a country develops, this sense of community disappears.

Do you have a sense of family?

Yes, we have. I like that because it doesn't happen any more here. Even in the country the young are leaving their family. The disintegration of families is due to, shall we say, material progress. When I was fourteen I earned five shillings a week. Well, I could not have a motorbike with that money and go to the big Pop Festival—I had to stay here. When I was nineteen I received fifteen shillings a week. It was still not enough—so, the only way to escape (not because of a quarrel but because of a natural urge to see the world) was to live on the road like a vagabond and play the violin to earn some more money. I was able to get away but many children could not or would not do as I did.

There was another link: religion. I think it helps, but in this country we have very little religious unity in the family now.

This separation has been accentuated by the gadget of television and the gadget of the discotheque from which no imaginative satisfaction is derived because no one is involved; they are purely passive. When the old father is watching television and the children are at the discotheque, they are yielding to the technological gadgets of isolation. They are not creative, they haven't learnt anything, they have merely bought a gadget and paid for it. Parents and children have formed no community. Watching television is not like going to the theatre; it is second-rate, passive: it is an isolation.

But in many other ways I can't help feeling that life is better now because the wives have been relieved of long centuries of drudgery, they have a better chance to be women.

Yes, but having more time people must be able to use that time and nothing is prepared to help them.

This is the major problem, the major dilemma of modern society. As leisure is increasing boredom is increasing, and boredom is destructive. Life is destroyed, time is wasted in trivial occupations which are imposed by commercial interests.

An art teacher at the Ladies' College and at the Secondary Modern School at the same time is facing this problem. From the girls of the Ladies' College he can't get really anything because he says they have lost their creative power, because they have been taught what to do and what to say and they don't know how to use their imagination. Whereas the girls from the Secondary Modern School are more primitive in some ways and more inclined to use their imagination.

> **My aim in writing was to celebrate myself and the fact of being alive. I haven't written novels, romances, but I have written about the life that I lived and I loved.**
>
> **—Laurie Lee**

Yes, imagination is the thing I would like to see preserved. In a way education destroys it. I don't think we should stay illiterate, but I know there is a certain sterile stage between complete illiteracy and a really cultivated mind. This middle region is a desert, because innocence has disappeared and you are just being given a non-education to destroy yourself. And indeed, if you are not educated at all you don't have access to all the trivial information; you are primitive but you still have a sense of wonder. Your own natural vocabulary may be limited but it has not been destroyed by journalistic influences, trivial mass media influences. Working men have been given a key to find in the Daily Mirror the golden places of the world blocked by the capitalist news operators. This may be tragic but I don't despair; I accept the modern world.

Style.

Virginia Woolf was a pure stylist. I wish I could read French because I would like to read Proust. There are good translations but it is not the same. Virginia Woolf had this attention to the complex line, the subtlety of inner life.

James Joyce was the Supreme innovator, the one who got caught in a swamp of his own creating, so there is no way forward, there is no way to develop, he is a phenomenon, an isolated phenomenon from which no one really can grow.

Why is that so?

Because he finished himself in *Finnegans Wake*. He wrote great short stories and *Ulysses* is a great book, but in *Finnegans Wake* he took his power of innovation to such extremes that he almost broke himself with verbal eccentricities.

Do you think it's style for style's sake?

No, I think style must say something and style is the machine; if you're going to fly in the upper air you have to design something that will take you there securely and with the power to stay aloft, to survive these rarefied visions. If the style is bad, you collapse and not only do you collapse but you have no means of communication. Style allows you to move into a world of your own but also allows you to communicate with the reader. If you ignore style, if you want to be idiomatic or colloquial, you suddenly find that in ten years you are old-fashioned.

Doesn't it reflect Modern Times?

Yes, I quite agree, but you see I am self-educated. My aim in writing was to celebrate myself and the fact of being alive. I haven't written novels, romances, but I have written about the life that I lived and I loved; so I feel the intensity, the extraordinary chance of being alive since I have no sense of immortality: I have no religious consolations. So all I can do is to celebrate (not in a religious way, in my own way) being alive. In order to celebrate it, I have to tell other people about it. This is how it was to me. My intention is to say "look, listen, it was like this". If I have any style, it's because I am trying to find always the right words—the words that cut into the other person's consciousness. That's why I write and re-write all the time. It is not easy. But it is the only thing I like to do.

Do you think of the person who is going to read your book?

Yes—I always have some people in my mind when I write, I think that "she", or "he" or "they" would be interested, or they would like this, or they would laugh. But I couldn't write about an abstraction, it's always about some living person or place.

Were you disappointed when your family reacted as they did?

Well, I was surprised. **Cider with Rosie** was written with my family in mind, and the neighbours. I chose to write about this little valley because I thought the neighbours, for example, would like that particular joke or incident, or be reminded of that particular day. It was not nostalgia, an escape; it was a *re-creation* of an intensity of life. I was trying to maintain a level of intensity. My sisters have forgiven me now, but they were shocked at first: "You shouldn't tell these things, it was a family secret that we were poor, that we hadn't anything to wear." It was not a family secret; living in a village, you know everybody's secret and they know yours.

What was your reaction after the success of **Cider with Rosie**?

When I was writing it, I had *some* people in mind. What astonished me was that this little story of a small village society seemed to have significance for *many* people. In fact what I did not know was that I was writing about not only a way of life but about many other people's lives—a time which should remind many people of their youth, of their past and roots, and also of certain inherited traditions which I knew and they knew and which was passing away.

Sylvia Secker   (review date 30 January 1976)

SOURCE: "Writer on the Move," in *The Times Literary Supplement,* No. 3855, January 30, 1976, p. 102.

[*In the following review, Secker offers a mixed appraisal of* I Can't Stay Long.]

Laurie Lee describes *I Can't Stay Long* as "on the whole a scrapbook of first loves and obsessions". He also records that some of the essays were written as long ago as twenty or thirty years. This no doubt accounts for the unevenness of the whole. In the [piece] called **"Love,"** for instance one has a curious sense of *déja vu*. This is written in what seems in places a modernized version of the style of Rom Landau, who used the same high-flown language, and who was much admired in the 1930s by one's maiden aunts. Here is Mr Lee: "Love approves, allows and liberates, and is not a course of moral correction, nor a penitential brainwash or a psychiatrist's couch, but a warm-blooded acceptance of what one is." There is, too, a slickness which sets the teeth on edge. In the same essay he writes of the "drug-fix of pop music (with its electronically erected virility)". Turning to the publisher's note at this point I read that some of these pieces have not appeared before except in the United States, which goes a long way to explaining the above but does not excuse it.

Yet when Lee drops his purple mantle he can write with a vivid, spare imagery that makes one realize how closely allied are the eyes of the poet and the painter: "the bright-backed cows standing along the dykes like old china arranged on shelves"; "motionless canals, full of silver light, lap the houses like baths of mercury". One is no longer reading but looking at the work of an old Dutch master, for it is of Holland that Mr Lee is writing. **"The Village That Lost Its Children"**, an account of the Aberfan disaster, is journalism at its best, factual and again vivid, the emotion directly conveyed through the words of the people of Aberfan. **"Hills of Tuscany"** is permeated with the heat and scents of the Italian countryside, and the evocation is such that the reader feels himself to be walking those fifty miles from Florence to Siena, drinking the black wine of Strada-in-Chianti, eating bread and fruit beside a valley stream and gratefully feeling its chill waters on his aching feet.

The genesis of *Cider with Rosie* is to be found in **"Writing Autobiography"**, beside Mr Lee's thoughts in general on this hazardous occupation. While allowing that there are many reasons for embarking on such a project, and were in his own case, he sees it mainly as an act of celebration and preservation. As to what is truth where autobiography is concerned, it is—for him—what you remember, with the rider that there is no pure truth, "only the moody account of witnesses". Which serves as a very precise description of *I Can't Stay Long,* which has however the added interest of showing the progress of the writer as writer over a span of some thirty years.

Robert Nye   (review date 6 April 1976)

SOURCE: "Laurie Lee's Poetry: English, Clean and—Well—Nice," in *The Christian Science Monitor,* April 6, 1976, p. 27.

[*Nye is a poet, critic, and essayist who lives in Scotland. In the review of* I Can't Stay Long *below, he notes that the most effective pieces in the collection revisit Lee's childhood and travels.*]

Laurie Lee is an underestimated English poet. He is underestimated because he has never gone out of his way to advertise himself or his work. Norman Cameron—another neglected poet—used to say of Mr. Lee that even when he wasn't very good, he was always clean. Mr. Lee's work, in verse and prose, speaks of a certain purity preserved or achieved at some cost in both eye and heart. He is also a generous and a good-humored writer.

Put all these qualities together, of course, and you have *Cider With Rosie* (1959), his masterpiece, that evocation of an English childhood now gone for ever, where a rare skill finds images to match a spirit of innocence and its evanescence.

I Can't Stay Long consists of all the occasional writings that he cares to preserve. He has put it together, he tells us, "partly as a means of clearing the barnacled chaos of my room but also as a way of revisting dimly remembered experiences and exercises." The volume contains pieces written over a period of 30 years. The author informs us that what they have in common is a "confident enthusiasm and unabashed celebration of the obvious."

With these credentials, you might expect *I Can't Stay Long* to be a slight book. It is partly so. Little in it is deeply thought or felt through—with the possible exception of an essay on the disaster of Aberfan, where many schoolchildren were killed in Wales when a slag heap slipped down the hill onto a little mining town. This piece sits uneasily amongst the others. I have mixed feelings about it. I cannot doubt the sincerity of Mr. Lee's response to the tragedy, but what I respect most is his feeling that nothing that he can say about it will do any good.

> Mr. Lee's work, in verse and prose, speaks of a certain purity preserved or achieved at some cost in both eye and heart. He is also a generous and a good-humored writer.
>
> —*Robert Nye*

In the circumstances, it might have been better to say nothing, and to have left it out of what is otherwise a very nice book, a very charming book, a scrapbook of things noticed and mostly loved by a poet. Nice is perhaps an appalling word, but it suits Mr. Lee. There is a niceness in him both in the old sense of being minutely and delicately precise, and in the modern colloquial sense of being agreeable. It shines through these pieces.

The first section revisits the days of *Cider With Rosie,* Mr. Lee's childhood in West Country England, in a village where there were no regular newspapers and of course no radio or television. "Such was my background," he declares, "and in some ways it still rules me." He celebrates the inheritance of an oral tradition of language, where the only literary influence came from the King James translation of the Bible. "I am made uneasy by any form of writing which cannot readily be spoken aloud."

The second section—dealing with abstractions, Love, Appetite, Charm, and so forth—is less immediately appealing. I had the feeling that Mr. Lee was straining to find something to say. I do not believe that this strain comes from Mr. Lee feeling ashamed of being obvious, but I could believe that it came from his feeling ashamed of having to write on subjects where it would be dishonest not to be obvious. His heart is in these essays, but it moves about uneasily amid the abstractions.

Part Three, I am glad to say, is quite a different kettle of fish. Indeed, it is several kettles of fish, all rather exotic, for here Mr. Lee has collected descriptions of places he has visited. In the Thirties, at a time when he was completely unknown save for a handful of poems published in periodicals, he wandered off to Spain with a violin for company, and picked up a living drifting from here to there and playing for his supper. In the present essays, he takes us with him in a similar spirit to Tuscany, to Mexico, and to Warsaw, Ibezia, and Ireland. Nowadays, instead of fidding for his supper, he writes essays that orchestrate his reminiscences and impressions. The effect is just as joyful as the fiddle music must have been.

Derek Stanford (review date August 1983)

SOURCE: A review of *Selected Poems*, in *Books and Bookmen*, No. 335, August, 1983, p. 28.

[*A fellow of England's Royal Society of Literature, Stanford is an English educator, poet, and critic who has frequently written about Muriel Spark, Christopher Fry, and Emily and Anne Brontë. In the review below, he offers praise for Lee's* Selected Poems, *noting the volume's nostalgic tone and subject matter.*]

Some of the purest poetry of sensuous perception that has been written this century comes from the pen of Laurie Lee whose ***Selected Poems*** are a pot-pourri of intense, yet almost antiquated, sweetness.

It is more detailed, less fantasticated, than the world of childhood which Dylan Thomas created in 'Fern Hill'. Thomas' was a retrospective vision (with all the nostalgia [of] time's passing occasions). Mr Lee, at his happiest, creates a sort of perennial immediacy—though it is one of myth fed by the present rather than realism, raw, refined or simple. Thus, he writes of the **'Village of Winter Carols'**:

> Village of winter carols
> and gaudy spinning tops,
> of green-handed walnuts
> and games in the moon.

Nostalgia is stated in a Foreword in which the poet tells us that these verses were "written by someone I once was and who is so distant to me now that I scarcely recognize him any more."

There is little here I can fault, though I do not like the italicised archaism in the second line—

> Fish and small birds
> do strike with diamond mouths

—which I would re-write "strike with their diamond mouths."

Most of the Imagist Movement poems dealt with urban or literary themes. I like to think of the spirits of Aldington, Flint and H.D. contemplating their rural inheritor.

An excerpt from *A Moment of War*

Once the planes had gone, there was little to be heard but the crackling of flames and the distant bells of a fire-engine. I was joined by two of my companions from the train, both silent, both fresh to this, as I was. A railway-man crossed the lines, groping about, bent double. We asked him if he was all right, and he said yes, but he needed help. He shone a torch on his left hand, which was smashed and bleeding, then jerked his head in the direction of the nearby street. We ran round the edge of the burning warehouse and found two little houses, also well alight. They were small working-class shops, blazing tents of tiles and beams from beneath which came an old man's cry.

'My uncle,' said the railwayman, tearing away at the smoking rubble with his one undamaged hand. 'I told him to sleep in the cinema.' The roofs collapsed suddenly, sending a skirt of sparks riffling across the road. The old man's cries ceased, and we staggered back while great curling flames took over. 'The fault is his,' said the railwayman. 'He would have been safe in the cine. He used to go there every afternoon.' He stood doubled up, staring furiously at the blazing ruin, his clothes smoking, his hands hanging black and helpless.

Walking back towards the station, we stumbled over a figure on the pavement, lying powdered white, like a dying crusader. His face and body were covered in plaster dust, and he shook violently from head to toe. We rolled him on to a couple of boards and carried him to the main platform, where several other bodies were already spread out in rows. A moaning woman held a broken child in her arms; two others lay clasped together in silence, while a bearded doctor, in a dingy white coat, just wandered up and down the platform blaspheming.

It was a small, brief horror imposed on the sleeping citizens of Valencia, and one so slight and routine, compared with what was happening elsewhere in Spain, as to be scarcely worth recording. Those few minutes' bombing I'd witnessed were simply an early essay in a new kind of warfare, soon to be known—and accepted—throughout the world.

Few acknowledged at the time that it was General Franco, the Supreme Patriot and Defender of the Christian Faith, who allowed these first trial-runs to be inflicted on the bodies of his countrymen, and who delivered up vast areas of Spain to be the living testing-grounds for Hitler's new bomber-squadrons, culminating in the annihilation of the ancient city of Guernica.

Laurie Lee, in his A Moment of War, *Viking, 1991.*

Angela Huth (review date 8 December 1983)

SOURCE: "Snake-bites of Farewell," in *The Listener*, Vol. 110, No. 2836, December 8, 1983, pp. 30-1.

[*Huth is an English novelist, playwright, journalist, critic, short story writer, and author of children's books. In the re-*

view below, she commends Lee for his ability to movingly combine photographs and text in Two Women, *an homage to his wife and daughter.*]

Two Women is a tribute by Laurie Lee to the most important forces in his life: his wife and daughter. It is primarily a picture book, revealing the author to be as magical a photographer as he is spinner of elegiac words. Mr Lee dismissively refers to his pictures as 'faded snapshots' he found shut away in a drawer. Assembled together (in beautiful layouts by Willie Landels) they evoke all the wonder of anyone's photograph album—how very quickly the past becomes amazing, funny, moving. But the quality of the photographs is far from that of the average album snapshot. With the instrument of his camera, as with his pen, Laurie Lee has the talent of capturing the essence of moments, so that years later it is that essence, rather than the reality, that still shines forth, pinned unfadingly there for ever like a pressed butterfly.

But the enchanted pictures of wife and daughter in Gloucestershire, for all their spirit, are not, you realise, the work of a professional. There is no cool calculation behind them. You cannot conceive that Laurie Lee has been fussing about with a light meter, suggesting that Cathy and Jessy move a bit this way or that. The composition is unstudied, often working brilliantly by chance. There's a preponderance of backlighting, so that hair dissolves to halos: out-of-focus flowers and grasses crowd many a foreground. Such softening devices, as the young Beaton discovered, lend charm to almost any subject. But in Laurie Lee's case it is hard to imagine that any such thoughts occurred to him as he pointed his camera: he probably would not call himself a photographer at all. The point is, he was there, recording private moments of mother and daughter through the years, along with fragments of rain, sun, icicles at windows, all trembling with those incandescent colours that are the ingredients of nostalgia to all who love the English countryside.

The text that accompanies the photographs is brief. It is the story of how Laurie Lee met his wife, daughter of a French fisherman, when she was a 'stumpy, wriggly, golden-curled little girl of five'. Picking him out of a crowd of friends, she sat on his knee, flattering him with her attentions. 'I don't know who she thought I was,' he writes, 'this crumpled 22-year-old stranger—but it was then, she swears, she decided to marry me.'

Twelve years later they began their life together, penniless, pigs' liver on toast, in an Earl's Court flat. Cathy, 'acquiescent and radiant', had by now become the sort of beauty who would have captivated Augustus John: fine eyes, sharp nose, bewitching mouth set in heart-shaped bones and undulating golden hair—all, later, inherited by her daughter. Laurie Lee remembers the 'locked-up London feeling we shared at the time . . . the seasons creaking themselves irrelevantly over the rooftops. . . . The need to go back to the west grew steadily stronger.' The move was made possible by the success of *Cider with Rosie*. Suddenly they were rich. To Gloucestershire they sped, the village of Laurie Lee's childhood. There, after 12 years of marriage, occurred 'just an ordinary miracle'—the birth of their daughter Jessy.

Laurie Lee, full of wonder, watched mother and daughter 'continuously, in their changing phases', starting with 'the child in the evening carried round like a candle illuminating her mother's face', to the moment of 'sad enchantment of seeing something about to take wing'. In recording what he saw and felt the author has dared to tread dangerous ground. The traps of sentimentality, and the smugness of nostalgia, await all those who venture to recall private, loving worlds. Mr Lee has avoided such pitfalls by ruthless compression. There is so much he has left unsaid: and yet, by just touching upon joys, fears, hopes, regrets, we can visualise the whole essence, again, of those abundant years. And although his book is a homage to peace and happiness, it is not a comfortable book. There lurks an edge of unease. He recognised he was 'merely the temporary keeper' of his daughter's helplessness: he is aware of ever-threatening endings. 'All love lives by slowly moving towards its end,' he says, 'and is sharpened by the snakebites of farewell within it.'

Brian Finney   (essay date 1985)

SOURCE: "Childhood," in his *The Inner I: British Literary Autobiography of the Twentieth Century,* Oxford University Press, 1985, pp. 117-37.

[*In the following excerpt, Finney discusses* Cider with Rosie *from a Jungian perspective, suggesting that Lee is* "attempting to describe the evolution of his individual psyche by relating it to . . . archetypal images."]

[Like Herbert Read, author of the autobiographical *The Innocent Eye,* Laurie] Lee sees his childhood as an idyll of the past to which he returns in memory for refreshment and renewal. Although longer, *Cider With Rosie* (1959) has the same air of simplicity verging on naivety which mirrors the child's vision of life. Yet [in his essay '**Writing Autobiography**' from *I Can't Stay Long*] he has subsequently written of its technical complexity. The book occupied him for two years and was written three times. For a start there was the whole problem of compression which brought him face to face with the question of autobiographical veracity. He found that in writing a childhood autobiography 'the only truth is what you remember'. Armed with the conviction that 'there is no pure truth', he found the confidence to distil his sisters' conversations over a period of twelve years to a few dozen phrases, five thousand hours at the village school into fifteen minutes' reading time, and a thousand days into 'a day that never happened' in '**The Kitchen**', although every incident in it happened on one of those thousand days.

The shape of the book was dictated largely by his purpose in writing it, 'to praise the life I'd had and so preserve it, and to live again both the good and the bad'. Lee was convinced that the end of his childhood 'also coincided by chance with the end of a rural tradition—a semi-feudal way of life which had endured for nine centuries, until war and the motor car put an end to it'. So he planned the book to start with the dawn of his childhood consciousness and gradually to widen its interest to include first his family, then Slad, the village in the Cotswolds where he spent his childhood, and finally the whole Gloucestershire valley in which Slad is situated. This may sound like the progressive abandonment of subjective for some kind of topographical autobiography. But Lee is well aware of the danger of allowing the autobiographical protagonist to become too much of a ghostly presence: 'The autobiographer's self can be a transmitter of life that is larger than his own—though it is best that he should be shown taking part in that life and involved in its dirt and splendours'. So the book ends on a personal note with an account of his first sexual experience with a girl, the Rosie of the title, and with his new adolescent sense of isolation as his horizons broaden beyond the confines of the valley. By ending on this note he anticipates his departure from home at the age of 19, a departure which he vividly describes in his second volume of autobiography, *As I Walked Out One Midsummer Morning* (1969).

Both these factors, compression and form, add a representative, more-than-personal element to Lee's portrait of his childhood which has helped to make the book a bestseller. *Cider with Rosie* is a celebration of the life of nature into which Lee was plunged as a child of three. It relates his early history to the history of the human race. His childhood begins with the experience of primeval man and ends with that of modern man living in a technological society. Deposited at the opening of the book into June grass taller than his three-year-old self, he is terrified by the experience of being lost amidst the seemingly primeval vegetation, 'thick as a forest' in which 'a tropic heat oozed up from the ground, rank with sharp odours'. For the first time in his life he finds himself cut off from the sight of other humans. The howl of terror that he lets out is like the cry of a newborn baby. This second birth that he experiences at the beginning of the book is into consciousness especially of the natural world of the countryside in which he is to spend his childhood. He and his family 'were washed up in a new land' which he sets out to explore, 'moving through unfathomable oceans like a South Sea savage island-hopping across the Pacific'. The images Lee uses are insistent in the parallels they draw between early man's experience of life on earth and his own childish exploration of his home and the surrounding countryside which he scarcely left up to the age of nineteen.

It is as if Lee were attempting to describe the evolution of his individual psyche by relating it to those archetypal images which according to Jung we inherit at birth. Jung argues that they constitute a form of racial memory which at the deepest level of the unconscious merges our unique experience with that of collective mankind. 'Childhood is important', Jung wrote late in life, 'because this is the time when, terrifying or encouraging, those far-seeing dreams and images appear before the soul of the child, shaping his whole destiny, as well as those retrospective intuitions which reach far back beyond the range of childhood experience into the life of our ancestors.' For the youthful Lee, the writer-to-be, those images connecting him to the beginnings of civilization are also destined to become the substance of his art and the basis for his essentially pastoral vision of life. Beginning with the landscape of his kitchen, he traces the way in which his childhood horizons gradually widen through exploration and experience. The outside world first manifests itself 'though magic and fear'

to this small boy who shares his 'wordless nights' with his mother in one bed. His heartbeats sound to him like the marching of demons and monsters. Old men live in the walls and floors of the house. The family is terrorized by Jones's goat, 'a beast of ancient dream', 'old as a god'. The village 'cast up beasts and spirits as casually as human beings'. During his first years in Slad Lee experiences the terrors of primitive man. When they experience a drought 'old folk said the sun had slipped in its course and that we should all of us very soon die', a superstitious fear given widespread religious sanction in ancient civilizations from Egypt to Peru. With the end of the drought 'terror, the old terror, had come again', in the form of torrential rain threatening to invade the family home. Terror is personified in the hysterical reactions of his mother whom he subsequently came to realize was exaggerating the situation out of all proportion to its danger. But by the time he had acquired this insight he had also inherited her primitive fear of heavy rain, a good instance of the power that experience during childhood holds over the thinking and reflecting adult.

Lee celebrates his childhood, despite its fears and terrors, as something shared with earlier civilization. The continuing link is nature which he animates and reveres. Repeatedly he employs language to show how he and his fellow villagers merge into the natural rhythm of life.

—Brian Finney

Lee's images of primeval life occur most frequently in the earlier part of the book. The valley, he writes, had 'been gouged from the Escarpment by the melting ice-caps some time before we got there'. Life in Slad is still in touch with the source of its existence, just as his childhood self is still connected to the origins of his species. When he is sent to the village school at the age of 4 he is confronted by hordes of savages, 'wild boys and girls from miles around' who 'swept down each day' like Vandals to rob him of his lunchtime potato. In no time he is pinching someone else's apple, thereby simultaneously becoming a member of society beyond his family and a part of the history of his race. As the book proceeds so the images evoke later more civilized phases of human history. His eldest sister who appears as 'a blond Aphrodite' serves as a representative of Greek civilization, while his youngest brother takes him into Christian times, being 'the one true visionary amongst us, the tiny hermit no one quite understood. . . .' Towards the end of the book the time scale advances to post-feudal Britain, still enjoying a basically agricultural mode of existence. His uncles, 'the true heroes of my early life . . . were bards and oracles . . . the horsemen and brawlers of another age', yet their 'lives spoke. . . of campaigns on desert marshes, of Kruger's cannon and Flanders mud. . . .' The child's natural hero worship is used to bring his development up to modern times and to place him within that context as the representative of the post-war generation.

Lee celebrates his childhood, despite its fears and terrors, as something shared with earlier civilization. The continuing link is nature which he animates and reveres. Repeatedly he employs language to show how he and his fellow villagers merge into the natural rhythm of life. At home all the children 'trod on each other like birds in hole'; they return to the house at night 'like homing crows'. His mother 'possessed an indestructible gaiety which welled up like a thermal spring'. She is a source as well as a product of nature, the personification of Mother Nature: 'I absorbed from birth, as I now know, the whole earth through her jaunty spirit'. Lee's childhood days were dominated by the change of the seasons. Yet because each season is distilled from a succession of years it acquires in the book a sense of timelessness. Remembering days spent with the Robinson children, he recalls their 'hide-out unspoiled by authority, where drowned pigeons flew and cripples ran free; where it was summer, in some ways, always'. Like Read, he makes overt his idealization as if to acknowledge and condone the adult's knowing falsification of the years of his childhood. For as an adult these moments have become timeless and therefore true to the adult's if not to the child's perception of that time.

Written after Lee had settled in London, the autobiography sets his personal loss within the wider context of the loss that Western civilization had sustained in the course of becoming urbanized and industrialized. In **'An Obstinate Exile'**, an essay written long after he had settled in London, Lee recognizes that there is no going back to the Slad of his childhood, that he is 'cut off from the country now in everything except heart'. He spends the latter half of the book mourning the disappearance of a way of life that nevertheless he chose voluntarily to abandon. Lee here illustrates what Edward Edinger has written of [in his 1973 *Ego and Archetype*] as the need for the adult to distinguish between a longing for the child's life of the unconscious, a state of nature, and childhood 'inflation' as he calls it, where the ego arrogates to itself the qualities of the larger total self. Edinger amplifies this distinction by citing the age-old controversy between man's yearning for the life of what Rousseau termed the 'noble savage' and his revulsion from primitivism, a revulsion such as Montaigne showed in his essay 'Of the Cannibals'. In Lee's autobiography the child's horizons no longer satisfy the growing young man. After the death of the village squire with its symbolic overtones, 'fragmentation, free thought, and new excitements' came 'to intrigue and perplex him'. This recognition of his voluntary participation in what he later came to see as a regrettable if irreversible process is what distinguishes Lee's from, for example, H. E. Bates's childhood autobiography, *The Vanished World* (1969). Bates shares Lee's sense of loss of the pastoral world of his early years but fails to acknowledge his own implication in the movement away from that world. For Bates the games they played, the fruit they picked, the days of harvesting were all better than today's. For him the present means drugs, violence, vandalism. His romanticized version of the past is never countered by any recognition that he is

not simply a victim of modern 'progress' but an active part of it.

Lee's account of his gradual detachment from the idyll of his country childhood, an idyll which continues to be a source of inspiration as well as of reproach to the mature writer, closely echoes Jung's account of life's natural cycle:

> The child begins its psychological life within very narrow limits, inside the magic circle of the mother and the family. With progressive maturation it widens its horizon and its own sphere of influence; its hopes and intentions are directed to extending the scope of personal power and possessions; desire reaches out to the world in ever-widening range; the will of the individual becomes more and more identical with the natural goals pursued by unconscious motivations. Thus man breathes his own life into things, until finally they begin to live themselves and to multiply; and imperceptibly he is overgrown by them.

This happens equally to individual man and to civilization at large, for, as Jung asserts, 'in our most private and most subjective lives we are not only private witnesses of our age, and its sufferers, but also its makers'. This is what Lee recognizes as he prepares to leave Slad, alone, drawn irresistably to London and then Spain. If one turns to *As I Walked Out One Midsummer Morning* one finds that he came to see his departure from Slad as a further birth into the wider world symbolized by his first awakening in the Spanish countryside: 'I felt it was for this I had come; to wake at dawn on a hillside and look out on a world for which I had no words, to start at the beginning, speechless and without plan, in a place that still had no memories for me.' In one sense Spain offers him everything missing from his cosy valley in the Cotswolds—vast vistas, alien customs, and a feeling of freedom with its 'anarchic indifference' to his presence there. Yet in another sense his experience of Spain is conditioned by his childhood immersion in the countryside and reproduces many of the dramas of his youth but in an adult form. Finally it is Spain that carries him out of the primeval past that Slad represented for him into the midst of the present, the horrors of a twentieth-century civil war. His active involvement in that war is a concrete realization of Jung's assertion that 'the life of the individual . . . alone makes history'.

Michael Glover (review date September-October 1991)

SOURCE: A review of *A Moment of War*, in *Books*, London, Vol. 5, No. 5, September-October, 1991, p. 26.

[*Glover is an English nonfiction writer who frequently focuses on historical events and themes. In the review of* A Moment of War *below, he finds Lee's autobiographical account of the Spanish Civil War "an affecting, engaging document."*]

Laurie Lee is one of the most popular and least prolific of our contemporary novelists: the sequence of autobiographical novels that began with the publication of *Cider with Rosie* in 1959—which has sold almost two million copies in paperback alone—will be continued this autumn with the appearance of *A Moment of War,* a fictional memoir of Lee's experiences as a volunteer in the Spanish Civil War in 1937.

The enduringly popular *Cider with Rosie* was rich—almost too rich, some might argue—with the sensuous, timeless details of a Gloucestershire childhood; by comparison, *A Moment of War* is a spare, often stark evocation of 'the stupefying numbness of war'—and a timely reminder of the fact that the heroism of war is seldom shared by its bewildered combatants.

Lee crossed over the Pyrenees from France into Spain with only a few books, a diary and a violin. He came as a volunteer, burning with idealism (like so many other recruits to the International Brigade), hopelessly optimistic, desperate to join the Republican forces in their ill-starred fight against the fascist battalions of Franco and his allies.

What he discovered was not a welcome but suspicion, hostility—and imprisonment. Instead of the ardour, the headiness, of battle, he experienced months of frustration, inertia and impotence in the teeth of a muddle-headed bureaucracy. And when eventually he got his chance to kill a man in self-defence, his thoughts were not of euphoria, but of guilt, confusion and self-doubt: 'Was this then what I'd come for—to smudge out the life of an unknown young man in a blur of panic which in no way could affect victory or defeat?'

A Moment of War does not rank amongst the masterpieces of war literature—it pales by comparison with George Orwell's partial, first-person account of that same war, *Homage to Catalonia,* for example—but it is an affecting, engaging document for all that, full of finely observed cameos of human suffering.

Valentine Cunningham   (review date 18 October 1991)

SOURCE: "On the Road to Teruel," in *The Times Literary Supplement,* No. 4620, October 18, 1991, pp. 11-12.

[*In the review of* A Moment of War *below, Cunningham describes Lee's autobiographical portrait as "momentous, extraordinary, [and] compelling."*]

Laurie Lee's account of what he did in the Spanish Civil War—momentous, extraordinary, compelling—reads like a confession. But it is a very belated one. *As I Walked Out One Midsummer Morning,* the second volume in what we are now to regard as the *Cider With Rosie* trilogy, ends with our author slipping through a gap in some frontier rocks and entering a Republican farmhouse with the greeting "I've come to join you." "I was back in Spain", he wrote, "with a winter of war before me." That was in 1969, thirty years after the Spanish War had ended. *A Moment of War* opens with just that event, those very words. But now we are in 1991. What, you can't help wondering, has kept Laurie Lee so long? After only a few pages, it's not difficult to guess that the terrible nature of what he has to relate is responsible for the conspicuously late showing.

This traveller still has innocences to shed. For a second time, he enters Spain as the naif, the idiot, a kind of baby holy fool. He had, of course, literally lost his virginity long since. In *As I Walked Out,* he, and we, met the motherly but sexy Concha in Madrid. There was also a tempestuous affair with a well-off woman up on the heights of Hampstead. She'd followed the building-site poet right to the French border. Now he carries a stash of her letters, detailing their doings in bed, hidden at the bottom of his pack. But still he is a kind of virgin. He claims not to have heard of prophylactics when the militia offers him some. A young zany of the road, laden with books, a camera and a startling violin, he remains a great puzzle to the International Brigade's hard men when he is called on to explain himself. To the pair of brutish Russian secret policemen and the clean-cut Bostonian killer, he is obviously a spy (that camera, for a start). But American Captain Sam is still wondering what Lee's "game" is right to the end of his stay in Spain. The Scottish proletarian Volunteer, Doug, thinks he's wet behind the ears—though he also thinks all Englishmen are softies. Marooned in the snows near Teruel, Lee and a pretty Portuguese boy are nearly shot by a fierce Welsh Brigadier with a huge and foully bandaged foot who takes them for a pair of "tarts". Part of the problem, clearly, is that although he is, by the normal standards of the International Brigade, a veteran of Spain, and is commonly taken by Spaniards to be French, Lee still wears a boyish sort of Englishness like some kind of spiritual suiting. His touchstones are boyhood and England. A bombed and burning house in Valencia, lit up from the inside, reminds him of a childhood turnip-lantern. A foul-tongued Catalan anarchist's pox-ravaged face looks stubbled like one of the English graveyards he knew in childhood. In a freezing hole in the Spanish earth, he thinks of the freezing cottage bedrooms of home, and feels not too badly off.

England haunts him like the five Chanel-scented English pound notes the Hampstead woman posted after him. (We hear a lot about these.) This particular Volunteer for Liberty was, as ever, led by the nose. And our Laurie Lee comes on still as the prose laureate of smells familiar to us from *Cider With Rosie* onwards.

> At my back was the tang of Gauloises and slumberous sauces, scented flesh and opulent farmlands; before me, still ghostly, was all I remembered—the whiff of rags and wood-smoke, the salt of dried fish, sour wine and sickness, stone and thorn, old horses and rotting leather.

In Spain, there are still fabulously scented erotic inductions to be invoked in that magically wide-eyed, synaesthetic prose: "Burning cold she was, close as a second skin, her mouth running across my chest. In spite of the cold, I smelt her unforgettable smell, something I'd never known in anyone else—a mixture of fresh mushrooms and trampled thyme, wood-smoke and burning orange." This is Eulalia, who turns out to be a sexual secret agent, a sort of Mata Hari, a practised lurer of men to death at the hands of the shadowy Republican gunmen, sent to keep an eye on him. And the collapse of Spanish good-times, allure and romance that she represents is central to the story—Lee's very potent version of a familiar narrative outline—of the collapse of between-the-wars ideals and idealism, the end of the great personal and collective leftist international Utopian romance of the 1930s that was prompted and then finished off by the Spanish Civil War.

> **Nobody has, I think, succeeded so well as Laurie Lee in dramatizing the wintry horrors—personal, political, military, geographical—when Spain's potential for sourness, sickness and rot took over completely.**
>
> **—*Valentine Cunningham***

In Lee's stunning account, the old Cervantick, edible, sunny Spain he has known, a country whose miseries and privations had a tolerable, even lovable grandeur and majesty, a land that had metamorphosed so easily into the great good place where a "grand gesture" against fascism felt necessary and appropriate, has been tragically degraded into an intolerably miserable scene, a freezing, hellish landscape, where the defenders of liberty are barely getting by on bits of donkey meat and sips of acorn coffee tasting of rusty buttons, and where the military and political gestures they make prove nearly as empty as their stomachs.

Over the years since the Spanish Civil War, we have, of course, heard a great deal from other Volunteer memorialists about the daft heroism and heroic daftness of the campaign, the farcical jamboree of non-training, the utter silliness of the *matériel*—jamming guns, ancient rifles, wrong ammunition—with which they had to confront fine modern German and Italian weapons; as well as the political mess, the empty words, the hollow rhetoric, the bizarre and scandalous incompetence of the command, high and low. And there have been many moving texts devoted to the sufferings of the men and women who flocked to the Republican side; not least poems about the terrible cold in the high sierras that proved such a shock to the people who thought Spain was sunny Spain all the year round. But nobody has, I think, succeeded so well as Laurie Lee in dramatizing the wintry horrors—personal, political, military, geographical—when Spain's potential for sourness, sickness and rot took over completely.

"God froze us", says one survivor of the terrible struggle for the snow-bound mountain fortress of Teruel, where the frozen corpses were stacked up like faggots. Lee's description of the desolation on those "frozen terraces" turns into one of those classic scenes of warfare going wrong in the snow—Napoleon's retreat from Moscow, or von Paulus's regiments at Stalingrad. In such a rebarbative climate, it's no surprise to find everyone and everything, people, animals, streets, towns, buildings, unremittingly ill. Everybody is tubercular, consumptive, sniffing, coughing. One fearfully skinny chap, about to be gunned down by Stalinist thugs in a back room, coughs weakly, "like a little dog". His plight is the general one.

What makes *A Moment of War* so mesmerizing is that Lee turns out to know at first hand as much about the skulduggeries in back rooms and up back streets as he does about freezing to death out on the high plains. And he knows about them as both patient and agent. Suspected of spying—his passport showed that he had been in Morocco just when the Franco-ists were plotting their coup—he twice escaped execution only by a whisker. The first time, he was kept two weeks in a freezing hole in the ground. When Dino the deserting *dinamitero* was taken out to be shot, Lee inherited his forage cap—the hat-band still warm and sweaty. His turn was next. The second time, he was put on death row in Albacete, and was granted the dubious last sexual rites, a "huffing, puffing" girl and a "wriggling" boy, as well as the final medical injection. Only the last-minute intervention of a mysterious Frenchman, who ushered him over the French border, saved his skin. Nor was this all. On his way out of Spain, given false papers, possibly deliberately, he was shut up for weeks in a Barcelona prison, alone, with no food except for a small sandwich got daily from a nun. Only the accident of Bill Rust, editor of the *Daily Worker,* hearing of this Englishman in prison, got him out.

Worse, though, than all of this, this perpetual victim of the Republican anxiety to hurt and kill was—seemingly as some sort of reward for having his life spared, or even as a weird test of loyalty—roped in by the Bostonian, Sam, to serve in a gang of internationalist night-time thugs, a special squad whose job was clandestinely to sort out suspects, to "get" alleged renegades and put the gun to the back of the neck of those pronounced disaffected. For a time, Laurie Lee was the kind of terror-monger Orwell's *Homage to Catalonia* is so shocked by.

Repeatedly, Lee's narrative confesses to the sort of moral sleaziness that infected this war—not only the "dark little games", the "malevolent jokes" of the nocturnal hit-men, but also the transgressions and blasphemies of war that Spain gave a special inflection to. Lee confesses to having been excited by the sight of bombing. Shame packs his narrative of the moment when in a sacked chapel he turned "petty violator", threw his kit on a desecrated altar to claim it as his bivouack, lay down on it and lit up a cigarette. By this action, "I believe I stained the rest of my life". Perhaps that is why it has taken almost the rest of his life to write about it.

In a bungling, "awkward, pushing, jabbing, grunting, swearing" hand-to-hand fight at Teruel he bayoneted a fascist soldier to death. The moment was so awful that he passed out, sick, hallucinating, paralysed, speechless. "Was this", he asks in a paragraph of Wilfred Owen-like intensity, "what I'd come for, and all my journey had meant—to smudge out the life of an unknown young man in a blur of panic which in no way could affect victory or defeat?" After such knowledge, what forgiveness? Back home, in Hampstead, the sense of moral staining spreads over his love-making: love, there, was "without honour". These are the book's last words.

Fortunately for us, as this book and a whole writing career marvellously reveal, the battlefield speechlessness did not last, and what Spain did for Laurie Lee was to bring home the importance of, and to enable, truthful words, truthful art, in the face of the liars, rhetoricians and propagandists. He played a part in the dubious subservience of art to propaganda. One time, the mephistophelean Boston Sam dragged him off to a cellar in Madrid to assist an obese Austrian and a pretty Spaniard in reading out some bad English translations of Machado in a vain short-wave broadcast beamed at the USA. As bombs hit the building, though, a broken-down fiddle was suddenly shoved at him, and he played some dances he'd learned on his first Spanish visit. This was by no means the "recital" Sam instantly announced it as, but the women sheltering in the room smiled. "Musica! . . . musica!" they indulgently assured their children. The zany was, after all, right to think a violin apt for a war. Violinists had their particular uses and truths. Especially writing ones.

In yet one more memorably described moment of telling absurdity, besuited Harry Pollitt, a bald pocket-minotaur fresh out from London's Communist Party headquarters, rouses the raggle-taggle troops who will soon perish at Teruel with his renowned stump oratory, so much so that for a moment they "howl for victory". Moments later, he's saying he can do "nowt" about getting sick volunteers repatriated. Memories like that starkly condition Lee's determination to tell it potently, but above all truthfully, however painful and belated the necessary owning up to transgressions past, his own and other people's, might be.

Hilary Corke   (review date 26 October 1991)

SOURCE: "My Enemy's Enemy Is Not My Friend," in *The Spectator,* Vol. 267, No. 8520, October 26, 1991, pp. 38-9.

[*Corke is an English educator, poet, editor, and translator. In the following review, Corke calls* A Moment of War *a "remarkable story."*]

In December 1937 Spain was tearing itself apart and Laurie Lee could no longer bear to remain outside the country that had given his mind its second birth. He was 'betraying the people of Spain'. Failing to convince the regular recruiters, he made himself into a one-man International Brigade and hiked over the Pyrenees. The closing page of *As I Walked Out* has him walking with his violin between the two rocks that marked the frontier and knocking at the first door. '*Pase usted.*'

That was published in 1969. Now, at last, 22 years later [in *A Moment of War*], we find out what happened next: which was that his apparently genial host couldn't believe that anyone could possibly be so romantic and impractical as to do what Lee said he had done. A violin! This Englishman was self-evidently a spy. So no sooner had he arrived there than the people of Spain popped him into, literally, an oubliette; where he remained for a fortnight in earshot of the firing-squads, until eventually suddenly released in apparently as inconsequential a manner as that in which he had been incarcerated.

> **Lee's great gift has always been, paradoxically, a negative one: he marvellously lacks the veils of hindsight and subsequent reflection that for most people falsify, even though they may embellish, their visions of their own past.**
>
> **—Hilary Corke**

For many of us that would have been enough. To escape by the skin of one's teeth summary death at the hands of the very people whom one has with the greatest difficulty and devotion come to help might well dampen the old ardour. Not Lee's. He was ever 'he who suffers and observes', and he shrugged it off as one of those things that happen in war, happen in Spain. It was not long before he had to shrug off the same again. Another paranoiac politico, another hell-hole jail, another firing-squad, again a miraculous intervention, no doubt by the literary guardian angel who was determined to preserve him to tell the tale. And then a third time; at which point it was decided that too much of the communist war-effort had already been devoted to not quite shooting Lee, and he was deported.

That is the mere frame of this remarkable story, but it is the canvas stretched on it that holds the attention. Lee's great gift has always been, paradoxically, a negative one: he marvellously lacks the veils of hindsight and subsequent reflection that for most people falsify, even though they may embellish, their visions of their own past. Between Lee at seventysomething and Lee at twentysomething there seems to be nothing but shiny air, not even a sheet of glass. He suggests little or nothing of what he feels about it now, that prismatically muddled violence, Looking-glass-land with vipers, that he happily epitomises as 'surrealist chess', though he leaves lying scattered clues from which we may well infer. At the time he simply accepted it as the pure essence of being alive, at that moment, in that place, for that person. He experiences, with brilliantly sympathetic clarity, but he doesn't, so far as the surface of his page is concerned, reflect.

That is therefore left for this moment, this place, and (at the present juncture) this person. And I note first that half the political affiliations in the world are based on the very questionable assumption that my enemy's enemy is my friend. He is not necessarily anything of the kind. Mutual enmity is not a binary and linear thing; it is just as possible for each of the three corners of a triangle to consume in hatred for the other two. Those splendidly idealistic young Englishmen who joined the International Brigade noted only that they had in their sights the grand enemy, Fascism, four years before the total conflict broke out. They hadn't worked out that at the same time they would be joining a vicious conspiracy of lefty riff-raff whose mental gamut ranged from the psychotically violent to the socially inadequate, and who spent more of their energy purging and slaughtering imagined heretics in their own ranks than they did Franco's Moors, who presented much less easy targets. In contradistinction it will be recalled that Evelyn Waugh's persona Guy Crouchback rejoiced at the Ribbentrop-Molotov pact, for now 'the enemy stood plain'; and mourned when the thieves fell out and the stirred moral picture became muddied again.

In that same year Louis Aragon and Nancy Cunard (some coupling!) circulated to authors a wondrously angled questionnaire:

> Are you for or against the legal government and the people of republican Spain? Are you for or against Franco and Fascism?

Waugh, in almost the sole dissenting voice, replied that

> If I were a Spaniard I should be fighting for Franco. As an Englishman I am not in the predicament of choosing between two evils.

Those who failed to perceive the existence of the predicament, and that in trying to suppress a Fascist Germany they were simultaneously attempting to set up a Cuba of Europe, may still occasionally be seen propping up the sad mahogany of certain seedy bars. Sooner or later a toady will indicate to you such a one, whispering that 'He was in Spain.' If that is an epigraph to *A Moment of War,* it is so in a very different spirit. Lee was 'in Spain' but it was a real Spain, of soil, snow, blood, pals, girls, not that dystopia of diseased politicking in the shadow of, in his own phrase, 'the deadly cynicism of Russia'. His fellow Englishmen, to say nothing of the other nationalities, were ex-convicts, alcoholics, wizened miners, dockers, noisy politicos and dreamy undergraduates busy scribbling manifestos and notes to boyfriends, but he did whatever the powers allowed him to do to aid them, for

> we shared something, unique to us at that time—the chance to make one grand, uncomplicated gesture of personal sacrifice and faith which might never occur again.

But everything between the lines of this excellent book denies the possibility that Lee gave any considered measure of intellectual assent. As to the toady in the watering-hole, perhaps the only comeback at this late date is a soft, 'Ah really? Benidorm?'

Albert Hoxie   (review date 2 May 1993)

SOURCE: "A Wide-Eyed Witness to War," in *Los Angeles Times Book Review,* May 2, 1993, pp. 3, 10.

[*Hoxie is an educator who specializes in history. In the review of* A Moment of War *below, he considers Lee's book to be essential for "anyone who wants to understand what war is actually like, when it is not being dramatized, hyped, heroized or propagandized."*]

Laurie Lee's memoirs are little known in the United States, though in English schools his first two volumes occupy about the same place that J.D. Salinger's *Catcher in the Rye* has filled here. *A Moment of War,* the third volume of Lee's story, had a substantial run on the British bestseller list last year—five decades after the first volume appeared.

Lee's prose has much the same kind of spare elegance and direct, heart-wrenching clarity of Lincoln's Gettysburg Address; and both Lincoln and Lee are dealing with that most painful of all types conflict: civil war. This book is Lee's account of his efforts to join the International Brigade in Spain in December of 1937.

Lee was born in 1914 in a village in Somerset. He has recounted the story of his adolescence in *Cider With Rosie,* a memoir of gentle humor and great charm. At 19, he walked out of Somerset with little money and a fiddle to confront the world, going first to London, where he managed to earn enough money to get himself to Vigo, Spain. From there, he walked across Spain in the blazing July that saw the beginnings of the Spanish Civil War. His account of that was called *As I Walked Out One Midsummer Morning,* published in 1969; he recorded the life he found in the villages of Spain, for it was in those that he spent most of his time, detailing indelibly the life and tone of a country poised on the brink of disaster. Now, almost a quarter of a century later, comes this memoir of the look and taste and feel of that disaster.

I don't know of any book that captures as clear-eyed and desolating a view of the realities of war. Christopher Isherwood in his *Berlin Stories* referred to himself as a camera, but Lee is far more genuinely just that. Lee is a poet (he has published verse along with his newspaper writings and memoirs), and he writes with the care of a poet who must weigh each word to find the precise one that will be the most telling and the most true. The language is always simple, direct and unornamented. In the entire work, there is not one cliche, no easy, borrowed phrase. Each word rings as true as though newly minted for this one purpose, fresh and clear as a winter morning.

There are no judgments, no romanticizing, no attempts to explain what is inexplicable. He simply records with the bleak honesty of a recording angel what he saw. Beside this work, George Orwell's account of this Civil War is angry and judgmental. Hemingway's is romantic and soft, for all of the Hemingway macho bravado. This is the reality of a land numbed by bitter cold, starvation and so much death that death no longer holds any meaning.

> **Laurie Lee's memoirs are little known in the United States, though in English schools his first two volumes occupy about the same place that J.D. Salinger's** *Catcher in the Rye* **has filled here.**
>
> **—Albert Hoxie**

Lee was then, and has remained, a Socialist, based on his absolute faith in the simple goodness of people; and it was that belief that led him to walk into Spain in December over the snow-covered Pyreness to the aid of the embattled Republicans, carrying a camera, which was taken from him immediately, and his violin, but no gun. He describes himself: "I was at that flush of youth which never doubts self-survival, that idiot belief in luck and a charmed life, without which illusion few wars would be possible." Knowing virtually nothing of the real situation in Spain, he arrives in a paranoid, brutalized, totally disorganized world with few means of simple survival, much less any hope of waging a war against an enemy that is fully equipped, organized and supported by massive aid from a Germany and an Italy eager to use the Civil War as a testing ground for the new weapons and tactics with which they will launch World War II.

Nothing is ever explained to him. At one point he is put in a prison cell to await execution as a spy, though for no reason ever given to him. There he spends three weeks, with one sandwich a day to keep him alive, only to be released as mysteriously as he had been arrested. He is shipped to Tarazona, close to the front at Teruel. There, now as a member of the Brigade, he is shown a photograph "of a slight, round-shouldered youth, with dark, fruity lips and the wide, dream-wet eyes of a student priest or a poet. His brow was smooth and babyish, his long chin delicately pointed." No one knew the name of the boy, so they called him Forteza, which was written on the back of the photograph.

Lee and another soldier are told only that the boy was a hero of the Barcelona uprising; a gunman, dynamiter and killer of three leading Trotskyists; had been kidnaped, tortured, condemned to death and had escaped and headed south. It is their job to find him and give him protection before any others find him, for he has lost his nerve. The boy is located, being cared for by a girl Lee has met before:

> On her rumpled bed, shaking with fear or fever, was the youth we instantly recognized from the photograph, except that the once smooth face of the priestlike dreamer was now savagely and bitterly scarred. When he saw Rafael and me, he shrank back on the bed, doubled up, and drew his knees to his chin. He broke into a paroxysm of coughing, while Eulalia soothed him, and wrapped a ragged blanket around him. . . . Forteza grew quiet, then pulled himself into a sitting position. He asked if we had any cognac. Rafael was carrying a flask and gave him some, which he drank in little birdlike sips. Then he smiled and let us draw him to his feet. Rafael grew hearty and wrapped his arm around Forteza's shoulders. "We were worried about you, man," he said, guiding him toward the door. "For God, why d'you take such risks?"
>
> I saw the panic slowly fade from Forteza's eyes as he struggled to find his balance. Eulalia lightly touched the back of his neck, then put her cold hand to my cheek. "He could be you, little brother," she said. We helped the lad down the stairs and supported him through the streets. Forteza's skeletal fame between us was as light as a bundle of sticks.
>
> When we got him back to the house, Kassell was drinking coffee by the fire. Jean and Pip left their chess game, the Dutchman stopped writing, and all joined Rafael and me by the door. Then Kassell got up and strode forward, crinkling in his

> black leather mackintosh, threw his arms around Forteza and kissed him.
>
> Forteza stood quiet, neither shivering nor coughing now. "Welcome, comrade," said Kassell, with his watery smile. "We thought something bad had happened to you." He ran his hands quickly over the boy's thin body, and led him into the inner room. Jean and Pip returned to their chess game, and the Dutchman to his writing. A little later we heard the sound of a shot.

There it is, a fair sample, no editorializing, no sentimentalizing, no excuses, a bleak report of a fragment of war. Lee was not yet a poet, or a writer, when he experienced these events, which were burned into his memory like a brand, still indelibly there to be written in this book more than 50 years later. It is a look at the kind of human tragedy that continues to exist today in places such as Bosnia; that seems to be eternal.

For anyone who wants to understand what war is actually like, when it is not being dramatized, hyped, heroized or propagandized, this is the book. For those who still cherish the beauty and the flexibility of the English language, this book and Lee's other two memoirs are a treasure.

[*A Moment of War* is] very much a "modern" presentation of war. The emphasis is not on the fighting and its possible significance but rather on the dirt and the difficulty of survival.

—*Peter Stansky, in his "Yesterday the Struggle," in* Book World—The Washington Post, *1 August 1993.*

Verlyn Klinkenborg   (review date 25 July 1993)

SOURCE: "One Poet's War," in *The New York Times Book Review,* July 25, 1993, p. 7.

[*Klinkenborg is an American editor and nonfiction writer. In the review of* A Moment of War *below, he discusses the contemporary relevance of Lee's autobiographical account of the Spanish Civil War.*]

For some artists and writers—I think of Goya or Michael Herr—war is a kind of fugue state, from which they return with a lingering vision in which you feel an expressive haste, a hysteria under flushed skin. These are the artists and writers for whom war retains a kind of esthetic sublimity, immoral to be sure and always undercut by the blatant ironies of combat, but with the mix of fear and beauty that Wordsworth could find in a mountain landscape unmolested by shellfire or that Byron could find in incest. The emotion with which such works are charged is a commentary on war and a gauge of authenticity. But there is another school of artists and writers for whom war obviates all commentary, for whom war, austerely depicted, is itself a commentary on human civilization. That is the school to which the English poet and memoirist Laurie Lee belongs.

Mr. Lee's new book, *A Moment of War: A Memoir of the Spanish Civil War,* is a bleak monument to a conflict that is remembered now mainly as an augury of World War II. But *A Moment of War* is also a reminder that irony, so debased in the ordinary way of speech, is something more than odd coincidence or amusing contradiction. Irony is the grim set of the mouth on a frozen corpse, a violent understatement.

Before crossing the Pyrenees into Spain in December 1937 at the age of 23, Laurie Lee had already walked to London from the Cotswold village in which he was raised. He had also walked across Spain on an earlier visit, supporting himself by playing violin in the streets. The life of Mr. Lee's native village and his foot travels are the subjects of his two earlier memoirs, *Cider With Rosie* (1959) and *As I Walked Out One Midsummer Morning* (1969), to which *A Moment of War* is the sequel. These are extraordinary books. Mr. Lee's prose is utterly distinctive, not least of all because one tends to read it as if it were somehow retroactive, a product not of the present age but of the late 1930's. It has Orwell's plainness without his didacticism. It can be called poetic, because its effects depend so much on Mr. Lee's use of metaphor, without ever falling into the kind of indulgence, the adjectival bog, you find in the memoirs of Patrick Leigh Fermor, who also happened to be walking across Europe about the same time as Mr. Lee. In Mr. Lee's prose, you can hear the maturity of the man and the writer, but across his pages there walks a youth whose thoughts are largely silent to the reader, whose footsteps echo in a landscape that in the mind of that independent young man, no one had ever seen before.

Mr. Lee's prose is utterly distinctive, not least of all because one tends to read it as if it were somehow retroactive, a product not of the present age but of the late 1930's.

—*Verlyn Klinkenborg*

It is hardly demeaning to say that when he left home at 19, Mr. Lee was an ignorant boy, a sophisticate only in the customs of rural living. But his ignorance made him adaptable, and it cushioned his sensitivity. When he returned to Spain in 1937 to join the Loyalists (his earlier trip had ended with his being plucked from the southern coast by a British destroyer at the outbreak of the civil war), Mr. Lee was arrested as a spy and imprisoned for two weeks in what was little more than a grave with an iron lid. Still, he writes, "my situation didn't disturb me too much . . . I was at that flush of youth which never doubts self-survival, that idiot belief in luck and a uniquely

charmed life, without which illusion few wars would be possible."

Certainly, illusion was the substance on which the Spanish Civil War fed. After being released from the grave (he was twice again imprisoned before leaving Spain), Mr. Lee found himself among a ragged company of volunteers—Russians, Frenchmen, Czechs, Americans—who drilled with wooden sticks and assaulted simulated machine guns (men beating rhythmically on oil drums). For anti-tank practice they hurled bottles at a pram. All this while Hitler was arming Franco.

The effect of military discipline is to suppress individuality, but in the preposterously unmilitary International Brigade, the collection of volunteers who flooded into Spain to fight in the Republican cause, individuality was never suppressed. "They were (as I was) part of the skimmed-milk of the middle-30's. You could pick out the British by their nervous jerking heads, native air of suspicion, and constant stream of self-effacing jokes. These, again, could be divided up into the ex-convicts, the alcoholics, the wizened miners, dockers, noisy politicos and dreamy undergraduates busy scribbling manifestos and notes to their boyfriends."

And in accounts of other wars—World War I, especially—you sense that behind the front lines there is an order that frays completely only where the trenches end and the barbed wire begins. You can hear the reflection of that order in, for instance, the rhythms of Sir Osbert Sitwell's memory of Ypres, in his memoir *Laughter in the Next Room*: "the broken and deserted city, the very capital of no man's land, extended its smashed streets and avenues of trees, black, angular shapes, sharp and ruthless, such as the contemporary gangs of Futurists would have wished to create had they been able to kidnap the God of Nature."

But in *A Moment of War,* you sense that there was no order anywhere in Spain and that a different kind of narrative is required, a story told in "gritty, throwaway lines—quietly savage, but with no dramatics." In paragraph after paragraph, scene after scene of this book, the reader comes upon terse non sequiturs, because the only pattern in Mr. Lee's experience of the Spanish Civil War was its lack of pattern. Even the climactic moment, the one scene of battle, expires in derangement: "I headed for the old barn where I'd spent my first night. I lay in a state of sick paralysis. I had killed a man, and remembered his shocked, angry eyes . . . I began to have hallucinations and breaks in the brain . . . Was this then what I'd come for, and all my journey had meant—to smudge out the life of an unknown young man in a blur of panic which in no way could affect victory or defeat?"

Other men, oppressed by what they learn of themselves in war, have also asked this question. Perhaps the greatest surprise in reading *A Moment of War,* published so late in this brutal century, is that Laurie Lee can still make us feel that question's implicit shame, first felt by him nearly 60 years ago in a barn outside the ruined city of Teruel.

Bernard Knox   (review date 22 December 1994)

SOURCE: "Poets of the Spanish Tragedy," in *The New York Review of Books,* Vol. XLI, No. 21, December 22, 1994, pp. 18, 20-2.

[*In the excerpt below, Knox examines Lee's account of the Spanish Civil War as presented in* A Moment of War.]

[Lee came to Spain] in the winter of 1937. He was twenty-three years old, and not yet widely known as a poet, though when in Spain he met Fred Copeman the commander of the British Battalion, who had been his strike leader when Lee worked as a builder's laborer in London, he was greeted with the words: "The poet from the buildings. Never thought you'd make it."

This was not his first visit to Spain. In the spring of 1936 he had sailed, with little more baggage than his fiddle, to Vigo on the northwest coast of Spain and made his way on foot, supporting himself by playing his fiddle to earn a few pesetas, across a country that Louis MacNeice, also a tourist in Spain that spring, though on a higher economic level, described [in his 1967 *Collected Poems of Louis MacNeice*] as "ripe as an egg for revolt and ruin." When the fighting broke out in July, Lee left for home, under the mistaken impression that the military coup had succeeded, but returned in the next year, to join the International Brigade. In 1969 he published a famous account of his summer journey, *As I Walked Out One Midsummer Morning*. And now, at the age of eighty, he has written an account of his second trip to Spain, *A Moment of War*.

It is not like any other account of the war written by a participant. For one thing, Lee was only in combat for a few moments of nightmare confusion outside Teruel, when, in a wild melee, he killed a man—he does not tell us exactly how.

> There was the sudden bungled confrontation, the breathless hand-to-hand, the awkward pushing, jabbing, grunting, swearing, death a moment's weakness or a slip of the foot away. Then we broke and raced off, each man going alone, each the gasping centre of his own survival.

This is a poet's prose: tense, economical, and suddenly illuminated by the unexpected but perfect word. Time and again the words on the printed page re-create the sharp reality of his surroundings and sensations, as in his description of the moment he realized, as he crossed the Pyrenees on foot, that France was now behind him and before him "all the scarred differences and immensities of Spain. At my back was the tang of Gauloises and slumberous sauces, scented flesh and opulent farmlands; before me, still ghostly, was all I remembered—the whiff of rags and woodsmoke, the salt of dried fish, sour wine and sickness, stone and thorn, old horses and rotting leather."

The story Lee has to tell is a grim one. Before his first experience of combat he was twice imprisoned as a spy. His first time in jail, or rather in an excavation in the frozen ground that was covered by an iron trapdoor, was in part due to his decision to cross the Pyrenees alone in December. "It was," he says, "just one of a number of idiocies I committed at the time." Volunteers normally came in

through a well-organized traffic—"some by boat, some by illegal train-shuttles from France, but most smuggled from Perpignan by lorry." The mountain peasant family at whose door he knocked fed him—on a "watery mystery that might have been the tenth boiling of the bones of a hare"—and next morning took him to the nearest village and handed him over to the police, saying: "We've brought you the spy."

After some time in the black hole—"it may have been a couple of days or but a few hours"—he was joined by another prisoner. "Now you've got a committee," the guard said as the newcomer was dropped in. He was a Spaniard, a deserter arrested trying to cross the mountains; his name was Dino. The two of them stayed together in the hole for about a week; Lee saw his fellow prisoner's face in "a brief glimmer of moonlight" only when "two dark shapes pulled him through the narrow entrance, and the manhole was closed again. I heard the clink of glasses, some moments of casual chatter, Dino's short laugh, then a pistol shot. . . ."

Lee expected the same fate, and when, a few days later, the grille was dragged open and a voice called "Hey, Rubio" (the Spanish for "blond") he was dragged out to see what he had expected—"the chair, the hand-cart, the plain wooden box, the sleepy officer with the bottle of coñac, the ragged soldiers lined up and looking at their feet—all were present." But not for him. "Another young man sat bound to a chair, smoking furiously and chattering like a parrot." Lee was taken to the Brigade reception center at Figueras.

Before he was executed, Dino had talked at length to Lee,

> laughing at the looking-glass difference between us. I was trying to get into the war and he was trying to get out of it, and here we were, stuffed into the same black hole. . . . and most certainly now, he said, we'd both be shot.

> And why not, indeed? The deserter appeared quite fatalistic about it. Patiently, drowsily, with no complaint or self-pity, my companion explained the situation to me. The Civil War was eighteen months old, and entering a bitter winter. The Republican forces were in retreat and could afford to take no chances. Franco's rebels were better armed, and had powerful allies abroad, while our side had few weapons, few friends, almost no food, and had learned to trust no one but the dead. What could you expect them to do with a couple of doubtful characters like us? They couldn't afford to keep us, feed us, or even turn us loose. Even less could they afford the luxury of a trial. So it was thought safer, and quicker, that anyone under suspicion should be shot, and this was being done regretfully as a matter of course.

Dino's explanation was not too far from the truth. "Almost no food" is exact; the Republic held the big cities, but Franco had occupied the food-bearing regions of Spain. Lee's narrative is rich in pungent evocations of the poor fare: coffee that "tastes of rusty buttons," a "glass of hot brown silt tasting of leather and rust," and "bean soup . . . with an interesting admixture of tar." And

Franco's recapture of Teruel in February 1938 was the beginning of a series of offensives that overwhelmed the Republic's heroic but outgunned and outmanned armies. The Spain Lee had seen on his first visit had changed almost beyond recognition. "Figueras had once been a fine hill town . . . War had shrivelled and emptied it, covering it with a sort of grey hapless grime so that even the windows seemed to have no reflections." At Madrid "there was little to be seen; rotting sandbags, broken roads, barricades of brick and bedsteads, shuttered windows, closed shops and bars."

Lee moves through a dark landscape eloquent of impending defeat from Figueras to Albacete, the base of the International Brigades, only to be imprisoned once again, this time with more than just suspicion against him. On his previous visit to Spain he had taken a short trip with a friend to Spanish Morocco; his passport showed that he had been there just at the time when the generals were readying the Foreign Legion and the Moorish *regulares* for the coup. Obviously, he must have been there for training and briefing for infiltration into the Brigades as a Franco agent. He was saved from the firing squad by the "crane-necked Frenchman" who had guided him to the frontier, and who turned up in Alabacete and vouched for him.

Lee was sent off to join the British volunteers for training at Tarazona. He found them quartered in a warehouse; they ate their meals in the church, which was

> bare as a barn—the walls and little chapels cleared of their stars and images, the altar stripped, all vestments gone. . . . Now the inside of Tarazona's own church had an almost medieval mystery and bustle, an absence of holy silences and tinkling rituals, and a robust and profane reoccupation by the people. . . .

> All over Republican Spain now such churches as this—which had stood for so long as fortresses of faith commanding even the poorest of villages, dominating the black-clad peasants and disciplining their lives and souls with fearsome liturgies, with wax-teared Madonnas and tortured Christs, tinselled saints and gilded visions of heaven—almost all were being taken over, emptied, torn bare, defused of their mysteries and powers, and turned into buildings of quite ordinary use, into places of common gathering.

On his first morning Lee was "awakened by the sound of a bugle—a sound pure and cold, slender as an icicle, coming from the dark winter outside. In spite of our heavy sleep and grunting longing for more, some of us began to love that awakening, the crystal range of the notes stroking the dawn's silence and raising one up like a spirit." After coffee ("its flavour was boiler grease") the company fell in on parade.

> The lines of men were not noticeably impressive, except that we displayed perhaps a harmonious gathering of oddities and a shared heroic daftness. Did we know, as we stood there, our clenched fists raised high, our torn coats flapping in the wind, and scarcely a gun between the three of us, that we had ranged against us the ris-

ing military power of Europe, the soft evasion of our friends, and the deadly cynicism of Russia? No, we didn't. Though we may have looked at that time, in our wantonly tattered uniforms, more like prisoners of war than a crusading army, we were convinced that we possessed an invincible armament of spirit, and that in the eyes of the world, and the angels, we were on the right side of this struggle. We had yet to learn that sheer idealism never stopped a tank.

Lee started training with a team on the Russian Maxim machine gun, but was soon pulled out for "special duty," which turned out to be service with the political police who had arrested him because of the entries in his passport. His boss, Kassell, was "thin as a peeled birch tree, with a starved face and feverish eyes." In a sequence of mysterious events—mysterious because Lee never knew what lay behind them and so neither do we—he took part in the capture of a young man called Forteza; according to Kassell, they were trying to rescue him. Forteza was snared by a young woman who had made love to Lee at Figueras but was now working for the police; Lee and a companion were sent to pick him up. When they carried him in, a sick boy whose

> skeletal frame . . . was as light as a bundle of sticks[,] . . . Kassell got up and strode forward, crinkling in his black leather mackintosh, threw his arms round Forteza and kissed him. Forteza stood quiet, neither shivering nor coughing now. "Welcome, comrade," said Kasell, with his watery smile. "We thought something had happened to you." He ran his hands quickly over the boy's thin body and led him into the inner room. . . . A little later we heard the sound of a shot.

Not long after this Lee was sent to the Teruel front, where he killed a man in his one and only contact with the enemy. It was not something he was proud of.

> I headed for the old barn where I'd spent my first night. I lay in a state of sick paralysis. I had killed a man, and remembered his shocked, angry eyes. There was nothing I could say to him now. . . . I began to have hallucinations and breaks in the brain. I lay there knowing neither time nor place. Some of our men found me, I don't know who they were, and they drove me back speechless to Tarazona.

The reader is not particularly surprised when the political commissar there told him he was to be sent back to London. To his protest the commissar replied: "You'd be more use to us there than here. After all, you're not much use to us here. You could write about us, make speeches. . . ." But Lee was not out of the woods yet. When he presented himself with his passport at police headquarters in Barcelona, they arrested him as a deserter and a spy. This time he was rescued by Bill Rust, the editor of the London *Daily Worker,* who eventually set him on the road to home and his lover in "high wealthy Hampstead. . . . I remember the flowers on the piano, the white sheets on her bed, her deep mouth, and love without honour."

Lee's experience in Spain was wildly eccentric, but though he did not share the long months of combat, interrupted only by death or wounds, that were the lot of the soldiers of the International Brigades, he admired them. Before he left Barcelona, Bill Rust set him to work sorting out the files he was keeping that were eventually to become the base for his book *Britons in Spain,* which appeared in January 1939. The files consisted of

> cards with the names and addresses of British and Irish volunteers. . . . There must have been five or six hundred of them. Many—more than half—were marked "killed in action" or "missing," at such fronts as Brunete, Guadalajara, the Ebro. Public schoolboys, undergraduates, men from coal mines and mills, they were the ill-armed advance scouts in the, as yet, unsanctified Second World War. Here were the names of dead heroes, piled into little cardboard boxes, never to be inscribed later in official Halls of Remembrance. Without recognition, often ridiculed, they saw what was coming, jumped the gun, and went into battle too soon.

FURTHER READING

Criticism

Berryman, John. "Waiting for the End, Boys." *Partisan Review* 15, No. 2 (February 1948): 254-67.
> Comparative review of several poetry collections. Offering a mixed assessment of *The Sun My Monument,* Berryman faults Lee's use of rhyme, but acknowledges that he is most effective when he focuses on love or the natural world.

Review of *I Can't Stay Long,* by Laurie Lee. *The New Yorker* LII, No. 1 (23 February 1976): 116.
> Favorable assessment of *I Can't Stay Long.*

Thwaite, Anthony. "Names and Images." *The Spectator,* No. 6944 (28 July 1961): 149.
> Comparative review of John Wain's *Weep before God,* Frederick Grubb's *Title Deeds,* Charles Olson's *The Distances,* and Lee's *The Sun My Monument.* Thwaite finds Lee's poems unimpressive and "slight."

Tomlinson, Charles. "Two Englands." *Poetry* 99, No. 1 (October 1961): 54-6.
> Discusses Lee's *The Edge of Day* and H. D.' s *Bid Me to Live,* noting each author's focus on England.

Additional coverage of Lee's life and career is contained in the following sources published by Gale Research: *Contemporary Authors,* **Vols. 77-80;** *Contemporary Authors New Revision Series,* **Vol. 33;** *Dictionary of Literary Biography,* **Vol. 27; and** *Major 20th-Century Writers.*

Alice McDermott

1953-

American novelist and short story writer.

The following entry provides an overview of McDermott's career through 1993.

INTRODUCTION

In her fiction McDermott frequently emphasizes the subjectivity of perception and the mutability of memory. She explores these issues by focalizing her narratives through the perspectives of multiple characters and by presenting their interrelated stories in an anti-chronological fashion. Children particularly interest McDermott, and her novels often focus on the events that vitiate their innocence, inducting them into an adult awareness of loss and death.

Biographical Information

McDermott was born to a middle-class family and raised in the suburbs of Long Island, New York. She earned a B. A. from the State University of New York at Oswego, then worked briefly as a clerk-typist for a New York vanity publisher before enrolling in the graduate writing program at the University of New Hampshire. After completing the program, McDermott published several short stories in various women's magazines. Her first novel, *A Bigamist's Daughter,* appeared in 1982. Following its publication, she began teaching creative writing at the University of California, San Diego, where she completed *That Night* (1987), which was nominated for a National Book Award. McDermott published her third novel, *At Weddings and Wakes,* in 1992. Currently, she teaches creative writing at American University.

Major Works

A Bigamist's Daughter concerns Elizabeth Connelly, the editor-in-chief of a New York vanity publishing house. Elizabeth becomes interested in her late parents' relationship when an author, Tupper Daniels, approaches her with a stalled manuscript celebrating the joys a bigamist brings to his scattered wives. The two become lovers, and as Tupper solicits Elizabeth's knowledge of her family history, he reworks it into his novel. Over the course of the story, it becomes apparent that Elizabeth's romantic expectations and the nature of her relationship with Tupper have been shaped by her perennially absent father, whom she suspects was a bigamist, and by a recent affair with a married man. The novel's third-person narrative is periodically interrupted by first-person passages in which Elizabeth recalls the sustained excitement she and her mother shared while waiting, respectively, for father and husband to return. *That Night* resembles *A Bigamist's Daughter* in that it, too, undermines conventional romanticism. Set in a lower-middle-class Long Island suburb during the early

1960s, McDermott's second novel opens with a description of the night in question, when the narrator, then a ten-year-old girl, witnesses the pivotal event of the novel. Rick, a teenage underachiever, and his friends lay siege to his girlfriend Sheryl's house, demanding to see her without realizing that she is pregnant and has been sent to stay with relatives in Ohio. Brandishing snow shovels and other "weapons," the neighborhood fathers confront the young mob; in the clumsy fight that follows, they vanquish Rick and his friends. As the novel unfolds, touching on events preceding and ensuing from this melee, the narrator reveals that she has long cherished romantic images of Sheryl and Rick. Moreover, she discloses that, like her, both have gone on to lead mundane adult lives which refute their—and her—adolescent belief in love's ability to triumph over adverse circumstances. *At Weddings and Wakes,* again set during the early 1960s, is also focalized largely through children to suggest how experience dispels innocence. Although the three Dailey children live on Long Island, their mother, Lucy Towne Dailey, frequently takes them to visit her widowed stepmother and three unmarried sisters in Brooklyn. The bulk of the novel's events occur in the Townes' dark, oppressively-furnished Brooklyn apartment, where the children observe their female relatives' melancholic commitment to remembering the dead and the departed. Because of the regularity of their visits, they also witness their Aunt May's long courtship, joyous wedding, and sudden death—events that catalyze their mature understanding of mortality and loss. Due to the third-person narrator's revelation early in the novel that May will die four days after her long-awaited nuptials, readers experience the wedding preparations with a mournful foreknowledge which intensifies McDermott's message that death permeates life.

Critical Reception

A Bigamist's Daughter received unusually widespread critical attention and high praise for a first novel. While several reviewers contended that the characters in this work are thinly developed, many praised McDermott's unflinching portrait of emotional and social isolation. Appreciating a similar lack of sentimentality in *That Night,* critics have commended McDermott's second novel's detailed evocation of life in lower-middle-class Long Island during the early 1960s and its realistic, generous characterization of Sheryl. Others, however, have questioned the relationship between McDermott's narrator and the thwarted teen lovers around whom *That Night* ostensibly revolves, wondering how such a young character could recall so much about the events in question as well as events she could not have witnessed. Like *That Night, At Weddings and Wakes* has been extolled for its rich period detail and for its insight into complex, often ambivalent, familial intimacies. Several critics have praised *At Weddings and Wakes*—indeed all of McDermott's works—as celebrating the ordinary. Many have observed her affinity for everyday language, noting that she favors complex syntactical patterns, constructing lengthy sentences in which short clauses proliferate to increasing emotional effect. Representative of the critics who applaud her for eschewing minimalism, David Leavitt has maintained that McDermott "gloriously rejects the notion that this betrayed and bankrupt world can be rendered only in the spare, impersonal prose that has become the standard of so much contemporary fiction." Instead, he has argued, she produces fiction "of almost 19th-century richness . . . [celebrating] the life of [the] suburban world at the same moment that [she] mourns that world's failures and disappointments."

PRINCIPAL WORKS

A Bigamist's Daughter (novel) 1982
That Night (novel) 1987
At Weddings and Wakes (novel) 1992

CRITICISM

Anne Tyler (review date 21 February 1982)

SOURCE: A review of *A Bigamist's Daughter,* in *The New York Times Book Review,* February 21, 1982, pp. 1, 28-9.

[*An American novelist, short story writer, critic, and editor, Tyler won a National Book Critics Circle Award for* The Accidental Tourist (1985) *and a Pulitzer Prize for her* Breathing Lessons (1988). *In the following, she offers a mixed assessment of* A Bigamist's Daughter *and maintains that, despite its occasionally fatuous characterization, the novel effectively demonstrates how childhood experiences determine adult expectations of love.*]

The heroine of Alice McDermott's first novel [*A Bigamist's Daughter*] is a young woman who works for a vanity press. In an office so bland and sleazy that it reminds her of an unlicensed electrolysis salon Elizabeth reads the summaries (but never the actual manuscripts) of books like *How to Win with Jesus During the Coming Holocaust* and *The Last Kiss of Love.* She murmurs a few words of extravagant enthusiasm into the author's ear, extracts a payment of $5,000 or more and keeps busy thereafter explaining why nothing much ever comes of the venture. Since Vista Books are often produced with the cheap labor available in India, there have been times when the galleys were delayed by monsoons. Dusty first editions, some with cruel, tongue-in-cheek jacket covers craftily designed to reflect the art director's disdain, are stacked in the storeroom unsold.

It is, Elizabeth reflects, a job that requires the one talent she developed in college—"how to look as if you're listening and sound as if you've done all the reading." Two years of this have made her a cynic, and when a young Southerner named Tupper Daniels shows up with a novel about a bigamist, she's more interested in the man himself than in the book he's peddling. This is a shame, since his book sounds as if it has distinct possibilities. Consider his description of the bigamist's wives, as imagined by the gossipy townsfolk:

> One, we would say, is fat, with curly hair, and she cries in her kitchen and wipes her eyes with a gingham apron, a small whimper always at her throat. Another is thin, sharp-nosed. She places long, bony fingers over her face and cries sitting on the edge of a cream-colored couch in a darkening living room. Another, we would tell one another, winking, smiling a little, is blond, shapely; she lies flung across her bed, crying with awful, shuddering sobs, one red slipper on the floor, the other still dangling from her polished toes.

Elizabeth and Tupper drift into a love affair, while at the same time Tupper seeks Elizabeth's professional advice on how to end his novel. Does the bigamist mend his ways? Does he wind up in court? Tupper has no idea.

It's here that *A Bigamist's Daughter* begins to draw the reader in. Elizabeth turns out to have had a most mysterious father—a man who was absent from his wife and daughter more often than he was home, a man whose profession was never explained to his daughter and whose real life seemed to be the one he led when away. As Elizabeth revives her memories of this man for the sake of Tupper's novel, she becomes more appealing; she loses the harshness and superficiality that initially alienate the reader. First-person chapters, scattered through the third-person story, describe the continual state of expectancy she and her mother enjoyed while waiting for the father's return; and the suffocatingly religious aura her mother's life took on for many years after the father's death; and the mother's own death, with all her secrets intact and the father's name on her lips even though she died in the arms of a devoted lover.

Was the father really a bigamist? At the outset, the question seems important, but in the end it hardly matters. What does matter is the issue of how a person's early view of love can shape—or deform—his whole life. For Elizabeth, the quintessential lover is one who is absent. She has had one serious affair with a man whose major appeal was his attachment to another woman; Elizabeth ended the affair when she realized that the other woman didn't mean so much to him after all. Tupper Daniels's steady, genuine care for her so abashes Elizabeth that she reinvents her old affair as a heroic myth—much as her mother, in mourning, tells and retells the story of how her husband flung himself on his knees at his very first glimpse of her.

This is not a flawless book. It's almost done in, at times, by the fatuousness of its two central characters—a serious problem if the reader is meant to care what happens to them. Tupper, though certainly likable, has an embarrassing habit of declaiming entire paragraphs from his novel-in-progress upon the slightest excuse. Elizabeth occasionally becomes so breathy and melodramatic with her talk of love that goes "beyond" and love that's "a spiritual life, like pure faith" that she seems merely silly And you can't help feeling impatient with her self-absorption. ("Talk to me," Tupper whispers in front of a romantic fire. "About my father?" Elizabeth asks. The reader groans.)

For the most part, though, *A Bigamist's Daughter* is impressive. There are spots where the writing is like very good sleight-of-hand. A certain conversation, for instance, takes place not just on one level or even two, but on three, while Tupper and Elizabeth ostensibly plot his novel's conclusion but are, beneath the surface, delving into the mysterious lives of Elizabeth's parents and arguing over her famous love affair. In another scene Elizabeth, after giving Tupper her fabricated version of this earlier affair, reflects upon other possible versions—meanwhile letting us know, in a subtle, seemingly unintentional way, which fabrication is actually the truth.

At such moments, Alice McDermott sounds like anything but a first-time novelist. She writes with assurance and skill, and she has created a fascinatingly prismatic story.

Stephen Harvey   (review date 23 February 1982)

SOURCE: A review of *A Bigamist's Daughter,* in *The Village Voice,* Vol. XXVII, No. 8, February 23, 1982, p. 43.

[*In the following positive review of* A Bigamist's Daughter, *Harvey commends McDermott's refusal to sentimentalize her characters' loneliness.*]

It's no disparagement of Alice McDermott's disturbing first novel [*A Bigamist's Daughter*] to note how much it resonates with the echo of Nathanael West's *Miss Lonelyhearts.* Young writers can't live in a literary vacuum; the best way they can render homage to the books they love is to find that strain in themselves which responds to those works, and channel it into something distinctively theirs. From commonplaces mined in so much undistinguished fiction—suburban girlhood replete with aloof Mommy and elusive Daddy, the Manhattan-singles life of studio apartments, frayed white-collar jobs and unassailable emotional defenses—McDermott has fashioned a tale which sounds, for a change, like truth. Her prose is spare and acidic, complementing her vision of people powerless to change the direction of their emotional lives, much less to understand how they got where they are in the first place. *A Bigamist's Daughter* is rare among recent books about sharp-witted unattached women because it doesn't succumb to the fancies that growth is everyone's birthright, and true love is still the best of everything. If McDermott has a pitch to make, it is that isolation endures beyond all else, but there's no need to become maudlin about that cheerless probability either.

As editor-in-chief at a vanity press and therefore confidant to the pitiable, her heroine Elizabeth has long since wised up. Her job is to encourage those willing to pay to encapsulate their torments in tomes with titles like *Gouged of Womanhood: Poems of Two Mastectomies.* ("If Edna St. Vincent Millay had had two mastectomies, she would have written poems like these," puffs the book jacket on this one.) A coworker notes, "They absolutely wrack their lives . . . squeeze out every little thing they've ever felt, and what pops out but a bad version of a fucking Hallmark card." Elizabeth understands this, but is unmoved. "If you can lie, assurance is no chore," is her motto. While these amateur scribes seek to exorcise their private histories by making them public, Elizabeth would much rather keep hers carefully submerged—until she comes across one misbegotten ms. which sets off reverberations of her own past. This is a novel by a softspoken southerner named Tupper, celebrating a polygamist whose wanderings brought joy to a disparate collection of spouses; Elizabeth's own childhood was punctuated by her father's protracted and unexplained absences, climaxing with his death in a car accident a thousand miles from home.

In a more conventional novel, Tupper would turn out to be the one unheralded genius lurking in the slush pile. Their subsequent affair would teach Elizabeth to face her family phantoms in order to slay them for good, and in the last chapter they'd join forces to found one of those small quality presses that publish serious stuff like Tupper's, leaving the penny-ante mendacity of "Vista Books" behind forever. But McDermott will have none of such jaunty illusions. In the wake of Elizabeth's recent troubles—her mother's slow estrangement and terminal illness, a long-thwarted affair, and the self-imposed isolation that followed—she just can't work up the treacly thrill of infatuation. Meeting Tupper's gaze in a gaudy restaurant he has chosen, she muses "they're nice eyes, but then most eyes are." After her long dry spell, sex with Tupper, though gratifying, is a reprise of "the slow downward movement, the saddest, the loneliest." Tupper's motives aren't exactly unsullied either, for all his relative naivete; he hopes Elizabeth's insights will elevate his book into the *chef d'oeuver* he knows it can be. When his prodding stirs her own curiosity, Elizabeth tries to excavate the truth about her father, and Tupper dutifully takes the intriguing fragments and turns them into pulp fiction.

These characters are not hateful in their selfishness; nor does McDermott exalt their myopic egoism into a masochistic fetish à la Joan Didion. She is more skeptic than misanthrope, and the matter-of-fact, contemplative tone of her writing never fails to convey the individual contours of her characters. McDermott has her doubts about the prospects for intimate contact between people; of her future as a novelist. I have none whatsoever.

Timothy J. Wood (review date April 1982)

SOURCE: A review of *A Bigamist's Daughter,* in *West Coast Review of Books,* Vol. 8, No. 2, April, 1982, p. 35.

[*In the following review, Wood praises McDermott's matter-of-fact depiction of love in* A Bigamist's Daughter, *but maintains that her secondary characters are underdeveloped.*]

[In *A Bigamist's Daughter*] Elizabeth Connelly, editor-in-chief of Vista Books, a vanity press, is the bigamist's daughter. Her interest in her father's bigamy becomes agitated by the appearance of Tupper Daniels, a southern novelist who has written a book about a bigamist in his hometown. Daniels' book has no ending, without which Elizabeth has no sales contract. Sensing their mutual needs and concerns, they become lovers; his interest in her father, a deceased travelling salesman, piques her own untapped curiosity and together they return to her roots on Long Island to discover more.

Daniels believes his book will be successful because "almost every woman has had a bigamist figure in her life." Elizabeth has had two: her father and her ex-lover Bill who has left her to return to his wife. Daniels' book will show the Elizabeths of the world "that their love for him (the bigamist) was noble and his leaving nothing personal. It will offer them a hope of his return."

In the end it is Elizabeth who is a bigamist. She leaves Daniels hanging and becomes a travelling editor for Vista. Her attitude is a page out of his book: there is nothing personal about this. She never develops anything personal for Daniels, he was merely a sharp corner to scratch her sexual and mental itching. Author McDermott's other characters serve as fillers. Elizabeth's father was a shadow, her mother a mystery, and her friends are props to bounce off of. This is the author's first novel and it is a very good one. The only flaws lie in her characterization.

An excerpt from *A Bigamist's Daughter*

"What did he look like, your father?"

She brushes back her hair. "Dark hair, like mine. Blue eyes, like mine. My nose exactly, I'm told. But his face was thinner and he had a mustache. A small one, like Clark Gable's."

"Was he tall?"

"Yes," she says. "And thin. Why are you so interested?"

He shrugs, rests his glass on his stomach. "I don't know; you get kind of defensive when you talk about him. I don't think you liked him."

"I was crazy about him," she cries. "I lived for the days he came home. Honestly, I think he spoiled me for any other man."

"Is that why you're not married?"

She laughs. "Could be. He's as good an excuse as any. If I need an excuse."

"There could be a correlation," he says, seriously. "If your father represented impermanence, then anyone who wanted to marry you would mean permanence, just the opposite."

"Very good, Mr. Freud," she says dryly, although, suddenly, her stomach is dancing, as if she were a child again, playing hide-and-seek, hiding in someone's dark, cool basement, feeling the searcher come near, stop, turn, walk away, and then walk back. "But not very original."

"No," he says, refusing to joke. "You should think about that. I should think about it too, if I'm going to get involved with you. I always look at a woman's father; it's usually a good indication of how she feels about men."

"Jesus," she says, laughing. "Do you want a character reference too? Birth certificate? Fingerprints?" She doesn't tell him that his basic premise, that they are to get "involved," is his first mistake.

"You see," he says calmly, pointing at her. "You get touchy when you talk about your father, even though you say you liked him. And you called him a bigamist."

"I was joking." Her voice is higher than she wants it to be. Sounds touchy.

"Yes, but you see," he says, "if you don't like your father, then it says something to me about how you feel about men like him."

Alice McDermott, in her A Bigamist's Daughter, *Perennial Library, 1988.*

Michiko Kakutani (review date 28 March 1987)

SOURCE: "Lost Illusions," in *The New York Times,* March 28, 1987, p. 10.

[*An American critic, Kakutani is a regular contributor to* The New York Times. *In the following mixed review of* That Night, *Kakutani asserts that while McDermott's failure to clarify the relationship between her narrator and the events she recounts proves confusing, this weakness does not diminish the novel's elegiac appeal.*]

The place is a Long Island suburb: one of those bedroom communities where the men go off to work each day, the women occupy themselves with neighborhood gossip and the kids pass the long summer evenings driving about in their cars and falling in love. The time is the early 1960's—roughly the same space of time chronicled, with such wit and affection, by the movie *American Graffiti.* It is a time that predates the dark revelations of Vietnam and the noisy rebellions of the late 60's—the last time, perhaps, when it could be said that America was truly innocent.

That Night the elegiac new novel by the author of the highly acclaimed *Bigamist's Daughter,* is concerned not only with that larger loss of innocence but also with the mundane disillusionments that go with adolescence and the rites of growing up. Indeed, the night referred to in the novel's title serves as a line of demarcation in the lives of Alice McDermott's characters. It is the night when they suddenly realize that their dreams of family love and safety are not inviolate, that violence and blood and loss play an equal role in the equation.

What exactly happened that fine summer evening? The facts themselves are fairly simple: one of the neighborhood boys named Rick has been trying to reach his girlfriend, Sheryl, for days. She has discovered that she is pregnant and her mother has summarily bundled her off to relatives out of state—she is to remain there, in seclusion, cut off from her former life. There is no opportunity for Sheryl to explain what has happened to Rick; and in his ignorance, he grows increasingly anxious and enraged. He and his friends begin circling the neighborhood in their cars, and they end by driving onto the lawn in front of Sheryl's house, where they threaten her mother with angry words and gestures. Neighbors rush to the scene, blows are exchanged and Rick winds up in jail.

The narrator of *That Night* witnesses this all as a child— she lives down the street from Sheryl, whom she's always looked up to as a savvy elder, wise in the ways of makeup and boys—and as she recalls the events from the vantage point of the future, they take on a symbolic resonance. "That night" comes to represent her own initiation into knowledge, into the mysteries of sex and the failures of love; and it comes to stand as a point of no return— beyond which lie only the disappointments and sobering realities of the grown-up world.

Until then, until "that night," the narrator—indeed, all the neighborhood kids and possibly their parents, too— have dwelled in a sort of prelapsarian state of romanticism and hope. Sheryl, especially, believes in the redemptive powers of love—her father has recently died and she sees her love for Rick as possessing the power of salvation; by loving him, she will save him and save herself. Nothing else matters, she tells him, not "friends, family, getting older, good luck or bad." The moment her mother succeeds in sending her away, however, she realizes that all those other things do in fact matter very much, that they have the capacity to undermine love, to erase it and slowly turn it into a dim memory.

Sheryl and Rick will go on to lead separate and altogether conventional lives, and their doomed affair will fade into a long list of disappointments and losses. Indeed, *That Night* leaves the reader with an indelible sense of the precariousness of daily life and the ephemerality of youth and passion. We see parents lose their children to death and anger; we see children lose their parents to madness and frustration, and we see lovers lose their idealism to the simple passage of time.

> **In *That Night* Ms. McDermott has succeeded in writing a novel that is, at once, mythic and personal—a novel that possesses the ability to make us remember our own youth and all that has vanished since.**
>
> **—Michiko Kakutani**

By the end of the novel, the narrator has traced both Rick and Sheryl's movement from rebellion into resignation, as well as her own passage into the melancholia of middle age. When we meet her, she has returned to her parents' house after a failed marriage. She and her husband, she observes, had reached the point "where we seemed to have lost our capacity for nostalgia, where what we'd shared, that part of our past together that had sustained us until now, had finally worn thin, and only an imagined history, or future, held any promise."

At times, Ms. McDermott's use of this narrator creates problems for the reader. We're never sure how much of the story has been distorted by nostalgia and the passage of time—perhaps we're not supposed to be. Not do we understand how the narrator is able to enter into the minds of Sheryl and Rick so readily and describe their emotions and dreams. It's possible that Ms. McDermott wants us to regard the entire book as a kind of imaginative projection on the part of the narrator—in this sense, Rick and Sheryl's actions possess no meaning in themselves; they serve, rather, as simple magnets for the narrator's own yearnings. If this is the case, however, Ms. McDermott fails to make it clear—and her novel consequently suffers from a certain narrative vagueness.

But while such matters may cause the reader to hesitate here or there, they in no serious way damage the emotional impact of *That Night*. By mixing up concrete details that anchor her story in a specific time and place (banlon shirts; pale, chalky lipstick; turquoise Chevys and the hum of lawnmowers on a summer evening) with a more lyrical sense of memory and desire, Ms. McDermott has succeeded in writing a novel that is, at once, mythic and personal—a novel that possesses the ability to make us remember our own youth and all that has vanished since.

David Leavitt   (review date 19 April 1987)

SOURCE: "Fathers, Daughters and Hoodlums," in *The New York Times Book Review,* April 19, 1987, pp. 1, 29-30.

[*Leavitt is an American novelist and short story writer. In the review below, he asserts that the "baroque richness of Ms. McDermott's sentences, the intellectual complexity of her moral vision, and the explicit emotion of her voice" distinguish* That Night *from other novels treating similar themes and incorporating suburban settings.*]

Suburbia has never had a very good rep in American literature. That man-made purgatory of our modern culture, situated at some precarious point halfway between the city with its violent grittiness and the small town with its long-kept secrets and fresh-bread smells, the suburb, for all its popular idealization, is usually frowned upon in the halls of high culture. Some notion of the decay of civilization— what Barbara Tuchman called "the decline of quality"—is attached to suburban life, for it's out there, after all, that high culture is being most visibly strangled by the overwhelming encroachment of television shows, junk food restaurants, rock videos, video games. And though John Cheever has wonderfully recounted the experience of suburban affluence—the great move out from the Sutton Place of the 1950's—it's only recently that any literature has begun to emerge that describes the experience of growing up in the television glow of the suburbs, particularly those suburbs that are both less affluent and less beautiful than Cheever's Shady Hill.

The literature that has emerged consists primarily of short stories rife with brand names, written in a spare, impersonal present tense that seems to have been chosen by the writers as perhaps singularly appropriate to this humble, even humiliated world. Much of this literature has been brilliant, cutting and important, but it is nonetheless written from a defensive position, as if the chronicler of suburbia must necessarily cultivate an anti-intellectual style, must wave the labels of his Franco-American Spaghettios cans in conscious defiance of high culture's urban disapproval.

Perhaps this is why *That Night,* the splendid second novel by Alice McDermott (her first was the highly praised *Bigamist's Daughter*), is such a surprise. This brief, lyrical novel is a kind of elegy, to both childhood in suburbia and the childhood of suburbia. "Enough, too much, has already been said about boredom in the suburbs, especially in the early sixties," the unnamed narrator tells us early on, and she is right to point out that excess of literary concentration. And yet *That Night,* for all the familiarity of its subject matter, is something new entirely. What distinguishes this novel from the mass of literature that takes on the barely middle-class suburban experience is the almost baroque richness of Ms. McDermott's sentences, the

intellectual complexity of her moral vision and the explicit emotion of her voice. *That Night* gloriously rejects the notion that this betrayed and bankrupt world can be rendered only in the spare, impersonal prose that has become the standard of so much contemporary fiction, and the result is a slim novel of almost 19th-century richness, a novel that celebrates the life of its suburban world at the same moment that it mourns that world's failures and disappointments.

The center of *That Night* is the narrator's recollection of the love affair between Sheryl, a teen-age girl who was her childhood neighbor, and Rick, the handsome, hoodish son of an eccentric local doctor and his schizophrenic wife. Their relationship is the subject of serious speculation among the younger girls of their Long Island neighborhood; in a scene of lyric intensity, Ms. McDermott describes the couple as they appeared to the narrator and her friend Diane Rossi, spying from a bedroom window across the street:

> Delicately, she turned her head, touching her cheek to his hair. She seemed to sigh or, with a dancer's grace, to softly lift her body and settle it down again with one breath. Then, abruptly, she threw her head back, his face still pressed to her breasts, and looked straight up at the sky. Some light from a neighbor's house seemed to penetrate the fine ends of her ratted hair, seemed to touch her throat and her forehead.

The crisis the novel's title alludes to is set in motion when Sheryl becomes pregnant and her newly widowed mother, having quickly dispatched Sheryl to an aunt's house in Ohio, tells a distraught and confused Rick that he must never call her daughter again. His self-described "overreaction" to Sheryl's disappearance is the starting point for the drama of "that night," the night around which the rest of the novel revolves.

That drama—a moonlit, late-summer battle between leather-jacketed hoodlums and T-shirt-clad fathers, a battle fought on one side with chains and on the other with baseball bats, hoes and garbage-pail lids—is rendered by Ms. McDermott with an almost operatic grandeur: a mysterious male rite to which the mothers and children of the neighborhood must bear witness. There is a moment late in the novel when the narrator, now an adult, briefly encounters the much-older Rick. The scene recalls Proust's madeleine: it brings back the memory of that night, and that memory, in turn, brings back a flood of recollections from both before and after. For the period that Ms. McDermott describes was a historically brief one: the transitory youth of the suburbs, those few years when the idea of suburban life seemed as new and promising as the shiny tract houses must have initially looked. "The suburb where we lived, like most, I suppose, was only one in a continuous series of towns and developments that had grown out from the city in the years after the Second World War," Ms. McDermott writes.

> They were bedroom communities, incubators, where the neat patterns of the streets, the fenced and leveled yards, the stop signs and traffic lights and soothing repetition of similar homes all helped to convey a sense of order and security

and snug predictability. And yet it seems to me now that those of us who lived there then lived nevertheless with a vague and persistent notion, a premonition or memory of possible if not impending doom.

That "premonition" of suburban decline extends to the families who live in the neighborhood as well; there's a sense of anxious foreboding sparked by the events of "that night," as well as by the fall of Rick and Sheryl, which presages for the other families inevitable future upheavals: "the scattering of sons, the restlessness of wives, the madness of daughters." We see this anxiety perhaps most acutely from the vantage point of Mrs. Carpenter, whose family has been relegated to her finished basement in order to protect a house that is simply "too beautiful to bear." Ms. McDermott might easily have painted Mrs. Carpenter as a figure of ridicule, but instead she has chosen to present her as a kind of displaced artist figure, a woman whose creative impulses have found expression only in the invention and protection of a breathtaking, perfect interior:

> She was not foolish. . . . Her pride in her small rooms, her rigorous house rules that no shoes should touch her carpet, no child spend more than ten waking minutes in his bedroom, no guest go unescorted, were merely part of a brave and determined effort to preserve what she knew of Beauty from the ravages of drink-spilling and ash-dropping Time. More artist than eccentric, then.

Appropriately, it is Mrs. Carpenter who sees in the tragedy of Sheryl's family "a glimpse into the future, a report from the uncharted frontier that their daily lives were slowly but inexorably moving toward."

That Night is a wonderfully unfettered, ample novel, one that celebrates voice, personality and feeling when so much fiction avoids those rewarding characteristics. Ms. McDermott has invested her novel with a strong sense of historical authority, rendering with sure clarity a time and place marked by both a cultural innocence and the premonition of its inevitable loss.

—*David Leavitt*

In sharp contrast to the story of the neighborhood is the story of Rick and Sheryl themselves. Sheryl particularly is a marvelous creation, a skinny, not terribly pretty girl whose somewhat sluttish appearance belies her almost mystic state of mind, and who has set herself in philosophical opposition to the old order of family life: "None of that matters to us," she tells the narrator, when asked if she and Rick plan to get married. "You know, getting married and having kids and buying a house. None of that

means anything to us." Sheryl's sources are modest—"the love songs of the Shirelles and Shangri-las, the auto accident/undying love poems printed in odd spaces in her teen magazines, the old-fashioned, heaven-saturated Catholicism of her grandmother"—but the power of her belief in love as a force strong enough even to overcome death is rendered with respect and empathy. She is transformed by Ms. McDermott from an unremarkable, sullen girl into a true heroine, possessing both strength of mind and a highly complex—though ultimately naive—sense of morality.

In one of the novel's most affecting scenes, the heavily made-up Sheryl approaches the young narrator and asks if she can help her dress her Barbie doll. In the course of their play, Sheryl explains the intensity of her love for Rick, as well as her assurance that it will transcend death, yet she's clearly still part child:

> "This your Barbie?" she asked.
>
> I said yes.
>
> "It's nice." She suddenly sat on the step just below mine and placed her books on her lap. I could see the initials she had written all over her loose-leaf binder with black magic marker, hers and Rick's. I noticed how the ink had bled a little into the fabric. I could have been glimpsing her garter belt, her diary, the initials seemed so adult and exotic, so indicative of everything I didn't know.
>
> Turning a little, she reached back to my doll-case and gently touched all the tiny dresses and skirts that were hanging there. Her fingers were thin and short and the edges of her nails pressed into her flesh as if she had only recently stopped chewing them. Then she touched the bare feet of the doll.
>
> "She needs shoes," she said.

It is Sheryl who, in the narrative's gritty denouement, invests *That Night* with its sense of almost Shakespearean tragedy, and it is Sheryl as well who is blessed with the novel's final, redemptive revelation, in a conclusion that opens beyond tragedy to suggest that what keeps us going is not anything we are conscious of, but rather a "blind, insistent longing . . . that this emptiness be filled again."

This is a novel of many small pleasures. It will be hard to forget Ms. McDermott's funny, touching description of her narrator's mother, a frustrated woman who, in her zeal to regain her "talent to conceive," resorts to "a kind of voodoo," standing on her head after intercourse or taking long baths in Epsom salts: or the mysterious midnight visit of a little-known, just-widowed neighbor, being led by his 4-year-old daughter from house to house to find and inform his dead wife's "girl friends"; or the remarkable moment in which Sheryl, asked by her well-meaning cousin which she would like to have, a boy or a girl, answers flatly, "I'd like to have a miscarriage." And there are many more scenes like these; throughout *That Night* Ms. McDermott writes with such consistent generosity and knowing intelligence that we quickly forgive her the book's occasional dramatic excesses. Indeed, in a decade that has seen the increasing popularity of fiction as reduced and intense as some nouvelle cuisine sauces, those excesses even come as a relief.

And that is perhaps what is most exciting about *That Night*; it is an original, a work that, in spite of its much-exploited subject, revels in a rich, discursive prose style that belongs entirely to Alice McDermott, and that stands completely out of sync with contemporary literary trends. In spite of its brevity, *That Night* is a wonderfully unfettered, ample novel, one that celebrates voice, personality and feeling when so much fiction avoids those rewarding characteristics. Ms. McDermott has invested her novel with a strong sense of historical authority, rendering with sure clarity a time and place marked by both a cultural innocence and the premonition of its inevitable loss.

Richard Eder   (review date 26 April 1987)

SOURCE: A review of *That Night*, in *Los Angeles Times Book Review*, April 26, 1987, p. 3.

[*An American critic, Eder received a 1987 Pulitzer Prize for Criticism and a 1987 citation for excellence from the National Book Critics Circle. In the following review of* That Night, *he lauds McDermott's fresh, detailed evocation of suburbia as well as the characterization of her female protagonist.*]

The deceptively ordinary elements of *That Night* are put together with such undercover art and such vigorously individual results that the book seems to be an act of germination more than an act of fiction. Alice McDermott nurtures her suburban pair of adolescent lovers as Mrs. Shelley, no doubt, nurtured a dozen ordinary pounds of Percy Bysshe.

That Night begins with an act of violence that is shocking, pathetic and funny at the same time; and goes on to relate what led up to it and what came afterward. It is voiced with musical economy by a narrator who was a preteen at the time, and who tells it years later.

One quiet summer evening in a Long Island suburb, with grass being watered and children playing on the sidewalks, three cars full of teen-age boys blast up onto a lawn. One of the boys advances to the door, followed by his companions, armed with chains. After talking a moment to the woman who answers the door, he pulls her roughly over the doorway and throws her to the ground. He steps back, looks up to the windows and howls desperately: "Sherry!"

The men on the block, who have rallied around, go for the intruders with baseball bats and snow shovels. It is a melee of awkward flailing; before long, the boys flee in their cars and the police arrive. Here is McDermott on the aftermath:

> There was the disappearing siren of the young cop's car, the approaching sirens of his reinforcements, little Jake screaming in his mother's arms. There were the other children, who had been blasted into the hedges and the grass by the escaping cars (and who were lying tragically now, unharmed but unwilling to stand until their own part in the adventure, their own brush with death, had been fully recognized). . . . It

seemed our whole neighborhood had raised its voice in one varied, inharmonious wail.

It is awful, of course, but the hint of wryness in McDermott's tone is telling us something else. Nobody has been seriously hurt; the boys are no better at swinging their chains than the men their snow shovels. Those children, "lying tragically now" are overplaying their role as war victims. So are the fathers, as defenders of civilization. So are the intruders, as young warriors helping Rick, their lovesick friend, rescue his princess from her tower.

Sheryl, the princess, is not in her tower. She is away in Ohio. Pregnant, she has been sent to stay with relatives. Her mother—the woman on the lawn—won't give Rick her address. Rick will be briefly arrested and wisely counseled. He will back away from his moment of glory, rejoin the world of adult expectations with a rueful "I guess I overreacted," get a suspended sentence and grow up to live a normal, unglorious life.

Sheryl, after her moment of grand passion, will have her baby out of town, and grow up to live a normal unglorious life. The torn-up lawn will be reseeded; families will move out and others move in. The children in the hedges will grow up, catch their own longings and passions that the suburbs are incapable of coping with, and leave.

Surely, we already know everything that McDermott is offering. In the first place, we have been told repeatedly that the American suburb is an aquarium more than an ecosystem; and that the creatures swimming in close proximity there have principally this present proximity in common, and derive very little past or future from each other. From the time they are ladled in, to the time they are ladled out, they are held together by something as fragile as a glass globe.

Second, we know that the young of the species, once they begin growing up, find little place there—economically, intellectually or emotionally.

Finally, we know that adolescents are in a state, anyway, where they make absolute and unsustainable claims on life in a seemingly hit-or-miss fashion that is agonizing for them and those close to them. The claims take the form of mortal and momentary love affairs, styles of dress, music and eating, and passions and loathings of all kinds.

These things should be as familiar as a television serial. But McDermott makes them seem new. We have never seen them before; and as with any new life, our own lives have to shift a little to make room for them.

The author's perceptions of suburban life have a rich detail of the quality of a Cheever or an Updike. Her wryness is only the reverse of tenderness; together, they make a voice that is closer to a lament than a denunciation.

The drama of Sheryl and Rick allows an assemblage of separate lives to think of itself, briefly, as a community; hence the overplaying on the evening of the fight. For a few days afterward, the men, who normally would get home after work and disappear into their houses and TV sets, hang about outside. It doesn't last; the suburbs have no facilities for transforming passions or death or even the

An excerpt from *That Night*

That night, as soon as I'd managed to break out of my mother's grip, I left our porch and went into the street. All the children were doing it, not even running but almost staggering, somewhat reluctantly, in our fathers' wakes, going only as far as what seemed to be the prescribed borders of the fight: about six feet or so from the cars and her lawn, which left us scattered across both sidewalks on either side and down the middle of the street. When the first police car approached, we merely turned our heads, stricken, I suppose, with that strange paralysis that seems to grip all crying and moaning children. Georgie Evers and I were the first two in his path, and it never occurred to us to step out of his way.

But by then the officer had seen the cars on the lawn and the brawl that took place beyond them.

He stopped, then turned on his siren and his lights, got out quickly and stood dumbfounded for a moment with one foot still in the car and his hand on the open door. He shouted, "You kids," waving his arm (still none of us moved), and then dove into his car again. He turned off the siren, made a call on his radio (the Meyer twins, who stood nearly at his elbow, claimed he said, Mayday! Mayday!), then leaped from the car again, the nightstick in his hand.

But the boys had begun a retreat as soon as they heard the siren. We saw them shaking our fathers from their legs and their arms, dropping their chains and even their jackets to the lawn if that was the only way to get rid of them. Some of the boys were bloodied, the blood black shadows that covered their mouths or their ears. They were shouting each other's names. I saw one of them was lifted and pushed into a car by the others. Car doors slammed. Even as the poor young officer jogged toward the fray, the first car, the one in Sheryl's driveway, the white one with the painted flourish, backed up with a screech and, turning its front wheels over the curb, headed out—passing within inches of some of the children who still stood crying or who, seeing the car come toward them, had leaped into bushes or onto the grass.

Again the cop turned to us and with another wide wave of his hand cried, "Get out of the street." But at the same time, the car that had led the procession did a sudden U-turn across Sheryl's lawn, its horn a staccato yell, and pulled out from her driveway. The next instant, I saw Rick. The light was on inside the remaining car, the one he had emerged from. I saw him through the back passenger window. I almost thought he was turning toward me, but he was simply curling forward in pain. He had lost his sunglasses. His hands, streaked with blood, were cupped over his face. I later learned his nose had been broken, but at the time I was certain he was crying. Then the door closed and the light went out.

Alice McDermott, in her That Night, *Farrar, Straus and Giroux, 1987.*

passage of time; their sustaining premise is an unbroken gentleness of surface.

Within this social portrait is McDermott's wonderful individual portrait of Sheryl, the transgressor and heartbreaking innocent. A few years earlier, her father had died; her orphan status and her mother's widow status make them awkward oddities in a community of families.

Sheryl seems older and wiser than her friends. Being an orphan allows her to discover the true faith. Love is a demonstration that the dead are not gone. As long as you love someone, that person can't be truly non-existent, she tells the narrator. "You don't end up loving air."

Meeting Rick, a high-risk, borderline youth with an insane mother and a withdrawn father, she finds a new field for her faith. Love will preserve them both, she tells him. Earlier, he had almost died in a car crash, driving with a friend. "Before me you would have been forgotten," she insists.

With pregnancy, the grown-ups take over. Sheryl's mission faces confiscation. Staying with a kindly cousin who wants to talk baby clothes and child care, she runs away. It is a short run; she finds herself without money or a place to go. In the restroom of a gas station, she faces her helplessness.

"To say that love could fade, that loss could heal, was to admit the possibility that there would be no return of the dead." But there is nothing more she can do for her father and Rick. "She could not both live and continue to keep them alive." Sheryl makes the feeble effort to kill herself, but when that fails, she chooses to have her baby and, later, to marry and have other babies.

McDermott has balanced her book so finely between the truth and the sadness of reality—the tears in things, as Virgil put it—that it would be wrong to say that Sheryl has chosen life. She has relinquished herself to life.

Rosellen Brown   (review date May 1987)

SOURCE: "Adolescent Angst," in *Ms.,* Vol. XV, No. 11, May, 1987, pp. 17-18, 20.

[*Brown is an American novelist, poet, and short story writer. In the excerpt below, she admires the tight construction of* That Night *as well as McDermott's poignant insistence on the inevitability of loss.*]

In *That Night,* Alice McDermott (author of the much-praised *A Bigamist's Daughter*) has centered her narrator's disillusion on one [dramatic and dangerous event]. . . . The speaker reconstructs an extraordinary confrontation that she witnessed as a 10-year-old suburban girl. A pregnant teenage neighbor, Sheryl, has been sent away to be separated from her demi-thug lover, Rick, and to have his baby out of sight. One night, as the little girl watches, Rick comes in search of Sheryl, bringing along a posse of friends who cruise the neighborhood in cars and finally erupt into a pitched battle with the fathers on the block, a pathetic and terrifying joust with chains against garbage can lids raised as shields, every householder wild with fury as he tries to protect the code of decency he stands for. There on the shorn lawns, fathers are fighting for their daughters' purity.

The novel is constructed as tightly as a rose with this incident at its center, the narrator's speculations spiraling out like petals around it. The story is a simple one made a great deal more circuitous by McDermott's attempt to convince us that the 10-year-old neighbor, her heart "stopped by the beauty of it all," saw and remembered many unlikely things and imagined the rest; probability is not the novel's strong suit. But we forgive McDermott the implausibility of this point of view because, to begin with, the speaker (now grown and eloquent) casts a forgiving and uncondescending eye on childhood in general and her neighborhood in particular:

> Enough, too much, has already been said about boredom in the suburbs, especially in the early sixties. . . . But I remember those nights as completely interesting, full of flux: the street itself a stage lined with doors, the play rife with arrivals and departures, offstage battles. . . .

Most of the story is her vicarious reconstruction of this neighborhood crisis. And as we near the end of her account of the painful tearing asunder of two sorrowing adolescents—the boy's mother is gently insane, the girl's father dies suddenly, leaving her bewildered and frightened; together their halved souls appear to make a shaky whole—we see that McDermott is really writing about Then and Now, or Early and Later, like the time designations in theater programs. *Then* it is clear to the lovers (who fling their bodies around in various urgent forms of action, fight for Rick, flight for Sheryl) that they will never survive the moment without each other.

But the narrator is too wise to be much impressed by the staying power of "the beauty of it all" anymore. She contemplates the capacity to go on—*Now*—and the forms that going on inevitably take: despair, compromise, the animal need to fill one's arms against emptiness yet again.

Thus another generation of householder evolves. Fathers, mothers, children hide their stifled passions behind suburban house facades. Grown herself, the narrator watches the daring hero, Rick, come back to the block where his unruly rage so long ago cut a swath across his girlfriend's lawn, and sees that he is, tragically, simply an adult now. He is awkward, distant from his old self, recovered—or permanently scarred but recovered nonetheless. As are they all, in their ways; as are we all.

McDermott writes of the poignancy of Then and Now with a grace and richness admirably unmuffled by the fashionable tendency to "minimalize" emotion.

> We had parents who spoke to us and to each other of the city streets where they had spent their childhoods as lost forever, wiped from the face of the earth by change; who said of their old neighborhoods, "You can't go there anymore," as if change had made a place as inaccessible as a time.

Of course her book is about the paralyzing hypocrisy of the "moral" code that would punish a pregnant girl with ostracism. . . . But . . . [it is] more profoundly occupied

with the tragic undertow, beyond changing mores, that takes the lives we hope for and think we deserve, and deforms them. Time and dailiness and then, to quote McDermott, "the cowardly incompetence of memory" wait for all of us, and unless we are rare exceptions, they are the forces that digest the sweetness of our dreams.

Karen Ahlefelder Watkins   (review date 25 May 1987)

SOURCE: "A Streetcar Named Syosset," in *The New Republic,* Vol. 196, No. 21, May 25, 1987, pp. 37-8.

[*In the following review, Watkins maintains that although McDermott's narrator often distracts readers from the characters whose story she is recounting,* That Night *powerfully represents the loss and longing that ensue from the aging process.*]

Sherrryyyyy! Young Marlon Brando-like Rick yells outside his girlfriend Sheryl's house, filling the neighborhood with the sound of his cry and creating the scene that dominates Alice McDermott's second novel, *That Night.* "He stood on the short lawn before her house, his knees bent, his fists driven into his thighs, and bellowed her name with such passion that even the friends who surrounded him, who had come . . . to murder her family if they had to, let the chains they carried go limp in their hands." This scene of violent passion is acted not in the stark setting of *A Streetcar Named Desire* but in the bucolic nest of the American Dream. The haunting cry of loss is set against the "staccato hum" of lawn mowers and "the collective gurgle of filters in backyard pools." These are suburbs transformed by love: "Venus was there," we are told, and what seems at first to be a teenage sex story turns into an engrossing tale about loss and fulfillment, memory and illusion.

Rick is bellowing outside Sheryl's house because he hasn't been able to see her. He and his friends have arrived in a convoy of "hot rods" to get Sheryl and "kill that old bitch" (Sheryl's widowed mother). Rick's mother has often unexpectedly left home to go into mental institutions, and Rick sees the same thing in Sheryl's disappearance: he fears she has changed into another person overnight. He doesn't know that Sheryl is pregnant and has been sent to relatives in Ohio to have the baby. At the sound of Rick's cry, the story's narrator (an unnamed woman, now an adult, looking back nostalgically on her childhood) says that her "ten-year-old heart was stopped by the beauty of it all."

McDermott's first novel, *A Bigamist's Daughter,* explored the way people use fictions to hide or transform the defeats and banalities of their lives. Elizabeth, an editor of a vanity press, tells her lover a story of a past love affair and attempts to transform herself and the affair through embellishments in her retelling. By the end of that novel, Elizabeth is more comfortable with unadorned reality. In *That Night* McDermott goes one step further and introduces a narrator who is both a character within and the creator of the story she tells, and who, also, embellishes her story in an attempt to transform the ordinary into the mythical—thereby revealing the transforming powers of memory and of stories themselves.

The narrator tells us: "It's nostalgia that makes me say it, . . . but there was no boredom in these suburbs." Yet behind the narrator's purple-tinted memories is routine. The "housebound and yardbound" men of the neighborhood cry out for something more. When Rick comes to take Sheryl, they emerge as protectors carrying makeshift weapons and clumsily battle the teenage boys. After the fight, pulled together in their new role, the men gather, "heady with the taste of their own blood," to "reenact in slow, stylized motion the blows they'd given, the blows they had received, adding now the grace that had been missing from the original performance, the witty dialogue, the triumph." Even the narrator is disappointed in their performance: she expected D'Artagnan.

The irony is sometimes cruel. McDermott seems closer to the women in her story: she takes us into their houses and exposes the painful realities of maintaining the dream of suburban life. The neighbors find a utopia in the home of Mrs. Carpenter's family. The upstairs of the Carpenter house, the "enchanted, mist-shrouded heights," is the model of suburban decoration. The family lives in the basement. Mrs. Carpenter ("more artist than eccentric") has created "Beauty" she hopes to save from "the ravages of . . . ash-dropping Time":

> The master bedroom was a sultan's palace, deep green and pink and silver with drapes hanging where there weren't even windows. Not a thing out of place, not a thing that didn't match. A gold swan spouting water in the bathroom sink, its wings Hot and Cold.

The narrator's mother comes back from a tour of the upstairs "holding her heart" and saying there is "nothing else like it in the world. The shine on the dining room table was blinding." Mrs. Carpenter sits in this pathetic paradise with "the bored distracted air of someone simply waiting to see how things turn out."

In *That Night* McDermott introduces a narrator who is both a character within and the creator of the story she tells, and who, also, embellishes her story in an attempt to transform the ordinary into the mythical—thereby revealing the transforming powers of memory and of stories themselves.

—*Karen Ahlefelder Watkins*

Sheryl's untimely pregnancy is set against some of the neighborhood women's pathetic attempts at conception, with their "voodoo" rituals—"hot water douches and citrus diets and intercourse performed with your head and throat hanging off the side of the bed." The narrator realizes that what her own mother is really attempting to conceive is "insurance" against the invalidity of her own existence. Leela, a friend of the narrator's mother, tries all of the above remedies, and says to her husband that if she fails she is "neither male nor female; I cannot know my worth."

While the women inside engage in their nightly gymnastics, Sheryl and Rick are making love in a park, a forest-like setting where, like Hawthorne's lovers in *A Scarlet Letter,* they can obliterate the world beyond. The narrator, as a child, is lucky enough to have a visit from the mysterious older Sheryl, who helps her dress a Barbie doll and who tells her, "I know all those things that other people think are important come down to nothing. They disappear." If Rick, Sheryl tells her, "had died before he met me, everybody . . . would have forgotten about him. . . . But I wouldn't forget." These words echo when the narrator lets us in on the scene in the park: "Sheryl would whisper, 'Before me you would have been forgotten.' " As the narrator tells it, these teenagers making love in a park are one with the natural world: "Perhaps by then he understood only that when she spoke of dying he should turn to her, loosen the scarf at her throat . . . gently push her back onto the grass." But reality breaks in on this idyll; later, in Ohio, Sheryl's cousin Pam, a plump, happily married housewife and mother, tells her that she too was in love like Sheryl, and that "what seems like a terrible loss to you now will only seem natural. . . ."

McDermott disappoints our expectations in the same way. The narrator takes us into the future beyond "that night" as the neighbors gather for a funeral. They look back wistfully at the young couple and the events of the night. Sheryl, a skinny girl with a flat round face—who wears Banlon sweaters, Woolworth scarves, and too much pancake makeup and black eyeliner, and who carries a turquoise comb in her pocket—is remembered as being as beautiful as a Miss America contestant. Though she ends up married with "two kids and a house and all," the women of the neighborhood "had hoped or imagined something more for Sheryl," more than "a life like theirs." Rick, whose youthful role has been that of passionate lover—a suburban Stanley Kowalski—grows to be an ordinary, nondescript family man with two kids.

Rick's cry, taken up by the whole neighborhood in "one, inharmonious wail," is the cry of loss answered by illusion. Suburbia has created its own romantic myth, one of cozy security: "Under the moon and the stars, there were identical rooftops and chimneys and TV antennas, no minarets or onion domes, and the trees that caught and muffled the lamplight were ordinary oak and maple." Yet things still happen there. Fathers die on their way to work, children are killed, and love is made powerless. On the way home from the hospital where Sheryl has left her baby behind, she gains comfort from the "blind, insistent longing that this emptiness be filled again."

The narrator provides potent ironies about the disillusionment of "coming of age," but her voice is sometimes a hindrance. It keeps us too distant from the other characters, too close to her, and at times the narrator's personal asides are more distraction than illumination. But this is minor, and doesn't diminish the novel's power significantly. McDermott's lyrical prose draws us along. The "howling wail" touches us too, and when the narrator says that these suburbs are not boring, we are lured into belief. Embellishing the night by telling us "Venus was there" seems heavy-handed; the moon perhaps would have sufficed. But like the narrator we accept the illusion of Venus and undying love. McDermott's suburbs are about the longing for an "irretrievable past," for the way life was before we knew there was a difference between the life of the basement and the one upstairs.

Whitney Balliett   (review date 17 August 1987)

SOURCE: "Families," in *The New Yorker,* Vol. LXIII, No. 26, August 17, 1987, pp. 71-2.

[*In the excerpt below, Balliett, an American critic who frequently writes about jazz, praises McDermott's use of language and pacing in* That Night.]

Novels were once panoramas, chronicles, labyrinths, whole subcontinents. A novel seemed to expand and multiply as it was read. But the movies have taken over those comprehensive tasks, and the novel has increasingly been made out of glimpses, incidents, small happenings. Its scope has become vertical rather than horizontal. Alice McDermott's *That Night* is centered on a single incident—a brief, dangerous, clumsy fight that takes place between some teen-agers and some grown men in a Long Island suburb in the early sixties. (American genre novels were once set on a variety of frontiers—the prairies, the lower East Side, the Maine woods, the upper East Side, and slow Southern dirt roads. But now they often take place on the last frontier—suburban housing developments.) The book plays with time. It begins with the fight, goes back a couple of hours, returns to the fight, moves forward several days, goes back a year, to the previous summer, then returns to the days following the fight, and, in due course, slides through the previous decade and the decade to come, always using the fight as its pivot. But there is nothing frenetic. The book goes along in an attractive slow motion—in the stately way that time itself moves.

Alice McDermott's writing has the same quality. She uses plain language, but she loves to string amplifying, overlapping clauses together:

> For after this, after the cars and the sudden spinning onto her lawn, the boys with their chains and the fight and the chilling sound of her boyfriend's cry, after this, no small scenes could satisfy us, no muffled arguments, no dinner-at-eight celebrations, no sweet, damaged child, could make us believe we were living a vibrant life, that we had ever known anything about love.

She is Henry James without the furbelows and bibelots and antimacassars.

The incident grows out of the relationship of two bleak high-school students—Sheryl (she is never given a surname) and Rick Slater. Separately, they are unfinished, even damaged, but as a pair they form a kind of whole. During the year before they start going together, Sheryl's father dies suddenly, of a heart attack, leaving her bereft but stoical and coolly melodramatic. She says to a neigh-

bor, "If you knew everybody you loved was just going to end up disappearing, you'd probably say, Why bother, right? . . . I mean how logical is it for you to love somebody and then they just die, like you never existed?" She tells Rick that she is not afraid of dying. He believes her, as he believes everything she says; she is the first person who has ever loved him. His father, once a distracted general practitioner, has let his practice go and works as an assistant in a medical laboratory, while his mother, crazed and diffused, spends most of her time in a state mental hospital. Alice McDermott's use of time builds a certain amount of suspense, and no more will be said of what happens to Sheryl and Rick, except that the battle in the opening pages is between Rick and his high-school friends and the men who live in Sheryl's neighborhood. The weapons are chains and baseball bats and snow shovels, and the engagement is useless and unheroic.

Alice McDermott's small, melancholy, lyrical book deals with life in the suburbs and with the old gulf between generations. But it is also about adolescent passion, which, despite the clichés surrounding it, is often so astonishing and empyreal that it is never matched, or even remembered properly, by its once dazzled victims. It is a passion that Sheryl and Rick can only circle.

Robert Towers   (review date 21 January 1988)

SOURCE: "All-American Novels," in *The New York Review of Books,* Vol. XXXIV, Nos. 21-2, January 21, 1988, pp. 26-7.

[*Towers is an American novelist. In the excerpt below, he commends the accuracy with which McDermott recreates a lower-middle-class Long Island town during the early 1960s as well as her focus on the ordinary in* That Night, *but he questions the book's merit as a contender for the National Book Award for Fiction.*]

That Night, a second novel by Alice McDermott, was a runner-up for the [National Book Award for Fiction]. Its subject is the love affair between two teen-agers, Rick and Sheryl, and its setting is a lower-middle-class, mostly Catholic, Long Island suburb in the early 1960s; more broadly, it is the story of the neighborhood's response to the violent termination of the affair as witnessed by a ten-year-old girl who has been following its progress with all of the rapturous curiosity of a child in love with the idea of love. That girl, now grown into wistful adulthood, recounts the events as she remembers them, imagines scenes involving Rick and Sheryl and their families which she did not witness, and comments ruefully on the changes wrought by time on all of the principals and bystanders, including herself. The result is a pleasant and readable piece of bittersweet Americana, scrupulously detailed and faithful to the spirit of its time and place.

Alice McDermott begins her novel at its most dramatic moment, when Rick, accompanied by his black-jacketed, chain-carrying friends, stands on the short lawn before Sheryl's house and—"with his knees bent, his fists driven into his thighs"—bellows her name. Unknown to him, Sheryl is pregnant, and her shamed mother and grandmother have shipped her off to relatives in Ohio, where, in accordance with the code of her class and religion, she is to bear her baby and give it up for adoption by a good Catholic family; she is never to see Rick again. All that Rick knows is that Sheryl has not answered his increasingly frantic telephone calls and that her mother has answered them in a frustratingly evasive way. The narrator remembers that, hearing that heartbroken cry, her own "ten-year-old heart was stopped by the beauty of it all."

> *That Night* **is a pleasant and readable**
> **piece of bittersweet Americana,**
> **scrupulously detailed and faithful to the**
> **spirit of its time and place.**
>
> *—Robert Towers*

Meanwhile the entire neighborhood has gathered outside on that early summer night. The fathers are armed with baseball bats and snow shovels to repel the invasion of "hoods," who, before pulling up in front of Sheryl's house, have slowly and menacingly driven though the neighborhood a number of times; the mothers and children are looking on in various states of excitement and alarm. When Rick pulls Sheryl's mother from her house, the men rush to her rescue and a melee ensues—chains against bats and shovels—that is ended by the arrival of the police. No one is seriously hurt, but for days afterward the fathers, who, unlike their wives and children, are not given to easy socializing within the neighborhood, meet to display their bruises and gashes and to boast about what they will do to the hoods if they ever come back. The narrator apostrophizes them:

> Our fathers. They were still dark-haired then, and handsome. Their bruised arms were still strong under their rolled shirt sleeves, their chests still broad under their T-shirts. They had fought wars and come home to love their wives and sire their children; they had laid out fifteen thousand dollars to shelter them. They had grown housebound and too cautious, . . . but now, heady with the taste of their own blood, . . . they were ready to take up this new challenge, were ready to save us, their daughters, from the part of love that was painful and tragic and violent, from all that we had already, even then, set our hearts on.

From this point the novel continues to deal with the aftermath of the invasion and follows Sheryl into exile in Ohio. At regular intervals the narrator interrupts her ongoing story to retrace the relationship between the two lovers. Both come from seriously disturbed situations at home. Rick, we learn, is the son of a failed doctor and a mentally ill, often suicidal mother; he does badly in school and hangs out with a tough gang of friends. Sheryl has been left raw and bleeding by the recent death of her young father, who had suffered a heart attack while driving to work. In *That Night*'s most moving episode, she is driven home by the high school principal, who breaks the news

to her, and arrives at the very moment that a policeman drives up in her father's car, returning it to the family. Convinced that there has been a mistake and that her father is alive, Sheryl "pushed wildly at the car door and then ran up the steps to her house. She seemed to be laughing and the women all up and down the block could hear her call to her father as she entered." At the time she takes up with Rick she is living at home with her bereaved, embittered mother and her Polish-speaking grandmother and longs for a love to replace her father's loss. There is a defiant edge to her grief.

Here is the way she looks:

> She was skinny, not very tall, with thin taffy-colored hair and light brown eyes. . . . Her mouth was small and seemed to hang a little too low in her round flat face. She wore pancake makeup and black eyeliner that itself was sometimes lined with white. She dressed as all the girls who went with hoods had dressed. To school, she wore tight skirts and thin, usually sleeveless sweaters made of some material like Banlon or rayon and meant to show off both her bra straps and her small breasts. She wore bangle bracelets and, later, Rick's silver ID bracelet and a delicate gold "slave chain" on her ankle, under her stocking.

Neither the story, the observations of character, nor the descriptions are in any way remarkable; the prose, while lucid, is hardly distinctive. Still, Alice McDermott deals honestly with her materials and does not try to wring from them any more poignancy or pathos than they warrant. Rick and Sheryl are ordinary kids, not a re-embodied Romeo and Juliet, and it is their ordinariness—and that of their suburban town—that are so affectionately recreated by the narrator. McDermott can be funny too, as in her account of the Carpenter family who live chiefly in the finished basement of their house—a basement equipped with a bathroom and a kitchenette—because the rest of the house, with its white and gold living room and a carpet that feels "like fur laid over clouds," is "too beautiful to bear."

The forward glances to the present, which allow us to see the decline of the neighborhood and the fear of crime that has replaced the old sense of security, are handled with considerable tact and a minimum of nostalgia. The final glimpse the author allows us of the adult Rick and his dejected family is, in its understated way, devastating.

That Night is, then, a small, decent work that succeeds within its limits. That it should have been nominated as one of the five best novels of the year must, I imagine, be nearly as surprising to its author as it is to this reviewer.

Michiko Kakutani   (review date 24 March 1992)

SOURCE: "The Lessons of Loss Learned in Childhood," in *The New York Times*, March 24, 1992, p. C15.

[*In the following review, Kakutani praises McDermott's use of children as narrators in* At Weddings and Wakes *and her thematic focus on loss.*]

Alice McDermott's last novel, the critically acclaimed *That Night,* used the story of a doomed teen-age romance to create a resonant portrait of suburban life in the early 1960's: a lyrical and haunting portrait that left the reader with an indelible sense of life's precariousness, the ephemerality of youth and passion and hope.

The same sense of lost innocence and betrayed dreams lingers in the wake of her latest book, *At Weddings and Wakes,* a beautifully wrought novel that depicts three generations of an Irish Catholic family in New York through the eyes of three young children. Though the child's point of view and the time frame—the early 60's, again—are reminiscent of *That Night,* the world portrayed in this volume feels light years removed from that earlier novel's leafy suburbs. It is a world where everyone goes to Mass on Sunday, the women wearing fur collars and hats, the men in dark, somber coats: a world where children dream of growing up to become nuns and priests; a world defined by holiday rituals and dozens of tiny domestic routines.

Though there are excursions to Long Island in *At Weddings and Wakes,* the novel takes place, for the most part, in Brooklyn, in the narrow, gloomy apartment of the Towne family, where Momma lives with her three unmarried stepdaughters: May, a kind, retiring woman, whose manners and clothes betray her former vocation as a nun; Veronica, a housebound spinster who drinks too much and spends too much time alone in her room, and Agnes, a bustling, efficient career woman, who prides herself on her knowledge of the world. ("She knew good china, fine cheese, the best seats at every Broadway theater. She knew the best stores, the best tailors, the proper way for a man's suit to fit.")

Their other sister, Lucy, is married and lives on Long Island, but she returns to the apartment twice a week, with her children, to visit Momma and complain about her unhappy marriage and her unfulfilled dreams. It is from the point of view of Lucy's three children—Margaret, Bobby and Maryanne—that we come to see the family and understand the ghosts that haunt its collective imagination.

Death, grief and disappointment: these are the lessons that Margaret, Bobby and Maryanne learn from the women in their family, the lessons that early on shatter their innocent apprehension of the world at large. Annie, Momma's sister—and the mother of Lucy and her sisters—died shortly after giving birth to Veronica. In time, Momma married Annie's husband, Jack, (and gave birth to a son named John), but it wasn't long before Jack, too, died suddenly, leaving Momma with an incradicable sense of loss and a lasting bitterness toward the world. John and Veronica have turned to alcohol as a solace from their own private failures, while Agnes, Lucy and May have tried to make a separate, it unsatisfying, peace with their circumscribed lives.

Then, suddenly, for a brief moment, May seems granted a chance at a second life: she falls in love with Fred, the local mailman. At first they speak awkwardly to each other about the weather, and their families, but one day, Fred takes May out to dinner. He starts sending her flow-ers every week—roses and daisies and violently colored gladioluses—and finally, after five years, he proposes.

At the wedding reception, the children look at May and Fred and realize that something indeed had happened in that hour since they'd left the church together.

> A consummation of sorts that had made them clearly husband and wife, made them so firmly husband and wife that it seemed for the moment that they could no longer be aunt, sister, stepdaughter, stranger, mailman, as well. They had shed, in the past hour, or perhaps only in the time since they entered this perfectly lit, hourless, seasonless place, everything about themselves but one another.

The marriage is short-lived. Four days after the wedding, May is dead: a startling, inexplicable death ("Something burst inside her"), as senseless and sudden as that of her mother and father.

This tragic event is mentioned by Ms. McDermott early in this elliptical novel, before we really understand the sad history of the Towne family, and it informs our reading of all that follows. We read about May's girlhood, her entry into and departure from the convent, her courtship and her wedding, all with the awful knowledge of her eventual fate.

For May's young nephew and nieces, her story will mark their initiation into "that current of loss after loss that was adulthood." Like the modern-day Romeo and Juliet story that stands at the center of *That Night,* the story of May's wedding and wake will become a kind of touchstone: it will forever divide the lives of Margaret, Bobby and Maryanne into a before and after.

In describing Margaret, Bobby and Maryanne's memories of their youth, Ms. McDermott rarely uses their names; they are usually referred to, simply, as "the children." Their perceptions, too, are invested with a certain timeless quality: a single afternoon at Momma's becomes a metaphor for all the afternoons spent there; a single Christmas becomes all holidays. As rendered through Ms. McDermott's rich, supple prose, and infused with her quiet, emotional wisdom, the story of these three children and their family assumes a kind of mythic resonance: it becomes a parable about all families and all families' encounters with love, mortality and sorrow.

Wendy Smith   (essay date 30 March 1992)

SOURCE: "Alice McDermott," in *Publishers Weekly,* Vol. 239, No. 16, March 30, 1992, pp. 85-6.

[*An American editor, Smith is the author of the 1990* Real Life Drama: The Group Theatre and America, 1931-1940. *In the following essay, based in part on conversations with McDermott, she provides an overview of McDermott's career as well as her insights into the writing process.*]

In 1979 a nervous graduate of the University of New Hampshire's writing program handed literary agent Harriet Wasserman's secretary a few short stories and 50 pages of an unfinished novel. Wasserman read them, called the writer and said, "I want you to give me everything you've got." Not too long after that, she invited Alice McDermott to her office and asked, "Would you like a male editor or a female one?"

The astonished 26-year-old, who would have been happy with "any living, breathing literary editor," wound up under the wing of Jonathan Galassi, then a rising star at Houghton Mifflin. She followed him to Random House, which in 1982 published her first novel, *A Bigamist's Daughter,* to the kind of critical enthusiasm most beginning writers only dream about. Next McDermott went with Galassi to Farrar, Straus & Giroux, which released *That Night* in 1987; it was nominated for a National Book Award and made into a film, which will be released later this spring.

Given this prompt and warm encouragement, it's surprising to discover that, for McDermott, "the hardest thing I had to do even to become a writer was believing that I had anything to say that people would want to read." She began with short stories, she explains, because "I felt I had to apologize for wanting to write fiction for a living, and with a short story there was this sense of, well, it's just a little bitty thing!"

On the eve of the April publication of her third novel, *At Weddings and Wakes,* the author, now 38, continues to display a certain diffidence about her work. Discussing the brevity of her books, none of which runs to much more than 200 pages, she comments, "I still have that sense of apology: Look, I'm not going to waste your time; I'm going to tell you what I need to tell you, then stop. When I'm composing something I'm always looking for that point where I feel everything I and the reader need to know is there, then that's enough. Sing your song and get off—before they bring out the hook!"

She traces the origins of this feeling to her childhood in suburban Long Island, "a place where writers were all dead people, not knowing anyone who was even close, who even worked as a secretary in a publishing house. It just seemed so remote. I remember discovering the *New York Times Book Review* when I was at Oswego [campus of the State University of New York], sitting out there on Lake Ontario with the *Times,* which we had started getting because we all realized we were going to have to begin thinking about jobs, and finding that they had this whole section about books!"

"We didn't have the *New York Times* around much at home. I think my family, with completely good intentions, discouraged me [from becoming a writer] because it seemed so removed to them; they saw me starving in a garret and tried to steer me away from it the same way they tried to steer me away from cocaine: 'I know it sounds very appealing right now, but believe me, you'll regret it!' Their big thing was that I should go to Katie Gibbs and learn shorthand: 'If you really love books, you can get a good job in publishing if you have your secretarial skills. Then maybe you can be an editor and if you really want to write, you can write at night. But you'll have health insurance!' "

> **If I was going to crusade for anything in literature, it would be that sometimes I worry that we're forgetting how to read fiction by relating it too much to real things, by saying, "How do you do this?" or "How autobiographical is it?"**
>
> **—Alice McDermott**

McDermott laughs without resentment as she mimics her parents' advice. She knows how tough a writer's life can be; after earning her B.A., she worked briefly as a clerk-typist at a vanity publisher, background she drew on for some hilarious but ultimately sad scenes in *A Bigamist's Daughter.* She was still uncertain enough about her choice of career when she enrolled in the University of New Hampshire's graduate writing program to declare, "I'm going to give myself these two years, and if I haven't published anything by the time I leave then I'll know I'm not a writer."

UNH gave her the confidence she needed. "For the first time in my life I was in a community of people who were writing, and that was wonderful. I don't want to make my family sound like a bunch of philistines; we always read at home, and books were important. But to be involved in the process in any way was remarkable to me—that people said 'I am a writer' without apologies. I went there filled with the idea of inspiration in the middle of the night: you jump out of bed and type for a while, then in the next scene you're at Sardi's. Here people read what I wrote, talked to me about it and told me what to do. It showed me how to be a working writer."

She credits her teacher Mark Smith with pushing her toward professionalism. "In my second year, he asked me what I had sent out. When I admitted I hadn't submitted anything, he said, 'Look, you've got the talent, but you've got to take yourself seriously. Is this a career, or just something that you're doing?' He treated me as a colleague, which was a wonderful confidence-builder; he helped me see myself as something other than apologetic about what I did."

All her talk about confidence-building and feeling apologetic may make McDermott sound neurotically self-deprecating, which she isn't. On the contrary, she's confident enough now to candidly reveal her insecurities and laugh gently at them, knowing that they're an inevitable part of the process. "One of the best things about New Hampshire was that when you said, 'This is really tough to do,' people said, 'Oh, yeah, I know.' Whereas once when I was home on vacation and all depressed about whatever I was working on—as I usually am when I'm writing—I came down to get a cup of tea and, when my mother asked me what was wrong and I said it was going really badly, she said, 'Well, don't do it!' "

Fortunately, McDermott didn't take her mother's advice.

She started sending out her short stories, which were published in *Redbook, Mademoiselle* and *Seventeen*. After *A Bigamist's Daughter* was released, she and her husband moved to the West Coast, where she taught at the University of California, San Diego, and completed *That Night.* Another transcontinental move, this time with a young son in tow, to Bethesda, Md., delayed work on a book that she eventually put aside to write *At Weddings and Wakes*.

"I had started a novel trying to deal somehow with Irish Catholic things, and I just wasn't settling into it right," she explains, seated in her publisher's downtown Manhattan offices. Her fair, faintly freckled skin and light brown hair suggesting her own Irish descent. She is relaxed and extremely articulate about the craft of writing as she discusses the genesis of her current book.

"I was sitting in my son's room, and he has that poster of *In the Night Kitchen* [Maurice Sendak's loving tribute to his native Brooklyn]. I thought, that sort of dark Brooklyn street, that's it exactly—clearly it's not an accurate drawing of any real place, but I liked that sense of giving an almost impressionistic feel, just the darkness and the strangeness of it. That gave me the idea for the opening chapter of *At Weddings and Wakes*."

That chapter describes the twice-weekly journey taken by the three Dailey children and their mother from their Long Island home to the Brooklyn apartment where their grandmother and aunts live—a vivid rendering so evocative in its use of physical and period detail (the time is the early 1960s) that the reader only gradually realizes that no specific subways, streets or neighborhoods have been identified.

That's the way the author wanted it; she had tried for the same impressionistic effect in *That Night,* which was set in a suburb most critics identified as Long Island but McDermott intended as "very much a generic suburb. I think when I write I take detail or image from absolutely wherever I can get it. I don't dare stop and think. It's just: 'That'll do. That'll do,'" she says, stretching out her hands to mime snatching individual "thats" out of the air. "It's only afterward that you sit back and say, 'Yes, this is that place.'"

McDermott, in fact, dislikes drawing those parallels. "If I was going to crusade for anything in literature, it would be that sometimes I worry that we're forgetting how to read fiction by relating it too much to real things, by saying, 'How do you do this?' or 'How autobiographical is it?'

"What really brought this home for me was when I went to the set of the movie of *That Night.* They took me into the room they had built for the girl who's the narrator. They had made this wonderful early '60s girl's bedroom: every detail was just right, things I hadn't thought of in years. And I had the feeling that all these details I had wrested from reality and tried to make something else entirely had been pulled back into reality.

"I think we have to remember that fiction is in its own world—it's a new world every time you open a book, and what its relationship is to the real world is almost beside the point. And isn't that wonderful? It's giving you an op-

portunity to see life not actually portrayed but as something else entirely. Not to get highfalutin, but it's a work of art that's complete in some way. The thing I took away from my morning on the movie set was that revelation: It's not that you remembered or found the right source to tell you what kind of advertising was in the subway in 1962—it's easy to find that out. It's what that advertisement means in the context of the whole work that's important."

I like that going over, seeing an event through other events that have occurred since, seeing it again and seeing it in a different way, from a different perspective as time goes on—to me that's very much what fiction does. I see so much of the process of fiction in memory, and I guess that appeals to me.

—*Alice McDermott*

When McDermott sets a novel in the past, as she has done with her two most recent books, evoking a particular period is not her primary interest. "The past gives you a perspective where you can see connections. I think with *A Bigamist's Daughter* I was resisting seeing connections—I said, 'No, there aren't any connections, goddammit,' and using the present was a way of proving that. Maybe just with age, I've started hoping there were connections, and it seemed that one way to find them was to look at some part of life as a whole. Generally that would be the past; that kind of closure seems to define the area you're working in. So it's a matter of trying to make sense rather than being proud of proving that there is no sense!"

Making sense of the past, for McDermott, involves a complex time structure in which the narrative circles around certain key events, which are not necessarily presented in chronological order. "That seems to me to be true to our experience about life; it's all seen through time. You don't look at the past just once, and you look at it with the knowledge of the present, which was the future. I like that going over, seeing an event through other events that have occurred since, seeing it again and seeing it in a different way, from a different perspective as time goes on—to me that's very much what fiction does. I see so much of the process of fiction in memory, and I guess that appeals to me."

"Also, I'm interested for my own writing in structure; I find myself more and more intrigued with the way novels are put together. Straight, realistic narrative seems to leave something out for me; I like the puzzle of it, the game of putting things together in unusual ways that somehow, I hope, come together. I guess this is why I've moved away from short-story writing. I remember saying in graduate school, although I'm not sure what I meant by it—I probably read it somewhere and thought it sounded good—'Life is lived in short stories; we live in moments.' Well, at 21 it feels like a short story, but the older I get, the more my life feels like a novel!"

With a three-year-old daughter and a six-year-old son demanding her attention, teaching responsibilities at American University and a new novel under way, McDermott's life is full enough for a Victorian three-decker. "The new novel is contemporary, but there are relatives to remind us of the past, and there's a sense of future as well—that's different, and that's what keeps me with it. The battle is always to keep yourself interested; I'm as easily distracted as the reader. My office is right through the laundry room, so I can always think of other things that need to be done! But a good thing that comes with having children and being busy is that it gives me energy, because it makes me use my time more efficiently."

Richard Eder   (review date 12 April 1992)

SOURCE: "Letting a Little Air In," in *Los Angeles Times Book Review,* April 12, 1992, pp. 3, 7.

[*In the following review, Eder appreciates McDermott's use of period detail and complex narration in* At Weddings and Wakes.]

Get the subatomics right and you get the universe right; get the quarks in line and the quintessentials fall into place. So modern physics tells us, pausing periodically to wonder if it is true.

There are a few American writers who use the homely details of people's lives and behaviors that way. They get these details absolutely right, not for the purpose of description, or classification, or—as with some of the minimalists—taxidermy, but to ignite the transformations inside them.

Ann Tyler does it frequently in her shabby-genteel Baltimore; Bobby Ann Mason did it at least once, in the small Kentucky town of *In Country;* Susan Minot did it, also once, with the troubled New England family of *Monkeys.* Alice McDermott did it with **That Night**. She got the movements and vacancies of an American suburb to work so exactly that, out of their clotted energy, she released a Tristan and an Iseult in the guise of two adolescent lovers.

McDermott does it once more in *At Weddings and Wakes*. A more constricted book in some ways, it is set, in the 1950s, among the stifled grievances of an Irish-American matriarch and her three spinster stepdaughters. Cooped up in the middle-class solidity of a Brooklyn apartment—Brooklyn was solid back then—they alternately fatten on rancorous memories and struggle ineffectually to escape them.

Mary Towne came over from Ireland in the 1920s to help with her sister's fourth childbirth. When the baby was born, the sister died; Mary stayed on to help the widower, and eventually to marry him. Briefly, there was a blaze of something like passion; then the widower died, leaving Mary to rule with the heavy hand of disappointed memory.

John, their son and her pride, turned into a drunk, moved away and comes back annually for a brief, angry visit. As for the stepsisters, the loving and sweet-tempered May entered a convent, found she loved its peace and quiet so much as to distract her from religion—a wonderful McDermott touch—and came home to live. At the end, she marries Fred, a postman, but it is a sadly brief escape. Agnes, with a good job as an executive secretary in Manhattan, returns each night to exercise her critical spirit and sharp tongue. Veronica, pock-marked and alcoholic, drifts woozily out of her bedroom long enough to locate an affront and carry it back in with her.

The Towne apartment—heavy furniture and Waterford crystal and starched Irish linen for holidays—is asphyxiating, and McDermott occasionally comes close to asphyxiating us with it. (It is a risk you take if you write well; describe a Camembert, and the reader has to open a window.) But essentially, her book transforms the oppressiveness.

The somber realism of the Towne menage is undermined by the little eyes that see it. They belong to the three children who visit dutifully twice a week during the summer from their home in the leafy green outskirts of Queens. Lucy, their mother, brings them; she is the fourth stepdaughter. Ostensibly, she has escaped; in fact, with her incessant visiting, her perpetual phone calls, her instant immersions into the latest round of Towne bickering, she is torn between two worlds.

The Brooklyn apartment is old-world memory troubled by the struggle of its prisoners. The new world and its possibilities are represented by Lucy's husband: kind, buoyant and with a talent for exploration and enjoyment. The children move forward with him, inevitably and fortunately, but at some sacrifice. McDermott makes us feel the health that lies in releasing memory's chains. She makes us feel the weight of the chains, but she makes us feel their piety as well, and the tug they exert even when cast off. Her book has a bewitching complexity.

The narration is part of the bewitchment. It belongs to the three children: kind Bobby, who at 12 or so still thinks he wants to be a priest; gawky and introspective Margaret, with a gloomy touch of her mother's "easy access to regret"; and Maryanne, the wide-eyed, melodramatic baby of the family. The narrative doesn't belong particularly to any one of them, though Margaret is the most likely, and it suggests both children seeing, and remembering as adults what they once saw.

This allows reflectiveness and immediacy; it allows a darting chronology. and a darting selection of events to be followed. It allows us, as children do, to change the subject. Its quickness and lightness do not lighten the heaviness of the Towne household, but they set it off like alternating tiles in a mosaic.

We read of the painful twice-weekly trip of Lucy and the children from Queens to Brooklyn: a 10-block walk in the July heat, a bus, then another bus, a subway and then another subway. Yet the painfulness—it lies not so much in the trip as in the quality of Lucy's dogged pilgrimage to her family's battles—is relieved by the freshness of the children's experiencing. They note Lucy's fuss with the front-door latch as they leave, her juggle with white gloves, handbag and the cigarette she lights up between buses and stamps out with the toe of her high heel pumps. In the crowded bus she stands, shielding them "in what might have been her shadow had the light been right, but was in reality merely the length that the warmth of her body and the odor of her talc extended."

After the long Brooklyn afternoon, their father arrives to take them home. They all perk up: the children, Lucy, her sisters, old Mrs. Towne. Gaiety has made an entrance, theatrical as the contrast between the masks of comedy and tragedy. The trip back in the family car is another contrast, a chariot ride after the morning's bus-and-subway ordeal.

Another chapter tells of the annual two-week beach holiday in a rented cabin on the eastern tip of Long Island. The Brooklyn visits are replaced by swimming, shell-collecting and fishing from a hired rowboat. It is the father's time. A slum child who remembers what a trip to the country meant to him, he insists on the two-week break to administer beauty as though it were a vitamin. Lucy enjoys it in a complaining sort of way; but each evening she treks to the public phone to plug back in to Brooklyn, and the quarrelsome remembrance that is her own vitamin.

There are stories of each of the Townes, and beautifully, lightly contrasting accounts of the children's own encounters at school and elsewhere. The most vivid and winning of the Towne stories is that of May, the ex-nun who timidly falls in love with Fred, the postman, and marries him. It is a lovely courtship, though it comes tragically late. The wedding and reception are a long and skillful set piece, but their awkward celebration and embarrassing emotional misfires belong to an all too familiar genre, and don't advance it much.

On the other hand, the story of Fred is one of the most rousing and moving things in the book. It uses familiar materials—he is an Irish-American bachelor who cares for his mother until her death—but his portrait continually takes on new and unexpected shadings. McDermott can make sadness exhilarating; she can make goodness as irresistible as venial sin.

The detail in *At Weddings and Wakes* is not painstaking but hallowing; as if specific descriptions were the wards of a key and lock that, fitted exactly, open the door to the perilous magic of the past.

Verlyn Klinkenborg   (review date 12 April 1992)

SOURCE: "Grief That Lasts Forever," in *The New York Times Book Review,* April 12, 1992, p. 3.

[Klinkenborg is an editor and nonfiction writer. In the following review, he provides a highly favorable assessment of At Weddings and Wakes.*]*

Alice McDermott's *At Weddings and Wakes* is her third novel in a decade. But after three books, her voice still has enough unfamiliarity to keep a reader slightly off balance. You're not quite sure what to expect of a McDermott

novel, and this is her own doing. For although they share some thematic constants, each of Ms. McDermott's books—*A Bigamist's Daughter, That Night* and now *At Weddings and Wakes*—seems to have fashioned, for her, a wholly new fictional manner of being.

We are used to speaking of a writer's growth, as if the increasing stature of each new book could be marked on a kind of critical doorjamb. But there is such a thing as utter transformation too, and that is harder to talk about. The effect of Ms. McDermott's extraordinary second novel, *That Night,* was not deducible in any way from the "promise" of *A Bigamist's Daughter.* And if *That Night* and *At Weddings and Wakes* feel like closer kin, it's only because Ms. McDermott has taught us to expect something extraordinary.

The much-refracted plot of *At Weddings and Wakes* concerns five women: four middle-aged sisters and their elderly stepmother, known simply as Momma. Lucy, the only married sister, whose three school-age children are the eyes through which the reader most often sees, has moved to the suburbs of Long Island, where her life, it is hinted, is undergoing a slow evisceration. Twice weekly, and on holidays, she makes the long trip to the Brooklyn apartment where she grew up, bringing her children with her, there to renew her marital lament among her family.

In that apartment, Momma still lives with Lucy's sisters: Agnes, a stern executive secretary; Veronica, an "unfortunate," an invalid; and May, a former nun whose wedding adorns one of the final sections of the novel. (Hers is also the wake.) There are men on the horizon too: "their father," as Lucy's husband is mostly known to us; Fred, the mailman who becomes May's husband and widower; and John, the only child of Momma's flesh, a drunkard. And there are the dead, of course.

To the extent that any novel's plot is a form of explanation, *At Weddings and Wakes* explains how the present is memorialized, how the three children's memories, as they will be understood many years later in adulthood, came into being. Though at one time or another Ms. McDermott uses the vantage point offered by almost every character in the novel, the children are her favorites, because what is customary for them has not yet been decided. She values the precariousness of their security, the way the unaccustomed springs up to terrify them. Collectively and individually, the children see the shadows and light behind every object, every habit, every murmur. Events are perceived as if they became, in the instant of that perception, memories that have long since given shape to the family's existence; the present seems to be the age-old past. Ms. McDermott is the kind of novelist who is likely to be described as transfiguring everyday life. But what is everyday life when memory has such power?

Ms. McDermott draws us into her novel by letting us be children again, allowing us to spy on an adult world where time is "draining itself from the scene in a slow leak." The Brooklyn apartment is as formal as the Irish grief it embodies; there is no accommodation for children. Once, when Lucy's children are left there alone with Momma, she begins to interrogate them about her stepdaughters'

> **After three books, McDermott's voice still has enough unfamiliarity to keep a reader slightly off balance. You're not quite sure what to expect of a McDermott novel, and this is her own doing.**
>
> **—Verlyn Klinkenborg**

failings, especially those of May, whose romance seems ludicrous to her. Of Momma's own husband, who died just outside the apartment door and who still seems to linger there, dying, she tells the children, "The only thing I ever held against him was that he made me believe the worst was over."

The children sit stunned at Momma's dining room table, intimidated by the cutlery and china, diminished by her reverie, "as near as they would ever come to the possibility of never seeing their mother again, of having been swept forever into that current of loss after loss that was adulthood." What they feel in that apartment is the permanence of female grief, a permanence to which much can be added but nothing taken away. Timelessness offers "no appeal to the children, since everything they wanted was in the future." But the future, seen from that apartment, is already tinged with sorrow, even at holidays: "Before the merry fog of [Christmas] had cleared they caught the stony shapes of Golgotha. The mournful part."

Yet against the stony shapes, Ms. McDermott portrays a beauty so heady that it requires all of Momma's anger, all of Agnes's brittleness and Lucy's self-absorbed lamentation, to balance it. Some of that joy belongs to the children, who have the naturally comic imaginations of those who have been suffocated by propriety: "In their secret hearts they wished to see [Aunt May] slip on one of the magazines, see her rise for one second into the air like a levitated woman (garters and bloomers showing) and then fall crashing back, their mother running in from the kitchen, Momma pulling open the bedroom door."

And it is right that the children should wish this upon Aunt May, for she is the one member of the family who would have stood up and laughed along with them. Her love (for the mailman! her sisters think) is that of an irrepressibly, though not stupidly, affectionate woman, a woman who left the convent because "she had come to love too dearly the life she was leading, the early Masses and the simple meals and, in those years she taught, the small faces of her students." As her marriage approaches, May finds herself "wondering if in order to bestow such a blessing—this blessing of romance, middle-aged romance at that—God was not sometimes as foolish, as childish, in his love for us as we are when we first discover our love for one another."

You may not be able to hear, from the few lines I've quoted, how remarkable Ms. McDermott's prose is. In *That Night* (a first-person novel) you could find, from time to time, a place where her rather clipped sentences began to

inhabit an architecture that wasn't quite vernacular but something more formal, more expressive. In *At Weddings and Wakes,* her sentences have been lengthened and elaborated, without becoming unduly sinuous, without losing their immediacy. They have a harmony all their own—grave, decorous, moving. They are put together like the music that plays at the end of May's wedding: "The notes of the organ seemed to build a staircase in the bleached air above their heads and then to topple it over as Aunt May and Fred walked down the steps, through the altar rail, and out over the white carpet to the door."

And the sentences of this beautiful novel are also like the low music that plays on the radio Lucy's husband listens to, in which he hears echoes of the sad speech of the women who surround him, "an undercurrent . . . that served as some constant acknowledgment of the lives of the dead."

Paul Baumann   (review date 22 May 1992)

SOURCE: "Imperishable Identities," in *Commonweal,* Vol. CXIX, No. 10, May 22, 1992, pp. 15-16.

[*In the following review, Baumann commends McDermott's evocation of daily life and family ties in* At Weddings and Wakes.]

Old Momma Towne, the widowed Irish matriarch of Alice McDermott's stunning new novel [*At Weddings and Wakes*], orchestrates the ceremonial gatherings of her four stepdaughters with a certain "papal dignity," the narrator tells us. She's a very Irish pope, to be sure. Of her daughter May's future husband's irritating habit of sending flowers, Momma Towne is as suspicious—and as unforgiving—as the proverbial Irish peasant. "Don't think I didn't notice," she announces in her brogue. "First of the month it's roses, last of the month daisies. . . . A man who runs out of money at the end of the month is no manager." Of the soon-to-be- married couple's unwary plans for the future—a future where inevitably every joy must be paid for in the hard currency of loss—Momma Towne is equally dismissive. "All of us moving out to Long Island with the grass and the trees. A regular vision of heaven," she says with her bitter wit. "It wouldn't hurt him to show a little more caution."

Weaned on Momma Towne's ruminative resentments, her stepdaughters—especially Lucy, mother of the three children whose wide eyes and sharp ears bring us into this enchanted world—can nurse a grievance with the same fierce devotion that their men milk a bottle of whiskey. Unsatisfactory marriage, alcoholism, disfigurement, and early death all haunt this stolid, intense, striving middle-class family. "My husband died right outside this apartment door," Momma Towne is fond of recalling, like a priest pronouncing the words of consecration. Her sister, her husband's first wife, died in childbirth in the same apartment. Her son John, handsome and fatally charming, has been exiled for his incorrigible drinking, relegated to an annual Christmas visit. So when Momma and her stepdaughters—Aunt May, Agnes, and Veronica still live at home—gather in her dark, cluttered Brooklyn apartment, there are many spirits to be appeased.

As a family the Towne women are a formidable and brooding presence. More than anything else, it is their "easy access to regret" that sets them apart and endows them with spiritual authority. That regret is also, irrevocably, a shared history and very much a corporate identity. Without it, they would be cut off both from what joy they can hope for as well as, paradoxically, from their deepest, most individual selves.

Bob Dailey, Lucy's husband, shrewdly evaluates the source of Momma's hurtful affections in telling the story of her prodigal son.

> Not, their father was now saying into the darkness as he drove, because of all the torment John had put Momma through in his wild days, oh no. That was not what had so thoroughly hardened her heart. What had done it, what had made her mad as hell, he said, was that the bastard had stopped. "She feels the same way about God."

McDermott is an elegant stylist who can tell a story from a variety of points of view, and she can get away with such luxurious sentiments and sentences. *At Weddings and Wakes* is a complex narrative that beguiles with the strong rhythm of its prose and the almost liturgical movement of its story. The novel opens with a bravado set piece in which the three young Dailey children are led by their fitful mother on the magical journey from their suburban home to Momma's fourth-floor walk-up. It is a journey in time and history as well as geography. Momma Towne's apartment is the focus of family life and lore, a shrine where a sacred creed is faithfully recited. As with the opening scene in McDermott's previous novel, *That Night,* which propels the reader into the lives of an otherwise unexceptional teen-age couple, *At Weddings and Wakes* immediately sweeps the reader into the numinous world of the Townes. McDermott turns the homely artifacts of everyday life—in this case Chiclets, butterscotch Life Savers, Syrian bread, the *Reader's Digest* and old *Playbill* magazines—into talismans and portents. While an unearthly light and shadow suffuse the streets and rooms, the smells, sounds, and voices of a familiar American landscape establish the thick texture of these lives.

Set in the early 1960s, the routines of the kitchen, followed by the small formalities of the "cocktail cart" anchor daily life. We are also given a glimpse of the strained intimacies of more traditional family gatherings. McDermott kneads this domestic experience in a way that seeks to hold seeming opposites—sisterly love and jealousy, motherly pride and resentment, transience and timelessness—in tension. The Townes do not so much rise above circumstance and history as they hallow them. McDermott is intent on evoking the timelessness present in every passing moment; on reclaiming the past that, though seemingly invisible, colors every present emotion and thing.

In this shadowy world lineage carries weight—we inherit both strengths and weaknesses, and often our strength is also our weakness. As Reynolds Price has written, "No-body under forty can believe how nearly everything's inherited." What the Townes inherit circumscribes their hopes, but is equally a gift—and can never be one without the other. It is unusual to read a contemporary novel so knowing in its acceptance of the boundedness of individual life and of life itself. "Love me, love my parents; love what I come from and what I will, with no more choice or volition, become," the narrator observed in *That Night. At Weddings and Wakes* seems an imaginative exploration of that sense of intergenerational identity, a turning away from the contemporary promise of self-determination toward the more lasting satisfactions of human connectedness and continuity. In so doing, the novel is eager to show how people are as much tied to one another by shared loss as by any transitory triumph or joy.

This is most poignantly realized in the penultimate chapter, where the wedding of May—a former nun who unexpectedly finds love in middle age—is refracted through the reader's increasingly focused knowledge of the bride's impending death.

There is nothing unique or particularly exhilarating about May's modest church wedding and reception. At the party, barely pubescent cousins sneak into the liquor, children scout out adult duplicities, the unwanted solicitousness of little-known relatives goes undeflected, mothers and fathers drink and dance with a youthful intimacy, and the dark corners of family history and the usual salacious gossip are given new life. All the familiar, sentimental songs are played and the traditional dances danced.

McDermott is meticulous with all the dowdy details of this unpretentious middle-class rite. At the same time, however, what is disconnected and incomplete about human love and life is miraculously made whole through the frame May's death imposes on the scene. Despite the brokenness and gentle absurdity of the individual lives involved, May's wedding/wake comes to transcend all temporal confusion. By allowing us to see May's ordinary happiness through the sharp focus of her death a mere four days away—a death as inexplicable as the love she had only recently found—McDermott returns us to the timelessness not of grand achievements, but of the humblest human desires, even failings.

This search for "what part of love remains" in the face of death and the erosion of time was a crucial theme in *That Night*. "Peace was annihilation and to say that love could fade, that loss could heal, was to admit forever that there would be no return of the dead," imagined one teenage protagonist. The dead are very much with us, thanks to the Towne women. Indeed, we are incomplete without them, or so thinks the otherwise gently skeptical Bob Dailey.

> But there was something they [the Towne women] gave him, too, with all their ghosts, something he couldn't deny: they provided his ordinary day, his daily routine of office, home, cocktails, dinner, homework, baths, and twenty minutes of evening news with an undercurrent—it was like the low music that now played on the kitchen radio—that served as some constant acknowledgement of the lives of the dead. He was

An excerpt from *At Weddings and Wakes*

At their windows her brother and her sister peered down into the street, to the shadowed door of the candy store they might get Aunt May to take them to, to the deserted playground of another elementary school that was closed for the summer where they might run, shoot imaginary baskets, hop through the painted squares for potsy which were now burning white in the city sun. There was another row of stores beyond the school's back fence, signless, mostly nondescript storefronts where, they had been told at various times, mattresses were made, ladies' lace collars, bow ties, church bulletins. . . .

In the dining room their mother said, "But who thinks of me?" Aunt May's reply was too soft for them to understand. "A little happiness," their mother said, and then said again, "I don't know. Some peace before I die. I don't know."

She didn't know. The children understood this much about her discontent, if nothing more. She didn't know its source or its rationale, and although she brought it here to Brooklyn twice a week in every week of summer and laid it like the puzzling pieces of a broken clock there on the dining-room table before them, she didn't know what it was she wanted them to do for her. She was feeling unhappy, she was feeling her life passing by. She hated seeing her children grow up. She hated being exiled from the place she had grown up in. She feared the future and its inevitable share of sorrow.

"The good things," they heard Aunt May tell her, and their mother replied that she'd counted the good things until she was blue in the face. Against the silence they heard the teacups being gathered and children shouting in the playground across the street.

Knowing the routine, they knew that when Aunt May next came into the room, holding her wrists in her hands although she no longer hid them under a nun's sleeves, it would be to tell them that Momma was coming in for her nap now, if they would please. And sure enough, just as the game outside was getting interesting, there she was with the old woman behind her, as white and broad as a god.

She was not their natural mother but the sister of the woman who had borne them and who had died with Veronica, the last. Momma had married the girl's father when Agnes, the oldest, was seven. He had died within that same year and so there had been no chance, the three children understood in their own adulthood, for any of the halfhearted and reluctant emotion that stepmothers are said to inspire to form between them: within the same year as her arrival she quickly became not merely a stranger to resent and accommodate but the only living adult to whom they were of any value.

Alice McDermott, in her At Weddings and Wakes,
Farrar Straus Giroux, 1992.

not so much unlike them, there were among the dead people he loved and missed and would not set his eyes on again, and the women's constant chorus of anger acknowledged that for him. . . .

At Weddings and Wakes reminded me of Joyce's great story "The Dead," with its haunting winter light and landscape, sharp social observation, and tribute to the bittersweet redemptions memory, desire, and longing afford. In "The Dead," the accident of hearing an old ballad calls a middle-aged woman back to the sharp passion of an adolescent love that ended in death. The dead never leave us, Joyce seems to be saying, for in our "last end" we all share a common fate and perhaps even an imperishable identity. "One by one they were all becoming shades. . . . His own identity was fading out into a grey impalpable world: the solid world itself which these dead had one time reared and lived in was dissolving and dwinding."

Alice McDermott takes us to very much the same place—even amid the tacky sincerity of suburban Long Island!—where the seemingly solid things of this world crumble before the elusive powers of human remembering and longing. At weddings and weakes we are allowed to say "forever."

Gail Pool   (review date August-September 1993)

SOURCE: "Peculiar Realism," in *The American Book Review,* Vol. 15, No. 3, August-September, 1993, p. 21.

[*In the following review, Pool praises McDermott's vivid depiction of family closeness and the mounting emotional power of her narrative in* At Weddings and Wakes *as well as the novel's inherent realism.*]

Critics have justly praised Alice McDermott as a young writer who has gone her own way. Even her first novel, *A Bigamist's Daughter,* which, like so many first novels, never quite found its footing, was highly individual. But in her second novel, *That Night,* she came into her own, finding the peculiar and peculiarly effective brand of realism she sustains in her third work, *At Weddings and Wakes*.

When we think of realistic fiction, we tend to think of straightforward narratives, well-developed characters, events laid out in chronological order. Alice McDermott's fiction turns these expectations around. No novels could be more true-to-life than *That Night* or *At Weddings and Wakes*. Yet, in both, her narratives are oblique, her characters selectively defined, her timeframes circular.

Reading *That Night* was, for me, a curious experience. A familiar tale of thwarted young love, the novel centers on Rick and Sheryl, a suburban teenage couple forced to separate when she becomes pregnant. Narrated by a woman who was a young girl when the story's main events take place, the book takes its title—which is frequently mentioned in the text—from a particular evening when Rick and his friends arrive at Sheryl's house to claim her, with violence if necessary.

Until well into the novel, I found myself annoyed with its slow pace, with its constant references to "that night," and with its narrow focus. But by the end, this slender book had conveyed a powerful impression of its characters' experience, an impression that lingered past the end. What McDermott did in this novel was to circle around her focal point—"that night"—with the economy and skill of a bird of prey. By tracking from a distance the life stories radiating out from that point, the book enabled us eventually to see not just Rick and Sheryl's lives, but the patterns of their lives within the context of suburbia and, more broadly, of life itself.

McDermott achieves something similar in *At Weddings and Wakes*. Once again, she takes up a familiar tale of American life. Once again, she tells her story mainly through the perspective—but not the voice—of youngsters. Once again, she establishes a focal point around which the novel revolves. And once again, she gives us a novel that moves very slowly, but gains emotional power by the end.

At Weddings and Wakes draws a portrait of an Irish-Catholic family, living in Brooklyn and Long Island, bound together by history, hostility, bitterness, and love. At the heart of the family is the strong matriarch Momma Towne, with the four stepdaughters she singlehandedly raised, the children of her dead sister, whose widower—also long dead—she herself married.

The Towne women include Agnes, who is overbearing, the only daughter who works outside the home; Veronica, who is scarred, reclusive, alcoholic; Lucy Dailey, who is the only daughter who left home to marry, and who has three children through whose eyes we observe the family and its goings-on. And finally there is the life-loving May, the Towne sister "most determined to be happy," who provides the novel with its focal point: an ex-nun now over forty, May falls in love and marries; four days after her wedding, she dies. This is the tale around which the book circles, the point toward which it leads.

McDermott lays the groundwork for her novel in her long first chapter, which takes us into the airless Brooklyn home where the sisters grew up, and where four Towne women and some family ghosts still reside. To this house, twice a week most weeks in summer, Lucy—dissatisfied with the suburbs, her husband, her life—brings her children: to visit Momma and her sisters, to talk as she never talks at home, "to determine her own fate, to resolve each time her own unhappiness or indecision." In this first chapter, McDermott deftly combines a sense of all the Daileys' visits and the specifics of a single occasion. Through the distancing perspective of the children, who only half-comprehend what they observe, we see the unvarying patterns of these "long and endless" afternoons.

When they arrive, May will throw down the key. She will sneak them various treats. Their mother will begin her lamentations. In time, the women will cook, they will drink cocktails before they eat, and then—though the children can never quite discern why or when—they will begin to fight. To the youngsters, this unaccountable anger seems "somehow prescribed, part of the daily and necessary schedule, merely the routine."

At last, the exquisite moment will arrive when their father comes to take them home.

In this beautifully choreographed chapter, McDermott introduces us to the novel's main relationships and themes; in subsequent chapters, she takes us back through the family's history and forward toward May's wedding and wake.

In various sections, we accompany the children with their tensely married parents on vacation, where they learn about May's death; we see the children in school, after her death; we move back to May's courtship and the family's response. Throughout, we learn the family stories going back to their arrival in this country from Ireland, the stories—already legends, myths—that have become, for the children, "part of everything they knew."

As McDermott winds her way back and forth through this family story, she describes people, places, perceptions in prose that feels as claustrophobic as the Towne family and their home. With zoom-lens intensity, she focuses on individual scenes, as in this description of the children's father when, at Christmas, he meets May's beau, the mailman, Fred:

> Their father liked him. They could tell by his own red cheek and his bright eyes as he carved the turkey, by the way he joked with the three of them, winking at the girls as he transferred the meat to their plates, and joked even with their aunts and Momma ("Mrs. Towne") as he piled their own plates high. The two men had discovered before dinner that they'd seen many of the same cities during the war and so there was that to give them their pleasure in each other, and, another discovery, a mutual youthful infatuation with basketball and crystal radios. There was the sense too, the children understood, that their father at last had someone from the outside to see him among these difficult women, someone who might see, as he sometimes asked his children to, what he was up against here. He spoke over the women's heads as he stood again to carve second helpings and his buoyancy seemed to include his anticipation of all future commiseration with this man, as well as his awareness of his own expertise, his experience. It would not be long before he would have the pleasure of telling him: I know these gals. Believe me.

Careful, intricately detailed, this writing engenders a feeling of closeness intensified by the narrow focus of the story and the limited view of the characters, whom we see almost only within family settings.

One result is that the book is slow going, at times tedious, as in the opening pages, which describe the stages of the children's journey with their mother from Long Island to Brooklyn.

On the other hand, McDermott's scenes, at once intensely described and stripped of extraneous, extrafamilial surroundings, become extremely vivid: they seem to stand out in relief. In time, we feel that we are seeing both incident and pattern. In the Towne family, we see all families caught in the tenacious hold of their affections and disaffections; in May's story, we feel the poignancy of all lives, subject to fate. In the end, the novel makes its impression, leading us toward a conclusion we learned almost at the beginning and managing to overtake us, to move us, with what we already know.

FURTHER READING

Criticism

Bawer, Bruce. "Of Families and Foreigners." *The Wall Street Journal* CCXIX, No. 85 (30 April 1992): A10.
　　Comparative review of McDermott's *At Weddings and Wakes* and Francine Prose's *Primitive People*. Bawer ac-

claims *At Weddings and Wakes* as a poignant and lyrical reminder of death's inevitability.

Gingher, Marianne. "First Love and Early Sorrow." *Washington Post Book World* XVII, No. 15 (12 April 1987): 1, 3.
　　Favorable review of *That Night*. Praising McDermott's focus on death and love, Gingher argues that the narrator's "uncanny omniscience" and contemplative voice, although at times disconcerting and intrusive, ultimately impart depth and wisdom to the novel.

Petroski, Catherine. "Life's Vital, Mysterious Family Rites." *Chicago Tribune Books* (29 March 1992): 1, 4.
　　Praises McDermott's use of characterization and her generous and complex portrayal of familial intimacies in *At Weddings and Wakes*.

Review of *That Night*, by Alice McDermott. *Time* 130, No. 4 (27 July 1987): 64.
　　Commends McDermott's depiction of intergenerational conflict in *That Night*.

Additional coverage of McDermott's life and career is contained in the following sources published by Gale Research: *Contemporary Authors,* Vol. 109; and *Contemporary Authors New Revision Series,* Vol. 40.

Brian Moore

1921-

(Also wrote under the pseudonyms Bernard Mara and Michael Bryan) Irish-born Canadian and American novelist, short story writer, nonfiction writer, and scriptwriter.

The following entry provides an overview of Moore's career. For further information on his life and works, see *CLC*, Volumes 1, 3, 5, 7, 8, 19, and 32.

INTRODUCTION

Moore is a prolific novelist who uses traditional narrative structures and an unadorned, straightforward prose style to examine what he calls defining "moments of crisis" in his protagonists' lives. Praised for absorbing plots, insightful characterization, and the skillful evocation of time and place, Moore's works often reflect his Roman Catholic background and investigate spiritual, psychological, and social issues. Lawrence Seanlan has written that Moore "has shown wonderful range . . . and asked important questions—of faith and passion, of ambition and solitude, of the writer's place in society."

Biographical Information

Born in Belfast, Northern Ireland, Moore was raised in a strict, religious household. Although he attended Catholic schools, he rejected his family's Catholicism and left school at the outbreak of World War II. After serving with the British Ministry of War Transit in North Africa, Italy, and France, Moore emigrated to Canada in 1948, living intermittently in Thessalon, Toronto, and Montreal. To support himself in Canada, he began writing—reporting for a Montreal newspaper, publishing several pulp novels, and selling short stories. Moore won literary acclaim with the publication of his first major novel, *Judith Hearne*, in 1955, and since then has steadily produced new works. Retaining his Canadian citizenship, Moore eventually moved to New York City and then to Malibu, California.

Major Works

Moore's early novels often draw upon his observations of society and religion in his native Belfast, as well as his experiences in Europe and Canada during the first years after he emigrated. Examining such psychological themes as self-awareness, delusion, and repression, he frequently explores the emotional effects of estrangement from community in his writings. For example, Judith Hearne, the eponymous heroine of Moore's first major novel, is an isolated Belfast spinster who finds solace in imagination and in alcohol. *The Feast of Lupercal* (1957) is also set in Belfast and focuses on Diarmuid Devine, a middle-aged virgin who dreams of love but does not allow himself to become involved with women. Moore also explores the emo-

tional consequences of alienation in subsequent novels that portray Irish émigrés struggling to negotiate the cultural differences between Ireland and their adopted countries. *The Luck of Ginger Coffey,* published in 1960, depicts the title character's struggle to earn a living and win social acceptance after transplanting his family to Montreal. In *An Answer from Limbo* (1962) an Irish-American magazine writer named Brendan Tierney decides to publish a novel, summoning his elderly mother from Ireland to care for his children while he works. The novel delineates the conflicts that arise between the fully assimilated and secularized Tierney, his American wife, and his traditional, staunchly Catholic mother. Further exploring the tension inherent in religious change, *Catholics* (1972) focuses on an insular monastic community considered heretical because its commitment to traditional Roman Catholic dogma is at odds with the greater social orientation of the contemporary Catholic Church.

During the late 1960s and 1970s, Moore also wrote several novels in which characters become painfully uncertain about their identities under changing circumstances. *I Am Mary Dunne* (1968) depicts a young woman who has been married three times, lived in Nova Scotia, Montreal, and

New York, and rejected her childhood Catholicism. Over the course of several days she contemplates the changes that have occurred in her life and becomes shaken in her sense of self-identity. Sheila Redden, the main character in *The Doctor's Wife* (1976), leaves Ireland for France, where she enters into a passionate, adulterous affair with a younger man. In *The Temptation of Eileen Hughes* (1981), a middle-aged businessman becomes infatuated with a twenty-year-old shopgirl whom he desires as an object of worship. In several works Moore compounds the ambiguities of identity by introducing supernatural events. In *Fergus* (1970), he represents the Irish memories that torment an émigré living in California as actual ghosts. *The Great Victorian Collection* (1975) demonstrates the difficulty of distinguishing between appearance and reality when a young historian awakens one morning to find the parking lot adjacent to his motel filled with the Victorian artifacts of the previous night's dream. *Cold Heaven* (1983) concerns a woman who witnesses her husband's death in a boating accident. The next day his body and personal effects disappear, suggesting that he has returned to life. Moore investigates spiritual themes and guilt as the woman attempts to interpret these events in light of both her religious convictions and her marital infidelity.

Moore's most recent works reflect a commitment to investigating the relationship between individual moral choices and their political and religious contexts. *Black Robe* (1985) traces the journey of Father Paul Laforgue, a seventeenth-century Jesuit, and the Native Americans who guide him from Quebec to a Huron settlement in western Canada. While the Indians do not resent Laforgue's efforts to convert them to Christianity, they are not eager to change their beliefs or behaviors. *The Color of Blood* (1987) is set in an unnamed Eastern European country where Cardinal Stephen Bem struggles with the ambiguous relationship between his Church and the country's totalitarian government. *Lies of Silence*, published three years later, is set in Northern Ireland and concerns a Belfast hotel manager, Michael Dillon, who must decide whether or not he will help the Irish Republican Army bomb his own hotel—if he complies, he will save his wife, whom IRA terrorists hold hostage; if he defies them, they will execute her. Complicating the moral and ethical implications of his choice are Dillon's plans to leave his wife for the BBC reporter with whom he has been having an affair. *No Other Life* (1993) portrays the relationship between Jeannot, a young, black messianic priest who espouses a politically active brand of religious vocation, and Father Paul Michel, the elderly white priest who mentors him. Narrated by Father Michel, the novel is set in a country reminiscent of Haiti, and Jeannot has often been compared to Father Jean-Bertrand Aristide.

Critical Reception

Judith Hearne brought Moore international attention, and some critics have characterized it as the best novel to emerge from Northern Ireland. The novel remains the most popular and acclaimed of Moore's early works, all of whose protagonists, Murray Prosky notes, "create

dream kingdoms to defend themselves against their fear that life has somehow passed them by." John Cronin, observing that anxiety and delusions also characterize Moore's exiled protagonists, considers him "the prose laureate of human mediocrity and embarrassment." Yet John Frayne believes that Moore's affinity for failures expresses a dour view of human potential, which has led several scholars to liken Moore to English poet Philip Larkin. Although the protagonists of Moore's most recent novels are generally stronger and more decisive, these works have received mixed reviews, with some critics faulting them for their reliance on thriller conventions and pacing at the expense of character development. However, most commentators laud Moore's ability to sustain narrative tension in these works and praise the detailed descriptions of diverse cultures in *Black Robe, The Color of Blood,* and *No Other Life.* Widely-read in Great Britain and Canada, Moore's readership has recently increased in the United States. A prominent figure in contemporary literature, Moore is respected for his skill in representing female characters, for his portraits of personal crises suffered by alienated individuals, and for his investigations of moral dilemmas that reflect and influence larger religious and political contexts.

PRINCIPAL WORKS

The Executioners (novel) 1951
Wreath for a Redhead (novel) 1951
French for Murder [as Bernard Mara] (novel) 1954
Bullet for My Lady [as Bernard Mara] (novel) 1955
Judith Hearne (novel) 1955; also published as *The Lonely Passion of Judith Hearne,* 1955
Intent to Kill [as Michael Bryan] (novel) 1956
This Gun for Gloria [as Michael Bryan] (novel) 1956
The Feast of Lupercal (novel) 1957; also published as *A Moment of Love,* 1965
Murder in Majorca [as Michael Bryan] (novel) 1957
The Luck of Ginger Coffey (novel) 1960
An Answer from Limbo (novel) 1962
*The Luck of Ginger Coffey (screenplay) 1964
The Emperor of Ice-Cream (novel) 1965
†Torn Curtain (screenplay) 1966
I Am Mary Dunne (novel) 1968
Fergus (novel) 1970
The Revolution Script (novel) 1971
Catholics (novel) 1972
Catholics (teleplay) 1973
The Great Victorian Collection (novel) 1975
The Doctor's Wife (novel) 1976
The Mangan Inheritance (novel) 1979
‡Two Stories (novellas) 1979
The Temptation of Eileen Hughes (novel) 1981
Cold Heaven (novel) 1983
§The Blood of Others [based on the novel *Le sang des autres* by Simone de Beauvoir] (screenplay) 1984
Black Robe (novel) 1985
The Color of Blood (novel) 1987
Lies of Silence (novel) 1990
**Black Robe (screenplay) 1991

No Other Life (novel) 1993

*This film was directed by Irvin Kershner.

†This film was directed by Alfred Hitchcock.

‡This work contains *Preliminary Pages for a Work of Revenge* and *Uncle T.*

§This film was directed by Claude Chabrol.

**This film was directed by Bruce Beresford.

CRITICISM

John Wilson Foster (essay date 1970)

SOURCE: "Passage Through Limbo: Brian Moore's North American Novels," in *Critique: Studies in Modern Fiction,* Vol. XIII, No. 1, 1970, pp. 5-18.

[*Foster is a Canadian critic and educator who has written extensively on Anglo-Irish literature. In the following essay, he examines the central characters in Moore's early novels who, after being expelled from their communities, attempt to gain admission into new social groups and struggle to maintain their identities.*]

Critics have persisted in forging similarities between Moore and his compatriot-in-exile, James Joyce. Jack Ludwig, for instance, saw Moore in 1962 as Joyce's heir in the genealogy of Irish fiction ["Brian Moore: Ireland's Loss, Canada's Novelist," *Critique* 5 (Spring-Summer 1962)]. Hallvard Dahlie, in a well-written and perceptive account of Moore's work, sees Joyce's progress from *Dubliners* to *Ulysses* reflected in Moore's own development from *The Lonely Passion of Judith Hearne* (1955) to *I Am Mary Dunne* (1968) [*Brian Moore: Studies in Canadian Literature* (Toronto, 1969)]. He perceives in both authors not only a shift from naturalistic techniques to experimentalism but a movement from despair to affirmation.

Such a comparison might pass muster if critics did not also assert that Moore's work, like Joyce's, is a fictionalization of the central dilemma facing man today. That dilemma has been capsulized for us by two Moore critics. According to Ludwig, Moore's characters "ask themselves *the* question facing twentieth-century man: knowing what he does about all things political and social how does man still get out of bed in the morning?" John Stedmond in his introduction to the Canadian edition of *Judith Hearne* claims that this novel "probes what David Daiches has called the central question in modern fiction: 'How is love possible in a world of individuals imprisoned by their own private consciousness?'"

These approaches to Moore are misguided. Moore's fiction strikes me as interesting and refreshing precisely because it does not focus upon an essentially twentieth-century predicament. The dilemma faced by Moore's important characters—with few exceptions—is in fact a primitive rather than modern dilemma. It is created by the characters' exclusion from the community and their sub-

sequent occupation of a ritual limbo through which they seek to pass as quickly and as successfully as possible. Though Moore occasionally diverges from this theme—most notably in *An Answer from Limbo*—each of his novels remains to greater or lesser degree a variation of it, but a variation that contributes to the pattern of the total canon. As I have tried to show elsewhere, Moore's two early Belfast novels explore ritual failure and the punishment and exclusion attendant upon such failure in a rigidly structured and provincial community ["Crisis and Ritual in Brian Moore's Belfast Novels," *Eire-Ireland,* Autumn, 1968, pp. 66-74]. Ritual failure I define as the inability to perform the rites of passage on the way to self-fulfilment within one's own group. This theme extends with variation into the North American novels, but later gives way to the cognate theme of ritual displacement which Moore exploits most fully in *I Am Mary Dunne*. Ritual displacement occurs when the individual is unwilling or unable to perform the rites of incorporation into a new society and thereby find happiness and fulfilment. Since Moore is a novelist and not a sociologist, I want to make it clear that I use the term "ritual" not in reference to specific rites and ceremonies, but rather to the rhythms of separation, initiation, and incorporation common to all societies and communities.

The Luck of Ginger Coffey, Moore's third novel, balances the two themes of ritual failure and displacement and is thus a pivotal work in the development of Moore's thematic concerns. Coffey does not fail sexually, as do Judith Hearne and Diarmuid Devine (in *The Feast of Lupercal*), but rather in his inability to carve out for himself a successful career in a world which deems professional success a desirable form of social advancement. As a result, he almost loses his wife and daughter to a more successful man.

Failure breeds failure for Ginger Coffey, creating in him a besieged state of mind in which paranoia can take root. The CRIPPLE MATE CASE he follows on newsstand headlines is a soap-opera fantasy of self-pity in which Coffey is the innocent victim of a conspiracy, guilty only of an incapacity he cannot help. Self-pity gives way to infantile regression during which he envies his child neighbor for living in a world of toys where no demands are made and no responsibilities are exacted. Moore presents a cruel symbol of this regression when he has Coffey find a job at Tiny Ones Inc., a Montreal diaper service.

The reversion to fantasy in the face of failure and bewilderment was a favorite resort, also, of Judith Hearne and Diarmuid Devine. There are other correspondences: in all three novels the social repercussions of failure are the same—exclusion from the community and the retraction of roles for the failure to play. Because he is unwilling to take a job unequal to his ambitions, Ginger Coffey finds his roles as husband and lover, father, and breadwinner challenged and for a time seriously threatened. As in the two previous novels, the failure is simple but the repercussions immense.

The Luck of Ginger Coffey, then, like its predecessors, is a novel about the price society exacts for failure. In each of the three novels, there is a climactic scene in which the confrontation between victim and society is brutally apparent. In *Judith Hearne* it is the scene in which Judith Hearne is forcibly ejected from the convent; in *Lupercal,* the scene in which Devine is caned. In *Ginger Coffey* it is the scene in which Coffey is booked on an indecent exposure charge after urinating in a doorway. In this scene, as in the other two, there is injustice at work as society misinterprets and overreacts—comically in this novel—to a minor transgression. Moore here bestows on Coffey, as he did on his two Belfast characters, something approaching the status of community scapegoat.

Though *Ginger Coffey* is structurally a much simpler novel than either of the earlier Belfast novels, in terms of Moore's work as a whole it represents a thematic advance. Ginger Coffey has been a failure in Ireland and, half-outcast, has withdrawn from the scene of battle. His failure within his own community is largely self-originating as was Judith Hearne's and Devine's. But when he emigrates to Canada, his subsequent failure becomes more complex and the responsibility for it less easy to assign. Coffey in Montreal is a stranger in a strange land and occupies the limbo of all newcomers. The dilemma of ritual failure has become the dilemma of ritual displacement; to the limitations of his own small talents is added the task of weathering the formidable if informal initiation rites facing him as a New Canadian. In terms of the ritual status of the individual, failure and displacement are two sides of the same coin: both result in exclusion and isolation, dangerous conditions of existence from which he struggles to extricate himself.

Coffey brings with him from Ireland the slap-happy heartiness, transparent manner and sheepskin jacket mentality of a bluffer who imagines himself a Dublin squire. He finds, alas, that these are flimsy credentials in a country preoccupied with hard talk, hard work, and equally hard cash. Only by lying can he survive and even then it is a precarious survival. In one sense, the novel is Ginger Coffey's education into the economic and social ways of Canada: it is no coincidence that the man to whom he almost loses his wife is a nattily-dressed, smooth-talking, get-ahead native Canadian against whom New Canadians have to compete. The novel is strewn with those who found the competition too stiff and who went under—old Billy the Irishman, for instance, in whom Coffey sees a terrifying prefiguration of himself.

And yet, in another sense, Coffey is Canada itself, uncertain, callow, occupying that limbo between Dominion and sovereign Republic, between the old country and the United States, between the promise and fulfillment of nationhood. Among the pub-frequenting proofreaders, this is a favorite if obscurely understood topic. "Poor old Canada," laments one, "not even a flag to call its own." "They sneeze in the States and we get pneumonia here," observes another. "Greatest mistake this country ever made was not joining the United States." The same men are willing to defend Canada vigorously when Coffey denigrates it, and thus exhibit what seems at times to amount to a national political schizophrenia.

Perhaps these two interpretations—Coffey as both hapless immigrant and as Canada herself—are not as far apart as they seem: the education of Coffey into the ways of a new

and brutal world might be seen as the education of Canada into such a world. I imagine that such a view might strengthen the claim that in *Ginger Coffey* Moore has produced Canada's best novel to date, a claim that ought not, however, to inflate the novel's reputation.

Part of Coffey's difficulty in adjusting to Canadian life is due to the fact that he has not separated himself fully or decisively from his past in Ireland. And so the mores of Irish provincialism continue to haunt him. They are even embodied for him in the figure of Eileen Kerrigan, the Irish immigrant who recognizes Coffey from the old country as he stands, mortified, in his Tiny Ones uniform. And the patronizing admonitions of his former parish priest (". . . if you burn your boats, you'll sink. You'll sink in this world and you'll sink in the next . . .") stay with him; little wonder, for they illustrate graphically the vicious parochialism of a people who both despise and envy those who attempt to shake off the spiritual and moral shackles that bind. The Irish exile is always admired, never forgiven.

But if Coffey cannot blot out the past, he can at least ensure a future. By the end of the novel Coffey has successfully performed the rites of incorporation—hardship, humiliation, temporary loss of social and personal identity—into Canadian society. The indecent exposure charge can be seen as the last "initiation rite" Coffey must endure before becoming a genuine Canadian, without the qualifier "New." The novel is thus more optimistic than the two previous novels because it ends, though Coffey may not recognize it, on a note of success.

But acceptance into Canadian society is only the beginning. In terms of Coffey's ability to forge a successful life within his new group, the ending is less optimistic. That is to say, he can begin afresh, and receives legal and emotional warrant to do so (having won back both his wife and his freedom), but he must drastically lower his standards. To this extent the ending spells resignation, though a healthier resignation than Judith Hearne's or Diarmuid Devine's. Their resignation is the abandonment of all hope whereas his refuses to countenance total defeat. "Life was the victory, wasn't it?" he asks, with characteristic melodrama. "Going on was the victory. For better for worse, for richer for poorer, in sickness and in health . . ." Like Judith Hearne and Devine, he has come to know his limitations. But his are fewer and less crippling. He has his wife and daughter and the genuine hope of a job befitting his meagre talents. He has stopped, acknowledged, and is ready to begin in a new way.

Only one of the three plotlines of Moore's fourth novel yields to a ritualistic interpretation, though it happens to be the most successfully handled of the three. Let me briefly mention the others.

Among other things, *An Answer from Limbo* is Moore's *Kunstlerroman*. The question whose answer echoes from limbo is that confronting Brendan Tierney the struggling writer: is he prepared to sacrifice anybody or anything for the sake of his work? He is, and the resulting emotional abandonment of his wife, children, and mother constitutes one of the main themes of the novel. Behind the question of emotional sacrifice is another: should he sacrifice integrity and quality in order to gain instant success on the popular market? Tierney's crisis is a legitimate imaging of limbo but is not the kind of ritual or social limbo with which I am here concerned. The ethical and aesthetic problems facing Tierney face every writer whether it be in Florence, Italy or Florence, Oregon. Since they do not spring directly from the mores of the writer's context and location, a ritualistic reading would be unilluminating.

For a similar reason I do not wish to spend any time on the second plotline of the novel: the lapse into infidelity and indignity of Jane Tierney during her search for a dark ravisher. This is the weakest part of the novel, for her dark ravisher, Vito Italiano, never in name or deed rises above the level of crude caricature. This might ironically reflect upon the kind of woman this frustrated writer's wife becomes, but no amount of intended irony could possibly compensate for over-simplified characterization, especially when genuine characters are being created alongside Italiano. The figure of Jane Tierney herself is interesting mainly because she seems in some respects to me a warm-up for a later creation, Mary Dunne.

It is the novel's third thematic strain that most forcefully links this work to the rest of Moore's canon: Mrs. Tierney's passage from Ireland and her subsequent destruction at the hands of an alien culture. Brendan's mother is the most successfully realized character in *Limbo* and after Judith Hearne perhaps Moore's happiest creation.

Mrs. Tierney, unlike the major characters of Moore's previous novels, is successful in worldly terms. She was pretty when younger, reflects Brendan at the close of the novel, married to a successful man, well-off, and widely loved. "Yet," he reminds himself, "she died alone in the limbo of a strange apartment and lay dead until, by accident, a stranger found her." Her isolation at the end is therefore contrasted to the fullness of her past life in Ireland.

Mrs. Tierney's material success is not the only difference between herself and Moore's previous heroes. While they attempt to escape the bondage of their past, she wishes strenuously to preserve hers and thus to prevent her absorption by an alien culture. Fittingly, her life ends with the ritual affirmation of her past in prayer and supplication, and in an implicit denial of the new world she finds so hostile. Yet Mrs. Tierney's career in the novel can still be seen as a passage through limbo, but a return passage through memory back to the ritual celebrations of her life—her children's births, her daughter's marriage, her husband's death.

Mrs. Tierney is a more admirable character than Ginger Coffey, if only because she makes an attempt to reestablish in New York the important values of her life in Belfast. This cannot be explained away simply in terms of her age and inflexibility set against Coffey's youth and adaptability. Coffey never did and never will have values that promote any kind of spiritual well-being. He is, as he says, "neither fish nor fowl, great sinner nor saint." This typically hand-me-down Coffey metaphor is as far as he is prepared to pursue the matter. On the other hand, Mrs. Tierney is a devout Catholic who suddenly finds herself in a Godless home and a Godless society. Intolerant and atavistic, she is the perfect foil to Brendan and Jane whose hypocritical and facile tolerance renders her less unattractive to the reader than she would otherwise appear.

Alarmed at the spiritual condition of her grandchildren, she surreptitiously baptizes them and the discovery of her act results in the final estrangement between mother and son. Neither her God nor her piety is welcome in the chic New York apartment and she goes off to die alone with her empty pleas for help and her invocations to an ancestral God. Her death—a familiar Moore victimization scene—three thousand miles from home in a strange apartment is a cruel irony for a woman who sets great store by the primitive delights of neighborliness and community. And it is an irony compounded by the fact that she dies at the feet of a blaring television set, as though it were some Christian or pagan divinity instead of the mass-producible apostle of amorality it actually is.

In Mrs. Tierney, Moore has abandoned the theme of ritual failure and concentrated upon the theme of ritual displacement. Like Ginger Coffey, Mrs. Tierney suffers the isolation of the newcomer which in her case proves fatal. As always, Moore appears critical of the community and society that victimizes his character. Mrs. Tierney is destroyed because she refuses to abandon both the past and its values in order to gain entrance to the world Brendan and Jane represent. This is not to say that Moore assents to her values: quite clearly he would reject them as he did in *Judith Hearne* and *Lupercal*. It is rather a matter of comparative evil, as if during his Greenwich Village stint Moore found something to fictionalize even worse than Irish-Catholic bigotry and intolerance—the wilful jettisoning of integrity, dignity and belief. And so, for once in Moore, provincialism becomes a virtue, a bulwark of sorts against the erosive hypocrisies of modern, cosmopolitan life.

How far the theme of ritual displacement can be taken is explored in Moore's sixth and best novel since *Judith Hearne*. In *I Am Mary Dunne*, Moore brings important thematic tributaries of his first five novels together in a fictional confluence and *tour de force*.

> The dilemma faced by Moore's important characters—with few exceptions—is a primitive rather than modern dilemma. It is created by the characters' exclusion from the community and their subsequent occupation of a ritual limbo through which they seek to pass as quickly and as successfully as possible.
>
> —*John Wilson Foster*

Moore establishes in his latest novel an analogical series of movements which represent, literally and metaphorically, the stages leading to the crisis of limbo. Mary's husbands and suitors—Jimmy Phelan, Ernie Truelove, Hatfield Bell, Terence Lavery—constitute the series of roles Mary has had to fill, and at the same time roughly parallel her wanderings from Nova Scotia to Toronto to Montreal to New York. These phases of her life she remembers during and after a day's activities that provide the chronology of her recollections in bed that same evening. **Mary Dunne** is therefore a cleverly wrought work and, less spacious than **An Answer from Limbo,** a return to the claustrophobic confines of a woman's fevered mind, where it all began for Moore. But the differences between Mary Dunne and Judith Hearne are several and large.

For one thing, whereas Judith Hearne is imprisoned in her past and her unchanging identity, Mary Dunne struggles throughout the novel to find one identity among many in which she can heave to and find refuge. This points up one crucial difference between ritual failure and displacement. The failures, Judith Hearne and Diarmuid Devine, find themselves unable to change and to move forward. Theirs is the limbo of stasis. Conversely, the displaced, Mrs. Tierney and Mary Dunne, find their continuum of identity splitting and strive to mend the breach, Mary Dunne through a neurotic recapitulation of the past, Mrs. Tierney through a sense of the past bolstered by her religious belief. Theirs is the limbo of instability. Ginger Coffey is the transitional figure in all this: the failure who forces himself to change by putting his identity up for grabs in a new country.

The threat to Mary Dunne's identity is much greater than that to Mrs. Tierney's. She is now Mary Lavery but she was Mary Bell and before that Mary Phelan. Each marriage required of her a different role to satisfy each husband:

> . . . I play an ingenue role, with special shadings demanded by each suitor. For Jimmy I had to be a tomboy; for Hat I must look like a model: he admired elegance. Terence wants to see me as Irish: sulky, laughing, wild. And me, how do I see me, who is that me I create in mirrors, the dressing-table me, the self I cannot put a name to in the Golden Door Beauty Salon?

Similarly, she accuses herself of obscuring her real identity behind a mask in each of her careers: ". . . weren't they just roles I acted out? Even acting itself." She has been student, writer, actress, provincialite, wealthy cosmopolite moving in sophisticated New York theatrical circles. She has cast off and put on so often that she seems to live between roles as frequently as she does within them.

Her upward social mobility is paralleled by a kind of upward sexual mobility. Two things haunt her: the memory of her father's death during an act of adultery, making her fear her own strong sexuality; secondly, her guilt-inducing treatment of her second husband, Hatfield Bell. Among the men, it is Bell who dominates the novel, eclipsing Mary's current husband as a character and a force in her life, though it is with Lavery that she claims to have found sexual and emotional happiness. Mary outsexed Bell as she did Phelan before him. This must be seen as a factor in Mary's insecurity before, and after, her marriage to Lavery. The inadequacies of her men she long believed were

due to her own unattractiveness, and the feeling persists in nightmare. Her movements from place to place and man to man can therefore be seen as a quest after sexual and emotional fulfillment.

But if Mary has achieved material and sexual success as Mary Lavery, why does she affirm her identity at the end of the novel, and after a symbolic as well as physical act of sexual intercourse with her husband, as Mary Dunne? Has she, like Mrs. Tierney, returned safely to her origins and thus resolved the identity crisis of the novel?

A proper reading of the end of the novel is crucial for an understanding of what Moore is trying to do. Mary's crisis apparently lasts but one day, but we are to assume I think that this identity crisis, though precipitated by premenstrual tension, is an accumulation of the smaller identity crises of her past. How we interpret the ending of the novel will therefore determine how successfully we think Mary, postmenstrually, will pull out of this biggest crisis of her life. Here is the last ringing sentence of the novel:

> . . . I know who I am, my mother said tonight that I am her daughter and while she lives I will be that, I will not change, I am the daughter of Daniel Malone Dunne and Eileen Martha Ring, I am Mary Patricia Dunne, I was christened that and there is nothing wrong with my heart or with my mind: in a few hours I will begin to bleed, and until then I will hold on, I will remember what Mama told me, I am her daughter, I have not changed, I remember who I am and say it over and over and over, I am Mary Dunne, I am Mary Dunne, I am Mary Dunne.

Dahlie sees this as an act of desperate affirmation, and elaborates:

> . . . in the act of remembering her past, she attains the identity spelled out by the book's title: the identities she had temporarily assumed as Mary Phelan, as Mary Bell, as Maria, and now as Mary Lavery, cannot obscure the only unchangeable fact about her, that she is, and always will be, Mary Dunne . . . no legal or social vicissitudes can alter what she was born—Mary Dunne.

Elsewhere he calls Mary Dunne's affirmation an "attainment of calm" ["Moore's New Perspective," *Canadian Literature,* Autumn, 1968].

Dahlie misses the central irony of the novel. We have to note that what looks like an affirmation is an *attempt* to affirm, which is not at all the same thing. Mary's repetition of her identity, in the anxiety of imminent menstruation, is like a captured soldier's repetition of his name, rank, and serial number—affirmation of a formalized, legal identity that satisfies neither himself nor his captors. Again, Mary's dependence upon what her mother has said in a brief telephone conversation testifies to her utter insecurity, not to any degree of certainty whatever. This "affirmation" caps the irony of the novel: in her current relationship with Lavery, Mary has found emotional satisfaction, as well as material success, yet in a crisis hearkens back to a past she cannot bother to recollect in detail.

For it is not Mary Dunne we come to know but rather

Mary Phelan and, supremely, Mary Bell. We know Mary Dunne only as the child who suggested that the Cartesian maxim, *cogito ergo sum,* might better be rendered as *memento ergo sum.* This is a curious emendation on the part of the child: we might even on the strength of it view Mary's subsequent life as a self-fulfilling prophecy, as if she had received philosophical license during childhood to wander whither and with whomever she pleased in the comforting knowledge that her identity remained safe at home in Butchersville, Nova Scotia. But even though she holds under duress of premenstrual tension to her Cartesian modification, her life and her recollections of that life disprove it. She is Mary Dunne, but is also each of her subsequent identities, not at once but successively. She is, in fact, the changeling she fears herself to be.

It is tempting to view Moore's North American fiction as more optimistic than his earlier Belfast fiction. The shift from parochial to cosmopolitan settings and from the burdensome piety of the chief Belfast characters to Mary Dunne's practical morality would seem to represent a movement from bondage to emancipation. It is almost as if Moore's novels trace the growing fortunes in a new continent of one hypothetical immigrant who has escaped Belfast's lower middle-class tedium. In accordance with this view, we might also see the characters of the North American novels as less constrained by ritual forces and community dogmas, making a ritualistic reading of the novels less pertinent.

Yet we should be careful not to oversimplify the direction Moore's work is taking. There are, we should remind ourselves, significant interruptions in the flow of the canon. ***Ginger Coffey*** is clearly more optimistic than ***Mary Dunne*** because one of its themes is ritual success. And Mrs. Tierney, an obviously sympathetic character, never in spirit leaves the restrictive Irish world Coffey flees in the preceding novel. Even more important than these interruptions is the discovery by Moore's latest characters that the absence of community dogmas is an even more terrifying predicament than their smothering presence. The world that Mrs. Tierney rejects is the world Mary Dunne inhabits: a faithless, structureless, impersonal world. Mary Dunne's response to this "emancipation" is to deny it by mistakenly stating that her identity resides in her beginnings. Yet it is clear to the reader that her problem, insofar as it is not simply premenstrual, can only be solved if she stays with Terence, establishes roots, forgets her past and constructs a future.

And so there is no suggestion in Moore's latest novel that happiness and identity lie outside ordinary human relationships and group values. Certainly Mary Dunne's plight cannot be construed as the "dreadful freedom" of the existentialists, or even as the plight of the twentieth-century man Stedmond and Ludwig are talking about. For the heroes of a great deal of contemporary fiction, neither society nor the community is desirable or possible as a lasting source of strength and identity. On the other hand, we sense that Mary Dunne's crisis is *her* failure, not society's. As a Nova Scotian woman who in thirty-two years has changed her social circumstances more often than most people do in a lifetime, she is clearly an atypical fig-

ure with an unrepresentative problem. She is the primitive outsider, a perpetual stranger who has denied herself the comforts of ritual and community. Whereas Ginger Coffey and Mrs. Tierney pass through limbo, one into death, the other into the life of the community, Mary Dunne's cry of false certainty barely masks the fear of eternal isolation.

An excerpt from *The Lonely Passion of Judith Hearne*

She scrabbled in the bureau drawer for the keys to the trunk and took them out with a hand that shook so the keys rattled. She unlocked it and found one bottle, wrapped in cheap brown paper. Then, apologetically, she clambered up on the bed and turned the Sacred Heart towards the wall. He looked at her, stern now, warning that this might be her last chance ever and that He might become the Stern Judge before morning came, summoning her to that terrible final accounting. No awakening to see James Madden, to walk ever in the city, to ever see him again. Tonight I may cast you down, He said. My Patience will not last for ever.

But the rage had started inside her, the pleasant urgency to open it, to fill a glass and sip it slowly, to feel it do its own wonderful work. So she turned the Sacred Heart to the wall, scarcely hearing the terrible warning He gave her.

Then she scrambled off the bed, shaking, took a glass from the trunk and scrabbled with her long fingers at the seal, breaking a fingernail, pulling nervously until the seal crumbled on the floor and the cork lay upended on top of the bedside table. She took off her clothes quickly, wise in the habits of it, because sometimes you forgot, later. She pulled on her night-dress and dressing-gown, sat quietly by the fire, shaking a little still, but with the rage, the desire of it. Then, while the bottle of cheap whiskey beat a clattering dribbling tattoo on the edge of the tumbler, she poured two long fingers and leaned back. The yellow liquid rolled slowly in the glass, opulent, oily, the key to contentment. She swallowed it, feeling it warm the pit of her stomach, slowly spreading through her body, steadying her hands, filling her with its secret power. Warmed, relaxed, her own and only mistress, she reached for and poured a tumbler full of drink.

Brian Moore, in his The Lonely Passion of Judith Hearne, *Little, Brown and Company, 1955.*

John A. Scanlan   (essay date Summer 1977)

SOURCE: "The Artist-in-Exile: Brian Moore's North American Novels," in *Eire-Ireland*, Vol. XII, No. 2, Summer, 1977, pp. 14-33.

[*In the following essay, Scanlan maintains that the protagonists of the novels Moore wrote between 1960 and 1971 are often Irish émigrés whose memories of the old country impede their efforts to establish new lives in North America.*]

The landmarks of Ulster, so prominent in Brian Moore's first novels, fade into the background of his later fiction until they are sometimes almost completely obliterated by time, distance, and the premeditated stratagems of art. Yet the passage from Belfast to the New World, detailed so persistently and in so many guises in each of Moore's works, from *The Luck of Ginger Coffey* (1960) to *Fergus* (1970), is no simple act of exorcism, a putting aside of old symbols of repression in favor of a new and freer life. For if St. Finbar's Church, St. Michan's School, and the Cenotaph have no literal place in the memories of characters like Coffey and Mary Dunne, close substitutes emerge as part and parcel of their common Irish heritage, and are reflected in the social, political, and religious institutions of the divided Canada where they spend a considerable portion of their lives. So abiding, in fact, is the memory of a tribal childhood, fenced in by all the proscriptions and antagonisms of the Belfast ghetto, that even in a late work like *The Revolution Script* (1971), overtly "non-fiction" and anti-autobiographical, ghosts of the IRA and the Sixth and Ninth Commandments stand at every window. In *An Answer From Limbo* (1962) and *Fergus,* however, the ghosts walk. And, thus, obsessed by their own feelings of guilt, the expatriate heroes of each are assaulted with hallucinations out of their own troubled past and find themselves incapable of fully distinguishing the imagined promise of New York or California from the remembered humiliations of Belfast.

Whatever the battle with the past signalled by Moore's own emigration and manifested in his fiction, then, its importance cannot be measured by any simple standard of success. Instead, in a fictional universe where every new experience recalls an old analogy or is threatened by the re-incarnation of half-forgotten years "over there . . . across the street" [*An Answer From Limbo*], the struggle to become something new attains its true significance only when it is recognized for what it truly is: a limited attempt to solve an infinite problem, a creative act conceived in opposition to the inexorable claims of memory. Seen in this light, Moore's fiction of exile is at least partially interpretable in terms of the similar difficulties his characters face when attempting to find fulfillment in their native culture or in some apparently freer substitute. For in both instances, self-expression is opposed to the stultifying power of tradition. Since self-imposed exile is evidently an attempt to evade that tradition, and since evasion is itself threatened by long tentacles of guilt having their source in unresolved conflicts with remembered principles of authority, nothing bars us from viewing Moore's North American fiction, at least in part, as an epoch in a Freudian quest for maturity.

Yet even an emphasis on the continuing interaction of communally defined forces of authority and a private need to revolt will tell us nothing about the characteristic form, and characteristic outcome, of that revolt in Moore's later fiction. For unlike earlier figures like Judith Hearne and James Madden, who apprehend the limits of their existence, but lack any appropriate language to confront them

in order to give life some additional meaning, all of Moore's permanent expatriates are given literary or thespian talents and ambitions. Thus, the most noteworthy difference between a character like Madden and one like Brendan Tierney is not simply the choice of exile, for we know that both once sought a more satisfactory life overseas; instead, it lies in the different perspectives on the past, present, and future that distinguish a writer's vision from that of a man desirous of selling hamburgers in Dublin. Similar distinctions separate the guilt-ridden, yet self-dramatizing Mary Dunne from Moore's first heroine, lost in the midst of her own introspective agony. For in *An Answer From Limbo* and *I Am Mary Dunne* (1968), as in all of Moore's fiction of irrevocable exile, art functions as the mirror that allows his central characters to understand their circumstances and gauge their own development.

By serving as the instrument for increased self-regard, art thus offers Moore's later spokesmen and spokeswomen an imaginative identity which precedes—and to a large extent, parallels—the self-confidence and freedom they seek in a new land. Yet because the same sensibility that actively seeks to create an alternative to the past is likely to be obsessed with it, an inherent contradiction quickly surfaces in Moore's treatment of the artist-in-exile. Thus memory, which is presented in several of his novels as an impetus to art and one of its major sources, is more often displayed as the chief enemy of creation, blighting every trace of individual talent with its cold traditional breath. Accruing its lethal force almost directly in proportion to the distance Moore's writers and actors put between themselves and the place of their birth, memory therefore possesses a negative significance that effectively puts to rest any overly-sanguine view of expatriation. For instead of moving toward creative apotheosis, Moore's artists drift inexorably westward toward emotional debilitation and expressive paralysis in California. In the first stages of their journey, though, they are still bouyed by their own sense of creative destiny. The Gavin Burke who chooses to leave Belfast at the end of *The Emperor of Ice Cream* (1965) walks with a jauntier air than a late figure like Fergus Fadden, whose name recalls both the land to which he is bound in memory and his own sense of diminution as he regards the personal history he has helped bring into being with his art.

By serving as the instrument for increased self-regard, art offers Moore's later spokesmen and spokeswomen an imaginative identity which precedes—and to a large extent, parallels—the self-confidence and freedom they seek in a new land.

—John A. Scanlan

In the strictest chronological sense, Gavin Burke is something of an anachronism. Appearing in Moore's fifth novel, a work depicting life in Belfast during the initial phases of World War II, his story is set in a personal and historical landscape apparently abandoned for good with the publication of *The Luck of Ginger Coffey* and *An Answer from Limbo*. Although *The Emperor of Ice Cream* does not address itself as directly to the problem of exile as either of its immediate predecessors, it gives us considerably more insight into the personality, circumstances, and ambitions of the nascent artist at the moment of his departure. Instead of beating an atavistic retreat back to the paternalism of Catholic Ulster, the novel employs Burke to trace expatriation back to its cultural and emotional roots, and center itself on the particular, aesthetically oriented sense of alienation that prompts its hero to divorce himself from his past. Thus, while all of the rest of Moore's fiction prior to *Catholics* (1972) treats departure from Ireland as an accomplished fact, only *The Emperor of Ice Cream* treats it as an untested hope. Gavin Burke, therefore, occupies the pivotal position in Moore's heroic pantheon, standing midway between the culturally repressed Judith Hearne and the culturally deracinated Fergus Fadden. His decision to forge a new life for himself divorces him irrevocably from the former, however, and places him at the beginning of the path trodden by Moore's other artists and writers.

Gavin Burke is Brian Moore's closest equivalent to the young Stephen Dedalus [From James Joyce's *Portrait of the Artist as a Young Man*], whose extreme sensitivity to his environment, coupled with a strong interest in language and poetry, leads finally to the conscious acceptance of a literary vocation pursued away from home. Yet Gavin is by no means so precocious as Stephen, and until comparatively late in the novel he lacks any trace of that arrogant self-assurance that allows Joyce's hero to confront the clergy, catechize his friends, and proclaim his ambitions in high mythological terms. At an age when Stephen has already experienced all of the pleasures of venery, has renounced his family and religion, and has sought to redefine Aristotle's aesthetic, Gavin is still uncertain of his own sexual and social maturity, only vaguely aware of the potential of the literary life, and only tentatively attracted to the freedom of London. And while *The Emperor of Ice Cream* does indicate that he gains sophistication, self-esteem, and a modicum of ambition in the course of his wartime apprenticeship, it never shows us a process of development as steadfastly revolutionary and literary as that manifested in *A Portrait of the Artist*. Instead, the Gavin we see at the end of the novel seems equally enamored of modern poetry, puppet theater, and socialist drama. He exits his father's house with vague hopes of becoming another Wallace Stevens, Ronald Colman, or David Garrick, and a half-formulated plan to go to England and join the R.A.E. Yet the handshake Gavin shares with his father at the close of *The Emperor of Ice Cream* is ultimately as decisive as Stephen Dedalus' refusal to please his mother and make his Easter duty. For despite its apparent rectitude, it signals a new interpretation of the present and a new vision of the future. In both instances, the novelty presents itself most obviously in the guise of personal freedom. But, as in Joyce, it is a freedom having its deepest sources in the creative imagination and, therefore, entails as one of its ends the production of art.

It is doubtful, though, if Gavin completely understands the motives behind his handshake, or completely perceives the relationship between his interest in poetry and drama and his desire to express his independence from an overbearing parent. Probably the only concrete feeling that accompanies his complex gesture of salutation, recognition, and farewell is a sense of relief, derived from the fact that he has indeed listened to a "new voice," that he has finally broken free of his "condemned house," and can now contemplate his changed situation without feeling guilt or courting recrimination. For in and of itself, the handshake serves merely to confirm a process that, in the course of the novel, has involved nearly every aspect of Gavin's personality, including his feelings about his own worth, his attitudes toward religion, politics, and art, and his relationship with parents, priests, male friends, and assorted members of the opposite sex. Gavin himself can sum up this process, as he does on the novel's first page when, in a monologue addressed to a statue of the Infant of Prague, he says: "I'm escaping from you and the likes of you." But in his role as talented adolescent, he lacks insight into the full dimensions of his desired escape, and does not consciously define the "new voice" that encourages it.

To the observant reader, though, it is apparent that the forces he wishes to escape are not simply religious, but include all of the stultifying and repressive experiences that have combined to shape his personality. Reacting against an authoritarian father, a parochial education, restrictive social mores, and the social divisions in Belfast, which set Catholics like Gallagher against Protestants like Craig, Gavin quite clearly faces the same basic problems confronting Moore's earlier Belfast protagonists. Although not sufficiently emphasized by any of the novel's earlier critics, it is almost equally clear that what distinguishes him from figures like Judith Hearne and Diarmuid Devine is his greater ability to visualize the forces arrayed against him, to dramatize them, and to resist them. Each of these talents derives from several sources, including his very different historical situation, his greater cultural sophistication, and his innate desire to regard particular experiences in terms of a more universal art.

We can, then, begin to explain Gavin's capacity to rebel by citing his youth. For, unlike Hearne or Devine, he appears before us as an adolescent, still malleable, still capable of paying heed to his instincts. And, as we learn from the novel's many references to masturbation and English girls "hot as coals," Gavin's instincts are by no means stunted and can speak to him every bit as persuasively as his censorious Catholic conscience. Similarly, his antagonism to his father's bullying and mother's complacency emerges, not as a pathetic consequence of arrested development, but as a simple attempt to achieve maturity according to the conventional Freudian pattern. Yet Moore's depiction of Belfast's social atmosphere typically centers on its resistance to change, its ability to thwart individual growth and to institutionalize the strictures of adolescence.

Indeed, one of Gavin's more significant insights is his recognition of this deep-rooted conservatism and its possible effect on his own development. Thus, even in the first phrases of *The Emperor of Ice Cream,* he is capable of observing the ageless, ambitionless, seemingly eternal social dependency of those that work beside him, and is moved to assert: "They and their condition are what I fear; they are my failing future." And later, in a scene reminiscent of Stephen Dedalus' visit to the medical college in Cork, he achieves a sort of negative epiphany while regarding a hospital portrait entitled "Medical Staff and Interns. 1930":

> He looked into the photograph and felt uneasy. Nothing had changed in this room since 1930. Nothing would change. Out there, in the world, governments might be overthrown, capitals occupied, cities destroyed, maps redrawn, but here, in Ireland, it made no difference. In convent parlors, all was still . . . [in the 1980's] this photograph would still be here. . . . Nothing would change. The care of this room would continue as would the diurnal dirge of Masses all over the land, the endless litanies of evening devotions, the annual pilgrimages to holy shrines, the frozen ritual of Irish Catholicism perpetuating itself in *secula, seculorum.*

To be successful in overcoming the force of "frozen ritual" in all of its religious and social manifestations, Gavin must therefore rely on something other than instinct. In this, he is aided by the special circumstances obtaining in Belfast during the years in which he approaches maturity. For as Hallivard Dahlie has indicated in *Brian Moore* (1968), in his chapter on *The Emperor of Ice Cream,* Gavin's "rebellion" is "buttressed by a significant historical event," namely, the opening phases of World War II, "which included the bombing of Belfast." Evaluating the significance of the novel's military backdrop, Dahlie argues persuasively that the external course of events influences Gavin's personal development even as it provides a symbolic representation of his shifting attitudes. Thus, we can accept without demurral Dahlie's contention that the phony war provides a lull in which values will naturally be questioned; and similarly, we can agree that "symbolically, the dropping of the bombs on Belfast indicates that nothing less than a total destruction of old values will suffice." For as Gavin himself indicates in the novel's first chapter, a passage quoted by Dahlie, "war was freedom, freedom from futures. There was nothing in the world so imposing that a big bomb couldn't blow it up."

Yet the literal explosion Gavin needs to achieve liberation, despite its major role in the novel, is only one manifestation of the war's far-reaching influence. For although Gavin joins his friend Freddy Hargreaves in a litany celebrating the destruction of the old order as they watch bombs falling on churches, shipyards, and residential neighborhoods, the atmosphere evoked by the war is not reducible to cynical joy "inspired by long awaited annihilation." And this is particularly true in Gavin's case, even though he considers himself a rebel and socialist and admires "the poets [who] knew the jig was up; [who] knew the rich and famous would crumble with the rest." For if, as Dahlie suggests, "his view of the world has been shaped in large part by a number of modern poets," it is equally true that his response to these poets has been largely conditioned by changes in the Belfast cultural atmosphere fos-

tered by the war. Those changes, while they have little effect on the majority of the population, seem to promote a fairly active creative life for the socially and artistically committed few.

There is considerable irony and not a totally negative irony, either, in Gavin's assertion: "I was just wondering how many pavement artists this war is going to produce." For although he regards "sidewalk" art with some scorn, judging it an instance of the failure he customarily fears, an avocation of broken-down old soldiers, an exercise in a corruptible medium, a debased form of self-expression characterized by ". . . coloring in horrid childish landscapes" and affixing sentimental legends, even this sort of drawing emerges as a sort of symbolic action promoted by the war, an act of creation arising out of destruction. And it is this second tendency that seems to spring up in Ulster during the period described by the novel. Thus, *The Emperor of Ice Cream* gives us isolated images of surprising cultural sophistication as it is evinced in the lives of soldiers as different as the "studious seeming private" reading *The New Statesman* and the drunken "Captain" listening to Bach. And similarly, Gavin's service in the ARP brings him into contact with the kindred spirit of Freddy Hargreaves, and hence, to "Jews, left-wing ministers, pansies, poets, boozers, puppeteers: this was a grown-up world, undreamed of in the St. Michan's school philosophy." The war thus threatens the past, not only with direct annihilation, but also with burial under an onslaught of new experiences. And it offers Gavin entry into this generally progressive, generally aesthetic world by giving him a role in a play by Clifford Odets at approximately the same time it gives him lessons in first aid and sexual maturity.

By transforming Gavin into a fledgling actor even as it dramatizes his break with the values of his parents, school, and religious and political compatriots, *The Emperor of Ice Cream* therefore suggests that the factor tipping the balance in favor of freedom is neither youth nor a simple sort of anarchic rebellion, but rather a sense of revolt tempered with art. For without poetry and without the theater, Gavin's life promises to be as empty and dissatisfying as the lives of his fictional predecessors. Inspired by a belief in art, however, he can look forward to a future informed by socialist ideals and brightened by a sense of personal ambition. But since socialism is only an ephemeral element in Gavin's personal makeup, since it is only one characteristic of many—but by no means all—of the writers he admires, and since nothing in *The Emperor of Ice Cream* suggests that Belfast is prepared to embark on a new political course, we would not be justified in considering the ideological promise of literature as the compelling element in the novel's essentially optimistic portrayal of art. Instead, the most important aspect of Gavin's aesthetic development seems to be internal and seems to depend not so much on the magnitude or permanence of any anticipated social change, as on the illumination provided by a personal, aesthetically heightened participation in history.

Gavin Burke in *The Emperor of Ice Cream* stands as Moore's archetypal romantic, striving with the aid of art to create a new life for himself even as he acts to destroy the old.

—*John A. Scanlan*

Gavin's interest in the Wallace Stevens' poem that supplies the title to the novel is indicative of this mode of viewing the world, since it weds an appreciation of the imagination refined to the point of hermeticism to a didactic interpretation of the poem's pragmatic import.

> . . . give thanks for this job which will grant you independence from your father's do's and don't's.

> Let be be finale of seem.
> The only emperor is the emperor of ice cream.

But if Stevens is ultimately a more important influence on Gavin than the Oxford Left poets, Yeats is ultimately a more important influence than Stevens. For it is Yeats who most explicitly links the historical processes of destruction to the romantic joy of personal expression; and it is Yeats who provides the specific metaphorical framework within which Gavin can attempt to achieve the same ideological reconciliation.

Thus, it is Yeats who assigns both political idealists and poets parts in the "casual comedy" and "tragic play" that constitute the two guises of life. And it is Yeats who insists that, in both instances, the assumption of the dramatic role "transfigures" history, and transforms the actor into the architect of a change that, however transitory, exists as something "terrible", "beautiful", even "gay." For Yeats, then, the decisive act is to choose history, to elucidate and celebrate one's own role in it, irrespective of final consequences. Yet, to choose history is precisely the difficulty of Moore's typically passive heroes and heroines, who lack any sense of active or willing participation in the world they occupy. And at the beginning of *The Emperor of Ice Cream,* this is Gavin's difficulty as well. Obsessed with the competing forces of superego and id, "White" and "Black angels," he feels doomed to failure. His most characteristic emotion is disgust at his own inability to act: "As usual, he had done nothing to save himself." And even as he matures and begins to achieve a degree of independence, he remains fearful that Yeats' qualified optimism is unwarranted: "Nothing would change." Yet after the bombing of Belfast, Gavin is able to conclude: "Tonight, all was changed." And his emotion upon watching Belfast burn is entirely consonant with Yeats' line, "A terrible beauty is born."

Admitting that this response is partially anarchistic, the natural consequence of Gavin's upbringing, it is still possible to assert that his new emotional state is largely creative, and signals the fruition in time of a commitment to action nurtured and directed by a relationship to the theater. Thus, Gavin's development both as an artist and as an individual is intimately connected with self-conscious role-playing. Initially, this role-playing is totally internal, a series of imaginary discussions with Black and White Angels and the Infant of Prague, and imaginary apologies to the angry Sally. Just as in *The Feast of Lupercal* (1957), however, a literal stage play brings the dramatic sense out into the open. But, while exposure ultimately crushes Devine, who is not strong enough to act out his fantasies, it affects Gavin in quite another way. For, as the Black Angel tells him, "So the play's not the thing, eh? It's your thing."

Indeed, as the novel progresses, that judgment proves increasingly true. For Gavin's development is ultimately confirmed by his ability to confront his experiences dramatically. Thus, relatively early in the novel, Gavin manages to accomodate himself to the ARP by performing in front of Sally:

> He told her. He told her all about Craig's mad drills and how the men hated him. He told her about the pub and what was said. He found himself standing up, acting different parts, imitating voices. When he had finished, he was quite pleased with his performance.

And later, he accommodates himself to his new, mature role in the morgue by dramatizing his courage: "Nonchalant, an actor on stage, he cut into the roast beef." His relationship to his family and his time is thus defined, finally, by his ability to transform the present into the moment in an ongoing play. The war contributes to this ability, even as it is interpreted in terms of it: "Tonight, history had conferred the drama of war on this dull, dead town in which he had been born." By moving from the "drama of war" to the drama of personal expression, as he does in the hand-shaking scene that brings the novel to a close, Gavin asserts his freedom from the limiting influence of his parents and Catholic upbringing, and moves inevitably in the direction of art awaiting its perfection in exile.

Gavin Burke stands as Moore's archetypal romantic, self-conscious, rebellious, who strives with the aid of art to create a new life for himself even as he acts to destroy the old. Gifted by history with the opportunity to demonstrate his emerging maturity to himself and others at the very moment he is attempting to shake off his past, he is able to celebrate change, to find joy in the creative impulse that emerges out of, and runs counter to, destruction. His thematic successors are not nearly so lucky. For although Ginger Coffey, Brendan Tierney, Fergus Fadden, and Mary Dunne all cut themselves off irrevocably from their native soil, and although the last three share many of Gavin's characteristics even to the extent of invoking art as a means of creating and confirming their new identities, each of these characters is forced to take a hard look at the psychological limits of a foreign existence. Lacking Gavin's youth and Gavin's opportunity for literal heroism, each stands further from impassioned adolescence; each is subject to more bitter memories, and each approaches the task of re-vitalizing the present burdened with a greater number of quotidian concerns. And each is faced with the necessity of generating a sense of personal worth single-handedly, without the aid of any transcendent world event or traditional audience. Therefore, for writers like Tierney and Fadden, and for a woman like Dunne who seeks to give dramatic or literary form to her life, self-imposed exile exists not only as the consequence of a long-standing desire to be free, but also as a condition that imposes its own strictures on creation. The task for each is thus to find a mode of expression manifesting a personal sense of accomplishment even in the presence of forces that continue to challenge the idea of identity and personal worth. Given their own evaluation of the troubled, often antithetical relationship between creativity and a sense of the self depending heavily on the remembrance of things past, it is difficult to imagine how any of the three can achieve a real measure of success.

Thus, *An Answer from Limbo* (1962), *Fergus* (1970), and *I Am Mary Dunne* (1968) all share a theme largely absent in *The Luck of Ginger Coffey* (1960), and which seems no longer relevant to Gavin Burke at the end of *The Emperor of Ice Cream* (1965). That theme, differently elaborated in each of the three novels, centers on the persistence of the past and on its ability to condition the present and hoped-for future even for those who have emotionally rejected memory in their attempt to find individual freedom.

The effect of the past on characters struggling to justify their lives is portrayed more directly and with more feeling in *Fergus* and *I Am Mary Dunne* than in *An Answer from Limbo*. Yet Brendan Tierney, although subject to fewer disturbing memories or moral qualms than Fadden and Dunne, is still portrayed as a man living in the shadow of his adolescence. And Moore forces us—and to a lesser extent, forces Tierney—to evaluate his present literary ambitions against that background. Brendan emerges in *An Answer from Limbo* as Moore's most promising artist, a man certain to "succeed" because he hungers after fame, has talent, and possesses a quality of ruthlessness, which his best friends recognize, a quality that enables him to put aside all familial and social responsibilities in favor of his writing. Several times he compares his appearance to that of Napoleon, but, as the novel makes clear, the comparison extends well beyond a "lock of hair over one eye" and "hard" "young" "accusatory eyes." For in terms of ego, Brendan has always been imperial. We learn that even as a child he proclaimed his ambition to be a great writer, that he considers his every word a manifestation of "genius," that he thinks his writing has religious significance, that he hopes to find his yet-to-be-written works placed reverently beside those of "Kierkegaard and Camus, Dostoyevsky and Gide." Finding himself in New York at the begining of the novel, he characterizes himself as a refugee from "provincial mediocrity" now resident "in the Rome of our day." It is apparently his desire to reign as literary emperor in the literary capital of the world.

His ambitions are grandiose, and fitting for one who wishes to assume the mantle of romantic artist. Brendan seems capable of fulfilling Gavin Burke's promise, of achieving that passionate intensity which is for Yeats, despite its moral ambiguity, the hallmark of all genuine creation. And as the novel progresses, we are given no reason to as-

sume that Brendan's ambitions will not bear actual fruit, for a book that will earn critical plaudits and substantial royalties seems clearly in the offing. Yet, despite the fact that he can look forward to all of this, his final perception of himself in *An Answer from Limbo* is bitter, perhaps despairing: "I have altered beyond all self-recognition. I have lost and sacrificed myself."

With this expression of self-awareness and disgust, we, as readers, cannot help agreeing. For long before Brendan has achieved any substantial insight into his charcter, we have had the opportunity to regard his literary aspirations in the light of their effect on his personal conduct. And because the novel employs a narrative approach giving not only Brendan's first-person account of things, but also a third-person omniscient account of how Brendan's wife and mother feel, we are able to judge that conduct on the basis of its consequences as they are amplified in the consciousness of its victims. The Faustian theme of the artist who sacrifices his happiness and security for his art is thus supplemented with a vision of that same artist blithely destroying the happiness of those who, in the past, have helped to give his life some meaning. Commenting on this tendency at his mother's funeral after he has finally been brought face-to-face with his own destructive egotism, and has thus gained some insight into his treatment of Jane, the much-neglected wife, Brendan recollects and underlines an earlier fantasy:

> *Standing by his wife's bedside watching her face contort, the better to watch her death agony. He can't help doing it. He's a writer. He can't feel: he can only record.*

Aware of his own responsibility for his mother's death and his wife's infidelity, and aware also that his always watchful, always calculating "stranger within" denies him the fulness of remorse and any possibility of change or absolution, Brendan perceives himself, at the end of *An Answer from Limbo,* much as we do.

Yet it is doubtful whether Brendan ever becomes fully aware of the broader implications of his mother's death, either as they relate to his characteristic treatment of her or to his particular status as a self-proclaimed "exile." For, throughout the novel, Brendan is drawn more persuasively by dreams of the future than he is by any conscious tie to the past. Indeed, his entire career seems dedicated to putting Ireland behind him. Thus, he tells us that he left Ireland not so much to fulfill his vague hope of becoming a writer, as to escape the religion of his youth. And the "need to run," which he describes, has led him to take an American wife and pursue fame in an American setting. From the moment that he sets foot on the channel steamer where bottles of whiskey and stout are being passed around and a girl is singing "Come Back to Erin," Brendan, gifted with a cynic's eye, becomes an outcast. Contemplating the mechanical landscape of a New York air terminal, he can proclaim as no other of Moore's Irish spokesmen can: "Exile now means . . . my Island is no longer my home."

And of course Brendan is partly right: he has achieved some sort of accommodation with New York; he no longer feels any conscious desire to return to "Erin." Yet the uneasiness that plagues him in the novel's last scene, when he becomes aware that he has "altered beyond all recognition," is more than a momentary recognition of selfishness and unconscious cruelty: it is also an insight into the emotional void he has created for himself by leaving the world of his childhood while lacking the means to enter completely into another world, sentient and fully alive. I would argue, then, that John Wilson Foster, generally a good reader of Moore and probably the most sensitive interpreter of Mrs. Tierney's role in *An Answer from Limbo*, nevertheless misses the point somewhat after he defines "ritual displacement" as the emotional dissatisfaction that "occurs when the individual is unwilling or unable to perform the rites of incorporation into a new society and thereby find happiness and fulfillment" ["Passage Through Limbo: Brian Moore's North American Novels," *Critique: Studies in Modern Fiction* XIII, 1 (1971)]. After identifying this sort of dislocation as the primary focus of Moore's North American novels, Foster fails to develop or apply his *aperçu* with regard to Brendan Tierney's situation. For while Foster is at least partly correct in stating that "the ethical and aesthetic problems facing Tierney face every writer whether it be in Florence, Italy, or Florence, Oregon," and while much of the appeal of *An Answer from Limbo* does derive from the universality of the crisis Brendan, as a writer, faces, given the novel's many references to exile, its many explicit and implicit comments on Brendan's sense of himself as a displaced Irishman, its extensive treatment of other Irish men and women adrift in America, and most importantly, its place in Moore's fictional canon, it is difficult to believe that at least some of Brendan's difficulties "do not spring directly from the mores of the writer's context and location."

Thus, while Brendan may have no conscious desire to return to Ireland, and may proclaim himself an agnostic and unalterable foe of paternal cant, there is no doubt that he continues to measure his present self against his parochial past. At times, this measurement is premeditated and overt, as when he calls upon his father to witness "that I am about to change my life," or defines his ambition in terms of the need to prove himself to his former teacher and classmates. At times, it is merely intuitive, "a sudden wash of nostalgia" that casts his contemporary image of himself into doubt:

> I forgot Jane, I forgot the present. Over there, just across the street, was the simple provincial life I had left behind. Over there Ted Ormsby waited, pint in hand, ready for an evening's talk. Over there. Home. Across the street.

But whether premeditated or instinctual, Brendan's need to find personal justification through the recollection of a past from which he has forever cut himself off situates him closer to his roots—and to his mother—than either he or Foster seems to recognize.

For Mrs. Tierney, like Brendan, the friend of stay-at-home Ted Ormsby, expresses in her antagonism to New York's spiritual wasteland and, in her lonely dreams, feelings that sometimes afflict her son, but which he has spent his entire adulthood trying to repress. In a sense, Brendan's situation is like Frank Finnerty's, the cousin and host in whose

apartment Mrs. Tierney dies. Frank is described as an emigrant who has lived 31 years in the United States and remembers almost nothing about Ireland except the potatoes. He does not even wear green on Saint Patrick's day, and dismisses the land of his birth as a "dead issue." Yet upon coming into contact with Mrs. Tierney and hearing her talk about Creeslough, he is brought in touch again with his memories of a waterfall, "the sound of home." And that memory produces for him both pleasure and pain, a fleeting sense of old values, a renewed recognition of his present treadmill existence, and of the loneliness accompanying it. Brendan, who attempts to escape this sort of recognition and who partially succeeds, does so only by putting his mother out of mind, by effectively killing her. But the price that he pays for his indifference is a sacrifice of integrity that is not only moral, but also cultural, historical, psychological. For, by choosing a literary career at the expense of his family, Brendan not only cuts himself off from home attachments, but also cuts himself off from a part of himself that once gave his life significance. More particularly, he cuts himself off from his Irish past and the faith and social codes against which he has always revolted, yet in which he has always found a standard capable of helping him achieve self-definition. His problem is, therefore, not simply the universal one of isolation and self-awareness which comes with art and age and introspection. Instead, it is that problem intensified by the extreme contrast between the standards and ideals of the Irish provinces and the "Rome of our day." Perceived in these terms, the antitheses between past and present, self and society are intensified until identity itself is threatened. Or, as Brendan says, prompted by the image of the Negro boy scouts boarding his subway train: ". . . if Scout Brendy Tierney were to sit down in the subway beside me, his merit badges sewn on his sleeve, what password could I give to prove our common identity?"

In terms of our study, that question is probably the most important raised in *An Answer from Limbo*. For it brings us back to the central problem Moore faces in his North American fiction, namely, the interrelationship of exile, freedom, and art. Since Gavin Burke essentially equates freedom with creation, and then creation with a vague ambition that can best be fulfilled by leaving Ireland, this problem really hardly troubles us when we read *The Emperor of Ice Cream*. It assumes more reality, however, when we discover that Brendan Tierney's exile does not completely free him from a concern with the past, even though it distances him from it. Will Brendan's guilt affect his writing, we are tempted to ask. And what, given Brendan's rejection of the past, his distaste for New York intellectuals, and his lack of interest in his immediate family, will he attempt to write about? *An Answer from Limbo* manages to sidestep both questions, however, by ascribing to Brendan the "ruthlessness" necessary to ignore guilt, and by telling us nothing at all about the subject of his uncompleted masterpiece. Thus, while more shadows gather on Brendan's horizon than on Gavin's, he is still portrayed as a figure moving toward conditional "success." It is apparently only when self-doubt becomes totally obsessive and when a regard for the judgments of the past interferes actively with the creation of a future that the bonds of exile become as onerous as the bonds of a traditional culture that has never been challenged. For Mary Dunne and Fergus Fadden, however, that limit is apparently reached. Both, despite substantial differences in their portrayal, emerge as artists of a sort who wage a losing battle with memory.

Of the two, Mary Dunne is the more unlikely artist, the more uncertain failure. Portrayed in the novel as a woman who once studied acting in Toronto and performed professionally for a year, she nevertheless disclaims any real talent, and dismisses her theatrical career as insignificant "enthusiasm"—mere role-playing. Similarly, after portraying herself as a person who would once have sought to turn her experiences into stories and after expressing her admiration for "Dostoevski, Proust, Tolstoi, [and] Yeats," she dissociates herself from the company of writers, saying, "They wrote, therefore they are, whereas I, sitting glum on that sofa, was nameless, lost, filled with shameful panic." What we are dealing with, then, is either someone who has made the belated discovery that she has no creative ability, and so has renounced all artistic ambition, or someone who has decided that her talent is an onerous gift, and so has decided to put it aside. Since Mary Dunne continues to identify her own actions throughout the novel as theater, characterized by "play-acting out on the fire escape" and a "frightening, unreal play going on inside my head," and since she serves, at least in memory, as the narrator of the novel bearing her name, it is the second answer that is obviously correct: she is afraid of her own literary and dramatic talents. And she is afraid because, even more than Brendan Tierney, she perceives her present in terms of her past and, in a manner very similar to his presentiment in the subway, she feels a radical, perhaps irremediable discontinuity between the person—or people—she once was and the person she is.

Her basic conundrum is expressed in the novel's Yeatsian epigraph, as Dahlie cogently suggests. But the impossibility of knowing "the dancer from the dance" is not necessarily reducible in her case to "an essential harmony existing between the various facets of her being." Rather, in this instance the image of dance and dancer intertwined seems to suggest the impossibility of disentangling any permanent identity from the rapidly changing circumstances of life. As Foster points out in his nearly definitive interpretation of the novel, her attempt at affirmation at its end is only an attempt, and "it is not Mary Dunne we come to know but rather Mary Phelan and, supremely, Mary Bell." And thus, as Foster again suggests, "She is Mary Dunne, but is also each of her subsequent identities, not at once but successively. She is, in fact, the changeling she fears herself to be."

Mary Dunne's problem with art is tied to her growing knowledge that drama or literature can confirm her fractured identity, but cannot mend it. For her sense of drama generates no apotheosis, but only the Mad Twin, a schizoid particle of her own personality, who has much in common with Judith Hearne's animate artifacts and Gavin Burke's Good and Bad Angels. Mary Dunne's attempt to explain herself by remembering every moment of her past is foredoomed by her prior realization that

> . . . when people say they can remember every-

thing that happened in their lives, they're deceiving themselves. I mean if I were to try to tell anyone the story of my life so far, wouldn't it come out as fragmentary and faded as those old snapshot albums, scrapbooks, and bundles of letters everyone keeps in some bottom drawer or other?

Thus memory, which she elevates at the beginning of her soliloquy as the source of all psychic value—"*memento, ergo sum*"—leads her to an awareness of all that she no longer is, and reminds her of her own mutability:

> I can no longer find my way back to the Mary Dunne I was in my schooldays, to that Mary Phelan who giggled and wept in the Blodgett's bedsitter, or to that girl who laughed long ago in a winter street when Hat cried "*Mange la merde,*" when I was Mary Bell. I will not even be able to go back to today when I am Mary Lavery, for today was a warning, a beginning. I mean forgetting my name, it was like forgetting my name that day, long ago, in Juarez, I will forget again. I will forget more often, it will happen to me every day and perhaps every hour.

Mary Dunne, who admires Yeats, and who echoes Molly Bloom and emulates Proust in her act of recollection, is, despite her literary heritage, incapable of saying "yes" to her personal history. By distancing her from her past, denying her transcendent faith in her art, and forcing her to contemplate the possibility that because she "cannot remember history" she may be "condemned to repeat it," Moore consigns her, not to Byzantium, but to the private "rag and bone shop" of her heart. In doing so, he is certainly expressing a universal theme, namely, the difficulty of maintaining a romantic image of the self in the face of experience and age. And by choosing to write about the life of a Canadian woman, he gives every indication of eschewing an obsessively autobiographical fiction, of expanding his geographical scope, and of further developing the insights into feminine psychology which served him so well in *The Lonely Passion of Judith Hearne*. Despite reservations we might have about the book's merit—it may well be too long, too repetitious, too replete with names and undramatic local references, too schematic and cruel in its portrayal of characters like Janice and Eunice, and it may well tell us too much about Hatfield Bell without, however, turning him into a compelling or totally realistic character—we can assent to Dahlie's assertion that "*Mary Dunne* emerges as a competent and promising departure from Moore's more traditional phase" (118).

Yet, even as a departure, *I Am Mary Dunne* continues to touch many of the same chords that Moore emphasizes in his portrayal of the specifically Irish exile. Perhaps the least important of these are the specifics of Mary's Irish ancestry, or the similarity of her response to Toronto and the response Burke and Tierney make to the Belfast they are intent on leaving. More significant seems to be the similarity of her obsessions to those of other characters who share an Ulster childhood. Thus, despite the fact that she comes from Butchersville, Ontario, and has never attended St. Michan's School, Mary Dunne's need to confront her past seems to stem from a continuing need to come to terms with her sexuality, her father, and her religion. Universal concerns all, their conjunction in *Mary Dunne* echoes the specifically Irish conjunction Moore has earlier tied to the prevailing social atmosphere of Ulster. In her identification of her father with the divine figure addressed in the "Our Father," in her hatred of that authoritarian figure and her fear that she may be too much like him, "promiscuous," doomed to live out the series of "naked" encounters "with naked men" about which she has so often dreamed, Mary Dunne seems to play an Irish Catholic Electra in the same hybrid play that features Brendan Tierney playing Oedipus.

But had Brendan broken up his lines to weep, Moore would have been capable of wheeling in another, somewhat higher-strung candidate for the part. For Fergus Fadden, hero of *Fergus,* recapitulates and brings to a logical close the theme of the displaced Irish artist who, having renounced his parochial upbringing, is, nevertheless, incapable of freeing himself from its debilitating effects. Probably Moore's worst novel—peopled with one-dimensional characters, who are physically present, and scores of hardly more credible apparitions, who enter and re-enter the novel with all the subtlety of Marley rattling his chains—*Fergus* unfortunately affords us few new insights beyond the obvious one that life, ever the servant of art, may finally have dealt with Moore as he, in his American novels at least, has been prone to deal with his characters. For Fergus, to put it briefly, is a writer who, because he is haunted by his parents, brothers, sisters, and an entire Belfast neighborhood replete with priests, theologians, dentists, and patriots, is unable to write anything in the United States except movie scripts. Either because he has some integrity left, or as seems more likely in view of the omnipresent, hectoring spirits, because he has completely lost the ability to organize his work, Fergus is in danger of losing even that limited skill. Concurrently, he worries about his divorce and his deteriorating relationship with Dani, his young and very "California" girlfriend. The same memory that destroys his ability to create contributes to a sense of guilt, and incomplete images of former sexual encounters deprive him of his present sexual satisfaction. Since the ghosts of everything past have put him on an unending windmill of Fellini-esque reminiscence, he has little hope, short of a heart attack, of stopping his downward slide. Only a vague recollection of some small gesture of goodwill toward a woman with the meticulously recorded name of Elaine Rosen promises Fergus anything beyond despair.

It would serve no useful purpose to speculate about Moore's personal reasons for writing *Fergus* (1970). Nor, despite its many obvious flaws, need we dwell on it and insist that *this,* after all, is what Brian Moore, the author of *The Lonely Passion of Judith Hearne* (1955), has inevitably come to. For *Catholics* (1972) and *The Great Victorian Collection* (1975), Moore's two most recent works, are both infinitely better novels, and strongly suggest that, when he turns his attention to a slightly different theme, Moore is still capable of producing excellent fiction. But that judgment carries us to the threshhold of another phase of Moore's career. What is important here is that *Fergus* is the ultimate expression of a theme that achieves its full definition in *An Answer from Limbo* (1962) and *The Emperor of Ice Cream* (1965), and which already

seems to be suffering from enervation and repetition in *I Am Mary Dunne* (1968). Seen in this light, the paralysis that afflicts Moore's later pilgrims, for whom nothing of significant psychological or creative value seems to exist except in an irredeemable past, seems finally to threaten Moore's own definition of himself as an artist. Lacking Joyce's willingness to yield himself entirely to his remembered adolescence, and unable or unwilling in much of his middle fiction to ignore, abstract, or romanticize the past, Moore courts disaster by producing re-cycled portraits of old influences and old antagonists. Unchanging, their predictability robs them of their vitality, and strips them of the power they once had to enlighten, to anger, and to shock.

An excerpt from *The Luck of Ginger Coffey*

Not even able to enjoy a bit of music. Bloody females! He lay back, entering a world where no earthly women were. In that world soft houris moved, small women of a Japanese submissiveness, administering large doubles and sweet embraces in rooms filled with comfortable club sofas and beds. In that world, men of thirty-nine were Elder Brothers, prized over any Greek stripling. In that world, a man no longer spent his life running uphill, his hope in his mouth, his shins kicked by people with no faith in him. In that world, all men had reached the top of the hill; there were no dull jobs, no humiliating interviews, no turndowns; no man was saddled with girning wives and ungrateful daughters, there were unlimited funds to spend, the food was plentiful and nonfattening, there were no Father Cogleys handing out warnings, no newspapers worrying you with atom bombs, no sneerers and mockers waiting to see you fail, no rents to pay, no clothes to buy, no bank managers. In that world you could travel into beautiful jungles with four Indian companions, climb a dozen distant mountain peaks, sail rafts in endless tropic seas. You were free. By flicking your fingers in a secret sign, you could move backwards or forwards in time and space, spending a day in any age that took your fancy, but as a leader of that age, the happiest man of that day. In that free world . . .

In that world, both quarts finished, Ginger Coffey fell asleep.

Brian Moore, in his The Luck of Ginger Coffey, *Little, Brown and Company, 1960.*

Bruce Stovel   (essay date Summer 1981)

SOURCE: "Brian Moore: The Realist's Progress," in *English Studies in Canada,* Vol. VII, No. 2, Summer, 1981, pp. 183-200.

[*In the following essay, Stovel argues that Moore shifted from "traditional social realism" to "impersonal" fiction to parables over the course of his first twelve novels, a transition which "recapitulates the major changes in fiction itself within the last century or so."*]

Brian Moore has written eleven novels in a career that now extends over a quarter-century. It is a distinguished body of work, and one distinguished, more than anything else, by its realism. Elusive as the term is, some sense of its meaning for Moore emerges from his own views on fiction. He has said, "I think we're in a sort of camp period with novels" [Richard B. Sale, "An Interview in London with Brian Moore," *Studies in the Novel,* vol. 1, No. 1, Spring, 1969] Calling himself "anti-*anti-roman,*" he believes most experimental writing fails because it does not portray actual life: "Life is all about very mundane things. It is all about ambition, jobs, worries about your children's health, fear of death. . . . There are no jobs in modern novels; everybody lives in some limbo." In fact, though, "most people still live in the old-fashioned world of the nineteenth-century novels" [quoted by Donald Cameron in "Brian Moore: Tragic Vein of The Ordinary," in *Conversations with Canadian Novelists,* 1973]. What makes the great novelists great for Moore is their realism: "Faulkner's gothic America is based on real people, real relationships between white and Negro, real feelings of hunters. . . . The finest things in *Ulysses* and in the *Portrait* rest on a naturalistic basis, on character and on [Joyce's] ability to write about ordinary people and ordinary—even banal—situations. I think that is strength; take that away and the books disappear" [quoted by Sale].

These beliefs are interesting, not so much in themselves, but for what they imply about Moore's plots and narrative methods. For realism is not a matter of content, nor a credo, but a formal term describing a certain kind of story told in a certain way. I would like to define Moore's realism in these terms and suggest the changing uses he has made of it. Moore's fiction does change in important ways. He employs a traditional social realism in his first five novels; the fifth, *The Emperor of Ice Cream* (1966), is highly autobiographical and seems to have laid many ghosts, formal as well as personal. The next two novels, *I Am Mary Dunne* (1968) and *Fergus* (1970), present a subjective realism new to Moore. After two works which reveal an uneasy compromise between parable and realism, *Catholics* (1972) and *The Great Victorian Collection* (1975), Moore returns, a little exhausted from his travels, perhaps, to traditional realism in his two most recent novels, *The Doctor's Wife* (1976), and *The Mangan Inheritance* (1979). Moore's growth from traditional realism to what Wayne Booth calls the impersonal novel to fable recapitulates the major changes in fiction itself within the last century or so; it also reflects our diminished belief in a shared reality. "The nineteenth-century novelist was a part of *his* community, a recorder of a world he knew and understood. But today's writer, particularly if he is an exile, tends to become what Mary McCarthy called a *machine à écrire*" [Brian Moore, "The Writer in Exile," *Canadian Journal of English Studies,* 2, 2 (1976)]. Moore is indeed an exile, in time as well as in space. He says defiantly, "I believe in a real world because I was brought up in it" (Sale), but time and change have made that world increasingly distant. Tracing this realist's progress, then, not only helps to understand Moore's fiction, but also offers some hints about the changing nature of realism itself.

> **The central drama in Moore's First Five novels lies in the conflicts between the characters' inner demands and the fixed social framework in which they find themselves.**
>
> **—Bruce Stovel**

Moore's first five novels all employ a traditional, objective realism. The central drama, in each case, lies in the conflicts between the characters' inner demands and the fixed social framework in which they find themselves. This framework, in other words, is necessary for presenting the dramatic movement from self-delusion to self-recognition and self-acceptance. Speaking in 1971, Moore said, "When I wrote most of my novels I was interested—I'm not sure that I'm much interested now—in presenting the moment in a person's life, the crucial few weeks or months, when one suddenly confronts the reality or unreality of one's illusions, because that, to me, is what the drama of a novel is" (Cameron). Each of these early novels is, as perhaps all works of traditional realism are, a *bildungsroman:* they trace the process of growing up, of changing from child to adult. Gavin Burke of *The Emperor of Ice Cream* has the delusions and discoveries of normal adolescence; he is not what Joyce called "a painful case." But all the other central characters are: they must make the transition in their thirties or early forties, an age when delusions have become habitual and change is much more painful. Judith Hearne, the spinster heroine of the first novel, *The Lonely Passion of Judith Hearne* (1955), is the classic instance: she penetrates, in the course of the novel, the genteel disguises she has erected to keep herself from recognizing her own desperate loneliness. If, as her crisis begins, she stands in line with the children for confession, she can sit before the mirror in the final chapter and say to herself, as she could not have a few weeks earlier, "That is an old woman." Diarmud Devine in *The Feast of Lupercal* (1957) sees in the final chapter that he has allowed himself to be caned by his fellow teacher, Tim Heron, as "a form of expiation" for being, metaphorically, a barren woman; Dev, too, has come a long way from the shame and indignation with which he rejected the overheard reference to himself as "that old woman." In *The Luck of Ginger Coffey* (1960), Ginger, a man who lives in boy's clothing and boy's dreams, exchanges his Alpine hat and hacking jacket for "the uniform, anonymous and humiliating," of a diaper deliverer; he is "aged white in one moment" by snow in the climactic scene. Brendan and Jane Tierney in *An Answer from Limbo* (1962), themselves parents, are presented as overgrown children, each absorbed in delusions of revenge and final triumph; the childishness appears in the words with which Jane expels her mother-in-law: "I didn't want you here, I never wanted you to come, life's miserable with you on top of us all the time and then you go interfering with my children, you sneaky, deceitful old—*poop.*" In the end, both Brendan and Jane are forced to face their delusions: "We have lost our dream," Jane reflects. When the emperor of ice cream comes to Belfast, Gavin Burke discovers what his favourite poems are really about: he can then let "be be finale of seem" [from the poem "The Emperor of Ice Cream" by Wallace Stevens] and move from indecision to decision, from subjection to his own guardian angels to guardianship of his own father.

In short, the fixed social setting of the novels is presented, not for its own sake, but as a means of dramatizing the protagonists' education—the process by which they are "led out of " themselves and into adult reality. This process is comic in nature, since the conflict of inner and outer is finally reconciled. Paradoxically, it is failure, not success, which produces the moral victory of self-knowledge, as Moore explains in an interview (Cameron). Devine is described at the start of *The Feast of Lupercal* as "a man whose appearance suggested some painful uncertainty"; Dev, like the other protagonists, is a child in his father's Victorian clothes, torn between allegiance to a reassuring past and the need to live in the present. By the end of the novel, his pains are at least known and accepted. Even *Judith Hearne,* that most sombre of novels, ends on a generic note of renewal and reconciliation. When Judith puts up her two ikons once more, she reflects that if her Aunt D'Arcy—whose opinions (delivered with a sniff of superiority) have always consoled her—is dead and gone, Aunt D'Arcy is still part of Judith's own persisting self; in the same way, she accepts the Sacred Heart as literally gone, but alive as part of her. In *An Answer from Limbo,* the presence and fate of Mrs. Tierney modify the inherently comic *bildungsroman* form; nevertheless, the novel takes its shape from Brendan's slow growth from painful uncertainty to painful certainty about the question, present in his mind from first to last, of whether he is willing to sacrifice himself to his writing. We should note that Brendan's ambition as a novelist, the moving force of the action, is presented throughout as a social and moral, not a literary, fact; Brendan indeed provides "A portrait of the young man as artist."

Objective realism is the key to understanding Moore's use of point of view in these five novels. Moore has described *Ginger Coffey* as "a first-person novel written in the third person" [quoted by Robert Fulford in "Robert Fulford Interviews Brian Moore," *Tamarark Review,* 23, 1962], and the phrase applies to all five early novels. In each, the action is experienced from within the central character (in *An Answer from Limbo,* from within three characters in rapid alternation); yet the central character is also presented to us as a social being, seen from outside. In fact, the hero of *The Feast of Lupercal* is, from first page to last, "Mr. Devine." The interplay between inner experience and fixed social reality is created largely by frequent shifts to the viewpoint of secondary or peripheral characters, especially at or just after moments of crisis. This device is Moore's signature on these early works. Judith Hearne's fellow boarders, the Rices, the O'Neill family, cashiers, clerks, taxi drivers, and Father Francis Xavier Quigley all punctuate and distance her harrowing drama. Similarly, dance instructors, tailors, amateur actors, schoolboys, Father McSwiney, and Dr. Keogh all provide a rhythm of crisis and relaxation, a blend of sympathy and detach-

ment, in *The Feast of Lupercal.* A clear instance of the effect of these shifts occurs in the final pages of *Ginger Coffey;* Ginger, drunk on straight self-pity and a mixture of sherry and Coca-Cola, is glimpsed first through the shocked eyes of the new man on the job, Mr. Rhodes, and later from the perspective of the constables who arrest him. The effect is to keep our view of Ginger external and ironic at his moment of greatest humiliation. In *An Answer from Limbo,* our distance is preserved by brief glimpses of the main action through the eyes of the children, Frank Finnerty (an Irish cousin), Ted Ormsby (Brendan's former friend), Vito and his pathetic sidekick, Lester, and, once more, the post-crisis policeman. Even Gavin Burke, the protagonist we sympathize with most directly, is kept at what Moore calls [in "Brian Moore: An Interview by Hallvard Dahlie," *Tamarack Review,* 46, 1968] "a very distinct remove" by extended scenes rendered from the viewpoint of his co-workers in the A.R.P. and by glimpses of Gavin as he is seen by his girlfriends and his mother.

If the purpose of these shifts in viewpoint is to give us an ironic grasp of the social situation and the protagonist's place within it, the shifts are merely one sign of Moore's prevailing attitude and strategy: irony. Moore's style artfully conveys ironic awareness to us, his readers, without interrupting our sympathetic participation in his protagonist's own experience. If we look at the extended passage early in *Judith Hearne* in which the heroine plays with her image in the mirror and then descends for the first time to the dim, over-furnished dining room of the boarding-house, we see that Judith's simple, hopeful perceptions are presented in a style that allows them to convey a great deal more to us than they do to her. Similarly, *Ginger Coffey* relies upon "his habitual processes of ratiocination" to convince himself that all is well; the phrase conveys both Ginger's trust in his own optimism and some less flattering implications. Many of the most memorable passages from these novels reveal, when examined, this flexible union of sympathy and judgment, of first-person experience and third-person awareness. Take, for example, the following:

> A drink would put things right. Drink was not to help forget, but to help remember, to clarify and arrange untidy and unpleasant facts into a perfect pattern of reasonableness and beauty. Alcoholic, she did not drink to put aside the dangers and disappointments of the moment. She drank to be able to see these trials more philosophically, to examine them more fully, fortified by the stimulant of unreason. (*Judith Hearne*)

Moore's irony is thus compassionate. If it reminds us that Judith's choices contain dimensions that she cannot understand, it also asks us to recognize her conflicts, if not her actions, as our own.

Ironic distance is also maintained by the use of two or more plots. In each of these books, Moore sets separate strands of action in motion; this forces reflective distance upon us; unexpected and suggestive patterns develop as the plots interact. Much of the art of *Judith Hearne,* for instance, lies in the way the social plot, in which Judith's lonely passion is a lonely romance, touches off a deeper, metaphysical plot, in which Judith's passion is a crucifixion. Losing the one passion throws her upon the thorns of the other. Ironically, the connection is thrust upon her by Bernie Rice, who intends to complete the rout of Madden in the social plot; he overreaches himself in that plot but, at the same time, begins Judith's torments by articulating her own doubts in the other. Devine's struggle for self-definition in *The Feast of Lupercal* is framed by the increasingly direct struggle between two priests for control of the Jesuit boys' school at which Dev teaches. His climactic confrontation with authority becomes merely an occasion for the old order, embodied in Dr. Keogh, to discomfit the sadistic careerist, Father McSwiney. Ginger Coffey's job worries and marriage worries are essentially separate, as his foolish pledge to base the fate of one upon the other underlines; when he is arrested, Ginger gives a false name, Gerald MacGregor, an amalgam of the two separate enemies who have, he thinks, brought him to this pass. Like Ginger, Gavin Burke finds himself "becalmed in indecision between adolescence and adult life" with both Sally Shannon and his career worries; the two plots conclude with matching, but separate, resolution scenes, in each of which "a new grown-up voice" informs Gavin that he is free of both Sally's and his father's demands. There are three plots in *An Answer from Limbo*— Brendan's struggle to become a recognized novelist, Jane's affair with Vito, Mrs. Tierney's missionary activities in the New World—and they interact intricately. Jane's rejection by Vito provokes her hysterical and guilty desire to punish Mrs. Tierney; Mrs. Tierney, by contrast, understands, sympathizes with, and helps Jane, rather than judges her. One of the novel's major ironies is that it is Mrs. Tierney, rather than Brendan or Jane, who shows tolerance; her harsh code is turned wholly upon her own life. Brendan, who has created this domestic hell, remains emotionally immune to both the women in his life; he lives in the limbo of those who refuse to choose.

These separate plots keep us at a reflective distance, since we must stand back if we are to see the plots counterpoint and converge. Ironic distance is a condition of another primary feature of these novels: humour. Here, again, the fixed social setting is instrumental; it throws into relief grotesques like Bernie Rice, Mr. Mountain, and Post Officer Craig. Ironic distance also allows us to see the comedy as well as the pathos in major scenes—for instance, in Judith Hearne's happiness in being at church with a good man beside her, while that man, James Madden, worries about his assault on the serving-girl the previous night and then falls asleep. Ginger Coffey is inflamed with desire for his own wife—once she has denied herself to him and he can imagine her infidelities with Gerry Grosvenor. The same sympathetic, yet humorous, irony prevails in *The Feast of Lupercal*. The quietest of the early novels, it is also very funny. Devine, a good Catholic, can only make love to his first girl by worshipping at the altar of her body: "But her mouth opened, her tongue probed. The reverence was profaned. He knelt back swiftly on his heels, hearing the short shocked gasp of his own breath." Dev then prays desperately for a miracle: "I will honour You all my life if only this will not come to pass." The final confrontation in Dr. Keogh's office mingles Dev's total humil-

iation with an exhilarating comic comeuppance for the hateful Father McSwiney.

The elements outlined so far can be found in almost all novels of objective realism. But Moore uses realism for one further purpose in these novels: to present a dramatic cycle of shame and self-pity. Other people are necessary for Moore's central characters, not so much to provide love (which all want and none receive), but to provide the judgment upon themselves that makes their own lives real. Ginger Coffey's dream of living for years in saintly renunciation of all human ties is rudely interrupted by the realization, "What good was it, doing something, if nobody in the whole world knew you were doing it?" Moore's characters are always and essentially aware of living before the eyes of others. Social and moral self-awareness is simply knowledge of the communal judgment. Judith Hearne turns her two household gods to the wall when she opens her bottles; Devine has the nervous habit of twisting his father's ring, seemingly consulting this symbol of bondage, in moments of crisis. Self-consciousness, in other words, consists of other people's real and imagined reactions to oneself; characters as different as Brendan Tierney and his mother illustrate this. Shame is thus, in these novels, much more powerful than guilt: Devine suffers less during and immediately after his sexual fiasco than he does when he sees the writing on the wall and "seemed to hear three hundred boyish voices chanting in eerie unison . . . *drawers down, drawers down.*"

Such dependence on what other people think is resented. Gavin Burke imagines being able to say to Sally, "Darling, you were right, I *am* ashamed of this job and I'm ashamed of being ashamed, if you know what I mean." Gavin's words hint that the first response to overwhelming shame is to try to escape it through self-pity: a person who cannot win esteem may still gain pity for his intense and abject suffering. Judith Hearne, Devine, Ginger Coffey, Gavin Burke, and, in more subtle ways, Brendan and Jane Tierney all seek refuge from shame in wild binges of self-pity. Of course, these binges only create further shame, as Father Quigley is quick to tell Judith. The characters' only hope of escaping this cycle lies in choosing to act in defiance of shame and self-pity, rather than simply suffering them; if Moore's protagonists do so, they find, to their surprise, that they can bear humiliation and not be annihilated.

Objective realism is necessary to convey this drama of shame and self-pity: the world around the characters is both the cause of their painful self-consciousness and the field in which it is tested. We feel Devine's shame so strongly, for instance, because we have been shown the strength of the social code he has violated. Here the demands of Moore's psychology coincide with the larger, formal patterns of realism. Shame and self-pity are, after all, adolescent emotions; the passage to adulthood, for Moore, can only be made by confronting them.

Moore was apparently anxious to turn to something very different after completing *The Emperor of Ice Cream* in 1966. In that novel, which he calls "my *Bildungsroman*" (Dahlie interview), he gives his most direct depiction of the Belfast world that he grew up in and believed to be real. At the same time, though, the novel's very realism may have seemed self-indulgent and evasive. In being true to his personal history, Moore wrote his only novel set in the past; Gavin's story is as much Moore's nostalgic *Goodbye to All That* [title of Robert Graves's autobiography] as his *bildungsroman*. Whatever the cause, Moore's impatience is evident in 1967; after stating that most experimental writing is camp and doesn't really work, he adds, "Yet at the same time I don't want to write realistic disguised autobiography" (Sale). He also speaks of personal reasons for a new departure: "*Emperor* was written at a crucial time in my life. . . . I started a new life half-way through the writing of it, I fell in love, remarried and so on. My new book was written and is being finished in this new happiness which is my present life" (Dahlie interview).

I Am Mary Dunne, Moore's "new book," indeed marks a new beginning. For the first time, Moore tells his story entirely in the first person. We never leave Mary's mind, as we did in the earlier novels, to gain distance and an ironic grasp of the actual situation; no larger, ironic consciousness conveys the action to us. Instead, like Mary, we must live with uncertainty. Is she going mad, in premenstrual depression, or in some intermediate state? Does her present husband, Terence, love her or does he protect her out of compassion for the wounded? Is she a moral monster, using and then betraying the people she has known, or is her life, as she would like to think, a series of successful struggles for fulfilment against those who would bind with briars her joys and desires? If she has sex on the brain, as her friend Janice charges, is she healthy or deformed thereby? Is she a Macbeth, as she fears, or is her role in her second husband's suicide that of stage-prop or even victim—Duncan and not Macbeth? Is her state of mind best explained by Catholicism as sin, by Freud as guilt about the sexuality her father bequeathed her, or by the Yeats epigraph as self-creation through the exercise of memory and imagination? Does she finally recover from her crisis or not? The novel's questions are left open: Moore now lets seem finale of be. As he said in 1967, "there's something onanistic about first person because you cannot really do anything with the character's own perceptions" (Sale). Judith's delusions, measured against a fixed actuality, give way to Mary's necessary illusions. If judgment is in abeyance, imaginative sympathy is now Moore's central aim: he means to make us feel as intensely as possible what it is to be his heroine. He says, and asks us to say after him, "I am Mary Dunne." We can measure the change by recalling the carefully-distanced use of first-person narration in *An Answer from Limbo;* there, only parts of the novel are told by Brendan Tierney, and the dramatic focus is not on Brendan's inner life.

Fergus, Moore's next novel, is a pale male version of a female *tour de force*, just as *The Feast of Lupercal* is an underplayed reworking of *Judith Hearne. Fergus,* like its predecessor, is the drama of an isolated person's confrontation with the ghosts of his past. The narration, though in the third person, never leaves the consciousness of Fergus Fadden, the aging novelist; in fact, almost all the other characters in the novel are incapable of seeing Fergus from

> **Moore means to make us feel as intensely as possible what it is to be his heroine. He says, and asks us to say after him, "I am Mary Dunne."**
>
> —*Bruce Stovel*

outside, since they are projections of his own mind. This subjectivism is the appropriate method of presenting a world in which, as Fergus's sister tells him, "You are your own god."

Time exists in both novels as a subjective medium, just as it does in, say, *Ulysses* and *The Sound and the Fury.* The present-tense action in each takes place within a single day, but, unlike Moore's earlier protagonists, who must have the courage to act, Mary and Fergus must have the courage to face their own thoughts. Thus there is no place for a double plot. The protagonist's mental life is a single, inescapable whole; present events provoke, and so contain, the persisting conflicts within Mary and Fergus. The plot in each case is subjective. Just as the thoughts of Quentin Compson or Leopold Bloom spiral inward, forming a mental journey that counterpoints the external events of a single day, so the minds of Mary and Fergus move obliquely toward a central recognition which they know and yet resist acknowledging. Mary's mind builds to, and finally contemplates, her discovery of her second husband's suicide. Fergus's mind must meet his own father, not as the all-too-convenient caricature of the novel's opening pages, but as the ground of his identity. Fergus's deepest self has demanded the climactic recognition scene with his father from the start; his father ended his ludicrous first appearance to his son with the words, "Yes, I'd be delighted about your writing. . . . But, your present life, well, that's another matter. Thank God I'm not around to make judgments on *that*. I should hope, though, that if I were, I'd be kinder to you than you are to me." In fact, one gauge of *Mary Dunne*'s structural superiority to *Fergus* is its greater unity of action. Mary's past and present are a seamless whole: confronting her guilty memories makes her feel even less worthy, even more unsure, of Terence's love, while his efforts to shield her remind her how much her past actions put her in need of protection. In *Fergus,* on the other hand, the present is dramatically inert: Fergus's ghosts neither affect not are affected by his relationship with young Dani and his decision not to revise his movie script.

In both novels, the subjective plot traces the sudden unravelling of a stable self. This is implicit in Mary's hysterical inability to remember what her name now is; Moore's working title for the novel, interestingly, was *A Woman of No Identity* (Dahlie interview). The final title, *I Am Mary Dunne,* suggests the counter-movement that occurs in each novel, the creation of a new and larger sense of self from the pieces. The epigraph to *I Am Mary Dunne* suggests that, like Yeats in "Among School Children," Mary ends by composing painfully separate selves into a single and connected image. By her own inner efforts she has achieved a persisting and coherent selfhood, one that she knows can fight her dooms. Similarly, Fergus ends up able to wave goodbye to the inner forces which have divided him, "releasing them"—and himself as well. The psychological integration of past and present replaces, in both novels, the *bildungsroman* reconciliation of inner and outer reality.

If these two novels have no fixed social framework, no outside views of the central figure, no ironic distance, and no counterpoint of separate plots, the humour of the early novels must be transformed—and it is. Characters and speeches that might earlier have been laughable are now more painful than ridiculous, since they hold too much power over the suffering protagonist. We might think, for instance, of the outpouring with which Hat Bell consigns Mary to "this poor Beatle bugger," an outpouring, which haunts Mary, or of the many pungent Irish voices which sound so vigorously from Fergus's past. An important change in perspective and texture has been made; once again, the 1967 interviews shed some light on Moore's achievement. Moore says that he wrote *I Am Mary Dunne* first in the third person, then "in the historical present," and finally in "first-person, non-historical present. . . . in one day with movements into the past." He explains that in the rewrite of the novel in its final form the last third of the book caused problems "because the character I introduce at the end, who has not been met up to then, is too grotesque. The first time around, I tended to emphasize his grotesque qualities, and now I'm trying to change him completely around" (Dahlie interview). The section Moore describes consists of one long, unbroken scene with Ernest Truelove, who *is* grotesque, even in name: his monstrous and tyrannizing self-pity in the name of love, his mixture of lust and chivalrous devotion, his clumsy attempts at sophistication which only make him "a professional hick"—everything about Ernie is ridiculous. But, as Moore implies, he is no grotesque to Mary, since he is the terrifying and stubborn embodiment of her own past; hence the treatment of him had to be shaded from grotesque humour, suitable for a James Madden or a Post Officer Craig, to a nightmare-like intensity suited to Moore's new subjective method of presentation.

In this new form of realism, Moore's dramatic cycle of shame and self-pity is replaced by a subjective cycle of guilt and depression. Mary Dunne, who believes in her amended version of Descartes, *memento ergo sum,* has no trouble rejecting the tenet of shame, "They saw it, therefore I am"; similarly, Fergus's ghosts appear in order to bewilder, not accuse, him. And if guilt is internalized shame, a feeling of self-defilement, the terror that Mary calls depression need not be caused by shameful action, as Mary realizes: "I do not know my fault, the Juarez dooms are not about real things, I do not think about Hat's suicide, I do not know what it is I have done, and so, not knowing, I cannot forgive myself." If guilt causes depression, depression only creates further guilt, and, since the cycle is a purely subjective one, action offers no release from it. Both protagonists can only resolve not to cease from mental fight against these inner enemies, but only after Mary has been driven to the brink of suicide and Fer-

gus to a heart attack. The real source of both guilt and depression is the fear of forgetting one's past; if identity is derived from memory, then to forget something is to die by so much. Mary realizes this from the outset: "As now, perhaps, I am beginning to die because some future me cannot keep me in mind." The moral struggle with memory, in which Mary and Fergus must face things which they are afraid to remember, is only part of a metaphysical struggle, in which both must face the terrors of forgetting. The climactic scene of *Fergus* turns on the hero's being able to recall a woman he can barely remember, a woman with whom he knows he did nothing shameful, simply because: "Don't you see? Forgetting is the most terrible thing that can happen to a person."

These two novels are still realistic, particularly if we follow W. J. Harvey and assume that a rich and complex presentation of character is the central feature of realism. But Moore's realism is now subjective, not objective; still, like the fiction of Joyce, Faulkner, Woolf, and other modernists, it extends, rather than repudiates, traditional realism. *I Am Mary Dunne* and *Fergus* present not those who are still children, but those who are adults and must renew contact with a childhood they fear they have lost; realism, though of a different kind, is still needed to tell this second kind of story, since both protagonists say, with their author, "I believe in a real world because I was brought up in it."

Fergus, like its autobiographical predecessor, *The Emperor of Ice Cream,* used up a body of material and a narrative method. The reader of Moore's earlier novels is familiar with its characters (Dr. Keogh) and its character types (the parents, the intellectual mentor), its scenes of ritual (the family rosary), and its dramatic moments (the missioner's hellfire). Technique, too, seems pushed to a point where it becomes obtrusive and redundant. Moore seems to have had an urge to put his realism to new uses after *Fergus;* at any rate, his next book, *The Revolution Script* (1971), is a "non-fiction novel" about the Quebec terrorist kidnappings of 1970. And his two subsequent works, *Catholics* (1972) and *The Great Victorian Collection* (1975), make realism subservient to parable, though the compromise is, in each case, an uneasy one. What Moore recently said of *The Great Victorian Collection* is true of both books: "I was writing against all the strengths I have" [quoted by Hubert de Santana in "Who Is Brian Moore?," *Books in Canada* 6, No. 8 (1977)].

Catholics is a fable set in the future and not quite a novel at all. It is less than half as long as Moore's other books and the only one not to treat relationships between men and women. Its status in Moore's eyes is perhaps indicated by the fact that it is his only book to date not dedicated to a person. Like his early novels, though, it contains two cleverly-connected plots and makes dramatic use of changes in viewpoint.

The first two-thirds of the novella is presented through the eyes of the calculating young careerist, James Kinsella, and depicts a social conflict between new and old Catholicism. This part of the novel is a dystopia, a satiric projection into the future of trends in contemporary experience; imaginative verve, not realistic texture, is the necessary means of conveying Moore's *reductio ad absurdum* of the strange paradoxes in modern culture. For instance, Kinsella takes heart from the words of his mentor, Hartmann: "You must show them that while you are the Revolution and they are the Tradition, the Revolution is the established faith and will prevail." Similarly, contemporary religion is presented as estranged from its own fixed and actual structures; in place of the stone walls of Muck Abbey, "that bareness which contains all the beauty of belief," we have Kinsella's new conception of community: "Today's best thinking saw the disappearance of the church building as a place of worship in favor of a more generalized community concept, a group gathered in a meeting to celebrate God-in-others." Moore's title, in short, contains a pun: all the world is about to become Catholic, since the word has regained its original meaning, all-embracing. But, of course, to be everything at once is to be nothing at all. As in most dystopias, the social forces satirized are those most hostile to imaginative activity; Moore, the realistic novelist, is threatened by all that Kinsella represents—loss of faith, loss of humility, denial of mystery and miracle, rejection of tradition as irrelevant, loss of community, even loss of individual identity.

Yet realism reappears, and with a vengeance, in the final section of the novella. There we switch to the viewpoint of Kinsella's opponent, the Abbot, who benefits from a cunning Lockwood-effect: Kinsella's rational secularism has been so limited that we sympathize all the more readily with the Abbot when we learn of his inner struggle for belief. The action thus moves, as it had in *Judith Hearne,* from a social plot to a metaphysical plot; Kinsella's triumph in one is only a means of producing the Abbot's spiritual triumph in the other.

But Moore's realism is too little and too late. The Abbot's character, as J. W. Foster says, is "sadly underdeveloped " [*Forces and Themes in Ulster Fiction,* 1974]. Compared to the agony of Judith Hearne, the Abbot's thoughts as he, like her, contemplates a tabernacle empty of God, seem simply that—thoughts. We think of him throughout as the Abbot, an official in the Church, rather than as Tomás O'Malley, the green-grocer's son; he has a spiritual history but no personal past. The Abbot, we may note, is born at the same date as his author; that is, he is a projection into the future of Moore himself. But the Abbot only symbolizes, and does not embody, Moore's real world of childhood.

The Great Victorian Collection is another uncertain mixture of parable and realism, though parable of a very different kind. Moore's model here is the most influential of contemporary anti-realists, Jorge Luis Borges. Moore recently said, "The idea of writing *The Great Victorian Collection* didn't come from Borges, but reading him gave me the courage to try" ["Interview: With Author Brian Moore," *Maclean's* (11 July 1977)]. But Moore's Borgesian fantasy, paradoxically, is an epistemological exploration of his own realism; speculations implicit in *Catholics* are taken up and developed here. The body of objects dreamed into existence by Anthony Maloney accurately reproduces the world he has known; the *objects d'art* are neither "original" nor copies of actual objects, but a

"wholly secular miracle." The first and all-important rule governing the Collection is that it is a unit: take any one object out of its place in the exhibit and it becomes a Japanese fake—a notion Aristotle would readily grasp. Maloney, like Moore himself, can only dream what he knows, the Victorian past; his agent and other self, Vaterman, turns on him with the charge, "Never mind whether you dreamed it up or not, have you ever listened to what serious people say about it? Why, they say it isn't relevant, it's completely out of date, it has nothing to do with our contemporary reality." That Maloney's creation should possess and finally destroy him is a special instance of a general truth for Moore: "People's lives change them" (Dahlie interview).

If the action consists of playful fantasy about realistic creation, the narrative method is similarly Borgesian and non-realistic. Events are presented from Maloney's point of view—we never see him through the eyes of another character—and yet not from within his own consciousness. This narrative perspective is new for Moore. It is pseudo-documentary, a mock-realism, as the following sentences from the opening pages illustrate: "He later said that when he entered the motel bedroom the blind was drawn and the bed was turned down. This has since been confirmed by Mrs. Elaine Bourget, wife of the proprietor, who customarily performs this service for guests." The realistic surface is ironic, but rather than conveying a larger than human meaning, the details convey their own lack of meaning. Much of the novel consists of transcripts, in documentary style, of TV interviews, researchers' reports, press conferences, and Maloney's own diary (as later published in a scholarly journal). The refusal to provide any omniscient framework is heightened by Moore's style, which often has the austere eloquence, the dramatic variation, of Borges: "Until then, he had believed that, by his actions, his inattention, his unworthiness, he could destroy this Collection he had so miraculously and fortuitously wrought. But what if the Collection, singular, faëry, false, had, with true artifice, begun to destroy him?"

As suits this parable, Maloney has little distinct personality. Like the Ancient Mariner, he is the blank, passive protagonist of a dream. He feels little, as his lack of response to the wife who has left him shows, and he sees even less—he has to be told by Mary Ann that Vaterman's belief that her father does follow her everywhere is false. In fact, as Maloney grasps, it is the very lack of any apparent source in his everyday life that makes his dream so remarkable: "I'm not a freak, I'm an ordinary person. It's what I've done that's extraordinary. . . . In fact, it's probably because I'm not interesting that I became a dreamer and dreamed up this stuff."

But Moore, inveterate realist that he is, fleshes out his parable with all the paraphernalia of realism. Maloney has a childhood and youth in Montreal, job worries, marital problems, a struggle for independence with his mother, shadowy memories of his dead father, and much more. A good deal of the novel is given over to developing elements superfluous in the parable. Maloney has, for instance, in dim and shadowy form, the inner life of shame and self-consciousness that we have seen in Moore's realistic fiction; early in the novel he examines his "Judas face" in the mirror in typical Moore fashion. These realistic elaborations jar with the prevailing narrative method. In the major scenes, Moore seems unable to decide which method to use; Maloney's desperate flight with Mary Ann presents fantasy, guilt, and self-pity as both dream-states and as realistic action. If Maloney's dream finally consumes him, Moore's own realistic imagination takes over and undermines his parable.

In his two latest novels, *The Doctor's Wife* (1976) and *The Mangan Inheritance* (1979), Moore has returned, at least ostensibly, to the objective realism of his first novels, just as Sheila Redden of *The Doctor's Wife* is once again from Belfast and even recalls the "Fairy" Rice of *Judith Hearne* from her days at university. Once more a social framework is used to present a story of maturation, "the crucial few weeks or months, when one suddenly confronts the reality or unreality of one's illusions." Sheila Redden ("Mrs. Redden" to us), a thirty-seven year old mother who is really still a child under her husband's care, has such a confrontation; her brother can see its effect at the novel's end: "Something had changed. He could not say, exactly, but she looked older." Once again, we have a story told primarily from within the heroine's own consciousness, but in the third person, with frequent shifts in viewpoint to other characters—her brother Owen, her husband, her friend Peg, even the casual voyeur, Mr. Balcer. Again, too, these shifts provide ironic distance: the novel's prologue, told from Owen's point of view after the major events have taken place, tells us in advance that the heroine's sexual idyll will not be permanent; Mr. Balcer takes over at the moments of greatest eroticism, forcing us to see the lovers from outside.

Moore's realism gives the novel its subtlety. The action builds to the heroine's decision; her sexual emancipation, which occupies the first half of the novel, serves this end, since it gives her faith that she can choose her own future. But choosing is such a painful state that she is soon referring to her new happiness in the past tense; finally, she is driven, like Mary Dunne and Maloney, to contemplate suicide as a release from conflict. Yet her decision, when made, shows that her growing pains have taught her to discriminate. She has decided not to return to her life with her husband in Belfast; she also sees that to be directed by her lover to a new life in America is not enough of a change from being managed by her husband. Furthermore, she must be sure that she has not used Tom Lowry, her younger American lover, merely as an instrument for her own liberation. From the start, her mind has recoiled from memories and dreams of raw horror in Belfast; even before she became involved with Tom, she was tempted to walk out of her life there, just like "those men you read about in newspaper stories who walk out of their homes saying they are going down to the corner to buy cigarettes and are never heard from again." If she must clarify her own motives, she must also give Tom a chance to test his; before she realizes fully what her question means, she asks him, "Supposing you were told you would never see *me* again. What would you do?" Moore's realistic presentation of character and conflict gives the decision its complex scrupulousness.

But the novel is raw romance as much as it is in Moore's earlier vein of realism. If the title alludes to Flaubert, it also suggests drug-store Bovarisme, a ladies' thriller. And if the setting is social, it is hardly fixed: with the help of planes and phones, we hop about glamorously from Belfast to Paris to the Mediterranean to Paris to London. This geographical fluidity corresponds to moral and psychological fluidity. There are no codes for the heroine to violate, no barriers to break through: "It seemed like another life," Sheila reflects, "that long-ago time or rules and rewards, when prayer and sin were real." Moore's heroine is, literally, shameless. As a result, her discoveries about herself—for instance, her realization that she married simply to escape life at home—occur abstractly and without dramatic force. Also, unlike the early novels, *The Doctor's Wife* has only one plot; this contributes to a lack of ironic distance from the central character. If secondary characters like Sheila's domineering husband and even more domineering sister-in-law provide a familiar kind of humour, there is no laughing when Sheila, like Devine earlier, falls to her knees in sexual worship. Tom Lowry, as a result, is too blandly and insubstantially good, a latter-day Will Ladislaw to our post-Freudian Dorothea; it is significant that he is the one main character whose point of view is not explored. Just as Sheila Redden is from Belfast, but not in it, so Moore can not simply return to his original domain, objective realism.

Realism and crude romance mingle even more strangely in *The Mangan Inheritance.* On the one hand, the opening situation is exactly that of the early novels: Jamie Mangan is a thirty-six-year-old painful case, a would-be poet and occasional journalist who has drifted through life directed by first his father and then his wealthy and famous wife. He is "lifelike, but not alive" until his wife jolts him by walking out and then by her death only days later in a car crash. Mangan, ironically, inherits her money: "at thirty-six he had been given a second chance." Moore once again contrasts North America and Ireland—in word and intonation, in ritual and belief, in kind of community—and we expect social texture to frame, once more, a plot tracing the movement from adolescent dreams to a facing of adult reality.

But this is not quite what happens. The money frees Mangan from worrying about his social identity—in that world of jobs, money, family ties that Moore had insisted was real—and allows him to embark, a latter-day Hawthorne hero, on an obsessive quest for the truth about his second inheritance, his Irish blood. The middle section of the novel, more than two-thirds of its length, is devoted to Mangan's search for his previous incarnations in southwest Ireland. If Sheila Redden was from a real Belfast, but not in it, Mangan comes back to Ireland, but as a stranger trying to penetrate a rainy Gothic mystery. And Gothic it is, for Mangan finds there his own eerie resemblance to past Mangans, an unspeakable family crime, the ruined ancestral home which draws and yet threatens, kindly warnings that he would be wiser to stop asking questions and go home, his involuntary and growing resemblance to his ancestors as he re-enacts their crimes, and a final revelation of the horrible act and its Grand Guignol punishment—a revelation made by the criminal himself in the ruins of a castle. And thus, if Sheila Redden's self-discoveries were inert, Mangan simply makes none at all: he has no self-deceptions to be exposed. He is more of a blank everyman, like his fellow Montrealer Tony Maloney, than a man with a personal past that affects his present. Suitably, his story is told without the shifting point of view that characterizes Moore's objective realism, and so without much irony or humour. Yet, unlike Mary Dunne and Fergus, the protagonists of Moore's subjective realism, Mangan lacks an intense and interesting inner life; though the story is told throughout from his point of view, he, like Tony again, is passive and motiveless (except for his one obsession). In the end, Mangan seems to have learned nothing from his adventures. He does make an im-

portant decision after hearing the criminal's confession and refusing benediction—but we don't know what that decision is. We hear that "a decision began to form in his mind," but news of his father's sudden illness recalls him to North America before he can disclose or act upon it. The six-page final section of the novel in Canada resolves neither the North American (realistic) nor the Irish (Gothic) plot strands, nor does it connect the two. It seems that Moore himself, like Mangan, has failed to integrate his two inheritances.

This analysis suggests that Moore has at least not been content to repeat his successes. It also suggests another reason for following his future work with interest: since his movement from objective realism to subjective realism to parable embodies in brief the history of the novel form, his next novels may well reveal the possibilities still open to realism itself.

Brian Moore with Bruce Meyer and Brian O'Riordan (interview date 1982)

SOURCE: An interview in *In Their Words: Interviews with Fourteen Canadian Writers,* Anansi, 1984, pp. 168-83.

[*In the following interview, conducted in 1982 during the James Joyce Centenary in Toronto, Canada, Moore discusses the treatment of political and religious issues in his novels, and explains why he prefers straightforward narrative to experimental fiction.*]

[*Meyer and O'Riordan*]: *We live in an age where often there is more attention paid to a writer's life than is paid to his work. Has this been a problem for you?*

[Moore]: There are people now reading biographies of W.H. Auden and Robert Lowell, who probably have read very little of their work. And then you have the examples of Mailer, Capote and Vidal, whose lives are of more interest to people than their work. So, in the case of a writer like myself, who has simply a private life and not a very colourful legend, the only things people can fasten onto are details like my nationality. I think it is irrelevant myself because with a writer it is what he writes that is of interest and not his life. If in my book I seem to be an Irish writer, then the reader thinks he's in the presence of an Irish writer. If he thinks I'm a Canadian, then he thinks he's in the presence of a Canadian writer. I think nationality is something Canadians worry about unduly. A good example is Nabokov, who at one time was a White Russian, then had British citizenship, and then became an American citizen. Then he left America when he had made enough money and went to live in Montreuil for the rest of his life. But the Americans always accepted him as an American author. In all the years I've lived in America, there's always been this question of whether or not I'm a Canadian author. Overall, though, I'm a writer who has no personal grievances because for the past twenty-five years I've been able to write what I wanted to write, and that makes me one of the lucky few.

Graham Greene has called you his favourite living writer. Do you return the compliment?

An excerpt from *The Emperor of Ice-Cream*

They danced, they danced past Bobby, who stood, barely moving, pressing against Imelda, his eyes shut, his wet lips open in a smile. "Kiss me," said Sheila Luddin. He kissed her. The whisky whirled in his head and he missed a dance step, he stumbled and she caught him. Dizzy, colored lights blurring in front of his eyes, he saw her face, a face which blurred into pinwheels of color. Then it came, hot, sudden and full, and he turned quickly from her, vomit rushing from his mouth. She took his hand, led him to the table and sat him down. "I told you," she said. "Better not grow up. Come on, I'll drive you home."

"I can't. Too soon. My father."

She laughed. "I remember that problem. All right, we'll go for a walk. You need air. Come on."

"No." He loved her, it was stupid to say so, but she was stunning, she was Bobby's captive and he loved her, you see, but there was vomit on his suit, he was sure he stank to high heaven of it and there was no point in her being with him now, he'd be ashamed to touch her, he was drunk and must be sober and this lovely other rotten, lost, damned soul, the only person in the whole world who understood him, must stay here and not see him reeling in the street outside. "I love you," he said. "Even though you're married. What's your phone number? May I ring you up?"

She bent over the table top, her red hair falling down to touch the teacups. She laughed and laughed and laughed. It was horrible. She looked up, still laughing, and said: "Just don't grow up. Don't grow up."

If only he could think of some crushing reply, if only he could pay her back for laughing at him, pay her back for mocking something very, very serious. But as he sat there, stiff with rage and shame, his stomach heaved. He bolted for the gents'. There, kneeling amid carbolic smells, he began his night's penance.

Brian Moore, in his The Emperor of Ice-Cream, *The Viking Press, 1965.*

Well, I've wondered if it is often the case that writers you like also like you. I admire Graham Greene's work and I've learned a lot from him. Greene and Waugh are the two pre-eminent English writers of their generation. They are pre-eminent in prose just as Larkin is in poetry. People that like Greene usually like Waugh. And people who like Waugh and Greene usually like Larkin. One tends to like writers in which one sees something of oneself. I'm very lucky that Graham Greene said that about me because it has helped my sales enormously. For instance, in faraway countries where they've never heard of anyone other than Graham Greene, his reference to me has been particularly useful. In one South American edition of **The Doctor's Wife,** Greene's quotation about me was used and it helped sell thirty-seven thousand copies. If I sold that many in the United States of a hardcover edition, I'd be very lucky.

Have you ever met Greene?

I met him once years ago in Montreal. It was only very briefly. I had only just finished my first novel and was introduced to him by the editor of *The Montreal Star* and we went out on the town together for the evening. I met him on one other occasion in Montreal when he passed through, but I can't really say that I know him.

Many of your novels don't deal directly with politics per se, except in the case of **The Revolution Script.** *In this sense you are also like Greene.*

Well, I started as a newspaperman and I learned from that that novelists can't possibly keep up with all the news and information today. For instance, if you set out to write a novel today about El Salvador, by the time it was published nine months later, it would probably be out-of-date. So I fear political subjects are very ephemeral. They are not a great subject for a novel today unless you have an exceptional experience like Solzhenitsyn. But to go and report on things journalistically, as novelists did in the nineteenth century, is a waste of time. Other media will cover these things much more accurately. Also, it is interesting that a political situation such as that in Northern Ireland has really not been touched directly by any major writer. Seamus Heaney doesn't write directly about it and neither does anyone else. My feeling about novels is that people are born, married, they fight and they die and various things happen to everyone—these are the subjects which interest me more rather than whether they were born on the right or wrong side of privilege.

Nevertheless, you did tackle a political subject in **The Revolution Script.**

That was a mistake. I wanted to do a non-fiction book and I started to do it out of a belief that Trudeau, in invoking the War Measures Act, was acting in the same way as the British had in Northern Ireland for twenty years. He was repressing liberty. And I saw too that the anglophone liberal people here were completely blind to that because they were afraid of the French. When I started to write the book I was trapped by the fact that I couldn't make direct contact with the terrorists. When the terrorists were allowed to flee to Cuba in the middle of my book, I had to make them fictional characters. I knew they weren't going to come back and sue me. (Laughter.) The book was

an experiment but I don't regard it as part of my work but rather as some journalistic exercise.

I'm interested in the moment in which one's illusions are shattered and one has to live without *the* faith, whatever that faith was.

—Brian Moore

You seem to write a great deal about the loss of faith in the face of personal adversity. You suggest that it is very important for one to develop some system of personal moral values, in order to stay sane, to have some constants and anchors in one's life. For instance, Judith Hearne has pictures of her aunt and the Sacred Heart and Ginger Coffey has his family. In traditional literature it is the artist, the intellectual, the aristocrat who has come to terms with the problems of faith in himself and in others. You seem to be more interested in the ordinary person's loss of faith. Do you see that as the common theme in your work?

There are certain continuing preoccupations in my novels, but, yes, I decided very early on that Joyce had written about an intellectual's loss of faith in *A Portrait of the Artist as a Young Man,* and I decided I couldn't compete with that. I also recognized, however, that Joyce himself, my great hero, had said that his work was a celebration of the commonplace, and I feel that my writing is also a celebration of the commonplace. I believe that the most interesting lives are the lives of ordinary people. Most of us can't relate to someone who is extraordinarily intelligent or extraordinarily dumb because most of us fall somewhere in between. I am interested in the point in ordinary people's lives when, like all of us, there's a carrot held out in front of them—like ambition. My novels often revolve around the moment in that person's life when to remove that carrot of ambition or desire, the person is forced, within a certain period of time, to re-evaluate their lives and make a decision about what they are going to do. I'm interested in the moment in which one's illusions are shattered and one has to live without *the* faith, whatever that faith was which originally sustained them. I also like in novels to start the clock ticking. I like the novel to take place within a certain time. I have to explain to the reader what made this particular time different. That to me is the natural moment of fiction, the natural moment of crisis. I do this in order to inject an element of suspense. I've come to have a greater interest in the element of suspense as I grow older. For instance, I will now look at Conrad's *The Secret Agent* in a way I would not when I was young. I look at the suspense in Graham Greene or Borges in a way which didn't interest me when I was younger. My new book, **Cold Heaven,** is a curious book in that for the first one hundred and fifty pages you believe you are reading a thriller because you don't know what's happening to the character. It moves very quickly, but on a rather mundane level, the way thrillers do, and then you discover, halfway through the book, that this isn't an ordinary thriller—it is a metaphysical thriller, about something more mysterious than that contained in an ordinary thriller. I don't think I would have written a book that way ten years ago. This is a culmination of my experiments along the same lines in **The Temptation of Eileen Hughes** and **The Mangan Inheritance. Cold Heaven** goes one step further. So, willy-nilly, I'm going through a cycle of books in the suspense genre. It is important to realize that what I'm trying to do is not write books that are detective stories, but rather are novels of suspense in the detective mode. The power of withholding information from the reader, but not dishonestly, the power of narrative, of unfolding a story by turning pages, builds narrative suspense, which is interesting for your writing because it forces you to write more leanly—in a direct, clear, clean way. My style has been evolving towards a more plain style. Reviewers have said that when I use a simile or metaphor it stands out. It is not simply piling on description. When I do finally say something about a character, it hits, it has a very big power. I think that is something which is the result of this very visual age we live in. People can't read in the way they used to because their mind's eye is making cinematic cuts. We see prose passages now as films because children are brought up looking at film all the time. I've always thought that the modern reader made jump-cuts just like directors in films. I think we could move fiction into the realm of short-takes, a way which has not really been attempted. Someday, someone will come up with a type of fiction which approximates the cinematic, and that will have a very interesting effect.

What about Kosinski and Robbe-Grillet?

There's no movement in Robbe-Grillet. He just pans around and looks at furniture, and as for Kosinski, he's just a bad writer, so I'm not the person to really discuss him. Whereas, if you take an older writer like Evelyn Waugh, he can take two men in a room and you can *see* exactly what they are doing, but in very understated prose. Similarly, Greene is one of the great scene-setters of all time. Their techniques are very cinematic. We tend to take cinematic as a pejorative word in writing, but I'm not using it that way at all.

You seem to be saying that the novel has a future.

I don't have any theories about "the novel". I find that experimental writing, unless it is truly experimental, is one of the most easily fakeable things in the world. One of the most truly experimental writers in the world is Flann O'Brien. The writing goes beyond Joyce into something that is absolutely brilliant. Borges is a truly experimental writer, also Gabriel Garcia Marquez. John Barth isn't. With these academic writers, it's all just Twenties' hokum revamped and regurgitated. It is unreadable and it is junk. I think most writers in their heart of hearts suspect that it is junk.

So when someone sits down to read a book of yours. . . .

I want them to read for pleasure, I want to move people. I find that unless I'm going to do better than *Ulysses,* I don't want to write an experimental novel. Although, I am among Joyce's greatest admirers, I think *Finnegans Wake*

is a great mistake. No one reads *Finnegans Wake* for pleasure, nor have they ever. The suspicious thing about most of this so-called experimental writing is that it is instantly teachable. The old, bad schlock writers like Irving Wallace and Robert Ludlum—all these people like the old storytellers, write in a very bad way, a very cliched way, but they write within a very strong framework of narrative, a strong framework of dream. Their books are wet dreams for college-educated people. They have that power. They are the obverse to me of the Barthian academic novelist, who is equally cliched and equally bored. I suffer from two things that prevent me from having a big audience. One is that I'm a nomad, and, two, I don't write the same book over and over again. There isn't a continuity to my books where people can say: "That's a Brian Moore". I have a continuing set of preoccupations, but I experiment with form. It is like what Greene said about me, I'm like a lion-tamer with the novel. It hasn't been a conscious strategy of mine to avoid being labelled English-Canadian or Irish-American because I would like to be claimed by everybody, and to have a readership in each of these places. I didn't have an Irish readership for a very long time because the clergy had my books banned in Ireland. Irish people thought for a long time that I was an American or a Canadian. The only good piece of luck I've had in this matter is that since my first book was published in England, the English always treated each book as a book by itself. So right from the very beginning in England, I've always had respectful, good reviews of my work. They are the only people who have never mentioned my nationality.

You mentioned that there were certain continuing preoccupations in your novels. Could you talk about some of them?

I suppose unlike most male novelists today, Catholicism continues to be something that I write about. I'm interested in the church as an organism. I'm interested in loneliness. I've always considered myself one of life's rejects. I came from a family of successful people—my father was a great achiever in examinations and things like that. I failed my examinations at school. I was very bad at math which in those days was the end—if you couldn't get math you couldn't get anything. I could never become a doctor because I was not good at chemistry. I was thirty before I wrote my first novel so I had quite a bit of experience at being a failure before I became a quasi-success.

Your novels tend to contain a rather bleak vision. . . .

I think that's true. I tend to try to examine the dichotomy between what people think they are and what they do. A wonderful book could be written about Hitler's image of Hitler. Hitler didn't see himself as he was and neither did Attila the Hun. It is interesting that monsters don't know they are monsters and to my mind everyone has a totally false notion of their own worth. Some people are modest to the point of not realizing their true worth, but they are a small minority.

Did you ever have a mentor or a particular teacher who influenced you or encouraged you when you were young?

Yes. When I was seven or eight, I remember the headmaster calling me in, and asking me to fill a notebook with essays on topics like what I did on my summer vacation. I was very flattered and happy to take the week off from studies to write for him. I wrote seven or eight essays and he used those essays for three or four years after. So, I was given this inflated notion of myself when I was very small. I wasn't as successful in any of my other subjects, so I got this notion of myself as a writer, but I was intimidated by other writers that I read and thought I could never equal them. So, I thought the next best thing I could do was to become a newspaper reporter. It was only after I had read a couple of bad books written by people that I knew that I decided I could do better than that. I thought that poor books were more important to read than Tolstoy.

Like Brendan Tierney in **An Answer from Limbo?**

Yes. I use that example. I seem to be at variance with most modern writers. When you read interviews with them they seem to say that writing is torture, that it is hell and how when they go through it they sweat blood and this sort of thing. I find that writing is torture. It is hell to get it right, but I'm only happy when I am writing. Why I write so much is that I'm happy when I am writing, not when I'm teaching or being interviewed. (Laughter.) I can live quite a solitary, monkish life because I'm not intimidated by the act of getting up in the morning and continuing to write a novel. I suppose that there are more writers like me, but they feel that it is impolitic to admit it.

When you were writing **The Mangan Inheritance** *you had a very severe illness, and you've said that the act of writing helped you to pull out of it. Has writing become something a little more special for you since then?*

I discovered during that period that I was too tired and too ill to read but I was able to write. So it had an influence. I was very close to death for quite a long time. That focussed my attention very closely on the years that I have left. Until I had the illness, I felt life was a perpetual party. After the illness I became aware that it might not be.

Also during the composition of **The Mangan Inheritance** *you switched genres from a novel of manners to a gothic horror. This was quite a gamble. Do you see yourself as a literary risk-taker?*

I do, indeed. For many reviewers and readers *The Mangan Inheritance* was too big a gamble. If I had a commercial mind, I would have written *The Mangan Inheritance* as a gothic horror and the book would have opened in Ireland. I would have had an enormously successful book because the whole Irish section is written in a more elevated, charismatic way, and the characters seem more interesting. The Canadian-American part of that book is written on a realistic level. One editor in fact suggested to me that I put the Canadian-American past in simply as a flashback. But I felt, as I always feel, that that would be a deception for the reader. The interest in *The Mangan Inheritance* should be that this is a person like you or me who is projected into this milieu. He should act as you or I would in a similar predicament. I knew I was taking risks, but I also knew that I would be cheating if I did it any other way.

> **I hate killing people in a novel because you don't go around indiscriminately killing people in real life. Death in a novel should be as momentous as it is in real life.**
>
> **—Brian Moore**

How does a novel start for you?

I start with a character and keep changing my opinion of him. By starting that way I feel I get to know him or her. It is like when you first meet a stranger. You have some fixed ideas about what they are like and gradually you get to know them and trust them. In my writing you trust to the instinct of the character which makes you know not to make them do something outré because they just wouldn't do that. That defines your plot. I hate killing people in a novel because you don't go around indiscriminately killing people in real life. Death in a novel should be as momentous as it is in real life.

You've never written a novel that was entirely a flashback, but you have indicated that you once thought of writing a screen-play for **Judith Hearne,** *which would have been almost entirely in flashback. Do you think in retrospect that the novel would have worked better as a flashback or did you simply think that, in cinematic terms, it would have worked better as a flashback?*

I must have been desperately trying to find some way to answer an interviewer's question. (Laughter.) I've talked to students about flashbacks in that way. Quite often when young writers start a story they start with a scene and the scene may last for two and a half pages, and then they decide I've got to tell the reader all about this person and they go into a flashback which lasts five and a half pages. I say to them, flashbacks should be small digressions. I have very strong feelings that you should never have a whole chapter in flashback because it can become another book. Either the narrative must keep moving forward and can't be interrupted or else the digression must neatly fit into the narrative. You can't be back-peddling. If you keep flashing back, then why should you go on?

Flashbacks take away from the element of building up suspense.

Yes, they do. You're damaging the narrative in that sense. The flashback is also a convention that was much more prevalent twenty years ago.

In both journalism and the cinema, one to a large extent is forced to shape the narrative in the present tense. Has your background as a journalist and as a screenwriter for John Huston and Alfred Hitchcock influenced you to write primarily in the present tense?

Yes, insofar as in the newspaper business you are concerned with the same questions that concern the novelist—who, what, when, why, where. Also, as a journalist, you get a microcosm of what is going on in society. You have to deal with present-day events—which bank was robbed today, that sort of thing.

How did you come to work with Alfred Hitchcock?

Alfred Hitchcock read my book, **The Feast of Lupercal,** and liked it. He had also gone to a Jesuit school and so identified with the setting of the novel. As a result of reading that book, he hired me to do the screenplay for **Torn Curtain** with Paul Newman and Julie Andrews.

How did you and Hitchcock get along?

The problem I had with Hitchcock was that he was a living legend. He'd done fifty films and I'd done zero, so I tended to take his word for everything. When we finished doing the script I thought it was very bad. I felt the characters were cardboard, and I made the mistake of telling him that. He was never a person who would have a confrontation with you to your face. He just simply hired two other screen-writers, and they were not able to change it. So I wound up getting sole credit for the script, which I'm not very proud of. I don't think I'm a Hitchcockian writer. I think by the time I met him he believed his own legend. It was hard to explain to him that these characters didn't seem real to me, that I didn't think it was going to work. One of the problems was that it was one of the most expensive films that Hitchcock ever made.

How about John Huston? He was also a legend by the time you met him.

Well, Huston was totally different. He is one of the few really brilliant people I've ever dealt with. He came to see me about my novel, **Catholics,** and suggested that I turn it into a film. He said, "It should only take you two or three weeks". Well, it almost killed me. These things take longer than that. He then called me and said that it would make a good television film, rather than a feature film. I thought, then, that he was kind of brushing me off, but actually he wasn't. He said he would direct it, but unfortunately the television network didn't see it that way because they felt he would be too expensive. He would have been a very interesting director to work with. You know he bought **Judith Hearne** at one point.

Katharine Hepburn was supposed to star in it wasn't she?

The studios didn't want her for the part. I had no say, of course, in that decision. This is one of the objections I have to working in film. The writer just has to do what he is told to do. I mean, the problem is that there is so much money involved. It is as if when you are writing a book you are told from the outset that this must sell 250,000 copies in paperback and be a Book-of-the-Month Club selection and be translated into eighteen foreign languages, or else it is a failure. There are too many masters to please in film. There's a confusion in people's minds today between art and commerce, which I think has made for a situation where even serious books are a risky business as compared to twenty-five years ago. When I first started being published it didn't cost very much for a novel to be published. You could live comfortably on five-thousand dollars a year. If you sold enough to cover the costs of a small paperback edition then everybody was happy, and you could

go on to the next book. I think it is very sad for the young writer today who has a first novel. He has to be an instant success so he doesn't really have time to develop as a writer.

Do you think the novel will go the way of poetry, in terms of substantially decreased sales and influence?

I would hate to think that. Part of the confusion is in our own minds. We do tend to equate, certainly the Americans do, literary with commercial success, even at the highest level. Can you think of a Canadian writer who is more highly regarded even though he has smaller sales than any of those who have the large sales? We tend to think of the successful writer as the one who sells a lot.

Did you ever write poetry?

No, not really. I would love to have had it in me.

Which Canadian writers do you read yourself?

I've read quite a lot of them. I think my favourite Canadian writer at the moment is Alice Munro. Once again, I like those people whose writing has some affinity with my own. Alice Munro, for me, captures a sense of Canada. I like Richard Wright. None of the writers I like are what I would call academics.

Can you tell us what you're working on now?

I've had to write five hours worth of a television script based on a book by Simone de Beauvoir and I had to invent new characters. I know the period and I know France well, so I had an advantage in that. The people who hired me were very enlightened, compared to the average movie people, in that they left me alone to work on it. I didn't have to attend a lot of meetings about it and I was able to get it done in time—in four months.

Are you ruthless with your time?

Yes, I have to be. I did meet with them yesterday and they agreed with my judgement that we had to cut it down by an hour. So that's what I'm doing now.

How did you feel about working with someone else's novel?

It is easier than working with your own, because you have already seen your novel as a novel. Someone else's work you can approach just as a story—this one is a love story, a period story about Vichy and the Jews.

One other thing we've noticed about your work, there are very few overt, literary references.

Yes, well I don't think of my work in Ph. D. thesis terms. I've always felt that if you can illuminate a particular situation, absolutely and truly, and if the situation is intrinsically of interest, that will become the archetypal situation. The mistake made in so much bad fiction is to try to take an archetypal situation and then try to get a character to fit the thesis of the novel—the novel written around a thesis. For instance, a writer decides, "I am going to write a novel about infidelity or about the loss of God". Well, my own approach would be: "What if so-and-so lost their faith? What would they think? How would they behave? What would they do?" I didn't realize it, but in **Judith Hearne** I was writing about the loss of faith, about the loss of faith in one ordinary person. But what I did without knowing it was write an archetypal model of a novel about lonely women. Of all my books it is the one that has stayed in print most constantly. It touched some very raw, sensitive nerve among women and especially among lonely women, or women who feared they would be lonely. It has outlived feminism and every faddish shade of opinion about women. If I had planned that the book should have this effect, it would be dead and forgotten—as would all my books.

Christopher Lehmann-Haupt (review date 25 March 1985)

SOURCE: A review of *Black Robe,* in *The New York Times,* March 25, 1985, p. C17.

[*In the following review, Lehmann-Haupt praises Moore's characterizations, his "unadorned but evocative prose," and his depiction of spiritual conflict in* Black Robe.]

As Brian Moore explains in an author's note that precedes the opening of his unusual new novel, *Black Robe*: "A few years ago, in Graham Greene's *Collected Essays,* I came upon his discussion of *The Jesuits of North America,* the celebrated work by the American historian Francis Parkman (1823-1893)."

A passage cited by Greene, about the extraordinary dedication of one particular 17th-century Jesuit Father, led Mr. Moore to read Parkman's great work and to discover that his main source was the *Relations,* the voluminous letters that the Jesuits sent back to their superiors in France. In the *Relations* themselves—and in "their deeply moving reports" revealing "an unknown and unpredictable world"—Mr. Moore found the inspiration for *Black Robe*.

If the route to his material is somewhat remote, the ground he arrives at will be familiar enough to anyone who has followed Brian Moore's fertile and inventive career as the author of 14 novels, among them *The Lonely Passion of Judith Hearne, The Luck of Ginger Coffey, The Emperor of Ice Cream, The Great Victorian Collection,* and his last, *Cold Heaven*. For it is understanding God's mysterious ways that concerns Mr. Moore in this imagined account of a dangerous trek through the wilderness north of Samuel de Champlain's Quebec settlement.

Whose version of the spiritual realm was more valid, Mr. Moore seems to be asking—"the Indian belief in a world of night and in the power of dreams" or "the Jesuits' preachments of Christianity and a paradise after death"? Could one set of beliefs be comprehended by followers of the other? What if Christianity was actually inimical to "Les Sauvages", as the Indians were collectively known to the French? What if the Jesuit fathers, or "Blackrobes," as the Indians called them, were corrupted by savage spirits?

If this summation makes *Black Robe* sound like thesis fiction, it is not altogether misleading. "This novel is an attempt to show," Mr. Moore concludes his introductory note, "that each of these beliefs inspired in the other fear, hostility, and despair, which later would result in the destruction and abandonment of the Jesuit missions, and the conquest of the Huron people by the Iroquois, their deadly enemy."

Yet if he is painting by the numbers, he has done an admirable job of modulating the colors within the spaces of his canvas. A reader is immediately intrigued with the figure of Father Laforgue, the guilt-infested missionary who is trying to reach an Indian community up north where disease has broken out and a priest has been murdered. Mr. Moore's unadorned but evocative prose creates a powerful sense of the lonely North American wilderness. "The day passed. The sun, high in the sky, dipped until it barely cleared the tops of the trees. A wind rippled the water into waves, a wind which numbed Laforgue's cheeks. He remembered what Father Bourque had told him of a second false summer which came in mid-October, bringing a few days of heat at the end of the autumnal season. That false summer was ending. Winter was near."

Mr. Moore has done a particularly good job of representing the Indians, succumbing to neither the noble-savage nor the lo-the-poor-Indian cliche, but instead representing what is known to have been their obscene and joshing banter with a liberal dollop of four-letter words. Most admirably of all, he has balanced perfectly the two spiritual worlds. When Laforgue recovers suddenly from an illness for which his Indian escorts are threatening to kill and ditch him, it might with equal plausibility be credited to the God to which he prays, or a hump-backed Indian sorcerer who is convinced Laforgue is possessed by a demon, or just plain chance.

The novel's realism breaks down only in the speed with which Laforgue and an Algonquin family recover from the tortures inflicted upon them by some Iroquois who capture them. It is a necessary part of Mr. Moore's grand design to illustrate both how and why the Indians "practiced ritual cannibalism and, for reasons of religion, subjected their enemies to prolonged and unbearable tortures." Yet having made his point—in scenes where the Iroquois "caress", their victims most horrifyingly—he hurries on a little hastily, and the reader must wince in sympathetic pain at what their injured persons are asked to perform.

But it is with spirits and not bodies that Brian Moore is ultimately concerned. And it is spirits that finally suffer the real and lasting damage in *Black Robe*. "We have become as bad as the Normans themselves," argues one Algonquin leader, referring of course to the French. "We have become greedy and stupid like the hairy ones."

And at the point where the plague-ridden Indians finally accept the offer of baptism out of fear that the priests have cast a spell on them, Laforgue reflects, "What are these baptisms but a mockery of the Church, of all the saintly stories we have read of saving barbarians for Christ?"

Yet despite these realizations both the Indians and the priests continue to work at cross purposes. The result is inevitable and tragic—the mutual destruction of their souls.

James Carroll   (review date 31 March 1985)

SOURCE: "The Ordeal of Father Laforgue," in *The New York Times Book Review,* March 31, 1985, p. 7.

[*An ex-Roman Catholic priest, Carroll is an American novelist, poet, nonfiction writer, and dramatist. In the following highly positive review of* Black Robe, *he argues that Moore encourages readers to recognize similarities between the seventeenth-century clash of cultures and ideologies represented in the novel and modern attempts "to divide the world into separate camps of good and evil."*]

Black Robe is an extraordinary novel. Part adventure story, part the life of a saint, part parable, it is an exemplary act of imagination in which Brian Moore has brought vividly to life a radically different world and populated it with men and women wholly unlike us. His novel's achievement, however, is that, through the course of its shocking narrative, these strangers become first figures of great sympathy and finally images of our own humanity. By the end of *Black Robe,* we recognize its fierce, awful world as the one we live in. We put Mr. Moore's novel down and look at ourselves and our places differently.

The novel is set in the wilds of North America in the early 17th century, and it concerns the journey of two Frenchmen from Champlain's Quebec to a besieged outpost in distant, unexplored and unfriendly territory. One of the Frenchmen is a Jesuit missionary, the Rev. Paul Laforgue, the Black Robe of the title and the novel's central character. A young man, new to America, drilled in his religious discipline and dependent on it for what steadiness and resolve he can muster in the face of a nightmare situation, the priest must survive betrayal by his Algonquin guides, torture by his Iroquois captors, abandonment by his fellow Frenchman, young Daniel Davost, the superstitious twisting of the meaning of their sacred mission by his Jesuit confrere, the ailing Rev. Fernand Jerome, whom he meets at the fever-ridden village of Ihonatiria, and the collapse of what he thinks is his faith in God.

Black Robe has an almost mythic purity. It is a classic dark-journey story, a passage through great difficulties in which a man's weaknesses are laid bare, his strengths discovered and for the first time claimed. But it is in no way high-flown. It has the essential elements of popular fiction—suspense, narrative drive, surprise and action. Despite the alien quality of the world it creates, the novel is so believable and consistent in its detail that the hazards and the consolations of the plot, unimaginable until now, seem natural, even familiar, to us as soon as Mr. Moore evokes them. Yet *Black Robe* depends not at all for its power on the stock images we have of such adventures and such characters. On the contrary, one of Mr. Moore's accomplishments is his original rendering of both the Indians and the priest.

It is no surprise that Mr. Moore can write compellingly about the interior conflict of a priest. He did it memorably in *Catholics,* and the collapse of faith is a main concern of several of his many novels. But Indians? And their interior conflicts? Their ways of speaking and eating and sleeping and courting and grieving? Their spirituality? Because it follows the early French usage, Mr. Moore calls

them "Savages" throughout his novel, but there is nothing pejorative in his attitude toward them. He shows us the horrifying aspects of their culture—their torturing of enemies, their cannibalism. But he shows us the touching aspects as well—the joyfulness of their sexuality, their generosity, their communality, their regard for the spirit world. One of the great pleasures of this novel is reading about the daily lives of these Algonquins, Hurons and Iroquois. It shocked me to realize how little I knew of these people about whom I've been hearing since childhood.

Of course, Mr. Moore's purpose in writing about the Indians is not anthropological, any more than his purpose in writing about a Jesuit missionary—one of those the Roman Catholic Church remembers as the North American Martyrs—is hagiographic. His subject is the collision of two cultures. Each culture is seen whole, with intelligence and sympathy, and considering the clichés that prevail about both Indians and priests, that alone makes *Black Robe* special. If Mr. Moore writes as a descendent of a culture that completely supplanted another, his story still is imbued with a sense of the profound tragedy it was for the Savages when they first had the Good News preached to them.

One can celebrate the arrival of Europeans in America and regard the worldwide missionary work of Jesuits as gallant and humanizing while also understanding the ambiguity of such things. The great mystery is not that evil exists but that it exists within the good, within civilization, even within the church. A vision that respects such complexity is hard to sustain, but it is more necessary now than ever, when the truly primitive impulse to divide the world into separate camps of good and evil is once again ascendant and so heavily armed. We can read *Black Robe* and see our own times in it. We can read it and remember that human beings can reach across vast divides to find one another. We can read it and understand that history, the endless story of colliding cultures, is tragic for everyone. Father Laforgue, the Black Robe, comes at last to the kind of wisdom, forbearance, humility and tolerance that in his view make him forever unworthy as a priest. But his view is what is primitive about his culture. He came to the New World to be a saint, and he failed because instead of "saving" the people he found there, he loved them.

Gerald Lynch   (review date Fall 1986)

SOURCE: "Blue Streaks," in *Canadian Literature,* No. 110, Fall, 1986, pp. 150-52.

[*In the following review, Lynch criticizes what he considers the sparse prose and often-underdeveloped characters of* Black Robe, *but praises Moore for suggesting that the Jesuit missionaries were in some respects as "savage" as the Native Americans they attempted to "civilize."*]

Black Robe is both an extension of and a departure from Moore's earlier work. It is an extension of explorations begun in earlier novels because it is concerned with a test of religious faith. It is a departure because its protagonist is a seventeenth-century Jesuit missionary in Canada, a man who cannot be labelled one of Moore's "ordinary people"; and it is a departure formalistically, being a historical romance of the kind written by Nathaniel Hawthorne.

Seemingly incongruous with its form, *Black Robe* is written in a pared-down style that Moore believes complements the self-sustaining power of suspenseful narratives. (This faith in narrative and concern with the appropriate style first emerged in *The Great Victorian Collection,* 1975.) [In *In Their Words: Interviews with Fourteen Canadian Writers,* 1984], Moore observed to [Bruce] Meyer and [Brian] O'Riordan that an overriding interest in narrative "forces you to write more leanly—in a direct, clear, clean way. My style has been evolving towards a more plain style." What such a style gains in narrative and poetic force it risks (in the hands even of such post-Hemingway adepts as Norman Levine and Moore) in verisimilitude and atmosphere; and with Moore we are talking of a writer who, as this quotation attests, values story. In Moore's recent novels, *Cold Heaven* (1983) and *The Temptations of Eileen Hughes* (1981), this plain style gains much and loses little. In *Black Robe* the writing is often flat, attenuated to dissipation, seemingly beaten in revision to too airy a thinness. For my taste, Brian Moore writes most splendidly when he imaginatively embeds his talents in the consciousness of his isolated protagonists and goes off in a white heat of defensive, offensive, and hopeful words, giving us characters such as Judith Hearne, Ginger Coffey, Brendan Tierney, Mary Dunne, and James Mangan. Surely a verbal dynamo can drive a narrative as well as does a plain style. Whatever, Moore has chosen the way of stylistic austerity, and an austere novel is what he has given us in *Black Robe*.

The narrative of *Black Robe* is the journey towards the Jesuit mission in Huronia (before the massacre there in 1640) of Father Laforgue, his young Norman assistant Daniel, and their Algonquin Indian guides, who abandon Laforgue and Daniel. The priest and young man are later rejoined by Daniel's alluring Indian lover and her family. But only Laforgue is credible as a character; and the details of the journey upriver convey the impression not of a voyage into the heart of darkness but of a glide down a Hollywood backlot. Nonetheless, nothing that Moore has written is without a centre of rich reward. And *Black Robe* rises to such levels of writing in its sustained positing of radical oppositions. The overarching opposition is that of civilization vs. nature, which opposition the novel expresses particularly in terms of European Christian vs. New World Savage. The European Christians are the original French Catholic explorers/exploiters of the area that became Quebec and Ontario. The New World Savages are Algonquins, Iroquois, and Hurons. Viewed thus, Moore can indeed be seen to have written a Canadian version not of *The Heart of Darkness* but of Hawthorne's *The Scarlet Letter*: the ancestral past and the tension of the spirit and the flesh are *Black Robe*'s true subject. (Moore's use of forest scenes especially brings Hawthorne to mind; I am not suggesting an indebtedness, though, but a remarkable, and I hope illuminating, similarity—in form, style, and intent.)

As deconstruction has reminded us, most binary oppositions are illusions that mask ideological prejudice. We are

also that which we exclude from our self-definitions and thereby oppose ourselves to. *Black Robe* shows the ways in which European Christians such as Daniel, tempted by lust and love, easily become the opposite to that with which they had identified themselves. *Black Robe*'s oft-mentioned scene of cannibalism, where a young boy is parboiled and eaten in front of his father and sister, nicely illustrates this concept of the elusiveness of radical distinctions. Although the Savages are shown to eat their victims ritualistically for a complexity of reasons, one of those reasons is to possess the threatening qualities of a valiant foe. At the risk of trivializing fundamental distinctions—the actual as opposed to the symbolic, for instance—and a myriad of all-important details, it is yet worth noting that one of Father Laforgue's sacred trusts is the Eucharist—the body and blood of Christ that is ritualistically eaten at the anti-climax of the central Catholic mystery. Thus do Cannibalism and Communion help to erase what had appeared to be one of *Black Robe*'s blackest lines of demarcation between Savage and Christian.

The Indians in *Black Robe* curse a blue streak (or "like nuns," as we used to say) in good Anglo-Saxon. Since other reviewers have made much both for and against the linguistic suitability of the device, I will add only that I

An excerpt from *I Am Mary Dunne*

Cogito ergo sum. I close my eyes and go back seventeen years. Mother Marie-Thérèse writes it on the blackboard. Her arm is bare to the elbow: the sleeve of her habit is rolled up to avoid chalk dust. "I think, therefore I am," she says. Where the Latin was just something to translate, the English jumps and my hand is up (unlike me, that) and when Mother sees me I ask wouldn't it have been more correct for him to have said *"Memento ergo sum"*?

"Memento?" —with that winter frost smile of hers.

"Yes, Mother. I remember, therefore I am."

She sends her smile searching among the other girls in the class. But no one has a comment. As for Reverend Mother's smile, it could mean "A silly girl has misunderstood Descartes," or "See how we have engaged the attention of Mary Dunne."

"And why would you say that?" she asks me.

"Because"—I am fifteen—"we are what we remember."

"Interesting," says Reverend Mother, but did she really think so? Did she remember our conversation an hour after class? I have remembered it seventeen years and now I wonder. If we are what we remember, did that girl I was die because I forgot her? As now, perhaps, I am beginning to die because some future me cannot keep me in mind.

Brian Moore, in his I Am Mary Dunne, *The Viking Press, 1968.*

think it works well. In any case, few readers who were raised Catholic will regret the purile thrill when the Savage asks the weeping Priest who had been lost in the forest, "What is wrong with you, you silly prick?"

Kerry McSweeney   (essay date Spring 1987)

SOURCE: "Sorceries," in *Essays on Canadian Writing*, No. 34, Spring, 1987, pp. 111-18.

[*In the following essay on* Black Robe, *McSweeney asserts that Moore could have represented Father Laforgue's crisis of faith more effectively by using "a self-conscious, intrusive narrator," but praises the novelist for depicting both the Native Americans and the missionaries "in ways that sharpen the reader's attention and intensify his response to the text."*]

"Few passages of history are more striking than those which record the efforts of the earlier French Jesuits to convert the Indians. Full as they are of dramatic and philosophic interest . . . it is wonderful that they have been left so long in obscurity." So wrote the American historian Francis Parkman in the preface to his *The Jesuits in North America in the Seventeenth Century* (1867), one of the most dramatically interesting volumes in his monumental *France and England in North America*. As Parkman explains, part of his puzzlement was owing to the copiousness of the available sources of information. Each year, long and detailed reports were sent back to Paris by the Jesuit missionaries and annually published in a series known as the *Relations,* which contains enormous amounts of information concerning the condition and character of the primitive inhabitants of North America. From the *Relations* and other written sources, Parkman fashioned an absorbing narrative of tremendous sweep. One of the geographical termini of the narrative was the rude Residence of Notre-Dame des Anges at Quebec, where a handful of exceptional men planned the conversion of the continent. Attempts were made to convert the nomadic Algonquins, whose existence during half the year was, says Parkman, "but a desperate pursuit of the mere necessaries of life under the worst conditions of hardship, suffering, and debasement." It was realized that little could be done to convert a nomadic tribe, and thus the attention of the Jesuits turned to the other geographical terminus: the land of the Hurons, who were a stationary people dwelling in small communities near the lake that bears their name. But this land was hundreds of miles from Quebec and could only be reached by an arduous canoe journey up the St. Lawrence and Ottawa rivers, along the Mattawa River, across Lake Nipissing, and down the French River into Georgian Bay. And, during the journey, travellers were vulnerable to attack by the ferocious Iroquois, whose war parties roamed northward from their base in what is now central New York State.

In an author's note to *Black Robe,* his fifteenth novel, Brian Moore explains that it was through reading an essay on Parkman's history by Graham Greene that he was led first to *The Jesuits in North America* and then to the *Relations.* It is particularly on the former that *Black Robe* depends—for its story line, for information about Indian customs, attitudes, and beliefs, and for innumerable small details. The novel's central character is a Jesuit priest, Paul Laforgue, "a slight, pale man, thin-bearded, intellectual, but with a strange determination in the eyes and narrow mouth," whose chance to serve on the front lines for the greater honour and glory of God comes when his superior at Quebec instructs him to journey to a Huron mission to assist its beleaguered incumbent, who, at last word, was at risk of being martyred.

For the first part of the journey, it is arranged that a party of Algonquins, on the way to their winter hunting grounds, will guide Laforgue, who is also accompanied by a young French layman, Daniel Davost, whose secret reason for wanting to make the journey is his oft-gratified lust for one of the Algonquins, a girl named Annuka. More than half the novel is devoted to this part of Laforgue's journey, which gives Moore ample opportunity to introduce a hunchback sorcerer named Mestigoit, describe a moose hunt in the snow, and detail features of the savage life-style, all of which are deeply repugnant to Laforgue: the nauseating stench inside the bark-covered shelters; the dogs that crawl over the bodies of the sleepers, looking for a place to lie and for something to eat; the promiscuous sex and foul language; the gluttonous feasts on half-cooked meat with pieces of fur still attached. This long first section of *Black Robe* ends when Laforgue, Daniel, Annuka, and her father Chomina are captured by the Iroquois, whose appalling tortures are explicitly described. After their escape, Laforgue eventually reaches Huronia, where the short second and concluding section of the novel takes place.

It is obvious that one of Moore's principal concerns in *Black Robe* is to describe the manners and mores of the Indians. It is just as clear that the novel's principal thematic intention is to contrast two different cultures, religions, and ways of being in the world—the savage and the civilized Christian. This is, of course, hardly an original undertaking. To speak only of white English-Canadian writers, there is a long tradition of imaginative response to Indian culture, as Leslie Monkman showed in his *A Native Heritage: Images of the Indian in English-Canadian Literature*. Until the contemporary period, most writers used the meeting of white man and red man to endorse, in one way or another, the values of the former. In recent decades, however, the response has grown more complex, and there has been a tendency to identify with the Indian world. In Margaret Atwood's *Surfacing,* for example, the white protagonist is reborn through discovering Indian gods residing in the landscape. *Black Robe* is a fresh example of this more complex contemporary attitude, though with a distinctive emphasis owing to the fact that, while he is a Canadian citizen, Brian Moore was educated in Ireland by the Jesuits and, unlike Parkman or E. J. Pratt, knows Roman Catholicism from the inside.

The "philosophic interest" of *Black Robe* is adumbrated by Moore when, at the end of his author's note, he speaks of "the strange and gripping tragedy that occurred when the Indian belief in a world of night and in the power of dreams clashed with the Jesuits' preachments of Christianity and a paradise after death. This novel is an attempt to show that each of these beliefs inspired in the other fear, hostility, and despair." The principal spokesman in the novel for the Indian point of view is the Algonquin Chomina. When Laforgue tells him that paradise will be open to him after death if he allows himself to be baptized, Chomina replies: "What paradise? A paradise for Normans? . . . Why would I want to go to a paradise where there are none of my people? No, I will die and go to another country where our dead have gone. There I will meet my wife and my son. Your god shits on me and mine." He also tells the priest:

> Look around you. The sun, the forest, the animals. This is all we have. It is because you Normans are deaf and blind that you think this world is a world of darkness and the world of the dead is a world of light. We who can hear the forest and the river's warnings, who speak with the animals and the fish and respect their bones, we know that is not the truth. If you have come here to change us, you are stupid. We know the truth. This world is a cruel place but it is the sunlight. And I grieve now, for I am leaving it.

And later, at the Huron mission, when Laforgue tells the Indians that to be baptized "You must give up those practices which offend Him. You must not cast off your wives, but keep them for life. You must not eat human flesh. You must not attend curing rituals or feasts of gluttony in which you become sick with eating. Above all, you must give up your belief in dreams," the eldest and wisest among them replies: "If we do these things and if we give up our belief in the dream, then the Huron life, the way we have always known, will end for us."

A particular concern of Moore's has been with the loss of religious belief and with what it is like to learn to live without God.

—*Kerry McSweeney*

This clash of beliefs in *Black Robe* is not merely stated; it is enacted in the consciousness of Laforgue, who undergoes a significant change during the course of his journey. To understand fully what happens to him, however, it is first necessary to consider an influence on *Black Robe* even more important than Parkman's *The Jesuits in North America*: the earlier novels of Brian Moore. As Moore has himself explained, the focal concern of his novels has always been "the moment in a person's life, the crucial few weeks or months, when one suddenly confronts the reality or unreality of one's illusions, because that, to me, is what the drama of a novel is" [quoted by Donald Cameron in "Brian Moore: The Tragic Vein of the Ordinary," in *Conversations with Canadian Novelists*, 1973]. A more particular concern has been with the loss of religious belief and with what it is like to learn to live without God. Loss of faith was the central precipitate of the crisis of Judith Hearne, the title character of Moore's first novel, and was

also movingly presented in the character of Tomás in *Catholics,* who, like Judith Hearne, came to the recognition that the tabernacle on the altar contained not the body of Christ, but only round wafers of unleavened bread. In the story of a few crucial months in the life of Paul Laforgue, Moore depicts this destabilizing rite of passage for the third time.

Ever since his order had granted his petition to be sent to New France, Laforgue has dreamed of the glory of martyrdom and, at the beginning of his journey, is certain that the hand of God is guiding his destiny. In a moment of spiritual exaltation, he feels that the dangers of the journey have been "transformed miraculously into a great adventure, a chance to advance God's glory here in a distant land." At one point he considers the *coureurs de bois* who have gone into the woods with the Algonquins and come back wild, corrupted, and promiscuous, and he wonders how they can so easily forget their civilization and their faith. But he does not begin seriously to doubt the mercy and providence of his God until after his harrowing experience as a captive of the Iroquois, during which, in addition to his own torments, he sees Chomina's young son have his throat slit, be hacked to pieces, have his bloodied limbs thrown into a cooking kettle, and, when parboiled, be passed among the warriors who had captured him. Laforgue now begins to feel "shut out from God's sight, as though he, like Chomina, was condemned to live forever in the darkness of this land." Like Tomás, he ceases to pray, while his mind stumbles into "thoughts of despair." Like Judith and Tomás, he comes to feel that "The hosts in the tabernacle were bread, dubbed the body of Christ in a ritual strange as any performed by these Savages." On the novel's last page, he baptizes a group of Hurons who have asked for the "water sorcery." It is not because he any longer believes in the efficacy of the sacrament, but for the same reason that at the end of *Catholics* Tomás leads his dispirited monks in prayer: because he loves them and wishes them well.

While its informing theme is closely similar to *Judith Hearne* and *Catholics, Black Robe* differs from them in being both an historical novel and an adventure story. Recently, the sixty-four-year-old novelist explained the reasons behind his growing interest in such comparatively popular fictional forms:

> "As I've become older I've become more interested in different forms of writing. I've discovered that the narrative forms—the thriller and the journey form—are tremendously powerful. They're the gut of fiction, but they're being left to second-rate writers because first-rate writers are doing curlicues and bringing the author into the novel and all these *nouveau roman* things."
>
> *Black Robe* is an effort to bring "that drive, that power, that commitment to holding the reader's attention which you find in Tolstoy and the other great Russians" back into the serious novel. Moore calls it a "heart of darkness story" about a journey into the wilderness which "moves forward but still contains ideas." [Robert Stewart, "The Literary Odyssey of Brian Moore," Montreal *Gazette,* 6 April 1985]

In the past, Moore has been an acute commentator on his own work; but in gauging the quality and distinction of *Black Robe,* I find the above remarks misleading. In the first place, the novel might well have been speculatively richer if Moore had brought into it, if not the author, at least the narrator, and had allowed him reflective and/or retrospective comments. This would have made unnecessary the unconvincing discussions between Laforgue and Chomina, during which the latter at times sounds more like Khalil Gibran than a foul-mouthed Algonquin. One is not asking for something as comparatively "curlicue" as Leonard Cohen's *Beautiful Losers,* the first-person narrator of which is an anthropologist specializing in North-American Indians and obsessed with the figure of Catherine Tekakwitha, the Iroquois virgin. But it is hard not to remember how successful John Fowles was in enriching the "philosophic" content of his historical novel, *The French Lieutenant's Woman,* through employing a self-conscious, intrusive narrator—a narratorial strategy that can hardly be called *avant garde,* since it was employed by several major nineteenth-century novelists.

As historical narrative, *Black Robe* cannot match the real thing—Parkman's *The Jesuits in North America in the Seventeenth Century.*

—Kerry McSweeney

One also wonders whether Moore is correct in implying that the power of *Black Robe* comes simply from its narrative drive, from its commitment to holding the reader's attention through story. At times one does turn the pages of the novel as eagerly as those of a thriller. But I should say the *artistic* strength of *Black Robe* lies less in its narrative drive than in its ability to defamiliarize its subject-matter in ways that sharpen the reader's attention and intensify his response to the text. This process can only occur at the expense of narrative drive, for the fresher and more unfamiliar the subjects are made, the more attention they draw to themselves, thus slowing the narrative pace. The most striking example of this process in *Black Robe* involves the language Moore has given the Indians to speak. In chapter 4 of *The Jesuits in North America,* Parkman reports that the expletives of the Algonquins "were foul words, of which they had a superabundance, and which men, women, and children alike used with a frequency and hardihood that amazed and scandalized" the Jesuits. Moore's artistic response to this narrative opportunity has been to make the Indians of *Black Robe* talk like the most linguistically debased contemporary anglophones, with particular prominence given to "shit" and to what, in their genteel moments, my seven-year-old son and his friends call "the f-word." The effect is startling and disconcerting, but does make the reader attentive to Moore's savages. To say that the constant stream of obscenity is gratuitous, ultimately *de trop,* and involves a de-

gree of stylization out of phase with the realistic postulates of the rest of the narrative, is to miss the point. As Victor Shklovsky, the Russian formalist who coined the term "defamiliarization" (*ostraneniye*), has explained, the artistic process of making strange involves an obvious display of the devices by which the effect is produced.

An equally impressive instance of defamiliarization in *Black Robe* is found in the presentation of Catholicism. In Tolstoy, Brian Moore finds narrative power; but there are other things to be found there also, one of which is well explained by Shklovsky: "Tolstoy described the dogmas and rituals he attacked as if they were unfamiliar, substituting everyday meanings for the customarily religious meanings of the words common in church ritual. Many persons were painfully wounded; they considered it blasphemy to present as strange and monstrous what they accepted as sacred." Something similar, if balder, happens in *Black Robe* when Catholic rituals and doctrines are observed from the savage point of view. At the beginning of chapter 2, for example, two Normans kneel before a third who "raised his right hand, the hand open like a knife. He made a downward movement, then a sideways movement. The two who knelt bowed their heads." "What are they doing?" asks one Indian. "It is some fucking sorcery," another replies. And, late in the novel, it is to the tabernacle and its sacred contents that a Huron is referring when he says: "I went into that place, shut off, where they keep pieces of a corpse in a little box, a corpse they brought from France."

While I am dubious about some of Moore's comments on *Black Robe,* I am in full agreement with his implicit conviction that it does have energy and drive and is a serious novel. It was not easy to think the same about three of Moore's last four novels. *The Doctor's Wife* (1976), *The Temptation of Eileen Hughes* (1981), and *Cold Heaven* (1983) were all slick romantic melodramas centring on adulterous passion, containing a spurious religious overlay, and littered with the tourist-eye detail of hotels, restaurants, and airports. As historical narrative, *Black Robe* cannot match the real thing—Parkman's *The Jesuits in North America in the Seventeenth Century.* As a "heart of darkness story" it lacks the intensity and resonant aura of Conrad's tale. But it is a strong and fresh addition to the canon of a distinguished contemporary novelist and evidence of its author's continued creative vigour.

Anne-Marie Conway (review date 2-8 October 1987)

SOURCE: "Under the Red Robe," in *The Times Literary Supplement,* October 2-8, 1987, p. 1073.

[*In the following positive review of* The Color of Blood, *Conway contends that, though character development suffers somewhat due to the demands of Moore's thriller format, the tautly paced novel nonetheless investigates "serious political and theological issues."*]

Black Robe, Brian Moore's last novel, and his first attempt at a historical theme, was a masterly exploration of the cultural abyss between the North American Indians and the Jesuit missionaries come in the name of God to "civilize" them. In *The Colour of Blood* the Jesuits again feature prominently and God is frequently invoked, but the time is the 1980s, the setting somewhere in the Eastern bloc (not Poland, although there are obvious similarities) and the style that of the political thriller.

Days before the bicentenary of the September Martyrs, an attempt is made on the life of the Catholic Primate, and the ensuing tension threatens to destroy the hard-won concordat between Church and State. The "raincoats"— as the much-hated Security Police are known—want to keep him in "protective custody", but he knows that his presence at the celebrations is essential to prevent a massive uprising. Shedding the red robes of his office for "the disguise of failure", Cardinal Bem goes on the run in a nightmarish world where even his own bishops are not to be trusted. Who are the instigators of this plot? Are they simple patriots, or right-wing fanatics backed by the CIA, or agents of a government fearful of that "larger neighbour" on its border and needing an excuse to stem the ever-growing power of the Church over the minds and hearts of the people? Only in the final chapters is the truth made clear.

The Revolution Script, Moore's imaginative reconstruction of the kidnapping, in 1970, of a British diplomat in Montreal, took us into the mind of the revolutionary left; in *The Colour of Blood* he invites us to consider the philosophical rather than the personal implications of political action. The thriller format becomes a vehicle to explore serious political and theological issues: the relationship between Church and State, the validity of "liberation theology", the meaning of "freedom" and "responsibility" under a totalitarian régime. In particular Moore questions the authenticity of a religious fervour too closely linked with political aspirations (the unstated parallels with the author's native Ireland spring first to mind, but the phenomenon is worldwide). Cardinal Bem personifies St Bernard's ideal of a man ruled by reason, balancing the demands of God and Caesar without ever losing sight of his priorities; in contrast, the Prime Minister, like Bem a graduate of the Jesuits, represents reason gone wrong, a leader prepared to countenance torture, detention, even murder, in the name of "the national good".

Always the consummate craftsman, Moore never allows the tension to slacken, reminding us that he is a writer who once worked with Alfred Hitchcock. From its opening sequence—a limousine speeding through the glistening streets of the capital towards the assassin's gun—to the spectacular finale in a cathedral glowing with candles and stained glass, this is a novel that cries out for cinematic treatment. Moore's prose is faultless, economical and elegant; and if the characterization is thinner than we have come to expect from the creator of Judith Hearne and Mary Dunne, it is only because it has been subordinated to more intellectual concerns.

Stefan Kanfer   (review date 2 November 1987)

SOURCE: "Lost in Greeneland," in *The New Republic,* Vol. 197, No. 18, November 2, 1987, pp. 47-8.

[*Kanfer is an American novelist, short story writer, dramatist, essayist, and journalist. In the following review, he as-*

serts that characterization in The Color of Blood *is superficial and that Moore rushes through issues which would have benefited from more extensive development.*]

Graham Greene should have no trouble entering the kingdom of heaven. It is on earth that he has much to answer for. Every paperback page-turner whose cover proclaims the coming of a new Existential Thriller ("He carried the war home with him like an infection!"), every fictive burnout in the CIA or the KGB ("Only he could tell the difference as the lines between the superpowers began to blur!"), every backdrop of mist, intrigue, and betrayal on the far side of civilization ("The 'infidels' knew truths that eluded the West!") owes its existence to the place that some wag dubbed Greeneland a half century ago.

Most of these works are ignored by the Master, but occasionally he displays pleasure when a disciple apes the famous trademarks: tongue-and-groove construction, political cynicism, and religious turmoil. John Le Carré has made a career of it, starting with *The Spy Who Came In from the Cold* ("The Best Spy Novel I Have Ever Read"— Graham Greene) and continuing through the let's-not-be-beastly-to-the-Palestinians theme of *The Little Drummer Girl.* The steadiest in a long, winding line of acolytes is Brian Moore, whose most appealing books are explorations of feminine psychology and a crisis of faith (*The Lonely Passion of Judith Hearne*), re-examinations of the past (*The Black Robe, The Great Victorian Collection:* "My favorite living novelist . . . treats the novel as a tamer treats a wild beast"—Graham Greene), and the sociology of theology (*Catholics:* "Funny, sad, and very moving"—Graham Greene). Moore's lesser works, "entertainments" in Greene's term, are thrillers written under the name of Michael Bryan. In his spare time the author has written screenplays, among them the moribund *Torn Curtain* for Alfred Hitchcock.

The Color of Blood fuses the high Moore and the low. It contains the dependable themes of prelate and thugs, foreign landscape and confusion of realms. This time out the cleric has escalated to cardinal, and the novelist has heightened the tempo. An assassination attempt occurs in the opening scene. Cardinal Bem, of a place very much like Poland, escapes with his life, but his loyal chauffeur is killed. Who would want to gun down the blameless Bem? His is the voice of compromise, attempting to reconcile the workers' movement with the demands of Marxist overlords. As it turns out, the marriage of Solidarity and the state is held at arm's length not only by the rulers but by the intransigent Archbishop Krasnoy. He plans to deliver a speech inciting the population to "an expression of national will," that is, counterrevolution. Red hat orders white hat to expunge all political content from his speech—or else. But Bem loses his authority when three officials appear at his residence and abduct him to a mysterious country house. Are they State Security men? Or are they forces within the Church itself? Bem makes many disheartening discoveries as he escapes into the hinterlands and finds himself at the whim and mercy of commoners with whom he had lost touch years ago.

This is Moore's 15th novel—perhaps one should say screenplay. It shows the practiced hand of a man who knows how to tighten suspense, provide chases and confrontations on cue, scatter ambiguities like bread crumbs along the way, and head toward what paperback publishers like to call a shattering climax.

But is it? Technically the author brings off his scenario. There is a sharply defined protagonist, plus narrow escapes and the classic *soupçons* of violence. But there are also instances of prepackaged cynicism: "Maybe it's true, as that knife grinder said, that the regime stuffs our mouth with sausage to keep us quiet. But what of the other world, the world that Henry Krasnoy calls free? Are the poor any better off there?" And there are unconvincing close-ups of

---

An excerpt from *Catholics*

Latin. The communion bell. Monks as altarboys saying the Latin responses. Incense. The old way.

"No Mass?" he said to the hotelkeeper. "But when they've come all this way, what do they do if there's no Mass?"

"Ah, now, Father, that's a grand thing to see. The pilgrims just stay there, kneeling and saying the rosary. They stay all day, waiting and praying."

"But don't some of them try to go out to the island itself?"

The hotelkeeper laughed, showing gap teeth. "No fear! No boat can land on Muck that doesn't know the trick of it. And the island boats will land nobody without the Abbot's permission. Besides," the hotelkeeper said, serious again. "These pilgrims do be good people. When the Abbot put up a sign in the church here in Cahirciveen saying 'Parishioners Only For Confession,' most of the pilgrims stopped bothering the monks. Mind you, the lines are still long. After Mass, on a Sunday, there do be three monks, hard at it in the church until it's time for them to take the boat back."

"But why do the confessions take so long?"

"We still have private confessions. One person at a time in the box."

Private confessions. *This* was not known in Rome. "What about public confessions?"

"Public confessions, Father?"

"Where the whole congregation stands before Mass and says an act of contrition?"

"Ah, that never took here."

Anger, sudden and cold, made Kinsella say: "It took everywhere else!" Ashamed, he saw the hotelkeeper bob his head, obedient, rebuked but unconvinced.

Brian Moore, in his Catholics, *McClelland and Stewart, 1972.*

---

the believer in crisis: " 'I don't know what the pope wants anymore,' the old man said. 'Where is the pope this week? Brazil? Japan? Who knows?' " And perfunctory glimpses of the Church undergoing alteration: "I admit that in the past, our priests have been as anti-Semitic as the rest of our people. But we are trying to change that." How "we" are trying remains offscreen. Perhaps Kurt Waldheim can enlighten us in a sequel.

All this might not have mattered if Moore had developed his plot and people. But *The Color of Blood* is 179 pages—the proper length for what film-makers call a treatment, but far too brief for the subjects introduced and then abruptly dismissed, as if the author was in a hurry to get on to his next project. A pity; Moore used to explore the mental and moral life of his characters en route. And when he played with symbols in the old days, he was never so obvious. In *The Color of Blood* he makes Bem the son of a stableman, and throughout his final days the cardinal cannot find a good place to lay his head. Although it would be unsporting to reveal the finale, no reader should be surprised to find grand tragedy at the fade-out. After all, this is a truly Christian leader who speaks the truth to uncomprehending souls.

As such he makes an appealing figure. One would have liked to see Cardinal Bem in a setting worthy of him, his anguish, and his author. Here Moore, who began so well some 30 years ago with the moving sorrows of a lonely spinster, seems to suffer from a form of literary anorexia. It may be the impatience of age—the author is 66—or the demands of a crowded schedule. Or it may be one more instance of too-close imitation. In that case, Moore has fallen long. *The Tenth Man,* Greene's latest, took just 156 pages to tell its tale.

Neal Ascherson   (review date 17 December 1987)

SOURCE: "Polish Nightmares," in *The New York Review of Books,* Vol. XXXIV, No. 20, December 17, 1987, pp. 44, 46, 48.

[*Ascherson is a Scottish-born English critic and journalist. In the following review, he praises Moore's astute, humane, and suspenseful depiction of Polish religious and political crises in* The Color of Blood.]

The Color of Blood, Brian Moore's latest novel, was on the short list for the Booker Prize, the main British fiction award. Though widely admired, it did not take the prize; the murmur in London was that it was "slight." A strange reservation. The book is certainly brief, and has the pace and economical structure of a thriller. But it is the work of a masterly writer now at the height of his powers: some of Graham Greene's "entertainments" were called slight when they first appeared, and those judgments seem today absurd. Nabokov's *Pale Fire* and *Lolita,* if one judges by length, are more rich and substantial than his briefer works, but *Laughter in the Dark,* which one can read on a short train journey, is among the most nearly perfect of Nabokov's fictions.

The scenery, physical and political, in Brian Moore's novel, reflects Poland's history. The Cardinal's name is

Stephen Bem (Cardinal Wyszyński's first name was Stefan, while Bem was a patriot general of the last century),
while the prime minister is named Urban (like the Polish
government spokesman), and the book contains many
other such allusions. But Moore also shows an uncanny
sensibility in penetrating to the heart of Polish moral dilemmas and nightmares. He achieves this penetration
largely through creating a fabulous, not-quite specific location, thereby freeing Polish debates from the supposedly
hermetic quality which encourages others to regard these
debates as idiosyncratic. He has released them into the
consciousness of all who have to seek the just path in
places where repression, nationalism, violence, and a religion of peace belong to present experience.

Years before the novel opens, in this Catholic nation ruled
by a Communist government and police, the cardinal has
signed a Church-State concordat with the prime minister,
one Francis Urban, who was once a fellow pupil of Bem's
at the same Jesuit school. But for some traditionalists in
the Church and in the Catholic laity, that compact with
foreign Marxism and its agents has amounted to national
betrayal. Now, as the tension between the people and the
regime is swelling toward a crisis, a plot has been laid between Catholic nationalists and some of Bem's own bishops to proclaim a popular insurrection. The proclamation
is timed for the great Catholic pilgrimage and rally at
Rywald (Moore's Czestochowa). But to give it a chance
of success, the workers and their underground trade
unions must be persuaded to call a general strike. And to
persuade the union leaders and the population as a whole
to move, the full authority of the Church must be put behind the appeal.

The obstacle is the personality of the cardinal-primate
himself, Stephen Bem. Unlike many of the plotters, he is
not a son of the aristocracy or the old officer caste. His father was a stableboy in a nobleman's palace, and this sets
him at a distance from the tradition of insurrections led
by the nobility. No less patriotic or anticommunist than
they, he sees more clearly than they do the futility of a rebellion that could only end in bloodshed and invasion by
Soviet armies. His task under God, as he sees it, is to ensure the survival of the nation and its true values, and his
faith is that the nation will outlive its oppressors. His
agreement with Urban, compromise as it was, has given
the Church the right to run its own schools, publish religious literature, and in general to carry on its duty of
maintaining the integrity of the nation. "Remember," he
says, "that, no matter which government rules us, we remain a free people, free in our minds, free in an unfree
state. That is the greater heroism." Cardinal Wyszyński,
too, put his name to such an agreement, and he, too, told
the Poles in 1956, on the brink of rebellion, that it was
sometimes harder to live for one's country than to die for
it.

Cardinal Bem will never approve the call for a rising. Yet
it cannot hope for success if he condemns it. The novel
opens as his car is ambushed by a group of Catholic fanatics, who can see no way to cut this knot beyond eliminat-
ing him. But Bem survives, although his driver and one
of the plotters are killed. Back at his palace, he is seized

> What compromises can a man make for
> his God? That Graham Greenean question
> lies at the heart of *The Color of Blood*.
>
> —*Neal Ascherson*

and abducted by men apparently from the security police,
who take him "for his own protection" to a guarded hide-
out in the countryside. (The location, Bem's relationship
with his custodians, and his own reflections owe much to
Wyszyński's own prison notebooks, published in English
under the title *A Freedom Within*, and it has been said that
Brian Moore's reading of that book was the novel's original inspiration.)

Bem contrives to escape, tries to find his way back to the
capital, and is caught once more. He realizes suddenly
that his captors are not the regime's men at all, but members of a Catholic underground conspiracy; his kidnapping has been staged in order to provide the final provocation which will justify the rising ("The Communists have
arrested the Primate") while gagging him at the crucial
moment. Again, Bem manages to break away and flee. He
is at last brought to a clandestine meeting with Jop, the
aging workers' hero who once led a free trade union struggle, and persuades him to throw his influence against the
coming strike. Jop is not sure if he will be obeyed. "We
don't count any more, the unions. . . . We can't afford
to speak out against the Church. If the people want this
demo and the Church is behind it, then we have to go
along." Here, expertly mirrored, is the real choice the Polish Church faced in August 1980: "If the people want this
strike and the working class is behind it, then we have to
go along."

Now Bem must somehow reach Rywald, before the bishop
there delivers the fatal sermon. But the real police, who
have been frantically searching for him, catch him on the
way. He is flown to the capital, as rumors of insurrection
begin to course through the nation, and is brought to confront Francis Urban himself.

At school, Urban was the rich boy, son of a landowner:
"It was natural for an Urban to become a general, even
a prime minister. What was not natural was his route to
this power." Before him is Stephen Bem, again the poor
boy now that he is no longer in robes but wears an ill-
fitting civilian disguise. They attack each other's credentials as a patriot: one is abused as an agent of Moscow and
the KGB, the other as the servant of Rome and the CIA.
When calm, though, both are forced to admit that they
have a common interest even though neither can confess
to being "on the same side." They say in Poland: "Nobody
knows what compromises a man can make for his country." Urban and Bem have both risked their careers for a
shabby concordat which was meant to save their country
from itself and from its neighbor. Bem knows that the
West will betray his people if they rise, as it has betrayed
them before. To save them, he must do the betraying him-

self, abort a great national and religious upsurge, and save the neck of this detestable government in the process. What compromises can a man make for his God? That Greenean question lies at the heart of this novel.

In the end, Cardinal Bem goes to Rywald. What happens there would be heartless for a critic to disclose. It's enough to say that this short novel maintains its physical and intellectual suspense to the last page, and the last line.

A great many ideas are carried by the characters of *The Color of Blood*. Not for a moment, however, do they cease to be unpredictable, genuine human beings. Cardinal Bem, lonely and steadfast, is afraid only of that moral darkness in which right and wrong begin stealthily to exchange places. I will remember him not only when thinking about Poland or Hungary, but also when I read about the travails of bishops in Latin America and South Africa, or—very particularly—about Bishop Edward Daly of Derry and Cardinal Tomas O Fiaich of Armagh.

It may be that Moore would not wish to be called a "Catholic novelist." But he shares with some other novelists who are Catholics (and some of the great Russians) the capacity to make characters who remain entirely convincing whatever burden of "significance" they carry. Muriel Spark, a convert, once took fright at her own sin of creating human beings without the power of saving themselves. If I have grasped this notion correctly, it means that when God understands, he does not so much forgive as extend mercy. A few novelists extend mercy of that kind to those they have imagined. Brian Moore is one of them.

Michael Paul Gallagher, SJ   (essay date Spring 1988)

SOURCE: "Religion as Favourite Metaphor: Moore's Recent Fiction," in *Irish University Review,* Vol. 18, No. 1, Spring, 1988, pp. 50-8.

[*In the following essay, Gallagher asserts that faith, both secular and religious, enables many of Moore's characters to survive crises.*]

> Searching for a language more honest than lying is the struggle of all spiritual life.
>
> —Jean Sullivan

> Although I'm not a religious writer, religion— the Catholic religion—has played a major role in many of my novels . . . I use religion as a metaphor.
>
> —Brian Moore

At a fairly early stage in *The Colour of Blood,* Cardinal Bem is allowed by his captors to speak by phone to the "Ministry of Religious Affairs". Although Bem is not aware of it at the time, the voice on the other end is another member of the nationalist faction of Catholics who have kidnapped him in this communist country. Nevertheless he senses the unreality of the situation:

> This conversation was like a dream; in dreams the most improbable threats are heavy with fearful plausibility.

That text and context could stand as a summary of the classic Brian Moore plot. In each of his books the central figure is forced out of his or her normal world into a state of being imprisoned in unreality, or at least in a reality that shakes all previous foundations. All of the protagonists encounter a radical fear for their own identity and are threatened by what seems like a dream. Thus, in *An Answer from Limbo* the obsessive writer, Brendan Tierney, came to ask "Am I, too, a prisoner of my dream?" and Maloney in *The Great Victorian Collection* likewise became "the prisoner of the new dream . . . prisoner of what he had wrought". "Dream" is again a key-word in *Black Robe,* which involves what Lawrence would call the "interdestruction" of the dreams of Indians and Jesuits alike. Hence one can discern a now familiar pattern in Moore's novels: a collapse of the previous securities of an individual through a journey into nightmare.

Although this ordeal is mainly psychological—and narrated with a traditional focus on the central consciousness—the novels tend to hint at epistemological and metaphysical concerns as well. It would be misleading, as he himself insists, to describe Brian Moore's work as religious fiction, and even more inaccurate to think of him in the old category of "Catholic novelist". Nevertheless a driving concern in his fiction has been with issues of faith, and faith in many senses. The main conflict for some of his central characters had to do with loss of a previously firm belief in a God of traditional Catholicism; one thinks of Judith Hearne of the first novel and of the Abbot of *Catholics*. Even when Moore moved away from explicitly religious settings for his crises of self-meaning, he still kept his sights on human faith-making. Thus in novels such as *Fergus* or *I am Mary Dunne* he was unsparing in exposing the vulnerability of secularist substitutes for faith, for what he called in *An Answer from Limbo* "the belief that replaces belief".

> **In each of Moore's books the central figure is forced out of his or her normal world into a state of being imprisoned in unreality.**
>
> **—Michael Paul Gallagher, SJ**

In this respect one might suggest a rough but workable distinction between "faith" and "Faith". The latter can point to explicit religious Faith, as explored in several of Moore's protagonists from Judith Hearne to Paul Laforgue and even Cardinal Bem. The term 'faith'—without the capital—can be applied to a wider range of signifying constructs which his characters use to find some stable anchorage for their lives. Indeed such a distinction, which Moore discovers in his own non-conceptual way, is commonplace in comtemporary theology. One of the best statements of a claim for a priority of 'faith' over 'Faith' comes from the literary scholar and theologian, William Lynch, who seeks to deconstruct the dominance of the cognitive in thinking about faith, and hence advocates "reversing our images" in order to recognize faith as "a colleague imagination":

> Let us hypothesize that faith is a first and primitive force in life; it is there, in a completely central and powerful way, from the beginning; it is not a sophisticated addition to knowledge, but a giant, universally operative force. [William F. Lynch, *Images of Faith: An Exploration of the Ironic Imagination,* 1973]

In a classic study of several years later [*Stages of Faith,* 1981], James Fowler rejected any automatic identification of 'faith' with religious categories and argued that faith is "a universal feature of human living"; for him faith is "a kind of imagination", a way of seeing life in relation to "a comprehensive image in the light of which we shape our responses". More recently, Roger Haight [in *An Alternative Vision,* 1985] has developed the same line of thinking in his account of "the psychological manifestations of faith" as a "centering act or attitude of the human personality", or as an integrating "stance toward life"; although such "faith" may be "expressed in some symbolic conceptual form", it is "not the same as belief ". These comments from three theological authors flesh out the distinction between "faith" and "Faith", and they also help to distinguish what is central to Moore's fictional concerns from what is secondary. In his novels "faith" is more fundamental than "Faith" but he has opted for "Faith" as a natural location for dramas of "faith". His central concern is neither with a crisis of creeds nor of explicit religious commitments but that more universal anchoring of personal existence in some ultimate "faith". In *The Lonely Passion of Judith Hearne* the world of "Faith" proved the best context for the more radical conflict of "faith", and the same was true of *Catholics*. Interestingly, in his three most recent novels, Moore has returned to the church contexts associated with explicit religious "Faith" as the best metaphor for his dramatizing the fragility of "faith" in its wider or humanistic sense. The "Faith" or church context stems from Moore's Irishness but from what he calls his "nomadic" experience outside Ireland he developed an acute sense for a collapse of any secure meanings as *the* crisis of today. In this sense Moore takes a metaphor from an Irish setting to confront a fundamental conflict of "faith" for individuals in Western society. One remembers that J. Hillis Miller once linked "the absence of God" with the dramatization of "subjectivism" as a major concern of modern literature [Miller, *The Disappearance of God,* 1965]; if so Brian Moore represents an Irish variant on this basic theme.

If the fifteen novels to date share this focus on a crisis of "faith", they also reveal recurring patterns over the years as well as some significant changes in horizon. The central figure is generally forced to move from presence to absence to difference. Presence in this sense means a set of self-securities sometimes associated with paternal authority (as in *Fergus* or *The Emperor of Ice-Cream*), and sometimes with a belief in the "real presence" in the tabernacle (a recurring image in Moore from *The Lonely Passion of Judith Hearne* to *Catholics* and *Black Robe*). Absence would point to the de-centering experiences that afflict

each main character: what seemed clear meanings or definite norms are now seen to be fragile metaphors. But in spite of that discovery of the fictiveness of "faith" and sometimes of "Faith", nearly every central figure has to live on, either crushed by or carrying the difference he or she has encountered. In a previous article I argued that Moore approaches "identity in terms of faith and faith in terms of identity" ["Brian Moore's Fiction of Faith," *Gaeliana,* 7 (1985)]. In this sense some earlier novels ended with a sense of blank failure (*Judith Hearne*), or dominated by guilt over the price paid for one's freedom (*An Answer from Limbo*), or with some surrender that spelt fundamental dishonesty (*Catholics*), but the capacity to cope with "difference" is presented in a notably serene manner in the last three novels. In these identity and faith come through the upheavals and seem able to survive. It is also in these three books that Moore has returned to overtly religious settings as vehicles or metaphors for his constant crisis of "faith".

Cold Heaven is a fascinating reversal of the classic plot of loss of religious belief: it is about the temptation of an atheist or agnostic to abandon her "faith" of "unFaith". Moreover, that temptation is double: Marie Davenport is disturbed not only by the preternatural happenings she experiences (visions of Our Lady on the coast of California, a husband who comes back to life having been pronounced dead) but more deeply by her contacts with an authentic mystic, Mother St Jude, in whom she sees "reverence mixed with overwhelming love". Out of the first temptation comes the epistemological and psychological drama of the book. Is Marie, rether like Mary Dunne, prone to paranoid interpretations? This is a real question not only for the reader of this spiritual thriller but for Marie herself, who vacillates between belief and unbelief of her own experiences. On the one hand "these unreal events were happening in this real, reassuringly ordinary world" and Moore's narratives are always magnificent in their creation of a credible context; on the other hand, "if I am imagining all this, I am inventing my own hell".

If there is a flaw in the inner logic of *Cold Heaven,* it is that it is so much easier for Marie to retain her atheism against the assaults of strange outer 'miracles' than to confront and reject the other miracle represented by Mother St Jude. She manages to resist "the defeat of my will" by the preternatural, with the result that at the end "she had refused and she had won". As a study in superstitious consciousness and in the cultural impossibility of religious faith, this novel is one of Moore's finest achievements. Like many of his central characters Marie Davenport moves through torment but is eventually "returned to ordinary life, to its burdens, its consequences". As a theological novel of sorts the core of the book is that "a miracle is only a sign; it does not complet belief ". Here the atheist under trial manages to retain her faith of unfaith, however battered, just as priest protagonists in Moore's next two novels will come through with their faith battered but somehow managing to survive. Like them Marie enters a zone of ambiguity at the end: she is a mixture of honesty (something has been seen and heard) and necessary dishonesty (she cannot admit this to anyone except herself). She can be secure in her rejection of what seems like superstitious religiousness, because she alone knows that the future shrine of the Virgin will be built literally on false grounds. But she herself suppresses the more destabilizing memory of Mother St Jude, whose "look she had never known from any other human being" and in whose presence she experienced "a larger feeling, a feeling of peace". Thus the fictional rhetoric of *Cold Heaven* seems faulty when the subversiveness of the mystic is evaded at the close.

With *Black Robe* and *The Colour of Blood,* it is as if Brian Moore has opted to revisit this spiritual dimension, which was left dangling in *Cold Heaven*. In that novel as part of her longest conversation with Marie, Mother St Jude tells the atheist young woman of her "anguish" of knowing that "because of my failure, God was absent", and how "the moment I saw you, God came back into my soul. It was true happiness". A strangely similar emergence from desolation into consolation occurs at the very end of the two subsequent novels about priest-believers. Although the historical contexts are totally different, ranging from a seventeenth-century Indian tribe in North America to a contemporary Eastern bloc country, each ending sees a priest giving a sacrament to the people and finding in this final moment both what seems to him as God's will and a new unburdened freedom within himself. For Father Laforgue in *Black Robe* "a prayer came to him, a true prayer at last" and for Cardinal Bem in *The Colour of Blood* "joy filled him. At last, he knew peace". This is more than a verbal coincidence; it is a clue to the different sense of an ending that Moore has given to all his novels of the 'eighties. What is here embodied in terms of a religious metaphor had its secular equivalent in the final situations of both Eileen Hughes and Marie Davenport, both of whom struggle through to a final sense of release from the turmoils they had encountered. At the close of *The Temptation of Eileen Hughes* we are told that she "hurried towards her freedom". All of Moore's protagonists undergo some temptation of their "faith" but few of the earlier ones arrived at the same degree of positive freedom, however tinged with ambiguity, that characterizes these four recent novels. In previous decades of Moore's career, liberating moments were strongest for Ginger Coffey and Gavin Burke but many of the other main characters ended in desolation of one kind or another.

It can be argued that the common pattern of these recent novels is from an initial self-security of "faith" through a series of threatening and nightmarish experiences to a moment of humbled return to a more fragile "faith" than before. And this return is marked by a surprising "joy" or "peace" or "love". This seems accurate so far as it goes, but it fails to mention another common element in Moore's recent fiction, his concern with "silence" and its ambiguities. On the more secular level, it seems to Marie in *Cold Heaven* that "they need my silence"; thinking of her whole brush with the incomprehensible "she would remember it in silence for the rest of her life". In the other two novels a concern with God's silence assumes a more central role. Thus even in the first page of *The Colour of Blood* Cardinal Bem's prayer is described as "withdrawing into that silence where God waited and judged". Then

at the end Bem is faced with his assassin at the communion rail:

> he saw the revolver that she had taken from her handbag and in that moment knew: This is God's will . . . The silence of God: would it change at the moment of his death?

The only indirect answer to that question is in the final sentence, when he "heard that terrible noise". The close of *Black Robe* had been less ambiguous and more affirmative. After an ordeal of much more horrifying proportions than that undergone by Cardinal Bem, Father Laforgue arrives at his final crisis. Like other Moore protagonists he confronts symbols of faith that for him have become emptied of their significance.

> He looked at the empty eyes of the statuette as though, in them, some hint might be given of that mystery which is the silence of God. But the statuette was wooden, carved by men. The hosts in the tabernacle were bread, dubbed the body of Christ in a ritual strange as any performed by these Savages . . . Here in this humble foolish chapel, rude as a child's drawing, a wooden box and a painted statuette could not restore his faith.

And yet his faith is in some way finally restored. How? Laforgue finds himself in disagreement with his fellow missioner, Father Jerome, who is happy to "use" an eclipse of the sun as an emotional lever on the Indians, pushing them towards communal baptism. But Laforgue is uneasy about this strategy and about the "accident of nature" over which he has "no sense of miracle". Father Jerome, by contrast, is quite blunt about his approach: for him "most Christians do not perform their duties because they love God, but because they fear Him". In the light of the seemingly positive ending of the book, this sentence assumes a certain importance: it would appear that Laforgue eventually decides to go ahead with the baptisms not out of fear but out of love.

Moore is too subtle a novelist to allow an up-beat ending to be the whole story; indeed his final pages are fraught with ironies and ambiguities.

—Michael Paul Gallagher, SJ

Moore is too subtle a novelist, however, to allow this up-beat ending to be the whole story; indeed his final pages are fraught with ironies and ambiguities. The turning point for Laforgue comes through a conversation with the Indian chief, in which Taretande ultimately asks him whether he is their enemy or whether he loves them. When Laforgue replies "yes" to the question about love, Taretande in turn says "Then baptize us". But we as readers know more than Laforgue about the tangle of motives underlying this request: they are a mixture of fear (that the plague is controlled by these blackrobes) and guile (seeming to obey but preserving their "dream"); only shortly before he had been in favour of killing the Jesuits. Nevertheless, when Laforgue in his struggle of decision turns again to encounter the silence of the tabernacle, he does so newly aware of the question about love.

> Had [his own] statement of belief in God any more meaning than Taretande's promise to do God's will? What *was* God's will? He looked at the tabernacle. He felt the silence.
>
> *Do you love us?*
>
> *Yes.*

Rather as Marie Davenport at the end of ***Cold Heaven*** turns from her brush with silence and strangeness to the "ordinary, muddled life of falling in love" and accepts an "imperfect existence", so a similar acceptance of flawed love seems evoked at the end of ***Black Robe***. Although his option for love is shot through with ambiguities, it is nevertheless in this way that Laforgue emerges from his morass of doubt and in the closing moment of the novel attains to "true prayer at last". The final words of the book are another repetition of *Do you love us? Yes.* Moore has always been suspicious of *anti-roman* sophistications and his latest novel, ***The Colour of Blood,*** keeps stubbornly to his pruned style of recent years and to a common-sense realism with its focus on the central character. With such an understated rhetoric, it might be possible to miss the ways in which this thriller echoes some of the Moore obsessions. A major change is that there is nothing of the overt crisis of faith in Cardinal Bem as was present in Father Laforgue; instead he is a credibly good man of solid if voluntarist faith. Although his God is a silent judge (as was already mentioned), Bem is not made to endure the same inner torment of faith as other recent protagonists. His outer ordeal involves a crisis of trust in his church colleagues but never to the point that it endangers his fundamental trust in God. Thus his questions are never the metaphysical doubts of Laforgue and others concerning the truth of the sacraments; rather he wonders about the abuse of religion in a political sense and ironically he becomes a martyr at the hands of right-wing Catholics who want—with echoes of Father Jerome—to "use" religion to incite a nationalist uprising against the communist regime. Here the drama seems more external than in other novels and one that is more concerned than before with the ambiguous relationship between religion and power.

Moore's handling of his religious metaphor in ***The Colour of Blood*** has shifted, one might say, from the paranormal of ***Cold Heaven*** to the paramilitary. Because of this many commentators may leap to the conclusion that he is writing some version of allegory about the North of Ireland, but this would seem naive in the light of the novel. Rather than offering a narrow parable of the North, it can be a study of the political underside of religion everywhere and in particular of the ambiguities of power struggles carried on in the name of religion. Indeed at one stage in this novel one has a confrontation between what we have been calling "faith" and "Faith", when the Cardinal meets with his old school companion, Francis Urban, now the communist prime minister. Hearing the phrase "the national good" on the latter's lips, Bem is drawn to reflect:

The national good. For Urban, there was no difference between the nation and the State. It was not the national good, but the preservation of the State, he served.

Where other novels took a crisis of psychological self-preservation as their focus, ***The Colour of Blood*** is inclined to explore the more political struggle for power within the religious structure of the Church (and to a lesser extent within the State). Throughout the novel Bem is presented as a conscientious leader, honest in his doubts about a situation where "religious beliefs have become inextricably entwined with political hatreds", as he says in his final address to the people. On his way to this pilgrimage site, he had a conversation with his priest secretary that seems strongly to echo the exchanges between Father Laforgue and Father Jerome in ***Black Robe.*** Voicing his anxieties about the driving force behind such popular "religious" events, the Cardinal says:

> 'I think our people are using religion now as a sort of politics . . . Are we filling the churches because we love God more than before? Or do we do it out of nostalgia for the past, or, worse, to defy the government? Because if we do, Kris, then God is mocked.'

One remembers that just before the final liberating moment in ***Black Robe*** Laforgue had asked himself, "Was this true baptism or a mockery?" This minor theme has now come to the centre of the stage in ***The Colour of Blood,*** a novel told from the perspective of a man trying not to abuse power but who finds himself thrust into a position where he is an important pawn in others' power games.

Although this latest novel shifts its attention from introspective crisis, nevertheless it communicates a liberalist suspicion of anything beyond the personal horizon: Bem may be authentic in his solitary conscience but all around him the bridges to public life are subject to traps and manipulations of power. If this is so, it would be in tune with Brian Moore's constant focus on the *individual* in crisis—even to the point of a distrust for social issues. If novels are the would-be epics of middle class culture, then Moore has accepted as his chosen limitation a specialization in subjectivity and isolated consciousness.

Our argument here has been that within his traditional territory, Brian Moore has increasingly focussed on something of a secular theology which might be summarized like this: God remains silent; the substitute dreams of humanity become destructive; religious signs can be manipulated; the mystic as inviting symbol can degenerate into churchy games of power and fear; and ordinary existence itself is a frail and fictive structure marred by egoisms. But the option that is called love, itself ambiguous and unsteady, seems the only foundation for "faith" (and even for "Faith"), or at any rate for the confessedly fragile self-meaning that is capable of emerging beyond crisis and becoming livable again.

An excerpt from *Black Robe*

Laforgue had never lived in an encampment of Savages. With the exception of Father Bourque, none of the priests now in the Québec residence had traveled as he would travel, sleeping outdoors or in Savage shelters, eating only Savage food. "It is travel of the most difficult sort," the Superior had warned him. "Yet it is also the most advantageous way in which to make the journey. For if you travel with a hunting party of men, women and children, there is always the chance that, if a child or an adult fall ill en route, a soul can be gained for God by a deathbed baptism. Father Brabant and others have written in the *Relations* that each time they journeyed to the Huron lands they had the great privilege of saving at least one soul in this manner. Remember, such a blessing will more than justify all the perils and discomforts you may suffer."

Now, remembering the Superior's words, Laforgue forced a smile as he endured the badgering of the Savage children: one tugging at the beads of his rosary as if to break them; another pulling at his beard and calling him a hairy dog, for the Savages were not bearded and pulled out their own sparse facial hair, considering it to be ugly. A third child, a giggling little girl, kept trying to slip her hand through the buttons of Laforgue's cassock and fondle his genitals. The Savages paid no attention to this, for it was unheard of for them to punish or restrain their children in any way. And so, as the little imp persisted, Laforgue lifted her up and put her aside, then tried to make his way clear of the crowd. But the Savage women laughingly restrained him and now, thinking longingly of his cell, where at this hour he would kneel alone in a time of prayer, he decided to invoke Captain Clock. Raising his hands as if to address the crowd, he shouted, "Wait! Captain Clock says I must go home. Captain says it is time for me to go.". . .

Chomina, the leader who had escorted Laforgue into the encampment, took him by the hand and cleared a passage for him among the laughing throng. "Go then, Nicanis," he said, using the name the Algonkin had given Laforgue. "Go home to the Captain and tell him that tomorrow, at first light, we await you here."

Brian Moore, in his Black Robe, *E. P. Dutton, 1985.*

Hallvard Dahlie   (essay date 1988)

SOURCE: "Brian Moore and the Meaning of Exile," in *Medieval and Modern Ireland*, edited by Richard Wall, Colin Smythe, 1988, pp. 91-107.

[*Dahlie is a Canadian critic and educator who has written extensively on Moore's works. In the following essay, originally presented at the International Conference of the Canadian Association for Irish Studies in February 1985 and subsequently revised, he discusses Moore's portrayal of exile in several of his novels, short stories, and essays.*]

Almost two thousand years ago, one of the earliest writers

sent into exile complained that he was compelled 'to dwell at the edge of the world, a land far removed from [his] own', a place where he had 'no interchange of speech.. . with the wild people [and was] understood by nobody' [Ovid, *Tristia* and *Epistulae ex Ponto*, translated by Arthur Leslie Wheeler, 1924]. Just over a decade and a half ago, another writer forced into exile, upon coming to his new habitation, was ecstatic about the kind of existence he found: 'the feeling of security, of an utter absence of that central European nightmare called the Doorbell-Ringing-At-Four-am' [Josef Skvorecky, 'A Country After My Own Heart', *Macleans*, March, 1974]. That Ovid uttered his words in Tomis, on the shores of the Black Sea, and Josef Skvorecky his in Toronto, on the shores of Lake Ontario, provides an interesting, but not all a significant, geographical juxtaposition, for there have been many exiles to Canada—notably Anna Jameson and Wyndham Lewis—who have seen Toronto as quite the equivalent of Ovid's place of punishment. Ovid's *Epistulae ex Ponto* and his *Tristia* communicated the belief, that was to last for centuries, that exile always meant punishment, a belief that was not to be significantly modified until the New World, in both fact and imagination, began to assume the dimensions of a possible Eden.

Between the two attitudes towards exile held by Ovid and Skvorecky—as a form of punishment and as a form of liberation—lies a whole range of meanings and perspectives, all of which, however, are implied by the two standard dictionary definitions—'enforced removal from one's native land according to an edict or sentence' and 'expatriation, prolonged absence from one's native land, endured by compulsion of circumstances or voluntarily undergone for any purposes'. The difficulty of arriving at any universally accepted definition of this term, or of such synonyms as expatriate and émigré, is reflected in the titles alone of the many books and articles which have examined this issue. Malcolm Cowley's *Exile's Return*, Ernest Earnest's *Expatriates and Patriots*, Terry Eagleton's *Exiles and Emigrés*, Thomas Farley's *Exiles and Pioneers*, Mary McCarthy's 'A Guide to Exiles, Expatriates and Internal Emigrés' all suggest the ambiguities and overlappings of these terms, and there are of course the more emotionally loaded synonyms of these words, like refugee, evacuee, displaced person, outcast, and remittance man. There are levels of respectability, too, attached to such terms: Mary McCarthy reminds us, for example, that if we are charitably raising funds for homeless Greeks, we are helping a group of refugees, but if a group of Greek writers abroad signs a manifesto, they are elevated to the status of writers-in-exile. And sometimes the whole question of rank lies within the exile's own mind and attitude: Vladimir Nabokov recalled in his *Speak Memory* how he and his fellow Russians in Western Europe viewed their new countrymen as 'perfectly unimportant strangers . . . in whose more or less illusory cities we, émigrés, happen to dwell', and in a statement that takes us right back to Ovid's attitude towards what he called 'the uncivilized Getae', he contritely confesses that 'we ignored them the way an arrogant or very stupid invader ignores a formless and faceless mass of natives'.

I think it is useful to see 'exile' as the most inclusive of all these terms, for in specific instances it can be applied to all of them, but within the context of this paper, it can quite accurately be distinguished from émigré and expatriate, the synonyms most frequently used when we are speaking of writers and artists. Nabokov and Skvorecky were originally émigrés—they were compelled to leave, on political and ideological grounds, a regime that, had they remained, would have proven hostile if not fatal, to their art. Theoretically, émigrés would return to their homelands once the political conditions make it artistically and morally justifiable to do so. If they remain in their new country, they undergo a kind of transformation or metamorphosis into the larger category of exile, and if they accommodate themselves completely to the social and cultural realities of their new nation, they would in effect become indistinguishable from that nation's indigenous writers.

Expatriates, for quite different reasons, are not totally or permanently committed to the idea of exile: they are little more than extended tourists who leave their homeland temporarily because they believe that certain possibilities for living or for art are more favourable elsewhere. 'They do things better in Europe: let's go there', was the cry of many of Malcolm Cowley's lost generation group, whose exploits he described so well in his book that should have been called *Expatriate's Return* rather than *Exile's Return*. For unlike the exile, they did go home again, and their initial hostility against what they saw as the hypocrisy and narrowness of North American life, was only a superficial revolt, derived in part from books like George Gissing's *The Private Papers of Henry Ryecroft* or George Moore's *Confessions of a Young Man*. 'Having come [to Europe] in search of values', Cowley remarks, 'they found valuta instead', and once that monetary advantage disappeared, they ceased being expatriates.

True exile derives from a much more profound and lasting impulse, and is essentially a more lonely and vulnerable position to assume than expatriation which, like the situation of the political émigré, is frequently attended by some kind of public attention. Exile is a process which both in its genesis and in its unfolding is irreversible, and there is a kind of inescapable definition that controls this term: because this displaced individual continues to be at odds with both the world he has rejected and the one he has moved into, he remains physically, spiritually, and intellectually an exile forever. In a talk that . . . was published in [The Canadian Association For Irish Studies's] journal a decade or so ago, the subject of this paper, Brian Moore, said that the exile cannot ever go home again, offering a useful distinction between the writer in exile, and the writer *as* exile ["**The Writer as Exile**," *Canadian Journal of Irish Studies*, Vol. 2, No. 2, December, 1976]. The former is, in effect, what I have defined here as the émigré or the expatriate, individuals who can and do return to their native land, whereas the writer *as* exile, in Moore's perspective, is permanently an outsider. It is this kind of exile that this paper is concerned with. . . .

In the literal sense, however, Moore has the perfect qualifications for what I have been defining as the exile: a native of one country, he is a citizen of a second, and a resident of yet a third, and since neither of these nations has un-

equivocally or exclusively claimed him, he is in more than a symbolic sense a man without a country. But of course the question of home is, explicitly or implicitly, a central concern of many exiles, and Moore's confession in that 1976 talk that he 'did not want to go home to Ireland' because in that land there was only a 'past, but no future', is transformed in much of his fiction into one of the major tensions experienced by his protagonists. The question that they in effect ask themselves is similar to the one that Malcolm Lowry's Kennish Drumgold Cosnahan asked himself in *Hear Us O Lord from Heaven Thy Dwelling Place:* 'But there was still this much of the European left in him, that he could ask the old question: how can a European feel himself American without first making his peace with Europe, without becoming, however deviously, reconciled with his home? Visiting Belfast in 1976, Moore saw the house of his birth as 'a monument, to a time, and a life, which is gone forever and will never be again', but this experience produced in him the kind of ambivalent vision that is central to any exile:

> I know only that once again, as has happened so often in my years of self exile, in countries far from the land of my birth—I stood balanced on that seesaw of emotion and memory which has been the fulcrum of my novels—the confrontation between now and then, between there and here, which was and is the fruit of my decision to choose exile. ["**The Writer as Exile**"]

When he did begin to write his serious fiction in the early 1950s, it was that Irish home and that Irish past that constituted his subject matter, rather than the superficially more dramatic events he had experienced by going into exile. And his first two serious fictional protagonists, Judith Hearne and Diarmuid Devine, locked forever in the restrictive and uncharitable world of deterministic Belfast, not only remain as two of Moore's most powerfully evoked and sensitively portrayed characters, but in their status as more or less normal representatives of that world, offer convincing justification for his going into exile in the first place. As far as making a personal commitment, therefore, about where and how to live, it was probably not difficult for Moore to sever his ties with Belfast, but in his artistic creations of his various fictional worlds, the protagonists who experience the strongest sense of dislocation and who have the most disturbing moral doubts are those exiled figures who in their pilgrimages to the New World have also abandoned the forces and values that shaped their early lives. This dilemma is central to a number of his North American novels, particularly *The Luck of Ginger Coffey* (1960), *An Answer from Limbo* (1962) and *Fergus* (1970), and in such finely-wrought short stories as '**Grieve for the Dear Departed**' and '**Uncle T**' published in 1959 and 1960 respectively. But it also constitutes a powerful strain in those Belfast novels whose protagonists have made, intellectually and emotionally, a break with that deterministic world, as reflected by Gavin Burke in *The Emperor of Ice-Cream* (1965) and by Sheila Redden in *The Doctor's Wife* (1976).

> The protagonists in Moore's fiction who experience the strongest sense of dislocation and who have the most disturbing moral doubts are those exiled figures who in their pilgrimages to the New World have also abandoned the forces and values that shaped their early lives.
>
> —*Hallvard Dahlie*

'Grieve for the Dear Departed' is set in Dublin, where a family is grieving for the dead father Daniel Kelleher, but its most important character is the absent son Michael who had gone off to America some sixteen years earlier, because of irreconcilable differences with his father. For this, his father had never forgiven him, but the grieving wife and mother knows that 'Dan's hate was mixed with pride', and on this belief she faked a telegram from Dan that would ensure Michael's return. The mother's grief is a double one: for her dead husband, but also for the absent son, the other 'dear departed' of this title, and added to her grief is her guilt over the betrayal she subsequently feels she has committed:

> I wrote out that cable never thinking, thinking only of me, of Michael, a child I wanted to see again, cold to my husband, cold to his paralyzed face, writing down what he could no longer stop me writing, taking from him the only thing he had left, his pride, his right to hate.

This is not an exile story in the sense that it juxtaposes one world against another in any specific scenes or situations, but rather in the sense that exile has divided a family against itself. Michael had attempted over the years to reconcile himself with his father, but one foresees in this story only the kind of delayed forgiveness that Fergus convinces himself he receives during the visitation of his dead parents. Throughout Moore's fiction, generational conflicts constitute a recurring theme, and frequently in novels like *The Emperor of Ice-Cream, Fergus,* and *The Doctor's Wife,* the accumulating levels of such conflicts suggest that not only households, but entire societies turn this kind of hatred in on themselves.

Moore's strongest short story, 'Uncle T', grows out of a situation similar to that which informed 'Grieve for the Dear Departed'. Here both Turlough Carnahan and his nephew, Vincent Bishop, are in exile in the United States and Canada respectively, and in both cases their anticlericalism and generally rebellious nature had caused their fathers to repudiate them. Strangers to each other until they meet now in New York, they nevertheless had formed mutually positive impressions of each other, and a belief in their likeness, through a three year exchange of letters. 'I have long thought that you—a rebel, a wanderer and a lover of literature—must be very much like me when I was your age', Uncle T had written, and it is this bond, along

with the possibility of working in his publishing firm, that Vincent had exploited to convince his new Canadian bride to accompany him to New York.

Barbara immediately detects and articulates truths about Uncle T's phoney character that Vincent is not willing to acknowledge, and as the evening drags on, both Irish husbands increasingly find themselves on the defensive against the realities about their situations relentlessly being revealed by their North American wives. 'I know you', Bernadette scolds Turlough as he makes one last desperate attempt to salvage the evening, 'it's your own fault, it's an old story, making yourself out to be something you never were'. Barbara and Bernadette are obviously more in touch with reality than their husbands are, but though they have logic and experience on their side, their attitudes nevertheless seem selfish and uncharitable. Vincent makes a response to his uncle at the end that his own father was unwilling to make to him, and perhaps because Turlough is such a loser, Moore convinces us that he deserves this acknowledgement. Vincent is clearly more like his uncle than he was prepared to admit at the outset, and for that reason his sudden glimpse of him from the taxi is a deeply troubling one:

> There, half-drunk on the pavement, stood a fat old man with dyed hair. Where was the boy who once wrote poems, the young iconoclast who once spoke out against the priests? What had done this to him? Was it drink, or exile, or this marriage to a woman twenty years his junior? Or had that boy never been?

The power of this scene derives from our realization that the questions Vincent meditates on might well one day be asked about himself, as foreshadowed by his dismissing Barbara and his joining his uncle in 'one for the road'. The story does not unequivocally lead to this conclusion, for Vincent and Barbara seem better equipped for life in the New World than Turlough and Bernadette: that a final resolution is left in abeyance is one measure of the skill and honesty with which Moore handles the realities of exile, a talent that becomes increasingly visible in his three main novels of exile set in the New World.

Turlough Carnahan's importance in Moore's vision of the New World at this time is suggested by the fact that the title figure of *The Luck of Ginger Coffey* is at the outset of that novel very much like him: James Francis Coffey, too, is a loser and an inveterate bluffer about the reality of his own personal situation. But Moore catches Ginger early enough (though in his crucial fortieth year) that he can make moves to offset the fact that his luck has just about run out, provided he is willing 'to abandon the facts of his life for the facts of the world'. His exile in the New World, deliberately chosen as an alternative to the dead ends of his existence in Dublin and Cork, provides him with the opportunity to do this, though it is not an easy process for him, and his basic mediocrity makes any spectacular improvement in his fortunes unlikely. For Carnahan, it is pathetically too late, and like James Madden of *Judith Hearne,* he appears doomed to fade into insignificance through alcoholism and bitterness; exile for him simply provided the opportunity to perpetuate his delusions in a world where he is virtually anonymous and where, without the talent and drive of a Brendan Tierney, he will very quickly go under.

In his carefully preserved image of a Dublin squire, Ginger walks blindly into this kind of situation on that first working day of a new year when he sets out, down to his last fifteen dollars and three cents, to make his mark on Montreal. That 'there wasn't a soul in Montreal who would say "There goes a man who's out of work" ', on the one hand reflects the kind of anonymity that protected Carnahan in New York, but on the other hand, it suggests that this city is prepared to honour this illusion while Ginger takes the opportunity to transform it into reality. For most of this first day, he tries to do just that, clinging to his belief in the 'rags to riches' cliché about the New World as opposed to the Old World, where, he muses, it 'was Chinese boxes, one inside the other, and whatever you started off as, you would probably end up as'. That he fails in all his attempts on that first day is due partly to his inflated opinion of himself, but also to the ingrained hostility of the officials he meets, who together constitute the entrenchment of class and privilege in Montreal. As a New Canadian, therefore, Ginger had not only to manipulate 'the facts of his life', but also to suffer the establishment's suspicions and prejudices barely disguised beneath the veneer of time-worn labels and clichés about the Irish.

It isn't until he is faced with the prospect of losing his wife and daughter that he is prepared to surrender his illusion about immediate success in the New World or his inflated image of himself. This process involves his inexorable descent from the *Executive and Professional* department of the Unemployment Office and from the Editorial floor of the *Tribune* to the subterranean proofreading room, and, as he loses Veronica and Paulie, to a basement room of the YMCA. By the time he has exchanged his Dublin squire's clothing for the 'anonymous and humiliating' delivery driver's uniform which, significantly, 'fitted him perfectly', he has attained the exile's ultimate position of isolation and anonymity, very much as Grove's Philip Branden did when he took on the lowly waiter's job in *A Search for America*. This point marks the beginning of Ginger's true self-awareness, and for the moment, since 'no one in the world knew where Ginger Coffey was', he is tempted to assume the ultimate state of exile: 'to retire from the struggle, live like a hermit, unknown and unloved in this faraway land', but he is too much a man of the flesh to pursue this notion seriously.

Ginger cannot remain anonymous for long, for his new identity is threatened when he is recognized by some former Dublin residents; but significantly, this recognition scene, where past reputation and present reality converge, produces an epiphany-like awareness in Ginger about his commitment to his exile: 'What did it matter? What did they matter, so long as he was not going home? And in that moment he knew that, sink or swim, Canada was home now, for better or for worse, for richer or for poorer, until death'. His formalizing of his commitment in the language of the marriage ceremony emphasizes the relationship between his two abiding concerns, the perserving of his family and the justifying of his exile to Canada in the

first place; it also suggests that his exile represented an existential protest against the closed order of the Old World, and a belief that one can only find his true nature through an individual and pragmatic testing of experience rather than through following prescribed rules and routines.

To dramatize Ginger's commitment to his exile and at the same time his lingering doubts and uncertainties about his action, Moore exploits a number of obligatory situations where we witness Ginger moving from private rationalizing through a grotesque initiation cermony to a final legal vindication of his new status. On that first day when he was still optimistic about his chances, he enters a church, ostensibly to keep warm, but in reality to justify his anti-clericalism: 'one of his secret reasons for wanting to get away to the New World was that, in Ireland, church attendance was not a matter of choice. Bloody well go, or else, tinker, tailor, soldier, sailor, rich man, poor man, you were made to suffer in a worldly sense. Here, he was free . . .'. And yet, he recalls the thunderous sermons of Father Cogley that seemed directed specifically at him, wherein he prophesied that unbelievers and adventurers would end up 'in some hell on earth, some place of sun and rot or snow and ice that no sensible man would be seen dead in'. His rejection of the church, therefore, is not entirely a comfortable decision, and certainly not an intellectual one, but rather, in keeping with his blustering optimism of that day, an impulsive and boastful manifestation of his pride.

But the next day he hits bottom as he joins a group of misfits who constitute his proofreading companions, and it is here, in a local tavern, where he undergoes a grotesque initiation ceremony into his Canadian experience, as the drunken Fox, in a bitter parody of the exile's dream, gives his vision of Canada as seen from the bottom:

> 'I have to explain the facts of life to our immigrant brother. Do you want to be remembered, Paddy? . . . Then you must bear in mind that in this great country of ours the surest way to immortality is to have a hospital wing called after you. Or better still, a bridge. We're just a clutch of little Ozymandiases in this great land. Nobody here but us builders . . . Remember that in this fair city of Montreal the owner of a department store is a more important citizen than any judge of the Superior Court. Never forget that, Paddy boy. Money is the root of all good here. One nation, indivisible, under Mammon that's our heritage.'

That the judge at Ginger's trial is humane and charitable in the sentence he hands down suggests that Fox is not entirely correct in his analysis of the Canadian dream, but Ginger, already having met such petty, self-serving individuals as Beauchemin, Kahn, and MacGregor, undoubtedly has some of his worst fears confirmed by this tirade. And as his fellow proofreaders hint that Ginger's promised promotion might never materialize, he begins to have serious doubts about his exile: 'Was it for this he had traveled across half a frozen continent and the whole Atlantic Ocean? To finish up as a galley slave among the lame, the odd, the halt, the old?'

Appropriately, the court room scene where he is finally recognized and vindicated follows immediately upon his self-confession in his cell, where he firmly acknowledges that whatever has happened to him is exclusively his fault, 'not God's, not Vera's, not even Canada's'. This *mea culpa* stance reflects the fundamental integrity that has always resided within Ginger (as we see, for example, in the Melody Ward episode), but that was frequently compromised because, in his concern for his family, he was always too eager to see himself as someone greater than he really was. It is this same concern that the judge takes into account as he sentences Ginger: 'I am dealing with you leniently, Coffey, because I am sorry for your family. To be alone in a new country, with their breadwinner in jail, seems to me a fate which your wife and child do not deserve'. The reconciliation with Veronica that follows constitutes a logical consequence both of his moral rebirth and of his legal recognition by Canada as a person deserving a further chance, a situation that stands in sharp contrast, for example, to the deterministic resolving of Judith's and Devine's personal dilemmas in their Belfast worlds.

The 'luck' that Ginger Coffey experiences in this process of transformation and reconciliation lies, ironically, in the fact that he is able to overcome that very stereotype of the Irish that various individuals parrot of him during that first long day of job-seeking. It is the Old World that has shaped him into the Dublin squire persona we meet initially, but it is the pragmatic New World that allows him to discard that image; therefore his 'luck' resides in the fact that *Executive and Professional* and the *Tribune*'s Editorial *did* turn him down, for from this moment on he can no longer rely on being 'at present a praiser of his own past', to borrow Stephen Dedalus's phrase about his father. From a sociological point of view, Ginger emerges as a valid representative of the post-war Irish immigrants, whom Moore described in an early interview as 'people who weren't doing very well at home . . . and got a terrible shock because they met a society that really wanted . . . work for money. And you had to know how to do something' ['Robert Fulford Interviews Brian Moore', *The Tamarack Review* 23, Spring, 1962]. Ginger unconsciously acknowledges that he is one of these people as he waits in a movie theatre to go through with the pre-arranged assignation with the call-girl—people who took on menial jobs for the sake of their families, just as he has done for Veronica and Paulie. 'Wasn't he one of them? Wasn't he a stranger here, never at home in this land where he had not grown up. Yes: he too'.

Moore quite properly emphasizes Ginger's isolation throughout this novel, for like all exiles, he is an outsider as far as both his worlds are concerned. Father Cogley's tirade against those who desert Ireland has its New World counterpart in the prejudices and hostility of those petty officials who see any immigrants as threats to their own secure world, so in both cases, Ginger has only himself to fall back on. Though he is by no means as articulate or as intellectually perceptive as Wyndham Lewis's Rene Harding, for example, he intuitively recognizes Harding's principle that 'there can be no consultation with others in a matter of conscience', and therefore he makes all his honest decisions about his fate in total isolation. He confronts in his imagination a terrifying void in these situations, for haunting him until the very end is his fear that

Veronica will remain with Grosvenor, abandoning him to a lonely existence in his new land; this spectre receives tangible shape when he goes to visit the sick proofreader, old Billy Davis who, he learns, also left Ireland to seek his fortunes in the larger world:

> Irish. *An immigrant, same as you.* A young wanderer, once travelling through this land of ice and snow, looking for the bluebird ERIN GO BRAGH. But was it really ERIN FOREVER? What trace of Erin was left on William O'Brien Davis save that harp and shamrock, that motto, faded as the old reminder that BILL LOVES MIN? Would Ginger Coffey also end his days in some room, old and used, his voice nasal and reedy, all accent gone?

Much as Vincent Bishop was disturbed by his vision of his Uncle T metamorphosed into a pathetic loser, so Ginger here is haunted by the spectacle of youthful hope betrayed, a situation obviously more frightening for the exile than for one secure in his own native land.

The progression from *Ginger Coffey* through *Limbo* to *Fergus* involves not only an increasing complexity in character, but also a corresponding complexity in the total settings in which the protagonists work out their dilemmas. Or perhaps it is more accurate to say that because the cities in question reflect the nature and compulsions of the individuals within them, the realistically perceived Montreal gives way to the increasingly surrealistic cityscapes of New York and Los Angeles. Brendan and Fergus are not only exiles, but writers-in-exile, and their dilemmas take on layers of complexity that did not obtain for Ginger, who essentially wanted only to be able to perserve his family intact, even if that meant surviving 'in humble circs.' For him, therefore, Montreal, in contrast to Dublin, is seen as a benign world, where a flexible pragmatism will sustain him from crisis to crisis, and where in a pinch he could always follow Wilson to Blind River. No such easy solutions or alternatives appear to be available for either Brendan or Fergus, whose artistic compulsions keep them in a kind of bondage to forces that recognized and encouraged them in the first place, and the abandoning of which in effect would amount to the abandoning of their careers as novelists. 'How easy it was to rationalize that first taste of corruption', Fergus recalls, as he rues his involvement with Boweri and Redshields, and it is a similar moral dilemma that keeps on troubling Brendan as well, beside which Ginger's survival problems seem quite minor and relatively easy to solve.

In *An Answer from Limbo,* the Old World and the New World meet most dramatically in the scene surrounding Brendan's meeting his mother at the airport, a scene that both literally and symbolically fulfills one of Moore's concerns while writing this novel: 'to put Irish Catholicism against the rootless wasteland of North America'. That these two worlds are fundamentally incompatible we have already surmised from our initial glimpses of Brendan and Mrs. Tierney in their separate worlds, and it is reinforced by the reservations of Ted Ormsby who, among other roles, acts out the remnants of Brendan's conscience back in Belfast: 'He was conscious . . . of the dangers to this woman in rejoining a son whose world and whose ways were so opposed to her own.' That they barely recognize each other at the airport after seven years apart clearly anticipates the gulf between them that grows wider as time goes on, for Brendan has, in spite of some lingering reservations, totally committed himself to his exile in the New World:

> Did I come to America because of my need to write, my need of Jane, or simply my old need to run? I do not know. But this morning, as I got off the bus at the airport . . . I knew that it is this world I care about, this world of moving staircases, electric eyes, efficient loudspeakers. Exile now means exile from this. My island is no longer home.

And, ironically, his earlier boast that he had escaped 'the provincial mediocrity' of his native land means he has abandoned, too, the values represented by his mother, whose 'lostness' as she enters the airport terminal is only the outward manifestation of how out of place she is in the New World.

But Brendan cannot entirely exorcise the forces of the Old World, any more than Ginger or Fergus can, for the paradox they all face is that it is these forces that have both shaped them and driven them into exile in the first place, and they all find themselves, to reverse the familiar epigram, between two worlds, one very much alive and the other powerless to die. 'Limbo is the modern condition: a place, neither heaven nor hell, a place of oblivion', Moore said in his working notes for this novel. But Brendan's isolation is not only cosmic, for his ambition and selfishness have made it a very human situation as well, as reflected in his inability to understand either Jane or his mother. By the end of *Limbo,* Brendan has fulfilled his primary reason for going into exile in the first place, for he has become a reasonably successful novelist, but in his personal relationships it has been a costly victory. Earlier we saw him asking himself about his real reason for exile, whether it was to pursue his ambitions to be a writer, or to pursue Jane, or simply to run away (reflecting Moore's own contention that it is frequently for mundane, rather than artistic, reasons that a writer goes into exile), but the course he consistently followed in the New World leaves no doubt about the priority of that first reason.

Where Ginger Coffey failed in his anticipated career, but succeeded in saving his family, the reverse holds true for Brendan and this, suggests Moore, is one of the penalties that some exiles are compelled to pay. *An Answer from Limbo* makes the point, too, that such a resolution does not elevate the exiled protagonist in any moral sense, but simply and unmistakably reminds him that the initial decision to go into exile produces all kinds of personal consequences that must at times seem to outweigh any artistic or professional advantages gained. Quite early in this novel, but after he has made his irreversible decision about the centrality of his novel, Brendan sincerely tries to resolve the human cost of what he is to do, in his poignant apostrophe to his dead father: 'I know only that if I were granted the wish to bring back to this world for one hour any human being I have known or read of, I would put in the call tonight for my father. . . . I wanted to prove to him that he was wrong, that I, of all his children, will

do him honour. O, Father, forgive me as I forgive you. Father, I am your son'.

This lament between father and son, as we have seen, constitutes a recurring note in Moore's exile fiction, but it is particularly important in *Fergus,* where it is Fergus's father who makes the first and the last of the visitations from the dead to break in upon his lonely existence on the Pacific. It isn't only geographically that Fergus is isolated, for he also feels vulnerable in a number of crucial personal relationships: with his youthful mistress, whom he is afraid of losing, with his Hollywood producers, threatening to cut him off if he won't change his novel to their liking, with his former wife, bleeding him for alimony and child support. In short, he is at that impasse where nothing in his present life is working out, and thus he wills into his consciousness all those forces of his past life that at one time had significance for him. When that long ordeal is over, he has achieved some victories, painful though some of them are, and he is able to dismiss the ghosts of the past as dawn breaks over the New World. Just before he had seen his father for the first time, he had stood looking over the Pacific, hearing the breakers pounding on the shore, and as his father leaves at the end, he becomes conscious of this recurring beat again. Thus, his earlier recollection of the refrain from Xenophon, *'Thalassa, Thalassa, the loud resounding sea, our great mother, Thalassa',* takes on a new significance, giving Fergus a kind of cosmic comfort, for like the Greek exiles who long ago sang the lament, he too, acquires both sadness and sustenance from beholding the sea in a world so far from his homeland.

Fergus on one level depicts Moore's ongoing fascination with communications of various sorts—fake telegrams ('Grieve for the Dear Departed'), unmade telephone calls (*Limbo*) delayed letters (*The Doctor's Wife*)—but in its unusual and unique way of showing how Fergus Fadden receives his messages from home, this novel dramatically personifies what the real cost of exile is. As a committed novelist, Fergus has to find out whether he, like Brendan Tierney, can get his revenge on the past 'by transforming it into a world of words', but his succession of visitors, from beyond the grave as well as from his immediate world, makes it impossible for him to find an easy or certain answer. He is misunderstood as an individual, harangued for his morals, berated for his selfishness, attitudes of the Old World that have been levelled not only against such deliberate exiles as Ginger and Brendan, but against such accidental ones as Sheila Redden in *The Doctor's Wife* or such imminent ones as Gavin Burke in *The Emperor of Ice-Cream.* Reinforcing the doubts that all these familiar charges resurrect are the threats emanating from his present California world, ranging from the impulsive petulance of his mistress, Dani, to the deliberate and obscene ultimatums coming from the Hollywood producers, Redshields and Boweri. In his past world Fergus did have a presence and a reality, even though he has tried to transform them, but in his present world, he is everyday aware of his insignificance. 'I could live here for a year and leave no mark on anything', he realizes. 'My presence would count for nothing'.

Fergus tries on one occasion to explain to his angry visitors why he has changed, but his explanation also underscores the kind of penalties one incurs in choosing a life of exile:

> Let me try to explain? Most people live their lives in one place, and they meet, essentially, the same people, year after year. But I've lived in Ireland, worked as a newspaperman in England and France, came to Amerca and worked on Long Island, then in New York, and now I'm here on the Pacific, I'm trying to say I've lived in so many places, it's impossible to remember . . . .

Here Fergus and Elaine, respectively an exile to the New World and a girl born in the New World, stand alone against the fury of the mob, simply for the reason that Fergus in his selfishness had forgotten her name and forgotten an earlier role he had played in her life. The Old World's unforgivingness and lack of charity, personified in Father Allen's hostile diatribes, unmistakably constitute a justification for Fergus's exile in the first place, but one can also understand, by the mob's accumulated fury, why it is that Fergus was not easily free of that legacy.

But Moore is not simplistic about the relative virtues or moralities of the Old and New Worlds in this novel. That California produces such monstrous figures as Boweri and Redshields, and such pathetic manipulators as Dani's mother, Dusty, helps make us uneasy about Fergus's future. For the moment, however, he has achieved a limited personal and moral victory: Dani has returned to him, he has refused to compromise his artistic convictions, and he has in effect cut off all further communication with all those, whether dead or living, who have tried to transform his life and his art. That it is a new dawn, too, rather than continuing darkness, that greets him as 'he walked toward the house' suggests his victory, though our final view of Fergus also spells out the kind of cosmic isolation that his exile has produced.

Doubts, fears, uncertainties—these are the emotions experienced by Moore's exiles in the New World, but at the same time they achieve an existential or experiential resolution of their dilemma that was not possible for such Old World protagonists as Judith or Devine.

—*Hallvard Dahlie*

In neither of these three North American novels does Moore impose a facile solution upon the dilemmas of his protagonists, and Brendan's agonizing questions at his mother's funeral—'Am I still my mother's son, my wife's husband, the father of my children? Or am I a stranger, strange even to myself?' —apply with very little modification to Ginger and Fergus as well. Brendan's epiphany is not unlike the observation made by Moore about the lost generation expatriates, that when they returned to Ameri-

ca, they experienced 'a terrifying realisation that the country of their boyhood is lost forever', [Brian Moore, **'The Crazy Boatloads'**, *Spectator,* 29 September 1961]. Doubts, fears, uncertainties—these are the emotions experienced by Moore's exiles in the New World, but at the same time they achieve an existential or experiential resolution of their dilemma that was not possible for such Old World protagonists as Judith or Devine. For Moore's New World exiles, the process of self-discovery and self-realization is a serious and somewhat frightening experience, with only Ginger reflecting occasionally the kind of rhapsodic acceptance of this world that attended such earlier exiles as Grove's Philip Branden or Lowry's Sigbjørn Wilderness. Unlike those writers, Moore is largely an urban novelist, and thus there is little evidence in his works of the notion of the New World as paradise, an idea that is tied largely to Canada's wilderness and rural aspects. For him such cities as Montreal, New York, and Los Angeles may provide opportunities that are unrealizable in Belfast or Dublin, but they are by no means free of corruption, favouritism, and hypocrisy, even though the determinism that exists in these New World cities is less pervasive and less inflexible than it is in the Old World.

With *The Doctor's Wife* Moore approaches the situation of exile in a different way, but presents a moral resolution that is quite as disturbing as Brendan's in *An Answer from Limbo.* Unlike him and the other New World protagonists, Sheila is only an accidental exile: her journey to France, on what was to be a second honeymoon, is merely part of a process of renewing and consolidating her normal existence as Mrs. Redden—that is, as the doctor's wife. Her transformation from permanent Belfast resident to homeless exile is sudden and frightening and, given the artistic shaping of this novel, totally inevitable. Sheila does what Judith and Devine should have done, and what Gavin Burke seems on the point of doing, but those two early protagonists had no external forces to compel them into action, as Sheila and Gavin did. But it isn't only the German bombings or the Irish troubles that operate in these latter cases—'you can't blame the Troubles for everything', Sheila argues—but clearly the forces of history coincide here with psychological crises to provide the atmosphere necessary for escape.

Sheila's decision to abandon home and family is precipitated both by the past—her recollections of her life as a student and of those lost opportunities, and by the present—the freedom that Paris offers, and her brief but intense sexual experience with Tom. But Tom's offer of a new life in America is no more a solution for her than is the medical and marital advice offered by her brother and her husband, and it is significant that she gives up all three men who are trying to regulate her life. In a very literal sense she has chosen the 'exile, silence, and cunning' stratagem of Stephen Dedalus, but she has applied it to a situation that is intensely personal and perhaps even selfish, compared to the larger spiritual, intellectual, and cultural problem that Joyce's protagonist was trying to solve. Exile *is* a selfish action, Moore seems to be suggesting, but it is also a painful one, and Sheila emerges as one of his strongest dramatizations of that fact. Socially she may find herself no father ahead at the end than was Judith or Devine, but psychologically she is far beyond them, and if nothing else, her act of falling in love with Tom compelled her to realize that she had to try to change what had become for her a futile and empty life. 'How did I get so bogged down in ordinariness that even this once I couldn't do the spontaneous thing, the thing I really wanted to do', she asks herself, as she leaves Tom to fly to Villefranche, and then anticipates the existential resolution she inevitably has to accept: 'The future is forbidden to no one. Unless we forbid it to ourselves'.

Her subsequent affair with Tom Lowry is the immediate, precipitating force that compels her to cut herself off from her Belfast home and family, but had her sexual satisfaction with him been the major factor, she would have found it an easy matter to accompany him to Vermont. Her exile has a much more profound and complex derivation, and in effect has been on hold ever since she was a youthful student in Paris. Her defining of herself to Tom by telling him of the past—'the excitement of coming from Belfast and Dublin to her first great foreign city'—is juxtaposed against what she has become since that time—'all that laundry list of events that had been her life since she married Kevin'. It is therefore appropriate that the break from that life be dramatized in precisely the same location—Room 450 of the Hotel Welcome at Villefranche—where her first honeymoon had initiated that life, and in this situation, her frenzied and joyous sexual aggressiveness with Tom is in part a response to the ordinariness that has characterized her sixteen years of marriage to Dr. Redden. Not that she understands completely what she is doing—her brother Owen is quite right when he concludes that 'that restless side of her was something that perhaps she didn't understand too well herself'—but as she explains to Peg, she is aware of a change in herself that all the old explanations will not satisfy:

> 'We put up with our lives, we don't try to change them. I didn't realize it, until I fell in love. What I'm doing now is supposed to be selfish. It's what people used to call sinful. But I'm happy, in a way I never was before. Is that a sin?'

Like Brendan Tierney, Sheila has learned, at painful cost to herself and those around her, something about the ultimate meaning of exile: virtual severance from the human community. Rejecting her husband, her lover, and her brother, all of woman have offered different solutions, she accepts her isolation at the end, 'and walked off down the street like an ordinary woman on her way to the corner to buy cigarettes', thus preparing to survive on her own terms in the anonymity of London. For Sheila, as for Moore's New World protagonists, exile clearly involves a combination of what we saw at the beginning with Ovid and Skvorecky: it is both punishment and liberation. All of Moore's exiles, as opposed to his protagonists who remain prisoners of Belfast's deterministic forces, seem to be able to say with Ginger Coffey that 'a man's life was nobody's fault but his own', and act decisively on that conviction, a realization that undoubtedly Moore himself came to long ago as he set out on his own life of exile. From his viewpoint of the writer *as* exile, he sees whatever society he is for the moment concerned with as an integral world with its own legitimate and demanding reality,

which must be re-created through the exiled writer's particular artistic and philosophical vision.

Jeanne A. Flood   (essay date Winter 1990)

SOURCE: *"Black Robe:* Brian Moore's Appropriation of History," in *Eire-Ireland,* Vol. XXV, No. 4, Winter, 1990, pp. 40-55.

[*Flood is an educator and critic. In the following essay on* Black Robe, *she criticizes Moore for misrepresenting Canadian Indians and the French Jesuit priests who attempted to "save" them. Flood also contends that Moore's strict reliance on the Jesuits' historical first-hand accounts both prevented him from fully utilizing his skills as a novelist and betrays his "oedipal" intentions to mock the Catholic Church.*]

Brian Moore's fifteenth novel, **Black Robe,** begins with a prefatory note. In it Moore gives as the genesis of his novel his reading of Graham Greene's essay on the American historian, Francis Parkman. Greene led Moore to Parkman's *The Jesuits in North America,* and Parkman led him to the *Jesuit Relations,* on which Parkman based his history. This was not the end of Moore's preparation for writing **Black Robe,** for he read "the works of anthropologists and historians who have established many facts about Indian behavior not known to the early Jesuits" and he consulted with various authorities whose names and academic affiliations he lists. Further, he visited Indian archives in Canada and also Huron Village, a reconstruction of a seventeenth century Huron settlement and Jesuit mission in Midland, Ontario. Moore is clearly anxious to establish a factual basis for his novel. This is a sound instinct, for **Black Robe** evokes protest. Two of its attributes are particularly disturbing: its lavish use of obscene language and the crude brutality of many of its scenes. Moore's preface, it seems to me, intends to justify these elements in the book. However, if we accept Moore's invitation to consider his book against its sources, we do not find justification for what he has done in the novel, but some very serious questions.

Moore begins his preface by quoting a passage from Parkman which appears in Greene's essay. It concerns Noel Chabanel, a Jesuit who hated his life among the Indians in Canada, but responded to a temptation to return to France by vowing to remain in Canada until he died. *"A solemn vow,"* Moore intones in italics. "A voice speaks to us directly from the seventeenth century, the voice of a conscience that I fear, we no longer possess." Moore's comment suggests his belief that moral certainty based on Christian faith is a historical relic, if an admirable one. This idea is reinforced by Moore's treatment of another historical relic, the belief of the Indians. He points out that Native Americans, too, had a religion and a moral code based upon it: "They were warlike; they practiced ritual cannibalism and, for reasons of religion, subjected their enemies to prolonged and unbearable tortures." His novel, he says, is an attempt to show how their conflicting beliefs and codes elicited from Jesuit and Indian alike "fear, hostility, and despair, which later would result in the destruction and abandonment of the Jesuit missions, and the conquest of the Huron people by the Iroquois, their deadly enemy." . . .

[This] preface not only attempt[s] to validate the realism of Moore's work, but to sugest as well that it is informed by a religious consciousness. Surely ascribing to Greene a kind of sponsorship of *Black Robe* suggests that Moore wants his readers to see his book as a religious novel— indeed, as a Catholic novel. But Moore is not writing in the tradition of Greene. As presented by Moore in *Black Robe,* Catholicism has nothing to do with religious belief or with human action informed by religious belief, which has often been Greene's subject. Catholicism in Moore is a system of instinctual repression, most perfectly expressed in the celibacy of the priesthood. The animistic belief of Moore's Indians has no more to do with a religion capable of informing human actions than does the Roman Catholicism of his Jesuit. In the novel, Indian religion is the exact antithesis of Catholicism. It is a system of instinctual gratification most fully expressed in the gross feeding of the Indian band. In *Black Robe,* contrary to the claim in his preface, Moore is writing neither about Jesuits nor about Native Americans. His concern is with power and submission, desire and fear, the ancient impasse between father and son. The most interesting aspect of the book is its insistence on the historical authenticity of the story it tells and its furious attack on the main source of knowledge and information on which that claim is based. The real energy in Moore's book is devoted to the degradation of the *Jesuit Relations.*

The protagonists or *Black Robe* are Paul Laforgue, a Jesuit priest, and his lay companion Daniel Davost. Most of the book, all but forty-one of its two-hundred-forty-six pages, is an account of the westward journey of the two from Quebec to a Jesuit mission at Ihonitaria in the territory of the Huron Indians. The two Frenchmen travel with a party of twenty-six Algonquin Indians who have been paid to guide them to their destination. Among the Algonquins is the passionate maiden Annuka, the object of Davost's enthusiastic lust and Laforgue's guilty desire. It is not overstating the case to say that Moore's account of the journey derives entirely from the *Jesuit Relations.* The only element in the action of *Black Robe* for which no source appears in the *Relations* is the lurid love triangle.

Not only do Moore's Jesuit sources supply most of the detail and incident of *Black Robe,* they also provide the authority for the most notable quality of the novel's language—its tedious scurrility. A footnote in Moore's preface attempts to justify this quality of the language:

> As for the obscene language used by natives at that time it was a form of rough banter and was not intended to give offense. I am aware that I have taken a novelist's license in the question of Algonkian understanding of Iroquoian speech.

The note, like the preface as a whole, is clearly intended to establish the factual basis of Moore's novel. Moore admits to a license that permits the depiction of mutual linguistic understanding between Indian tribes whose difference is defined by language. Leaving aside the possibility that such a course is less an indication of the novelist's cre-

ative freedom than of a failure of invention, we should note that Moore makes no apology for the way in which he represents Indian language; rather, he justifies the method he has devised for doing so: the unrelenting repetition of the four-letter words that comprise the working obscene vocabulary of modern English-speakers.

> In *Black Robe,* contrary to the claim in his preface, Moore is writing neither about Jesuits nor about Native Americans. His concern is with power and submission, desire and fear, the ancient impasse between father and son.
>
> — *Jeanne A. Flood*

As we have noted, Moore uses the footnote on language in the preface to justify this particular strategy. If we accept his invitation to check his novel against its sources, however, we do not come away with an impression of Moore's historical accuracy, but rather with a sense of his inability to create a style worthy of the languages described by those who heard and studied them in the seventeenth century. In fact, Parkman does note the use of obscene language by the Indians. Parkman's authority is Father Paul Le Jeune's account in the *Jesuit Relation* of 1634 of the habits and customs of the Montagnais tribe with whom he had passed the winter of 1633-34. Le Jeune does comment on certain qualities of Indian speech. "I do not believe that there is a nation under heaven more given to sneering and bantering than that of the Montagnais," he notes. The savages "are slanderous beyond all belief," speaking ill even of their close relatives. Le Jeune accounts for this behavior:

> The reason of this is, it seems to me, that their slanders and derision do not come from malicious hearts or from infected mouths, but from a mind which says what it thinks in order to give itself free scope, and which seeks gratification from everything, even from slander and mockery.

Though Le Jeune first remarks on the Indian use of insult, he goes on to write about obscenity in Indian speech.

> In place of saying, as we do very often, through wonder, "Jesus! what is that? My God! Who has done that?" these vile and infamous people pronounce the names of the private parts of man and woman. Their lips are constantly foul with these obscenities; and it is the same with the little children. So I said to them, at one time, that if hogs and dogs knew how to talk, they would adopt their language.

This passage constitutes the ultimate justification for the use of obscene language in Moore's novel. We may take it as certain, on the authority of Le Jeune, that native Americans in the seventeenth century did not express themselves with the restraint acceptable to a French Jesuit. But we can also take it as certain on the same authority that the impoverished argot assigned to the Indian characters in **Black Robe** is not a reasonable representation of Indian speech. The Jesuits were fascinated by Indian languages; their accounts of their efforts to learn them offer many possible strategies for the creation of a style that might suggest Indian speech.

Descriptions of Indian language abound in the *Jesuit Relations*. Le Jeune in the *Relation* of 1633 notes that the Montagnais language "is very poor and very rich," poor in having no names "for thousands of things which are in Europe," rich "because in the things of which they have a knowledge, it is fertile and plentiful." In the *Relation* of 1634, he greatly expands this insight. Here Le Jeune takes an interest not so much in the deficiencies of the language as in the richness with which, he says, it is "fairly gorged." He notes "an infinite number of proper nouns" that can be explained only by circumlocutions in French. He finds a dazzling complexity and precision in verb forms and a similar amplitude in adjectival usage. Le Jeune is bewildered and frustrated by this richness:

> . . . I am almost led to believe that I shall remain poor all my life in their language. When you know all the parts of Speech of the languages of our Europe, and know how to combine them, you know the languages; but it is not so concerning the tongue of our Savages. Stock your memory with all the words that stand for each particular thing, learn the knot or Syntax that joins them together, and you are still only an ignoramus. . . .

Jean de Brebeuf in the *Relation* for 1635 remarks on the abundance in the language of the Hurons, writing that he will have to study for a long time with the savages "so prolific is their language." In 1636 he writes that "the key to the secret" of Huron language is its great variety and specificity of nouns, which he calls "compound words," and which in French would be expressed not as a noun, but as an adjective and a noun. Brebeuf notes further that Hurons cannot use a noun expressing a personal relationship without qualifying that relationship. For example, Hurons could not say "father," but had to say "my father, your father, his father."

The *Jesuit Relations* present Indian languages as rich, various, and precise. Their descriptions of the languages offer obvious strategies for representing seventeenth century Native American speech. Moore chooses to ignore all of these possibilities in **Black Robe**. Only the obscenity of Indian speech interests him. In the *Relation* for 1633, Le Jeune remarked that the authority of a Montagnais chief is based upon his skill as an orator:

> There is no place in the world where Rhetoric is more powerful than in Canada, and nevertheless, it has no other grab than what nature has given it; it is entirely simple and without disguise; and yet it controls all these tribes, as the Captain is elected for his eloquence alone, and is obeyed in proportion to his use of it, for they have no other law than his word.

This is the way in which Moore presents an Algonquin chief deliberating with his people on the proper course of action in a difficult situation. In pursuit of Annuka, Daniel Davost has left Laforgue, whom the Indians call "Nicanis," to join the Indians. The Indians must decide what to do with Davost.

> "That is shit," Neehatin said, and laughed to show he was not angry. "Look, you assholes, let's not have any bad words now. We have reached the hunting place. We're safe. We have meat to eat tonight. I'm going to send that boy back to Nicanis. I'll tell him that unless he leaves tomorrow, he'll get a present from me: a hatchet in his skull."

Le Jeune and Brebeuf painfully learned complex and elaborately nuanced Indian languages. We have Le Jeune's testimony that the speakers of Algonquin were given to obscene raillery and insult, but we also have his testimony on the eloquence of their language. Moore takes from the *Jesuit Relations* permission to write obscenity, but not permission to invent a style that could represent a language such as Le Jeune and Brebeuf described.

As I have noted, the *Jesuit Relations* contribute a great deal more to **Black Robe** than certification for the scatalogical excess to which its Indian characters are addicted. Moore depends heavily on Le Jeune's narrative of 1634 as a source for the experiences of Laforgue and Davost during their journey to Ihonitaria. Le Jeune wrote at great length about the social customs, religious beliefs, domestic habits, and daily routine of the Montagnais with whom he lived as they moved through the forest all winter in pursuit of game. Moore makes extensive use of this information. He describes the repellent eating habits of Laforgue's Algonquins: "The Savages ate gluttonously from the kettles, stopping from time to time to wipe their greasy fingers on their hair or on the coats of their dogs, which ran barking around the fires in search of discarded scraps." Le Jeune is the source: "As to them, they wipe their hands upon their hair, which they allow to grow very long, or else, upon their dogs." Moore presents a meal in the Algonquin camp after a successful hunt:

> Then, as the first pieces of half-cooked meat were taken from a pot, Neehatin rose, cut a slice from a haunch of deer, and came to Laforgue holding it on his knife. "Here, Nicanis," he said. "Eat this. Now you will truly eat."
>
> This was the Savage phrase of hospitality. Laforgue took the greasy meat in his hands. Hair and skin still adhered to it. "Now I will truly eat," he said and, conquering his nausea, bit into the half-cooked flesh.

Le Jeune supplies justification for every detail of this description. He writes that after a meal, the bark plates of the Indians are "covered with grease, the fur of the Moose, and hair." Le Jeune says of the serving of the food at an Indian meal that "one of them takes down the kettle from the fire and distributes to each one his share; sometimes presenting the meat at the end of a stick." He writes that the phrase for expressing one's pleasure in food is *"tapoué nimitison,* 'I am really eating.' " In the *Relation* for 1633 he notes that meat is taken out of the cooking kettles when it is only half- cooked.

Laforgue has many of the experiences and makes many of the observations that Le Jeune did, and Le Jeune's thoughts also turn up as those of Moore's Father Bourque, Laforgue's immediate religious superior and an authority on native Americans, having spent a winter living with them. Laforgue interprets Indian behavior on the authority of Father Bourque:

> Laforgue looked at the tall girl, who was picking fleas from her mother's hair and eating them. The Savages ate these insects not from appetite but as a revenge against the fleas for having been bitten by them. That was what Father Bourque had told him. He said it was part of their feelings toward their enemies. An enemy must be shown no mercy. He must be crushed.

Here is Le Jeune:

> I have shown in my former letters how vindictive the Savages are toward their enemies, with what fury and cruelty they treat them, eating them after they have made them suffer all that an incarnate fiend could invent. . . . I have said that they eat the lice they find upon themselves, not that they like the taste of them, but because they want to bite those that bite them.

These instances typify the closeness of the correspondence between *Black Robe* and the *Jesuit Relations*. The degree of that closeness can hardly be exaggerated. On the basis of Le Jeune's experience, the Algonquin Neehatin offers Laforgue warm and dry mittens, and advises him that Indian hunters will not take care of those who cannot withstand the rigors of the winter. On the basis of Jean de Brebeuf's report that the Hurons of Ihonitaria were fascinated by a chiming clock which they thought to be animated by a spirit, Moore's savages gather to admire the clock in the Jesuit house in Quebec. Le Jeune's Montagnais built a winter camp, a process which he described. When Moore's Laforgue travels with the Algonquins, they build a winter camp, and in doing so they exactly follow the sequence of actions presented by Le Jeune. Le Jeune writes that the Indians of Quebec thought that the first European ships which they saw were floating islands, and that the wine and biscuits which the Europeans offered them were blood and wood. Thinking of Indian duplicity, Moore's Davost reflects that the first Indians to see a European ship at Quebec thought it was a floating island, and that Europeans "drank blood and ate dry bones." In *Black Robe,* Moore presents a speech in which Champlain commends Laforgue to the Algonquins. Its language and its concepts echo the speech Le Jeune reports, in the *Jesuit Relations,* that Champlain made to the Hurons in 1633 when the Jesuits Jean de Brebeuf, Antoine Daniel, and Ambroise Davost were vainly attempting to go with them to the Huron country.

The scenes of brutality and sadism in *Black Robe* also derive from the *Jesuit Relations,* usually with the addition of the obscene language that so fascinates Moore. A case in point is the account of the torture of Laforgue and Davost by Iroquois children. The two Frenchmen, An-

nuka, and her family have been captured. After various vile deeds are perpetrated against the prisoners, the Iroquois turn the survivors over to the children, who command them to dance and sing while naked.

> "Sing," cried one child.
>
> They began the Ave Maria.
>
> "Be quiet," cried a second child.
>
> They stopped singing. The first child, the one who had ordered them to sing, at once went to the fire and, picking up a burning brand, held it close to Daniel's penis. "I told you to sing," the child yelled.
>
> Daniel began to sing.
>
> "Stop!" cried the second child, approaching, also waving a burning brand.

The source of this scene is Joseph Bressani's account of his torture by the Iroquois. Traveling with a party of Hurons and a young Frenchman to the Huron country, the Italian Jesuit was captured in 1644. When the torture began, Bressani and his fellow prisoners were stripped, beaten, and burned. They were also placed at the mercy of everyone in the tribe.

> It was necessary to obey the very children, and that in things little reasonable, and often contrary. "Get up and sing" said one. "Be quiet," said the other; and if I obeyed one, the other ill-used me. "Here, give thy hand, which I will burn for thee;" and the other burned me because I did not extend it to him.

Bressani's statement about the actions of the children is embedded in his report of what he suffered from the young Iroquois warriors, who tore out his beard and tortured him with fire. In Bressani, the target of the assault by fire is the hands. In Moore, as we have seen, Iroquois children assault the penis. However, even this is not quite a pure invention, for we can find a sort of authority in Bressani, who wrote that some of his tortures, though not by children, involved sexual abuse: "Six or seven nights they tormented me in such fashion, and in such places, that I could not describe these things, nor could they be read, without blushing." Moore closes his scene with a little girl, whose command over obscenity is every bit as good as that of her elders, pulling hard on the unfortunate Laforgue's beard.

Every detail in the scene of torture by children comes out of the *Jesuit Relations;* only in the arrangement of the details does Moore make use of his "novelist's license." To a reader who might find the language and action of this scene lurid to the point of incredibility, the *Jesuit Relations* supply a defense. Such actions as this actually happened and were reported by those who suffered them. Moore imports the authority for what he has written from his sources; the novel does not generate its own authority. For this reason, there is a persistent hollowness in *Black Robe,* an emotional flatness, a lack of conviction. These qualities make the scene we have just considered, but they are everywhere in the novel. Here is a description of Lafor-

> **The preface of *Black Robe* exists to dissociate the novel's crude excess from the author and to assign ultimate responsibility for it to history as the seventeenth-century Jesuits reported it. This claim is the reason for the novel's existence, as well as the reason for its failure.**
>
> **— *Jeanne A. Flood***

gue's consciousness after the Iroquois have cut off the joint of one of his fingers and thrown it in the cooking pot which contains the body of Annuka's brother:

> In excruciating pain, Laforgue fell to his knees and then, in a scene so terrible that it surpassed horror or pity or forgiveness or rage, he saw three older women take from the cooking kettle the limbs of the dead child and pass them, parboiled, to the warriors who had captured Chomina's party.

This is rhetorical excess in the absence of any genuine imagining. The single crude detail "parboiled" syntactically misplaced, does not convey credible realism, but the straining toward some emotion that the passage, indeed, the novel as a whole cannot support.

The preface of *Black Robe* exists to dissociate the novel's crude excess from the author and to assign ultimate responsibility for it to history as the seventeenth-century Jesuits reported it. This claim is the reason for the novel's existence, as well as the reason for its failure. *Black Robe* is not, as the preface suggests, a nostalgic homage to Jesuits dead three hundred years and to moral commitment based on religious conviction. Nor does it fulfill its second claim: to present an understanding of the Indian ethos that was beyond the Jesuits and, thus, to convey a truer version of the story they told. The real energy of *Black Robe* is directed, as I have tried to demonstrate, toward the subversion of the *Jesuit Relations.* However, the masking of this destructive energy in a realism that claims to represent historical actuality, rather than discrediting the *Jesuit Relations,* issues in the strange inauthenticity of *Black Robe* itself.

The obscene language of *Black Robe* illustrates this dynamic. The historical fact that Le Jeune expressed shock at Montagnais obscenity becomes Moore's obligation and opportunity to write obscenity. But he does not stand behind these words. Rather, they are presented as a necessity imposed upon him by the desire to create a style faithful to history as certified by the Jesuits. Where the novelist should be is Le Jeune's *Relation*. The obscenity of *Black Robe*—first a shock, then an irritation, finally an embarrassment—fails to create the illusion of realism. If the disbelieving reader accepts the invitation implicitly extended in the preface to check the novel against its sources on the issue of language, he finds both historical authority for the

strategy Moore adopted *and* a sense of how seriously that strategy misrepresents what the sources have to say. In the end, the obscenity of *Black Robe* seems perverse naughtiness—neither a valid representation of historical reality nor an expression of the novelist's creative freedom.

Subversive, too, is the appropriation of what the writings of Le Jeune and Bressani report for the experiences and reflections of Paul Laforgue. Their narratives show Le Jeune and Bressani to have been physically courageous men, strong in body and spirit. They were resourceful, capable of great endurance, deeply centered in their religious belief. Although in the novel Laforgue bears the Indian name "Nicanis" associated with Le Jeune in the *Relations,* he lacks any qualities that suggest basic adult competence, let alone the cheerful common sense and fortitude that distinguish Le Jeune in his appearances in the *Relations*. Indeed, Laforgue lacks physical and emotional power to a remarkable degree: pitifully weak and inept in body, he displays the emotions of a cowardly child. His spiritual life, so long as he is a believer, consists of compulsive worry about the technicalities of penitential and baptismal ritual, while his intellectual life seems vacuous. Typical of Laforgue's inadequacy is an incident in which he gets lost in the forest. When he is rescued, he embraces one of the Indians and begins to cry. The quality of his reflections on this event, as well as his tears, typify his astonishing childishness: "I might have died here, alone in this wilderness. I did not welcome death as a holy person should. I was afraid." So much for the renowned spiritual discipline of the Jesuits.

As we have noted, very few scenes in *Black Robe* cannot be traced to the *Jesuit Relations.* The most important of these invented scenes present Laforgue in blind panic as he witnesses sexual encounters between Davost and Annuka, which he does on several occasions since he is given to voyeurism. In the first incident, wildly excited as he thinks of Annuka giving to him "the same delight she had just given to the boy," Laforgue masturbates. Horrified at himself, he runs into the woods: "He stood sobbing in that wild place, bereft of all hope, beyond all forgiveness." Then he scourges himself until "his flayed back was purpled as the sky above." The next night, although the priest has recalled this scene and cried even as he again became sexually excited, he goes into the woods to spy on the lovers, but leaves deciding that he is "no longer fit to be a priest." In the third repetition of the voyeur-lovers scene, Laforgue, again in tears interrupts the passionate pair *in medias res* and then kneels down and begins to pray aloud. The ensuing display of contempt and anger by the young lovers is one of the more convincing moments of the novel.

In the lengthy journey section of *Black Robe,* Laforgue is a pathetic coward, a voyeur, and a hysteric. In the second part of the novel, he is without religious belief. This condition comes upon him quite suddenly. It has nothing to do with his sexual guilt, which never comes into his consciousness again after the final voyeuristic crisis. It has nothing to do with his torture by the Iroquois, which disappears from his consciousness and from any significance in the book as soon as the torture scene ends. Nevertheless, when Laforgue at last reaches Ihonitaria, he reflects that "he has ceased to pray." This seems very strange, since he is presented as punctilious, not to say relentless, about carrying out such priestly duties as come his way in the first part of the novel, and he is never once shown to entertain the slightest doubt. However, after being saved by a timely eclipse from being tortured to death by the population of Ihonitaria, Laforgue is in full blown spiritual crisis. In fact, his position is exactly that articulated by Moore in his preface: "What error has come upon me so that, today, that eclipse of the sun seemed to me a phenomenon which, were I to believe in it as the hand of God, would leave me in the same murk of superstition as the Savages themselves?" Apparently Laforgue is as baffled as the reader by this unexpected development in his spiritual life. Nevertheless, in the final scene of *Black Robe,* the unbelieving Laforgue prepares to baptize the unbelieving Indians: "What are the baptisms but a mockery of all the days of my belief, of all the teachings of the Church, of all the saintly stories we have read of saving barbarians for Christ?"

A character created through the appropriation of the *Jesuit Relations,* Laforgue casts doubt on the *Jesuit Relations.* Here again appears the bad faith that permeates *Black Robe*. The mockery of saintly stories is not in the character's contemplated sacramental action, but in the novelist's creation of the character. To impose on the narratives the Jesuits wrote of their own lives Laforgue's contemptible timidity, sexual panic, and lack of faith is not to take a novelist's freedom to create a different kind of story with its own laws and its own authenticity. Rather, *Black Robe* attempts to devalue and mock the Jesuit stories, by almost slavishly imitating their account of the externals of circumstance and action while also denigrating the qualities of mind and spirit of those long dead priests to whom, after all, the experiences narrated in the *Relations* belong. The ambiguous pieties of the preface establish this denial as the keynote of the text. The claim there that *Black Robe* presents a realistic illusion that is uniquely faithful to historical actuality is the means by which Moore conceals the aggressive desire that generates the story and by which he detaches the fiction from the novelist by assigning responsibility for the narrative to other agencies. The preface attempts to suggest that Moore is not creating a story but, rather, reporting from a position of weary objectivity on a complex even which those who enacted it and wrote its history did not understand and, therefore, misrepresented.

Black Robe, which appropriates the stories of dead fathers to mock them, is an assault on the oedipal father. I have argued elsewhere that Moore has always seen the creation of fiction as such an attack and, therefore, as an action both guilty and dangerous [in *Brian Moore,* 1974 and "*The Doctor's Wife:* Brian Moore and the Failure of Realism," *Eire-Ireland* XVIII, No. 2, 1983]. *Black Robe* differs from his more successful novels, such as *The Lonely Passion of Judith Hearne,* or *The Feast of Lupercal,* or *An Answer from Limbo,* in that Moore has not been able to create through the characters an expression of that defiance. Indeed, the oedipal dynamic as enacted within *Black Robe* is notably confused and muddled. Thus, Laforgue and Davost play the roles of both father and son to each other. The insistence on Davost's boyishness suggests his filial

status as does the fact that he calls Laforgue "father." On the other hand, Laforgue's hysteria at witnessing Davost and Annuka in intercourse belongs not to the father but to the son as witness of the primal scene. Further, in *Black Robe* virtually the only mark of Laforgue's priestly fatherhood is his power to hear confessions; however, even as he urges Davost to submit to that power by confessing his sexual sins to him, he confesses to Davost, saying that both "boy" and priestly father are guilty of the same sin with the same woman.

The confused conflict over sex and confession between Laforgue and Davost ends when the two are captured and tortured by the Iroquois. It is the Indians, those obscene talkers, historically known as priest-killers, who enact the aggressive rage of the son against the father within the novel. The purported understanding of the seventeenth-century Indian mind acquired by Moore from the anthropologists does not, in fact, issue in a credible set of Indian characters. Moore's Indians do not express the ethos and sensibility of a culture with its own central myth, logic, and coherence. Rather, they bear the mark that has distinguished those characters in Moore's novels who express the rebellion of the son-artist; they believe in dreams rather than in a reality sponsored by figures of paternal authority. However, the foul-mouthed, dirty, murderously vicious "Savages" are certified to be so by Jesuit testimony, not created to be so by the necessity of the novel in which they appear.

No matter their setting, no matter the fictive citizenship of their characters, all of Brian Moore's novels involve a transaction between an Ireland of the mind and a Canada of the mind. The defining characteristic of Moore's mental Ireland is a powerful patriarchal authority rooted in traditional Roman Catholic belief and providing a sturdy structure of meaning and value on which all human experience can be located. For Moore, the negative aspect of this inner Ireland is its merciless repression of sexual energy and, by extension, of the creative energy of the artist. Moore's Canada, on the other hand, is the New World, where desire may be enacted without devastating punishment and, consequently, a spiritual wasteland where gratification and, indeed, life itself lacks meaning. A seventeenth-century French Jesuit bearing the name of a nineteenth-century French poet, Laforgue is a psychic Irishman in terms of Moore's mental geography: childlike in relation to spiritual authority, terrified of the body, consumed by guilt. When he comes to Canada, all that Laforgue is and all that he believes becomes nullified by the native Canadians whose lives are guided by dream and ferocious desire. The Catholicism of Moore's Davost shows that he, too, belongs to that same psychic Ireland, but when he encounters the Canadian Indians, he quickly abandons his past. Like the Indians, Davost sees what he wants and takes it. In Canada, his experience is strictly of the moment, connecting neither to the past nor the future, referring to nothing outside itself. There is no obstacle to his desire. Unlike Laforgue, he becomes a success in Canada—indeed, at the end of *Black Robe,* he is indistinguishable from the Indians.

Brian Moore has defined himself as an Irish novelist in

Canada. This fact is played out, I suggest, in the dynamic of his novels, in the endless struggle between the Old World and the New, between the father's traditional provenance and the spiritually diminished but physically and materially gratifying territory claimed by the son. In two of his least successful novels Moore seems compelled to examine the interaction between these worlds by quite literally appropriating incidents from Canadian history for his own purposes. *Black Robe* is one of these works, and the other is *The Revolution Script* (1971). *The Revolution Script* presents the 1970 kidnapping of two government officials, James Cross and Pierre Laporte, and the subsequent murder of Laporte by a group of young French Canadian terrorists. In *The Revolution Script,* as in *Black Robe,* Moore recounts a story of men in authoritative positions within a powerful patriarchal institution who are brutalized and defeated by native Canadians. Both novels begin with a preface pointing out the historical basis of Moore's narrative and suggesting that the novels that follow are less inventions than factual reports.

Both *Black Robe* and its documentary predecessor suggest that Moore's mental Canada is the necessary counterpart of his mental Ireland. Without the New World of murderous desire and energy, the Old constricted but morally and spiritually substantial Old World of *The Lonely Passion of Judith Hearne* and *The Feast of Lupercal* would not exist. However, there is a price in guilt that Moore has never ceased to pay for becoming a novelist, which for him meant leaving Ireland and becoming Canadian in both the public, literal and the private, metaphorical meaning of the term. Coming almost twenty years after *The Revolution Script, Black Robe* is also a Canadian story of the assault upon the symbolic father that comes to us claiming to be not an invention but a report, thus in some sense negating and denying Moore's power and identity as a novelist. Coexisting with the appropriation and distortion of the Jesuits' Canadian stories, such a denial affirms the spiritually rooted, patriarchal world of his own interior Ireland. However, when, as novelist, Moore so relentlessly distances himself from the rebellious oedipal desire that creates *Black Robe,* he also distances himself from his own power as a novelist. It is this distance that weakens *Black Robe* as a credible work of fiction.

Seamus Deane (review date 20-26 April 1990)

SOURCE: "In the Firing Line," in *The Times Literary Supplement,* No. 4542, April 20-26, 1990, p. 430.

[*Deane is an Irish poet, essayist, critic, and educator. In the following negative review of* Lies of Silence, *he contends that, although there "are few better living novelists than Brian Moore," his representation of the crisis in Northern Ireland is stereotypical and inaccurate.*]

There are few better living novelists than Brian Moore, but one would find little support for that statement in this book. Since the publication of *Catholics* in 1972, he has consistently found ways of bringing the secular world into collision with metaphysical or religious phenomena and of allowing the subsequent reverberations to shake the foundations of both. There has always been an investigative,

sleuth-like aspect to his writing. We can detect that something is wrong because the symptoms of unease are so marked. The source of the wrong is often found to be rooted in the very assumptions on which the investigation itself was based. The diverse worlds of his fiction—Belfast, Toronto, New York, California, Eastern Europe, seventeenth-century Canada, a future world off the south-west Irish coast—are painstakingly fumigated of all illusion but the disinfectant clarity that results may itself be the most powerful illusion of all. The withering economy of Moore's prose, the sardonic observation of social and political systems, are indications of a highly cultivated detachment that ostensibly accepts no reality that cannot be directly experienced in and through the body.

Of course, since he is a novelist, this "belief" undergoes its own subversion; worlds work in slippery ways, stories are acts of interpretation as well as acts of reportage. By emphasizing the reportage, he can appear to subdue the interpretive element. But when sheer reportage threatens to enforce interpretations that would question the narrowly solid world we know by our senses, then a heat tremor seizes everything and renders it insecure. Earlier novels such as *The Great Victorian Collection* (1975), *The Mangan Inheritance* (1979) and *Cold Heaven* (1983) absorb this insecurity into their rhetoric and narrative; the more recent *Black Robe* (1985) and *The Colour of Blood* (1987) privatize it. It is not, in them, a question of a consciousness that doubts its capacity to know the world; rather, it is a question of a consciousness that cannot know itself. The only recourse in these instances is to silence. It may be a dark fate but it's also a chaste one. On the other hand, those who are full of certainties are ready to make whatever noise is necessary to assert their claims. The loudest noises are made by weapons. A gunshot ends Moore's last novel, *The Colour of Blood,* and his new one, *Lies of Silence*.

There the resemblance ends. The lies of silence are told by just about everyone—the British Government, the Christian Churches, the general populace. For here we are in Northern Ireland, specifically in Belfast, and the story concerns a crisis of conscience in a man, Michael Dillon, who has to make two crucial decisions. One is to identify a member of the IRA to the police; the other is to tell his wife he is leaving her for another woman. The first decision has two phases; first he contacts the police to tell them that there is a bomb at the hotel he manages, even though he is thereby risking his wife's safety, since the IRA unit involved is holding her as hostage. Second, he has to decide to identify a young IRA man who had unwittingly let Dillon see his face during the takeover of the Dillon household. Despite the urgings of a slimy Catholic priest, Dillon decides to go ahead with the identification. But, even though he has by now got out of Belfast to London, the IRA have (through the priest) tracked him down, and kill him as he telephones the police in Northern Ireland. Phase two of his decision made, he is silenced.

The meaning of the connection between the two choices involved here escapes me. Moreover, since Moore takes the opportunity to launch a series of punctual tirades against all who have conspired to produce the Northern

Irish crisis, it seems improbable that any deep morality is involved in bearing witness against the IRA or against a corrupt system. The IRA men are the usual stereotypes—rough, tough, never nervous, plagued by acne and a poor education. Indeed everyone involved is stereotypical, except that the IRA is in Moore's firing line, and all his blank ammunition reverberates around them. The strain of his tendentious account of the political crisis shows in uncharacteristics slips—a university degree ceremony at 8.00 in the morning, an IRA unit going to the trouble of making a hit in London, given a legal system that has long dispensed with the need for evidence; a Catholic priest complicit with the IRA in a manner that is improbable in itself and inaccurate as a representation of the relationship between the two organizations. This is the first time I have read a Moore novel that was willing to risk improbability for the sake of making a propagandistic point. The lies of silence are in what this novel does not say about the

---

An excerpt from *The Color of Blood*

The Prime Minister leaned down and fondled the Dalmatian's neck. After a long moment, he looked up and said [to Cardinal Bem], "For once, I think—I want to think—that we are on the same side. Tell me who *you* believe is behind this. It might help my decision as to whether or not I should let you go."

"First of all, you have no right to detain me. Secondly, we will never be on the same side. Years ago you went to the Soviet Union as a prisoner, arrested after a student demonstration. Five years later you were a Soviet officer in a crack military school. You, whose ancestors fought for this country's independence. It sickens me to hear you talk of the national good. You know your regime is hated and feared by most of your countrymen."

"You don't understand patriotism as I do," the Prime Minister said. "Remember, no matter what you think of me, I am trying to hold this country together. And only I can do it. I am willing to accept that I am disliked."

"You are trying to hold this country together as a satellite of a foreign power. Therefore you are not a patriot, but an agent of that power."

"And Rome?" the Prime Minister said. "Isn't Rome a foreign power? Isn't your true allegiance to Rome and, ultimately, to the West?"

"I do not trust the West any more than you do. We both know that for the West this country is a pawn in a larger game. The West does not care about us and will not help us."

"Well, to Rome, then," the Prime Minister said, irritably.

"My orders do not come from Rome!"

Brian Moore, in his The Color of Blood, *E. P. Dutton, 1987.*

North. Otherwise it is a satisfactory summary of all the clichés. It may be a relief to Moore to have got it all off his chest, but he might have done better to write a letter to the editor of the *Daily Telegraph*—like that he would have been in the land of fiction without pretending that he was also in the land of art. Perhaps the next novel will be one of his miracles; then this one can be left in its own, sad silence.

Francine Prose (review date 2 September 1990)

SOURCE: "The Reluctant Terrorist," in *The New York Times Book Review,* September 2, 1990, pp. 1, 23.

[*Prose is an American novelist, short story writer, and educator. In the following excerpt, she commends the suspenseful plotting, austere prose, and "thematic weight" of* Lies of Silence.]

Nothing cheers a writer so little as well-intentioned commiseration for not having attained the vast readership admirers think one deserves. And yet there are certain authors whose gifts so exceed their renown that their situation inevitably inspires this sort of unhelpful puzzlement and indignation.

One such writer is Brian Moore, whose 16th novel, *Lies of Silence,* is characteristically first rate. The recipient of major awards in Canada and Britain, Mr. Moore has so far failed to achieve what the pollsters succinctly call "name recognition" in the United States, perhaps because his work ranges so widely, from intense novels of sensibility (*The Lonely Passion of Judith Hearne*) to suspenseful, ingeniously plotted thrillers with moral and metaphysical themes (*Cold Heaven, The Color of Blood*). Perhaps the problem is that Mr. Moore's nationality involves multiple hyphenation—born in Belfast, he has spent much of his life in Canada and now resides in Southern California. Or the problem may even lie with the estimable qualities that are found in his diverse books. This is not, after all, an era of fevered acclaim for the quietly controlled, the intelligent, the spiritually minded and unassuming.

Paradise for the reader, purgatory for the critic, the plot of *Lies of Silence* is one that only a spoiler would reveal—and risk ruining the surprises that detonate throughout the novel like cleverly hidden and elegantly designed incendiary devices. (The notion of "unbearable suspense" is, of course, a cliché, but I found that I kept briefly putting down the novel to postpone the moment when I had to face what might happen next.)

Set in contemporary Northern Ireland, *Lies of Silence* centers on Michael Dillon, the manager of a grand old Belfast hotel, an establishment to which families traditionally come for graduation luncheons and where, on a morning just after the novel begins, a well-known Protestant rabble-rouser is scheduled to address a convention of the Canadian Orange Order. In Dillon's Belfast version of a normal life, the "Troubles" and the presence of British soldiers are a daily fact; body checks and bomb threats have come to seem routine: "A queue of cars was waiting to be admitted to the hotel grounds. Security was tight, for the hotel had been bombed last year. The occupants of each car must get out and go into the adjoining hut for a body search, while the car itself was checked over by the outside guards."

Dillon is one of those Irishmen one recognizes fondly from the work of Sean O'Faolain, Frank O'Connor and William Trevor; we know, even upon first meeting them, that these men are not destined for great happiness, that even the small pleasures life offers them will sadly come to nothing. As the novel opens, Dillon is tormenting himself over the (one might think) straightforward choice between his shrill, unstable wife and his loving mistress, a young BBC reporter whose imminent transfer to London triggers the first of the personal crises that set the plot in motion.

Although to Dillon these difficulties seem singularly oppressive, they strike us as neither exceptional nor uncommon until, in the course of one frightening night, he unwillingly becomes involved in a violent I.R.A. terrorist plot. Suddenly his domestic difficulties are both heightened and dwarfed by an almost impossible moral dilemma that transforms his private life into the sensational stuff of the evening news. The effect on Dillon is seismic, and soon there are aftershocks—a succession of ethical temptations and decisions that sends him fleeing to London and changes forever his notions of heroism, of the possibility of escape.

Graham Greene has called Brian Moore his "favorite living novelist." Although the two writers are significantly different, Mr. Greene's remark does suggest the affection we often feel for those whose interests and virtues remind us warmly of our own. . . . Both write brilliantly about how various sorts of spiritual and historical struggles (crises of faith; political, moral, romantic crises) can overlap and complicate one another—and in the end turn out to be separate manifestations of a single human condition. Finally, both Graham Greene and Brian Moore write spare, swiftly plotted fiction that is capable of supporting considerable thematic weight.

So, too, *Lies of Silence* has immense tensile strength. One is struck by how austere its sentences are—and yet by how much the novel embraces, how much disturbance it generates without ever stooping to theatrics, how daringly it approaches and eludes the clutches of melodrama. It is possible to read this book purely for the pleasantly unsettling angst its dramatic plot induces. But it is more rewarding to pause and admire its flashes of depth and the nervy way in which Mr. Moore takes textbook-case ethical quandaries (the good of one versus the good of many, the right to a private life versus social responsibility) and uses the techniques of fiction to give them an agonizing, provocative spin. Certain scenes—Dillon's wife's conversation with a jumpy, teen-age I.R.A. volunteer and, later, his own confrontation with a manipulative Catholic priest—can be read as paradigms of how to create tension and surprise while remaining convincing and without contrivance.

Over his long career, Brian Moore has mastered the literary magic trick of making the weighty seem graceful, making the dense and complex seem effortless and unadorned. One hopes that *Lies of Silence* will inspire more readers

to discover Mr. Moore's earlier work, to experience the range and agility of this fine writer's sleight of hand.

Richard Eder   (review date 9 September 1990)

SOURCE: "Challenging the Acquiescence of Ulster," in *Los Angeles Times Book Review,* September 9, 1990, pp. 3, 10.

[*Eder is an American critic and journalist. In the following review, he praises Moore's suspenseful plotting in* Lies of Silence *but contends that some of his characters are underdeveloped and serve merely as political mouthpieces.*]

It is all there, perhaps too plainly there, in the title. Brian Moore has written an angry political novel that is also a novel of suspense. The suspense is intricately tangled in an impossible moral choice, faced by a Northern Irishman who struggles to resign from his country's conflict, and cannot.

Impossibility is the curse of the politics that has made Ulster's history a strangled gyre that grinds away, decade after decade, sinking but never sinking through. And it is the focus of Moore's anger.

Moore is a prolific novelist who has written on a variety of themes since he got out of his native Belfast, young, in 1948. Belfast—Catholic Belfast, specifically—is not out of him, though. *Lies of Silence* is his phrase for the mental and moral excusing and evading that allow the Irish Republican Army to operate out of the Catholic community, even though Catholics will deplore its violence, or at least, the seeming hopelessness of its violence.

Acquiescence in the face of evil is the charge Moore brings against the minority population of the North. He barely mentions the Protestant majority, and the British appear only in the form of a cool and barely glimpsed security official. The author's quarrel is with the sentimentality that allows his Catholics to wink at present atrocities in the name of past heroics. His target is Mother Machree. She'll kill you, the message goes; and in *Lies of Silence,* she does.

Michael Dillon is civilized and apolitical, the successful manager of a Belfast hotel that is owned by an American chain. He hopes for promotion to one of the chain's London hotels; he cannot wait to get out of the city he was born and reared in.

London means a decent life and escape. Escape, also, because he will leave Moira, his gloomy and sub-hysteric Belfast wife, and go live with uncomplicated Andrea, a researcher for the BBC. Escape, finally, out Europe's last medieval war, and into Europe of the Common Market and no-fault history.

Just as Michael is about to take off, his house is seized by an IRA gang. With Moira as their hostage, and under threat of death, Michael must drive a bomb-rigged car into his hotel parking lot—as manager, he will not be searched—where a time-device is to detonate and kill a lot of people, including an Ian Paisley-like Protestant extremist who is attending a lunch.

Lies of Silence is tightly, sometimes breathtakingly, constructed around the dilemmas that ensue. If Michael warns the police, he threatens Moira's life. If he does not, he risks the lives of dozens of others. (One of the ingenious half-turns on this dilemma is that he cannot be sure if there is a dilemma. The IRA itself may or may not have given a warning; his captors will not say.)

The painful but undoubtedly correct choice is to sacrifice one life—perhaps—instead of many—perhaps. Except that Moira's death would also be highly convenient. And Michael twists in the arid scruples of choice and conscience of a sort that Graham Greene wrote about more finely in *The Heart of the Matter* and *The Power and the Glory.*

It is Moore's skill to give a living answer to this moral puzzle. No normal human being, much less a scrupulous one, could abide doing nothing, however finely balanced the choices. The hotel is bombed; its guests are evacuated in time.

A moral dilemma, however, now turns political as well. Moira, too gruesomely whiny up to now to matter much, suddenly becomes real. She and Michael, Catholics but uninvolved, must make new choices. He will go to London, the longed-for escape now justified by police warnings that he is in danger.

Moira, on the other hand, refuses "to let them push me out." She will stay and denounce the IRA on television. In the book's most effective confrontation, she lets Michael know that if he was willing to see her die to stand up against the terror, she is willing to lose him to another woman to do the same thing.

Even in London, though, Michael is not free. He had recognized one of the gunmen; the police ask him to make the identification. A priest with IRA connections comes over, ostensibly to plead mercy for the son of a parishioner. "A lovely woman," he calls her. As for the youth: "You know what these lads are like, they're just kids." As if mercy were all that was at stake, and the duty of any Catholic, even a sophisticate, was to exercise it exclusively with other Catholics.

But the priest brings an unspoken message as well. The IRA will kill Michael if he talks. And he must decide finally whether he can escape the war and its choices.

In a number of ways, *Lies of Silence* succeeds remarkably. On the level of sheer suspense, for example. It is marvelously canny. And if there is contrivance in using this suspense, and the dilemmas that nourish it, to open up a larger political and moral dimension, it seems well justified.

Moore will be criticized for making his exclusive targets the IRA and the failure of most Catholics to confront the kind of choice that Moira and Michael are brought to. But he is not writing an overview of Northern Ireland; he has chosen, as is his right, to focus upon one aspect of its tragedy. If the chicken of majority oppression has laid the egg of minority violence—which, in turn, hatches a violent Protestant chicken, and so on—why, Moore has decided to tell an egg story. He tells it well.

On the other hand, he can be plodding in his prose. When

Michael and Andrea arrive in London and enjoy a few days of happiness, Moore writes: "They were here. Everything had changed. Everything."

He can also be crude in his characters, manipulating actions and discourse to make political points. The priest is oily and repulsive. Moore has cast a role instead of writing a character.

It is all too convenient when Michael, driving the bomb-rigged car after the night of terror in his hijacked home, passes the Catholic school where he was taught to hate Protestants. It was "run by priests whose narrow sectarian views perfectly propagated the divisive bitterness which led to the events of last night."

As the protagonist, Michael has moments of real substance when he truly embodies the dilemmas he is in. But he is given too much to do, to feel, to think; the agony that is the heart of the book is a busy agony, and the busy-ness weakens it.

John Banville   (review date 6 December 1990)

SOURCE: "In Violent Times," in *The New York Review of Books,* Vol. XXXVII, No. 19, December 6, 1990, pp. 22-5.

[*Banville is an acclaimed Irish novelist, short story writer, and critic whose works include* Long Lankin *(1970),* Mefisto *(1986), and* Ghosts *(1993). In the following review, Banville offers a negative appraisal of* Lies of Silence, *asserting that the novel's thinly developed characters "are made to mouth extended disquisitions on the Northern Ireland troubles."*]

Lies of Silence is, by my reckoning, Brian Moore's seventeenth novel. In the past he has produced some marvelous books—my own favorites are his first, the heartbreaking *The Lonely Passion of Judith Hearne,* and the very frightening *Cold Heaven* (1983)—and for this reason if for no other one would wish to find warm words for his latest. However, *Lies of Silence* (. . . on the short list for this year's Booker Prize) is thin stuff, an anecdote spun out to novel-length and peopled, if that is the word, not with characters but character sketches. I picked it up with some excitement and put it down with a heavy heart. The publisher describes it as "a culmination of an extraordinary literary career"; one trusts there will be higher points than this in Mr. Moore's writing life.

Brian Moore was born in Belfast, and in this novel he has returned to his native city. He still knows the place, or perhaps it is more accurate to say that he has learned to know it anew, for the Belfast of today is very different from the one in which he grew up, despite the persistence of the entrenched attitudes of the fanatics on both sides of the religious and political divides. The gunmen of the 1940s and 1950s were ruthless amateurs; their present-day descendants are ruthless and professional. Moore is an enemy of the IRA, seeing them for what they are: at best misguided, at worst sectarian murderers bent on destroying the two Irish states and setting up in their place a new, "pure," fascist Ireland. Yet for all the forthrightness of its denunciation of violence, *Lies of Silence* does not succeed in catching . . . the precise shade of murderousness that has broken out at intervals again and again in Ireland since the 1920s.

Michael Dillon is the manager of a large and successful hotel in Belfast. He is middle-aged, trapped in an unhappy marriage, and engaged in an affair with Andrea, a young Canadian woman who works for the BBC in Belfast. On the day on which the novel opens Andrea brings the news that she has been offered a transfer to London, and Dillon decides finally to break with his wife Moira, and move to "the mainland" and start a new life there with Andrea. He has lived in London before, and been happy there, and came back to Belfast only to please Moira. He cares nothing—or thinks he cares nothing—for the North and its immemorial hatreds.

Dillon is oddly anomalous. We are told that in his youth he had aspired to be a poet; since Brian Moore has pared his narrative to the bone, cutting out all but the most necessary information, one assumes this poetic streak is meant to be significant, but if so, the significance has failed to register with this reader, at least. Is it that the author feels that a girl as young and pretty as Andrea could not love a mere hotel manager unless there was a touch of the poet in him? Or that only a "cultured" person would be sensitive enough to perceive the subtleties of the moral dilemma into which the plot pitches Michael Dillon?

This dilemma is meant to be the crux of the book, but even here there is a curious slackness. Dillon returns home determined to break the news to Moira that he is going to leave her. He puts off the fearful moment, and in the middle of the night the house is invaded by a gang of IRA men intent on assassinating a bigoted Protestant clergymen. The IRA plan to place a bomb in Dillon's car, which in the morning he will drive to the hotel where the clergyman is due to speak. To ensure his cooperation, Moira will be held hostage at the house, and will be killed if Dillon alerts the police.

Dillon drives the car to the hotel, but then, unable to countenance the likely loss of many innocent lives, he telephones the police, and the building is cleared before the bomb goes off. Despite his fears, Moira has not been harmed—the gang, somewhat implausibly, left the house before the bomb was due to go off—but she is deeply wounded by Dillon's decision to save the lives of strangers and leave her to the mercy of the gunmen.

By now Brian Moore must be sick of hearing repeated his statement that his unconscious method in his novels is "to find the moment of crisis." Certainly the choice which Dillon has to face (or choices, one should say: there is a lot of plot packed into this short book) is a critical one. Somehow, though, we do not feel for him, or with him, as we should. There is an unfocused quality in the portrayal of this man; here and there, at the "moments of crisis," he fades before our eager gaze, grows attenuated to the point of transparency. This is the danger of using the thriller form, as Moore does; in order for the plot to progress at a satisfactorily cracking pace, character must give way before the demands of action. *Lies of Silence* is wonderfully exciting to read; the trouble is, for the most part it seems little more than that.

There are surprising lapses. The accents of working-class characters and of the terrorists are indicated by the dropping of final *g*s in feminine endings ("Mornin', Mr. Dillon"; "Get inside, you, or I'll fuckin' kill you," etc.). Certain events from early on in the book have no apparent consequences; for instance, on page 38 Dillon is punched in the stomach and kicked on the shin by one of the terrorists, but if these assaults leave a mark, none is mentioned, and Dillon is able to go through his day seemingly without feeling even a twinge from his innards or his bruised shinbone.

There is something amateurish too in the way that the characters are made to mouth extended disquisitions on the Northern Ireland troubles:

> "You're not fighting for anybody's freedom [Dillon's wife tells one of the terrorists]. Not mine, not the people of Northern Ireland's, not anybody's. The only thing you're doing is making people hate each other worse than ever. Maybe that's what you want, isn't it? [sic] Because if the Catholics here stopped hating the Prods, where would the IRA be?"

Perhaps, writing from Dublin, I am unfair to criticize Moore for providing these explanatory passages for the benefit of his international readership, but they jar. Worse, however, is the thinness of characterization. While the solidity of the portrait of Dillon waxes and wanes, figures such as Andrea are granted no more than a flickering existence, and seem mere ciphers put there to progress the plot. The exception is Moira; she is the best portrait in the book, a tough, vivid, sexy woman with a mind and a will of her own; it is a pity the novel was not built around her instead of her less convincing husband.

Brian Moore once worked with Hitchcock. *Lies of Silence* has that air of drab menace which the director brought to even the least of his films. The priest who comes to Dillon supposedly to plead for reasonableness in the matter of identifying one of the gunmen, but who in reality is carrying a death threat from the IRA, is spendidly horrible in a Hitchcockian way (and reminiscent, too, of the sinister priest who "helps" the heroine of *Cold Heaven*).

I wish I could like this novel. It is a courageous (no one should underestimate the vengefulness or the long reach of the IRA) attempt to give non-Irish readers a true picture of how things are now in Northern Ireland. However, right-mindedness has never been a guarantee of good or convincing fiction. *Lies of Silence* reads less like a novel than a film treatment.

Crystal Gromer   (review date 11 January 1991)

SOURCE: "A Land of Password," in *Commonweal*, Vol. CXVIII, No. 1, January 11, 1991, pp. 24-5.

[*In the following review, Gromer criticizes Moore's use of "stick figures, stock figures" in* Lies of Silence, *which she considers a "tautly told" yet insubstantial thriller.*]

"Whatever you say say nothing," the title of a poem in Seamus Heaney's 1975 volume *North,* could serve as apt epigraph for Brian Moore's new novel, *Lies of Silence,*

An excerpt from *Lies of Silence*

'What do you want?' He heard the fear in his voice.

'IRA. Where's your wife?'

'She's upstairs, asleep.'

As he spoke, there was a sound of footsteps in the kitchen. Two more masked intruders came through the kitchen into the hall. One of them was very tall and carried a walkie-talkie. Both were armed. They went into the darkened sitting-room, then came out again. The tall one shut off his walkie-talkie, which had been making a crackling sound.

'Go up and bring her down,' the one with the flashlight told Dillon, then turned and pointed to the smallest member of the group. 'Volunteer, you go with him.'

The small one kept his revolver pointed at Dillon's back as they went upstairs. When they reached the landing, Dillon said to him, 'Wait here, would you? I don't want to frighten her.'

Blue eyes white-circled by the holes of the balaclava studied him for a moment. 'Is there a phone in there?'

'Yes.'

'Then I have to come in with you.'

Dillon switched on the landing light which permitted him to see into the bedroom. She was still asleep. He went into the bedroom and, as he did, she sat up.

'Oh!' she called in a half-shriek as though wakened from a frightening dream.

At once he ran to the bed and caught hold of her. 'It's all right, Moira, it's all right. It's me.'

'Oh, Christ,' she said. 'What are you doing up at this hour?'

Suddenly, the bedroom light came on. Standing by the switch was the small masked intruder, pointing his revolver at them. 'Ohh!' Moira gasped, but Dillon held her, pressing her tightly to him.

'Shsh! It's all right.'

She stared over his shoulder at the masked man, and then, surprisingly, eased herself out of Dillon's embrace. 'Who's he? What's he doing here?' she said in an aggrieved voice.

'Get up,' said the masked man.

'What do you want from us?' she said. She did not sound afraid.

Brian Moore, in his Lies of Silence, *Bloomsbury, 1990.*

which takes him—perhaps as reluctantly as his main character—back to Belfast, his birthplace.

For the lies that Moore sees raging in Ulster, "lies told over the years to poor Protestant working people about the Catholics, lies to poor Catholic working people about the Protestants, lies from parliaments and pulpits, lies at rallies and funeral orations"—are not only sins of commission, but at their worst, they are lies of silence, the lies that come of saying nothing, and sins of omission as well. Most guilty are those in Westminister who turn a blind eye to Ulster and its injustices.

The Northern habit of survival rests in silence. "Smoke-signals are loud-mouthed compared with us," Heaney says, and fifteen years later, the characters in Moore's Belfast agree; when they dissent, their act of speech is rained upon by violence or by the threat of it. Perhaps only the Middle East, for many of the same causes—some even having the same agents, Lloyd George, Alfred Balfour, their double-sided negotiating in the first decades of this century, and timeless imperial greed among them—seems as hopeless of resolution as Northern Ireland. "Another martyr for the cause?" a mother, exasperated, questions her daughter in Moore's novel. Weary, she continues, "A united Ireland? Have some sense. The South of Ireland doesn't want us and couldn't take care of us if we were handed to them on a plate tomorrow. It's all madness, this, madness, and don't you be going and getting mixed up in it."

Whatever you say, say nothing: the mother's theme. Brian Moore's theme, however, is not only about the costs of saying nothing in that slippery grey Ulster Heaney calls a "land of password, handgrip, wink and nod," but also about the costs of getting mixed up in it all the same and finding oneself unable to say nothing. That is what happens to Michael Dillon. On the night he has come home ready to tell his wife that he is leaving her for another woman (just as he is leaving Belfast for London), on the night he has gathered together his courage and his passport, he encounters not visions of his new life, but four frighteningly young terrorists of the IRA. Hooded in woolen balaclavas, armed, they force Michael and Moira Dillon to get up from bed and wait for dawn in their living room, watched over by first one guard, then another. Their plan is to place a bomb in Michael's car, and then have him drive it to the hotel he manages, where an Ian Paisley figure named Dr. Pottinger is to address a breakfast audience. As the hotel manager, Dillon will pass through the security guard and park his car in his accustomed spot, just under the windows where Pottinger is to speak. So the assassination is to go, without warning. Moira remains behind in the living room, hostage to the plan's success.

On his drive through the streets of Belfast that morning, Michael Dillon observes details with the hypersensitivity of the newly condemned: three boys rushing and shouting on their way to school, the equestrian statue showing King William in victory at the Boyne, the Victorian houses around Queen's University, alight that day with the festivities of graduation. All these things are almost unbearably alive to him on a drive that seems interminable, packed as it is with the observations of a lifetime, packed as it is with a bomb. The hotel is an eternity and a second away. He parks his car. Overhead, he hears a tour group discussing the benefits of eating up a good breakfast, already paid for, since lunch is both unknown and uncovered. You'll be dead by lunchtime, Michael Dillon thinks in the isolation of his secret knowledge. Don't worry about the Ulster fry.

Dillon, however, decides to tip off the police; the dining room of the Clarence Hotel is damaged, but no one is injured. Neither is Moira, for the teenage terrorists had fled from her living room even before the bomb was due to go off. The daughter of a Catholic butcher on the Falls road, Moira understands lies of silence. She knows in an instant that her husband bartered her life for other lives, just as she knows, without his having said anything, that he will leave her for another woman.

"So, it's better you say nothing," Detective Inspector Harry Randall counsels the estranged couple. But Moira goes on a campaign. Within hours she's on television.

Why does she do this? Why does she break the taboo of the tribe? Is it for those reasons she announces histrionically at dinner when her mother admonishes her to have sense? "It's people like us who're the only ones who can stop them," Moira says, agreeing with her father's outburst against the IRA. "I should tell the whole world what happened to us last night. I should tell the way they treated us. . . . My husband had to choose between saving his wife's life or saving the life of the likes of Pottinger. We should stand our ground. And then, if we're shot, the whole world will know why we're being shot."

Or is it that Moira gets caught up in her own rightness, and that the injury she's suffered is more personal than political? Her speech comes, at least in part, in bitter retaliation to her husband's silence after the bombing, his betrayal of her during it. Or is it simply that she enjoys the fuss of being the celebrity of the moment, rushed into makeup and onto the air? "Did you see me on the news?" she asks Michael. "Am I all right? My face, I mean?" she asks the producer of the newscast. Moira is not one to forego the careful application of eyeliner, even if it is under the nervous eye of a young IRA gunman.

It's not Brian Moore's intention to show why Moira—or Michael or any of the other characters in *Lies of Silence*—do what they do. For though Moore has written wonderful novels that portray people of complexity and pathos, the characters in this novel are very little fleshed out, as though stick figures, stock figures, will do for the purpose he has at hand. That purpose is to make us turn pages, quickly, apprehensively; plot is the driving force of our fear. *Lies of Silence* is a thriller; it is a good thriller, tautly told, chilling. But it makes for disappointing reading nonetheless. It is too spare, too much itself a victim of Northern reticence. It feels shallow, as though with four films of previous novels behind him, Moore was writing it more with an eye to a film than to a reading audience. There is nothing here you couldn't learn in a two-hour movie. The genre of violence does violence to a complex, if contentious, history.

"Is there life before death?" Seamus Heaney quotes a graf-fiti slogan at the conclusion of his poem. There is not enough life in Brian Moore's new novel for us to care about the deaths which close it.

Hallvard Dahlie   (review date Spring 1992)

SOURCE: "Held Hostage," in *Canadian Literature*, No. 132, Spring, 1992, pp. 184-86.

[*In the following review, Dahlie praises the suspenseful plotting in* Lies of Silence *and commends Moore's insistence that individual moral choices produce social consequences.*]

[*Lies of Silence* is] a masterful novel of suspense, in which individuals' moral crises are convincingly tied in with the social, political, and religious conflicts that have beset Ulster, seemingly forever. Moore has exploited these issues in many of his earlier works, but in *Lies of Silence* the protagonists do not merely suffer or endure these bigotries: they are forcibly conscripted into the terrorist activities that these behavioural patterns make inevitable. By playing on the connotations of the title words, Moore shows how an ordinary individual gets caught up in this dilemma: "Dillon felt anger rise within him, anger at the lies which had made . . . [Belfast] sick with a terminal illness of bigotry and injustice, . . . lies from parliaments and pulpits, . . . and above all, the lies of silence from those in Westminster. . . . " When he has these thoughts, he has been transformed from a private, non-political person with a soluble moral crisis (to tell his wife that he is leaving her) into a public, political figure, held hostage by the IRA, with a moral crisis that in effect is insoluble (saving the lives of dozens of innocent individuals, or saving his wife).

In this ten-chapter novel, Dillon's immediate moral situation occupies only the first chapter, but there is sufficient foreshadowing here to give hints of the other nine-tenths of that world, like some gigantic invisible iceberg moving into place: "a police armoured car came towards him, lopsided, like a damaged cardboard carton"; "the left side of Teddy's head was matted with blood, the jaw crushed as though it had been hit by a car." And at the end of this chapter, the "traitor's kiss" that he gives Moira both spells out his own failure to act decisively when he had the chance, and foreshadows that his moral situation will become increasingly difficult to resolve.

That Dillon cannot tell Moira about leaving her for Andrea Baxter is only one of the "lies of silence" that he commits over the succeeding few days of this crisis. With or without Andrea, with or without the IRA, it is likely that his marriage to the bulimic Moira would not have lasted, for he knows that he had married her chiefly for her physical beauty. But the IRA crisis reveals how incompatible they are: she grows in strength and determination, and becomes very much her own person, a role that was denied her as Michael's wife. She speaks out on radio and television—no "lies of silence" from her—while Michael veers back and forth between silence and speaking. That she survives this ordeal may be Moore's way of suggesting that there *might* be a solution to the Irish problem. "It's people like us who're the only ones who can stop them." she argues to her parents and Michael. "And we're not going to stop them by letting them run our lives."

But that is as far as Moore goes. What he gives us in *Lies of Silence* is a disturbing depiction of how individuals and societies behave when held hostage by forces both uncontrollable and unpredictable. As in his earlier novels, the "moment of crisis" from which he works may seem uncomplicated, but the strength of Moore's fiction, including this superb novel, resides in the ways he reveals that this is inevitably a delusion, and that individual actions always have ever-widening moral implications.

Terry Eagleton   (review date 8 April 1993)

SOURCE: "Lapsing," in *The London Review of Books,* Vol. 15, No. 7, April 8, 1993, p. 15.

[*Eagleton is a prominent English critic, essayist, novelist, and playwright. Written from a Marxist perspective, his critical works include* Exiles and Emigrés: Studies in Modern Literature *(1970),* Walter Benjamin; or, Towards a Revolutionary Criticism *(1981), and* Literary Theory: An Introduction *(1983). In the following review, he contends that* No Other Life *presents a formulaic view of third-world political dynamics.*]

There are no ex-Catholics, only lapsed ones. A lapse, as the light little monosyllable suggests, is a mere temporary aberration, an ephemeral error which can always be retrieved; and even the more ominous sounding 'excommunication' can always be undone by a quick bout of repentance. Leaving the Catholic church is as difficult as resigning from the Mafia; for the Church in its wisdom has artfully anticipated such renegacy and created within its ranks the special category of 'lapsed', wedged somewhere between saints and clergy. Like every authoritarian institution, the church incorporates its own outside into itself, so that to lapse is to enjoy a privileged relationship with it, to be counted among an honourable company of ruined Jesuits, inverted metaphysicians, loose-living Dubliners and Latino leftists. Indeed if religious devotion survives anywhere in these secular times, it is in the negative theology of these Oedipal offspring of Mother Church, who hammer their fists on her bosom with all the passionate intensity of the true believer.

In any case, being a Catholic is as much a cultural as a religious affair: to abandon the church altogether would be like changing your accent or taste for curried eggs. The Catholic faith is not something to be brooded over in some access of Kierkegaardian angst; it is just something you are born into, like the Isle of Man or the aristocracy. A former Cardinal Archbishop of Westminster, who happened to our mutual embarrassment to be a relative of mine, once announced on television that he had never had a moment's doubt about his faith; but while some found this odiously complacent, we cognoscenti understood that his faith was just not the kind of thing you could have

doubts about—that his style of believing no more accommodated the notion of doubt than his style of walking.

Leaving Ireland is as difficult as deserting the church. For two groups of the Irish population—artists and the poor— the central question about Ireland was always how to get out of it. Exile and emigration are as much Irish pursuits as hurling and poteen-brewing, and living abroad as much a modality of Irishness as living on Aran. In the 19th century, more Irish lived outside the country than in it; leaving Ireland became part of what it meant to live there. If it hadn't been for the contributions of the New York police force or the Chicago building industry, whole villages in Kerry and Donegal would have sunk without trace. The Irish population was haemorrhaging like an open wound, forced out by the threat of starvation and the dreariness of colonial life; so that if the Irish are an international race, they have the British to thank for it. As for the writers, it was more spiritual than material poverty which drove them to Trieste or Toronto, in flight from clerical oppression, sectarian wrangling and dearth of usable cultural traditions. There is a wry irony in the recruitment of the Wildes, Joyces and Becketts to the English literary canon: having helped to reduce their country to a stagnant colonial enclave, the English then coolly appropriated those Irish artists who took to their heels to escape this dire condition.

Brian Moore took off from Northern Ireland to North America many years ago, but this, as with Joyce, was just a way of putting some daylight between himself and the place in order the more effectively to engage with it. All writing distances what it draws closer, displaces the object it re-creates. Writing is a way of possessing the world at long distance, but thus of fleshing it to more vivid presence; so it is a suitable sort of trade for the exile, who is able from this long perspective to grasp his or her homeland as a distinctive entity in a way more difficult for the natives. From his vantage-point in Canada or California, Moore has re-invented Ireland over and over again, and it is hard not to see his fiction as among other things a set of elaborate strategies for rationalising his reluctance to live there. *The Mangan Inheritance* takes the old cliché of the Irish-American sentimentally in search of his roots and submits it to savage parody: its hero returns to the land of his fathers only to discover a kind of Cork version of Cold Comfort Farm, a gruesome landscape of incest, failed poets and dipsomaniac dwarfs, a place where you are more likely to have your cock cut off than be gathered to the bosom of your long-lost cousins. The Catholicism of *Black Robe* is a creed thrust upon vital native Americans by fanatical Jesuit missionaries; this allows Moore to fantasise an Edenic time when religion never was, and to view the whole business as an alien imposition from above. But this can never be true in Belfast, where theology is at the root of what you are, and where the old joke that when religion starts interfering with your daily life it's time to give it up is likely to fall peculiarly flat. *Lies of Silence* is Moore's novel of the Northern Irish Troubles, and the remote perspective of the exile shows up in its artistic thinness, and its failure to dislodge a single stereotype. The IRA have acne and shout a lot, and the only way out of this tribal warfare is a one-way air ticket.

> Just as *Lies of Silence* failed to transform the outsider's stereotyped perceptions of Northern Ireland, so *No Other Life* is as depressingly schematic about the Third World.
>
> —*Terry Eagleton*

There is more to Moore, however, than the bemused middle-class liberal. He springs, after all, from a notoriously ill-used community, if from a fairly well-heeled bit of it, and his Greene-like affinity with the dispossessed has a Catholic, communitarian feel to it. (As far as his personal standing with the Almighty goes, he escapes the honorific category of 'lapsed' since he claims never to have believed in the first place, an astonishing spiritual achievement for the child of a Belfast Catholic family and something of a theological phenomenon all in itself). Moore has the sympathy of a small, inconsiderable nation for small, inconsiderable people, for the poignant Judith Hearnes and cruelly exploited Eileen Hughes's of this world; and in *No Other Life* the downtrodden, superstitious, politically wracked country of his childhood is magnified a hundredfold and imaginatively recreated as the desolate Caribbean island of Ganae. The narrator, the missionary priest Paul Michel, tells the tale of Jean-Paul Cantave, an outcast black urchin who enters holy orders, gains a PhD in Paris and returns to lead his destitute people against American capital, the spectacularly corrupt local elite and the alarmed reactionaries of the Vatican. Cantave is a charismatic if peculiarly inept revolutionary; his uncompromising political rhetoric (somewhat portentously rendered in blank verse) drives his followers to their deaths; but by the end of the novel he has disappeared Zapata-like into heroic legend, and displays rather more political promise as a corpse than he ever did alive.

Just as *Lies of Silence* failed to transform the outsider's stereotyped perceptions of Northern Ireland, so this novel is as depressingly schematic as the Third World political logic (dictator—liberator—liberator-turned-dictator) it seeks to chart. It is a remorselessly two-dimensional work, grippingly dramatic in its action but strikingly impoverished in its inner life. The blurb presents Cantave as some tantalising enigma, but that is the last thing he is: he is just a stock type of the priest turned guerrilla fighter, who adds little imaginative enrichment to that now familiar figure. The narrator is one of a long line of agonised Moore liberals, as attracted to Cantave as he is alarmed by him; and though some psychologically complex subtext is struggling to break out of this ambivalent cleric, it comes to as little as the casual loss of faith which has taken place at some elusive point in the narrative. Greene would have handled him incomparably better, just as Naipaul has in his time churned out a more impressive species of Cantave.

There is an excellent Moore novel in the tension between Michel and Cantave; but *No Other Life* is regrettably not

it. For Michel represents the Californian liberal pragmatist in his author, just as Cantave stands for the Catholic absolutist; and if Moore writes as finely as he does, it is partly because this tension is one he is productively unable to resolve. Like Michel, he is wary of political violence; but because he shares something of Cantave's solidarity with the poor, he knows that oppression runs deeper than the reformist can handle. Moore detests the IRA; but as a Northern Irish Catholic he has a feel for the history of injustice which gave birth to it, as many English liberals do not. It is just that, in this latest novel, this tragic impasse shrinks to the stalemate signalled by its fatalistic title. The title means both 'no life after death' and 'no possibility of change on earth'; but even Moore must agree that the latter proposition is a good deal more implausible than the former, and that it belongs to the religious false consciousness he opposes to believe that the second statement follows logically from the first.

Henry Louis Gates, Jr.   (review date 12 September 1993)

SOURCE: "The Sword and the Saviour," in *The New York Times Book Review,* September 12, 1993, pp. 1, 34.

[*Gates is an American critic and educator who has written extensively on African-American and third-world black literature. In the following highly positive review of* No Other Life, *he compares Moore's fictional Father Jeannot of Ganae to Father Jean-Bertrand Aristide of Haiti and asserts that, by using a white narrator to provide a retrospective account of Jeannot's career, Moore allows his novel to be read "as an allegory of the relationship of the first world to the third."*]

Political exile gives birth to its own mythology—tales of injustice and desire that the survivors tell one another to assuage their guilt, to keep faith with the past, to cast light into the shadows that define the state of exile itself. For the Haitian taxi drivers who queue each day at Harvard Square, one sentence repeats like the Kyrie, regardless of the time of day: "Papa is returning. . . . Papa is returning." Despite its ironic echoes of the elder Duvalier, "Papa" in Haitian Creole connotes the Father, the Messiah, Jesus. And Papa is how his followers refer to Jean-Bertrand Aristide, Haiti's first democratically elected President, a Roman Catholic priest who for the past two years has embodied a government in exile.

Father Aristide's dramatic ascension to the presidency in 1991, his uncompromising quest to end two centuries of misrule, corruption, neocolonialism and color-as-class prejudice within Haiti, and his expulsion by his own religious order, the Salesians, for exalting class struggle have caught the attention of those eager to see democracy sweep through the whole of the Caribbean and black Africa. Indeed, the mythologizing of the man's life and works has taken a multitude of forms: a flattering account of his life and thoughts in a book by Amy Wilentz (*The Rainy Season: Haiti Since Duvalier*), a collection of his sermons and writings (*In the Parish of the Poor*) and a compelling autobiography (*Aristide: An Autobiography*) have added to the haunting, telegenic image of a frail black priest, seemingly accountable solely to God.

Now, in *No Other Life,* Brian Moore has drawn on Father Aristide's curious drama to give us—just seven weeks before his scheduled return to power—the first fictionalized account of this messianic 40-year-old Catholic priest's rise and fall from power.

Mr. Moore knows exile from the inside. Born in Belfast in 1921, he emigrated to Canada in 1948 and now lives in Los Angeles. Despite having produced 18 novels praised by the critics and his peers (Graham Greene called him his favorite living novelist) he has remained a somewhat shadowy figure on the literary landscape. Although his last book, *Lies of Silence,* was a finalist for the Booker Prize in 1990, Mr. Moore has never enjoyed the readership his work deserves.

Like Greene, Mr. Moore excels, I believe, in describing internal exile—the conflict between religious faith and the exigencies of lived experience—and the crisis of belief that can result from that exile. In *No Other Life,* he combines his capacity to depict diverse cultures in convincing detail (displayed in the Native Americans in *Black Robe,* his novel about Jesuit missionaries in 17th-century Canada) with the interior turmoil of a Catholic priest (as he did in *Catholics*). The result is a brilliant meditation on spiritual indeterminacy, on the struggle between religious and temporal faith—on the question of how (or even whether) religious belief should be expressed in the political realm. For Mr. Moore, the political and the spiritual enfold each other like the sides of a Möbius strip.

Like Graham Greene, Mr. Moore excels in describing internal exile—the conflict between religious faith and the exigencies of lived experience.

—Henry Louis Gates, Jr.

The dangers of writing a novel about a Caribbean country that is and is not Haiti, and a beatific visionary who is and is not Father Aristide, are legion. What saves this book from the perils of hagiography is the presence of the black protagonist's white double, Father Paul Michel, a French Canadian missionary. Father Paul, the novel's narrator, is 65 years old when he looks back in time to tell us the story of his protégé, Jeannot, a 13-year-old orphan whom he lifted out of a life of rural poverty to be a scholarship student at his elite secondary school in the island's capital city.

The relationship between Jeannot and Father Paul suggests a further danger Mr. Moore has deftly avoided, that of writing yet another neocolonial travelogue in which a European rediscovers himself in the mirror of the other. In fact, it is the subtle interdependency between colonial and postcolonial, teacher and pupil, white and black—and

especially between the wavering agnosticism of the increasingly wary Father Paul and the single-minded belief of the man whose political career he has fostered—that makes *No Other Life* so much more than that oxymoron, the "contemporary historical novel." Mr. Moore's book can be read as an allegory of the relationship of the first world to the third and, ultimately, a study of the interpenetration of the spiritual and the political.

Recent history has made the plot all too familiar: Father Paul Michel, the last white principal of an elite prep school, the Collège St. Jean, on the destitute Caribbean island of Ganae, presents us with a memoir of his relationship to a revolutionary Catholic priest, Jean-Paul Cantave, whom the islanders come to know as their political savior, Jeannot. As a boy, Jeannot, a dark-skinned *noir* like the nation's president, is brilliant, quick and charismatic; when he grows to adulthood, he will inspire as much mistrust among the church hierarchy and the *mulâtre* ruling class as worship among the black peasantry. Jeannot is sent to France to complete his education, then returns to lead his life as a simple parish priest in the slum called La Rotonde. But his parish soon swells to include the entire nation as Ganae's dictator stages a massacre in Jeannot's ramshackle church.

Jeannot's rise from pamphleteer among his classmates to spontaneous leader of the island's dispossessed is seamlessly portrayed, and it is to Mr. Moore's credit as a storyteller that the rebel priest's reach for power—and his almost inevitable downfall—are drawn with great suspense. Jeannot battles with the military, with his enemies in the mulatto ruling class, with his superiors at the Vatican. But as Father Paul watches these struggles, he is unable to shake his fear that Jeannot's actions amount to hubristic despotism, that Jeannot's intransigence might lead to the murder of his innocent followers. This tension increases as the political crisis worsens, culminating in a magnificently rendered chase that ends with the two men alone together, fleeing through the countryside on a motorbike as Jeannot's recorded words are broadcast to the nation.

It is the transformation of Father Paul's religious faith into the temporal creed of his apt pupil that forms the parallel plot to that of Jeannot's political fortunes. Although Father Paul has helped in Jeannot's mission to the poor, he has stayed away from politics—until Jeannot runs for the presidency and Father Paul's association with him becomes, in the eyes of the church and the entrenched establishment of Ganae, a liability. Secretly summoned to consult at the Vatican after a hasty flight to Canada to pray for his dying mother, Father Paul returns to Ganae, and a meeting of Jeannot's followers, deeply unsure of his own true mission:

"What *was* my duty? Was it, as the Cardinal said, to save these people's immortal souls, or was it to help Jeannot relieve their mortal misery? And as I stood there . . . seeing the happiness in the faces of those who crowded around the tables to eat the simple food prepared for them, into my mind came that quiet but deadly sentence: *There is no other life.*"

Even in the secular world, however, Father Paul discovers that there is no surety: "The poor of Ganae believed in Jeannot as their Messiah, a Jesus come amongst them. The Kingdom of God is founded on faith. Faith is reason's opposite. Jeannot believed that God had chosen him. Now he would use that belief to change the lives of others. At that moment I was besieged by doubts. But I had faith in him. And so, I hoped to change things."

Like Father Aristide, who stood firm against the ruling class that remained in Haiti after the death of Papa Doc Duvalier and the departure of his son, Jeannot is forced into exile. But, unlike Father Aristide's, his exile is not to a foreign country. He simply vanishes, a move that makes him a deity to the followers he has left behind—but also deals a final blow to Father Paul's certainty of belief, in God and in man.

And what of the reader's belief? Mr. Moore's cunning tale makes palpable the profound ambivalence that lies at the root of our own modernity. And it suggests that our once-firm convictions about the consequences of religious doctrine and the efficacy of good deeds may be more captivating in death than in life: when Jeannot is no longer on the scene, the complexities and contradictions of the living man and his cause can be shrouded in pieties, held at a safe distance. This irony is suggested by Father Paul's description of the curious funeral of one of Jeannot's martyred followers, which he and Jeannot, fleeing from an Army-backed coup, stumble across in the countryside:

> The dead man was seated at a table dressed, as was the custom, in his best clothes, a clean white shirt, denim trousers, sandals. His old felt fedora was perched jauntily on his head. On the table was a funerary wreath fashioned from white frangipani and red immortelles. A dish of plantains, beans and rice had been set before him and an unlit cigarette drooped from his lips. He was a peasant in his 30's, scarecrow thin, as were most of the others in the room. And then I saw the bullet hole in his temple. The blood had been cleaned away.

In a manner reminiscent of Valentin Mudimbe's *Between Tides,* the story of an African priest who exchanges the dogma of the church for that of Marxism, *No Other Life* is a powerful rendering of our loss of faith in the gods we choose to live by, and a vivid evocation of the spiritual and physical struggle that takes place as a result of that loss. It is a tribute to Brian Moore's craft that he has explored this subtle theme within a stormy drama based on real-life political travails. The greatest achievement of his novel is to have located the metaphysical in the political without diminishing our horror at the brutality both of the evils we seek to combat and those that can be unleashed in response our best-intentioned actions.

William Weaver   (review date 19 September 1993)

SOURCE: "One Step Away From Fanaticism," in *Los Angeles Times Book Review,* September 19, 1993, pp. 3, 11.

[*Weaver is an American critic, translator, and travel writer who has written extensively on music and the theater. In the following review, he praises the economical style and engaging pace of* No Other Life.]

"Only one step separates fanaticism from barbarism." In his new and disturbing novel Brian Moore quotes this line of Diderot and later, to underline its importance, he repeats the quotation. In fact, the *pensée* does illuminate a large part of the story, but—as the story further reminds—there is also only one step between saintly devotion and destructive fanaticism; and *No Other Life* is concerned also with the ambiguities of the whole process. How does a bright boy on a backward island, rescued from the endemic grinding poverty, succeed in becoming first a brilliant priest, then a potent political leader, then a quasi-dictator and—finally—a legend? Through a first-person narrator—at times the varied narrative strands observer, at other times participant—Moore interweaves into a glowing fabric of changing colors. Public life alternates with the profoundly private, secular with religious past with present and black with white.

Moore gives his Caribbean island the name Ganae. Readers of Graham Greene's novel *The Comedians* or Ian Thomson's remarkable autobiographical travel book *Bonjour Blanc* will probably identify Moore's setting with Haiti, though the corrupt political life, the Papa-Doc figure, the Tonton Macoute, the disease and unemployment and hunger could belong to other Third World areas. As in Haiti, race is the fundament of Ganae's society: the narrator is white, an elderly French-Canadian priest; the young protagonist is black; the antagonists are largely mix-ancestry, light-skinned aristocrats, members of the powerful caste who run the country, control the army and the church (and in some cases, also traffic in drugs, accumulating immense fortunes.)

The real political struggle in Ganae—as in Haiti—has traditionally been between the Creole-speaking blacks, exploited, deliberately kept uneducated, underpaid, underfed, and the French-speaking mulattoes, who shop in Paris, send their sons in the College St. Jean, the one local institution where boys can learn something, and, from there, go on to the Sorbonne or Oxford or Princeton. At the opening of the book, Father Paul Michel is retiring as headmaster and leaving the island where he has spent most of his adult life. Before going away, he decides to write down the account of the central experience of his years in Ganae.

Not long after Father Michel's arrival there, in a characteristic political upset, a young black country dentist was elected president, encouraged by the army, who assumed he would become their puppet. Instead, he becomes their terror. In his public speeches, he promises advantages for the black populace but they are soon his victims as much as their mixed-race enemies. As a token gesture, however, the prestigious College St. Jean decides to admit a few more blacks, to indicate goodwill to the dictator, who has been fulminating against elitist education. The newcomer, Father Michel is soon sent out to round up a few promising black students. "The following day I rode on mule back over a road never traveled by motor vehicles, up to a mud-walled mountain shack on land denuded by 300 years of ignorant and relentless agriculture." There he meets a woman, as worn and wasted as the land around her; a widow, she is raising four of her own children as well as two orphaned nephews. It is one of these, Jean-Paul Cantave, "Jeannot," who takes over the book and Father Michel's life. His aunt "gave him into my care as casually as she would give away a puppy from a litter."

Father Michel's account is for the most part, unemotional, even laconic. Naturally, this tone only heightens the drama, as the Canadian priest attempts through all the conflicts and violence, to maintain his detachment and, at the same time, his loyalties.

The boy Jeannot quickly elects Father Michel his role-model and determines to become a priest. Michel's mild do-good attitude, however, quickly becomes an overpowering social commitment in the boy. And when after an absence abroad, Pere Cantave returns to Ganae and is assigned to a poor parish where he quickly and compellingly voices his indignation, the disinherited rally behind him not just because he is outspoken in their defense, but also because they believe he is a saint or, indeed, God. *Jeannot ce Messiah*—Jeannot is the Messiah—becomes a popular cry.

If this Messianic role disturbs Jeannot's old mentor, it creates genuine alarm in religious circles (the higher prelates of Ganae are all the dictator's appointees). The young priest is not defrocked, but he is removed from his parish—after thugs have burned the church—and forbidden to say Mass. For a dedicated priest, this is a terrible punishment, and the author sensitively conveys Jeannot's suffering. At the same time the youth continues his active fight against injustice and—on the death of the dictator—Jeannot is elected president, supported by the opposition parties. The wicked generals flee to Paris; the humble priest—and some of the less transparent advisers he has now attracted—are installed in the incongruous kitsch presidential mansion.

On short notice, Michel has to fly to Canada, to his mother's deathbed. For a moment, the reader might think this is digression, but in a surprising and delicate, deftly-drawn scene with the dying woman, questions are raised which color the rest of the story from Canada, and Michel is summoned to the Vatican, where the political implications of Jeannot's case are subtly debated. Here Moore shows a grasp of ecclesiastical policies as firm as his control of Caribbean plots and country-plots.

No Other Life is not a political novel, nor is it an abstract debate without power, corruption and sanctity. For much of its course it reads like a superior thriller. There are massive crowd scenes worthy of Greene himself, and there is a hair-raising chase sequence that allows Moore in a page, or even in a paragraph, to introduce and define minor characters, whose responses to Jeannot's request for help contribute to the moral debate while maintaining the taut suspense.

Moore is a fertile writer of wide-ranging interests; but no matter how varied in subject and setting, his books all reflect an enduring concern with questions of morality, responsibility, and, always, he knows how to create charac-

ters—priests and lay—in convincing situations of trial and achievement.

An excerpt from *No Other Life*

I am one of the last white priests on this island and the last foreign principal of the Collège St Jean. At the ceremonies on Tuesday night, this was not mentioned. But yesterday, alone in the sitting room of our residence, watching the videotape which they have made for me, I saw myself as they must now see me. The ceremony was held in the college auditorium. Priests, nuns, students and dignitaries, all were mulatto or black. On the wall behind the microphones and the podium there was a large photograph of our new Pope, himself a man of mixed blood. And then, walking towards the podium, a ghost from the past, this stooped white man in a frayed cassock, incongruous as the blackamoor attendant in a sixteenth-century painting of the French court. I am a reminder of a past they feel is best forgotten. They are happy to see me go.

And yet, on the videotape, they weep, they embrace me. Some profess love for me. One of my former students, now the Minister for Foreign Affairs, praised me in his address for my efforts to bring the benefits of higher education to scholarship students from city slums and rural backwaters. There was applause when he said it, but how many in his audience thought of Jeannot at that moment? Jeannot, the most important milestone of my life, is nowhere mentioned in this farewell ceremony. On the video screen, surrounded by smiling faces, I cut slices from a large cake. The videotape, like the gold watch of other days, attests that I lived and worked with these people for most of my adult life. It is a memento.

But what sort of memento? I am a member of the Albanesians, a Catholic teaching Order, founded in France. Unlike lay people who retire, I have no family, no children, or grandchildren, no link with normal life. My brother and my sister are strangers I have not seen for many years. When a religious retires it is as though he is struck down with a fatal illness. His earthly task is over. Now he must prepare himself for death. In another age it was a time of serenity, of waiting to be joined with God and those who have gone before. But, for me, death is a mystery, the answer to that question which has consumed my life.

Brian Moore, in his No Other Life, *Doubleday, 1993.*

William Trevor **(review date 21 October 1993)**

SOURCE: "Lives of the Saints," in *The New York Review of Books,* Vol. XL, No. 17, October 21, 1993, pp. 3, 6.

[*Trevor is an acclaimed Irish short story writer, novelist, dramatist, and memoirist. In the following review, he commends the subtly detailed evocation of time and place and the insightful characterizations in* No Other Life.]

The lives of the saints make fascinating reading. Saint Patrick, a slave on a lonely Irish mountainside, escaped from his bondage only to find himself overwhelmed by a sacred destiny that was as confining as any serfdom. Converting the people of the island where he had tended sheep, he gave his life to their spiritual well-being, made the locally ubiquitous shamrock the emblem of the Trinity, and rid the land of snakes.

Saint Ursula, child of tenth-century royalty in England, spurned the advances of a pagan king, wishing to remain a virgin, unwed and holy. Granted a generous period of grace, she took to the open sea with ten ladies-in-waiting who in turn were accompanied by a multitude of female servants and companions. For three years they sailed the seas in eleven vessels, until winds blew them up the Rhine to Cologne and on to Basel, where they disembarked, immediately making for Rome to pray at the tombs of the apostles. On the way back, unwilling to deny their Christian faith to godless captors, they were massacred.

Saint Joan left the plough to lead the armies of France. Scavenging dogs turned away from the corpse of Saint Bibiana, fearful of its sanctity. The Blessed Lucy endured a loss of blood through her stigmata every Wednesday and Friday for three years. The twin saints, Cosmas and Damian—moneyless doctors who took no fees for their services—defied death by water, fire, and crucifixion before they were beheaded.

So at least, in all these cases, it is said. There may be some other reason for the absence of snakes in Ireland, and for the fact that shamrock grows wild there while withering on the neighboring island. The voices that told Joan of Arc to save France may have been no more than the voices that today communicate with young schizophrenics. The martyrdom of Saint Ursula and her eleven thousand virgins is treated with reserve in the Roman liturgy. The dogs, when they nosed out poor Saint Bibiana, may have already scavenged their fill that day. Stigmata are not uncommon, nor is the defiance of death.

Yet these saints are venerated. They are real because people have made them so, their long vanished feature alive in the imaginations they nourish, their strength the faith of the faithful, the marvels of their lives an inspiration. And somewhere in the entanglements of exaggeration and myth there is a whispering insistence that human goodness is what matters most of all: however faint, it's a sound to honor with the benefit of the doubt.

Such goodness, though, is notoriously tricky territory for the fiction writer; trickier still to keep disbelief at bay when saintliness is possibly involved and the miraculous has a part to play. Yet novelists have to take chances and Brian Moore has always prospered by doing so. With the truth as its target, the obsession of the storyteller has repeatedly led him to difficult terrain: hot spots attract him. In his last novel, *Lies of Silence,* the hell-hole he explored was contemporary Northern Ireland, which could certainly do with another visit from Saint Patrick. The grimmest patch in Western Europe, with its gray, thudding helicopters and army check-points, its bloody Sundays and careless murderers, it is a place of lies: "lies told over the years to poor Protestant working people about the Catholics,

lies told to poor Catholic working people about the Protestants, lies from parliaments and pulpits, lies at rallies and funeral orations, and, above all, the lies of silence from those in Westminster who did not want to face the injustices of Ulster's status quo."

In Moore's first novel, *The Lonely Passion of Judith Hearne,* the hell-hole is his heroine's daily existence. It is riddled with the consoling lies that soften reality for the credulous, and the happy little lies that blossom so warmly after one drink too many. Lost among them, Miss Hearne is as trapped by the ordinary circumstances of her life as the people of Belfast are by the misfortunes of history. And no saint comes to the rescue here, either.

The hot spot of *No Other Life* is a Caribbean island, corrupt, poverty-stricken, its beach fronts fouled, its priests and its people exploited, the weak and humble easy prey for roving gangs of uniformed bullies. Moore's Ganae strongly resembles contemporary Haiti, and there are recognizable parallels between Haiti's recent history and some, at least, of the events that occur in this novel. The warm, bright sunshine of Ganae illuminates nothing; darkness rules, and "the night is never silent. In the slums . . . there are no cars or trucks and so the noises of night are medieval. Voices quarrel, shout, sing drunken songs. Dogs bark. Roosters, wakened untimely, crow in darkness. Footsteps sound loud in the narrow, filthy streets."

The population of Ganae is made up of *noirs,* mulattos, and a few whites, the mulattos being the elite class. Creole and French are spoken, and the local dictator is Doumergue, appearing to the outside world as a meek, well-intentioned black man who has promised to fight illiteracy and provide decent schools. At official audiences in the presidential place his grubby suit doesn't fit properly, his battered black Homburg is handed apologetically to a bemedaled military aide before he mounts the throne that is the presidential chair. He states himself to be "the living incarnation of the people's wish to better their lives." In fact, he is a thug who has no wish to see anyone's life bettered except his own. Armed with old-fashioned Lee-Enfield rifles, his *bleus*—similar thugs, who take their title from their blue seersucker overalls—rob and intimidate. The army does what it's told.

Brian Moore has written nothing as subtle, or as perfectly sustained as *No Other Life.*

—*William Trevor*

The eyes through which the many images of Ganae under this dictatorship are observed belong to Father Paul Michel, a white Canadian priest who tells the story from the vacuum of retirement, looking back over twenty years to what Brian Moore has elsewhere called "the moment of crisis," although in Ganae it is one of many moments, crises being endemic there. One of the last white priests on the island, the last principal of the Collège St. Jean, Father Michel will end his days in a retreat house in Cuba.

He is given, before he goes, instead of a gold watch, a videotape of his long Caribbean sojourn. One of his former students, now the minister for foreign affairs, "praised me in his address for my efforts to bring the benefits of higher education to scholarship students from city slums and rural backwaters." And it's natural, Father Michel reflects, mulling over his flickering video at some later time, that one student in particular doesn't feature in it: Jeannot is best forgotten, best obliterated by simply not being there.

He found him in Doumergue's time, in a mud shack at the end of a mule track, a thirteen-year-old orphan, small and delicate, in a dirty denim shirt, patched trousers, and wooden-soled clogs. His teacher said he was brilliant; the aunt who looked after him—"a woman with the flayed face and wasted body of those who live on the rim of starvation"—was glad to be rid of that extra mouth to feed. Given into the priest's care with relief, Jeannot becomes a boarder at the Collège St. Jean.

In time he, too, enters the priesthood, inspired in his vocation by the misery of life in the slums of the town, its "black, swollen heart." Here, there is more than the poverty he knew among the mule tracks: a stench of sewage, no running water, no electric light, twelve-year-old girls selling themselves on the sidewalks, cripples, deformed children, starving babies, women covered in sores, the blind, the dumb, beggars who have never been anything else and never will be. This is the parish Jeannot chooses. Here he begins his imitation of Christ.

In Father Michel he engenders a father's pride. "I have failed in most of the things that I set out to do," the elderly priest confesses, but when the memory returns to him of his protégé offering the Mass in his crowded church, some of that failure dissipates. An old, well-used image of the Church of the Incarnation—as ugly as a garage, with its grim dun-colored walls and rough stucco—lightens his melancholy. It isn't at all a place where "one would expect to be caught in the magic and mystery of the Mass. And yet as we knelt, looking up at Jeannot, frail and childlike in a surplice that seemed to have been made for someone twice his size, it was as though he led us into a world from which all other worlds were shut out. As he raised the communion chalice, and in that solemn moment changed bread and wine into the body and blood of Christ, we, who watched, were filled with the certainty that he, by the grace of God, performed a miracle at the altar. I, who have said Mass for forty years, . . . felt that, truly, God had come down among us."

And there's the memory, too, that when Jeannot preached it was with a voice so compelling that the congregation was transfixed:

> Brothers and sisters.
> Today I want to raise you up.
> The Church is not far away in
> Rome.
> The Church is not archbishops

> and popes.
> The Church is us—you and I—
> And we who are the Church have
> a duty to speak out . . .
> But I warn you
> If you speak out you will receive
> blows.
> St. Paul received blows because he
> told the truth.
> But he endured them.
> As you will endure them,
> As I will endure them . . .

The prediction is a sound one. In no time at all the blows are falling as relentlessly as the rain that seasonally mocks the plywood shelters and tin-roofed hovels. Shots disturb the Mass in the Church of the Incarnation; blood and death are there, where a moment ago there was peace, and hope. Then two of Doumergue's gangsters turn their attention to the figure at the altar.

> Suddenly, it was as though all of us were figures in a painting, frozen in a frame. Jeannot did not flinch. He stood facing the killers, his arms outstretched as if to embrace them. His face showed love, not fear. . . . Again the two assassins raised their rifles and fired. They were not more than thirty feet from their target, but the bullets went wide. The upraised arm of a statue to the right of Jeannot shattered and fell on the altar steps.

The finished priest, alone in old age with his memories and his videotape, might be memories and his videotape, might be forgiven if his recall mercifully becomes faulty here. A miracle has occurred. *"Mesiah!"* the crowd cries out. *"Mesiah, Mesiah!"* A saint is sanctified while everyone watches, while everyone is a witness. That surely should be the end: let the legends accumulate. In fact, it is only the beginning.

"I had long believed," Father Michel records, "that Jeannot was a saintly person, possibly a saint. If that were true, it was conceivable that God had saved him. . . . I had seen the assassins miss, firing at close range."

Whatever he is, however he is protected from on high, Jeannot is a nuisance now. All over the island it is already believed that he is a prophet, that God has sent him to save Ganae. His church is burnt to the ground by Doumergue's minions, he is censured by his archbishop for continuing to preach his provocative sermons, the papal nuncio orders him to abandon his parish. In his name, the people defy the dictatorship; he himself defies his Church. He believes, with the political priests of South America, that the true Church is the people's church. "God will avenge us!" is his dangerous rallying cry.

Two processes occur in the making of a novel, either simultaneously or consecutively, depending upon the novelist's idiosyncrasy and method. There is the creation of raw material—events and people gathered together in as higgledy-piggledy a muddle as they are in life—and the ordering of this accumulation, the trimming and shaping so that it takes the form of a story. In *No Other Life,* before the destruction of Jeannot's church, Moore concentrates on establishing an authenticity, a feeling of documentary or newspaper reportage. His backdrop is cunningly detailed so that it becomes believably snagged in the reader's imagination, and it is firmly in place before he permits his storyteller's curiosity to poke about in the world that is the backdrop's extension, before the search for truth begins in the make-up of fiction.

The action of this novel seems almost to write itself, but this impression is a deceptive one. Smoothly, quietly, everything is managed, and the puppet-master's strings aren't visible for an instant. Jeannot's sermons become speeches:

> One hot meal a week.
> Yes, that is what the people eat in
>   Cap Nord and Cap Sud . . .
> Work all day in the fields and
>   come home to eat plantains at
>   night.
> But here in Port Riche.
> What do the rich eat?
> The rich who hold power thanks
>   to the generals.
> What do they eat?
> Fine French food. Imported meats.
> What do they drink?
> Fine French wine. Champagne.

But you have power too, Jeannot reminds the people who are increasingly his. Act, he urges them; but before they can do so Ganae's dictator dies. Immediately there is an opportunity for the revolution to be a bloodless one. For the first time in the island's history there can be democratic elections; and even though the Pope has forbidden priests to run for political office, Jeannot is persuaded to offer himself as the next president. Overwhelmingly he is voted in.

It is then that the bit-part player, Father Michel, begins to shed his peripheral role. The fiery young president inaugurates his program of reform, but the teacher-priest who led him by the hand from his mountain desert, who awoke in him an awareness of the ugly status quo, has to answer now for the turmoil that freedom and justice trail in their wake. It is he who is summoned to Rome, to explain, if he can, the disobedience of his protégé.

Father Michel travels, as well, to Canada, where his mother is dying. She is an old woman who has prayed diligently all her life, who has unwaveringly believed in God and the Church, and in her own immortal soul. Now, sensing the odor of death, as the dying are said to, she believes that no heaven awaits her, that nothing does. "You . . . have wasted your life," she sorrowfully chides her son, "telling people something which isn't true."

Is this some cruel senility speaking, or has the odor of death brought the truth with it? Is the firebrand who now rules Ganae right to insist that politics make more sense than priests? Is he right, while personally helping to clean the streets of years of filth, to insist that the priestly life without politics, without action, is nothing? Trapped between the denials of two generations in two different places and in different circumstances, Father Michel feels lost. Are his mother's children and grandchildren the only continuation of her life? Is the man he loves as a son in-

spired by vengeance for the past as much as by hope for the future? Everywhere there are questions without answers.

Yet as he listens to Jeannot's radio speeches as once he listened to his sermons, he still wonders if this is how the voice of a hated agitator was once heard in a remote province of the Roman Empire. A rabble-rousing, fanatical president Jeannot may be, but no one could call him evil, as his predecessor was. He is foolish. He is politically naive. His boys are the new *bleus.* Suspicious of a parliament to which, as yet, they owe no gratitude, the president's followers demonstrate against it and would prefer the dictatorship of the leader they trust. "Justice time" is the expression used, and there is killing again in Ganae. Yet somehow, Father Michel believes, it may all come right.

Peering back from the shadows to that particular time, he sees that it never did. Things fell apart, again, in Ganae. The saint whose destiny he was certain about was an ersatz saint, flawed because he did not possess the gift of wisdom. When, in turn, Jeannot was deposed he was led back to obscurity by his childhood rescuer and the two passed through a village in which a wake was in progress. More vivid than anything on Father Michel's videotape, there is the remembered image of the dead man—another victim of politics—seated at a table in his best clothes, an unlit cigarette drooping from his lips, an old fedora jauntily on his head. There were drums and a *mandoline* that day, a wreath of frangipani and red immortelles. Grouped around the upright corpse, the mourners ceased their chanting dirge when they recognized the fleeing Jeannot. They touched his clothes, and wept, and smiled, and bowed in holy veneration.

The cry of joy— *"C'e Mesiah! C'e Mesiah!"* —heard then for the last time in Ganae, and absent of course from Father Michel's videotape—mocks him from his more truthful memory. As does the girl he once desired on a street somewhere, and the face of another girl, and the mulatto beauty he desired in middle age, and his mother dying. Such uneasy images and echoes are what kept him company, but at least they're better than the official lies of silence.

For the elderly priest pondering his life, there is no pattern, no gleam of illumination in his weariness, only confusion and bewilderment, and his own wild thought that, yes, perhaps his mother was right. In the midst of so much distortion, so much misreading of diving promise and intention, it seems more likely now that eternal life can only be begged for, and is not guaranteed. He can be sure only of the story he tells, of the saint that never was and the drama of an innocence that ignominiously failed, leaving behind even less meaning than there appeared to be originally.

No Other Life is a beguiling, marvelously readable account of a good priest's vocation. As all successful novels do, it reverberates and haunts, its intensity lingering long after the book has come to an end. Brian Moore has written nothing as subtle, or as perfectly sustained.

Jack Miles   **(essay date 13 November 1994)**

SOURCE: "The Epiphanies of Love and Loss," in *Los Angeles Times Book Review,* November 13, 1994, pp. A, G.

[*In the following essay, written to commemorate Moore's reception of the Robert Kirsch Award, Miles praises the psychological acuity and moral profundity of Moore's fiction, commending, in particular, his portrayal of women, priests, and artists.*]

The anonymous judge for the Robert Kirsch Award noted that among the many distinguished authors living in or writing about the American West, there is "only one inescapable candidate" for *The Times'* highest literary honor—Brian Moore.

Moore, a resident of Malibu since shortly after World War II, is certainly the most distinguished novelist living on the West Coast of the United States, although his reputation is international. In fact, the judge noted, Moore is "like the prophet without honor in his own country," celebrated with many literary prizes in England, Canada and his native Ireland, but never here.

From his first novel, *The Lonely Passion of Judith Hearne,* which developed the cult status among British students that *Catcher in the Rye* did in the United States, the judge observed that he has had a loyal and discerning following that reaches beyond the reputation of being "a novelist's novelist" by which he is also known.

Though none of his 18 novels is quite like any of the others, he writes for the most part in a traditional novelistic manner; the judge offered a comparison to author Graham Greene, whose work Moore admires and who in turn designated Moore as the contemporary novelist he most admired.

"Like Greene," the Kirsch judge commented, "Moore has written novels of the kind Greene called his 'entertainments'—serious thrillers which in Moore's case even more than in Greene's have a marked psychological and moral interest—though the bulk of his fiction, like Greene's, is concerned with the most profound and reverberating moral questions, such as the dilemmas of Catholic faith, of the uniquely isolated individual in a hostile society, of passionate but unrequited love.

"When I think of the problem of the serious writer in our time, who works in the shadow of mass catastrophes that threaten to overwhelm the imagination, I think of Moore and his ability to find a context and a scale for the individual life through which he can engage the great questions of politics, faith, and conscience, and I am grateful that he lives among us."

Moore's Judith Hearne is a literary triumph of a very rare sort, for she is the sort of woman in whom virtually no man—and no male writer—would take an interest. (Her failure with men is, in fact, one of the themes of the book.) The challenge of drawing a believable character of the opposite sex is one of the largest any novelist faces. Male novelists usually overcome it by creating a larger-than-life spectacle of a woman or, if the woman must be ordinary, moving her through a set of extraordinary events. In this

novel, Moore makes Judith compelling without resorting to either of those ploys.

In several of Moore's novels, including *I Am Mary Dunne, The Doctor's Wife* and *The Temptation of Ellen Hughes,* his fascination with the kind of woman who holds up half of heaven but rarely merits literary attention returns to the fore. Married or not, the Moore heroine is the little woman, small because she has never been allowed to grow; but he notices her with a kind of love, as an attentive teacher might notice a child sitting a bit too quietly in the corner. She interests him in the very plainness of her character. He draws her out and makes us interested in her without ever tricking her out in quirky characterological adornment. There is something, finally, quite dazzling about this feat.

Brian Moore is a Northern Irish ex-Catholic who has spoken gratefully of the upper-class Protestant family who opened to him the larger world of English literature and secular British culture. He eventually left the British Isles for, initially, Canada (he remains a Canadian citizen) and then the United States.

But rather than a migration from one country to the next, this movement has been a concentric enlargement with Belfast ever at its center. Quite literally, Moore divides his time among the several countries to which he owes some emotional allegiance, among which France—as for so many Irish intellectuals—must also be numbered. If he is not in flight, he may be said to be in a particular kind of exile, taking his place in the history of distinguished European writers who for personal or political reasons chose to live at this far western edge of the western world. Among the recognizable varieties of California writer, the European in exile is unquestionably one.

The late Graham Greene, an Englishman who was in spiritual and often enough physical exile from England for much of his life, had something in common with Moore, Greene fled from England toward (if not quite to) the Church, Moore from the Church toward (if not quite to) England. Each stalled a bit short of his destination, and in the no-man's-land between belief and unbelief and between the British Isles and Everywhere Else they have been fellow travelers. "Greeneland," as critics eventually called it, was the generic Third World outpost where the inadequacies—above all the spiritual inadequacies—of the First World could be seen stripped of the bright costume that concealed them back home. "Mooritania," as we might call it, overlaps with Greeneland, notably in Moore's most recent novel, *No Other Life,* which is set in a place very like Haiti. But Moore's Ireland, post-colonial and as seedy and corrupt as any tropical venue, offers in its way all that Haiti offers.

A priest in any of these settings is an interesting character, a failed or spoiled priest often the most interesting character of all. As something of a failed or spoiled priest myself, I am not above being a bit touchy about fictional versions of the type. But what troubles all us believers or near-believers or former believers or nostalgic unbelief-refusers about "blasphemous" fiction is never the blasphemy proper. There is, if anything, something off-putting about the writer who fancies he has shocked you when he hasn't come close. It is rather the pretension one trips over all too often that art or story—telling or, God help us, film-making is somehow ultimate and therefore sacred.

Neither Greene nor Moore ever wraps himself in those flowing robes, but of the two it is Moore who has always seemed to me to have the greater self-conscious control of the issue. Moore's *The Mangan Inheritance* is, for me, the ultimate ruination of the sacred untruth that the writer is not as other men.

Finally, a brief word on style. Partly because of his penchant for failed characters (success, he once told an interviewer, dilutes character, failure distills it) and for characters without rich resources of culture or education, Moore's style is sometimes quite plain. He writes, so to speak, close to his characters' impoverished bone. But once in a great while, he steps outside his always meticulously constructed narrative and allows himself a passage of rich, lyrical description. These passages are always few, they always leave the reader crying for more. Like Shakespeare's songs, they become an element in the suspense: never guaranteed but always possible and always a delight when provided. One looks back on them with pleasure and forward to them with hope.

Let that appreciative and expectant mood stand in lieu of any more searching characterization of the body of work for which, at 73, Brian Moore receives this award. The Kirsch Award judge called himself "grateful" that Moore lives among us. A good enough word, but the position that most of Moore's readers assume when they think about him is not, I suspect, the abashed and dutiful posture of the indebted but the cockier, slightly self-congratulatory pose of the lucky. For those fortunate enough to have found their way to him, Brian Moore is a wonderful piece of luck.

FURTHER READING

Bibliography

McIlroy, Brian. "A Brian Moore Bibliography: 1974-1987." *Irish University Review* 18, No 1 (Spring 1988): 106-33.

> Bibliography which includes Moore's novels first published after 1974, earlier novels reprinted after 1974, and scripts. McIlroy also lists secondary sources including interviews, whole books and chapters, dissertations, articles, and reviews.

Criticism

Banville, John. "Honest-to-God Alarms." *The Times Literary Supplement,* No. 4690 (19 February 1993): 22.

> Praises the sustained tension and "existential terror" that the critic finds in *No Other Life.*

Bradbury, Patricia. "Moore Shatters Illusion in the Search for Spiritual Survival." *Quill & Quire* 53, No. 8 (August 1987): 29.

> Favorable review of *The Color of Blood.* Bradbury ad-

mires both the novel's gripping plot and its emphasis upon "personal forgiveness and honesty."

Breslin, John R. "The Savage Mission." *Commonweal* CXII, No. 10 (17 May 1985): 313-14.

> Praises Moore's depiction in *Black Robe* of the ambiguities in both Native American and Jesuit culture.

Coren, Michael. "Brian Moore's Love among the Ruins of Belfast." *Quill & Quire* 56, No. 4 (April 1990): 28.

> Admires the structural complexity of *Lies of Silence* and Moore's astute analysis of the strife in Northern Ireland.

Cosgrove, Brian. "Brian Moore and the Price of Freedom in a Secular World." *Irish University Review* 18, No. 1 (Spring 1988): 59-73.

> Analyzes *The Lonely Passion of Judith Hearne* and *The Doctor's Wife* in terms of George Lukacs's theory that the novelistic form developed in response to the disappearance of God in an increasingly secular world. According to Cosgrove, both Judith Hearne and Sheila Redden exemplify Lukacs's claim that, in such a world, individuals must construct their own meaning.

Craig, Patricia. "Moore's Maladies: Belfast in the Mid-Twentieth Century." *Irish University Review* 18, No. 1 (Spring 1988): 12-23.

> Characterizes Moore as a "strong social critic" who analyzes some of the social, sexual, and intellectual problems that trouble Belfast in *The Lonely Passion of Judith Hearne, The Feast of Lupercal,* and *The Emperor of Ice Cream.*

Cronin, John. "The Resilient Realism of Brian Moore." *Irish University review* 18, No. 1 (Spring 1988): 24-36.

> Provides an overview of Moore's career, focusing on his shift away from the lonely and conflicted Irish exiles who figure prominently in his early novels to the "new, un-Irish fables which are proving impressively effective vehicles for his enduring speculations about the human condition."

Dahlie, Hallvard. "*Black Robe:* Moore's 'Conradian' Tale and the Quest for Self." *Irish University Review* 18, No. 1 (Spring 1988): 88-95.

> Identifies similarities between Marlow, Joseph Conrad's narrator in *Heart of Darkness* (1902), and Laforgue, Moore's protagonist in *Black Robe.*

Eder, Richard. Review of *Black Robe,* by Brian Moore. *The Los Angeles Times Book Review* (7 April 1985): 1.

> Asserts that while Moore's effort to represent seventeenth-century Native-American culture is often strained, his depiction of the Indians is more substantial and realistic than his portrayal of Father Laforgue.

Flanagan, Thomas. "Dangerous Amusements." *The Nation* (New York) 245, No. 10 (3 October 1987): 345-46.

> Examines the varied novelistic settings in which Moore has explored what Flanagan considers his central concern in *The Color of Blood,* "the fragility of the self." Flanagan also discusses a Canadian Broadcast Corporation documentary on Moore's career.

Foster, John Wilson. "Crisis and Ritual in Brian Moore's Belfast Novels." *Eire-Ireland* III, No. III (Autumn 1968): 66-74.

> Maintains that both Diarmuid Devine in *The Feast of Lupercal* and the title character in *The Lonely Passion*

of Judith Hearne confront "a primitive rather than a twentieth-century dilemma": how to live when rejected by a "compassionless community."

Frayne, John P. "Brian Moore's Wandering Irishman—The Not-So-Wild Colonial Boy." In *Modern Irish Literature: Essays in Honor of William York Tindall,* edited by Raymond J. Porter and James D. Brophy, pp. 215-34. New York: Twayne Publishers, 1972.

Overview of Moore's first seven novels. Frayne discusses Moore's depiction of the conflict between Irish and American values and argues that his belief in failure as a distiller of personality produces "static" and "self-defeating" characters.

Leahy, David. "History: Its Contradiction and Absence in Brian Moore's *The Revolution Script* and *Black Robe.*" *World Literature Written in English* 28, No. 2 (Autumn 1988): 308-17.

Challenges the claim, advanced by Moore and many of his critics, that Moore's realism is "ideologically innocent." Leahy argues that *The Revolution Script* and *Black Robe,* by ignoring contextual complexities and suppressing subversive voices, re-inscribe hegemonic values.

Long, J. V. "The Cardinal's Virtues." *Commonweal* CXIV, No. 19 (6 November 1987): 634-36.

Lauds Moore's characterization of Cardinal Bem, the central character in *The Color of Blood,* as a spiritual innocent who nonetheless demonstrates the "shrewd practice of virtue" during a complex political crisis.

McIlroy, Brian. "Displacement in the Fiction of Brian Moore." *English Studies in Canada* XV, No. 2 (June 1989): 214-34.

Uses psychoanalytic and postcolonial theory to assert that Moore's Irish characters play language games reflecting their status as colonized subjects and participation in "the mediation of repression in Moore's fiction."

McSweeney, Kerry. "Brian Moore's Grammars of the Emotions." In his *Four Contemporary Novelists: Angus Wilson, Brian Moore, John Fowles, V. S. Naipaul,* pp. 56-99. Quebec: McGill-Queen's University Press, 1983.

Asserts that the settings in Moore's fiction reflect his own circumstances and divides the novels into categories: those set in Belfast, those set in Europe and Canada, and those set in the United States. McSweeney also notes similarities between the novelist and English poet Philip Larkin.

O'Connell, Shaun. "Brian Moore's Ireland: A World Well

Lost." *The Massachusetts Review* XXIX, No. 3 (Fall 1988): 539-55.

Examines the ways in which Moore's early novels represent Ireland as repressive and limiting. O'Connell further proposes that the Irish émigrés depicted in later novels often prove unable to progress beyond the paralysis that characterized their lives in Ireland.

O'Donoghue, Jo. *Brian Moore: A Critical Study.* Dublin: Gill and MacMillan, 1990, 266 p.

Analyzes Moore's fiction according to geographic and thematic categories, for example: novels set in Belfast, "novels of exile and escape," novels that explore the consequences of rejecting God, and novels that explore "politics as morality."

Ricks, Christopher. "The Simple Excellence of Brian Moore." *The New Statesman* 71 (18 February 1966): 227-28.

Commends Moore's early fiction, asserting that his focus on ordinary emotional experiences renders the novels widely accessible.

Roberts, Paul. "*Black Robe:* A Terrible and Touching Beauty." *Quill & Quire* 51, No. 6 (June 1985): 38.

Praises the verisimilitude and objectivity of *Black Robe.*

Shepherd, Allen. "The Perfect Role of the Outsider: Brian Moore's *No Other Life.*" *New England Review* 16, No. 3 (Summer 1994): 164-67.

Praises Moore's "creation of a multiplicity of perspectives on Jeannot," the main character in *No Other Life,* and asserts that the novel succeeds more because it is absorbing than because it is topical.

Sigal, Clancy. "Cardinal Bem on the Run." *The New York Times Book Review* (27 September 1987): 11.

Favorable review of *The Color of Blood,* which Sigal admires because, within an absorbing thriller format, Moore explores the complexities of the relationship between church and state in Eastern Europe.

Turbide, Diane. "Bombs and Betrayal." *Maclean's* 103, No. 25 (18 June 1990): 66.

Praises *Lies of Silence* for fusing detailed characterization with suspenseful plotting.

Interview

Sale, Richard B. "An Interview in London with Brian Moore." *Studies in the Novel* 1, No. 1 (Spring 1969): 67-80.

Relates Moore's observations regarding his childhood, the authors who influenced him, and various techniques he has employed in his fiction.

Carol Muske

1945-

(Full name Carol Anne Muske; also publishes under married name Carol Muske-Dukes) American poet and novelist.

The following entry presents an overview of Muske's career through 1994.

INTRODUCTION

Muske's work is praised for its insights into daily life and close familial relationships. Generally writing from a feminist perspective, Muske is noted for her carefully constructed sentences, unique metaphors, and the use of autobiographical elements in her work. Holly Prado has written that Muske's "contemplation of experience is personal yet moves further, into the spiritual and philosophical."

Biographical Information

Born in St. Paul, Minnesota, Muske began writing poetry when she was six years old. After earning her undergraduate degree at Creighton College in 1967, she received an M. A. in English and creative writing from San Francisco State College in 1970. Muske then continued her education at the University of Paris where she studied French literature; during this time she joined a travelling production of the musical *Hair* (1967) and toured throughout Europe and Russia. When she returned to the United States the following year, Muske settled in New York City where she attended poetry writing workshops, taught creative writing to inmates in New York prisons, and became an assistant editor at the literary journal *Antaeus.* Her first book of poetry, *Camouflage,* was published in 1975. The recipient of several prestigious awards and grants, Muske has also lectured and taught English at numerous universities throughout the United States.

Major Works

The obliquely autobiographical verse of *Camouflage* reflects Muske's attention to word choice and unique turns of phrase. The poems in this volume deal primarily with the ways in which the speaker's "outer self" is shaped by the perceived need to conceal her tumultuous inner emotional life. Muske's second collection, *Skylight* (1981), examines ambivalent feelings in intimate relationships, using her own life—particularly her divorce from her first husband—as the source for poems that chart the love-hate nature of a marriage that ultimately dissolves. Portraying the significance of Muske's mother and grandmother, the poems in the first section of *Wyndmere* (1985) focus on the various bonds that united the three generations of women. In the book's later poems, Muske addresses such present-day concerns as her new marriage, the creative process, and the birth of her daughter. Although Muske uses

slightly more abstract language in *Applause* (1989), the volume continues the examination of what are considered her signature themes: her past; the inner significance of her interpersonal relationships; and the need to appreciate beauty in a world beset by pain and suffering, which in many of the poems in this volume is represented by death from AIDS. Muske's first novel, *Dear Digby* (1989), tells the comic and poignant story of Willis Jane Digby, the Letters editor of a feminist magazine, who comes to identify with two of her more eccentric, perhaps "crazy," correspondents. The novel asserts that distinctions between "crazy" and "sane" are ultimately untenable and that everyone is more or less "insane." In the poetry collection *Red Trousseau* (1993), Muske uses witches and the Salem witch hunts of the 15th century as metaphorical devices with which she discusses the emotional vicissitudes of intimate relationships, attitudes toward abortion, and political protest. The poems both represent and examine the ways in which personal and political issues are inextricably bound. Muske's second novel, *Saving St. Germ* (1993), deals comically with serious themes. The story concerns a biochemist whose comfortable life in her laboratory and in the abstract realm of advanced scientific theory is disrupted by the dissolution of her marriage and the ensuing court battle for custody of her daughter. Muske's main theme in this work is the difficulty of integrating mind and body, intellect and emotions, interior life and the "real" world.

Critical Reception

Muske's works have received generally favorable critical assessments. Most critics consider her mastery of form and her ability to convey both passion and self-analysis as among her strengths as a poet. Her early works, notably *Camouflage,* displayed her formal talent and earnestness, but not yet the integration of form with subject matter. *Choice* magazine suggested that her first volume showed "a wealth of promise, but . . . one looks forward to the next collection." Her later poetry builds on these strengths and adds a more sophisticated political dimension, examining the ways public reality and private inner life intersect and influence one another. Wayne Koestenbaum, in his highly favorable review of *Applause,* argued that the only fault he could find in her mature work is her "reliance on a vocabulary that gives too little tonal pleasure and on a stumbling, start-and-stop tempo. Some might call it concision; to me, it seems a refusal to leap. . . . I long to hear a phrase tumble beyond its limit." Reception of her novels has likewise been very positive, with reviewers praising her prose style but faulting some of her structural decisions. For example, while most commentators praise *Dear Digby* for its comic touches and its poignant depictions of quietly desperate lives, some critics have detected a certain ambivalence in the combination of approaches. Linsey Abrams asserted that "one wishes she had decided to write either a flat-out comic novel . . . or [a] more serious, psychologically acute story." Similarly, Tom De Haven has suggested that *Saving St. Germ* is an excellent novel marred only by a pat happy ending. He has argued that the novel's resolution is "an artistic false move by the otherwise rigorously unsentimental Ms. Muske Dukes."

PRINCIPAL WORKS

Camouflage (poetry) 1975
Skylight (poetry) 1981
Wyndmere (poetry) 1985
Applause (poetry) 1989
*Dear Digby (novel) 1989
Red Trousseau (poetry) 1993
*Saving St. Germ (novel) 1993

*These works were published under the name Carol Muske-Dukes.

CRITICISM

Choice (review date January 1976)

SOURCE: A review of *Camouflage,* in *Choice,* Vol. 12, No. 11, January, 1976, p. 1447.

[*In the following review, the critic points to the strengths and weaknesses of* Camouflage.]

First collections of poetry are always fascinating. Generally, there is a measure of promise as well as all the faults that occur when a complex art is newly explored by a novice. This is particularly true of Muske's collection [*Camouflage*]. Her prime gift at this stage is a strong feeling for vocabulary and an instinct for strong phrasing. What she must continue to develop is the concept of structure and the fusion of idea and form. Two of the works in the "Ice" sequence, **"Freezing to death"** and **"A yoga class,"** demonstrate what she can do when her poetic elements come together in harmony. There is also a feel for characterization, particularly in **"Swangsong"** (perhaps the best work in this collection). The title poem may be a stanza short of fully working out a significant concept. The long sequence, "Salad days: Nebraska, 1964," busily entangles autobiographical swatches and adjectival phrases to the reader's severe disadvantage. At this point, Muske has a wealth of promise, but then so do a host of other currently published poets; one looks forward to the next collection.

Sherod Santos (review date Spring 1982)

SOURCE: A review of *Skylight,* in *Western Humanities Review,* Vol. XXXVI, No. 1, Spring, 1982, pp. 54-8.

[*Santos is an American poet and educator. In the following excerpt, he praises* Skylight *for its focus on love relationships between men and women.*]

The two major concerns of [*Skylight*]—the revelation (both personal and didactic) of a feminist argument, and the painful exegesis of the love relationship between men and women—account for much of its anger and frustration, and for almost all of its best poems. It is a strong will that wrote much of this book, but it is also a poet who is not less interested in those moments when the will has been subsumed by what she calls, in one of her more moving poems, "the familiar carnage of love."

There are several poems which do not touch on either of those concerns, but they tend to be much less important by comparison. There is one cluster near the middle of the book—containing titles like **"Real Estate," "Golden Retriever"** and **"Women's House"**—which is, at best, only a humorous and witty digression from what is this book's really more serious intent. Lines such as "slide // with each slide of the old trombone, / be good to the bald, press up against / the ugly duck-like"—and these from a poem about life inside a women's prison, "Juanita talks / like a lady to a lady prisoner / who cut her baby up. Night struts in with night: / in a sequined dress, in tits, in the body of a man // a woman"—these lines tend to feel out of place when set against the fervor and compulsion of this book's strongest poems.

Much of the authority of *Skylight* derives from its systematic use of assertion and confrontation. One of its recurrent arguments is that the history of western civilization has been one-sided—there is, in the poet's terminology, his story and her story, and the former, the canonized version, only tells half (his half) of the truth, while the second, the as-yet-unwritten version, is still enmeshed "in a language we have yet to translate." Attaching her idea, in **"Short Histories of the Sea,"** to what is, perhaps, the most appropriate metaphor, Muske locates the geographic (that is, psychological) nature of that schism: "What was beneath / had nothing to do with history // as they invented it: / sailor / warrior / king. // . . . *in the sea / she is historian.*" The poem then proceeds to explicate its thesis:

> Above, we've never learned very well
> what makes us famous—
> the past turning up
> in the genes
> spontaneously
>
> with nothing to say
> about loving ourselves
> as fish
> or feminine gesture
>
> and no mention
> of this other history writing itself
> in the body's tides
> in spite of us.

The structure of *Skylight* is geared for a descent into that submarine world, into the world of memory ("they're the same, / memory and worry") and the world of speculation ("Just this moment. Two women. The future of the world"). There are repeated images of a struggle with speech, with that untranslated language, and there are numerous poems designed to enact that previously forbidden gesture of "loving ourselves": there is a moving tribute to the poet's mother (**"Coral Sea, 1945"**), to a Catholic nun who was her teacher in grade school (**"Worry"**), to a close woman friend on some unspecified "political" mission in Cyprus, and to Delmira Augustini, the turn-of-the-century Uruguayan poet who was murdered by her husband. All of these poems are demonstrations, in the Wordsworthian sense, of the ways in which the basic dogmatic assertions within the text are, in fact, an indistinguishable part of the poet's autobiography, indistinguishable, that is, until the poet wrests them from experience for the sake of her, and our, instruction.

But the poems I keep coming back to in this collection are of that second concern, those dealing with the love relationship between men and women. One critic recently called this book "asexual," a comment which seems to me now rather petulant, since behind almost every poem collected here (and I can find only two exceptions) there looms the explicit, and usually threatening, presence of a physical sexual identity. As the poet herself remarks in a poem about the childhood discovery of that identity, there is "Nowhere to hide the body!" It is a presence she even recognizes as powerful enough to threaten the very structure of her political ideas, dissolving rhetoric before the "brilliant manifesto of your hair." Still, the psychic terrain of these poems is much more complicated than just that,

and one of the reasons I find these the strongest poems is because they are less decided, the lines of distinction are more ambiguously drawn. It is also because the poet is now implicated in "the crime," as she calls it, and what that gives rise to is a poem of greater urgency, surprise and self-discovery: the poet is no longer standing off in the wings always certain of the poem's outcome.

In **"Fireflies,"** a central poem addressed to the poet's ex-husband, Muske looks back on a major instance of failed love, to that moment when the couple begins to recognize the futility of their attempt to restore the relationship. The poem (a Shakespearean sonnet, rare in the repertoire of young poets these days) is masterful in its restraint, in its refusal to fall back on personal blame or guilt, in its exquisite surrender to the rather ominous destiny which now surrounds them both:

> **"Fireflies"**
>
> We walked together up that country road.
> It was dark. Vermont. Another season.
> Then, looking up, we saw the sky explode
> with fireflies. Thousands, in one frisson
> of cold light, scattered in the trees, ablink
> in odd synchrony. That urgency,
> that lightening pulse, would make us stop, think
> of our own lives. The emergency
>
> that brought us here. The city, separation
> and the pain between us. Your hands that heal
> can't make us whole again; this nation
> of lovestruck bugs can't change that. Still, we feel
> the world briefly luminous, the old spark
> of nature's love. Around us now, the dark.

A less skillful or more sentimental poet would have found some way of ending this poem on the penultimate sentence, but Muske seems to harbor few illusions about love or romantic idealism—she is too smart, and experienced, to believe that the spark at the end of the poem (is it nostalgia? or romance?) is anything more enduring than the fireflies' blink.

More often than not Muske finds love played out on a kind of battlefield where the dialectic can be tested through the senses. The following lines are from an allegorical poem called **"War Crimes,"** a poem in which the poet intentionally confuses the torturer and lover as each performs his private ritual on the peculiarly passive (though still responsive) body of the woman, until:

>   the great nerve
> which runs from head to pelvis
> which makes us courteous
> shy
> scrupulous
> makes us touch one another with gentleness
>
> would tremble
> till it was plucked
> held in the pliers
> then in the fire
>
> shrivelling in that little violence
> of heat and light
>
> which in another form

we often refer to
as love.

But unlike **"Fireflies," "War Crimes"** is finally unconvincing, not only because the central conceit is slightly facile and the last strophe pre-emptive, but also because the
"victim" seems such a mindless, if unwitting, accomplice—she seems somehow reduced to that "great nerve
/ which runs from head to pelvis."

But it is not to be in such a bleak allegorical landscape, nor
in the domesticated landscape of Vermont, that Muske is
to realize the most important insights into her theme—
rather, it is in the much less clearly defined world of India,
in that world where the dead float on the surface of the
Ganges, where Untouchables linger outside hotels in
which tourists "rise in glass elevators," where gardens are
"built / by one lover for another in shapes / of perfect neurosis." It is in that world of contiguous antinomies that the
poet finds the perfect setting (and now the perfect metaphor) for her own circumspect meditations: "The moon's
on trial in its own courtroom." This is Diana she is referring to, we can be sure, and the verdict is, we find out, unequivocal, "guilty, guilty again." But just as she discovers
in India that it is love itself that is culpable, so, too, she
discovers there the possibility for a pure and selfless act
of love. And it is a sign of Muske's bitter sense of irony
that she only allows that discovery within such a tragic
scenario, in the gesture of an old man in Benares lifting
the body of his dead wife onto a ghat to be burned:

> In my time on earth
> I have seen few acts of true chivalry
> or reverence
> of man for woman.
>
> But the memory of him
> with her
> in the cradle of his arms
> placing her just so in the fire
> so she would burn faster
> so the kindling of the stretcher
> would catch—
> is enough for me now,
> will suffice
> for what remains on this earth
> a gesture of bereavement
> in the familiar carnage of love.

It may be that certain of the poems in *Skylight* overreach
themselves, but that is, it would seem, the price any poet
must pay who writes with a heart and mind as heavy with
truth as Muske's best poems seem to show. And perhaps
because of her vulnerability to an explicit notion of truth,
Skylight is a book which is ultimately tortured by its own
ideas: almost every assertion that it attempts is confronted
in a later poem by some contradiction within the poet's
own experience, so that the whole edifice of belief and conviction is contravened by an inner life at once passionate
and vertiginous. And yet, in some wonderful, almost heroic way, Muske manages to hold onto both those worlds,
and to assert the integrity and validity and autonomy of
each.

Jean Gould   (essay date 1984)

SOURCE: "Carol Muske," in *Modern American Women
Poets,* Dodd, Mead & Company, 1984, pp. 320-29.

[*Gould was an American biographer and author of children's literature. In the following essay, she discusses the
ways in which Muske's life is reflected in her work.*]

Like Freya Manfred, Carol Muske comes from Minnesota, where she was born on December 17, 1945, in St. Paul;
and she, too, is of Czech origin on her mother's side, and
partially Germanic-Scandinavian on her father's. However, the similarity between the backgrounds of these two
poets has no bearing on their respective work. Indeed,
considering the fact that both their maternal and paternal
ancestries are so much alike, the contrast in the poetry of
Manfred and Muske is amazing, and points up the individuality of each poet.

Carol Muske, according to her first volume, *Camouflage,*
claims to regard her poetry "as a kind of protective coloration," and it is true that the reader catches only brief
glimpses of her personal life, often obliquely, as in the title
poem: not until the last stanza does the poet reveal herself,
troubled, transforming her outer self into "a new species"
to conceal the suffering of her inner being. There is a sense
of power, of passion held in check by strong emotional
control, by restraint in revealing all, which in turn lends
an aura of mystery to her poems, luring the reader to return a second and third time to discover the full meaning.
As a result, one experiences a feeling of suspense and
drama in her lines such as is never found in the outpour-
ings of so-called "confessional" poetry.

For example, a poem entitled, **"Coral Sea, 1945,"** concerns the advent of her emergence from her mother's
womb, designated, "For my mother," and told in terms
of the circumstances just prior to her actual birth a week
later. After descriptive passages of her mother's walk to
the beach during the final stage of pregnancy; of the tropical waters whose reef holds "a small fleet awaiting the end
of the world"; and an imaginative passage of strange sights
and events occurring in the Coral Sea, the poet draws a
parallel between these unbelievable scenes and the equally
unbelievable image of herself in the final stage of gestation,
her body burning inside her mother's, "in the coral sea /
near the reef of her lungs." The poem concludes: "In the
year the war ended / the world opened, / ending for me
/ with each slow tremor / cold / invisible as snow / falling
/ inside the volcano." The last line is a reference to one
of the unbelievable things cited in the above-mentioned
passage, and is a striking evocation of the strange, stressful, mysterious, and awesome phenomenon of birth.

In her childhood, small Carol attended a primary parochial school of the Catholic church, called "School of the
Holy Spirit." Designated, "For Sister Jeanne D'arc," a
poem entitled, **"Worry,"** depicts the little six-year-old girl
carrying the first lilacs to the teacher she always was to
call "John Dark," to her an ominous-sounding name. As
a confirmed Catholic, she had been taught, and believed
that Christ would hold up the fallen; but at six, she lay
awake worrying about the bough that breaks in the traditional lullaby. And carrying the lilacs wrapped in a cocoon

of gauze, she worried for fear their necks would break before the bouquet was safely in the nun's hands. There were other classroom concerns to trouble a sensitive six-year-old, but Sister John Dark never knew; in a way it was heaven-on-earth to present the limp lilacs to her revered teacher, but somehow the posibility of danger lurked behind the "Dark."

At eight, in the company of twenty bored girls about her age, Carol took toe dancing from an elderly erstwhile Russian prima ballerina, who attempted to teach, through a vale of tears, in a Minneapolis basement studio, the art she had lost when a cab crushed her great toe eons before, in Dubrovnik. It is her story that the poet tells in a few tense stanzas, evoking the sympathy of the reader for the sad one who weeps as she sips brandy while instructing her pupils, sometimes "nodding when the needle stuck / on a crack in *Romeo and Juliet*." The pathos of the poem entitled, **"Swansong,"** is heightened by the neutral note at the end: "Those days we stood on ceremony: / mute sisters of the dance, we froze / holding second position till six / when the mothers came."

There were many scenes that left a mark, but the one that made an indelible impression on Carol Muske as a child was the sight of a prison—Stillwater Prison in St. Paul. She was no more than eight or nine when, on a Sunday afternoon drive, her father pointed out to the children the huge fortresslike structure holding the state's criminal offenders behind bars. Formidable, gray, and dreary, it produced in Carol a feeling of horror mixed with sympathy for people locked up behind those walls. The picture of that grim place remained in her mind, and was to become an influence in one of the engrossing, rewarding interests of her adult creative life.

She began to feel the urge to write poetry when she entered Our Lady of Peace High School, which had a remarkably broad program in literature and the arts. Her first poems appeared in the high school publication, and by her junior year she was poetry editor, then editor of the paper. She read poetry avidly, from the classics to the romantics and the moderns, and tentatively tried her hand at her own verses, encouraged by the sisters in the English department. At graduation, they urged her to continue her studies of literature in higher education. Unfortunately, Creighton College in Nebraska, to which Carol was sent with one of her brothers who was studying engineering, placed more emphasis on science than the arts; and as a result, there was a hiatus in her poetry writing.

However, she did make an important alliance, one that influenced both her life and work. She fell in love and became engaged to Edward Healton, a pre-med student majoring in neurology, tendrils of which eventually found their way into the poet's lines. Through Edward's sisters, who lived in California, she learned that the State University of San Francisco had an excellent program in English and creative writing, and persuaded her parents to let her go there for a Masters degree. It was a fortuitous choice: her advisor for her Master's thesis was Kay Boyle, then teaching at Berkeley, but connected with San Francisco State. Still the rebel and champion of many causes as well as free verse in modern poetry, Kay Boyle was then involved with the protest movement against the Vietnam War; she was as outspoken as the vociferous Berkeley students and did not hesitate to join the marches. Besides critical advice on Muske's Master's thesis, she gave the young poet a strong sense of social consciousness, which in a few years was to bear fruit in a different area.

Following graduation, Carol had an opportunity to go to the University of Paris on a student visa, and her father, as a present, made it possible for her to accept. She was there a year, taking courses in French language and literature, and for a time was a member of the travelling company of *Hair,* which toured Europe and Russia. On her return, she decided to stay in New York, city of excitement and center of the publishing world. Edward was entering his internship in neurology at Columbia Presbyterian Hospital, and the thought of going back to Minnesota was inconceivable. New York was in the throes of the turmoil over Attica in 1970-1971, and the poet, remembering Stillwater, was immediately drawn into the struggle for rehabilitation of the unfortunate prisoners fighting for the right to regain some kind of a decent life, to express their feelings as human beings, and not to be treated as animals in an iron cage.

"*Attica* was more than a prison uprising," Muske said in 1982. "It was an organized movement—a metaphor signifying prison reform as a matter of principle." Joining the general surge of poets and writers who were sympathetic to the prisoners' cause, she conceived the idea of starting a poetry workshop at the Women's House of Detention on Riker's Island. She received permission from the court authorities to carry out her plan; but opposition unexpectedly came from the matrons, who seemed to resent the poet's presence as an intrusion of their territory, a threat to their authority. One of them tried to discourage Carol with hard-nosed prison warden logic. "Most of those girls can't even read or write," she said. "They're not going to turn out for some poetry class." But Carol argued, "I think they will. Let me put the notice up on the bulletin board and we'll see. . . ."

The matron agreed grudgingly, and the response was almost a complete turnout of the inmates. They came bringing diaries, notebooks, letters, filled with their attempts at self-expression, eager for instruction. The trial project was so successful it received support from the National Endowment for the Arts, New York Council for the Humanities, Poets and Writers, other organizations and foundations, and expanded to include all the arts. First called "Free Space," the title was changed to "Art Without Walls," extending to classes in poetry, fiction, graphic arts, dance, and videotape throughout the New York State prison system. Eighteen New York prisons formed an "inside circuit" for a lecture series on location to discuss prison reform from sentencing to cell conditions, the victimless crimes (drugs and gambling), and the overall subject of "Women and Violence." Among those who took part in the program were Adrienne Rich, Toni Morrison, and several other colleagues in the world of modern poets active in the feminist movement.

It was inevitable that the absorbing task of teaching poetry to prison inmates evoked poems of her own, some of which were published in Carol Muske's first volume, which did not appear until 1975. In the meantime, she was married to Edward Healton, and hired by Daniel Halpern, poet and editor of *Antaeus,* as his assistant after several of her poems appeared in the magazine. Her marriage to Edward did not work out, but they parted amiably, and are still friends. And the influence of his profession on her poetry is readily apparent in her imagery, not only in her first volume—which was dedicated, "For my mother and father For Daniel and . . . For Edward"—but in her second, *Skylight* . . . ; and even in her scheduled third, *Wyndmere,* one finds references to the basic structure of the body, with emphasis on the nervous system. In **"War Crimes,"** dealing with the love-hate syndrome of war, she speaks of "the great nerve / which runs from head to pelvis / which makes us courteous / shy / scrupulous / makes us touch one another with gentleness," turning the tortured victim of war toward pity for his torturers through the power of "the brain in the body." The "great nerve" then would tremble "till it was plucked," as if hot, held in pliers then in fire; in conclusion, "shriveling in that little violence / of heat and light / which in another form / we often refer to / as love." The striking metaphor of the poem, first published in *The New Yorker,* caused more than one reader to comment on its unique, strong character. The words "bone," "muscle," as well as "nerve" (or "nerves") appear often in Muske's lines.

It is the ability to transform the small incidents of daily living into matters of consequence that infuses Muske's lines with force and an element of surprise in her imagery.

—Jean Gould

"Fireflies," the poem that follows **"War Crimes,"** is marked, "For Edward Healton," and was obviously written when they were separating. It speaks of the pain between them, and says, "Your hands that heal / can't make us whole again." For an instant, the sky above them had "exploded in a shower of cold light from a nation of fireflies," like a brief, blatant reminder of "the old spark / of nature's love." And then the sky over Vermont, where they had come on an emergency, was suddenly dark. On this dim note, presaging a dark future for further life together, the poem ends. There are other instances of references to this brief marital union and its dissolution, notably the title poem, **"Skylight,"** which seems to symbolize the reach for happiness that never materialized. "Ex-friend, there's an elevator / that never stops rising," a ladder that leads to the sky beyond "the scaffold of passion," are all figures indicating a rueful loss.

Skylight is offered "for Curtis Catherine Ingham and Thomas Lux," two people who were closest to her during the trying period of separation and divorce from Edward. Poet Lux, whose work bears the mark of muscular meta-

phor, directness of statement, and wry humor, was among the kindred spirits Carol met at the MacDowell Colony, where she received residencies in 1973 and 1974; she shared her life with him for a time. Both secured teaching posts to finance their poetry writing. Besides continuing as co-director of the Art Without Walls Program in New York State prisons, Carol Muske has taught or held the post of visiting lecturer at the New School for Social Research, New York University, YMHA Poetry Center, Columbia University, University of New Hampshire, George Washington University, and the University of California at Irvine, in the Graduate Creative Writing Program. She has received awards from the National Endowment for the Arts, the New York State Council on the Arts, The Poetry Society of America (the Alice Fay di Castagnola Award for a manuscript-in-progress), and has had her poetry published in anthologies as well as the leading literary magazines. She has given many readings at main universities.

The daily life of two poets may have proved a strain, although there was no actual rivalry between Carol Muske and Tom Lux; each admired the other's work and was willing to accept criticism. For whatever reason, however, they separated after little more than a year together. And soon after her appointment as visiting poet at Irvine in California, she met and fell in love with actor David Dukes, who was equally drawn to the poet. With her large, expressive hazel eyes, the broad planes of her face, her slightly retroussé nose above a long lip of her well-formed mouth, Carol Muske is an extremely attractive young woman. She has the eloquence of a dramatic actress in her features, yet when she smiles it is the smile of a sunny-tempered, loving little girl. She can be vivacious yet meditative in the space of half an hour. She laughs easily, but when concerned about someone or some cause she is fighting for, she becomes formidably serious.

It was not long before she and David decided to cast their lot together; their professions complemented each other and were regarded with mutual admiration by both of them. One of the leading poems in Muske's third volume, *Wyndmere,* entitled, **"White Key,"** first published in the 1982 summer issue of *The American Poetry Review,* is marked "for David," and contains several passages that reveal the core of their harmonious relationship, not the least of which stated in a few words: "You're sure / of yourself, friend, and I like that." A poem of evaluation, of meditation during a plane flight—another frequent theme of this poet's work—it asks the question, "What do we deserve on this earth?" and answers (in italics) *"Not to be lied to by the mind:* the body bent / by that conscious wind into habits of the cage." As the plane hovers above its landing site, she observes: "We wake up so few times in our lives. / The wheels touch—we lean up into love, / *white on white,* a key unseen / in a cylinder of entry. . . ."

In another poem, **"Afterwards,"** the poet derives philosophic import from a comparison of two plane flights, the first short but rough, the second long but smooth, yet she did not fall asleep as she had during the first, because she was no longer in the arms of her beloved: each had to take a separate plane to "opposite ends of the country." It is only "afterwards" that the poet is able to analyze the cause and effect on her psyche of those two flights, and observes, "It has something to do with the power of loss, / how it opposes itself at the last moment. / . . . how falling together / our lives seemed the only constant objects in the sky, how impossible it seemed that thin air / would ever begin to displace us."

Carol Muske and David Dukes were married on January 29, 1983, and the following fall a daughter was born, to whom they gave the first name Anne, and the surname of both parents, Muske-Dukes, thus preserving the identity of the poet as well as the actor.

In **"Panus Angelicus"** and **"Coming Over Coldwater"**— also published in *The American Poetry Review* prior to her third volume—Muske views with maturity some of the liturgical lessons learned by rote in primary school. By herself in Italy, the sight of a man selling *pani d'angeli*—bread of angels—recalls her childhood when they learned it in Latin: *Panis angelicus,* the host they "balanced on their tongues till it didn't seem like swallowing God." They would ask a blessing on their swallowing, but only now, as an adult, is the poet, as she admits, "learning patience, struggling each day / to swallow what I'm given and, in that order, to bless it." **"Coming Over Coldwater,"** a metaphysical poem, reveals the religious thought pattern of the poet while she is driving alone across Coldwater Canyon in California at night, again recalling the lessons and customs of school days, like swearing off sweets, then eating with extra delight at "Lent's end." And only then does she realize the significance of Christ's promise of Paradise to the good thief, and his murmuring, "Sitio"—I thirst—still desiring life, still drinking in the earth. She relates it to her own desire for "cold water / and light, love preserved as Paradise." It serves as a signal to her to "hit the low beams" to preserve her life as she drives out of the canyon.

It is this blending of the physical with the transcendental that distinguishes Carol Muske's poetry. She can be pragmatic and mystical in her attitude toward life, and it is this ability to transform the small incidents of daily living into matters of consequence that infuses her lines with force and an element of surprise in her imagery. It is this distinctive quality that caused Carrolyn Kizer to write: "On a dark day, when I've read too much, and all the poets start turning into each other, I like to think about Carol Muske, who only turns into more wonderful versions of herself. Her dazzle and virtuosity are one of a kind: Mozartean. That's as high as I know how to go." Such enthusiasm from a fellow poet and critic who is well qualified to judge is obviously justified. And the applause of audiences whenever Carol Muske makes a public appearance at leading universities and libraries across the country accents the accolades of her peers. Here is a young poet whose bright future is undoubtedly assured.

Carolyn Kizer   (review date 3 November 1985)

SOURCE: "Motherhood, Magic, and Lavender," in *The New York Times Book Review,* November 3, 1985, p. 13.

[*Kizer is an American poet who won the 1985 Pulitzer Prize*

for her collection Yin *(1984). In the following excerpt, she presents a largely positive review of* Wyndmere *and suggests that the volume may be a preliminary step prior to a truly great work.*]

The first poems in Carol Muske's **Wyndmere** are concerned with her mother, a grandmother, a grandfather, in the new light of what it means to her to be a parent. This is a lighter book than **Skylight,** her previous work, not just in its length, but in that it doesn't contain those glittering arias that made us sit up and take notice. One senses the poet marking time as she stretches to her full stature. If Miss Muske *takes* her time, her next book will show the flowering. This one opens with **"Wyndmere, Windemere"**—Wyndmere the place in North Dakota where her mother was born. "Windemere," meaning "wind-mother," a lovely conceit, expresses the fragile and volatile nature of this most profound human tie—we know her intimately; we shall never know her.

> The world's wrong, mother,
> Shelley said it when, at the end,
> he got it right. And you, who knew
> every word of his by heart, agreed.
>
> The washed dresses stood on thin air.
> You plucked them with distracted grace,
> a wind-mother. . . .
> *you held me close, you let me go.* . . .
> Poetry's the air we drown in together. . . .
> In the wind, on the back step,
> I heard the words of poets
>
> who got it right again and again,
> in a world so wrong,
> it measures only loss
> in those crosses of thin air,
>
> in the blowdown and ascent
> of the separator, the mother,
> whose face catches once,
> then turns from me, again and again.

The next poem picks up on the theme of separateness— her grandfather was "a Separator Man, / harvesting the wheat." His threshing machine separated

> strong from weak . . .
> My grandfather died
> rich and didn't know it.
> No one told him.
>
> By then,
> he was too good
> at separating—
>
> his wife ten years dead,
> his children gone away.
> No one to give something to,
>
> no one to witness how
> what was taken away
> stayed with him—

Next, her grandmother, her brother, a school friend who was raped—handled with a tact that precludes voyeurism, unlike the majority of poems on that anguishing topic. Then Miss Muske dances off into the world of lovers, books, Italy—particularly felicitous, these last—and a fine love poem involving John Tyndall's theory of sight (impurities in the air allow us to see light). She ends with two poems about her daughter. In **"August, Los Angeles, Lullaby,"** as she holds her baby she sees what her mother must have intended for her:

> watching her suck as she
> dreamed of sucking, lightheaded
> with thirst as my blood flowed
>
> suddenly into tissue that
> changed it to milk. No matter
> how close I press, there is a
>
> texture that moves between me
> and whatever might have injured
> us then. Like the curtain's sheer
>
> opacity, it remains drawn
> over what view we have of dawn
> here in this onetime desert,
>
> now green and replenished,
> its perfect climate
> unthreatened in memory—
>
> though outside, as usual,
> the wind blew, the bough bent,
> under the eaves, the hummingbird
>
> touched once the bloodcolored hourglass,
> the feeder, then was gone.

The linkage of blood and blood; the hummingbird, symbol of all that is luminous, swift and ephemeral; the light, sure touch—these are characteristic of Carol Muske's art.

Sandra M. Gilbert   (review date December 1985)

SOURCE: A review of *Wyndmere,* in *Poetry,* Vol. CXLVII, No. 3, December, 1985, pp. 163-64.

[*Gilbert is an American poet, critic, and educator. In the following excerpt, she argues that despite its strengths,* Wyndmere *does not display Muske's full ability as a poet.*]

Ironic yet sincere, meditative but oblique, "leaping" through "confessional," [Carol Muske] does what I suppose they tell young writers to do at Iowa (and I don't know whether or not she went there): she's never bombastic, isn't too self-consciously literary, understands form, doesn't make syntactic blunders, and is sparing in her use of adjectives. Surprisingly, however, despite such trendy credentials, she's much of the time very good. **Wyndmere** includes pieces on many standard recent *topoi*—the mother poem, the grandmother poem, the husband poem, the newborn child poem, the feminist revision of a fairytale, the poem to a former lover, the poem(s) about foreign travel, and so forth—but the works we encounter in this volume aren't just smoothly finished, they're often freshly imagined.

In section I of the book, for example, Muske associates her own initiation into poetry with her literary mother, who, when "The washed dresses stood on thin air, / . . . plucked them with distracted grace"; she associates her own growth with, that is, a punningly defined "wind-mother" who explained " 'I'm a tough farm girl / from Wyndmere, nothing fazes me.' " Then, in section III, she

celebrates the birth of her own daughter, attending suavely to "The pure amnesia of her face" and its expression that is "pure / figurative, resembling no one." Throughout, her explorations of often, by now clichéd encounters (the raped friend, the wedding ceremony) are consistently interesting and lively. Most frequently, moreover, what makes them so is a carefully cultivated gift for phrase-making that converts accurate observation into decisive declaration. The poem **"Surprise,"** for instance, examines different facets of that experience to conclude:

> . . . recall your horror once
> opening the front door, on your birthday, on seeing the faces
> of your friends disfigured by the weight of occasion.
> You thought the ones who liked you least
> screamed loudest:
> Surprise!

And a piece called **"From the Arsonist,"** in the sequence "Three Letters," pronounces—acutely, in view of its subject—that "Hell is the absence of metaphor."

Even in her use of literary history, Muske is controlled and cool compared to, say, [Amy] Clampitt. If her **"Illness as Metaphor"** (itself owning a self-consciously allusive title drawn from Susan Sontag) deals with the fate and fatality of John Keats, it is emphatically no vulgar *John Keats Story.* Imagining a revision of the poet's life so that he becomes, momentarily, a contemporary hippie—

> Sign here, John Keats, you'll like
> your new apartment; great view
> of the Spanish Steps, best dope
>
> in Rome

—Muske struggles to define the historical distinctions that make the author of "The Ode on a Grecian Urn" our nervously admired hero:

> Ah, the twentieth century, ah the nineteenth.
> One heartless, the other literal-
> minded about love. You guessed which
>
> was which as you lay above, coughing
> your lungs into a cup. . . .

Moreover, the last line of her book's final poem (**"Soundings,"** about her newborn daughter) is Yeatsian in its ambitious conception of

> the soul rung forward into image,
> as metal is stunned into coin,
> as the hammer sounds against its resistance:
>
> the gold unblinking eye of the forge.

Why, then, given this level of accomplishment, do I wish Muske weren't quite so "Iowa," quite such a dutiful embodiment of work-shopping virtues? Maybe, despite her decorum, I suspect she's capable of longer leaps, more imaginative inventions—and I wish that her musing "wind-mother" would blow her in their direction.

Holly Prado   (review date 1 December 1985)

SOURCE: A review of *Wyndmere,* in *Los Angeles Times Book Review,* December 1, 1985, p. 11.

[*Prado is an American poet and novelist. In the following review, she lauds Muske's ability to combine technical literary skill with the passion needed to write vital, risk-taking poetry.*]

Ah, that wonderful, rare thing: a poet who has the ability to deepen the secrets of experience even while revealing them. Carol Muske's third book of poems, **Wyndmere,** enchants—not with the sweetness of an unconscious sleeping beauty but with the glint and magic of a highly skilled writer who uses her knowledge deftly, pulling us in until we're thoroughly immersed in the alchemical brew of real poetry.

One of Muske's strengths is her ease in merging autobiographical detail with the inner realm of thought and feeling. Her contemplation of experience is personal yet moves further, into the spiritual and philosophical; then it belongs not only to the poet but to all of us. The first section of the book deals primarily with the past, emphasizing the importance of a mother and grandmother. Muske is less interested in simple influences on behavior than on powerful psychic exchanges: " . . . I read / because you said to . . . Poetry's the air we drown in together, / mother, poetry's the turning room, / the clear field mined with words / you read first. . . ." Again and again, she returns to the effect of poetry on spirit: "Hell is the absence of metaphor," and " . . . souls drift in permanent / transience, in the light-distance of God's photograph, / which some call Poetry." As the writing progresses, the past opens into the present, which includes travel, literature, loves, and culminates with the birth of a daughter.

Muske has developed a reputation as a poet, winning prizes and grants, teaching at the University of Southern California. There's a temptation to believe that poets who do well for themselves in the world don't take risks in their writing, have become careful in order to be accepted. Muske's work does show her training—these poems are honed and consciously crafted. But rather than diminishing the heat of the writing, her educated containment and grace increase it. She's discovered a way to work magic within the boundaries of technical achievement. That's quite an accomplishment.

Stephen McCauley   (review date 16 April 1989)

SOURCE: "Love Letters from the Mad," in *The New York Times Book Review,* April 16, 1989, p. 13.

[*McCauley is an American novelist, educator, and critic. In the following review, he explains why* Dear Digby *"doesn't add up to the sum of its many appealing parts."*]

Life is no picnic for Willis Jane Digby. The heroine and narrator of Carol Muske-Dukes's entertaining first novel, **Dear Digby,** edits the letters column for *Sisterhood* magazine ("a bimonthly cross between a feminist *Time* and a liberated *Ladies Home Journal* with an all-woman staff"); lately the letters, particularly those from both male and female crazies, have begun to drive her, well, crazy. She's begun to see something of herself and her own perceptions of the world in letters from, for example, a woman who puts cat food in her husband's cereal every morning, or a woman who writes to complain of being sexually harassed by the bald man on the label of a cleaning product. Digby, like Nathanael West's Miss Lonelyhearts, her literary ancestor, finds these missives from the outer limits of sanity less and less amusing; she begins to take them seriously. On days when she's feeling "in the mood to respond to the Loonies," she dons a tuxedo and a pair of floppy rabbit ears. The outfit makes her feel "like a radio tower . . . I pull everybody in" and, at the same time, protected. "People look, laugh uncertainly, then watch their step with me."

There's a lot in Digby's personal life that makes her responsive to the off-center letters. She's unsuccessfully married to a successful, vain actor. ("I abandoned *you?*" she admonishes during one fight. "You abandoned me every time we entered a room with a mirror.") She's recently had a miscarriage and still talks to the baby she's lost. And most of all, the shadow of a childhood friend's accidental death, for which Digby has been held responsible since age 12, looms large over all her life.

But trouble—and the novel's wacky plot—really begin when Digby decides to publish some of the more disturbed letters in the magazine, along with her pithy, sometimes cutting responses. "Why can't our magazine also be for the woman who's gone a little crackers," she asks at a staff meeting, "alone in the rec room at ten A.M., eating Ding Dongs, getting weird?" Thus commences her involvement with a disfigured mental patient named Iris Moss, who claims she's being raped in her hospital bed, and with a sociopathic voyeur who signs his letters The Watcher. "Something has hurt you," he writes. "I can tell as I watch you. . . . I wish I knew what has hurt you." As it turns out, of course, he does know.

Dear Digby is a blend of social satire, war between the sexes and mystery thriller. In part, the book is a paean to the virtues of having a "crazy safety valve," particularly for women. The unusual letters Digby publishes are intended to show how women who are "not on the political barricades" have found ways to deal with their frustrations. "Male crazies," Digby explains, "come in predictable (often boring) wrappers, but the women are chattier, more distracted from the solemnity of dementia . . . weirdly *hopeful* in a hopeless world."

Ms. Muske-Dukes, the author of four books of poetry, has written a novel full of sharp insights and surprising images. At its best (the opening chapter, for example) **Dear Digby** is driven by a zany comic gusto. She is particularly good at writing amusing hit-and-run portraits: there's Minnie White-White-Goldfarb, the hyper, hyphenated *Sisterhood* receptionist who's trying to "annex a personal history," and Digby's mother, a failed artist whose paintings are rejected, even by a gallery burglar.

Unfortunately, however, the social satire of the novel gets diluted by some of the more difficult aspects of the plot. An extended confrontation with The Watcher and a courtroom drama revolving around the plight of the mental patient, Iris Moss, are both unconvincing. Ms. Muske-Dukes's originality and wit, so much in evidence elsewhere, fail her in these scenes. The irony of the early chapters gives way to sentimentality.

If the whole of the novel doesn't add up to the sum of its many appealing parts, *Dear Digby* does, in its best scenes, throb with oddball life. Digby herself is a winning character—acid-tongued and, of course, more than a little batty.

Linsey Abrams   (review date 21 May 1989)

SOURCE: "Miss Lonelyhearts Meets the Feminine Mystique," in *Los Angeles Times Book Review*, May 21, 1989, p. 3.

[*Abrams is an American novelist whose works include* Charting by the Stars *(1979) and* Double Vision *(1984). In the following review of* Dear Digby, *she argues that the novel's half-comic, half-serious style undermines the reader's identification with the protagonist.*]

Dear Digby, the poet Carol Muske-Dukes' first novel, makes its most obvious literary reference to Nathanael West's *Miss Lonelyhearts.* The impossible predicament of he, or in this case she, who must answer in print the painful *cries de coeur* of strangers is one of enduring interest. It's a story with a built-in irony: that mortals can petition only other mortals to redress life's wrongs. But the greater irony lies in the predicament of the respondent, who by definition is inadequate to the task. Inevitably, the story is his or hers.

Willis Jane Digby is the Letters editor for *SIS* (read *Ms. Magazine*), a glossy feminist bimonthly, whose staff biographies taken together read like a compendium of the women's movement in its heyday. We learn immediately, from Digby's first-person narration, illustrated by several of the spicier letters she receives (here termed "Ink Theater"), that a lot of the correspondence is from "crazy" people, many of them sexually fixated. (Where else would such people write but to *SIS Magazine,* forum for sexual politics, to discuss such matters as hypnotic rape, seminal fluid, and jock straps?) Of course, such letters are never actually printed in the magazine . . . that is, until Digby decides to intersperse them with the "you-are-doing-such-a-fine-job-for-women" and "write-your-congressperson-about-daycare" letters, written by the supposedly sane readers of *SIS.*

In both its structure, in which the lives of Willis Digby and two certifiably "crazy" people who regularly write her, meet, and in its expressed themes, the novel plays out the idea that we are all more or less crazy. As Willis Digby describes her column, "I see [it] as a kind of demilitarized zone where these two impulses—the desire of the sane to go crazy and the desire of the crazy to be sane—converge." It turns out, as the editor's own past is revealed through a series of flashback chapters that illuminate a particularly harrowing incident from childhood, and two later painful episodes of adulthood, that Digby has personal reasons for identifying with her "crazy" correspondents, the women in particular.

The brilliance of *Miss Lonelyhearts* lies in its disturbing redefinition of an American vocabulary. What we had called Manifest Destiny, rugged individualism, freedom . . . was by another name, loneliness, alcoholism, the edge of madness. It is clear from her novel's inscription, William Carlos Williams' "The pure products of America go crazy—" that Muske-Dukes claims this same literary territory. But she does so, with a twist. This novel has an unmistakably female vision—both in its sexual politics and its ultimate insistence on community.

Muske-Dukes is a fine stylist. Her sculpted images and energetic prose make her storytelling vivid and compelling. Yet one wishes she had decided to write either a flat-out comic novel about the battle of the sexes, as narrated by a feminist survivor, or the more serious, psychologically acute story of a woman who responds to the pain and craziness in other people because of the pain and craziness in herself. The problem here [in *Dear Digby*] is that the reader is asked to respond to Digby alternately as a stand-up comedian and as a character with a painful past. Her quite funny one-liners have the effect, at times, of undermining the reader's identification with her predicament, which is really everyone's.

Wayne Koestenbaum   (review date 24 September 1989)

SOURCE: "Distortions in the Glass," in *The New York Times Book Review,* September 24, 1989, pp. 50-1.

[*Koestenbaum is an American poet, critic, and educator. In the following excerpt, he praises* Applause *and Muske's ability to combine simplicity and complexity, straightforwardness and abstraction.*]

Many contemporary poems stage a war between simple and complex styles—a battle in which "simplicity" incarnates the virtues of nature, and "complexity" bears the curse of the sterile and the insincere. Carol Muske, however, nimbly negotiates between these two poles. Though she tends to be straightforward, her fourth poetry collection, *Applause* also risks artifice, relinquishes plainness and reaches toward the rhetorical. She tempers glib candor with a recognition that language is inevitably impeded and enriched by all that resists easy saying.

Even the volume's first sentence shows Ms. Muske's desire to place poems at an oblique angle to her own "I," to disembody her voice, to speak and to watch herself speaking: "It's my old apartment, Gramercy Park, / but then it's not." The divisions that trouble her are sometimes metaphysical—"little 'you's and 'me's, / estranged suddenly from the vanity of their motion"—and sometimes historical. In **"Monk's House, Rodmell,"** for example, she confirms (and questions) her own poetic vocation by visiting Virginia Woolf's house, where, echoing John Ashbery, she sets

> a convex mirror on a stand,
> so that when the visitor
>
> looked in
> expecting to see the familiar
> line of lip and brow,

what appeared instead
was the head up-ended—
the mouth a talking wound

More often, Ms. Muske's fleet changes of perspective occur when first and third worlds, rich and poor, healthy and sick, collide. In **"August 1974: A Tapestry,"** she watches an 8-year-old boy in Kashmir, whipped by his foreman, weave a rug. Clearly, the weaver represents the artist, whose artifact is stained blood-red by history. Ms. Muske implies that because poems, however elegant, sometimes have ugly contexts, poets must answer to the unhappiness that surrounds them and learn to harness their lovely images to argument.

"In the perfect center of the glass," she writes, "there is resistance to the image." Sometimes she should resist the image more strenuously. My favorite phrase in the book is "Nile-green Nile"—precisely because it avoids verisimilitude, offering instead a tautological emptiness (the Nile looks like the Nile) exactly where we expect literal description. Sometimes Ms. Muske uses images that clip unruliness into shape too succinctly: "Outside, the green August shade deepened, / grew burnished as a brass samovar." The poem that most successfully resists a pat, unexamined relation to the image is the volume's title [piece], **"Applause,"** a sustained meditation on what it means to behold, to appreciate—particularly in the context of suffering. The poem's specific pain is death from AIDS. That immensity makes Ms. Muske's tone bleak, philosophically expansive: "Applause has no opposite, contains its own poles."

I enjoy her abstractions—such phrases as "the exquisite, denatured vision / of invention." They counter her reliance on a vocabulary that gives too little tonal pleasure and on a stumbling, stop-and-start tempo. Some might call it concision; to me, it seems a refusal to leap. The ideas come in small clusters, tight sentences that often lack propulsion. I long to hear a phrase tumble beyond its limit, for the shorter poems to achieve the momentum reached in **"Applause."** And yet terseness brings rewards. Ms. Muske writes, wryly, "It is not night. / It is California." Here an idea casts a shadow; she reaches past anecdote. Such flashes of wit give her work its distinctive, dry taste.

Tom De Haven   (review date 11 April 1993)

SOURCE: "For Love of a Protein Sequence," in *The New York Times Book Review,* April 11, 1993, p. 18.

[*De Haven is an American novelist, screenwriter, and author of children's literature. In the following review of* Saving St. Germ, *he explains that the novel's "unconvincing, hurried conclusion can't spoil what in all other respects is a truly original work of fiction."*]

"I've always believed that science requires its practitioners be in a state of despair, informed despair," says Esme Charbonneau Tallich, the narrator of Carol Muske Dukes's second novel, **Saving St. Germ.** The Harvard-trained biochemist is proof of her own hypothesis. For someone who longs only to "putter or theorize," and who often forgets she has a body as well as a mind, a job as well

as a calling, a family as well as an advanced degree, the laboratory of daily life can almost seem like a torture chamber.

In Esme, Ms. Muske Dukes, the author of five books of poetry and a previous novel, **Dear Digby,** has created a character as likable as she is off-putting, with habits, quirks and observations that startle you with their strangeness but always feel true. Here's a woman who mentally builds "the chemical architecture of nicotine" when she craves a cigarette and "the skeletal structure of Tylenol" if she has a headache, a woman who likens marriage to "an unremitting gaze" and strolls home from work "immersed in contemplation of immunodetection of tyrosine phosphorylation on protein 70K"—unlike most of us, who just wonder if there's any pot roast left in the refrigerator.

Hired by the University of Greater California, in Los Angeles, to "do something flashy, fund-attracting," Esme remains stubbornly academic, openly hostile to the "social enlightenment"—the medical applications—of genetic research: "I don't believe I can save everybody. . . . I *want* them saved but *I* can't do it." She'd rather work on "saving St. Germ. Some tiny little organism, some protein sequence that's going to change the quality of human life, but only intellectually, only as a model for *thought.*" In other words, give her a computer and a paycheck on Friday—and please shut the door on your way out. Dream on, Esme.

While her mulishness at U.G.C. rankles both faculty members and fast-track doctoral students, Esme's "emotional reluctance" at home infuriates, then finally estranges, her husband, Jay, a technical director for a television show and an aspiring stand-up comic. ("The fact was," says his coolly objective wife, "almost *anybody* I knew was funnier than Jay.") Though he's willing, almost, to forgive Esme her complete lack of interest in Hollywood history, stars and gossip—the stuff that lends texture to *his* life—he won't forgive her total (and, to his mind, practically criminal) acceptance of their daughter's alarming eccentricities.

A 5-year-old given to speech that sounds feverish, even Dadaistic ("This light is too *loud*"; "This air in my hand, in this minute, is not blue"; "I am talking in the red language"), Ollie walks around the house wearing a carboard box on her head—when she isn't twirling in circles or staring off into space. Her doctor suspects "emotional dysfunction, with hints of (but not) autism." Esme, however, insists that Ollie is an "unprecedented being" who is merely preoccupied, "thinking hard." When she refuses to take Ollie for psychiatric testing, Jay leaves her, suing for divorce and asking the court for custody of the child.

That crisis—along with her suspension for absenteeism from the university and the distinct possibility that an admired colleague is about to plagiarize her research—provokes Esme to become, reluctantly and clumsily, something she's always avoided being: an actor in the human drama. "I'd been unstable, unrepentant, heartless, single-minded about my goal," she thinks. "But somehow I'd had faith; the world of theory is touched by God, it had provided me a halo tunnel—I'd felt blessed, invincible. Now the walls were starting to fall and there was no longer that sense of invincibility, the giddiness of privileged vision."

After suffering an abrupt, and abbreviated, emotional collapse that sends her wandering numbly around the seedier precincts of Los Angeles, an integrated mind-body Esme emerges. That's fine for her, but an artistic false move by the otherwise rigorously unsentimental Ms. Muske Dukes. And yet her novel's unconvincing, hurried conclusion can't spoil what in all other respects is a truly original work of fiction, something fresh—the exploration of a subculture that's baffling, often intimidating, to most of us, and usually ignored by American literary novelists. Esme's lucid "Imaginary Lectures"—with subjects that range from theoretical chemistry and the "handedness" of the universe to the historical plight of women scientists and the exuberance of unfettered thought ("It's like chinning yourself on the topmost rung of the ladder to heaven")—are enough to make this reader, who managed somehow to graduate from college using oceanography and meteorology to fulfill his science requirements, wish that he'd had the guts, way back then, to get down and dirty with some tetrahedral molecules.

Sandra M. Gilbert   (review date April 1994)

SOURCE: "Family Values," in *Poetry*, Vol. CLXIV, No. 1, April, 1994, pp. 39-53.

[*In the following excerpt, Gilbert faults the narrative obscurity of many poems in* Red Trousseau, *but praises the ways in which Muske "analyzes the politics and poetics of the family."*]

[Carol] Muske is a writer of prose fiction besides being a poet; she has published two accomplished novels. So I'm particularly bemused when the basic plots, as it were, of some of the most ambitious pieces in this book [*Red Trousseau*] elude me in places: portions of the often powerful series of "Unsent Letters" with which the collection concludes baffle me because I'm sure I'm not grasping the situations out of which the works arise, and even the story line of the beautiful title poem, **"Red Trousseau,"** could be clarified and sharpened. Yes, the latter piece begins with a man and a woman talking, and it isn't surprising that it turns into a meditation on witchburning since it features an epigraph from the notorious fifteenth-century treatise on that subject entitled the *Malleus Maleficarum* (*Witches' Hammer*). Nonetheless, the opening section strikes me as needlessly (albeit perhaps stylishly) provisional in its delineation of a relationship that is mysteriously central to the poem:

> Because she desired him,
> and feared desire, the room
> readied itself for judgment:
> though they were nothing to
> each other, maybe friends,
> maybe a man and a woman
> seated at a table
>   beneath a skylight
> through which light poured,

interrogatory.

Nor is this relationship more dramatically developed later on. It never becomes clear to me, for instance, why we're told in the next section that

> Because his face always appears to her
> half in shadow,
>   she chooses finally
> to distrust him and her seared memory. . . .

That said, however, I should acknowledge my admiration for the technical *brio* and political passion underlying this work's powerful conclusion, with its ambivalently pained and prayerful vision of witchburning:

> I admit now that I never felt sympathy for her,
> as she stood there burning in the abstract. . . .
> I suspected her mind of collaboration,
> apperceptive ecstasy, the flames wrapped
> about her like a red trousseau, yes,
> the dream of immolation.
>
> But look at the way her lips move. . . .
> God, tell me there was a moment
> when she could have willed herself into language,
> just once, into her own stammering, radical defense:
>
> *I am worth saving*
>
> before the flames breathed imperious at her feet
> before her mouth, bewitched, would admit to anything.

More, I should note that the energy charging this strong passage derives . . . from a profound awareness of the complicated web into which the personal and the political, the familial and the feminist are often woven.

Poems in *Red Trousseau* where such interweavings function most triumphantly include **"Frog Pond,"** a meditation on abortion that gains admirable complexity from its agonized portrait of a Right-to-Lifer ("My advice: don't / take her on" although she is "split cell, sister, / the raw fixed light in her face set to mine"); **"Prague: Two Journals,"** a sequence commemorating "Jan Palach, a Czech student [who] burned himself to death protesting the 1968 Soviet invasion of Prague" in which the speaker returns with her young daughter to the Czech city she'd visited as a student and speaks to "the girl who was Jan Palach's lover" (as he burned, "He kept touching himself, she said. / Over and over as if he was a newborn, finding / his body for the first time. Then he began to bow, / growing transparent"); and **"Barra de Navidad: Envoi,"** which broods on a luminous epiphany of a "young man with an infant's white coffin / on his head" and "his wife's sudden keening, / spreading like blood unpent beneath the heat's surface" and rises to a rueful realization:

> So little remains in this feeble re-telling:
>   his regal stride
>   her single cumulative note . . .
>
>   grief following its image,
>   grief's true color vanishing:
>   snow on the sleeping volcano.

But for me the centerpiece of the collection, and the one

that most vividly analyzes the politics and poetics of the family, is the splendid sequence "My Sister Not Painting, 1990." Here the art of the sister—sister*s*, really, for the speaker's verse is in a sense as much at issue as her sibling's painting—is shown to be centrally engaged with the madness and sexuality of "Uncle, drunk," who disgraces himself "by telling his awful story," a tale of the terror of war, of social scandal that becomes inextricable from both the scandal of gender and family scandal:

> He was back in the World War, last one left
> in his regiment, wintry Alps, everyone dead around
> him.
>
> He buried no one, but waited days and days to be
> saved.
>
> He dreamed they were alive in a different way. He
> sang.
>
> Suddenly he saw a young man in a military uniform,
> standing
> before him in a bright light. Then the youth's clothes
> melted away and the boy became a woman.
>   Uncle desired him,
> desired to lie down with her among the dead bodies
> of all his friends who had died for our country.
> Then the man-woman turned away, then faced him
> again,
> revealing the Sacred Heart burning in its cage
>   of neon thorns.
>
> Carried at last down the mountain
> to the hospital, he could not stop

seeing this, telling this.

> So Christ was a woman
> and he longed to fuck her. God is the two
> sexes joined, he cried, spilling,
> don't you see, one sex! joined at the heart!

FURTHER READING

Criticism

deCrinis, Mona. "You've Come a Long Way, Baby!" *West Coast Review of Books* 14, No. 5 (May-June 1989): 18-23.
    Omnibus review of contemporary novels by women, including positive remarks on *Dear Digby.*

Review of *Saving St. Germ,* by Carol Muske. *Kirkus Reviews* LX, No. 23 (1 December 1992): 1462.
    Positive review in which the critic faults Muske only for being too obvious with her affection for the protagonist.

Seaman, Donna. Review of *Saving St. Germ,* by Carol Muske. *Booklist* 89, No. 9 (1 January 1993): 790.
    Brief, highly positive review.

———. Review of *Red Trousseau,* by Carol Muske. *Booklist* 89, No. 13 (1 March 1993): 1151.
    Positive review of *Red Trousseau.*

Solomon, Charles. Review of *Dear Digby,* by Carol Muske, *Los Angeles Times Book Review* (15 September 1991): 10.
    Brief review arguing that, despite "flashes of first-rate writing," the novel "fails because the author attempts to tell too many stories in too few pages."

Additional coverage of Muske's life and career is contained in the following sources published by Gale Research: *Contemporary Authors,* Vols. 65-68 rev. ed.; and *Contemporary Authors New Revision Series,* Vol. 32.

Luis Omar Salinas

1937-

American poet and editor.

The following entry provides an overview of Salinas's career through 1988.

INTRODUCTION

Salinas is generally regarded as a distinguished figure in contemporary Chicano poetry. Described by critics as highly creative and evocative, his verse frequently employs surrealistic images and metaphors, and discusses such traditional themes as alienation, loneliness, death, and honor. As noted Chicano poet Gary Soto has written, "Salinas possesses a powerful imagination, a sensitivity toward the world, and an intuitive feel for handling language."

Biographical Information

Born in Robstown, Texas, Salinas emigrated with his family to Mexico at the age of three, and shortly after their arrival Salinas's mother died of tuberculosis. Salinas's father returned to Robstown and, saddled with bills related to his wife's sickness and death, sent his children to live with relatives who soon adopted them. Separated from his father and his younger sister, Salinas and his new family eventually moved to California. An excellent student—he learned to read and write at an early age—Salinas was fluent in English and became avidly interested in the adventure stories of American novelist Jack London. In high school, he became a practicing Catholic and was active in athletics. Serving in the United States Marines Reserves and attending Bakersfield City College, Salinas eventually reunited with his father and settled in Los Angeles. Beginning in 1958, he attended California State College, studying history, drama, and literature, but working full-time and attending college part-time proved too much for him and he soon suffered a mental breakdown. Diagnosed as schizophrenic—it has since been determined that he is manic-depressive—he was hospitalized for eleven months, during which time he attempted suicide; Salinas has noted that it was around this time that he also began writing poetry. Continuing to receive medical supervision, he returned to his studies in 1963, enrolling first at East Los Angeles Community College and, the following year, at California State University, Los Angeles. Coping with mental illness and the demands of various odd jobs, Salinas was hardly a model student and frequently missed or dropped out of classes. Inspired by the work of the Spanish poet Gustavo Adolfo Becquer, however, he eventually took a creative writing class taught by Henri Coulette. Relocating to the agricultural Fresno Valley with his father, Salinas began classes at Fresno State where he suffered additional nervous breakdowns. Despite the pressures of a workshop atmosphere, Salinas took several writing class-

es, working under the direction of such renowned American poets as Philip Levine and Peter Everwine. At Fresno, Salinas was also asked to teach in the Ethnic Studies Department. That same year he published *Crazy Gypsy* (1970), a collection of verse that largely explores the painful sense of alienation and loneliness resulting from the death of a mother. Although *Crazy Gypsy* was rushed into production—early editions are full of spelling and grammatical errors—the volume was a commercial and critical success. Nevertheless, Salinas waited ten years to publish his second volume of verse, *Afternoon of the Unreal* (1980). He has since released *Prelude to Darkness* (1981), *Darkness under the Trees/Walking behind the Spanish* (1982), and *The Sadness of Days* (1987). He was awarded the Stanley Kunitz Award from *Columbia Magazine* in 1980 and continues to write and publish extensively in journals and anthologies. He is also the coeditor of *From the Barrio* (1973), an anthology of Chicano writings. A new collection of work, tentatively titled *Sometime Mysteriously,* awaits publication.

Major Works

Alternately characterized as romantic, political, dark, and

brooding, Salinas's poetry addresses the chaotic nature of human existence or, as he puts it, "the strange fullness of the unreal." Replete with unusual and fascinating imagery similar to the surrealist poetry of Federico García Lorca, Míguel Hernández, César Vallejo, and Pablo Neruda, Salinas's verse—which is often marked by ambiguity and disjointed sentence structure—is considered both highly emotive and striking. For example, in "Sunday . . . Dig the Empty Sounds" from *Crazy Gypsy,* a frantic youngster searches for his mother amidst an array of such frightening symbols as "the blood of children and the clouds with mouths." Much of Salinas's poetry is distinguished by this focus on alienation and abandonment—feelings he associated with the death of his mother and his separation from his sister and father. For instance, in "Poem for Olivia," a piece dedicated to his mother that appears in *Afternoon of the Unreal,* he writes: "I didn't come to this world / to be frightened / yet your death sticks / in my stomach / and I must clean the kitchen / with my hands / and I wander on / into the night of leavened bread / and pursue truth / like a tube needing air." Salinas also explores the pain of unrequited love in such collections as *Prelude to Darkness* and *Darkness under the Trees/Walking behind the Spanish.* The latter, which is comprised of two separate collections, contains new and old work. In the first part of the volume, his focus is largely autobiographical and emphasizes such themes as love, insanity, and loneliness. The second portion of the book is more political in nature, honoring, in part, poets and anti-Fascist revolutionaries who were active in the Spanish Civil War. Politics is likewise central to several of the pieces in *Crazy Gypsy*—which includes protest chants Salinas wrote while at Fresno State and poems about Vietnam and the Argentine revolutionary Che Guevara—and to *The Sadness of Days,* which is also known for its focus on philosophical issues. In one poem from *The Sadness of Days,* he offers an analysis of the work of photographer Ansel Adams: "Grandeur is always the subject: shards / of sunlight splitting clouds; rubble of lost / boulders under a heaven of cliff face and cumuli; / a tiny cemetery—crosses like picket fences— / near the ghostly town under the mountains / flooding with white, the moon above / like some Platonic ideal."

Critical Reception

Although Salinas's work has been well-received, it has engendered minimal critical commentary. Following the publication of *Crazy Gypsy,* reviewers initially focused on the social message of Salinas's poetry, largely ignoring its surrealist dimensions and influences. As Eliezar Risco Lozada and Guillermo Martinez wrote in the introduction to *Crazy Gypsy:* "There is a degree of surrealism in Omar's highly personalized juxtaposition of images. But we can't allow that superficial surrealism to distract us from the deeper reality of the poems." In recent years, however, scholars have asserted that the form and content of Salinas's work are inseparable, arguing that the poetry's distinctive features—economy of expression, syntactical ambiguity, and ingenious placement of symbols—have a specific thematic function. While some have faulted his verse as ungrammatical and poorly crafted, most have agreed that Salinas succeeds in creating a poetry that simultaneously defines and preserves the Chicano experience within an Anglo-American culture. Salinas, for his part, has stated that although his poetry contains abstract elements, his work remains grounded in the reality of the human condition, his family history, and his Chicano ancestry.

PRINCIPAL WORKS

Crazy Gypsy (poetry) 1970
From the Barrio: A Chicano Anthology [editor, with Lillian Faderman] (anthology) 1973
I Go Dreaming Serenades (poetry) 1979
Afternoon of the Unreal (poetry) 1980
Prelude to Darkness (poetry) 1981
Darkness under the Trees/Walking behind the Spanish (poetry) 1982
The Sadness of Days: Selected and New Poems (poetry) 1987

CRITICISM

Eliezar Risco Lozada and Guillermo Martinez (essay date 1970)

SOURCE: An introduction to *Crazy Gypsy,* Origenes Publication, 1970, pp. 7-11.

[*In the following essay, Risco Lozada and Martinez note thematic and stylistic aspects of Salinas's work, including an emphasis on surrealism, women, loneliness, and Chicano identity.*]

Omar is the Crazy Gypsy. Omar is the whistler of tunes. Omar is the dreamer of stoics, of nightingales, of moons, of bellies, of stars, and of death. Omar is the poet of somnambular beginnings . . . amazed by his own trickery at finding the right words to say to the virgin. Omar is the claimer of bodies . . . undertaker of America. Omar is the son of Aram the happy money man. Omar is the repairman of corazones. Who is Omar?

For those who know Omar, he is a man without guile, drinking companion, listener of Mexican discos, tripster, friend . . . But, who is that other (and the same) Omar who comes alive in the "I" of these poems?

The Omar of these poems [in *Crazy Gypsy*] is, first of all, lonely. Lonely, with an abysmal loneliness not bound by psychological theories. The loneliness of Omar is a deep, metaphysical loneliness. It is the loneliness of one who translates into cosmic and universal terms the existential despair of the Chicano in the southwest. Like Omar says, "a distinct passenger in who knows what train."

Omar, the persona in these poems, was born in Robstown. Where is Robstown? Omar says it is in Texas, but, in reality we have all lived there. Robstown, where "La Llorona is . . . or so the people say." Robstown where the sun rises "at 6:15" and where they drive "drunk Mexicans . . . out of town." Robstown, where "Anita's brother has a congressional . . . and they wouldn't serve him. . . ." Robstown, where we "go to the rosary at San Antonio and pray."

If we look at these phrases, only a Chicano would have experienced such a reality and expressed it thus. "A little town," un pueblito, is where we were all born, and even if the name of it has the word town—like in Robstown—we still have to repeat it in saying "little town." The kind of awareness of separateness expressed in the lives, "Mother . . . why do they look at us like that." All of these reflect the unique experience of the chicano, and his bicultural self.

In **"MEXICO age four,"** again we find the same bicultural self as Omar contemplates the painted walls—the same walls that "crumble and fall" in **"Crazy Gypsy"**—of a cemetery in Saltillo. The dog that barks at doctors and policemen. But, more importantly the "torn hair and blood . . . on the paving stones" that make it possible for Omar to say "how ugly the air smells (que feo huele)." The "hungry beggars," the "leaky rooftops," the "stoic leaves of autumn," and

> "sighs of love
> as deep
> as pig grunts
> silenced by their masters."

Omar, in his loneliness, weaves a tapestry of far out symbolism and concrete imagery, **"The River,"** where the Llorona is "or so the people say," becomes alive, "a friend and a great comforter," and the same River is

> "an asylum
> where people
> knit dreams,
> a child's clothing for the sky."

That is why Omar tells us so much about dreams, "child's clothing for the sky." Omar has the tenderness of the child. He sees himself writing songs to his dead mother . . . or shedding tears with the songs of Pedro Infante . . . or living with "Aram, his dog and his thirteen year old wife," because "I'm his son."

There is a degree of surrealism in Omar's highly personalized juxtaposition of images. But we can't allow that superficial surrealism to distract us from the deeper reality of the poems. In **"Cold Rain,"** we might be tempted to let "a world of oysters and dreams," "the belly of hemorrhaged nightmare," the "panthers clawing at the wind," and the "pretty artichoke smiles," distract us from the presentation of the persona as a "callous guardian of a utopian of sorts."

> The Omar of *Crazy Gypsy* is, first of all, lonely. Lonely, with an abysmal loneliness not bound by psychological theories. The loneliness of Omar is a deep, metaphysical loneliness. It is the loneliness of one who translates into cosmic and universal terms the existential despair of the Chicano in the southwest.
>
> —*Eliezar Risco Lozada and Guillermo Martinez*

Omar weaves his poetry, self-amused at his "own trickery" but always mindful of "the umbilical cord of words" that ties him to the virgin, "a vision, a rose in an afternoon of silence."

This is the same virgin that "sleeps covetously" in the train where strange women travel incognito "running from the scandal of neurosis" because "they heard tell of a great psychiatrist who cures bad dreams."

There are very few men in Omar's poetry. There is Aram, Pedro Infante, Quetzalcoatl, Cortez, su amigo Phil, the dead Mexican in Vietnam, Bob with his "Jewish butterflies," and Guevara. Instead there are plenty of women.

There is his mother, either going to pray at San Antonio, or the dead mother he sings to. There is the virgin, "in a world of oysters and dreams." The fearless girls telling him their troubles, his "loneliness bottled up in their tummies." There is Madame Ungerum, with "the kingdom and the andurfum. . . ." There is his drunk gypsy girlfriend. The women who make "love pugnaciously in rooms around alleyways" and "fat women on a corner" selling tacos. There is La Llorona, the "dense . . . female companionship," and "the lungs of a young girl."

Consistently the women are not concretely identified, while the men are. The men are individuals with names, while the women remain anonymous, background to the drama on stage.

These are not all the poems Omar has written, but nearly everything is here. This vision of social reality of the chicano is here, entire.

Here we find the "horrible pain that keeps me silent," "the roads as empty containers . . . and the neighbors . . . working in hell for low pay," the blood and the dreams.

And, at the end, we find Omar "sonador de las estrellas," "en el abrigo de la ilusion." Or, as he would say in the last lines of **"Guevara,"** Guevara,

> "with a smell as fresh
> as yesterdays fallen snow."

Gary Soto   (review date 1980)

SOURCE: A review of *Crazy Gypsy,* in *Parnassus: Poetry in Review,* Vol. 8, No. 2, 1980, pp. 229-34.

[*A distinguished Chicano poet, essayist, memoirist, short story writer, and educator, Soto was the editor of Salinas's 1987* The Sadness of Days. *In the review below, he assesses the strengths and weaknesses of* Crazy Gypsy.]

I remember reading somewhere that happy literature has no history; it has no place among serious letters. As a child moves toward maturity, begins to see and feel the world as if for the first time, he throws aside the happy literature—comic books and adventure novels—and turns to the shelf where lie the works of Flaubert, Cervantes, Anderson. . . . Through literature he learns to weep for everything beautifully temporary, and learns that everywhere there is a potential threat, that cat with dirty claws, those cars speeding through red lights, and even your own mother cutting meat with an unwashed knife. He learns through literature, if he is sensitive and keen-minded, to see the world in a different light and at a different angle.

Crazy Gypsy by Luis Omar Salinas is a serious book, a collection of poems by a Chicano who speaks privately of what it is to be a man wind-blown in a rush of experience. The book wears several masks—the romantic, the political, and most visibly, that of loneliness. When reading these poems I ask myself how a man, through his trying years, could endure the loneliness that is so often a framework of his poems—a loneliness that sidesteps racial lines to speak for others. Perhaps only the sensitive, the truly observant, can contend with it, rise each morning with its sourness in his mouth, while the indifferent eat their meals in peace, sit numbly before reruns of *Donna Reed* or *Gunsmoke,* and when it's time to die simply fall into a grave, never wondering what it was all about. Omar, on the other hand, comes to terms with his isolation through poetry; it is a therapeutic act to plead for understanding to a piece of typing paper, as it must have been in **"Nights and Days":**

> I am alone
> and with me
> the roads
> as empty containers
>
> if you become
> saddened
> by suffering
> butterflies
> look to the right
> and you see a town
> on the other side
> where the neighbors
> hide themselves
> like a swallow
> working in hell
> for low pay
>
> I could have
> imagined this
> a world before
> but not this
> night of darkness
> not this night

Here, with a scaffold of spare but intense images, he says to the "you," who is possibly a friend touched sentimentally by the "suffering" of small things, that there are places where the pain is *real:* not poetic pain, not adolescent grimace, not anguish of the psyche over the failure of a baseball team—but pain that occurs from factory or field work. How, then, does loneliness play a part of the poem? It surfaces because priorities are reversed: instead of being touched by human suffering, Omar sees the "you" moved by the flutter of hurt butterflies. He could have imagined a dark world but not where one throws emotion on the wrong creature.

> ***Crazy Gypsy* is a serious book, a collection of poems by a Chicano who speaks privately of what it is to be a man wind-blown in a rush of experience.**
>
> **—*Gary Soto***

There are poems in which women are magical, some virginal, others not nearly so, but all seemingly blessed with the simple dust of the roads. They are, in fact, the archetype of the woman propped up, for better or worse, on a pedestal—a being not to be manhandled or abused, and with whom love is scattered roses, mirrors, and a cleansing rain. Omar's stance in his poems, as in life, is romantic, musing over the women because they are innocent and unattainable, an arm's length away:

> Lonely, bespectacled
> looking for the right words
> to say to the virgin,
> I am amazed by my own trickery.
>
>   . . . . .
>
> She is a vision
>   a rose in an afternoon
>   of silence
>   and there is nothing
>   we can do
>   there is nothing
>   we can say
>
> Like the night of petty artichoke smiles
>   I leave her
>   and walk with cold rains
>   the night calling,
>   facing itself
>   in the mirror.
>
>   ("**Cold Rains**")

Political poems, as everybody has noted, are difficult to write well, though rewarding if executed with craft and a mature statement. They are often simplistic in their utterances, banal in their vision, offering no solution to injustice other than "Let's unite on a common front of brotherhood." Granted, it is necessary to reassure a communion among us Chicanos, to formulate an articulated goal in which to end injustice in "the home of the free"; political poems, however, which are "pat" with lines that verge on propaganda, never call on the reader to consider intently what he is reading. Poetry, after all, should demand attention. Omar's political poems are uneven, general where specifics are needed, silly where seriousness is called for. Omar, I feel, is not travelling in familiar territory when politics come into play; he is much more illuminating when he concerns himself with things from the heart. An exemplary failure is **"Stand Up,"** a chant poem in which he leads a cheer for those radical Fresno State faculty whose contracts, in the late '60s, were under attack from then President Falk:

> Fresno State
> stand up and fight.
>
> Poets
> defend your lives.
>
> America
> stand still
>
> look to the young
> revolution
> and stars.
>
> Fresno State
> stand up and
> fight.

Other weak poems, those I am sure Omar wishes would grow wings and vanish from the pages, are **"The River,"** **"Teran,"** and ***"Las Canciones, Los Versos y Las Luchas del Corazon."*** Nothing is redemptive in them or demands a second reading. The creative spark simply fails to flash. There are, however, several political poems with the power to move a reader to action. They are **"Guevara,"** **"Through the Hills of Spain,"** and the horrific **"Death of Vietnam,"** which is quoted here in its entirety:

> the ears of strangers
>   listen
> fighting men tarnish the ground
>   death has whispered
>   tales to the young
> and now choir boys are ringing
>   bells
>   another sacrifice for America
>
>   a Mexican
>   comes home
> his beloved country
>   gives homage
> and mothers sleep
>   in cardboard houses
>
>   let all anguish be futile
> tomorrow it will rain
> and the hills of Viet Nam
> resume
>   the sacrifice is not over

Something could be said about the poem's structure and tone, the jutting line breaks, the apparent ease of its composition, or the quasi-Latin American stance that leans toward melodrama. These qualities could be examined, but they could draw away from the point, which is one of opposites: that friends are deaf and strangers attentive; that a soldier's return is a return to destitution; that it is O.K.

to shrug one's shoulders and blame the dead for being futile; and that with the verb "resume," there is the suggestion that the hills are mechanistic and far from a communion with nature.

> Luis Omar Salinas has studied the work of Lorca, Hernandez, Vallejo, and Neruda, as a young artist feasts upon the paintings of O'Keeffe or Picasso, and has come away with values to apply to his poetry and, exclusively in his own voice, make into art.
>
> —*Gary Soto*

But the poems which capture our attention, mesmerize us more than others, are those forged and twisted with head-scratching images. They compel us to sit there, perplexed but alert, counting our fingers to see if, indeed, we are on the right planet. What could he mean by "the clouds go berserk," "the reckless noise of stars," or "the earth surrenders to an anarchy of cows"? Obviously Omar has studied, brilliantly and at great length, Spanish and Latin American poetry, taking into consideration the works of Lorca, Hernandez, Vallejo, and Neruda, who all wrote a poetry, at one stage of development or another, marked with surrealism. He has studied their work, as a young artist feasts upon the paintings of O'Keeffe or Picasso, and has come away with values to apply to his poetry and, exclusively in his own voice, make into art. These poems include **"Aztec Angel," "Saturday," "Crazy Gypsy," "Take a Look at the Horizon,"** among others. My favorite is **"Sunday . . . Dig the Empty Sounds,"** which ends with one of the most frightening images I have yet read:

> I survive the rain
> dreaming, lost, frowning
> the shoes of my mother
> talking
> to the children in Africa
> to the crazy dogs
> that huddle in corners
> starving
> empty of sound.

Crazy Gypsy has been out of print [since 1972]. I, as do others, think this is a shame. Here is a book that is important for more than historical reasons, unlike much of Chicano poetry written during the late '60s, and it can't find a publisher, though the author has been searching for one for some time. Three years ago, while browsing through a rare-books store on Telegraph Avenue in Berkeley, a friend spotted *Crazy Gypsy,* squeezed between the good company of Rexroth and Shelley, selling for $12.50, exactly $10.85 more than the original price. He said it was worth every penny, and I would have to agree.

Luis Omar Salinas (essay date 26 February 1982)

SOURCE: A chapter in *Partial Autobiographies: Interviews with Twenty Chicano Poets*, edited by Wolfgang Binder, Palm & Enke, 1985, pp. 147-49.

[*In the following essay, originally composed in 1982, Salinas discusses his life, his literary influences, and poetry writing.*]

I was born June 27th, 1937, in a small town by the name of Robstown, Texas. Christened and baptized in the Catholic Church Luis Omar Salinas. The son of Rosendo Valdez Salinas and Olivia Treviño Salinas. My father was born in the States and my mother in Paraz, Mexico. Before I was age four my mother died of tuberculosis, and I have vague recollections of her. My father worked in farms. At age four I was legally adopted by my uncle and aunt, Alfredo C. Salinas and Oralia Campos Alvarado Salinas. My second father was a clerk in a clothing store and my second mother a housewife. I gained entrance into a lower middle-class family having been born into the peasantry. At age three I lived in Mexico with my sister Irma [who is] a year younger than I [with] my father and mother. My most terrible memory of my childhood was there in Monterrey where we lived next to a madhouse. The screams and strange behavior baffled and scared me. My father had a small business there, and survival was uppermost in our mind then. In the poem **"Mexico Age Four"** I describe that experience. This experience made a lasting impression on me. I could not understand why they were all locked up. And treated so inhumanly. Many years later at the age of twenty I, too, would experience madness. I must have moved about two or three times in my childhood. My fondest memory was during Christmas when I was eight years old and received a bicycle for Christmas. I was out on the street by six a. m. trying out my new bicycle. It came as quite a surprise. I adjusted to my new home on U.S. soil, yet the wounds of my mother's death had not left. They would surface later in the most critical period of my life at age twenty. By age four I was tutored at home by one of my aunts and learned to read and write at that early age. At age five I started school [at] St. Anthony's Grammar School in Robstown, Texas. I was more influenced by my parents than by any of the nuns. I do remember I was an excellent student. At the top of my class. I grew to like old Mexican films where I managed to get a distorted picture of sex, love and *machismo*. They entertained, however, but served mostly as an escape from the real world. What was the real world? I was fearful, bright, a quiet child with very good manners. I guess it was about that age that I grew conscious of being Mexican American. What more to add to man's inhumanity to man. The white world was alien to me. Most of it was bigoted and indifferent. Yes, Luis, there would be forms of evil which could not and would not be understood. I was like in a world with Victor Hugo and his character John Val jailed for stealing a loaf of bread to five years of prison.

I grew up speaking Spanish, today I am rather fluent in both English and Spanish. I don't remember when I wrote my first poem. It must have been while I was in the sanatorium. I must have written it to get a better sense of self, to get some kind of illumination into my life. I do remember at age twenty-one writing poems on paper napkins. I had no knowledge of the craft. My first published poems were published by the Cal State University at Los Angeles *Literary Magazine*. Of course then I had visions of making a lot of money. But I was to find out later poetry is not written with money in mind. It is almost the sacred art of illumination and growth of one's mind. The most rewarding compensation for my poetry has not been money, but a closeness of being. A feeling of speaking to the Gods. One of refinement and culture. Also one of discovery and exploration into the vastness of human experience.

I love to read my poetry in public. For here is a gauge as to how you are doing. The testing ground so to speak. I'm a private person but need the stimulation of groups and intellectual discourse. I love conversation, especially when the subject deals with the arts. I could not function as a hermit.

When I was first going to Los Angeles State College, I found a poet in Spanish by the name of Gustavo Bécquer. It was Adolfo's *Rimas* which actually got me started. If there would be a spiritual father it would have to be him. Later with my education I would add Miguel Hernández and César Vallejo.

I seem to have a strong kinship with the Hispanic and Spanish poets. Having studied so many of them I feel my voice in my poems seems to have been influenced tremendously by them. My work is definitely existential.

The Chicano poets I like most are Gary Soto and José Montoya. I like Soto's work primarily because of his skill. I appreciate Montoya's earthiness also because he does things I don't do. Of the mainstream poets I like Philip Levine and Peter Everwine, two poet teachers of mine.

Of my own poems the ones I like are **"Going North,"** **"Poem for Olivia,"** and **"Through The Hills of Spain."** **"Going North"** I like because of its simplicity. And also it seems to state some Chicano themes. **"Olivia"** I like for its associations and its directness. A poem dealing with someone's death is doubly difficult and I think I handled the language well. **"Through The Hills of Spain,"** I kind of wrote this poem about Miguel Hernández as an observer. This poem [is] about such a magnificent poet and tumultuous period in history, with all the tragic overtones of war. The movement also I feel is excellent. Certainly one of my better inspired poems.

Usually, if I can think of the first line to a poem, I can continue and finish a poem. I've gone through periods with a lot of editing. Sometimes I would rewrite a poem some four times. However, for the most part I write a poem in one sitting. Maybe I'll change a word here and there.

A poet, I see myself like a shoemaker or carpenter. It is certainly the most important and interesting part to my life. For the most part it is the poet's job to focus in a historical sense but in a larger universal sense. Fifty years from now Chicanos and anyone, really, will have a framework of poetry to discuss and find relevant. There is a kind of immortality to literature and its author, and time may make this literature more valuable.

In one poem I remember, to paraphrase, a man can go

mad with too many dreams or be mad for not having any at all. So in my work *Afternoon of the Unreal* I tried to write somewhat after Cervantes. The theme of madness and dream. And the underlying hardfaced reality staring at us constantly. I think it was a conscious effort on my part to deal with the subject of dreams. Most poets are dreamers by nature. Or else why would he be writing poetry, which in the material world is so little esteemed and respected?

I write poetry for selfish reasons. To get recognition. Taste a bit of fame in my time. Also it is a good for one's balance as a human being.

I am not too familiar with Mexico but what I do feel stems from my early childhood and tragedy. I'm really a little afraid when I think of Mexico. Its tremendous poverty. I guess one can find corruption and degradation almost anywhere but I feel Mexico from a one-sided stance, much like a man trying to catch fish in a stream of sand.

The U.S.A. —my thoughts of the States are mostly good. We Chicanos would not be here if we didn't appreciate man's opportunities.

When I wrote the poem **"Many Things of Death,"** I wasn't aware the poem would succeed so well and be received so well critically. In my unfortunate childhood death meant bereavement, and shock, and pain.

Now I see my death as being another experience in a chain of events. As a sort of respite from life. Maybe one seems to look forward to it. No one has written anything from the beyond. It's the last goodbye.

Gary Soto (essay date Summer 1982)

SOURCE: "Luis Omar Salinas: Chicano Poet," in *MELUS,* Vol. 9, No. 2, Summer, 1982, pp. 47-82.

[*In the following excerpt, in part based on interviews conducted with Salinas and his teachers and publishers, Soto examines various poems from Salinas's oeuvre, noting their underlying melancholy and incorporation of surrealistic imagery and political concerns. Much of the unexcerpted portion of the essay provides a biographical overview of Salinas's life, particularly his childhood, adolescence, and college years.*]

Crazy Gypsy is an uneven book of 39 poems, some of which are ungrammatical, scattered in thought, and poorly crafted, while others are a bit silly, as the poem **"Ass"** illustrates:

> Yesterday
> I thought
>   myself a prince
>   rode horseback
>   beside a river
> and fell on my ass
>
> Walked beside her ladyship
>   and fell on my ass
> the kingdom is talking
>   my kingdom
> Salinas fell on his ass
> on the way to mass

The book was so rushed into production that no one person had the opportunity to pencil in corrections and revised lines, thus editing the book for the better. Instead, Luis gathered his poems from drawers, tattered folders, and friends who had kept copies and turned them over to [his publishers] Risco Lozado and Martinez in hopes of making a book. Because of this rush the book was printed with run-on sentences, comma splices, misused pronouns, and confusing subject/verb agreements.

But these problems aside, what we find are many deeply felt, highly imaginative and psychologically true and vulnerable poems, which in part rise from a frightening sense of alienation and loneliness that issues from the death of [Salinas's] mother. As [his teacher Philip] Levine mentioned, nearly all his poems in his first class (Fall, 1965) [at Fresno State] were, in one way or another, about her death. In many respects Luis was trying to exorcise his complex feelings of guilt and fear through writing. If he wrote poems—pages, volumes, shelves—the pains would lessen, become miniscule against a backdrop of other problems, like finding a job, good friends, etc. He had to keep turning over the fact that she was dead and perhaps then, and only then, would his predicament become less tragic, as these lines from **"The Train,"** which was written in 1966 in Levine's class, suggest:

> I must keep overwhelming my mind
> with the mad memory
>   of strange women
> who travel with me incognito
>   running from the scandal of neurosis.

The effect of his mother's death was deep-seated, a catastrophe that was at the center of his life. From this psychological wound came remarkable poems written with an apparent ease. They are direct, evocative, and succinct—qualities that are characteristic of mature writing. Moreover, they are remarkable for their integrity and their propensity to deal directly with facts. Luis would feel that it would be dishonest to fake emotion or, worse, avoid an actual pain. All one could possibly do was to live to some purpose, and his was to write as well as he could and to contend with his loneliness before a typewriter, as he did in writing **"Nights and Days":**

> I am alone
> and with me
> the roads
> as empty containers
>
> if you become
> saddened
> by suffering
> butterflies
> look to the right
> and you see a town
> on the other side
> where the neighbors
> hide themselves
> like a swallow
> working in hell
> for low pay
>
> I could have
> imagined this
> a world before

but not this
night of darkness

not this night

Here, with a scaffold of spare but intense images, he says to the "you," who is possibly a friend touched sentimentally by the "suffering" of small things, that there are places where the pain is *real:* not poetic pain, not adolescent grimace, but pain that occurs from factory or field work. Thus, a paradox exists because priorities are reversed: instead of being touched by human suffering, Luis sees the "you" moved by the flutter of hurt butterflies. He could have imagined a dark world but not one in which someone expends emotion on the wrong creature.

Often Luis wrote his best poems in a state of demonic frenzy in a world of contradictions in which reality is not the one most people wake up to.

—*Gary Soto*

In the title poem, **"Crazy Gypsy,"** which was written in 1967, we find Luis defining his character. He is "nimble footed and carefree," writing "songs / to my dead mother." We find him "end(ing) up in jail / eating powdered eggs," which is a reference to 1960 when he was arrested for breaking a window at the drive-in in Los Angeles. In section three of this five part poem, he rushes through a catalogue of surprising images:

My spine shakes
  to the songs
    of women

I am heartless and lonely
  and I whistle a tune
    out of one of my dreams
      where the world
        babbles out loud
          and Mexican hat check girls
            do a dance composed
              by me in one
                of my nightmares
                  and sold
                    for a bottle
                      of tequila.

The poem continues and what we discover is that he is not one person but many; his disposition may be one of love on Tuesday and hate on Wednesday:

I am Omar
  the Mexican gypsy
. . . .
    I speak of love
      as something
        whimsical and aloof
          as something

I speak of death
  as something inhabiting

the sea
  awkward and removed

I speak of hate
  as something
    nibbling my ear . . .

This poem was praised by Levine in class—its images, humanity, power—so much so in fact that Luis attempted another similar in structure and theme called **"Aztec Angel,"** which would become popular with commercial publishers and the general poetry-reading public. As in **"Crazy Gypsy,"** what makes this poem succeed is its exciting images and unpredictable associations, as sections three and five illustrate:

I am the Aztec angel
  fraternal partner
    of an orthodox
      society
  where pachuco children
    hurl stones
      through poetry rooms
  and end up in a cop car
    their bones itching
      and their hearts
        busted from malnutrition

Drunk
  lonely
    bespectacled
  the sky
      opens my veins
        like rain
      clouds go berserk
        around me
      my Mexican ancestors
        chew my fingernails
I am an Aztec angel
    offspring
  of a woman
    who was beautiful

Interestingly, Luis did not favor this poem, despite the success it received in class and out. He felt that it was a parody, a mere facade of the true emotion that came in writing its twin, **"Crazy Gypsy."** He told Bonnie Hearn, "I wrote **'Aztec Angel'** because I wanted to write another **'Crazy Gypsy.'** It didn't work. I'd already done it."

In turn, there are Luis' political poems which are, for the most part, obviously willed. They are often simplistic in their utterances, banal in their vision, and dependent upon "pat" lines to move the reader. Moreover, they are often general where specifics are needed, silly where seriousness is called for, as the poem **"Stand Up"** [illustrates].

There are, however, some remarkable poems; one of the most impressive is the horrific **"Death in Vietnam":**

the ears of strangers
    listen
fighting men tarnish the ground
  death had whispered
        tales to the young
and now choir boys are ringing
      bells
    another sacrifice for America
  a Mexican

comes [home]
his beloved country
    gives homage
and mothers sleep
        in cardboard houses

let all anguish be futile
tomorrow it will rain
and the hills of Viet Nam
resume
        the sacrifice is not over

Again, as in **"Nights and Days,"** there exists a paradoxical situation of opposites: friends are deaf and strangers attentive; a soldier's return is a return to destitution; it's O.K. to shrug one's shoulders and blame the dead for being futile; and with the very word "resume," there is a suggestion that the hills are mechanistic and far from a communion with nature. The world is confused and its priorities unjustly reversed.

One of Luis' gifts is his ability to conjure exciting images; they are wholly original and perplexing perceptions that rise out of his mind's keen eye, ordering the world in a different light.

—Gary Soto

In many ways his most finished poem is **"Sunday . . . Dig the Empty Sounds,"** which was written in 1968 while he slouched in an all night cafe in Berkeley with Paul Aloujian. The poem is a search for his mother, and it maneuvers through a desolate landscape and a catalogue of bizarre images:

It is Sunday, and I look for you
a meteor wandering, lazy,
simple as dust. I've encountered life here,
a single shadow discovering the breast.
I bake the joys of afternoons in the sun,
with the blood of children
running weakly through the street
struck dumb by dark.
The human eyes of women loiter
here like stars on the cobblestones—
water of the oppressed
standing still on the horizon
caught like a fish in the narrow heart of
    mice . . .

The human mouths of clouds
go by here
running thieves in the sunlight

I survive the rain
dreaming, lost, frowning
while the shoes of my mother
talk
to the children of Africa
to the crazy dogs
that huddle in corners
starving

empty of sound.

What is striking is that Luis wrote this poem, as well as many others, while under a self-induced trance: he hadn't slept in more than forty-eight hours, he was wired on countless cups of sugared coffee, and his conversation with Paul was short-circuited nonsense. Often Luis wrote his best poems in a state of demonic frenzy in a world of contradictions in which reality is not the one most people wake up to. In the poem there are strange intuitive associations such as "the human mouths of clouds" and "caught like a fish in the narrow heart / of mice. .." as well as associations in other poems that are equally striking:

tongues hang in the wind
    and I've got to shout
        to be heard

                "Quixotic Expectation"

I can be a nurse,
a nun
or perhaps
an orange
that will bite
your tongue

                                "Woman"

. . . this corner of the earth
surrenders to the anarchy of cows

                                "Saturday"

As these lines suggest, one of Luis' gifts is his ability to conjure exciting images; they are wholly original and perplexing perceptions that rise out of his mind's keen eye, ordering the world in a different light. Wherever he turns there is a possibility of a new experience through the juxtaposition of "things," for the stimuli he faces daily are forever in transition, a landscape most people do not take in. That is, where one may see shoes under a table and a dog sleeping in the corner, Luis witnesses a contrasting scene:

The shoes of my mother
talk
to the children of Africa
to the crazy dogs
that huddle in corners
starving
empty of sound.

Some may say that these perceptions are wholly surrealistic, but this hints at an aesthetic assumption; that Luis is embracing a literary device or school. Granted, Luis has studied both the French and Spanish surrealists—affinities that will be mentioned in the coming pages—but I feel that Luis' waking world is extraordinarily lush, a fact due, in part, to his sensitivity and appreciation for life in general. In other words, his viewing experience is broader and even deeper, which makes for a different poetry, one in which the images are "tuned" and perplexing. Interestingly, even his ability to read is altered by the way he sees. [One of Salinas's former professors, Peter] Everwine notes:

Luis has the strangest reading of every literary text I have ever heard in my life. He reads a text according to nothing while everyone I know reads to some literary assumptions. But not Luis. Every text is absolutely exotic, to be read

in different ways. And that's terrific . . . but it's
also spooky.

Again, one of Luis' abilities is to turn images that are exciting and often frightening. They are compelling for their
stark perceptions and, furthermore, in their suggesting the
inner workings of his mind—a mind brimming with impressions that are wonderfully alien.

Still, an exciting image alone does not make a poem. It is
one element among several which lead to the complete
poem. If we look again at our initial comments about his
work—the feeling of alienation and loneliness—we discover what is at the heart of his work. Luis is a poet of feeling, and binding this emotion with imagination, complexity, and craft, he produces art in which his central idea is
universal: man caught in a rush of harsh realities. It is a
dark world, chaotic and unfair. Hence poems in which
men and women shoulder their way through unjust sta-
tions of poverty and grim circumstances:

> How ugly the air smells in this town
> as if torn hair and blood
>   were on the paving stones,
> and taxi drivers asleep on their meters,
>   sluts
> drink iced-tea through the shattered
>   windows
>   I see only
>   hungry beggars and sheep
>   on their knees.
>
>   "Mexico Age Four"

Consequently these are poems in which his political notions are for his *raza* and a new world order. Interestingly,
unlike the early Chicano poets (Corky Gonzales, Alurista,
Abelardo Delgado, and the one-poem-poets who have
vanished), Luis did not depend upon a loudly propagandistic voice, but on one that was less assuming, quieter, but
equally convincing. He had studied that with Levine for
three years, and Luis knew that you should not beg for
pity or milk an emotional response from the reader. He
had learned "to show, not tell," a basic notion about writing Levine hammered into his students' minds, often
through a combination of embarrassment, intimidation,
and affection. Thus, through apt instruction and initial
years of what may be seen as a apprenticeship, Luis was
able to write some of his best poems in which his emotion
registered when the subject was loosely political. They are
believable, sincere, and mature, as in these stanzas from
"Guevara":

> Guevara . . . Guevara
>   there is hunger in Bolivia
>   and children mumble on the hilltops
>   with your lips
>   (the river is strewn with dead communists
>   Guevara)
>
> and that mystery that talks of you
>   on that damp earth
>   waiting for that troubled sea
>   to chant
>   Guevara . . . Guevara
>   we have found you
>   your blood fills our throats
>   or lungs

> our bellies
> with a smell as fresh
> as yesterday's fallen snow

and in these stanzas from an elegy for Miguel Hernandez:

> the night is hushed
> mockingbirds listen
> to the tirades of men
> wounded in battle
>
> blood of your blood
> senseless death in the air
> the wind swallows birds
>
> Hernandez . . . Hernandez
>
> There is death caught by the nostrils
>   of the sky
>   there is death everywhere
> the sea calling to forlorn travelers
>
>   Hernandez . . . Hernandez
>   your wound leaves the redness of
>   sky never conquered
>   untouched, virginal
>
> Oh, yawning tenderness
> lust on the wheels of a train
> blood on the faces of bulls
> soil calloused by murder
> homicide of undertakers
> and children
>
>   **"Through the Hills of Spain"**

As these poems suggest, as well as the many others, Luis
had in fact carefully read the surrealists. In the mid-
sixties, just prior to studying under [Henri] Coulette [at
Cal State Los Angeles], he had come across French Surrealist poets [André] Breton and [Paul] Eluard, and what
amazed him was their use of images, many of which did
not make sense but were elegantly distorted and chaotic.
He rolled them through his mind, wrote them on school
folders, and typed them out to see how they appeared on
typing paper. He was charmed by these poets, as well as
by "the beats" whom he had discovered at about the same
time, and began to imitate them, poem after poem—
although none has been saved, except for **"Menagerie."** It
wasn't until 1967, while enrolled in Philip Levine's writing
class, that he was introduced to Spanish and Latin American poets—Vallejo, Hernandez, Lorca, Neruda, and Jimenez. He was taken with these poets because he saw himself
in them and because of their deep generosity toward mankind. He was touched by Vallejo and Hernandez' rise from
the peasant class; by Lorca's fear of the city and its multi-
tudes; by Neruda's belief in the common place; by Jimenez' momentary passion.

He studied their work in Levine's class as well as in the
translation classes he took from Jose Elgorriaga, professor
of Foreign Languages. He carried their books about campus, showing friends poems he especially admired. Even
when he was well and when he was recovering in hospitals,
he kept their books at hand. I remember once when I visited him, he had the complete works of Hernandez open on
the night stand, ready for those who might listen.

This influence is not strictly one of style but also of spirit.

Luis is a poet of feeling, and binding this emotion with imagination, complexity, and craft, he produces art in which his central idea is universal: man caught in a rush of harsh realities. It is a dark world, chaotic and unfair.

—Gary Soto

He saw them as touchstones against an unjust world—poets who lived to some purpose. They were blessed with a profound sense of community, and this is what attracted Luis to them. What they gave to the world, Luis returned by writing poems that affirmed that their lives had been significant. Later, Luis would "walk" behind these poets and their sensibilities, and his vision of this world would become better defined as the result of his further descent into loneliness.

Luis Omar Salinas with Cindy Veach (interview date 1982)

SOURCE: An interview in *Northwest Review,* Vol. 20, Nos. 2 & 3, 1982, pp. 238-41.

[*In the interview below, Salinas relates his interest in death and its import in his poetry as well as his literary influences.*]

"Many Things of Death"
Death today
smells
of apples
worms chewing
their gums

a child with mud
on his hands

today it has
the mouth of an insect
crawling through
the avenues

it has the nightmares
of fish
drunk
on rain

it has the footsteps
of a gardener
wanting to murder
a chair

it has nonsense
in its eyes
a dog barking
at a cloud

a woman opening
an awkward door

it has the stubbornness

of an owl hatching
its eggs

it has the elegance
and laughter
of clowns

many things of death
in the taciturn
protest
of ants

in the unrest of flies

[*Veach*]: *The Spanish term* duende *implies an intensification of the senses as if in the presence of death. Your poem seems to possess* duende, *written as if brushing past death in every line. Do you feel an urgency and intensity, such as this, when you write?*

[Salinas]: I believe in poetry as mystery and would like to think of *duende* as a sort of magic captivating the poet in a kind of intoxication of the senses. It's as if someone were writing the poems for me. I remember writing the poem, **"Many Things of Death,"** in one sitting with little or no editing. I remember the emotion of anger. I followed my intuition like always. I didn't have to think in terms of structure or strategy. It's as if I were talking directly to death, saying, "Stay away." My first experience with death was at age four with the death of my mother, who died at 27. So, in a sense, I had about forty years to prepare the poem.

Could you talk a little about rapid association of images and its importance to your work? Would you consider such associations a technique or do you think it is possible for association alone to be the content of a poem?

Rapid associations are a key to my kind of poetry. In my first book, ***Crazy Gypsy,*** I had a lot of dazzling and striking images. In my second book, ***Afternoon of the Unreal,*** I made a conscious effort at toning down imagery. I am not a poet of the Surreal, yet there are elements of Surrealism in my poetry. One can get lost in Surrealism. My best poems have a directness and a kind of urgency seen, for example, in a line like, "Poverty is the smile from a turtle." I can work with this line since I have already set the way in which the poem is to go. Yet it leaves me with a lot of freedom. Here is the poem to illustrate the way I write:

Poverty is the smile from a turtle,
It is my kin and I entering a river,
It is my nephew telling jokes, feeling
pangs of puberty. Poverty you have me
by the fingers. Mother poverty you have
things well in hand. The nite and you
are twins. When we meet to talk
over supper you never fail to appear.
Yet your handshake is reminiscent
of a promiscuous wench. The door
is open please leave.

In Leaping Poetry, *Robert Bly describes the leap as a jump from the conscious to the unconscious and then back to the conscious mind. To perform these leaps, he feels, the poet must be writing with great spiritual energy. What are your thoughts on such arcs of association? When you deal with the unknown, as you do here, do you feel you have leaped into the unconscious?*

In the poem, **"What is Poverty,"** there is a leap from the first line to the second. Definitely I am going from the conscious to the unconscious. We have a lot of poetry in the unconscious. In fact, I feel, most of our poems are already prepared for us. It is a matter of assimilation.

The clarity and swiftness of this poem reminds me of poets like Lorca, Vallejo and Neruda. Who and what have been the major influences on your writing?

Poets like Lorca, Vallejo and Neruda have been a definite influence on my poetry. In fact, I hold them in awe and reverence. They opened so many doors for me. My first influence was the late romantic Gustavo Adolfo Becquer. I like his sense of being haunted. I still love Becquer's poetry, though it's outdated. Lorca, Vallejo and Neruda made me see the incredible and the tragic. Of course, the great commotion and turmoil of the civil war filled Lorca and Vallejo with a kind of doom. Yet they faced the madness and wrote great poetry. I do feel the major influence in my life has been my mother's death. At age four I was sort of predestined to a tragic vision of life. Also, when madness came at age twenty I was the offspring of pain, fear, rejection. It has been one long battle with madness. These two events nailed me with no reason whatsoever. Yet poetry became like a kind of saving grace. I owe much to contemporary poets like Philip Levine and Peter Everwine.

In "Many Things of Death" death seems always to be just over one's shoulder; not the sober deity of the underworld, but a child, a gardener, an owl. Would you discuss your thoughts concerning death?

Death woke me early. The only way to be somewhat victorious over death is for one to reach somewhat of a state of immortality. Sometimes I feel like Miguel Unamuno. Why should we die. If God dreamt us up, He is going to have to dream us up again after we die. Maybe we will come back like birds. I wouldn't mind being a colorful bird, and my friends as well. There is so much beauty. To spend it in a grave would be a waste. Sometimes I get the feeling I've lived before and that I will live again. Then again, it could be *finis*. But I have great religious energy. We will all meet again in a better place. We might even get a chance to meet Shakespeare, Shelley, Byron, Cervantes. Who knows where the dead go? Maybe the ghosts of great writers go to the *Corrida* on Sundays. The Catholic nuns told me it will be a fine place. Maybe I'll come back as a bullfighter. But I do see greatness in this life. And of late I feel a great lust for life. Maybe we're in heaven already and don't know it. Little miracles in my life tell me a lot. And people capable of great kindness and compassion speak a true language. I feel whatever happens will be for the best.

John Addiego   (review date 1983)

SOURCE: A review of *Darkness Under the Trees,* in *Northwest Review,* Vol. 21, No. 1, 1983, pp. 150-51.

[*In the review below, Addiego commends Salinas's* Darkness under the Trees, *observing that his verse has a dark,* *brooding quality typically associated with Spanish literature.*]

There's a fierce humor in the personal cosmos Salinas creates in his new book, ***Darkness Under the Trees: Walking Behind the Spanish.*** Beneath the humor a compassionate, lonely person is looking squarely at death; the grotesque characters (polite hunchbacks, pregnant barmaids, mad people) are compared to the speaker, whose tonal leaps from the supplicant to the bawdy make him seem equally absurd, and equally genuine:

> Evening becomes evening,
> and I'm not letting up, God.
> I'm still sleeping
> with my neighbor's wife
> on Sundays—
> and sometimes drive nails
> into flowers out of boredom
> and bump into beggars
> when morning goes dead.

This is the voice of someone who doesn't fit easily into society, a person who sympathizes with those who live alone and those on society's fringes. The speaker seems to be drifting outside of time and culture, and his observations often dance along an exuberant edge of madness, as they do in **"Poem Before a Tremendous Drunk":**

> I venture forth onto the avenue
> like an avocado picker in search
> of a woman. I am in an indelicate
> cerebral mood, and the toxic
> whispers of the starlings
> keep my feet in bombastic
> condition. I wish for once
> to come upon this incredible
> world and catch it by the nose,
> toss it to the ground
> and bedevil the evening
> with young sarcasm.

Salinas dedicates several poems to the victims of the Spanish Civil War, as well as to other revolutionary heroes and poets. But this "walking behind the Spanish," speaking to the ghosts of his ancestry, is more evident in several of the more personal, self-exploratory poems than in the "homages." A spirit in synch with the ancestral Spanish *duende* shapes these lines:

> The prostitute is eyeing her nipples,
> they are defenseless, the men come to her
> like fishermen who never go fishing.
> A young man I know has slashed his throat.
> The night grows in America.
> A spider makes its web over my head.
> I light a cigarette,
> a dog barks.
> It is getting cold.

Reminiscent of some of James Wright's American imagery, these poems probe a darkness edged with sensuality. Federico Garcia Lorca [in his "The *duende:* Theory and Divertissement," in *The Poet's Work,* 1979] has defined the "black sounds" of *duende* in Spanish and Mexican expression this way: "These black sounds are the mystery, the roots that probe through the mire that we all know of and do not understand, but which furnishes us with whatever is sustaining in art."

The sensual, amused style of Salinas' poetry has a shadow of darkness over it which seems to descend from this Spanish source. In this new collection his heartfelt delivery and imagination are fashioned to their finest tuning.

Charlotte M. Wright (review date May 1988)

SOURCE: A review of *The Sadness of Days: Selected and New Poems,* in *Western American Literature,* Vol. XXIII, No. 1, May, 1988, p. 91.

[*In the review below, Wright examines the evocative power of* The Sadness of Days.]

The poems in **The Sadness of Days** are not for the faint of heart. Full of anger, blood, spittle, and venom, these poems speak of the clashes of the world: between young and old, between rich and poor, between educated and uneducated, between living and dead. Luis Omar Salinas's poetic voice expresses itself in the language of darkness. Consider these poems as examples: **"Prelude to Darkness," "As Evening Lays Dying," "Darkness Under the Trees," "I Live Among the Shadows," "It Will be Darkness Soon,"** and **"In the Thick of Darkness."** Don't look in this book for "have a nice day" sentiment. What you'll find in these pages is raw, unpolished, angry, and confused emotion.

Gary Soto (review date July-August 1988)

SOURCE: "Voices of Sadness & Science," in *The Bloomsbury Review,* Vol. 8, No. 4, July-August, 1988, p. 21.

[*In the following, Soto offers a generally favorable assessment of* The Sadness of Days.]

The Chicano protest poets of the sixties and early seventies have put down their pens and have gone into real estate or, if they haven't gone off to make a living, to raise a family, to do the best they can, then they have continued to write just as loudly but with fewer willing listeners. In their place, a number of literate poets have surfaced who speak more quietly, but just as urgently, and with a greater expanse of ideas—poets like Alberto Rios, Lorna Dee Cervantes, Jimmy Santiago Baca, Juan Felipe Herrera, Ray Gonzalez, and Cherrie Moraga. It's not that their work is void of political commentary (at times the work *is* political), but they are far more passionate about their feelings, more faithful to their ideas, and more exploratory for themes.

Luis Omar Salinas, probably the most highly respected Chicano poet writing today, was one of those protest poets who managed to write poetry that was political yet artful—not sloppy ramblings. And now we have his major effort, **The Sadness of Days: Selected and New Poems,** a generous collection from five previous books, the earliest being **Crazy Gypsy** (1978).

Salinas is a poet who wears the coat of Don Quixote and the muddy boots of Shelley, a poet placed in an unjust world who muses over his sadness that things never seem right. The world is temporary for Salinas, often dreamy, insecure, and romantic. Yes, romantic. Even the titles suggest his preoccupation with unattainable love: **"Romance in the Twilight," "Lover in a Mad World," "Women Like Taverns I've Dreamt," "Salinas Sees Romance Coming His Way,"** and **"The Woman Follows Me Home As I Walk."** And if the titles aren't romantic, then they are large in their metaphysical implications: **"The Road of El Sueno by the Sea," "I Surrender in the March of My Bones," "Rosita, the Future Waits with Hands of Swans," "When the Stars Get Angry and Coo Above Our Heads,"** among so many others.

> **Salinas is a poet who wears the coat of Don Quixote and the muddy boots of Shelley, a poet placed in an unjust world who muses over his sadness that things never seem right. The world is temporary for Salinas, often dreamy, insecure, and romantic.**
>
> **—Gary Soto**

His literary affiliation lies with Spanish and Latin American poets. We see a bit of Neruda and Hernandez in his work, some Lorca, some Vallejo, but not so much as to trouble us into thinking that he is an imitator. Just as we see a bit of French in Wallace Stevens, and a bit of Whitman in Allen Ginsberg, we live with it. We can certainly live with Salinas' poetry which is lyrical, lush in detail, imaginative, tender one moment and comical the next.

Salinas' central concern, one which resonates in every poem, is visible in the poem **"The Odds."** He says: "Even animals / have customs; I only wish / they could ask a perfect / question like, What time is it?" Salinas would like to hear questions from the animal world he could answer. The questions that men and women raise are large. What could he possibly answer about religion or philosophy, music or literature?

"On the Photographs of Ansel Adams"

Grandeur is always the subject: shards
of sunlight splitting clouds; rubble of lost
boulders under a heaven of cliff face and cumuli;
a tiny cemetery—crosses like fence pickets—
near the ghostly town under the mountains
flooding with white, the moon above
like some Platonic ideal. Always this grandeur,
the abstractions light makes beneath
the imperturbable glacier-wrought peaks.
Nothing of the feminine. Always the implied
movement towards perfection. Climax
of will and the willed vision. Always
the mind and the eye and the mind's eye.
The iceberg yielding to the avarice
of gravity. The river at peak flow
and not after. Desert sand brawling
with sunlight and wind. Not delicate may-apple
or seed husk but fulminating surf. Not

the moment but the moment's passing:
the marsh grass, Glacier Bay, '48, bending
and bent with the attentions of rain.

Salinas addresses the issue of existence, but with a poet's
fondness for image, not a philosopher's gray language. We
have poems where women are "bitches" and, on the next
page, they are "forgotten madonnas." We have compassion for the poor, then hatred for them; landscapes that
are frighteningly dark, then pleasant; seriousness, then
utter comedy. Salinas is particularly noted for his imagination. He has that rare ability to conjure strange but effective images that, at first glance, strike the reader as surreal. It is not surrealism, but a mad way of looking at the
world, because, as he says, "Someone is chasing me up my
arm." *The Sadness of Days* is an important collection of
poetry. Not all the poems are completely successful, but
they are not flat or dull. Salinas certainly deserves a wider
audience.

FURTHER READING

Criticism

Review of *From the Barrio: A Chicano Anthology,* edited by
Luis Omar Salinas and Lillian Faderman. *Choice* 10, No. 9
(November 1973): 1377.
> Praises the editors for including mostly new work in
> *From the Barrio,* arguing that this "book will best be put
> to use as a reader for the general public."

de Ortego y Gasca, Felipe. "An Introduction to Chicano Poetry." In *Modern Chicano Writers: A Collection of Critical Essays,* edited by Joseph Sommers and Tomás Ybarra-Frausto,
pp. 108-16. Englewood Cliffs, N.J.: Prentice-Hall, Inc., 1979.
> General overview discussing thematic aspects and the
> origins of Chicano poetry. The critic briefly cites work
> by Salinas and others, including Ricardo Sánchez, Ro-
> dolfo Gonzales, and Abelardo Delgado.

McKesson, Norma Alarcón. Review of *From the Barrio: A
Chicano Anthology,* edited by Luis Omar Salinas and Lillian
Faderman. *Revista Chicano-Riqueña* 2, No. 2 (Spring 1974):
53-4.
> Notes *From the Barrio*'s value for both Chicano and
> non-Chicano readers, arguing that the volume is themat-
> ically characterized by a "strident identity crisis."

Additional coverage of Salinas's life and career is contained in the following sources
published by Gale Research: *Contemporary Authors,* Vol. 131; *Dictionary of Literary
Biography,* Vol. 82; *Hispanic Literature Criticism;* and *Hispanic Writers.*

Vikram Seth

1952-

Indian novelist, poet, travel writer, and author of children's books.

The following entry provides an overview of Seth's career through 1995. For further information on his life and works, see *CLC*, Volume 43.

INTRODUCTION

Lauded for his versatility, Seth has experimented with such forms as the verse novel in *The Golden Gate* (1986) and produced works in prose and poetry that remark on such diverse places as China, California, and India. Critics have praised his wit and humor and his ability to evoke a sense of the cultures about which he is writing.

Biographical Information

Born in Calcutta, India, Seth spent part of his youth in London. Returning to his homeland in 1957, Seth received his primary and secondary education in India. He then studied philosophy, politics, and economics at Corpus Christi College, Oxford, where he developed an interest in poetry and learned Chinese. After leaving Oxford, Seth moved to California to work on a graduate degree in economics at Stanford University. There he met poet Timothy Steele, who profoundly influenced his work—Seth later dedicated his verse novel, *The Golden Gate,* to him. Seth also spent two years at Nanjing University in China. While there, he published his first collection of poetry, *Mappings* (1980), and hitchhiked across China and Tibet to India, a journey recounted in *From Heaven Lake* (1983), for which he received Britain's most prestigious travel-writing award, the Thomas Cook Prize. Eventually returning to Stanford, Seth took a break from his graduate work to write *The Golden Gate,* which he followed with another collection of poetry, a book of animal fables, and the prose novel *A Suitable Boy* (1993), for which he spent eight years in New Delhi writing and researching.

Major Works

From Heaven Lake is a travelogue describing Seth's experiences on a trip from Nanjing University to his home in Calcutta via Tibet. Rather than merely discussing places to stay or sights to see, he demonstrates the value of cultural adaptability and sensitivity as he describes the land, the people he met, and the fragility of Tibet's cultural heritage in the wake of China's Cultural Revolution. His next work, the poetry collection *The Humble Administrator's Garden* (1985), centers on Seth's life in India and his experiences as a student at Oxford, Nanjing, and Stanford. Claude Rawson noted that the poems are "observant of pathos, of ironies of behaviour, and of the unexpected small exuberances of life." Modeled after Alexander Pushkin's

Yevgeny Onegin (1833; *Eugene Onegin*), *The Golden Gate* is a verse novel composed of nearly six hundred sonnets written in iambic tetrameter. Set in San Francisco, California, during the early 1980s, the story centers on the interactions of three young professionals and their friends and explores issues related to religious guilt, the nuclear arms race, sexuality, love, and death. One of the longest books ever written in English, *A Suitable Boy* has drawn favorable comparisons to the novels of Jane Austen, George Eliot's *Middlemarch* (1872), and Salman Rushdie's *Midnight's Children* (1981). Set in India during the early 1950s, the story centers on two characters: Lata Mehra, for whom her mother actively seeks a husband; and Maan Kapoor, who is searching for meaning in his life. The novel, however, is considered more than an exercise in character study; containing numerous subplots, it provides a vivid and lavishly detailed portrait of India's diverse society and culture.

Critical Reception

Critics have commended Seth's sensitivity to Chinese culture in *From Heaven Lake* and his ability to accurately convey that culture to readers. *The Golden Gate* elicited enthusiastic critical response, with commentators praising it as a work of technical virtuosity suffused with wit and accessible language that moves from elevated literary allusion to colloquial speech. Although a number of reviewers have argued that Seth overemphasized rhyme to the detriment of the story's depth and character development, *The Golden Gate* is generally regarded as a bold achievement at a time when strict adherence to meter and rhyme goes largely unheeded by most poets. D. J. Enright commented: "*The Golden Gate* is a technical triumph, unparalleled (I would hazard) in English. We may not have scorned the sonnet, but we shall hardly have thought it capable of this sustained sequentiality, speed, elegance, wit and depth of insight." David Lehman concurred, arguing that in *The Golden Gate* "Seth makes us care about his characters, proposes a moral criticism of their lives and captures his California setting with a joyous wit little seen in narrative poetry this side of Lord Byron." Critical reaction to *A Suitable Boy* has been mixed. Numerous reviewers have found the length burdensome and the wealth of detail overwhelming in comparison to what they regarded as the slightness of the story's insight and dramatic action. Rhoda Koenig, for instance, has argued that *A Suitable Boy*'s depth "may not trouble readers who seek nothing more than the acquaintance of some agreeable characters and a travelogue of postcolonial India. Those, however, who want to be rewarded with some insight, drama, and artistry . . . may feel that 'quite pleasing' is an insufficiently enticing justification." Most commentators, however, have praised the novel for providing an in-depth treatment of Indian culture. Commenting on the writing in *A Suitable Boy,* Schuyler Ingle stated: "It is absolutely seamless. There are no impediments placed between the reader and the story and the intimate lives of the characters. The reader's immersion in Indian life is so complete that by the time *A Suitable Boy* comes to its successful conclusion, aspects of Indian life that seem exotic—like the idea of arranging a marriage for a daughter—make perfect sense to a Western reader."

PRINCIPAL WORKS

Mappings (poems) 1980
From Heaven Lake: Travels through Sinkiang and Tibet (travel essay) 1983
The Humble Administrator's Garden (poems) 1985
The Golden Gate (verse novel) 1986
All You Who Sleep Tonight (poetry) 1990
Beastly Tales from Here and There (fables) 1992
A Suitable Boy (novel) 1993
Arion and the Dolphin (juvenilia) 1995

CRITICISM

Eve Siegel   (review date Spring 1984)

SOURCE: A review of *From Heaven Lake: Travels Through Sinkiang and Tibet,* in *San Francisco Review of Books,* Spring, 1984, pp. 22-3.

[*In the following review, Siegel compares* From Heaven Lake *to Lawrence Durrell's essays on Greece, arguing that both writers excel in describing the culture, history, and physical qualities of their subjects.*]

Most accounts about the Republic of China in the general market these days are by old China hands: authors like Theodore White, Ross Terrill, and others who have spent large part of their careers as bona-fide sinologists. But here is a first book by a young man quite new to "China watching." Whatever Vikram Seth may lack in years or experience, however, he makes up for [in ***From Heaven Lake***] with his fresh, literary reportage on the people and day-to-day life of contemporary China.

Seth is an Indian, albeit one educated at Oxford and at Stanford University, who provides some striking insights gleaned from his two-year stint as a student at Nanjing into Asia's two largest and most populous nations as they struggle toward modernity. He makes no pretense, however, at being expert in either nation's social, political, or economic problems (though he does predict, in his capacity as a nascent demographer, that China will achieve zero population growth within the next 50 years).

Seth's journal, which he kept during a 1,500-mile hitchhike through northwest China and Tibet enroute home to his native India, is very light on academic analysis of any kind. Nor does he rush into print with the names of his favorite guest houses for overnighting along the way to Lhasa, provide maps with precise locations of truck transport yards that are so essential to catching a successful lift, or tell the reader where to get the best yak-butter tea. There are few, if any, choices in these matters in China's hinterlands. What Seth does over and over again, though, is demonstrate how to be culturally adaptable and sensitive. Not only does he employ these anthropological tools with great skills in dealing with whatever circumstances turn up; he also brings to bear considerable charm, wiles, and a hefty dose of good karma as he slips past Chinese bureaucracy. In this respect, Seth is more akin to travelers of yore who passed this way on the Silk Routes than to today's student tourist.

If Seth's book, enchantingly titled, ***From Heaven Lake: Travels through Sinkiang and Tibet,*** is not a hitchhiker's guide to China's remote regions, it is a fine collection of essays on the people he meets and the lives they lead. There is old Wang, a unit leader at a truck depot in Liuyuan who baffles Seth with his obvious annoyance at Seth's missing a ride that left Lhasa the day before Seth even arrived at the ". . . dusty terminus . . . that is the start of the road south to Tibet. . . ."

And there is Lao Sui, the chain-smoking, 35-year-old driver who gives Seth his first ride from near the Mongolian border to a forlorn spot some 150 kilometers from the Tibetan capital, where the truck gets stuck up to its chassis in mud. Sui not only drives this arduous, bumpy, hazardous, and nerve-wracking route with all the aplomb of an American milkman making his neighborhood rounds, but stops along the way to gossip, haggle with hawkers for the best watermelons at the lowest price, deliver presents and essential goods to friends—and take orders for more the next time he's coming through.

Seth's most intimate Tibetan contact—with Norbu and his family—provides haunting insight into the lives of people who suffered in the throes of China's Cultural Revolution. The arrest and imprisonment of Norbu's father, the death of his mother, and a pervasive feeling of persecution keeps the entire family looking over its shoulder long after the father has been released and the massive internal anarchy has subsided.

Throughout the journey Seth brings a poet's eye, wry humor, and a gifted linguist's love for nuance to his interactions. He is drawn to China, and especially Tibet, more by a longing to know the roots of his cultural and literary heritage than by mere wanderlust. He isn't making this journey to see strange and distant lands, but to absorb their ancient traditions and modern values, and to be near their mystic powers. Hence, he "cannot speak at all" when he sees the Potala Palace for the first time; and his frequent references to the effects of the Chinese Cultural Revolution upon people and their revered traditions convey a poignant message about the fragility of ancient heritage in our times:

> This day Zhi Xiong came to the old
>   temple.
> He came from far away with no other
>   intention
> Than to see the ancient temple,
> And he saw it and wept.

Though Seth is quoting a Chinese poem he found scribbled on the ruins of a temple just outside Dunhuang, the words appear to capture the real motivation lurking in Seth's own heart for this odyssey.

Seth's inspiration for travel through Tibet and his style of writing is perhaps best compared to Lawrence Durrell's essays and articles on Greece. As Greece provided a primal source of religious mythology and literary inspiration for the British author, so Tibet does for the Indian. Both men—poets, multi-lingual, passionately literate—could not fail to be compelled by countries whose geographical borders represent, as Durrell said of Greece, only "a state of mind." Like the Mekong, Yangtze, Indus, and Bramaputra rivers—which Seth notes have their headwaters in Tibet—Seth is seeking out the sources of those legends, fables, and stories that have helped shape his own culture.

Yet, for both writers, the universal mysteries take their place as casual though omnipresent backdrops to the warmth, humor, and frustrations of daily life in these respective countries. Adopted by local people during his time in Corfu as a young man, Durrell, like Seth, marvelled at the native hospitality about which "there is nothing to do but surrender yourself." Like Durrell, Seth possesses an uncanny ability to become part of his surroundings. His English and American friends sing their songs and the Chinese applaud politely; Seth sings the theme song from *Awara,* an Indian love film with enormous popularity throughout China, and the Chinese not only sing along with him—in Hindi, no less—but also recognize him as one of their own. As an Asian traveling through Asia, Seth is accepted by people from every strata of Chinese society in a way that few *waibin* (foreign guests) from Western countries could be.

At another time Seth is hauled out of bed at 3:15 am by the police and grilled about what he is doing in this town, since it is not among those listed on his precious travel pass. *"Guiding shi guiding"* (regulations are regulations), the police rave—until they notice a photograph of Seth's family, taken in their New Delhi home. Asiatic civility returns at the sight of this photo, and Seth is escorted back to his room with apologies for the inconvenience.

Like Durrell's "travel writings," in which, if the reader never sets foot on a Greek island, he will know the smells, sounds, and tastes of it, *From Heaven Lake* shows that Seth has a similar power to unfold distant landscapes with sensual clarity and render them immediate with instinctive rapport for other peoples. He dedicates the book to "the people I met along the way," suggesting an affinity with the philosophy of Lao-tzu. For the receptive traveler, then, "the way" may well become the "tao," or the path to self-knowledge. "Because water excels in benefitting the myriad creatures without contending with them and settles where none would like to be, it comes close to the way," wrote Lao-tzu some 2,400 years ago. *From Heaven Lake* moves Vikram Seth, traveler, like a flow of water down distant mountains, inexorably towards the "tao," where lovers of fine writing are welcome to join him.

David Lehman   (review date 14 April 1986)

SOURCE: "A Sonnet to San Francisco," in *Newsweek,* Vol. CVII, No. 15, April 14, 1986, pp. 74-5.

[Lehman is an American poet and critic. In the following review of The Golden Gate, *he praises Seth for revitalizing the novel in verse.]*

Vikram Seth is scarcely your conventional first novelist. Born in Calcutta 34 years ago, educated at Oxford, he's the author of a "Tibetan travel book" titled *From Heaven Lake* and is currently completing a dissertation at Stanford University on the economic demography of China. But nothing about his background will quite prepare you for *The Golden Gate,* Seth's utterly original and utterly delightful novel about Yuppiedom in "light-pearled, / Fog-fingered" San Francisco, "the loveliest city in the world." What distinguishes the novel from any other you'll pick up this year is its form. Inspired by Pushkin's *Eugene Onegin, The Golden Gate* consists of close to 600 sonnets. Everything from the dedication, acknowledgments and contents pages to the author's bio is written in a sprightly iambic tetrameter.

In setting out to revitalize verse as a storytelling medium, Seth fulfills all the requirements of first-rate fiction. He writes with the fluidity and directness of prose but with a buoyancy and intensity available only in verse. The effect is a little like that of a comic opera, with lyric arias punctuating the recitative. It begins when John, a workaholic Silicon Valley engineer, sheepishly bares his lonely heart to his ex-girlfriend Jan, a sculptor who doubles as the drummer in a rock band called Liquid Sheep. Here's how they talk between bites of Chinese food:

> "I'm young, employed, healthy,
>   ambitious,
>   Sound, solvent, self-made,
>   self-possessed.
> But all my symptoms are pernicious.
>   The Dow-Jones of my heart's
>   depressed.
> The sunflower of my youth is wilting.
>   The tower of my dreams is tilting.
> The zoom lens of my zest is blurred.
>   The drama of my life's absurd.
> What is the root of my neurosis?
>   I jog, eat brewer's yeast each day,
> And yet I feel life slip away.
>   I wait your sapient diagnosis.
> I die! I faint! I fail! I sink!"
>   "You need a lover, John, I think."

Jan's solution is to advertise John's plight (*"Young handsome yuppie, 26 . . ."*) in the personal columns of the *Bay Guardian.* A plot full of plausible complications ensues. What begins in whimsy leads to romance (John meets Liz Dorati, a recent product of Standford Law) and then to a chain reaction of romantic reversals and realignments. Long before the novel's unhappy but poetically just ending, we begin to recognize John's personal ad as an improbable but no less effective metaphor for characters who are afflicted with loneliness but persist in "lusting for love."

The San Francisco these Yuppies inhabit is an ever-ever land of microchips and macrobiotics, "holistic / Modes of ingestion" and peaceniks. Seth gently satirizes the antinuke demonstration that drastically changes his characters' lives: against a backdrop of "an inflated / Blue whale with *Save the Humans* scrawled / Across its side," Phil, John's college roommate, runs into Liz wheeling her cat, Charlemagne, in a baby carriage. Seth's playful wit works as easily to elevate the humble (Charlemagne is an inveterate scene stealer) as to mock human pomp and arrogance. But for all the comic set pieces, the novel's ultimate morality is severe. Crucially, it's the bisexual and idealistic Phil, a "good atheist Jew" who quit his job at Datatronics to join the peace movement, who ends up favored by fortune while priggish, homophobic John emerges with his initial desolation intact.

None of this may have worked in prose; in verse it's a nonstop pleasure. Seth makes us care about his characters, proposes a moral criticism of their lives and captures his California setting with a joyous wit little seen in narrative poetry this side of Lord Byron. A scene in which kids and cats cavort around a piano evokes this characteristic fusion of puns and literary allusions: "Thus the young yahoos coexist / With whoso list to list to Liszt." Readers looking for an antidote to the trendy nihilism on display in so many first novels these days need look no further.

Bruce King   (review date Summer 1986)

SOURCE: "A Satirical Neoformalist," in *The Sewanee Review,* Vol. XCIV, No. 3, Summer, 1986, pp. lxiv-lxvi.

[*An American educator and critic, King has written extensively on Indian poetry. In the following review, he discusses* The Humble Administrator's Garden *in relation to postmodernism.*]

There was a radical populist form of postmodernism in the 1960s in which modernist high art was seen as the enemy of immediacy, self-expression, and fulfillment; more recently a conservative neoformalism has challenged modernist poetics. Vikram Seth, whose *The Humble Administrator's Garden* won the new Commonwealth Poetry Prize for Asia, reports on surfaces and the trivia of life in purposefully clichéd language, stereotyped ideas, using such forms as the sonnet, quatrain, and epigrammatic couplet. While some poems are written in free verse, Seth usually writes a monosyllabic, regularly stressed line. A refusal to look inward, a celebration of simple pleasures and of survival, and a half-serious resort to platitude and pastiche for amusement and as defense make Seth a poet of our time, when eclecticism, historicism, and self-aware artifice are associated with postmodernism.

The Humble Administrator's Garden is divided into poems about China, where Seth studied for two years; India, where he was born and raised; and California, where he now lives. Images of national trees and leaves are used both to unify the volume and to suggest different cultural styles. China appears to be a place to discover universal brotherhood despite cultural differences, India is a land of memories and lost relations, but America despite all its comforts and pleasures is lonely and dangerous. While the Chinese poems are imagistic and atmospheric, tendencies toward *chinoiserie* are held in check by rigid western stanzaic forms and by worldly wisdom. Often the poems offer analogies to the poetics of their creation. In the title poem ["**The Humble Administrator's Garden**"], a sonnet, there is a "plump gold carp," a "lily pad," a "Fragrant Chamber," a "Rainbow Bridge," a "willow," a "lotus," and "half a dozen loquats"; but such beauty has been unscrupulously achieved: "He may have got / The means by somewhat dubious means." Administrative practicality creates the self-satisfying poetic art of the garden: "He leans against a willow with a dish / And throws a dumpling to a passing fish."

The personality offered is of a social observer with little revealed inner life; the manner controls such emotions as fear, isolation, envy, and boredom. The California poems refer to loneliness, old letters, former loves, absence, and nostalgia for a foreign (European) past, presumably when Seth was a student at Oxford before coming to America. Emotions are mocked by expressing them platitudinously: "The fact is, this work is as dreary as shit. / I do not like it a bit." "There is so much to do / There isn't any time for feeling blue." Pastiche, rhyme, stanzaic structure, and controlled comedy contribute to a conscious formalism, a display of artifice that purposely lowers the pressure. As in the poetry of Philip Larkin, the lexis is varied to invigorate an unreverberant diction.

Although some of the poems are so laid-back as to be teasingly close to triviality, there is often a threat to survival even when the tone shifts among wit, comedy, humor, and satire to celebrate West Coast American popular culture. The ten six-line stanzas of **"Abalone Soup"** narrate an evening when friends were diving for abalone in the Pacific ("Eight thirty. Where are they? At nine o'clock / I'll call up next of kin. 'How do you do— / Mrs. Gebhart? Your son was lost at sea, / A martyr to cuisine.' Ah, abalone"). Seth's sense of exile, of being a world traveler and an East Indian settled in California, must contribute to his awareness of the incongruities of life in contemporary America.

There is a high but eclectic intertextuality in **"Ceasing upon the Midnight,"** which begins with the absurdity of: "He stacks the dishes on the table. / He wants to die, but is unable"; moves through memories of other countries and cultures; and returns to an unromantic alcoholic present: "The bottle lies on the ground. / He sleeps. His sleep is sound." Deftly and ironically maneuvering its way through obvious echoes, the poem imitates the structure, movement, and psychology of the typical grand romantic ode, which is undermined by witty but bland irony, part of a very unromantic poetic: "the rules / of metre, shield him from / Himself." Consequently "To cease upon / / The midnight under the live-oak / Seems too derisory a joke." The style holds off destructive emotions.

The final poem in **The Humble Administrator's Garden** is **"Unclaimed,"** which epigrammatically comments upon a passing sexual encounter: "To make love with a stranger is the best. / There is no riddle and there is no test." The throw-away manner, like the theme, is a demonstration of a defensive position, "not aching to make sense." Claiming "That this is all there is," Seth controls by deflating romantic urges; he aims at being relaxed, unengaged.

The dampening of emotions, the simultaneous parody and celebration of stereotypes and clichés, has been a fashionable stance in sophisticated pop music. That one of Seth's poems has already been recorded, while others are written in song forms, shows that postmodernists make little distinction between high and mass culture.

While his ideas and style resemble those of Timothy Steele, a poet whom he admires, Seth is less tense, and less metaphysical. For those educated on modernist literature, Seth's poetry can seem shockingly slight and pseudo-traditional; but with familiarity the poems deepen to reveal an unexpectedly original contemporary writer.

Alan Hollinghurst   (review date 4 July 1986)

SOURCE: "In the Onegin Line," in *The Times Literary Supplement*, No. 4344, July 4, 1986, p. 733.

[*Hollinghurst is an English novelist, editor, and critic. In the following review, he praises* The Golden Gate *for its technical virtuosity but complains that the form lacks the subtlety of prose.*]

The Pushkin stanza is a wonderfully self-renewing form. Fourteen lines long, it gathers together two kinds of quatrain and three couplets into tight units which are none the less full of movement and contrast, fleeter and less architectonic than sonnets, the closure of the quatrains offset by the forward-moving couplets at the centre, and brought to epigrammatic poise by the couplet at the end. It is a form whose inner counterpoint gives it both gravity and levity, and it is hard to imagine a better vehicle for social verse narrative which aims to be both reflective and lightly comic. Its small but perceptible vogue in recent English poetry, boosted perhaps by Charles Johnston's acclaimed translation of *Eugene Onegin* in 1977, has not always reflected its particularly Pushkinian qualities: Peter Levi's *Ruined Abbeys* (1968) set subject perversely at odds with medium; Andrew Waterman's *Out for the Elements* (1981), though full of lexical ingenuity, had too little narrative, too much bragging confessional; John Fuller's *The Illusionists* (1980), on the other hand, a tale which exposed an innocent's progress through the machinations of the London art world, and centred on a forged Hogarth picture of *The Rape of the Lock,* reconnected the form to historic tradition, and exploited its potential for Byronic digression as well as Augustan concision.

Vikram Seth's **The Golden Gate,** a verse novel of modern Californian life over 8,000 lines long, is not so funny, or so digressive. It does not draw such attention to the difficulties of the stanza or make such ostentatious comedy of solving them: it raises a smile rather than a laugh. But it is a technical *tour de force.* Seth has gone as far as can be imagined towards ease of diction, and at its best his stanza seems an entirely natural medium, through which he moves, for page after page, with effortless fluency. To be sure, there is a certain amount of waxing, doffing and inditing, half-obsolete short cuts to rhymes or metrical evenness. And the main characters—priggish yuppie John, glamorous barrister Liz, gay, conscience-racked Ed, feminist sculptor Jan, sexy dropout Phil and his son Paul—tirelessly fill out short lines with their conveniently monosyllabic names: " 'Phil, don't / Defend her . . .' 'John, I don't care greatly / whose side I'm taking' " is a typical exchange. Perhaps the air of manic sociability and bristling egos that results is a deliberate part of Seth's portrait of his adoptive California.

Certainly there is something essential that goes unexplained behind this bizarre book. In a way it calls for more authorial intrusion *à la* Pushkin, more pointers to the author's relation with his material. Seth doesn't appear *in propria persona* until Chapter Four, when he has got Ed and Phil into bed together, and with slightly arch propriety steps forward to draw a veil over what they do. In Chapter Five he plays blandish homage to *Onegin* and Johnston ("Sweet-watered, fluent, clear, light, blithe") and records the horror of a publisher, met at a party, at the idea of a verse novel. But we would like Seth to socialize with us far more often. The sleekness of the whole accomplishment intensifies the enigma: why has he undertaken the project in the first place? What is it about these people that merits his or our extended attention?

The impetus seems to be partly satirical and polemical: the

faddishness of Californian life is paraded and indulged; and the novel centres persuasively on an anti-nuclear protest and an eloquent speech made at a demonstration outside "Lungless Labs". It is also affectionate and romantic, with abundant descriptions of the beauty of the country and a sense of Californian *douceur de vivre.* The characterization of Phil is the most inward and interesting, as he looks back with pain on a marriage a year dead, answers his little boy's questions, follows his own heart and mind into rejection of Reaganite society and into two love affairs. And there are passages of real poignancy about the deaths of one or two of the characters. Something rather disturbing and perhaps unintended happens, though, when all these concerns are treated in the ambiguous ethos of the Pushkin stanza, especially if the author abstains from his role as guide and prompt. The effect is in part of an up-market version of Cyra McFadden's *The Serial,* of scintillating technique brought to bear on evidently banal material, of soap transmogrified. Yet at the same time the verse, for all its suaveté, seems to trap its protagonists in artificial attitudes, serving them up in a light *blanquette* of general and motiveless irony. It is by no means the same as writing in prose. Time and again in **The Golden Gate** one sees how the form has prevented the subtlety, the economic naturalness of prose narrative, and in turn invested everything that is described with an air of faint but irreducible fatuity. Just as they are made to matter one discovers that one doesn't care about Seth's characters after all.

It is very hard in the end to say what one thinks of this book—except that such sharp-eyed and sophisticated talent can only go on to do something even more extraordinary; perhaps something which strikes more unhesitatingly to the heart of the matter.

Whitney Balliett   (review date 14 July 1986)

SOURCE: "John and Liz, Phil and Ed," in *The New Yorker,* Vol. LXII, No. 21, July 14, 1986, pp. 82-3.

[*Balliet is an American journalist, nonfiction writer, and critic. In the following review, he remarks favorably on* The Golden Gate.]

During the last half of the nineteenth century, the long poem (epic, narrative, meditative, pastoral), entrenched for almost three hundred years, was slowly dispossessed by the Victorian novel. The long poem has made sporadic returns—in the work of Eliot, Pound, Auden, Spender, Betjeman, John Berryman, Robert Penn Warren, and Alfred Corn, and in the cousinly verse novels and verse plays of the Benét brothers, Christopher La Farge, Maxwell Anderson, Christopher Fry, and Eliot. And now we have, like the reappearance of the ivory-billed woodpecker, Vikram Seth's verse (and first) novel, **The Golden Gate**. Some essential statistics: The book has five hundred and ninety-four stanzas, including a stanza each for acknowledgments, dedication, table of contents, and a note about the author. The stanzas are patterned on the sonnetlike form developed by Pushkin in *Eugene Onegin,* which was published in 1833. They are in iambic tetrameter, and the rhyme scheme is aBaBccDDeFFeGG. The lowercase letters denote feminine rhymes (a two-syllable rhyme, with

the accent on the first syllable, as in "wilting" and "tilting"), and the uppercase denote masculine rhymes (a stressed terminal-syllable rhyme, as in "day" and "away"). Seth was born in Calcutta in 1952, graduated from Oxford, and is working toward a Ph.D. in economic demographics at Stanford. He has published a travel book and a book of poems, and he lives in San Francisco.

The Pushkin stanza was designed more for speed than for emotional content, and it is surprising how much Seth packs into it. The book's technical aplomb, pleasing bits of wit, and general hustle very nearly conceal its keening and sorrow. (Separated from the elegance and ease of his verse, Seth's story sounds almost maudlin.) It is 1980, and John, a clever twenty-six-year-old Silicon Valley executive, is

> Gray-eyed, blond-haired, aristocratic
> In height, impatience, views, and face,
> Discriminating though dogmatic,
> Tender beneath a carapace
> Of well-groomed tastes and tasteful
>   grooming.

He is also bored, lonely, and sorry for himself. He telephones a former girlfriend, Janet Hayakawa, a sculptor and a drummer in a rock band called Liquid Sheep, and they have lunch. Unbeknownst to John, Janet then places a lonely-hearts ad for him in a newspaper, and John, angered at first, finds Miss Right—a handsome and irresistible lawyer named Liz Dorati. John and Liz fall in love, and John comes (unpleasantly) to life. Plot Two appears. Phil Weiss, an old friend of John's, has been deserted by his Wasp wife, who has gone back East to marry someone else, leaving Phil with their only child, Paul. John and Liz move into an apartment, and at their house-warming Phil meets Ed, Liz Dorati's younger brother. Phil and Ed fall in love. Ed, who keeps a pet iguana named Schwarzenegger, is younger than Phil, and his religious views inhibit him, and the two men break up. The story continues to startle us—not always persuasively—and no more should be said of it except to point out that John, for all the misery he brings down on his difficult self, becomes comprehensible, and even affecting, by the end of the book.

It takes Seth a while to get his tetrameters going. Here is Chapter One, Verse 7:

> A linkless node, no spouse or sibling,
> No children—John wanders alone
> Into an ice cream parlor. Nibbling
> The edges of a sugar cone
> By turns, a pair of high school lovers
> Stand giggling. John, uncharmed, discovers
> His favorite flavors, Pumpkin Pie
> And Bubble Gum, decides to buy
> A double scoop; sits down; but whether
> His eyes fall on a knot of three
> Schoolgirls, a clamorous family,
> Or, munching cheerfully together,
> A hippie and a Castro clone,
> It hurts that only he's alone.

By Verse 36 of the same chapter, he has begun to take hold:

> Time sidles by: on television

The soaps dissolve, the jingles change.
Defeat or pity or derision
Constricts our hearts. Our looks grow
   strange
Even to us. The grail, perfection,
Dims, and we come to view rejection
As an endurable result
Of hope and trial, and exult
When search or risk or effort chances
To grant us someone who will do
For love, and who may love us too—
While those who wait, as age advances,
Aloof for Ms. or Mr. Right
Weep to themselves in the still night.

Halfway through the book, a Catholic priest makes an anti-nuclear speech at a rally which lasts nine pages, and it is eloquent and passionate:

Killing is dying. This equation
Carries no mystical import.
It is the literal truth. Our nation
Has long believed war was a sport.
Unoccupied, unbombed, undying,
While "over there" the shells were flying,
How could we know the Russian dread
Of war, the mountains of their dead?
We reveled in acceleration
At every level of the race;
And even now we're face to face
With mutual extermination
We talk as blithely as before
Of "surgical strikes" and "limited war."

But before we get this far Seth, who directly addresses the reader, is busy laughing at himself. He tells a book editor at a party that he is writing a novel—in verse:

. . . He turned yellow.
"How marvelously quaint," he said,
And subsequently cut me dead.

Two stanzas later, Seth says to us:

How do I justify this stanza?
These feminine rhymes? My wrinkled muse?
This whole passé extravaganza?
How can I (careless of time) use
The dusty bread molds of Onegin
In the brave bakery of Reagan?
The loaves will surely fail to rise
Or else go stale before my eyes.

But they don't; Seth pulls off his feat with spirit, grace, and great energy. He reaches a perfect level in his verse—somewhere just below poetry and to the right of the song lyrics of Lorenz Hart, Cole Porter, and Johnny Mercer. But, unlike them, he has no music to lean against.

Marjorie Perloff (review date November-December 1986)

SOURCE: " 'Homeward Ho!': Silicon Valley Pushkin," in *The American Poetry Review,* Vol. 15, No. 6, November-December, 1986, pp. 37-46.

[*An Austrian-born American educator and critic, Perloff has written extensively on modern poetry. In the following excerpt from a review of* The Golden Gate, *she asserts that*

Seth's concern with rhyme weakens the novel's characterization, plot, and satirical force.]

The big news is that rhyme is back. More specifically, that after almost a century of free-verse dominance the long narrative poem written in rhyming metered stanzas is back. "Compose," said Ezra Pound in 1912, "in the sequence of the musical phrase, not in sequence of a metronome." And again, "Do not retell in mediocre verse what has already been done in good prose." Self-evident as these twin propositions seemed to the great American Modernists from Pound, Williams, and H.D. to Lowell and Bishop, Merwin and Kinnell, O'Hara and Ashbery, Creeley and Levertov, James Wright and Charles Wright, we are now witnessing a renewed interest in what we might call an unabashed metronomism, coupled with a desire somehow to "retail" in verse the most prosaic of suburban tales. Or so it would seem from the wide-spread enthusiasm, indeed euphoria, generated by the publication of *The Golden Gate*.

Vikram Seth's "novel in verse" is divided into thirteen books of variable length. Its stanza (there are 590 in all) is that of Pushkin's *Eugene Onegin* (1823-31), which is to say an iambic tetrameter stanza of fourteen lines, rhyming AbAbCCddEffEgg, where the capital letters indicate feminine rhymes. The fourteen-line stanza recalls, of course, both the Shakespearean and the Petrarchan sonnet: we can read it as an octave (Shakespearean quatrain plus two couplets) followed by a sestet (Petrarchan quatrain plus final couplet). But the *Onegin* stanza avoids strong medial division in the interest of flexibility, and indeed, the closest English counterpart to Seth's verse unit is the ottava rima stanza of Byron's *Don Juan,* which similarly drapes its syntax over a series of lines (ababab), only to come down hard on the clinching couplet. In Seth's hands, the resulting stanza looks like this:

The food arrives as soon as ordered.
Impressed and ravenous, John relents.
His chopsticks fasten on beef bordered
With broccoli. Enticing scents
Swim over the noise, the greasy table.
Two bottles each of beer enable
Small talk and large, in cyclic waves,
To wash their shores, and John behaves
At last less stiffly if not sadly.
"How are the cats?" "Just fine." "And you?"
"Great." "And the sculpture?" "Yes, that too."
"Your singing group?" "Oh, not so badly.
But I came here to hear your song.
Now sing!" "Jan, I don't know what's wrong."

The scene is an inexpensive Chinese restaurant in San Francisco: John Brown (the Silicon Valley microchip/defense-contract hero) is having lunch with Janet Hayakawa (an ex-lover and lover-again-to-be, who is a sculptress by avocation and earns a living playing the drums with a rock group called "Liquid Sheep"); the purpose of the lunch is to discuss John's "problem," which is that he needs a girl. In what follows, Jan helps him find one (by means of an ad in the "Personals" column of the local paper), and the plot, such as it is, takes off from there. Boys get girls (John gets a lawyer named Liz Dorati) or sometimes boys (Phil Weiss, deserted by Claire

Weiss, gets Ed Dorati), boys lose girls (John loses Liz) and get others (Jan), boys and girls go to parties, restaurants, concerts, and antinuclear rallies; girls have pet cats, with names like Charlemagne (Liz's) or Cuff and Link (Jan's), that sometimes come between lovers.

What makes this material interesting? Bruce Bawer, in a glowing review for *The New Criterion* [(May 1986)], writes:

> Let me begin by making it clear what *The Golden Gate* . . . is not. It isn't poetry: it doesn't have (or attempt to have) the requisite depth or density; it isn't rich in metaphor or other poetic devices. . . . Nor is *The Golden Gate* a great novel: there can be little doubt but that had it been written in prose, its characters would have come across as rather insignificant, its plot as less than compelling.
>
> What this book *is* however, is an extraordinarily accomplished work of narrative verse. . . .

And Bawer goes on to praise Seth's "charming story," its "marvelous wit" that "has given new life to a genre that, for no good reason, has in the present literary climate come to be considered passé, retrograde, even infantile." "The result of [Seth's] efforts," Bawer concluded, "is one of the most delightful new books in recent memory."

How a book that has neither poetic nor novelistic value can nevertheless be an exemplary verse narrative isn't clear to me, these being distinctions we would never make in the case of its parent texts, *Don Juan* and *Eugene Onegin*. Bawer's encomium is, in any case, echoed by John Hollander in *The New Republic* [(21 April 1986)]:

> . . . this brilliantly fashioned tale of life among a number of Bay Area yuppies is never anything less than quaintly, and most unqualifiedly, marvelous. . . . The use of expertly controlled verse to give moral substance and extraordinary wit and plangency to a far from extraordinary tale is an astonishing achievement in its own right.

Again, X. J. Kennedy (*Los Angeles Times Book Review*, 6 April 1986) says of Seth's versification, "Such fluency probably hasn't been heard in English since Alexander Pope went around letting heroic couplets effortlessly tumble from his lips." This curiously Romanticized reference to Pope suggests that in the late twentieth century rhyming has become so exotically remote that we find the sheer utterance of like sounds cause for veneration. Even a critic as stringent and austere as Susan Sontag compares *The Golden Gate* to *Eugene Onegin* in its "particular mix of wit, sagacity, and rue" and praises Seth's poem as "a thrilling, subtle literary achievement."

What poem or book of poems in recent memory has earned such praise? And what does the extravagance of the critics' praise tell us about the current situation in poetry? It is the latter question that especially concerns me here. Let me begin by looking at the way rhyme works in Seth's long "novel in verse."

At its most elementary level, rhyme affords us the pleasure of discovering similarity in dissimilarity and vice-versa. For example:

Little Miss Muffett
Sat on her tuffet
Eating her curds and whey.
Along came a spider
And sat down beside her
And frightened Miss Muffett away.

"Muffett" and "tuffet," "whey" and "away," "spider" and "-side her"—in each of these pairs, words of quite different meaning (and, in the case of the second and third rhymes, different syntactic function) are unexpectedly—and thus pleasurably—brought together by sound. Advertising slogans ("Winston tastes good / like a cigarette should"), political aphorisms ("I like Ike"), jump-rope jingles ("All in together, girls! / How do you like the weather, girls?"), football cheers—these elementary verse forms answer to our most basic yearning for both repetition and difference.

Secondly, and more important, rhyme plays a significant role as a metrical and rhetorical marker, signalling the ends of lines and organizing lines into larger stanzaic units. Again, the pleasure produced is that of sameness in difference: the syntax of a given stanza propels us forward even as the metrical repetition and rhyming pulls us back and makes us aware of the verse unit itself. Consider the following stanza from *Don Juan*, in which Byron's narrator supplies us with a devastating account of the hero's prudish mother, Donna Inez:

> Perfect she was, but as perfection is
>   Insipid in this naughty world of ours,
> Where our first parents never learn'd to kiss
>   Till they were exiled from their earlier bow-
>   ers
> Where all was peace, and innocence, and bliss
>   (I wonder how they got through the twelve
>   hours),
> Don Jose, like a lineal son of Eve,
> Went plucking various fruit without her leave.

This ottava rima stanza is made up of a single sentence, with heavy compounding and subordination and a comic parenthetical aside in the seventh line. But even as the syntax propels us over the line breaks, heading for the conclusion of the period after "leave," the rhymes create a kind of counterpoint, forcing the sentence, so to speak, into reverse. "Perfect she was but as perfection is"—the line break between "is" and "Insipid" suggests that line 1 is a self-contained clause on the analogy of "Perfect is as perfect does." Furthermore, the contrast of this "is" with the "kiss" and "bliss" denied to the likes of the prudish Donna Inez sets up its own pattern, in counterpoint to the narrator's overt statement. At the same time, the movement that takes us from "ours" to "bowers" is undercut by the narrator's cynical aside, "I wonder how they got through the twelve hours." All is now set up for the couplet which presents us with the "forbidden fruit" of Inez's bogus "paradise": "Don Jose, like a lineal son of Eve, / Went plucking various fruit without her leave."

Take away the rhymes from such a stanza and it loses its life blood. Pushkin's *Eugene Onegin* (Seth cites Charles Johnston's "luminous translation" of *Onegin* as his source) resembles the Byronic model in its brilliant foregrounding of the narrator as *improvisatore*, advising and cajoling the reader, making witty asides, commenting on the actions of his characters and participating in their every thought and gesture. The resultingly fluid narrative structure is played off against the stability of the tetrameter stanza, with its complex rhyme scheme. Here, for example, is the poet's comic account of the difficulties the writing a love letter posed to Tatyana:

> I see another problem looming:
> to save the honour of our land
> I must translate—there's no presuming—
> the letter from Tatyana's hand:
> her Russian was as thin as vapour,
> she never read a Russian paper,
> our native speech had never sprung
> unhesitating from her tongue,
> she wrote in French . . . what a confession!
> what can one do? as said above,
> until this day, a lady's love
> in Russian never found expression,
> till now our language—proud, God knows—
> has hardly mastered postal prose.

Even in translation, this stanza conveys the poem's extraordinary agility, its seemingly effortless passage through a series of difficult rhymes, all the while shifting from narration to interpolated commentary and back again, until, with the articulation of the final couplet, the improvisatore lands safely on his feet, driving home the absurd notion that Russian aristocrats can express themselves in elegant language—as long as that language is not their own!

But what cannot be translated, here and elsewhere in *Eugene Onegin,* is what the Russian Formalists called the "semantic transfer" of which rhyme is capable, that is to say, the "orientation" of a given rhyming unit toward its partner so as to produce a meaning not otherwise present in the sentence or phrase in question. When, for example, Pope writes in *The Rape of the Lock:*

> One speaks the glory of the British Queen
> And one describes a charming Indian screen

the rhyming of "British Queen" and "Indian screen" obviously tells us something about this society's values. Or when, in "Sailing to Byzantium," Yeats writes:

> That is no country for old men. The young
> In one another's arms, birds in the trees
> —Those dying generations—at their song,
> The salmon-falls, the mackerel-crowded seas,
> Fish, flesh, or fowl, commend all summer long
> Whatever is begotten, born, and dies.

the *a* rhyme of the ottava rima ("young"—"song"—"long") is ironically qualified when the b rhyme on "trees" and "seas" culminates in the off-rhyme of "dies," as if to explain why the poet must leave the natural world behind and prepare himself for "the artifice of eternity."

It is well known that Yeats usually began a poem by jotting down a set of rhyme words and then filling in the lines; for him, as for no other twentieth-century poet writing in English, rhyme was the pivot that set the poem in motion. The tradition was carried on by poets like Auden and Frost, but, as I remarked at the outset of this essay, for most Modernist and Postmodernist poets, rhyme be-

came the exception rather than the rule, an ordering device too confining and restrictive to allow for the delicate curve of the poet's lyric emotion. Indeed, by midcentury both rhyme and meter were increasingly subsumed under the category "closed form," which came to be equated with all things authoritarian, narrowly traditionalist, rule bound—a straitjacket to be avoided like the plague in the quest for freedom, which is to say "open form." The classic statement of this position is probably Robert Lowell's confession, in his 1961 *Paris Review* interview, that "I couldn't get my experience into tight metrical forms. . . . I felt that the meter plastered difficulties and mannerisms on what I was trying to say to such an extent that it terribly hampered me." Given the fact that Lowell was not exactly a radical in the larger scheme of postwar American poetics, this renunciation set the stage for two decades of so-called "open form," with its corollary view of meter and especially of rhyme as quaint exotica.

No wonder, then, that what has been called "the new formalism" of such young poets as Gjertrud Schnackenberg, Brad Leithauser, Mary Jo Salter, and now Vikram Seth should generate interest. But how does it work out in practice? Is Seth's recreation of the Pushkin stanza more than an exercise in ingenuity? Here is a fair sample from Book I, in which John is fighting off the boredom and loneliness of bachelorhood:

> He goes home, seeking consolation
> Among old Beatles and Pink Floyd—
> But "Girl" elicits mere frustration,
> While "Money" leaves him more annoyed.
> Alas, he hungers less for money
> Than for a fleeting Taste of Honey.
> Murmuring, "Money—it's a gas! . . .
> The lunatic is on the grass,"
> He pours himself a beer. Desires
> and reminiscences intrude
> Upon his unpropitious mood
> Until he feels that he requires
> A one-way Ticket to Ride—and soon—
> Across the Dark Side of the Moon.

Having set up the "listening to old records" theme, Seth seems to be at a loss. He has his stereotypical hero "hunger less for money / Than for a fleeting Taste of Honey"—a rhyme that, despite the allusion to the pop song, seems merely cute as is the subsequent "Money—it's a gas! . . . / The lunatic is on the grass." It is not just that "taste of honey" and "it's a gas" are too obviously alien to John's own speech habits, but that, to carry conviction, the rhyme would have to show that "money" and "honey," far from being opposites are, in the consciousness of a Silicon Valley type like John, inextricably intertwined. It is the sort of thing Cole Porter did brilliantly:

> You've got those ways
> Those certain ways
> That make me go down to Cartier's
> For a wedding ring.
> You've got that thing.

A girl's "ways"/"Cartier's"—don't they go together? Or again:

> You're the top!
> You're Mahatma Gandhi

You're the top!
You're Napoleon brandy,
You're the purple light
Of a summer night in Spain
You're the National Gall'ry
You're Garbo's sal'ry
You're cello-phane.

For the café society that Porter satirized so fondly, cellophane (newly invented when he wrote the song in 1934) was about on a par with "nights in Spain," just as the National Gallery and Garbo's salary fall into the same zone of "People are talking about. . . ." It is the sort of wit Seth strives for and too frequently muffs:

Janet picks up her fortune cookie,
Then puts it down, turns to her friend:
"Don't bank too much on youth. Your rookie
Season is drawing to an end."

Or again:

Two mornings after Janet fires
Her postal charge, she's roused from sleep.
A chilled voice on the phone inquires:
"You sent it? Janet, you're a creep."

Janet, as Seth presents her, wouldn't use the word "rookie," any more than John would, in this particular context, call Janet a "creep." Nor can we attribute these words to the poem's narrator, as we would in the case of *Don Juan* or *Eugene Onegin,* because Seth's narrator does not really function as a character in this "novel," nor is it evident that his attitudes and values are in any serious way superior to or critical of his characters. No, in **The Golden Gate,** John calls Janet a creep because "creep" rhymes with "sleep," and Jan calls John a "rookie" because "rookie" rhymes with "fortune cookie." Young men call Liz Dorati "a cutie" because "cutie" rhymes with "beauty"; her law firm is called "Cob and Kearny" so as to get a rhyme for "attorney." At Phil Weiss's alfresco breakfast, evidently the setting for characteristic California Sunday brunch-fare, "Anne Gunn, the artist wields her fork / With graphic verve, impaling pork." The serving and consumption of pork at a California brunch strikes me as completely implausible—but then "pork" does rhyme with "fork." And so on.

But isn't this to put too much weight on rhyme qua rhyme? Isn't it sufficient that rhyme acts as a rhetorical and metrical marker (the second function defined above), acting to control the flow of Seth's "idiomatic" (X.J. Kennedy's designation) speech rhythms? "In practice," says John Hollander, "the reader is made aware not of the structure of [the] intricate framework, but of what is being woven onto it." But what *is* being woven onto it? Here is a stanza describing John's second date with Liz:

Cut to dessert. An apt potation
Of amaretto. They forgo
The cinema for conversation
And hand in hand they stroll below
The fog-transfigured Sutro Tower
A masted galleon at this hour,
Adjourn for ice cream, rich and whole,
At Tivoli's, near Carl and Cole;
Next for a drive—refreshing drama

Of changing streets and changeless bay
And, where the fog has cleared away,
The exquisite bright panorama
Of streetlights, sea-lights, starlight spread
Above, below, and overhead.

Do the rhyme words here function as rhetorical and metrical markers, foregrounding the narrative itself or are they distracting? The shift in the opening line from contemporary colloquialism ("Cut to dessert") to literary quaintness ("An apt potation") strikes me as merely cute, as if to say, Look, reader, I know my way around poetic diction, I know (line 6) what a "masted galleon" is and can compare it to the "fog-transfigured Sutro Tower." The cuteness continues as the emphatic rhymes fall like a deck of cards on what is mere filler. What, for example, can ice cream be but "rich and whole"? Diluted and made in sections? Thin and watery? Does the in-house reference to "Carl and Cole" characterize the scene? And why is the drive the couple takes a "refreshing drama," except for the fact that "drama" is about to rhyme with the "exquisite bright panorama"? As for the final couplet, rather than giving Seth's predictable little vignette of Bay Area dining and dating a bit of a lift, it falls as flat as the pancakes these wheat-germ eating young professionals despise:

Of streetlights, sea-lights, starlight spread
Above, below, and overhead.

All that is now needed—and we get it in the next stanza—is that our lovers

. . . stand, half-shivering, half still,
Below the tower on Telegraph Hill.

No wonder they're cold, what with all that ice cream they've eaten. Again, I turn to Cole Porter for comic relief:

If you're ever in a jam
Here I am.
If you're ever in a mess,
S.O.S.
If you've ever lost your teeth and you're out to
      dine,
Borrow mine.

But the decorum of **The Golden Gate** allows for no such absurdity. The morning after her first night with John:

Liz enters with a coffee tray
In negligible negligée.
She pours two cups. Without embracing
They sit, their eyes infused with sleep
And love, and drink the potion deep.

And from thereon out, things jog along predictably enough to the Friday office routine, the response of both lovers' bosses to their absent-mindedness (of course people in love can't concentrate!), and so on. Indeed, the twists and turns of the ensuing plot are as predictable as if they had been programmed on one of the computers our hero himself had built.

As an Indian, educated at Oxford and hence having the vantage point of the outside witness on the California scene, Vikram Seth has been praised all around for his sharp eye for social nuance. "If this writer's ear for rhymed verse is perfect," says John Hollander, "so is his ear for colloquial discourse, for the inadvertent ironies of commercial product-naming, for the tonalities of callow and sincere self-expression. And so is his almost John O'Hara-like eye and ear for the cultural fact and the revealing detail."

Reading such commentary, one's expectations are naturally high. Here is a fair sample of Seth's treatment of freeway culture:

> The freeway sweeps past humming pylons
> Past Canterbury Carpet Mart,
> Warehouses, ads displaying nylons
> On shapely legs that make John start.
> A cigarette ad, sweet and suborning,
> Subverts the Surgeon General's warning:
> A craggy golfer, tanned, blue-eyed,
> Insouciantly stands beside
> A Porsche-caged blonde; coolly patrician,
> He puffs a menthol-tipped King-size.
> John tries to curb his vagrant eyes
> And heed the poet's admonition:
> "Beneath this slab John Brown is stowed.
> He watched the ads and not the road."

One can learn a great deal about Flaubert's *mot juste,* about Pound's "exact treatment of the thing," from reading this or related stanzas in *The Golden Gate*. Take the reference to "nylons" in line 3. The fact is that ads haven't displayed "nylons / On shapely legs" for many a year because women no longer wear "nylons"; they wear *panty hose,* with further designations like "control top" or "stretch sheer"—designations that actually might have afforded Seth some good fun—and panty hose are made out of a variety of synthetic fabrics but not out of nylon. As for "pylons," these unsightly strings of telephone poles have long been tucked out of sight; one still sees them along streets but not along freeways. Their "humming," in any case, is a phenomenon no freeway driver would so much as perceive.

Are these inaccuracies merely trivial and is it nitpicking to point them out? Why, after all, must Seth's satire be based on documentary observation? Because, so I would argue, the social irony of this particular situation depends upon the specificity of the satirist's target. To submit stereotypes to satiric treatment is to fail to transcend them. Thus the stanza in question plays upon a well-worn cliché that goes something like this: Oh, those crazy California freeways with their monstrous and distracting billboards, their crass materialism and vulgar pop culture. Look at those giant carpet marts with bogus medieval names like Canterbury! But of course the carpet mart is the Californian's true religious sanctuary. And so on.

How much sting can such a cartoon cliché have? The reality is much more interesting. Billboards, to begin with, are designed to be scanned quickly so that no one need ever take his or her eyes off the road so as to "read" them. Further, to be a freeway commuter is to become so acclimatized to billboards and neon road signs that one all but looks through them. Which is not to say that their messages don't act as hidden persuaders, entering our consciousness and dictating, in subtle ways, our thought processes. But the idea that John would almost swerve off the road because he is so taken with the ads "displaying ny-

lons / On shapely legs" or the "Porsche-caged blonde" ("caged" strikes me as precisely the wrong word here) and her "craggy golfer, tanned, blue-eyed," is about on the same par as the very ads it claims to satirize. Its version of "California on wheels" reminds me of the British Airways version of "London," with Robert Morley, his Burberry slung over his arm, his slightly rumpled but perfectly tailored suit and neat umbrella, silhouetted against the Houses of Parliament and urging us to take the package tour.

Indeed, as a social document, *The Golden Gate* is closer to Neil Simon than to Pushkin. Here is Pushkin describing the reading habits of his Romantic heroine:

> Seeing herself as a creation—
> Clarissa, Julie, or Delphine—
> by writers of her admiration,
> Tatyana, lonely heroine,
> roamed the still forest like a ranger,
> sought in her book, that text of danger,
> and found her dreams, her secret fire,
> the full fruit of her heart's desire;
> she sighed, and in a trance coopted
> another's joy, another's breast,
> whispered by heart a note addressed
> to the hero that she'd adopted.
> But ours, whatever he might be,
> ours was no Grandison—not he.

Tatyana is, of course, characterized by her reading, her longing to be a Romantic heroine like Rousseau's Julie or Mme de Staël's Delphine, and to win the heart of a Richardsonian lover. But the ironies of Pushkin's narrative are multiple. At one level, Tatyana suffers from *Bovarysme;* she is just a provincial girl who will eventually be taken to the marriage market in Moscow and auctioned off to the highest bidder. At another level, Tatyana's world is quite as Romantic as the one of her reading: the man she loves fights a duel with and kills the landowner-poet Lensky, who is in love with her sister Olga. Moreover, after Tatyana is married, the tables are turned: Onegin now woos her as ardently and passionately as she ever wooed him and she has the privilege of rejecting him. But then again, if this is the Romantic note, Pushkin's "novel" is also realistic in its treatment of Tatyana's marriage. Not only does this young girl not pine away for her lost lover; she seems, in her arranged marriage, composed, serene, and relatively quite satisfied. Her behavior, in other words, can be construed in a variety of ways. The fond narrator seems to know no more about her than we do:

> Tatyana's letter, treasured ever
> as sacred, lies before me still.
> I read with secret pain, and never
> can read enough to get my fill.
> Who taught her an address so tender,
> such careless language of surrender?
> Who taught her all this mad, slapdash,
> heartfelt, imploring, touching trash
> fraught with enticement and disaster?
> It baffles me.

So convincing are the narrator's words that we almost forget that, in point of fact, the person who "taught her all this . . . touching trash" is the poet himself.

It is, of course, less than fair to compare Vikram Seth to the greatest of Russian poets, but since he himself invokes Pushkin's tutelary spirit, and since the great redeeming feature of *The Golden Gate* is that it does send us back to Pushkin and to Byron (no mean feat!), it may be helpful to use the Pushkin frame. Take the question of John's reading—or Phil's or Ed's—as a mode of depicting the social norms of San Francisco yuppiedom. In Book I, we learn that John "Enjoys his garden, likes to read / Eclectically from Mann to Bede," but nothing John ever says or does throughout the poem suggests that he would have so much as heard of the Venerable Bede, much less read Thomas Mann. As for Ed, Liz's twenty-year-old brother who embarks on a gay liaison with Phil (later Phil will marry Ed's sister Liz as a surrogate), his messy room is described as follows:

> A Bible, an unopened packet
> Of guitar strings, a saxophone,
> Shaving cream, razor and cologne. . . .
> A commentary on Aquinas
> Rests on the floor, while on a shelf
> Lies the august *Summa* itself,
> Next to (in order) *Conquering Shyness,
> The Zen of Chess, The Eightfold Way,
> Theories of Film,* and the *Pensées.*

Pascal? St. Thomas? To define Ed, whose conversation consists mostly of one-liners like "this coffee really gets you wired," as a reader of anything more complicated than *The Eightfold Way* is stretching things a bit. What, in any case, are such "telling details" meant to show? That Ed is intellectually pretentious? That he is well-educated and these books are the hangovers from his college days? That he hankers after religious truth? That he is worthy of the intellectual Phil Weiss's attentions? Or is Seth simply engaging in a bit of showing off?

To my mind, the documentary detail used throughout the "novel" is of this order, the characters remaining pure paper dolls. And faceless paper dolls at that. Even on the daytime serials there is greater individuation. We know that *The Young and the Restless'* Ashley Abbott comes from one of Genoa City's leading families and has "class" whereas Nicky Reed, her rival for the favors of tycoon Victor Newman, was once a stripper and remains something of a dumb blonde. No one could ever mistake Ashley for Nicky. But Liz Dorati and Janet Hayakawa are, despite their ethnic names (names never permitted on the Soaps), made of the identical mold. The reason we cannot tell them apart is that Seth never thinks of them as anything but Representative Yuppies. As such, their reading is not likely to go much beyond *Newsweek*.

Stereotypical Bay Area types have stereotypical parents. It is here that *The Golden Gate* falters most notably. What sort of mother would a Liz Dorati, a twenty-seven-year-

---

> **The Golden Gate speaks to the nostalgia that characterizes the not-so-golden late 1980s. As the millenium approaches, as Apocalyptic images come to haunt our fictions, as political and military decisions become increasingly complex and problematic, there is inevitably a longing for the Old Poetry, poetry written before the fall into free rhythms and abstruse, often seemingly prosaic locutions.**
>
> **—*Marjorie Perloff***

---

old lawyer (Stanford LL.B.), whose father owns vineyards in Sonoma County and who "was brought up marinading / Near the jacuzzis of Marin," be likely to have? Mrs. Dorati might be a health-food and exercise freak, spending her time at the gym or lunching with her friends at the salad bar. She might have affairs with younger men. She might be into gardening or pottery or horses. She might be a lawyer or real estate agent. She might be on drugs. Certainly, there are many Marin County alternatives. In the cartoon world of *The Golden Gate,* however, Moms are Moms:

> "Liz, dear, it's been just lovely meeting
> Your friends, and John; what a nice boy.
> We hope that soon. . . . " Without complet-
>   ing
> Her exhortation to enjoy
> A copula more sacramental
> (Resulting in the incidental
> Production of grandchildren—three
> Seems best—to dandle on her knee),
> Mrs. Dorati hugs her daughter
> And drives off with rheumatic care.
> Liz stands and breathes the sharp night air,
> While from the house keen squeals of slaughter
> And wrath attend that Liquid Sheep
> Have just commenced to rant and weep.
>
> So much for the Vivaldi. Thinking,
> "Mom's got out in the nick of time,"
> Liz turns back. . . .

Who is this Hallmark Card Mother who refers to a twenty-seven-year-old man as "a nice boy" and is already anticipating the grandchildren she will "dandle on her knee"? Who is this fifty-odd-year-old who "drives off with rheumatic care" and must be spared the horrors of loud rock? No television sitcom could get away with so tired a cliché. Here is Mrs. Dorati, soon to die of cancer, "In raptures / About her flesh-and-blood grandchild" (the offspring of Liz and Phil):

> "Look at that nose, Mike—it recaptures
> My father's nose. Look, look, he smiled. . . .
> Oh, what a darling—what a beauty—

What name have you . . . oh, what a cutie! . . .
What name have you decided on?"
Liz says: "We think we'll call him John."

In the stanza preceding this one, the narrator himself expresses a different opinion: "How ugly babies are! How heedless / Of all else than their bulging selves— / Like sumo wrestlers, plush with needless / Kneadable flesh—like mutant elves. . . ." In thus framing the portrait of the doting grandmothers (Mrs. Weiss has also appeared on the scene), Seth is being, not ironic, but merely patronizing. And indeed, the novel is characterized throughout by a tone of arch superiority. For Byron, Juan and the other characters are the means by which the hypocrisies and follies of Regency England (and, beyond these, of mankind in general) are unmasked. Pushkin's dramatis personae are more complex: seen as they are through the eyes of a narrator who is one of them, they remain enigmatic just as our friends do in real life. We can attribute this or that motive to Onegin and Tatyana, Lensky and Olga, but it is by no means clear whether, say, Onegin is primarily a sympathetic character (a victim, perhaps, of the failure of the Decembrist revolt) or whether he is meant to be viewed as the archetypal superfluous dandy of the post-Napoleonic era.

But what are Seth's themes? Bruce Bawer is probably right when he says, "Affection . . . is what his book is all about. Its ultimate lessons are wonderfully simple ones: that love and friendship are the finest things on earth; that life being short, youth evanescent, and the world unstable, human attachments should be cherished, not repudiated. . . . In *The Golden Gate,* even the nuclear-weapons issue is secondary to love and friendship." Secondary, one wants to ask, for whom? Can the contemporary poet, in Seth's own words, "use / The dusty bread molds of Onegin / In the brave bakery of Reagan"? Or do these cream puffs, made with synthetic eggs, fail to rise?

Like the series of dramas on colonial subjects currently featured on *Masterpiece Theatre,* like the two-day network coverage of the Royal Wedding, *The Golden Gate* speaks to the nostalgia that characterizes the not-so-golden late 1980s. As the millenium approaches, as Apocalyptic images come to haunt our fictions, as political and military decisions become increasingly complex and problematic, there is inevitably a longing for the Old Poetry, poetry written before the fall into free rhythms and abstruse, often seemingly prosaic locutions. Before the Imagist-Vorticist revolution, so this line of reasoning goes, poems were things one could memorize and recite—think of Yeats's "Easter 1916" or Frost's "Desert Places"—but who can memorize even one of the shorter poems of William Carlos Williams, let alone the poems of Frank O'Hara or Robert Duncan or Leslie Scalapino? Furthermore, stanzaic poems like Oscar Wilde's "Ballad of Reading Gaol" were coherent thematically as well as formally: they weren't just coterie poems designed for classroom consumption. In the same vein, *The Golden Gate* can be read by the fireside of an evening—indeed, it can (and will) be read by the very Phil Weisses and Liz Doratis who are its subject. And such a reading, far from being disquieting, will be as reassuring as a cup of hot cocoa. As John imagines the deceased Janet telling him at the end of the novel:

"I'm with you, John. You're not alone.
Trust me, my friend; there is the phone.
It isn't me you are obeying.
Pay what are your own heart's arrears.
Now clear your throat; and dry these tears."

Which is to say, in the words of the ubiquitous AT&T ad that might be Seth's epigraph, "Reach out and touch someone!"

But nostalgia is not the whole story either. In a narrower literary sense, the new cult of rhyme, of straightforward verse narrative and "transparent" language, has everything to do with the increasing dominance of theory in the English curriculum, the publishing houses, and the leading periodicals, both in the United States and in Britain. It is no coincidence, for example, that Vikram Seith's "novel in verse" has been hailed as heralding the New Dispensation precisely at the same time that John Ashbery's *Selected Poems,* published by Viking just a few months earlier, has received its share of hostile newspaper reviews. . . .

In accounting for his boredom with Ashbery's *Selected Poems,* James Fenton [writing in *The New York Times Book Review* (29 December 1985)] says facetiously, "I was approaching the book under a certain misconception, that it was asking to be, well, *read.*" Instead, Fenton suggests, here is "the exorbitantly demanding poet, asking of the reader impossible feats of attention, taxing our patience, yielding only a minimum of reward. . . ." What a relief, then, to turn from these "hinting[s] at a profundity of philosophical insight which is designed to make a nonphilosopher uneasy," to Vikram Seth's unabashedly denotative language in *The Golden Gate:*

"I'll drive you home. Come back tomorrow
To fetch—" "I live near Stanford, Ed."
"Oh . . . well, in that case, share my bed—
Just don't try driving!—You can borrow
My toothbrush too. Come on, let's go—
Good night, Liz—Bye, John—Homeward ho!"

Nothing "designed to make a nonphilosopher uneasy" here. The words mean what they say, no more nor less. And the regular beat of the tetrameter is reassuring, neatly chiming as it does on "tomorrow"/"borrow," "Ed" and "bed," "go" and "ho."

"Homeward ho!" The longing to build Pushkin's or Byron's Jerusalem in California's green and pleasant land is surely an understandable one. But the realities of living in the late twentieth century are bound to cast a shadow. When asked, "What is the place of Bertolt Brecht in your theater?" the Polish director and critic Jan Kott said: "We do him when we want Fantasy. When we want Realism, we do 'Waiting for Godot.' " In the same spirit, I offer in response to Seth's "Homeward ho!" the opening page of Beckett's most recent poetic fiction, *Worstward Ho* (1983):

On. Say on. Be said on. Somehow on. Till
    nohow on. Said nohow on.
Say for be said. Missaid. From now say for be
    missaid.
Say a body. Where none. No mind. Where
    none. That at least. A place. Where
none. For the body. To be in. Move in. Out of.

Back into. No. No out. No back. Only in.
Stay
  in. On in. Still.
All of old. Nothing else ever. Ever tried. Ever
  failed. No matter. Try again. Fail again.
Fail
  better.

Beckett's fictions have always been poetic, but here, in the late work, the permutation of a very few repeated particles ("on" / "no" / "none" / "nohow"; "in" / "on"; "Say" / "said" / "stay / "missaid") creates the rhythm of medieval chant, a strange liturgical echo that strikes with the force of a hammer blow. Beckett's drama of the self trying to inhabit a body virtually stops us in our tracks.

The sounding of language, as *Worstward Ho* reminds us, is just as integral to poetry as are its tropes and its lyric conventions. It is to Vikram Seth's credit that, in his own fashion, he has called for a renewed attention to the role of sound in poetry. But surely, now that we have this tour de force, the next step is to "Try again. Fail again. Fail better."

Rowena Hill   (review date 1986)

SOURCE: "Vikram Seth's *The Golden Gate*: A Quick Look," in *The Literary Criterion,* Vol. XXI, No. 4, 1986, pp. 87-90.

[*In the following review, Hill complains that the values in* The Golden Gate *are flawed but praises the novel's balanced structure.*]

Judging by his novel **The Golden Gate,** it is hard to see how Vikram Seth can be considered an Indian writer, except by accident of birth. There are a few Indian references in the text, such as the "Taste of Honey" and the charioteer metaphor, and the non-violent attitude of the peace marchers has obvious Gandhian connections ("As evidence of our sincerity / We won't resist"), but there is nothing here that California has not possessed for a long time. The same could be said of the attitude of acceptance of contrasts that the book reveals at moments. This is, in fact, a totally Californian novel. What does perhaps result from the author being an adopted son of that state is a dose of gloating (the insistence of the accepted outsider on his belonging) in his celebrations of the Californian way of life, which can be irritating to anyone who has been exposed to the Californian claim to represent the vanguard of humanity in awareness and knowhow.

As a novel, the book is successful. It is carefully structured and balanced in its episodes. All the characters are clearly identified and followed through according to their importance—The pace is rapid without loss of depth. All the detail is credible and vivid: the Californian activities, picnics and walks, good food, music, pastimes like scrabble, the pets (even an animal lover can get fed up with the fuss about the cat Charlemagne, although American critics have singled him out for praise), the college reminiscences, the feministic reactions, the way people generally talk, advise, confess to, feel and care about each other.

In the author's vision of his people there is both irony and compassion. Straightforward compassion is revealed in the passages about Chuck, the little boy who loses both parents in an accident, or old Mrs. Dorati: "She stares / Down at her mottled skin, her lonely / Bent Hands. She thinks: 'Don't weep. Don't pray. / It's pain. It can't be wished away.' " But the sympathy is not lost when we come to the more complex characters: Ed, with his incapacity to adjust the claims of sense and religious duty, Janet, with her eccentricities, her ferocity against 'men' and her great understanding and generosity, Liz, who suffers at not being able to stick to her commitments, the versatile Phil, and, above all, John. Seth calls nuclear plant employees "Those who devised these weapons, decent / Adjusted, family-minded folk", and he has chosen for his main character (it is John who opens and closes the book) a man opposed to the peace campaigners, who "kneels bareheaded and unshod / Before the Chip, a jealous God". John's refusal to consider fully the implications of his job (except momentarily near the end of the book, when he seems to have found happiness), his surly temper and his "self-damned, self-banished" loss of Liz, are at least partially justified by his being an "emotional waif" who has never known a mother's love, and he is always treated with understanding.

However, the doubt may arise on reflection whether, perhaps beyond the author's conscious intentions, John's loss of everything he cares for, his "depleted" condition at the end, is not a kind of punishment for some of his attitudes, his scorn of those who fight for nuclear disarmament, and his condemnation of homosexuality. The winner in the book is Phil, John's friend, rival and enemy, whose "self-accepting psychic bounce" allows him to give up his job in Silicon valley to work for peace, and to love sexually, with no qualms, both women and men. Liz says of him "I couldn't better / Hope for a better half, / A good kind man who makes me laugh", and at the end he is head of a family of survivors of the plot's mishaps.

This contrast between John and Phil and their destinies leads us to what is arguably the greatest flaw in the book, a flaw in values. The central chapter shows us the march of the protesters against the Lungless Labs where nuclear bombs are produced, and nineteen poems are dedicated to an impassioned speech, from the mouth of Father O'Hare, against nuclear war. The diction is simple and serious and the whole sermon is very moving and convincing: "Well, we have gathered here this morning / In disparate but harmonious voice / To show that we have made our choice; / That we have hearkened to the warning / That hate and fear kill; and are here. Confronting death and hate and fear." Elsewhere in the book, Phil also speaks movingly about the results of nuclear warfare: "And then, when the soft radiation. Descends on what's not been destroyed— Trees, whales, birds, wolves—the birthless void-Think how the crown of earth's creation / Will murder that which gave him birth. / Ripping out the slow womb of earth." In the chapter following the peace march, we have Phil's insistent effort to convince Ed to carry on their homosexual affair, with some strongly persuasive lines: "While in its sweet maturity / Your lovely body dries unused? / Ed, if that's so, you'll have abused / Your self— and God's gift—far more truly. / Than any flagrant sensualist". It is not necessary to be unsympathetic to homosexuals, or even to deny validity to such arguments that in a different context, in order to be disturbed by the equivalence implied between the plea for peace and human survival and the plea for homosexual enjoyment. 'Make love not war' is much too simplistic an equation, and we object to the proportions in your scale of values, O California!

> The self-consciousness of the form and language itself is what gives *The Golden Gate* its quality. It is, to start with, a remarkable feat to write a readable novel in 590 sonnets of completely regular rhyme scheme.
>
> —*Rowena Hill*

The intervention of the author's 'I' in the novel is also doubtfully successful. The comments on the foolishness of lovers and the ugliness of babies are silly, though what we are told about the origin of the book ("I may as well have fun and try it") is interesting. The self-consciousness of the form and language itself is what gives this book its quality. It is, to start with, a remarkable feat to write a readable novel in 590 sonnets of completely regular rhyme scheme. This sonnet (a lighter sonnet than the classical, with one foot truncated) is extremely versatile. It can be slack and colloquial in the dialogues, terse and biting in rage against critics, full of compressed insights ("but Paul is smiling, / Floating on a slow tide of Brahms, / Back in his absent mother's arms"), mellow in descriptions. But it also plays with itself, using echoes of older authors (Shakespeare, Marvell, Kipling), inventing absurb rhymes (sunrise / bun rise) and enjoying sound effects ("Alas, unlathered by her blathering, / Phil concentrates on olive-gathering"). And it rises at intervals to high poetry, in the description of a lover's happiness at waking, or the statement of the nihilistic point of view ("What after all is earth's creation? / A virus in the morgue of space"), in many celebrations of nature ("Outside, the red sky dyes the river / That murmurs down the valley, where / The leafless weeping willows quiver / And where at dusk a shivering hare / May be seen poised or crouched or bounding").

The lives of the characters in [*The Golden Gate*] do not really participate in the grandeur and beauty of their natural surroundings (or even the impressiveness of their Golden Gate Bridge), as the poet sometimes seems to want to suggest. The people are not of mythological stature; they are too small, too human-centred. Only at the end, the death of Liz's mother and the birth of her son coincide to give us a sense of universality of experience. If we forgive Vikram Seth his Californian complacency it will be for his human compassion, which is beautifully expressed near the end of the novel in a sonnet addressed to St. Francis: "O San Francisco, saint of love. / Co-sufferer in searing pity / Of all our griefs . . . who, blind at noon, / Opened your heart and sang in darkness—And where it was,

sowed light, look down. / Solace the sorrows of your town."

R. T. Smith (review date Winter 1988)

SOURCE: A review of *The Golden Gate,* in *The Southern Humanities Review,* Vol. XXII, No. 1, Winter, 1988, pp. 96-8.

[*In the following review, Smith praises* The Golden Gate's *pace and style but laments its simplistic characterization and lack of depth.*]

One Sunday I luxuriated, moving from hammock to canvas captain's chair and back, from *sombre* to *sol* and again, with Pepsi at noon and gin by twilight, the whole time entertained by Vikram Seth's **The Golden Gate,** which author and publisher have named a novel, but which I would call a light verse epic in a minor key.

In 594 (counting dedication, acknowledgements, table of contents and author's bio note) tetrameter fourteeners with the unlikely rhyme scheme of *abbaccddeffegg,* Seth has woven, through game and gambit and gesture worthy of Pope or Pushkin, a narrative of five central and a dozen other characters occupying the trendy, dreamlike landscape of hi-tech around San Francisco. His style is glib, crisp, zesty and facile, qualities which might damage a more serious work, but this performance is not serious for the most part. Very little seems at stake through most of the conflicts as pro- and antagonists scrimmage for egosalve and hedonistic pleasure in a manner both intoxicated and intoxicating. The central character is the author's language and pleasantly intrusive consciousness, and we yield to the spell, not the weight.

The dramatis personae include hi-tech John, a sad lone ranger wishing for a mate who will tolerate his defense work at Lungless Labs. Bookish and sometimes petty, John is a yuppie with a vengeance, and he suffers for it. Jan, on the other hand, is a sculptor and drummer for Liquid Sheep, another sad case, a matchmaker who subordinates her needs to John's until all else fails. Her demise in the tale seems Seth's most arch trick.

And **The Golden Gate** is a nest of tricks, gimmicks, stunts. The central purpose seems to be an articulate twisting of language in this all-embracing style that accommodates with equal gusto and bliss: reviews, bumper stickers, protest speeches, legal briefs, scrabble, dialogue, corporate babble, meditations, chess strategies, narration, lyric apostrophes, "personals" ads, and an invocation to the muse. Seth somehow manages to assimilate it all and process it toward a witty-pithy tone that is at once gymnastic and aloof. No small accomplishment, as this gestural outline of a novel explores contemporary sexuality, aesthetics, finance, and leisure with insights that occasionally seem to transcend the stylistic template that owes much to MTV glitz and PC facility. I would call it a code, rather than a style, were it not so inclusive and deft.

Yet it's not too difficult to guess at the limitations of such a production. The cleverness is often unresonant, seemingly invoked to bridge from one composition dilemma to the next. The characters are caricatures, albeit sparkling ones

I enjoyed seeing pulled through their paces. Even the iguana Schwarz (short for Arnold) has charm. Even the wicked cat Charlemagne. But they are no less foils and strategies than the people. Whether chatting at a party or tossing in a lusty bed, confronting a dying mother or avoiding an old lover, these people are silhouettes with simple outlines, like the puppets in shadow shows. The author really doesn't render them with high seriousness, which dooms (or promotes) his effort to the realm of amusement as a kind of masterpiece in a minor key with only a tithe of heft, a chamber suite meant to be followed by domestic white wine. My greatest regret is that the characters talk so much alike, so much like the narrator, no small problem in any sort of "novel."

This does not, however, mean that I would dismiss **The Golden Gate,** for the taste lingers and is worth some savoring. Here is an example of Seth's outrageously swift and inviting characterization from early in the book, where his style has not faltered yet by straining for much depth of characterization. The subject is Liz Dorati, daughter of a vintner and a grandchildless matron who is dying of cancer:

> 2.30
> Though Liz was brought up marinading
> Near the jacuzzis of Marin,
> She never reveled in parading
> Her heart, her knowledge, or her skin.
> She bloomed unhardened to her beauty,
> Immune to "Lizzie, you're a cutie!"
> Though doting aunt and bleating beau
> Reiterated it was so.
> Her mother, anxious, loving, rigid,
> Said, "Liz, a pretty girl like you
> Ought to be thinking of . . . " "Et tu?"
> Sighed Liz, "Mom, do you think I'm frigid?
> Just let me get my law degree
> Out of the way—and then, I'll see."

Surprises of enjambment and caesura keep the writer on his mark, and who would mourn the lack of depth when the pace is so exhilarating? Even the rhymes are boldly playful, the "army . . . salami" and "nonpareil . . . zinfandel" reminiscent of Byron's "intellectual . . . hen pecked you all." Therefore:

> Who would label anaesthetic
> This California epic verse
> That darts so slyly? Any critic
> Who cannot abide swift wit's terse
> Characters should not deride it
> Until he's given in, tried it
> And labored in vineyards less vatic
> Than Barth or Barthelme, manic
> As Mailer but omnivorous
> Enough to merge tofu, protest,
> Cancer, an omelet for breakfast,
> A monkish gay, an orphan's trust.
> Who won't admit Seth's deft sorcery
> Has Pen Envy, the First Degree.

William Grimes (review date 26 January 1988)

SOURCE: "And So Tibet," in *The Village Voice,* Vol. XXXIII, No. 4, January 26, 1988, p. 48.

[*In the following review of* From Heaven Lake, *Grimes praises Seth's attention to human behavior and cultural difference.*]

It is early August, and Vikram Seth, one of three passengers wedged into the cab of a Chinese truck, is rumbling along the road to Lhasa. He is suffering from altitude sickness. The landscape—and there's lots of it—is monotonous and almost theatrically harsh: "Every few kilometers or so, a large and glossy raven sits perched on a telegraph pole, karking desolately." Gyanseng, a young Tibetan who has sat virtually silent for the entire trip, turns loquacious as the border nears; he begins singing, off-key, a number of Tibetan and Chinese favorites, including "Do Re Mi," "Jingle Bells," and "Red River Valley." This is a fairly convincing version of hell.

Seth's [*From Heaven Lake*] makes a strong case for letting other people travel to Tibet for us. There comes a point—probably the third rousing chorus of "Jingle Bells"—when even the most adventurous have to ask: Is the punishment worth it? Seth, of course, was more or less ensured a tough trip; his status as a foreign student at Nanjing University made independent travel immediately suspect and open to official challenge every step of the way. As if that weren't enough, he chose hitchhiking over air travel in a cost-cutting move. His convoluted journey thus became—apart from the occasional stunning vista or Buddhist temple—an unenticing potpourri of frustrating bureaucratic encounters, physical torment, and paralyzing boredom.

Seth dedicates **From Heaven Lake** "to the people I met along the way," and quite rightly. In the end, the chance encounters with ordinary Chinese and Tibetans are what animate the book. It comes as an anticlimax when he reaches his semimythic destination, Lhasa, an enigma wrapped inside a cliché (how long before visitors are greeted by a billboard that reads, "Welcome to the World's Most Spiritual City"?). Take Sui, the Chinese trucker who plies the 1800-kilometer route between Lhasa and Liuyuan—"a dusty, treeless, godforsaken depot"—and sportingly squeezes Seth into his cab, at substantial cost to his own comfort and schedule. A chain-smoker and omnivorous reader (he sinks into a kind of trance when picking up a comic book), he has, over the years, built up a social network along his route that is both a vital supply line and a relief from monotony. The innumerable little detours and pit stops, sometimes for barter, sometimes just for a bit of conversation, permit Seth to observe how average Chinese citizens get along and fiddle the system.

Seth was ideally equipped to take advantage of such opportunities. Fluency in Chinese helped, of course, but far more valuable was the curiosity about human behavior, the sympathy for all manner of human foibles, that makes **The Golden Gate,** his dazzling novel in verse, more than a technical tour de force. If the book's descriptions of landscape and temples tend toward blandness, its miniature character studies are memorable. They attest not only to the author's sharp eye (and ear), but to his unfeigned interest in how and why people act the way they do.

The admirable spirit of "nothing human is alien to me" undergoes a test of sorts near Lhasa, where Seth witnesses a peculiar burial ritual. On a flat rock outside the Sera monastery, butchers carve up human corpses, mince the meat, and mix it with barley meal. When a group of arrogant Han Chinese approach the dead, making jokes, an infuriated butcher chases them off, waving a severed leg over his head. Atop a sheer cliff, enormous eagles watch with interest, impatient for feeding time to begin.

Disturbed, Seth later talks over what he has seen with a Tibetan, who confesses that at his uncle's burial he grew queasy when it came time to crush the skull. Seth nods in sympathy, then characteristically reflects, "Of course, we Hindus also break the skull during the ceremony of cremation." This tolerant, understanding spirit makes Seth a superior tour guide, regardless of the destination. A trip to deepest Nebraska would work just as well.

Lachlan Mackinnon   (review date 21 September 1990)

SOURCE: "Brief and Bald," in *The Times Literary Supplement,* No. 4564, September 21, 1990, p. 1007.

[*In the following review, Mackinnon asserts that the short poems in* All You Who Sleep Tonight *do not give Seth room to express his voice and finds the book full of "humdrum sentiments and linguistic inertia."*]

Even the acknowledgements, dedication, contents and biographical note to Vikram Seth's *The Golden Gate* (1986) were cast into Pushkin's *Onegin* stanza. This both suggested the form's infinite capacity and flaunted the author's virtuosity. Everything was swept into an aesthetic world, but such a world as could contain everything. Vikram Seth's skill was not uniform: *The Golden Gate* has bumpy lines and passages, but the poem gets away with them because of its narrative impulse.

The skills needed for conducting a long narrative are, obviously, unlike those required by short forms. *All You Who Sleep Tonight* collects seven years' poems, some of them presumably contemporary with *The Golden Gate.* They are contained in five sections, "Romantic Residues", about love, "In Other Voices", "In Other Places", the epigrammatic "Quatrains" and the thoughtful "Meditations of the Heart". Although the poems are occasional in origin, they have been arranged in a way which suggests both similarity of subject and the author's versatility. The book feels a little like a huckster showing his wares.

In "Equals", an uneasy intimacy is recorded. "It's evening. I lack courage" the poem begins, ending in the belief that "We are, at least in hope, unequal equals, / If not in deed". The second stanza is:

> I sit down. I am tired.
> To speak my mind's beyond my power to do.
> I have no warranty against the vision
> I have of you.

The implausible "warranty" may be taken as a contrast to an implicit insured bureaucratic order, though it sounds a register touched nowhere else, but the second line is a disaster: the redundant "to do" is clearly there only for the rhyme's sake, and a poem of sixteen lines does not easily forgive such padding.

Seth writes, with reference to Mozart, that

> He never like the great Beethoven thunders,
> 'My stomach's aching and my heart is breaking
> And you will hear me,' yet to hear him is
> To suffer all heartbreak, to assume all sorrow
> And to survive.

"Adagio" celebrates music, but these lines must call Seth's ear in question. The first is very hard to read and a metrical nightmare created by the poem's preceding four lines, which have settled uneasily to a pentametric norm. The internal rhyme booms out jauntily in the second line to contradict the monotonous egotism described, while the closing lines say more than they can, however stumblingly, show. "All sorrow"? One had thought this Christ's prerogative. We can see what Seth means, but cannot be made to feel it by the bald assertion.

Such local misgivings arise from most pages of this collection. A wider worry has to do with sensibility. The best poems are slight in form, as with **"Heart"**, which ends

> Above all, to my heart I'm true.
> It does not tell me what to do.
> It beats, I live, it beats again.
> For what? I wish I knew it knew.

Hypochondriac insomnia is delightfully conveyed by this sense of the body's otherness. However, Seth's "Quatrains" too often fall flat because of their commonplaceness. In **"Malefic Things"**,

> Imagining the flowerpot attacked it,
> The kitten flung the violets near and far.
> And yet, who knows? This morning, as I backed it,
> My car was set upon by a parked car.

It's an old joke barely revived by the too evident exigency of rhyme, but in no way the gnomic wisdom it wishes itself to be.

The humdrum sentiments and linguistic inertia of *All You Who Sleep Tonight* remind me of Byron, perhaps only moved by sour thoughts of his wife to find a personality in short form. *The Golden Gate,* like *Don Juan,* depends much on its narrator's voice. The dramatic monologues in the present collection afford that voice no room: like Byron, Seth needs a demanding, expansive form to think in, and the short poem inhibits both the variety and the digressiveness which are his natural gifts.

John Oliver Perry   (review date Summer 1991)

SOURCE: A review of *All You Who Sleep Tonight,* in *World Literature Today,* Vol. 65, No. 3, Summer, 1991, pp. 549-50.

[*Perry is an American educator and critic. In the following review, he complains that the poems in* All You Who Sleep Tonight *are drab and uninspired.*]

Even a thin volume of thin poems could be enough to keep the reading public aware of Vikram Seth after the "phenomenal success" of his Byronesque, semisatiric, semiromantic novel in verse, *The Golden Gate,* five years ago.

The longest piece here (twenty-eight four-line stanzas) is termed "a pendant (as it were)" to that work, but it is neither cast in a similar vein (except for a final clever quip) nor marked with a similar narrative verve, being instead rather drably descriptive, uninspired historical and moral commentary. It is surely a mistake to ask for repeat performances from writers. Still, in form the poems of *All You Who Sleep Tonight* continue to rhyme and to make particular points—"to effect closure"—as Seth has always done. The opening poem, **"Round and Round,"** tells how the fantasy of a returned love is punctured; sad letdowns, in one way or another, dominate in the next eight anecdotes of failed love affairs.

The next section, "In Other Voices," renders in verse several horror stories drawn from various sources: quandaries of a Nazi-raped Lithuanian Jew, **"Ghalib, Two Years after the Mutiny,"** an AIDS patient to his lover, an Auschwitz commandant's complaint, and, most harrowing (though weakened by the pentameter couplets), **"A Doctor's Journal Entry for August 6, 1945."** Stripped naked himself by the Hiroshima blast, he is dismayed to see in the streets a woman with a child, "Both naked. Had they come back from the bath?" But climactically, when he then sees another naked man, "the thought arose / That some strange thing had stripped us of our clothes. / The face of an old woman on the ground / Was marred with suffering, but she made no sound. / Silence was common to us all. I heard / No cries of anguish, or a single word." Successive readings also weaken, rather than deepen, these final perceptions and feelings, which matter and form require should be ultimate.

Among "Other Places" appear several poems set in China, **"Lion Grove, Suzhou"** being the most clever and moving. It is based on an effective and most affecting conceit: that the "far more than playful and far less than sane" intelligence which laid out this cryptic garden parallels (and pleases) that of runaway children, who "gulp with shocking glee," and their parents, "too pleased for anger when they're found." The extra twists of ideational complexity here intensify the feeling and load the eight lines appropriately, despite the descriptive requirements. No similar enrichment, unfortunately, touches the twenty "quatrains," eleven of which are, in fact, paired couplets, but clearly these are meant as briefly clever epigrams, quite successful in a light Roman manner.

The poems in the final section, "Meditations of the Heart," more often than not draw on a similar vein of wit, though more saddened by loss, death, solitude. Without the pressure for snappy rhyme, the blank-verse **"Poet— For Irina Ratushinskaya,"** imprisoned for six years, nevertheless ends, "Her poems she memorized line by line and destroyed. / The Contents were what was difficult to remember." Unless fairly ordinary ideas are very sharply formulated, they remain ordinary and become even less if pressure is slackened by a padded phrase or feeling is trimmed out of callousness or to be cool or witty. These dangers are perhaps exemplified in the title poem [**"All You Who Sleep Tonight"**], where the tone might possibly have been deepened if the penultimate line read, "Some for more nights than one."

All you who sleep tonight
Far from the ones you love,
No hand to left or right,
And emptiness above—

Know that you aren't alone,
The whole world shares your tears,
Some for two nights or one,
And some for all their years.

It is a tribute to the poems of *All You Who Sleep Tonight* that often they can sound a bit like Frost or Hardy. There is little to remind us that the poet has returned to his native India, where, we are teased, he "is working on a novel (not in verse) set in post-Independence India." Perhaps that prospect is what occasioned the present publication, only eleven poems being previously printed.

Pico Iyer   (review date 19 March 1993)

SOURCE: "India Day by Day," in *The Times Literary Supplement*, No. 4694, March 19, 1993, p. 20.

[*Iyer is an English journalist and travel writer. In the following review, he contends that parts of* A Suitable Boy *are more satisfying than the whole and that the novel would have been stronger if it had been shorter.*]

In the house of English letters, Indian writers have often admitted us to the kitchen, with its hot spices, odd condiments and strange terms; and to the bedroom, not only for its obvious seductions, but also for the wild dream-flights entertained there. The event-infused city, the superstitious village, the polymorphous forms of Indian films are all by now familiar parts of the Indian scenery. But what Vikram Seth has tried to do, in his quietly monumental new novel, is to usher India into the drawing-room, to make it seem as everyday and close to us as nineteenth-century St Petersburg, say, or Regency Bath. His is a novel of the parlour and the breakfast-table, and one that passes like a long morning, and afternoon and evening, with the family.

A Suitable Boy is, on the face of it, simply a tale of a "nice, quiet girl" called Lata, nineteen years old, living in northern India in 1950, and trying to find a husband. Meanwhile, around her, the world's largest democracy is preparing for the first General Election in its young history. At its heart a story of four intertwined families, and their universal anxieties and affections, the novel is also a portrait of India, three years after Partition, trying to find a suitable future for itself, and struggling to keep the customs that steady while shedding the ones that stultify. It is the story of the passing of an era, of the last strains of a rarefied world of *ghazals* and nawabs, and the first approaches of a new, industrial age; of how the elegant Rajput miniature, you might say, is being replaced by the news-photo.

The distinguishing feature of the novel, though, may simply be its uneventfulness, its surpassing dailiness, the way in which Seth catches a life-sized, human, unextraordinary India. He sets his book, after all, not during the tumult of Independence, but in the uncertain interregnum that came after. And his purpose seems to be to rescue the country from melodrama and exoticism, and to show that if Dickens, with his volubility and humour and affection, is one natural chronicler of India, Jane Austen is another. As in E.M. Forster (another obvious precedent), traumas pass between the lines, and death is something that happens off-stage. In that sense, *A Suitable Boy* could almost be said to be a novel about things not happening: when a drunken boy drives a car too fast late at night, he brakes before he hits a lamp-post or a child; when a boy is rejected by his beloved, he does not kill himself, but goes off to the country for a month; when a child is lost in a murderous riot, he is, somehow, found.

This benign refusal of block capitals is ideally suited to Seth's gentle pacing and to the admirable directness and lucidity of his prose. None the less, the sheer bulk of the book comes as a surprise. For Seth's has always seemed a light, an almost glancing sensibility; his seemed a kind of Noël Coward talent. Charm is his calling-card, and sunniness his forte; playfulness is a large part of his attraction (evident here, before one even begins, in a rhyming Table of Contents, and two contradictory epigraphs from Voltaire about the *longueurs* of long novels). His last book, of poems, was one of the slimmest of the year; this one promises to be the longest. The question it raises is what happens to light comedy when it is extended across half a million words. Can an epic be built on charm alone?

There are, increasingly, two strands of Indian fiction, that of compassionate realism (exemplified by R. K. Narayan and, recently, Rohinton Mistry), and that of pinwheeling invention (the mode of Salman Rushdie, Shashi Tharoor and I. Allan Sealy). Seth firmly allies himself with the former, and he attempts here what might be regarded as a counter-Rushdie epic: relatively secluded and old-fashioned where Rushdie is determinedly topical and international, somewhat conservative in style and temper where Rushdie is wilfully radical (Seth writes a classic English prose, and the most tender and touching marriage of all in this book about marriages is an arranged one). Most of all, Seth is a peace-maker, where Rushdie is a belligerent, and there are those, of the Rushdie camp, who will find his openness—"It is best to be on good terms with everyone", thinks one character, early on—too mild-mannered.

For me, though, the singular appeal of *A Suitable Boy* lies in its fondness, and in its evocation of an unhurried, gossipy, small-talking India as teasing and warm as every family reunion I've ever attended. His is the charmed world of the privileged middle classes, as Indian as their love of P.G. Wodehouse and Charlie Chaplin, as Indian as their college productions of *Twelfth Night* and boating trips on Windermere. Scattering movie-ads, greeting-card jingles and excerpts from law books through his narrative, Seth catches something thoroughly and unmistakably Indian, in the soft spot for numbers, the riddles, the quips about "making hail while the sun shines". Here are absent-minded professors, bored beauties and feckless boys who say things like "Nothing I've ever done seems to have happened." Here too are Dickensian processions of repetitious lawyers, stutterers and eccentrics (and even a character consistently called Uriah).

Seth clearly loves his people, and he passes that love on to us. He shows them selfish, quarrelsome and idle, yet never without sympathy; indeed, much of the sweetness of the main plot comes from the fact that all three of Lata's shadow suitors are entirely engaging. Even a family that speaks largely in doggerel, composes poems to its dog Cuddles and keeps reminding one how lovably eccentric it is, becomes likeable. There is in all this an occasional trace of self-delight, and not every reader will find himself won over by the boyish witticisms ("Curiosity is a curious thing" and "No fait is ever accompli until it's accompli"), or the little jokes (characters called Dr Matthew Evans and Sir David Gower). But it must be said that the only ill-tempered character in the book is the one called Seth.

Seth makes of his affections, moreover, a central point; the one strain running through the long narrative is a determination to see India through particulars and people, and a complete rejection of those besetting Indian vices, pomposity and abstraction. (In one bravura passage, Seth throws off a host of sparkling generalities—India is like the Square, like the Trinity, like a Duality, like a Oneness, like a Zero—so as, in effect, to show that anything you might say about this huge and contradictory place is true, and meaningless.) And at every turn he shows us, in the Forsterian way, how individuals can go beyond the divisions created by institutions, and friendship can conquer communalism. Thus a Hindu crosses religious lines to befriend a Muslim, and later stabs him—for reasons that have nothing to do with their religions. At the same time, Seth is worldly enough to see how idealism can undermine the people it would try to help; to show how undoing an unjust system can mean undoing the innocent people who are beneficiaries; and to catch the heart of that age-old Indian riddle of compassion and corruption, that a man is damned if he tries to tamper with the law to save a renegade son, and damned if he does not.

Seth is at his finest in his portrayal of the people most unlike himself—like Muslims, say, or women. He evokes with great sensitivity the plight—and the strength—of women in the constricting space of a zenana, and in an age when a man may say, "I had six children and six daughters too." One of the book's most powerful scenes is an episode of sexual threat, seen from the woman's point of view. He writes of children, and dogs and parakeets, with an uncle's fondness.

By its end, in fact, the novel has found a place for almost every possible position: even that of the foreigner who finds Indians "face-flattering, back-biting, name-dropping, all-knowing, self-praising, power-worshipping . . ." (having lived half his life abroad, Seth can temper an insider's knowledge with an outsider's amusement). *A Suitable Boy* is, in its unobtrusive way, panoramic: it gives us Muslim festivals and Hindu ones, courtesans and court-rooms, villages and cities and towns. What he does not know, he has researched, and, with his economist's training, Seth shows us all the details of how a Czech shoe-factory in India works; with his position as the son of a High Court judge, he covers in commanding detail the debate about land ownership. He describes Nehru's coup against himself, and issues as current as Hindu temples in

Muslim areas. And though these passages occasionally seem a little tacked on, to give the novel epic status, there is not a detail that I found unconvincing or false.

But is it worth the weight? In *The Golden Gate,* as Gore Vidal saw it, Seth wrote "the Great California Novel", and his new one (handicapped, for some readers, by the Rushdie-like £1 million in advances it has received) is clearly an attempt to write the Great Indian one. In *The Golden Gate,* he was so much at home in his Pushkin stanzas that he made one forget (and so forgive) his virtuosity; here, attempting a 1,400-page novel on his first go at prose fiction, that is not so clearly the case. Over the course of the novel, he gives us any number of analogies for the book we are reading: it is like the Ganges, with its "tributaries and distributaries", it is like a banyan tree, with its slowly exfoliating roots; it is like a musician's *raag,* starting slowly but picking up speed.

Every single page of *A Suitable Boy* is pleasant and readable and true; but the parts are better crafted, and so more satisfying, than the whole. At times, it almost feels as if Seth is following his story more than leading it, and I could not help but think of his *alter ego* Amit (an Oxford-educated poet, and son of a High Court judge, embarked on an enormous first novel) saying that the reason his book was so long was that it was "very undisciplined". In places, the book feels more like a serial than an epic, and it is not immediately evident that its some 1,400 pages make it four times better than it would have been at 350. Indeed, its central love-story is so compelling that I found myself thinking that inside that fat novel, a much stronger thin one was struggling to get out.

Its publishers have likened the book, with its spacious realism, to Tolstoy and George Eliot. For me, though, *A Suitable Boy* is closest to Tanizaki, in his *Makioka Sisters.* For it is, like the Japanese novel, at its heart an elegy as well as a comedy of manners, about a traditional society in a time of change, and about a leisurely world of graces giving way to a new, more democratic time. Like Tanizaki, Seth locates these changes in the woman's curtained world of rituals, and uses a rich family's search for a husband as a way of making history intimate and human. Like Tanizaki, he writes winningly of everything domestic, especially women and their children. And like Tanizaki, he has given us that unlikeliest of hybrids, a modest *tour de force.*

John Oliver Perry (review date Spring 1993)

SOURCE: A review of *Beastly Tales from Here and There,* in *World Literature Today,* Vol. 67, No. 2, Spring, 1993, pp. 447-48.

[*In the following review, Perry lauds* Beastly Tales from Here and There.]

On reading the delightful animal fables gathered in *Beastly Tales from Here and There,* it is tempting to exclaim, "Aha, now Vikram Seth's talent for rhyming wit has at last found its proper form!" To say that much, however,

one would have to reexamine closely at least *The Humble Administrator's Garden* and *The Golden Gate* as well as especially the light Roman "quatrains" in *All You Who Sleep Tonight.* The issues for a critical reader in those previous books, however, stretch far beyond their formal pleasures, for they arouse moralistic questions about the exact nature of the feelings moving their diverse rhythms and anthropological questions about the accuracy of their supposedly keen, often witty observations, most dubiously of California gay culture. No such doubts cloud the immediate or the meditated experience of these ten tales of animal encounters, set (mostly reset) in brightly rollicking tetrameter couplets.

The first two tales, **"The Crocodile and the Monkey"** and **"The Louse and the Mosquito,"** are drawn from Indian lore; two more each are from China, Greece (Aesop), and the Ukraine, while the final two "came directly to me," Seth says, "from the Land of Gup." With these resources, quite naturally much of the reader's meditative pleasure (i. e., after the sheer joy in the verbal play) consists in the special cultural twists of plot, character, and moral. **"On the Ganga's greenest isle"** Kuroop the uxorious crocodile is ready to sacrifice his monkey friend and benefactor to the unbridled whimsical tastes of his mate (hilariously rendered in color on the jacket, but Ravi Shankar's line drawings inside are great fun too). However—the usual fabular ironic reversal—the crocodile's very unquestioning faith in love that prompted this encounter allows the monkey to trick his friend by professing an equal desire to please the pampered wife and thus to escape. In the second tale, somewhat unexpectedly but no less inevitably and thus most meaningfully, the instigator of a passionate crime—the Mosquito sharply stings the sleeping King—flies away while the kindly, reluctantly facilitating Louse, an exceedingly careful bloodsucker, is exterminated with all his lousy clan.

The shortest tale is the only one framed by its supposed source—an event seen by Mr. Yang and commemorated as **"The Faithful Mouse"** by "his friend the poet Chang," who "in couplets sad and stoic / celebrates her acts heroic"—and adding a supposed moral, "Acts that prove that shock and pain, / Death and grief are not in vain," which Seth briskly closes off: "Which fine lines, alive or dead, / Neither of the mice has read." Thus, just as deft play with various forms of rhyming closures (masculine and feminine, noun with verb, zeugma and chiasmus, et cetera) and of run-on lines underlies the veral and metrical wit, so do the narrative endings titillate and play havoc with our expectations, including those about poetry.

Probably the most notable moral reversal is in, and here of, the famous Aesopian fable **"The Hare and the Tortoise."** An astonishingly vain and garrulous hare—whom, characteristically, Seth makes archetypically (?) female—is indeed just barely bested in the race by the tortoise's "hard work and regularity. / Silly creature! Such vulgarity! / Now she'll learn that sure and slow / is the only way to go." The slangy certainty should warn us of a modern twist. For not the first or last time in these tales the press comes into animal affairs: "Stories of her quotes and capers / Made front page in all the papers— / . . . / Soon she saw her name in lights, / Sold a book and movie rights, / . . . / And her friends, when they played Scrabble / . . . / Let her spell 'Compete' with K. / / Thus the hare was pampered rotten / And the tortoise was forgotten." Surely Seth's experiences with *The Golden Gate* have fed this poem well.

Still, such inversions and juxtapositions do not always produce successful wit, much less neat satiric jabs at contemporary morality. The final and longest tale expounds upon planet-threatening issues in man's greedy environmental plundering and degradation, nominally of the animals' Bingle Valley, most specifically for Indians alluding to the hugely controversial Narmada Valley power, flood-control, and irrigation project. Perhaps the issues are too complex; though twenty-four pages ought to have given ample scope, they seem merely to prolong the debacle. The previous entirely made-up fable **"The Nightingale and the Frog,"** however, is both of normal length (five pages) and, despite its obviously self-serving self-referentiality—about traditional poets' mistakenly seeking a more powerful voice and a more appreciative audience—makes its depressing ironic point "with panache," but not like that claimed by "the foghorn of the frog / [That b]lared unrivalled through the bog." Which reminds us that effective satire requires established cultural norms, but can still manage with a minimal self-awareness: e. g., that human society is commonly dominated by incompetent boors employing their own pompous rules, again including poetry as a primary human endeavor.

The genre of retold and newly imagined animal tales has a long and brilliant history, encompassing sometimes coarse folk ballads, La Fontaine's sophisticated seventeenth-century "Fables Choisis," translations of the latter by Marianne Moore, and T. S. Eliot's "Cats," and, famously in prose, animal sagas by both the imperialist Kipling and the antiauthoritarian Orwell. Evidently they have often been not only formally or esthetically but socially, culturally, and morally successful through their witty indirection with animalized characters. It would be silly, then, to recommend these poems as essentially "children's literature," though, insofar as such stories must appeal to the grown-ups reading them aloud, there can be little doubt that these will delight audiences at the widest age ranges. The sheer sound of the lines and rhymes will catch any ear, the play of language please any user of words, and the humorous animals and their mock-heroic deeds meet the stricter demands of social and psychological analysis. Yet it is never as children's tales or even as necessarily women's lore that these sorts of fables arise in folk cultures to give shape to human experience, and we can thus suppose more solid underlying motivations for these than a hot day in Delhi when Seth "could not concentrate on . . . work [and] decided to write a summer story involving mangoes and a river." Given a new oral form here in Vikram Seth's flexible verbal imagination, we can readily imagine that these "Beastly Tales" will have a longer shelf life among literate English-using families than most other, more highly acclaimed, more immediately serious literary work—whether Seth's or someone else's.

John Lanchester   (review date 22 April 1993)

SOURCE: "Indian Summa," in *London Review of Books,* Vol. 15, No. 8, April 22, 1993, p. 9.

[*In the following review, Lanchester remarks favorably on* A Suitable Boy, *praising the novel as a "portrait of Indian life" that possesses remarkable structural clarity.*]

Forests have been slain, not only in the manufacture of *A Suitable Boy,* but in the production of its review coverage. An unusual amount of the publicity has been statistical, with journalists dwelling on the size of the book (1349 pages), its weight (an uncompromising 1.5 kilos), the size of the advances received ('2.6 crore rupees'), and its status as the longest one-volume novel in the English language. (*Clarissa* is longer and is now published in one volume, but wasn't written that way.) The Indian reviews are generally rupee-driven, and widely acclamatory; one magazine says that Seth 'has become India's answer to Pearl S. Buck and Tolstoy'. The English reviews are also rupee-driven, and are more acclamatory still; the favourite comparison is with *Middlemarch.* Salman Rushdie writes to the papers to deny a rumour that he had dismissed the novel as a soap-opera: he says he's two hundred pages in and going strong. On the other hand, the first American review calls the book 'a cream puff'.

Proust somewhere says that Balzac is more vulgar than life itself. A wonderful compliment, and one that comes to mind not only about all this publication kerfuffle (which has been something that Balzac wouldn't have minded putting in a novel) but about *A Suitable Boy,* too. It has the Balzacian unembarrassedness about money and class as primary human motivations; it has the qualities Auden praised in Jane Austen's work, when he wrote (in 'Letter to Lord Byron') that

> You could not shock her more than she shocks
> me;
> Beside her Joyce seems innocent as grass.
> It makes me most uncomfortable to see
> An English spinster of the middle class
> Describe the amorous effect of 'brass',
> Reveal so frankly and with such sobriety
> The economic basis of society.

A Suitable Boy is, like the novels of Jane Austen, structured around the institution of the arranged marriage. The novel is set in Brahmpur, fictional capital of the fictional state of Purva Pradesh; one of the novel's many technical triumphs is that no non-Indian would guess that these aren't real places. (When they first met, Seth's English editor asked him if he had written the book in Brahmpur—another wonderful compliment.) The action takes place in 1951 and 1952. It opens with the wedding of Savita Mehra, eldest daughter of the good-natured but none-too-bright Mrs Rupa Mehra, to Pran Kapoor, lecturer in English at Brahmpur University: " 'You too will marry a boy I choose,' said Mrs Rupa Mehra firmly to her younger daughter.' The younger daughter is the attractive Lata, a student at Brahmpur University, and one of the two central characters in the novel; the other is Maan, Pran's happy-go-lucky younger brother, the son of Mahesh Kapoor, the Revenue Minister of Purva Pradesh. At the wedding, Lata and Maan are spotted chatting by a friend:

> 'Who was that Cad you were talking to?' she asked Lata eagerly.
>
> This wasn't as bad as it sounded. A good-looking young man, in the slang of Brahmpur University girls, was a Cad. The term derived from Cadbury's chocolate.

Lata's search for a husband—a suitable boy—and Maan's search for something to do with his life are the two main strands of the novel. Around them Seth constructs a miraculously vivid and diverse portrait of Indian life. For instance: one of the multiply-ramifying plot themes concerns a Bill being put through the Purva Pradesh legislative assembly by Mahesh Kapoor, father of Pran and Maan. The new law will abolish the system of *zamindari,* or the feudal ownership of land; among those who will be grievously affected by this are the Nawab Sahib, the great Muslim landlord of Purva Pradesh, who spends all his time in his library preparing an edition of the Urdu poet Mast—and who also happens to be Mahesh Kapoor's closest friend.

We see Kapoor struggling to get the Bill through the legislative assembly, harassed, on the one hand, by the outraged representatives of the *zamindari* class and, on the other, by the Socialist party, who are enraged that the new law doesn't go far enough; we watch a challenge to the Bill in the state Supreme Court; and we see its effect on people's lives when Maan is sent to the impoverished countryside for a few months, allegedly to learn Urdu, in fact as a break to cool off from the sweaty affair he is having with famous Muslim courtesan Saeeda Bai—a period of semi-voluntary rustication that is to have unexpected consequences when his father, disgusted by creeping corruption in the ruling Congress Party, resigns his ministerial post and (partly on the basis of demographic calculations made by Bhaksar, his ten-year-old mathematical-genius nephew) tries to re-enter the state parliament from a new, rural, constituency.

That summary, however, leaves out a wide variety of interlinked characters and stories, like that of Rasheed, Maan's Urdu tutor, with whom Maan travels into the immiserated village life of Purva Pradesh, and through whose eventual psychological disintegration we get a glimpse of 'the tragedy of the countryside, of the country itself'; or the story of Waris, the rustic tough who works first as Mahesh Kapoor's election agent, then as his most bitter rival; or of another of Rasheed's pupils, Tasneem, Saeeda Bai's beautiful younger sister—or is she?; or the story of Prime Minister Nehru himself, at loggerheads with the party he is leading into the General Election of 1951—the first Indian election staged under universal suffrage and the 'largest election ever held anywhere on earth', involving a sixth of the world's population. And all this is only one of the book's several focuses of attention.

> If *A Suitable Boy* has a model it is less the 19th-century masterpieces with which it has been compared than the country of India itself—a country whose variety of life and livings provides the writer with a pattern and a challenge.
>
> —*John Lanchester*

Seth spent a decade at Stanford, studying for a PhD in economics and writing his verse-novel about *la vita Californiana, The Golden Gate.* The training in economics shows up in *A Suitable Boy,* one of whose many virtues is a strong sense of how the world actually works. This is as apparent in the uproarious pastiche of parliamentary debate as it is in scenes like the one in which Pran is trying to get Joyce into the Brahmpur University English syllabus, despite the opposition of his departmental head, the portly and malevolent Professor Mishra:

> 'It is heartening to come across a young man—a young lecturer'—Professor Mishra looked over at the rank-conscious reader, Dr Gupta—'who is so, shall I say, so, well, direct in his opinions and so willing to share them with his colleagues, however senior they may be . . . We are already hardpressed to teach 21 writers in the time we allot this paper. If Joyce goes in, what comes out?'
>
> 'Flecker,' answered Pran without a moment's hesitation.
>
> Professor Mishra laughed indulgently. 'Ah, Dr Kapoor, Dr Kapoor . . .' he intoned,
>
> 'Pass not beneath, O Caravan, or pass not singing. Have you heard
> That silence where the birds are dead yet something pipeth like a bird?
>
> James Elroy Flecker, James Elroy Flecker.'
> That seemed to settle it in his mind.

But this is to over-emphasise the public aspects of the novel at the expense of its portrayal of the private life, as treated through the dilemmas of Lata as she decides between her three suitors. There is hunky Kabir Durrani, whom she deeply fancies, but who is rendered definitively ineligible by being—to Mrs Rupa Mehra's ineffable horror—a Muslim. (When Mrs Mehra finds out that Kabir's mother has had a breakdown, she isn't slow to use the ammunition against him: 'Muslim and mad.') There is her brother-in-law, the Oxford-educated and ultra-eligible Amit Chatterji, poet and darling of Calcutta literary society, at work on a thousand-page novel about the Bengal famine. And finally there is Haresh Khanna, who makes up for deficiencies in glamour (he's short, speaks English badly and works for a shoe company) by his energy, amiability and uncomplicated affection for Lata. The ending is happy, but not idiotically or unreflectingly so; several characters have been visited by tragedy, and there's even an undercurrent of melancholy in the fact that Lata can only choose one of her suitors. The tone is not unlike that caught by Empson in his essay on Gray's 'Elegy': 'It is only in degree that any improvement of society could prevent wastage of human powers; the waste even in a fortunate life, the isolation even of a life rich in intimacy, cannot but be felt deeply, and is the central feeling of tragedy.'

If *A Suitable Boy* has a model it is less the 19th-century masterpieces with which it has been compared than the country of India itself—a country whose varity of life and livings provides the writer with a pattern and a challenge. In its attempt to incorporate India into itself the novel resembles an ostentatiously different book, *Midnight's Children*. Seth's imagination and Rushdie's are not so far apart: the work of both writers is informed by liberal, pluralistic values, and *A Suitable Boy* is, among other things, a political book. The violence and degradation consequent on extreme poverty are present in the novel, which is concerned throughout with the threat India faces from 'the systemic clutch of religious fundamentalism'. At one point, a group of fanatics attempt to dismantle a mosque, in order to build a temple on the site; a sadly accurate prediction of the events at Ayodhya.

The style of *A Suitable Boy* is as astonishing as its content. Seth has striven for complete transparency: all his energies are concentrated on making the prose a vehicle for the characters and the action. Virtuoso effects are confined to often comic moments of parody and impersonation, as when Dr Makhijani reads his deliriously terrible 'Hymn to Mother India' to the Brahmpur Literary Society ('Mahatma came to us like summer "andhi", / Sweeping the dungs and dirt, was M.K. Gandhi'). Kingsley Amis has famously remarked that in reading his son's books he feels the lack of simple declarative sentences, along the lines of 'having nothing more to say, they finished their drinks and left.' He should like *A Suitable Boy,* which contains no other kind of sentences, and which has a studied lack of fastidiousness about people saying things 'firmly', or 'confidently', or 'wryly', or any-other-adverbially.

The prose is intended not to distract. The resulting structural clarity is remarkable—you never don't know what's happening, why, where and to whom. (Compare this to *One Hundred Years of Solitude,* which calls for the construction of maps, home-made wallcharts and plot-flow diagrams.) It's a considerable technical feat, which draws no attention to itself—in fact, the only aspect of *A Suitable Boy* which draws attention to itself is its length. Seth has taken his own advice: in an essay published in this journal in 1988, he wrote of the requirement to balance the injunction to 'load every rift with ore' with the contervailing admonition to 'allow the poem to breathe'. *A Suitable Boy* breathes, all right; the unfakable, unmistakable breath of life.

Michele Field   (essay date 10 May 1993)

SOURCE: "Vikram Seth," in *Publishers Weekly,* Vol. 240, No. 19, May 10, 1993, pp. 46-7.

[*In the following essay based on an interview with Seth,* *Field and Seth discuss his literary career and the writing and publishing of* A Suitable Boy.]

Vikram Seth ("Seth" is pronounced to rhyme with "fate") has always set records. His first prose book, *From Heaven Lake,* was about walking through Tibet, and it set a record as the only book in 11 years which Chatto & Windus had found in the slush pile and published. (In 1983 it went on to win Britain's most prestigious travel-writing award, the Thomas Cook Prize.) Seth's much-celebrated first novel, *The Golden Gate,* was written in verse. And his second novel, *A Suitable Boy,* coming this month from Harper-Collins, is the longest single-volume work of English fiction since Samuel Richardson's *Clarissa* was published in 1747.

But Seth is also one of those rare men who is "unaccountably" regarded as a genius by people who have not read any of his three book-length works. (He also publishes his own poetry and translations of Mandarin poets.) One wonders how Vikram Seth has held on to this reputation while spending the last eight years at his parents' home in a suburb of Calcutta. Or why he turned his back on Britain (Oxford, 1971-1975) and California (Stanford, 1975-1984), the places where word-of-mouth first made him famous, and returned to India. "I had been away a long time, 14 years or something, and I thought I'd like to go back—not be called back by some family emergency," he says. "Though research for *A Suitable Boy* necessitated my being in India for quite a while, the actual writing could have been done anywhere."

A Suitable Boy is a social history, but it is also a domestic history of parents and children set in the early 1950s, shortly after India gained its independence. (Seth was born in 1952.) Is that why he decided to reinstate himself in a real-life situation that must have made him feel like a child again?

"No, I didn't make a particular effort to put myself back," Seth replies, "though I like mealtimes with the family. A drink of scotch with my father in the evening is a ritual." (He halts the conversation to write a note about a malt whiskey he wants to buy his father.) Seth is short, and because he still wears the kind of sharp-creased trousers favored by schoolboys, sweaters which ride up his wrists, and orange knapsacks, it is easy to forget that he's past 40, not 14.

Publishers Weekly is speaking with Seth in London; interviewer and interviewee both have the flu. Paracetamol tablets are popped, and tea is drunk (his heavily sugared—he would prefer lukewarm champagne), and when strength fails, the conversation collapses into whispers. Seth has such a seductive personality that one can hardly remember the disarray with which he dresses or his receding hairline; instead, what lingers in the mind are eyes as deep as a dolphin's, and the wholly ironic inflection in his answers, whatever the question. If there were a Nice Author award on a par with the Booker Prize, this year Seth would win both.

Was it a little difficult to write with his family around him? "No, I am quite selfish, I suppose, and my family is correspondingly generous," he answers. "They know that I have lived by myself for many years abroad and that [working] *is* difficult unless I have some measure of privacy." Still, he says, "while my characters were, novelistically speaking, 'young,' other people were a distraction. My characters are so wraith-like at the beginning, so *un*imaginable, that I have to make an effort to imagine them. And real people are a tremendous distraction because they're so real."

Seth does not dismiss autobiographical analogies with the same vehemence as other novelists. His father was in the shoe-manufacturing business, as is Haresh, one of the characters who courts Lata, the novel's central character—a marriageable young woman who, studying law, most resembles Seth's mother (a magistrate). "That's a weird one," Seth concedes. "But anybody who tries to read Oedipal complexes into this novel . . . would be doing the Freudian thing which I am trying to avoid. Freud is a fashion and a fact, but I think he explains very little of the world."

Seth seems to eschew all theories, whether Freudian, philosophical, or economic—which is surprising, if only because he studied politics, philosophy and economics at Oxford and demographic economics at Stanford. Certainly the nuts and bolts of political demographics run through *A Suitable Boy,* but we get nothing of the theory. "This book is hopelessly 'reactionary' in that sense, but I think it is hopelessly 'modern' in that it tells a plain story," Seth laughs.

He explains, "*The Golden Gate* got, by and large, generous reviews. But there was one school of thought which said that stylistically speaking it was deliciously avantgarde; and another school which said it was dreadfully reactionary because it goes back to Pushkin and rhyming meter. As far as content went, some people said it was wonderful: it talks about gay rights and women's rights and the anti-nuclear movement. And yet, another school said it had the happy families of the typical, antiquated, silly Victorian novel. So whether it is reactionary or distastefully trendy, who cares?"

Seth may be more difficult to explain than his characters. Are their lives simple compared to his? Amit, the character in *A Suitable Boy* who is most like Seth, still seems much simpler. "Maybe, possibly," the novelist replies. Seth is discreet, even mysterious, about his personal life and his wide-ranging interests; his characters seem more focused, more "Victorian." He smiles. "Yes, it is unlikely that Amit would have been able to swim with dolphins." Seth is referring to his hands-on experience with Dingle Bay dolphins last June as part of his research for an opera libretto about dolphins commissioned by the English National Opera—a project Seth tackled between the writing of the novel and its revision.

In parts, *A Suitable Boy* is almost like a script—and since Seth seems interested in turning from poems and fiction to playwriting (and is considering a commission from the Royal Shakespeare Company), one wonders if his facility for conversation isn't the common factor in all his work. At this, he raises his eyebrows and answers with a quote: " 'But what's the use of a book, said Alice, without pictures and conversation?' " If conversation is like glass, letting characters speak directly to us, then the stanzas of *The Golden Gate* are stained glass, while the style of *A Suitable Boy* is clear, clean windowpane.

Despite the popularity of Seth's books (*A Suitable Boy* is on bestseller lists in India, where it was published in February, and in Britain, where it was published in March), most of his fans, he believes, probably follow him for one book only. "I don't know who followed me from *Heaven Lake* to *The Golden Gate,* and I don't know who will follow me from the *Gate* to *A Suitable Boy.* I write what I want to write, and leave the rest to whomever publishes the book."

Yet Seth is famous for controlling his own literary affairs. After his first luck with finding a British publisher for *Heaven Lake* (though it found no American publisher then; it was published by Random and Vintage on the heels of his success with *The Golden Gate*), Seth faced frustration in seeking publication for *The Golden Gate.* Without an agent, he dispatched the *Gate* himself to every poetry editor in America. "It was rejected by every one— dozens! And then a fiction editor took it up, someone who'd received it from a friend of a friend. Suddenly, within one week, Knopf, Random House and Viking all wanted to publish it. Amazing."

The ragged course of Seth's early publishing career made him rather hard-nosed when it came to *A Suitable Boy.* He knew he needed an agent, and began searching for one in the same manner he'd adopted previously when pursuing publishers—he asked everybody and settled on the best option.

In 1986, he came to London and interviewed all the agents about whom he'd heard a good word; he not only talked with them one-on-one, but met whole agencies in conference. Finally, he selected Giles Gordon as his chief agent (and Irene Skolnick from Curtis Brown in New York— "though she couldn't be more different from Giles"). Gordon, of the Sheil Land agency, is famous as the Royal family's literary agent—as Prince Charles's agent, in particular—and he seemed an unlikely choice for Seth. But because Seth manages to treat Gordon in an aptly lordly manner, and is naturally eccentric in a style that Gordon relishes, it looks like a marriage made in heaven.

Still, Gordon hardly understood what Seth was doing in Calcutta until, in the summer of 1991, the 5000 pages of typescript—the first draft of *A Suitable Boy*—landed on his desk. Undaunted, Gordon drew up a list of nine possible British publishers, and Seth insisted upon coming to London and talking to all nine—two a day over a five-day period. The Seth-Gordon "game," waged for the good of the novel, has already gone down in the annals of London literary history: they won it with an advance of £250,000 from Orion, the largest ever paid for a "first novel" in Britain.

The next challenge to be met was rather different: since Seth felt that *A Suitable Boy* was a distinctly Indian novel, he wanted the novel to be published initially in India—and to be typeset there. "This was a grueling business," he admits. However, in recounting it, Seth is characteristically discreet, and barely complains about a phase that nearly killed him. "I was in Calcutta, and I knew I wanted the novel to be typeset once—once only. I couldn't bear to proofread a book of this length for three different English-language publishers: I would have hated it by the end. I decided to do it in India to show that we *could.*"

The Indian edition, which Seth has with him in his nylon knapsack, is lovely, printed on the type of paper one associates with Bibles—thin but opaque, and lying flat at the spine. It is more expensive paper than is generally used in the West, and produces a lighter-weight book. "This is the kind of edition I imagined I might have 20 years down the line," Seth exults. "I certainly didn't imagine that the first commercial edition in India would be as nice as this," he says, caressing a page.

There is now room in the top echelon of Indian writers: the generation of Narayan, Naipaul and Desai has become the "older" one, and in the younger generation Seth has been placed nose-to-nose with Salman Rushdie. Of course, Seth would not have been considered to be in the running for best-young-Indian-novelist if he had stayed in California or London, "but now they *have to* [consider me]," he says, with a twinkle in his eye. The only aspect of this which seems to exasperate him is the implied rivalry with Rushdie.

"It is ridiculous, and very unfair to Salman. He is supposed to have made a comment about [*A Suitable Boy* as] my 'soap opera.' That is something which he may have said to his friends, but he didn't say it to me. What he said to me was, 'I hear you've written a book,' and from that people have tried to pretend that he was in some sense denigratory."

But the betting is on, even though Rushdie couldn't have written *A Suitable Boy*—and probably wouldn't have wanted to. Seth probably wouldn't have wanted to write *The Satanic Verses;* he's dismissive even of James Joyce. However, like Joyce, Seth throws himself into extremely eccentric books which, in the long run, prove more than feasible commercially. He is equally like Joyce in his talent for foreign languages and his "back-water-comes-forward" biography: Joyce's Dublin seems merely a few blocks away from Seth's Calcutta and his imaginary city, in *A Suitable Boy,* of Brahmpur.

What Joyce didn't have to manage is the year now facing Seth, who is living in several different countries while promoting *A Suitable Boy,* and finally leaving his parents' home for a second time. The first line of *A Suitable Boy* has Lata's mother saying to her younger daughter, "You too will marry a boy I choose." Joyce's mother might have said something similar, but Joyce didn't obey her. Seth, still unmarried, may not, either.

Robert Worth   (review date 21 May 1993)

SOURCE: "India—All of It," in *Commonweal,* Vol. CXX, No. 10, May 21, 1993, pp. 25-6.

[*In the following review of* A Suitable Boy, *Worth laments that Seth's concern with moderation and fairness in his por-trayal of India weakens the novel's story and leaves the reader longing for more action and a faster pace.*]

Vikram Seth has become something of a literary hero in recent months, both in his native India and in England. Newspapers have touted the million-pound advance he received for his monumental novel, set in early 1950s' India, and his publishers have trumpeted comparisons with Dickens, George Eliot, and Tolstoy. Seth is one of several brilliant and increasingly visible young Indian writers, and his aspirations match the recent trend (espoused by Tom Wolfe, among others) toward lengthy and ambitious "social" novels in the model of the nineteenth-century masters. Seth appears, in other words, to be riding a wave of expectation for something like a Great Indian Novel. The renewed outbreaks of religious and ethnic violence in India over the last few months make his *magnum opus,* which describes remarkably similar episodes in the years just after independence, all the more timely. Nor will this novel provoke any *fatwas.* Seth's grand (perhaps too grand) ambition has been to fit all of India into a novel without offending anybody.

On the surface, *A Suitable Boy* describes the lives of four large, extended Indian families linked by marriage and friendship. One of those families, the Khans, belong to the *zamindari* aristocracy, whose feudal privileges were being swept away by land reforms at the time of the novel's setting. Another family, the Brahmin Chatterjis, contains the first Indian High Court justice; the third is fathered by a powerful minister of revenue who is also a member of the national Legislative Assembly. The fourth family, lacking such obvious distinctions, nonetheless contains one of the first Indian executives (a "brown Sahib") in a high-profile British management firm. Seth grounds his fiction, in other words, in some of the most important political and social issues of the day. Nehru himself becomes a character (albeit a minor one) and lengthy speeches from the Legislative Assembly are quoted *verbatim.*

Nonetheless, Seth's novel is far less concerned with political struggles than with the smaller dramas of everyday life. The story is set, after all, not during the struggle for independence but afterwards, during a period of relative peace and stability. There are crises, for the four families of *A Suitable Boy,* but none of them explodes into melodrama. An adulterous affair threatens chaos, but then fizzles out peacefully; a heartbroken young man considers suicide, but ends up spending a month in the country instead. Seth appears to be bent on showing us the interstices of social change, the way that life and love will go on no matter what history may be up to. It is hardly surprising when Lata, the novel's central character, does indeed find a suitable boy to marry.

This emphasis on the redeeming aspects of private life is in keeping with Seth's prior work. His first novel, *The Golden Gate,* described the joys and sorrows of three twenty-something characters in San Francisco. Far more limited in scope than *A Suitable Boy,* it was nevertheless an ambitious book: the prospect, Seth tells us, of a novel composed of sequential sonnets was enough to send both editors and friends away in disgust. But the critics raved; Gore Vidal promptly dubbed it "the great Californian novel." Seth's verbal gift was supple enough to capture even the most fragmentary conversations, and to range in tone from charming doggerel at the outset to redemptive tragedy in the novel's final pages.

In *A Suitable Boy* Seth appears to have bitten off more than he can chew. His plot, weaving back and forth toward India's first general election, insists on taking a glimpse of almost every issue that might conceivably have a bearing on that event: religion, law, business, changing cultural traditions. Even the drudgeries of life in a remote northern village are given their fullest possible expression. But the farther Seth roams from his central, high-caste characters, the more his prose tends to sound like a museum-tour: dry, passionless, and analytical.

To some extent these failings are the result of Seth's desire to be fair, to offer a balanced portrait of the nation that will respect all the parties involved. He could not be more different, in this respect, from Salman Rushdie, whose 1980 novel *Midnight's Children* also takes postindependence India as its subject, and Indian family life as its vehicle. *Midnight's Children* shuttles wildly back and forth in time, presenting a feverish, supernatural vision of Indian life and society. The narrator, who was born at the very second of independence, literally *becomes* the voice of modern India; he has none of the calm detachment that marks Seth's novel. He is cursed, wounded, and finally castrated by the forces that were set in motion at his birth, and the magical realism of his narration represents a desperate effort to make sense of those forces. That effort ends, with the novel, in a terrifying vision of apocalypse. The book makes no effort, in other words, to build bridges or to present a "balanced" view. Its very form would appear to mock that possibility in a country so torn by extremism and hatred. Rushdie leaves us, in the end, with nothing more than a painfully vivid impression.

If *A Suitable Boy* fails to achieve such vividness, that is probably because Seth is after different quarry. A former doctoral student in economics who abandoned demography for literature, Seth treats his characters with a gentle concern, and is unwilling to sacrifice them (or their future) to blazing language or dramatic conclusions. *A Suitable Boy* makes no effort to shock its readers, or even to dazzle them. It aims instead at a vast, comprehensive unity; and it focuses on those aspects of life that hold society together rather than those that tear it apart. In that sense Seth seems to have moved self-consciously beyond the jarring, fragmentary aesthetics of most "postmodern" fiction. All the same, it's hard to get through *A Suitable Boy* without wishing for more action, a faster pace, and a stronger story. Moderation and fairness are necessary virtues in India's current crisis; but they are not of much value in a novel.

Schuyler Ingle   (review date 23 May 1993)

SOURCE: "A Family of 900 Million," in *Los Angeles Times Book Review,* May 23, 1993, pp. 4, 11.

[*In the following review, Ingle lauds* A Suitable Boy.]

It is no wonder that when Vikram Seth finished writing the rather simple story of Mrs. Rupa Mehra's search for a suitable boy to marry her lovely young daughter, Lata, he had produced a novel over 1,300 pages long. The author, you see, left nothing out.

He chose to tell the whole story, producing for all time the whole world of Lata Mehra, with all the intermingled levels of North Indian culture, including entangled and intertwined families, a plethora of castes and religions, levels of education, and political and economic aspirations. And sex and violence, as well as poetry and puns and jokes.

In a land of 900 million people, Seth seems to be saying, no one person can possibly be singled out: Their connections must be taken into account as well.

And yet, this is not a bloated text. In fact, it is spare. In a magnificent display of artistic control as well as compassion for his reader, Vikram Seth disappears. And in an odd way, so too does his writing. It is absolutely seamless. There are no impediments placed between the reader and the story and the intimate lives of the characters. The reader's immersion in Indian life is so complete that by the time *A Suitable Boy* comes to its successful conclusion, aspects of Indian life that seem exotic—like the idea of arranging a marriage for a daughter—make perfect sense to a Western reader.

The tale takes place in a mythical city, Brahmpur, capital of a mythical state, Purva Pradesh, in the very real Northern India of the early 1950s. Of the many events that play through the text, one is the general election of newly independent India in 1951. Another is the struggle to push through the state assembly a bill that would strip feudal landlords of their holdings. Seth takes the fallout of such momentous change right down to the village level.

A Suitable Boy begins with the marriage of Pran Kapoor to Lata Mehra's older sister, Savita. The basic cast of characters the reader will follow through a year of politics, religious strife, love affairs, suicides, attempted murders, debauchery, courtship, festivals, strikes, Shakespeare productions, horse races, cricket matches, human stampedes, births and deaths all pretty much appear at this first wedding: Mehras, Kapoors, Chatterjis and Khans. The author is kind enough to provide family trees at the front of the book, but the story is so clearly told the reader will rarely refer to them.

Make no mistake about it: This is a book about India and Indians. The first white men, a couple of British twits, appear at about page 400; they make some silly, ignorant remarks about the local culture, then quickly disappear. The next white men appear somewhere around page 1,000. They are Czech overseers at a shoe factory. They, too, disappear. And by the time they do, the reader can describe the making of shoes from the tanning of the hides through the final polishing of the brogues. The level of relevant detail Seth weaves through his text—whether numbers theory or political machination or academic maneuvering or farming or classical musicianship or natural history or cultural anthropology—is astonishing for the way it comforts the reader and draws him in closer and closer to the many characters at hand.

If Seth consciously worked from models or with a literary strategy, he settled on the great, sweeping novels of the 19th Century. Tolstoy comes to mind without too much prodding (though Seth never succumbs to lecturing his readers). The 19th Century masters may well have had grand literary aspirations in mind when they set to work, and no doubt Vikram Seth did as well. But they also wrote to entertain, to fill an evening, to offer an informed distraction at the end of the day. And so does Vikram Seth.

There are no impediments in *A Suitable Boy* placed between the reader and the story and the intimate lives of the characters. The reader's immersion in Indian life is so complete that by the time *A Suitable Boy* comes to its successful conclusion, aspects of Indian life that seem exotic make perfect sense to a Western reader.

—*Schuyler Ingle*

His struggle, however, is far greater than Tolstoy's or George Eliot's, for he writes against the impact of television and film, those modern doses of spoonfed entertainment that make few demands as they quickly come and go. Seth writes against a reader's busy life and reduced attention span. Like *Middlemarch,* though, *A Suitable Boy* is a page-turner, and the page-turning must go on night after night. I found myself getting edgy as the evenings wore on, hoping dinner guests would leave earlier than normal so I could get down to reading. I left dishes in the sink until morning so I could get back to reading; put off the writing of letters and the paying of bills so I could get back to reading. To close the door, pull down the shade, slip between the sheets and balance this weighty tome against my knees became the driving force of my days.

In time I found myself talking back to this book, as though it were alive. I found myself laughing through pages. And very much to my surprise, I found myself reading through tears at the death of an important though rather minor character, if the weight of characters can be measured in quantities of ink.

I also found myself more frightened in fewer measured words than I ever thought possible at the scene in which Lata suddenly comprehends the incestuous relationship between a relative and his daughter. She faces the evil alone, unprotected, and it is an absolutely chilling two or three pages.

A Suitable Boy is a book that pays readers back, and richly, for their nightly effort.

Anita Desai   (review date 27 May 1993)

SOURCE: "Sitting Pretty," in *The New York Review of Books,* Vol. XLI, No. 10, May 27, 1993, pp. 22-6.

[*Desai is an Indian novelist, short story writer, and author of books for children. In the following review, she examines character and style in* A Suitable Boy.]

The character Vikram Seth chooses in his novel *A Suitable Boy* to represent himself is not one of the central characters; it is Amit the poet who "was sitting pretty in his father's house and doing nothing that counted as real work," which happens to be the writing of an historical novel. In an uncharacteristically confiding moment, he compares writing fiction to Indian music.

> I've always felt that the performance of a raag resembles a novel—or at least the kind of novel I'm attempting to write. You know . . . first you take one note and explore it for a while, then another to discover its possibilities, then perhaps you get to the dominant, and pause for a bit, and it's only gradually that the phrases begin to form and the tabla joins in with the beat . . . and then the more brilliant improvisations and diversions begin, with the main theme returning from time to time, and finally it all speeds up, and the excitement increases to a climax.

He is cut short by an acerbic critic, Dr. Ila Chattopadhyay, who interrupts, "What utter nonsense. . . . Don't pay any attention to him. . . . He's just a writer, he knows nothing at all about literature." So Amit tries again and the next time round he compares his work to a banyan tree:

> It sprouts, and grows, and spreads, and drops down branches that become trunks or intertwine with other branches. Sometimes branches die. Sometimes the main trunk dies, and the structure is held up by the supporting trunks. When you go to the Botanical Garden you'll see what I mean. It has its own life—but so do the snakes and birds and bees and lizards and termites that live in it and on it and off it. Of course, it's also like the Ganges in its upper, middle and lower courses—including its delta—of course.

Both—or all three—comparisons imply the slow and ample growth of an entity that gains impressive dimensions through size, longevity, and intricacy of design. One has to agree they are apt comparisons for a novel about four large families and the social and political life of northern India in the 1950s which fills nearly 1,400 pages.

Engagingly, the author is also capable of downplaying the book's scope and achievement. After a reading at the Brahmpur Literary Society, Amit is pursued by the usual questions: "Why is it that you do not write in Bengali, your mother tongue?" and "Why do you use rhyming?" and also the one that Seth will have been asked with monotonous regularity over the last few months: "Why is it . . . so long? More than a thousand pages!" He replies:

> Oh, I don't know how it grew to be so long. I'm very undisciplined. But I too hate long books. . . . And I have my own way of reducing that bulk. . . . Well, what I do is to take my pen-knife and slit the whole book into forty or so fascicles . . . And when I'm wandering around—in a cemetery, say—I can take them

out and read them. It's easy on the mind and on the wrist. I recommend it to everyone.

"Everyone" is appalled. "Mr. Nowrojee looked as if he were about to faint dead away. Amit appeared pleased with the effect." Vikram Seth alias Amit Chatterji clearly enjoys creating such effects. His last literary success was a novel he wrote entirely in verse, *The Golden Gate.* Much was made of the fact that the verse form was the tetrameter sonnet employed by Pushkin in *Eugene Onegin.* Here the analogy was unfortunate, for *The Golden Gate* was, for all its technical achievement, essentially light verse closer in spirit to John Betjeman and Ogden Nash than to Pushkin's ferocious and satirical wit. It was precisely this that made readers who ordinarily "never read poetry" find it painless and enjoyable. Seth employs the same facility for light rhyming verse to leaven the bulk and weight of his gigantic novel, and in his "Word of Thanks" addresses:

> Gentle reader, you as well,
> The fountainhead of all
>   remittance.
> Buy me before good sense insists
> You'll strain your purse and
>   sprain your wrists.

Equally enticing is his "Table of Contents," also listed in verse:

> 1 Browsing through books, two
>   students meet one day.
>   A mother mopes; a medal melts
>   away.
>
> 2 A courtesan sings coolly
>   through the heat.
>   A hopeful lover buys a parakeet.
>
> 3 A couple glides down-river in a
>   boat.
>   A mother hears that mischief is
>   afloat. . . .

—and the charm of the rhyming couplets eases us into the formidable river of prose. Light verse on the one hand, the prosy mass of a family saga on the other: How are the two to be bridged? Seth may have had in mind the Sanskrit epic in which, through all the digressions and diversions, the thread of narrative is maintained and imprinted on the memory of their readers—or, in the days when epics were composed, on their listeners—by frequent recourse to rhyming couplets and song, more memorable than rambling prose.

It is not possible to carry this analogy any further: the verse is extraneous, an embellishment, not a literary device of the author's. Seth's affection is for the ordinary and the everyday: he creates neither heroes nor villains of mythical proportions, nor does he build historical events into ahistorical legends. The epic belongs to an oral tradition beyond resurrection in an age of technological communication, and Seth's novel must be fitted into the modern literary tradition, which is essentially Western. He himself claims—or his publishers claim on his behalf—that his novel belongs to the nineteenth-century tradition created by Tolstoy, Dickens, George Eliot, and Jane Aus-

ten. One would like to think that the assertion is enough to bring a blush to the cheek of even so phenomenally successful an author as Vikram Seth.

Seth's touch is feather-light and airy; one can ascribe to it neither the great dark weight of Tolstoy's searching meditations nor the flashing satiric swordplay of Jane Austen's pen. The great Victorian zeal for reform that inspired so much of Dickens's and Eliot's work can hardly be said to be Seth's purpose: he is too fond and too tolerant of his characters to want to transform them. Although, in their rash youth, they might be tempted by the possibilities of change, defiance, and the unknown, they learn their lessons and return, chastened, to the safety and security of the familiar and the traditional, represented here, in the Indian fashion, by the great god Family.

We are left with the undeniable length of the book—a family saga stretched to the point when "Victorian" does become an apt adjective: one thinks of the Albert Memorial in London, the Victoria Memorial in Calcutta, of Victorian skirts and Victorian meals and Victorian furniture as other examples of such amplitude and substance. How did the author of such delicately proportioned verse as in *The Humble Administrator's Garden* and *All You Who Sleep Tonight* get drawn into a prose project on such a scale? At times one might even find oneself asking *why*. Surely the story of Lata being maneuvered by her mother into choosing between three suitors, or the story of the Hindu boy Maan's friendship with the Muslim boy Firoz, or of the Urdu teacher Rasheed's desire to bring change to his unchanging village, would have made a more shapely story in itself, of a more conventional length of two to three hundred pages.

Yes, but one soon sees that such a story would have been slight, and negligible in itself (and has often been written, by others): it is precisely by interweaving all their tales with such skill into patterns of such intricacy that Seth achieves his effect of bulk and mass impossible to overlook. His intention was clearly to reproduce India on a scale in keeping with its history, its population, its diversity, and abundance of life. Neither two inches of ivory nor the more sizable stretch of a Victorian oil painting in a heavy gilt frame would have suited his purpose, and if his novel has an artistic equivalent then it is the folk painting on a village wall, a mural in a cave, or a stitched and embroidered quilt patiently patched together and embellished by that multiplicity of detail that gives it density and richness. In *The Speaking Tree: A Study of Indian Culture and Society* Richard Lannoy termed such art a display of "the unified field awareness" which involves a disregard of a single focal point, an even distribution of emphasis, a giving of importance to both foreground and background by flattening perspective, and the resulting cyclical effect that makes possible a study that begins at any point and ends at any point and yet covers all the territory.

The canvas is provided by the fictitious state of Purva Pradesh in north India (which bears a very close resemblance to present-day Uttar Pradesh, now commonly known as the Hindi Belt, or the Cow Belt, being the home of Hindu fundamentalism) in the year 1951. Not a year that is particularly memorable in modern Indian history, yielding up not even one momentous event to memory. By choosing it rather than another, Seth again displays his proclivity for the commonplace and quotidian, and he is able to convince his reader of its historical accuracy by means of thorough research and the painstaking reproduction of the politics of the time—the beginnings of disillusionment with Nehru, who only four years before had led India from colonial rule to independence, the beginnings of the rift in the ruling Congress Party between those who continued to support him and those who had become impatient for change, and the preparations for the first general election held in independent India:

> And then finally it would be the voters who mattered, the great washed and unwashed public, sceptical and gullible, endowed with universal adult suffrage, six times as numerous as those permitted the vote in 1946. It was in fact to be the largest election ever held anywhere on earth.

Nevertheless it could not have held the reader's interest if Seth had not created characters who are personally involved in these public affairs, and for this purpose he employs the services of four large, sprawling families that live in the dusty environs of Brahmpur, the state capital, and the more sophisticated city of Calcutta—the Mehras, the Chatterjis, the Kapoors, and the Khans. The first three, being Hindu, are related by marriage; the last, being Muslim, only by friendship. To the first two are given all the lighter roles—they provide us with amusement and laughter; to the latter two are given the darker ones—they provide the drama, and the melodrama.

For all the breadth and the scope of the author's intention, there is at the heart of his work a modesty that one would have thought belonged to the miniature, not the epic scale. The characters are not heroes or villains, and we see them involved in the usual affairs of love and business. They are so numerous that Seth runs the risk of seeming to skim over the surface of their lives; occasionally one finds oneself wishing he would pause and give us a moment to reflect. No, no, we must get to our feet and rush on regardless—scarcely has Pran the college lecturer had his heart attack than his wife Savita has her baby; no sooner have we dispatched with Maan's court case then it is time to get Lata married.

This leaves Seth little space to develop his characters. They come to us extremely well-equipped with easily recognizable characteristics: in the Mehra family, the matriarch Mrs. Rupa Mehra is identified by her capacious black handbag, her collection of greeting cards that she cannibalizes to commemorate every new family occasion (on the birth of her new granddaughter she chooses one that reads, "A Lady Baby came today!—what words are quite so nice to say?"), frequent recourse to tears, and constant reference to her dead husband; her son Arun by his pompous and officious ways; and her son Varun by his cringing evasiveness.

In the Chatterji family Amit the poet is reclusive and difficult to draw out, Dipankar is spiritual and discourses on profound matters with the Grande Dame of Culture ("'. . . not Unity, not Unity, but Zero, Nullity itself, is

the guiding principle of our existence' "), Kakoli talks almost exclusively in rhyming couplets, and the frivolous Meenakshi divides her time between canasta at the Shady Ladies Club in the mornings and casual promiscuity in the afternoons. At the end of the book they have progressed no further in any new directions.

If, in spite of their predictability, we become so engaged in their lives and even devoted to them, it is because of the author's skill in providing them with details we find recognizable and true, and in this he goes to tireless lengths. Arun Mehra is only a minor character but one is given all the information one could want about the management agency for which he works and which controls trade and commerce in "Abrasives, Air Conditioning, Belting, Brushes, Building, Cement, Chemicals and Pigments, Coal, Coal-Mining Machinery, Copper & Brass . . . " and so on down the alphabet to "Tea, Timber, Vertical Turbine Pumps, Wire Rope," thereby giving Arun the aplomb that informs his every gesture:

> He got out of the car, leaving his briefcase behind, and protecting himself with the *Statesman*. His peon, who had been standing in the porch of the building, started when he saw his master's little blue car. It had been raining so hard he had not seen it until it had almost stopped. Agitated, he opened the umbrella and rushed out to protect the sahib. He was a second or two too late.
>
> "Bloody idiot."
>
> The peon, though several inches shorter than Arun Mehra, contrived to hold his umbrella over the sacred head as Arun sauntered into the building. He got into the lift, and nodded in a preoccupied manner at the lift-boy.
>
> The peon rushed back to the car to get his master's briefcase, and climbed the stairs to the second floor of the large building.

Unerring as is his eye for the telling detail, the method works best in humorous scenes and is less successful in portraying the darker, more sweeping passions, which are often rendered as bathos. Maan's infatuation with the Muslim courtesan, Saeeda Bai, and its effects are analyzed in a perfunctory manner: when Maan's mother, Mrs. Mahesh Kapoor, "saw Maan so drunk and unsteady she was very unhappy. Though she did not say anything to him, she was afraid for him. If his father had seen him in his present state he would have had a fit." The Hindu boy discovers his best friend, Firoz, in Saeeda Bai's drawing room, misinterprets his intentions and attacks him in a blind rage, then staggers off, dripping with blood, into a dark and misty night. This scene belongs to melodrama, complete with a slowly clopping tonga horse. The courtroom scene in which Firoz withdraws his accusation and Maan is acquitted is one in which Seth feels so ill at ease that he winds it up in one page and hurriedly tidies it out of sight. The revelation made about the true ancestry of Saeeda Bai's "sister" Tasneem ("the child she had conceived in terror, had carried in shame, and had borne in pain") rings false—it is not a moment of truth but merely a device of the plot.

Seth himself seems to be on the side of Maan's father,

Mahesh Kapoor, who slaps Maan when he comes home drunk: " 'Love?' cried his father, his incredulity mixed with rage . . . 'Get out! Out!' " and he seems positively relieved when Maan sees the folly of his ways and rejects Saeeda Bai:

> So shattering had been his mother's death, Firoz's danger, his own disgrace, and his terrible sense of guilt that he had begun to suffer a violent revulsion of feeling against himself and Saeeda Bai. Perhaps he saw her too as a victim. . . . "I am to blame for all that has happened." "You don't love me—don't tell me you do—I can see it—" she wept. "Love—" said Maan. "Love?" Suddenly he sounded furious.

Lata Mehra, the charming young heroine of the book, whose mother in the opening scene declares her plans for her—" 'You too will marry a boy I choose,' said Mrs. Rupa Mehra firmly to her younger daughter," and in the final chapter brings off this highly desirable ending—Lata, too, less dramatically but equally soberly, abandons youth's dreams of passion and gives up her unsuitable Muslim suitor so as not to distress her mother. Both she and Maan sacrifice romance in the name of family and stability. Lata tells her appalled friend Malati, "If that's what passion means, I don't want it. Look at what passion has done to the family." When Malati protests, "You are mad—absolutely mad. How could you do it?" Lata tries to explain. Being modern and "Westernized," a student of English literature at Brahmpur University, she does so by quoting Clough:

> " 'There are two different kinds, I believe, of human attraction. One that merely excites, unsettles, and makes you uneasy; the other that—' Well, I can't remember exactly, but he talks about a calmer, less frantic love, which helps you to grow where you were already growing, 'to live where as yet I had languished. . . .' "

Her mother, who begins each day by reading two pages of the *Bhagavad Gita,* would have quoted instead: "He who can withstand the impulse of lust and anger even here [in this life], before he is separated from the body, is steadfast and truly a happy man."

If any philosophy is being expounded here it appears to be that of Aristotle's golden mean—the avoidance of excess, the advisability of moderation, the wisdom of restraint, temperance, and control. Whenever these rules are flouted, grief results.

Even changing the rules can cause a dangerous imbalance. Mahesh Kapoor, as revenue minister, is largely responsible for the Zamindari Abolition Bill that proposes to dispossess such landlords as Firoz's father, the nawab of Baitar, of their land. Many landlords, less noble and generous than the old nawab, act quickly to remove tenant farmers from their lands before the bill can turn them into virtual owners. Maan's Urdu teacher Rasheed who passionately hates the old feudal system and longs to bring about reform in his ancestral village, sees the risk to the peasant Kaccheru on his father's property. He marches into the village patwari's office to insist that the family land holdings be changed in favor of Kaccheru who has worked so loyally for his family through the years. For this he is punished severely: his family denounces him for his meddling zeal, he is unable to help a single person in the slumberous, mosquito-ridden village, and he loses his mind and commits suicide (a scene so distasteful to the author that it is the shortest in the book).

These dangerous and fraught involvements actually take up the lesser amount of space: more is given to the lighthearted and the pleasurable in which Seth is clearly more in his element. Some of the set pieces are on the grand scale, rendered either in the detailed informative manner of official reports, for example, the Pul Mela (the gigantic fair held on the banks of the Ganga)—

> The roads on the Pul Mela sands were packed with people. . . . Men, women and children, old and young, dark and fair, rich and poor, brahmins and outcastes. Tamils and Kashmiris, saffron-clad sadhus and naked nagas, all jostled together. . . .

—or in more lurid descriptive prose as in the raising of the Shiva-linga, the phallic symbol of the god Shiva, from the riverbed and its inadvertent descent:

> It kept rolling on, down, down, swifter and swifter towards the Ganga, crushing the pujari who now stood in its downward path with arms upraised, smashing into the burning pyres of the cremation ghat, and sinking into the water of the Ganga at last, down its submerged stone steps, and onto its muddy bed.

> The Shiva-linga rested on the bed of the Ganga once more, the turbid waters passing over it, its bloodstains slowly washed away . . .

—a description which resembles nothing so much as one of those grim steel engravings of the Mutiny of 1857 that expressed the British colonial nightmare.

Fortunately there are the lesser activities, at once so busy and so leisurely in the distinctively Indian way, that occupy the four families—a boat ride on the river at dawn, feeding monkeys with fruit under a banyan tree, a courtesan's recital of Urdu love poetry, a tea party at which three matrons discuss their grandchildren, the making of mango pickles and the dangers of allowing young daughters too much freedom (" 'You see, it is like this,' said Mrs. Mahesh Kapoor gently, 'please look after your daughter, because someone saw her walking with a boy on the bank of the Ganga near the dhobi-ghat yesterday morning' "), a discussion with a gardener over a matter of sloping lawns and pond herons, and a good many eminently civilized games of cricket played on dusty university fields by handsome young men showing off with bat and ball while demure wives sit in the sun with their knitting.

With the glee of an anthropologist let loose among Pacific islanders, Seth describes for us all the festivals of the Indian calendar year, from the colorful spring festival when characters stagger through the canna lilies in a happy haze of bhang—on that day not merely permitted but prescribed—and then are dunked in tubs of pink water, through Rakhi when brothers and sisters swear loyalty to each other by the tying of pretty wrist bands and gifts of sweets and money; Janamashtmi to celebrate the birth of the baby Krishna; Bakr-Id celebrated by Muslims by the slaughter of goats and the feasting on their flesh; Karva Chauth at which good wives fast to ensure long lives for their husbands; and winding up with Christmas and New Year's Eve with plum pudding and brandy sauce in the clubs of Calcutta, that haven for boxwallahs left over from the heyday of the East India Company. (Inexplicably, the greatest festival of the Hindu year, Diwali, is left out.) So ardently are these celebrated by one set of citizens or the other that when the Hindu festival of Ramlila, commemorating Rama and Sita's triumphant return to their kingdom after fourteen years of wrongful exile, occurs on the same day as the Muslims are conducting the Mohurrum procession of the funerary tazias of the Prophet's murdered nephews, Hasan and Hosain, through the city toward the mosque, a slight delay on the part of one leads to what police and politicians had dreaded—a bloody clash accompanied by knives, fires, riots, and deaths. Even when Hindus are celebrating the Pul Mela by themselves, with processions of sadhus taking turns at bathing in the holy waters of the Ganga they manage to contrive a colossal tragedy.

For the most part, however, the celebrations are affectionate and enjoyable as family life is. If there are bad experiences, few are so bad that they cannot be put right by a basket of ripe mangoes, or a timely song. When shadows loom, Seth steps forward to drive them away with a flap of his hands; if the schoolboy Tapan has been traumatized by the cruelties of his schoolfellows in the British-style public school Jheel (Seth himself studied in one called Doon), a rescue is quickly devised by his resourceful brothers and no lingering effects such an experience might have had on the boy are shown us. There is only one truly nasty character in the whole book—Uncle Sahgal, who plods quietly down the corridor to his daughter's bedroom at night and then tries to slip into Lata's—but he is seen as a figure in a nightmare: daylight drives him into oblivion and no more is made of his sinister vice.

> When Mr. Sahgal, her uncle from Lucknow, approached them with a repellent smile, she held Haresh's hand tightly. . . . Lata had closed her eyes. He looked at her face, at the lipstick on her lips, with a slight sneer, before moving away.

It is the last we see of him and the wedding celebrations go on apace.

Critics have remarked on the remarkable absence of Freud from the book, which is written as if Freud's theories had never filtered down into the bazaars of Brahmpur, and, in fact, the vast majority of Indians have never heard of them and feel they do not need to—everything has surely already been portrayed in the *Mahabharata,* the *Ramayana* . . .

If Seth displays an old-fashioned regard for the "normal," and an unpoetic one for anti-romanticism, so does he show himself an admirer of another old-fashioned virtue: work. He is surely redressing a common lapse on the part of novelists when he ascribes more space to his characters' trades and professions than he does to their looks, dress, or love lives, and thereby accords them an unexpected dignity. He

transforms Lata's most humble suitor, Haresh Khanna, something of an upstart in his flashy silk shirts and two-tone shoes that so distress her, into a kind of hero, for he is devoted to his work in the far-from-sweet-smelling shoe trade. So that we may know exactly how Haresh rises from rung to rung of it, Seth takes us on a tour from the fetid open-air tanneries, where low-caste chamars stand in pits soaking the flayed skins, to the Czech empire of Prahapore (closely resembling the ubiquitous Bata Shoe Company and Batanagar). So intense is his involvement with his profession that on the morning after his wedding, he proposes to visit the local shoe factory: he is obtuse enough to invite his bride to accompany him. She demurs. On the train carrying them to their new home in Prahapore, he is so exhausted that he falls asleep, leaving her to entertain herself by feeding the monkeys at the railway station with a somewhat pensive air.

Not a romance in the Western sense, or even the Eastern. To which hemisphere then, and to what era, does Seth belong? By virtue of his age and nationality, to a generation of Indian writers born after Independence and now in their forties, who have attracted attention abroad and even made the reading and writing of novels a respectable pursuit in India. Yet he has little in common with them in any literary sense: he writes as if Salman Rushdie had never written *Midnight's Children* or *The Satanic Verses,* firmly turning his back upon the unconfined imagination and dangerous fantasy. He does not have Amitav Ghosh's taste for fine shadings and subtleties, or for the historical satire marked out by Shashi Tharoor and Alan Sealy as their territory. Seth has refused to either equal or outdo his contemporaries. He is quoted in interviews as having said that he wished to strip fiction of ideas and style, suggesting these only get in the way of a reader's enjoyment.

Yet it is impossible for a writer of either prose or poetry to disregard an essential element of style: language, especially troubling to an Indian writing in a non-Indian language, English. Novelists of an earlier generation—Raja Rao, R. K. Narayan, and Mulk Raj Anand—found their own individual solutions to the problem, but that did not obviate the need for experimentation on the part of the younger generation. Seth, with his cheerful disregard for anything that proposes to be "a problem," has decided to throw together all their experiments and all their solutions: some of his characters are fluent users of the English idiom ("How fearfully dowdy!" and "A bit of a bounder, I'd say"), some in a more laborious schoolroom English ("Your superstitious mother will start panicking if they miss the correct configuration of stars"), and others in the casual multilingualism common to urban Indians ("So you're his sala," "I'll be kutti with you," "You can't be kutti with your uncle"). There are also passages in the babu English in which British satirists used to delight, at its most hilarious in a meeting of the Brahmpur Literary Society at which a Dr. Makhijani reads an interminable patriotic poem:

> Let me recall history of heroes
>   proud,
> Mother-milk fed their breasts,
>   who did not bow.
> Fought they fiercely, carrying

worlds of weight,
Establishing firm foundation of
Indian state.

At times Seth helps clarify matters by telling us, "His conversation with his father had been in Hindi, hers with her mother in English." At other times he leaves us to draw our own conclusions: for example, the courtesan's dialogue with her admirers is so courtly, allusive, and elaborate, it can only be in Urdu, e.g., "Sit down and illumine our gathering." Seth provides no glossary for non-Hindi-speaking readers, counting upon the energy of his prose to help them over any hurdles of speech, and in this his instinct seems to have been right, for the text moves at an unencumbered pace, leaving his readers amazed at their ability to read some 1,400 pages so easily, and awed, of course, by Seth's having written them with seemingly equal ease.

Awe, too, is what Seth's labor inspires in the reader. At the end it is as if one had listened to a raag played by a musician with skill, dexterity, and charm. It may seem ungrateful, then, to wish there had also been moments of silence, of stillness, in the midst of such a buzz of words and actions, when one might have heard the great resounding *boum* emerge from the heart of the cave, the dark heart of even the most ordinary man or woman.

There is little in *A Suitable Boy* of the darker aspects of Indian married life: none of his female characters is married against her will, or burned alive because she or her dowry is deemed insufficient. Yet, the happy spirit of the novel seems neither sentimental nor blind. It is a natural gift of the author, who never mocks or dismisses his characters.

—*John Bemrose, in "Full-lotus Fiction," in* Maclean's, *31 May 1993.*

Robert Towers   (review date 1 June 1993)

SOURCE: A review of *A Suitable Boy,* in *The New York Times Book Review,* June 1, 1993, pp. 3-4.

[*Towers is an American educator, novelist, and critic. In the following review, he asserts that* A Suitable Boy *addresses an important era in Indian history but is not successful as a novel.*]

Indian poet Vikram Seth's novel *A Suitable Boy* begins with a lavishly detailed set piece devoted to a Hindu wedding and, more than 1,300 pages later, ends with another. One might well see the book itself in terms of a coupling (an odd one), for Mr. Seth—known in America as the author of a well-received novel in verse, *The Golden Gate*—has joined an essentially tidy, Jane Austen-like main plot with an attempt to re-create the multitudinous life of post-

British India on a scale unequaled since Salman Rushdie's *Midnight's Children.* Apart from their predilection for vast and crowded canvases, however, it would be hard to imagine two writers less alike than the wildly inventive and ferociously satirical Mr. Rushdie and the amiable Mr. Seth, a sentimental "bourgeois" realist with a taste for scrupulous documentation.

This novel, which is set in the early 1950's, opens on a scene of triumph: Mrs. Rupa Mehra, a middle-aged widow of good family, has found a suitable boy for her elder daughter, Savita, and "the cream of Brahmpur society" is present to witness the performance of the Sanskrit marriage rites. It is true that her new son-in-law, Pran Kapoor, is darker than she would like and not in the best of health, but he is "a good, decent, cultured khatri boy" of 30. The term "khatri," as the reader will soon deduce, applies to the high caste to which both the Mehras and the Kapoors belong. The warmhearted, superstitious and excitable Mrs. Rupa Mehra can now focus her attention on her younger daughter, Lata. But the virginal Lata is dismayed at the thought of the nuptial night her sister must undergo and blurts out to her mother that she doesn't think she ever wants to get married. Mr. Seth continues:

> Mrs. Rupa Mehra was too wearied by the wedding, too exhausted by emotion, too softened by Sanskrit, too cumbered with congratulations, too overwrought, in short, to do anything but stare at Lata for 10 seconds. What on earth had got into the girl? What was good enough for her mother and her mother's mother and her mother's mother's mother should be good enough for her. Lata, though, had always been a difficult one, with a strange will of her own, quiet but unpredictable. . . . But Mrs. Rupa Mehra too had a will, and she was determined to have her own way, even if she was under no illusions as to Lata's pliability.

This passage, which illustrates the conventionality of the novel's language and sentiment, sets into motion what will become the reader's main concern: will Lata submit to Mrs. Rupa Mehra's arrangements, or will she exercise that spirit of her own even if it means defying not only her mother but also the prohibitions of caste and religion? Three candidates eventually present themselves. One of them, a handsome cricket-playing fellow named Kabir, strongly attracts Lata, but he is a Muslim and therefore out of the question as far as her mother is concerned. Then there is Amit Chatterji, a poet and a member of a Calcutta Brahmin family related by marriage to the Mehras. And finally there is Haresh, a brisk young man determined to make a career for himself in the shoe-manufacturing industry.

But the marrying off of Lata provides only the main plot line, which often drops from sight for 50 pages at a time while Mr. Seth pursues one of his numerous, almost equally important subplots. These involve the Congress Party politician Mahesh Kapoor, who is the father of Pran and of another son, the indolent and troubled Maan; the Nawab Sahib of Baitar, an aristocratic Muslim zamindar, or landowner, and his son Firoz Khan, whose estates are likely to be expropriated under the Zamindari Abolition

Act, sponsored by the Nawab's old friend Mahesh Kapoor; and the rich but somewhat feckless Chatterjis, one of whom, the selfish and adulterous Meenakshi, is married to Lata's snobbish older brother Arun. (Genealogical tables for each of these families are provided as a reader's aid in the front and back of the book.)

To me, the most moving of the subplots concerns the infatuation of Maan with an imperious Muslim singer-courtesan and his drunken stabbing of his dear friend (and, by implication, onetime lover) Firoz Khan, whose life he earlier saved during a Hindu-Muslim riot; here the suspense hangs on the question of whether Maan will have to stand trial (and a possible life sentence) for the almost fatal stabbing.

The above barely begins to suggest the multitude of characters and events that throng *A Suitable Boy.* Although Mr. Seth takes what might be called an avuncular interest in his characters, he seems more passionately concerned to offer his Western readers as thick—and as multilayered—a slice of Indian life in the 1950's as this huge novel can hold. The setting moves back and forth between the cities of Brahmpur (which is fictional) and Calcutta, with excursions to New Delhi, Kanpur and Lucknow and to a remote country village where Maan spends a month in exile. Each major setting is elaborately documented in terms of its social and demographic components, with the domestic routines of the various families lovingly recounted.

In Calcutta, where both the spirit and the customs of the recent British Raj still prevail some three or four years after independence, we join the frivolous Chatterjis at dinner in their Ballygunge mansion, go to cocktail parties given by British executives and to races at the Tollygunge Club.

In the city of Brahmpur, a state capital on the banks of the Ganges, we attend meetings of the legislative assembly and hearings in the high court, visit the university, listen to technically described performances of Indian classical music, venture into foul-smelling slums where the low-caste leatherworkers scrape the fat from rotting hides, follow the election campaign of Mahesh Kapoor, participate in the Hindu festivals of Holi and Ramlila and the Muslim celebration of Muharram.

It is the religious festivals that provide Mr. Seth with the occasion for his most striking displays of narrative energy. During the Pul Mela festival, as hundreds of thousands of pilgrims converge on Brahmpur to bathe in the Ganges at the time of the full moon, the pressure of the crowd trying to descend a ramp to the river produces a catastrophe:

> Some people at the edges of the ramp tried to slip through the bamboo barricades and scramble down to the ditches on either side. But last night's storm had made these steep slopes slippery, and the ditches themselves were filled with water. About a hundred beggars were sheltering by the side of one of the ditches. Many of them were cripples, some were blind. The injured pilgrims, gasping for breath and clawing for a foothold on the slope, now came tumbling onto them. Some of the beggars were crushed to

> death, and some tried to flee into the water, which soon turned to a bloodied slush as more of those who were trapped on the ramp sought this, their only route of escape, and fell or slid onto the screaming people below.

Within 15 minutes more than a thousand people are dead.

Though many pages of *A Suitable Boy* are devoted to religious rites, processions, myths and beliefs, Mr. Seth's own attitude toward these phenomena seems determinedly secular—as if one of his aims is to demystify India, to counteract the Western notion of wonder-working holy men and gurus of profound spirituality. The swamis and their devotees in the novel are presented in mildly comic terms. "It is rare," he writes,

> for religious feeling to be entirely transcendent, and Hindus as much as anyone else, perhaps more so, are eager for terrestrial, not merely post-terrestrial, blessings. We want specific results . . . whether to insure the birth of a son or to find a suitable match for a daughter. We go to a temple to be blessed by our chosen deity before a journey, and have our account books sanctified by Kali or Saraswati.

What Mr. Seth does not play down is the tragic interweaving of religion and politics, the ancient rivalry between Hindu and Muslim, the undying suspicion and resentment that can be blown into flame at any moment by unscrupulous office-seekers or bigoted religious leaders. In this respect, as in so many others, Vikram Seth's re-creation of the India of 1950 provides an accurate preview of the India of today.

Is this vast novel, which confidently aspires to the panoramic sweep of 19th-century fiction, an important work of literary art? *A Suitable Boy* is a Book-of-the-Month Club selection; it has received extensive prepublication publicity and has, in England at least, inspired comparisons to *War and Peace* and *Middlemarch.* Such claims are hyperbolic, to say the least. Mr. Seth's novel contains no Natashas or Pierres, no Dorothea Brookes or Lydgates. In his drive toward inclusiveness, he has sacrificed intensity. He does not stick with any one character long enough—even the most promising or interestingly troubled—or probe deeply enough to achieve the kind of impassioned empathy that renders a character unforgettable. Though he refers several times to Jane Austen's novels and seems to have modeled Mrs. Rupa Mehra to a considerable degree on Mrs. Bennet in *Pride and Prejudice,* he settles for a genial, soft-edged treatment of this often foolish and intrusive woman and thus deprives her of the comic absurdity with which Austen endows her matchmaking mamma.

Similarly, Lata is a pleasant ingenue whose love for the unsuitable Kabir is made to seem hardly more profound than a schoolgirl's crush; she is no Lizzie Bennet. The other characters are conventionally conceived, well drawn and sufficiently interesting in their social and familial roles; none, I predict, will continue to haunt our memories. Despite a number of vigorously written scenes, the narrative as a whole is diffuse, often overwhelmed by long (and sometimes tedious) passages devoted to the processes involved in shoe manufacture or to verbatim campaign speeches or debates in the legislative assembly. In the end, *A Suitable Boy* succeeds less as a novel than as a richly detailed documentary focused upon a crucial era in the history of an endlessly fascinating country.

Richard Jenkyns (review date 14 June 1993)

SOURCE: "As the Raj Turns," in *The New Republic,* Vol. 208, No. 24, June 14, 1993, pp. 41-4.

[*Jenkyns is an English educator and critic. In the following review, he argues that* A Suitable Boy *lacks fully developed characters and that the domestic and public dimensions of the book have not been integrated.*]

In *The Golden Gate,* the brilliant verse novel about life in California that made his name, Vikram Seth tells us that he started rhyming (in English) at the age of 3. The whole of that book is written in tetrameter sonnets, including the dedication, the table of contents and the author's biography at the back. Since his name is pronounced something like "sate," he has made even the title page rhyme: *The Golden Gate / by Vikram Seth.* The literary taste behind this is delightfully broad and unpretentious; Belloc's *Cautionary Tales for Children* are quoted as much as, if not more than, Shakespeare and Marvell.

The passion for versification, and especially for gladly silly versification, spills over into *A Suitable Boy.* It is mixed in with an engagement with English literature, shared between Seth and most of his main characters, which also ranges from the sublime to the absurd. The boisterous Chatterji family improvises doggerel couplets at the breakfast table. Seth's contents page summarizes the subject of each chapter in couplets, the style of which will recall to English children—and I suspect to middle-class Indian children too—the adventures of Rupert Bear. Mrs. Rupa Mehra, the heroine's voluble and sentimental mother, cuts out the verses in greetings cards, and finds the emotions stirred in her by the birth of her granddaughter summed up in a more than usually emetic poem by Wilhelmina Stitch (" 'A Lady Baby came to-day—' / What words are quite so nice to say . . ."). Her family, which includes a lecturer in English at the local university and a student in the same department, adopts these verses as a running joke.

In perhaps the best scene in the book—certainly in its most amusing scene—the heroine, Lata, and her boyfriend attend a meeting of the Brahmpur Literary Society (next week: Professor Mishra on "Eliot: Whither?"), where Mr. Nowrojee reads his formally exact triolets and Dr. Makhijani his "Hymn to Mother India," babu English mated with the muse of William McGonagall:

> Let me recall history of heroes proud,
> Mother-milk fed their breasts, who did not bow.
> Fought they fiercely, carrying worlds of weight,
> Establishing firm foundations of Indian state.

Lata is advised by a friend to read P. G. Wodehouse when her love life is going wrong. Jane Austen is a recurrent

name in the book: Lata sits in a train reading *Emma* and looking out at the burning plains of north India; Seth quotes several sentences. One of her suitors is Amit Chatterji, poet and novelist, whose sister remarks, "Jane Austen is the only woman in his life."

Not only English literature but also British values are an ever present background. Mothers looking for suitable matches for their children are concerned to find good spoken English and a light complexion: Haresh Khanna, one of Lata's suitors, has the advantage of having studied in England, the disadvantage of having gone to a Midlands technical college, unlike Amit Chatterji, who was at Cambridge. But he scores off the pushy anglophile Arun Mehra, whose knowing chat about London shops and theaters turns out to be entirely secondhand.

In some senses, then, this is a postcolonial novel. It is set at the start of the 1950s and mainly follows the lives of four connected families over a period of two years. There is no single story line and no central character, but a loose framework is provided by Mrs. Mehra's search for a suitable boy to marry Lata—hence the book's rather weak title. It is free, however, of the covert nationalism that is often hidden in the postcolonial novel.

The best of the postcolonial novelists—perhaps the best novelist of our time—was Patrick White. He is commonly seen as hostile to modern Australia, but his scorn is really nationalism frustrated: he is angry with his country for being prosperous, contented and suburban, when it should be grand and tragic. Salman Rushdie is not so different; in *Midnight's Children* he is cross because India ought to have the attributes of a world power but does not, and in *Shame* he is furious with Pakistan for not being India. The novels set in V. S. Naipaul's native Trinidad are straightforwardly colonial, yet he too, in a more muted way, has perhaps a streak of Indian nationalism, to judge from *India: A Wounded Civilization,* which castigates a country that, judged by reasonable standards, has done pretty well in appallingly difficult conditions. Seth, by contrast, has no ax to grind about India, no thesis to argue: he simply lays the life of his characters expansively before us. That, in itself, is fine. The question is whether he has anything much to say.

Is *A Suitable Boy* meant to be the Great Indian Novel? It is certainly a publishing phenomenon. Though there are some scenes of mass violence and death, it is mostly an uneventful narrative of the ordinary lives of middle-class people, and it is 1,350 pages long. Yet publishers have been falling over themselves to buy it. A huge amount of money seems to be riding on this book: the galleys sent to reviewers boast of the "100,000-Copy First Printing," "12-City National Author Tour" and "Extraordinary Three-Dimensional Single-Copy Counter Display." "Destined to become a monumental best seller . . . an international publishing event": we have become used to films that the motion-picture industry decrees shall be colossal box-office successes (the public, in a curious way, seems to have no say), and now it is happening to a novel.

It is true that very large books tend to get favorable reviews, for several reasons. Contrary to what writers believe, reviewers are quite softhearted people; faced with the prospect of rubbishing the result of many years' labor, they long to be in a kindlier line of business, like seal-culling or the white slave trade. More cynically, one may suspect that many reviewers will skip a lot of a very long book, and it is dangerous to condemn what you have not read. But there is also a subtler temptation: to suppose that a huge book can only be spoken of, whether for praise or blame, in superlatives. Amit Chatterji, the poet who has turned to writing a historical novel about India more than 1,000 pages long (no prizes for guessing who he is based on), remarks that he hates long books:

> The better, the worse. If they're bad, they merely make me pant with the effort of holding them up for a few minutes. But if they're good, I turn into a social moron for days, refusing to go out of my room, scowling and growling at interruptions, ignoring weddings and funerals and making enemies out of friends. I still bear the scars of *Middlemarch.*

This, offering no middle ground, seems like a bid for our approbation: since *A Suitable Boy* is not obviously a bad book, it must be a marvel. What we do not expect, with something so massive, is to speak in neutral, colorless terms: pleasant, mostly unpretentious, some pale charm, some gentle humor, readable but a bit flat and dull. But such, I think, is the judgment that we should return on this book. It is certainly a surprising thing to come from the bravura performer of *The Golden Gate.*

"A story as big as India, as intimate as the heart"—thus the publicity, describing precisely what the book is not. For it is lacking in both largeness and in *le petit fait significatif,* which Stendhal thought to be the essence of the novel. In an effort to be epic, Seth includes four violent scenes: a communal riot resulting in death; a religious festival that goes wrong, causing a thousand deaths; a communal riot bringing many deaths; a religious event that goes wrong, causing death (one notices a certain lack of invention). These episodes are poorly narrated, but in any case they are stuck on inorganically: in between, life trickles quietly on.

Since the novel is essentially a domestic saga, these misjudgments are comparatively unimportant. Much more damaging is the lack of intimacy. The problem is partly that almost all the characters, unlike the "extraordinary counter display," are two-dimensional, the chief exception being the small businessman Haresh Khanna, one of the suitors, a well-observed mixture of awkwardness, passion, dullness and persistence. Lata never comes alive at all. Other people describe her mostly, we note, in negatives: "unaffected," "intelligent without arrogance" and "attractive without vanity." Fifty pages from the end she rejects one suitor because "his moods veer and oscillate as wildly as mine"; we have seen no sign of this alleged temperament.

Seth seems unable to realize inner experience. Perhaps the most intimate moment in the whole novel comes near the beginning, when Lata and a boyfriend go up river to see the Barsaat Mahal (not described, but presumably we are to imagine a Taj Mahal transferred from the banks of the Jumna to the banks of the Ganges):

> "Now sit and watch for five minutes," said the boatman. "This is a sight you will never forget in your lives."
>
> Indeed it was, and neither of them was to forget it. The Barsaat Mahal, site of statesmanship and intrigue, love and dissolute enjoyment, glory and slow decay, was transfigured into something of abstract and final beauty. Above its sheer river-wall it rose, its reflection in the water almost perfect, almost unrippled. They were in a stretch of the river where even the sounds of the old town were dim. For a few minutes they said nothing at all.

That is not badly written (except for the helpless sentence, "Indeed it was, and neither of them was to forget it"). But it is not very well written, either. The Barsaat Mahal is not realized; we have to take its beauty on trust. And anyway, what a cop-out to wheel on this tourist-poster backdrop as a substitute for the exploration of the interior life.

That is meant to be a particularly charged passage. Much more of *A Suitable Boy* is like this:

> At the stroke of ten, from behind the dull scarlet hangings to the right of Courtroom Number One of the High Court of Judicature at Brahmpur, the five white-turbaned red-liveried gold-braided ushers of the judges emerged. Everyone rose to his feet. The ushers stood behind the tall-backed chairs of their respective judges and, at a nod from the Chief Justice's usher—who looked even more magnificent than the others owing to the insignia of crossed maces across his chest—pulled them back to give the judges room.
>
> All eyes in the packed courtroom had followed the ushers as they moved toward the bench in what was almost a procession. Normal cases required a single judge or a bench of two, and cases of great importance and complexity might be assigned to three judges. But five judges implied a case of exceptional moment, and here were the heralds of the five in all their resplendent regalia.

Again, that is not positively bad writing, but it lacks any positive quality. It just rambles on inertly, with what Austen called "too many particulars of right hand and left." Sometimes the proliferation of pointless detail becomes absurd. Consider this, about a character who will appear for only a page or two:

> He had on an open shirt and fawn trousers. His coat was hanging across his chair. He was a well-proportioned man, about 5 feet 9 inches in height, and extremely soft-spoken. He was unsmiling and unbending and hard as nails. . . . His eyes were penetrating.

The book is like a soap opera, or to take a more literary comparison, like a Victorian serial novel, in that it often seems to go on simply because there is time or space to be filled. A mother has a baby; the delivery is painful; then the mother is happy. So what? And when invention runs out, there are doublet episodes. Lata is threatened with sexual abuse, but escapes; the youngest Chatterji is threatened with sexual abuse, but is rescued. Maan Kapoor gets drunk and misbehaves in a way that threatens his elder brother's career; his father turns him out of the house. Varun Mehra gets drunk and threatens his elder brother's career; his brother turns him out of the house. Sometimes Seth seems to be inspired by the schoolteaching technique of Waugh's Paul Pennyfeather: "There will be a prize of half a crown for the longest essay, irrespective of any possible merit."

The publicity material describes *A Suitable Boy* as "passionate and teeming," and compares the author to Dickens, Tolstoy, Austen and George Eliot. Actually, Seth seems somewhat distrustful of passion: readers can compare the decisions of Lata and of the heroine of *The Golden Gate* about their marriages (it would be unkind to potential readers to say more). "Teeming" gives us two clichés in a single word—one about India, another about long novels. If Seth is trying to teem, he fails; but perhaps it is fairest to judge the book as an epic of domestic life. This is no *War and Peace,* not least because Seth does not adequately fit together his story's public and private dimensions. Thanks to translations, we may have the subconscious impression that the great Russians all wrote the same decent, colorless prose; that, alas, is *A Suitable Boy's* nearest resemblance to Tolstoy. It lacks not only Dickens's genius but also his energy and his comic gusto (there is a clumsy chapter in which an old retainer is pushed onto the stage to mangle the English language in a series of comic malapropisms). Nor is this the Indian *Middlemarch*: Seth lacks not only George Eliot's psychological penetration but her sense that life is a matter of moral choices. Surprisingly, moral drama is absent from *A Suitable Boy*—or almost. True, the politician Mahesh Kappor decides to leave the Congress Party. Then he decides to rejoin. It is impossible to care.

The comparison with Austen is the one that Seth himself seems most to court. Indeed, the opening of the book, with a garrulous, silly mother looking for husbands for her daughters, the elder docile and beautiful, the younger more lively: Does this not recall the start of *Pride and Prejudice*? But within a page Austen has moved from the famous generalization of her first sentence into the heart of the Bennets' lifeless marriage, with a funny but terrible picture of a clever man, tied to a foolish woman, consoling himself by making jokes at her expense that he knows she is not smart enough to understand. Few writers, to be sure, could match that.

A Suitable Boy is a rather likable book, beneficent toward almost all its characters. We are constantly being told how high-minded, kindly or popular so- and-so is. This occasionally pooterish amiability extends to the smallest walk-on parts: " 'Would you take down a letter, Miss Christie?' he said to his secretary, an exceptionally discreet and cheerful young Anglo-Indian woman"—and one who will barely last a paragraph. In a similar spirit of benevolence, Seth seems unwilling to hurt his characters, and this is ultimately debilitating to the novel: if you prick his people, they do not bleed.

Thus Pran Kapoor's standing with his boss is wrecked by

his brother, but he expresses no anger. Lata is removed to Calcutta by her mother to get her away from her unsuitable Muslim boyfriend, but she continues to behave toward her with the same unruffled amiability. Mahesh Kapoor the politician is pushing through a bill to expropriate the lands of his old friend the Nawab, but the Nawab does not let this mar the friendship. Eventually the book lurches, unexpectedly, into novelettish melodrama, and two of the characters are very nearly murdered by a third; but despite their grave injuries they cheerfully forgive their almost-killer. One does not feel that this shows their nobility. They suffer no pain because there is nothing inside them except stuffing.

Near the end of the book Lata chooses between her three suitors. I had thought that I would be indifferent to the decision, but this was not so; her best friend's distressed belief that she has married the wrong man raises a genuine issue. The book ends, as it began, with a wedding; the close is mildly touching, mildly amusing—it goes against the grain to speak of so vast a novel in such unemphatic terms, but it seems right. *A Suitable Boy* is, of course, preposterously too long, but the publishers were probably right on commercial grounds not to cut it, for there is nothing prodigious about it except its length. Were it 600 pages shorter, it would be obvious for what it is: a decent, unremarkable, second-rate novel. As it is, after 1,300 pages the feeling still persists that it is a little thin.

Ben Downing   (review date 1993)

SOURCE: "Big City, Long Poem," in *Parnassus: Poetry in Review,* Vol. 17, No. 2, 1993, pp. 219-34.

[*In the following excerpt, Downing complains that the individual sonnets in* The Golden Gate *lack intensity and that the story lacks depth.*]

Vikram Seth is mad about sonnets. *The Golden Gate* consists of a staggering five hundred and ninety of them strung together to form a verse novel. Even the bio page, acknowledgments, dedication, and table of contents are written in sonnet form. Seth's sonnets depart, however, from the traditional English line laid down by Wyatt and Surrey in that they rarely aspire to be, in Rossetti's phrase, a "moment's monument." Rather, they trace their ancestry back to Pushkin, placing high value on wit and effervescence. To achieve these effects, Seth favors quick, playful tetrameter over the more ponderous pentameter. Here Seth, anticipating the inevitable clamor of objections to his atavistic approach, cannily issues a preemptive apology:

> How do I justify this stanza?
> These feminine rhymes? My wrinkled muse?
> This whole passé extravaganza?
> How can I (careless of time) use
> The dusty bread molds of Onegin
> In the brave bakery of Reagan?

If the pairing of Onegin with Reagan (or the odious metaphor that frames it) made you wince, *The Golden Gate* is not your book. Yet I would add, in limited defense of Seth, that the kind of crass collision exemplified by this rhyme is what *The Golden Gate* is largely about. Set in San Francisco circa 1980, it is a yuppie epic at once celebrating and satirizing the city's cultural pretensions. Enraptured lovers, who meet through a singles ad, "In phrase both fulsome and condign / Sing praise of California wine." Liz works as an attorney, John in Silicon Valley where he "kneels bareheaded and unshod / Before the Chip, a jealous God." Other characters spend weekends pickling olives or haunting cafés through which strains of Bach are eternally wafting. Homer's sea suffers a change into a lawyer's "wine-dark suit." Cats are given chardonnay to drink, pet iguanas quiche to nibble on.

All this might be funnier if it weren't so dated. Seven years after its publication, *The Golden Gate* already seems like a mildly amusing artifact of that excessive time when (in its own words) "the syndrome of possessions" reached epidemic proportions, and when AIDS had yet to cast the darkest portion of its shadow over San Francisco. Seth's sonnets are best suited to light subjects and mock-heroic catalogues, as in this blithe romp through contemporary materialism:

> John looks about him with enjoyment.
> What a man needs, he thinks, is health;
> Well-paid, congenial employment;
> A house; a modicum of wealth;
> Some sunlight; coffee and the papers;
> Artichoke hearts adorned with capers;
> A Burberry trench coat; a Peugeot;
> And in the evening, some Rameau
> Or Couperin; a home-cooked dinner,
> A Stilton, and a little port;
> And so to duvet . . .

Or here, where the responses John receives to his singles ad amount to a compendium of Bay Area perversities:

> Yes, why describe the louche lubricious
> Dreams of a Daly City Dame,
> The half-enticing, subtly vicious
> Burblings of Belle from Burlingame,
> And then from Eve of San Francisco,
> "Six novel ways of using Crisco,"
> Or the Tigress of Tiburon
> Who waits to pounce on hapless John.

These passages are pleasing in the clever way they comically enact the velocity, skittishness, and empty plenitude of urban America. But when Seth turns his attention to weightier matters, the results can be disastrous. In his long diatribe against nuclear weapons, Seth's sophistication on the subject rarely rises above the level of an average shrill rock 'n' roll band. Quoting these lines, I am truly embarrassed for him:

> It takes a great deal of moral clarity
> To see that it is right to blitz
> Each Russian family to bits
> Because their leader's muscularity
> —Quite like our own—on foreign soil
> Threatens our vanity, or 'our' oil.

Thankfully, such patches of wretched writing are relatively scarce, as are the obvious instances where Seth scrambles clumsily to complete a rhyme—"Sulawesi" laboring to chime with "crazy," or "et al." forced under the yoke with "Senegal." Given the book's length and formal constraints, a certain number of glaring surface imperfections

are nearly inevitable, perhaps even forgivable. In fact, Seth is to be partially commended for his overall fluency; the sonnets slide in and out of each other with scarcely a hitch.

Ironically, it is just this fluency that most damages *The Golden Gate.* The scathing review received by one of the book's characters, a sculptor, seems to mirror Seth's own fear of critical persecution:

> . . . the languid tedium
> Of lines too fluid to show pains
> Reflect this artist's dated chains:
> Derivative, diluted passion,
> A facile versatility . . .

For smoothness has been achieved only at great expense. In order to accommodate novelistic sweep, the poetry has been stripped of its focused intensities; very few individual sonnets could stand on their own foundations. Equally, the fiction has been severely simplified and reduced to fit into the sonnets's fourteen-line containers.

Despite Seth's ambition, *The Golden Gate* is neither good poetry nor good fiction. In attempting to bridge two genres, it falls between them. Instead of buttressing and enabling each other, the verse tends to hobble the narrative, the narrative to compromise the verse.

—*Ben Downing*

The plot, by the way, is really too innocuous to warrant much discussion. Suffice it to say that couples couple, uncouple, and then recouple in curious combinations; spirits, like the seasons, rise and fall; with two deaths and a birth in the final pages, tragic and uplifting elements mingle mawkishly. More interesting than the story itself is the fact that Seth chooses to parcel it out into such small packages. I suspect at least a few of his reasons for doing so are mimetic in nature. The use of sonnets *says something* about contemporary San Francisco: that many of the city's residents would like to think of their lives as the experiential equivalents of sonnets, as classically trim little epiphanies marching happily—ABAB—toward the well-heeled, tidy closure of GG. "Life's a sonnet!" might be the motto for yet another of those bumperstickers of which Californians are inordinately fond. Naturally, the characters' desire for shapely order is constantly crossed and frustrated in *The Golden Gate* by the world's inescapable vicissitudes (break-ups, death, bad reviews) and this tug of fantasy against reality is effectively heightened by the use of sonnets: Form remains stable while content veers toward entropy.

Yet despite Seth's ambition, *The Golden Gate* is neither good poetry nor good fiction. In attempting to bridge two genres, it falls between them. Instead of buttressing and enabling each other, the verse tends to hobble the narrative, the narrative to compromise the verse. The genres, in Seth's hands at least, are like an arranged marriage: not deeply compatible. One is nearly always conscious of the story straining against its poetic leash. In turn, the poetry is given free reign only during brief lyric interludes (encomia for landscape, an invocation of the city's patron saint) before being retethered to the plot. Like the game of Scrabble played in Chapter 8, *The Golden Gate* is limited by rules of its own devising. It moves deftly enough about its board; unfortunately, that board is a small one.

FURTHER READING

Criticism

Bell, Pearl K. Review of *A Suitable Boy,* by Vikram Seth. *Partisan Review* LXI, No. 1 (Winter 1994): 82-4.
> Contends that *A Suitable Boy* lacks a "controlling sense of selection and discrimination."

Brunet, Elena. Review of *From Heaven Lake,* by Vikram Seth. *Los Angeles Times Book Review* (10 January 1988): 14.
> Praises *From Heaven Lake* for its vivid portrayal of China and Tibet.

Corey, Stephen. Review of *All You Who Sleep Tonight,* by Vikram Seth. *The Ohio Review,* No. 47 (1991): 132-39.
> Faults the poems of *All You Who Sleep Tonight* for being sophomoric and singsongy.

Davis, Dick. "Obliquities." *The Listener* 114, No. 2938 (5 December 1985): 33-4.
> Praises *The Humble Administrator's Garden,* arguing that its tone is "modest, ordered, well-mannered and well-planned, with a trace of deprecatory self-pity."

Review of *Arion and the Dolphin,* by Vikram Seth. *The Economist* 333, No. 7891 (26 November 1994): 101.
> Remarks favorably on *Arion and the Dolphin.*

Gupta, Santosh. "*The Golden Gate*: The First Indian Novel in Verse." In *The New Indian Novel in English: A Study of the 1980s,* edited by Viney Kirpal, pp. 91-100. New Delhi: Allied Publishers Limited, 1990.
> Discusses character, style, and theme in *The Golden Gate.* Gupta asserts that the work is not great poetry but is a delightful evocation of life in San Francisco.

King, Bruce. "Postmodernism and Neo-formalist Poetry: Seth, Steele, and *Strong Measures.*" *The Southern Review* 23, No. 1 (Winter 1987): 224-31.
> Compares *The Golden Gate* to Timothy Steele's *Sapphics against Anger, and Other Poems,* noting the place of both works in modern poetry.

Koenig, Rhoda. "Whoa, Boy." *New York* 26, No. 20 (17 May 1993): 84-5.
> Negative review of *A Suitable Boy.* Koenig argues that the novel lacks depth, insight, and drama.

Mehta, Nina. "A Saga of Four Families in India." *The Christian Science Monitor* 85, No. 162 (19 July 1993): 13.
> Remarks on Seth's depiction of 1950s India in *A Suitable Boy.*

Mungo, Raymond. "Modern Love in Rhythm and Rhyme." *The New York Times Book Review* (11 May 1986): 11.
> Favorably reviews *The Golden Gate.* Mungo writes the essay entirely in rhyme.

Interview

Woodward, Richard B. "Vikram Seth's Big Book." *New York Times Magazine* (2 May 1993): 32-6.
> Essay based on a conversation with Seth in which the author discusses the ways in which *A Suitable Boy* mirrors his life.

Additional coverage of Seth's life and career is contained in the following sources published by Gale Research: *Contemporary Authors,* Vols. **121, 127;** *Contemporary Literary Criticism,* Vol. **43;** and *Dictionary of Literary Biography,* Vol. **120.**

Jane Urquhart

1949-

(Born Jane Carter) Canadian novelist, poet, and short story writer.

The following entry provides an overview of Urquhart's life and career through 1995.

INTRODUCTION

Considered one of Canada's most promising writers, Urquhart is known for works that reflect her fascination with literary Romanticism and the Victorian Era. Often emphasizing the theme of estrangement, her writing is noted for its focus on place and landscape, memory and history, and the creative process. Urquhart's novels, for which she is best known, frequently employ parallel story lines and often incorporate historical figures and events.

Biographical Information

Born in northern Ontario, Urquhart was raised in the small mining settlement of Little Long Lac until she was five or six years old, at which time she moved with her family to Toronto. As a child, she was a voracious reader, and she has cited Emily and Charlotte Brontë, Robert Louis Stevenson, L. M. Montgomery, Frances Hodgson Burnett, and Charles Dickens as among her favorite authors. Attending junior college in Vancouver in the late 1960s, Urquhart eventually returned to Ontario where she received a B. A. in English in 1971 from the University of Guelph. At Guelph she also met and married artist Paul Keele. Following the death of Keele in a car accident, Urquhart resumed her academic career, earned a B. A. in art history, and, in the mid-1970s, married artist Tony Urquhart. In addition to the demands posed by her role as a mother, Urquhart began to pursue a writing career in 1977, initially working as a poet and then turning to fiction.

Major Works

Urquhart's debut novel, *The Whirlpool* (1986), is set near Niagara Falls in late nineteenth-century Canada. Considered Gothic in its tone and outlook, the novel opens and closes with descriptive pieces detailing the death of English poet Robert Browning. The remainder of the novel, drawn in part from Urquhart's second husband's family history, concerns a widowed undertaker, who fishes victims and debris out of the whirlpool under the falls, and her young "mute" son. A lovesick poet and the object of his desire—a woman filled with Romantic notions of the natural world and an ardent admirer of Browning's verse—are also central to the plot. Emphasizing the fluidity of language and desire, *The Whirlpool* employs a circular structure and story line, which are reinforced by the novel's central image of the whirlpool. Urquhart's next

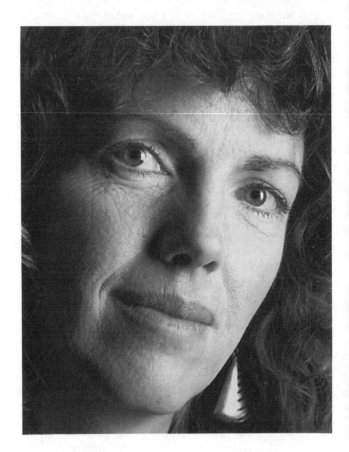

novel, *Changing Heaven* (1990), similarly features a renowned literary figure as a character. Juxtaposing the tumultuous love affair between a nineteenth-century balloonist and her manager with that of a twentieth-century Canadian scholar named Ann and an art historian, the multilayered *Changing Heaven* recounts scenes from Ann's life and includes passages in which the ghost of Emily Brontë discusses her Gothic romance *Wuthering Heights* (1847) and the nature of love. In her explication and retelling of *Wuthering Heights,* Urquhart continues Brontë's examination of passion and betrayal, obsession, nature, and the creative process. In *Away* (1993) Urquhart explores Canadian history and her own Irish heritage. Spanning four generations of women and infused with Celtic myth and folklore, the novel is a family saga relating the experiences of an Irish woman and her descendants in both Ireland and Canada. Thematically, *Away* presents issues related to immigration, time, "otherness" and identity, and the oral tradition.

Urquhart's verse collections, *False Shuffles* (1982), *I Am Walking in the Garden of His Imaginary Palace* (1982), and *The Little Flowers of Madame de Montespan* (1983), similarly reveal a focus on the past and frequently incorporate references to historical figures and other literary texts. In *The Little Flowers of Madame de Montespan,* for example, Urquhart examines issues related to love, power, and memory, often speaking in the voice of Madame de Montespan, a mistress of King Louis XIV of France and a prominent figure at the court of Versailles. Focusing on problems of language, meaning, and communication, Urquhart argues in *False Shuffles* that there is a relationship between poets and magicians, making numerous allusions to a twentieth-century book on the art of prestidigitation. *False Shuffles* also shares similarities with Urquhart's novels: the volume contains poems that are set in Niagara Falls, some in which an undertaker's wife speaks, and a number of pieces featuring a young woman who relates the stories of her female relatives and ancestors. The short story collection *Storm Glass* (1987) likewise has elements in common with Urquhart's other writings. Noted for its surrealist aspects and focus on estrangement, pain, death, and foreign settings, the collection includes "The Death of Robert Browning," which appeared as the prologue and epilogue to *The Whirlpool,* and the critically acclaimed title piece. A tale of domestic and sexual conflict, "Storm Glass" revolves around a married couple's debate concerning the correct name for shards of glass that have been made smooth by their exposure to the elements. The pieces in *Storm Glass* have been praised by Patricia Bradbury as "poetry made long, not fiction rendered short."

Critical Reception

Best known for her fiction, Urquhart is often noted for her complex narrative structures, her emphasis on Gothic themes and the supernatural, and her meticulous attention to time and place. At times faulting Urquhart's use of parallel and circular story lines in her novels, reviewers have occasionally argued that Urquhart often values plot and setting over characterization. She has also been castigated by some critics for her inclusion of Browning and Brontë in *The Whirlpool* and *Changing Heaven;* while applauding her use of these writers as characters, some commentators argued that Urquhart's combination of fact, folklore, and literary analysis was heavy-handed. Nevertheless, Urquhart is highly regarded in her homeland and abroad. She has been the recipient of several awards, including France's Prix pour le meilleur livre étranger for *The Whirlpool* as well as Ontario's Trillium Award.

PRINCIPAL WORKS

False Shuffles (poetry) 1982
I Am Walking in the Garden of His Imaginary Palace (poetry) 1982
The Little Flowers of Madame de Montespan (poetry) 1983
The Whirlpool (novel) 1986
Storm Glass (short stories) 1987
Changing Heaven (novel) 1990
Away (novel) 1993

CRITICISM

Joyce Wayne (review date March 1983)

SOURCE: A review of *False Shuffles,* in *Quill and Quire,* Vol. 49, No. 3, March, 1983, p. 66.

[*In the following positive review, Wayne briefly discusses stylistic and thematic aspects of* False Shuffles.]

Once in a very long while a book of poetry appears that is so strong and original it signals the discovery of a remarkable new talent.

Jane Urquhart's second book of poetry, **False Shuffles,** is one of these occasions. Filled with the lives of small-town eccentrics, Niagara Falls daredevils, undertakers' brides, and beer-hall waitresses, the book is both expertly crafted and emotionally compelling.

At its heart, **False Shuffles** is about the power of magic as the poet, portrayed as magician, explores a surrealistic world. Illusion takes precedence over reality, and the odd, the eccentric, and the ghostly mean more than the daily news.

The language is intensely private and the imaginative landscape is highly charged with passion and memory. It's a shadowy, eerie landscape Urquhart creates where a turn-of-the-century bride records the number of bodies drowned in Niagara Falls and another girl dismantles a tombstone in search of a dead woman's clothes.

The poems are written mainly as tales, in a voice deceptively straightforward but always alert, tense, and often on the verge of some ghastly discovery. It is a voice that rips open the surface of the ordinary to reveal the magic and horror lurking beneath the commonplace, a voice that has chosen, almost reluctantly, to tell the stories of her own ancestors as if they were concealed treasure in an abandoned graveyard.

These poems will clutter your dreams with their dark, illuminating vision, for they are, as Urquhart describes them: "loose bits of paper carried by the wind / caught for a moment / on the fence around this time."

Rhea Tregebov (review date May 1984)

SOURCE: A review of *The Little Flowers of Madame de Montespan,* in *Quill and Quire,* Vol. 50, No. 5, May, 1984, p. 35.

[*In the following mixed review, Tregebov asserts that* The Little Flowers of Madame de Montespan *"is a well-written little book . . . that reveals a poet who could do more if she wanted to."*]

Madame de Montespan's 10-year career as mistress of Louis XIV (he built the Petite Trianon at Versailles for her) ended in scandal. She was implicated in the poisoning scare that raged through the court in the late 1670s. Madame *had* administered love potions to Louis, but greater mischief was not proved conclusively: Louis himself destroyed the trial records to preserve her name. If more such facts had been noted somewhere in Jane Urquhart's book of poems, it would be more easily appreciated.

Nonetheless, this is a well-written little book (illustrated with some very fine photos by Ottawa artist Jennifer Dickson) that reveals a poet who could do more if she wanted to. Urquhart has chosen to speak in the voice of Mme de Montespan, recounting a glistening world of surfaces where the sun (king) "polishes your tables / his brilliance clings to cutlery / till spoons become large / bright incisions / all across the grain". In portraying the circumscribed life of a woman whose existence is dependent on the eye of the beholder—"the hours filled with / preservation of her flesh"—the poems themselves, too often, are constrained, even slight.

The prose poems, however, expand both subject and scope, and Versailles becomes a metaphor for human will. These poems demonstrate that Urquhart is a poet of depth and intelligence.

Lola Lemire-Tostevin   (review date Spring 1985)

SOURCE: "Museum & World," in *Canadian Literature,* No. 104, Spring, 1985, pp. 134-36.

[*In the following excerpt, Lemire-Tostevin offers a thematic discussion of* The Little Flowers of Madame de Montespan.]

Jane Urquhart has chosen a museum as the setting for her third book. The poems of *The Little Flowers of Madame de Montespan* hover in and out of the rooms and gardens of Versailles in the persona of Montespan who was for a while a favourite mistress of Louis XIV. They pause over catalogued items and saved artifacts like "loose fragments drawn into new configurations." They shift behind windows and over brocade coverings of baroque beds; they witness and conjure devious plots; they settle in glass coffins or the frozen ground under lifeless monuments and leafless trees of the carefully kept winter gardens. The six photographs of Versailles by Jennifer Dickson are very effective in both capturing and adding to the mood of the book.

The Little Flowers is in the same sleight of hand spirit as Urquhart's second book *False Shuffles*. Where it engaged the author's own history, *The Little Flowers* suggests behind-the-scene machinations of social life when the Sun King held court "dressed in a hundred diamonds." The games, costumes, and disguises prevalent in Urquhart's poetry serve less to conceal than dis/guise and capture the deceptive space, the absent revolving around the obvious. Historical fragments are gathered (like little flowers?) and through the author's imagination new configurations are drawn (a garden?). Dialectical tension between past and present, between historical characters and author makes it difficult to discern between voices, as in the Anonymous Journal "entries" where someone walking in the garden is making "new marks . . . new boundaries."

Within the artificial structure of the poem/garden/journal the reality of the subject is caught. As the trap of the poem/garden closes in, the subject matter is the only reality that lingers on. Where the theme of this book revolves around love (and hate) as means to the king, and the king as means to love; in fact love is presented to us less as a human reality than an historical construct organized around strategies of power. As Michel Foucault so brilliantly demonstrated in *The History of Sexuality,* it is a construct which still has far reaching effects today.

While I don't find Urquhart's poetry uniformly strong, there are some poems, such as **"Le Roi S'Amuse,"** that draw me again and again:

> The man who touches you
> without love
>
> . . . .
>
> he is the death
> of the child in you
> the beginning of dark
>
> . . . .
>
> the mouth he puts to yours
> contains a brutal statement
> your limbs become machinery
> to the limits he enforces
>
> . . . .
>
> his breath remains
> forever at your throat
>
> remember him

[Urquhart] is less interested in the account of her characters' movements than in the complex drift of their unconsciousness.

—Alberto Manguel, in his "Brevity, Soul and Wit," in Maclean's, 21 September 1987.

Ian Sowton   (review date Fall 1985)

SOURCE: "Sleight of Tongue," in *Canadian Literature,* No. 106, Fall, 1985, pp. 112-15.

[*In the following excerpt, Sowton discusses intertextual aspects and influences of* False Shuffles.]

One very fine effect of the intertextualities at play in *False Shuffles* (among cards/book of tricks/Urquhart's poems) is the witty problematization of a three-generation history: grandmother, mother, narrating daughter. The interleaved lexicon—of false shuffle: transparent swizzle stick: magician: sleight: tricks—genially but persistently interrogates our shaky everyday equilibriums between narration and what is narrated, between verbal signs and their purported herstorical referents. Consider this gem from [*Blackstone's Tricks Anyone Can Do*] which Urquhart deals in just before the section on "False Shuffles": "This is a real false shuffle. It will require considerable practice to render it deceptive"; in their earlier site these remarks are straight; here, in their later site, they undergo a deep intertextual seachange and glow with gorgeous multiple equivocations. The semiotics of *False Shuffles* is very subtle; as a sign system this deck of texts offers not only citations that function simultaneously as thematic epigraphs, equivocating commentary, and *caveat lectors,* but also the bonus of Tony Urquhart's visual representations of playing cards, including a delicious 9 of Clubs in which signifiers for clubs also signify trees in a suitably enigmatic landscape. Documents and documentations, too, are extremely important in the weave of this text. Old documents, scraps of family or district records, bits of local lore are, as it were, edited—recovered, ordered, and re-narrated as an equivocal but indispensable context, or pretext, of the narrator's own life story. She documents her own brief career as a failed barmaid; the reason she fails is precisely because she is a documenter; her colleagues who stay and make it can do so because "they were living it / just living it / documenting nothing."

The section "False Shuffles" is all the more interesting in that the relationship the teller is trying to recount actively resists even the compromised certainties of documentation—as well it might, being a surreal relationship to a shape-changer, a spellbinding, illusionist-magician. The shouted injunction at the end of **"Party Game,"** "remember these objects / AND WRITE THEM ALL DOWN," is a major pretext for this whole collection. This writer-down has a very nice sense of all the sleights endemic to remembering and writing, her calibrations of that slightest of twists between a genuine shuffle and a false one.

Jane Urquhart with Geoff Hancock (interview date 13 December 1985)

SOURCE: An interview in *The Canadian Fiction Magazine,* No. 55, 1986, pp. 23-40.

[*The editor of* The Canadian Fiction Magazine, *Hancock is a Canadian journalist and critic who has edited several books about and anthologies of Canadian literature. In the following interview, originally conducted in late 1985, Urquhart discusses her life, art, and influences.*]

Jane Urquhart was born in northern Ontario, and now lives near Waterloo, Ontario. She is an accomplished creative writer of both poetic and prose forms. Her poems are collected in *False Shuffles; The Little Flowers of Madame de Montespan;* and *I Am Walking In The Garden of His Imaginary Palace,* a deluxe limited edition done in collaboration with her husband, artist Tony Urquhart. Her first novel, with a working title of *The Whirlpool Dream House,* is scheduled for publication with McClelland & Stewart's new Signature series in 1986. She is currently working on a collection of short stories, several of which have previously appeared in *Canadian Fiction Magazine,* as well as a novel located in Brontë country.

Jane Urquhart's work has wit, flair, and zaniness combined with a passion for her subjects. Her writing contains a vision unique in contemporary Canadian creative writing. While polished in style, she looks for the bizarre underside of our own history. Whether her work is situated at turn of the century Niagara Falls, the palace of Versailles, or in a confessional based on one of her husband's drawings, she reveals that conflict between order and chaos, that split between the old world and the new that is in the Canadian psyche.

The following interview took place Dec. 13, 1985 in Toronto's Bond Place Hotel, and was later revised. That is to say, most of the jokes, quips, one liners, and quick repartee was deleted or toned down.

. . . . .

[*Hancock*]: *How do you feel about being interviewed?*

[Urquhart]: Being interviewed by you is preferable to being interviewed by the R.C.M.P.

Tell me about your childhood, and how that contributed to your sense of history as it appears in your fiction.

My childhood contributed enormously to my writing. Two geographical and historical factors were strong in my childhood, I suppose I should say three; S. E. Rural Ontario, Toronto, and the North Woods. I was born in a tiny mining town, about two hundred miles north of Thunder Bay, Ontario, a place called Little Long Lac. This spot was pure Robert Service. There were brothels run by ladies called Backwoods Bessie, Kirkland Lake Annie, and Coffee Annie. Men called Pipefitter Slim and Hardrock Sam. My parents, and other professionals living there, mingled with these people from the mid 1930s on. The mine closed in the mid 1950s, when I was five or six years old and my family then left that place for the lights of Toronto. But an already established Northern Mythology moved with us in the form of anecdotes about the people and events of that community. Sitting around the dining table, listening to my father and my godfather tell prospecting stories, knowing they were 2/10ths fact and 8/10ths embellishment got me interested in fiction. It was the Canadian Oral Tradition at work.

My mother's family was an extended, Irish tribal unit, two generations removed from the old sod . . . farmers in S. Eastern rural Ontario. That side of the family also spent a lot of time keeping the oral tradition alive. When I was with them I heard all kinds of stories about strong willed grandmothers, town drunks, various babies that died of awful childhood diseases, brides that died on the bed in their wedding gowns, magic lantern shows. Some of these tales appear in my fiction, now, and also in my poems. It seems that I spent a great deal of my childhood just listening, seeing the stories in my mind. This produced a visual landscape that didn't necessarily exist in the real world. It's that kind of landscape I use in my stories and poetry now.

Also, the books I read as a child still influence me the most. I am still, for instance, very interested in the work of the Brontës. I read *Jane Eyre* and *Wuthering Heights* when I was nine and I feel precisely the same way about those books today as I did then.

Did you write when you were young?

I wrote a lot. More than I do now. I kept endless, desperate diaries from the ages nine to twenty. As a small child I wrote poems, stories, plays, notes to friends in class, letters to myself to be opened when I was twenty-one. I kept most of this material in a suitcase which was given to me as a Christmas present when I was ten. Maybe my parents were hoping I would leave home. The suitcase had a key and I could lock it up. A strange thing happened to me when I decided I was going to send some material out as an adult. I realized that I was actually opening that suitcase, for someone other than myself, for the first time. That was a crisis I had to go through and overcome. Writing was a private act, not confessional necessarily, but all mine. My own world. I could creep in and stay in and no one else knew about it.

My mother discovered my diaries a few times. That was so traumatic than I began to keep two diaries; one for my mother and one for myself. One was total fiction, the other total reality. You can guess which was which.

Did she encourage you to write?

She certainly encouraged me to read. When you read a lot as a child you also want to write. My mother was, and is a voracious reader. Unlike me, she reads a lot of non-fiction, as well as fiction; history, politics, etc. She is still the person most likely to keep me in touch with the world outside. She provided me with books which I literally lived inside for months at a time; Francis Hodgson Burnett's *Little Princess, The Secret Garden,* Robert Louis Stevenson's *A Child's Garden of Verses* as well as novels such as *Treasure Island.* All of Dickens, Louisa May Alcott, and L. M. Montgomery's books. The latter stamped the Canadian rural landscape indelibly on my brain and gave that landscape a time frame—late nineteenth, early twentieth century. I'll simply never be able to look at it any other way, despite suburbs, shopping malls and McDonalds. Also L. M. Montgomery's *Family of New Moon, Emily Climbs* and *Emily's Quest* are books about a young girl who wants to be, and eventually becomes, a writer and this young girl is a *Canadian.* It was wonderful for me. It felt so familiar.

My father, on the other hand, read little. Even after we moved to Toronto he spent a great deal of time in the bush; staking claims, looking for mines. He was most at home on Duncan Campbell Scott's *Height of Land.*

You've published three books of poetry, and you've completed a novel. . . . How have you fared with the critics?

I am pleased by any response to my published writing. Moving that privacy into the public arena can be disorientating and I'm always surprised to discover that there is someone else, even if it's only one person out there reading and thinking about something I have written. The thinking, in particular, stuns me.

Academic literary criticism, however, was something I avoided for a long time. I do have a B.A. in English Literature, but, interestingly enough, while I was at university I wrote absolutely nothing creative. I think now that, at that time, I was boggled by literary criticism, by a second hand response to literature, by having to perceive literature as something that needed to be explained . . . translated as if it were a foreign language. That stopped me for quite a while. I kept on reading but didn't start to write again until I was twenty-nine or thirty.

But recently I have become very excited by some of the criticism I have been reading; Fanny Ratchford's amazing study of the Brontës as children, *The Brontës Web of Childhood* or Margaret Lane's *Drug-Like Brontë Dream* . . . also Sandra Gilbert and Susan Guber's *The Madwoman in the Attic* is, I think, a very important book. What these books taught me, apart from the obvious, factual information that I might have gleaned from them, is that criticism itself, is or can be, a creative act. All these women care passionately about their subjects . . . emotion literally leaps off the page. It's very moving.

Now that the "new criticism" seems to be the "old criticism" there's more of an emphasis on literature as a philosophy in and of itself. The idea that literature itself is a conceptual problem to be dealt with. Do you find yourself now a critic of your own work-in-progress?

Not as much as I'd like to be, or, at least, not immediately. I'm better after a time-space of a year or so. I take what I've written, put it in a drawer, forget it, then look at it much later. That seems to work for me. When I'm involved in the process of writing a first draft of a story, or novel, or series of poems I am so close to it that I can't see it clearly.

I must say that, though I am a staunch Canadian Nationalist, and I am fond of Canadian writers and Canadian Literary Heritage, I have no real idea of what the Canadian Short Story Tradition is. But whatever the case I can only write about what I want to write about and whether or not it fits into the Canadian Literary Tradition seems, somehow irrelevant.

—Jane Urquhart

Do you ever show your work-in-progress to anyone?

Yes, I do, but not until it's nearly finished or at least at the stage of the first completed draft. At that stage I might show it to friends who are also writers, and friends who I believe will give it a sympathetic reading. A negative response early on can simply stop me dead. Two people who have been extremely helpful and encouraging and who live reasonably close are the poet and librarian Stuart MacKinnon and the artist and writer Virgil Burnett. They are close enough to me to have a clear understanding of both my imagination and my voice and are therefore able to direct me from the inside rather than the outside.

How do you feel about the relationship between a writer and an editor?

It's an extremely important relationship, and, as you know, an editor can come in many different shapes and sizes. An editor such as yourself who is willing to take chances and encourage new visions and voices while at the same time supporting those who are more established is extraordinarily valuable. I remember how thrilled I was when you accepted my first stories for CFM, . . . how that reinforcement produced a kind of energy, made me want to do *more*.

Susan Clark at Press Porcépic really taught me how to construct a book of poetry, how one poem enhances another, how to dispose of unnecessary verbiage. I worked with Joe Rosenblatt on my second book of poetry and that was not only instructive but also fun. As a result we became close friends.

Most recently I've been working with Ellen Seligman at McClelland and Stewart. She is a great nurturer, a great coaxer. Again, I believe that she has the extraordinary ability of being able to understand the whole vision, the whole imagination of the writers that she deals with. She looks from the inside of the writer out, rather than the other way around. This ensures that, no matter what happens, the book will always belong to the writer. With her I find myself coming up with solutions to problems that I didn't know existed.

Many of these are what I call translation problems . . . the difficulty of describing my own tiny perfect inner world to the reader. The important thing is not to change that world but to somehow give the reader access to it.

How many drafts would you take your work through?

That is difficult to answer. I revise certain sections countless times. Some parts more than other. By the time I've finished the first draft, or what I might call the first draft, sentences, paragraphs, lines, verses may have altered drastically.

Do friends and family ever appear in your work? Do you draw upon your autobiographical past?

Yes, I suppose that I do in that I have two autobiographical pasts; the actual and the imaginary. For some reason my memories of what I was imagining in the past are much clearer than whatever events [were] taking place. This *imagining* was often, though not always, triggered by events and, of course, there were times when events became so significant that there was no need, no time for imaginative embellishment.

Because almost any story or anecdote that someone else tells acts itself out in my own inner theater while I am listening I have a tendency to use other people's pasts more than my own. I'm a great thief in that regard. I have consistently stolen from my husband, for instance. He grew up as part of an undertaker's family in Niagara Falls, Ontario. One of the main characters in my recent novel is based on his grandmother who actually ran the business. My interest in her began with the discovery of a little notebook among my husband's papers. In this notebook Tony's grandmother had written descriptions of the various bodies, and parts of bodies, that were found in the Niagara River from 1909 to 1938. I immediately began to wonder about and then to mentally construct the character of this woman I had never met. From there the book evolved.

What's it like living with a well known artist like Tony Ur-

quhart? By that I mean do you have to set high standards for yourself?

Well, I don't *have* to set high standards for myself. He doesn't insist that I excel in any particular activity or anything like that. On the other hand just watching him over the last decade or so has changed the way I feel about time. He is a compulsive worker. During the day if he's not teaching, he's in the studio working. It is as simple as that. Nothing stops him, *absolutely* nothing. When I first met him he was living alone with his two daughters who were small children at the time. He was doing all the washing, cooking, housekeeping, working full time at the university, attending various art functions in Toronto and sitting on Canada Council juries etc. Even so, his output was enormous. That taught me that if you really want to create something there are no excuses for not creating it. It is something that just *has* to happen regardless of circumstances.

Do you find an overlap between your writing and the visual arts?

Tony and I produced one book together; *I Am Walking in the Garden of His Imaginary Palace,* a long narrow book with a long narrow title, long narrow poems and long narrow Urquhart drawings. We did not, however, pre-conceptualize that book in any way. It was a case of synchronicity. We looked at each other's work one evening, realized we were dealing with the same subject matter and said, "Hey, why don't we make a book together?"

The visual arts and my writing do overlap in other ways. I completed two undergraduate degrees at university; one in English and one in Art History and I'm inclined to think that the one in Art History has helped me the most. Learning to see and visual memory are really so important. Learning how to compose a landscape, for instance, to eliminate what doesn't need to be there and to add what does. Almost any painting is a combination of memory, fantasy and actuality in varying degrees. Exactly the same thing is true of writing.

Is your fiction a mirror of your self?

It depends on the definition of "self." It may be a reflection of my inner self but I'm not even sure that is true. I think that very little of my writing is confessional, or, at least it's not a reflection of my daily life.

What makes a work boring for you?

I wonder if you mean something I am working on or literature in general? Very little bores me but if I do get bored its usually by a form of grim reporting of untransformed events. I have a much more reflective than active mind. I find myself more interested in what characters are thinking and imagining than what they are doing or how they are behaving.

Many of my stories are travel stories probably because strange things happen to people emotionally when they are en-route, while they are in the state of passing from their ordinary geography into one where they feel less comfortable. People can often see themselves better in a foreign geography . . . out of context.

—Jane Urquhart

Do you find that it's to your advantage to live in a small town?

Absolutely. Particularly my small town; Wellesley, Ontario. It's about ninety miles west of Toronto, near Kitchener-Waterloo. Like all small towns its mythology is exact and manageable. The archetypal figures of post-mistress, librarian, mayor, handy man, village idiot, grocer, are all there playing out their archetypal roles. It is pure theater. Since I am not really part of it I am able to assume the role of spectator.

My small town is also in the center of a strong Mennonite community which gives me direct access to the North American 19th century. I couldn't live anywhere else in the world and have that. As I sit writing or reading in my porch room, horses and buggies go by the windows, or cutters in winter complete with sleigh bells. All the things that happened in 19th century rural Ontario are still happening in Wellesley; quilting bees, box socials, fall fairs, church teas.

I don't have any desire to become part of all that but I want it to exist and I want to be able to watch it exist.

You have the added bonus of being near an academic community at the University of Waterloo.

I haven't had all that much to do with the university as such except for the Department of Fine Arts where my husband teaches. The faculty of this little Department is interesting in that they are all professional visual artists as well as academic teachers and some of them, like Virgil Burnett and Nancy-Lou Patterson are writers as well.

The one aspect of the university that I could not live without is the Arts Library. The poet, Stuart MacKinnon that I mentioned before, works there as collection's manager and in many ways I feel as if he is my own private librarian. He shares my interest in Canadian History, including Canadian Literary History, and is always willing to bring interesting books to my attention.

I love libraries, I always have. I'm an incurable browser. I spend a great deal of time just wandering through the stacks, letting certain books call to me from the shelves; not necessarily great literary works of art but other, odder things such as *Nineteenth Century Missionary Tracts, A Dictionary of Disasters and Shipwrecks, A History of Museums, Second Sight in The Scottish Highlands, A Collection*

of the Letters between Jonathan Swift and Vanessa, An Encyclopaedia of Sins. These are the kind of books I find by strolling and looking . . . books I never could have discovered any other way.

There is another side of the university that has been of some value to me and that is the Writer-in-Residence program at St. Jerome's College. Susan Musgrave was writer-in-residence there for the last two years so it was marvelous to have access to her. Unlike me, she is a confessional writer, so as I got to know her it was fascinating for me to watch how the emotions of her life became re-ordered and transformed into poetry on the page.

What other writers do you admire and learn from?

I don't think I've ever read anything that I haven't learned from . . . if that were the case I would have stopped reading, which, of course I haven't. In Canada I've been most interested in the work of Michael Ondaatje and Alice Munro . . . the former because of the strange leaps he takes between the ordinary and the surreal; the latter, because, in her early work at least, she explores the dark side of the Canadian Pioneer Rural Myth. Robertson Davies' *Deptford Trilogy* had a great effect on me some years ago, at a time when I wasn't writing. It made me wish, for some reason, that I was. Timothy Findley, *The Wars* in particular, and probably because of the combination of history and imagination . . . the ever present archive.

For a long time I found myself attracted to nineteenth, early twentieth century writing, Flaubert, Turgenev, Zola, the poetry of Emily Dickinson, but recently I have found myself delighted by certain contemporary novels; Julian Barnes' *Flaubert's Parrot,* and an American novel called *House Keeping* by Marilyn Robinson, all of John Cheever's novels started to appeal to me and an English book called *Waterland* by a writer called Graham Swift. What these books all have in common is the effect of history upon the imagination; not necessarily history in the formal sense . . . smaller histories from smaller archives . . . things told and passed down . . . things documented. Tangible ghosts in a way . . . the lure of the past.

I also like to read writers of the unreal; Angela Carter's black fairy tales, my friend Rikki's darkly funny books; *Butcher's Tales* and *The Stain* . . . her's is a voice and a vision uniquely her own, Italo Calvino's richly visual writings and, of course, the ever present South Americans though I'm not sure that what they are writing about could be classified as "unreal." These last writers were important to me in that they taught me that you *could* write fiction where imagination and actuality changed places, moved back and forth, where the borders blurred.

Do you have an ideal writer?

Apart from myself and a few friends not really. Perhaps I would like my nine year old daughter to be my ideal future reader.

Do you work with plot first, or character, or situation, or language, in your fiction?

I would have to say, that of those four, situation is the closest, in that when I begin to write, I really have no preconceived method of approach. It's most often a visual image that triggers me, or sometimes a remembered emotion. I have had the experience of the first line which came to me in the middle of the night and forced me into my freezing little porch room. But that doesn't often happen.

Does your poetry begin in the same way?

Usually a visual image, or a remembered visual image, or a remembered imaginary image begins a poem for me. The first poems I wrote as an adolescent were lyrical/confessional; a different discipline than the one I involve myself in now. At present, it seems, that I have to write in series. I am much more comfortable with something I can think about over a long period of time; weeks, months . . . even years. This means that when I return to the poems I am always returning to the same general geography.

You are more drawn to fiction of imagination than fiction of fact. Are you also drawn to similar experimentation in fiction?

I really don't think about things like that when I'm working. My work doesn't feel experimental to me. I think I am writing in a fairly conservative form. Certainly, my language is conventional. Subject matter is another story. Perhaps, from that point of view, it might be possible for some people to perceive my writing as experimental.

How do you go back, reconstruct the past, draw upon documentary evidence and combine it with your imaginative processes?

The imagination comes into play at odd and unexpected moments. Part of an anecdote my grandmother told me can combine with pure imagination and historical research can combine with a contemporary emotion. Or imaginary emotion can combine with a contemporary anecdote. I have, however, used my own emotions in my writing to help me get inside and experience my characters.

How do you create your characters?

They seem to just happen to me, or, at least so far that has been the case. Often, when I begin to write I feel as though I already know them very well, but that, as in any relationship, I feel as though I would like to get to know them better. So I begin to explore.

Could you tell me about the genesis and working out of the two sequences of stories, the wheelchair pieces and the Seven Confessions.

The idea for the Wheelchair Sequence came to me while I was looking at a series of drawings my husband had completed of six Victorian wheelchairs. I began to believe that each and every one of the wheelchairs should have a story connected to it. I didn't want the wheelchair to be the main character, necessarily, but I felt that it might be noticed in passing or be used in some manner during the narrative. Almost every human being, after all is crippled in some way or another and, if they aren't yet, they will be soon.

The Seven Confessions began in a similar way. Tony had made a drawing (only one this time) of a Catholic Confessional Box which is really a very sinister looking piece of furniture. I began to be fascinated, as I moved farther and farther away from confessional poetry, about the act of confession itself . . . not only Catholic confession . . . but the process of sitting down and relating a story in the first person that concerns the self and is of great emotional importance. I decided that there should be seven stories in the sequence; one for each of the seven deadly sins.

Two sloths were hanging in a tree. One says to the other, why can't we just be lust and greed? Moving right along here, your style and subject matter in these pieces doesn't fit into the Canadian Short Story tradition.

I must say that, though I am a staunch Canadian Nationalist, and I am fond of Canadian writers and Canadian Literary Heritage, I have no real idea of what the Canadian Short Story Tradition is. Maybe that's a typically Canadian remark. But whatever the case I can only write about what I want to write about and whether or not it fits into the Canadian Literary Tradition seems, somehow irrelevant.

Does a story for you have a certain pace, a quick beginning, or, what makes a story interesting for you?

I am not consciously aware of pace when I'm writing but I would say that my stories are more passive than active. More reflective. A certain male writer-in-residence at the University of Waterloo told me a few years ago that one of my stories was, in fact, not a story because nothing took place in it. "Nothing is happening here," he said, "there are no hunters or grizzly bears or baseball games." I said, "The woman in this story is dying and something is happening to her emotionally! The story is inside her head." But he said, "It's so passive, laid back. Why don't you put a few events into it?" I couldn't do it. The story was the event.

Memory plays a large part in your writing.

Yes, but, as I've already said, not just my memories, other memories as well. The past is a memory but it is a memory that is alive.

I was in contact with nineteenth century rural Ontario as a child because I spent a great deal of time at my Grandmother's house. Her parlour was total Victoriana . . . doilies and bric-a-brac. For her, memory was also the environment she moved around in every day, so, in fact it was the present. And for me, when I was there it was the present as well; just a few degrees removed because it belonged to her. The stories she told, which were memories, also applied to the objects that surrounded her daily. In one way or another you take history with you. You can't help it.

So other people's memory stories appear in my poetry and prose, after they have been filtered through the listener who then, in turn, becomes the next narrator. When I hear a story I visually construct the house where the story occurred, the garden outside the house, the road that passes by the front door, the town the house is in and so on. It's a combination of fact and fabrication. The beginning of legend. Very important, I think, for a country like Canada with such a short past and such a slim history. In my own case the combination of hearing about and imagining the past tells me who I am right now.

Do you use notebooks and diaries to recall the past?

I use notebooks only when I'm travelling, when I'm not in my own room every day, with access to my typewriter and I don't want to let anything go by . . . or when I'm doing research.

Could you tell me about your collage diary?

That book started out as a travel diary about twelve years ago and has gradually evolved into a true collage. Not only have I worked on it but so have several others. The visual artist Hugh MacKenzie has done drawings in it as have Ted Godwin, Mieke Bevelander . . . even Michael Ondaatje has scribbled a couple of drunken portraits of Tony and myself in it. Several people have written remarks in it. In a way it's really like an annotated scrapbook complete with absurd photographs, wine labels, dinner party reports, theater stubs, newspaper clippings, post cards etc. But it is also fiction in that I occasionally record the events of my life there in an altered form. It's really meant to amuse myself at some later date.

Is travel important to you?

Very. Many of my stories are travel stories probably because strange things happen to people emotionally when they are en-route, while they are in the state of passing from their ordinary geography into one where they feel less comfortable. People can often see themselves better in a foreign geography . . . out of context.

Passing aquaintances, met when I'm travelling, often appear in my fiction. I remember an Englishman we met on the terrace of a pension just outside of Florence who was obsessed by lizards. He spent all morning scuttling around the terrace looking for them, sort of rounding them up. He was very annoyed if anyone scattered his lizard collection. He ended up in a section of the novel. I might not have even noticed him if I had not been removed from my own usual surroundings. Being out of place heightens perception.

Which places are important to you? Where do you go when you travel?

France has been important to me . . . particularly Versailles. I discovered through the landscape of the gardens there almost everything I wanted to know about power. The grounds of the Palace are gorgeous, but they have been controlled to such an extent by a single individual, Louis the XIV, that they are frightening. It's the difference between chaos and order, which is negative and which is positive. At Versailles the idea seems to be that everything has to be under control: the paths have to be straight, nothing, except monuments and certain trees can grow higher than three feet, all the flower beds have to be the same flower, the same colour. This goes on for *acres*. This fascinated and kind of appalled me and triggered two collections of poems. Being born in Northern Canada, where very little of nature is under control gave me a certain set of expectations in terms of landscape. Versailles really shook those expectations up.

The idea of order versus chaos began to interest me to such as extent that I started to direct my travels in order to observe it more closely. I must be moving into the disordered stage because my most recent travels have been to the Yorkshire Moors . . . Brontë country. The moors are open, natural and wild . . . totally exposed to the elements. A town, on the other hand, or even a house, is built and ordered and controlled by man. Storm and calm are two basic unresolved issues in *Wuthering Heights* . . . issues that I continue to be interested in.

Do you need emotional stability to deal with chaos?

I need both stability and uncertainty . . . not just to cope, but to write. Poetry probably is emotion recollected in tranquility, as Wordsworth suggested, but the hard part is to find some sort of balance between the two. Without the emotion there is no creative energy but without the tranquility you can't possibly work. Trying to work this out I spend a great deal of time rushing back and forth from one polarity to another.

How do you do this? A special room, a special time of the day?

Yes, I do have a special room, and I tend to work mostly during the daylight hours. I also live in Wellesley; surrounded by trees, lawns and quiet. If I lived in Toronto I fear I'd be permanently seduced into emotion . . . there just wouldn't be any tranquility. The enforcement of the family also helps . . . children, in some crazy way help me to write, rather than hinder, in that they have schedules that *have* to be followed for reasons of survival. They make demands at specific times of the day; they have to go to school, or to bed at eight o'clock, and they have to eat. I give myself allotments of time between those demands so that writing becomes a reward.

My husband once told me that when his daughter Robin was very small he went into her room to wake her up from her afternoon nap and she said; "My dreams come up to me and I have to say them." How's that for a definition of poetry?

—*Jane Urquhart*

How do you know when a story or poem or the novel is finished?

I keep on working until it stops feeling good. Then I know it's finished. It may not be perfect or a great work of art but it's finished for me. As long as I'm obsessed by it, then I know it's not finished. It's entirely intuitive.

Do you like the idea that a writer, like a visual artist, invents forms?

I like the idea but I'm not sure it is entirely true. Certainly, in my case, I borrowed the forms that I use. Sequential stories and poems have been written by plenty of others before me. My work *does* often stem from a visual experience but visual art operates a little differently. Goya's *Disasters of War;* the great series of etchings, do tell a story, or expose a sequence of stories, but they also have an immediate visual impact that is impossible to produce when you are using words. The immediate impact is brought about by using different tools; colour, form, composition.

Do you feel a sense of power over the page? Or do your characters simply come through you and you have to be true to them?

Tony once told me that when his daughter Robin was very small he went into her room to wake her up from her afternoon nap and she said; "My dreams come up to me and I have to say them." How's that for a definition of poetry?

I don't think that I am consciously in control of the characters though I do have a vague idea of where I want them to go and what I want them to do. Often I feel that I, myself, am having some sort of dialogue with them. I become quite emotionally involved.

Does that also happen when you get strong characters like the poet Robert Browning?

I have always adored Robert Browning's poetry and so I had great fun with his character. He was sort of like a stuffy old uncle with a heart of gold. Oddly enough I didn't read any Browning biographies until I was finished with that part of the novel. I just intuited, through reading the poetry, that Browning was likely to be an ordered variety of individual who might, in some far corner of himself, wish that he wasn't. That led me to think that, while he was dying, a well ordered death in bed, he might be envious of Shelley's death which was much more wild and emotional. As you know, Shelley drowned when his small sailboat was caught in a freak storm off the coast of Italy.

Was Browning set up to be a counterpart to wild Canada?

That was part of it but there were other factors at work as well. I knew that the Canadian poet in the novel was going to drown so what I was initially looking for was an old world poet who would also drown. I wanted to set the story in 1889. Part of the reason that late nineteenth century Canadian poets were having problems, or at least in my opinion, was that they were trying to impose Wordsworth's daffodils in the total disorder of the Canadian landscape. Anyway, I was looking for an English poet and remembered that Browning died in Venice in 1889. He did not drown but was certainly surrounded by water and he was thinking about Shelley . . . who did drown.

All your work has those old world/new world connections.

I suppose it has to do with nature and childhood. The old world is culture and the new world is nature. That must have been a concept that any person from the old world would have to think about, if only practically, when they encountered the new world. In *The Little Flowers of Madame de Montespan* I have Louis the XIV, that great orderer of the landscape, stumbling through the forest at the edge of Niagara Falls in a nightmare. I just knew that that particular geography would be a nightmare for a man like that. In *Whirlpool Dream House* a young man with an old

world idea of what a poet should be is trying to live out that fantasy in nineteenth century Canada.

False Shuffles *is an important book to you. You have the three generations of women; the grandmother, the mother and the narrating daughter . . .*

It connects again to my interest in the past. The narrating daughter is the speaker and the oral tradition plays, and has played, an enormous role in that both the grandmother and the mother have passed their interpretation of events down to the narrating daughter. I was dealing with the idea that in many works of literary art, a thousand stories have filtered down to the person who has either the skills or the inclination to record, after they have passed it through their own imagination, what they have heard of the past.

Your writing might also be seen as about the difficulties between memory and writing, or that gap between narrating and what's being narrated.

I don't see it so much as a difficulty. It's more like a state of grace. It's always the altering of the orally narrated tale that turns it into a work of art. That sense of it passing from fact, through the imagination, into writing.

The gap might be the most important part of all. The gap, after all, is where the imagination comes in.

False Shuffles *is about magic and illusion and shape changing.*

Yes. You think something is this way, but, by the time I get finished with it, you are going to see it some other way. That's what creative writing is all about.

But the magic part of it is also the documenting of a relationship.

True. The difficulties of making yourself heard and making yourself known, and the difficulties of language and how it doesn't always fulfil its promise. How much can you really even know about another person through the medium of language, which is all we really have? Language is metaphor and symbol. It makes me wonder how we manage to communicate at all.

What links all your books?

The idea of 'the story' certainly links all my books. There is some magic moment of transition when experience stops being experience and starts becoming a combination of remembered and imagined experiences, and then later, in some cases, documented or told experience.

Do women have different sensibilities as writers?

I've always believed that women are at least as capable as men in all fields and in creative areas we may be slightly better off. The Jungian concept of animus/anima is interesting in that the anima is the creative spirit in the human psyche and it is also the feminine spirit. So, in a way, we have an edge on men already.

However, I hate and resent segregation on any level. What I hope feminism has done for me is that it has allowed me access to the male of the species as people and as thinkers in a way that is not confused by sexual issues.

> The idea of "the story" links all my books. There is some magic moment of transition when experience stops being experience and starts becoming a combination of remembered and imagined experiences, and then later, in some cases, documented or told experience.
>
> —*Jane Urquhart*

Your work has a lyrical quality which I associate with the Broadway musical or is this just a lucky guess?

Geoff, you're so perceptive! When I was a child I was obsessed by Broadway musicals. My parents took me to New York when I was ten years old. We saw three Broadway musicals. I thought I had entered the Kingdom of Heaven! Now I realize that my writing has to do with that moment when words stop being factual and start being lyrical. In the best musicals you can hardly tell where the transition comes between straight dialogue and song. And it is possible in a musical, to sing about anything and everything. That's the way writers should be. When the moment is correct they should just effortlessly break into song.

Do you have an agenda for future projects?

I have some plans and ideas. I'll be spending a couple of months in Yorkshire this spring and hope to work on another novel set in that location. I'm also writing a series of poems loosely connected to the Brontës. It's hard to say, at this point, how all of this will work out, but that's part of the lure. I like to believe that, like Emily Dickinson;

> I dwell in possibility
> A fairer house than prose.

Brent Ledger   (review date November 1986)

SOURCE: A review of *The Whirlpool*, in *Quill and Quire*, Vol. 52, No. 11, November, 1986, p. 25.

[*In the following review, Ledger offers a highly negative assessment of* The Whirlpool.]

[*The Whirlpool*] is a dissertation masquerading as a novel and as deceptions go, it's not terribly successful. Pity the poor reader who, lured by the Signature Series' romance-style covers, opens the book and looks for a story. 'Twould be in vain: there's no plot, little characterization, next to no dialogue, and certainly no drama.

Urquhart is after a berth in the CanLit pantheon. The three major characters in her novel live beside the whirlpool in 19th-century Niagara Falls. They live in separate solipsistic bubbles, seldom talking, almost never touching. In each case, the character's major relationship is with nature. It's that golden oldie, that cherished Canuck chestnut: man against nature or, will we survive with our garrison mentality intact? Maude the undertaker lives in peace-

ful co-existence with the whirlpool, making a living by burying its victims. Fleda lives on Whirlpool Heights where she views the Canadian landscape through the filter of Wordsworth and Browning (and looks in vain for a Canadian Heathcliff). Patrick the poet sees the whirlpool as a metaphor and tries to skim meaning from it by swimming the vortex. He dies. That's the most exciting event in the book and it occurs off camera. When it comes to this sort of theme, Edgar Rice Burroughs did it better.

The only fun in Urquhart territory is dry and intellectual, a sort of academic party game: plucking trendy themes from Urquhart's impeccable but ultimately boring prose. There's lots of them, and most of them you've heard before: the Canadian view of nature, the effect of social mythologies on personal action, the stupefying effects of domestic drudgery on women, the arbitrary nature of signs. It's as if Margaret Atwood had co-authored a book with Roland Barthes—and left her wit behind. An ill-digested mess of Canadian cultural criticism and French linguistic theory, *The Whirlpool* is a novel with a couple of heads but no heart.

Nancy Wigston   (review date 6 December 1986)

SOURCE: "Eccentrics in a Luminous Maelstrom," in *The Globe and Mail,* Toronto, December 6, 1986, p. E21.

[*In the positive review below, Wigston relates the story line of* The Whirlpool, *noting Urquhart's focus on history and eccentric characters.*]

The Whirlpool is a jewel of a book: its finely polished facets are full of light, yet suggest numerous depths. The depths are real, for the story takes place in late nineteenth-century Niagara Falls, and much of the action focuses on the mystery of the huge cataract and its adjacent whirlpool. But the depths here equally serve to illuminate the collective identity of a people.

Jane Urquhart brings her poetic sensibility to bear on the psyches of an eccentric set of Ontarians, bracketing their tales with a portrait of poet Robert Browning on the final day of his life, in Venice. Watery Venice gives way to watery Niagara during the closing days of a flu epidemic. Maud Grady, the undertaker's wife, sits in her house with the corpses of her husband and parents-in-law lying in the bedrooms overhead. The prose crackles with the texture of the imprisoning black crepe that Maud dons for the mandatory mourning period, which lasts years. Death exerts an almost erotic magnetism for many of the characters in this book—as it did for many true nineteenth-century romantics. And it's with increasing pleasure that we watch Maud emerge through layers of black to grey and lilac and finally to triumphant yellow—back to life.

Others in Urquhart's eccentric pantheon aren't so lucky. The poetic Patrick, sent down from Ottawa while recovering from an attack of pneumonia that had left him weak and "in a state of perpetual despair," is drawn inexorably toward the whirlpool and away from the physicality of life and love.

Fleda McDougal, wife of Major David, lives independently in a tent in the woods, near the whirlpool, which she thinks of as being "like memory, like obsession. .. like a mystical pyramid."

Right she is. Like the ancient Egyptians, this is a society obsessed with death and its houses. Urquhart has opened a window on a past few will recognize, but all will believe in.

As Fleda waits for her husband to build their house in the woods, she is stalked by the idealization of womanhood common to Victorian men. The convalescing Patrick sees her as a dark vision, still and silent in a moving world. Her husband, obsessed with the War of 1812 and the nefarious Americans, sees her as a somewhat inadequate version of his beloved heroine, Laura Secord.

Joining in the danse macabre is the endless population of "floaters," the drownings that crop up regularly every spring, as well as the more spectacular challengers of the mighty falls, rushing to their deaths in contraptions of their own design. Urquhart fills in the blanks in our bland history with the color and pageantry of one such event—Buck O'Connor shoots the rapids in a container of moose hides and antlers. Even more intriguing are the notes based on an actual "death-log" of anonymous drownings kept by an undertaker's wife, an ancestor by marriage of author Urquhart. The fictional Maud looks at her conscientious notes on one unclaimed corpse, wondering, "Who was the keeper of his memories? There was something tragic, not about his battered body, necessarily, but about his blue polka dot handkerchief, his Fashion smoking tobacco, his Peterson pipe."

Rarely has our history been served so well, yet this is by no means a "historical" novel, dishing up yet another helping of gooey romanticism. No, Urquhart's moody, incisive and shimmering prose, her cleverness and wit soar beyond that. In, but not of, Victorian times, *The Whirlpool* is both old and new. As the sweetly crazed patriot Major McDougal puts it in one of the book's best lines: "Thinking Canadian is a very lonely business, my boy, and don't forget it." Jane Urquhart's luminous maelstrom ensures that we won't.

Sherie Posesorki   (review date January-February 1987)

SOURCE: A review of *The Whirlpool,* in *Books in Canada,* Vol. 16, No. 1, January-February, 1987, p. 26.

[*In the following, Posesorki provides a mixed assessment of* The Whirlpool.]

The person and poetics of Robert Browning cast a giant shadow over Jane Urquhart's ambitious first novel *The Whirlpool.* In her prologue Urquhart presents the elderly Browning in Venice, overwhelmed by his recollections of the poet Shelley and by portents of his death. This romantically morbid vignette introduces the major *leitmotivs* of her novel: dreams, obsessions, death, and their relationship to the production of art.

Browning wrote, "Throughout life, 'tis death makes life live. Gives it whatever the significance." That is the premise Urquhart dramatizes through the lives of her charac-

ters, who all are cocooned in the mourning of their death-related obsessions and livelihoods. Maud Grady, the undertaker's widow, spends her days tenderly tending the dead, and her nights dreaming of her late husband. She ignores her autistic son in favour of her "dolls"—dead young girls that she prepares for embalming. Military historian David McDougall marries a woman who resembles the spectre who haunts his dreams—Laura Secord—and neglects her in his pursuit of his studies. His wife Fleda, preoccupies herself with compulsive rereadings of Browning by the edge of a whirlpool, where Patrick, a poet, spies on her, then takes her as his muse.

Urquhart's prose is clear and vivid, and her characters' obsessions have a brooding power. Nonetheless, the pulleys of her ideas have more force and drama than the lives of her characters. They don't embody and enact her concepts: rather, they ride them, like children on a carousel. What is missing from *The Whirlpool* is the fictional alchemy that transforms the dead matter of fiction into the warm flesh of life.

William French   (review date 25 June 1987)

SOURCE: A review of *Storm Glass,* in *The Globe and Mail,* Toronto, June 25, 1987, p. D1.

[*French is a Canadian editor and critic. In the favorable review below, he surveys several of the stories collected in* Storm Glass.]

Glib generalizations won't do in any discussion of Jane Urquhart's fiction. Just when she seems to be establishing a pattern in this first collection of 17 short stories [entitled *Storm Glass*], she darts off in another direction and ambushes our expectations.

But it can be said, without fear of contradiction, that she has impressive talent. There's nothing simple and obvious here; concentric circles of meaning ripple out from the stories, and the prose shimmers like reflections in a deep pool. (Her frequent use of water imagery is contagious.) If Urquhart occasionally strives too hard for complexity, that's always a risk for writers who press against the limits of the conventional short story.

Urquhart, who was born in Northern Ontario and came of age in Toronto, has published three volumes of poetry, and her poetic sensibility is much in evidence here (as it was in her first novel, *The Whirlpool,* published last fall).

Urquhart (whose husband, artist Tony Urquhart, provides some appropriate drawings) observes in a preface to *Storm Glass* that most of the stories are about other places. She adds: "It seems to me now that the word 'other' is important in that it was an attraction to the mysterious 'other' that started me writing short fiction in the first place: that wild desire to explain, if only to myself, a landscape, an era, a human being, an event, about which I had little knowledge and to which I had limited access."

Thus several of the stories are set in Italy and France. They're mostly about tourists who make unexpected discoveries about themselves. One of these stories, **"Italian Postcards,"** may be the best in the collection. (It has already been published in Oberon's *Best Canadian Stories 86.*) Set in Assisi, it describes an almost eerie parallel between the experience of a woman tourist and a priest, and the woman who became Santa Chiara and her mentor, St. Francis. The story illustrates one of Urquhart's recurring themes, the close interaction of two people—in this case, husband and wife—who remain isolated.

Another excellent story, **"Forbidden Dancés,"** is worthy of Alice Munro, but with an added prismatic effect that gives it an extra dimension. The narrator recalls her childhood encounters with her grandmother, who had been forbidden to dance by her father. There was good reason, as it turns out, as the granddaughter, no longer protected by the innocence of childhood, discovers for herself.

Five related stories are grouped under the general title of "Five Wheelchairs." A wheelchair does indeed appear in each, sometimes as a symbol of a crippled spirit and maimed emotions, but sometimes in an unexpected context. If there is a linking theme, it's the corrosive effects of boredom. In one story, it's the boredom of a burned-out marriage; in another, small-town boredom leads a woman to get her excitement from funerals. When not enough people die, she invents their deaths.

Another story involves a woman in a wheelchair and a man who frequently dances for her with a glass of wine on his forehead. We're not sure whether he does it to entertain her or to satisfy his own vanity, until the sudden surrealist twist at the end.

Another set of stories is grouped under the heading, "Seven Confessions." Each of the stories illustrates one of the seven deadly sins, but usually in an unexpected way. Lust, for example, describes the reaction of a woman to a hunchback in the foreign town where she has sought anonymous exile. As she watches him from her window, he innocently intrudes on her neutrality until, sympathy aroused, she tries vainly to communicate her affection by emulating him.

Perhaps the most imaginative story is **"The Death of Robert Browning,"** in which Urquhart gets inside the head of the poet as he nears death in Venice. He has constant unbidden thoughts of Shelley, and realizes he had kept the drowned poet out of his thoughts because he subconsciously realized Shelley was the better poet. The shimmering quality that is a hallmark of Urquhart's prose is much in evidence here, as is the recurring imagery of water. This story formed the opening and closing of Urquhart's novel, *The Whirlpool,* but it can stand firmly on its own.

The title piece is a gently effective look at a woman who has resisted being dominated by her strong-minded husband. But, in the process, the sharp edges of her character have become rounded, just like pieces of glass found on the beach. This glass becomes a symbol of their differences; he insists they're called storm glass, but she knows them as beach glass or water glass.

Urquhart is the kind of writer who makes us wonder, with a sense of pleasurable anticipation, what in the world she'll do next.

Timothy Findley   (review date June-July 1987)

SOURCE: "Through the Looking Glass," in *Books in Canada,* Vol. 16, No. 5, June-July, 1987, p. 14.

[*Findley is a renowned Canadian novelist, playwright, and scriptwriter. In the following review, he praises Urquhart's focus on and striking evocation of character, time, and place in* Storm Glass.]

In 1986, Jane Urquhart published her first novel, *The Whirlpool,* to almost universal critical acclaim. When it met with a negative response, it tended to offend or bemuse because of its imaginative content. In *The Whirlpool,* Urquhart treated reality with contempt. She was clearly a courageous stylist with a unique vision—and such writers rarely escape without raising a few hackles. Now, with *Storm Glass,* the courage of the stylist is confirmed and the uniqueness of the vision is expanded.

Though most of the stories here predate the writing of *The Whirlpool,* the reader is given the chance, once again, to explore the territory of dreams and memory so vividly established in that book. Clearly, this is a milieu in which Urquhart excels.

The author herself describes her work as "escape writing" and certainly there is an air of creative freedom in the stories that make up *Storm Glass.* People walk in and out of one another's dreams and cross with alarming ease from the present into the past. In one story—**"The Drawing Master"**—an artist encounters a pile of Victorian wheelchairs dumped unceremoniously out of someone else's dream in a previous story. Discarded on the one hand by their owners and on the other by the woman in whose dream they first appeared, the wheelchairs represent for the artist the perfect image of an abiding sadness he could not, till then, articulate.

In the title story [**"Storm Glass"**], a dying woman who has lost—over time—her sense of bonding with her husband comes to terms with what divided them. And she does this by exploring the view from her window through his eyes. At first, she holds fast to the view—which presents the shores of a lake—by means of her own determined understanding of what is there. Slowly, she veers as far away from that interpretation of reality as she dares, by trying to understand what she sees through her children's eyes. In her mind, she walks with her children around the shores of the lake, picking up the bits of broken coloured glass that lie in amongst the stones thrown up by storms. She has always called these shards either *water glass* or *beach glass,* but her husband insists it is *storm glass,* smoothed and worn by the violence of wind and waves. This imagery of broken glass—and the characters' harsh insistence on what it must be called—provides the ground on which the woman and her husband come to terms with their lives together. Its simplicity is worth noting. Few writers would get away with achieving this sort of profound reconciliation over a piece of glass, but Urquhart does it wonderfully well.

One of the stories in *Storm Glass* has already served as prologue and epilogue for *The Whirlpool.* This is **"The Death of Robert Browning,"** but it bears rereading because of its evocation of another time and place—and equally because of its extraordinary evocation of what might be called creative regret. Browning, dying, cannot rid himself of the image of Shelley drowning and he wishes he were worthy of dying more splendidly himself; as if his death were all he had to leave posterity.

Other times and other places lend their colour to most of the stories in this collection. Windows and glass are also prominent. Some of the characters have no names and all of them are dreamers, though what they dream is hardly the stuff of which good sleep is made. *Storm Glass* is exhilarating precisely because the dreams of which it tells are so disturbing: disturbingly real and disturbingly familiar. Most readers will recognize the impulse here to wake up and escape the dream, but most will also recognize the tantalizing magic of dreams that keeps us going back for more. Certainly, most who read this book will hope Jane Urquhart goes back for more again and again.

Patricia Bradbury   (review date July 1987)

SOURCE: "Jane Urquhart's Short Stories in the Landscape of the Poet," in *Quill and Quire,* Vol. 53, No. 7, July, 1987, p. 64.

[*In the review below, Bradbury discusses* Storm Glass, *its imagery and symbolism, its poetic quality, and its similarities to the works of the Romantics.*]

"It was an attraction to the mysterious 'other'," says poet and novelist Jane Urquhart, "that started me writing short fiction . . . that wild desire to explain, if only to myself, a landscape, an era, a human being, an event, about which I had little knowledge and to which I had but limited access. . . . Writing fiction can be, you see, the most satisfying form of armchair travel. . . . And as I look out my window to the white of the field, the diagonals of the rail fence and the horizontals of the winter trees, I'm grateful, also, that my armchair is situated where it is."

This introduction to Urquhart's new and very beautifully designed collection of short stories, *Storm Glass,* is ordinary enough. Most writers describe their fictional impulses in these terms: the desire to catch the particulars of other people and things, the need to draw alien landscapes. What is not at all ordinary is Urquhart's result: rich imagery drawn meticulously in complex colour alongside character and plot in pale outline.

In the title story ["**Storm Glass**"], particulars are rather few. A woman is dying, we know not for what reason. She has children who are grown and a husband who is non-intellectual; she has a room, with two windows, which she cannot leave. More than just being herself, the woman is representative of storm glass—broken glass thrown into large bodies of water, like lakes, and gradually eroded by storms, "robbed by time of one of its more important qualities, the ability to cut". Her husband, on the other hand, represents fresh shards. He is forced to ignore death to remain "sharp, dangerous, alive".

A beautiful dualism is evoked, but is this a short story? I would call it more a contemplation, for it expresses the desire of the writer to explore an image, not to analyse a

character or tell a tale. The story "**Pride**" follows a similar structure. People exist—or so it seems—to allow the author to express the symbolic significance of a boat, a boat that once held a family of hopeful immigrants but is now sadly empty and washed up from the sea.

In spite of constant shifts to different countries and eras, we do not have a feeling of multiplicity in *Storm Glass,* but the sense that we've entered *one* landscape, *one* time zone, in which imagery, from story to story, is remarkably the same. It's as if we've arrived in a symbolic universe, where language is never jarring or casual. We're in the landscape, it seems, of the poet.

> Most writers describe their fictional impulses in these terms: the desire to catch the particulars of other people and things, the need to draw alien landscapes. What is not at all ordinary is Urquhart's result: rich imagery drawn meticulously in complex colour alongside character and plot in pale outline.
>
> *—Patricia Bradbury*

"Limp and drifting," says the author, describing the poet Percy Shelley in "**The Death of Robert Browning**", "the drowned man looked as supple as a mermaid, arms swaying in the current, hair and clothing tossed as if in a slow, slow wind. His body was losing colour, turning from pastel to opaque, the open eyes staring, pale, as if frozen by an image of the moon. Joints unlocked by moisture, limbs swung easily on their threads of tendon, the spine undulating and relaxed." How appropriate this language is for Robert Browning. But it's a bit of a shock to find, in "**Forbidden Dances**", a young girl sharing the great poet's imagery. Ophelia, she thinks, "always looked to me like beautiful refuse in the water, bright bits of garbage, everything trailing and coming apart at the seams. Hair, shawls, arms, fingers." In "**Pride**", we find echoes of this language again when a business-oriented grandfather describes the above-mentioned boat. It was "injured, wrecked—with sand and water spilling into its hull and its sail dragging behind it like long, drowned hair". One cannot help but think that, in spite of Urquhart's words to the contrary, her "armchair travel" does not take us outside to other identities as much as inside to her own highly developed system of symbols that different characters, as masks, set free. There is little here of the social historian or commentator. There is often little here of the plot maker. What we're experiencing in *Storm Glass* is poetry made long, not fiction rendered short.

Many moments in the collection are perfectly marvellous: a grandmother's sudden confession in "**Forbidden Dances**"; an evocative exchange of crippledness in "**Shoes**". The book is about the exploration of pain, the kind that is "permanent, incorruptible, unable to decay", like that on the face of St. Chiara in the story **"Italian Postcards"**. People's boredom and routine are broken up, repeatedly, not by joy but by death or personal suffering. In **"Gift"**, a Mr. Delacour gives his bored wife a wheel-chair to facilitate her need to invent an "awe-inspiring" disease. Only death makes Robert Browning take note of his life and realize that he's responded to some of the world's most exotic scenery "with the regularity of a copy clerk". Death invades the ordered couple in **"Pride"** only briefly, after which they return to their regular schedule. The man reads the stock reports, his wife packs the cooler, both ignoring, by choice, the delicious although disturbing beauty of death in the sea. In another story, **"Lust"**, an ex-tended metaphor for the process of writing, a woman mimics the degradation of a hunchback, accepting agonies to get closer to a man who will ignore her. It is this endless indifference, like that of a priest in **"Italian Postcards"**, that "sets him apart. Rejection without object, without malice, a kind of healing rejection; one that causes a cleansing ache".

This notion of cleansing through a reduction of the self forms an obvious link to the poetry of the Romantics, who yearned for a suspension between life and death, an arrest-ed disintegration. Various images of skeletons dance through these pieces, themselves "suspended somewhere between being and non-being". Like the storm glass, they are relics "of that special moment when the memory and the edge of the break softened and combined in order to allow preservation".

Urquhart seems to be searching for these relics in herself, the part, like Shelley's heart, that will not burn. She wears away images through endless examination, trying, per-haps, to wear away her own "crippledness" of unknowing. Such seems to be the purpose of her carefully tuned "sto-ries"—in the end, a talented poet's purpose.

Geraldine Sherman on Urquhart's place in Canadian literature:

Many of [Jane Urquhart's] characters have remarkable visual memories; discussions of paintings go on for pages, animated talk that's uncommon in Canadian fic-tion. Still, Jane acknowledges she might be part of a group of writers identified by Margaret Atwood as southern Ontario Gothic; James Reaney, Graeme Gib-son, Timothy Findley (at times), and Atwood herself. They find the supernatural in the commonplace: sudden death, unexpected storms, graveyards.

Geraldine Sherman, in her "Urquhart's Victorian Fascination with the Elements," in Quill and Quire, *January, 1990.*

Russell Brown   (review date May-June 1988)

SOURCE: "A Gathering of Seven," in *The American Book Review,* Vol. 10, No. 2, May-June, 1988, pp. 10, 21.

[An educator and critic, Brown has served as co-editor of anthologies of Canadian literature. In the excerpt below, he reviews The Whirlpool *and* Storm Glass. *Although fault-ing Urquhart's ability to effectively sustain narrative move-ment in her works, he extols the precision of her prose style.]*

Jane Urquhart, Janice Kulyk Keefer, and Paulette Jiles are three fiction writers who began as poets, and their fic-tion remains rooted in poetry. Although that poetic quali-ty is part of the attractiveness of their writing, at times it is achieved at the cost of the traditional strengths of narra-tive. In particular, Urquhart provides a wonderful group of nearly Gothic characters in *The Whirlpool,* makes fas-cinating use of historical background (Niagara Falls at the end of the nineteenth century) there, and manages to sug-gest intriguing symbolic depths—but her novel remains static. Still, the writing in *The Whirlpool* is so precisely etched and extraordinary that the book is always reward-ing. And the lack of an ongoing forward movement may be intentional; certainly it is appropriate to the novel's central image:

> In one sense the whirlpool was like memory; like obsession connected to memory, like history that stayed in one spot, moving nowhere and endlessly repeating itself.

Urquhart seems more comfortable in the brief stories that are collected in *Storm Glass,* because there she can avoid the problem of narrative movement while exploring the lyric possibilities of prose. These stories (like many today) resolve the way poems do. The conclusion of **"The Draw-ing Master"** suggests the strengths of this fiction:

> The drawing master approached [the student] and bent over his shoulder to offer his usual words of quiet criticism—perhaps a few words about light and shade, or something about tex-ture. He drew back, however, astonished. There before him on the paper was a perfectly drawn skeleton of a bird, and surrounding that and sometimes covering it or being covered by it, in a kind of crazy spatial ambiguity, drawn in by the student with the blunt ends of a pocketful of crayons, was the mad, turbulent landscape. It shuddered and heaved and appeared to be ger-minating from the motionless structure of the bird whose bones the young man had sensed be-neath dust and feathers. It needed no glass to protect it, no frame to confine it. And it was as confused and disordered and wonderful as ev-erything the master had chosen to ignore.

But if Urquhart herself is one who does not ignore the mad and turbulent landscape, it is not so much the turbulence itself that interests her as the products of it, the emblems of which are the "storm glass" of her title story, those beautiful fragments that have been smoothed and shaped by ocean waves. The stories in this collection, like the crys-tal-bead chapters strung together in *The Whirlpool,* are such objects: small, hard-edged, frequently beautiful.

An excerpt from *Changing Heaven*

Ann sits, now, out on the West Yorkshire moors on a rock, under a leaden sky and thinks, *I'll never be free of this*. She thinks, *let me in, let me in*. She who has only recently managed to get herself out.

She has memorized the words of the first scene in *Wuthering Heights*. She cannot shake its weather, cannot stop responding to the descriptions.

"Merely the branch of a fir tree that touched my lattice as the blast wailed by," and "the gusty wind, the driving of the snow." *I was,* she thinks, *mistaken. I was misperceived as a harmless piece of vegetation tapping on the glass that separated us.* The word "merely" bruises her. The words "detected the disturber" bring tears to her eyes. *I was a disturber,* she thinks, *then more than that . . . and then the full fury of the nightmare was upon him.*

It is as if thinking of that early scene at this moment, when she has left Arthur and has dragged her limping self out into the weather, identifies it, surely, as his; as if he had taken one of his immaculately sharpened pencils and had drawn a fine line beside the passage to bring it to her attention. "Look, here we are, you and I," he might have said, "This is the nature of our relationship: you trying to get in, me trying to keep you out. The war, the constant war between us."

She rises now to continue her walk on the narrow path that crosses the moor. Now and then she passes an abandoned farm whose buildings are so black they appear to have been burnt by a mysterious, indifferent fire. . . . Ann has already seen several rotting carcasses, remnants of those animals who, for one reason or another, were unable to survive the winter. Unable to survive exposure.

The thing about weather, thinks Ann . . . is that you either embrace it or you shelter yourself from it. Either way, it can extinguish the flame, with wind and rain on the one hand, or, if you run from it, if you hide in a closed space, the fire suffocates from lack of oxygen.

God, this sky, she thinks, *this uncertain earth.* Her feet slide on mud and press into boggy places. Overhead marches platoon after platoon of clouds bringing who knows what kinds of storm fronts, snow, or hail, an abrupt change of season. Bringing, for certain, nothing soft or warm. A consecutive series of polar statements.

She passes the Brontë waterfall, which has become a meaningless trickle since the reservoir was created late in the last century. She crosses Sladen Beck. *There is water too,* she thinks, *and it changes with weather.* The rain begins and Ann opens her black umbrella, which is almost immediately snatched from her by the wind. She pauses momentarily to watch it tumble over the heather, a wounded bat trying unsuccessfully to reassemble the mechanism necessary for flight. Then she laughs aloud. Perhaps out here everything will be blown away from her and she will return to her rented cottage and eventually to Canada, light, unencumbered, without any burdens at all.

Jane Urquhart, in her Changing Heaven, *David R. Godine, Publisher, Inc., 1993.*

Katherine Ashenburg   (review date March 1990)

SOURCE: "Inside Stories," in *Saturday Night*, Vol. 105, No. 2, March, 1990, pp. 53-5.

[*In the following excerpt, Ashenburg discusses the prominent role of Emily Brontë's* Wuthering Heights (1847) *in* Changing Heaven.]

The desire to read or reread the hero's work is a strange but real measure of success in this genre. Judged by this yardstick (as well as by others), Jane Urquhart's second novel, ***Changing Heaven,*** succeeds superbly. Urquhart, who bracketed her first novel, ***The Whirlpool,*** with scenes of Robert Browning's dying in Venice, has created a tartly level-headed ghost of Emily Brontë for the presiding genius of her new book.

At first Brontë seems peripheral to the main action, which is shared by two sets of lovers—a Victorian balloonist whose professional name is Arianna Ether and her manager, and a contemporary Canadian scholar named Ann Frear who is having an affair with a married art historian. Only gradually, as the two pairs struggle to reconcile obsession with everyday life, storm with calm, and the appeal of two-in-oneness with its horror, does it become clear that ***Changing Heaven*** is a sustained meditation on the themes of *Wuthering Heights*. Just as the child Ann Frear discovered the story of Heathcliff and Cathy during a Toronto hurricane and never recovered (as an adult she is writing a book about *Wuthering Heights* and weather), so the Victorian novel informs virtually every page of Urquhart's. As Ann Frear points out, there is only one scene in *Wuthering Heights* that registers zero on the wind scale. Similarly, Jane Urquhart's beautifully written book throbs with the storm and wind of passion and the bitter cold of its withdrawal.

Changing Heaven unpeels its solutions to the problem of writing about a writer layer by layer. It tackles not only the content of *Wuthering Heights* but the connection between Brontë's life and her work—the question, as Ann Frear sees it, "of how a woman so withdrawn can also be so engaged with life." In a novel remarkable for its freshness and originality, the character of Emily Brontë is the most unexpected touch of all. Utterly focused and pragmatic, she loves only two things: her imagination and her brother Branwell. Although she describes her life's work as "inventing angry love affairs," she declines these "extended tantrums" for herself. The problem with men is that they "only interfere with the inventing."

Changing Heaven presents Emily Brontë as both stunningly ordinary woman and consummate artist. The meagre facts of her life count for very little: it's her work that deserves contemplation, argument, attention. ***Changing Heaven*** is a portrait of a mind that harks back again to T. S. Eliot, who in "Tradition and Individual Talent" also wrote that emotions a poet had never experienced would serve as well as the most familiar feelings. He claimed, "It is not in his personal emotions, the emotions provoked by particular events in his life, that the poet is in any way remarkable or interesting. . . . The emotion of art is impersonal." Jane Urquhart's Emily Brontë would have approved. So, probably, would Jane Urquhart. It's a tough, unpopular thesis that novelists might contemplate before beginning a book about a writer.

Jane Urquhart on the writing process:

I think a kind of practice element comes in, almost like playing the piano. The more you write—you hope—the better you get in terms of technical things. But each book dictates its own style, so stylistically things are changed enough that you have to learn all over again how to use the language in relation to the subject-matter. There's a type of music that goes along with the style, and if I don't hear it then I know there's something the matter.

Jane Urquhart, in Stephen Smith's "Writing Away: *Allowing the Imagination to Fill in the Blanks,"* in Quill and Quire, *August, 1993.*

Thomas M. Disch (review date 18 March 1990)

SOURCE: "Niagara Falls Gothic," in *The New York Times Book Review,* March 18, 1990, p. 16.

[*Disch is an American novelist, short story writer, poet, editor, librettist, and author of books for children. He has also written under the name Leonie Hargrave and the joint pseudonyms Thom Demijohn and Cassandra Kyne. In the following, he provides a negative review of* The Whirlpool.]

Jane Urquhart's new book, ***The Whirlpool,*** is an almost perfect example of the first novel in the common, and pejorative, sense of the term. Of course, there are as many types of first novels as there are types of novels, and the type the Canadian poet Jane Urquhart has aspired to is one of the more modest: a genteel historical novel with Gothic overtones (but nothing overtly or vulgarly horripilating) concerning the inactions of abnormally sensitive individuals. There are three separate strands of plot, which are never braided, and more symbols than you can shake a stick at.

The principal symbol is, as you might expect, the whirlpool of the title, which is, in reality, the whirlpool at the base of Niagara Falls. It represents almost anything the author supposes attractive, complex, mysterious, inexorable or deathly, and it is always there, just at the threshold of hearing, all through the novel.

The main plot concerns a sensitive young poet, Patrick, who, loitering about Niagara Falls in the summer of 1889, espies a young married woman, Fleda, who is permanently encamped in a private glade overlooking the falls and spends all her time reading the poetry of Robert Browning (who also figures, for his sins, as a character in the book). Patrick rather fancies Fleda, but in the world of ***The Whirlpool*** young poets don't make advances on young matrons (though it might be desired of them). No, Patrick is infected with Fleda's fascination with the symbolic whirlpool and decides that, in lieu of indelicately making overtures to her, he will swim across it, with foreseeable consequences.

Meanwhile, in the same general area (but rarely interacting with the doomed nonlovers), the widow Maud looks after the undertaking business she inherited when her husband and in-laws died in an epidemic. The epidemic spared her young son, but it had left him tetched and quite strange. First the toddler refuses to speak a word, and then very quickly he develops a kind of echolalia and, soon after, an uncanny knack for word association games of a symbolic character. And I quote:

> "What's nothing?" asked Patrick.
>
> "Noth-ing," said the child, carefully enunciating both syllables.
>
> "Yes, but where?"
>
> "Be-reavement," said the child.
>
> "Whose bereavement?" asked Patrick, surprised.
>
> "Sorrow," replied the child with a bored sigh, something close to a yawn. "Wheelbarrow?"
>
> "Have you lost your wheelbarrow?"
>
> The child stroked his toy and looked absently around the yard. "Floater," he said vaguely.

Vagueness is another specialty of the author, as of many other first novelists, who find that quality so much more evocative than specificity. Boredom often accompanies vagueness, as it did above and does again here: "The vague anger that he had felt towards the American Regiments when he had sat down to write had been replaced by boredom." A reader with postmodern sensibilities can't help hearing a self-reflective echo in this conjunction of vagueness, anger and boredom with the act of writing. First novelists are often geniuses of unconscious self-revelation.

To be fair, Ms. Urquhart has some writerly oddities all her own, especially a mechanistic conception of the human mind as a kind of VCR that replays both memories and imaginings as it ordains. Here is Robert Browning in such a moment of automatic recall:

> He quickened his steps, hoping that if he concentrated on physical activity his mind would not subject him to the complete version of Shelley's "Lines Written Among the Euganean Hills." But he was not to be spared. The poem had been one of his favourites in his youth and, as a result, his mind was now capable of reciting it to him, word by word, with appropriate emotional inflections, followed by a particularly moving rendition of "Julian and Maddalo" accompanied by mental pictures of Shelley and Byron galloping along the beach at the Lido.

If Ms. Urquhart could sustain that tone of naïve misapprehension, ***The Whirlpool*** might have been one of those counterclassics of literature, which are common enough in poetry (Think of the great Scottish bard, William McGonagall! Think of the Sweet Singer of Michigan, Julia Moore!) but much rarer among novels (at least those that come to be published). But Ms. Urquhart's bizarre model of human memory is more a first novelist's convenience than a genuine lunacy: it is there because it allows her a marvelous expository ease. Whenever she must fill us in on the background of her characters, the VCR of involuntary memory simply reels it off.

What is Robert Browning, who appears in a prologue and an epilogue, doing in the book? Since these framing vignettes have no connection to the Canadian chapters (except for his being Fleda's favorite poet), this is a real poser. My guess is that (1) he is dying in Venice, an essentially romantic activity, and (2) his presence authenticates the novel's claim to being literature, a higher critical realm in which it may be accounted a mark of seriousness to be dull and portentous.

It may be, of course, that I am entirely mistaken. Critics can be. Critics in Canada, whence this book comes to us, have hailed its "moody, incisive and shimmering prose" and its "elaborated density of theme and pattern," and proclaimed it to be "a powerful and accomplished work." They may be right—or they may simply be Canadian and very loyal to one of their own. If the latter is the case, a wonderful possibility has opened up for unpublished first novelists from this country who share Jane Urquhart's disposition and gifts. Emigrate!

Janice Kulyk Keefer   (review date April 1990)

SOURCE: "Stormy Weather," in *Books in Canada,* Vol. IXX, No. 3, April, 1990, pp. 31-2.

[*Keefer is a Canadian poet, short story writer, novelist, and critic. In the review below, she praises the prose style and originality of* Changing Heaven, *but faults the novel's structure and Urquhart's attempts to "demystify" Emily Brontë.*]

Like her first novel, **The Whirlpool,** Jane Urquhart's latest work of fiction plunges us into a world of passions and marvels and intricate obsessions. **Changing Heaven** opens with a meditation on wind and weather, invoking those tempests of mind and heart without which we cannot achieve our full stature or understand our true nature as human beings. Urquhart's new novel is, in large part, a love affair with another novel, *Wuthering Heights,* one of the strangest, most powerful texts in the English language. At crucial moments in **Changing Heaven,** climactic scenes from Emily Brontë's novel are echoed: lightning strikes, windows are wrenched open to let whirling blizzards in, the wild winds of the Yorkshire moors river through the hair and heads of those whose souls are large enough to welcome them.

Within this doubled structure, Urquhart develops two interrelated love affairs: that between a 19th-century balloonist, Polly Smith (a. k. a. Arianna Ether), and her Svengali, the Arctic-enamoured Jeremy Unger, and that between a 20th-century, would-be Catherine Earnshaw, Ann Frear, and her elected Heathcliff, an obsessed art historian named Arthur Woodruff. During the painful work-

ing out of her passion for Arthur, Ann also becomes involved with John Hartley, a Yorkshireman who combines a love of Greek and carpentry: eventually the two establish a temporary idyll similar to that enjoyed by Catherine Heathcliff and Hareton Earnshaw at the end of *Wuthering Heights.*

Yet to complement the elemental, infinite, and eternal "weather" of Emily Brontë's novel, Urquhart creates an "ordinary" fictive world, giving us vignettes of Ann's girlhood and adolescence in the Toronto of Hurricane Hazel, and evoking the desperate but dreary world of motel-room trysts on the outskirts of Toronto the Good. She is uncannily good in her illumination of the densely furnished recesses of certain characters' minds. Her account of the genesis of Arthur's passion for Tintoretto is as much a *tour de force* as her depiction, in **The Whirlpool,** of the extraordinary coming-into-speech of the undertaker's child; in one of **Changing Heaven's** most powerful extended metaphors, Arthur burns his hands in his attempt to emulate Tintoretto's techniques and vision, and subsequently loses the capacity to feel and touch, if not to hold. It is Ann's misfortune to fall violently in love with the married Arthur (during an electrical storm, of course) and to attempt to make him into that soul mate for whom she's yearned since her girlhood devouring of *Wuthering Heights.*

Urquhart's prose is poetic, in Virginia Woolf's definition of that term: it is not lyrical so much as metaphysical, concerned with "that side of the mind which is exposed in solitude . . . its thoughts, its rhapsodies, its dreams." Urquhart is a master of perceptual realization; remarkable for the fineness as well as the acrobatic quality of her intelligence. But as far as the actual structure of her novel is concerned (its ability to support and carry through the magnificence of her conceptions), important doubts must be raised. For this reader, at least, one aspect of this novel that simply doesn't work is the sequence of interludes between the ghosts of the rather bubble-headed Arianna Ether and an Emily Brontë who has been stripped of her fierceness and mystery, and turned into something of a girlish prattler, expounding on the writing of *Wuthering Heights* and the queer twists of her family life. For anyone unfamiliar with the mystique of the Brontës, and with the tantalizingly small amount that is known of Emily in particular, the information Urquhart's Emily provides will undoubtedly be interesting. It may be useful for appreciating those resonances of *Wuthering Heights* that Urquhart has worked into her own fiction about the effect of Emily Brontë's fiction on Ann and her lovers. But those acquainted with the exemplary power and scope of Brontë's vision in *Wuthering Heights,* and its concentrated focus, may end by being puzzled and dissatisfied with the ghosts raised by Urquhart in **Changing Heaven.** Perhaps she is trying to demystify the figure of Emily Brontë, to make her an approachable *semblable* and Beatrice figure not only for the rather slow-witted Polly/Arianna but for the reader as well. But the demystification of Emily Brontë is an uphill, and I would think self-defeating task, one which seriously weakens the structure, and therefore the power of **Changing Heaven.**

Urquhart is a master of perceptual realization; remarkable for the fineness as well as the acrobatic quality of her intelligence.

—Janice Kulyk Keefer

Ingmar Bergman's enormous admiration for Andrei Tarkovsky derived from the Russian director's ability to move with superb ease in and out of "the room of dreams." The secret of Tarkovsky's genius, Bergman suggests, is that he never *explained;* that in works of the highest imaginative order, the logic of image and desire is such that explanation is superfluous and diminishing. Having Emily Brontë explain to Polly and the reader so much of what is already implicit in Urquhart's re-envisioning and invoking of *Wuthering Heights* is a substantial miscalculation. In addition, the detail and arcana that Urquhart pours out in the course of an increasingly freighted narrative, as well as the fictions-within-this-fiction prompted by another fiction—the stories told by that rustic *beau-idéal,* John Hartley—may strike the reader as unnecessary amplifications and as digressions instead of developments. One may feel that Urquhart failed to be sufficiently selective in her use of that wealth of material she uncovered in the course of writing her novel: that by simplifying or compressing the structure of her novel, she might have achieved a form to match her splendid vision.

Yet the intricacy and ardour of Urquhart's prose combined with the dazzling ambition of her imaginative conception; her preoccupations with aesthetics—for example, the arrangement of objects on a windowsill, the play of light on surfaces—as well as with our darker and deeper emotions, make her one of the most compelling and accomplished voices in contemporary Canadian fiction. She is a writer who not only takes enormous risks; she offers us, as well, extraordinary rewards.

Bin Ramke   (review date May-June 1990)

SOURCE: A review of *The Whirlpool,* in *The Bloomsbury Review,* Vol. 10, No. 3, May-June, 1990, p. 21.

[*In the following review, Ramke, an American poet and educator, praises* The Whirlpool *for the feeling of poetry it conveys.*]

The events of Jane Urquhart's first novel [*The Whirlpool*] take place on various borders; not merely the geographical and geological border between the United States and Canada (on the Canadian side of Niagara Falls), but also on borders between married couples, between those with language and those without, even between the living and the dead. The characters include Maud Grady, the widow of the town's deceased undertaker, a widow about to shed her mourning, whose skin has been next to crepe (milled in Halstead, England, "on secret looms in secret factories,") so long it is now stained a deathly gray. Her child,

who "progresses" from his early absolute quiet, to speaking words at random, to attaching particular words to the wrong objects or events:

> "Onion," said the boy.
>
> "Nickel," said Patrick.
>
> The child was not to be moved. He retaliated with the word "shovel."
>
> The child stroked his toy and ignored the coin. "Salad fork!" he sang as the trolley, making a great deal of noise, rolled by. "Ri-ver."

And there is the poet, Patrick, taking a rest in Niagara. If the book sometimes has the feel and freedom of poetry, even of surrealistic poetry, this may have something to do with Jane Urquhart's excellence as a poet—she is the author of three books of poems, including the amazingly beautiful *I Am Walking in the Garden of His Imaginary Palace,* illustrated by artist Tony Urquhart. But Urquhart's first novel *is* a novel, and it tells a fascinating story, although it is difficult to say exactly whose story. In the end, it is not the story of the widow of the undertaker, nor of her son (who, still having no apparent grasp of the meaning of any single word, is finally able to mimic the tone and reproduce exactly the conversations of all adults around him—a devastating talent); nor of the married couple, nor of the poet, Patrick, who spies on the wife, then leaves her in horror when she shows an interest in him; nor is it the story of the man who, like some perversion of St. Peter, becomes a fisher of men, pulling the bodies of suicides and daredevils of the whirlpool below the Falls in exchange for whiskey; nor is it the story of the Canadian-military-historian in all his nationalistic fervor. Maybe it is the story of the river, and of the devastation wrought by beautiful natural events which power their way through and between human lives, inevitably eroding, leaving a mark. Or in a marvelously misdirecting sort of way, the protagonist could be poetry (but don't worry—you don't have to actually *read* any), as the book is bracketed by a few pages of marvelous mock-documentary/ stream of consciousness of Robert Browning in his last days. And each of the characters is a sort of poet, in a peculiar or perverse sort of way. Poetry is often explicable simply as the act of naming, and this book is filled with naming: "Going to the display room . . . Sweet repose, Journey's End, Gone Before, she murmured, reciting the familiar names of the various coffins" or, to return to that fascinating child, a sort of *idiot savant* of language:

> . . . these words, disconnected from their sources, began to astound Patrick, to set up ridiculous yet poetic associations. All at once he was certain that, when he visited the river in the future, he would be unable to do so without conjuring streetcars in his imagination. Likewise, from this day on, he supposed that journeys on streetcars would include water moving behind his forehead. Finally, this idea delighted him . . .

As the idea, and this book, will delight anyone who has the good sense to read it. We could consider it Canada's latest gift.

> [The Whirlpool] is strongly Canadian in flavour, set firmly in the Victorian sensibilities of the late 19th century.
>
> —*Val Ross, in "Urquhart Wins a Top Award in France—Marquez, Singer Honoured in Past," in* The Toronto Globe and Mail, *17 March 1992.*

Elìn Elgaard   (review date Summer 1991)

SOURCE: A review of *The Whirlpool*, in *World Literature Today*, Vol. 65, No. 3, Summer, 1991, p. 487.

[*In the following review, Elgaard discusses characterization in* The Whirlpool.]

Set in the (Canadian) Niagara of the 1880s, Jane Urquhart's first novel portrays characters who seek life rather than live it. Patrick, the poet, observes landscape—and the woman "mysteriously" inhabiting it—as perfect, ethereal architecture, not to be sullied by the mundane (i. e., flesh-and-blood vulnerability). Fleda, the dreamer, reads and breathes Browning's poetics, soon Patrick's as well, with a tenderness—for his *reality*—that he cannot countenance: "Patrick began to shake. He felt his privacy, his self, had been completely invaded—How dare she? he thought as if she, not he, had been the voyeur—She was not supposed to be aware of the lens he had fixed on her." David, Fleda's husband and a history researcher, is obsessed by the ghost of Laura Secord, supposed to have made a journey on foot (with one cow) to Indian territory; his collections of fact seem to Patrick mere "documented rumours" and, to Fleda, metaphors for other things.

Nominally on the sidelines is Maud, the undertaker's widow who, with the Old River Man, picks up the pieces of anonymous lives after annual stunts through the Falls—and springtime's desperate drownings in the river. Through her son, however, she achieves near-centrality: that taciturn small child's capacity for life working in "an echo, then a spiral," which, contrary to reader expectation, wants to *save* the living rather than (like the titular whirlpool's magnetism) take them. With Patrick, the boy celebrates words, attaching himself to the maudlin poet, repeating fragments of his remarks till a game is set in motion, rhythmic and self-generating like childhood's first: "talking / walking / stalking / gawking—the laughter had taken hold of them both by now, shaking their rib-cages and rattling their windpipes." Later he invades his mother's closet of carefully kept "unidentifieds" (found on drowned victims over the years) and classifies them, stone with stone, et cetera. She wakes to see him truly:

> —he was standing in the doorway gazing at her—Lit from behind his hair like a brilliant halo—and Maud perceived he was the possessor of all the light—Now the child had caused all the objects that surrounded her, the relics she catalogued, to lose their dreadful power.

It is clear that child's intense, associative world is the one recommended; and after Patrick's tragic end—his only way of becoming one with a nature he fears—Fleda realizes this: "Nobody understood. It wasn't the message that was important. It was the walk. The journey—Setting forth."

The same journey is seen in Fleda's dreamy whirlpool games—little vessels made from birch bark and pushed into the currents, a complete revolution meaning a long life. Patrick, on the other hand, could only play "Poohsticks" with a difference, trying to *understand* the current, using field glasses to account for every one. The child's "pool" of thought is a word expanded, for dangerous sun *as well as* warm water; his lack of fear is seen as a sinister "lack of emotion" only by an adult world forgetful of visionary origins.

Jeffrey Canton   (essay date 1991)

SOURCE: "Ghosts in the Landscape," in *paragraph*, Vol. 13, No. 2, 1991, pp. 3-5.

[*In the following essay, based on an interview with Urquhart, Canton reveals Urquhart's thoughts on the writing process and the role of landscape and the fantastic in her work.*]

"I had explored the graveyard outside the Bronte parsonage," explains Jane Urquhart, "but on my way out to the moors, I noticed another graveyard, slightly newer. Wandering through it, I saw a tombstone engraved with a balloon, and a woman's name and dates. It's one of the most terrifying graveyards that I've been in. When I went to live in Yorkshire, in the village of Stanbury, which is as close to the site of *Wuthering Heights* as you can get, I asked about this grave, and was told that the woman buried there had been a stunt performer. She took off over the Bronte moors as part of a village gala, and parachuted from the balloon over the moors; but the parachute didn't open and she was killed."

"I thought to myself—of all places to come crashing down, the Bronte moors are probably the best. You might become a ghost, and this would be a terrific place to haunt. You might run into another ghost, and that's basically how the novel began in my mind."

In Toronto to read at Harbourfront and launch her second novel, *Changing Heaven*, Urquhart, in conversation, is as provocative as the fiction she writes. The wild, wuthering atmosphere of *Changing Heaven* seems almost to hover above us. She is constantly shifting about, moving, gesturing, bursting with a restless energy that outraces speech, weaving a web of thoughts and ideas intricately about us.

The tombstone of Lucy Cove that triggered *Changing Heaven*, Urquhart explains, is the kind of image that usually sets her off on her fictional travels. "The idea for a novel," she says, "usually precedes the actual writing. It's something that I carry around with me—I read around it, think about it, visit the landscape. When I was writing *The Whirlpool*, I spent a great deal of time in the forest which is above the Niagara River whirlpool itself. And, I read, among other things, the diary of a woman called Julia

Cruickshank, who was married to a military historian who was supposed to be building her a house in this landscape. That was certainly part of the genesis of that novel."

"In addition, my husband Tony comes from the oldest undertaking family in Canada. His family had a little book that belonged to his grandmother, wherein she recorded items found on bodies retrieved from the Niagara River. Like a character in that novel, she also dug up cannonballs and buttons and things when she was gardening; and the funeral home was located on the battleground of Lundy's Lane. I never met Tony's grandmother, and my imaginary concept of this woman was probably very different from the woman she might have been, though I discovered subsequently that I wasn't that far off. Tony's mother also told me stories about what it was like to grow up in that particular environment, so it was real, it was given to me."

Urquhart is bent on exploring fictional worlds, and *Changing Heaven* leads us into the midst of Emily Bronte's fantastic high Gothic masterpiece, *Wuthering Heights.* The spirit of Emily Bronte herself roams the moors in Urquhart's book, landscaping them to fit her moods, and she is joined by the spirit of 19th century balloonist Arianna Ether. Not a spiritualist herself, Urquhart nonetheless adores ghosts. "There is something about the literature of the 19th century that suggests a more viable atmosphere for ghosts. It's probably the inheritance of writers like Edgar Allen Poe."

"As far as believing in them—I haven't decided. I'm not the sort of person who belongs to psychic research societies. If I were, no doubt my ghosts might be more ponderous individuals."

She is careful to add, "The ghosts in *Changing Heaven* are ghosts on a metaphorical level as well as on an actual level. In a way, they haunt the book. I like to think of Emily Bronte as haunting her own presence in the story. Emily and Arianna don't manifest themselves as howling, shrieking phantoms dragging their chains behind them. They are not out to drive anyone mad with fear; the ghost of Emily Bronte is very much against haunting. On the whole, they are lighthearted ghosts—but they do talk about serious issues, particularly about women and men and how they regard each other."

Urquhart admits that she is obsessed with *Wuthering Heights.* "I chose Emily Bronte," she says, "partly because of my great admiration for her work, and, accidentally, because of the discovery of Lucy Cove's grave. I wanted to hear, I suppose, what Emily would have had to say about romantic love, for example—a topic that one chooses these days at one's own risk when writing a novel. I didn't have a preconceived plan about what shape her character was going to take, and I was surprised to discover that she became so pragmatic."

Urquhart adamantly maintains, "I wasn't interested in writing a fictional biography of Emily Bronte based on a transcription of 19th century letters and diaries. I wanted her to develop in my own mind. I feel that she was a strong character, a little bossy and with an enormous imaginative scope. Not an ethereal, Emily Dickinson type, but robust—she did spend enormous amounts of time tramping

about the moors with her vicious dog, Keeper." *Changing Heaven* also has autobiographical elements. Urquhart makes it clear that Ann Frears, the protagonist of the novel, is not a fictional stand-in for Jane Urquhart; the childhood sections of Ann's story have parallels in Urquhart's life. "If there is any part of *Changing Heaven* that is autobiographical, it's Ann's obsession with *Wuthering Heights.* I read it when I was 9 or 10 years old. I didn't necessarily understand it—I wasn't that precocious—but I certainly found myself fascinated by the concept of this out of control passion that, in the novel, is totally reflected in the landscape. I'm sure that Emily Bronte chose the name Heathcliff because the combination of those two words, heath and cliff, dominate the land there."

"In *The Whirlpool,*" she explains, "landscape operates in the same way that the weather does in *Changing Heaven.* The landscape is in a state of turbulence and flux. Granted, that is also to some degree true of the moors, but the moors are earthbound, and the changes and fluctuations that take place on the moors are dependent on atmospheric conditions. Not so with Niagara Falls. That's my husband's part of the world, a part of the world that I visited often. I found that the Niagara region and that river, in particular, were so resonant with meaning. I have a feeling that landscape reflects personality more than we perhaps give it credit. When I looked at the river for the first time, it astounded me."

"I need more than a superficial connection with the landscape I'm going to discuss in a novel," Urquhart adds. "I need to actually live in the place for a while. When I lived near Haworth, for example, I would take long walks on the moors—not because I thought that I was a reincarnation of Emily Bronte and could experience everything she did by being out there—but so as to be able to pick up details of the world surrounding me. You know when you are on the moors that these are Emily Bronte's moors. In *Changing Heaven,* Emily's ghost discusses creating the moors with Arianna, and, in a sense, she really did create them for the rest of us—we will never see them in any other way. They are hers, they belong to her."

Obsession is the stuff of Jane Urquhart's fiction.

—Jeffrey Canton

Changing Heaven blends the fantastic and the fabulous with the dailiness of contemporary life in Toronto. Part of the novel is three stories that Bronte scholar Ann Frears is told when she stays in Yorkshire. To Urquhart, "Telling stories is an important part of the human psyche. Wanting to shape the events of our lives, to give them order. Transforming our daily lives into the stuff of myth."

"In Stanbury, I lived with my husband and daughter in a little cottage much like the one in the novel, and we met the most wonderful people. Very strong and rich, spiritually rich. They have had incredibly difficult lives, the Yorkshire people, yet they have held onto their sense of self in the most remarkable way. And they are born story-tellers, once they get over their reticence about your being a stranger. The stories in *Changing Heaven* are based on fragments that I heard in 'The Friendly Pub,' although they developed into something entirely different from the stories that I heard."

"The Yorkshire people are very practical and down to earth, yet they have a strong streak of magic in them, similar to the Irish. They know what their landscape is, they know their community, and they like to add myths to their lives. When I finished *Changing Heaven,* it struck me that the Brontes were probably the wonderful writers they were because they came out of that tradition of Yorkshire storytelling."

"These people in Stanbury," she tells me, "are the grand-children of the Reverend Patrick Bronte's parishioners. They talk about the Brontes as part of the community that their grandparents knew—'Oh, that Bramwell, he was a bad lot.' There was one woman who told me, 'The trouble with those girls was they never got married. Because shoes wouldn't and clogs dasn't.' And that meant that people who wore shoes were of a higher class than that of a simple parson and his daughters, while clogs were working class and that class dared not communicate with the parson's daughters on a romantic level. So the Brontes were in a kind of limbo between classes."

Obsession is the stuff of Jane Urquhart's fiction. It is a theme that she explores not only in *Changing Heaven* but in her earlier novel, *The Whirlpool,* as well. "I don't think many authors can write without being obsessed," she explains. "Unless you care deeply about your material, you are not going to have the emotional impulse to pull your-self all the way through the book. An enormous amount of time goes into writing a novel, and usually I'm obsessed from the day I first sit down to write the first sentence until I finish the tenth draft. I'm obsessed with obsessions. I have to be obsessed with the subject and I'll hold it in my mind for long periods of time. And think about it, play with it, talk about it. My friends know exactly where I am in the writing of my next book—I'm boring them all to death talking about the Irish potato famines of the 19th century. Interest in the subject isn't enough for me—I really have to know it. Reading and research are only tools—I couldn't have written *Changing Heaven* if I hadn't lived in Stanbury, experienced the landscape, walked it for miles and miles."

Urquhart's next project "centres in part around the whole kind of extended family that I grew up in—this extended Irish family that immigrated to Canada around the time of the potato famine. It will be a new experience for me because it involves many kinds of characters which I haven't dealt with in my fiction to date."

"I want to explore the myth of that Ireland which the im-migrants brought with them, that culminated in the ro-manticization of that land, and that became stronger as the generations moved forward and further away from it. I heard stories when I was growing up that had been liter-ally handed down from my great-great-great-grandfathers! Stories that focused on all kinds of real and imagined injustices, and the difficulty of keeping your sense of self when there's a great imperialist power loom-ing over you. Which I think we can relate to looking south of the border."

"The other side of the book—there are always two sides to my books—has to do with magic. I'm very curious about the concept that the Irish have of a person who is *away*—someone who has been touched by the supernatu-ral world. When such a person returns to the cottage kitchen, that person is not really *back*. The Irish some-times believe that if a certain person has been touched by the supernatural, that what you have in that cottage kitch-en is a supernatural being who has been disguised as that individual."

"I'm hoping to work that concept of being *away* in a su-pernatural sense with the concept of immigration to a new land. When you are there, *away* from the homeland, the homeland then takes on the aspect of a myth."

Susan Macfarlane   (review date Spring 1992)

SOURCE: "Train & Balloon," in *Canadian Literature,* No. 132, Spring, 1992, pp. 209-10.

[*In the following excerpt, Macfarlane praises Urquhart's "tight interlacing of metaphor, structure and theme" in* Changing Heaven.]

Changing Heaven is a novel apparently fragmented into individual stories telling of separate characters in the nine-teenth and twentieth centuries. . . . [T]hese stories are linked through theme and recurrent images, but the char-acters, too, begin to merge into each other's stories. Ar-thur and Ann, two twentieth-century academics, have at first separate chapters, but their stories converge as they become enmeshed in an increasingly stormy affair. The story of two nineteenth-century balloonists parallels *Wu-thering Heights* in some aspects and the ghost of Emily Brontë figures in their tale, told intratextually by a moor-land sage Ann is coming to love. In this intense and com-plicated structure, time is spatialized to bring the stories of these characters together under the (internal) storytell-er's control in a frenzied, storm-tossed chapter. These winding stories show the wind to be the book's theme. The academics intellectualize the wind and see it, in art, as a metaphor of passion: Ann associates it with the passion of *Wuthering Heights*; Arthur is obsessed with the tempest-tossed angels in Tintoretto. One of many angels, fallen or otherwise, who link the narrative levels of the novel is the balloonist Arianna who falls to her death at the start of the novel.

The reader is enthralled not by plot but by the tight inter-lacing of metaphor, structure and theme: it is not only the wind which aspires to change heaven, controlling destiny, but each of the characters reflects this thematic desire to shape and control as well. Urquhart explores this theme from a variety of perspectives and narrative levels. The convergence in the climax is overwhelming; . . . I look forward to reading more of Urquhart.

Nancy Wigston   (review date August 1993)

SOURCE: A review of *Away*, in *Quill and Quire*, Vol. 59, No. 8, August, 1993, p. 28.

[In the following review, Wigston offers a favorable assessment of Away.*]*

In Jane Urquhart's fictional renderings of the Canadian past, history is transformed into a series of fluid images. The title of her new novel, *Away*, reverberates with meaning. First, it indicates the mysterious condition suffered by Irish peasant women who have encountered a daemon lover from the "other world," the enchanted realm that now and then collides with this one. Second, it refers to the forced migration of the Irish to Canada, forced when the deadly scythe of the potato famine cut them down without mercy.

Urquhart's book juggles an ambitious sweep of history, myth, and geography, from County Antrim to the environs of Belleville and Port Hope (in what is now Ontario) in the early years of the Canadian union. Inevitably, some myths travel better than others. Little in the book is more powerful than the opening scene, when a woman called Mary witnesses a quirky miracle on an Irish beach: a storm pushes quantities of cabbages, silver teapots, and barrels of whiskey towards shore. The sea's last gift? A half-drowned sailor. For Mary, nothing will ever again be the same.

Although Mary is "away," she marries Brian O'Malley, the local schoolmaster, and has a child, Liam. They emigrate to Canada when her second child, Eileen, is born. But a strange destiny calls Mary, more magnetic than her short-lived prosperity in the new world. Her children grow up in the forest, her husband retreats to a bitter memory of nationhood, surrounded by his foes from the Protestant Orange Lodge.

The book examines the way ethnic hatreds seeded themselves in the minds of settlers—a timely message for today. The music and poetry of the Celts are a sensuous delight, but turn poisonous when mixed into a Fenian political stew. With its unerring sense of place and enduring portraits of Irish-Canadians, *Away* makes a lyrical, passionate case for respect for the land and its myths, whether they be Celtic or Ojibway, or best of all, a blending of the two.

Elizabeth Grove-White   (review date 11 September 1993)

SOURCE: "A Dazzling Novel of Home and Away," in *The Globe and Mail*, Toronto, September 11, 1993, p. C22.

[In the following review, Grove-White praises Urquhart's evocation of time and place in Away, *noting that despite the specificity of its locale, the novel has universal relevance.]*

For anyone who believes that Canadians, or at least Canadians of European descent, are soulless, sexless creatures who inhabit not so much a landscape as a bottom line, Jane Urquhart should be required reading. Like Michael Ondaatje in Toronto and Jack Hodgins on Vancouver Is-

land, Urquhart dreams our history for us, peopling the countryside around Lake Ontario with revenants born in memory, in imagination, in that enigmatic place where history and geography overlap.

Away, Urquhart's ambitious, dazzling new novel, recounts an alternative history of Canada lived through several generations of an Irish family who settle in Southern Ontario. Beginning in Ireland in the final years of the old Celtic world, the story, told by the family's women, brings us to present-day Lake Ontario, to an equally endangered landscape. The novel opens with Mary, the young Gaelic-speaking storyteller whose life changes forever when she falls in love with the dying sailor she finds washed ashore on her remote island. Driven away from her land by the potato famine, she survives the deadly Atlantic crossing and the horrors of Grosse Isle's quarantine station to die mysteriously on the shores of a Canadian lake.

Her Canadian-born daughter Eileen picks up the story's thread, moving us to the bustling new Ontario town of Port Hope, the flooded streets of Montreal's Irish shantytown and finally to Ottawa, where her passion for a young dancer joins private and public histories together in a fateful encounter with Thomas D'Arcy McGee.

From the family farm on the shores of Lake Ontario, Eileen's granddaughter Esther, the family's final witness, moves the story to the present day. The house, charged with memory, is part of a countryside being consumed by industry. Desperate to preserve memory, Esther fills the house with unintelligible notes stuck to objects and furniture recording their history and her own. It is Esther's voice, the voice of the last storyteller invoking the family's ghosts, that weaves these fragments into a coherent saga spanning the generations.

Urquhart has, however, less in common with Mazo de la Roche or John Galsworthy that she has with those great lyrical storytellers, Emily Bronte and Thomas Hardy. Like them, she is preoccupied, not by the minutiae of day-to-day experience, but by moments of lived intensity. The everyday lives of the characters—the usual stuff of generational novels—happen out of sight; what remains are moments of such luminous, piercing vision they bring tears to the eyes—the sweet curve of a man's sleeping body, the complete world that is hidden in a rockpool, the rapture of a dance. *Away* is a necklace of such moments, strung together on the serviceable thread of familiar family saga.

Like Hardy and Bronte, Urquhart claims kinship with a much older tradition of bards, dream weavers and myth makers, no mere entertainers, but the living memories and maps of their people and the land they lived on. In *Away*, as in the older stories, time erodes inessential detail, weathering characters so that what remains are less individuals than impersonal, elemental types, forces of history and landscape.

Ultimately time and place are *Away*'s main characters, reminding us of a truth we forget at our peril: we are, in an old Gaelic phrase, the tenants of time and place, not their colonizers. They possess us, not we them.

Like all great storytellers, Urquhart is rich in language,

An excerpt from *Away*

Late the next morning Aidan and Eileen awoke to the smell of mildew and dissolved wallpaper paste; odours they had ignored the night before. They dressed and descended the damp stairs to assess the damage to the rest of the house. A film of pale brown mud covered all the furniture that had not been taken to higher ground and stained the cracked walls and warped floorboards. Detritus was everywhere: handbills, twigs, newspapers, hair ribbons, one glove, a toy boat and, in a first-floor room, a trout, imprisoned, drowned by air, flopping feebly in the half inch of water that remained. . . .

"They'll be back soon," he said, "to clean this up."

"They?"

"The ones that live here." He took Eileen's hand and led her to a small room at the north end of the central hall. "This is where my father died," he said darkly, "though there's nothing of him left here at all . . . nothing at all."

"When did he die?"

"Last year." Aidan rubbed dirt from the surface of one window pane, revealing a view of a narrow plot of mud surrounded by a broken board fence. "He was forty-eight. Died in his sleep. Heart failure."

"Do you have brothers and sisters?"

"Not any more. Only my father and I survived the emigration. My sister died on the boat and then my mother and brothers were taken to the fever sheds. We never saw them again."

"I don't remember my mother," said Eileen, "alive." . . .

"My father worked on the bridge out there," Aidan said, waving his arm towards the south, "and once when they were sinking a piling they came to some bones, and then more bones, and more bones. They'd found the mass grave, you see, where thousands of us were thrown. Everyone working on the bridge was Irish, so it was their own brothers and children and wives they were uncovering. They wouldn't go on with it"—he coughed—"they *couldn't* go on with it . . . no matter what the bosses said. There were fights. Some of the men sat down and wept. No one would turn another inch of soil."

He cleared his throat and looked away from Eileen. "They moved the location of the bridge, then, Misters Brassey and Betts."

"Out of respect?"

"There was *no* respect, Eileen, there is never any respect. You've come to the wrong place if you're looking for that. They did it because the men wouldn't work and there's no labour cheaper than Irish labour."

She noticed that his right hand was clenched.

"They pulled a huge rock out of the river the next week and the men decided it should be a memorial. So there it stands—one great Jesus rock and six thousand Irish under it. That's where my family is."

Jane Urquhart, in her Away, *Viking, 1994.*

spending it generously and fiercely. Her Gaelic voices avoid the top-o'-the-morning, faith-and-Begorrah Synge-song that passes for too often for the Irish voice. In the Irish sections her language sounds miraculously close to that of the great elegiac Gaelic poets of the 17th and 18th centuries. The style serves content: her syntax conjures the bustling optimism of 19th-century Ontario no less than the slow, muffled heartbeat of our own dying landscapes.

Book designer Stephen Kenny has done full justice to *Away,* creating a book that gives as much pleasure to hold as to read. The Burne-Jones painting on the cover might well have been expressly commissioned, the type is clear, unfussy, and the smell of the rich, silky paper reminds us that reading can be as much a sensuous as a cerebral delight. More shame then that the book's copy editors failed to lavish equal care on their work. Punctuation in several places is eccentric without being charming, and in a jarring and unintentionally funny typo, the words "resolution" and "revolution" are confused.

Away gives the lie to reviewers fond of complaining about the unbridgeable division between today's popular fiction and great art. You don't need to be an academic to savour this book. You don't even have to be Irish or Canadian. No: Written by a major novelist at the height of her considerable powers, *Away* is for all of us, for anyone who has ever gone away, and for everyone who comes from away.

Gale Harris   (review date Fall 1993)

SOURCE: "Art and Revelation," in *Belles Lettres: A Review of Books by Women,* Vol. 9, No. 1, Fall, 1993, pp. 23, 43.

[*In the excerpt below, Harris relates Urquhart's focus on art, creation, and obsessive love in* Changing Heaven.]

The relationship between art, the artist, and the appreciation of art has long intrigued writers of fiction. This theme is explored brilliantly in new novels by [Jane Urquhart and other] emerging but already masterful authors who freely transcend boundaries between centuries, life and death, and reality and memory. . . .

In *Changing Heaven,* Jane Urquhart weaves together stories about Victorian and modern couples as she explores obsessive love and the role of imagination in art. . . .

For the three protagonists of Urquhart's second novel, *Changing Heaven,* creation is as disturbing, changeable, and haphazard as emotions or weather. A turn-of-the-century balloonist, Arianna Ether, creates the illusion of an angel's purity and weightlessness when she floats, with the help of a parachute, to earth like the silk of a milkweed pod. Emily Brontë's ghost roams the moors of Arianna's last descent and recalls the "spontaneous combustion" of her childhood fantasies. Ann, a modern-day Brontë scholar, constructs her first book using memories, "their patterns ripped so haphazardly they are impossible to identify."

Arianna and Ann are trapped in obsessive love affairs that unleash a chaos in which the outside world becomes meaningless. They crave intimacy and details to provide a context for their relationships, but their lovers cling to separateness and distance from the color and scenery of life. Emily Brontë's ghost dismisses love as an effort to invent the plot of one's own life story and declares that real men "only interfere with the inventing." When the three women, living and dead, meet on Haworth moor, Urquhart's tumultuous rhapsody to love, remembrance, and creation is brought to a beautifully orchestrated and moving conclusion.

In *Changing Heaven,* Jane Urquhart weaves together stories about Victorian and modern couples as she explores obsessive love and the role of imagination in art.

—Gale Harris

Changing Heaven is a complex book filled with capricious weather, the storms of love, and the ardor of voices telling stories to keep memories and dreams alive. Urquhart's sensuous, inventive prose weaves a spell that catches us in "the perfect balance of *here* and *gone*." She teaches us the value of disturbances and things that change but never disappear. We discover with Ann that the antidote to obliteration can be simple, honest words that act as "a microscope directed at [the] heart and placed there for the purpose of total revelation." . . .

Urquhart [celebrates] the power of creativity not only for the artist but also individuals who lose themselves in works of art. The miracle of artistic creation does not end with weaving a story into a tapestry or carving it into a landscape. It continues to unlock human consciousness. . . . Urquhart's novel, with its imaginative richness, exalts the clarifying winds of change and creation.

Janet McNaughton   (review date October 1993)

SOURCE: "Magically Real," in *Books in Canada,* Vol. XXII, No. 7, October, 1993, p. 44.

[*In the following, McNaughton offers praise for* Away.]

Jane Urquhart's *Away* is a complex layering of ideas about emotions and emotions about ideas. If that sounds too intellectual, *Away* is also one of those novels that moves in and takes over your life. Urquhart writes on a very large canvas, spanning more than a century and two continents. The book begins in pre-famine Northern Ireland, when

beautiful young Mary pulls a drowning man from a sea awash with cabbages, silver teapots, and casks of whisky. The man dies in Mary's arms. Ever after he is regarded as Mary's demon lover and she is thought to be not of this world—"away."

The novel describes what happens to Mary and Brian, the sceptical, self-educated schoolteacher she marries, and to their children, Liam and Eileen. When the famine comes, the family is given passage to Canada by their twin Protestant landlords Osbert and Granville Sedgewick. The sincere and totally ineffectual efforts of these two characters to somehow connect with their Catholic tenants give the narrative a broad comic thread. But beneath the humour, Urquhart conveys the Sedgewicks' sense of loss because they can never feel at home in the country where they were born.

In Canada, the story focuses on Eileen. Mary abandons her family just after this child is born, and Eileen embodies the worst flaws of both parents: Mary's mystic attachment to things she cannot possess, and Brian's bitterness about the wrongs visited upon the Irish. It would be unfair to reveal the way in which these traits shape Eileen's life, but her story is compelling. At the periphery of Eileen's story, Urquhart places D'Arcy McGee, the only political figure to have been assassinated in Canada. Urquhart uses this assassination to explore what it meant to be Irish and Catholic in 19th-century Canada, the nature of nationalism, and the wisdom of nursing old political wounds in a new land. She makes some important points in the process, but her prose never degenerates into polemic.

Urquhart has a way of playing with romance and romanticism that, in her earlier novels, sometimes left the reader (at least this reader) uncertain of her intent. I found it difficult to know if *Changing Heaven* (1990) was a romance, or a novel that explored how the conventions of romance can distort women's lives. In *Away,* Urquhart does not reveal her ideas about Eileen's character, emotions, and politics until the final pages of the book, but when she does, her intent is clear and will take most readers by surprise.

Away is enjoyable not only for its complexity of ideas and subtle characterization, but also for the sheer power of Urquhart's writing. Magic realism is a driving force in this book, but it almost always connects seamlessly with reality. The only concept that seemed incredible to me was that of trying to express a political message by dancing. Everything else, from demon lover to talking crow, rang true. *Away* is simply a great novel.

Barbara Holliday   (review date 17 August 1994)

SOURCE: "Multigenerational Tale Adds Poetic Lift to Women's Issues," in *Detroit Free Press,* Section D, August 17, 1994, p. 3.

[*Holliday is an American critic. In the following review, she relates the story line of* Away.]

Jane Urquhart is an Irish Canadian who writes with the lilt of the Old Sod. Her third novel, *Away,* brings alive an old superstition linked to today's consciousness.

Away is the story of four generations of women, three of whom, in the author's words, are women of extremes. They either stay young into old age or age very young. They thrive near water. Men, states of mind, come and go. In the end, these bright, engaging women describe themselves as being "away."

The writing is poetic, musical, enhanced by the occasional Gaelic phrase. The message is mixed. At times it seems a plea for women's equality; again, it sees love as a fickle male domain, expressed in the words of an old Irish saying: "The most short-lived traces: the trace of a bird on a branch, the trace of a fish on a pool, the trace of a man on a woman."

Esther O'Malley Robertson, 82, is recalling the family history as she heard it at 12 from her grandmother, Old Eileen.

It starts in 1842 when the girl, Mary on Rathlin Island off the north Ireland coast, falls in love with a drowned sailor and, true to superstition, falls into the state of "away," the victim as it were, of the faerie daemons. Only we know of her quickness of mind, her avid curiosity.

In time, she weds the schoolmaster Brian O'Malley, gives him a son Liam and they flee the potato famine to the Canadian wilderness, creating "an acre of light" in the harsh terrain.

Overseas, Mary falls back into her old state after the birth of a daughter, Eileen, and vanishes in the forest, seeking "the darlin' one." Seven years later her frozen body is returned by Exodus Crow and his fellow Ojibway who had befriended the beautiful woman with the red-gold hair.

Eileen eventually falls under the sway of the charismatic nationalist Aidan Lanighan. He leaves her with the memory of his embrace and a gun for safe-keeping.

To the young Esther who will not always heed her words, Old Eileen confessed, "I've been away all my life. . . . If I were you I would be where I stand. . . . No more drifting."

But at another place, we hear the saddest words in this novel of knowledge-seeking women and wrong-footed love. Aidan is explaining to the young Eileen why he dances alone, that he has no partner.

> "There's me," she said . . . "I danced with you once."
>
> "Yes," he admitted, whirling away, "but you didn't know the steps."

Revolutions, one likes to think, have been fought for less.

Kelly Hewson   (review date Winter 1995)

SOURCE: A review of *Away,* in *World Literature Today,* Vol. 69, No. 1, Winter, 1995, pp. 143-44.

[*In the following, Hewson offers a highly favorable assessment of* Away, *noting Urquahart's focus on story and voice.*]

The title of Jane Urquhart's third novel [*Away*] is not just a reference to Mary, an intriguing character who, on a remote island off the northern coast of Ireland, gets taken by a daemon lover, renamed, and claimed by the "otherworld." Rather, the condition of being "away" resonates as a metaphor, reminding us how a writer must feel when she is writing or a reader when she is engaged by fiction, unwilling or unable to leave completely the world of the book, its entrancing geography interrupting the mundane here and now; or how one functions when overcome by passion for another, drifting, as if spellbound, in a dreamlike fog. Urquhart has always been superb at rendering intense states of being, and *Away* offers plenty of such renderings.

This is also a novel about story and voice. Eileen, daughter of the one who went away, tells her mother's and her own story to her granddaughter Esther. She is telling the stories to Esther as warnings—about the hazards of passion and the dangers of change. Mary's story, which traces the hardships endured by the Catholic peasant class in Ireland circa 1840, is the most captivating. Once she and her family migrate to Canada, her story becomes one of abject abandonment, that, through the character of Exodus Crow, Urquhart miraculously manages to make a skeptical reader and Mary's deserted family understand. When the focus of the novel shifts from Mary to Eileen, it engages less intensely. Mary's story is, after all, a hard one to match. Though her voices come from the land she is in—Canada—Eileen drinks from the pool of stories of Ireland's sorrows that her father tells her and takes the voice of an Irish nationalist, a choice for which she gets a cruel comeuppance. Her folly—making up a story about her lover because he won't tell her his—leads to her story's climax and its moral: "All interpretations are misinterpretations."

Although some readers may find the later pace of *Away* sluggish, where Urquhart is consistently superlative is in the crafting of minute, remarkably intense scenes, the power of which cannot be revealed in this short space. What follows is a sample of the author's lyricism and sensitivity as she outlines a desperate community's response to a song heard in the final moments of a bleak wedding celebration.

> There was great sorrow in the song and great joy, also, that the privilege of sorrow had not yet been cast from the people who sang it. The land they stood on had heard such songs as this before and it would hear them again, for it was the music that could not be starved out of it. The women knew that their bones would sing in the earth after their flesh had gone, and the men, who now joined them, knew that the song would make its way through the coming generations.

Early in the novel, one of Urquhart's characters bemoans the tyranny of the English over the Irish—their repression of the Irish language, of Irish voices and stories. In one sense *Away* can be read as an answer to his lament, for in writing it, Urquhart retrieves, in her daring, beautiful fashion, some of the poetry, voices, and stories he has feared cast from his people.

Jane Urquhart with Elaine Kalman Naves   (interview date 7 February 1995 and 2 March 1995)

SOURCE: An interview in *Books in Canada,* Vol. XXIV, No. 4, May, 1995, pp. 7-13.

[*In the following interview, which was conducted over the course of a few weeks in early 1995, Urquhart discusses her life and her art.*]

Jane Urquhart began her literary career as a poet, publishing three collections: *I Am Walking in the Garden of His Imaginary Palace* (1982), *False Shuffles* (1982), and *The Little Flowers of Madame de Montespan* (1983). She has also written a book of short stories—*Storm Glass* (1987)—but she is best known for her novels, all published by McClelland & Stewart: *The Whirlpool* (1986), *Changing Heaven* (1990), and *Away* (1993), which was a co-winner of Ontario's Trillium Award.

This interview has been fused together out of two separate conversations with Jane Urquhart, one by phone on February 7, 1995 and the other in person on March 2 in Ottawa, the day after her husband had received the Order of Canada.

. . . . .

[*Naves*]: *This has been quite a year for you, winning the Marian Engel Award last fall and sort of taking up permanent residence on the* Globe's *best-seller list, not to mention invitations to read in Australia and being published in Germany. What's this all doing to your life and writing?*

[Urquhart]: It's made me schizophrenic, in a way. Because obviously the events that you take part in that are outside of your writing room are outer-life events. I sort of divide my life into inner life and outer life. And fortunately I've had a fair amount of practice doing that most of my life as a result of my ability to be distanced, shall we say, in certain situations. Like schoolrooms and places like that.

Meaning?

Meaning that I was a terrible day-dreamer as a child, as any one of my report cards would attest to.

So you've had experience in what they call splitting?

Yes, I think that must be it! Undoubtedly I should be undergoing severe psychiatric treatment.

Seriously, do you have time to write?

Yes, because the nature of my life has changed quite dramatically since I started writing. When I began to write, I was looking after two stepchildren full time, Tony [Urquhart, her husband]'s two daughters were living with us and they were about 14 and 16. And also I had a small baby, a little girl called Emily, whom Tony and I had shortly after we got married. And Tony's other two children, two boys, came to visit us almost every weekend. And so my domestic life was very, very full. But since then, everyone has grown up. Including me. As a result, the house is a lot calmer and I have great open periods of time that just never existed 10 years ago. I can remember a period when I was doing six loads of laundry a day. But,

in fact, the necessity of me being at home actually contributed to my writing. I think it was a good situation.

That's an interesting spin on the lot of the woman writer, which is something I wanted to ask you about.

I still think it's difficult for some women writers. I was fortunate in that my husband was very supportive of what I was doing, financially as well as emotionally. Which may or may not be a good thing in the eyes of certain feminist groups. But the real truth is it provided me with a little time and security, and that was what I needed to really be able to get into my inner life. Had I been a single woman it might have been a whole different story, in the sense that the big issue is the financial issue. How do you combine the need to write novels—which take an enormous amount of time and an enormous amount of space within that time—with the need to eat? It's not going to support you financially, and even if it eventually does, it's certainly not going to do that in the beginning.

But you have received grants, too, haven't you?

Oh, yes, over the years. Which is another thing that I've learned as a side effect of travelling as an author. The discovery of just how lucky we really are as Canadians. I know that we have a tendency to complain and carry on about cutbacks in grants, but I've been to many countries where there are no grants, where people are astonished that here the government will give certain authors a subsistence level income for a year.

What countries are you speaking about now?

Well, France for instance. It does have certain programs that support the arts and obviously they're terribly interested in the arts. Which is always wonderful and encouraging and perhaps—I'm not sure about this—it might be easier to make a living in France as a writer. Because one of the things I noticed in France is that when you walk into a café, everyone is either reading something or writing something. [*laughing*] And there are wonderful bookstores everywhere. But from what I understand from French authors, the kind of government support that exists in Canada does not exist there.

> **As a child, I learned so much listening to my mother and my aunt talk about what was happening, not only to them but to people around them. They were talking out of real interest and emotional engagement.**
>
> **—Jane Urquhart**

To change the subject a bit, I'm going to be a bit of a devil's advocate with this question. **The Whirlpool, Changing Heaven,** *and* **Away:** *why always the 19th century?*

I think there are a number of reasons for that. One of the most important ones is that I feel in a way as if I grew up in the 19th century. I think that had to do with the fact that my extended family, the Quinn family, my mother's side, the side of the family that I knew best as a child, were mostly agricultural people and they really did live on farms. With woodstoves. And they had horses. They didn't have buggies, obviously they were driving cars, but life had not changed that much since the 19th century. And also when I was a child, and even now, though less and less, sadly, the landscape is the landscape that was created in the 19th century. For better or worse. That's what we had: rail fences and farms and barns and houses, all of which had been constructed in the 19th century. So that the world that I remember most vividly as a child was a sort of 19th-century world that had been adapted to deal with the 20th century.

Another reason was that as a child I spent huge amounts of time reading 19th-century novels, so that there were two realities at work. There was the reality of my extended family operating in the way that their ancestors in Canada had, and the reality of even the books that I read: *The Secret Garden, The Little Prince,* all of Dickens, L. M. Montgomery. And that was a 19th-century world. Another thing, I think, is that it's over, so that you can look back at it and see it. Perhaps incorrectly, but at least you can pretend to see it in a state of completion.

I think that that's the attraction about writing about the past for me. I find it so hard to figure out what's going on today. I marvel at people who can write fiction about contemporary life.

I do, too. I think it's a great gift. But I personally don't have it. I think it's partly because I feel a bit cut off from what's going on today.

Because you live in the country? [In a small village in southern Ontario.]

Partly, and also because of the way I live. I'm fortunate enough, to my mind anyway, that I'm not out there in an office dealing with contemporary life as it seems to exist.

I don't think you've ever had a day job, or have you?

Oh, yes, I have! I used to be the assistant to the information officer for the Royal Canadian Navy! [*laughter*] This was shortly after I'd graduated from university and when I was living with my first husband, who died—I only add that because if I don't people assume that I was divorced.

You were married at 19 and widowed when you were 24, I think.

Yes. My husband was attending the Nova Scotia College of Art and Design and I had already graduated, so I had to get a job and so there it was. I had attended the University of Guelph and graduated with a general degree in English and then we went off to Halifax. That was just a fabulous job. And I've had other day jobs—I was a waitress once, that was a night job in fact, shortly before I married Tony. I think that was the way I made the money for our honeymoon.

Michel Tremblay once told me that his training as a writer consisted in listening to the women who lived in his house-

hold. His mother and aunts and so on. I have the impression that you also were a great listener as a child.

Oh, yes, and under perfect conditions—with thousands of female relatives around. It is true, the women are the people who pass the stories down through the generations in any family. Occasionally, one of the men would tell a story. When they did, it was a very exciting event, and it was often war-related. But the women were constantly gossiping. I've always been a great believer that gossip is not an evil thing. I see it as an investigation of human nature and I think it's absolutely lovely, as long as it's not malicious.

As a child, I learned so much listening to my mother and my aunt talk about what was happening, not only to them but to people around them. They were talking out of real interest and emotional engagement. And then there were the stories that I wasn't supposed to listen to. But that was not a big problem because there was a hot-air grate in my grandmother's house. And when you were sent upstairs— the grate was right over the kitchen table—you could hear everything that was going on in the kitchen.

Now tell me, was this up in Little Long Lac, in Northern Ontario, where you were born, or in Loughbreeze Beach where **Away** *is partially set?*

This was in Northumberland County where Loughbreeze Beach is situated. And all of that side of the family, the Quinns, lived in that area on Ontario farms. I would go there every summer, for the whole summer.

It must be wonderful to have that connection to the land. Although I've read that it's changing very rapidly.

Yes. In fact right at this very moment I'm beginning to be involved in a debate with a developer. I just see the southern Ontario landscape, the agricultural landscape, disappearing. It's terribly sad because it's the second rape of the land as far as I'm concerned. The first being of course the cutting of all of the trees and the clearing of the land to change it from forest to agricultural land. And now we're going to pave all of Ontario! It's very disturbing. It's also disturbing given how little agricultural land there is. The Canadian Shield comes down so far. Mississauga exists on what is some of the best agricultural land in Ontario. It's upsetting to see it disappearing at the rate that it is.

> **I don't think I ever confuse my own identity with the identity of my characters. But that world is very real to me when I'm working on it, which is probably why it's fairly depressing to finish a book, because you let that world go.**
>
> *—Jane Urquhart*

Away *very definitely conveys the sense of loss of that coun-*

tryside. But where do the Celtic legends come into it, and the sense of the occult? Was there a tradition of that in your own family?

There was a tradition of a kind of prescience, particularly among the women of the family, but I was not told Celtic legends as a child or anything like that. There were legends associated with the family and a lot of generational tale-telling. For instance, we would be told stories about our great-grandparents or great-aunts and -uncles as if those people were somehow still with us and alive and functioning. These were almost morality tales in some cases and so I think that was very similar to the Irish experience in the section of the book set in Ireland. These were basically part of the family myth. But as far as Irish folk-tales are concerned, that folkloric side didn't surface in my family. I heard about the history of Ireland and how dreadful the British were. And we were certainly instructed in the evil ways of the Orange Lodge. [*laughing*]

So it was a Catholic family?

Well, in fact, no. They were Catholics in the beginning. I was told over and over again when I visited Ireland that Quinn is a Gaelic name and there's no possibility that the family could have been anything but Catholic. But what seems to have happened—for all I know this may be myth, too—is that when they came to Canada, they changed their religion because they settled in a tiny village called Castleton, which is still there. And there was only one church, so if they wanted to be part of the community, there it was. But all the rest of it stayed in place. All the other children, for instance, were able to go to the Orange Parade, but not the Quinn kids. That was highly disapproved of. And there was great suspicion of the Family Compact and monarchy and all that. It's fascinating to see what does hang on in a family and what disappears.

The figure of Mary-Moira, the great-grandmother with the demon lover, she's all creation, isn't she?

She is completely fictional. I knew that I wanted to write a book about Ireland and the Irish experience, partly from the point of view of Canadians who are of Irish descent and because of my own family's obsession with things Irish. I found it fascinating that they were so many generations removed from the old country and yet so emotionally attached to a place they'd never seen. So I wanted to explore that. But the opening of the book came to me after I'd spent some time in that landscape. I'd been to Rathlin Island and I'd spent a lot of time on the northern coast because my family came from County Antrim. It's one of the most gorgeous landscapes in the world, just stunning and moving and rough. There's a kind of toughness about it, it's not a sentimental landscape, not Wordsworth's "Daffodils" at all. It's very solid and threatening in some ways and very powerful. And after I came back, I was just daydreaming and suddenly the image of the almost completely drowned man floating in on the waves came into my mind and then I knew that I had the opening of the book.

And had you heard of the concept of "away"?

I had, when I was in Northern Ireland.

So this was not something that was in the family?

No, it wasn't. It was an idea that I had as a result of hearing about the concept and wanting to explore "awayness" in terms of both immigration and the idea of being separated from the self. And then the book sort of unfolded from the narrative point of view, like a road that rose to meet me. It was quite lovely.

So how much of this stuff do you actually believe?

I believe it in a fictional sense. When I'm writing it I believe it.

So it came to you and then you had to explore what it would be like to be this woman—

Not even so much as what it would be like to be her, but to be able to be conscious in that world. I don't think I ever confuse my own identity with the identity of my characters. But that world is very real to me when I'm working on it, which is probably why it's fairly depressing to finish a book, because you let that world go.

What were you trying to do with the character of Exodus Crow in the story?

Exodus Crow is a mixed Native character who is very important to the book in ways that are difficult to describe. One of the things that I learned by creating him—he may or may not be accurate (who's ever to say what an accurate example of any particular race is?) —was how similar the Ojibway systems of belief were and are to the Celtic systems of belief. There's an incredible commonality of spiritual experience there. I found that pretty exciting.

I'm curious about your decision not to use dialect in the story.

I made a conscious choice about that. First of all, I wouldn't have had the skill to pull it off. But I also felt that I didn't want it to be one of those "Faith and Begorrah" cute little quaint Irish books. Because it's really a Canadian book, it's about Canada and not Ireland as such. And even when I say it's about Canada, I hope it's much more than that, too. I also think that one of the last stereotypes that appears to have not yet died is that of the staggering, brogue-riven, drunken, cute, funny Irishman. If someone such as myself started to use Irish dialect, it just wouldn't work.

> I think what's interesting about autobiography and fiction for me is that they're so often unconscious. In fact, people will bring things to my attention and I will go "Of course! That's where it came from."
>
> —*Jane Urquhart*

Tell me about your reading habits as a child.

Well, I would say compulsive. I read every *word* that L. M. Montgomery wrote at least three and maybe four times. But I was also reading Louisa May Alcott and Dickens to a great extent. And *Wuthering Heights,* of course.

When did your great interest in the Victorian poets begin?

That began fairly early because my mother had been quite interested in Victorian poetry as a young woman as a result of studying it in high school. She wasn't able to go to university because in her time, of course, if anyone was going to university in a farm family, it certainly wasn't going to be a girl and there were six boys in her family. This was just not an alternative for her. She introduced me to Browning, in particular, when I was 10 or 11. When she was being educated, children were required to memorize poetry and so she knew an awful lot. She could recite all of "My Last Duchess" for instance. Or "Andrea del Sarto." And [*laughing*] she did. I think that was partly what led me to Victorian poets. And of course later on in university I studied them.

Isn't there a story about how your mother wanted to be a novelist when she was a child?

When she was a child, she and her friend decided to collaborate on a novel. So they borrowed the only typewriter in the village, which was at the bank. And the bank manager actually allowed them to take it home for the weekend. They were going to write the novel on the weekend! They had to walk about two miles with this great huge heavy Underwood from the village to the farm. I don't know what happened to that novel. She has never divulged the exact subject of it.

She didn't become a writer, she—

Became a reader. A really serious reader. Shortly after she married my father and they moved to Little Long Lac, where a gold mine was opening. My father had just graduated from mining engineering school at the University of Toronto in 1934 and there were no roads in there at that time and very little getting in and out, except by bushplane. Nevertheless, my mother was able to get the *New Yorker* and the Book-of-the-Month-Club selections. I was telling some people in Australia when I was there that my mother had actually read the novels of Eleanor Dark, whose house I was staying in. (Eleanor Dark has recently been re-released from Virago, a wonderful rediscovered Australian writer.) And my mother was reading works of that nature in Little Long Lac!

At what time did you realize that you wanted to be a writer?

Oh, at about the same time as I realized that I wanted to be a ballet dancer and a star of the Broadway stage. Those three came together at the age of about seven. I think I started to take myself seriously after my daughter was born and I think that's because I lost my child status. One can no longer pretend to be a child when one has a child. This, as I mentioned before, was when things were domestically rather wild with two full-time and two part-time stepchildren and one baby. But it also organized me in a way, I think, to have a baby who was on a certain schedule and who later went to school and came home at certain times. So that I was able to carve out a period of time to myself. For instance, when she was napping. I think I was

able to get two hours a day at that time. And I was fierce about it. I took the two hours regardless of circumstances.

I think a lot of writing comes from the unconscious and in my case usually the best of my writing comes out of the unconscious. I'm not too aware of what I'm doing and I try to somehow remain unaware.

—*Jane Urquhart*

I think you have said that when you were writing **The Whirlpool** *you never expected it to be published?*

I couldn't have written it, I think, if I had allowed myself to believe that it would be published, because it was based on two very real stories. One was the story of Julia Cruikshank, who was the wife of Ernest Cruikshank, the first president of the Ontario Historical Society and a military historian. And the other one was based on my husband's grandmother, who ran the oldest funeral home in Niagara Falls. I never met her personally—she was dead before I met Tony. Nevertheless, I was dealing with his family history. It was so fascinating, I just couldn't help myself. And his parents were alive! I think had I admitted to myself that I was going to try to get the book published, I would have felt terribly inhibited. So I convinced myself that the book was far too weird, no one would ever publish it anyway, so I could just . . . I had to write it really, it was a story that had to be written.

It was about your husband's grandmother, I know, but she was a young widow in the story. And you had been a young widow, too.

Yes, that's true, I hadn't thought about any of that until long after the book was finished. I think what's interesting about autobiography and fiction for me is that they're so often unconscious. In fact, people will bring things to my attention and I will go "Of course! That's where it came from." Not long ago, my mother was talking about a schoolhouse in Northumberland County that she and several other members of the family gave to one of my uncles as a Christmas present, if you can believe it, because it was for sale for $100 and it was the schoolhouse where he began to teach. And I suddenly remembered going up to that schoolhouse as a child about the time that they were going to buy it, and I realized when my mother told me that story that the schoolhouse that I was describing in *Away,* the schoolhouse that existed in Canada, was that schoolhouse. I hadn't thought about it until my mother mentioned it, and she hadn't thought about it either. And then I realized, "That's right. That's where it came from."

I think a lot of writing comes from the unconscious and in my case usually the best of my writing comes out of the unconscious. I'm not too aware of what I'm doing and I try to somehow remain unaware. It works better for me, especially in the first draft, than if I were to sit down and become very conscious of where the narrative was going, what kind of imagery I wanted to use.

I guess also writing in this fey, sometimes supernatural way that you—

I think it would be very self-conscious if I were too aware of what I was doing. Too manipulative somehow.

What do you mean by that?

Formula. I think a formula exists to manipulate the reader and I'm not interested in doing that. I'm more interested in, I suppose, selfishly entertaining myself. [*laughing*]

You've spoken in the past of how art history helped teach you to see. Can you talk a little bit about visual memory—for instance, when you went to Northern Ireland to do research for **Away,** *how did you store away the landscape in your mind so that you could write about it in Canada? Or did it just stay there?*

Well, if I'm very fortunate, it will stay there. For me the best way to remember a landscape is to walk it. When I was in Yorkshire, for instance, before I wrote **Changing Heaven,** I began to do some serious walking. It had nothing to do with any interest in physical health—I'm not really a very athletic person. But with a five-mile distance from the little cottage where I lived to the alleged site of *Wuthering Heights,* I was required to walk because there was no other way of getting there. And I discovered that I just loved it. The experience of walking a landscape is very, very important. And also it's essential that I do it alone. Because if someone else is with me, I'm going to be talking.

So I've done an awful lot of walking in various landscapes, alone. Now, that applies to landscapes I'm not already familiar with. The landscapes of my childhood seem to be just there, I can call them up almost at any time. I can pretty well do almost stone by stone the whole walk home from school. But it's really essential for me to know the landscape that I'm going to be writing about. I have to be able to see where I am when I am writing.

FURTHER READING

Criticism

Fitzgerald, Judith. Review of *I Am Walking in the Garden of His Imaginary Palace,* by Jane Urquhart. *Quill & Quire* 48, No. 10 (October 1982): 33.

> Praises *I Am Walking in the Garden of His Imaginary Palace* as "an extraordinarily well-designed and meticulously crafted book," but laments the quality of the verse.

Houston, Gary. "Symbolism Swirls around Images." *Chicago Tribune* (21 March 1990): section 5: 3.

> Mixed review in which the critic lauds the prose style and symbolism of *The Whirlpool,* but faults the narrative as lacking dramatic interest.

Manguel, Alberto. "Northern Lights: Canada Heats Up." *Village Voice* 33, No. 42 (18 October 1988): 52-3, 101.

> Discusses the genre of the short story in Canada, briefly mentioning Urquhart's work as reflected in the pieces collected in *Storm Glass.* The critic also discusses work by Rohinton Mistry, Sandra Birdsell, and Graeme Gibson.

Ross, Val. "Going for the Magical Is Dangerous." *The Toronto Globe and Mail* (27 September 1993): C1.

> Feature article written on the occasion of the publication of *Away.* Ross discusses Urquhart's emphasis on place, identity, and obsession in her novels.

Seaman, Donna. "Love and Art." *Booklist* 89, No. 14 (15 March 1993): 1296.

> Compares Urquhart's *Changing Heaven* to Barbara Anderson's *Portrait of the Artist's Wife.* Seaman states that both novels "are about the entanglement of love and art, but while [Anderson's is] about creation and fulfillment, the other explores obsession and isolation."

Additional coverage of Urquhart's life and career is contained in the following sources published by Gale Research: *Contemporary Authors,* Vol. 113; *Contemporary Authors New Revision Series,* Vol. 32; and *DISCovering Authors: Canadian Edition 2.0.*

Wendy Wasserstein

1950-

American playwright, scriptwriter, and essayist.

The following entry provides an overview of Wasserstein's career through 1994. For further information on her life and works, see *CLC,* Volumes 32 and 59.

INTRODUCTION

Wasserstein is best known for *The Heidi Chronicles* (1988), winner of several prizes including a Tony Award, a New York Drama Critics Circle Award, and a Pulitzer Prize for Drama. Her plays tend to be humorous and typically concern well-educated women who came of age during the 1960s and 1970s and who must choose between professional careers and the traditional roles of wife and mother.

Biographical Information

Born in Brooklyn, New York, Wasserstein and her family moved to Manhattan in 1962, where she attended private schools. Her interest in the theater began as a child when she was chosen to perform in school plays; later, she turned to playwriting when she discovered that she could be excused from physical education classes by writing musicals for her school's annual mother-daughter fashion show. After graduating from high school, Wasserstein attended Mount Holyoke College in South Hadley, Massachusetts, a private school for women. Wasserstein did not become seriously involved with the theater until her junior year when she took a drama course and acted in several plays. Graduating in 1971, Wasserstein eventually returned to New York City and attended City College, studying creative writing under playwright Israel Horovitz and novelist Joseph Heller before earning her M.A. in 1973. That same year, *Any Woman Can't* (1973), a bitter farce about a woman who tries to secure independence in a male-dominated world, became her first play to be produced professionally. Wasserstein applied to two prestigious graduate programs—Columbia Business School and Yale University School of Drama—was accepted by both, and opted for Yale, where she eventually earned an M.F.A. in 1976. At Yale she received direction from renowned American drama critic Robert Brustein, and met classmates Christopher Durang, Albert Innaurato, and Meryl Streep, all of whom, like Wasserstein, would successfully establish themselves in the theater and the motion picture industry.

Major Works

Noted for their simple story lines, complex characters, and witty dialogue, Wasserstein's plays explore how and why women choose marriage, a career, or a particular way of life, and the feelings of anguish, confusion, and libera-

tion associated with such decisions. Her *Uncommon Women and Others* (1975) focuses on five women approaching their thirties who reunite six years after graduating from Mount Holyoke College. Contrasting the carefree optimism of the characters' college years with their present confusion and disappointment, the play depicts the majority of them as still undecided about what they want to do with their lives. In her next play, *Isn't It Romantic* (1981), Wasserstein concentrates on two women in their thirties—Janie Blumberg, an intelligent and slightly overweight Jewish writer, and her friend Harriet, a beautiful and sophisticated WASP business executive who marries a man she does not love—and their relationships with their mothers. Similar to *Uncommon Women* in many respects, *Isn't It Romantic* focuses on intergenerational conflict, the institution of marriage, and the notion that some women marry simply because it is expected of them. In *The Heidi Chronicles* Wasserstein sharpened her dramatic focus on feminist concerns by examining the social and intellectual development of a single character, an unmarried art historian named Heidi Holland. The play spans approximately 25 years, relating events from Heidi's personal life and professional career. Central to Heidi's development are her relationships with two men and her friendship with a group of women who inspire her involvement with the feminist movement of the 1960s and 1970s. By the 1980s, however, many of her peers have adopted the materialism that they once denounced; consequently, Heidi, who has maintained her commitment to feminist principles, is left disillusioned and feeling isolated. At an alumnae luncheon, which some critics consider the climax of the play, Heidi delivers a long monologue, confessing her feelings of abandonment and her disappointment with contemporary women, explaining, "I thought that the whole point was we were all in this together." Nonetheless, the play ends on an optimistic note with Heidi finding fulfillment as the single parent of a newly adopted daughter. Centering on three conspicuously different middle-aged sisters who share similarities with Wasserstein and her own siblings, *The Sisters Rosensweig* (1992) examines the complicated process of balancing a professional career with romantic relationships. Some reviewers have suggested, however, that this play's most significant theme concerns Jewish identity and the problem of assimilation with mainstream culture.

Critical Reception

While Wasserstein has achieved some success as an essayist and a screenwriter, she is primarily known as one of America's most popular playwrights. Commentators have lauded Wasserstein's *Uncommon Women and Others* for its uncompromising wit and focus on women's issues. Although some reviewers have argued that its episodic structure obscures narrative perspective and dramatic focus, others have found that its plot is far less important than its characters and dialogue, which have been praised as both original and amusing. Commentators generally faulted early versions of *Isn't It Romantic* for its heavy reliance on wisecracks and one-liners; they argued that while such devices provide some genuinely humorous moments, they detract from the somber issues presented in the work. Wasserstein, however, has defended the play's humor, noting that her protagonist uses it as a form of self-defense. The revised version of *Isn't It Romantic,* which was first staged in 1983, was praised for containing sharper characterizations and a clearer focus on mother-daughter relationships. Despite its numerous awards, overall critical reaction to *The Heidi Chronicles* has been mixed. Although some reviewers considered aspects of the play unmotivated and implausible, many found Wasserstein's portrait of Heidi's generation poignant and well-observed. Linda Winer asserted: "[*The Heidi Chronicles*] is a wonderful and important play. Smart, compassionate, witty, courageous, this one not only dares to ask the hard questions . . . but asks them with humor, exquisite clarity and great fullness of heart." William A. Henry III, however, has argued that the "play is more documentary than drama, evoking fictionally all the right times and places but rarely attaining much thorny particularity about the people who inhabit them." Still other commentators have faulted Heidi as an uninteresting character, and many, such as Gayle Austin, have argued that the work provides a disservice to women and the cause of feminism: "The trouble with this play is that although it raises issues, Wasserstein undercuts serious consideration through fac-

ile supporting female characters, sit-com humor, and a passive heroine who forms an absence at the center of the play." Although John Simon has suggested that *The Sisters Rosensweig* is technically Wasserstein's best play to date, most commentators have found it too dependent on situational humor and the contemporaneity of such emotionally-charged social issues as homosexuality, AIDS, and single motherhood. Nevertheless, Wasserstein continues to be recognized for her acute social observations, witty one-liners, and perceptive insights into contemporary society. Furthermore, she has been credited with influencing the direction of American drama by greatly expanding women's roles and by offering significant alternatives to the conventional happy endings of dramatic comedy.

PRINCIPAL WORKS

Any Woman Can't (drama) 1973
Happy Birthday, Montpelier Pizz-zazz (drama) 1974
Uncommon Women and Others: A Play about Five Women Graduates of a Seven Sisters College Six Years Later (drama) 1975; revised version, 1977
When Dinah Shore Ruled the Earth [with Christopher Durang] (drama) 1975
Uncommon Women and Others (screenplay) 1978
The Sorrows of Gin [adaptor; from the short story "The Sorrows of Gin" by John Cheever] (screenplay) 1979
Isn't It Romantic (drama) 1981; revised version, 1983
Tender Offer (drama) 1983
The Man in a Case [adaptor; from the short story "The Man in a Case" by Anton Chekhov] (drama) 1986
Miami (musical) 1986
**The Heidi Chronicles* (drama) 1988
Bachelor Girls (essays) 1990
The Heidi Chronicles, and Other Plays (dramas) 1990
The Sisters Rosensweig (drama) 1992

**The Heidi Chronicles* was adapted for and aired on cable television in 1995.

CRITICISM

Edith Oliver (review date 5 December 1977)

SOURCE: A review of *Uncommon Women and Others,* in *The New Yorker,* Vol. LIII, No. 42, December 5, 1977, p. 115.

[*Oliver began her career as an actress, television writer, and producer, and joined the* New Yorker *in 1948, where she became the off-Broadway theater critic in 1961. In the following review, she lauds* Uncommon Women and Others *for its well-drawn characterizations and humor but suggests that there is an "underlying sadness" in the play as the women "try to cope with the times and with what is expected of them."]*

Uncommon Women and Others, Wendy Wasserstein's funny, ironic, and affectionate comedy. . .is about five seniors—close friends—at Mount Holyoke College, and about their prissy housemother; a deadpan, silent freshman; a former friend who has more or less left the clique; and a square type who combines cheerful rhymed chatter about elves and Piglet with practical arrangements for fixing other girls up with Yale men for weekends. That these satellites—the "Others" of the title—may indeed be more uncommon than the women of the constellation is just one of many jokes in this refreshing show. It opens with a prologue set in a restaurant, where the five heroines meet for the first time since their graduation, six years earlier, and where, amid hugs and shrieks and kisses, each of them reports on her activities up to now. Under the laughter there is in almost every instance a feeling of bewilderment and disappointment over the world outside college, which promised so much, and with their own dreams, which seem to have stalled. "When we are forty, we will be *incredible,*" says Swoosie Kurtz, as Rita—the bold one, the ringleader, the buccaneer. (During their undergraduate years, the age of incredibility was first twenty-five and then thirty.) But so far none of them has children, only two are married, and only one has taken the first steps into a career. For some reason I've forgotten, they clink glasses and sing a song that has a special meaning for them, and then we are back in college and in the dormitory, where (except for an epilogue, also set in the restaurant) all the action takes place.

The action is a collage of small scenes (there is no play, or, if there is one, I couldn't find it), and many of them are preceded by the voice of a man making a speech about the attributes of a liberal-arts college and the uncommon women it produces; the pompous voice-overs punctuate the show and give it much of its ironic point. In the episodes, the girls appear in twos and threes, and sometimes all together, to talk of men and sex and men's colleges and ambitions, as girls have always done, but these girls live in the new time of the Liberated Woman, and there are allusions to Germaine Greer and Simone de Beauvoir, to *Ms.* and "A Room of One's Own" and "The Group." These are their touchstones. In spite of their bluntness and candor in talking about their feelings and, above all, about sex, there is some confusion and underlying sadness as they try to cope with the times and with what is expected of them. Miss Wasserstein is always aware of these feelings, yet they never impede her wonderful, original comedy. It is the girls and the games they play and their conversations that make the show, and every moment is theatrical. "We are all allowed one dominant characteristic," somebody says. That is not entirely true. The characters are never allowed to become types, and, for all their funny talk and behavior, they are sympathetically drawn.

The acting, under Steven Robman's direction, is in every instance as right and satisfying as the script, and it more than makes up for any dramatic lapses. Miss Kurtz has never been funnier or more in command as she presides over many of the games and conversations, and never more touching as she lets us see her confidence beginning to crack at the end. Jill Eikenberry gives a sensitive performance as a Phi Beta worried about getting into law school, and even more worried about the sort of woman she may turn into if she does. Ann McDonough plays a girl who falls in love with one man, is content to marry him and take care of him, and is delighted to announce her pregnancy to her friends at the end. Josephine Nichols is the housemother, who is given to small talk and recitations of Emily Dickinson's poems (as the girls mimic her behind her back), but who reveals, in one speech, a remarkable streak of independence in her past, and some quite unorthodox behavior. Alma Cuervo is a Jewish girl at her most appealing when she finally gets up the courage to make a long-distance call (which comes to nothing) to a young doctor whom she met for one moment in the Fogg Museum. Anna Levine is the freshman, oblivious of all the chatter, whose ambition is to "get Wittgenstein on film," and who crams for her typing exam to the Hallelujah Chorus—very funny character, very funny acting. The others, just as good, are Ellen Parker, Cynthia Herman, and Glenn Close. Miss Wasserstein is an uncommon young woman if ever there was one. Jennifer von Mayrhauser's costumes are exceptionally witty, too.

John Simon   (review date 12 December 1977)

SOURCE: "The Group," in *New York* Magazine, Vol. 10, No. 50, December 12, 1977, p. 103.

[*A distinguished American drama and film critic, Simon is the author of* Uneasy Stages: A Chronicle of the New York Theatre, 1963-1973 *(1976) and* Singularities: Essays on the Theatre, 1964-1974 *(1976). Here, he contends that* Uncommon Women and Others *is well-written and enjoyable but adds that the subject matter of the play is too familiar to be especially interesting.*]

Uncommon Women begins with five Holyoke alumnae meeting in a restaurant six years after graduation. They comment on their respective development or nondevelopment, reminisce about absent friends and foes, and are presently transported back into their college days, only to return to the present at play's end. The prologue-play-epilogue construction is highly conventional, and, indeed, there is nothing uncommon about ***Uncommon Women and Others.*** In fact, Miss Wasserstein's problem is a very common one among young playwrights writing memory plays about themselves and friends when younger yet: Nothing much has happened to them, and what has is far from unusual. Still, it matters to them, and they cannot see why it should not be equally fascinating to the rest of the world. But it isn't. When older authors, with more experience and greater perspective, look back at their pasts, they can find purposeful structures along with universal significance that would have eluded their less mature and distanced selves.

Miss Wasserstein has a chortlingly mischievous sense of outer and inner dialogue, of what these collegians said or merely thought; and she observes her characters, one of whom must be herself, with a nice blend of sympathy and unsentimentality. But there is no shape, no sense of direction, no purpose here, except recording something for memory's sake, which is all too private a pursuit. These girls, giggling, straining, wisecracking, or brazening their way through college and the last remnants of their childhood, are recognizable and likable creatures, but, give or take a bit, we know them already too well—even their existential surprises hold little dramatic surprise for us.

Yet the dialogue is brisk and sassy, the characters are mettlesome, giddy, and richly absurd. Only Susie Friend, the goody-goody one, and Carter, the weirdo, are exaggerated—though this may be more the director's doing than the author's; the others ring true, individually and together, but no larger, collective truth emerges. There is also a certain fuzziness about period: Anachronisms pop up here and there. What is greatly to Wasserstein's credit, however, is that Mrs. Plumm, the housemother, does not come out as a caricature: While kidding her, the playwright does not rob her of her humanity. And Josephine Nichols plays her to perfection, funnily but not ludicrously.

Almost all the acting is a joy. Mind you, most of these characters do not require immense imaginative leaps by their interpreters; still, how often do we not see actors unable to play even closer roles? Swoosie Kurtz is marvelous as the comic hedonist, an oversexed hellion not without the pathos of oversexed hellions. Her quizzical inflections and out-of-left-field timing are a delight. Jill Eikenberry, as the stunner and overachiever who is basically insecure, is superb. It is not easy to embody smoothly contrary extremes, but Miss Eikenberry, one of our loveliest and most gifted actresses, does it with a tremulous, humorless assiduity that is just right and obviously requires a great deal of humor and intelligence to achieve.

Everybody else is good, too, though I was especially pleased with Ellen Parker and Ann McDonough, both of them new to me, and both very able to infuse considerable refinement into parts that lent themselves to obviousness. Would that Steven Robman had directed with a slightly more acute sense of pacing, but no matter: The fun, though small-scale, was genuine.

Harold Clurman   (review date 17 December 1977)

SOURCE: A review of *Uncommon Women and Others,* in *The Nation,* New York, Vol. 225, No. 1, December 17, 1977, pp. 667-68.

[*Highly regarded as a director, author, and longtime drama critic for* The Nation, *Clurman was an important contributor to the development of the modern American theater. In 1931, with Lee Strasberg and Cheryl Crawford, he founded the Innovative Group Theater, which served as an arena for the works of new playwrights and as an experimental workshop for actors. Strasberg and Clurman introduced the Stanislavsky method of acting—most commonly referred to as "Method" acting—to the American stage. Based on the dramatic principles of Russian actor and director Konstantin Stanislavsky, the method seeks truthful characterization through the conveyance of the actor's personal emotional experiences in similar situations. In the re-*

view below, Clurman offers a mixed assessment of Uncommon Women and Others.]

Perhaps the most suitable reviewer for Wendy Wasserstein's *Uncommon Women and Others* would be a young woman who went to college in the early 1970s. This play by a recent graduate of the Yale School of Drama is sympathetically entertaining and if we take her at her word, authentic. I cannot be sure as to the authenticity, but if we grant it that merit, it is also revealing.

The play deals with a group of students (whose average age is 21) at Mt. Holyoke. As with most of the plays by younger writers, there is more description of a condition than development of a situation: there is no "story." Rita (Swoosie Kurtz) is eccentric, possibly promiscuous, and given to bold sexual allusion and confession. Samantha (Ann McDonough) is a virgin who looks forward to marriage and offspring, a state of mind which Rita envies. Holly (Alma Cuervo), imaginative, witty, in her eagerness for love makes playful long-distance advances to men she has casually met.

After graduation, Muffet (Ellen Parker), who yearns for a hero and perfect mate, will regretfully find employment in an insurance office. Kate (Jill Eikenberry), who has had more lovers than Rita and remains cold withal, will become a lawyer. Leilah (Glenn Close) is interested in anthropology and goes off to Iran where she marries a native. Carter (Anna Levine), the freshman who falls in with the group, appears semi-catatonic, serves as an "ear" to several others. She aims to master typing. Mrs. Plumm (Josephine Nichols), as general supervisor, reads Emily Dickinson at parents'-day meetings; she seems wholly unaware of the intimate life and thoughts of her "girls."

Except for the uncommunicative Carter, all these students are extraordinarily and brightly articulate. They have a special gift for epigrammatic (frequently funny) sallies in sophisticated slang. What they talk about for the most part in sweeping vocabulary of four-letter specificity is sex. The keynote and the pathos of the play are in Rita's farewell as her friends on graduation take leave of one another: "When we're 30 we'll all be fucking amazing." She bethinks herself and repeats the phrase, each time advancing the term of their amazing future to 35, 40 and 45. It is a realization of deep insecurity she shares with all the others as they are about to face the world beyond the campus.

The "girls" have studied Nietzsche, Wittgenstein, Wallace Stevens: in short, their college curriculum has been thoroughly "serious." But none of this education seems to have rubbed off on them. There is no talk at all about social affairs, art, literature, theatre, politics. Except for the aforementioned anthropologist, there is no sign of a belief in, or commitment to, anything. Is this typical or true? If it is, let us look to it or woe betide us all!

The cast in the main is wonderfully attractive and talented. Still I had the impression that, though the actors were all giving excellent performances, I did not always believe in them as persons. This may be due to the expert but rather too meticulous direction. Actors who are too thoroughly controlled by a director tend to lose the freedom which fosters individuality, spontaneity, truth.

Erika Munk (review date 27 December 1983)

SOURCE: " 'Tis the Reason . . ." in *The Village Voice,* Vol. XXVIII, No. 52, December 27, 1983, pp. 109-10.

[*Munk is an American editor and critic. Below, she likens Wasserstein's revised version of* Isn't It Romantic *to popular television drama, suggesting that the play's characterizations are weak and its plot lacks real dramatic conflict, but adds that the acting in* Isn't It Romantic *is excellent.*]

Peculiar as it may seem, live theater for the upper middle class is tending more and more to become a replica of the TV drama that same class creates to pacify the rest of us: punchy little scenes moving from living room to bedroom to office; neat little characterizations relying heavily on racial and cultural type, psychologized plots about mild generational conflict and not too passionate romance, powdered saccharine slowly sifting over everything at the end, and never a glimmer of the world outside.

TV writers know that their prime function is to fill time between one commercial and the next; what Wendy Wasserstein—who seems talented, serious, and surely perhaps alas, not cynical—thinks she's doing is to entertain us very, very lightly with the theme of women's self-determination. The commercials are there, however, selling upper middle-class reconciliation.

In ***Isn't It Romantic*** Janie, a would-be writer, tries to declare some independence from her mother, Tasha (father is marginally in tow), by getting her own apartment, taking a part-time job writing for *Sesame Street,* and refusing to move in with the young doctor she loves. Janie's story is paralleled by her friend Harriet, who rebels against her super-executive mother, Lillian, by getting married. Tasha wants Janie to settle down with a "nice" (meaning wealthy) man, so she refuses; Lillian wants Harriet to concentrate on work (meaning corporate success), so she doesn't. Both mothers take their daughters' rebellions with grace, after a brief moment's grousing; so we have a happy ending on the status quo, with opening positions merely reversed.

The parallels and oppositions, not to mention much of the humor, are shaped by one fact alone: Janie's Jewish, Harriet's WASP. So of course Janie is warm, disorganized, and has fat thighs, and Harriet is tall, thin, and put together, while Tasha is vulgar, meddlesome, and lovable, and Lillian is elegant, straightforward, and cool. Because everyone's rich, however, the entire gamut of Jewish-intellectual-radical stereotypes is left out. And because this is a TV play at heart, both Judaism and Protestantism are stripped of all religious and ethical meanings. Believe me, they're missed.

The first act sets the story up in a series of jokes; a few are wonderfully wicked about bourgeois feminism (Janie gets a rejection message on her phone machine: "Our readers feel you haven't experienced enough woman's pain to stimulate our market"), others are eccentrically and delightfully local (like the one about the Four Brothers restaurants), and most of the rest, as mentioned, are about Jewishness. The only portrait unblunted by affection, however, is the figure of Paul Stuart, Harriet's married lover, who—like Lillian and Harriet herself, I guess it's a Protestant trait—keeps saying, "Everything in life's a negotiation," and acting unbelievably, hilariously swinish. The others, however exaggerated, are too nice for satire, too human for farce, too thin for comedy.

The second act gets more and more sentimental and conciliatory, as if Wasserstein had "satire is what closes on Saturday" engraved on her heart, and "politics is what closes on Friday" engraved on her brain. Banal dialogues—"I want it all," "You have to set priorities"—increasingly edge up on the funny parts, emotions emerge palely from the mouths of cartoons, and the fact that there's nothing there becomes the only notable presence.

Too bad, because the cast is terrific. Cristine Rose's Janie is earnest, rowdy, and—horrid overused word—vulnerable; I'd believe in her as a writer, if she'd been given the chance to play one. Lisa Banes, more mannered, has a less believable transition to make, but manages. Betty Comden is so spiffy as mother Tasha that the point of Janie's rebellion almost disappears—it's clear she'll never lose her mother's love, so what's the danger? And Jo Henderson takes a part that might be a comic version of Marlene in *Top Girls* and makes it so sympathetic, though rational, that Harriet's rebellion also loses point. Chip Zien exactly captures the simultaneous niceness and suffocating patronizing of Janie's lover ("The Jewish family should always have three children"). But Jerry Lanning's Paul, boorish, twitchy, arrogant, and blissfully unaware, gets the acting honors, perhaps because he's the one character Wasserstein felt no compunction about.

> I've always loved going to the theater. I figured I wasn't likely to become a dancer or an actress, so it seemed to me that writing plays was the way to be part of this world I loved.
>
> —*Wendy Wasserstein, in an interview in* Harper's Bazaar, *June, 1984.*

Sylviane Gold (essay date 7 February 1984)

SOURCE: "Wendy, the Wayward Wasserstein," in *The Wall Street Journal,* February 7, 1984, p. 30.

[*In the following article, Gold profiles Wasserstein's life and career up to the production of* Isn't It Romantic.]

One Wasserstein arranges mergers and acquisitions for First Boston. Another runs the communications division of American Express. The third is married to a doctor. And the youngest—well, the youngest Wasserstein writes plays.

However, aberrant her behavior may seem in the context of her family, Wendy Wasserstein appears perfectly normal to the people who concoct lists of promising young American playwrights. Her first play, ***Uncommon Women*** *and Others,* has had more than 1,000 productions on college campuses across the country and has reached an even larger audience on public television. Her second, *Isn't It Romantic,* is currently a hit off-Broadway, at Playwrights Horizons.

But like the other Wassersteins, who, she says, had originally hoped she'd "marry a lawyer, live in Scarsdale and do plays at the community center," Ms. Wasserstein sees the peculiarity of her situation. "Who," she asks with sincere amazement, "goes out into the world to become a playwright?"

This particular one was born in Brooklyn, in 1950, to a textile manufacturer—"My father invented velveteen," she says—and his wife—"a mother and a dancer"—who'd come here from Poland. Raised on the profits from velveteen amid that trio of overachieving siblings, Ms. Wasserstein has turned, in her plays, to the problems of bright, well-educated young women with a wealth of options and no way of deciding among them. "Sometimes," she says, "I write to kind of figure out what I'm thinking."

In *Uncommon Women,* Ms. Wasserstein explored with uncommon humor the perplexities of a group of Mount Holyoke students six years after graduation. When the play was produced in New York, in 1977, she was herself six years out of Holyoke, and the play was very much a reflection of her own state of mind at the time. "I was very confused. I just didn't know what I wanted, and it didn't seem to me that my friends knew, either."

Isn't It Romantic, she says, sprang initially from her strong emotions when she learned that a friend of hers was getting married. And, indeed, it's about two women approaching 30 without husbands, and the various ways in which they deal with that crucial fact. But after several re-writes, Ms. Wasserstein explains, the play grew to include a more generalized reaction "to being told how to live your life, with the dictum changing every six months."

Although her plays are unquestionably comedies, Ms. Wasserstein takes their concerns quite seriously. "In a large sense," she says, "*Isn't It Romantic* is a political play. It deals with life choices for women-that's political to me. I don't think you can bring people into the theater by doing it didactically. . . . You don't have to have a woman riding a tractor, or an alcoholic prostitute, or someone who's mad as hell. And I wouldn't want to sit at the typewriter writing that. But sometimes I think that comedy is written by the *most* serious people: You take it so seriously that you have to put a pin in it."

With her mop of tousled black hair and calculatedly casual dress, Ms. Wasserstein looks only half serious. In fact, she resembles one of the uncommon women she describes in her first play: "Hair disheveled, yet well cut. She wears expensive clothes that don't quite match, . . . because she doesn't want to try too hard. That would be too embarrassing." The same kind of non-nonchalance is evident as she fills you in on her background.

She began writing plays, she says, at prep school, "because I figured out that you could get out of gym if you wrote

the mother-daughter fashion show." Of such stuff come promising young playwrights!

Ms. Wasserstein has turned, in her plays, to the problems of bright, well-educated young women with a wealth of options and no way of deciding among them. "Sometimes," she says, "I write to kind of figure out what I'm thinking."

—Sylviane Gold

At college, she majored in Intellectual History. ("Don't be impressed," she laughs—she laughs a lot; "it means you don't have to memorize the dates.") And one summer, on her way to becoming a congressional intern, she was sidetracked by a friend, who said, "Why don't you take playwrighting with me at Smith? And then afterwards we can shop!"

The shopping may or may not have worked out. But the playwrighting course was a turning point. "I realized you could seriously grow up to be a playwright," says Ms. Wasserstein. Still, when she graduated she was in the same fix as so many of her characters: She didn't know what to do. She applied to several law schools, but was rejected, so she returned to New York and took odd jobs and writing courses at City College, with playwright Israel Horovitz and novelist Joseph Heller.

After two years, she felt the time had come to get serious. So she applied to the Columbia Business School and the Yale Drama School. "I got into both," she says, "and I decided to take the risk of trying something I really wanted to do." It was at Yale that she wrote the first version of *Uncommon Women.* She did more work on it when it was selected for production at the Eugene O'Neill Theater Center in Connecticut, in 1976. And in the fall of 1977, she watched it open—and close—in New York.

Although it ran for only 2½ weeks, the play did put Ms. Wasserstein on that list of up-and-comers. So she got a little TV work and a little film work. On the money she earned from those, she wrote a first draft of *Isn't It Romantic.* She was able to rewrite it, and get started on a musical, because of a grant from the Guggenheim Foundation. And with *Isn't It Romantic* ensconced at Playwrights Horizons for a comfortable run, she may earn enough money to finish her musical.

She seems philosophical about her precarious financial situation—"It goes up and down a lot," she shrugs. And she doesn't seem to mind that her name isn't in lights on a big Broadway marquee. What she does seem to resent is that she and her colleagues, like her Yale classmates Albert Innaurato and Christopher Durang, are still ranked among the "promising" by those list makers.

"There has to be a new generation of popular playwrights," she says. "The people who go to see Bernard

Slade and Neil Simon—they'd *like* our plays. We're not Bohemians, with bongo drums and guitars and smoke. We're writers, and we write for audiences. And we do good work."

Even her parents, Ms. Wasserstein says, have grudgingly come around to that opinion. And if her mother still responds occasionally to the query "How's Wendy?" with a mournful "Wendy! Wendy's not a lawyer. Wendy's not married to a lawyer. Wendy's writing *plays!*" Ms. Wasserstein needn't worry—she can always find a spot for the line in her next one.

Walter Kerr   (review date 26 February 1984)

SOURCE: "Are Parents Looking Better on Stage?" in *The New York Times,* February 26, 1984, pp. 7, 36.

[*Kerr is an American playwright, director, and highly respected drama critic for the* New York Times *who was awarded the 1978 Pulitzer Prize for Drama Criticism. A conservative critic whose likes and dislikes have often coincided with those of Broadway audiences, Kerr strongly believes that good theater is popular theater. In the following review, Kerr lauds the revised version of* Isn't It Romantic *for its improved characterizations.*]

The older and younger generations are still having at it, but I think I detect a shift in the wind towards fairness. Even a scrupulous fairness. Am I wrong?

Take a look at Wendy Wasserstein's *Isn't It Romantic,* which you will want to do anyway since it's an altogether delightful business. Miss Wasserstein started out, several years ago, to write a funny but not exactly evenhanded little comedy about two independent young women, Janie and Harriet, who were hard and fast chums pursuing rather different goals. Harriet wanted to be as independent as her mother and Janie wanted to be independent *of* her mother. That's for starters.

When the play was first done at the Phoenix in 1981, the youngers were pretty solidly there. We felt we knew Janie first shot out of the box. Janie, now played by Cristine Rose, is a sort of conscientious mess, I mean a mess on principle. She announces, before too many words have snapped by, that she looks like an extra in *Potemkin.* If I disagree with that, it is only because the extras in *Potemkin* look as though they belong to the clothes they are wearing whereas Janie seems not even to have been introduced to hers. She seems to have borrowed them outright from that Dutch boy whose image used to appear on cans of paint (perhaps it still does, I haven't painted anything lately). I am, of course, thinking of a *used* can of paint. And Janie is thinking of more than her outfit when she tells us "I have fat thighs and I want very badly to be someone else without going through the effort of actually changing myself into someone else."

Janie does have certain psychological and emotional problems. For instance, she doesn't want to be nice, and that's difficult. In fact, when she falls in love with a young Jewish doctor who seems to be wearing a nest of robins in his hair, and possibly in his beard, she runs right into a kind of incompatibility of nicenesses. As she ruefully says, looking

deeply into his soul and ditching him forever in the same moment of crisis, "I'm so sweet, I never say what I want, and you're so sweet, you always get what you want." (Chip Zien, who plays the doctor and who does *not* get the girl he wants, is both touching and helplessly macho in the same bittersweet leavetaking.)

This leaves Janie alone in her new apartment, trying to become herself—whoever that may be—while friend Harriet romps off into an affair with her boss's boss, to be followed by a proper marriage and children and career and oh, everything a young woman could wish for and fail to manage. (Harriet is blithely, twittily played by Lisa Banes, and author Wasserstein has even given the boss's boss, Jerry Lanning, a defiant speech of his own: Really a howl of pain over the male's inability to know what's expected of him now that he's been turned into a wife.)

Alone in her apartment—and never alone because her mother is on the doorstep by 7 A.M. daily, cartons of coffee in hand—Janie works out the things she resents, the job she might aim for, the absurdities of the world as it is presently constituted. She is given to strong opinions: "Jean Harris's mistake was stopping with Hy, she should have taken care of all of them—Dr. Atkins, Dr. Pritikin, the nut in Beverly Hills who says it's good to live on papaya." She harbors resentments, too: "I resent having to pay the phone bill, be nice to the super, find meaningful work, fall in love, get hurt, all of it I resent deeply."

There is nothing, however, she resents so deeply as that mother, who is by this time not only at the door but through it. The mother—Jewish, doting, undefatigable— simply cannot grasp her chick's endless flight from an overflowing love. "My daughter," she complains, "thinks I call her in the morning to check up on her—yesterday she answered the phone and said 'Hello, Mother, this morning I got married, lost 20 pounds and became a lawyer.'"

In short, Janie knows just what is expected of her and is determined to evade it. And, between Janie and Harriet, playwright Wasserstein has quite tidily accounted for the upcoming generation, witty and only occasionally woebegone as it is. That particular accounting, however, was nearly complete in the play as it originally stood. Where matters had been enormously improved is in her handling of the less-than-golden oldies, the two mothers. In the original form of the piece, as I remember it, Janie's mother was straight off the ethnic stockpile while Harriet's was as chilly and brittle as the icicles we've been stamping off the garage gutters these past weeks. The two weren't really real enough to engage in a fair contest with their offspring.

That's been changed. I saw Betty Comden play Janie's maternal nemesis, ever-ready with a guiding push ("Just a little one"). And Miss Comden was no joke. She was funny, all right. Funny when demonstrating a time-step that didn't exactly make her the neighborhood Pavlova, but established her credentials as a "modern woman," practically an *artiste.* Funnier still explaining how Richard Nixon "did all right for himself." (You'll have to see the show to pick up the payoff; my lips are sealed.)

But in the reworked version at Playwrights Horizons, we

were instantly aware of a decidedly complicated woman behind Miss Comden's worried, ravishing smile. This woman, now in the hands of actress Marge Kolitsky, is solidly present in the text itself. She has antennae of her own, picks up more than the morning gossip or rumors circulated by park bench. She hears Janie and a whole generation, hears them when she's not even there, hears them in ways that hurt. "You know what's sad?" she asks abruptly. "Not sad like a child is ill or something. But a little sad to me. My daughter never thinks I call because I miss her."

She is also able, once again abruptly, to speak up for herself firmly, betraying only a trace of uncertainty—no more than a twist of lemon, say—as she comes to a coda. She has told Janie boldly that she isn't dependent upon her, doesn't *need* her to fill up her life: "I'm an independent woman, a person in my own right." The spunk is of course gratifying to all of us. What is moving is a swift turn to her husband, the barest hint of alarm, as she asks without pause: "Am I right, Simon?" A new dimension unfolds as we watch, catching us quite off guard.

With Jo Henderson, as the poised and canny executive Harriet's mother has become, the attack must be different though the ultimate vitamin-enriched effect is much the same. (Daughter Harriet is an executive now, too, which means that she and her mother can only communicate through secretaries. Of course, their secretaries can arrange for them to meet for lunch once in a while.) Miss Henderson is efficient, but not hard; her bleached repose is almost soothing; she has grown content with authority and no longer feels the need to be wary.

An immaculate presence at a restaurant table that is no doubt permanently hers, she doesn't in the least mind speaking openly and without regret on the choices she's had to make. Confronted, quite a while back, with a husband, an infant and a job, she swiftly recognized that she could not manage all three: "The first thing that had to go was pleasing my husband because he was a grownup and could take care of himself." Plain and clear as that.

Nor, in her unemotional slyboots way, is she willing to take the rap for the child who might have missed her: "Harriet, you can't blame everything on me—I wasn't home enough for you to blame everything on me." Miss Henderson has a knack for winning contests either way, yet there isn't a trace of caricature in the writing or in the relaxed, even friendly, performing. We don't wind up thinking her heartless; she goes away with what might be called our blessing, and without begging for it.

Susan L. Carlson (essay date December 1984)

SOURCE: "Comic Textures and Female Communities 1937 and 1977: Clare Boothe and Wendy Wasserstein," in *Modern Drama*, Vol. XXVII, No. 4, December, 1984, pp. 564-73.

[*In the following excerpt, Carlson asserts that Wasserstein's innovative treatment of female roles in* Uncommon Women and Others *has contributed to the advancement of dramatic comedy, not only by diffusing old prejudices*

against women, but also by addressing serious issues without detracting from the play's overall humor and wit.]

Wendy Wasserstein's 1977 comedy *Uncommon Women and Others* mirrors [Clare] Boothe's [1937 comedy *The Women*] in its all-female world and picaresque plot; and it borrows the earlier play's superstructure of five main characters playing out social roles against a backdrop of clearly typed characters. But the crucial difference is that Wasserstein shows how a comedy full of women no longer needs to be a bitter dead end.

As her subtitle documents, Wasserstein's text is "A Play About Five Women Graduates of a Seven Sisters College Six Years Later." While it begins and ends "Six Years Later" with the five women gathered at a restaurant for lunch, most of the action is a replay of scenes during the characters' senior year at Mount Holyoke. There is no plot. Instead of events and suspense, Wasserstein gives her characters time and peer audiences. As they drift in and out of the play's seventeen episodes, the five main characters set their own paces and create a dramatic forum in which they can leisurely, continually mold, test, and retest their lives and those of their friends. Wasserstein may have discarded the comic plotting that confined Boothe, even in her loosely plotted play, but the later dramatist has not discarded comedy. In a new mode, she presents the same comic search for a resolution, for the comfort of a happy ending.

Sometimes boldly, sometimes fearfully, the five Mount Holyoke seniors relentlessly confront their futures. Kate, a Phi Beta Kappa who loves trashy novels, collects men, and is headed for law school, is the other women's image of success, their Katharine Hepburn. Although she is well on her way to becoming the successful career woman already typed by her friends, Kate has doubts about the "role" she has chosen for herself. She fears becoming "a cold efficient lady in a grey business suit" and laments, "I don't want my life to simply fall into place." "Six Years Later," Kate is still fighting against the constraints of her role as the career woman; she realizes that she has sacrificed as much as she has gained, but she remains admirable in her constant, honest battle within and against a role which isolates her.

Kate's bold insecurity is matched by Rita's willful perverseness. A mouthy, playfully radical feminist preoccupied with tasting her menstrual blood and lecturing her friends on the dangers of a society "based on cocks," Rita refreshes the spirits of the others while restlessly searching for the experiences and feelings that will make her feel whole. Her constant, soon haunting refrain is to proclaim how amazing this group of women will be at ages twenty-five or thirty or forty-five—or somewhere down the road. Pressing achievement conveniently always just out of reach in the future, Rita squares her hope with her disappointments. With her unabating hatred of roles, Rita has not let society pigeonhole her, but she has not yet found a way to fashion a world without the old pigeonholes.

Muffet's and Holly's searches for their futures are less frenetic than either Kate's or Rita's. They wander in and out of Wasserstein's scenes, trying—in their more subdued ways—to fashion their lives somehow out of the old roles which remain the only ones they know and the undefined new ones no one else can describe for them. Wishing for the direction of a Kate or a Rita, Holly slips and slides between the despair and elation of growing up. Her long-distance telephone conversation "to" a man she has only casually met in a museum is touching evidence of her need for a man and her confusion over her preference for the comforting presence of Rita or Kate. Muffet confesses a similar need for men, and like Holly fears planning for the future as much as meeting it.

Holly and Muffet are openly insecure about a future they cannot seem to pattern for themselves; Kate and Rita are much less secure than they know they seem. Yet all four consciously confront a world in which women's roles have become ambiguous and confusing. Unlike theirs, Samantha's position recalls Boothe's simpler, albeit harsher female world. Like Boothe's women, Sam opts for a very traditional marriage, one in which she can dedicate herself to her husband, Robert. She feels no shame about giving herself to her husband and, in fact, radiates self-confidence and contentment that the others all envy. Sam chooses life akin to the values and conditions Boothe traced in *The Women,* but hers promises happiness that life in *The Women* could not. Because she consciously chooses a traditional marriage as one of many options open to her, Sam has the potential of being happy as a satellite in Robert's world. The others envy her not because she can so easily choose an established role, but because she can fit into it: they could not. Wasserstein does not make the mistake of preaching that "new" types like Rita and Kate are any more acceptable than "old" types like Sam; she simply provides a context where all such roles coexist and can be studied, challenged, accepted, altered, or dropped.

Wasserstein's expansive plot, her concentration on characters and roles, and her weaving of texture are not unique. Any number of comic playwrights (and many great ones) have preceded her with such mixtures, yet usually without her success in transforming comedy's women. Although in time Wasserstein's transformations will come to seem a matter of degree and not radical alterations, the still significant difference between Wasserstein and predecessors like Boothe is consciousness. Wasserstein *is aware* that comedy's built-in easy answers to women's problems are deceptive and dangerous; she *is aware* that comic conventions in and of themselves pressure characters into a limited number of roles. And for now, her ability to translate this awareness to a comic practice that focuses on characters (not roles) and allows these characters to create unified female communities must be viewed as significant. For in creating her community, Wasserstein diffuses comic prejudice against female friendship. Sifting through her treasure chest of Mount Holyoke scenes and characters, Wasserstein allows real female friendships to develop, friendships that have been rare in comedy. Freed from the requirement that they bond only with men (and produce the traditional happy ending), Wasserstein's women can choose to bond with each other.

In the final scene of Act I, Rita—coordinating the others

as usual—asks them which one woman they would marry if they could, if women married women. A joyous communal dance grows out of the touching, honest exchange that follows and is our cue that Act I is over. While there are many other direct comments on female friendships in the play, none surpasses this marriage scene in its creation of believable, lasting relationships. Its direct substitution of female-female marriage for the traditional male-female kind must be read as a challenge to a world and comedy that expect otherwise. It is almost as if Wasserstein knew her play could not end this way, so she indulged her dreams and her characters' dreams of togetherness in this wish-fulfilling pseudo-ending. She provides enough evidence elsewhere that her female community is no utopia, for this group of women has its tensions and defections along with its Bacchic idylls.

> Wasserstein *is aware* that comedy's built-in easy answers to women's problems are deceptive and dangerous; she *is aware* that comic conventions in and of themselves pressure characters into a limited number of roles. In creating her community of women, Wasserstein diffuses comic prejudice against female friendship.
>
> *—Susan L. Carlson*

Wasserstein deals directly with the fragility of such happy communes by creating two very distinct communities in the play. We focus on the five women who will meet again six years later in the restaurant frame of the play—Kate, Rita, Holly, Muffet, and Sam. Yet in our peripheral vision other students remain—Susie Friend, Carter, and Leilah—who are set off not only by their absence from the reunion, but also by the one-dimensional nature of their roles in the Mount Holyoke community. These misshapen shadows of outsiders and failed friendships keep Wasserstein's play from deteriorating into a facile celebration of sorority. Like the hairdressers, the cooks and the attendants in *The Women,* who offered a background chorus of roles, these three outsiders put a damper on the soaring aspirations of the "uncommon women" by stubbornly reminding them of a world that is still not all that different from Boothe's.

The closing of ***Uncommon Women and Others*** is Wasserstein's final statement about these women's roles, as well as her final transformation of comedy. Because the playwright wants it this way, there is no end, only a stopping point. The indeterminateness of her ending is indicated both by the age of Wasserstein's matured women—still only twenty-seven—and by the constant transition they have learned, for better or worse, to accept in their lives. The stopping point of the end is marked as a pause also by Sam's announcement that "Robert and I are having a baby." Sam's announcement is not intended as a parody of the traditional ending of comedy with marriage and the implicit future promise of babies; her solid, lovable character ensures that we respond to her news as warmly as the other women do. Moreover, in Sam's announcement, Wasserstein does not simply embrace the comfortable comic ending which returns the world to an established social order. By making Sam's future as a mother only one part of an otherwise diffuse ending, Wasserstein extracts the joy and assurance of the traditional comic ending without the encumbrance of comedy's predictable return to the status quo. In other words, Wasserstein protects against the reactionary power of the traditional comic ending by setting Sam's future in the context of four other, much less defined futures. All five women, like Wasserstein, know that the happy endings promised in comedy are illusive, but that comedy's joy is not. In this they are uncommon.

Forming her characters as a social unit in a comedy of textures, Wasserstein demonstrates how the delicate relations of women to social roles may be best studied, may be *only* studied, in an altered comic form. Boothe's comedy about women generated bitterness, complaints, and brittle laughter; Wasserstein's comedy about women nurtures faith, concern, and warm, easy laughter. Community.

Wendy Wasserstein with Esther Cohen (interview date August 1987)

SOURCE: An interview in *Women's Studies: An Interdisciplinary Journal,* Vol. 15, No. 3, 1988, pp. 257-70.

[*In the following interview, Wasserstein talks about her plays* Uncommon Women and Others *and* Isn't It Romantic, *and shares her views on humor and feminism.*]

Challenged by my esteemed editor to write a printable article on women writers and humor in theatre (try to imagine a scene from *The Front Page,* only in an Indian restaurant—"Esther, get me that article, and pass the poori!"), I decided that I had nothing to say that one such writer couldn't say for herself. Thus, with the lure of a bottle of Diet Coke and the promise of being quoted in an academic journal, Wendy Wasserstein agreed to be interviewed for this article. I met Wendy, the noted playwright, author of **Uncommon Women and Others, Isn't It Romantic?** and **Miami,** and a contributing editor to *New York Woman,* while working as a stage manager on **Isn't It Romantic?** and I knew her to be a witty, straightforward and eminently quotable woman. Eager to hear her views on humor, in both her work and her life, I met with Wendy on a sweltering afternoon in August, 1987.

. . . . .

[*Cohen*]: *I guess my first question is, when did you decide you liked to write? When did writing become something that you liked to do?*

[Wasserstein]: I remember as a child thinking that my family was very funny. I think this was because my mother was somewhat eccentric. And I do remember watching shows like *Make Room for Daddy* and thinking that those kids were pretty boring. And I actually thought, like Rusty Hammer and Angela Cartwright, they are such good kids, and I thought "no one's family is really like this." And actually I thought our family was far more entertaining than that. So I think partially from that, though I didn't really write those things.

I wrote in high school. I went to school in New York City at Calhoun, and I figured out that one of the ways I could get out of gym was if I wrote something called the Mother-Daughter Fashion Show. I know very little about fashion, but they used to have this Mother-Daughter Fashion Show once a year at the Plaza Hotel, and you got to leave school to go to the fashion show. But if you wrote it you didn't have to go to gym for like two or three weeks, it was fantastic. So, I started writing those.

So you were always an observer of people—watching your family, watching your friends.

Yeah, I think so. I think that's true.

What did you write in these fashion shows?

I don't know. I remember writing some song to "King of the Road" about "Miss Misunderstood." I don't know *what* I wrote.

So did you write in college?

Uh huh. I went to Holyoke and one of my best friends told me—I was taking a course to go become a Congressional intern, and I used to read the Congressional Digest at the Holyoke library and fall asleep, I just couldn't do it—and then she said to me "Well why don't you come to Smith and take playwriting with me, and then we could shop." So she said the magic word and the duck came down, and I said "Yes, I'll go shop." So we went up to Smith and I had a wonderful teacher. I started writing plays for him, really. And that's how that all happened. But I grew up going to the theatre and I used to dance, I used to go to dancing school at the June Taylor School of the Dance. It was never somewhat intellectual theatre, never had that sort of bent.

But was it always funny, was it always comedy?

Yeah, it always was sort of comic. It's kind of interesting. I think what happened to me, the real bend in the road for me, was that after my senior year in college I went to California with some friends of mine to Long Beach State to a summer dance program, which is really crazy of me to have done, and we had odd jobs. I mean one of my friends worked at a Union 76 station, and I had some job in some sweet shop. It was crazy. But I had thought that I would maybe stay in California and try to write television. And instead, I hated California so much—I think it was because I couldn't drive; I just loathed it—that I came home back to New York and applied to drama school.

And I think I'd be a very different writer, very different person, if I had stayed in California.

Do you think living in New York itself has affected the kind of writing you do?

Yes I think so. Because when I dream or think, I think in terms of the rhythm of theatrical comedy. It's not—I mean it's certain kinds of theatrical comedy because it's what you're around. I mean as a kid I used to go to those Neil Simon plays. By the time I got to drama school, those

Albert Innaurato/Chris Durang plays. So it depends, what comes into your brain.

Do you find, as you're writing, that your humor comes more out of the situation that you're writing about, or are the characters themselves funny?

Sometimes the characters are funny. I mean, sometimes I like to do bright colors, and then they can be quite funny. Sometimes, you know—I haven't learned to use a computer, so I still type, and it's such a pain in the neck—sometimes I just retype scenes and start putting in things. I couldn't believe it—I'm writing a play right now about twenty years of peoples' lives, and this girl is telling this boy how unhappy she is, and for some reason I started writing Yasser Arafat jokes. For no reason. Because it's so boring retyping this stupid thing. But, you know sometimes it's funny to see. I think for myself, I'm slightly shy actually, and sometimes it's fun for me to write some character that's larger than life. That would say things I would never say but I know they're funny. And I like to do that a lot. And I also think, to get further into humor and women, that a lot of comedy is a deflection. If you look at *Isn't It Romantic?*, Janie Blumberg is *always* funny, so as not to say what she feels. And so, I think you use it— you use it to get a laugh, but you use it deliberately too. I mean, the best is when you use it deliberately.

Do you think that your women characters are more prone to doing it that way—using their humor as a deflection?

Sometimes, yes, the women use it more as a defense, I think.

Do you think that—among your friends, people you know—do women use their humor in different ways than the men do?

Yes, I think they do. I think sometimes, men sometimes top each other. Women don't do that. Women know how to lay back and have a good time, you know, and the gossip is great. Great!

The best. The best.

The best! Exactly! I mean, that's delightful. Nothing could be better. And I love it when it's people you absolutely don't know, whom I don't know a thing about. I mean, people call here and tell me about John Updike's personal life. I don't know him!

But you know more about him than he does.

I'm sure I know more about him than he would ever know about me! But I think that that—so that's kind of different too. And I don't mean it in a bitchy way, it's just different. It's kind of like sitting around.

I think that—certainly in my relationships with my women friends—life is just funny between us, and we share those sort of humorous moments. We're not always telling each other jokes.

No, and I don't even know how to tell a joke. But, you know, if you come home from a bad date, or something's happened, you know, and you've been fired—you know, you've just lost your job to some 21-year-old girl who's blond and can't do anything, but the boss . . . You know

that if you go home and tell your story to somebody, you will make it funny. And it will release the pain from you of whatever it is. Because you can't take that nonsense seriously.

Do you try to incorporate that way of reacting to people in your plays? In **Uncommon Women** *I thought the characters really reacted naturally to each other, and in* **Isn't It Romantic?** *they had real relationships, and that humor sort of showed.*

It's a little different than the one I'm doing now, but I think that's part of them, it's part of the relationship. People who are funny—I mean, one of my very best friends ever is Chris Durang, and there's nothing like a conversation with Christopher, because he's so funny! He's just wonderful. And when he's funny, he's hilarious. Just hilarious. And that's a wonderful thing. I mean, that's like a riff, almost. It's a great comfort. So, it's hard. But there are different kinds of humors, too. I don't like mean humor very much. I find nastiness is difficult for me, a little bit.

What's nice about plays is they're about words, and they can get long, and they can be your feelings, and I think that's wonderful. It's very joyous.

—Wendy Wasserstein

In the plays that you've written, do you think of them as being "women's" plays or written from a "women's" perspective? Or are they more written from your *perspective?*

I guess it's from my perspective, although sometimes I do think those stories have to be told. And if they're not, if I don't tell them, I mean someone else will tell them, that's for sure. But sometimes I look at these girls and I think I want to put them on the stage. I used to have great pleasure when I would see the audiences come to *Isn't It Romantic?* sometimes. Like you'd see five women together going out, and I thought that's great. There should be something for them. There really should be. And I think the thing is the women I write about are kind of middle class, upper middle class people, who have good jobs and they're good looking, and there's no problem. I mean, they're not Philip Barry people, but they're not sort of working class. So they're not the people one would tend to dramatize. Because there's nothing tragic there. And there's nothing romantic there. So I think that's why they're interesting to write about.

Because you can relate to them.

Because you can relate to them. It's like someone you knew in college. And I think that to make those people theatrical is interesting. I hope.

How do you choose what to write about?

It depends. I think that writing a play is such a long and

arduous task that it has to be something you care about pretty much, that's going to interest you longer than twenty pages. They're long, plays, they're like 90 pages, and it's a lot of typing!

And you have to live with them while they're running, too, for two years or. . . .

Yeah, you do, so I think it's got to be something that interests you enough. There are different things that interest you in different times. The play I'm writing right now is very personal. I have an idea for a musical after this that's based on a 19th century American play, just because I'd like to lose myself in something that's foreign to me.

It depends on where you're at at that particular moment. You haven't just written plays. You've written articles and TV screenplays. Is it different writing for the different media?

Very different. Sure it is. It's like one time I adapted a Cheever story for television that was called "The Sorrows of Gin," and the climax was the child realized the adult world was tattered like a piece of burlap. Well, you can't, like in a play, have the kid pick up the burlap and say "Gee Dad, tattered like the adult world." I mean, what you do is bring the camera in on the kid. Just like in a play you can't have people drive along—you know, you can't do it. Television is a close-up medium. You go in for the face, and they don't have to talk. I just wrote a TV movie that's going to be done in the fall about Teri Garr learning to drive, because I just learned to drive.

And you always pictured yourself as being Teri Garr.

Exactly, exactly. We're very similar. But anyway, at the end—she's this terrible driver, terrible terrible driver, and she finally passes her test by dressing up as Catherine Bach in *The Dukes of Hazzard*. When she passes her test, she's like the millionth person in her town to pass the test. There's this high school band that comes out and starts playing *The Little Old Lady from Pasadena*, because she passed, I mean it's crazy. But see, you could never do that on the stage. I mean, there's no way you could go to Playwrights Horizons and say "And now I'd like a high school band."

On an Equity salary.

What's nice about plays is they're about words, and they can get long, and they can be your feelings, and I think that's wonderful. It's very joyous.

How about writing for a nonperformance medium? Like articles. Do you have a different emotional reaction to writing those than to writing something that's being performed?

I've been writing some for a magazine called *New York Woman* recently. And it's fun. It's different though. You know what it is? I remember as a kid someone once told me that I had to learn to postpone gratification. And the thing about magazine things is it gets published pretty quickly. I mean, a play you can write and two years from then maybe you'll work it out. And I think magazine, because it's a shorter form, you can get—like I just wrote an article about manicures. I'd never write a play, a two hour

play about manicures unless, you could do it quite artistically I guess with dancing fingers and stuff.

And Tommy Tune. . .

And Tommy Tune, right, right. So that was fun to do for the magazine. I mean, I like that, I find it a release. You know why? Because I think of myself as a playwright, so I hold that very important to me. And when something's that important to you, you get scared of it. Whereas magazine writing doesn't scare me that much, because what's the worst they'll say? Wendy, you're not a magazine writer. And I'll say, that's right. But actually, I've enjoyed this magazine writing.

Does your humor translate the same way in each of these different media?

It depends. I mean, the magazine I wrote for sent me off to meet Philipe de Montebello at the Met. It was pretty funny. But in these magazine things I always use "I", first person, and there's a persona that I elect to use. You know, there's an "I" that's always talking about how I wish I wore leather miniskirts and I hate pantyhose and things like that. I don't do that so much in the plays. I mean, what's fun about plays is you can divide yourself into a lot of characters and hide yourself in different places.

But you really consider yourself a playwright. That's really what you enjoy.

I think so. Yeah, I mean I hope so.

Even though you're not on the stage, do you enjoy that audience feedback?

I do. I mean, when it works, it's great. When a production goes wrong, it is hell. It's really hell, it's so painful. That's the other thing. I mean, so you write an article and people don't like it. Or you write an article and they never call you again and they don't publish it. It's not the same pain, it's really not. From the word go, from the no actors are available to the director doesn't show up, to the show doesn't work and no one's laughing, to you pick up some terrible review—I mean, all of that is devastating. It's just terrible. It's enough to give you a sense of humor. I mean, it's really awful! I'm writing this play here and I can't even think about all that stuff. It's just too awful.

Well, it's such a process.

It's a real process. And you don't know what's going to happen. You just don't know.

It's true, it's not just your imput that will make it in the end. There are so many other factors and people involved.

Exactly.

Is that intimidating, that there are so many other people who influence?

When it works, like with Gerry Gutierrez [director of] ***Isn't It Romantic?,*** it's fantastic. Because, there you were giving birth to something alone in your room and then you've got a partner. And when that happens, it's great, because they . . . I mean, I'm not a director, I have no sense of visuals, nothing! I'll do anything to tell a joke.

There's this story about *Isn't It Romantic?* There was something about, there was some joke about three hundred running Hasidic Jews, or something, that Gerry Gutierrez kept telling me to cut because I should stay on the through line of the play. And I cut things like someone's mother being the last white woman to shop at Klein's—jokes like that. And I kept cutting them. But the running Hasidic Jews I really didn't want to cut. And so finally, I lit a cigarette and I turned to Gerry and I said "do you know, Gerry, it's not just the joke. It's the zeitgeist of the play. When the hubris of the character . . ." I don't know what the hell I was talking about. All I wanted to do was keep my joke. So I thought if I can talk to this man in the most high-faluting terms I can possibly pull out . . . I was talking about anecnorisises of the audience, I didn't know what I was saying. But I just wanted to keep my joke. But I think that, when you have someone with you who's on the same line as you are, and can take you further, that's a thrill. If you're an artist, you want someone to challenge you, and extend you. But you can also simultaneously have somebody who cripples you. And that's hard, it's so painful. It's just terrible.

Is it the same in film?

I think film is different, because film—I think the pain is up front. Just cutting the deal is painful. And then you know it's a director's medium. And it belongs to the producer. Unless you're going to direct your film or produce it, it's not the same thing. It's not your baby, it's their's. You're like a hired hand. You know, they can hire six different writers to do one of these things.

Do you consider yourself funny?

I can't tell a joke. And I am shy. I mean I can go to a meal and not say anything. I have that unique capability of, if I'm scared of someone, I won't say anything. But sometimes I can be funny. I can be funny with a girlfriend. I can be very sarcastic. So yes, I have that ability to make people laugh, I always have. I know how to make friends and get on with people because I could be funny. Not funny in like stick my tongue out with food on it, but sort of funny in a nonthreatening, likable way.

Were you always funny? Were you funny as a child, do you think?

I think I was, yeah. Or pleasing, in a way. There's a line about Janie in *Isn't It Romantic?* I think Harriet says "That's the thing about Janie, she's not threatening to anybody. That's her gift." I think that's somewhat similar with me.

You said your family was funny. How were they funny?

Well, my mother's very eccentric. She's like the woman in *Isn't It Romantic?* Her name is Lola, she goes to dancing classes six hours a day, she's—I won't say her age—but she's a very eccentric woman. She's very lively, very colorful. She's quite amusing, actually.

Did you have to compete with that as a child?

She's kind of an Auntie Mame figure. I think as a child you think it's very colorful. Then when you get sort of shy, you know, when you get to sixth grade and everyone's

mother is showing up in a suit, and they've got a station wagon, and your mother pulls in with a Carmen Miranda hat, you've got to think, "Oh God." I think that's a little difficult.

You've said before that you have humor with your friends and that a friend like Chris Durang is very funny. Do you think Chris is the funniest person you know? Who do you think is?

He's a pretty funny guy. Yeah. Actually, he might be the funniest person I know. Although you can meet Chris, you know you can have dinner with Chris and he can decide not to talk, too. So you know, you can have a lovely meal with both of us and we could both not talk. But actually I do think he's very funny. You know who's terrible funny too? Paul Rudnick. He wrote a novel called *Social Disease.* He's a dear friend of mine, and he is hilarious. The other day I was chatting up a friend and she was telling us about some man who was reading Boswell's *Life of Johnson,* and Paul Rudnick said "Of Don Johnson?" Which I thought was so funny. Terribly funny. He's quite witty. I mean, Christopher is so brilliant and imaginative that he just gets, you know, large, it's just wonderful. Yes, I would say they were the funniest people I knew.

I know Chris and he is brilliant and imaginative. But he's also sly.

Yes, he's very sly. He's witty. I mean, I don't like sort of locker room jockey humor. I've absolutely no interest in it. And I don't like sort of sex jokes either. Actually, because I don't get them.

Would you say humor is important in your relationship with people?

Yeah, very. Very. I think it's sort of how I get by. I giggle a little too much. But yes I think so, because one it makes one entertaining, two it deflects, and also it's a way of commenting on things. So yeah, I think it's very important to me.

It's a point of view on life.

It is a point of view. It really is. And it sort of pricks a hole in things, too, keeps things in line. And then also it helps you deal with things which are overwhelmingly tragic, which are undealable with. I mean the bad things are just horrendous. They're not funny at all, so you might as well make fun of everything else.

When you're writing, whether you're writing a screenplay or a play or an article, do you think about the audience that it's aimed for?

I don't think about the audience. You do think of the rhythm of the things and people laughing. You don't think about the audience per se. I mean, sometimes you think about [it], you don't want to—I don't like to be offensive, really. I know some people don't mind that at all.

In fact, aim for it.

Aim for it, right. But it depends. No, I don't mind offending peoples', you know, moral grounds. Fuck 'em. But you wouldn't want to write a character as offensive that you didn't want to be offensive. That's what I meant. But do

I think about the audience that it's for? Not really. Not really. Sometimes.

Does it sometimes surprise you who ends up being the audience for your play? Or the reader?

Yes. I just saw *Isn't It Romantic?* in Tokyo. You know, that's a play that I can't get done in London, no one has wanted to do it. But for some reason that show really worked in Japan. So, yes, that's a shocker.

Why do you think that was? Did they relate to the family-ness of it?

I think they related to the family-ness of it, and also, in Japan a woman who's over 25 who isn't married is known as a wedding cake after Christmas. Actually it was very interesting because this play worked almost as a political play. So that was quite interesting. But in terms of, one is always shocked who likes their plays and who doesn't. The person that you think will most like your play doesn't like it, and then someone else will like it. It's usually some maniac, some mass murderer; David Berkowitz will say "oh you're my favourite playwright."

Have you gotten reactions from your plays that surprised you? Interpretations that blew you over?

Sometimes, or you see a bad production that doesn't make any sense.

Do you have a specific emotional reaction to your plays? I mean, do you feel differently about **Uncommon Women** *say, than* **Isn't It Romantic?**

Yes you do. Well, yeah you do. Because you're so close to them that you do. I. . . It's funny, I have a real love I think for *Uncommon Women.* I really, I find it very dear. I think because whoever wrote it really cared a lot. There's a lot of raw emotion there. That monologue of Holly's is very raw, and dear. I admire *Isn't It Romantic?* because it's better crafted. It's very clean, that play. Sometimes I thought that people didn't take play as seriously as I would have liked them to. Because I thought there were very serious things being slyly discussed there. That's what was interesting about Japan. The director told me that he did my play because he was a revolutionary. That's like saying you did *Barefoot in the Park* because you're a revolutionary. But I found that very moving. I wrote this musical *Miami* that's not finished that I have to finish. And because it went through a difficult workshop production, I have a difficult relationship with it. So it all depends. What's nice about writing a new play is we don't know each other that well yet. So you do have different feelings about things.

This is a question I wanted to ask you. Do you think the 1980's are funny?

No. I was just writing about them. I really don't like the 1980's very much. I don't. It's all sort of retro-'50 or retro-'60. You know what it is? It's commenting. Or as Gerry Gutierrez would say, indicating. I do think they're funny. I mean Ronald Reagan and "I can't remember" is hilarious. I mean, someone must do something with that. What, you can't remember? I mean things like that are outra-

> **As soon as you start playacting in your writing or in your life, there's trouble, a little bit. Especially in your writing. Because what works is going to be whatever's honest to you.**
>
> —*Wendy Wasserstein*

geous. So, a man can't become president because he slept with a model, but you can start your own CIA and become a hero? That's nuts!

But maybe not inherently amusing.

But not amusing. No, I don't find it funny. Do you find it funny?

Well, I asked this only because a friend of mine and I were discussing political humor the other day. And saying how it seemed the 1980's were ripe for political humor, except that it was all so awful that the humor is sort of different. It's not like '60's humor.

It's true. You know what's sort of funny? When I was in London, all these people said to me, "How come you people don't write anything about the government? I mean, about Ronald Reagan. Why are there no plays about this? I mean, look at him." And in some ways, Mrs. Thatcher is funnier. Because she's so fucking dour and has no sense of humor that you want to lance her right away. I mean you just look at her and you want her to put her panty hose on her head. I mean she's just, she's horrible. Ronald Reagan is slightly different.

Well, George Carlin once said "If a stupid person goes senile, how can you tell the difference?" Your plays are not topical humor plays, but some of your pieces obviously in newspapers must treat topical matters. How do you approach that differently than in a play?

Well it's different with a play because the newspaper thing gets published right away so you can reflect off of the topicality of it. In a play I try to go more through the character of it. If I'm writing now about Reagan it would be as filtered through the characters who lived through that period. *Uncommon Women* is in a way about feminism. It's just as filtered through the people who were participating in it at that time.

Do you find that women have a different reaction to your writing than men?

Sometimes. It can go either way. They can either take me more seriously and see what's there, and have connection to it, or—you know, everybody has an opinion, and you know the opinion of "well, we know all of this already, and we've moved beyond this." So you get a little bit of that too. You know, one time I was at a bar in Westport, Connecticut, waiting for the train, which was late, and some little girl with brown curly hair and glasses, and looked sort of sad, came up to me and recognized me, and said she loved my play, and I thought "she is the saddest girl in the room. Of course she loves my plays! Anywhere you go, you look for the saddest girl with the brown curly hair and they're the ones who like my play!" I thought, "I bet Beth Henley gets like good looking blonde girls, nice and thin, coming up to her and saying they liked her play. They don't have those sad eyes."

Do you think that men always get it when they see your pieces?

I think sometimes they do. I think sometimes they don't. I mean, sometimes they might think they're trivial, I think. But no, I don't think that much, really. I don't think so. I hope not.

Do you think that, when you say trivial, do you think that smaller things are more important to women?

No, but I also don't think that women write plays like "Fuck you, fuck me, fuck you, fuck you, fuck the duck, fuck the dog, fuck a this, fuck a that. Goodbye." I mean you don't, that's not how you hear it. And if that's what's good and taut, well then, I don't write good or taut. You know, I think there's room for everything. Because there are women who can write like that, too. I don't, but there are people who do, and do it well, and do it brilliantly. I mean, Caryl Churchill's new play is wonderful. It's a tough piece of work, you know. But it's, it's good.

Do you find it's a small community of women writers? Or is it just a small community of known *women writers?*

I think maybe known. It's funny, I was on the NEA [National Endowment for the Arts] panel the other year, playwriting panel, and we gave grants. I think the grants went to 60% women writers. I think there are more and more women writers. Definitely more and more. And wonderful writers, too. And when you think about Marsha Norman and Beth Henley, all those people, they're terrific.

Do you think it's hard for women to get started? To get funding, to get. . .

You know what's hard? It's hard to keep one's confidence. It's hard to keep yourself in the middle, not to be a nice girl and not to be a tough girl, you know, but somehow to be yourself. That's hard. And as soon as you start play-acting in your writing or in your life, there's trouble, a little bit. Especially in your writing. Because what works is going to be whatever's honest to you. So I think in that way, yes, there's somewhat of a problem. But, I mean, I think the most important thing is that decent women write and get those plays out. I think that's very important.

But you see more women now, I mean, nobody goes into shock when a Marsha Norman play is done.

No. I don't think any play does not get done because [it's by] a woman. I mean, I'm a product of the O'Neill and Playwrights Horizons, Yale Drama School; these aren't specifically women's institutions. When you write plays and you're a woman writer, you get these questions like, are you a feminist? She's a dear writer. She's a tough writer. You don't get this stuff when you're a man.

He's just a writer.

He's a writer, right, it's not he's tough, he's dear, he's a feminist, she's a sweetie. I mean, what is this? You know? She's got balls? The men, they all have balls. They don't have this problem! So, I mean, that's sort of, that's hard.

Is it hard to take emotionally?

Yeah, I think that is hard, a little bit. Yeah, I do.

You say you're not a joke teller, but do you have a favorite joke?

I don't. I can't tell a joke. I can't, I don't know any jokes. I forget them. People tell me them and I can't remember. I can't remember topical jokes like Chernobyl jokes about Chicken Kiev, I can't remember them. I just don't. I don't know how to write one, or tell one. There was even a joke character, I mean a comedian in *Miami* and I had a hard time telling his jokes. Because the comedy for me comes out of character. If I had to write, not somebody who's a comedian but someone, if it came out of their character, I could do that. But that's different jokes. And I always think whoever makes up those jokes that get spread around so quickly must be terribly bright.

What makes you laugh?

I don't know. Rubber chickens. It depends, there's a variety of things. I think when Ricky Ricardo shows up and Lucy has a baby and he's dressed in his voodoo outfit for the Club Tropicana—I think that is so funny. I have a bit of a whimsical sense of humor. I like puncturing things, though. I think that that's quite funny. And verbal play, too, I think is very funny. I don't like slapstick very much. But I think other people do, I just don't care for it very much. Although some things I think are very funny. I know there's a Woody Allen movie, is it *Take The Money and Run* where his parents are both wearing Groucho glasses? That's *very* funny. Very funny. You know why? Sometimes funny things are almost like the fantasy, and then it comes real.

It's sort of like trying to find the fine line between the completely absurd and the everyday.

That's right, that's right. Or seeing it. Seeing the completely absurd *in* the everyday.

It's sort of the description of my life.

Yes, it's true. Mine too. So, Esther . . . ?

So darling. Well thank you, darling, very much.

Oh, darling, a pleasure.

Wendy Wasserstein with Kathleen Betsko and Rachel Koenig (interview date 1987)

SOURCE: An interview in *Interviews with Contemporary Women Playwrights*, Beech Tree Books, 1987, pp. 418-31.

[*Below, Wasserstein discusses the characters, language, and humor of her* Uncommon Women and Others *and* Isn't It Romantic *as well as her views about being a woman playwright and the future of American theater in general.*]

[*Interviewer*]: *Your plays are very funny. Will you talk a lit-*

tle about comedic writing in general, and then specifically about women's comedy?

[Wasserstein]: Well, there's always that old Woody Allen joke: When you write comedy you sit at the children's table, and when you write tragedy you sit at the adult table. But I'm not sure that's true. It's very satisfying for me to hear the audience laugh. The audience is alive, it's *there*. What's interesting about my plays is that they are comedies, but they are also somewhat wistful. They're not *happy,* nor are they farces, which is odd because I've been given offers to write sit-coms for television, and I don't think I'd be good at it. There's an undercurrent in my work.

Christopher Durang is a very dear friend, and a brilliant writer. We've collaborated on a film [*When Dinah Shore Ruled the Earth*] and it's interesting how our voices merge at a point. Mine tends to be more warm, and his is more startling. There's a give and take, but I'm still interested in that warmth. Collaboration is also a matter of stretching oneself, trying to get out into other forms. Chris talks about moving toward more warmth, and I find myself moving toward something darker. When we wrote the movie, we met every day, and wrote the whole script on one notepad. The writing became *one* voice. It was very interesting.

Do you think it is more natural for you to write "warm"?

I wouldn't say that. It's hard, talking about a female aesthetic. Best put, I once heard Marsha Norman say that women writing plays had secrets they wanted to tell. When I wrote *Uncommon Women and Others,* I wanted to write an all-woman play. Now given that, what am I going to write? My characters rafting down the Colorado River? It just happens that the men I've known have not gone to girls' schools for eight years. They have not had the pleasure of a course on "Gracious Living." They also did not grow up—and hopefully this has changed—with having to hear "Be a sweet girl, be a good girl." That's different nowadays. I was writing *Uncommon Women* from an experience I had. I don't know if that gets down to an aesthetic. When you're talking about an aesthetic, you're also talking about language.

How would you describe your stage language?

The people in my plays talk circularly. They do not talk directly. I don't know if that's women or that's Wendy. It's probably Wendy. But Wendy is a woman writer, and *Uncommon Women* comes from a woman's experience. It's *about* women sitting around talking. It's reflective. I do agree with Marsha Norman in that I think there are stories to tell that haven't been told. But you're not only telling them for women, hopefully.

You said that in working on **Isn't It Romantic** *you were interested in the ways in which your characters became trapped by their own humor.*

Janie Blumberg, the main character, is totally trapped by her own sense of humor. Some people seeing the first version of the play thought it was composed of very witty one-liners, but I felt it was how Janie talks. Janie is a char-

acter who has a problem expressing her feelings and she desperately wants to be liked.

Is Janie's humor a way of protecting herself?

It's a protection, but it's a vulnerability as well. I think that may be very female. Janie in *Isn't It Romantic* tells joke, joke, joke and then finally explodes. Finally, she discovers her own strength. And furthermore, there is a strength in being comedic. It's a way of getting on in the world, of taking the heat out of things. Humor is a life force.

It seemed that many of the critics missed the irony of **Isn't It Romantic** *in its original production.*

Women playwrights fall into a trap because the audience goes in expecting a "woman's play," with a feminist sensibility. Nobody goes into a man's play and thinks, "I want a man's point of view on this." They don't expect to discover the male playwright's political feeling about the sexes. That is never asked of men. For example, when Janie in *Isn't It Romantic* doesn't marry the doctor, it's not because she's a grand feminist, or because she loves her career, or wants to ride off on a tractor. He isn't right for her. As a playwright, first and foremost you must be true to your characters. It's the character's motivation; not me speaking for womankind. Even *Uncommon Women* doesn't say, "This is what I feel about women." Basically what it's saying is "I'm very confused." The characters are confused; they're also dear and kind and funny. The play asks: "Why are they so confused?" I want to *show* you their confusion. But it's not saying I have any answers. And what it's really not saying is "Fuck you."

Didn't you once say that **Isn't It Romantic** *is about being funny?*

Janie Blumberg's humor gives her the ability to distance herself from situations. But she simultaneously endears herself to people by being amusing. The play is about her difficulty in communicating. She's so verbal, and yet she can't talk. It's a play about speech—about the ability to speak and not to speak at the same time, which comes from the pressure women are under to be a good girl, a smart girl, and a warm girl, simultaneously.

As a playwright, first and foremost you must be true to your characters. It's the character's motivation; not me speaking for womankind.

—*Wendy Wasserstein*

Is **Isn't It Romantic** *about the price of being a good, smart, warm and funny girl?*

Yes, I think so.

Is Janie willing to pay the price?

Janie is strong, but she doesn't know it. Maybe she secretly knows she's strong and is frightened by it. It's not going to be easy for Janie, but she is able to move from feeling and that's interesting. In fact, that's character. Janie is stronger than her friend Harriet who has all the externals. . . . Harriet could be a cover on *Savvy* magazine. The girl who "has it all." You know, the person who gets up at eight o'clock in the morning, spends twenty minutes with her daughter and ten minutes with her husband, then they jog together, she drives to work, comes home to her wonderful life, studies French in the bathtub, and still has time to cry three minutes a day in front of the mirror.

What's troublesome, from my point of view, about the Women's Movement is that there are *more* check marks to earn nowadays. More pressure. What's really liberating is developing from the inside out. Having the confidence to go from your gut for whatever it is you want. Janie is able to do that.

The character of Janie's mother in ***Isn't It Romantic*** runs around saying, "I like life, life, life." She's a bit of a crackpot, but she *does* have a spirit. The comedy itself is a spirit. It's not an application form, a resume, it's life. This life spirit creates a current, a buoyancy, which, getting back to drama, is very important. It's important to reach the essence of that spirit in what you create. That, to me, is heroic.

In the Phoenix production of **Isn't It Romantic** *most of the critics were upset by the fact that in the end, Janie rejected the nice Jewish doctor as a husband.*

If the Jewish doctor had been a creep, and Janie decided not to marry him, the play would be a feminist statement: Good for her, see how strong she is. I wanted to write a nice man. And the play's not about the fact that she doesn't marry. I don't feel one way or another about marriage per se, though I'd like to get married one of these days. . . .

The doctor isn't really perfect, is he?

He's not perfect at all! He tells her he wants to make alternate plans, he calls her "monkey," he buys an apartment without telling her. If these are people's ideals, after the play they should see a marriage counselor. And Janie's not scared. He is a Jewish doctor, he is darling and funny and dear, but Janie has a right to her decisions. She has a right, even if that means she's going to be alone. Even if she's *wrong* in her choice. Even if she's going to sit in her apartment and cry every night, if that's what she wants to do. . . .

Since the emergence of women's issues, men's behavior has been under close scrutiny. You seem to have taken an ironic swipe at the "new male" in drawing your character, Paul Stuart [from **Isn't It Romantic**], *whose behavior is old hat—despite his liberated rhetoric.*

Things have gotten very confusing. It's true that men can exploit the new rhetoric. My character Paul Stuart is very smart when he says that when he got married, women didn't know they could have careers. He says, "Now you girls have careers and *you* want a wife." He's pretty much figured things out. The fact that *he* still gets to have a wife is interesting. . . .

Your plays bear the message that women can't *"have it all." Helen Gurley Brown says that women* can *have it all, if only they learn the right strategies.*

I've never been one for strategies, really. Because I can't make one for myself. What should you do? Take colored index cards for everything you want, put them on a bulletin board: baby on the pink card, job on the blue? I never understood how those things work. I know there are women who have careers *and* babies. They work very hard. More credit to them. But the whole notion of "having it all" is ridiculous. It's a ridiculous phrase. Who's determining what "it all" is? Helen Gurley Brown? That's not fair. No man has had the pressure during the past ten years of having a different article come out every two weeks dictating how he should live his life. It changes every two weeks!

There isn't any formula for happiness. The very basic expectations of being a "good girl," a "nice girl," and a "kind girl" are still being put upon us. This is confusing because there's nothing wrong with wanting to be kind, unless it hurts you, or keeps you from doing what you want to do.

Who is responsible for this malaise? The media? The theater? The government?

I don't know. You *do* want to work *and* have children *and* be gorgeous. But until there's a dictum for men that says, "Have it all," it's not fair for women to feel they should. Even with all the media talk about the "new father" and "time-sharing" I've yet to see the male "have it all" article come out.

As far back as **Uncommon Women** *you seemed to have an awareness of the way the "new male" was absorbing the liberated woman's language. Rita says, "The only problem with menstruation for men is that some sensitive schmuck could write about it for the* Village Voice *and become the new expert on women's inner life."*

I guess to be fair, things have changed. . . .

Doesn't it sometimes seem things have regressed?

Well, I went back to Mt. Holyoke in 1979 to see a production of **Uncommon Women.** I asked some of the students there what they thought about the play. One of them said, "Well, we think it's a nice *period* piece." I said, "Who do you think I am, Sheridan?" I mean, I had been studying there only eight years before! Then the women told me that unlike my characters, they knew what they wanted: to go to business school, or earn Ph.D.s or get married. I did think to myself, "This is becoming like Amherst College during the fifties." What's so great about that?

Can we go back to the critics for a moment? Not many of them were kind about your rather broad character, Susie Friend, the cheerful organizer in **Uncommon Women.** *Shakespeare was allowed a few clowns, why not Wendy Wasserstein?*

Lots of women I know have grown up with Susie Friends. Now that's a woman's story! There have always been these

> **I tend to go on big canvases. My favorite authors are Russian: Tolstoy, Chekhov . . . the whole idea of presenting a social life and a personal life interests me.**
>
> —*Wendy Wasserstein*

little organizers in women's colleges. Of course, now they're organizing in banks!

Is it okay for her to be a little less than three-dimensional because she is a peripheral character?

Susie Friend was a device. If you see *Uncommon Women* as a spectrum of women: on one end, there's Susie Friend, and on the other, there's Carter, the intellectual. That's all.

You've said that the character of Tasha Blumberg in Isn't It Romantic *was close to your mother in some ways.*

Well, she is and she isn't. When you base a character on someone in real life, you are always condensing, as well as trying to keep the tone consistent. Tasha is not totally like my mother. Although my mother *is* a danseur! There is also an assumption that every mother you write is your own mother. That's not necessarily true. You have different things to say about a mother-daughter relationship at different times of life and in different kinds of plays.

You've also said that it was easier for you to write the character Lillian, Harriet's mother, in Isn't It Romantic *than Tasha Blumberg. Why is that?*

Harriet's mother is an intriguing character. She was a more interesting woman to write because, of all the women in *Isn't It Romantic,* she is the most modern.

Some of the critics saw Lillian as bitter. Do you agree?

Lillian is not hard or bitter. She is not Faye Dunaway in *Network.* But she's tough. In terms of comedy, she was fun to write because her sense of humor is very different from the other characters I have written. She has a little inflection, she's very wry and dry, and that was good for me because sometimes all of my characters have similar senses of humor. Lillian knows of the world and her own life. She has made her choices and has come to terms with them. In her life, there was not room for a man. She could not "have it all." She did pay a price and what's tragic is that her daughter is now going to pay another price.

What is the price for Lillian?

Lillian had a bad marriage with a selfish man. Maybe with a more understanding man, she would have been fine. Who knows what the problem was? But in her life, she could not work it out. It wasn't worth it to her. Lillian is not a romantic. Lillian is fair. She is modern because she faces herself. What she has to say is honorable: "You tell

me who has to leave the office when the kid bumps his head or slips on a milk carton." If she has to go home, time and time again, then why should she be with a man anyway? From Lillian's point of view, there is no reason to have *two* babies, your husband and your child. What's interesting is that Lillian, in her own way, is also a "good girl." She is not doing anything wrong. She is very American. A good mother, a hard worker . . .

Be more specific as to what was more difficult about writing Tasha Blumberg, the character most nearly like your own mother.

I'll tell you why she was harder to write than Lillian. I've always thought that *Uncommon Women* was me split into nine parts, in terms of characters. But the truth is, what was always the hardest in *Uncommon Women* was writing Holly, who, autobiographically, is closest to me, though there are parts of me in all of the characters. That play is twofold. First, it's a play about Holly and Rita, which examines the fact that the Women's Movement has had answers for the Kates of the world (she becomes a lawyer), or the Samanthas (she gets married). But for the creative people, a movement can't provide answers. There isn't a specific space for them to move into. Holly was the hardest to write because I thought, "That's Wendy," or people will think, "THAT'S WENDY! There's the hips, there she is." And I also didn't want to self-congratulatize when drawing that character. So I find it difficult to write autobiographical characters. There aren't good guys and there aren't villains in my plays. If I were to say there's a problem with my writing, it's typified by the line in *Uncommon Women* when one character says, "Sometimes it's difficult having sympathy with everyone's point of view." I have been accused of being too generous to the other, less autobiographical characters in my plays, but in fact, it is hardest for me to be generous to the character that is closest to me.

You feel you have to humble yourself?

Yes. I think so. When someone said to me, "You're a playwright, why use a confused persona to represent yourself in a play? *You* know what you're doing. Why shouldn't the character?" I said, "I'm a playwright *because* I don't know everything. Because I am trying to figure things out." You do divide yourself up when you are writing. Marty Sterling, the doctor in *Isn't It Romantic* has the sweetest speech about marriage. Why doesn't Janie have that speech?

So Tasha Blumberg was harder to write than Lillian because she was more autobiographical?

Tasha is closer to my mother, that is true. I find my mother very funny. My mother dances six hours a day. She's, as she says, twenty-one plus, and she has not gone to Mt. Holyoke, but she is very sharp. Sometimes I find her humor funnier than my own. I saw my mother on the street the other day. I was in a taxi, and I stopped. She jumped in and said, "Oh, it's so wonderful to have children, honey. It's so wonderful to see you and I only hope that by the time you have children, you take a fertility pill and have five." Then she looked at me and said, "And that's going into the play, isn't it?" I thought, there is no way I could write anything as good as that. And she knew it. I haven't finished with my mother yet. That is the truth of all this.

Will you write about it someday?

Maybe it's where my writing is going. I don't know. Although I am proud of the last scene in *Isn't It Romantic,* the play doesn't deal with the pain of that subject. The real reason for comedy is to hide the pain. It is a way to cope with it. A way of staying "up." It's a privacy. You are there, and you are not there. You don't share equally about every topic. That's the truth of language, the truth of dialogue. If you did, you wouldn't be writing language, you wouldn't be writing what you are hearing, how people really talk. . . .

So humor creates subtext?

Yes and it is also part of the delight of writing itself. When you come up with a good line, you make yourself laugh, right there at the typewriter. It gives you pleasure.

I want to say that the other reason Lillian was easier to write than Tasha was that Lillian was someone on my mind. She is contemporary. She's an image that is closer to, if not me, then me ten years from now. She reflects a conflict that I think about a lot. Men and children. Having children alone, and whether or not that's possible. Tasha Blumberg—forget my mother—is from another world, a different time, which is harder to capture. Lillian is closer to my world. I have considered writing plays about the young Tasha at Radio City, the dancer. And at one point in *Isn't It Romantic,* Janie gets up and starts to tap dance. There is an image of a person alone, who dances. Janie's mother is a dancer, and that is the gift from mother to daughter.

You studied dramatic writing at Yale. Were there other women in the playwriting program?

Susan Nanons was there, Sharon Stockard-Martin, Grace McKeaney . . . they are all very talented women. But no, the playwriting program was not overflowing with women.

Did you take a lot of flak for writing **Uncommon Women,** *a play with an all-female cast?*

I made the decision to write a play with all women after seeing all that Jacobean drama, where a man kisses the poisoned lips of a woman's skull and drops dead. I thought, "I can't identify with this." I wanted to write a play where all the women were alive at the curtain call. And I had seen my friend, Alma Cuervo, whom I love dearly, have to play the pig-woman in *Bartholomew Fair,* a panda in *General Gorgeous* . . . I thought, What's going on?

Were people shocked by **Uncommon Women?**

Well, the play was not in as good a shape as it is now. I do remember someone who saw the Yale production saying that I was a "subset" of Christopher Durang. Chris came to my defense and said, "When I write my play about an all woman's college, you can call me." It was shocking to me.

You said in an interview that the point of view at Yale was that "the pain in the world is a man's pain."

Though women are often said to write "small tragedies," they are *our* tragedies, and therefore large, and therefore legitimate. They deserve a stage.

Why didn't **Uncommon Women,** *with all of its success, move to Broadway?*

We had one offer, which is an interesting story. The producer told me that at the end of the play things should be different. He said the play was too wistful. He thought, that at the end, when everyone asks Holly, "What's new with you?" she should pull out a diamond ring and say, "Guess what? I'm going to marry Dr. Mark Silverstein." I thought, "Well, she'd have to have a lobotomy, and I'd have to have a lobotomy too." So the play never went to Broadway. It does stick in my craw because *Uncommon Women* is a very good play and it had such an amazing cast. But sometimes you've opened a door, and when you go to the next work, people listen. Don't I sound old and wise? The play should have moved to Broadway!

Is **Uncommon Women** *a political play?*

It's political because it is a matter of saying, "You must hear this." You can hear it in an entertaining fashion, and you can hear it from real people, but you must know and examine the problems these women face. It all comes from the time I was in college, which was a time of great fervor. There used to be pieces in that play that were very political. The most political part was when Mark Rudd came to Mt. Holyoke. In that version, Susie Friend had a strike speech and even organized a strike for Mark Rudd.

Why did you take that out?

Well, I took it out because I thought that it would open the play up to all the questions of Vietnam, and that's another play. I really wanted to do something so that women's voices could be heard. I'm happy I did that. I can remember the 1969 Cambodia strike. Simultaneously, Amherst College was accepting women for the first time. There were twenty-three women and twelve hundred men. That was a glorious experience. I didn't go to the dining hall for two weeks. I was scared to death! The first night I was there, the men were rating us! I remember going to the student-faculty meeting and saying, "You have to let us stay here." The speaker seemed to think this was a very selfish issue. He said, "We have Kent State, we have Cambodia . . . what's the big deal about a little girl wanting to stay at Amherst College?" I thought, "This is one of the most important things happening in terms of long-range changes for women." In fact, Amherst College went coed two years later. That's just an isolated incident. I do think that that whole period has not yet been resolved. Maybe things *are* regressing. I try to find answers to these issues through my plays.

Your character Leilah in **Uncommon Women,** *says, "Sometimes I think I just need to live in a less competitive culture." How do you think that relates to being an artist in America?*

When I was at Yale, I was frightened to death. I remember

years later telling Christopher Durang that I felt like I was going from platform to platform, trying to catch the train to Moscow. I went from platform six to platform seven and I kept missing the train. I had no idea what I was doing at drama school. Everyone else I knew was going to law school or marrying lawyers, except for my immediate friends, who seemed as cuckoo as me. I really couldn't explain my feelings to anyone. If you tell someone you are a playwright, they say, "So what do you do for a living?" Or, if you're a successful playwright, they say, "Gee, isn't that glamorous?" You think, "Yeah, it's real exciting. I sit in a room alone every day and I write. Thrilling!" Either way, you are in an odd spot. It doesn't place you in the margins, but you are not in the mainstream of society. It certainly doesn't make for a secure life. But it does at least make for a life of doing what you want to do. I feel very lucky to be able to do that.

You seem to make a plea for community in your work. . . .

Yes. Or at least, a plea to establish your own kind of family. Maybe my family is Chris Durang and Ted Talley and André Bishop. It could well be, but again, that's pretty marginal. You can't go to weddings and say "My family is Chris Durang, and Ted Talley and André Bishop. . . ."

Would you tell us something about Playwrights Horizons?

I am very lucky because that theater is my home, and it has made a tremendous difference to me, having someplace that I know I can work out of. I've had a long association with the people there. Life is competitive, but Playwrights Horizons is not. It is a community, and that has always been very important to me.

The theater is the home of the individual voice—at least in dramatic form. It is not in movies or television. For myself, I am trying to work on structure, on comedy, and on being able to create a feeling of community. That can only happen in the theater.

—*Wendy Wasserstein*

What happens when you are in rehearsal with a play? Are you able to maintain sufficient artistic control over your work?

It depends on the production and on the play. I was there through everything with **Uncommon Women.** I was at the [Eugene] O'Neill [National Playwrights Conference], the Phoenix Theatre, and when they did the television production for PBS. I had a good relationship with the director, Steve Robman.

You felt your intentions were given enough attention?

Yes. But subsequently, I have seen productions of **Uncom-**

mon Women around the country and I can't tell you the sort of horrifying things I've seen. It's unbelievable.

How do you react to a bad production?

It depends on whether you've been involved in the actual production. Sometimes you just go to see the play. That's taught me that there is a point at which you have to let a play go. It was hard for me to let **Uncommon Women** go because it had such a short run in New York. I like to be able to go to a theater for more than a two-and-a-half-week run.

You don't experience anger in rehearsal? You've never had to fight for your intentions?

Well, yes, sure I have. Rehearsal is a very important time to learn not to be such a good girl. I think you have to learn to speak up, because the point is, it's your play, and you *do* know something about it. It is very important to pick the right director. That is step one. And you can't be a good girl about picking a director either. You can't pick somebody just so everyone will like you. You have to pick someone you respect and who will be right for the play.

Have you ever worked with a woman director?

Susan Dietz directed **Uncommon Women** in California.

Did you feel she brought any special insights to the work?

I did like the production a lot. I don't know how to answer that question because I was assigned Steve Robman at the O'Neill and he stayed with the production throughout. It wasn't a conscious choice for a male director or against a female director. It is very important that there be more women directors, and that more women directors are encouraged, which goes all the way back to the question of how many women directing students there are at Yale. I do think what you want is a *good* director.

What did you mean, earlier, when you spoke of "letting go" of the play?

I told Chris the other night that I've had the sensation, with both **Uncommon Women** and **Isn't It Romantic** of waiting for the play to embrace me. I keep waiting for the play to give back what I've given. And it cannot happen. You can get depressed. Because if you're a good writer, you're generous and you give it everything and people laugh and applaud—but still, the play is inanimate. It cannot reach out and embrace you. That's hard to come to terms with. You can follow a play around the country waiting for that to happen. But it can't—and finally, you have to separate from it and just send it out.

Is the closest you can get to that embrace hearing the spontaneous laughter from the audience?

Maybe. But during **Uncommon Women,** there was something special among those actresses and me. I can remember being in the dressing room with Swoosie Kurtz and Jill Eikenberry and Alma Cuervo, and Anna Levine, Glenn Close and Ellen Parker and there was the sense of embracing, a sense of all starting out together . . . again, that feeling of community. And I would say I feel it more at the laughter than at the applause.

Why did you decide to study playwriting at Yale instead of attending Columbia Business School, where you had also been accepted?

You know, I even sent Columbia a deposit! When I graduated from Mt. Holyoke I came to New York and took writing courses at City College. I studied with Israel Horovitz and Joseph Heller. While studying playwriting with Israel, I had my first play done at Playwrights Horizons—this was back when it was at the YMCA on Fifty-second Street. I applied to both programs because I felt "I've *got* to make a living." I was living at home at the time. I thought I'd go to business school, then get a job in Chicago and everything would be fine. But when I got into Yale School of Drama, I thought, "Playwriting is something I really want to do. It's worth a shot." But it was hard. It took me a long time to take myself seriously. I mean, it still takes me a long time to take myself seriously. . . .

Did Durang and Talley have difficulty taking themselves seriously?

I don't know. I don't think they thought something was wrong with them because they weren't in law school or married to a lawyer. I thought something was wrong with me. I thought I was a Ford Pinto. Now, I've gotten used to it. I'm used to living a life of eighty percent security.

Does a Guggenheim Fellowship help with that feeling of eighty percent security?

Yes. That was the best thing since **Uncommon Women.** It is a certified "We believe in you." I have a funny story about that. In October, my father said, "So what are you doing?" I said, "Applying for a Guggenheim." He said, "What's that?" I told him it was a foundation that gives artists money to finish their work. Then he said, "No daughter of mine's going on welfare!" I'm the only person whose parents are going to disinherit her for winning a Guggenheim!

Did you see **Uncommon Women** *as a "non-play," as some of the reviewers did?*

Uncommon Women is not a conventionally structured play. On a simple level, it moves through the seasons of the year. I do not see that play as presentational. It's like an odd sort of documentary. I am more interested in content than form. **Uncommon Women** is episodic. I don't know what actually *happens* in that play . . . they graduate.

Quite a lot happens. . . .

But it is an emotional action. And I tend to go on big canvases. My favorite authors are Russian: Tolstoy, Chekhov . . . the whole idea of presenting a social life and a personal life interests me. I also love Ibsen.

There's much reference recently to "The new woman playwright"—Mel Gussow's article in The New York Times Magazine *[May 1, 1983], for example. Is it really that women are newcomers to playwriting, or is it the attention that's new?*

I think it's the attention that's new. I do think there are women who open doors, like Marsha Norman. I don't know if her play 'night, Mother could have won a Pulitzer Prize twenty years ago. So maybe there is a little more attention nowadays. But at the same time, when I saw that article, I thought, "Where is Corinne Jacker?" And that article also brings up the whole issue of whether women playwrights are a separate category. We are all playwrights. I think that is very important. But for now, any minority group must be labeled. Our idea of a playwright is a white male—then all the others are separated into subsets: black playwrights, gay playwrights, women playwrights, and so on. The point is, we are all in it together. But I listen to my plays, and as I hear them, I distance myself, and I still think, "A woman wrote this."

Are female playwrights becoming less political than they were in the sixties and seventies?

It depends on what you see as political. Politics on the largest level is *from each according to their ability.* Nine girls taking a curtain call can be seen as political. It's important in terms of feeling legitimate. So is the fact that men can come to my plays and laugh, and that some girl from New Jersey comes to the play and says, "This is my story." And if my story can reach her, maybe *she* can tell *her* story. That is very important. Comedy does not segregate the political.

Do you feel that British women playwrights are more likely to be overt in their politics?

That could be true. It could have to do with being brought up in a society where feminism has been connected to broader political issues. Maybe feminism has taken a different shape there. Caryl Churchill is a wonderful playwright. Her *Top Girls* was great. The way she took the larger political scope and then looked at the personal was fantastic.

I believe in comedy, in its spirit, and in its ability to lift people off the ground. And the personal level, to me, is somewhat comedic.

—Wendy Wasserstein

Can you give us a summation?

It is very important that women keep writing plays for many reasons. The theater is the home of the individual voice—at least in dramatic form. It is not in movies or television. I think the work of women in America is evolving. For myself, I am trying to work on structure, on comedy, and on being able to create a feeling of community. That can only happen in the theater.

Are you optimistic about the state of American theater?

Oddly enough, I am. Because you do not write by committee in theater. The way that artists are discriminated against does have an effect on your pocketbook. Getting a Guggenheim helped this year, but you know, I am not making millions. The Guggenheim is not the money you would make as a first-year lawyer. That's how our society works. It makes you feel marginal. But, as somebody who believes in the individual voice, I still believe in the theater and what can happen there. I believe in comedy, in its spirit, and in its ability to lift people off the ground. I also think there are stories to tell, and as a woman writer, I want to tell those stories, to work out those conflicts. I want to take these conflicts from the political down to the personal. And the personal level, to me, is somewhat comedic. I hope to write a play that is going to be a history of the Women's Movement, which is a serious thing to take on. I want to write about someone who went through it and how it affected them personally—I want to explore the reverberations. Because I want to understand, and sometimes I understand better by writing. . . .

Graydon Carter   (review date March 1989)

SOURCE: "East Side Stories," in *Vogue,* Vol. 179, No. 3, March, 1989, p. 266B.

[*In the following unfavorable review, Carter characterizes* The Heidi Chronicles, *as "Off-Broadway lite" and reminiscent of television sitcoms.*]

Wendy Wasserstein's **The Heidi Chronicles** and Richard Greenberg's *Eastern Standard* are both comedic attempts to humanize the anxieties and dreams of bloodless yuppie existence. Drenched in soppy good intention, both plays have moved from venturesome Off Broadway, where they didn't really belong, to the commercial houses of Broadway, where they do. . . . In **The Heidi Chronicles** [Wasserstein] exhumes an old but promising device—picking up the lives of characters at dramatic junctures over a prolonged period—only to cruelly effect a sort of dramatic euthanasia on it. Central to this theme are the character and career of Heidi Holland, played by Joan Allen.

Heidi's life is sketched out in eleven vignettes over the course of some twenty-three years. Along the way we are introduced to the two men in her life, Scoop Rosenbaum, a cocky, too-smart magazine editor played by Peter Friedman (who, in the course of researching his role, spent some time with me; he must have learned the cockiness elsewhere), and Peter Patrone, an awkward but acid-tongued gay pediatrician played by Boyd Gaines. It would be fun and delightfully voyeuristic to drop in on Heidi's life like this, if she weren't so unconnected with what is going on around her. Heidi, alas, is profoundly uninteresting, a lifeless, moody dishrag. Against all evidence to the contrary, everyone nevertheless seems to be mad about her.

Heidi's world is a catalog of baby-boomer clichés. Sensitive men become homosexuals. Independent women become lesbians. Heterosexuals marry but are unhappy. Homosexuals get AIDS. Former radicals become TV producers. Sixties anarchists become eighties capitalists. One young woman, sketched as a mid-1980s, on-the-go professional, is dressed, get this: *in a boxy business suit, with a*

white shirt, floppy red bow tie, and white running shoes and socks. This is social satire on a par with television's *Who's the Boss?*

You feel like you've seen it all before. And if you grew up in front of the television set, chances are you have. This is Off-Broadway lite, theater written for couch potatoes in the Esperanto of cocooning—sitcom language. At one point in **The Heidi Chronicles,** one character informs another that they have "charisma. [Beat.] *I hate charisma!*" A decade before, Lou Grant told Mary Richards: "You have spunk, Mary. [Beat.] *I hate spunk.*" Scoop Rosenbaum (devilishly clever, nicknaming a magazine editor "Scoop"), just married, and having difficulty getting out the word *wife,* says, "My waa . . . waaa . . . [slaps his face] *wife!*" Ted Baxter similarly stumbled over the word "marr . . . marrr . . . marriage" when he proposed to Georgette. Oh, but **The Heidi Chronicles** brings back such memories. Really, intermission felt more like a station break.

Gerald Weales   (review date 5 May 1989)

SOURCE: "Prize Problems: 'Chronicles' & 'Cocktail Hour'," in *Commonweal,* Vol. CXVI, No. 9, May 5, 1989, pp. 279-80.

[*An American novelist and drama critic, Weales is the author of such books as* American Drama since World War II *(1962) and* The Jumping-Off Place: American Drama in the 1960s *(1969). In the following excerpt from a review of a Broadway performance of* The Heidi Chronicles, *he comments on the play's major weaknesses, particularly centering on the character of Heidi, whom he considers both unconvincing and lacking in dramatic interest.*]

Wendy Wasserstein's **The Heidi Chronicles** began as a workshop production at the Seattle Repertory Theatre; then, shepherded by the Seattle Rep's Daniel Sullivan, it moved to a well-received off-Broadway debut and then to Broadway; it has now been blessed by the Pulitzer Prize committee. It is a typical American-theater success story of the 1980s, but I have trouble working up much enthusiasm for its triumphant journey.

The Heidi of the title is an art historian, a presumably intelligent and sensitive woman who moves from 1965 to 1989, picking her way through the ideational thickets of those years, only to find that the goal of her generation, to become an independent woman in a male world, brings emptiness with it. The audience follows Heidi's progress in brief scenes that teeter on the edge of broad satire and sometimes, as in the consciousness-raising meeting, fall over completely. Heidi remains pretty much the same throughout the fifteen years—concerned, but a little cold, a little distant, her involvement tinged with self-irony. On her stroll down memory lane, she is accompanied by the two men closest to her—a homosexual doctor who remains her best friend (and incidentally provides an excuse to bring in AIDS as an item in Wasserstein's cultural catalogue) and a fast-talking charmer, sometimes her lover, an intellectual conman who plays the main chance and persists in confusing the fashionable with the significant. Heidi's oldest woman friend, the only other important character in the play, is a Wasserstein joke, a chameleon who becomes whatever the moment requires: a ditsy sexpot, a jargonesque feminist, a member of an ecological commune, a power-lunch paragon in the entertainment business.

The chief weakness of the play is that it has no dramatic center. Heidi is so muted in her behavior that she serves as little more than a foil for the more animated characters—a kind of wall on which Wasserstein can hang her snapshots. Joan Allen is one of the finest reactors among American performers (consider last year's Tony-winning performance in *Burn This*), but however fascinating it is to watch Allen work, Heidi remains flaccid. We are supposed to understand the distress within the character, which surfaces primarily in runs of nervousness and in one unlikely overt moment in which she turns a speech at an alumnae gathering into a high whine of generational regret. At the end of the play, she has adopted a child and the suggestion is that she has found a certain solidity as a single mother, but nothing in the play or the character makes motherhood look like anything but an occasion for Heidi's next disappointment. The ending is as arbitrary as that of Wasserstein's earlier hit, *Isn't It Romantic,* in which the heroine decides for no very clear reason not to marry the man she loves; perhaps she had been to see *My Brilliant Career* at her local moviehouse.

If Heidi as activist and Heidi as unrealized lover are a bit difficult to accept in her *Chronicles,* Heidi as art historian is impossible. She is supposed to be an expert on female artists, correcting the sexual imbalance in the history of art, and we see her in lectures at the beginning of each act. Her manner is oddly frothy, her disclosure decorated with what I think of as wee academic jokies. The wee academic jokie, of which there are far too many on campuses, is not funny if it sounds as though it were written into the lecture, if it is taken out of the classroom context, if it makes the speaker sound as though she were apologizing for her subject matter. So it is with all of Heidi's jokies. Her lectures diminish the whole enterprise of rethinking the female presence in art. In part, that is a product of the unanchored Heidi described in the paragraph above. In part, it grows out of the play's tendency to trivialize the genuine concerns of women in particular, radicals in general, by emphasizing the fashionable patina on social change. As a comic writer, Wasserstein can see what is ludicrous in the convoluted social history of the last fifteen years. On the serious side, *The Heidi Chronicles* is one of those gee-it-didn't-turn-out-the-way-we-expected plays, another offspring of *The Big Chill.*

Richard Hornby (review date Autumn 1989)

SOURCE: A review of *The Heidi Chronicles,* in *The Hudson Review,* Vol. XLII, No. 3, Autumn, 1989, pp. 464-65.

[*An educator, critic, and nonfiction writer, Hornby teaches and writes about drama. In the following, he offers a negative assessment of* The Heidi Chronicles.]

Wendy Wasserstein's *The Heidi Chronicles* is a lifeless, vulgar play, rendered all the more irritating by the many awards that this non-playwright has won simply because she is a woman, writing on fashionable issues. Wasserstein does not even begin to know how to construct a play. Her characters are automatons, set in motion as targets for crude ridicule; her plots are aimless; her ideas are trite; her dialogue is pretentiously witless.

Heidi, originally performed at Playwrights Horizons, was transferred to Broadway last March in a surprisingly lavish production, starring the superb Joan Allen in a role well beneath her talent. In thirteen scenes, the play takes its title character from 1965 until today, purporting to depict the problems of an intelligent, single woman in contemporary society. Heidi encounters two men in her youth: A bright boy she first meets at a prep school dance, who eventually becomes a pediatrician, and who turns out to be a homosexual; and a smart-ass womanizer she meets at a McCarthy-for-President rally, who becomes a successful magazine publisher. She becomes the long-term friend of the former, despite his mercurial temperament, and the long-term lover of the latter, despite his many affairs and even his marriage to another woman. She takes a doctorate in art history; dabbles in feminism; becomes a professor; and finally, in 1989, when it is clear that she will probably never marry, she adopts a baby.

Joan Allen, tall, intelligent, beautiful, and charming, was marvelous last year as the dancer in Lanford Wilson's *Burn This.* That character became involved in a destructive sexual relationship similar to those in *Heidi,* but she was also articulate and energetic. This character does give two art history lectures in the play that are interesting and humorous in a low-key way, but when speaking with other characters she mostly hems and haws, and an extemporary talk to her finishing school alumnae degenerates into free-associative drivel. Heidi is so passive that she seems to be going through life in a daze. I could never understand why she doesn't tell the stereotypical folk who seem forever to be nagging her—the radical lesbian, the inane TV hostess, the Jewish American Princess, plus Heidi's two loudmouth boyfriends—simply to go to hell. Nor could I understand why a woman as attractive as Joan Allen should be limited to a homosexual and a compulsive philanderer when it comes to men.

The tacked-on, upbeat ending where Heidi adopts a baby (a girl, of course) also seemed implausible, a *dea ex machina* intended to demonstrated that a woman can find happiness and fulfillment without a husband. Thousands of American couples would like to know how a single, fortyish woman managed quickly to adopt a healthy white infant who, we are told, is intelligent and beautiful. In terms of the drama, moreover, *I'd* like to know how a character who has so far seemed totally unassertive suddenly found the courage and drive to adopt a child. It takes a lot of time and effort; you don't just pick them up at Bloomingdale's.

I liked Thomas Lynch's set designs early in the play, when he achieved a wide range of locales with simple means—a few hanging streamers to suggest the prep school dance, the bottom half of a huge museum banner to suggest the front of the Art Institute of Chicago. As the scenes progressed, however, the settings became ever more elaborate and mechanized, with revolving *periaktoi* (three-sided prisms) and sliding floor panels shifting walls and furniture about, until the stage floor seemed as cluttered and busy as a railway station. The growing ponderousness was a visual synecdoche for the play itself, which might have been a simple, unpretentious treatment of a young woman's life, but which turned into a cumbrous morality play about Everywoman in the Eighties.

Phyllis Jane Rose   (essay date October 1989)

SOURCE: "Dear Heidi: An Open Letter to Dr. Holland," in *American Theatre,* Vol. 6, No. 7, October, 1989, pp. 26-9, 114-16.

[*Rose was the founder of the Roses International Women's Theater and Softball Syndicate. In the excerpt below, written in the form of a letter dated 1 October 1989 to the protagonist of* The Heidi Chronicles, *she accuses the play's eponymous heroine of complicitly participating in the oppression of women and challenges her to actively oppose the patriarchal ways of contemporary society.*]

Oct. 1, 1989

South Adelaide, Australia

Dear Heidi,

I came to Australia to spend six months learning about women and the arts here. I arrived on the other side of the earth on April Fool's Day. I saw your **Chronicles** twice before I left the States, once at Playwrights Horizons and once on Broadway. I've been thinking about you ever since.

You haven't met me. I'm writing because you said you felt "stranded." I understand the feeling. I work in the theatre. Your field is art history. We both study images. We both work to create positive images of women.

Let me recount for you a dozen images I saw onstage in **The Heidi Chronicles.** Then you'll know if I missed something, and other readers will understand my references. The play's the thing. I don't presume that these snapshots are a substitute.

· · · · ·

1. You're 40 years old, and somewhat shy behind a lectern in a Columbia University classroom. Pleasant and softly sardonic, you explicate slides of little-known paintings by women from centuries past. Lily Martin Spencer's 19th-century canvas *We Both Must Fade* reminds you of "one of those horrible high school dances," the kind where "you sort of want to dance, and you sort of want to go home, and you sort of don't know what you want. So you hang around, a fading rose in the exquisitely detailed dress, waiting to see what might happen."

2. You're 16, at a high school dance in Chicago. You're with your best friend Susan, who knows exactly what the boy/girl rules are and loves playing the game. You're both on the sidelines. When "ladies' choice" is announced, Susan gets herself a partner. You sit down and read *Death Be Not Proud.* Peter Patrone comes in. Impressed that you're reading, he initiates a B-movie cruise fantasy and

asks you to marry him. "I covet my independence," you reply. "I want to know you all my life," he counters. "If we can't marry, let's be great friends." Peter teaches you to dance the hully-gully to "The Shoop Shoop Song."

3. You're 19, a student at Vassar, off the dance floor (again) at a Eugene McCarthy rally, when you're accosted by Scoop Rosenbaum, founder and editor of *The Liberated Earth News.* "You're obviously a liberal," Scoop challenges, "or you wouldn't be here." "I came with a friend," you dodge. Scoop one-ups you with his quick wit. "Lady, you better learn to stand up for yourself," he taunts, but when you do, he puts you down. You are intrigued with the challenge of beating Scoop at his own game. You accept his invitation to bed.

4. Now 21 and a student at Yale, you're visiting still-best-friend Susan, who's joined a feminist consciousness-raising group while attending law school. You tag along reluctantly and sit outside the circle: Jill, a recovering housewife; Becky, an abandoned adolescent; Fran, a passionate lesbian. Cajoled to speak, you tell them, "My interest is images of women from the Renaissance Madonna to the present." "A feminist interpretation?" Fran wonders. "Humanist," you specify. You talk about Scoop. "I allow him to make me feel valuable," you confess. "And the bottom line is I know that's wrong." Then, in a scene that hovers between ridicule and reverence, you join the circle and plead with the group, "Becky, I hope our daughters never feel like this. I hope all our daughters feel so fucking worthwhile. Do you promise we can accomplish that much, Fran?" At the end of the session, while the rest of you sing a campfire song in a circle, Fran puts on Aretha's "R-E-S-P-E-C-T," full volume.

5. Now 25 and writing your dissertation, you're demonstrating outside the Art Institute of Chicago to demand equal representation for women artists. Peter Patrone arrives chanting, "No more master-penises!" You tell him Susan has become a "radical shepherdess/counselor." He tells you he's become a "liberal homosexual pediatrician." You don't want to hear it, but you do. When Peter's lover arrives, the three of you march off chanting, "Women in Art!"

6. You're 28, and attending Scoop's wedding to Lisa. Peter and Susan are there, but you're not feeling social. Finally alone with Scoop, you tell him, "I'm writing a book of essays on women and art. . . . It's sort of humorous. Well, sort of social observation. I mean, it's sort of a point of view." Is it Scoop's decisiveness that makes you so indecisive? "We're talking life choices," he reminds you. "I haven't made them yet," you object. "Yes you have," he contradicts, "or *we'd* be getting married today." The lights fade as you and Scoop slow-dance to Sam Cooke's "You Send Me." You do not close your eyes. You seem to be somewhere else.

7. You're 31, and arrive late for the shower for Scoop and Lisa's first baby. You and Peter had gone to the memorial rally for John Lennon in Central Park, where you saw Scoop philandering. Everyone keeps this secret from Lisa. Susan has just accepted a film production job in L.A., "targeting films for the 25-to-29-year-old female audi-

ence." Scoop's successful magazine *Boomer* has just done a cover story on Peter Patrone, "The Best Pediatrician in New York under Forty." Nobody's happy. "I like men," another woman confesses, "but they're not very nice." You all toast, "To John. And Ringo, and Paul, and George, forever!"

8. You're 33 and appearing on "Hello, New York," a TV show about baby-boomers in the '80s. April, the media-ditz host, introduces you as an "essayist, curator, feminist." You are seated between Peter and Scoop. They monopolize the show, even when the questions are directed at you. Afterwards, you're angry. "You're clutching your purse," Scoop observes. "I have valuables," you retort. "I'm very late." Tight-lipped, you leave.

9. You're 35, and meeting Susan and a colleague in a trendy New York restaurant. Susan is visiting from Hollywood to offer you a job as consultant for a new TV series about women in the arts. You're sad because this is a power lunch, not a chance to reconnect. "I'm not political anymore," Susan asserts. "I mean, equal rights is one thing, equal pay is one thing, but blaming everything on being a woman is just passé." Spotting movie stars across the room, Susan and friend rush off. They accept your "no" to the TV offer, but they don't hear you.

10. You're 37, and your keynote address to the "Women, Where Are We Going?" luncheon at the Plaza Hotel turns into an extemporaneous nervous breakdown. Out pours a flood of apologies—for your unhappiness, for feeling worthless, for feeling superior. "I feel stranded," you confess, in embarrassment and humiliation. "And I thought the whole point was that we wouldn't feel stranded. I thought the point was we were all in this together."

11. You're 38 and you're moving. It's Christmas Eve, and you've brought all your records and books to donate to Peter's new AIDS ward for children (partially funded by Susan's new TV series about women and art). You've been offered a teaching position in the Midwest. "I've been sad for a long time," you tell Peter. "I don't want to be sad anymore." "Unfortunately, things are for real here," Peter counters, telling you about community violence against immune-deficient children and tallying up the number of friends' funerals he's had to go to. "A sadness like yours seems a luxury," he concludes. You reply, "I understand." And you stay, giving up the teaching job. The two of you reprise your B-movie cruise fantasy to "The Shoop Shoop Song."

12. You're 39, and you've bought an apartment. You're reading, alone, when Scoop appears, antic as always, to tell you that he's decided to sell *Boomer* and go into politics. Peter has helped you adopt a baby from Panama. You name her Judy, after *A Date with Judy*. Now your dream is in the future. If your daughter and Scoop's son ever get together, you muse, "He'll never tell her it's either/or, baby. And she'll never think she's worthless unless he lets her have it all. And maybe, just maybe, things will be a little better." Scoop calls you "a mother for the '90s." After he's gone, you awkwardly pick up Judy and say to her, "A heroine for the 21st." You rock her and croon Sam Cooke's "You Send Me," and we see the final slide:

you holding Judy on the steps of the Metropolitan Museum of Art under the banner for the Georgia O'Keeffe exhibition.

. . . . .

Since I've been in Australia, Heidi, *The Heidi Chronicles* (and your playwright, Wendy Wasserstein) have garnered numerous prestigious awards, including the Susan Smith Blackburn Prize (awarded to "a woman who deserves recognition for having written a work of outstanding quality for English-speaking theatre"), the Dramatists Guild's Hull Warriner Award (presented annually by other dramatists to an "American play dealing with contemporary political, religious or social mores"), the Pulitzer Prize in drama (for "excellence") and the Tony award (for best play of the season).

You've also gathered raves from most mainstream critics, female and male: "An enlightening portrait of a generation" (Mel Gussow, *The New York Times*), "Not just a funny play, but a wise one" (Howard Kissel, *The Daily News*), "A wonderful and important play, gloriously well-written and staged" (Linda Winer, *Newsday*). On the other hand, Frank Lipsius did call you a "milquetoast" in *The Financial Times,* and Jacques le Sourd (*Gannett Westchester Newspapers*) thought the play could be called *Memoirs of a Wallflower,* which I understand, given your physical positioning at dances, your propensity to sidestep and dodge direct opinion, and your reliance on the qualifier "sort of."

Two thoughtful feminist critics were caustically critical. Alisa Solomon in *The Village Voice* found *The Heidi Chronicles* "an unbearably clever play," "just the kind of show Susan would love to produce. It assures us that [intelligent, educated women] are funny for the same traditional reasons women have always been funny: They hate their bodies, can't find a man, and don't believe in themselves."

In her review for *Fresh Air* on National Public Radio, Laurie Stone accused the playwright of "newspeak," of "trivializing" protest, of "purport[ing] to portray feminists" although Heidi "rejects the word feminist in favor of humanist—as if fighting for women's rights were a diminishment." In response to your implication that the women's movement has left you stranded, Stone asks, "Would anyone dare suggest that the Civil Rights Movement promised minorities too much and is therefore to blame for middle-aged disappointment black people may feel?"

Good question.

Heidi, I *am* writing to you because you said you feel stranded.

If I were able to paint an image of *The Heidi Chronicles,* the composition would target Peter and Scoop in the center. At the outer edges I'd wash a shadow circle of anonymous male suitors. You would be trapped between the inner and outer circles, "hanging around," "waiting to see what might happen." The image doesn't change at the end of the play. You simply carry Judy with you because, even with Judy, you're "waiting" for a future when Scoop's son and your daughter might meet, "And she'll never think she's worthless unless he lets her have it all." I don't understand that last sentence, Heidi, but whatever it means, a man is still at the center, still in control of a woman feeling all right about herself.

It is because of this image that I write to you, Heidi. You *are* stranded, but not where and by whom you think. You have cut yourself off from us. You have barricaded yourself in a closed circle with men and, as someone said at Scoop and Lisa's shower, "They're not very nice."

Peter is wrong. You sadness is not a "luxury." Your sadness speaks of the dis-ease of half the population on earth.

Do you know that in the history of western European dramatic literature—until the 1970s—there are no images of women confronting the world as whole and unique persons? Until the 1970s, there are no roles for women in which her behavior does not center around the actions of a man.

The absence from the stage of images of women acting on their own beliefs in truth, beauty or justice implies that women do not act in this way in the world. Or, if they do, it is not important enough to be dramatized. In your *Chronicles,* your struggle for women artists, your professed dedication to content over form, are secondary to your relationships with men. Your intelligence becomes wit in their presence. Your imagination settles for fantasy.

As you know, Aeschylus' *Oresteia* trilogy is one of the oldest stories in the library of Western European drama. I want to retell you the story from a feminist (not a humanist) point of view.

In the first play, Clytemnestra kills Agamemnon, who has sacrificed their 13-year-old daughter Iphegenia so the weather will clear and his navy can sail, sack Troy and reclaim Helen (his wife's sister and his brother's wife).

In the second play, Orestes, encouraged by Apollo and by his sister Electra, kills his mother to avenge his father's murder.

As the third play opens, The Furies, defenders of mothers and matriarchy ("dark," "ugly," "despicable"), are "hounding" Orestes, demanding he be punished for the most heinous of crimes: matricide. Apollo, Orestes' defense lawyer, calls Athena to judge whether The Furies are right. Athena asks 12 citizens to be the jury. If the vote is tied, Athena will cast the deciding vote.

When I was in school, the play was taught as a record of the birth of "civilized" democracy, as demonstrated in the appointment of the first citizen jury and in the victory of Persuasion (Athena) over Violence (The Furies). I used to teach the play this way myself.

The setting is Ares Hill, where the Amazons camped, built their fortresses and were defeated. Iphegenia's murder is never discussed. Apollo argues that killing the father is a much worse crime than killing the mother because "the mother is no parent of that which is called her child, but only nurse of the new planted seed that grows. The parent is he who mounts."

The men of the jury are deadlocked. Athena casts her vote with Orestes—against The Furies and against matriarchy—because, she says, "There is no mother anywhere who gave me birth. I am always for the male."

Athena then "persuades" The Furies to go underground where they are to renounce their anger, "sit on shining chairs before the hearth," become household goddesses, preside over marriages, and change their names to The Kindly Ones.

If this is the beginning of Western democracy, it is also the end of justice and self-determination for women. A gynocentric value system has been officially buried. Calling The Furies "The Kindly Ones" is a newspeak trick. The future is male-centered.

Men declared war on women centuries before Aeschylus wrote *The Oresteia.* Male institutions effectively silenced independent women in public places long before the male-identified Athena (played by a male actor) assured the chorus of Greek citizens (land-owning men, played by male actors) that "I am always for the male." Rights of matrilinear descent were dead even as Athena sent The Furies underground to renounce their anger.

Still influenced by the Greeks, traditional Western theatre continues to define and delimit the nature and value of women's roles. In opera and mainstream theatre, when there are roles for women (including Shakespeare), women die, go mad, are banished or get married. The classical definition of "comedy" is a play that ends in marriage, effectively sending the "virgin" (she who is not possessed) to the hearth and male dominion.

Twentieth-century American musical comedies are direct descendants of this tradition. They continue to tame the wildness out of women. Consider *My Fair Lady. The Sound of Music, South Pacific.* In each, a witty, energetic, independent, optimistic young woman saves a middle-aged man from despair. Then they get married.

If I were able to paint an image of *The Heidi Chronicles,* the composition would target Peter and Scoop in the center. At the outer edges I'd wash a shadow circle of anonymous male suitors. Heidi would be trapped between the inner and outer circles, "hanging around," "waiting to see what might happen." The image doesn't change at the end of the play.

—*Phyllis Jane Rose*

Somehow, Heidi, you've gone to the hearth and male dominion all by yourself. As if you've made a new decision. As if, in Laurie Stone's words, "reaction is revolution." As if "surrendering independence is a measure of independence."

We cannot afford this complicity, Heidi. It matters—not only who paints the pictures and who writes the plays, but what the images are and who benefits from them.

The fact is, all art is political. It either supports the status quo or challenges it. Just as in Apollo's time, the status quo values what is white, male, heterosexual and capitalist. (Scoop gets another "A.") Art which supports the status quo is celebrated by establishment reviewers as "humanist" or "important" or "universal." Art which challenges status quo values is diminished as "feminist" or "special interest" or "political."

In the United States, between 1974 (when you were picketing the Art Institute of Chicago) and 1988 (when you adopted Judy), audiences of Native Americans, African-Americans, Hispanics, Asian-Americans, poor people of both genders as well as women of all races and ages began to see positive images of themselves presented by cultural workers who looked like them and who experienced life in ways audience members recognized. "Nontraditional" audiences entered theatres, some for the first time, eager to have their struggles for self-definition and self-determination validated on the public stage. . . .

All colonized peoples are fighting the same war, Heidi. "He Who Mounts," in Apollo's phrase, has colonized not only all women and children but all men of cultures and colors different from his own. He has colonized the earth itself. "The earth is our Mother," say indigenous peoples. But He Who Mounts has declared himself a single parent. Unless we continue to do battle, our mother the earth will die. Matricide will be global this time.

Your work, my work, our work can create images to empower out communities to prevent it. But we have to act. We cannot *sort of . . . hang around . . . waiting to see what might happen. Especially* when we feel stranded.

I fly back to the States today. Can we meet for coffee? Toast The Furies instead of The Beatles?

Respectfully yours,

Phyllis Jane Rose

Kent Black   (review date March 1990)

SOURCE: "The Wendy Chronicles," in *Harper's Bazaar,* Vol. 123, No. 3339, March, 1990, pp. 154, 162.

[*In the following review, Black offers praise for* Bachelor Girls.]

"I think one of the reasons I took up writing is my need to make order out of disorder . . . that and this problem I have of remembering everything that has ever happened and been said to me," says playwright Wendy Wasserstein, settling down with a cup of coffee in her cluttered apartment to discuss her new book of essays *Bachelor Girls,* due out next month. "You know, I might have made my mother truly happy and become a lawyer if a friend of mine at Mt. Holyoke college hadn't suggested we take playwriting over at Smith . . . the reason being that there was much better shopping in Northampton than in South Hadley."

It is a telling comment for the 39-year-old writer. In her plays, characters often struggle between traditional values and the goals they have set for themselves. Though the conflicts are serious, both for the characters and their creator, Wasserstein's instinct is to employ her considerable sense of irony to help gain perspective.

One essay that typifies her indefatigable wit and depth is entitled **"Jean Harlow's Wedding Night."** It concerns the author's recollection of flying to Paris to meet a man she loves. The affair proves to be a disaster and Wasserstein's reaction when the man tells her that he has fallen for another woman is to battle rejection with humor and anecdote. Though her ex-lover's indifference moves her to tears, she ends her sobbing in the Jardin des Tuileries by walking to the Jeu de Paume to see a Degas exhibit. "I even hummed a little Cole Porter on the way. I am, after all, a resourceful person, and I love Paris in the springtime."

Wasserstein, a product of Brooklyn and Manhattan's Upper East Side, fondly remembers her childhood filled with dance lessons at the June Taylor School followed by Broadway matinees. Her mother Lola, "a perpetual dance student even at age 70," has figured prominently in her life and art. Not only was she the inspiration for the archetypal Jewish mother in her second play *Isn't It Romantic,* but is also at the core of the struggle that gives her daughter's work such resonance. "No matter how successful I become as a playwright," says Wasserstein, "my mother would still be thrilled to hear me tell her I'd just lost 20 pounds, gotten married and become a lawyer."

In her three major plays to date, *Uncommon Women and Others, Isn't It Romantic* and *The Heidi Chronicles*— winner of both a 1989 Pulitzer Prize and Tony Award— the characters must all address the changing roles of women in the last two decades: career or family, feminism or June Cleaver's values. It is a dilemma best summed up by a character in *The Heidi Chronicles* who says, "Either you shave your legs or you don't."

Bachelor Girls illustrates familiar themes. As a contributing editor to *New York Woman,* Wasserstein wrote these pieces for her column for more immediate gratification "since it usually takes at least two years to get a play on stage . . . if ever." She also admits that the essay form allows her to develop some of the ideas she employs on the stage. "I like plays because they are live, and no matter how funny something is, if the audience doesn't laugh, then it doesn't work," she says. "But there are no characters to hide behind in the essays. They are much tougher to write in some ways because of their directness."

Indeed, Wasserstein draws on personal experience in all of the pieces in this collection. True to her claim of "remembering everything," she connects moments of her youth to those of her adulthood. In **"A Phone of Her Own,"** she recollects wonderfully those pivotal "phone" conversations in a young girl's life: from the world-shaking calls of pre-adolescence when grownups have the nerve to make a youngster hang up after only an hour, to the heart-stopping LDs (long distance) on the college dormitory pay phone, to its hated position in the adult world when every ring brings yet another unwanted intrusion.

To her credit, however, the punch in these essays is delivered by more than bittersweet memories and pointed one-liners. Behind the "know-what-I-mean" posturings are Wasserstein's studies of her generation's convolutions through the '60s, '70s and '80s, her musings about women who have traded in NOW values for Volvos and kiddie car seats.

Though labels such as "important writer of her generation" often arouse suspicions, Wasserstein may actually deserve the mantle. She is not only attuned to her peers but also to women of any generation. "I was lecturing recently at a college and I met these young women who told me they had it all planned out: family, profession, political affiliations, everything," she recalls. "But there seemed to be a problem with that, too. Being so reasonable about life at 19, weren't they missing out on a certain passion?"

There are sketches in **Bachelor Girls** that will cause audible laughter; in fact, comparisons to Woody Allen are not entirely fatuous. There is a decidedly regional flavor to Wasserstein's humor and the mercurial shifts in perspective from superiority to inferiority are best expressed in essays like **"Perfect Women Who are Bearable,"** in which she categorizes chimp-ologist Jane Goodall as "bearable." ("It would be helpful to talk with Jane about where to meet available men.") Finally, there is the pathos present throughout all of Wasserstein's work. Yes, she is a witty writer, but she never fails to show that comedy is serious business, a perspective earned by sometimes funny, sometimes sad, sometimes tough encounters with life.

"I am always interested in exploring the ideas behind the experiences with my own tortured adolescence, my Aunt Florence's son's bar mitzvah or my mother's eccentricity. Of course, every time I would finish one of these essays and send it off to my editor," she laughs, "I would immediately call her up and scream, 'Wait a minute, you can't print that!'"

Gayle Austin   (review date March 1990)

SOURCE: A review of *The Heidi Chronicles*, in *Theatre Journal*, Vol. 42, No. 1, March, 1990, pp. 107-08.

[*In the following review, Austin discusses characterization in* The Heidi Chronicles *and feminist reaction to the play. She notes that although the play has been lauded by some feminists for its focus on women, others argue that the work portrays women in traditional roles and has the potential to "become part of the system that oppresses women and so highly rewards their creative expressions when they aid in its purposes."*]

The Heidi Chronicles is a rare play for Broadway. Written by a woman, its central character is an unmarried professional woman. It won the Pulitzer, Tony, N.Y. Drama Critics Circle, Drama Desk, Outer Critics Circle, Hull-Warriner, and Susan Smith Blackburn awards. Ostensibly a triumph for women, **Heidi** is instead a problematic example of how the male-dominated production system of

commercial theater maintains its control over women, in this case with the complicity of a woman playwright.

Heidi follows a single woman through three decades, from high school in the 1960s and feminist activities in the 1970s to a career as an art historian who rediscovers "lost" women painters and chooses to become a single mother in the 1980s. Like Wasserstein's previous plays, **Uncommon Women and Others** (1977) and **Isn't It Romantic** (1983), **Heidi** is topical and episodic, placing a few serious, poignant moments within a comic form.

Joan Allen brought her intelligent and vulnerable presence to the character as the first Heidi in the Broadway production. Having described herself as a "highly informed spectator," Heidi appears in the prologues of both acts showing slides to her college classes and commenting on the women artists who made the paintings. But Heidi is also a nearly silent spectator in her own life. In almost every scene her major action is watching the activities of the other characters on or offstage. She has relatively little dialogue in these scenes. In one, she begins to speak during a TV talk show, only to be literally interrupted by the two men in her life, who are seated on either side of her. The only time Heidi has a substantial speaking role is in monologues during the two slide-show prologues and during Act II, scene 4, in which Heidi speaks to women from her old high school. This speech, which comes at the climatic point of the play, is one in which Heidi departs from her prepared lecture text to question her life and the feminist movement. She says, "I feel stranded" and "I thought the point was we were all in this together." The point is that Wasserstein portrays Heidi's women friends as trivial and her men friends as serious and has Heidi blame the women's movement for that situation.

Wasserstein keeps women at a spectatorial distance in this play and focuses most of Heidi's attention on her two male friends, love-interest Scoop and gay pediatrician Peter. The two scenes in which groups of women appear together, consciousness raising in Ann Arbor in 1970 and a baby shower in New York a decade later (played by the same three actresses), are near caricatures of group female behavior. The play shows that the women she knows do not form part of Heidi's support network while the men do. Her disappointment with women is made to seem "natural," given these women, rather than part of a larger pattern in which women are taught that they are "stranded" from each other and can only rely on men for support.

The final two scenes of the play show Heidi working out her primary relationships, first with Peter, then with Scoop. Neither man is a satisfactory life partner for her, however, and the final moment of the play shows Heidi singing the same song to her daughter that she danced to at the end of Act I with Scoop. The closure of the play is based on her substitution of one bond for another: mother for lover. Her work and women friends are absent. No wonder the play has been received less than enthusiastically by many feminists.

To some, mainly liberal feminists, the play's acceptance into the mainstream is a source of pride and represents a step forward for all women playwrights. But for materialist feminists, who look at its circumstances of production and reception, the price for attaining that status is far too high. The very factors that allowed this play to achieve its privileged position are the same factors that prevent plays with more threatening messages to cross the line into the canon. To reach this point of visibility, a play must have a commercial production in New York City. Given the power structure of this mode of production, any message that threatens to disrupt male privilege will not succeed. *Heidi* does not unsettle men. It not only reassures them, it gives them all the best lines.

The difficulties of forming satisfactory relationships with men, of balancing personal life and career, and of having children are real issues in women's lives and are all too rarely dealt with in any manner on the stage. Although there is a limit to how much the play can be blamed for what it is not, it is valid to consider the effects of the way some of its most problematic actions are carried out on-stage. Some women may identify with Heidi, but others chafe at the entire representational frame the play places around her. The realism it employs makes invisible the real difficulties a woman in Heidi's position encounters, such as the costs of the transactions in the play. The adoption of a baby, at the conclusion of the play, would have financial costs that are never addressed. Heidi's decision to stay in New York because of Peter's need for her is shown as a simple, emotional decision, with no relevance to her career or economic implications. The trouble with this play is that although it raises issues, Wasserstein undercuts serious consideration through facile supporting female characters, sit-com humor, and a passive heroine who forms an absence at the center of the play.

The biggest danger to women posed by the play is its future influence. As *Heidi* enters the canon of plays that are widely produced, it will be published, anthologized, criticized, and taught as a prime example of the work of a woman playwright. It would have additional influence as a film; one can even imagine it as a television series. Scenes from the play will echo through audition halls for decades to come. The "I thought we were all in this together" monologue will be memorized and repeated, enacted and absorbed by thousands of aspiring young actresses. In this way the play will become part of the system that oppresses

women and so highly rewards their creative expressions when they aid in its purposes.

Thomas E. Luddy   (review date 1 May 1990)

SOURCE: A review of *The Heidi Chronicles, and Other Plays,* in *Library Journal,* Vol. 115, No. 8, May 1, 1990, p. 89.

[*In the following review, Luddy favorably assesses* The Heidi Chronicles, and Other Plays.]

Wasserstein has made the cultural territory of the American experience since the 1960s her own. She is its most articulate theatrical chronicler. This collection of her recent work, *Uncommon Women and Others, Isn't It Romantic,* and the Pulitzer Prize-winning *The Heidi Chronicles,* traces that experience through three decades of changing styles, mores, life objectives, and intellectual challenges. She examines her characters and their times with great good humor, complexity, depth of feeling, and a firm refusal to accept trite and easy images. She writes the truth about people and their lives without blinking. She teaches us all what it was like to live through a period of great turmoil and confusion.

Ray Olson   (review date 1 June 1990)

SOURCE: A review of *The Heidi Chronicles, and Other Plays,* in *Booklist,* Vol. 86, No. 19, June 1, 1990, p. 1872.

[*In the following review of* The Heidi Chronicles, and Other Plays, *Olson compares Wasserstein's plays to the work of Mary McCarthy and Philip Barry.*]

[Wendy Wasserstein's *The Heidi Chronicles, and Other Plays* contains the] 1989 Pulitzer Prize winner and two earlier comic dramas by, if you will, the Baby Boomers' Mary McCarthy. Less acerbic and intellectual, more sentimental and emotional, Wasserstein has the same ambition McCarthy exercised in *The Group.* She tries to limn a stratum of society consisting for her as for McCarthy of her fellow matriculants of the elite "Seven Sisters" colleges. In *Uncommon Women and Others* (1977), she actually apes *The Group,* setting the formative college experiences of a circle of women within the framing device of a reunion. Similarly, *The Heidi Chronicles* (1988) sandwiches 25 years of its art historian heroine's development, especially her relations with the man who loves her and the other man she loves, between slices of a lecture on women artists. The middle play, *Isn't It Romantic?* (1983), concerns two young businesswomen's struggles to live up to and give up on their parents' expectations. The focal character in all three is habitually undecided and standoffish but arrives at some self-understanding by the final curtain. All three read more somberly than they play, much like the dramas of Philip Barry (*Holiday, The Philadelphia Story*), whose peer Wasserstein certainly is.

J. K.   (review date Autumn 1990)

SOURCE: A review of *Bachelor Girls,* in *West Coast Review of Books,* Vol. 15, No. 4, Autumn, 1990, pp. 44-5.

<hr>

Michael Coveney on Wasserstein's "Yale" origins and connections:

Along with fellow playwrights Christopher Durang, Ted Talley and Albert Innaurato, and the producer Rocco Landesman, who runs the powerful Jujamcyn conglomerate of theatres, Wasserstein was one of a remarkable group who graduated from Yale Drama School in the late Seventies. The group were all pupils and friends of the influential critic Robert Brustein, and all believe that serious new work can flourish in the commercial sector.

Michael Coveney, in his "Taking Supper with Hillary,"
in The Observer, *24 July 1986.*

[In the following positive review, the critic discusses the humor and satire of the essays contained in Bachelor Girls.*]*

This collection of essays [*Bachelor Girls*] by Tony Award-winning playwright Wendy Wasserstein includes enjoyable, funny reading as well as satirical social commentary that is short and gossipy enough to keep even the most skeptical reader interested.

Wasserstein's view of the world includes everything from the stark and serious, such as her anxiety-ridden trip to Rumania—to the satirical, such as in her article **"The Sleeping Beauty Syndrome: The New Agony of Single Men"** a riotous takeoff on the horrible clamor that was created in the media during the mid-'80s regarding single women and their reduced chances of finding husbands. She's turned this around, saying, "Forty-year-old men are more likely to have a Pan Am 747 land on their head (than get married)!"

Other witty pieces include some personal ones about a relative's Bar Mitzvah, a humorous/serious tribute to the author's mother, Lola, and a wonderful trip Wasserstein took to Japan to view a Japanese version of her play, *Isn't It Romantic.* One unforgettable scene in her essay **"Winner Take All"** shows her sitting at her typewriter in her bathrobe, feeling incredibly sorry for herself when the phone rings and she's informed that she's just won a Pulitzer Prize for her play, *The Heidi Chronicles.*

Wasserstein also writes about women—she scathingly criticizes such things as fashion, private girls' schools, the shaving of legs and the manicuring of nails, and, of course, dieting, of which Wasserstein laments, "weight is the bane of my existence."

Two of the funniest essays in the book include **"Perfect Women Who Are Bearable,"** in which Wasserstein gives us alternative lists of famous women who she either can't stand or who she admires—and **"The World's Worst Boyfriends,"** a list that includes Rasputin. (It also includes Mel Gibson, but only because "he's a happily married family man. The impossible dream.")

A lot of Wasserstein's charm stems from her Brooklyn background, and she loves to talk about New York in general, comparing it to much more hideous places such as Los Angeles (she's uncomfortable on the West Coast.) Her chatty use of language reminds one of the hysterically funny cut-up in the girls' dorm (which she apparently once was), and her use of the term Bachelor Girl (she's unmarried and 40—God! Such a stigma!) throughout the book is her way of avenging those who are disdainful of or embarrassed for the unmarried (yet successful) woman. Readers familiar with Wasserstein through her essays on her plays will easily understand and enjoy this book. New readers will be entertained and, at the same time, pick up some clever insights.

Wendy Wasserstein (essay date 1990)

SOURCE: "Winner Take All," in *Bachelor Girls,* 1990. Reprint by Vintage Books, 1991, pp. 193-97.

[In the essay below, Wasserstein discusses her reaction to winning the Pulitzer Prize for The Heidi Chronicles.*]*

I dreamed I accepted the Tony Award wearing a CAMP EUGENE O'NEILL sweatshirt. It was an odd dream for two reasons. First, because my friend William Ivey Long, the costume designer, had made me a dress for the occasion; and, second, because until 1989 the only thing I'd ever won was a babka cake at a bakery on Whalley Avenue in New Haven.

My world view has always been from the vantage point of the slighted. I am the underachiever who convinces herself that it's a source of pride *not* to make the honor roll. Still, for the rest of my life I will remember the name of all those people who *did.* I am a walking Where Are They Now column. I'm perpetually curious as to what happened to all those supposed prodigies who were singled out while I and my coterie of far more interesting malcontents passed on.

As a child, on the eve of any school evaluation, I would inform my parents which of my teachers "hated me." In retrospect, it seems doubtful that I was offensive enough to evoke my teacher's animosity, but I certainly wasn't diligent enough in my schoolwork to earn their admiration, either. So, having fashioned a life based on anticipated exclusion—my date left with the blond; they gave the prize to the boy; the woman in the Anne Klein suit and the legs got the job—it came as a genuine surprise, a shock, when, for the first time ever, the winner was me.

On a gray March afternoon, I'm sitting in my bed, looking at my typewriter and thinking about how my life hasn't changed significantly since I was sixteen. I'm working up to a frothy, self-recriminating how-have-I-gone-wrong when the phone rings. On days when I'm building up to substantial negativity, I usually don't pick up the receiver but instead just listen as the messages are recorded. This time, though, the voice belongs to Marc Thibodeau, the press agent for my play *The Heidi Chronicles,* and I like him, so I pick up.

"Wendy, you just won the Pulitzer Prize."

And you, Mr. Thibodeau, are the king of Rumania.

"It's a rumor, Marc. It's just a rumor!" I begin hyperventilating. I am a woman in her thirties wearing a quilted bathrobe, half working, half lying in bed in a room cluttered with assorted stuffed animals. I am not a Pulitzer Prize winner. Edward Albee is a Pulitzer Prize winner.

Mr. Thibodeau informs me that I should call a reporter from the Associated Press. Also, I must call my mother. I begin to dial gingerly. It's possible I am having delusions of grandeur. It's possible I might shortly be calling the *Times* as Eleanor of Aquitaine. Michael Kuchwara, the AP reporter, accepts my call, however, and validates the story. Suddenly I remember sitting in our living room with my mother and watching an episode of the TV series *The Millionaire.* I recall how my mother knocked on the television screen to encourage a delivery to our Brooklyn address. "Mother," I want now to shout, "Michael Anthony called *me.* John Beresford Tipton is giving me the Pulitzer Prize!"

Immediately, *everything* changes. The phone rings with the constancy of the American Stock Exchange. Flowers and champagne arrive in competitive quantities. (Since that day I have, in fact, become an expert on the comparative floral arrangements of Surroundings, Twigs, and the Sutton East Gardens.) My doormen are more than taken aback by the flow of deliveries to my apartment. One of them asks me when I'm getting married; another expresses amazement that so many of my friends have remembered my birthday. Eventually, my sister telephones to say that not only has my mother called my aunts to inform them that I've won the Nobel Prize, but my cousins have already begun asking when I'm going to Stockholm.

I will never forget that day. Although I consider myself a professional malcontent, I can't deny at least this one experience of pure, unadulterated happiness. I take a cab to the theater to see the cast of my play, and the whole process of creating the production flashes in front of me. I remember rewriting scenes between bites of cheeseburger as I sat alone at a coffee shop on Forty-second Street. There's something soothing about such inauspicious beginnings. If I concentrate on the coffee shop, I convince myself, I will not be overwhelmed by what is happening to me.

Joan Allen, our leading lady, suggests that I come onstage at the end of the performance. I tell her it's impossible, I'm much too shy. I've never taken a curtain call. I want an *Act One* experience. I want to be watching from the back of the theater.

At intermission, however, I find myself in the lobby face to face with Edward Albee. We know each other from the Dramatists Guild and have friends in common. He embraces me and asks me whether I'll be taking a curtain call. I shake my head. I giggle. Edward then tells me to be a person, to take off my coat and seize the moment.

Walking out onto the stage at the Plymouth Theater I become a character in someone else's script. A part of me imagines that I'm Carol Channing—I want to enter with my arm stretched to the ceiling, shouting, "Dolly will never go away again!" Another part of me has no idea what to do onstage while the audience is applauding. I begin to kiss every actor in my play. As long as I'm moving, I won't have to speak or, heaven forbid, cursty. That night the audience gives us a standing ovation.

Nineteen eighty-nine was my favorite year so far. Perhaps it is all attributable to the astral plane, Libra in orbit, or Maggie Smith's inability to open as scheduled in *Lettice & Lovage* (which freed the Plymouth Theater for *The Heidi Chronicles*). For whatever reason, I spent the greater part of the spring of 1989 winning awards, as if to counteract on a massive front any remnants of ironic negativity. At the Outer Critics Circle Awards, my escort, the actress Caroline Aaron, whispered to me toward the end of the evening, "Wendy, it's just you and Baryshnikov left." Frankly, I would never have suspected that the two of us might be on a double bill.

Of course, there's also the down side. Will anything this wonderful ever happen to me again? How many people are now going to hate me? Where do I take all these things to be framed? Is it gauche to put them up on the walls in my apartment? What happens if Werner Kulovitz at Barbara Matera's, a theatrical costume shop, has stopped importing that feather-light apparatus to "lift and separate" when I need my next formal? And the nagging "Can *I* ever do it again?"

I haven't actually counted the awards, but I'm sure that if I did I could psych myself into some new form of anxiety over them. In the past I've given my parents every diploma or certificate I've received for them to display in their den. But this time I've been selfish—the awards are still resting in a corner of my study. Some days I ignore them in a concerted effort to get back to my life and work, to return to the point of view of the slighted. But, truthfully, there are times when I wander in and take a surreptitious peek at that corner. Nothing is quite as gratifying as recognition for work one is truly proud of.

As for next year, I will be very hurt if I don't win the Heisman Trophy.

Helene Keyssar   (essay date March 1991)

SOURCE: "Drama and the Dialogic Imagination: 'The Heidi Chronicles' and 'Fefu and Her Friends'," in *Modern Drama*, Vol. XXXIV, No. 1, March, 1991, pp. 88-106.

[*In the following excerpt, Keyssar expresses her disappointment with the tremendous success of* The Heidi Chronicles. *She contends that, according to Mikhail Bakhtin's definition of meaningful theater, in which drama is "simultaneously entire unto itself and part of the whole culture,"* The Heidi Chronicles *is "aggressively monologic" and "self-contained," thus alienating large segments of society.*]

The Heidi Chronicles was first workshopped in April 1988 by the Seattle Repertory Theatre; on 12 December 1988 it opened at Playwrights Horizons in New York City; three months later, it transferred to the Plymouth Theatre on Broadway, where it quickly became one of the major hits of the season. Awards have poured down upon the play and its author: in addition to the Pulitzer Prize for drama and the Tony for best play of the season, *The Heidi Chronicles* won the Susan Smith Blackburn prize (a prize specifically meant to recognize outstanding work by women playwrights) and the Dramatists Guild Hull Warriner award which selects "the best American play dealing with contemporary political, religious or social mores." While my experience as a spectator is that audiences take the play lightly—they laugh, giggle and chat briefly after the performance about their own experiences growing up from the sixties to the eighties, experiences that the play recalls—both the wealth of awards and the passionately mixed reviews it provoked suggest that *The Heidi Chronicles* commands serious attention.

Working with the same kinds of characters she has created in previous dramas (*Uncommon Women and Others; Isn't It Romantic*), Wasserstein takes us along for the ride on a twenty-five year journey from adolescence to adulthood of two men and a woman, all bright, upper-middle-class people who begin to come to consciousness in the mid-sixties. (Heidi's friend, Susan, also makes the journey, but she is always a foil or adjunct to the affairs of the central three characters.) Heidi, who becomes an art historian, is ostensibly the protagonist of the drama (she appears in each of the play's eleven scenes and two prologues), although she is often dominated, dramatically and politically, by the two men in her life: Peter Patrone, a caring, intelligent man who becomes "a liberal homosexual pediatrician"; and Scoop Rosenbaum, already an aggressive entrepreneur at nineteen who rises to become editor of *Boomer* magazine.

In a series of eleven "anecdotes," these characters repeatedly re-encounter each other, at each instance addressing the vicissitudes of their own lives in the context of the changing values and mores of their society. None of these three main characters ever changes, but the play does build towards and away from two quasi-recognition scenes. In the first of these (Act Two, Scene 4), Heidi loses control of the keynote address she is delivering to a luncheon gathering at the Plaza Hotel and rambles towards a conclusion in which she confesses to the audience that she is "just not happy," that she feels "stranded" and disillusioned because she thought that the whole point of the women's movement "was that we were all in this together." In the next scene, Heidi visits Peter at a children's hospital ward on Christmas Eve, and Peter reveals that he, the most prominent pediatrician in New York City, is living in an increasingly narrow world because so many of his friends are dying of AIDS. He confesses to Heidi that he is hurt because she does not understand him and is not authentically there for him as a friend. She immediately responds that she could "become someone else next year." The two briefly transcend their differences and embrace, but if there is recognition of self or other here, some traditional movement from ignorance to knowledge, the moment is explicitly presented as transitory and private. Heidi's offer to "become someone else" is not a step towards a transformation of self but more like a proposal to wear a different dress tomorrow. Heidi neither knows what it means to "become someone else" nor does she know what kind of person she would will herself to become. Her offer to "become someone else next year" would be a good laugh line—even, perhaps, a parody of a dramatic transformation—were it not uttered in the context of Peter's suffering.

Gender—its roles and consciousnesses—provides the thematic thread that links the episodes in the twenty-five-year time line of *The Heidi Chronicles.* Since there is neither beauty in the language nor surprise in the events or characters of this play, I can only surmise that it is the topical interest in gender issues that has called forth so much critical attention, both positive and negative. Those who praised *The Heidi Chronicles* found it to be "enlightening" (Mel Gussow, *The New York Times*), "wise" (Howard Kissel, *The Daily News*), and "important" (Linda Winer, *Newsday*) in its depiction of feminism and feminists, and of men's and women's relations to each other. Negative commentary on the play, most thoroughly and bitingly presented in a long piece by Phyllis Jane Rose in *American Theatre* [October 1989], also focused on gender issues. "The absence from the stage of images of women acting on their own beliefs in truth, beauty or justice implies that women do not act in this way in the world,"

writes Rose in her letter to Heidi. "Or, if they do," Rose continues, "it is not important enough to be dramatized. In your *Chronicles,* your struggle for women artists, your professed dedication to content over form, are secondary to your relationships with men. Your intelligence becomes wit in their presence. Your imagination settles for fantasy."

The Heidi Chronicles is all that, or worse than, Rose contends. And here [Mikhail] Bakhtin comes to my aid in understanding why I find this drama—and its mostly celebratory public reception—so disturbing. It is precisely because this drama does not re-present the heteroglossia of the world, precisely because it is aggressively monologic, self-contained, a seemingly perfect picture without loopholes of a particular historic moment that is so pleasing to some and distressing to others. Heidi does an adequate job of recuperating women artists, but even when she speaks of her subjects it is in the monologic discourse of professional academia. On the one occasion—a television talk show—where Heidi is explicitly positioned to speak her own different voice, she is silenced by the voices of two men, Scoop and Peter, her old friends who also appear on the show. Afterwards she is angry, but even in her anger we are given no sense of what her own voice might sound like. And if we are meant to see this scene as a dramatization of difference as absence, as an assault on patriarchical monology, such a vision is quickly undercut by the subsequent scene, a meeting among Heidi and her women friends, where the women's talk and ideologies are indistinguishable from that of Scoop and Peter. Heidi only briefly finds an alternative voice during her rambling speech at the women's luncheon, and that utterance is inaccessible because it is framed as the self-pitying ramblings of a woman in the process of a nervous breakdown.

The characters in *The Heidi Chronicles* neither acknowledge each other as other—indeed, their persistent attempt is to be like each other—nor do they, to use once more a Bakhtinian term, "interanimate" each other. The world they comprise is coherent, consistent and stable, despite superficial changes from involvement in leftist politics and the women's movement to a kind of mushy humanism. Reaction is not revolution, as Rose urges, quoting Laurie Stone, and the world of *The Heidi Chronicles* is adamantly one of reaction, not revolution or change. When we meet Heidi for the last time, with her newly-adopted baby, she is "waiting" for something, perhaps for a new world and new generation in which her baby daughter's voice will be different and will be heard. Her world is not provocatively open, unfinalized; Heidi and her baby are just sitting there rocking, bathed in the nostalgia of an old fifties song. As my twelve-year-old daughter commented immediately after seeing the production, the play could have ended at any of several of its last few scenes. Had it done so, it would not have made any difference—to those on stage or in the audience.

In "Discourse in the Novel," an essay that is central to Bakhtin's reflections, Bakhtin urges that this "verbal-ideological decentering will occur only when a national culture loses its sealed-off and self-sufficient character, when it becomes conscious of itself as only one among *other* cultures and languages" [*The Dialogic Imagination*]. In its refusal of such a "decentering," **The Heidi Chronicles** reveals a national culture that remains "sealed-off," "authoritarian," "rigid" and unconscious of itself as only one among other cultures and languages. And it does so to a dangerous degree. There is no place in the world of this drama for the voices of women and men who can speak the discourses of feminism; there is no room in this drama for the poor, the marginalized, the inarticulate, for those who are not successes in the terms of the eighties, for those who wish to transform and not react. If this is what drama today is at its best, then it is less than that which Bakhtin claimed it to be initially.

Charles Solomon   (review date 25 August 1991)

SOURCE: A review of *Bachelor Girls,* in *Los Angeles Times Book Review,* August 25, 1991, p. 10.

[*In the following, Solomon offers praise for* Bachelor Girls.]

In [the comic collection of essays entitled **Bachelor Girls,**] originally published in *New York Woman,* the author of **The Heidi Chronicles** reflects on the problems of being an intelligent female and less than gorgeous in contemporary America. Numerous writers, from Erma Bombeck to Cathy Guisewite (of the comic strip "Cathy"), have exploited the humorous potential of these topics, but Wasserstein writes with unusual perception and wit. She acknowledges her predilection for junk food, recalling the day she discovered she belonged to the biological class of "cupcakivores," but she balances that confession with a touching description of the mixed emotions she experienced when she won the Pulitzer Prize. The result is a satisfying and very funny blend of self-deprecation, pride and bemusement.

John Simon   (review date 2 November 1992)

SOURCE: "The Best So Far," in *New York* Magazine, Vol. 25, No. 43, November 2, 1992, pp. 100-01.

[*In the following review, Simon praises* The Sisters Rosensweig *for its convincing characters and humorous dialogue, asserting that the work is Wasserstein's best to date.*]

The Sisters Rosensweig is Wendy Wasserstein's most accomplished play to date. It is through-composed, with no obtrusive narrator haranguing us. Its central, but not hypertrophic, character is the eldest sister, Sara Goode, divorced from her second husband. An expatriate in London, she is celebrating her fifty-fourth birthday, for which her younger sister Gorgeous Teitelbaum has flown in from Boston, where she dispenses personal advice over the airwaves. From farthest India, the youngest sister, Pfeni Rosensweig, has jetted in; now a travel writer, she is shirking her mission, a study of the lives of women in Tajikistan. Equitably, all three sisters end up sharing center stage, both literally and figuratively.

Gorgeous, who, we are told, is happily married with four children, is group leader of the Temple Beth-El sisterhood of Newton, Massachusetts, on a visit to London; Pfeni is here to touch base with her lover, the famous stage direc-

tor Geoffrey Duncan, whom she has converted to heterosexuality and may soon be marrying. Here, too, is a friend of Geoffrey's, the New York *faux* furrier and genuine mensch Mervyn Kant. Rounding out the cast are Tess, Sara's precocious teenager; Tom Valiunus, Tess's dopey but good-natured punker boyfriend, with whom she is planning a political-protest trip to his ancestral Lithuania; and Nicholas Pym, a British banker, stuffed shirt, and suitor to Sara.

Wasserstein is surely one of our wittiest one-liner writers, but under the bubbles and eddies of her wit are real people in deep water, resolutely and resonantly trying to keep from drowning.

—John Simon

This is the stuff of Anglo-American comedy, more specifically Anglo-Jewish-American drawing room comedy, in which some related but diverse mores and some diverse but trying-to-become-related people are playing off one another. Sara, a banker herself, is high-powered, smart, and sex-starved. Pfeni and the ebullient but labile heterosexual Geoffrey are having difficulties. And the ostensibly contented Gorgeous is there to stick her bobbed but nosy nose into everybody's business.

A seasoned theatergoer may well guess several plot developments, though there are also a few surprises. But plot is far less important than character and dialogue, both of which Miss Wasserstein does handsomely and humorously. She is surely one of our wittiest one-liner writers, but under the bubbles and eddies of her wit are real people in deep water, resolutely and resonantly trying to keep from drowning. And she is able to orchestrate the interaction of her disparate characters into a complex, convincing polyphony. There may be a touch of the arbitrary here and there; mostly, however, the play flows, entertains, and liberally dispenses unpompous wisdom about ourselves.

Particularly pleasing is that **Sisters** manages to be both of its time, 1991, and of all time, unless human nature changes radically, which for these 5,000 years it hasn't. The three Rosensweig sisters are by no means unworthy descendants of a famed earlier sisterly trio, to whom an occasional quotation in the text alludes. If I have any problem with the play, it is that several of its characters have a propensity for bursting into song and dance at the slightest, or even no, provocation. In a straight play, this can be as unsettling as long spoken passages in a musical.

It is to the skilled cast's credit that every last drop of humor is extracted easefully, even as the no-less-germane modulations into seriousness are achieved with gearshifts a Lexus or Infiniti might envy. Jane Alexander's Sara is one of the most memorable of this stylish actress's creations; here is perfect timing backed up with the subtlest changes of intonation and incomparable facial play. Without effort or undue emphasis, Miss Alexander's diaphanous face reveals the playground of ideas and battleground of emotions; it is as if the countenance itself had repartee, soliloquies, and tirades at its wordless disposal.

Madeline Kahn, as Gorgeous, is once again her special blend of philosopher and fool, shrewd observer and egocentric, outrageous jokester and wistful waif—a ditsy Diotima whom none could improve on. Frances McDormand is saddled with the autobiographical character whom most playwrights either overwrite or, as in this case, slightly underwrite. But she does Pfeni gamely and touchingly, opposite John Vickery's dazzlingly campy and exquisitely English-theatrical Geoffrey. Robert Klein's Mervyn is all we expect from this sovereign clown: exuberantly wisecracking, irrepressibly amorous, impudently ingratiating. And Patrick Fitzgerald's affably preposterous Tom has no lack of assurance and authenticity.

I am less taken with Julie Dretzin's Tess and, especially, Rex Robbins's Nicholas, but they do not gum up the works. Daniel Sullivan's direction is as painterly as it is musicianly: everything in the right place and tempo. John Lee Beatty's set is devilishly right, and Pat Collins's lighting and Jane Greenwood's costumes collude with it cunningly. You will not be bored here.

Edith Oliver (review date 2 November 1992)

SOURCE: "Chez Rosensweig," in *The New Yorker,* Vol. LXVIII, No. 37, November 2, 1992, p. 105.

[*In the following review, Oliver offers praise for* The Sisters Rosensweig.]

Admirers of Wendy Wasserstein (fan club may be more like it) will be relieved to know that she is as romantic as ever, and that her head is in the right place, too, while her tongue remains safely in her cheek. I use the word "romantic" because her new play, **The Sisters Rosensweig,** at the Mitzi Newhouse, is more in tune with her **Isn't It Romantic,** of some years ago, than with the recent **Heidi Chronicles. The Sisters Rosensweig** takes place in the elegant London sitting room of Sara Goode, née Rosensweig, a twice-divorced American Jew who is the European director of the Hong Kong & Shanghai Bank. (It's interesting to note that the small stage of the Mitzi can, under the right auspices, seem as spacious and lavish as any in town; in this instance, the auspices are John Lee Beatty's, and the exquisite lighting is by Pat Collins.) The occasion that launches the action is the celebration of Sara's fifty-fourth birthday, and her two younger—but not much younger—sisters are coming to her house to celebrate. They are Pfeni, a free-lance travel writer, and Gorgeous, a wife and mother who is about to embark on a personal-advice TV program but at the moment is shepherding a group of Jewish ladies on a pilgrimage to the Crown Jewels. (She bears a more than incidental resemblance, by the way, to Dr. Ruth.) We begin with Pfeni's arrival: Sara asks her to "talk to" her rebellious daughter, who plans to leave for Lithuania with her left-wing working-class boyfriend as soon as the party is over. Then Pfeni's beau, a bright bisexual director, brimming with high spirits and bitchy anecdotes, arrives; he, in turn, has invited an associate of his

from America. The associate is a hearty, noisy Jewish manufacturer of fake fur who, once established as a guest, refuses to budge, determined to crash this family occasion. He is also determined to woo and win Sara, who, although her career is moving successfully along, feels she has come to a personal stop.

The funny incidents and the funny lines fly by, so quickly that one is almost unaware that a story is being told, and the laughter is all but continuous until Pfeni's beau confesses that he misses men ("So do I," she says), and their inevitable breakup leaves her disheartened. By the end of the play, Sara, having secretly crept up to bed with the brash visiting American—"How was it?" asks each of her sisters the morning after—realizes that many emotional possibilities are still open. Nothing is over—not even life with daughter. Pfeni pulls herself together, and cheerfully lights out for foreign parts, ready to resume her career; and dear Gorgeous, having been presented with a pink outfit from Chanel by her grateful ladies, decides to cash it in and go home to that TV program and her husband and children. The mood is warm and *gemütlich* but never foolish. Jean Kerr once described a kind of play that gave her a pain as "an Irish aren't-we-adorable?" *The Sisters Rosensweig* is not a Jewish "aren't-we-adorable?" There isn't a sentimental key in Wendy Wasserstein's typewriter.

The performance, under the direction of Daniel Sullivan, is superb. Jane Alexander is remarkable as Sara Goode; Frances McDormand and Madeline Kahn are Pfeni and Gorgeous. Robert Klein, a one-man explosion of sex and mirth, is the visiting American furrier; John Vickery is a blithe spirit if ever there was one; Patrick Fitzgerald is almost irresistible as the boyfriend, his words lightly tinged with brogue; Rex Robbins is an upper-class diplomat invited for the festivities; and Julie Dretzin, making her theatre debut, is Sara's daughter. (Welcome!) The casting is fine throughout and, in the case of Miss Alexander, inspired. Who would have thought the lady to have had so much comedy in her?

Jack Kroll (review date 2 November 1992)

SOURCE: "You Gotta Have Heart," in *Newsweek,* Vol. CXX, No. 18, November 2, 1992, p. 104.

[*In the following review of* The Sisters Rosensweig, *which premiered at New York's Lincoln Center under the direction of Daniel Sullivan, Kroll maintains that Wasserstein's female characters are poorly developed and that the play's humor, while entertaining, evades rather than confronts serious issues.*]

There's a fine borderline between entertaining an audience and ingratiating oneself with it. In her new play **The Sisters Rosensweig** Wendy Wasserstein violates that border. Wasserstein, who won the 1989 Pulitzer Prize for her play **The Heidi Chronicles,** has dealt deftly with the thorny ironies of the young feminist middle class. But in her new play she settles for—no, insists on—the clever laugh, the situation that charms rather than challenges. The play deals with three Jewish-American sisters celebrating the 54th birthday of the eldest, Sara, in London, where she's become a big-shot banker. Sara (Jane Alexander) has been on the cover of *Fortune,* but her emotional life is in a spiritual safe-deposit box. Pfeni (Frances McDormand) is a travel writer who restlessly ricochets between the world's flash points. Gorgeous (Madeline Kahn) is a housewife who's embarked on a radio career as Dr. Gorgeous, a kind of non-Teutonic Dr. Ruth. Consider the possibilities.

Wasserstein considers them, evokes them and then gaily abandons them with gags and banter that use her undoubted comedic gifts to evade rather than confront. The breakup of the Soviet Union, the American recession, the plight of the homeless, the question of Jewish identity, the problem of bisexuality—all these are embodied in specific situations, and all are disposed of with a winsome superficiality that would look one-dimensional in sitcom land.

Mervyn Kane (Robert Klein), a faux furrier who falls for Sara, speaks of the anti-Semitism he's encountered in his travels. So? So nothing, there's no follow-through—Wasserstein can't wait to get to a party scene where she dispenses shop-worn gossip about hanky-panky between Laurence Olivier and Danny Kaye. Pfeni's improbable affair with a bisexual English director ends even more improbably when he informs her that a lecture he gave to a women's club made him realize that "I miss men." Wasserstein even commits the mortal sin of betraying her own characters. In a cheap-laugh scene, she has Tess (Julie Dretzin), Sara's idealistic daughter, give up her "revolutionary" zeal, putting on the Bergdorfian baubles of her aunt Gorgeous.

Such japery demeans the work of this gifted writer. In her collection of essays, *Bachelor Girls,* she confesses that "being funny for me [has] always been just a way to get by, a way to be likable yet to remain removed." Director Daniel Sullivan and a notable cast can't conquer the play's final effect of likability smothering substance. Wasserstein's most appealing character is Merv the furrier, played with fine wit and heart by comic Robert Klein. It's nice to see a feminist writer show her pivotal female character saved by a real *mensch.*

Robert Brustein   (review date 7 December 1992)

SOURCE: "The Editorial Plan," in *The New Republic,* Vol. 207, No. 24, December 7, 1992, pp. 33-4.

[*A highly respected American drama critic, Brustein was formerly Wasserstein's teacher. He is noted for his controversial views regarding the theater and for his commitment to quality. In the following review, he finds Wasserstein's* The Sisters Rosensweig *endearing but considers the work a regression to her earlier plays.*]

Wendy Wasserstein's *The Sisters Rosensweig,* newly opened at Lincoln Center, has quickly been announced for Broadway, where it should have opened in the first place. It is the female equivalent of *Conversations with My Father,* Neil Simon for the college set, a sit-com *Three Sisters,* already destined for Critics Circle Awards and anthologies like *Best American Plays of the Year.* My heart sank a little when the witty one-liners began popping ("Multiple divorce is a splendid thing, you get so many names to choose from"; "Love is love, gender is merely spare

parts"). I had hoped, after *The Heidi Chronicles,* that my very gifted former student was shaking her witticism habit. *The Sisters Rosensweig* has a lot of charm, but it is a regression. I guess it's hard, in the precarious circus of American theater, to give up your trapeze.

Wasserstein's wit is not cruel, which makes her play at the same time endearing and somewhat toothless. Her technique is to create a character who looks at first like a stereotype, then to show the more complicated workings of the human heart. One can't help liking the person who creates this kind of material, even when it seems thin and predictable, so by its own internal measure, which is to be likable, *The Sisters Rosensweig* is a success. People will be entertained and will leave the theater feeling warm and wise, which are the requisites of a commercial hit.

The play is primarily about Jewish identity. Three sisters gather together in London to celebrate the eldest's fifty-fourth birthday. Sara (Jane Alexander) is a haughty, loveless banker who, scorning her religious background, is now seeing a vaguely anti-Semitic Englishman. Gorgeous (Madeline Kahn) is a New England housewife from West Newton, currently "schlepping the sisterhood around London." Pfeni (Frances McDormand), the youngest, is an activist journalist in love with a bisexual English stage director. Of these only Gorgeous is remotely satisfied with her sexual lot. The main action concerns Sara's reluctant attraction to a shamelessly Jewish furrier named Mervyn from Roslyn (Robert Klein) who prefers to call her Sadie. Although Pfeni's stage director eventually decides he prefers men, Sara gets to sleep with Mervyn ("That furrier has some very special skills—just call it fun fur"). And the character who once called herself "a cold bitter woman who has turned her back on her family, her religion, and her country" finally gets to acknowledge her Jewish roots.

> **Wasserstein's wit is not cruel, which makes her *The Sisters Rosensweig* at the same time endearing and somewhat toothless. Her technique is to create a character who looks at first like a stereotype, then to show the more complicated workings of the human heart.**
>
> **—Robert Brustein**

The director, Daniel Sullivan, has mismatched three actresses who really don't seem like sisters, which makes the simulated Moscow Art Theater poses appear even more artificial. But the performances are creditable enough—in the case of Kahn even wonderful. Edgy, nervous, and slightly hysterical, with a voice that slides into bat shrieks, she invariably finds both the comedy and the poignancy in a character who could easily have become a suburban housefrau caricature. I found Alexander's Sara, though womanly, a trifle too coiffed, but so is the role. And his colorful character tempted John Vickery's English stage director into too much show-biz rodomontade. Klein's Mervyn, on the other hand, was a congenial loud mouth, a good-natured version of Alan King. But, oh, Wendy Wasserstein, after you've picked up all your awards, won't you throw away your safety net?

Stefan Kanfer   (review date 5-19 April 1993)

SOURCE: "The Trivial, the Traumatic, the Truly Bad," in *The New Leader,* Vol. LXXVI, No. 5, April 5-19, 1993, pp. 22-3.

[*Kanfer is an educator, critic, editor, novelist, playwright, and nonfiction writer who has written for television. In the following excerpt, he discusses the weaknesses of* The Sisters Rosensweig, *noting its focus on Jewish identity and assimilation, and its allusions to Anton Chekhov's 1901* Tri sestry (Three Sisters).]

Sisterhood is powerful. Take Chekhov's *The Three Sisters.* Wendy Wasserstein did. The playwright transported a trio of siblings from imperial Russia to present-day England, gave their yearnings a feelgood spin, and diluted them with gags. Result: a demand for tickets so great that *The Sisters Rosensweig* recently moved from a modest space in Lincoln Center to the full-sized Ethel Barrymore Theater.

Happily, Jane Alexander is still in the role of Sara, a fast-track international banker. To celebrate her 54th birthday, Sara's two younger siblings arrive simultaneously at her sumptuous London house. Pfeni, née Penny (Christine Estabrook), is a travel writer; Gorgeous (Madeline Kahn) is a tornado in the guise of a housewife, mother of four, and host of a Boston call-in radio program.

At first, all three women seem busy and fulfilled. But as the play develops, each turns out to be as needy as a poster child. Divorced twice, Sara has assumed a gloss of English hauteur. Men find her threatening, and stay away in herds. In reaction to the ice-cold Sara, her teenage daughter Tess (Julie Dretzin) has fallen passionately in love with an unkempt prole, Tom (Patrick Fitzgerald). The two spend their hours driving Sara up the rose-patterned walls, demonstrating for Lithuanian independence and dining exclusively on "primary color food." Pfeni keeps on the move because she cannot set down physical or emotional roots. The one man in her life, Geoffrey (John Vickery), is a self-absorbed bisexual director. "Love is love," he declares. "Gender is merely spare parts." Gorgeous boasts about her multiplaned life, but in many ways she is the saddest of the siblings, stuck with an unresponsive—and unemployed—husband, deriving her satisfaction from nonstop chatter and constant changes of wardrobe.

Into this hothouse world comes Mervyn (Robert Klein), a middle-aged American merchant who stops by for a moment, and stays for dinner. Mervyn appears to be a Bronx Babbitt; then, as the evening progresses, he reveals an intellectual bent and a natural irony. ("My daughter teaches semiotics. That means she screens *Hiroshima Mon Amour* once a week.") He is the first man in years to evince an interest in Sara. Will she succumb to his advances? Is Yitzchak Rabin Jewish? Of course she will. The more important question is: Are the Rosensweigs Jewish? That is not so certain.

Identity is Wasserstein's subtext, and from time to time she considers the price of assimilation as well as the many ways of being an expatriate from one's spiritual home. When Gorgeous insists on lighting Sabbath candles, Sara, who has been fleeing her origins since adolescence, takes it as a personal affront. When Pfeni becomes obsessed with the travails of the Kurds, she recovers the social conscience of her late mother—a conscience rekindled in Tess. At such moments *Sisters* edges toward a real theme. But 90 per cent of the evening is concerned with situation comedy. Some of it is sharply observed ("What a pleasure," says Sara, "to live in a country where our feelings are openly repressed"). Much of it is as cheap as Gorgeous' junk jewelry. The New England yenta hears Mervyn talking about Metternich and the Concert of Europe. "What concert?" she yaps. "I must have missed that one on the tour." Jackie Mason has turned down better material.

In the playwright's uncertain hands, events rarely happen organically; they occur because she wants them to occur. Vickery, for example, is a skilled and energetic performer, but all he offers here is a collage of eccentricities and one-liners. Nothing he says or does suggests that he would be attractive to any woman, and his farewell to Pfeni ("I miss men") is as unsurprising as her reply ("So do I"). Similarly, young Tess ceaselessly tells her family how committed she is to the Cause; she and Tom plan to fly off to Vilnius. Toward the end of Act Two she announces that she isn't going after all. At a London rally, she suddenly felt like "an outsider" and decided to stay home. The real reason Tess didn't go is much simpler. Wasserstein needed her to make a very debatable point about Jews being on the periphery of world events.

Given this shallow, brittle work, several actors perform miracles. Alexander, under the bright direction of Daniel Sullivan, lends *Sisters* an intelligence and flair that are not in the script. Kahn and Klein, both experienced comedians, are alternately poignant and show-stopping hilarious. The rest of the cast varies between slick and competent, abetted by John Lee Beatty's sumptuous set and Jane Greenwood's witty costumes.

It may seem unfair to compare Wasserstein with Chekhov—who could stand against the Master? But she invites the comparison: One of the sisters even quotes Masha's famous line about yearning for Moscow. And in the *Playbill,* the American makes a point of bringing the Russian onstage: "I've always been a big fan of Chekhov," recalls Wasserstein, "so I thought the idea of three sisters would be a novel one for a play." It *was* novel, back in 1901. Today it requires something more. A big fan creates a lot of breeze, but very little fresh air.

Alex Raskin   (review date 30 May 1993)

SOURCE: A review of *The Sisters Rosensweig,* in *Los Angeles Times Book Review,* May 30, 1993, p. 6.

[In the following review, Raskin offers a mixed assessment of The Sisters Rosensweig.*]*

One reason Wendy Wasserstein's characters are so compelling is that they have been invented by such a half-breed: a feminist playwright who can't seem to ignore the enticing call of the comfy Jewish suburban family. You can hear this call in the play that won her the Pulitzer Prize, *The Heidi Chronicles,* which ended happily when the heroine adopts a baby to raise on her own. And you can feel it intimately in the relationship at the center of this play. Sara, a 54-year-old British financier with "the biggest balls at the Hong Kong/Shanghai bank," "no longer sees the necessity for romance" until she meets Merv, a 58-year-old furrier ("Shhh! Please, synthetic animal covering," he tells progressive clients). Vintage Wasserstein, their courtship is one of passion thinly concealed by pugnaciousness. Sara: "How many support groups did you join when Roslyn died? I'm sorry that was cruel." Merv: "No, but it was in surprisingly bad taste. I joined two." Sara: "And what did you learn about yourself?" Merv: "That I couldn't write poetry."

Just as marriage seems inevitable, though, Wasserstein steers the romance askew by having Sara limit their relationship to a friendship. Cynics will say that Wasserstein—remembering how prominent feminists upbraided her for suggesting in *The Heidi Chronicles* that a woman needs a baby to be happy—is simply going against the natural emotional drift of her play in order to be PC. But the plot diversion is actually central to Wasserstein's message, which is that nesting must be counterbalanced by questing. Not coincidentally, this is similar to the message of Chekov's *The Three Sisters.* But the success of Wasserstein's characters at heeding it is all the more remarkable because their bi-coastal, bisexual lives are infinitely more disorienting than those in Tsarist Russia.

Richard Hornby (essay date Summer 1993)

SOURCE: "English Versus American Acting," in *The Hudson Review,* Vol. XLVI, No. 2, Summer, 1993, pp. 365-71.

[In the following excerpt, Hornby discusses characterization in The Sisters Rosensweig.*]*

Wendy Wasserstein's new play, *The Sisters Rosensweig,* like her earlier *Heidi Chronicles,* is a pseudo-feminist piece that will no doubt eventually be performed in every college theatre in the country. The three eponymous sisters at first give the impression of being independent women, but soon reveal a predilection for inadequate men, who nonetheless manage to dominate their lives.

The oldest sister, Sara, heads an international bank. The second, amusingly named "Gorgeous," is the wife of a corporate lawyer from Newton, Massachusetts, and a radio personality herself. The youngest is Pfeni, a globe-trotting journalist. As the play begins, all three gather in London for Sara's fifty-fourth birthday. Sara, who has been married three times, in the course of the play has a one-night affair with a furrier who talks like a second-rate Jewish comic. Gorgeous reveals that her corporate lawyer husband is actually unemployed and playing at being a *film noir* detective, supported by her income as a radio purveyor of advice. Pfeni breaks up with the man in her life, a homosexual stage director. Sara's daughter, Tess, breaks up with *her* young man, an Irishman dedicated to the unlikely cause of Latvian independence.

Thus the four women, for all their supposed liberation, are defined by their relationship with men. Sara is supposed to be a big-time banker, but we see her spending no time at all on what in real life would be an all-consuming profession; in the course of the play she cooks a meal, sleeps with a man, and chats with her sisters and daughter, all traditional female activities. Gorgeous' radio work, though lucrative, is revealed to be utterly bogus; her principal obsession is elegant clothing. Pfeni, like the title character in *The Heidi Chronicles,* is hooked on a male homosexual, who leaves her because he misses men. If this is supposed to be a *feminist* play, I would hate to see one in which Wasserstein was being traditionalist!

The Broadway production of *The Sisters Rosensweig* succeeded because of superlative performances by two of the three leads. (If nothing else, Wasserstein can attract fine actresses.) Jane Alexander, who in real life is WASP to the core, played the role of Sara with a perfect balance of Jewishness and elegance, strongly mixed with intelligence and humor. Nevertheless, Madeline Kahn, the funniest American actress since Fannie Brice, managed to surpass her. Her Jewish inflections, perfect comic timing, and boundless energy made her performance a joy. At one point, the furrier brings Gorgeous the genuine Chanel suit she has always dreamed of wearing; Kahn's reaction with surprise, delight, and near-sexual ecstasy was worth the price of admission.

As Pfeni, Christine Estabrook was the weakest of the three sisters, but part of the problem was in the writing; for a hot-shot international journalist, Pfeni seems surprisingly staid and passive. John Vickery brought energy and charm to the role of the gay director; the rest of the cast were unremarkable. Daniel Sullivan directed with pace and subtlety; Jane Greenwood's costumes were, as usual, superb, as was John Lee Beatty's elegant setting, a Queen Anne style living room, bright and diverse, with beautiful white flowered wallpaper. One of Beatty's great strengths as a designer is his ability to suggest a world beyond what we see. Here, his gracefully angled setting, with its many levels and areas, not only made for lovely, constantly changing stage pictures, but led us imaginatively to the remainder of the sumptuous townhouse, and the genteel quarter of London in which it is situated. Finally, Pat Collins' lighting . . . perfectly suggested the cool, misty, shifting light of soggy London.

Michael Coveney (review date 14 August 1994)

SOURCE: A review of *The Sisters Rosensweig,* in *The Observer,* August 14, 1994, p. 11.

[In the following review, Coveney offers a mixed assessment of a London production of The Sisters Rosensweig, *but praises Wasserstein for her "clever mix of emotional comedy and old-fashioned Broadway wise-cracking."]*

Wendy Wasserstein's *The Sisters Rosensweig* is a well-wrought comedy about growing older without sex and learning to live with your family. Some folks around me were not sure about 'schtupping' but they soon caught on; we've all seen *She Schtups to Conquer,* after all, and that's how Sara Goode (Janet Suzman) proceeds with her fake furrier (Larry Lamb), 'the furrier who came to dinner.'

As an American comedy set in London, the play's jaundiced squint at Jewish displacement in middle-class life was always deliberate: the idea of withering roots and values is absorbed in a comfortable, creamy Holland Park apartment, enticingly well designed by Lez Brotherston. And Suzman's tense and throatily intoned Sara is easily the match of Jane Alexander's in New York; Sara, the twice-divorced European head of the Hong Kong and Shanghai Bank, celebrates her 54th birthday in September 1991 and provides a gloriously irrelevant social flashpoint while Russia crumbles and Lithuania declares its independence.

Wasserstein's confection, with its nods towards Chekhov, Moss Hart and George S Kaufman, is a clever mix of emotional comedy and old-fashioned Broadway wise-cracking. Lynda Bellingham is fine as the younger, journalist sister. But Maureen Lipman spoils a winning performance as the daffy sibling by coarse clowning. On Broadway, when Madeline Khan tried on her surprise gift of a pink Chanel suit, she was both touching and hilarious as she inquired, 'Do I look like Catherine Denoove?' Ms Lipman crashes around with a lampshade on her head and asks, without the slightest hope of a positive reply, 'Do I look like Audrey Hepburn?' Michael Blakemore's direction is otherwise impeccable.

FURTHER READING

Criticism

Corliss, Richard. "Broadway's Big Endearment." *Time* 122, No. 27 (26 December 1983): 80.
Favorably assesses *Isn't It Romantic,* noting that although Wasserstein writes about Jews and "WASPs," she does so without "a tincture of sitcom condescension, finding poignant similarities in perpendicular lives."

Hoban, Phoebe. "The Family Wasserstein." *New York* 26, No. 1 (4 January 1993): 32-7.
Feature article profiling Wasserstein, her parents, and siblings, noting her family's influence on her work.

Ruling, Karl G. *"The Heidi Chronicles:* A Production Casebook." *TCI* 27, No. 3 (March 1993): 40-3.
Discusses various productions of *The Heidi Chronicles,* focusing, in particular, on set designs and budgets.

Interview

"The More Decade." *Harper's Bazaar* 117, No. 3268 (June 1984): 146-47, 180.
Relates Wasserstein's thoughts on success, aging, independence, and motherhood. Comments from journalist Diane Sawyer, film critic Janet Maslin, and photographer Annie Leibovitz are also included.

Additional coverage of Wasserstein's life and career is contained in the following sources published by Gale Research: *Contemporary Authors,* Vols. 121, 129; *Contemporary Authors Bibliographic Series,* Vol. 3; *Contemporary Literature Criticism,* Vols. 32, 59; and *Drama Criticism,* Vol. 4.

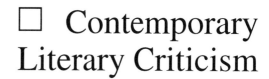 Contemporary
Literary Criticism

Indexes

Literary Criticism Series
Cumulative Author Index
Cumulative Topic Index
Cumulative Nationality Index
Title Index, Volume 90

How to Use This Index

The main references

> Calvino, Italo
> 1923-1985.....CLC 5, 8, 11, 22, 33, 39,
> 73; SSC 3

list all author entries in the following Gale Literary Criticism series:

BLC = *Black Literature Criticism*
CLC = *Contemporary Literary Criticism*
CLR = *Children's Literature Review*
CMLC = *Classical and Medieval Literature Criticism*
DA = *DISCovering Authors*
DC = *Drama Criticism*
HLC = *Hispanic Literature Criticism*
LC = *Literature Criticism from 1400 to 1800*
NCLC = *Nineteenth-Century Literature Criticism*
PC = *Poetry Criticism*
SSC = *Short Story Criticism*
TCLC = *Twentieth-Century Literary Criticism*
WLC = *World Literature Criticism, 1500 to the Present*

The cross-references

> See also CANR 23; CA 85-88;
> obituary CA 116

list all author entries in the following Gale biographical and literary sources:

AAYA = *Authors & Artists for Young Adults*
AITN = *Authors in the News*
BEST = *Bestsellers*
BW = *Black Writers*
CA = *Contemporary Authors*
CAAS = *Contemporary Authors Autobiography Series*
CABS = *Contemporary Authors Bibliographical Series*
CANR = *Contemporary Authors New Revision Series*
CAP = *Contemporary Authors Permanent Series*
CDALB = *Concise Dictionary of American Literary Biography*
CDBLB = *Concise Dictionary of British Literary Biography*
DLB = *Dictionary of Literary Biography*
DLBD = *Dictionary of Literary Biography Documentary Series*
DLBY = *Dictionary of Literary Biography Yearbook*
HW = *Hispanic Writers*
JRDA = *Junior DISCovering Authors*
MAICYA = *Major Authors and Illustrators for Children and Young Adults*
MTCW = *Major 20th-Century Writers*
NNAL = *Native North American Literature*
SAAS = *Something about the Author Autobiography Series*
SATA = *Something about the Author*
YABC = *Yesterday's Authors of Books for Children*

Literary Criticism Series
Cumulative Author Index

Barbusse, Henri 1873-1935 . . . . **TCLC 5**
See also CA 105; DLB 65

Barclay, Bill
See Moorcock, Michael (John)

Barclay, William Ewert
See Moorcock, Michael (John)

Barea, Arturo 1897-1957 . . . . **TCLC 14**
See also CA 111

Barfoot, Joan 1946- . . . . **CLC 18**
See also CA 105

Baring, Maurice 1874-1945 . . . . **TCLC 8**
See also CA 105; DLB 34

Barker, Clive 1952- . . . . **CLC 52**
See also AAYA 10; BEST 90:3; CA 121;
129; MTCW

Barker, George Granville
1913-1991 . . . . **CLC 8, 48**
See also CA 9-12R; 135; CANR 7, 38;
DLB 20; MTCW

Barker, Harley Granville
See Granville-Barker, Harley
See also DLB 10

Barker, Howard 1946- . . . . **CLC 37**
See also CA 102; DLB 13

Barker, Pat 1943- . . . . **CLC 32**
See also CA 117; 122

Barlow, Joel 1754-1812 . . . . **NCLC 23**
See also DLB 37

Barnard, Mary (Ethel) 1909- . . . . . . **CLC 48**
See also CA 21-22; CAP 2

Barnes, Djuna
1892-1982 . . . **CLC 3, 4, 8, 11, 29; SSC 3**
See also CA 9-12R; 107; CANR 16; DLB 4,
9, 45; MTCW

Barnes, Julian 1946- . . . . **CLC 42; DAB**
See also CA 102; CANR 19; DLBY 93

Barnes, Peter 1931- . . . . **CLC 5, 56**
See also CA 65-68; CAAS 12; CANR 33,
34; DLB 13; MTCW

Baroja (y Nessi), Pio
1872-1956 . . . . **TCLC 8; HLC**
See also CA 104

Baron, David
See Pinter, Harold

Baron Corvo
See Rolfe, Frederick (William Serafino
Austin Lewis Mary)

Barondess, Sue K(aufman)
1926-1977 . . . . **CLC 8**
See also Kaufman, Sue
See also CA 1-4R; 69-72; CANR 1

Baron de Teive
See Pessoa, Fernando (Antonio Nogueira)

Barres, Maurice 1862-1923 . . . . **TCLC 47**
See also DLB 123

Barreto, Afonso Henrique de Lima
See Lima Barreto, Afonso Henrique de

Barrett, (Roger) Syd 1946- . . . . **CLC 35**

Barrett, William (Christopher)
1913-1992 . . . . **CLC 27**
See also CA 13-16R; 139; CANR 11

Barrie, J(ames) M(atthew)
1860-1937 . . . . **TCLC 2; DAB**
See also CA 104; 136; CDBLB 1890-1914;
CLR 16; DLB 10, 141, 156; MAICYA;
YABC 1

Barrington, Michael
See Moorcock, Michael (John)

Barrol, Grady
See Bograd, Larry

Barry, Mike
See Malzberg, Barry N(athaniel)

Barry, Philip 1896-1949 . . . . **TCLC 11**
See also CA 109; DLB 7

Bart, Andre Schwarz
See Schwarz-Bart, Andre

Barth, John (Simmons)
1930- . . . . . . **CLC 1, 2, 3, 5, 7, 9, 10, 14,
27, 51, 89; SSC 10**
See also AITN 1, 2; CA 1-4R; CABS 1;
CANR 5, 23, 49; DLB 2; MTCW

Barthelme, Donald
1931-1989 . . . . . . **CLC 1, 2, 3, 5, 6, 8, 13,
23, 46, 59; SSC 2**
See also CA 21-24R; 129; CANR 20;
DLB 2; DLBY 80, 89; MTCW; SATA 7;
SATA-Obit 62

Barthelme, Frederick 1943- . . . . **CLC 36**
See also CA 114; 122; DLBY 85

Barthes, Roland (Gerard)
1915-1980 . . . . **CLC 24, 83**
See also CA 130; 97-100; MTCW

Barzun, Jacques (Martin) 1907- . . . . **CLC 51**
See also CA 61-64; CANR 22

Bashevis, Isaac
See Singer, Isaac Bashevis

Bashkirtseff, Marie 1859-1884 . . . **NCLC 27**

Basho
See Matsuo Basho

Bass, Kingsley B., Jr.
See Bullins, Ed

Bass, Rick 1958- . . . . **CLC 79**
See also CA 126

Bassani, Giorgio 1916- . . . . **CLC 9**
See also CA 65-68; CANR 33; DLB 128;
MTCW

Bastos, Augusto (Antonio) Roa
See Roa Bastos, Augusto (Antonio)

Bataille, Georges 1897-1962 . . . . **CLC 29**
See also CA 101; 89-92

Bates, H(erbert) E(rnest)
1905-1974 . . . . . . **CLC 46; DAB; SSC 10**
See also CA 93-96; 45-48; CANR 34;
MTCW

Bauchart
See Camus, Albert

Baudelaire, Charles
1821-1867 . . . . . **NCLC 6, 29; DA; DAB;
PC 1; SSC 18; WLC**

Baudrillard, Jean 1929- . . . . **CLC 60**

Baum, L(yman) Frank 1856-1919 . . . **TCLC 7**
See also CA 108; 133; CLR 15; DLB 22;
JRDA; MAICYA; MTCW; SATA 18

Baum, Louis F.
See Baum, L(yman) Frank

Baumbach, Jonathan 1933- . . . . . . **CLC 6, 23**
See also CA 13-16R; CAAS 5; CANR 12;
DLBY 80; MTCW

Bausch, Richard (Carl) 1945- . . . . . . **CLC 51**
See also CA 101; CAAS 14; CANR 43;
DLB 130

Baxter, Charles 1947- . . . . **CLC 45, 78**
See also CA 57-60; CANR 40; DLB 130

Baxter, George Owen
See Faust, Frederick (Schiller)

Baxter, James K(eir) 1926-1972 . . . . **CLC 14**
See also CA 77-80

Baxter, John
See Hunt, E(verette) Howard, (Jr.)

Bayer, Sylvia
See Glassco, John

Baynton, Barbara 1857-1929 . . . . . . **TCLC 57**

Beagle, Peter S(oyer) 1939- . . . . **CLC 7**
See also CA 9-12R; CANR 4; DLBY 80;
SATA 60

Bean, Normal
See Burroughs, Edgar Rice

Beard, Charles A(ustin)
1874-1948 . . . . **TCLC 15**
See also CA 115; DLB 17; SATA 18

Beardsley, Aubrey 1872-1898 . . . . . **NCLC 6**

Beattie, Ann
1947- . . . . **CLC 8, 13, 18, 40, 63; SSC 11**
See also BEST 90:2; CA 81-84; DLBY 82;
MTCW

Beattie, James 1735-1803 . . . . **NCLC 25**
See also DLB 109

Beauchamp, Kathleen Mansfield 1888-1923
See Mansfield, Katherine
See also CA 104; 134; DA

Beaumarchais, Pierre-Augustin Caron de
1732-1799 . . . . **DC 4**

**Beauvoir, Simone (Lucie Ernestine Marie
Bertrand) de**
1908-1986 . . . . **CLC 1, 2, 4, 8, 14, 31, 44,
50, 71; DA; DAB; WLC**
See also CA 9-12R; 118; CANR 28;
DLB 72; DLBY 86; MTCW

Becker, Jurek 1937- . . . . **CLC 7, 19**
See also CA 85-88; DLB 75

Becker, Walter 1950- . . . . **CLC 26**

Beckett, Samuel (Barclay)
1906-1989 . . . . . . **CLC 1, 2, 3, 4, 6, 9, 10,
11, 14, 18, 29, 57, 59, 83; DA; DAB;
SSC 16; WLC**
See also CA 5-8R; 130; CANR 33;
CDBLB 1945-1960; DLB 13, 15;
DLBY 90; MTCW

Beckford, William 1760-1844 . . . . **NCLC 16**
See also DLB 39

Beckman, Gunnel 1910- . . . . **CLC 26**
See also CA 33-36R; CANR 15; CLR 25;
MAICYA; SAAS 9; SATA 6

Becque, Henri 1837-1899 . . . . **NCLC 3**

Beddoes, Thomas Lovell
1803-1849 . . . . **NCLC 3**
See also DLB 96

Bedford, Donald F.
See Fearing, Kenneth (Flexner)

Beecher, Catharine Esther
    1800-1878 .... NCLC 30
    See also DLB 1

Beecher, John 1904-1980 .... CLC 6
    See also AITN 1; CA 5-8R; 105; CANR 8

Beer, Johann 1655-1700 .... LC 5

Beer, Patricia 1924- .... CLC 58
    See also CA 61-64; CANR 13, 46; DLB 40

Beerbohm, Henry Maximilian
    1872-1956 .... TCLC 1, 24
    See also CA 104; DLB 34, 100

Beerbohm, Max
    See Beerbohm, Henry Maximilian

Beer-Hofmann, Richard
    1866-1945 .... TCLC 60
    See also DLB 81

Begiebing, Robert J(ohn) 1946- ..... CLC 70
    See also CA 122; CANR 40

Behan, Brendan
    1923-1964 .... CLC 1, 8, 11, 15, 79
    See also CA 73-76; CANR 33;
    CDBLB 1945-1960; DLB 13; MTCW

Behn, Aphra
    1640(?)-1689 ...... LC 1, 30; DA; DAB;
                        DC 4; PC 13; WLC
    See also DLB 39, 80, 131

Behrman, S(amuel) N(athaniel)
    1893-1973 .... CLC 40
    See also CA 13-16; 45-48; CAP 1; DLB 7,
    44

Belasco, David 1853-1931 .... TCLC 3
    See also CA 104; DLB 7

Belcheva, Elisaveta 1893- .... CLC 10
    See also Bagryana, Elisaveta

Beldone, Phil "Cheech"
    See Ellison, Harlan (Jay)

Beleno
    See Azuela, Mariano

Belinski, Vissarion Grigoryevich
    1811-1848 .... NCLC 5

Belitt, Ben 1911- .... CLC 22
    See also CA 13-16R; CAAS 4; CANR 7;
    DLB 5

Bell, James Madison
    1826-1902 .... TCLC 43; BLC
    See also BW 1; CA 122; 124; DLB 50

Bell, Madison (Smartt) 1957- ...... CLC 41
    See also CA 111; CANR 28

Bell, Marvin (Hartley) 1937- ..... CLC 8, 31
    See also CA 21-24R; CAAS 14; DLB 5;
    MTCW

Bell, W. L. D.
    See Mencken, H(enry) L(ouis)

Bellamy, Atwood C.
    See Mencken, H(enry) L(ouis)

Bellamy, Edward 1850-1898 ...... NCLC 4
    See also DLB 12

Bellin, Edward J.
    See Kuttner, Henry

Belloc, (Joseph) Hilaire (Pierre)
    1870-1953 .... TCLC 7, 18
    See also CA 106; DLB 19, 100, 141;
    YABC 1

Belloc, Joseph Peter Rene Hilaire
    See Belloc, (Joseph) Hilaire (Pierre)

Belloc, Joseph Pierre Hilaire
    See Belloc, (Joseph) Hilaire (Pierre)

Belloc, M. A.
    See Lowndes, Marie Adelaide (Belloc)

Bellow, Saul
    1915- ...... CLC 1, 2, 3, 6, 8, 10, 13, 15,
        25, 33, 34, 63, 79; DA; DAB; SSC 14;
                                        WLC
    See also AITN 2; BEST 89:3; CA 5-8R;
    CABS 1; CANR 29; CDALB 1941-1968;
    DLB 2, 28; DLBD 3; DLBY 82; MTCW

Belser, Reimond Karel Maria de
    See Ruyslinck, Ward

Bely, Andrey .... TCLC 7; PC 11
    See also Bugayev, Boris Nikolayevich

Benary, Margot
    See Benary-Isbert, Margot

Benary-Isbert, Margot 1889-1979 ... CLC 12
    See also CA 5-8R; 89-92; CANR 4;
    CLR 12; MAICYA; SATA 2;
    SATA-Obit 21

Benavente (y Martinez), Jacinto
    1866-1954 .... TCLC 3
    See also CA 106; 131; HW; MTCW

Benchley, Peter (Bradford)
    1940- .... CLC 4, 8
    See also AAYA 14; AITN 2; CA 17-20R;
    CANR 12, 35; MTCW; SATA 3

Benchley, Robert (Charles)
    1889-1945 .... TCLC 1, 55
    See also CA 105; DLB 11

Benda, Julien 1867-1956 .... TCLC 60
    See also CA 120

Benedict, Ruth 1887-1948 .... TCLC 60

Benedikt, Michael 1935- .... CLC 4, 14
    See also CA 13-16R; CANR 7; DLB 5

Benet, Juan 1927- .... CLC 28
    See also CA 143

Benet, Stephen Vincent
    1898-1943 .... TCLC 7; SSC 10
    See also CA 104; DLB 4, 48, 102; YABC 1

Benet, William Rose 1886-1950 ... TCLC 28
    See also CA 118; DLB 45

Benford, Gregory (Albert) 1941- .... CLC 52
    See also CA 69-72; CANR 12, 24, 49;
    DLBY 82

Bengtsson, Frans (Gunnar)
    1894-1954 .... TCLC 48

Benjamin, David
    See Slavitt, David R(ytman)

Benjamin, Lois
    See Gould, Lois

Benjamin, Walter 1892-1940 ...... TCLC 39

Benn, Gottfried 1886-1956 .... TCLC 3
    See also CA 106; DLB 56

Bennett, Alan 1934- ..... CLC 45, 77; DAB
    See also CA 103; CANR 35; MTCW

Bennett, (Enoch) Arnold
    1867-1931 .... TCLC 5, 20
    See also CA 106; CDBLB 1890-1914;
    DLB 10, 34, 98, 135

Bennett, Elizabeth
    See Mitchell, Margaret (Munnerlyn)

Bennett, George Harold 1930-
    See Bennett, Hal
    See also BW 1; CA 97-100

Bennett, Hal .... CLC 5
    See also Bennett, George Harold
    See also DLB 33

Bennett, Jay 1912- .... CLC 35
    See also AAYA 10; CA 69-72; CANR 11,
    42; JRDA; SAAS 4; SATA 41;
    SATA-Brief 27

Bennett, Louise (Simone)
    1919- .... CLC 28; BLC
    See also BW 2; DLB 117

Benson, E(dward) F(rederic)
    1867-1940 .... TCLC 27
    See also CA 114; DLB 135, 153

Benson, Jackson J. 1930- .... CLC 34
    See also CA 25-28R; DLB 111

Benson, Sally 1900-1972 .... CLC 17
    See also CA 19-20; 37-40R; CAP 1;
    SATA 1, 35; SATA-Obit 27

Benson, Stella 1892-1933 .... TCLC 17
    See also CA 117; DLB 36

Bentham, Jeremy 1748-1832 ..... NCLC 38
    See also DLB 107

Bentley, E(dmund) C(lerihew)
    1875-1956 .... TCLC 12
    See also CA 108; DLB 70

Bentley, Eric (Russell) 1916- .... CLC 24
    See also CA 5-8R; CANR 6

Beranger, Pierre Jean de
    1780-1857 .... NCLC 34

Berendt, John (Lawrence) 1939- .... CLC 86
    See also CA 146

Berger, Colonel
    See Malraux, (Georges-)Andre

Berger, John (Peter) 1926- ...... CLC 2, 19
    See also CA 81-84; DLB 14

Berger, Melvin H. 1927- .... CLC 12
    See also CA 5-8R; CANR 4; CLR 32;
    SAAS 2; SATA 5

Berger, Thomas (Louis)
    1924- .... CLC 3, 5, 8, 11, 18, 38
    See also CA 1-4R; CANR 5, 28; DLB 2;
    DLBY 80; MTCW

Bergman, (Ernst) Ingmar
    1918- .... CLC 16, 72
    See also CA 81-84; CANR 33

Bergson, Henri 1859-1941 .... TCLC 32

Bergstein, Eleanor 1938- .... CLC 4
    See also CA 53-56; CANR 5

Berkoff, Steven 1937- .... CLC 56
    See also CA 104

Bermant, Chaim (Icyk) 1929- ...... CLC 40
    See also CA 57-60; CANR 6, 31

Bern, Victoria
    See Fisher, M(ary) F(rances) K(ennedy)

Bernanos, (Paul Louis) Georges
    1888-1948 .... TCLC 3
    See also CA 104; 130; DLB 72

Bernard, April 1956- .... CLC 59
    See also CA 131

Berne, Victoria
    See Fisher, M(ary) F(rances) K(ennedy)

Bernhard, Thomas
    1931-1989 . . . . **CLC 3, 32, 61**
    See also CA 85-88; 127; CANR 32;
    DLB 85, 124; MTCW

Berriault, Gina   1926- . . . . **CLC 54**
    See also CA 116; 129; DLB 130

Berrigan, Daniel   1921- . . . . **CLC 4**
    See also CA 33-36R; CAAS 1; CANR 11,
    43; DLB 5

Berrigan, Edmund Joseph Michael, Jr.
    1934-1983
    See Berrigan, Ted
    See also CA 61-64; 110; CANR 14

Berrigan, Ted . . . . **CLC 37**
    See also Berrigan, Edmund Joseph Michael,
    Jr.
    See also DLB 5

Berry, Charles Edward Anderson   1931-
    See Berry, Chuck
    See also CA 115

Berry, Chuck . . . . **CLC 17**
    See also Berry, Charles Edward Anderson

Berry, Jonas
    See Ashbery, John (Lawrence)

Berry, Wendell (Erdman)
    1934- . . . . **CLC 4, 6, 8, 27, 46**
    See also AITN 1; CA 73-76; DLB 5, 6

Berryman, John
    1914-1972 . . . . . . **CLC 1, 2, 3, 4, 6, 8, 10,**
                          13, 25, 62
    See also CA 13-16; 33-36R; CABS 2;
    CANR 35; CAP 1; CDALB 1941-1968;
    DLB 48; MTCW

Bertolucci, Bernardo   1940- . . . . **CLC 16**
    See also CA 106

Bertrand, Aloysius   1807-1841 . . . . **NCLC 31**

Bertran de Born   c. 1140-1215 . . . . . **CMLC 5**

Besant, Annie (Wood)   1847-1933 . . . **TCLC 9**
    See also CA 105

Bessie, Alvah   1904-1985 . . . . **CLC 23**
    See also CA 5-8R; 116; CANR 2; DLB 26

Bethlen, T. D.
    See Silverberg, Robert

Beti, Mongo . . . . **CLC 27; BLC**
    See also Biyidi, Alexandre

Betjeman, John
    1906-1984 . . . **CLC 2, 6, 10, 34, 43; DAB**
    See also CA 9-12R; 112; CANR 33;
    CDBLB 1945-1960; DLB 20; DLBY 84;
    MTCW

Bettelheim, Bruno   1903-1990 . . . . . . **CLC 79**
    See also CA 81-84; 131; CANR 23; MTCW

Betti, Ugo   1892-1953 . . . . **TCLC 5**
    See also CA 104

Betts, Doris (Waugh)   1932- . . . . **CLC 3, 6, 28**
    See also CA 13-16R; CANR 9; DLBY 82

Bevan, Alistair
    See Roberts, Keith (John Kingston)

Bialik, Chaim Nachman
    1873-1934 . . . . **TCLC 25**

Bickerstaff, Isaac
    See Swift, Jonathan

Bidart, Frank   1939- . . . . **CLC 33**
    See also CA 140

Bienek, Horst   1930- . . . . **CLC 7, 11**
    See also CA 73-76; DLB 75

Bierce, Ambrose (Gwinett)
    1842-1914(?) . . . . . . **TCLC 1, 7, 44; DA;**
                           SSC 9; WLC
    See also CA 104; 139; CDALB 1865-1917;
    DLB 11, 12, 23, 71, 74

Billings, Josh
    See Shaw, Henry Wheeler

Billington, (Lady) Rachel (Mary)
    1942- . . . . **CLC 43**
    See also AITN 2; CA 33-36R; CANR 44

Binyon, T(imothy) J(ohn)   1936- . . . . **CLC 34**
    See also CA 111; CANR 28

Bioy Casares, Adolfo
    1914- . . . **CLC 4, 8, 13, 88; HLC; SSC 17**
    See also CA 29-32R; CANR 19, 43;
    DLB 113; HW; MTCW

Bird, Cordwainer
    See Ellison, Harlan (Jay)

Bird, Robert Montgomery
    1806-1854 . . . . **NCLC 1**

Birney, (Alfred) Earle
    1904- . . . . **CLC 1, 4, 6, 11**
    See also CA 1-4R; CANR 5, 20; DLB 88;
    MTCW

Bishop, Elizabeth
    1911-1979 . . . . . . **CLC 1, 4, 9, 13, 15, 32;**
                             DA; PC 3
    See also CA 5-8R; 89-92; CABS 2;
    CANR 26; CDALB 1968-1988; DLB 5;
    MTCW; SATA-Obit 24

Bishop, John   1935- . . . . **CLC 10**
    See also CA 105

Bissett, Bill   1939- . . . . **CLC 18**
    See also CA 69-72; CAAS 19; CANR 15;
    DLB 53; MTCW

Bitov, Andrei (Georgievich)   1937- . . . **CLC 57**
    See also CA 142

Biyidi, Alexandre   1932-
    See Beti, Mongo
    See also BW 1; CA 114; 124; MTCW

Bjarme, Brynjolf
    See Ibsen, Henrik (Johan)

Bjornson, Bjornstjerne (Martinius)
    1832-1910 . . . . **TCLC 7, 37**
    See also CA 104

Black, Robert
    See Holdstock, Robert P.

Blackburn, Paul   1926-1971 . . . . . . **CLC 9, 43**
    See also CA 81-84; 33-36R; CANR 34;
    DLB 16; DLBY 81

Black Elk   1863-1950 . . . . **TCLC 33**
    See also CA 144; NNAL

Black Hobart
    See Sanders, (James) Ed(ward)

Blacklin, Malcolm
    See Chambers, Aidan

Blackmore, R(ichard) D(oddridge)
    1825-1900 . . . . **TCLC 27**
    See also CA 120; DLB 18

Blackmur, R(ichard) P(almer)
    1904-1965 . . . . **CLC 2, 24**
    See also CA 11-12; 25-28R; CAP 1; DLB 63

Black Tarantula, The
    See Acker, Kathy

Blackwood, Algernon (Henry)
    1869-1951 . . . . **TCLC 5**
    See also CA 105; DLB 153, 156

Blackwood, Caroline   1931- . . . . **CLC 6, 9**
    See also CA 85-88; CANR 32; DLB 14;
    MTCW

Blade, Alexander
    See Hamilton, Edmond; Silverberg, Robert

Blaga, Lucian   1895-1961 . . . . **CLC 75**

Blair, Eric (Arthur)   1903-1950
    See Orwell, George
    See also CA 104; 132; DA; DAB; MTCW;
    SATA 29

Blais, Marie-Claire
    1939- . . . . **CLC 2, 4, 6, 13, 22**
    See also CA 21-24R; CAAS 4; CANR 38;
    DLB 53; MTCW

Blaise, Clark   1940- . . . . **CLC 29**
    See also AITN 2; CA 53-56; CAAS 3;
    CANR 5; DLB 53

Blake, Nicholas
    See Day Lewis, C(ecil)
    See also DLB 77

Blake, William
    1757-1827 . . . . **NCLC 13, 37; DA; DAB;**
                            PC 12; WLC
    See also CDBLB 1789-1832; DLB 93;
    MAICYA; SATA 30

Blake, William J(ames)   1894-1969 . . . **PC 12**
    See also CA 5-8R; 25-28R

Blasco Ibanez, Vicente
    1867-1928 . . . . **TCLC 12**
    See also CA 110; 131; HW; MTCW

Blatty, William Peter   1928- . . . . **CLC 2**
    See also CA 5-8R; CANR 9

Bleeck, Oliver
    See Thomas, Ross (Elmore)

Blessing, Lee   1949- . . . . **CLC 54**

Blish, James (Benjamin)
    1921-1975 . . . . **CLC 14**
    See also CA 1-4R; 57-60; CANR 3; DLB 8;
    MTCW; SATA 66

Bliss, Reginald
    See Wells, H(erbert) G(eorge)

Blixen, Karen (Christentze Dinesen)
    1885-1962
    See Dinesen, Isak
    See also CA 25-28; CANR 22; CAP 2;
    MTCW; SATA 44

Bloch, Robert (Albert)   1917-1994 . . . **CLC 33**
    See also CA 5-8R; 146; CAAS 20; CANR 5;
    DLB 44; SATA 12; SATA-Obit 82

Blok, Alexander (Alexandrovich)
    1880-1921 . . . . **TCLC 5**
    See also CA 104

Blom, Jan
    See Breytenbach, Breyten

Bloom, Harold   1930- . . . . **CLC 24**
    See also CA 13-16R; CANR 39; DLB 67

Bradford, Gamaliel 1863-1932..... **TCLC 36**
See also DLB 17

Bradley, David (Henry, Jr.)
1950-................. **CLC 23; BLC**
See also BW 1; CA 104; CANR 26; DLB 33

Bradley, John Ed(mund, Jr.)
1958-...................... **CLC 55**
See also CA 139

Bradley, Marion Zimmer 1930-..... **CLC 30**
See also AAYA 9; CA 57-60; CAAS 10;
CANR 7, 31; DLB 8; MTCW

Bradstreet, Anne
1612(?)-1672 ...... **LC 4, 30; DA; PC 10**
See also CDALB 1640-1865; DLB 24

Brady, Joan 1939- .... **CLC 86**
See also CA 141

Bragg, Melvyn 1939- .... **CLC 10**
See also BEST 89:3; CA 57-60; CANR 10,
48; DLB 14

Braine, John (Gerard)
1922-1986 .... **CLC 1, 3, 41**
See also CA 1-4R; 120; CANR 1, 33;
CDBLB 1945-1960; DLB 15; DLBY 86;
MTCW

Brammer, William 1930(?)-1978 .... **CLC 31**
See also CA 77-80

Brancati, Vitaliano 1907-1954..... **TCLC 12**
See also CA 109

Brancato, Robin F(idler) 1936- ..... **CLC 35**
See also AAYA 9; CA 69-72; CANR 11,
45; CLR 32; JRDA; SAAS 9; SATA 23

Brand, Max
See Faust, Frederick (Schiller)

Brand, Millen 1906-1980 .... **CLC 7**
See also CA 21-24R; 97-100

Branden, Barbara .... **CLC 44**
See also CA 148

Brandes, Georg (Morris Cohen)
1842-1927 .... **TCLC 10**
See also CA 105

Brandys, Kazimierz 1916- .... **CLC 62**

Branley, Franklyn M(ansfield)
1915- .... **CLC 21**
See also CA 33-36R; CANR 14, 39;
CLR 13; MAICYA; SAAS 16; SATA 4,
68

Brathwaite, Edward Kamau 1930-... **CLC 11**
See also BW 2; CA 25-28R; CANR 11, 26,
47; DLB 125

Brautigan, Richard (Gary)
1935-1984 .... **CLC 1, 3, 5, 9, 12, 34, 42**
See also CA 53-56; 113; CANR 34; DLB 2,
5; DLBY 80, 84; MTCW; SATA 56

Braverman, Kate 1950- .... **CLC 67**
See also CA 89-92

Brecht, Bertolt
1898-1956 ...... **TCLC 1, 6, 13, 35; DA;
DAB; DC 3; WLC**
See also CA 104; 133; DLB 56, 124; MTCW

Brecht, Eugen Berthold Friedrich
See Brecht, Bertolt

Bremer, Fredrika 1801-1865 ..... **NCLC 11**

Brennan, Christopher John
1870-1932 .... **TCLC 17**
See also CA 117

Brennan, Maeve 1917-............. **CLC 5**
See also CA 81-84

Brentano, Clemens (Maria)
1778-1842 .... **NCLC 1**
See also DLB 90

Brent of Bin Bin
See Franklin, (Stella Maraia Sarah) Miles

Brenton, Howard 1942-........... **CLC 31**
See also CA 69-72; CANR 33; DLB 13;
MTCW

Breslin, James 1930-
See Breslin, Jimmy
See also CA 73-76; CANR 31; MTCW

Breslin, Jimmy .... **CLC 4, 43**
See also Breslin, James
See also AITN 1

Bresson, Robert 1901-............ **CLC 16**
See also CA 110; CANR 49

Breton, Andre 1896-1966... **CLC 2, 9, 15, 54**
See also CA 19-20; 25-28R; CANR 40;
CAP 2; DLB 65; MTCW

Breytenbach, Breyten 1939(?)- .. **CLC 23, 37**
See also CA 113; 129

Bridgers, Sue Ellen 1942- .... **CLC 26**
See also AAYA 8; CA 65-68; CANR 11,
36; CLR 18; DLB 52; JRDA; MAICYA;
SAAS 1; SATA 22

Bridges, Robert (Seymour)
1844-1930 .... **TCLC 1**
See also CA 104; CDBLB 1890-1914;
DLB 19, 98

Bridie, James.................... **TCLC 3**
See also Mavor, Osborne Henry
See also DLB 10

Brin, David 1950-................ **CLC 34**
See also CA 102; CANR 24; SATA 65

Brink, Andre (Philippus)
1935-................... **CLC 18, 36**
See also CA 104; CANR 39; MTCW

Brinsmead, H(esba) F(ay) 1922- .... **CLC 21**
See also CA 21-24R; CANR 10; MAICYA;
SAAS 5; SATA 18, 78

Brittain, Vera (Mary)
1893(?)-1970 .... **CLC 23**
See also CA 13-16; 25-28R; CAP 1; MTCW

Broch, Hermann 1886-1951....... **TCLC 20**
See also CA 117; DLB 85, 124

Brock, Rose
See Hansen, Joseph

Brodkey, Harold 1930-........... **CLC 56**
See also CA 111; DLB 130

Brodsky, Iosif Alexandrovich 1940-
See Brodsky, Joseph
See also AITN 1; CA 41-44R; CANR 37;
MTCW

Brodsky, Joseph .. **CLC 4, 6, 13, 36, 50; PC 9**
See also Brodsky, Iosif Alexandrovich

Brodsky, Michael Mark 1948- ..... **CLC 19**
See also CA 102; CANR 18, 41

Bromell, Henry 1947-............. **CLC 5**
See also CA 53-56; CANR 9

Bromfield, Louis (Brucker)
1896-1956 .... **TCLC 11**
See also CA 107; DLB 4, 9, 86

Broner, E(sther) M(asserman)
1930-...................... **CLC 19**
See also CA 17-20R; CANR 8, 25; DLB 28

Bronk, William 1918-............. **CLC 10**
See also CA 89-92; CANR 23

Bronstein, Lev Davidovich
See Trotsky, Leon

Bronte, Anne 1820-1849......... **NCLC 4**
See also DLB 21

Bronte, Charlotte
1816-1855 .... **NCLC 3, 8, 33; DA;
DAB; WLC**
See also CDBLB 1832-1890; DLB 21

Bronte, Emily (Jane)
1818-1848 .... **NCLC 16, 35; DA; DAB;
PC 8; WLC**
See also CDBLB 1832-1890; DLB 21, 32

Brooke, Frances 1724-1789 .... **LC 6**
See also DLB 39, 99

Brooke, Henry 1703(?)-1783 .... **LC 1**
See also DLB 39

Brooke, Rupert (Chawner)
1887-1915 .... **TCLC 2, 7; DA; DAB;
WLC**
See also CA 104; 132; CDBLB 1914-1945;
DLB 19; MTCW

Brooke-Haven, P.
See Wodehouse, P(elham) G(renville)

Brooke-Rose, Christine 1926-...... **CLC 40**
See also CA 13-16R; DLB 14

Brookner, Anita
1928- .... **CLC 32, 34, 51; DAB**
See also CA 114; 120; CANR 37; DLBY 87;
MTCW

Brooks, Cleanth 1906-1994 ..... **CLC 24, 86**
See also CA 17-20R; 145; CANR 33, 35;
DLB 63; DLBY 94; MTCW

Brooks, George
See Baum, L(yman) Frank

Brooks, Gwendolyn
1917- ...... **CLC 1, 2, 4, 5, 15, 49; BLC;
DA; PC 7; WLC**
See also AITN 1; BW 2; CA 1-4R;
CANR 1, 27; CDALB 1941-1968;
CLR 27; DLB 5, 76; MTCW; SATA 6

Brooks, Mel.................... **CLC 12**
See also Kaminsky, Melvin
See also AAYA 13; DLB 26

Brooks, Peter 1938-.............. **CLC 34**
See also CA 45-48; CANR 1

Brooks, Van Wyck 1886-1963...... **CLC 29**
See also CA 1-4R; CANR 6; DLB 45, 63,
103

Brophy, Brigid (Antonia)
1929-.................. **CLC 6, 11, 29**
See also CA 5-8R; CAAS 4; CANR 25;
DLB 14; MTCW

Brosman, Catharine Savage 1934-.... **CLC 9**
See also CA 61-64; CANR 21, 46

Brother Antoninus
See Everson, William (Oliver)

Broughton, T(homas) Alan 1936- ... **CLC 19**
See also CA 45-48; CANR 2, 23, 48

Broumas, Olga 1949-.......... **CLC 10, 73**
See also CA 85-88; CANR 20

Brown, Charles Brockden
1771-1810 . . . . **NCLC 22**
See also CDALB 1640-1865; DLB 37, 59,
73

Brown, Christy 1932-1981 . . . . **CLC 63**
See also CA 105; 104; DLB 14

Brown, Claude 1937- . . . . **CLC 30; BLC**
See also AAYA 7; BW 1; CA 73-76

Brown, Dee (Alexander) 1908- . . **CLC 18, 47**
See also CA 13-16R; CAAS 6; CANR 11,
45; DLBY 80; MTCW; SATA 5

Brown, George
See Wertmueller, Lina

Brown, George Douglas
1869-1902 . . . . **TCLC 28**

Brown, George Mackay 1921-. . . . **CLC 5, 48**
See also CA 21-24R; CAAS 6; CANR 12,
37; DLB 14, 27, 139; MTCW; SATA 35

Brown, (William) Larry 1951-. . . . . . **CLC 73**
See also CA 130; 134

Brown, Moses
See Barrett, William (Christopher)

Brown, Rita Mae 1944-. . . . . **CLC 18, 43, 79**
See also CA 45-48; CANR 2, 11, 35;
MTCW

Brown, Roderick (Langmere) Haig-
See Haig-Brown, Roderick (Langmere)

Brown, Rosellen 1939-. . . . . **CLC 32**
See also CA 77-80; CAAS 10; CANR 14, 44

Brown, Sterling Allen
1901-1989 . . . . **CLC 1, 23, 59; BLC**
See also BW 1; CA 85-88; 127; CANR 26;
DLB 48, 51, 63; MTCW

Brown, Will
See Ainsworth, William Harrison

Brown, William Wells
1813-1884 . . . . **NCLC 2; BLC; DC 1**
See also DLB 3, 50

Browne, (Clyde) Jackson 1948(?)-. . . **CLC 21**
See also CA 120

Browning, Elizabeth Barrett
1806-1861 . . . . . **NCLC 1, 16; DA; DAB;
PC 6; WLC**
See also CDBLB 1832-1890; DLB 32

Browning, Robert
1812-1889 . . **NCLC 19; DA; DAB; PC 2**
See also CDBLB 1832-1890; DLB 32;
YABC 1

Browning, Tod 1882-1962 . . . . **CLC 16**
See also CA 141; 117

Brownson, Orestes (Augustus)
1803-1876 . . . . **NCLC 50**

Bruccoli, Matthew J(oseph) 1931- . . **CLC 34**
See also CA 9-12R; CANR 7; DLB 103

Bruce, Lenny . . . . **CLC 21**
See also Schneider, Leonard Alfred

Bruin, John
See Brutus, Dennis

Brulard, Henri
See Stendhal

Brulls, Christian
See Simenon, Georges (Jacques Christian)

Brunner, John (Kilian Houston)
1934- . . . . **CLC 8, 10**
See also CA 1-4R; CAAS 8; CANR 2, 37;
MTCW

Bruno, Giordano 1548-1600 . . . . **LC 27**

Brutus, Dennis 1924- . . . . **CLC 43; BLC**
See also BW 2; CA 49-52; CAAS 14;
CANR 2, 27, 42; DLB 117

Bryan, C(ourtlandt) D(ixon) B(arnes)
1936- . . . . **CLC 29**
See also CA 73-76; CANR 13

Bryan, Michael
See Moore, Brian

Bryant, William Cullen
1794-1878 . . . . . . **NCLC 6, 46; DA; DAB**
See also CDALB 1640-1865; DLB 3, 43, 59

Bryusov, Valery Yakovlevich
1873-1924 . . . . **TCLC 10**
See also CA 107

Buchan, John 1875-1940 . . . **TCLC 41; DAB**
See also CA 108; 145; DLB 34, 70, 156;
YABC 2

Buchanan, George 1506-1582 . . . . **LC 4**

Buchheim, Lothar-Guenther 1918- . . . **CLC 6**
See also CA 85-88

Buchner, (Karl) Georg
1813-1837 . . . . **NCLC 26**

Buchwald, Art(hur) 1925-. . . . . **CLC 33**
See also AITN 1; CA 5-8R; CANR 21;
MTCW; SATA 10

Buck, Pearl S(ydenstricker)
1892-1973 . . . . **CLC 7, 11, 18; DA; DAB**
See also AITN 1; CA 1-4R; 41-44R;
CANR 1, 34; DLB 9, 102; MTCW;
SATA 1, 25

Buckler, Ernest 1908-1984. . . . . **CLC 13**
See also CA 11-12; 114; CAP 1; DLB 68;
SATA 47

Buckley, Vincent (Thomas)
1925-1988 . . . . **CLC 57**
See also CA 101

Buckley, William F(rank), Jr.
1925- . . . . **CLC 7, 18, 37**
See also AITN 1; CA 1-4R; CANR 1, 24;
DLB 137; DLBY 80; MTCW

Buechner, (Carl) Frederick
1926- . . . . **CLC 2, 4, 6, 9**
See also CA 13-16R; CANR 11, 39;
DLBY 80; MTCW

Buell, John (Edward) 1927-. . . . . **CLC 10**
See also CA 1-4R; DLB 53

Buero Vallejo, Antonio 1916- . . . **CLC 15, 46**
See also CA 106; CANR 24, 49; HW;
MTCW

Bufalino, Gesualdo 1920(?)-. . . . . **CLC 74**

Bugayev, Boris Nikolayevich 1880-1934
See Bely, Andrey
See also CA 104

Bukowski, Charles
1920-1994 . . . . **CLC 2, 5, 9, 41, 82**
See also CA 17-20R; 144; CANR 40;
DLB 5, 130; MTCW

Bulgakov, Mikhail (Afanas'evich)
1891-1940 . . . . **TCLC 2, 16; SSC 18**
See also CA 105

Bulgya, Alexander Alexandrovich
1901-1956 . . . . **TCLC 53**
See also Fadeyev, Alexander
See also CA 117

Bullins, Ed 1935- . . . . **CLC 1, 5, 7; BLC**
See also BW 2; CA 49-52; CAAS 16;
CANR 24, 46; DLB 7, 38; MTCW

Bulwer-Lytton, Edward (George Earle Lytton)
1803-1873 . . . . **NCLC 1, 45**
See also DLB 21

Bunin, Ivan Alexeyevich
1870-1953 . . . . **TCLC 6; SSC 5**
See also CA 104

Bunting, Basil 1900-1985. . . . **CLC 10, 39, 47**
See also CA 53-56; 115; CANR 7; DLB 20

Bunuel, Luis 1900-1983 . . **CLC 16, 80; HLC**
See also CA 101; 110; CANR 32; HW

Bunyan, John
1628-1688 . . . . . . **LC 4; DA; DAB; WLC**
See also CDBLB 1660-1789; DLB 39

Burckhardt, Jacob (Christoph)
1818-1897 . . . . **NCLC 49**

Burford, Eleanor
See Hibbert, Eleanor Alice Burford

Burgess, Anthony
**CLC 1, 2, 4, 5, 8, 10, 13, 15, 22, 40, 62,
81; DAB**
See also Wilson, John (Anthony) Burgess
See also AITN 1; CDBLB 1960 to Present;
DLB 14

Burke, Edmund
1729(?)-1797 . . . . **LC 7; DA; DAB; WLC**
See also DLB 104

Burke, Kenneth (Duva)
1897-1993 . . . . **CLC 2, 24**
See also CA 5-8R; 143; CANR 39; DLB 45,
63; MTCW

Burke, Leda
See Garnett, David

Burke, Ralph
See Silverberg, Robert

Burney, Fanny 1752-1840 . . . . **NCLC 12**
See also DLB 39

Burns, Robert 1759-1796. . . . . **PC 6**
See also CDBLB 1789-1832; DA; DAB;
DLB 109; WLC

Burns, Tex
See L'Amour, Louis (Dearborn)

Burnshaw, Stanley 1906-. . . . . **CLC 3, 13, 44**
See also CA 9-12R; DLB 48

Burr, Anne 1937- . . . . **CLC 6**
See also CA 25-28R

Burroughs, Edgar Rice
1875-1950 . . . . **TCLC 2, 32**
See also AAYA 11; CA 104; 132; DLB 8;
MTCW; SATA 41

Burroughs, William S(eward)
1914- . . . . **CLC 1, 2, 5, 15, 22, 42, 75;
DA; DAB; WLC**
See also AITN 2; CA 9-12R; CANR 20;
DLB 2, 8, 16, 152; DLBY 81; MTCW

Burton, Richard F. 1821-1890. . . . **NCLC 42**
See also DLB 55

Busch, Frederick 1941- ... **CLC 7, 10, 18, 47**
See also CA 33-36R; CAAS 1; CANR 45;
DLB 6

Bush, Ronald 1946- .... **CLC 34**
See also CA 136

Bustos, F(rancisco)
See Borges, Jorge Luis

Bustos Domecq, H(onorio)
See Bioy Casares, Adolfo; Borges, Jorge
Luis

Butler, Octavia E(stelle) 1947- ..... **CLC 38**
See also BW 2; CA 73-76; CANR 12, 24,
38; DLB 33; MTCW

Butler, Robert Olen (Jr.) 1945-..... **CLC 81**
See also CA 112

Butler, Samuel 1612-1680 .... **LC 16**
See also DLB 101, 126

Butler, Samuel
1835-1902 ...... **TCLC 1, 33; DA; DAB;
WLC**
See also CA 143; CDBLB 1890-1914;
DLB 18, 57

Butler, Walter C.
See Faust, Frederick (Schiller)

Butor, Michel (Marie Francois)
1926- .... **CLC 1, 3, 8, 11, 15**
See also CA 9-12R; CANR 33; DLB 83;
MTCW

Buzo, Alexander (John) 1944-...... **CLC 61**
See also CA 97-100; CANR 17, 39

Buzzati, Dino 1906-1972 .... **CLC 36**
See also CA 33-36R

Byars, Betsy (Cromer) 1928-....... **CLC 35**
See also CA 33-36R; CANR 18, 36; CLR 1,
16; DLB 52; JRDA; MAICYA; MTCW;
SAAS 1; SATA 4, 46, 80

Byatt, A(ntonia) S(usan Drabble)
1936- .... **CLC 19, 65**
See also CA 13-16R; CANR 13, 33;
DLB 14; MTCW

Byrne, David 1952-............... **CLC 26**
See also CA 127

Byrne, John Keyes 1926-
See Leonard, Hugh
See also CA 102

Byron, George Gordon (Noel)
1788-1824 ..... **NCLC 2, 12; DA; DAB;
WLC**
See also CDBLB 1789-1832; DLB 96, 110

C. 3. 3.
See Wilde, Oscar (Fingal O'Flahertie Wills)

Caballero, Fernan 1796-1877..... **NCLC 10**

Cabell, James Branch 1879-1958 ... **TCLC 6**
See also CA 105; DLB 9, 78

Cable, George Washington
1844-1925 .... **TCLC 4; SSC 4**
See also CA 104; DLB 12, 74

Cabral de Melo Neto, Joao 1920-... **CLC 76**

Cabrera Infante, G(uillermo)
1929- .... **CLC 5, 25, 45; HLC**
See also CA 85-88; CANR 29; DLB 113;
HW; MTCW

Cade, Toni
See Bambara, Toni Cade

Cadmus and Harmonia
See Buchan, John

Caedmon fl. 658-680............. **CMLC 7**
See also DLB 146

Caeiro, Alberto
See Pessoa, Fernando (Antonio Nogueira)

Cage, John (Milton. Jr.) 1912- ..... **CLC 41**
See also CA 13-16R; CANR 9

Cain, G.
See Cabrera Infante, G(uillermo)

Cain, Guillermo
See Cabrera Infante, G(uillermo)

Cain, James M(allahan)
1892-1977 .... **CLC 3, 11, 28**
See also AITN 1; CA 17-20R; 73-76;
CANR 8, 34; MTCW

Caine, Mark
See Raphael, Frederic (Michael)

Calasso, Roberto 1941- .... **CLC 81**
See also CA 143

Calderon de la Barca, Pedro
1600-1681 .... **LC 23; DC 3**

Caldwell, Erskine (Preston)
1903-1987 .... **CLC 1, 8, 14, 50, 60;
SSC 19**
See also AITN 1; CA 1-4R; 121; CAAS 1;
CANR 2, 33; DLB 9, 86; MTCW

Caldwell, (Janet Miriam) Taylor (Holland)
1900-1985 .... **CLC 2, 28, 39**
See also CA 5-8R; 116; CANR 5

Calhoun, John Caldwell
1782-1850 .... **NCLC 15**
See also DLB 3

Calisher, Hortense
1911- .... **CLC 2, 4, 8, 38; SSC 15**
See also CA 1-4R; CANR 1, 22; DLB 2;
MTCW

Callaghan, Morley Edward
1903-1990 .... **CLC 3, 14, 41, 65**
See also CA 9-12R; 132; CANR 33;
DLB 68; MTCW

Calvino, Italo
1923-1985 ..... **CLC 5, 8, 11, 22, 33, 39,
73; SSC 3**
See also CA 85-88; 116; CANR 23; MTCW

Cameron, Carey 1952-............ **CLC 59**
See also CA 135

Cameron, Peter 1959-............. **CLC 44**
See also CA 125

Campana, Dino 1885-1932........ **TCLC 20**
See also CA 117; DLB 114

Campbell, John W(ood, Jr.)
1910-1971 .... **CLC 32**
See also CA 21-22; 29-32R; CANR 34;
CAP 2; DLB 8; MTCW

Campbell, Joseph 1904-1987 .... **CLC 69**
See also AAYA 3; BEST 89:2; CA 1-4R;
124; CANR 3, 28; MTCW

Campbell, Maria 1940-............ **CLC 85**
See also CA 102; NNAL

Campbell, (John) Ramsey
1946- .... **CLC 42; SSC 19**
See also CA 57-60; CANR 7

Campbell, (Ignatius) Roy (Dunnachie)
1901-1957 .... **TCLC 5**
See also CA 104; DLB 20

Campbell, Thomas 1777-1844 .... **NCLC 19**
See also DLB 93; 144

Campbell, Wilfred................. **TCLC 9**
See also Campbell, William

Campbell, William 1858(?)-1918
See Campbell, Wilfred
See also CA 106; DLB 92

Campos, Alvaro de
See Pessoa, Fernando (Antonio Nogueira)

Camus, Albert
1913-1960 .... **CLC 1, 2, 4, 9, 11, 14, 32,
63, 69; DA; DAB; DC 2; SSC 9; WLC**
See also CA 89-92; DLB 72; MTCW

Canby, Vincent 1924-............. **CLC 13**
See also CA 81-84

Cancale
See Desnos, Robert

Canetti, Elias
1905-1994 .... **CLC 3, 14, 25, 75, 86**
See also CA 21-24R; 146; CANR 23;
DLB 85, 124; MTCW

Canin, Ethan 1960-............... **CLC 55**
See also CA 131; 135

Cannon, Curt
See Hunter, Evan

Cape, Judith
See Page, P(atricia) K(athleen)

Capek, Karel
1890-1938 ...... **TCLC 6, 37; DA; DAB;
DC 1; WLC**
See also CA 104; 140

Capote, Truman
1924-1984 ...... **CLC 1, 3, 8, 13, 19, 34,
38, 58; DA; DAB; SSC 2; WLC**
See also CA 5-8R; 113; CANR 18;
CDALB 1941-1968; DLB 2; DLBY 80,
84; MTCW

Capra, Frank 1897-1991.......... **CLC 16**
See also CA 61-64; 135

Caputo, Philip 1941-.............. **CLC 32**
See also CA 73-76; CANR 40

Card, Orson Scott 1951- .... **CLC 44, 47, 50**
See also AAYA 11; CA 102; CANR 27, 47;
MTCW; SATA 83

Cardenal (Martinez), Ernesto
1925- .... **CLC 31; HLC**
See also CA 49-52; CANR 2, 32; HW;
MTCW

Carducci, Giosue 1835-1907....... **TCLC 32**

Carew, Thomas 1595(?)-1640........ **LC 13**
See also DLB 126

Carey, Ernestine Gilbreth 1908- .... **CLC 17**
See also CA 5-8R; SATA 2

Carey, Peter 1943-............. **CLC 40, 55**
See also CA 123; 127; MTCW

Carleton, William 1794-1869...... **NCLC 3**

Carlisle, Henry (Coffin) 1926-...... **CLC 33**
See also CA 13-16R; CANR 15

Carlsen, Chris
See Holdstock, Robert P.

Chandler, Raymond (Thornton)
    1888-1959 .... TCLC **1, 7**
    See also CA 104; 129; CDALB 1929-1941;
    DLBD 6; MTCW

Chang, Jung 1952- .... CLC **71**
    See also CA 142

Channing, William Ellery
    1780-1842 .... NCLC **17**
    See also DLB 1, 59

Chaplin, Charles Spencer
    1889-1977 .... CLC **16**
    See also Chaplin, Charlie
    See also CA 81-84; 73-76

Chaplin, Charlie
    See Chaplin, Charles Spencer
    See also DLB 44

Chapman, George 1559(?)-1634 ...... LC **22**
    See also DLB 62, 121

Chapman, Graham 1941-1989 ...... CLC **21**
    See also Monty Python
    See also CA 116; 129; CANR 35

Chapman, John Jay 1862-1933 ..... TCLC **7**
    See also CA 104

Chapman, Walker
    See Silverberg, Robert

Chappell, Fred (Davis) 1936- .... CLC **40, 78**
    See also CA 5-8R; CAAS 4; CANR 8, 33;
    DLB 6, 105

Char, Rene(-Emile)
    1907-1988 .... CLC **9, 11, 14, 55**
    See also CA 13-16R; 124; CANR 32;
    MTCW

Charby, Jay
    See Ellison, Harlan (Jay)

Chardin, Pierre Teilhard de
    See Teilhard de Chardin, (Marie Joseph)
    Pierre

Charles I 1600-1649 .... LC **13**

Charyn, Jerome 1937- .... CLC **5, 8, 18**
    See also CA 5-8R; CAAS 1; CANR 7;
    DLBY 83; MTCW

Chase, Mary (Coyle) 1907-1981 ...... DC **1**
    See also CA 77-80; 105; SATA 17;
    SATA-Obit 29

Chase, Mary Ellen 1887-1973 .... CLC **2**
    See also CA 13-16; 41-44R; CAP 1;
    SATA 10

Chase, Nicholas
    See Hyde, Anthony

Chateaubriand, Francois Rene de
    1768-1848 .... NCLC **3**
    See also DLB 119

Chatterje, Sarat Chandra 1876-1936(?)
    See Chatterji, Saratchandra
    See also CA 109

Chatterji, Bankim Chandra
    1838-1894 .... NCLC **19**

Chatterji, Saratchandra .... TCLC **13**
    See also Chatterje, Sarat Chandra

Chatterton, Thomas 1752-1770 .... LC **3**
    See also DLB 109

Chatwin, (Charles) Bruce
    1940-1989 .... CLC **28, 57, 59**
    See also AAYA 4; BEST 90:1; CA 85-88;
    127

Chaucer, Daniel
    See Ford, Ford Madox

Chaucer, Geoffrey
    1340(?)-1400 .... LC **17**; DA; DAB
    See also CDBLB Before 1660; DLB 146

Chaviaras, Strates 1935-
    See Haviaras, Stratis
    See also CA 105

Chayefsky, Paddy .... CLC **23**
    See also Chayefsky, Sidney
    See also DLB 7, 44; DLBY 81

Chayefsky, Sidney 1923-1981
    See Chayefsky, Paddy
    See also CA 9-12R; 104; CANR 18

Chedid, Andree 1920- .... CLC **47**
    See also CA 145

Cheever, John
    1912-1982 ...... CLC **3, 7, 8, 11, 15, 25,
        64**; DA; DAB; SSC **1**; WLC
    See also CA 5-8R; 106; CABS 1; CANR 5,
        27; CDALB 1941-1968; DLB 2, 102;
        DLBY 80, 82; MTCW

Cheever, Susan 1943- .... CLC **18, 48**
    See also CA 103; CANR 27; DLBY 82

Chekhonte, Antosha
    See Chekhov, Anton (Pavlovich)

Chekhov, Anton (Pavlovich)
    1860-1904 ..... TCLC **3, 10, 31, 55**; DA;
        DAB; SSC **2**; WLC
    See also CA 104; 124

Chernyshevsky, Nikolay Gavrilovich
    1828-1889 .... NCLC **1**

Cherry, Carolyn Janice 1942-
    See Cherryh, C. J.
    See also CA 65-68; CANR 10

Cherryh, C. J. .... CLC **35**
    See also Cherry, Carolyn Janice
    See also DLBY 80

Chesnutt, Charles W(addell)
    1858-1932 .... TCLC **5, 39**; BLC; SSC **7**
    See also BW 1; CA 106; 125; DLB 12, 50,
        78; MTCW

Chester, Alfred 1929(?)-1971 .... CLC **49**
    See also CA 33-36R; DLB 130

Chesterton, G(ilbert) K(eith)
    1874-1936 .... TCLC **1, 6**; SSC **1**
    See also CA 104; 132; CDBLB 1914-1945;
        DLB 10, 19, 34, 70, 98, 149; MTCW;
        SATA 27

Chiang Pin-chin 1904-1986
    See Ding Ling
    See also CA 118

Ch'ien Chung-shu 1910- .... CLC **22**
    See also CA 130; MTCW

Child, L. Maria
    See Child, Lydia Maria

Child, Lydia Maria 1802-1880 .... NCLC **6**
    See also DLB 1, 74; SATA 67

Child, Mrs.
    See Child, Lydia Maria

Child, Philip 1898-1978 .... CLC **19, 68**
    See also CA 13-14; CAP 1; SATA 47

Childress, Alice
    1920-1994 .. CLC **12, 15, 86**; BLC; DC **4**
    See also AAYA 8; BW 2; CA 45-48; 146;
        CANR 3, 27; CLR 14; DLB 7, 38; JRDA;
        MAICYA; MTCW; SATA 7, 48, 81

Chislett, (Margaret) Anne 1943- .... CLC **34**

Chitty, Thomas Willes 1926- .... CLC **11**
    See also Hinde, Thomas
    See also CA 5-8R

Chivers, Thomas Holley
    1809-1858 .... NCLC **49**
    See also DLB 3

Chomette, Rene Lucien 1898-1981
    See Clair, Rene
    See also CA 103

Chopin, Kate
    .... TCLC **5, 14**; DA; DAB; SSC **8**
    See also Chopin, Katherine
    See also CDALB 1865-1917; DLB 12, 78

Chopin, Katherine 1851-1904
    See Chopin, Kate
    See also CA 104; 122

Chretien de Troyes
    c. 12th cent. - .... CMLC **10**

Christie
    See Ichikawa, Kon

Christie, Agatha (Mary Clarissa)
    1890-1976 ...... CLC **1, 6, 8, 12, 39, 48**;
        DAB
    See also AAYA 9; AITN 1, 2; CA 17-20R;
        61-64; CANR 10, 37; CDBLB 1914-1945;
        DLB 13, 77; MTCW; SATA 36

Christie, (Ann) Philippa
    See Pearce, Philippa
    See also CA 5-8R; CANR 4

Christine de Pizan 1365(?)-1431(?) .... LC **9**

Chubb, Elmer
    See Masters, Edgar Lee

Chulkov, Mikhail Dmitrievich
    1743-1792 .... LC **2**
    See also DLB 150

Churchill, Caryl 1938- ... CLC **31, 55**; DC **5**
    See also CA 102; CANR 22, 46; DLB 13;
        MTCW

Churchill, Charles 1731-1764 .... LC **3**
    See also DLB 109

Chute, Carolyn 1947- .... CLC **39**
    See also CA 123

Ciardi, John (Anthony)
    1916-1986 .... CLC **10, 40, 44**
    See also CA 5-8R; 118; CAAS 2; CANR 5,
        33; CLR 19; DLB 5; DLBY 86;
        MAICYA; MTCW; SATA 1, 65;
        SATA-Obit 46

Cicero, Marcus Tullius
    106B.C.-43B.C. .... CMLC **3**

Cimino, Michael 1943- .... CLC **16**
    See also CA 105

Cioran, E(mil) M. 1911- .... CLC **64**
    See also CA 25-28R

Cisneros, Sandra 1954- ...... CLC **69**; HLC
    See also AAYA 9; CA 131; DLB 122, 152;
        HW

Clair, Rene .... CLC **20**
    See also Chomette, Rene Lucien

Clampitt, Amy 1920-1994 .... **CLC 32**
See also CA 110; 146; CANR 29; DLB 105

Clancy, Thomas L., Jr. 1947-
See Clancy, Tom
See also CA 125; 131; MTCW

Clancy, Tom..................... **CLC 45**
See also Clancy, Thomas L., Jr.
See also AAYA 9; BEST 89:1, 90:1

Clare, John 1793-1864 ...... **NCLC 9; DAB**
See also DLB 55, 96

Clarin
See Alas (y Urena), Leopoldo (Enrique Garcia)

Clark, Al C.
See Goines, Donald

Clark, (Robert) Brian 1932-........ **CLC 29**
See also CA 41-44R

Clark, Curt
See Westlake, Donald E(dwin)

Clark, Eleanor 1913- .... **CLC 5, 19**
See also CA 9-12R; CANR 41; DLB 6

Clark, J. P.
See Clark, John Pepper
See also DLB 117

Clark, John Pepper
1935- .... **CLC 38; BLC; DC 5**
See also Clark, J. P.
See also BW 1; CA 65-68; CANR 16

Clark, M. R.
See Clark, Mavis Thorpe

Clark, Mavis Thorpe 1909- .... **CLC 12**
See also CA 57-60; CANR 8, 37; CLR 30;
MAICYA; SAAS 5; SATA 8, 74

Clark, Walter Van Tilburg
1909-1971 .... **CLC 28**
See also CA 9-12R; 33-36R; DLB 9;
SATA 8

Clarke, Arthur C(harles)
1917- ...... **CLC 1, 4, 13, 18, 35; SSC 3**
See also AAYA 4; CA 1-4R; CANR 2, 28;
JRDA; MAICYA; MTCW; SATA 13, 70

Clarke, Austin 1896-1974........ **CLC 6, 9**
See also CA 29-32; 49-52; CAP 2; DLB 10, 20

Clarke, Austin C(hesterfield)
1934- .... **CLC 8, 53; BLC**
See also BW 1; CA 25-28R; CAAS 16;
CANR 14, 32; DLB 53, 125

Clarke, Gillian 1937- .... **CLC 61**
See also CA 106; DLB 40

Clarke, Marcus (Andrew Hislop)
1846-1881 .... **NCLC 19**

Clarke, Shirley 1925-............ **CLC 16**

Clash, The
See Headon, (Nicky) Topper; Jones, Mick;
Simonon, Paul; Strummer, Joe

Claudel, Paul (Louis Charles Marie)
1868-1955 .... **TCLC 2, 10**
See also CA 104

Clavell, James (duMaresq)
1925-1994 .... **CLC 6, 25, 87**
See also CA 25-28R; 146; CANR 26, 48;
MTCW

Cleaver, (Leroy) Eldridge
1935- .... **CLC 30; BLC**
See also BW 1; CA 21-24R; CANR 16

Cleese, John (Marwood) 1939- ..... **CLC 21**
See also Monty Python
See also CA 112; 116; CANR 35; MTCW

Cleishbotham, Jebediah
See Scott, Walter

Cleland, John 1710-1789 .... **LC 2**
See also DLB 39

Clemens, Samuel Langhorne 1835-1910
See Twain, Mark
See also CA 104; 135; CDALB 1865-1917;
DA; DAB; DLB 11, 12, 23, 64, 74;
JRDA; MAICYA; YABC 2

Cleophil
See Congreve, William

Clerihew, E.
See Bentley, E(dmund) C(lerihew)

Clerk, N. W.
See Lewis, C(live) S(taples)

Cliff, Jimmy..................... **CLC 21**
See also Chambers, James

Clifton, (Thelma) Lucille
1936- .... **CLC 19, 66; BLC**
See also BW 2; CA 49-52; CANR 2, 24, 42;
CLR 5; DLB 5, 41; MAICYA; MTCW;
SATA 20, 69

Clinton, Dirk
See Silverberg, Robert

Clough, Arthur Hugh 1819-1861.. **NCLC 27**
See also DLB 32

Clutha, Janet Paterson Frame 1924-
See Frame, Janet
See also CA 1-4R; CANR 2, 36; MTCW

Clyne, Terence
See Blatty, William Peter

Cobalt, Martin
See Mayne, William (James Carter)

Cobbett, William 1763-1835 ..... **NCLC 49**
See also DLB 43, 107

Coburn, D(onald) L(ee) 1938- ...... **CLC 10**
See also CA 89-92

Cocteau, Jean (Maurice Eugene Clement)
1889-1963 .... **CLC 1, 8, 15, 16, 43; DA;
DAB; WLC**
See also CA 25-28; CANR 40; CAP 2;
DLB 65; MTCW

Codrescu, Andrei 1946- .... **CLC 46**
See also CA 33-36R; CAAS 19; CANR 13, 34

Coe, Max
See Bourne, Randolph S(illiman)

Coe, Tucker
See Westlake, Donald E(dwin)

Coetzee, J(ohn) M(ichael)
1940- .... **CLC 23, 33, 66**
See also CA 77-80; CANR 41; MTCW

Coffey, Brian
See Koontz, Dean R(ay)

Cohan, George M. 1878-1942 ..... **TCLC 60**

Cohen, Arthur A(llen)
1928-1986 .... **CLC 7, 31**
See also CA 1-4R; 120; CANR 1, 17, 42;
DLB 28

Cohen, Leonard (Norman)
1934-..................... **CLC 3, 38**
See also CA 21-24R; CANR 14; DLB 53;
MTCW

Cohen, Matt 1942-................ **CLC 19**
See also CA 61-64; CAAS 18; CANR 40;
DLB 53

Cohen-Solal, Annie 19(?)- .... **CLC 50**

Colegate, Isabel 1931- .... **CLC 36**
See also CA 17-20R; CANR 8, 22; DLB 14;
MTCW

Coleman, Emmett
See Reed, Ishmael

Coleridge, Samuel Taylor
1772-1834 .... **NCLC 9; DA; DAB;
PC 11; WLC**
See also CDBLB 1789-1832; DLB 93, 107

Coleridge, Sara 1802-1852....... **NCLC 31**

Coles, Don 1928- .... **CLC 46**
See also CA 115; CANR 38

Colette, (Sidonie-Gabrielle)
1873-1954 ...... **TCLC 1, 5, 16; SSC 10**
See also CA 104; 131; DLB 65; MTCW

Collett, (Jacobine) Camilla (Wergeland)
1813-1895 .... **NCLC 22**

Collier, Christopher 1930-......... **CLC 30**
See also AAYA 13; CA 33-36R; CANR 13,
33; JRDA; MAICYA; SATA 16, 70

Collier, James L(incoln) 1928- ..... **CLC 30**
See also AAYA 13; CA 9-12R; CANR 4,
33; CLR 3; JRDA; MAICYA; SATA 8,
70

Collier, Jeremy 1650-1726.......... **LC 6**

Collier, John 1901-1980........... **SSC 19**
See also CA 65-68; 97-100; CANR 10;
DLB 77

Collins, Hunt
See Hunter, Evan

Collins, Linda 1931-.............. **CLC 44**
See also CA 125

Collins, (William) Wilkie
1824-1889 .... **NCLC 1, 18**
See also CDBLB 1832-1890; DLB 18, 70

Collins, William 1721-1759 .... **LC 4**
See also DLB 109

Colman, George
See Glassco, John

Colt, Winchester Remington
See Hubbard, L(afayette) Ron(ald)

Colter, Cyrus 1910- .... **CLC 58**
See also BW 1; CA 65-68; CANR 10;
DLB 33

Colton, James
See Hansen, Joseph

Colum, Padraic 1881-1972........ **CLC 28**
See also CA 73-76; 33-36R; CANR 35;
CLR 36; MAICYA; MTCW; SATA 15

Colvin, James
See Moorcock, Michael (John)

D'Annunzio, Gabriele
1863-1938 . . . . **TCLC 6, 40**
See also CA 104

d'Antibes, Germain
See Simenon, Georges (Jacques Christian)

Danvers, Dennis 1947- . . . . **CLC 70**

Danziger, Paula 1944- . . . . **CLC 21**
See also AAYA 4; CA 112; 115; CANR 37;
CLR 20; JRDA; MAICYA; SATA 36,
63; SATA-Brief 30

Da Ponte, Lorenzo 1749-1838 . . . . **NCLC 50**

Dario, Ruben 1867-1916 . . . . **TCLC 4; HLC**
See also CA 131; HW; MTCW

Darley, George 1795-1846 . . . . **NCLC 2**
See also DLB 96

Daryush, Elizabeth 1887-1977 . . . . **CLC 6, 19**
See also CA 49-52; CANR 3; DLB 20

**Dashwood, Edmee Elizabeth Monica de la
Pasture** 1890-1943
See Delafield, E. M.
See also CA 119

Daudet, (Louis Marie) Alphonse
1840-1897 . . . . **NCLC 1**
See also DLB 123

Daumal, Rene 1908-1944 . . . . **TCLC 14**
See also CA 114

Davenport, Guy (Mattison, Jr.)
1927- . . . . **CLC 6, 14, 38; SSC 16**
See also CA 33-36R; CANR 23; DLB 130

Davidson, Avram 1923-
See Queen, Ellery
See also CA 101; CANR 26; DLB 8

Davidson, Donald (Grady)
1893-1968 . . . . **CLC 2, 13, 19**
See also CA 5-8R; 25-28R; CANR 4;
DLB 45

Davidson, Hugh
See Hamilton, Edmond

Davidson, John 1857-1909 . . . . **TCLC 24**
See also CA 118; DLB 19

Davidson, Sara 1943- . . . . **CLC 9**
See also CA 81-84; CANR 44

Davie, Donald (Alfred)
1922- . . . . **CLC 5, 8, 10, 31**
See also CA 1-4R; CAAS 3; CANR 1, 44;
DLB 27; MTCW

Davies, Ray(mond Douglas) 1944- . . **CLC 21**
See also CA 116; 146

Davies, Rhys 1903-1978 . . . . **CLC 23**
See also CA 9-12R; 81-84; CANR 4;
DLB 139

Davies, (William) Robertson
1913- . . . . . **CLC 2, 7, 13, 25, 42, 75; DA;
DAB; WLC**
See also BEST 89:2; CA 33-36R; CANR 17,
42; DLB 68; MTCW

Davies, W(illiam) H(enry)
1871-1940 . . . . **TCLC 5**
See also CA 104; DLB 19

Davies, Walter C.
See Kornbluth, C(yril) M.

Davis, Angela (Yvonne) 1944- . . . . . . **CLC 77**
See also BW 2; CA 57-60; CANR 10

Davis, B. Lynch
See Bioy Casares, Adolfo; Borges, Jorge
Luis

Davis, Gordon
See Hunt, E(verette) Howard, (Jr.)

Davis, Harold Lenoir 1896-1960 . . . . **CLC 49**
See also CA 89-92; DLB 9

Davis, Rebecca (Blaine) Harding
1831-1910 . . . . **TCLC 6**
See also CA 104; DLB 74

Davis, Richard Harding
1864-1916 . . . . **TCLC 24**
See also CA 114; DLB 12, 23, 78, 79

Davison, Frank Dalby 1893-1970 . . . **CLC 15**
See also CA 116

Davison, Lawrence H.
See Lawrence, D(avid) H(erbert Richards)

Davison, Peter (Hubert) 1928- . . . . . **CLC 28**
See also CA 9-12R; CAAS 4; CANR 3, 43;
DLB 5

Davys, Mary 1674-1732 . . . . **LC 1**
See also DLB 39

Dawson, Fielding 1930- . . . . **CLC 6**
See also CA 85-88; DLB 130

Dawson, Peter
See Faust, Frederick (Schiller)

Day, Clarence (Shepard, Jr.)
1874-1935 . . . . **TCLC 25**
See also CA 108; DLB 11

Day, Thomas 1748-1789 . . . . **LC 1**
See also DLB 39; YABC 1

Day Lewis, C(ecil)
1904-1972 . . . . **CLC 1, 6, 10; PC 11**
See also Blake, Nicholas
See also CA 13-16; 33-36R; CANR 34;
CAP 1; DLB 15, 20; MTCW

Dazai, Osamu . . . . **TCLC 11**
See also Tsushima, Shuji

de Andrade, Carlos Drummond
See Drummond de Andrade, Carlos

Deane, Norman
See Creasey, John

**de Beauvoir, Simone (Lucie Ernestine Marie
Bertrand)**
See Beauvoir, Simone (Lucie Ernestine
Marie Bertrand) de

de Brissac, Malcolm
See Dickinson, Peter (Malcolm)

de Chardin, Pierre Teilhard
See Teilhard de Chardin, (Marie Joseph)
Pierre

Dee, John 1527-1608 . . . . **LC 20**

Deer, Sandra 1940- . . . . **CLC 45**

De Ferrari, Gabriella 1941- . . . . **CLC 65**
See also CA 146

Defoe, Daniel
1660(?)-1731 . . . . **LC 1; DA; DAB; WLC**
See also CDBLB 1660-1789; DLB 39, 95,
101; JRDA; MAICYA; SATA 22

de Gourmont, Remy
See Gourmont, Remy de

de Hartog, Jan 1914- . . . . **CLC 19**
See also CA 1-4R; CANR 1

de Hostos, E. M.
See Hostos (y Bonilla), Eugenio Maria de

de Hostos, Eugenio M.
See Hostos (y Bonilla), Eugenio Maria de

Deighton, Len . . . . **CLC 4, 7, 22, 46**
See also Deighton, Leonard Cyril
See also AAYA 6; BEST 89:2;
CDBLB 1960 to Present; DLB 87

Deighton, Leonard Cyril 1929-
See Deighton, Len
See also CA 9-12R; CANR 19, 33; MTCW

Dekker, Thomas 1572(?)-1632 . . . . **LC 22**
See also CDBLB Before 1660; DLB 62

Delafield, E. M. 1890-1943 . . . . **TCLC 61**
See also Dashwood, Edmee Elizabeth
Monica de la Pasture
See also DLB 34

de la Mare, Walter (John)
1873-1956 . . . . **TCLC 4, 53; DAB;
SSC 14; WLC**
See also CDBLB 1914-1945; CLR 23;
DLB 19, 153; SATA 16

Delaney, Franey
See O'Hara, John (Henry)

Delaney, Shelagh 1939- . . . . **CLC 29**
See also CA 17-20R; CANR 30;
CDBLB 1960 to Present; DLB 13;
MTCW

Delany, Mary (Granville Pendarves)
1700-1788 . . . . **LC 12**

Delany, Samuel R(ay, Jr.)
1942- . . . . **CLC 8, 14, 38; BLC**
See also BW 2; CA 81-84; CANR 27, 43;
DLB 8, 33; MTCW

De La Ramee, (Marie) Louise 1839-1908
See Ouida
See also SATA 20

de la Roche, Mazo 1879-1961 . . . . . . **CLC 14**
See also CA 85-88; CANR 30; DLB 68;
SATA 64

Delbanco, Nicholas (Franklin)
1942- . . . . **CLC 6, 13**
See also CA 17-20R; CAAS 2; CANR 29;
DLB 6

del Castillo, Michel 1933- . . . . **CLC 38**
See also CA 109

Deledda, Grazia (Cosima)
1875(?)-1936 . . . . **TCLC 23**
See also CA 123

Delibes, Miguel . . . . **CLC 8, 18**
See also Delibes Setien, Miguel

Delibes Setien, Miguel 1920-
See Delibes, Miguel
See also CA 45-48; CANR 1, 32; HW;
MTCW

DeLillo, Don
1936- . . . . . **CLC 8, 10, 13, 27, 39, 54, 76**
See also BEST 89:1; CA 81-84; CANR 21;
DLB 6; MTCW

de Lisser, H. G.
See De Lisser, Herbert George
See also DLB 117

De Lisser, Herbert George
1878-1944 . . . . **TCLC 12**
See also de Lisser, H. G.
See also BW 2; CA 109

Doerr, Harriet 1910- .... **CLC 34**
See also CA 117; 122; CANR 47

Domecq, H(onorio) Bustos
See Bioy Casares, Adolfo; Borges, Jorge
Luis

Domini, Rey
See Lorde, Audre (Geraldine)

Dominique
See Proust, (Valentin-Louis-George-Eugene-)
Marcel

Don, A
See Stephen, Leslie

Donaldson, Stephen R. 1947-....... **CLC 46**
See also CA 89-92; CANR 13

Donleavy, J(ames) P(atrick)
1926- .... **CLC 1, 4, 6, 10, 45**
See also AITN 2; CA 9-12R; CANR 24, 49;
DLB 6; MTCW

Donne, John
1572-1631 .. **LC 10, 24; DA; DAB; PC 1**
See also CDBLB Before 1660; DLB 121,
151

Donnell, David 1939(?)-.......... **CLC 34**

Donoghue, P. S.
See Hunt, E(verette) Howard, (Jr.)

Donoso (Yanez), Jose
1924- .... **CLC 4, 8, 11, 32; HLC**
See also CA 81-84; CANR 32; DLB 113;
HW; MTCW

Donovan, John 1928-1992 .... **CLC 35**
See also CA 97-100; 137; CLR 3;
MAICYA; SATA 72; SATA-Brief 29

Don Roberto
See Cunninghame Graham, R(obert)
B(ontine)

Doolittle, Hilda
1886-1961 ..... **CLC 3, 8, 14, 31, 34, 73;**
DA; PC 5; WLC
See also H. D.
See also CA 97-100; CANR 35; DLB 4, 45;
MTCW

Dorfman, Ariel 1942-.... **CLC 48, 77; HLC**
See also CA 124; 130; HW

Dorn, Edward (Merton) 1929-... **CLC 10, 18**
See also CA 93-96; CANR 42; DLB 5

Dorsan, Luc
See Simenon, Georges (Jacques Christian)

Dorsange, Jean
See Simenon, Georges (Jacques Christian)

Dos Passos, John (Roderigo)
1896-1970 ..... **CLC 1, 4, 8, 11, 15, 25,**
34, 82; DA; DAB; WLC
See also CA 1-4R; 29-32R; CANR 3;
CDALB 1929-1941; DLB 4, 9; DLBD 1;
MTCW

Dossage, Jean
See Simenon, Georges (Jacques Christian)

Dostoevsky, Fedor Mikhailovich
1821-1881 ...... **NCLC 2, 7, 21, 33, 43;**
DA; DAB; SSC 2; WLC

Doughty, Charles M(ontagu)
1843-1926 .... **TCLC 27**
See also CA 115; DLB 19, 57

Douglas, Ellen .... **CLC 73**
See also Haxton, Josephine Ayres;
Williamson, Ellen Douglas

Douglas, Gavin 1475(?)-1522....... **LC 20**

Douglas, Keith 1920-1944 .... **TCLC 40**
See also DLB 27

Douglas, Leonard
See Bradbury, Ray (Douglas)

Douglas, Michael
See Crichton, (John) Michael

Douglass, Frederick
1817(?)-1895 ...... **NCLC 7; BLC; DA;**
WLC
See also CDALB 1640-1865; DLB 1, 43, 50,
79; SATA 29

Dourado, (Waldomiro Freitas) Autran
1926- .... **CLC 23, 60**
See also CA 25-28R; CANR 34

Dourado, Waldomiro Autran
See Dourado, (Waldomiro Freitas) Autran

Dove, Rita (Frances)
1952- .... **CLC 50, 81; PC 6**
See also BW 2; CA 109; CAAS 19;
CANR 27, 42; DLB 120

Dowell, Coleman 1925-1985....... **CLC 60**
See also CA 25-28R; 117; CANR 10;
DLB 130

Dowson, Ernest Christopher
1867-1900 .... **TCLC 4**
See also CA 105; DLB 19, 135

Doyle, A. Conan
See Doyle, Arthur Conan

Doyle, Arthur Conan
1859-1930 .... **TCLC 7; DA; DAB;**
SSC 12; WLC
See also AAYA 14; CA 104; 122;
CDBLB 1890-1914; DLB 18, 70, 156;
MTCW; SATA 24

Doyle, Conan
See Doyle, Arthur Conan

Doyle, John
See Graves, Robert (von Ranke)

Doyle, Roddy 1958(?)-............ **CLC 81**
See also AAYA 14; CA 143

Doyle, Sir A. Conan
See Doyle, Arthur Conan

Doyle, Sir Arthur Conan
See Doyle, Arthur Conan

Dr. A
See Asimov, Isaac; Silverstein, Alvin

Drabble, Margaret
1939- ... **CLC 2, 3, 5, 8, 10, 22, 53; DAB**
See also CA 13-16R; CANR 18, 35;
CDBLB 1960 to Present; DLB 14, 155;
MTCW; SATA 48

Drapier, M. B.
See Swift, Jonathan

Drayham, James
See Mencken, H(enry) L(ouis)

Drayton, Michael 1563-1631........ **LC 8**

Dreadstone, Carl
See Campbell, (John) Ramsey

Dreiser, Theodore (Herman Albert)
1871-1945 ...... **TCLC 10, 18, 35; DA;**
WLC
See also CA 106; 132; CDALB 1865-1917;
DLB 9, 12, 102, 137; DLBD 1; MTCW

Drexler, Rosalyn 1926- .... **CLC 2, 6**
See also CA 81-84

Dreyer, Carl Theodor 1889-1968.... **CLC 16**
See also CA 116

Drieu la Rochelle, Pierre(-Eugene)
1893-1945 .... **TCLC 21**
See also CA 117; DLB 72

Drinkwater, John 1882-1937...... **TCLC 57**
See also CA 109; DLB 10, 19, 149

Drop Shot
See Cable, George Washington

Droste-Hulshoff, Annette Freiin von
1797-1848 .... **NCLC 3**
See also DLB 133

Drummond, Walter
See Silverberg, Robert

Drummond, William Henry
1854-1907 .... **TCLC 25**
See also DLB 92

Drummond de Andrade, Carlos
1902-1987 .... **CLC 18**
See also Andrade, Carlos Drummond de
See also CA 132; 123

Drury, Allen (Stuart) 1918-........ **CLC 37**
See also CA 57-60; CANR 18

Dryden, John
1631-1700 .... **LC 3, 21; DA; DAB;**
DC 3; WLC
See also CDBLB 1660-1789; DLB 80, 101,
131

Duberman, Martin 1930-.......... **CLC 8**
See also CA 1-4R; CANR 2

Dubie, Norman (Evans) 1945-..... **CLC 36**
See also CA 69-72; CANR 12; DLB 120

Du Bois, W(illiam) E(dward) B(urghardt)
1868-1963 ...... **CLC 1, 2, 13, 64; BLC;**
DA; WLC
See also BW 1; CA 85-88; CANR 34;
CDALB 1865-1917; DLB 47, 50, 91;
MTCW; SATA 42

Dubus, Andre 1936- ... **CLC 13, 36; SSC 15**
See also CA 21-24R; CANR 17; DLB 130

Duca Minimo
See D'Annunzio, Gabriele

Ducharme, Rejean 1941- .... **CLC 74**
See also DLB 60

Duclos, Charles Pinot 1704-1772 ..... **LC 1**

Dudek, Louis 1918- .... **CLC 11, 19**
See also CA 45-48; CAAS 14; CANR 1;
DLB 88

Duerrenmatt, Friedrich
1921-1990 ...... **CLC 1, 4, 8, 11, 15, 43**
See also CA 17-20R; CANR 33; DLB 69,
124; MTCW

Duffy, Bruce (?)-................. **CLC 50**

Duffy, Maureen 1933- .... **CLC 37**
See also CA 25-28R; CANR 33; DLB 14;
MTCW

Dugan, Alan 1923- .... **CLC 2, 6**
See also CA 81-84; DLB 5

du Gard, Roger Martin
See Martin du Gard, Roger

Duhamel, Georges 1884-1966 .... **CLC 8**
See also CA 81-84; 25-28R; CANR 35;
DLB 65; MTCW

Dujardin, Edouard (Emile Louis)
1861-1949 .... **TCLC 13**
See also CA 109; DLB 123

Dumas, Alexandre (Davy de la Pailleterie)
1802-1870 .. **NCLC 11; DA; DAB; WLC**
See also DLB 119; SATA 18

Dumas, Alexandre
1824-1895 .... **NCLC 9; DC 1**

Dumas, Claudine
See Malzberg, Barry N(athaniel)

Dumas, Henry L. 1934-1968 ..... **CLC 6, 62**
See also BW 1; CA 85-88; DLB 41

du Maurier, Daphne
1907-1989 .... **CLC 6, 11, 59; DAB;
SSC 18**
See also CA 5-8R; 128; CANR 6; MTCW;
SATA 27; SATA-Obit 60

Dunbar, Paul Laurence
1872-1906 ...... **TCLC 2, 12; BLC; DA;
PC 5; SSC 8; WLC**
See also BW 1; CA 104; 124;
CDALB 1865-1917; DLB 50, 54, 78;
SATA 34

Dunbar, William 1460(?)-1530(?) .... **LC 20**
See also DLB 132, 146

Duncan, Lois 1934-.............. **CLC 26**
See also AAYA 4; CA 1-4R; CANR 2, 23,
36; CLR 29; JRDA; MAICYA; SAAS 2;
SATA 1, 36, 75

Duncan, Robert (Edward)
1919-1988 .... **CLC 1, 2, 4, 7, 15, 41, 55;
PC 2**
See also CA 9-12R; 124; CANR 28; DLB 5,
16; MTCW

Duncan, Sara Jeannette
1861-1922 .... **TCLC 60**
See also DLB 92

Dunlap, William 1766-1839 .... **NCLC 2**
See also DLB 30, 37, 59

Dunn, Douglas (Eaglesham)
1942- .... **CLC 6, 40**
See also CA 45-48; CANR 2, 33; DLB 40;
MTCW

Dunn, Katherine (Karen) 1945-..... **CLC 71**
See also CA 33-36R

Dunn, Stephen 1939- .... **CLC 36**
See also CA 33-36R; CANR 12, 48;
DLB 105

Dunne, Finley Peter 1867-1936.... **TCLC 28**
See also CA 108; DLB 11, 23

Dunne, John Gregory 1932-........ **CLC 28**
See also CA 25-28R; CANR 14; DLBY 80

**Dunsany, Edward John Moreton Drax
Plunkett** 1878-1957
See Dunsany, Lord
See also CA 104; 148; DLB 10

Dunsany, Lord................. **TCLC 2, 59**
See also Dunsany, Edward John Moreton
Drax Plunkett
See also DLB 77, 153, 156

du Perry, Jean
See Simenon, Georges (Jacques Christian)

Durang, Christopher (Ferdinand)
1949- .... **CLC 27, 38**
See also CA 105

Duras, Marguerite
1914- ...... **CLC 3, 6, 11, 20, 34, 40, 68**
See also CA 25-28R; DLB 83; MTCW

Durban, (Rosa) Pam 1947-........ **CLC 39**
See also CA 123

Durcan, Paul 1944-........... **CLC 43, 70**
See also CA 134

Durkheim, Emile 1858-1917 ...... **TCLC 55**

Durrell, Lawrence (George)
1912-1990 .... **CLC 1, 4, 6, 8, 13, 27, 41**
See also CA 9-12R; 132; CANR 40;
CDBLB 1945-1960; DLB 15, 27;
DLBY 90; MTCW

Durrenmatt, Friedrich
See Duerrenmatt, Friedrich

Dutt, Toru 1856-1877.......... **NCLC 29**

Dwight, Timothy 1752-1817...... **NCLC 13**
See also DLB 37

Dworkin, Andrea 1946- .... **CLC 43**
See also CA 77-80; CAAS 21; CANR 16,
39; MTCW

Dwyer, Deanna
See Koontz, Dean R(ay)

Dwyer, K. R.
See Koontz, Dean R(ay)

Dylan, Bob 1941- ...... **CLC 3, 4, 6, 12, 77**
See also CA 41-44R; DLB 16

Eagleton, Terence (Francis) 1943-
See Eagleton, Terry
See also CA 57-60; CANR 7, 23; MTCW

Eagleton, Terry .... **CLC 63**
See also Eagleton, Terence (Francis)

Early, Jack
See Scoppettone, Sandra

East, Michael
See West, Morris L(anglo)

Eastaway, Edward
See Thomas, (Philip) Edward

Eastlake, William (Derry) 1917-..... **CLC 8**
See also CA 5-8R; CAAS 1; CANR 5;
DLB 6

Eastman, Charles A(lexander)
1858-1939 .... **TCLC 55**
See also NNAL; YABC 1

Eberhart, Richard (Ghormley)
1904- .... **CLC 3, 11, 19, 56**
See also CA 1-4R; CANR 2;
CDALB 1941-1968; DLB 48; MTCW

Eberstadt, Fernanda 1960-........ **CLC 39**
See also CA 136

Echegaray (y Eizaguirre), Jose (Maria Waldo)
1832-1916 .... **TCLC 4**
See also CA 104; CANR 32; HW; MTCW

Echeverria, (Jose) Esteban (Antonino)
1805-1851 .... **NCLC 18**

Echo
See Proust, (Valentin-Louis-George-Eugene-)
Marcel

Eckert, Allan W. 1931- .... **CLC 17**
See also CA 13-16R; CANR 14, 45;
SATA 29; SATA-Brief 27

Eckhart, Meister 1260(?)-1328(?) .. **CMLC 9**
See also DLB 115

Eckmar, F. R.
See de Hartog, Jan

Eco, Umberto 1932-........... **CLC 28, 60**
See also BEST 90:1; CA 77-80; CANR 12,
33; MTCW

Eddison, E(ric) R(ucker)
1882-1945 .... **TCLC 15**
See also CA 109

Edel, (Joseph) Leon 1907-...... **CLC 29, 34**
See also CA 1-4R; CANR 1, 22; DLB 103

Eden, Emily 1797-1869 .... **NCLC 10**

Edgar, David 1948-.............. **CLC 42**
See also CA 57-60; CANR 12; DLB 13;
MTCW

Edgerton, Clyde (Carlyle) 1944- .... **CLC 39**
See also CA 118; 134

Edgeworth, Maria 1768-1849... **NCLC 1, 51**
See also DLB 116; SATA 21

Edmonds, Paul
See Kuttner, Henry

Edmonds, Walter D(umaux) 1903- .. **CLC 35**
See also CA 5-8R; CANR 2; DLB 9;
MAICYA; SAAS 4; SATA 1, 27

Edmondson, Wallace
See Ellison, Harlan (Jay)

Edson, Russell .... **CLC 13**
See also CA 33-36R

Edwards, Bronwen Elizabeth
See Rose, Wendy

Edwards, G(erald) B(asil)
1899-1976 .... **CLC 25**
See also CA 110

Edwards, Gus 1939- .... **CLC 43**
See also CA 108

Edwards, Jonathan 1703-1758.... **LC 7; DA**
See also DLB 24

Efron, Marina Ivanovna Tsvetaeva
See Tsvetaeva (Efron), Marina (Ivanovna)

Ehle, John (Marsden, Jr.) 1925-.... **CLC 27**
See also CA 9-12R

Ehrenbourg, Ilya (Grigoryevich)
See Ehrenburg, Ilya (Grigoryevich)

Ehrenburg, Ilya (Grigoryevich)
1891-1967 .... **CLC 18, 34, 62**
See also CA 102; 25-28R

Ehrenburg, Ilyo (Grigoryevich)
See Ehrenburg, Ilya (Grigoryevich)

Eich, Guenter 1907-1972 .... **CLC 15**
See also CA 111; 93-96; DLB 69, 124

Eichendorff, Joseph Freiherr von
1788-1857 .... **NCLC 8**
See also DLB 90

Eigner, Larry .... **CLC 9**
See also Eigner, Laurence (Joel)
See also DLB 5

Eigner, Laurence (Joel) 1927-
See Eigner, Larry
See also CA 9-12R; CANR 6

Eugenides, Jeffrey 1960(?)- .... **CLC 81**
See also CA 144

Euripides c. 485B.C.-406B.C. .... **DC 4**
See also DA; DAB

Evan, Evin
See Faust, Frederick (Schiller)

Evans, Evan
See Faust, Frederick (Schiller)

Evans, Marian
See Eliot, George

Evans, Mary Ann
See Eliot, George

Evarts, Esther
See Benson, Sally

Everett, Percival L. 1956- .... **CLC 57**
See also BW 2; CA 129

Everson, R(onald) G(ilmour)
1903- .... **CLC 27**
See also CA 17-20R; DLB 88

Everson, William (Oliver)
1912-1994 .... **CLC 1, 5, 14**
See also CA 9-12R; 145; CANR 20; DLB 5,
16; MTCW

Evtushenko, Evgenii Aleksandrovich
See Yevtushenko, Yevgeny (Alexandrovich)

Ewart, Gavin (Buchanan)
1916- .... **CLC 13, 46**
See also CA 89-92; CANR 17, 46; DLB 40;
MTCW

Ewers, Hanns Heinz 1871-1943 ... **TCLC 12**
See also CA 109

Ewing, Frederick R.
See Sturgeon, Theodore (Hamilton)

Exley, Frederick (Earl)
1929-1992 .... **CLC 6, 11**
See also AITN 2; CA 81-84; 138; DLB 143;
DLBY 81

Eynhardt, Guillermo
See Quiroga, Horacio (Sylvestre)

Ezekiel, Nissim 1924- .... **CLC 61**
See also CA 61-64

Ezekiel, Tish O'Dowd 1943- .... **CLC 34**
See also CA 129

Fadeyev, A.
See Bulgya, Alexander Alexandrovich

Fadeyev, Alexander. .... **TCLC 53**
See also Bulgya, Alexander Alexandrovich

Fagen, Donald 1948- .... **CLC 26**

Fainzilberg, Ilya Arnoldovich 1897-1937
See Ilf, Ilya
See also CA 120

Fair, Ronald L. 1932- .... **CLC 18**
See also BW 1; CA 69-72; CANR 25;
DLB 33

Fairbairns, Zoe (Ann) 1948- .... **CLC 32**
See also CA 103; CANR 21

Falco, Gian
See Papini, Giovanni

Falconer, James
See Kirkup, James

Falconer, Kenneth
See Kornbluth, C(yril) M.

Falkland, Samuel
See Heijermans, Herman

Fallaci, Oriana 1930- .... **CLC 11**
See also CA 77-80; CANR 15; MTCW

Faludy, George 1913- .... **CLC 42**
See also CA 21-24R

Faludy, Gyoergy
See Faludy, George

Fanon, Frantz 1925-1961 ..... **CLC 74; BLC**
See also BW 1; CA 116; 89-92

Fanshawe, Ann 1625-1680 .... **LC 11**

Fante, John (Thomas) 1911-1983 ... **CLC 60**
See also CA 69-72; 109; CANR 23;
DLB 130; DLBY 83

Farah, Nuruddin 1945- ...... **CLC 53; BLC**
See also BW 2; CA 106; DLB 125

Fargue, Leon-Paul 1876(?)-1947 ... **TCLC 11**
See also CA 109

Farigoule, Louis
See Romains, Jules

Farina, Richard 1936(?)-1966 .... **CLC 9**
See also CA 81-84; 25-28R

Farley, Walter (Lorimer)
1915-1989 .... **CLC 17**
See also CA 17-20R; CANR 8, 29; DLB 22;
JRDA; MAICYA; SATA 2, 43

Farmer, Philip Jose 1918- .... **CLC 1, 19**
See also CA 1-4R; CANR 4, 35; DLB 8;
MTCW

Farquhar, George 1677-1707 .... **LC 21**
See also DLB 84

Farrell, J(ames) G(ordon)
1935-1979 .... **CLC 6**
See also CA 73-76; 89-92; CANR 36;
DLB 14; MTCW

Farrell, James T(homas)
1904-1979 .... **CLC 1, 4, 8, 11, 66**
See also CA 5-8R; 89-92; CANR 9; DLB 4,
9, 86; DLBD 2; MTCW

Farren, Richard J.
See Betjeman, John

Farren, Richard M.
See Betjeman, John

Fassbinder, Rainer Werner
1946-1982 .... **CLC 20**
See also CA 93-96; 106; CANR 31

Fast, Howard (Melvin) 1914- ...... **CLC 23**
See also CA 1-4R; CAAS 18; CANR 1, 33;
DLB 9; SATA 7

Faulcon, Robert
See Holdstock, Robert P.

Faulkner, William (Cuthbert)
1897-1962 ..... **CLC 1, 3, 6, 8, 9, 11, 14,
18, 28, 52, 68; DA; DAB; SSC 1; WLC**
See also AAYA 7; CA 81-84; CANR 33;
CDALB 1929-1941; DLB 9, 11, 44, 102;
DLBD 2; DLBY 86; MTCW

Fauset, Jessie Redmon
1884(?)-1961 .... **CLC 19, 54; BLC**
See also BW 1; CA 109; DLB 51

Faust, Frederick (Schiller)
1892-1944(?) .... **TCLC 49**
See also CA 108

Faust, Irvin 1924- .... **CLC 8**
See also CA 33-36R; CANR 28; DLB 2, 28;
DLBY 80

Fawkes, Guy
See Benchley, Robert (Charles)

Fearing, Kenneth (Flexner)
1902-1961 .... **CLC 51**
See also CA 93-96; DLB 9

Fecamps, Elise
See Creasey, John

Federman, Raymond 1928- ...... **CLC 6, 47**
See also CA 17-20R; CAAS 8; CANR 10,
43; DLBY 80

Federspiel, J(uerg) F. 1931- .... **CLC 42**
See also CA 146

Feiffer, Jules (Ralph) 1929- .... **CLC 2, 8, 64**
See also AAYA 3; CA 17-20R; CANR 30;
DLB 7, 44; MTCW; SATA 8, 61

Feige, Hermann Albert Otto Maximilian
See Traven, B.

Feinberg, David B. 1956-1994 ...... **CLC 59**
See also CA 135; 147

Feinstein, Elaine 1930- .... **CLC 36**
See also CA 69-72; CAAS 1; CANR 31;
DLB 14, 40; MTCW

Feldman, Irving (Mordecai) 1928- .... **CLC 7**
See also CA 1-4R; CANR 1

Fellini, Federico 1920-1993 ..... **CLC 16, 85**
See also CA 65-68; 143; CANR 33

Felsen, Henry Gregor 1916- .... **CLC 17**
See also CA 1-4R; CANR 1; SAAS 2;
SATA 1

Fenton, James Martin 1949- .... **CLC 32**
See also CA 102; DLB 40

Ferber, Edna 1887-1968 .... **CLC 18**
See also AITN 1; CA 5-8R; 25-28R; DLB 9,
28, 86; MTCW; SATA 7

Ferguson, Helen
See Kavan, Anna

Ferguson, Samuel 1810-1886 ..... **NCLC 33**
See also DLB 32

Fergusson, Robert 1750-1774 .... **LC 29**
See also DLB 109

Ferling, Lawrence
See Ferlinghetti, Lawrence (Monsanto)

Ferlinghetti, Lawrence (Monsanto)
1919(?)- .... **CLC 2, 6, 10, 27; PC 1**
See also CA 5-8R; CANR 3, 41;
CDALB 1941-1968; DLB 5, 16; MTCW

Fernandez, Vicente Garcia Huidobro
See Huidobro Fernandez, Vicente Garcia

Ferrer, Gabriel (Francisco Victor) Miro
See Miro (Ferrer), Gabriel (Francisco
Victor)

Ferrier, Susan (Edmonstone)
1782-1854 .... **NCLC 8**
See also DLB 116

Ferrigno, Robert 1948(?)- .... **CLC 65**
See also CA 140

Feuchtwanger, Lion 1884-1958 ..... **TCLC 3**
See also CA 104; DLB 66

Feuillet, Octave 1821-1890 ...... **NCLC 45**

Feydeau, Georges (Leon Jules Marie)
1862-1921 . . . . **TCLC 22**
See also CA 113

Ficino, Marsilio 1433-1499 . . . . **LC 12**

Fiedeler, Hans
See Doeblin, Alfred

Fiedler, Leslie A(aron)
1917- . . . . **CLC 4, 13, 24**
See also CA 9-12R; CANR 7; DLB 28, 67;
MTCW

Field, Andrew 1938- . . . . **CLC 44**
See also CA 97-100; CANR 25

Field, Eugene 1850-1895 . . . . **NCLC 3**
See also DLB 23, 42, 140; MAICYA;
SATA 16

Field, Gans T.
See Wellman, Manly Wade

Field, Michael . . . . **TCLC 43**

Field, Peter
See Hobson, Laura Z(ametkin)

Fielding, Henry
1707-1754 . . . . . . **LC 1; DA; DAB; WLC**
See also CDBLB 1660-1789; DLB 39, 84,
101

Fielding, Sarah 1710-1768 . . . . **LC 1**
See also DLB 39

Fierstein, Harvey (Forbes) 1954- . . . **CLC 33**
See also CA 123; 129

Figes, Eva 1932- . . . . **CLC 31**
See also CA 53-56; CANR 4, 44; DLB 14

Finch, Robert (Duer Claydon)
1900- . . . . **CLC 18**
See also CA 57-60; CANR 9, 24, 49;
DLB 88

Findley, Timothy 1930- . . . . **CLC 27**
See also CA 25-28R; CANR 12, 42;
DLB 53

Fink, William
See Mencken, H(enry) L(ouis)

Firbank, Louis 1942-
See Reed, Lou
See also CA 117

Firbank, (Arthur Annesley) Ronald
1886-1926 . . . . **TCLC 1**
See also CA 104; DLB 36

Fisher, M(ary) F(rances) K(ennedy)
1908-1992 . . . . **CLC 76, 87**
See also CA 77-80; 138; CANR 44

Fisher, Roy 1930- . . . . **CLC 25**
See also CA 81-84; CAAS 10; CANR 16;
DLB 40

Fisher, Rudolph
1897-1934 . . . . **TCLC 11; BLC**
See also BW 1; CA 107; 124; DLB 51, 102

Fisher, Vardis (Alvero) 1895-1968. . . . **CLC 7**
See also CA 5-8R; 25-28R; DLB 9

Fiske, Tarleton
See Bloch, Robert (Albert)

Fitch, Clarke
See Sinclair, Upton (Beall)

Fitch, John IV
See Cormier, Robert (Edmund)

Fitzgerald, Captain Hugh
See Baum, L(yman) Frank

FitzGerald, Edward 1809-1883 . . . . **NCLC 9**
See also DLB 32

Fitzgerald, F(rancis) Scott (Key)
1896-1940 . . . . . . **TCLC 1, 6, 14, 28, 55;
DA; DAB; SSC 6; WLC**
See also AITN 1; CA 110; 123;
CDALB 1917-1929; DLB 4, 9, 86;
DLBD 1; DLBY 81; MTCW

Fitzgerald, Penelope 1916-. . . **CLC 19, 51, 61**
See also CA 85-88; CAAS 10; DLB 14

Fitzgerald, Robert (Stuart)
1910-1985 . . . . **CLC 39**
See also CA 1-4R; 114; CANR 1; DLBY 80

FitzGerald, Robert D(avid)
1902-1987 . . . . **CLC 19**
See also CA 17-20R

Fitzgerald, Zelda (Sayre)
1900-1948 . . . . **TCLC 52**
See also CA 117; 126; DLBY 84

Flanagan, Thomas (James Bonner)
1923- . . . . **CLC 25, 52**
See also CA 108; DLBY 80; MTCW

Flaubert, Gustave
1821-1880 . . . . **NCLC 2, 10, 19; DA;
DAB; SSC 11; WLC**
See also DLB 119

Flecker, (Herman) James Elroy
1884-1915 . . . . **TCLC 43**
See also CA 109; DLB 10, 19

Fleming, Ian (Lancaster)
1908-1964 . . . . **CLC 3, 30**
See also CA 5-8R; CDBLB 1945-1960;
DLB 87; MTCW; SATA 9

Fleming, Thomas (James) 1927- . . . . **CLC 37**
See also CA 5-8R; CANR 10; SATA 8

Fletcher, John Gould 1886-1950 . . . **TCLC 35**
See also CA 107; DLB 4, 45

Fleur, Paul
See Pohl, Frederik

Flooglebuckle, Al
See Spiegelman, Art

Flying Officer X
See Bates, H(erbert) E(rnest)

Fo, Dario 1926-. . . . . **CLC 32**
See also CA 116; 128; MTCW

Fogarty, Jonathan Titulescu Esq.
See Farrell, James T(homas)

Folke, Will
See Bloch, Robert (Albert)

Follett, Ken(neth Martin) 1949- . . . . **CLC 18**
See also AAYA 6; BEST 89:4; CA 81-84;
CANR 13, 33; DLB 87; DLBY 81;
MTCW

Fontane, Theodor 1819-1898 . . . . . **NCLC 26**
See also DLB 129

Foote, Horton 1916-. . . . . **CLC 51**
See also CA 73-76; CANR 34; DLB 26

Foote, Shelby 1916- . . . . **CLC 75**
See also CA 5-8R; CANR 3, 45; DLB 2, 17

Forbes, Esther 1891-1967. . . . . **CLC 12**
See also CA 13-14; 25-28R; CAP 1;
CLR 27; DLB 22; JRDA; MAICYA;
SATA 2

Forche, Carolyn (Louise)
1950- . . . . **CLC 25, 83, 86; PC 10**
See also CA 109; 117; DLB 5

Ford, Elbur
See Hibbert, Eleanor Alice Burford

Ford, Ford Madox
1873-1939 . . . . **TCLC 1, 15, 39, 57**
See also CA 104; 132; CDBLB 1914-1945;
DLB 34, 98; MTCW

Ford, John 1895-1973. . . . . **CLC 16**
See also CA 45-48

Ford, Richard 1944- . . . . **CLC 46**
See also CA 69-72; CANR 11, 47

Ford, Webster
See Masters, Edgar Lee

Foreman, Richard 1937-. . . . . **CLC 50**
See also CA 65-68; CANR 32

Forester, C(ecil) S(cott)
1899-1966 . . . . **CLC 35**
See also CA 73-76; 25-28R; SATA 13

Forez
See Mauriac, Francois (Charles)

Forman, James Douglas 1932-. . . . . . **CLC 21**
See also CA 9-12R; CANR 4, 19, 42;
JRDA; MAICYA; SATA 8, 70

Fornes, Maria Irene 1930-. . . . . . **CLC 39, 61**
See also CA 25-28R; CANR 28; DLB 7;
HW; MTCW

Forrest, Leon 1937- . . . . **CLC 4**
See also BW 2; CA 89-92; CAAS 7;
CANR 25; DLB 33

Forster, E(dward) M(organ)
1879-1970 . . . . . **CLC 1, 2, 3, 4, 9, 10, 13,
15, 22, 45, 77; DA; DAB; WLC**
See also AAYA 2; CA 13-14; 25-28R;
CANR 45; CAP 1; CDBLB 1914-1945;
DLB 34, 98; DLBD 10; MTCW;
SATA 57

Forster, John 1812-1876 . . . . **NCLC 11**
See also DLB 144

Forsyth, Frederick 1938-. . . . . . **CLC 2, 5, 36**
See also BEST 89:4; CA 85-88; CANR 38;
DLB 87; MTCW

Forten, Charlotte L. . . . . **TCLC 16; BLC**
See also Grimke, Charlotte L(ottie) Forten
See also DLB 50

Foscolo, Ugo 1778-1827. . . . . **NCLC 8**

Fosse, Bob . . . . **CLC 20**
See also Fosse, Robert Louis

Fosse, Robert Louis 1927-1987
See Fosse, Bob
See also CA 110; 123

Foster, Stephen Collins
1826-1864 . . . . **NCLC 26**

Foucault, Michel
1926-1984 . . . . **CLC 31, 34, 69**
See also CA 105; 113; CANR 34; MTCW

Fouque, Friedrich (Heinrich Karl) de la Motte
1777-1843 . . . . **NCLC 2**
See also DLB 90

Fourier, Charles 1772-1837 . . . . . . **NCLC 51**

Fournier, Henri Alban 1886-1914
See Alain-Fournier
See also CA 104

Fournier, Pierre 1916- .... **CLC 11**
See also Gascar, Pierre
See also CA 89-92; CANR 16, 40

Fowles, John
1926- ...... **CLC 1, 2, 3, 4, 6, 9, 10, 15,**
33, 87; DAB
See also CA 5-8R; CANR 25; CDBLB 1960
to Present; DLB 14, 139; MTCW;
SATA 22

Fox, Paula 1923- .... **CLC 2, 8**
See also AAYA 3; CA 73-76; CANR 20,
36; CLR 1; DLB 52; JRDA; MAICYA;
MTCW; SATA 17, 60

Fox, William Price (Jr.) 1926- ..... **CLC 22**
See also CA 17-20R; CAAS 19; CANR 11;
DLB 2; DLBY 81

Foxe, John 1516(?)-1587 .... **LC 14**

Frame, Janet .... **CLC 2, 3, 6, 22, 66**
See also Clutha, Janet Paterson Frame

France, Anatole .... **TCLC 9**
See also Thibault, Jacques Anatole Francois
See also DLB 123

Francis, Claude 19(?)- .... **CLC 50**

Francis, Dick 1920- .... **CLC 2, 22, 42**
See also AAYA 5; BEST 89:3; CA 5-8R;
CANR 9, 42; CDBLB 1960 to Present;
DLB 87; MTCW

Francis, Robert (Churchill)
1901-1987 .... **CLC 15**
See also CA 1-4R; 123; CANR 1

Frank, Anne(lies Marie)
1929-1945 .. **TCLC 17; DA; DAB; WLC**
See also AAYA 12; CA 113; 133; MTCW;
SATA-Brief 42

Frank, Elizabeth 1945- .... **CLC 39**
See also CA 121; 126

Franklin, Benjamin
See Hasek, Jaroslav (Matej Frantisek)

Franklin, Benjamin
1706-1790 .... **LC 25; DA; DAB**
See also CDALB 1640-1865; DLB 24, 43,
73

Franklin, (Stella Maraia Sarah) Miles
1879-1954 .... **TCLC 7**
See also CA 104

Fraser, (Lady) Antonia (Pakenham)
1932- .... **CLC 32**
See also CA 85-88; CANR 44; MTCW;
SATA-Brief 32

Fraser, George MacDonald 1925- .... **CLC 7**
See also CA 45-48; CANR 2, 48

Fraser, Sylvia 1935- .... **CLC 64**
See also CA 45-48; CANR 1, 16

Frayn, Michael 1933- ...... **CLC 3, 7, 31, 47**
See also CA 5-8R; CANR 30; DLB 13, 14;
MTCW

Fraze, Candida (Merrill) 1945- ..... **CLC 50**
See also CA 126

Frazer, J(ames) G(eorge)
1854-1941 .... **TCLC 32**
See also CA 118

Frazer, Robert Caine
See Creasey, John

Frazer, Sir James George
See Frazer, J(ames) G(eorge)

Frazier, Ian 1951- .... **CLC 46**
See also CA 130

Frederic, Harold 1856-1898 ...... **NCLC 10**
See also DLB 12, 23

Frederick, John
See Faust, Frederick (Schiller)

Frederick the Great 1712-1786 ...... **LC 14**

Fredro, Aleksander 1793-1876 ..... **NCLC 8**

Freeling, Nicolas 1927- .... **CLC 38**
See also CA 49-52; CAAS 12; CANR 1, 17;
DLB 87

Freeman, Douglas Southall
1886-1953 .... **TCLC 11**
See also CA 109; DLB 17

Freeman, Judith 1946- .... **CLC 55**
See also CA 148

Freeman, Mary Eleanor Wilkins
1852-1930 .... **TCLC 9; SSC 1**
See also CA 106; DLB 12, 78

Freeman, R(ichard) Austin
1862-1943 .... **TCLC 21**
See also CA 113; DLB 70

French, Albert 1943- .... **CLC 86**

French, Marilyn 1929- ...... **CLC 10, 18, 60**
See also CA 69-72; CANR 3, 31; MTCW

French, Paul
See Asimov, Isaac

Freneau, Philip Morin 1752-1832 .. **NCLC 1**
See also DLB 37, 43

Freud, Sigmund 1856-1939 .... **TCLC 52**
See also CA 115; 133; MTCW

Friedan, Betty (Naomi) 1921- ...... **CLC 74**
See also CA 65-68; CANR 18, 45; MTCW

Friedlaender, Saul 1932- .... **CLC 90**
See also CA 117; 130

Friedman, B(ernard) H(arper)
1926- .... **CLC 7**
See also CA 1-4R; CANR 3, 48

Friedman, Bruce Jay 1930- .... **CLC 3, 5, 56**
See also CA 9-12R; CANR 25; DLB 2, 28

Friel, Brian 1929- .... **CLC 5, 42, 59**
See also CA 21-24R; CANR 33; DLB 13;
MTCW

Friis-Baastad, Babbis Ellinor
1921-1970 .... **CLC 12**
See also CA 17-20R; 134; SATA 7

Frisch, Max (Rudolf)
1911-1991 ..... **CLC 3, 9, 14, 18, 32, 44**
See also CA 85-88; 134; CANR 32;
DLB 69, 124; MTCW

Fromentin, Eugene (Samuel Auguste)
1820-1876 .... **NCLC 10**
See also DLB 123

Frost, Frederick
See Faust, Frederick (Schiller)

Frost, Robert (Lee)
1874-1963 .... **CLC 1, 3, 4, 9, 10, 13, 15,**
26, 34, 44; DA; DAB; PC 1; WLC
See also CA 89-92; CANR 33;
CDALB 1917-1929; DLB 54; DLBD 7;
MTCW; SATA 14

Froude, James Anthony
1818-1894 .... **NCLC 43**
See also DLB 18, 57, 144

Froy, Herald
See Waterhouse, Keith (Spencer)

Fry, Christopher 1907- .... **CLC 2, 10, 14**
See also CA 17-20R; CANR 9, 30; DLB 13;
MTCW; SATA 66

Frye, (Herman) Northrop
1912-1991 .... **CLC 24, 70**
See also CA 5-8R; 133; CANR 8, 37;
DLB 67, 68; MTCW

Fuchs, Daniel 1909-1993 .... **CLC 8, 22**
See also CA 81-84; 142; CAAS 5;
CANR 40; DLB 9, 26, 28; DLBY 93

Fuchs, Daniel 1934- .... **CLC 34**
See also CA 37-40R; CANR 14, 48

Fuentes, Carlos
1928- ...... **CLC 3, 8, 10, 13, 22, 41, 60;**
DA; DAB; HLC; WLC
See also AAYA 4; AITN 2; CA 69-72;
CANR 10, 32; DLB 113; HW; MTCW

Fuentes, Gregorio Lopez y
See Lopez y Fuentes, Gregorio

Fugard, (Harold) Athol
1932- .... **CLC 5, 9, 14, 25, 40, 80; DC 3**
See also CA 85-88; CANR 32; MTCW

Fugard, Sheila 1932- .... **CLC 48**
See also CA 125

Fuller, Charles (H., Jr.)
1939- .... **CLC 25; BLC; DC 1**
See also BW 2; CA 108; 112; DLB 38;
MTCW

Fuller, John (Leopold) 1937- .... **CLC 62**
See also CA 21-24R; CANR 9, 44; DLB 40

Fuller, Margaret .... **NCLC 5, 50**
See also Ossoli, Sarah Margaret (Fuller
marchesa d')

Fuller, Roy (Broadbent)
1912-1991 .... **CLC 4, 28**
See also CA 5-8R; 135; CAAS 10; DLB 15,
20

Fulton, Alice 1952- .... **CLC 52**
See also CA 116

Furphy, Joseph 1843-1912 .... **TCLC 25**

Fussell, Paul 1924- .... **CLC 74**
See also BEST 90:1; CA 17-20R; CANR 8,
21, 35; MTCW

Futabatei, Shimei 1864-1909 ...... **TCLC 44**

Futrelle, Jacques 1875-1912 ...... **TCLC 19**
See also CA 113

Gaboriau, Emile 1835-1873 ...... **NCLC 14**

Gadda, Carlo Emilio 1893-1973 .... **CLC 11**
See also CA 89-92

Gaddis, William
1922- ..... **CLC 1, 3, 6, 8, 10, 19, 43, 86**
See also CA 17-20R; CANR 21, 48; DLB 2;
MTCW

Gaines, Ernest J(ames)
1933- .... **CLC 3, 11, 18, 86; BLC**
See also AITN 1; BW 2; CA 9-12R;
CANR 6, 24, 42; CDALB 1968-1988;
DLB 2, 33, 152; DLBY 80; MTCW

Gaitskill, Mary 1954- .... **CLC 69**
See also CA 128

Galdos, Benito Perez
See Perez Galdos, Benito

Gale, Zona 1874-1938 . . . . **TCLC 7**
See also CA 105; DLB 9, 78

Galeano, Eduardo (Hughes) 1940-. . . **CLC 72**
See also CA 29-32R; CANR 13, 32; HW

Galiano, Juan Valera y Alcala
See Valera y Alcala-Galiano, Juan

Gallagher, Tess 1943-. . . . **CLC 18, 63; PC 9**
See also CA 106; DLB 120

Gallant, Mavis
1922- . . . . **CLC 7, 18, 38; SSC 5**
See also CA 69-72; CANR 29; DLB 53;
MTCW

Gallant, Roy A(rthur) 1924- . . . . **CLC 17**
See also CA 5-8R; CANR 4, 29; CLR 30;
MAICYA; SATA 4, 68

Gallico, Paul (William) 1897-1976 . . . **CLC 2**
See also AITN 1; CA 5-8R; 69-72;
CANR 23; DLB 9; MAICYA; SATA 13

Gallup, Ralph
See Whitemore, Hugh (John)

Galsworthy, John
1867-1933 . . . . . . **TCLC 1, 45; DA; DAB;**
WLC 2
See also CA 104; 141; CDBLB 1890-1914;
DLB 10, 34, 98

Galt, John 1779-1839 . . . . **NCLC 1**
See also DLB 99, 116

Galvin, James 1951- . . . . **CLC 38**
See also CA 108; CANR 26

Gamboa, Federico 1864-1939. . . . . . **TCLC 36**

Gandhi, M. K.
See Gandhi, Mohandas Karamchand

Gandhi, Mahatma
See Gandhi, Mohandas Karamchand

Gandhi, Mohandas Karamchand
1869-1948 . . . . **TCLC 59**
See also CA 121; 132; MTCW

Gann, Ernest Kellogg 1910-1991. . . . **CLC 23**
See also AITN 1; CA 1-4R; 136; CANR 1

Garcia, Cristina 1958- . . . . **CLC 76**
See also CA 141

Garcia Lorca, Federico
1898-1936 . . . **TCLC 1, 7, 49; DA; DAB;**
DC 2; HLC; PC 3; WLC
See also CA 104; 131; DLB 108; HW;
MTCW

Garcia Marquez, Gabriel (Jose)
1928- . . . . **CLC 2, 3, 8, 10, 15, 27, 47, 55,**
68; DA; DAB; HLC; SSC 8; WLC
See also AAYA 3; BEST 89:1, 90:4;
CA 33-36R; CANR 10, 28; DLB 113;
HW; MTCW

Gard, Janice
See Latham, Jean Lee

Gard, Roger Martin du
See Martin du Gard, Roger

Gardam, Jane 1928- . . . . **CLC 43**
See also CA 49-52; CANR 2, 18, 33;
CLR 12; DLB 14; MAICYA; MTCW;
SAAS 9; SATA 39, 76; SATA-Brief 28

Gardner, Herb. . . . . **CLC 44**

Gardner, John (Champlin), Jr.
1933-1982 . . . . . **CLC 2, 3, 5, 7, 8, 10, 18,**
28, 34; SSC 7
See also AITN 1; CA 65-68; 107;
CANR 33; DLB 2; DLBY 82; MTCW;
SATA 40; SATA-Obit 31

Gardner, John (Edmund) 1926-. . . . . **CLC 30**
See also CA 103; CANR 15; MTCW

Gardner, Noel
See Kuttner, Henry

Gardons, S. S.
See Snodgrass, W(illiam) D(e Witt)

Garfield, Leon 1921-. . . . . **CLC 12**
See also AAYA 8; CA 17-20R; CANR 38,
41; CLR 21; JRDA; MAICYA; SATA 1,
32, 76

Garland, (Hannibal) Hamlin
1860-1940 . . . . **TCLC 3; SSC 18**
See also CA 104; DLB 12, 71, 78

Garneau, (Hector de) Saint-Denys
1912-1943 . . . . **TCLC 13**
See also CA 111; DLB 88

Garner, Alan 1934-. . . . . **CLC 17; DAB**
See also CA 73-76; CANR 15; CLR 20;
MAICYA; MTCW; SATA 18, 69

Garner, Hugh 1913-1979 . . . . **CLC 13**
See also CA 69-72; CANR 31; DLB 68

Garnett, David 1892-1981 . . . . **CLC 3**
See also CA 5-8R; 103; CANR 17; DLB 34

Garos, Stephanie
See Katz, Steve

Garrett, George (Palmer)
1929- . . . . **CLC 3, 11, 51**
See also CA 1-4R; CAAS 5; CANR 1, 42;
DLB 2, 5, 130, 152; DLBY 83

Garrick, David 1717-1779 . . . . **LC 15**
See also DLB 84

Garrigue, Jean 1914-1972 . . . . **CLC 2, 8**
See also CA 5-8R; 37-40R; CANR 20

Garrison, Frederick
See Sinclair, Upton (Beall)

Garth, Will
See Hamilton, Edmond; Kuttner, Henry

Garvey, Marcus (Moziah, Jr.)
1887-1940 . . . . **TCLC 41; BLC**
See also BW 1; CA 120; 124

Gary, Romain . . . . **CLC 25**
See also Kacew, Romain
See also DLB 83

Gascar, Pierre . . . . **CLC 11**
See also Fournier, Pierre

Gascoyne, David (Emery) 1916- . . . . **CLC 45**
See also CA 65-68; CANR 10, 28; DLB 20;
MTCW

Gaskell, Elizabeth Cleghorn
1810-1865 . . . . **NCLC 5; DAB**
See also CDBLB 1832-1890; DLB 21, 144

Gass, William H(oward)
1924- . . . **CLC 1, 2, 8, 11, 15, 39; SSC 12**
See also CA 17-20R; CANR 30; DLB 2;
MTCW

Gasset, Jose Ortega y
See Ortega y Gasset, Jose

Gates, Henry Louis, Jr. 1950-. . . . . . **CLC 65**
See also BW 2; CA 109; CANR 25; DLB 67

Gautier, Theophile
1811-1872 . . . . **NCLC 1; SSC 20**
See also DLB 119

Gawsworth, John
See Bates, H(erbert) E(rnest)

Gaye, Marvin (Penze) 1939-1984 . . . **CLC 26**
See also CA 112

Gebler, Carlo (Ernest) 1954-. . . . . . . **CLC 39**
See also CA 119; 133

Gee, Maggie (Mary) 1948-. . . . . **CLC 57**
See also CA 130

Gee, Maurice (Gough) 1931-. . . . . . . **CLC 29**
See also CA 97-100; SATA 46

Gelbart, Larry (Simon) 1923- . . . **CLC 21, 61**
See also CA 73-76; CANR 45

Gelber, Jack 1932-. . . . . **CLC 1, 6, 14, 79**
See also CA 1-4R; CANR 2; DLB 7

Gellhorn, Martha (Ellis) 1908- . . **CLC 14, 60**
See also CA 77-80; CANR 44; DLBY 82

Genet, Jean
1910-1986 . . . **CLC 1, 2, 5, 10, 14, 44, 46**
See also CA 13-16R; CANR 18; DLB 72;
DLBY 86; MTCW

Gent, Peter 1942-. . . . . **CLC 29**
See also AITN 1; CA 89-92; DLBY 82

Gentlewoman in New England, A
See Bradstreet, Anne

Gentlewoman in Those Parts, A
See Bradstreet, Anne

George, Jean Craighead 1919-. . . . . . **CLC 35**
See also AAYA 8; CA 5-8R; CANR 25;
CLR 1; DLB 52; JRDA; MAICYA;
SATA 2, 68

George, Stefan (Anton)
1868-1933 . . . . **TCLC 2, 14**
See also CA 104

Georges, Georges Martin
See Simenon, Georges (Jacques Christian)

Gerhardi, William Alexander
See Gerhardie, William Alexander

Gerhardie, William Alexander
1895-1977 . . . . **CLC 5**
See also CA 25-28R; 73-76; CANR 18;
DLB 36

Gerstler, Amy 1956-. . . . . **CLC 70**
See also CA 146

Gertler, T. . . . . **CLC 34**
See also CA 116; 121

Ghalib 1797-1869 . . . . **NCLC 39**

Ghelderode, Michel de
1898-1962 . . . . **CLC 6, 11**
See also CA 85-88; CANR 40

Ghiselin, Brewster 1903- . . . . **CLC 23**
See also CA 13-16R; CAAS 10; CANR 13

Ghose, Zulfikar 1935-. . . . . **CLC 42**
See also CA 65-68

Ghosh, Amitav 1956- . . . . **CLC 44**
See also CA 147

Giacosa, Giuseppe 1847-1906 . . . . . . **TCLC 7**
See also CA 104

Gibb, Lee
See Waterhouse, Keith (Spencer)

Gordimer, Nadine
    1923- .... CLC 3, 5, 7, 10, 18, 33, 51, 70;
        DA; DAB; SSC 17
    See also CA 5-8R; CANR 3, 28; MTCW

Gordon, Adam Lindsay
    1833-1870 .... NCLC 21

Gordon, Caroline
    1895-1981 ... CLC 6, 13, 29, 83; SSC 15
    See also CA 11-12; 103; CANR 36; CAP 1;
        DLB 4, 9, 102; DLBY 81; MTCW

Gordon, Charles William   1860-1937
    See Connor, Ralph
    See also CA 109

Gordon, Mary (Catherine)
    1949- .... CLC 13, 22
    See also CA 102; CANR 44; DLB 6;
        DLBY 81; MTCW

Gordon, Sol   1923-................ CLC 26
    See also CA 53-56; CANR 4; SATA 11

Gordone, Charles   1925-.......... CLC 1, 4
    See also BW 1; CA 93-96; DLB 7; MTCW

Gorenko, Anna Andreevna
    See Akhmatova, Anna

Gorky, Maxim........ TCLC 8; DAB; WLC
    See also Peshkov, Alexei Maximovich

Goryan, Sirak
    See Saroyan, William

Gosse, Edmund (William)
    1849-1928 .... TCLC 28
    See also CA 117; DLB 57, 144

Gotlieb, Phyllis Fay (Bloom)
    1926- .... CLC 18
    See also CA 13-16R; CANR 7; DLB 88

Gottesman, S. D.
    See Kornbluth, C(yril) M.; Pohl, Frederik

Gottfried von Strassburg
    fl. c. 1210- .... CMLC 10
    See also DLB 138

Gould, Lois .... CLC 4, 10
    See also CA 77-80; CANR 29; MTCW

Gourmont, Remy de   1858-1915.... TCLC 17
    See also CA 109

Govier, Katherine   1948-.......... CLC 51
    See also CA 101; CANR 18, 40

Goyen, (Charles) William
    1915-1983 .... CLC 5, 8, 14, 40
    See also AITN 2; CA 5-8R; 110; CANR 6;
        DLB 2; DLBY 83

Goytisolo, Juan
    1931-........... CLC 5, 10, 23; HLC
    See also CA 85-88; CANR 32; HW; MTCW

Gozzano, Guido   1883-1916 .... PC 10
    See also DLB 114

Gozzi, (Conte) Carlo   1720-1806 .. NCLC 23

Grabbe, Christian Dietrich
    1801-1836 .... NCLC 2
    See also DLB 133

Grace, Patricia   1937-............ CLC 56

Gracian y Morales, Baltasar
    1601-1658 .... LC 15

Gracq, Julien .... CLC 11, 48
    See also Poirier, Louis
    See also DLB 83

Grade, Chaim   1910-1982 .... CLC 10
    See also CA 93-96; 107

Graduate of Oxford, A
    See Ruskin, John

Graham, John
    See Phillips, David Graham

Graham, Jorie   1951-............. CLC 48
    See also CA 111, ⌐LB 120

Graham, R(obert) B(ontine) Cunninghame
    See Cunninghame Graham, R(obert)
        B(ontine)
    See also DLB 98, 135

Graham, Robert
    See Haldeman, Joe (William)

Graham, Tom
    See Lewis, (Harry) Sinclair

Graham, W(illiam) S(ydney)
    1918-1986 .... CLC 29
    See also CA 73-76; 118; DLB 20

Graham, Winston (Mawdsley)
    1910- .... CLC 23
    See also CA 49-52; CANR 2, 22, 45;
        DLB 77

Grant, Skeeter
    See Spiegelman, Art

Granville-Barker, Harley
    1877-1946 .... TCLC 2
    See also Barker, Harley Granville
    See also CA 104

Grass, Guenter (Wilhelm)
    1927- ..... CLC 1, 2, 4, 6, 11, 15, 22, 32,
        49, 88; DA; DAB; WLC
    See also CA 13-16R; CANR 20; DLB 75,
        124; MTCW

Gratton, Thomas
    See Hulme, T(homas) E(rnest)

Grau, Shirley Ann
    1929- .... CLC 4, 9; SSC 15
    See also CA 89-92; CANR 22; DLB 2;
        MTCW

Gravel, Fern
    See Hall, James Norman

Graver, Elizabeth   1964-.......... CLC 70
    See also CA 135

Graves, Richard Perceval   1945- .... CLC 44
    See also CA 65-68; CANR 9, 26

Graves, Robert (von Ranke)
    1895-1985 ...... CLC 1, 2, 6, 11, 39, 44,
        45; DAB; PC 6
    See also CA 5-8R; 117; CANR 5, 36;
        CDBLB 1914-1945; DLB 20, 100;
        DLBY 85; MTCW; SATA 45

Gray, Alasdair (James)   1934- ...... CLC 41
    See also CA 126; CANR 47; MTCW

Gray, Amlin   1946- .... CLC 29
    See also CA 138

Gray, Francine du Plessix   1930-.... CLC 22
    See also BEST 90:3; CA 61-64; CAAS 2;
        CANR 11, 33; MTCW

Gray, John (Henry)   1866-1934 .... TCLC 19
    See also CA 119

Gray, Simon (James Holliday)
    1936- .... CLC 9, 14, 36
    See also AITN 1; CA 21-24R; CAAS 3;
        CANR 32; DLB 13; MTCW

Gray, Spalding   1941-............. CLC 49
    See also CA 128

Gray, Thomas
    1716-1771 ...... LC 4; DA; DAB; PC 2;
        WLC
    See also CDBLB 1660-1789; DLB 109

Grayson, David
    See Baker, Ray Stannard

Grayson, Richard (A.)   1951-....... CLC 38
    See also CA 85-88; CANR 14, 31

Greeley, Andrew M(oran)   1928-.... CLC 28
    See also CA 5-8R; CAAS 7; CANR 7, 43;
        MTCW

Green, Brian
    See Card, Orson Scott

Green, Hannah
    See Greenberg, Joanne (Goldenberg)

Green, Hannah .... CLC 3
    See also CA 73-76

Green, Henry.................... CLC 2, 13
    See also Yorke, Henry Vincent
    See also DLB 15

Green, Julian (Hartridge)   1900-
    See Green, Julien
    See also CA 21-24R; CANR 33; DLB 4, 72;
        MTCW

Green, Julien .... CLC 3, 11, 77
    See also Green, Julian (Hartridge)

Green, Paul (Eliot)   1894-1981...... CLC 25
    See also AITN 1; CA 5-8R; 103; CANR 3;
        DLB 7, 9; DLBY 81

Greenberg, Ivan   1908-1973
    See Rahv, Philip
    See also CA 85-88

Greenberg, Joanne (Goldenberg)
    1932- .... CLC 7, 30
    See also AAYA 12; CA 5-8R; CANR 14,
        32; SATA 25

Greenberg, Richard   1959(?)-....... CLC 57
    See also CA 138

Greene, Bette   1934- .... CLC 30
    See also AAYA 7; CA 53-56; CANR 4;
        CLR 2; JRDA; MAICYA; SAAS 16;
        SATA 8

Greene, Gael .... CLC 8
    See also CA 13-16R; CANR 10

Greene, Graham
    1904-1991 .... CLC 1, 3, 6, 9, 14, 18, 27,
        37, 70, 72; DA; DAB; WLC
    See also AITN 2; CA 13-16R; 133;
        CANR 35; CDBLB 1945-1960; DLB 13,
        15, 77, 100; DLBY 91; MTCW; SATA 20

Greer, Richard
    See Silverberg, Robert

Gregor, Arthur   1923-............. CLC 9
    See also CA 25-28R; CAAS 10; CANR 11;
        SATA 36

Gregor, Lee
    See Pohl, Frederik

Gregory, Isabella Augusta (Persse)
    1852-1932 .... TCLC 1
    See also CA 104; DLB 10

Gregory, J. Dennis
    See Williams, John A(lfred)

Haley, Alex(ander Murray Palmer)
    1921-1992 .... **CLC 8, 12, 76; BLC; DA;**
                                        DAB
    See also BW 2; CA 77-80; 136; DLB 38;
    MTCW

Haliburton, Thomas Chandler
    1796-1865 .... **NCLC 15**
    See also DLB 11, 99

Hall, Donald (Andrew, Jr.)
    1928- .... **CLC 1, 13, 37, 59**
    See also CA 5-8R; CAAS 7; CANR 2, 44;
    DLB 5; SATA 23

Hall, Frederic Sauser
    See Sauser-Hall, Frederic

Hall, James
    See Kuttner, Henry

Hall, James Norman   1887-1951 ... **TCLC 23**
    See also CA 123; SATA 21

Hall, (Marguerite) Radclyffe
    1886(?)-1943 .... **TCLC 12**
    See also CA 110

Hall, Rodney   1935- .... **CLC 51**
    See also CA 109

Halleck, Fitz-Greene   1790-1867 .. **NCLC 47**
    See also DLB 3

Halliday, Michael
    See Creasey, John

Halpern, Daniel   1945- .... **CLC 14**
    See also CA 33-36R

Hamburger, Michael (Peter Leopold)
    1924- .... **CLC 5, 14**
    See also CA 5-8R; CAAS 4; CANR 2, 47;
    DLB 27

Hamill, Pete   1935- .... **CLC 10**
    See also CA 25-28R; CANR 18

Hamilton, Alexander
    1755(?)-1804 .... **NCLC 49**
    See also DLB 37

Hamilton, Clive
    See Lewis, C(live) S(taples)

Hamilton, Edmond   1904-1977 ...... **CLC 1**
    See also CA 1-4R; CANR 3; DLB 8

Hamilton, Eugene (Jacob) Lee
    See Lee-Hamilton, Eugene (Jacob)

Hamilton, Franklin
    See Silverberg, Robert

Hamilton, Gail
    See Corcoran, Barbara

Hamilton, Mollie
    See Kaye, M(ary) M(argaret)

Hamilton, (Anthony Walter) Patrick
    1904-1962 .... **CLC 51**
    See also CA 113; DLB 10

Hamilton, Virginia   1936- .... **CLC 26**
    See also AAYA 2; BW 2; CA 25-28R;
    CANR 20, 37; CLR 1, 11; DLB 33, 52;
    JRDA; MAICYA; MTCW; SATA 4, 56,
    79

Hammett, (Samuel) Dashiell
    1894-1961 .... **CLC 3, 5, 10, 19, 47;**
                                        SSC 17
    See also AITN 1; CA 81-84; CANR 42;
    CDALB 1929-1941; DLBD 6; MTCW

Hammon, Jupiter
    1711(?)-1800(?) .... **NCLC 5; BLC**
    See also DLB 31, 50

Hammond, Keith
    See Kuttner, Henry

Hamner, Earl (Henry), Jr.   1923- ... **CLC 12**
    See also AITN 2; CA 73-76; DLB 6

Hampton, Christopher (James)
    1946- .... **CLC 4**
    See also CA 25-28R; DLB 13; MTCW

Hamsun, Knut .... **TCLC 2, 14, 49**
    See also Pedersen, Knut

Handke, Peter   1942- .. **CLC 5, 8, 10, 15, 38**
    See also CA 77-80; CANR 33; DLB 85,
    124; MTCW

Hanley, James   1901-1985 ... **CLC 3, 5, 8, 13**
    See also CA 73-76; 117; CANR 36; MTCW

Hannah, Barry   1942- ...... **CLC 23, 38, 90**
    See also CA 108; 110; CANR 43; DLB 6;
    MTCW

Hannon, Ezra
    See Hunter, Evan

Hansberry, Lorraine (Vivian)
    1930-1965 ...... **CLC 17, 62; BLC; DA;**
                                        DAB; DC 2
    See also BW 1; CA 109; 25-28R; CABS 3;
    CDALB 1941-1968; DLB 7, 38; MTCW

Hansen, Joseph   1923-............. **CLC 38**
    See also CA 29-32R; CAAS 17; CANR 16,
    44

Hansen, Martin A.   1909-1955..... **TCLC 32**

Hanson, Kenneth O(stlin)   1922- .... **CLC 13**
    See also CA 53-56; CANR 7

Hardwick, Elizabeth   1916- .... **CLC 13**
    See also CA 5-8R; CANR 3, 32; DLB 6;
    MTCW

Hardy, Thomas
    1840-1928 ...... **TCLC 4, 10, 18, 32, 48,**
    53; DA; DAB; PC 8; SSC 2; WLC
    See also CA 104; 123; CDBLB 1890-1914;
    DLB 18, 19, 135; MTCW

Hare, David   1947- .... **CLC 29, 58**
    See also CA 97-100; CANR 39; DLB 13;
    MTCW

Harford, Henry
    See Hudson, W(illiam) H(enry)

Hargrave, Leonie
    See Disch, Thomas M(ichael)

Harjo, Joy   1951- .... **CLC 83**
    See also CA 114; CANR 35; DLB 120;
    NNAL

Harlan, Louis R(udolph)   1922-..... **CLC 34**
    See also CA 21-24R; CANR 25

Harling, Robert   1951(?)- .... **CLC 53**
    See also CA 147

Harmon, William (Ruth)   1938-..... **CLC 38**
    See also CA 33-36R; CANR 14, 32, 35;
    SATA 65

Harper, F. E. W.
    See Harper, Frances Ellen Watkins

Harper, Frances E. W.
    See Harper, Frances Ellen Watkins

Harper, Frances E. Watkins
    See Harper, Frances Ellen Watkins

Harper, Frances Ellen
    See Harper, Frances Ellen Watkins

Harper, Frances Ellen Watkins
    1825-1911 .... **TCLC 14; BLC**
    See also BW 1; CA 111; 125; DLB 50

Harper, Michael S(teven)   1938- .. **CLC 7, 22**
    See also BW 1; CA 33-36R; CANR 24;
    DLB 41

Harper, Mrs. F. E. W.
    See Harper, Frances Ellen Watkins

Harris, Christie (Lucy) Irwin
    1907- .... **CLC 12**
    See also CA 5-8R; CANR 6; DLB 88;
    JRDA; MAICYA; SAAS 10; SATA 6, 74

Harris, Frank   1856(?)-1931....... **TCLC 24**
    See also CA 109; DLB 156

Harris, George Washington
    1814-1869 .... **NCLC 23**
    See also DLB 3, 11

Harris, Joel Chandler
    1848-1908 .... **TCLC 2; SSC 19**
    See also CA 104; 137; DLB 11, 23, 42, 78,
    91; MAICYA; YABC 1

Harris, John (Wyndham Parkes Lucas)
    Beynon   1903-1969
    See Wyndham, John
    See also CA 102; 89-92

Harris, MacDonald .... **CLC 9**
    See also Heiney, Donald (William)

Harris, Mark   1922- .... **CLC 19**
    See also CA 5-8R; CAAS 3; CANR 2;
    DLB 2; DLBY 80

Harris, (Theodore) Wilson   1921-.... **CLC 25**
    See also BW 2; CA 65-68; CAAS 16;
    CANR 11, 27; DLB 117; MTCW

Harrison, Elizabeth Cavanna   1909-
    See Cavanna, Betty
    See also CA 9-12R; CANR 6, 27

Harrison, Harry (Max)   1925- ...... **CLC 42**
    See also CA 1-4R; CANR 5, 21; DLB 8;
    SATA 4

Harrison, James (Thomas)
    1937- .... **CLC 6, 14, 33, 66; SSC 19**
    See also CA 13-16R; CANR 8; DLBY 82

Harrison, Jim
    See Harrison, James (Thomas)

Harrison, Kathryn   1961- .... **CLC 70**
    See also CA 144

Harrison, Tony   1937-............. **CLC 43**
    See also CA 65-68; CANR 44; DLB 40;
    MTCW

Harriss, Will(ard Irvin)   1922-...... **CLC 34**
    See also CA 111

Harson, Sley
    See Ellison, Harlan (Jay)

Hart, Ellis
    See Ellison, Harlan (Jay)

Hart, Josephine   1942(?)- .... **CLC 70**
    See also CA 138

Hart, Moss   1904-1961 .... **CLC 66**
    See also CA 109; 89-92; DLB 7

Harte, (Francis) Bret(t)
1836(?)-1902 . . . . **TCLC 1, 25; DA;**
SSC 8; WLC
See also CA 104; 140; CDALB 1865-1917;
DLB 12, 64, 74, 79; SATA 26

Hartley, L(eslie) P(oles)
1895-1972 . . . . **CLC 2, 22**
See also CA 45-48; 37-40R; CANR 33;
DLB 15, 139; MTCW

Hartman, Geoffrey H. 1929- . . . . **CLC 27**
See also CA 117; 125; DLB 67

Hartmann von Aue
c. 1160-c. 1205 . . . . **CMLC 15**
See also DLB 138

Haruf, Kent 19(?)- . . . . **CLC 34**

Harwood, Ronald 1934- . . . . **CLC 32**
See also CA 1-4R; CANR 4; DLB 13

Hasek, Jaroslav (Matej Frantisek)
1883-1923 . . . . **TCLC 4**
See also CA 104; 129; MTCW

Hass, Robert 1941- . . . . **CLC 18, 39**
See also CA 111; CANR 30; DLB 105

Hastings, Hudson
See Kuttner, Henry

Hastings, Selina . . . . **CLC 44**

Hatteras, Amelia
See Mencken, H(enry) L(ouis)

Hatteras, Owen . . . . **TCLC 18**
See also Mencken, H(enry) L(ouis); Nathan,
George Jean

Hauptmann, Gerhart (Johann Robert)
1862-1946 . . . . **TCLC 4**
See also CA 104; DLB 66, 118

Havel, Vaclav 1936- . . . . **CLC 25, 58, 65**
See also CA 104; CANR 36; MTCW

Haviaras, Stratis . . . . **CLC 33**
See also Chaviaras, Strates

Hawes, Stephen 1475(?)-1523(?) . . . . . **LC 17**

Hawkes, John (Clendennin Burne, Jr.)
1925- . . . . . . **CLC 1, 2, 3, 4, 7, 9, 14, 15,**
27, 49
See also CA 1-4R; CANR 2, 47; DLB 2, 7;
DLBY 80; MTCW

Hawking, S. W.
See Hawking, Stephen W(illiam)

Hawking, Stephen W(illiam)
1942- . . . . **CLC 63**
See also AAYA 13; BEST 89:1; CA 126;
129; CANR 48

Hawthorne, Julian 1846-1934 . . . . . **TCLC 25**

Hawthorne, Nathaniel
1804-1864 . . . . **NCLC 39; DA; DAB;**
SSC 3; WLC
See also CDALB 1640-1865; DLB 1, 74;
YABC 2

Haxton, Josephine Ayres 1921-
See Douglas, Ellen
See also CA 115; CANR 41

Hayaseca y Eizaguirre, Jorge
See Echegaray (y Eizaguirre), Jose (Maria
Waldo)

Hayashi Fumiko 1904-1951 . . . . . . **TCLC 27**

Haycraft, Anna
See Ellis, Alice Thomas
See also CA 122

Hayden, Robert E(arl)
1913-1980 . . . . . **CLC 5, 9, 14, 37; BLC;**
DA; PC 6
See also BW 1; CA 69-72; 97-100; CABS 2;
CANR 24; CDALB 1941-1968; DLB 5,
76; MTCW; SATA 19; SATA-Obit 26

Hayford, J(oseph) E(phraim) Casely
See Casely-Hayford, J(oseph) E(phraim)

Hayman, Ronald 1932- . . . . **CLC 44**
See also CA 25-28R; CANR 18; DLB 155

Haywood, Eliza (Fowler)
1693(?)-1756 . . . . **LC 1**

Hazlitt, William 1778-1830 . . . . . . **NCLC 29**
See also DLB 110

Hazzard, Shirley 1931- . . . . **CLC 18**
See also CA 9-12R; CANR 4; DLBY 82;
MTCW

Head, Bessie 1937-1986 . . . **CLC 25, 67; BLC**
See also BW 2; CA 29-32R; 119; CANR 25;
DLB 117; MTCW

Headon, (Nicky) Topper 1956(?)- . . . **CLC 30**

Heaney, Seamus (Justin)
1939- . . . . **CLC 5, 7, 14, 25, 37, 74; DAB**
See also CA 85-88; CANR 25, 48;
CDBLB 1960 to Present; DLB 40;
MTCW

Hearn, (Patricio) Lafcadio (Tessima Carlos)
1850-1904 . . . . **TCLC 9**
See also CA 105; DLB 12, 78

Hearne, Vicki 1946- . . . . **CLC 56**
See also CA 139

Hearon, Shelby 1931- . . . . **CLC 63**
See also AITN 2; CA 25-28R; CANR 18,
48

Heat-Moon, William Least . . . . **CLC 29**
See also Trogdon, William (Lewis)
See also AAYA 9

Hebbel, Friedrich 1813-1863 . . . . . **NCLC 43**
See also DLB 129

Hebert, Anne 1916- . . . . **CLC 4, 13, 29**
See also CA 85-88; DLB 68; MTCW

Hecht, Anthony (Evan)
1923- . . . . **CLC 8, 13, 19**
See also CA 9-12R; CANR 6; DLB 5

Hecht, Ben 1894-1964 . . . . **CLC 8**
See also CA 85-88; DLB 7, 9, 25, 26, 28, 86

Hedayat, Sadeq 1903-1951 . . . . **TCLC 21**
See also CA 120

Hegel, Georg Wilhelm Friedrich
1770-1831 . . . . **NCLC 46**
See also DLB 90

Heidegger, Martin 1889-1976 . . . . . . **CLC 24**
See also CA 81-84; 65-68; CANR 34;
MTCW

Heidenstam, (Carl Gustaf) Verner von
1859-1940 . . . . **TCLC 5**
See also CA 104

Heifner, Jack 1946- . . . . **CLC 11**
See also CA 105; CANR 47

Heijermans, Herman 1864-1924 . . . **TCLC 24**
See also CA 123

Heilbrun, Carolyn G(old) 1926- . . . . . **CLC 25**
See also CA 45-48; CANR 1, 28

Heine, Heinrich 1797-1856 . . . . **NCLC 4**
See also DLB 90

Heinemann, Larry (Curtiss) 1944- . . **CLC 50**
See also CA 110; CAAS 21; CANR 31;
DLBD 9

Heiney, Donald (William) 1921-1993
See Harris, MacDonald
See also CA 1-4R; 142; CANR 3

Heinlein, Robert A(nson)
1907-1988 . . . . . . **CLC 1, 3, 8, 14, 26, 55**
See also CA 1-4R; 125; CANR 1, 20;
DLB 8; JRDA; MAICYA; MTCW;
SATA 9, 69; SATA-Obit 56

Helforth, John
See Doolittle, Hilda

Hellenhofferu, Vojtech Kapristian z
See Hasek, Jaroslav (Matej Frantisek)

Heller, Joseph
1923- . . . . **CLC 1, 3, 5, 8, 11, 36, 63; DA;**
DAB; WLC
See also AITN 1; CA 5-8R; CABS 1;
CANR 8, 42; DLB 2, 28; DLBY 80;
MTCW

Hellman, Lillian (Florence)
1906-1984 . . . . . . **CLC 2, 4, 8, 14, 18, 34,**
44, 52; DC 1
See also AITN 1, 2; CA 13-16R; 112;
CANR 33; DLB 7; DLBY 84; MTCW

Helprin, Mark 1947- . . . . . **CLC 7, 10, 22, 32**
See also CA 81-84; CANR 47; DLBY 85;
MTCW

Helvetius, Claude-Adrien
1715-1771 . . . . **LC 26**

Helyar, Jane Penelope Josephine 1933-
See Poole, Josephine
See also CA 21-24R; CANR 10, 26;
SATA 82

Hemans, Felicia 1793-1835 . . . . . . **NCLC 29**
See also DLB 96

Hemingway, Ernest (Miller)
1899-1961 . . . . **CLC 1, 3, 6, 8, 10, 13, 19,**
30, 34, 39, 41, 44, 50, 61, 80; DA; DAB;
SSC 1; WLC
See also CA 77-80; CANR 34;
CDALB 1917-1929; DLB 4, 9, 102;
DLBD 1; DLBY 81, 87; MTCW

Hempel, Amy 1951- . . . . **CLC 39**
See also CA 118; 137

Henderson, F. C.
See Mencken, H(enry) L(ouis)

Henderson, Sylvia
See Ashton-Warner, Sylvia (Constance)

Henley, Beth . . . . **CLC 23**
See also Henley, Elizabeth Becker
See also CABS 3; DLBY 86

Henley, Elizabeth Becker 1952-
See Henley, Beth
See also CA 107; CANR 32; MTCW

Henley, William Ernest
1849-1903 . . . . **TCLC 8**
See also CA 105; DLB 19

Hennissart, Martha
See Lathen, Emma
See also CA 85-88

Henry, O. . . . . TCLC **1, 19; SSC 5; WLC**
See also Porter, William Sydney

Henry, Patrick 1736-1799 . . . . LC **25**

Henryson, Robert 1430(?)-1506(?). . . . LC **20**
See also DLB 146

Henry VIII 1491-1547 . . . . LC **10**

Henschke, Alfred
See Klabund

Hentoff, Nat(han Irving) 1925- . . . . . CLC **26**
See also AAYA 4; CA 1-4R; CAAS 6;
CANR 5, 25; CLR 1; JRDA; MAICYA;
SATA 42, 69; SATA-Brief 27

Heppenstall, (John) Rayner
1911-1981 . . . . CLC **10**
See also CA 1-4R; 103; CANR 29

Herbert, Frank (Patrick)
1920-1986 . . . . . . CLC **12, 23, 35, 44, 85**
See also CA 53-56; 118; CANR 5, 43;
DLB 8; MTCW; SATA 9, 37;
SATA-Obit 47

Herbert, George
1593-1633 . . . . LC **24; DAB; PC 4**
See also CDBLB Before 1660; DLB 126

Herbert, Zbigniew 1924- . . . . CLC **9, 43**
See also CA 89-92; CANR 36; MTCW

Herbst, Josephine (Frey)
1897-1969 . . . . CLC **34**
See also CA 5-8R; 25-28R; DLB 9

Hergesheimer, Joseph
1880-1954 . . . . TCLC **11**
See also CA 109; DLB 102, 9

Herlihy, James Leo 1927-1993 . . . . . . CLC **6**
See also CA 1-4R; 143; CANR 2

Hermogenes fl. c. 175- . . . . CMLC **6**

Hernandez, Jose 1834-1886 . . . . . . NCLC **17**

Herrick, Robert
1591-1674 . . . . . LC **13; DA; DAB; PC 9**
See also DLB 126

Herring, Guilles
See Somerville, Edith

Herriot, James 1916-1995 . . . . CLC **12**
See also Wight, James Alfred
See also AAYA 1; CA 148; CANR 40

Herrmann, Dorothy 1941- . . . . CLC **44**
See also CA 107

Herrmann, Taffy
See Herrmann, Dorothy

Hersey, John (Richard)
1914-1993 . . . . . . CLC **1, 2, 7, 9, 40, 81**
See also CA 17-20R; 140; CANR 33;
DLB 6; MTCW; SATA 25;
SATA-Obit 76

Herzen, Aleksandr Ivanovich
1812-1870 . . . . NCLC **10**

Herzl, Theodor 1860-1904 . . . . TCLC **36**

Herzog, Werner 1942- . . . . CLC **16**
See also CA 89-92

Hesiod c. 8th cent. B.C.- . . . . CMLC **5**

Hesse, Hermann
1877-1962 . . . . CLC **1, 2, 3, 6, 11, 17, 25,
69; DA; DAB; SSC 9; WLC**
See also CA 17-18; CAP 2; DLB 66;
MTCW; SATA 50

Hewes, Cady
See De Voto, Bernard (Augustine)

Heyen, William 1940- . . . . CLC **13, 18**
See also CA 33-36R; CAAS 9; DLB 5

Heyerdahl, Thor 1914- . . . . CLC **26**
See also CA 5-8R; CANR 5, 22; MTCW;
SATA 2, 52

Heym, Georg (Theodor Franz Arthur)
1887-1912 . . . . TCLC **9**
See also CA 106

Heym, Stefan 1913- . . . . CLC **41**
See also CA 9-12R; CANR 4; DLB 69

Heyse, Paul (Johann Ludwig von)
1830-1914 . . . . TCLC **8**
See also CA 104; DLB 129

Heyward, (Edwin) DuBose
1885-1940 . . . . TCLC **59**
See also CA 108; DLB 7, 9, 45; SATA 21

Hibbert, Eleanor Alice Burford
1906-1993 . . . . CLC **7**
See also BEST 90:4; CA 17-20R; 140;
CANR 9, 28; SATA 2; SATA-Obit 74

Higgins, George V(incent)
1939- . . . . CLC **4, 7, 10, 18**
See also CA 77-80; CAAS 5; CANR 17;
DLB 2; DLBY 81; MTCW

Higginson, Thomas Wentworth
1823-1911 . . . . TCLC **36**
See also DLB 1, 64

Highet, Helen
See MacInnes, Helen (Clark)

Highsmith, (Mary) Patricia
1921-1995 . . . . CLC **2, 4, 14, 42**
See also CA 1-4R; 147; CANR 1, 20, 48;
MTCW

Highwater, Jamake (Mamake)
1942(?)- . . . . CLC **12**
See also AAYA 7; CA 65-68; CAAS 7;
CANR 10, 34; CLR 17; DLB 52;
DLBY 85; JRDA; MAICYA; SATA 32,
69; SATA-Brief 30

Higuchi, Ichiyo 1872-1896 . . . . NCLC **49**

Hijuelos, Oscar 1951- . . . . . . CLC **65; HLC**
See also BEST 90:1; CA 123; DLB 145; HW

Hikmet, Nazim 1902(?)-1963 . . . . . . CLC **40**
See also CA 141; 93-96

Hildesheimer, Wolfgang
1916-1991 . . . . CLC **49**
See also CA 101; 135; DLB 69, 124

Hill, Geoffrey (William)
1932- . . . . CLC **5, 8, 18, 45**
See also CA 81-84; CANR 21;
CDBLB 1960 to Present; DLB 40;
MTCW

Hill, George Roy 1921- . . . . CLC **26**
See also CA 110; 122

Hill, John
See Koontz, Dean R(ay)

Hill, Susan (Elizabeth)
1942- . . . . CLC **4; DAB**
See also CA 33-36R; CANR 29; DLB 14,
139; MTCW

Hillerman, Tony 1925- . . . . CLC **62**
See also AAYA 6; BEST 89:1; CA 29-32R;
CANR 21, 42; SATA 6

Hillesum, Etty 1914-1943 . . . . TCLC **49**
See also CA 137

Hilliard, Noel (Harvey) 1929- . . . . . . CLC **15**
See also CA 9-12R; CANR 7

Hillis, Rick 1956- . . . . CLC **66**
See also CA 134

Hilton, James 1900-1954 . . . . TCLC **21**
See also CA 108; DLB 34, 77; SATA 34

Himes, Chester (Bomar)
1909-1984 . . . . CLC **2, 4, 7, 18, 58; BLC**
See also BW 2; CA 25-28R; 114; CANR 22;
DLB 2, 76, 143; MTCW

Hinde, Thomas . . . . CLC **6, 11**
See also Chitty, Thomas Willes

Hindin, Nathan
See Bloch, Robert (Albert)

Hine, (William) Daryl 1936- . . . . CLC **15**
See also CA 1-4R; CAAS 15; CANR 1, 20;
DLB 60

Hinkson, Katharine Tynan
See Tynan, Katharine

Hinton, S(usan) E(loise)
1950- . . . . CLC **30; DA; DAB**
See also AAYA 2; CA 81-84; CANR 32;
CLR 3, 23; JRDA; MAICYA; MTCW;
SATA 19, 58

Hippius, Zinaida . . . . TCLC **9**
See also Gippius, Zinaida (Nikolayevna)

Hiraoka, Kimitake 1925-1970
See Mishima, Yukio
See also CA 97-100; 29-32R; MTCW

Hirsch, E(ric) D(onald), Jr. 1928- . . . CLC **79**
See also CA 25-28R; CANR 27; DLB 67;
MTCW

Hirsch, Edward 1950- . . . . CLC **31, 50**
See also CA 104; CANR 20, 42; DLB 120

Hitchcock, Alfred (Joseph)
1899-1980 . . . . CLC **16**
See also CA 97-100; SATA 27;
SATA-Obit 24

Hitler, Adolf 1889-1945 . . . . TCLC **53**
See also CA 117; 147

Hoagland, Edward 1932- . . . . CLC **28**
See also CA 1-4R; CANR 2, 31; DLB 6;
SATA 51

Hoban, Russell (Conwell) 1925- . . CLC **7, 25**
See also CA 5-8R; CANR 23, 37; CLR 3;
DLB 52; MAICYA; MTCW; SATA 1,
40, 78

Hobbs, Perry
See Blackmur, R(ichard) P(almer)

Hobson, Laura Z(ametkin)
1900-1986 . . . . CLC **7, 25**
See also CA 17-20R; 118; DLB 28;
SATA 52

Hochhuth, Rolf 1931- . . . . CLC **4, 11, 18**
See also CA 5-8R; CANR 33; DLB 124;
MTCW

Hochman, Sandra 1936- . . . . CLC **3, 8**
See also CA 5-8R; DLB 5

Hochwaelder, Fritz 1911-1986 . . . . . . CLC **36**
See also CA 29-32R; 120; CANR 42;
MTCW

Hochwalder, Fritz
See Hochwaelder, Fritz

Johnson, B(ryan) S(tanley William)
1933-1973 . . . . **CLC 6, 9**
See also CA 9-12R; 53-56; CANR 9;
DLB 14, 40

Johnson, Benj. F. of Boo
See Riley, James Whitcomb

Johnson, Benjamin F. of Boo
See Riley, James Whitcomb

Johnson, Charles (Richard)
1948- . . . . **CLC 7, 51, 65; BLC**
See also BW 2; CA 116; CAAS 18;
CANR 42; DLB 33

Johnson, Denis 1949- . . . . **CLC 52**
See also CA 117; 121; DLB 120

Johnson, Diane 1934- . . . . **CLC 5, 13, 48**
See also CA 41-44R; CANR 17, 40;
DLBY 80; MTCW

Johnson, Eyvind (Olof Verner)
1900-1976 . . . . **CLC 14**
See also CA 73-76; 69-72; CANR 34

Johnson, J. R.
See James, C(yril) L(ionel) R(obert)

Johnson, James Weldon
1871-1938 . . . . **TCLC 3, 19; BLC**
See also BW 1; CA 104; 125;
CDALB 1917-1929; CLR 32; DLB 51;
MTCW; SATA 31

Johnson, Joyce 1935- . . . . **CLC 58**
See also CA 125; 129

Johnson, Lionel (Pigot)
1867-1902 . . . . **TCLC 19**
See also CA 117; DLB 19

Johnson, Mel
See Malzberg, Barry N(athaniel)

Johnson, Pamela Hansford
1912-1981 . . . . **CLC 1, 7, 27**
See also CA 1-4R; 104; CANR 2, 28;
DLB 15; MTCW

Johnson, Samuel
1709-1784 . . . . . **LC 15; DA; DAB; WLC**
See also CDBLB 1660-1789; DLB 39, 95,
104, 142

Johnson, Uwe
1934-1984 . . . . **CLC 5, 10, 15, 40**
See also CA 1-4R; 112; CANR 1, 39;
DLB 75; MTCW

Johnston, George (Benson) 1913- . . . **CLC 51**
See also CA 1-4R; CANR 5, 20; DLB 88

Johnston, Jennifer 1930- . . . . **CLC 7**
See also CA 85-88; DLB 14

Jolley, (Monica) Elizabeth
1923- . . . . **CLC 46; SSC 19**
See also CA 127; CAAS 13

Jones, Arthur Llewellyn 1863-1947
See Machen, Arthur
See also CA 104

Jones, D(ouglas) G(ordon) 1929- . . . . **CLC 10**
See also CA 29-32R; CANR 13; DLB 53

Jones, David (Michael)
1895-1974 . . . . **CLC 2, 4, 7, 13, 42**
See also CA 9-12R; 53-56; CANR 28;
CDBLB 1945-1960; DLB 20, 100; MTCW

Jones, David Robert 1947-
See Bowie, David
See also CA 103

Jones, Diana Wynne 1934- . . . . **CLC 26**
See also AAYA 12; CA 49-52; CANR 4,
26; CLR 23; JRDA; MAICYA; SAAS 7;
SATA 9, 70

Jones, Edward P. 1950- . . . . **CLC 76**
See also BW 2; CA 142

Jones, Gayl 1949- . . . . **CLC 6, 9; BLC**
See also BW 2; CA 77-80; CANR 27;
DLB 33; MTCW

Jones, James 1921-1977 . . . . **CLC 1, 3, 10, 39**
See also AITN 1, 2; CA 1-4R; 69-72;
CANR 6; DLB 2, 143; MTCW

Jones, John J.
See Lovecraft, H(oward) P(hillips)

Jones, LeRoi . . . . **CLC 1, 2, 3, 5, 10, 14**
See also Baraka, Amiri

Jones, Louis B. . . . . **CLC 65**
See also CA 141

Jones, Madison (Percy, Jr.) 1925- . . . **CLC 4**
See also CA 13-16R; CAAS 11; CANR 7;
DLB 152

Jones, Mervyn 1922- . . . . **CLC 10, 52**
See also CA 45-48; CAAS 5; CANR 1;
MTCW

Jones, Mick 1956(?)- . . . . **CLC 30**

Jones, Nettie (Pearl) 1941- . . . . **CLC 34**
See also BW 2; CA 137; CAAS 20

Jones, Preston 1936-1979 . . . . **CLC 10**
See also CA 73-76; 89-92; DLB 7

Jones, Robert F(rancis) 1934- . . . . **CLC 7**
See also CA 49-52; CANR 2

Jones, Rod 1953- . . . . **CLC 50**
See also CA 128

Jones, Terence Graham Parry
1942- . . . . **CLC 21**
See also Jones, Terry; Monty Python
See also CA 112; 116; CANR 35

Jones, Terry
See Jones, Terence Graham Parry
See also SATA 67; SATA-Brief 51

Jones, Thom 1945(?)- . . . . **CLC 81**

Jong, Erica 1942- . . . . **CLC 4, 6, 8, 18, 83**
See also AITN 1; BEST 90:2; CA 73-76;
CANR 26; DLB 2, 5, 28, 152; MTCW

Jonson, Ben(jamin)
1572(?)-1637 . . . . **LC 6; DA; DAB; DC 4;
WLC**
See also CDBLB Before 1660; DLB 62, 121

Jordan, June 1936- . . . . **CLC 5, 11, 23**
See also AAYA 2; BW 2; CA 33-36R;
CANR 25; CLR 10; DLB 38; MAICYA;
MTCW; SATA 4

Jordan, Pat(rick M.) 1941- . . . . **CLC 37**
See also CA 33-36R

Jorgensen, Ivar
See Ellison, Harlan (Jay)

Jorgenson, Ivar
See Silverberg, Robert

Josephus, Flavius c. 37-100 . . . . . **CMLC 13**

Josipovici, Gabriel 1940- . . . . **CLC 6, 43**
See also CA 37-40R; CAAS 8; CANR 47;
DLB 14

Joubert, Joseph 1754-1824 . . . . **NCLC 9**

Jouve, Pierre Jean 1887-1976 . . . . . . **CLC 47**
See also CA 65-68

Joyce, James (Augustine Aloysius)
1882-1941 . . . . . . **TCLC 3, 8, 16, 35, 52;
DA; DAB; SSC 3; WLC**
See also CA 104; 126; CDBLB 1914-1945;
DLB 10, 19, 36; MTCW

Jozsef, Attila 1905-1937 . . . . **TCLC 22**
See also CA 116

Juana Ines de la Cruz 1651(?)-1695 . . . **LC 5**

Judd, Cyril
See Kornbluth, C(yril) M.; Pohl, Frederik

Julian of Norwich 1342(?)-1416(?) . . . . **LC 6**
See also DLB 146

Juniper, Alex
See Hospital, Janette Turner

Just, Ward (Swift) 1935- . . . . **CLC 4, 27**
See also CA 25-28R; CANR 32

Justice, Donald (Rodney) 1925- . . **CLC 6, 19**
See also CA 5-8R; CANR 26; DLBY 83

Juvenal c. 55-c. 127 . . . . **CMLC 8**

Juvenis
See Bourne, Randolph S(illiman)

Kacew, Romain 1914-1980
See Gary, Romain
See also CA 108; 102

Kadare, Ismail 1936- . . . . **CLC 52**

Kadohata, Cynthia . . . . **CLC 59**
See also CA 140

Kafka, Franz
1883-1924 . . . . **TCLC 2, 6, 13, 29, 47, 53;
DA; DAB; SSC 5; WLC**
See also CA 105; 126; DLB 81; MTCW

Kahanovitsch, Pinkhes
See Der Nister

Kahn, Roger 1927- . . . . **CLC 30**
See also CA 25-28R; CANR 44; SATA 37

Kain, Saul
See Sassoon, Siegfried (Lorraine)

Kaiser, Georg 1878-1945 . . . . **TCLC 9**
See also CA 106; DLB 124

Kaletski, Alexander 1946- . . . . **CLC 39**
See also CA 118; 143

Kalidasa fl. c. 400- . . . . **CMLC 9**

Kallman, Chester (Simon)
1921-1975 . . . . **CLC 2**
See also CA 45-48; 53-56; CANR 3

Kaminsky, Melvin 1926-
See Brooks, Mel
See also CA 65-68; CANR 16

Kaminsky, Stuart M(elvin) 1934- . . . **CLC 59**
See also CA 73-76; CANR 29

Kane, Paul
See Simon, Paul

Kane, Wilson
See Bloch, Robert (Albert)

Kanin, Garson 1912- . . . . **CLC 22**
See also AITN 1; CA 5-8R; CANR 7;
DLB 7

Kaniuk, Yoram 1930- . . . . **CLC 19**
See also CA 134

Kant, Immanuel 1724-1804 . . . . . . **NCLC 27**
See also DLB 94

Kantor, MacKinlay 1904-1977 . . . . . . CLC 7
See also CA 61-64; 73-76; DLB 9, 102

Kaplan, David Michael 1946- . . . . . . CLC 50

Kaplan, James 1951- . . . . CLC 59
See also CA 135

Karageorge, Michael
See Anderson, Poul (William)

Karamzin, Nikolai Mikhailovich
1766-1826 . . . . NCLC 3
See also DLB 150

Karapanou, Margarita 1946- . . . . CLC 13
See also CA 101

Karinthy, Frigyes 1887-1938 . . . . . . TCLC 47

Karl, Frederick R(obert) 1927- . . . . . CLC 34
See also CA 5-8R; CANR 3, 44

Kastel, Warren
See Silverberg, Robert

Kataev, Evgeny Petrovich 1903-1942
See Petrov, Evgeny
See also CA 120

Kataphusin
See Ruskin, John

Katz, Steve 1935- . . . . CLC 47
See also CA 25-28R; CAAS 14; CANR 12;
DLBY 83

Kauffman, Janet 1945- . . . . CLC 42
See also CA 117; CANR 43; DLBY 86

Kaufman, Bob (Garnell)
1925-1986 . . . . CLC 49
See also BW 1; CA 41-44R; 118; CANR 22;
DLB 16, 41

Kaufman, George S. 1889-1961 . . . . . CLC 38
See also CA 108; 93-96; DLB 7

Kaufman, Sue . . . . CLC 3, 8
See also Barondess, Sue K(aufman)

Kavafis, Konstantinos Petrou 1863-1933
See Cavafy, C(onstantine) P(eter)
See also CA 104

Kavan, Anna 1901-1968 . . . . . . CLC 5, 13, 82
See also CA 5-8R; CANR 6; MTCW

Kavanagh, Dan
See Barnes, Julian

Kavanagh, Patrick (Joseph)
1904-1967 . . . . CLC 22
See also CA 123; 25-28R; DLB 15, 20;
MTCW

Kawabata, Yasunari
1899-1972 . . . . . CLC 2, 5, 9, 18; SSC 17
See also CA 93-96; 33-36R

Kaye, M(ary) M(argaret) 1909- . . . . . CLC 28
See also CA 89-92; CANR 24; MTCW;
SATA 62

Kaye, Mollie
See Kaye, M(ary) M(argaret)

Kaye-Smith, Sheila 1887-1956 . . . . . TCLC 20
See also CA 118; DLB 36

Kaymor, Patrice Maguilene
See Senghor, Leopold Sedar

Kazan, Elia 1909- . . . . CLC 6, 16, 63
See also CA 21-24R; CANR 32

Kazantzakis, Nikos
1883(?)-1957 . . . . TCLC 2, 5, 33
See also CA 105; 132; MTCW

Kazin, Alfred 1915- . . . . CLC 34, 38
See also CA 1-4R; CAAS 7; CANR 1, 45;
DLB 67

Keane, Mary Nesta (Skrine) 1904-
See Keane, Molly
See also CA 108; 114

Keane, Molly . . . . CLC 31
See also Keane, Mary Nesta (Skrine)

Keates, Jonathan 19(?)- . . . . CLC 34

Keaton, Buster 1895-1966 . . . . CLC 20

Keats, John
1795-1821 . . . . NCLC 8; DA; DAB;
PC 1; WLC
See also CDBLB 1789-1832; DLB 96, 110

Keene, Donald 1922- . . . . CLC 34
See also CA 1-4R; CANR 5

Keillor, Garrison . . . . CLC 40
See also Keillor, Gary (Edward)
See also AAYA 2; BEST 89:3; DLBY 87;
SATA 58

Keillor, Gary (Edward) 1942-
See Keillor, Garrison
See also CA 111; 117; CANR 36; MTCW

Keith, Michael
See Hubbard, L(afayette) Ron(ald)

Keller, Gottfried 1819-1890 . . . . . . NCLC 2
See also DLB 129

Kellerman, Jonathan 1949- . . . . CLC 44
See also BEST 90:1; CA 106; CANR 29

Kelley, William Melvin 1937- . . . . . . CLC 22
See also BW 1; CA 77-80; CANR 27;
DLB 33

Kellogg, Marjorie 1922- . . . . CLC 2
See also CA 81-84

Kellow, Kathleen
See Hibbert, Eleanor Alice Burford

Kelly, M(ilton) T(erry) 1947- . . . . . . CLC 55
See also CA 97-100; CAAS 22; CANR 19,
43

Kelman, James 1946- . . . . CLC 58, 86
See also CA 148

Kemal, Yashar 1923- . . . . CLC 14, 29
See also CA 89-92; CANR 44

Kemble, Fanny 1809-1893 . . . . NCLC 18
See also DLB 32

Kemelman, Harry 1908- . . . . CLC 2
See also AITN 1; CA 9-12R; CANR 6;
DLB 28

Kempe, Margery 1373(?)-1440(?) . . . . . LC 6
See also DLB 146

Kempis, Thomas a 1380-1471 . . . . . . LC 11

Kendall, Henry 1839-1882 . . . . . . NCLC 12

Keneally, Thomas (Michael)
1935- . . . . . . CLC 5, 8, 10, 14, 19, 27, 43
See also CA 85-88; CANR 10; MTCW

Kennedy, Adrienne (Lita)
1931- . . . . CLC 66; BLC; DC 5
See also BW 2; CA 103; CAAS 20; CABS 3;
CANR 26; DLB 38

Kennedy, John Pendleton
1795-1870 . . . . NCLC 2
See also DLB 3

Kennedy, Joseph Charles 1929-
See Kennedy, X. J.
See also CA 1-4R; CANR 4, 30, 40;
SATA 14

Kennedy, William 1928-... CLC 6, 28, 34, 53
See also AAYA 1; CA 85-88; CANR 14,
31; DLB 143; DLBY 85; MTCW;
SATA 57

Kennedy, X. J. . . . . CLC 8, 42
See also Kennedy, Joseph Charles
See also CAAS 9; CLR 27; DLB 5

Kenny, Maurice (Francis) 1929- . . . . CLC 87
See also CA 144; CAAS 22; NNAL

Kent, Kelvin
See Kuttner, Henry

Kenton, Maxwell
See Southern, Terry

Kenyon, Robert O.
See Kuttner, Henry

Kerouac, Jack . . . . . CLC 1, 2, 3, 5, 14, 29, 61
See also Kerouac, Jean-Louis Lebris de
See also CDALB 1941-1968; DLB 2, 16;
DLBD 3

Kerouac, Jean-Louis Lebris de 1922-1969
See Kerouac, Jack
See also AITN 1; CA 5-8R; 25-28R;
CANR 26; DA; DAB; MTCW; WLC

Kerr, Jean 1923- . . . . CLC 22
See also CA 5-8R; CANR 7

Kerr, M. E. . . . . CLC 12, 35
See also Meaker, Marijane (Agnes)
See also AAYA 2; CLR 29; SAAS 1

Kerr, Robert . . . . CLC 55

Kerrigan, (Thomas) Anthony
1918- . . . . CLC 4, 6
See also CA 49-52; CAAS 11; CANR 4

Kerry, Lois
See Duncan, Lois

Kesey, Ken (Elton)
1935- . . . . . . CLC 1, 3, 6, 11, 46, 64; DA;
DAB; WLC
See also CA 1-4R; CANR 22, 38;
CDALB 1968-1988; DLB 2, 16; MTCW;
SATA 66

Kesselring, Joseph (Otto)
1902-1967 . . . . CLC 45

Kessler, Jascha (Frederick) 1929-. . . . CLC 4
See also CA 17-20R; CANR 8, 48

Kettelkamp, Larry (Dale) 1933- . . . . CLC 12
See also CA 29-32R; CANR 16; SAAS 3;
SATA 2

Keyber, Conny
See Fielding, Henry

Keyes, Daniel 1927- . . . . CLC 80; DA
See also CA 17-20R; CANR 10, 26;
SATA 37

Khanshendel, Chiron
See Rose, Wendy

Khayyam, Omar
1048-1131 . . . . CMLC 11; PC 8

Kherdian, David 1931- . . . . CLC 6, 9
See also CA 21-24R; CAAS 2; CANR 39;
CLR 24; JRDA; MAICYA; SATA 16, 74

Khlebnikov, Velimir . . . . TCLC 20
See also Khlebnikov, Viktor Vladimirovich

Khlebnikov, Viktor Vladimirovich   1885-1922
 See Khlebnikov, Velimir
 See also CA 117

Khodasevich, Vladislav (Felitsianovich)
  1886-1939 .... **TCLC 15**
 See also CA 115

Kielland, Alexander Lange
  1849-1906 .... **TCLC 5**
 See also CA 104

Kiely, Benedict   1919-......... **CLC 23, 43**
 See also CA 1-4R; CANR 2; DLB 15

Kienzle, William X(avier)   1928- .... **CLC 25**
 See also CA 93-96; CAAS 1; CANR 9, 31;
  MTCW

Kierkegaard, Soren   1813-1855.... **NCLC 34**

Killens, John Oliver   1916-1987..... **CLC 10**
 See also BW 2; CA 77-80; 123; CAAS 2;
  CANR 26; DLB 33

Killigrew, Anne   1660-1685.......... **LC 4**
 See also DLB 131

Kim
 See Simenon, Georges (Jacques Christian)

Kincaid, Jamaica   1949- ... **CLC 43, 68; BLC**
 See also AAYA 13; BW 2; CA 125;
  CANR 47

King, Francis (Henry)   1923- ..... **CLC 8, 53**
 See also CA 1-4R; CANR 1, 33; DLB 15,
  139; MTCW

King, Martin Luther, Jr.
  1929-1968 .... **CLC 83; BLC; DA; DAB**
 See also BW 2; CA 25-28; CANR 27, 44;
  CAP 2; MTCW; SATA 14

King, Stephen (Edwin)
  1947- ...... **CLC 12, 26, 37, 61; SSC 17**
 See also AAYA 1; BEST 90:1; CA 61-64;
  CANR 1, 30; DLB 143; DLBY 80;
  JRDA; MTCW; SATA 9, 55

King, Steve
 See King, Stephen (Edwin)

King, Thomas   1943-.............. **CLC 89**
 See also CA 144; NNAL

Kingman, Lee...................... **CLC 17**
 See also Natti, (Mary) Lee
 See also SAAS 3; SATA 1, 67

Kingsley, Charles   1819-1875 ..... **NCLC 35**
 See also DLB 21, 32; YABC 2

Kingsley, Sidney   1906-1995....... **CLC 44**
 See also CA 85-88; 147; DLB 7

Kingsolver, Barbara   1955-...... **CLC 55, 81**
 See also AAYA 15; CA 129; 134

Kingston, Maxine (Ting Ting) Hong
  1940-.................. **CLC 12, 19, 58**
 See also AAYA 8; CA 69-72; CANR 13,
  38; DLBY 80; MTCW; SATA 53

Kinnell, Galway
  1927-.......... **CLC 1, 2, 3, 5, 13, 29**
 See also CA 9-12R; CANR 10, 34; DLB 5;
  DLBY 87; MTCW

Kinsella, Thomas   1928- .... **CLC 4, 19**
 See also CA 17-20R; CANR 15; DLB 27;
  MTCW

Kinsella, W(illiam) P(atrick)
  1935-................... **CLC 27, 43**
 See also AAYA 7; CA 97-100; CAAS 7;
  CANR 21, 35; MTCW

Kipling, (Joseph) Rudyard
  1865-1936 ...... **TCLC 8, 17; DA; DAB;**
           PC 3; SSC 5; WLC
 See also CA 105; 120; CLR 39; DLB 19, 34,
  141, 156; MAICYA; MTCW; YABC 2

Kirkup, James   1918- .... **CLC 1**
 See also CA 1-4R; CAAS 4; CANR 2;
  DLB 27; SATA 12

Kirkwood, James   1930(?)-1989 ...... **CLC 9**
 See also AITN 2; CA 1-4R; 128; CANR 6,
  40

Kirshner, Sidney
 See Kingsley, Sidney

Kis, Danilo   1935-1989 .... **CLC 57**
 See also CA 109; 118; 129; MTCW

Kivi, Aleksis   1834-1872 .... **NCLC 30**

Kizer, Carolyn (Ashley)
  1925-................. **CLC 15, 39, 80**
 See also CA 65-68; CAAS 5; CANR 24;
  DLB 5

Klabund   1890-1928.............. **TCLC 44**
 See also DLB 66

Klappert, Peter   1942-............. **CLC 57**
 See also CA 33-36R; DLB 5

Klein, A(braham) M(oses)
  1909-1972 .... **CLC 19; DAB**
 See also CA 101; 37-40R; DLB 68

Klein, Norma   1938-1989 .... **CLC 30**
 See also AAYA 2; CA 41-44R; 128;
  CANR 15, 37; CLR 2, 19; JRDA;
  MAICYA; SAAS 1; SATA 7, 57

Klein, T(heodore) E(ibon) D(onald)
  1947- .... **CLC 34**
 See also CA 119; CANR 44

Kleist, Heinrich von
  1777-1811 .... **NCLC 2, 37**
 See also DLB 90

Klima, Ivan   1931-................ **CLC 56**
 See also CA 25-28R; CANR 17

Klimentov, Andrei Platonovich   1899-1951
 See Platonov, Andrei
 See also CA 108

Klinger, Friedrich Maximilian von
  1752-1831 .... **NCLC 1**
 See also DLB 94

Klopstock, Friedrich Gottlieb
  1724-1803 .... **NCLC 11**
 See also DLB 97

Knebel, Fletcher   1911-1993........ **CLC 14**
 See also AITN 1; CA 1-4R; 140; CAAS 3;
  CANR 1, 36; SATA 36; SATA-Obit 75

Knickerbocker, Diedrich
 See Irving, Washington

Knight, Etheridge
  1931-1991 .... **CLC 40; BLC**
 See also BW 1; CA 21-24R; 133; CANR 23;
  DLB 41

Knight, Sarah Kemble   1666-1727 ..... **LC 7**
 See also DLB 24

Knister, Raymond   1899-1932...... **TCLC 56**
 See also DLB 68

Knowles, John
  1926-........... **CLC 1, 4, 10, 26; DA**
 See also AAYA 10; CA 17-20R; CANR 40;
  CDALB 1968-1988; DLB 6; MTCW;
  SATA 8

Knox, Calvin M.
 See Silverberg, Robert

Knye, Cassandra
 See Disch, Thomas M(ichael)

Koch, C(hristopher) J(ohn)   1932-- ... **CLC 42**
 See also CA 127

Koch, Christopher
 See Koch, C(hristopher) J(ohn)

Koch, Kenneth   1925- .... **CLC 5, 8, 44**
 See also CA 1-4R; CANR 6, 36; DLB 5;
  SATA 65

Kochanowski, Jan   1530-1584....... **LC 10**

Kock, Charles Paul de
  1794-1871 .... **NCLC 16**

Koda Shigeyuki   1867-1947
 See Rohan, Koda
 See also CA 121

Koestler, Arthur
  1905-1983 .... **CLC 1, 3, 6, 8, 15, 33**
 See also CA 1-4R; 109; CANR 1, 33;
  CDBLB 1945-1960; DLBY 83; MTCW

Kogawa, Joy Nozomi   1935-........ **CLC 78**
 See also CA 101; CANR 19

Kohout, Pavel   1928-.............. **CLC 13**
 See also CA 45-48; CANR 3

Koizumi, Yakumo
 See Hearn, (Patricio) Lafcadio (Tessima
  Carlos)

Kolmar, Gertrud   1894-1943...... **TCLC 40**

Komunyakaa, Yusef   1947-........ **CLC 86**
 See also CA 147; DLB 120

Konrad, George
 See Konrad, Gyoergy

Konrad, Gyoergy   1933- ...... **CLC 4, 10, 73**
 See also CA 85-88

Konwicki, Tadeusz   1926-..... **CLC 8, 28, 54**
 See also CA 101; CAAS 9; CANR 39;
  MTCW

Koontz, Dean R(ay)   1945-......... **CLC 78**
 See also AAYA 9; BEST 89:3, 90:2;
  CA 108; CANR 19, 36; MTCW

Kopit, Arthur (Lee)   1937- .... **CLC 1, 18, 33**
 See also AITN 1; CA 81-84; CABS 3;
  DLB 7; MTCW

Kops, Bernard   1926-.............. **CLC 4**
 See also CA 5-8R; DLB 13

Kornbluth, C(yril) M.   1923-1958.... **TCLC 8**
 See also CA 105; DLB 8

Korolenko, V. G.
 See Korolenko, Vladimir Galaktionovich

Korolenko, Vladimir
 See Korolenko, Vladimir Galaktionovich

Korolenko, Vladimir G.
 See Korolenko, Vladimir Galaktionovich

Korolenko, Vladimir Galaktionovich
  1853-1921 .... **TCLC 22**
 See also CA 121

Landwirth, Heinz 1927-
See Lind, Jakov
See also CA 9-12R; CANR 7

Lane, Patrick 1939- .... **CLC 25**
See also CA 97-100; DLB 53

Lang, Andrew 1844-1912 .... **TCLC 16**
See also CA 114; 137; DLB 98, 141;
MAICYA; SATA 16

Lang, Fritz 1890-1976 .... **CLC 20**
See also CA 77-80; 69-72; CANR 30

Lange, John
See Crichton, (John) Michael

Langer, Elinor 1939- .... **CLC 34**
See also CA 121

Langland, William
1330(?)-1400(?) ...... **LC 19; DA; DAB**
See also DLB 146

Langstaff, Launcelot
See Irving, Washington

Lanier, Sidney 1842-1881 .... **NCLC 6**
See also DLB 64; MAICYA; SATA 18

Lanyer, Aemilia 1569-1645 ...... **LC 10, 30**
See also DLB 121

Lao Tzu .... **CMLC 7**

Lapine, James (Elliot) 1949- .... **CLC 39**
See also CA 123; 130

Larbaud, Valery (Nicolas)
1881-1957 .... **TCLC 9**
See also CA 106

Lardner, Ring
See Lardner, Ring(gold) W(ilmer)

Lardner, Ring W., Jr.
See Lardner, Ring(gold) W(ilmer)

Lardner, Ring(gold) W(ilmer)
1885-1933 .... **TCLC 2, 14**
See also CA 104; 131; CDALB 1917-1929;
DLB 11, 25, 86; MTCW

Laredo, Betty
See Codrescu, Andrei

Larkin, Maia
See Wojciechowska, Maia (Teresa)

Larkin, Philip (Arthur)
1922-1985 .... **CLC 3, 5, 8, 9, 13, 18, 33,
39, 64; DAB**
See also CA 5-8R; 117; CANR 24;
CDBLB 1960 to Present; DLB 27;
MTCW

Larra (y Sanchez de Castro), Mariano Jose de
1809-1837 .... **NCLC 17**

Larsen, Eric 1941- .... **CLC 55**
See also CA 132

Larsen, Nella 1891-1964 ..... **CLC 37; BLC**
See also BW 1; CA 125; DLB 51

Larson, Charles R(aymond) 1938- ... **CLC 31**
See also CA 53-56; CANR 4

Las Casas, Bartolome de 1474-1566 .. **LC 31**

Lasker-Schueler, Else 1869-1945 .. **TCLC 57**
See also DLB 66, 124

Latham, Jean Lee 1902- .... **CLC 12**
See also AITN 1; CA 5-8R; CANR 7;
MAICYA; SATA 2, 68

Latham, Mavis
See Clark, Mavis Thorpe

Lathen, Emma .... **CLC 2**
See also Hennissart, Martha; Latsis, Mary
J(ane)

Lathrop, Francis
See Leiber, Fritz (Reuter, Jr.)

Latsis, Mary J(ane)
See Lathen, Emma
See also CA 85-88

Lattimore, Richmond (Alexander)
1906-1984 .... **CLC 3**
See also CA 1-4R; 112; CANR 1

Laughlin, James 1914- .... **CLC 49**
See also CA 21-24R; CAAS 22; CANR 9,
47; DLB 48

Laurence, (Jean) Margaret (Wemyss)
1926-1987 .. **CLC 3, 6, 13, 50, 62; SSC 7**
See also CA 5-8R; 121; CANR 33; DLB 53;
MTCW; SATA-Obit 50

Laurent, Antoine 1952- .... **CLC 50**

Lauscher, Hermann
See Hesse, Hermann

Lautreamont, Comte de
1846-1870 .... **NCLC 12; SSC 14**

Laverty, Donald
See Blish, James (Benjamin)

Lavin, Mary 1912- ...... **CLC 4, 18; SSC 4**
See also CA 9-12R; CANR 33; DLB 15;
MTCW

Lavond, Paul Dennis
See Kornbluth, C(yril) M.; Pohl, Frederik

Lawler, Raymond Evenor 1922- .... **CLC 58**
See also CA 103

Lawrence, D(avid) H(erbert Richards)
1885-1930 .... **TCLC 2, 9, 16, 33, 48, 61;
DA; DAB; SSC 4, 19; WLC**
See also CA 104; 121; CDBLB 1914-1945;
DLB 10, 19, 36, 98; MTCW

Lawrence, T(homas) E(dward)
1888-1935 .... **TCLC 18**
See also Dale, Colin
See also CA 115

Lawrence of Arabia
See Lawrence, T(homas) E(dward)

Lawson, Henry (Archibald Hertzberg)
1867-1922 .... **TCLC 27; SSC 18**
See also CA 120

Lawton, Dennis
See Faust, Frederick (Schiller)

Laxness, Halldor .... **CLC 25**
See also Gudjonsson, Halldor Kiljan

Layamon fl. c. 1200- .... **CMLC 10**
See also DLB 146

Laye, Camara 1928-1980 ... **CLC 4, 38; BLC**
See also BW 1; CA 85-88; 97-100;
CANR 25; MTCW

Layton, Irving (Peter) 1912- ..... **CLC 2, 15**
See also CA 1-4R; CANR 2, 33, 43;
DLB 88; MTCW

Lazarus, Emma 1849-1887 .... **NCLC 8**

Lazarus, Felix
See Cable, George Washington

Lazarus, Henry
See Slavitt, David R(ytman)

Lea, Joan
See Neufeld, John (Arthur)

Leacock, Stephen (Butler)
1869-1944 .... **TCLC 2**
See also CA 104; 141; DLB 92

Lear, Edward 1812-1888 .... **NCLC 3**
See also CLR 1; DLB 32; MAICYA;
SATA 18

Lear, Norman (Milton) 1922- ...... **CLC 12**
See also CA 73-76

Leavis, F(rank) R(aymond)
1895-1978 .... **CLC 24**
See also CA 21-24R; 77-80; CANR 44;
MTCW

Leavitt, David 1961- .... **CLC 34**
See also CA 116; 122; DLB 130

Leblanc, Maurice (Marie Emile)
1864-1941 .... **TCLC 49**
See also CA 110

Lebowitz, Fran(ces Ann)
1951(?)- .... **CLC 11, 36**
See also CA 81-84; CANR 14; MTCW

Lebrecht, Peter
See Tieck, (Johann) Ludwig

le Carre, John .... **CLC 3, 5, 9, 15, 28**
See also Cornwell, David (John Moore)
See also BEST 89:4; CDBLB 1960 to
Present; DLB 87

Le Clezio, J(ean) M(arie) G(ustave)
1940- .... **CLC 31**
See also CA 116; 128; DLB 83

Leconte de Lisle, Charles-Marie-Rene
1818-1894 .... **NCLC 29**

Le Coq, Monsieur
See Simenon, Georges (Jacques Christian)

Leduc, Violette 1907-1972 .... **CLC 22**
See also CA 13-14; 33-36R; CAP 1

Ledwidge, Francis 1887(?)-1917 ... **TCLC 23**
See also CA 123; DLB 20

Lee, Andrea 1953- .... **CLC 36; BLC**
See also BW 1; CA 125

Lee, Andrew
See Auchincloss, Louis (Stanton)

Lee, Don L. .... **CLC 2**
See also Madhubuti, Haki R.

Lee, George W(ashington)
1894-1976 .... **CLC 52; BLC**
See also BW 1; CA 125; DLB 51

Lee, (Nelle) Harper
1926- ..... **CLC 12, 60; DA; DAB; WLC**
See also AAYA 13; CA 13-16R;
CDALB 1941-1968; DLB 6; MTCW;
SATA 11

Lee, Helen Elaine 1959(?)- .... **CLC 86**
See also CA 148

Lee, Julian
See Latham, Jean Lee

Lee, Larry
See Lee, Lawrence

Lee, Laurie 1914- .... **CLC 90; DAB**
See also CA 77-80; CANR 33; DLB 27;
MTCW

Lee, Lawrence 1941-1990 .... **CLC 34**
See also CA 131; CANR 43

Lewisohn, Ludwig 1883-1955...... **TCLC 19**
See also CA 107; DLB 4, 9, 28, 102

Lezama Lima, Jose 1910-1976 ... **CLC 4, 10**
See also CA 77-80; DLB 113; HW

L'Heureux, John (Clarke) 1934-.... **CLC 52**
See also CA 13-16R; CANR 23, 45

Liddell, C. H.
See Kuttner, Henry

Lie, Jonas (Lauritz Idemil)
1833-1908(?) .... **TCLC 5**
See also CA 115

Lieber, Joel 1937-1971............ **CLC 6**
See also CA 73-76; 29-32R

Lieber, Stanley Martin
See Lee, Stan

Lieberman, Laurence (James)
1935-.................... **CLC 4, 36**
See also CA 17-20R; CANR 8, 36

Lieksman, Anders
See Haavikko, Paavo Juhani

Li Fei-kan 1904-
See Pa Chin
See also CA 105

Lifton, Robert Jay 1926-......... **CLC 67**
See also CA 17-20R; CANR 27; SATA 66

Lightfoot, Gordon 1938-.......... **CLC 26**
See also CA 109

Lightman, Alan P. 1948- .... **CLC 81**
See also CA 141

Ligotti, Thomas (Robert)
1953- .... **CLC 44; SSC 16**
See also CA 123; CANR 49

Li Ho 791-817.................... **PC 13**

Liliencron, (Friedrich Adolf Axel) Detlev von
1844-1909 .... **TCLC 18**
See also CA 117

Lilly, William 1602-1681.......... **LC 27**

Lima, Jose Lezama
See Lezama Lima, Jose

Lima Barreto, Afonso Henrique de
1881-1922 .... **TCLC 23**
See also CA 117

Limonov, Edward 1944-.......... **CLC 67**
See also CA 137

Lin, Frank
See Atherton, Gertrude (Franklin Horn)

Lincoln, Abraham 1809-1865..... **NCLC 18**

Lind, Jakov .... **CLC 1, 2, 4, 27, 82**
See also Landwirth, Heinz
See also CAAS 4

Lindbergh, Anne (Spencer) Morrow
1906-...................... **CLC 82**
See also CA 17-20R; CANR 16; MTCW;
SATA 33

Lindsay, David 1878-1945 .... **TCLC 15**
See also CA 113

Lindsay, (Nicholas) Vachel
1879-1931 .... **TCLC 17; DA; WLC**
See also CA 114; 135; CDALB 1865-1917;
DLB 54; SATA 40

Linke-Poot
See Doeblin, Alfred

Linney, Romulus 1930- .... **CLC 51**
See also CA 1-4R; CANR 40, 44

Linton, Eliza Lynn 1822-1898.... **NCLC 41**
See also DLB 18

Li Po 701-763................. **CMLC 2**

Lipsius, Justus 1547-1606 .... **LC 16**

Lipsyte, Robert (Michael)
1938-................. **CLC 21; DA**
See also AAYA 7; CA 17-20R; CANR 8;
CLR 23; JRDA; MAICYA; SATA 5, 68

Lish, Gordon (Jay) 1934-.. **CLC 45; SSC 18**
See also CA 113; 117; DLB 130

Lispector, Clarice 1925-1977...... **CLC 43**
See also CA 139; 116; DLB 113

Littell, Robert 1935(?)- .... **CLC 42**
See also CA 109; 112

Little, Malcolm 1925-1965
See Malcolm X
See also BW 1; CA 125; 111; DA; DAB;
MTCW

Littlewit, Humphrey Gent.
See Lovecraft, H(oward) P(hillips)

Litwos
See Sienkiewicz, Henryk (Adam Alexander
Pius)

Liu E 1857-1909................ **TCLC 15**
See also CA 115

Lively, Penelope (Margaret)
1933-.................. **CLC 32, 50**
See also CA 41-44R; CANR 29; CLR 7;
DLB 14; JRDA; MAICYA; MTCW;
SATA 7, 60

Livesay, Dorothy (Kathleen)
1909-.................. **CLC 4, 15, 79**
See also AITN 2; CA 25-28R; CAAS 8;
CANR 36; DLB 68; MTCW

Livy c. 59B.C.-c. 17 .... **CMLC 11**

Lizardi, Jose Joaquin Fernandez de
1776-1827 .... **NCLC 30**

Llewellyn, Richard
See Llewellyn Lloyd, Richard Dafydd
Vivian
See also DLB 15

Llewellyn Lloyd, Richard Dafydd Vivian
1906-1983 .... **CLC 7, 80**
See also Llewellyn, Richard
See also CA 53-56; 111; CANR 7;
SATA 11; SATA-Obit 37

Llosa, (Jorge) Mario (Pedro) Vargas
See Vargas Llosa, (Jorge) Mario (Pedro)

Lloyd Webber, Andrew 1948-
See Webber, Andrew Lloyd
See also AAYA 1; CA 116; SATA 56

Llull, Ramon c. 1235-c. 1316..... **CMLC 12**

Locke, Alain (Le Roy)
1886-1954 .... **TCLC 43**
See also BW 1; CA 106; 124; DLB 51

Locke, John 1632-1704 .... **LC 7**
See also DLB 101

Locke-Elliott, Sumner
See Elliott, Sumner Locke

Lockhart, John Gibson
1794-1854 .... **NCLC 6**
See also DLB 110, 116, 144

Lodge, David (John) 1935-........ **CLC 36**
See also BEST 90:1; CA 17-20R; CANR 19;
DLB 14; MTCW

Loennbohm, Armas Eino Leopold 1878-1926
See Leino, Eino
See also CA 123

Loewinsohn, Ron(ald William)
1937-...................... **CLC 52**
See also CA 25-28R

Logan, Jake
See Smith, Martin Cruz

Logan, John (Burton) 1923-1987..... **CLC 5**
See also CA 77-80; 124; CANR 45; DLB 5

Lo Kuan-chung 1330(?)-1400(?)...... **LC 12**

Lombard, Nap
See Johnson, Pamela Hansford

London, Jack.. **TCLC 9, 15, 39; SSC 4; WLC**
See also London, John Griffith
See also AAYA 13; AITN 2;
CDALB 1865-1917; DLB 8, 12, 78;
SATA 18

London, John Griffith 1876-1916
See London, Jack
See also CA 110; 119; DA; DAB; JRDA;
MAICYA; MTCW

Long, Emmett
See Leonard, Elmore (John, Jr.)

Longbaugh, Harry
See Goldman, William (W.)

Longfellow, Henry Wadsworth
1807-1882 ...... **NCLC 2, 45; DA; DAB**
See also CDALB 1640-1865; DLB 1, 59;
SATA 19

Longley, Michael 1939-.......... **CLC 29**
See also CA 102; DLB 40

Longus fl. c. 2nd cent. - .... **CMLC 7**

Longway, A. Hugh
See Lang, Andrew

Lopate, Phillip 1943- .... **CLC 29**
See also CA 97-100; DLBY 80

Lopez Portillo (y Pacheco), Jose
1920-.................... **CLC 46**
See also CA 129; HW

Lopez y Fuentes, Gregorio
1897(?)-1966 .... **CLC 32**
See also CA 131; HW

Lorca, Federico Garcia
See Garcia Lorca, Federico

Lord, Bette Bao 1938-............ **CLC 23**
See also BEST 90:3; CA 107; CANR 41;
SATA 58

Lord Auch
See Bataille, Georges

Lord Byron
See Byron, George Gordon (Noel)

Lorde, Audre (Geraldine)
1934-1992 .... **CLC 18, 71; BLC; PC 12**
See also BW 1; CA 25-28R; 142; CANR 16,
26, 46; DLB 41; MTCW

Lord Jeffrey
See Jeffrey, Francis

Lorenzo, Heberto Padilla
See Padilla (Lorenzo), Heberto

Loris
See Hofmannsthal, Hugo von

Loti, Pierre .... **TCLC 11**
See also Viaud, (Louis Marie) Julien
See also DLB 123

Louie, David Wong 1954- .... **CLC 70**
See also CA 139

Louis, Father M.
See Merton, Thomas

Lovecraft, H(oward) P(hillips)
1890-1937 .... **TCLC 4, 22; SSC 3**
See also AAYA 14; CA 104; 133; MTCW

Lovelace, Earl 1935-.............. **CLC 51**
See also BW 2; CA 77-80; CANR 41;
DLB 125; MTCW

Lovelace, Richard 1618-1657........ **LC 24**
See also DLB 131

Lowell, Amy 1874-1925 .. **TCLC 1, 8; PC 13**
See also CA 104; DLB 54, 140

Lowell, James Russell 1819-1891 .. **NCLC 2**
See also CDALB 1640-1865; DLB 1, 11, 64,
79

Lowell, Robert (Traill Spence, Jr.)
1917-1977 ... **CLC 1, 2, 3, 4, 5, 8, 9, 11,
15, 37; DA; DAB; PC 3; WLC**
See also CA 9-12R; 73-76; CABS 2;
CANR 26; DLB 5; MTCW

Lowndes, Marie Adelaide (Belloc)
1868-1947 .... **TCLC 12**
See also CA 107; DLB 70

Lowry, (Clarence) Malcolm
1909-1957 .... **TCLC 6, 40**
See also CA 105; 131; CDBLB 1945-1960;
DLB 15; MTCW

Lowry, Mina Gertrude 1882-1966
See Loy, Mina
See also CA 113

Loxsmith, John
See Brunner, John (Kilian Houston)

Loy, Mina .... **CLC 28**
See also Lowry, Mina Gertrude
See also DLB 4, 54

Loyson-Bridet
See Schwob, (Mayer Andre) Marcel

Lucas, Craig 1951- .... **CLC 64**
See also CA 137

Lucas, George 1944-.............. **CLC 16**
See also AAYA 1; CA 77-80; CANR 30;
SATA 56

Lucas, Hans
See Godard, Jean-Luc

Lucas, Victoria
See Plath, Sylvia

Ludlam, Charles 1943-1987..... **CLC 46, 50**
See also CA 85-88; 122

Ludlum, Robert 1927- .... **CLC 22, 43**
See also AAYA 10; BEST 89:1, 90:3;
CA 33-36R; CANR 25, 41; DLBY 82;
MTCW

Ludwig, Ken..................... **CLC 60**

Ludwig, Otto 1813-1865.......... **NCLC 4**
See also DLB 129

Lugones, Leopoldo 1874-1938 ..... **TCLC 15**
See also CA 116; 131; HW

Lu Hsun 1881-1936 ...... **TCLC 3; SSC 20**
See also Shu-Jen, Chou

Lukacs, George .... **CLC 24**
See also Lukacs, Gyorgy (Szegeny von)

Lukacs, Gyorgy (Szegeny von) 1885-1971
See Lukacs, George
See also CA 101; 29-32R

Luke, Peter (Ambrose Cyprian)
1919-1995 .... **CLC 38**
See also CA 81-84; 147; DLB 13

Lunar, Dennis
See Mungo, Raymond

Lurie, Alison 1926-........ **CLC 4, 5, 18, 39**
See also CA 1-4R; CANR 2, 17; DLB 2;
MTCW; SATA 46

Lustig, Arnost 1926-.............. **CLC 56**
See also AAYA 3; CA 69-72; CANR 47;
SATA 56

Luther, Martin 1483-1546 .... **LC 9**

Luzi, Mario 1914-................ **CLC 13**
See also CA 61-64; CANR 9; DLB 128

Lynch, B. Suarez
See Bioy Casares, Adolfo; Borges, Jorge
Luis

Lynch, David (K.) 1946-.......... **CLC 66**
See also CA 124; 129

Lynch, James
See Andreyev, Leonid (Nikolaevich)

Lynch Davis, B.
See Bioy Casares, Adolfo; Borges, Jorge
Luis

Lyndsay, Sir David 1490-1555 ...... **LC 20**

Lynn, Kenneth S(chuyler) 1923- .... **CLC 50**
See also CA 1-4R; CANR 3, 27

Lynx
See West, Rebecca

Lyons, Marcus
See Blish, James (Benjamin)

Lyre, Pinchbeck
See Sassoon, Siegfried (Lorraine)

Lytle, Andrew (Nelson) 1902-...... **CLC 22**
See also CA 9-12R; DLB 6

Lyttelton, George 1709-1773........ **LC 10**

Maas, Peter 1929- .... **CLC 29**
See also CA 93-96

Macaulay, Rose 1881-1958 ..... **TCLC 7, 44**
See also CA 104; DLB 36

Macaulay, Thomas Babington
1800-1859 .... **NCLC 42**
See also CDBLB 1832-1890; DLB 32, 55

MacBeth, George (Mann)
1932-1992 .... **CLC 2, 5, 9**
See also CA 25-28R; 136; DLB 40; MTCW;
SATA 4; SATA-Obit 70

MacCaig, Norman (Alexander)
1910- .... **CLC 36; DAB**
See also CA 9-12R; CANR 3, 34; DLB 27

MacCarthy, (Sir Charles Otto) Desmond
1877-1952 .... **TCLC 36**

MacDiarmid, Hugh
.... **CLC 2, 4, 11, 19, 63; PC 9**
See also Grieve, C(hristopher) M(urray)
See also CDBLB 1945-1960; DLB 20

MacDonald, Anson
See Heinlein, Robert A(nson)

Macdonald, Cynthia 1928-...... **CLC 13, 19**
See also CA 49-52; CANR 4, 44; DLB 105

MacDonald, George 1824-1905..... **TCLC 9**
See also CA 106; 137; DLB 18; MAICYA;
SATA 33

Macdonald, John
See Millar, Kenneth

MacDonald, John D(ann)
1916-1986 .... **CLC 3, 27, 44**
See also CA 1-4R; 121; CANR 1, 19;
DLB 8; DLBY 86; MTCW

Macdonald, John Ross
See Millar, Kenneth

Macdonald, Ross..... **CLC 1, 2, 3, 14, 34, 41**
See also Millar, Kenneth
See also DLBD 6

MacDougal, John
See Blish, James (Benjamin)

MacEwen, Gwendolyn (Margaret)
1941-1987 .... **CLC 13, 55**
See also CA 9-12R; 124; CANR 7, 22;
DLB 53; SATA 50; SATA-Obit 55

Macha, Karel Hynek 1810-1846.. **NCLC 46**

Machado (y Ruiz), Antonio
1875-1939 .... **TCLC 3**
See also CA 104; DLB 108

Machado de Assis, Joaquim Maria
1839-1908 .... **TCLC 10; BLC**
See also CA 107

Machen, Arthur.......... **TCLC 4; SSC 20**
See also Jones, Arthur Llewellyn
See also DLB 36, 156

Machiavelli, Niccolo
1469-1527 .... **LC 8; DA; DAB**

MacInnes, Colin 1914-1976...... **CLC 4, 23**
See also CA 69-72; 65-68; CANR 21;
DLB 14; MTCW

MacInnes, Helen (Clark)
1907-1985 .... **CLC 27, 39**
See also CA 1-4R; 117; CANR 1, 28;
DLB 87; MTCW; SATA 22;
SATA-Obit 44

Mackay, Mary 1855-1924
See Corelli, Marie
See also CA 118

Mackenzie, Compton (Edward Montague)
1883-1972 .... **CLC 18**
See also CA 21-22; 37-40R; CAP 2;
DLB 34, 100

Mackenzie, Henry 1745-1831 .... **NCLC 41**
See also DLB 39

Mackintosh, Elizabeth 1896(?)-1952
See Tey, Josephine
See also CA 110

MacLaren, James
See Grieve, C(hristopher) M(urray)

Mac Laverty, Bernard 1942-....... **CLC 31**
See also CA 116; 118; CANR 43

MacLean, Alistair (Stuart)
1922-1987....... **CLC 3, 13, 50, 63**
See also CA 57-60; 121; CANR 28; MTCW;
SATA 23; SATA-Obit 50

Maclean, Norman (Fitzroy)
1902-1990 . . . . CLC 78; SSC 13
See also CA 102; 132; CANR 49

MacLeish, Archibald
1892-1982 . . . . CLC 3, 8, 14, 68
See also CA 9-12R; 106; CANR 33; DLB 4,
7, 45; DLBY 82; MTCW

MacLennan, (John) Hugh
1907-1990 . . . . CLC 2, 14
See also CA 5-8R; 142; CANR 33; DLB 68;
MTCW

MacLeod, Alistair   1936- . . . . CLC 56
See also CA 123; DLB 60

MacNeice, (Frederick) Louis
1907-1963 . . . . . . CLC 1, 4, 10, 53; DAB
See also CA 85-88; DLB 10, 20; MTCW

MacNeill, Dand
See Fraser, George MacDonald

Macpherson, James   1736-1796 . . . . . . LC 29
See also DLB 109

Macpherson, (Jean) Jay   1931- . . . . . . CLC 14
See also CA 5-8R; DLB 53

MacShane, Frank   1927- . . . . CLC 39
See also CA 9-12R; CANR 3, 33; DLB 111

Macumber, Mari
See Sandoz, Mari(e Susette)

Madach, Imre   1823-1864 . . . . NCLC 19

Madden, (Jerry) David   1933- . . . . CLC 5, 15
See also CA 1-4R; CAAS 3; CANR 4, 45;
DLB 6; MTCW

Maddern, Al(an)
See Ellison, Harlan (Jay)

Madhubuti, Haki R.
1942- . . . . CLC 6, 73; BLC; PC 5
See also Lee, Don L.
See also BW 2; CA 73-76; CANR 24;
DLB 5, 41; DLBD 8

Maepenn, Hugh
See Kuttner, Henry

Maepenn, K. H.
See Kuttner, Henry

Maeterlinck, Maurice   1862-1949 . . . TCLC 3
See also CA 104; 136; SATA 66

Maginn, William   1794-1842 . . . . . . NCLC 8
See also DLB 110

Mahapatra, Jayanta   1928- . . . . CLC 33
See also CA 73-76; CAAS 9; CANR 15, 33

Mahfouz, Naguib (Abdel Aziz Al-Sabilgi)
1911(?)-
See Mahfuz, Najib
See also BEST 89:2; CA 128; MTCW

Mahfuz, Najib . . . . CLC 52, 55
See also Mahfouz, Naguib (Abdel Aziz
Al-Sabilgi)
See also DLBY 88

Mahon, Derek   1941- . . . . CLC 27
See also CA 113; 128; DLB 40

Mailer, Norman
1923- . . . . . . CLC 1, 2, 3, 4, 5, 8, 11, 14,
28, 39, 74; DA; DAB
See also AITN 2; CA 9-12R; CABS 1;
CANR 28; CDALB 1968-1988; DLB 2,
16, 28; DLBD 3; DLBY 80, 83; MTCW

Maillet, Antonine   1929- . . . . CLC 54
See also CA 115; 120; CANR 46; DLB 60

Mais, Roger   1905-1955 . . . . TCLC 8
See also BW 1; CA 105; 124; DLB 125;
MTCW

Maistre, Joseph de   1753-1821 . . . . NCLC 37

Maitland, Sara (Louise)   1950- . . . . . . CLC 49
See also CA 69-72; CANR 13

Major, Clarence
1936- . . . . CLC 3, 19, 48; BLC
See also BW 2; CA 21-24R; CAAS 6;
CANR 13, 25; DLB 33

Major, Kevin (Gerald)   1949- . . . . . . CLC 26
See also CA 97-100; CANR 21, 38;
CLR 11; DLB 60; JRDA; MAICYA;
SATA 32, 82

Maki, James
See Ozu, Yasujiro

Malabaila, Damiano
See Levi, Primo

Malamud, Bernard
1914-1986 . . . . . . CLC 1, 2, 3, 5, 8, 9, 11,
18, 27, 44, 78, 85; DA; DAB; SSC 15;
WLC
See also CA 5-8R; 118; CABS 1; CANR 28;
CDALB 1941-1968; DLB 2, 28, 152;
DLBY 80, 86; MTCW

Malaparte, Curzio   1898-1957 . . . . . TCLC 52

Malcolm, Dan
See Silverberg, Robert

Malcolm X . . . . CLC 82; BLC
See also Little, Malcolm

Malherbe, Francois de   1555-1628 . . . . . LC 5

Mallarme, Stephane
1842-1898 . . . . NCLC 4, 41; PC 4

Mallet-Joris, Francoise   1930- . . . . . . CLC 11
See also CA 65-68; CANR 17; DLB 83

Malley, Ern
See McAuley, James Phillip

Mallowan, Agatha Christie
See Christie, Agatha (Mary Clarissa)

Maloff, Saul   1922- . . . . CLC 5
See also CA 33-36R

Malone, Louis
See MacNeice, (Frederick) Louis

Malone, Michael (Christopher)
1942- . . . . CLC 43
See also CA 77-80; CANR 14, 32

Malory, (Sir) Thomas
1410(?)-1471(?) . . . . LC 11; DA; DAB
See also CDBLB Before 1660; DLB 146;
SATA 59; SATA-Brief 33

Malouf, (George Joseph) David
1934- . . . . CLC 28, 86
See also CA 124

Malraux, (Georges-)Andre
1901-1976 . . . . . . CLC 1, 4, 9, 13, 15, 57
See also CA 21-22; 69-72; CANR 34;
CAP 2; DLB 72; MTCW

Malzberg, Barry N(athaniel)   1939- . . . CLC 7
See also CA 61-64; CAAS 4; CANR 16;
DLB 8

Mamet, David (Alan)
1947- . . . . CLC 9, 15, 34, 46; DC 4
See also AAYA 3; CA 81-84; CABS 3;
CANR 15, 41; DLB 7; MTCW

Mamoulian, Rouben (Zachary)
1897-1987 . . . . CLC 16
See also CA 25-28R; 124

Mandelstam, Osip (Emilievich)
1891(?)-1938(?) . . . . TCLC 2, 6
See also CA 104

Mander, (Mary) Jane   1877-1949 . . . TCLC 31

Mandiargues, Andre Pieyre de . . . . . . CLC 41
See also Pieyre de Mandiargues, Andre
See also DLB 83

Mandrake, Ethel Belle
See Thurman, Wallace (Henry)

Mangan, James Clarence
1803-1849 . . . . NCLC 27

Maniere, J.-E.
See Giraudoux, (Hippolyte) Jean

Manley, (Mary) Delariviere
1672(?)-1724 . . . . LC 1
See also DLB 39, 80

Mann, Abel
See Creasey, John

Mann, (Luiz) Heinrich   1871-1950 . . . TCLC 9
See also CA 106; DLB 66

Mann, (Paul) Thomas
1875-1955 . . . . TCLC 2, 8, 14, 21, 35, 44,
60; DA; DAB; SSC 5; WLC
See also CA 104; 128; DLB 66; MTCW

Manning, David
See Faust, Frederick (Schiller)

Manning, Frederic   1887(?)-1935 . . . TCLC 25
See also CA 124

Manning, Olivia   1915-1980 . . . . . . CLC 5, 19
See also CA 5-8R; 101; CANR 29; MTCW

Mano, D. Keith   1942- . . . . CLC 2, 10
See also CA 25-28R; CAAS 6; CANR 26;
DLB 6

Mansfield, Katherine
. . . . . TCLC 2, 8, 39; DAB; SSC 9; WLC
See also Beauchamp, Kathleen Mansfield

Manso, Peter   1940- . . . . CLC 39
See also CA 29-32R; CANR 44

Mantecon, Juan Jimenez
See Jimenez (Mantecon), Juan Ramon

Manton, Peter
See Creasey, John

Man Without a Spleen, A
See Chekhov, Anton (Pavlovich)

Manzoni, Alessandro   1785-1873 . . NCLC 29

Mapu, Abraham (ben Jekutiel)
1808-1867 . . . . NCLC 18

Mara, Sally
See Queneau, Raymond

Marat, Jean Paul   1743-1793 . . . . LC 10

Marcel, Gabriel Honore
1889-1973 . . . . CLC 15
See also CA 102; 45-48; MTCW

Marchbanks, Samuel
See Davies, (William) Robertson

Marchi, Giacomo
See Bassani, Giorgio

Margulies, Donald . . . . CLC 76

Marie de France   c. 12th cent. - . . . . CMLC 8

Marie de l'Incarnation   1599-1672 . . . . LC 10

Mauriac, Claude 1914-............ CLC 9
See also CA 89-92; DLB 83

Mauriac, Francois (Charles)
1885-1970 .... CLC 4, 9, 56
See also CA 25-28; CAP 2; DLB 65;
MTCW

Mavor, Osborne Henry 1888-1951
See Bridie, James
See also CA 104

Maxwell, William (Keepers, Jr.)
1908-...................... CLC 19
See also CA 93-96; DLBY 80

May, Elaine 1932- .... CLC 16
See also CA 124; 142; DLB 44

Mayakovski, Vladimir (Vladimirovich)
1893-1930 .... TCLC 4, 18
See also CA 104

Mayhew, Henry 1812-1887 ...... NCLC 31
See also DLB 18, 55

Mayle, Peter 1939(?)-............ CLC 89
See also CA 139

Maynard, Joyce 1953-............ CLC 23
See also CA 111; 129

Mayne, William (James Carter)
1928-...................... CLC 12
See also CA 9-12R; CANR 37; CLR 25;
JRDA; MAICYA; SAAS 11; SATA 6, 68

Mayo, Jim
See L'Amour, Louis (Dearborn)

Maysles, Albert 1926- .... CLC 16
See also CA 29-32R

Maysles, David 1932-............ CLC 16

Mazer, Norma Fox 1931- .... CLC 26
See also AAYA 5; CA 69-72; CANR 12,
32; CLR 23; JRDA; MAICYA; SAAS 1;
SATA 24, 67

Mazzini, Guiseppe 1805-1872 .... NCLC 34

McAuley, James Phillip
1917-1976 .... CLC 45
See also CA 97-100

McBain, Ed
See Hunter, Evan

McBrien, William Augustine
1930-...................... CLC 44
See also CA 107

McCaffrey, Anne (Inez) 1926-...... CLC 17
See also AAYA 6; AITN 2; BEST 89:2;
CA 25-28R; CANR 15, 35; DLB 8;
JRDA; MAICYA; MTCW; SAAS 11;
SATA 8, 70

McCall, Nathan 1955(?)-.......... CLC 86
See also CA 146

McCann, Arthur
See Campbell, John W(ood, Jr.)

McCann, Edson
See Pohl, Frederik

McCarthy, Charles, Jr. 1933-
See McCarthy, Cormac
See also CANR 42

McCarthy, Cormac 1933-..... CLC 4, 57, 59
See also McCarthy, Charles, Jr.
See also DLB 6, 143

McCarthy, Mary (Therese)
1912-1989 ... CLC 1, 3, 5, 14, 24, 39, 59
See also CA 5-8R; 129; CANR 16; DLB 2;
DLBY 81; MTCW

McCartney, (James) Paul
1942-.................... CLC 12, 35
See also CA 146

McCauley, Stephen (D.) 1955- ..... CLC 50
See also CA 141

McClure, Michael (Thomas)
1932-.................... CLC 6, 10
See also CA 21-24R; CANR 17, 46;
DLB 16

McCorkle, Jill (Collins) 1958-...... CLC 51
See also CA 121; DLBY 87

McCourt, James 1941-............ CLC 5
See also CA 57-60

McCoy, Horace (Stanley)
1897-1955 .... TCLC 28
See also CA 108; DLB 9

McCrae, John 1872-1918........ TCLC 12
See also CA 109; DLB 92

McCreigh, James
See Pohl, Frederik

McCullers, (Lula) Carson (Smith)
1917-1967 .... CLC 1, 4, 10, 12, 48; DA;
DAB; SSC 9; WLC
See also CA 5-8R; 25-28R; CABS 1, 3;
CANR 18; CDALB 1941-1968; DLB 2, 7;
MTCW; SATA 27

McCulloch, John Tyler
See Burroughs, Edgar Rice

McCullough, Colleen 1938(?)-...... CLC 27
See also CA 81-84; CANR 17, 46; MTCW

McDermott, Alice 1953- .... CLC 90
See also CA 109; CANR 40

McElroy, Joseph 1930- .... CLC 5, 47
See also CA 17-20R

McEwan, Ian (Russell) 1948- ... CLC 13, 66
See also BEST 90:4; CA 61-64; CANR 14,
41; DLB 14; MTCW

McFadden, David 1940-.......... CLC 48
See also CA 104; DLB 60

McFarland, Dennis 1950- .... CLC 65

McGahern, John
1934-.......... CLC 5, 9, 48; SSC 17
See also CA 17-20R; CANR 29; DLB 14;
MTCW

McGinley, Patrick (Anthony)
1937-...................... CLC 41
See also CA 120; 127

McGinley, Phyllis 1905-1978 ...... CLC 14
See also CA 9-12R; 77-80; CANR 19;
DLB 11, 48; SATA 2, 44; SATA-Obit 24

McGinniss, Joe 1942-............ CLC 32
See also AITN 2; BEST 89:2; CA 25-28R;
CANR 26

McGivern, Maureen Daly
See Daly, Maureen

McGrath, Patrick 1950-.......... CLC 55
See also CA 136

McGrath, Thomas (Matthew)
1916-1990 .... CLC 28, 59
See also CA 9-12R; 132; CANR 6, 33;
MTCW; SATA 41; SATA-Obit 66

McGuane, Thomas (Francis III)
1939-................CLC 3, 7, 18, 45
See also AITN 2; CA 49-52; CANR 5, 24,
49; DLB 2; DLBY 80; MTCW

McGuckian, Medbh 1950-........ CLC 48
See also CA 143; DLB 40

McHale, Tom 1942(?)-1982....... CLC 3, 5
See also AITN 1; CA 77-80; 106

McIlvanney, William 1936-........ CLC 42
See also CA 25-28R; DLB 14

McIlwraith, Maureen Mollie Hunter
See Hunter, Mollie
See also SATA 2

McInerney, Jay 1955- .... CLC 34
See also CA 116; 123; CANR 45

McIntyre, Vonda N(eel) 1948- ..... CLC 18
See also CA 81-84; CANR 17, 34; MTCW

McKay, Claude
.... TCLC 7, 41; BLC; DAB; PC 2
See also McKay, Festus Claudius
See also DLB 4, 45, 51, 117

McKay, Festus Claudius 1889-1948
See McKay, Claude
See also BW 1; CA 104; 124; DA; MTCW;
WLC

McKuen, Rod 1933-............. CLC 1, 3
See also AITN 1; CA 41-44R; CANR 40

McLoughlin, R. B.
See Mencken, H(enry) L(ouis)

McLuhan, (Herbert) Marshall
1911-1980 .... CLC 37, 83
See also CA 9-12R; 102; CANR 12, 34;
DLB 88; MTCW

McMillan, Terry (L.) 1951-..... CLC 50, 61
See also BW 2; CA 140

McMurtry, Larry (Jeff)
1936-.......... CLC 2, 3, 7, 11, 27, 44
See also AAYA 15; AITN 2; BEST 89:2;
CA 5-8R; CANR 19, 43;
CDALB 1968-1988; DLB 2, 143;
DLBY 80, 87; MTCW

McNally, T. M. 1961- .... CLC 82

McNally, Terrence 1939-...... CLC 4, 7, 41
See also CA 45-48; CANR 2; DLB 7

McNamer, Deirdre 1950-.......... CLC 70

McNeile, Herman Cyril 1888-1937
See Sapper
See also DLB 77

McNickle, (William) D'Arcy
1904-1977 .... CLC 89
See also CA 9-12R; 85-88; CANR 5, 45;
NNAL; SATA-Obit 22

McPhee, John (Angus) 1931- ...... CLC 36
See also BEST 90:1; CA 65-68; CANR 20,
46; MTCW

McPherson, James Alan
1943-.................... CLC 19, 77
See also BW 1; CA 25-28R; CAAS 17;
CANR 24; DLB 38; MTCW

McPherson, William (Alexander)
1933-...................... CLC 34
See also CA 69-72; CANR 28

Mead, Margaret 1901-1978........ CLC 37
See also AITN 1; CA 1-4R; 81-84;
CANR 4; MTCW; SATA-Obit 20

Mirbeau, Octave 1848-1917...... **TCLC 55**
See also DLB 123

Miro (Ferrer), Gabriel (Francisco Victor)
1879-1930.................. **TCLC 5**
See also CA 104

Mishima, Yukio
.... **CLC 2, 4, 6, 9, 27; DC 1; SSC 4**
See also Hiraoka, Kimitake

Mistral, Frederic 1830-1914...... **TCLC 51**
See also CA 122

Mistral, Gabriela........... **TCLC 2; HLC**
See also Godoy Alcayaga, Lucila

Mistry, Rohinton 1952-........... **CLC 71**
See also CA 141

Mitchell, Clyde
See Ellison, Harlan (Jay); Silverberg, Robert

Mitchell, James Leslie 1901-1935
See Gibbon, Lewis Grassic
See also CA 104; DLB 15

Mitchell, Joni 1943-.............. **CLC 12**
See also CA 112

Mitchell, Margaret (Munnerlyn)
1900-1949.................. **TCLC 11**
See also CA 109; 125; DLB 9; MTCW

Mitchell, Peggy
See Mitchell, Margaret (Munnerlyn)

Mitchell, S(ilas) Weir 1829-1914 .. **TCLC 36**

Mitchell, W(illiam) O(rmond)
1914-.......................... **CLC 25**
See also CA 77-80; CANR 15, 43; DLB 88

Mitford, Mary Russell 1787-1855.. **NCLC 4**
See also DLB 110, 116

Mitford, Nancy 1904-1973........ **CLC 44**
See also CA 9-12R

Miyamoto, Yuriko 1899-1951..... **TCLC 37**

Mo, Timothy (Peter) 1950(?)-...... **CLC 46**
See also CA 117; MTCW

Modarressi, Taghi (M.) 1931-...... **CLC 44**
See also CA 121; 134

Modiano, Patrick (Jean) 1945-..... **CLC 18**
See also CA 85-88; CANR 17, 40; DLB 83

Moerck, Paal
See Roelvaag, O(le) E(dvart)

Mofolo, Thomas (Mokopu)
1875(?)-1948........... **TCLC 22; BLC**
See also CA 121

Mohr, Nicholasa 1935-...... **CLC 12; HLC**
See also AAYA 8; CA 49-52; CANR 1, 32;
CLR 22; DLB 145; HW; JRDA; SAAS 8;
SATA 8

Mojtabai, A(nn) G(race)
1938-.............. **CLC 5, 9, 15, 29**
See also CA 85-88

Moliere
1622-1673..... **LC 28; DA; DAB; WLC**

Molin, Charles
See Mayne, William (James Carter)

Molnar, Ferenc 1878-1952....... **TCLC 20**
See also CA 109

Momaday, N(avarre) Scott
1934-........ **CLC 2, 19, 85; DA; DAB**
See also AAYA 11; CA 25-28R; CANR 14,
34; DLB 143; MTCW; NNAL; SATA 48;
SATA-Brief 30

Monette, Paul 1945-1995......... **CLC 82**
See also CA 139; 147

Monroe, Harriet 1860-1936...... **TCLC 12**
See also CA 109; DLB 54, 91

Monroe, Lyle
See Heinlein, Robert A(nson)

Montagu, Elizabeth 1917-........ **NCLC 7**
See also CA 9-12R

Montagu, Mary (Pierrepont) Wortley
1689-1762.................... **LC 9**
See also DLB 95, 101

Montagu, W. H.
See Coleridge, Samuel Taylor

Montague, John (Patrick)
1929-.................... **CLC 13, 46**
See also CA 9-12R; CANR 9; DLB 40;
MTCW

Montaigne, Michel (Eyquem) de
1533-1592...... **LC 8; DA; DAB; WLC**

Montale, Eugenio
1896-1981........ **CLC 7, 9, 18; PC 13**
See also CA 17-20R; 104; CANR 30;
DLB 114; MTCW

Montesquieu, Charles-Louis de Secondat
1689-1755.................... **LC 7**

Montgomery, (Robert) Bruce 1921-1978
See Crispin, Edmund
See also CA 104

Montgomery, L(ucy) M(aud)
1874-1942.................. **TCLC 51**
See also AAYA 12; CA 108; 137; CLR 8;
DLB 92; JRDA; MAICYA; YABC 1

Montgomery, Marion H., Jr. 1925-.. **CLC 7**
See also AITN 1; CA 1-4R; CANR 3, 48;
DLB 6

Montgomery, Max
See Davenport, Guy (Mattison, Jr.)

Montherlant, Henry (Milon) de
1896-1972................. **CLC 8, 19**
See also CA 85-88; 37-40R; DLB 72;
MTCW

Monty Python
See Chapman, Graham; Cleese, John
(Marwood); Gilliam, Terry (Vance); Idle,
Eric; Jones, Terence Graham Parry; Palin,
Michael (Edward)
See also AAYA 7

Moodie, Susanna (Strickland)
1803-1885................ **NCLC 14**
See also DLB 99

Mooney, Edward 1951-
See Mooney, Ted
See also CA 130

Mooney, Ted.................... **CLC 25**
See also Mooney, Edward

Moorcock, Michael (John)
1939-.................. **CLC 5, 27, 58**
See also CA 45-48; CAAS 5; CANR 2, 17,
38; DLB 14; MTCW

Moore, Brian
1921-...... **CLC 1, 3, 5, 7, 8, 19, 32, 90;
DAB**
See also CA 1-4R; CANR 1, 25, 42; MTCW

Moore, Edward
See Muir, Edwin

Moore, George Augustus
1852-1933........... **TCLC 7; SSC 19**
See also CA 104; DLB 10, 18, 57, 135

Moore, Lorrie.............. **CLC 39, 45, 68**
See also Moore, Marie Lorena

Moore, Marianne (Craig)
1887-1972.... **CLC 1, 2, 4, 8, 10, 13, 19,
47; DA; DAB; PC 4**
See also CA 1-4R; 33-36R; CANR 3;
CDALB 1929-1941; DLB 45; DLBD 7;
MTCW; SATA 20

Moore, Marie Lorena 1957-
See Moore, Lorrie
See also CA 116; CANR 39

Moore, Thomas 1779-1852....... **NCLC 6**
See also DLB 96, 144

Morand, Paul 1888-1976.......... **CLC 41**
See also CA 69-72; DLB 65

Morante, Elsa 1918-1985........ **CLC 8, 47**
See also CA 85-88; 117; CANR 35; MTCW

Moravia, Alberto....... **CLC 2, 7, 11, 27, 46**
See also Pincherle, Alberto

More, Hannah 1745-1833....... **NCLC 27**
See also DLB 107, 109, 116

More, Henry 1614-1687............. **LC 9**
See also DLB 126

More, Sir Thomas 1478-1535....... **LC 10**

Moreas, Jean.................... **TCLC 18**
See also Papadiamantopoulos, Johannes

Morgan, Berry 1919-.............. **CLC 6**
See also CA 49-52; DLB 6

Morgan, Claire
See Highsmith, (Mary) Patricia

Morgan, Edwin (George) 1920-..... **CLC 31**
See also CA 5-8R; CANR 3, 43; DLB 27

Morgan, (George) Frederick
1922-....................... **CLC 23**
See also CA 17-20R; CANR 21

Morgan, Harriet
See Mencken, H(enry) L(ouis)

Morgan, Jane
See Cooper, James Fenimore

Morgan, Janet 1945-............. **CLC 39**
See also CA 65-68

Morgan, Lady 1776(?)-1859...... **NCLC 29**
See also DLB 116

Morgan, Robin 1941-.............. **CLC 2**
See also CA 69-72; CANR 29; MTCW;
SATA 80

Morgan, Scott
See Kuttner, Henry

Morgan, Seth 1949(?)-1990........ **CLC 65**
See also CA 132

Morgenstern, Christian
1871-1914.................. **TCLC 8**
See also CA 105

Morgenstern, S.
See Goldman, William (W.)

Moricz, Zsigmond 1879-1942..... **TCLC 33**

Morike, Eduard (Friedrich)
1804-1875................ **NCLC 10**
See also DLB 133

Naipaul, Shiva(dhar Srinivasa)
1945-1985 . . . . CLC **32, 39**
See also CA 110; 112; 116; CANR 33;
DLBY 85; MTCW

Naipaul, V(idiadhar) S(urajprasad)
1932- . . . . . CLC **4, 7, 9, 13, 18, 37; DAB**
See also CA 1-4R; CANR 1, 33;
CDBLB 1960 to Present; DLB 125;
DLBY 85; MTCW

Nakos, Lilika 1899(?)- . . . . CLC **29**

Narayan, R(asipuram) K(rishnaswami)
1906- . . . . CLC **7, 28, 47**
See also CA 81-84; CANR 33; MTCW;
SATA 62

Nash, (Frediric) Ogden 1902-1971 . . CLC **23**
See also CA 13-14; 29-32R; CANR 34;
CAP 1; DLB 11; MAICYA; MTCW;
SATA 2, 46

Nathan, Daniel
See Dannay, Frederic

Nathan, George Jean 1882-1958 . . . TCLC **18**
See also Hatteras, Owen
See also CA 114; DLB 137

Natsume, Kinnosuke 1867-1916
See Natsume, Soseki
See also CA 104

Natsume, Soseki . . . . TCLC **2, 10**
See also Natsume, Kinnosuke

Natti, (Mary) Lee 1919-
See Kingman, Lee
See also CA 5-8R; CANR 2

Naylor, Gloria
1950- . . . . CLC **28, 52; BLC; DA**
See also AAYA 6; BW 2; CA 107;
CANR 27; MTCW

Neihardt, John Gneisenau
1881-1973 . . . . CLC **32**
See also CA 13-14; CAP 1; DLB 9, 54

Nekrasov, Nikolai Alekseevich
1821-1878 . . . . NCLC **11**

Nelligan, Emile 1879-1941 . . . . TCLC **14**
See also CA 114; DLB 92

Nelson, Willie 1933- . . . . CLC **17**
See also CA 107

Nemerov, Howard (Stanley)
1920-1991 . . . . CLC **2, 6, 9, 36**
See also CA 1-4R; 134; CABS 2; CANR 1,
27; DLB 5, 6; DLBY 83; MTCW

Neruda, Pablo
1904-1973 . . . . . CLC **1, 2, 5, 7, 9, 28, 62;**
DA; DAB; HLC; PC 4; WLC
See also CA 19-20; 45-48; CAP 2; HW;
MTCW

Nerval, Gerard de
1808-1855 . . . . . NCLC **1; PC 13; SSC 18**

Nervo, (Jose) Amado (Ruiz de)
1870-1919 . . . . TCLC **11**
See also CA 109; 131; HW

Nessi, Pio Baroja y
See Baroja (y Nessi), Pio

Nestroy, Johann 1801-1862 . . . . . . NCLC **42**
See also DLB 133

Neufeld, John (Arthur) 1938- . . . . . . CLC **17**
See also AAYA 11; CA 25-28R; CANR 11,
37; MAICYA; SAAS 3; SATA 6, 81

Neville, Emily Cheney 1919- . . . . . . CLC **12**
See also CA 5-8R; CANR 3, 37; JRDA;
MAICYA; SAAS 2; SATA 1

Newbound, Bernard Slade 1930-
See Slade, Bernard
See also CA 81-84; CANR 49

Newby, P(ercy) H(oward)
1918- . . . . CLC **2, 13**
See also CA 5-8R; CANR 32; DLB 15;
MTCW

Newlove, Donald 1928- . . . . CLC **6**
See also CA 29-32R; CANR 25

Newlove, John (Herbert) 1938- . . . . . CLC **14**
See also CA 21-24R; CANR 9, 25

Newman, Charles 1938- . . . . CLC **2, 8**
See also CA 21-24R

Newman, Edwin (Harold) 1919- . . . . CLC **14**
See also AITN 1; CA 69-72; CANR 5

Newman, John Henry
1801-1890 . . . . NCLC **38**
See also DLB 18, 32, 55

Newton, Suzanne 1936- . . . . CLC **35**
See also CA 41-44R; CANR 14; JRDA;
SATA 5, 77

Nexo, Martin Andersen
1869-1954 . . . . TCLC **43**

Nezval, Vitezslav 1900-1958 . . . . . . TCLC **44**
See also CA 123

Ng, Fae Myenne 1957(?)- . . . . CLC **81**
See also CA 146

Ngema, Mbongeni 1955- . . . . CLC **57**
See also BW 2; CA 143

Ngugi, James T(hiong'o) . . . . CLC **3, 7, 13**
See also Ngugi wa Thiong'o

Ngugi wa Thiong'o 1938- . . . . . CLC **36; BLC**
See also Ngugi, James T(hiong'o)
See also BW 2; CA 81-84; CANR 27;
DLB 125; MTCW

Nichol, B(arrie) P(hillip)
1944-1988 . . . . CLC **18**
See also CA 53-56; DLB 53; SATA 66

Nichols, John (Treadwell) 1940- . . . . CLC **38**
See also CA 9-12R; CAAS 2; CANR 6;
DLBY 82

Nichols, Leigh
See Koontz, Dean R(ay)

Nichols, Peter (Richard)
1927- . . . . CLC **5, 36, 65**
See also CA 104; CANR 33; DLB 13;
MTCW

Nicolas, F. R. E.
See Freeling, Nicolas

Niedecker, Lorine 1903-1970 . . . . CLC **10, 42**
See also CA 25-28; CAP 2; DLB 48

Nietzsche, Friedrich (Wilhelm)
1844-1900 . . . . TCLC **10, 18, 55**
See also CA 107; 121; DLB 129

Nievo, Ippolito 1831-1861 . . . . NCLC **22**

Nightingale, Anne Redmon 1943-
See Redmon, Anne
See also CA 103

Nik. T. O.
See Annensky, Innokenty Fyodorovich

Nin, Anais
1903-1977 . . . . . . CLC **1, 4, 8, 11, 14, 60;**
SSC 10
See also AITN 2; CA 13-16R; 69-72;
CANR 22; DLB 2, 4, 152; MTCW

Nissenson, Hugh 1933- . . . . CLC **4, 9**
See also CA 17-20R; CANR 27; DLB 28

Niven, Larry . . . . CLC **8**
See also Niven, Laurence Van Cott
See also DLB 8

Niven, Laurence Van Cott 1938-
See Niven, Larry
See also CA 21-24R; CAAS 12; CANR 14,
44; MTCW

Nixon, Agnes Eckhardt 1927- . . . . . . CLC **21**
See also CA 110

Nizan, Paul 1905-1940 . . . . TCLC **40**
See also DLB 72

Nkosi, Lewis 1936- . . . . CLC **45; BLC**
See also BW 1; CA 65-68; CANR 27

Nodier, (Jean) Charles (Emmanuel)
1780-1844 . . . . NCLC **19**
See also DLB 119

Nolan, Christopher 1965- . . . . CLC **58**
See also CA 111

Norden, Charles
See Durrell, Lawrence (George)

Nordhoff, Charles (Bernard)
1887-1947 . . . . TCLC **23**
See also CA 108; DLB 9; SATA 23

Norfolk, Lawrence 1963- . . . . CLC **76**
See also CA 144

Norman, Marsha 1947- . . . . CLC **28**
See also CA 105; CABS 3; CANR 41;
DLBY 84

Norris, Benjamin Franklin, Jr.
1870-1902 . . . . TCLC **24**
See also Norris, Frank
See also CA 110

Norris, Frank
See Norris, Benjamin Franklin, Jr.
See also CDALB 1865-1917; DLB 12, 71

Norris, Leslie 1921- . . . . CLC **14**
See also CA 11-12; CANR 14; CAP 1;
DLB 27

North, Andrew
See Norton, Andre

North, Anthony
See Koontz, Dean R(ay)

North, Captain George
See Stevenson, Robert Louis (Balfour)

North, Milou
See Erdrich, Louise

Northrup, B. A.
See Hubbard, L(afayette) Ron(ald)

North Staffs
See Hulme, T(homas) E(rnest)

Norton, Alice Mary
See Norton, Andre
See also MAICYA; SATA 1, 43

Norton, Andre 1912- . . . . CLC **12**
See also Norton, Alice Mary
See also AAYA 14; CA 1-4R; CANR 2, 31;
DLB 8, 52; JRDA; MTCW

Orris
See Ingelow, Jean

Ortega y Gasset, Jose
1883-1955 . . . . **TCLC 9; HLC**
See also CA 106; 130; HW; MTCW

Ortese, Anna Maria 1914- . . . . **CLC 89**

Ortiz, Simon J(oseph) 1941- . . . . **CLC 45**
See also CA 134; DLB 120; NNAL

Orton, Joe . . . . **CLC 4, 13, 43; DC 3**
See also Orton, John Kingsley
See also CDBLB 1960 to Present; DLB 13

Orton, John Kingsley 1933-1967
See Orton, Joe
See also CA 85-88; CANR 35; MTCW

Orwell, George
. . . . . **TCLC 2, 6, 15, 31, 51; DAB; WLC**
See also Blair, Eric (Arthur)
See also CDBLB 1945-1960; DLB 15, 98

Osborne, David
See Silverberg, Robert

Osborne, George
See Silverberg, Robert

Osborne, John (James)
1929-1994 . . . . . **CLC 1, 2, 5, 11, 45; DA;**
DAB; WLC
See also CA 13-16R; 147; CANR 21;
CDBLB 1945-1960; DLB 13; MTCW

Osborne, Lawrence 1958- . . . . **CLC 50**

Oshima, Nagisa 1932- . . . . **CLC 20**
See also CA 116; 121

Oskison, John Milton
1874-1947 . . . . **TCLC 35**
See also CA 144; NNAL

Ossoli, Sarah Margaret (Fuller marchesa d')
1810-1850
See Fuller, Margaret
See also SATA 25

Ostrovsky, Alexander
1823-1886 . . . . **NCLC 30**

Otero, Blas de 1916-1979 . . . . **CLC 11**
See also CA 89-92; DLB 134

Otto, Whitney 1955- . . . . **CLC 70**
See also CA 140

Ouida . . . . **TCLC 43**
See also De La Ramee, (Marie) Louise
See also DLB 18, 156

Ousmane, Sembene 1923- . . . . **CLC 66; BLC**
See also BW 1; CA 117; 125; MTCW

Ovid 43B.C.-18(?) . . . . **CMLC 7; PC 2**

Owen, Hugh
See Faust, Frederick (Schiller)

Owen, Wilfred (Edward Salter)
1893-1918 . . . . . . **TCLC 5, 27; DA; DAB;**
WLC
See also CA 104; 141; CDBLB 1914-1945;
DLB 20

Owens, Rochelle 1936- . . . . **CLC 8**
See also CA 17-20R; CAAS 2; CANR 39

Oz, Amos 1939- . . . **CLC 5, 8, 11, 27, 33, 54**
See also CA 53-56; CANR 27, 47; MTCW

Ozick, Cynthia
1928- . . . . **CLC 3, 7, 28, 62; SSC 15**
See also BEST 90:1; CA 17-20R; CANR 23;
DLB 28, 152; DLBY 82; MTCW

Ozu, Yasujiro 1903-1963 . . . . **CLC 16**
See also CA 112

Pacheco, C.
See Pessoa, Fernando (Antonio Nogueira)

Pa Chin . . . . **CLC 18**
See also Li Fei-kan

Pack, Robert 1929- . . . . **CLC 13**
See also CA 1-4R; CANR 3, 44; DLB 5

Padgett, Lewis
See Kuttner, Henry

Padilla (Lorenzo), Heberto 1932- . . . **CLC 38**
See also AITN 1; CA 123; 131; HW

Page, Jimmy 1944- . . . . **CLC 12**

Page, Louise 1955- . . . . **CLC 40**
See also CA 140

Page, P(atricia) K(athleen)
1916- . . . . **CLC 7, 18; PC 12**
See also CA 53-56; CANR 4, 22; DLB 68;
MTCW

Paget, Violet 1856-1935
See Lee, Vernon
See also CA 104

Paget-Lowe, Henry
See Lovecraft, H(oward) P(hillips)

Paglia, Camille (Anna) 1947- . . . . **CLC 68**
See also CA 140

Paige, Richard
See Koontz, Dean R(ay)

Pakenham, Antonia
See Fraser, (Lady) Antonia (Pakenham)

Palamas, Kostes 1859-1943 . . . . **TCLC 5**
See also CA 105

Palazzeschi, Aldo 1885-1974 . . . . **CLC 11**
See also CA 89-92; 53-56; DLB 114

Paley, Grace 1922- . . . . **CLC 4, 6, 37; SSC 8**
See also CA 25-28R; CANR 13, 46;
DLB 28; MTCW

Palin, Michael (Edward) 1943- . . . . . **CLC 21**
See also Monty Python
See also CA 107; CANR 35; SATA 67

Palliser, Charles 1947- . . . . **CLC 65**
See also CA 136

Palma, Ricardo 1833-1919 . . . . **TCLC 29**

Pancake, Breece Dexter 1952-1979
See Pancake, Breece D'J
See also CA 123; 109

Pancake, Breece D'J . . . . **CLC 29**
See also Pancake, Breece Dexter
See also DLB 130

Panko, Rudy
See Gogol, Nikolai (Vasilyevich)

Papadiamantis, Alexandros
1851-1911 . . . . **TCLC 29**

Papadiamantopoulos, Johannes 1856-1910
See Moreas, Jean
See also CA 117

Papini, Giovanni 1881-1956 . . . . **TCLC 22**
See also CA 121

Paracelsus 1493-1541 . . . . **LC 14**

Parasol, Peter
See Stevens, Wallace

Parfenie, Maria
See Codrescu, Andrei

Parini, Jay (Lee) 1948- . . . . **CLC 54**
See also CA 97-100; CAAS 16; CANR 32

Park, Jordan
See Kornbluth, C(yril) M.; Pohl, Frederik

Parker, Bert
See Ellison, Harlan (Jay)

Parker, Dorothy (Rothschild)
1893-1967 . . . . **CLC 15, 68; SSC 2**
See also CA 19-20; 25-28R; CAP 2;
DLB 11, 45, 86; MTCW

Parker, Robert B(rown) 1932- . . . . . . **CLC 27**
See also BEST 89:4; CA 49-52; CANR 1,
26; MTCW

Parkin, Frank 1940- . . . . **CLC 43**
See also CA 147

Parkman, Francis, Jr.
1823-1893 . . . . **NCLC 12**
See also DLB 1, 30

Parks, Gordon (Alexander Buchanan)
1912- . . . . **CLC 1, 16; BLC**
See also AITN 2; BW 2; CA 41-44R;
CANR 26; DLB 33; SATA 8

Parnell, Thomas 1679-1718 . . . . **LC 3**
See also DLB 94

Parra, Nicanor 1914- . . . . **CLC 2; HLC**
See also CA 85-88; CANR 32; HW; MTCW

Parrish, Mary Frances
See Fisher, M(ary) F(rances) K(ennedy)

Parson
See Coleridge, Samuel Taylor

Parson Lot
See Kingsley, Charles

Partridge, Anthony
See Oppenheim, E(dward) Phillips

Pascoli, Giovanni 1855-1912 . . . . . . **TCLC 45**

Pasolini, Pier Paolo
1922-1975 . . . . **CLC 20, 37**
See also CA 93-96; 61-64; DLB 128;
MTCW

Pasquini
See Silone, Ignazio

Pastan, Linda (Olenik) 1932- . . . . . . **CLC 27**
See also CA 61-64; CANR 18, 40; DLB 5

Pasternak, Boris (Leonidovich)
1890-1960 . . . . . . **CLC 7, 10, 18, 63; DA;**
DAB; PC 6; WLC
See also CA 127; 116; MTCW

Patchen, Kenneth 1911-1972 . . . **CLC 1, 2, 18**
See also CA 1-4R; 33-36R; CANR 3, 35;
DLB 16, 48; MTCW

Pater, Walter (Horatio)
1839-1894 . . . . **NCLC 7**
See also CDBLB 1832-1890; DLB 57, 156

Paterson, A(ndrew) B(arton)
1864-1941 . . . . **TCLC 32**

Paterson, Katherine (Womeldorf)
1932- . . . . **CLC 12, 30**
See also AAYA 1; CA 21-24R; CANR 28;
CLR 7; DLB 52; JRDA; MAICYA;
MTCW; SATA 13, 53

Patmore, Coventry Kersey Dighton
1823-1896 . . . . **NCLC 9**
See also DLB 35, 98

Paton, Alan (Stewart)
1903-1988 . . . . . . **CLC 4, 10, 25, 55; DA; DAB; WLC**
See also CA 13-16; 125; CANR 22; CAP 1; MTCW; SATA 11; SATA-Obit 56

Paton Walsh, Gillian 1937-
See Walsh, Jill Paton
See also CANR 38; JRDA; MAICYA; SAAS 3; SATA 4, 72

Paulding, James Kirke 1778-1860 . . **NCLC 2**
See also DLB 3, 59, 74

Paulin, Thomas Neilson 1949-
See Paulin, Tom
See also CA 123; 128

Paulin, Tom . . . . **CLC 37**
See also Paulin, Thomas Neilson
See also DLB 40

Paustovsky, Konstantin (Georgievich)
1892-1968 . . . . **CLC 40**
See also CA 93-96; 25-28R

Pavese, Cesare
1908-1950 . . . . . **TCLC 3; PC 13; SSC 19**
See also CA 104; DLB 128

Pavic, Milorad 1929- . . . . **CLC 60**
See also CA 136

Payne, Alan
See Jakes, John (William)

Paz, Gil
See Lugones, Leopoldo

Paz, Octavio
1914- . . . . **CLC 3, 4, 6, 10, 19, 51, 65; DA; DAB; HLC; PC 1; WLC**
See also CA 73-76; CANR 32; DLBY 90; HW; MTCW

Peacock, Molly 1947- . . . . **CLC 60**
See also CA 103; CAAS 21; DLB 120

Peacock, Thomas Love
1785-1866 . . . . **NCLC 22**
See also DLB 96, 116

Peake, Mervyn 1911-1968 . . . . . . **CLC 7, 54**
See also CA 5-8R; 25-28R; CANR 3; DLB 15; MTCW; SATA 23

Pearce, Philippa . . . . **CLC 21**
See also Christie, (Ann) Philippa
See also CLR 9; MAICYA; SATA 1, 67

Pearl, Eric
See Elman, Richard

Pearson, T(homas) R(eid) 1956- . . . . **CLC 39**
See also CA 120; 130

Peck, Dale 1967- . . . . **CLC 81**
See also CA 146

Peck, John 1941- . . . . **CLC 3**
See also CA 49-52; CANR 3

Peck, Richard (Wayne) 1934- . . . . . . **CLC 21**
See also AAYA 1; CA 85-88; CANR 19, 38; CLR 15; JRDA; MAICYA; SAAS 2; SATA 18, 55

Peck, Robert Newton 1928- . . . . **CLC 17; DA**
See also AAYA 3; CA 81-84; CANR 31; JRDA; MAICYA; SAAS 1; SATA 21, 62

Peckinpah, (David) Sam(uel)
1925-1984 . . . . **CLC 20**
See also CA 109; 114

Pedersen, Knut 1859-1952
See Hamsun, Knut
See also CA 104; 119; MTCW

Peeslake, Gaffer
See Durrell, Lawrence (George)

Peguy, Charles Pierre
1873-1914 . . . . **TCLC 10**
See also CA 107

Pena, Ramon del Valle y
See Valle-Inclan, Ramon (Maria) del

Pendennis, Arthur Esquir
See Thackeray, William Makepeace

Penn, William 1644-1718 . . . . **LC 25**
See also DLB 24

Pepys, Samuel
1633-1703 . . . . . **LC 11; DA; DAB; WLC**
See also CDBLB 1660-1789; DLB 101

Percy, Walker
1916-1990 . . . . **CLC 2, 3, 6, 8, 14, 18, 47, 65**
See also CA 1-4R; 131; CANR 1, 23; DLB 2; DLBY 80, 90; MTCW

Perec, Georges 1936-1982 . . . . **CLC 56**
See also CA 141; DLB 83

Pereda (y Sanchez de Porrua), Jose Maria de
1833-1906 . . . . **TCLC 16**
See also CA 117

Pereda y Porrua, Jose Maria de
See Pereda (y Sanchez de Porrua), Jose Maria de

Peregoy, George Weems
See Mencken, H(enry) L(ouis)

Perelman, S(idney) J(oseph)
1904-1979 . . . **CLC 3, 5, 9, 15, 23, 44, 49**
See also AITN 1, 2; CA 73-76; 89-92; CANR 18; DLB 11, 44; MTCW

Peret, Benjamin 1899-1959 . . . . **TCLC 20**
See also CA 117

Peretz, Isaac Loeb 1851(?)-1915 . . . **TCLC 16**
See also CA 109

Peretz, Yitzkhok Leibush
See Peretz, Isaac Loeb

Perez Galdos, Benito 1843-1920 . . . **TCLC 27**
See also CA 125; HW

Perrault, Charles 1628-1703 . . . . **LC 2**
See also MAICYA; SATA 25

Perry, Brighton
See Sherwood, Robert E(mmet)

Perse, St.-John . . . . **CLC 4, 11, 46**
See also Leger, (Marie-Rene Auguste) Alexis Saint-Leger

Perutz, Leo 1882-1957 . . . . **TCLC 60**
See also DLB 81

Peseenz, Tulio F.
See Lopez y Fuentes, Gregorio

Pesetsky, Bette 1932- . . . . **CLC 28**
See also CA 133; DLB 130

Peshkov, Alexei Maximovich 1868-1936
See Gorky, Maxim
See also CA 105; 141; DA

Pessoa, Fernando (Antonio Nogueira)
1888-1935 . . . . **TCLC 27; HLC**
See also CA 125

Peterkin, Julia Mood 1880-1961 . . . . **CLC 31**
See also CA 102; DLB 9

Peters, Joan K. 1945- . . . . **CLC 39**

Peters, Robert L(ouis) 1924- . . . . **CLC 7**
See also CA 13-16R; CAAS 8; DLB 105

Petofi, Sandor 1823-1849 . . . . **NCLC 21**

Petrakis, Harry Mark 1923- . . . . **CLC 3**
See also CA 9-12R; CANR 4, 30

Petrarch 1304-1374 . . . . **PC 8**

Petrov, Evgeny . . . . **TCLC 21**
See also Kataev, Evgeny Petrovich

Petry, Ann (Lane) 1908- . . . . . . **CLC 1, 7, 18**
See also BW 1; CA 5-8R; CAAS 6; CANR 4, 46; CLR 12; DLB 76; JRDA; MAICYA; MTCW; SATA 5

Petursson, Halligrimur 1614-1674 . . . . **LC 8**

Philips, Katherine 1632-1664 . . . . **LC 30**
See also DLB 131

Philipson, Morris H. 1926- . . . . **CLC 53**
See also CA 1-4R; CANR 4

Phillips, David Graham
1867-1911 . . . . **TCLC 44**
See also CA 108; DLB 9, 12

Phillips, Jack
See Sandburg, Carl (August)

Phillips, Jayne Anne
1952- . . . . **CLC 15, 33; SSC 16**
See also CA 101; CANR 24; DLBY 80; MTCW

Phillips, Richard
See Dick, Philip K(indred)

Phillips, Robert (Schaeffer) 1938- . . . **CLC 28**
See also CA 17-20R; CAAS 13; CANR 8; DLB 105

Phillips, Ward
See Lovecraft, H(oward) P(hillips)

Piccolo, Lucio 1901-1969 . . . . **CLC 13**
See also CA 97-100; DLB 114

Pickthall, Marjorie L(owry) C(hristie)
1883-1922 . . . . **TCLC 21**
See also CA 107; DLB 92

Pico della Mirandola, Giovanni
1463-1494 . . . . **LC 15**

Piercy, Marge
1936- . . . . **CLC 3, 6, 14, 18, 27, 62**
See also CA 21-24R; CAAS 1; CANR 13, 43; DLB 120; MTCW

Piers, Robert
See Anthony, Piers

Pieyre de Mandiargues, Andre 1909-1991
See Mandiargues, Andre Pieyre de
See also CA 103; 136; CANR 22

Pilnyak, Boris . . . . **TCLC 23**
See also Vogau, Boris Andreyevich

Pincherle, Alberto 1907-1990 . . . **CLC 11, 18**
See also Moravia, Alberto
See also CA 25-28R; 132; CANR 33; MTCW

Pinckney, Darryl 1953- . . . . **CLC 76**
See also BW 2; CA 143

Pindar 518B.C.-446B.C. . . . . **CMLC 12**

Pineda, Cecile 1942- . . . . **CLC 39**
See also CA 118

Pinero, Arthur Wing 1855-1934 . . . **TCLC 32**
See also CA 110; DLB 10

Pinero, Miguel (Antonio Gomez)
1946-1988 . . . . **CLC 4, 55**
See also CA 61-64; 125; CANR 29; HW

Pinget, Robert 1919- . . . . **CLC 7, 13, 37**
See also CA 85-88; DLB 83

Pink Floyd
See Barrett, (Roger) Syd; Gilmour, David;
Mason, Nick; Waters, Roger; Wright,
Rick

Pinkney, Edward 1802-1828 . . . . . **NCLC 31**

Pinkwater, Daniel Manus 1941- . . . . **CLC 35**
See also Pinkwater, Manus
See also AAYA 1; CA 29-32R; CANR 12,
38; CLR 4; JRDA; MAICYA; SAAS 3;
SATA 46, 76

Pinkwater, Manus
See Pinkwater, Daniel Manus
See also SATA 8

Pinsky, Robert 1940- . . . . **CLC 9, 19, 38**
See also CA 29-32R; CAAS 4; DLBY 82

Pinta, Harold
See Pinter, Harold

Pinter, Harold
1930- . . . . . **CLC 1, 3, 6, 9, 11, 15, 27, 58,
73; DA; DAB; WLC**
See also CA 5-8R; CANR 33; CDBLB 1960
to Present; DLB 13; MTCW

Pirandello, Luigi
1867-1936 . . . . . . **TCLC 4, 29; DA; DAB;
DC 5; WLC**
See also CA 104

Pirsig, Robert M(aynard)
1928- . . . . **CLC 4, 6, 73**
See also CA 53-56; CANR 42; MTCW;
SATA 39

Pisarev, Dmitry Ivanovich
1840-1868 . . . . **NCLC 25**

Pix, Mary (Griffith) 1666-1709 . . . . **LC 8**
See also DLB 80

Pixerecourt, Guilbert de
1773-1844 . . . . **NCLC 39**

Plaidy, Jean
See Hibbert, Eleanor Alice Burford

Planche, James Robinson
1796-1880 . . . . **NCLC 42**

Plant, Robert 1948- . . . . **CLC 12**

Plante, David (Robert)
1940- . . . . **CLC 7, 23, 38**
See also CA 37-40R; CANR 12, 36;
DLBY 83; MTCW

Plath, Sylvia
1932-1963 . . . . . **CLC 1, 2, 3, 5, 9, 11, 14,
17, 50, 51, 62; DA; DAB; PC 1; WLC**
See also AAYA 13; CA 19-20; CANR 34;
CAP 2; CDALB 1941-1968; DLB 5, 6,
152; MTCW

Plato
428(?)B.C.-348(?)B.C. . . . . **CMLC 8; DA;
DAB**

Platonov, Andrei . . . . **TCLC 14**
See also Klimentov, Andrei Platonovich

Platt, Kin 1911- . . . . **CLC 26**
See also AAYA 11; CA 17-20R; CANR 11;
JRDA; SAAS 17; SATA 21

Plick et Plock
See Simenon, Georges (Jacques Christian)

Plimpton, George (Ames) 1927- . . . . . **CLC 36**
See also AITN 1; CA 21-24R; CANR 32;
MTCW; SATA 10

Plomer, William Charles Franklin
1903-1973 . . . . **CLC 4, 8**
See also CA 21-22; CANR 34; CAP 2;
DLB 20; MTCW; SATA 24

Plowman, Piers
See Kavanagh, Patrick (Joseph)

Plum, J.
See Wodehouse, P(elham) G(renville)

Plumly, Stanley (Ross) 1939- . . . . . . **CLC 33**
See also CA 108; 110; DLB 5

Plumpe, Friedrich Wilhelm
1888-1931 . . . . **TCLC 53**
See also CA 112

Poe, Edgar Allan
1809-1849 . . . . . **NCLC 1, 16; DA; DAB;
PC 1; SSC 1; WLC**
See also AAYA 14; CDALB 1640-1865;
DLB 3, 59, 73, 74; SATA 23

Poet of Titchfield Street, The
See Pound, Ezra (Weston Loomis)

Pohl, Frederik 1919- . . . . **CLC 18**
See also CA 61-64; CAAS 1; CANR 11, 37;
DLB 8; MTCW; SATA 24

Poirier, Louis 1910-
See Gracq, Julien
See also CA 122; 126

Poitier, Sidney 1927- . . . . **CLC 26**
See also BW 1; CA 117

Polanski, Roman 1933- . . . . **CLC 16**
See also CA 77-80

Poliakoff, Stephen 1952- . . . . **CLC 38**
See also CA 106; DLB 13

Police, The
See Copeland, Stewart (Armstrong);
Summers, Andrew James; Sumner,
Gordon Matthew

Polidori, John William
1795-1821 . . . . **NCLC 51**
See also DLB 116

Pollitt, Katha 1949- . . . . **CLC 28**
See also CA 120; 122; MTCW

Pollock, (Mary) Sharon 1936- . . . . . . **CLC 50**
See also CA 141; DLB 60

Polo, Marco 1254-1324 . . . . **CMLC 15**

Pomerance, Bernard 1940- . . . . **CLC 13**
See also CA 101; CANR 49

Ponge, Francis (Jean Gaston Alfred)
1899-1988 . . . . **CLC 6, 18**
See also CA 85-88; 126; CANR 40

Pontoppidan, Henrik 1857-1943 . . . **TCLC 29**

Poole, Josephine . . . . **CLC 17**
See also Helyar, Jane Penelope Josephine
See also SAAS 2; SATA 5

Popa, Vasko 1922-1991 . . . . **CLC 19**
See also CA 112; 148

Pope, Alexander
1688-1744 . . . . . . **LC 3; DA; DAB; WLC**
See also CDBLB 1660-1789; DLB 95, 101

Porter, Connie (Rose) 1959(?)- . . . . . **CLC 70**
See also BW 2; CA 142; SATA 81

Porter, Gene(va Grace) Stratton
1863(?)-1924 . . . . **TCLC 21**
See also CA 112

Porter, Katherine Anne
1890-1980 . . . . . . **CLC 1, 3, 7, 10, 13, 15,
27; DA; DAB; SSC 4**
See also AITN 2; CA 1-4R; 101; CANR 1;
DLB 4, 9, 102; DLBD 12; DLBY 80;
MTCW; SATA 39; SATA-Obit 23

Porter, Peter (Neville Frederick)
1929- . . . . **CLC 5, 13, 33**
See also CA 85-88; DLB 40

Porter, William Sydney 1862-1910
See Henry, O.
See also CA 104; 131; CDALB 1865-1917;
DA; DAB; DLB 12, 78, 79; MTCW;
YABC 2

Portillo (y Pacheco), Jose Lopez
See Lopez Portillo (y Pacheco), Jose

Post, Melville Davisson
1869-1930 . . . . **TCLC 39**
See also CA 110

Potok, Chaim 1929- . . . . **CLC 2, 7, 14, 26**
See also AAYA 15; AITN 1, 2; CA 17-20R;
CANR 19, 35; DLB 28, 152; MTCW;
SATA 33

Potter, Beatrice
See Webb, (Martha) Beatrice (Potter)
See also MAICYA

Potter, Dennis (Christopher George)
1935-1994 . . . . **CLC 58, 86**
See also CA 107; 145; CANR 33; MTCW

Pound, Ezra (Weston Loomis)
1885-1972 . . . . . . **CLC 1, 2, 3, 4, 5, 7, 10,
13, 18, 34, 48, 50; DA; DAB; PC 4; WLC**
See also CA 5-8R; 37-40R; CANR 40;
CDALB 1917-1929; DLB 4, 45, 63;
MTCW

Povod, Reinaldo 1959-1994 . . . . **CLC 44**
See also CA 136; 146

Powell, Adam Clayton, Jr.
1908-1972 . . . . **CLC 89; BLC**
See also BW 1; CA 102; 33-36R

Powell, Anthony (Dymoke)
1905- . . . . **CLC 1, 3, 7, 9, 10, 31**
See also CA 1-4R; CANR 1, 32;
CDBLB 1945-1960; DLB 15; MTCW

Powell, Dawn 1897-1965 . . . . **CLC 66**
See also CA 5-8R

Powell, Padgett 1952- . . . . **CLC 34**
See also CA 126

Powers, J(ames) F(arl)
1917- . . . . **CLC 1, 4, 8, 57; SSC 4**
See also CA 1-4R; CANR 2; DLB 130;
MTCW

Powers, John J(ames) 1945-
See Powers, John R.
See also CA 69-72

Powers, John R. . . . . **CLC 66**
See also Powers, John J(ames)

Pownall, David 1938-............ **CLC 10**
See also CA 89-92; CAAS 18; CANR 49;
DLB 14

Powys, John Cowper
1872-1963 .... **CLC 7, 9, 15, 46**
See also CA 85-88; DLB 15; MTCW

Powys, T(heodore) F(rancis)
1875-1953 .... **TCLC 9**
See also CA 106; DLB 36

Prager, Emily 1952-.............. **CLC 56**

Pratt, E(dwin) J(ohn)
1883(?)-1964 .... **CLC 19**
See also CA 141; 93-96; DLB 92

Premchand..................... **TCLC 21**
See also Srivastava, Dhanpat Rai

Preussler, Otfried 1923-.......... **CLC 17**
See also CA 77-80; SATA 24

Prevert, Jacques (Henri Marie)
1900-1977 .... **CLC 15**
See also CA 77-80; 69-72; CANR 29;
MTCW; SATA-Obit 30

Prevost, Abbe (Antoine Francois)
1697-1763 .... **LC 1**

Price, (Edward) Reynolds
1933- .... **CLC 3, 6, 13, 43, 50, 63**
See also CA 1-4R; CANR 1, 37; DLB 2

Price, Richard 1949- .... **CLC 6, 12**
See also CA 49-52; CANR 3; DLBY 81

Prichard, Katharine Susannah
1883-1969 .... **CLC 46**
See also CA 11-12; CANR 33; CAP 1;
MTCW; SATA 66

Priestley, J(ohn) B(oynton)
1894-1984 .... **CLC 2, 5, 9, 34**
See also CA 9-12R; 113; CANR 33;
CDBLB 1914-1945; DLB 10, 34, 77, 100,
139; DLBY 84; MTCW

Prince 1958(?)-................. **CLC 35**

Prince, F(rank) T(empleton) 1912-.. **CLC 22**
See also CA 101; CANR 43; DLB 20

Prince Kropotkin
See Kropotkin, Peter (Aleksieevich)

Prior, Matthew 1664-1721.......... **LC 4**
See also DLB 95

Pritchard, William H(arrison)
1932-.......................... **CLC 34**
See also CA 65-68; CANR 23; DLB 111

Pritchett, V(ictor) S(awdon)
1900- .... **CLC 5, 13, 15, 41; SSC 14**
See also CA 61-64; CANR 31; DLB 15,
139; MTCW

Private 19022
See Manning, Frederic

Probst, Mark 1925- .... **CLC 59**
See also CA 130

Prokosch, Frederic 1908-1989.... **CLC 4, 48**
See also CA 73-76; 128; DLB 48

Prophet, The
See Dreiser, Theodore (Herman Albert)

Prose, Francine 1947-............ **CLC 45**
See also CA 109; 112; CANR 46

Proudhon
See Cunha, Euclides (Rodrigues Pimenta) da

Proulx, E. Annie 1935- .... **CLC 81**

Proust, (Valentin-Louis-George-Eugene-)
Marcel
1871-1922 .... **TCLC 7, 13, 33; DA;**
DAB; WLC
See also CA 104; 120; DLB 65; MTCW

Prowler, Harley
See Masters, Edgar Lee

Prus, Boleslaw 1845-1912 .... **TCLC 48**

Pryor, Richard (Franklin Lenox Thomas)
1940- .... **CLC 26**
See also CA 122

Przybyszewski, Stanislaw
1868-1927 .... **TCLC 36**
See also DLB 66

Pteleon
See Grieve, C(hristopher) M(urray)

Puckett, Lute
See Masters, Edgar Lee

Puig, Manuel
1932-1990 ... **CLC 3, 5, 10, 28, 65; HLC**
See also CA 45-48; CANR 2, 32; DLB 113;
HW; MTCW

Purdy, Al(fred Wellington)
1918-................ **CLC 3, 6, 14, 50**
See also CA 81-84; CAAS 17; CANR 42;
DLB 88

Purdy, James (Amos)
1923-............ **CLC 2, 4, 10, 28, 52**
See also CA 33-36R; CAAS 1; CANR 19;
DLB 2; MTCW

Pure, Simon
See Swinnerton, Frank Arthur

Pushkin, Alexander (Sergeyevich)
1799-1837 ..... **NCLC 3, 27; DA; DAB;**
PC 10; WLC
See also SATA 61

P'u Sung-ling 1640-1715 .... **LC 3**

Putnam, Arthur Lee
See Alger, Horatio, Jr.

Puzo, Mario 1920-......... **CLC 1, 2, 6, 36**
See also CA 65-68; CANR 4, 42; DLB 6;
MTCW

Pym, Barbara (Mary Crampton)
1913-1980 .... **CLC 13, 19, 37**
See also CA 13-14; 97-100; CANR 13, 34;
CAP 1; DLB 14; DLBY 87; MTCW

Pynchon, Thomas (Ruggles, Jr.)
1937- ..... **CLC 2, 3, 6, 9, 11, 18, 33, 62,**
72; DA; DAB; SSC 14; WLC
See also BEST 90:2; CA 17-20R; CANR 22,
46; DLB 2; MTCW

Qian Zhongshu
See Ch'ien Chung-shu

Qroll
See Dagerman, Stig (Halvard)

Quarrington, Paul (Lewis) 1953-.... **CLC 65**
See also CA 129

Quasimodo, Salvatore 1901-1968 ... **CLC 10**
See also CA 13-16; 25-28R; CAP 1;
DLB 114; MTCW

Queen, Ellery................. **CLC 3, 11**
See also Dannay, Frederic; Davidson,
Avram; Lee, Manfred B(ennington);
Sturgeon, Theodore (Hamilton); Vance,
John Holbrook

Queen, Ellery, Jr.
See Dannay, Frederic; Lee, Manfred
B(ennington)

Queneau, Raymond
1903-1976 .... **CLC 2, 5, 10, 42**
See also CA 77-80; 69-72; CANR 32;
DLB 72; MTCW

Quevedo, Francisco de 1580-1645.... **LC 23**

Quiller-Couch, Arthur Thomas
1863-1944 .... **TCLC 53**
See also CA 118; DLB 135, 153

Quin, Ann (Marie) 1936-1973....... **CLC 6**
See also CA 9-12R; 45-48; DLB 14

Quinn, Martin
See Smith, Martin Cruz

Quinn, Simon
See Smith, Martin Cruz

Quiroga, Horacio (Sylvestre)
1878-1937 .... **TCLC 20; HLC**
See also CA 117; 131; HW; MTCW

Quoirez, Francoise 1935-........... **CLC 9**
See also Sagan, Francoise
See also CA 49-52; CANR 6, 39; MTCW

Raabe, Wilhelm 1831-1910 .... **TCLC 45**
See also DLB 129

Rabe, David (William) 1940-... **CLC 4, 8, 33**
See also CA 85-88; CABS 3; DLB 7

Rabelais, Francois
1483-1553 ...... **LC 5; DA; DAB; WLC**

Rabinovitch, Sholem 1859-1916
See Aleichem, Sholom
See also CA 104

Racine, Jean 1639-1699 .... **LC 28; DAB**

Radcliffe, Ann (Ward) 1764-1823 .. **NCLC 6**
See also DLB 39

Radiguet, Raymond 1903-1923 .... **TCLC 29**
See also DLB 65

Radnoti, Miklos 1909-1944 .... **TCLC 16**
See also CA 118

Rado, James 1939-............... **CLC 17**
See also CA 105

Radvanyi, Netty 1900-1983
See Seghers, Anna
See also CA 85-88; 110

Rae, Ben
See Griffiths, Trevor

Raeburn, John (Hay) 1941-........ **CLC 34**
See also CA 57-60

Ragni, Gerome 1942-1991 .... **CLC 17**
See also CA 105; 134

Rahv, Philip 1908-1973 .... **CLC 24**
See also Greenberg, Ivan
See also DLB 137

Raine, Craig 1944-............... **CLC 32**
See also CA 108; CANR 29; DLB 40

Raine, Kathleen (Jessie) 1908- ... **CLC 7, 45**
See also CA 85-88; CANR 46; DLB 20;
MTCW

Rainis, Janis 1865-1929.......... **TCLC 29**

Rakosi, Carl..................... **CLC 47**
See also Rawley, Callman
See also CAAS 5

Raleigh, Richard
  See Lovecraft, H(oward) P(hillips)

Raleigh, Sir Walter 1554(?)-1618 .... **LC 31**
  See also CDBLB Before 1660

Rallentando, H. P.
  See Sayers, Dorothy L(eigh)

Ramal, Walter
  See de la Mare, Walter (John)

Ramon, Juan
  See Jimenez (Mantecon), Juan Ramon

Ramos, Graciliano 1892-1953 ..... **TCLC 32**

Rampersad, Arnold 1941- .... **CLC 44**
  See also BW 2; CA 127; 133; DLB 111

Rampling, Anne
  See Rice, Anne

Ramsay, Allan 1684(?)-1758 .... **LC 29**
  See also DLB 95

Ramuz, Charles-Ferdinand
  1878-1947 .... **TCLC 33**

Rand, Ayn
  1905-1982 ...... **CLC 3, 30, 44, 79; DA; WLC**
  See also AAYA 10; CA 13-16R; 105; CANR 27; MTCW

Randall, Dudley (Felker)
  1914- .... **CLC 1; BLC**
  See also BW 1; CA 25-28R; CANR 23; DLB 41

Randall, Robert
  See Silverberg, Robert

Ranger, Ken
  See Creasey, John

Ransom, John Crowe
  1888-1974 .... **CLC 2, 4, 5, 11, 24**
  See also CA 5-8R; 49-52; CANR 6, 34; DLB 45, 63; MTCW

Rao, Raja 1909- .... **CLC 25, 56**
  See also CA 73-76; MTCW

Raphael, Frederic (Michael)
  1931- .... **CLC 2, 14**
  See also CA 1-4R; CANR 1; DLB 14

Ratcliffe, James P.
  See Mencken, H(enry) L(ouis)

Rathbone, Julian 1935- .... **CLC 41**
  See also CA 101; CANR 34

Rattigan, Terence (Mervyn)
  1911-1977 .... **CLC 7**
  See also CA 85-88; 73-76; CDBLB 1945-1960; DLB 13; MTCW

Ratushinskaya, Irina 1954- .... **CLC 54**
  See also CA 129

Raven, Simon (Arthur Noel)
  1927- .... **CLC 14**
  See also CA 81-84

Rawley, Callman 1903-
  See Rakosi, Carl
  See also CA 21-24R; CANR 12, 32

Rawlings, Marjorie Kinnan
  1896-1953 .... **TCLC 4**
  See also CA 104; 137; DLB 9, 22, 102; JRDA; MAICYA; YABC 1

Ray, Satyajit 1921-1992........ **CLC 16, 76**
  See also CA 114; 137

Read, Herbert Edward 1893-1968.... **CLC 4**
  See also CA 85-88; 25-28R; DLB 20, 149

Read, Piers Paul 1941- ...... **CLC 4, 10, 25**
  See also CA 21-24R; CANR 38; DLB 14; SATA 21

Reade, Charles 1814-1884 .... **NCLC 2**
  See also DLB 21

Reade, Hamish
  See Gray, Simon (James Holliday)

Reading, Peter 1946- .... **CLC 47**
  See also CA 103; CANR 46; DLB 40

Reaney, James 1926- .... **CLC 13**
  See also CA 41-44R; CAAS 15; CANR 42; DLB 68; SATA 43

Rebreanu, Liviu 1885-1944 .... **TCLC 28**

Rechy, John (Francisco)
  1934- .... **CLC 1, 7, 14, 18; HLC**
  See also CA 5-8R; CAAS 4; CANR 6, 32; DLB 122; DLBY 82; HW

Redcam, Tom 1870-1933 .... **TCLC 25**

Reddin, Keith. **CLC 67**

Redgrove, Peter (William)
  1932- .... **CLC 6, 41**
  See also CA 1-4R; CANR 3, 39; DLB 40

Redmon, Anne .... **CLC 22**
  See also Nightingale, Anne Redmon
  See also DLBY 86

Reed, Eliot
  See Ambler, Eric

Reed, Ishmael
  1938- ... **CLC 2, 3, 5, 6, 13, 32, 60; BLC**
  See also BW 2; CA 21-24R; CANR 25, 48; DLB 2, 5, 33; DLBD 8; MTCW

Reed, John (Silas) 1887-1920 ...... **TCLC 9**
  See also CA 106

Reed, Lou. . . . . **CLC 21**
  See also Firbank, Louis

Reeve, Clara 1729-1807 .... **NCLC 19**
  See also DLB 39

Reich, Wilhelm 1897-1957 .... **TCLC 57**

Reid, Christopher (John) 1949- ..... **CLC 33**
  See also CA 140; DLB 40

Reid, Desmond
  See Moorcock, Michael (John)

Reid Banks, Lynne 1929-
  See Banks, Lynne Reid
  See also CA 1-4R; CANR 6, 22, 38; CLR 24; JRDA; MAICYA; SATA 22, 75

Reilly, William K.
  See Creasey, John

Reiner, Max
  See Caldwell, (Janet Miriam) Taylor (Holland)

Reis, Ricardo
  See Pessoa, Fernando (Antonio Nogueira)

Remarque, Erich Maria
  1898-1970 .... **CLC 21; DA; DAB**
  See also CA 77-80; 29-32R; DLB 56; MTCW

Remizov, A.
  See Remizov, Aleksei (Mikhailovich)

Remizov, A. M.
  See Remizov, Aleksei (Mikhailovich)

Remizov, Aleksei (Mikhailovich)
  1877-1957 .... **TCLC 27**
  See also CA 125; 133

Renan, Joseph Ernest
  1823-1892 .... **NCLC 26**

Renard, Jules 1864-1910 .... **TCLC 17**
  See also CA 117

Renault, Mary. . . . . **CLC 3, 11, 17**
  See also Challans, Mary
  See also DLBY 83

Rendell, Ruth (Barbara) 1930- .. **CLC 28, 48**
  See also Vine, Barbara
  See also CA 109; CANR 32; DLB 87; MTCW

Renoir, Jean 1894-1979 .... **CLC 20**
  See also CA 129; 85-88

Resnais, Alain 1922-.............. **CLC 16**

Reverdy, Pierre 1889-1960 .... **CLC 53**
  See also CA 97-100; 89-92

Rexroth, Kenneth
  1905-1982 ...... **CLC 1, 2, 6, 11, 22, 49**
  See also CA 5-8R; 107; CANR 14, 34; CDALB 1941-1968; DLB 16, 48; DLBY 82; MTCW

Reyes, Alfonso 1889-1959 .... **TCLC 33**
  See also CA 131; HW

Reyes y Basoalto, Ricardo Eliecer Neftali
  See Neruda, Pablo

Reymont, Wladyslaw (Stanislaw)
  1868(?)-1925 .... **TCLC 5**
  See also CA 104

Reynolds, Jonathan 1942- .... **CLC 6, 38**
  See also CA 65-68; CANR 28

Reynolds, Joshua 1723-1792 .... **LC 15**
  See also DLB 104

Reynolds, Michael Shane 1937- .... **CLC 44**
  See also CA 65-68; CANR 9

Reznikoff, Charles 1894-1976 .... **CLC 9**
  See also CA 33-36; 61-64; CAP 2; DLB 28, 45

Rezzori (d'Arezzo), Gregor von
  1914- .... **CLC 25**
  See also CA 122; 136

Rhine, Richard
  See Silverstein, Alvin

Rhodes, Eugene Manlove
  1869-1934 .... **TCLC 53**

R'hoone
  See Balzac, Honore de

Rhys, Jean
  1890(?)-1979 .... **CLC 2, 4, 6, 14, 19, 51; SSC 21**
  See also CA 25-28R; 85-88; CANR 35; CDBLB 1945-1960; DLB 36, 117; MTCW

Ribeiro, Darcy 1922- .... **CLC 34**
  See also CA 33-36R

Ribeiro, Joao Ubaldo (Osorio Pimentel)
  1941- .... **CLC 10, 67**
  See also CA 81-84

Ribman, Ronald (Burt) 1932- .... **CLC 7**
  See also CA 21-24R; CANR 46

Ricci, Nino 1959- .... **CLC 70**
  See also CA 137

Rice, Anne   1941- .... **CLC 41**
See also AAYA 9; BEST 89:2; CA 65-68;
CANR 12, 36

Rice, Elmer (Leopold)
1892-1967 .... **CLC 7, 49**
See also CA 21-22; 25-28R; CAP 2; DLB 4,
7; MTCW

Rice, Tim(othy Miles Bindon)
1944- .... **CLC 21**
See also CA 103; CANR 46

Rich, Adrienne (Cecile)
1929- .... **CLC 3, 6, 7, 11, 18, 36, 73, 76;**
PC 5
See also CA 9-12R; CANR 20; DLB 5, 67;
MTCW

Rich, Barbara
See Graves, Robert (von Ranke)

Rich, Robert
See Trumbo, Dalton

Richard, Keith .... **CLC 17**
See also Richards, Keith

Richards, David Adams   1950- ...... **CLC 59**
See also CA 93-96; DLB 53

Richards, I(vor) A(rmstrong)
1893-1979 .... **CLC 14, 24**
See also CA 41-44R; 89-92; CANR 34;
DLB 27

Richards, Keith   1943-
See Richard, Keith
See also CA 107

Richardson, Anne
See Roiphe, Anne (Richardson)

Richardson, Dorothy Miller
1873-1957 .... **TCLC 3**
See also CA 104; DLB 36

Richardson, Ethel Florence (Lindesay)
1870-1946
See Richardson, Henry Handel
See also CA 105

Richardson, Henry Handel .... **TCLC 4**
See also Richardson, Ethel Florence
(Lindesay)

Richardson, Samuel
1689-1761 ...... **LC 1; DA; DAB; WLC**
See also CDBLB 1660-1789; DLB 39

Richler, Mordecai
1931- ...... **CLC 3, 5, 9, 13, 18, 46, 70**
See also AITN 1; CA 65-68; CANR 31;
CLR 17; DLB 53; MAICYA; MTCW;
SATA 44; SATA-Brief 27

Richter, Conrad (Michael)
1890-1968 .... **CLC 30**
See also CA 5-8R; 25-28R; CANR 23;
DLB 9; MTCW; SATA 3

Ricostranza, Tom
See Ellis, Trey

Riddell, J. H.   1832-1906 .... **TCLC 40**

Riding, Laura .... **CLC 3, 7**
See also Jackson, Laura (Riding)

Riefenstahl, Berta Helene Amalia   1902-
See Riefenstahl, Leni
See also CA 108

Riefenstahl, Leni .... **CLC 16**
See also Riefenstahl, Berta Helene Amalia

Riffe, Ernest
See Bergman, (Ernst) Ingmar

Riggs, (Rolla) Lynn   1899-1954 .... **TCLC 56**
See also CA 144; NNAL

Riley, James Whitcomb
1849-1916 .... **TCLC 51**
See also CA 118; 137; MAICYA; SATA 17

Riley, Tex
See Creasey, John

Rilke, Rainer Maria
1875-1926 .... **TCLC 1, 6, 19; PC 2**
See also CA 104; 132; DLB 81; MTCW

Rimbaud, (Jean Nicolas) Arthur
1854-1891 ..... **NCLC 4, 35; DA; DAB;**
PC 3; WLC

Rinehart, Mary Roberts
1876-1958 .... **TCLC 52**
See also CA 108

Ringmaster, The
See Mencken, H(enry) L(ouis)

Ringwood, Gwen(dolyn Margaret) Pharis
1910-1984 .... **CLC 48**
See also CA 148; 112; DLB 88

Rio, Michel   19(?)- .... **CLC 43**

Ritsos, Giannes
See Ritsos, Yannis

Ritsos, Yannis   1909-1990 ..... **CLC 6, 13, 31**
See also CA 77-80; 133; CANR 39; MTCW

Ritter, Erika   1948(?)- .... **CLC 52**

Rivera, Jose Eustasio   1889-1928 ... **TCLC 35**
See also HW

Rivers, Conrad Kent   1933-1968 ...... **CLC 1**
See also BW 1; CA 85-88; DLB 41

Rivers, Elfrida
See Bradley, Marion Zimmer

Riverside, John
See Heinlein, Robert A(nson)

Rizal, Jose   1861-1896 .... **NCLC 27**

Roa Bastos, Augusto (Antonio)
1917- .... **CLC 45; HLC**
See also CA 131; DLB 113; HW

Robbe-Grillet, Alain
1922- ...... **CLC 1, 2, 4, 6, 8, 10, 14, 43**
See also CA 9-12R; CANR 33; DLB 83;
MTCW

Robbins, Harold   1916- .... **CLC 5**
See also CA 73-76; CANR 26; MTCW

Robbins, Thomas Eugene   1936-
See Robbins, Tom
See also CA 81-84; CANR 29; MTCW

Robbins, Tom .... **CLC 9, 32, 64**
See also Robbins, Thomas Eugene
See also BEST 90:3; DLBY 80

Robbins, Trina   1938- .... **CLC 21**
See also CA 128

Roberts, Charles G(eorge) D(ouglas)
1860-1943 .... **TCLC 8**
See also CA 105; CLR 33; DLB 92;
SATA-Brief 29

Roberts, Kate   1891-1985 .... **CLC 15**
See also CA 107; 116

Roberts, Keith (John Kingston)
1935- .... **CLC 14**
See also CA 25-28R; CANR 46

Roberts, Kenneth (Lewis)
1885-1957 .... **TCLC 23**
See also CA 109; DLB 9

Roberts, Michele (B.)   1949- .... **CLC 48**
See also CA 115

Robertson, Ellis
See Ellison, Harlan (Jay); Silverberg, Robert

Robertson, Thomas William
1829-1871 .... **NCLC 35**

Robinson, Edwin Arlington
1869-1935 .... **TCLC 5; DA; PC 1**
See also CA 104; 133; CDALB 1865-1917;
DLB 54; MTCW

Robinson, Henry Crabb
1775-1867 .... **NCLC 15**
See also DLB 107

Robinson, Jill   1936- .... **CLC 10**
See also CA 102

Robinson, Kim Stanley   1952- ...... **CLC 34**
See also CA 126

Robinson, Lloyd
See Silverberg, Robert

Robinson, Marilynne   1944- .... **CLC 25**
See also CA 116

Robinson, Smokey .... **CLC 21**
See also Robinson, William, Jr.

Robinson, William, Jr.   1940-
See Robinson, Smokey
See also CA 116

Robison, Mary   1949- .... **CLC 42**
See also CA 113; 116; DLB 130

Rod, Edouard   1857-1910 .... **TCLC 52**

Roddenberry, Eugene Wesley   1921-1991
See Roddenberry, Gene
See also CA 110; 135; CANR 37; SATA 45;
SATA-Obit 69

Roddenberry, Gene .... **CLC 17**
See also Roddenberry, Eugene Wesley
See also AAYA 5; SATA-Obit 69

Rodgers, Mary   1931- .... **CLC 12**
See also CA 49-52; CANR 8; CLR 20;
JRDA; MAICYA; SATA 8

Rodgers, W(illiam) R(obert)
1909-1969 .... **CLC 7**
See also CA 85-88; DLB 20

Rodman, Eric
See Silverberg, Robert

Rodman, Howard   1920(?)-1985 ..... **CLC 65**
See also CA 118

Rodman, Maia
See Wojciechowska, Maia (Teresa)

Rodriguez, Claudio   1934- .... **CLC 10**
See also DLB 134

Roelvaag, O(le) E(dvart)
1876-1931 .... **TCLC 17**
See also CA 117; DLB 9

Roethke, Theodore (Huebner)
1908-1963 ...... **CLC 1, 3, 8, 11, 19, 46**
See also CA 81-84; CABS 2;
CDALB 1941-1968; DLB 5; MTCW

Rogers, Thomas Hunton   1927- ..... **CLC 57**
See also CA 89-92

Savan, Glenn 19(?)- .... **CLC 50**

Sayers, Dorothy L(eigh)
1893-1957 .... **TCLC 2, 15**
See also CA 104; 119; CDBLB 1914-1945;
DLB 10, 36, 77, 100; MTCW

Sayers, Valerie 1952- .... **CLC 50**
See also CA 134

Sayles, John (Thomas)
1950- .... **CLC 7, 10, 14**
See also CA 57-60; CANR 41; DLB 44

Scammell, Michael .... **CLC 34**

Scannell, Vernon 1922- .... **CLC 49**
See also CA 5-8R; CANR 8, 24; DLB 27;
SATA 59

Scarlett, Susan
See Streatfeild, (Mary) Noel

Schaeffer, Susan Fromberg
1941- .... **CLC 6, 11, 22**
See also CA 49-52; CANR 18; DLB 28;
MTCW; SATA 22

Schary, Jill
See Robinson, Jill

Schell, Jonathan 1943- .... **CLC 35**
See also CA 73-76; CANR 12

Schelling, Friedrich Wilhelm Joseph von
1775-1854 .... **NCLC 30**
See also DLB 90

Schendel, Arthur van 1874-1946 ... **TCLC 56**

Scherer, Jean-Marie Maurice 1920-
See Rohmer, Eric
See also CA 110

Schevill, James (Erwin) 1920- .... **CLC 7**
See also CA 5-8R; CAAS 12

Schiller, Friedrich 1759-1805 .... **NCLC 39**
See also DLB 94

Schisgal, Murray (Joseph) 1926- ..... **CLC 6**
See also CA 21-24R; CANR 48

Schlee, Ann 1934- .... **CLC 35**
See also CA 101; CANR 29; SATA 44;
SATA-Brief 36

Schlegel, August Wilhelm von
1767-1845 .... **NCLC 15**
See also DLB 94

Schlegel, Friedrich 1772-1829 .... **NCLC 45**
See also DLB 90

Schlegel, Johann Elias (von)
1719(?)-1749 .... **LC 5**

Schlesinger, Arthur M(eier), Jr.
1917- .... **CLC 84**
See also AITN 1; CA 1-4R; CANR 1, 28;
DLB 17; MTCW; SATA 61

Schmidt, Arno (Otto) 1914-1979 .... **CLC 56**
See also CA 128; 109; DLB 69

Schmitz, Aron Hector 1861-1928
See Svevo, Italo
See also CA 104; 122; MTCW

Schnackenberg, Gjertrud 1953- ..... **CLC 40**
See also CA 116; DLB 120

Schneider, Leonard Alfred 1925-1966
See Bruce, Lenny
See also CA 89-92

Schnitzler, Arthur
1862-1931 .... **TCLC 4; SSC 15**
See also CA 104; DLB 81, 118

Schopenhauer, Arthur
1788-1860 .... **NCLC 51**
See also DLB 90

Schor, Sandra (M.) 1932(?)-1990 ... **CLC 65**
See also CA 132

Schorer, Mark 1908-1977 .... **CLC 9**
See also CA 5-8R; 73-76; CANR 7;
DLB 103

Schrader, Paul (Joseph) 1946- ...... **CLC 26**
See also CA 37-40R; CANR 41; DLB 44

Schreiner, Olive (Emilie Albertina)
1855-1920 .... **TCLC 9**
See also CA 105; DLB 18, 156

Schulberg, Budd (Wilson)
1914- .... **CLC 7, 48**
See also CA 25-28R; CANR 19; DLB 6, 26,
28; DLBY 81

Schulz, Bruno
1892-1942 .... **TCLC 5, 51; SSC 13**
See also CA 115; 123

Schulz, Charles M(onroe) 1922- .... **CLC 12**
See also CA 9-12R; CANR 6; SATA 10

Schumacher, E(rnst) F(riedrich)
1911-1977 .... **CLC 80**
See also CA 81-84; 73-76; CANR 34

Schuyler, James Marcus
1923-1991 .... **CLC 5, 23**
See also CA 101; 134; DLB 5

Schwartz, Delmore (David)
1913-1966 ... **CLC 2, 4, 10, 45, 87; PC 8**
See also CA 17-18; 25-28R; CANR 35;
CAP 2; DLB 28, 48; MTCW

Schwartz, Ernst
See Ozu, Yasujiro

Schwartz, John Burnham 1965- .... **CLC 59**
See also CA 132

Schwartz, Lynne Sharon 1939- ..... **CLC 31**
See also CA 103; CANR 44

Schwartz, Muriel A.
See Eliot, T(homas) S(tearns)

Schwarz-Bart, Andre 1928- .... **CLC 2, 4**
See also CA 89-92

Schwarz-Bart, Simone 1938- .... **CLC 7**
See also BW 2; CA 97-100

Schwob, (Mayer Andre) Marcel
1867-1905 .... **TCLC 20**
See also CA 117; DLB 123

Sciascia, Leonardo
1921-1989 .... **CLC 8, 9, 41**
See also CA 85-88; 130; CANR 35; MTCW

Scoppettone, Sandra 1936- .... **CLC 26**
See also AAYA 11; CA 5-8R; CANR 41;
SATA 9

Scorsese, Martin 1942- .... **CLC 20, 89**
See also CA 110; 114; CANR 46

Scotland, Jay
See Jakes, John (William)

Scott, Duncan Campbell
1862-1947 .... **TCLC 6**
See also CA 104; DLB 92

Scott, Evelyn 1893-1963 .... **CLC 43**
See also CA 104; 112; DLB 9, 48

Scott, F(rancis) R(eginald)
1899-1985 .... **CLC 22**
See also CA 101; 114; DLB 88

Scott, Frank
See Scott, F(rancis) R(eginald)

Scott, Joanna 1960- .... **CLC 50**
See also CA 126

Scott, Paul (Mark) 1920-1978 .... **CLC 9, 60**
See also CA 81-84; 77-80; CANR 33;
DLB 14; MTCW

Scott, Walter
1771-1832 .... **NCLC 15; DA; DAB;
PC 13; WLC**
See also CDBLB 1789-1832; DLB 93, 107,
116, 144; YABC 2

Scribe, (Augustin) Eugene
1791-1861 .... **NCLC 16; DC 5**

Scrum, R.
See Crumb, R(obert)

Scudery, Madeleine de 1607-1701 ..... **LC 2**

Scum
See Crumb, R(obert)

Scumbag, Little Bobby
See Crumb, R(obert)

Seabrook, John
See Hubbard, L(afayette) Ron(ald)

Sealy, I. Allan 1951- .... **CLC 55**

Search, Alexander
See Pessoa, Fernando (Antonio Nogueira)

Sebastian, Lee
See Silverberg, Robert

Sebastian Owl
See Thompson, Hunter S(tockton)

Sebestyen, Ouida 1924- .... **CLC 30**
See also AAYA 8; CA 107; CANR 40;
CLR 17; JRDA; MAICYA; SAAS 10;
SATA 39

Secundus, H. Scriblerus
See Fielding, Henry

Sedges, John
See Buck, Pearl S(ydenstricker)

Sedgwick, Catharine Maria
1789-1867 .... **NCLC 19**
See also DLB 1, 74

Seelye, John 1931- .... **CLC 7**

Seferiades, Giorgos Stylianou 1900-1971
See Seferis, George
See also CA 5-8R; 33-36R; CANR 5, 36;
MTCW

Seferis, George .... **CLC 5, 11**
See also Seferiades, Giorgos Stylianou

Segal, Erich (Wolf) 1937- .... **CLC 3, 10**
See also BEST 89:1; CA 25-28R; CANR 20,
36; DLBY 86; MTCW

Seger, Bob 1945- .... **CLC 35**

Seghers, Anna .... **CLC 7**
See also Radvanyi, Netty
See also DLB 69

Seidel, Frederick (Lewis) 1936- ..... **CLC 18**
See also CA 13-16R; CANR 8; DLBY 84

Seifert, Jaroslav 1901-1986 ..... **CLC 34, 44**
See also CA 127; MTCW

Sei Shonagon c. 966-1017(?) ...... **CMLC 6**

Selby, Hubert, Jr.
1928- . . . . CLC 1, 2, 4, 8; SSC 20
See also CA 13-16R; CANR 33; DLB 2

Selzer, Richard   1928- . . . . CLC 74
See also CA 65-68; CANR 14

Sembene, Ousmane
See Ousmane, Sembene

Senancour, Etienne Pivert de
1770-1846 . . . . NCLC 16
See also DLB 119

Sender, Ramon (Jose)
1902-1982 . . . . CLC 8; HLC
See also CA 5-8R; 105; CANR 8; HW;
MTCW

Seneca, Lucius Annaeus
4B.C.-65. . . . . CMLC 6; DC 5

Senghor, Leopold Sedar
1906- . . . . CLC 54; BLC
See also BW 2; CA 116; 125; CANR 47;
MTCW

Serling, (Edward) Rod(man)
1924-1975 . . . . CLC 30
See also AAYA 14; AITN 1; CA 65-68;
57-60; DLB 26

Serna, Ramon Gomez de la
See Gomez de la Serna, Ramon

Serpieres
See Guillevic, (Eugene)

Service, Robert
See Service, Robert W(illiam)
See also DAB; DLB 92

Service, Robert W(illiam)
1874(?)-1958 . . . . . . TCLC 15; DA; WLC
See also Service, Robert
See also CA 115; 140; SATA 20

Seth, Vikram   1952- . . . . CLC 43, 90
See also CA 121; 127; DLB 120

Seton, Cynthia Propper
1926-1982 . . . . CLC 27
See also CA 5-8R; 108; CANR 7

Seton, Ernest (Evan) Thompson
1860-1946 . . . . TCLC 31
See also CA 109; DLB 92; JRDA; SATA 18

Seton-Thompson, Ernest
See Seton, Ernest (Evan) Thompson

Settle, Mary Lee   1918- . . . . CLC 19, 61
See also CA 89-92; CAAS 1; CANR 44;
DLB 6

Seuphor, Michel
See Arp, Jean

Sevigne, Marie (de Rabutin-Chantal) Marquise
de   1626-1696 . . . . LC 11

Sexton, Anne (Harvey)
1928-1974 . . . . CLC 2, 4, 6, 8, 10, 15, 53;
DA; DAB; PC 2; WLC
See also CA 1-4R; 53-56; CABS 2;
CANR 3, 36; CDALB 1941-1968; DLB 5;
MTCW; SATA 10

Shaara, Michael (Joseph, Jr.)
1929-1988 . . . . CLC 15
See also AITN 1; CA 102; 125; DLBY 83

Shackleton, C. C.
See Aldiss, Brian W(ilson)

Shacochis, Bob . . . . CLC 39
See also Shacochis, Robert G.

Shacochis, Robert G.   1951-
See Shacochis, Bob
See also CA 119; 124

Shaffer, Anthony (Joshua)   1926- . . . . CLC 19
See also CA 110; 116; DLB 13

Shaffer, Peter (Levin)
1926- . . . . . . CLC 5, 14, 18, 37, 60; DAB
See also CA 25-28R; CANR 25, 47;
CDBLB 1960 to Present; DLB 13;
MTCW

Shakey, Bernard
See Young, Neil

Shalamov, Varlam (Tikhonovich)
1907(?)-1982 . . . . CLC 18
See also CA 129; 105

Shamlu, Ahmad   1925- . . . . CLC 10

Shammas, Anton   1951- . . . . CLC 55

Shange, Ntozake
1948- . . . . CLC 8, 25, 38, 74; BLC; DC 3
See also AAYA 9; BW 2; CA 85-88;
CABS 3; CANR 27, 48; DLB 38; MTCW

Shanley, John Patrick   1950- . . . . CLC 75
See also CA 128; 133

Shapcott, Thomas W(illiam)   1935- . . CLC 38
See also CA 69-72; CANR 49

Shapiro, Jane . . . . CLC 76

Shapiro, Karl (Jay)   1913- . . CLC 4, 8, 15, 53
See also CA 1-4R; CAAS 6; CANR 1, 36;
DLB 48; MTCW

Sharp, William   1855-1905 . . . . TCLC 39
See also DLB 156

Sharpe, Thomas Ridley   1928-
See Sharpe, Tom
See also CA 114; 122

Sharpe, Tom. . . . . CLC 36
See also Sharpe, Thomas Ridley
See also DLB 14

Shaw, Bernard . . . . TCLC 45
See also Shaw, George Bernard
See also BW 1

Shaw, G. Bernard
See Shaw, George Bernard

Shaw, George Bernard
1856-1950 . . . TCLC 3, 9, 21; DA; DAB;
WLC
See also Shaw, Bernard
See also CA 104; 128; CDBLB 1914-1945;
DLB 10, 57; MTCW

Shaw, Henry Wheeler
1818-1885 . . . . NCLC 15
See also DLB 11

Shaw, Irwin   1913-1984. . . . . . CLC 7, 23, 34
See also AITN 1; CA 13-16R; 112;
CANR 21; CDALB 1941-1968; DLB 6,
102; DLBY 84; MTCW

Shaw, Robert   1927-1978 . . . . CLC 5
See also AITN 1; CA 1-4R; 81-84;
CANR 4; DLB 13, 14

Shaw, T. E.
See Lawrence, T(homas) E(dward)

Shawn, Wallace   1943- . . . . CLC 41
See also CA 112

Shea, Lisa   1953- . . . . CLC 86
See also CA 147

Sheed, Wilfrid (John Joseph)
1930- . . . . CLC 2, 4, 10, 53
See also CA 65-68; CANR 30; DLB 6;
MTCW

Sheldon, Alice Hastings Bradley
1915(?)-1987
See Tiptree, James, Jr.
See also CA 108; 122; CANR 34; MTCW

Sheldon, John
See Bloch, Robert (Albert)

Shelley, Mary Wollstonecraft (Godwin)
1797-1851 . . NCLC 14; DA; DAB; WLC
See also CDBLB 1789-1832; DLB 110, 116;
SATA 29

Shelley, Percy Bysshe
1792-1822 . . NCLC 18; DA; DAB; WLC
See also CDBLB 1789-1832; DLB 96, 110

Shepard, Jim   1956- . . . . CLC 36
See also CA 137

Shepard, Lucius   1947- . . . . CLC 34
See also CA 128; 141

Shepard, Sam
1943- . . . . CLC 4, 6, 17, 34, 41, 44; DC 5
See also AAYA 1; CA 69-72; CABS 3;
CANR 22; DLB 7; MTCW

Shepherd, Michael
See Ludlum, Robert

Sherburne, Zoa (Morin)   1912- . . . . . . CLC 30
See also AAYA 13; CA 1-4R; CANR 3, 37;
MAICYA; SAAS 18; SATA 3

Sheridan, Frances   1724-1766. . . . . LC 7
See also DLB 39, 84

Sheridan, Richard Brinsley
1751-1816 . . . . NCLC 5; DA; DAB;
DC 1; WLC
See also CDBLB 1660-1789; DLB 89

Sherman, Jonathan Marc. . . . . CLC 55

Sherman, Martin   1941(?)- . . . . CLC 19
See also CA 116; 123

Sherwin, Judith Johnson   1936- . . . CLC 7, 15
See also CA 25-28R; CANR 34

Sherwood, Frances   1940- . . . . CLC 81
See also CA 146

Sherwood, Robert E(mmet)
1896-1955 . . . . TCLC 3
See also CA 104; DLB 7, 26

Shestov, Lev   1866-1938 . . . . TCLC 56

Shiel, M(atthew) P(hipps)
1865-1947 . . . . TCLC 8
See also CA 106; DLB 153

Shiga, Naoya   1883-1971. . . . . CLC 33
See also CA 101; 33-36R

Shih, Su   1036-1101. . . . . CMLC 15

Shilts, Randy   1951-1994 . . . . CLC 85
See also CA 115; 127; 144; CANR 45

Shimazaki Haruki   1872-1943
See Shimazaki Toson
See also CA 105; 134

Shimazaki Toson . . . . TCLC 5
See also Shimazaki Haruki

Sholokhov, Mikhail (Aleksandrovich)
1905-1984 . . . . CLC 7, 15
See also CA 101; 112; MTCW;
SATA-Obit 36

Shone, Patric
See Hanley, James

Shreve, Susan Richards 1939- ...... **CLC 23**
See also CA 49-52; CAAS 5; CANR 5, 38;
MAICYA; SATA 46; SATA-Brief 41

Shue, Larry 1946-1985 .... **CLC 52**
See also CA 145; 117

Shu-Jen, Chou 1881-1936
See Lu Hsun
See also CA 104

Shulman, Alix Kates 1932- ...... **CLC 2, 10**
See also CA 29-32R; CANR 43; SATA 7

Shuster, Joe 1914- .... **CLC 21**

Shute, Nevil .... **CLC 30**
See also Norway, Nevil Shute

Shuttle, Penelope (Diane) 1947- ..... **CLC 7**
See also CA 93-96; CANR 39; DLB 14, 40

Sidney, Mary 1561-1621 .... **LC 19**

Sidney, Sir Philip
1554-1586 .... **LC 19; DA; DAB**
See also CDBLB Before 1660

Siegel, Jerome 1914- .... **CLC 21**
See also CA 116

Siegel, Jerry
See Siegel, Jerome

Sienkiewicz, Henryk (Adam Alexander Pius)
1846-1916 .... **TCLC 3**
See also CA 104; 134

Sierra, Gregorio Martinez
See Martinez Sierra, Gregorio

Sierra, Maria (de la O'LeJarraga) Martinez
See Martinez Sierra, Maria (de la
O'LeJarraga)

Sigal, Clancy 1926-................ **CLC 7**
See also CA 1-4R

Sigourney, Lydia Howard (Huntley)
1791-1865 .... **NCLC 21**
See also DLB 1, 42, 73

Siguenza y Gongora, Carlos de
1645-1700 .... **LC 8**

Sigurjonsson, Johann 1880-1919... **TCLC 27**

Sikelianos, Angelos 1884-1951 .... **TCLC 39**

Silkin, Jon 1930- .... **CLC 2, 6, 43**
See also CA 5-8R; CAAS 5; DLB 27

Silko, Leslie (Marmon)
1948- .... **CLC 23, 74; DA**
See also AAYA 14; CA 115; 122;
CANR 45; DLB 143; NNAL

Sillanpaa, Frans Eemil 1888-1964... **CLC 19**
See also CA 129; 93-96; MTCW

Sillitoe, Alan
1928- .... **CLC 1, 3, 6, 10, 19, 57**
See also AITN 1; CA 9-12R; CAAS 2;
CANR 8, 26; CDBLB 1960 to Present;
DLB 14, 139; MTCW; SATA 61

Silone, Ignazio 1900-1978 .... **CLC 4**
See also CA 25-28; 81-84; CANR 34;
CAP 2; MTCW

Silver, Joan Micklin 1935- .... **CLC 20**
See also CA 114; 121

Silver, Nicholas
See Faust, Frederick (Schiller)

Silverberg, Robert 1935- .... **CLC 7**
See also CA 1-4R; CAAS 3; CANR 1, 20,
36; DLB 8; MAICYA; MTCW; SATA 13

Silverstein, Alvin 1933- .... **CLC 17**
See also CA 49-52; CANR 2; CLR 25;
JRDA; MAICYA; SATA 8, 69

Silverstein, Virginia B(arbara Opshelor)
1937- .... **CLC 17**
See also CA 49-52; CANR 2; CLR 25;
JRDA; MAICYA; SATA 8, 69

Sim, Georges
See Simenon, Georges (Jacques Christian)

Simak, Clifford D(onald)
1904-1988 .... **CLC 1, 55**
See also CA 1-4R; 125; CANR 1, 35;
DLB 8; MTCW; SATA-Obit 56

Simenon, Georges (Jacques Christian)
1903-1989 .... **CLC 1, 2, 3, 8, 18, 47**
See also CA 85-88; 129; CANR 35;
DLB 72; DLBY 89; MTCW

Simic, Charles 1938-... **CLC 6, 9, 22, 49, 68**
See also CA 29-32R; CAAS 4; CANR 12,
33; DLB 105

Simmons, Charles (Paul) 1924-..... **CLC 57**
See also CA 89-92

Simmons, Dan 1948-.............. **CLC 44**
See also CA 138

Simmons, James (Stewart Alexander)
1933- .... **CLC 43**
See also CA 105; CAAS 21; DLB 40

Simms, William Gilmore
1806-1870 .... **NCLC 3**
See also DLB 3, 30, 59, 73

Simon, Carly 1945-.............. **CLC 26**
See also CA 105

Simon, Claude 1913-....... **CLC 4, 9, 15, 39**
See also CA 89-92; CANR 33; DLB 83;
MTCW

Simon, (Marvin) Neil
1927- .... **CLC 6, 11, 31, 39, 70**
See also AITN 1; CA 21-24R; CANR 26;
DLB 7; MTCW

Simon, Paul 1942(?)- .... **CLC 17**
See also CA 116

Simonon, Paul 1956(?)- .... **CLC 30**

Simpson, Harriette
See Arnow, Harriette (Louisa) Simpson

Simpson, Louis (Aston Marantz)
1923- .... **CLC 4, 7, 9, 32**
See also CA 1-4R; CAAS 4; CANR 1;
DLB 5; MTCW

Simpson, Mona (Elizabeth) 1957-... **CLC 44**
See also CA 122; 135

Simpson, N(orman) F(rederick)
1919- .... **CLC 29**
See also CA 13-16R; DLB 13

Sinclair, Andrew (Annandale)
1935- .... **CLC 2, 14**
See also CA 9-12R; CAAS 5; CANR 14, 38;
DLB 14; MTCW

Sinclair, Emil
See Hesse, Hermann

Sinclair, Iain 1943-............... **CLC 76**
See also CA 132

Sinclair, Iain MacGregor
See Sinclair, Iain

Sinclair, Mary Amelia St. Clair 1865(?)-1946
See Sinclair, May
See also CA 104

Sinclair, May .... **TCLC 3, 11**
See also Sinclair, Mary Amelia St. Clair
See also DLB 36, 135

Sinclair, Upton (Beall)
1878-1968 ...... **CLC 1, 11, 15, 63; DA;**
DAB; WLC
See also CA 5-8R; 25-28R; CANR 7;
CDALB 1929-1941; DLB 9; MTCW;
SATA 9

Singer, Isaac
See Singer, Isaac Bashevis

Singer, Isaac Bashevis
1904-1991 .... **CLC 1, 3, 6, 9, 11, 15, 23,**
38, 69; DA; DAB; SSC 3; WLC
See also AITN 1, 2; CA 1-4R; 134;
CANR 1, 39; CDALB 1941-1968; CLR 1;
DLB 6, 28, 52; DLBY 91; JRDA;
MAICYA; MTCW; SATA 3, 27;
SATA-Obit 68

Singer, Israel Joshua 1893-1944 ... **TCLC 33**

Singh, Khushwant 1915-........... **CLC 11**
See also CA 9-12R; CAAS 9; CANR 6

Sinjohn, John
See Galsworthy, John

Sinyavsky, Andrei (Donatevich)
1925- .... **CLC 8**
See also CA 85-88

Sirin, V.
See Nabokov, Vladimir (Vladimirovich)

Sissman, L(ouis) E(dward)
1928-1976 .... **CLC 9, 18**
See also CA 21-24R; 65-68; CANR 13;
DLB 5

Sisson, C(harles) H(ubert) 1914-..... **CLC 8**
See also CA 1-4R; CAAS 3; CANR 3, 48;
DLB 27

Sitwell, Dame Edith
1887-1964 .... **CLC 2, 9, 67; PC 3**
See also CA 9-12R; CANR 35;
CDBLB 1945-1960; DLB 20; MTCW

Sjoewall, Maj 1935-.............. **CLC 7**
See also CA 65-68

Sjowall, Maj
See Sjoewall, Maj

Skelton, Robin 1925-............. **CLC 13**
See also AITN 2; CA 5-8R; CAAS 5;
CANR 28; DLB 27, 53

Skolimowski, Jerzy 1938-......... **CLC 20**
See also CA 128

Skram, Amalie (Bertha)
1847-1905 .... **TCLC 25**

Skvorecky, Josef (Vaclav)
1924-................. **CLC 15, 39, 69**
See also CA 61-64; CAAS 1; CANR 10, 34;
MTCW

Slade, Bernard................. **CLC 11, 46**
See also Newbound, Bernard Slade
See also CAAS 9; DLB 53

Slaughter, Carolyn 1946-.......... **CLC 56**
See also CA 85-88

Slaughter, Frank G(ill) 1908- . . . . . . CLC 29
See also AITN 2; CA 5-8R; CANR 5

Slavitt, David R(ytman) 1935-. . . . CLC 5, 14
See also CA 21-24R; CAAS 3; CANR 41;
DLB 5, 6

Slesinger, Tess 1905-1945 . . . . TCLC 10
See also CA 107; DLB 102

Slessor, Kenneth 1901-1971. . . . . . . CLC 14
See also CA 102; 89-92

Slowacki, Juliusz 1809-1849 . . . . . NCLC 15

Smart, Christopher
1722-1771 . . . . LC 3; PC 13
See also DLB 109

Smart, Elizabeth 1913-1986. . . . . . . CLC 54
See also CA 81-84; 118; DLB 88

Smiley, Jane (Graves) 1949- . . . . CLC 53, 76
See also CA 104; CANR 30

Smith, A(rthur) J(ames) M(arshall)
1902-1980 . . . . CLC 15
See also CA 1-4R; 102; CANR 4; DLB 88

Smith, Anna Deavere 1950-. . . . . . . CLC 86
See also CA 133

Smith, Betty (Wehner) 1896-1972. . . CLC 19
See also CA 5-8R; 33-36R; DLBY 82;
SATA 6

Smith, Charlotte (Turner)
1749-1806 . . . . NCLC 23
See also DLB 39, 109

Smith, Clark Ashton 1893-1961 . . . . CLC 43
See also CA 143

Smith, Dave. . . . . CLC 22, 42
See also Smith, David (Jeddie)
See also CAAS 7; DLB 5

Smith, David (Jeddie) 1942-
See Smith, Dave
See also CA 49-52; CANR 1

Smith, Florence Margaret 1902-1971
See Smith, Stevie
See also CA 17-18; 29-32R; CANR 35;
CAP 2; MTCW

Smith, Iain Crichton 1928- . . . . CLC 64
See also CA 21-24R; DLB 40, 139

Smith, John 1580(?)-1631 . . . . LC 9

Smith, Johnston
See Crane, Stephen (Townley)

Smith, Lee 1944-. . . . . CLC 25, 73
See also CA 114; 119; CANR 46; DLB 143;
DLBY 83

Smith, Martin
See Smith, Martin Cruz

Smith, Martin Cruz 1942-. . . . . CLC 25
See also BEST 89:4; CA 85-88; CANR 6,
23, 43; NNAL

Smith, Mary-Ann Tirone 1944-. . . . . CLC 39
See also CA 118; 136

Smith, Patti 1946- . . . . CLC 12
See also CA 93-96

Smith, Pauline (Urmson)
1882-1959 . . . . TCLC 25

Smith, Rosamond
See Oates, Joyce Carol

Smith, Sheila Kaye
See Kaye-Smith, Sheila

Smith, Stevie . . . . CLC 3, 8, 25, 44; PC 12
See also Smith, Florence Margaret
See also DLB 20

Smith, Wilbur (Addison) 1933-. . . . . CLC 33
See also CA 13-16R; CANR 7, 46; MTCW

Smith, William Jay 1918- . . . . CLC 6
See also CA 5-8R; CANR 44; DLB 5;
MAICYA; SATA 2, 68

Smith, Woodrow Wilson
See Kuttner, Henry

Smolenskin, Peretz 1842-1885. . . . NCLC 30

Smollett, Tobias (George) 1721-1771 . . LC 2
See also CDBLB 1660-1789; DLB 39, 104

Snodgrass, W(illiam) D(e Witt)
1926- . . . . CLC 2, 6, 10, 18, 68
See also CA 1-4R; CANR 6, 36; DLB 5;
MTCW

Snow, C(harles) P(ercy)
1905-1980 . . . . CLC 1, 4, 6, 9, 13, 19
See also CA 5-8R; 101; CANR 28;
CDBLB 1945-1960; DLB 15, 77; MTCW

Snow, Frances Compton
See Adams, Henry (Brooks)

Snyder, Gary (Sherman)
1930- . . . . CLC 1, 2, 5, 9, 32
See also CA 17-20R; CANR 30; DLB 5, 16

Snyder, Zilpha Keatley 1927- . . . . . . CLC 17
See also AAYA 15; CA 9-12R; CANR 38;
CLR 31; JRDA; MAICYA; SAAS 2;
SATA 1, 28, 75

Soares, Bernardo
See Pessoa, Fernando (Antonio Nogueira)

Sobh, A.
See Shamlu, Ahmad

Sobol, Joshua. . . . . CLC 60

Soderberg, Hjalmar 1869-1941 . . . . TCLC 39

Sodergran, Edith (Irene)
See Soedergran, Edith (Irene)

Soedergran, Edith (Irene)
1892-1923 . . . . TCLC 31

Softly, Edgar
See Lovecraft, H(oward) P(hillips)

Softly, Edward
See Lovecraft, H(oward) P(hillips)

Sokolov, Raymond 1941-. . . . . CLC 7
See also CA 85-88

Solo, Jay
See Ellison, Harlan (Jay)

Sologub, Fyodor . . . . TCLC 9
See also Teternikov, Fyodor Kuzmich

Solomons, Ikey Esquir
See Thackeray, William Makepeace

Solomos, Dionysios 1798-1857 . . . NCLC 15

Solwoska, Mara
See French, Marilyn

Solzhenitsyn, Aleksandr I(sayevich)
1918- . . . . . . CLC 1, 2, 4, 7, 9, 10, 18, 26,
34, 78; DA; DAB; WLC
See also AITN 1; CA 69-72; CANR 40;
MTCW

Somers, Jane
See Lessing, Doris (May)

Somerville, Edith 1858-1949 . . . . . . TCLC 51
See also DLB 135

Somerville & Ross
See Martin, Violet Florence; Somerville,
Edith

Sommer, Scott 1951- . . . . CLC 25
See also CA 106

Sondheim, Stephen (Joshua)
1930- . . . . CLC 30, 39
See also AAYA 11; CA 103; CANR 47

Sontag, Susan 1933-. . . CLC 1, 2, 10, 13, 31
See also CA 17-20R; CANR 25; DLB 2, 67;
MTCW

Sophocles
496(?)B.C.-406(?)B.C. . . . . CMLC 2; DA;
DAB; DC 1

Sordello 1189-1269. . . . . CMLC 15

Sorel, Julia
See Drexler, Rosalyn

Sorrentino, Gilbert
1929- . . . . CLC 3, 7, 14, 22, 40
See also CA 77-80; CANR 14, 33; DLB 5;
DLBY 80

Soto, Gary 1952-. . . . . CLC 32, 80; HLC
See also AAYA 10; CA 119; 125; CLR 38;
DLB 82; HW; JRDA; SATA 80

Soupault, Philippe 1897-1990 . . . . . . CLC 68
See also CA 116; 147; 131

Souster, (Holmes) Raymond
1921-. . . . . CLC 5, 14
See also CA 13-16R; CAAS 14; CANR 13,
29; DLB 88; SATA 63

Southern, Terry 1926- . . . . CLC 7
See also CA 1-4R; CANR 1; DLB 2

Southey, Robert 1774-1843 . . . . NCLC 8
See also DLB 93, 107, 142; SATA 54

Southworth, Emma Dorothy Eliza Nevitte
1819-1899 . . . . NCLC 26

Souza, Ernest
See Scott, Evelyn

Soyinka, Wole
1934- . . . . CLC 3, 5, 14, 36, 44; BLC;
DA; DAB; DC 2; WLC
See also BW 2; CA 13-16R; CANR 27, 39;
DLB 125; MTCW

Spackman, W(illiam) M(ode)
1905-1990 . . . . CLC 46
See also CA 81-84; 132

Spacks, Barry 1931-. . . . . CLC 14
See also CA 29-32R; CANR 33; DLB 105

Spanidou, Irini 1946-. . . . . CLC 44

Spark, Muriel (Sarah)
1918- . . . . CLC 2, 3, 5, 8, 13, 18, 40;
DAB; SSC 10
See also CA 5-8R; CANR 12, 36;
CDBLB 1945-1960; DLB 15, 139; MTCW

Spaulding, Douglas
See Bradbury, Ray (Douglas)

Spaulding, Leonard
See Bradbury, Ray (Douglas)

Spence, J. A. D.
See Eliot, T(homas) S(tearns)

Spencer, Elizabeth 1921-.......... **CLC 22**
See also CA 13-16R; CANR 32; DLB 6;
MTCW; SATA 14

Spencer, Leonard G.
See Silverberg, Robert

Spencer, Scott 1945-............. **CLC 30**
See also CA 113; DLBY 86

Spender, Stephen (Harold)
1909-............ **CLC 1, 2, 5, 10, 41**
See also CA 9-12R; CANR 31;
CDBLB 1945-1960; DLB 20; MTCW

Spengler, Oswald (Arnold Gottfried)
1880-1936 .... **TCLC 25**
See also CA 118

Spenser, Edmund
1552(?)-1599 .... **LC 5; DA; DAB; PC 8;
WLC**
See also CDBLB Before 1660

Spicer, Jack 1925-1965 ...... **CLC 8, 18, 72**
See also CA 85-88; DLB 5, 16

Spiegelman, Art 1948-............ **CLC 76**
See also AAYA 10; CA 125; CANR 41

Spielberg, Peter 1929-............. **CLC 6**
See also CA 5-8R; CANR 4, 48; DLBY 81

Spielberg, Steven 1947-........... **CLC 20**
See also AAYA 8; CA 77-80; CANR 32;
SATA 32

Spillane, Frank Morrison 1918-
See Spillane, Mickey
See also CA 25-28R; CANR 28; MTCW;
SATA 66

Spillane, Mickey .... **CLC 3, 13**
See also Spillane, Frank Morrison

Spinoza, Benedictus de 1632-1677 .... **LC 9**

Spinrad, Norman (Richard) 1940-... **CLC 46**
See also CA 37-40R; CAAS 19; CANR 20;
DLB 8

Spitteler, Carl (Friedrich Georg)
1845-1924 .... **TCLC 12**
See also CA 109; DLB 129

Spivack, Kathleen (Romola Drucker)
1938-........................ **CLC 6**
See also CA 49-52

Spoto, Donald 1941-.............. **CLC 39**
See also CA 65-68; CANR 11

Springsteen, Bruce (F.) 1949- ...... **CLC 17**
See also CA 111

Spurling, Hilary 1940-............ **CLC 34**
See also CA 104; CANR 25

Spyker, John Howland
See Elman, Richard

Squires, (James) Radcliffe
1917-1993 .... **CLC 51**
See also CA 1-4R; 140; CANR 6, 21

Srivastava, Dhanpat Rai 1880(?)-1936
See Premchand
See also CA 118

Stacy, Donald
See Pohl, Frederik

Stael, Germaine de
See Stael-Holstein, Anne Louise Germaine
Necker Baronn
See also DLB 119

**Stael-Holstein, Anne Louise Germaine Necker
Baronn** 1766-1817 .... **NCLC 3**
See also Stael, Germaine de

Stafford, Jean 1915-1979... **CLC 4, 7, 19, 68**
See also CA 1-4R; 85-88; CANR 3; DLB 2;
MTCW; SATA-Obit 22

Stafford, William (Edgar)
1914-1993 .... **CLC 4, 7, 29**
See also CA 5-8R; 142; CAAS 3; CANR 5,
22; DLB 5

Staines, Trevor
See Brunner, John (Kilian Houston)

Stairs, Gordon
See Austin, Mary (Hunter)

Stannard, Martin 1947-........... **CLC 44**
See also CA 142; DLB 155

Stanton, Maura 1946- .... **CLC 9**
See also CA 89-92; CANR 15; DLB 120

Stanton, Schuyler
See Baum, L(yman) Frank

Stapledon, (William) Olaf
1886-1950 .... **TCLC 22**
See also CA 111; DLB 15

Starbuck, George (Edwin) 1931-.... **CLC 53**
See also CA 21-24R; CANR 23

Stark, Richard
See Westlake, Donald E(dwin)

Staunton, Schuyler
See Baum, L(yman) Frank

Stead, Christina (Ellen)
1902-1983 .... **CLC 2, 5, 8, 32, 80**
See also CA 13-16R; 109; CANR 33, 40;
MTCW

Stead, William Thomas
1849-1912 .... **TCLC 48**

Steele, Richard 1672-1729 .... **LC 18**
See also CDBLB 1660-1789; DLB 84, 101

Steele, Timothy (Reid) 1948-....... **CLC 45**
See also CA 93-96; CANR 16; DLB 120

Steffens, (Joseph) Lincoln
1866-1936 .... **TCLC 20**
See also CA 117

Stegner, Wallace (Earle)
1909-1993 .... **CLC 9, 49, 81**
See also AITN 1; BEST 90:3; CA 1-4R;
141; CAAS 9; CANR 1, 21, 46; DLB 9;
DLBY 93; MTCW

Stein, Gertrude
1874-1946 ...... **TCLC 1, 6, 28, 48; DA;
DAB; WLC**
See also CA 104; 132; CDALB 1917-1929;
DLB 4, 54, 86; MTCW

Steinbeck, John (Ernst)
1902-1968 ...... **CLC 1, 5, 9, 13, 21, 34,
45, 75; DA; DAB; SSC 11; WLC**
See also AAYA 12; CA 1-4R; 25-28R;
CANR 1, 35; CDALB 1929-1941; DLB 7,
9; DLBD 2; MTCW; SATA 9

Steinem, Gloria 1934-............ **CLC 63**
See also CA 53-56; CANR 28; MTCW

Steiner, George 1929-............. **CLC 24**
See also CA 73-76; CANR 31; DLB 67;
MTCW; SATA 62

Steiner, K. Leslie
See Delany, Samuel R(ay, Jr.)

Steiner, Rudolf 1861-1925........ **TCLC 13**
See also CA 107

Stendhal
1783-1842 .... **NCLC 23, 46; DA; DAB;
WLC**
See also DLB 119

Stephen, Leslie 1832-1904 .... **TCLC 23**
See also CA 123; DLB 57, 144

Stephen, Sir Leslie
See Stephen, Leslie

Stephen, Virginia
See Woolf, (Adeline) Virginia

Stephens, James 1882(?)-1950...... **TCLC 4**
See also CA 104; DLB 19, 153

Stephens, Reed
See Donaldson, Stephen R.

Steptoe, Lydia
See Barnes, Djuna

Sterchi, Beat 1949-.............. **CLC 65**

Sterling, Brett
See Bradbury, Ray (Douglas); Hamilton,
Edmond

Sterling, Bruce 1954-............. **CLC 72**
See also CA 119; CANR 44

Sterling, George 1869-1926....... **TCLC 20**
See also CA 117; DLB 54

Stern, Gerald 1925- .... **CLC 40**
See also CA 81-84; CANR 28; DLB 105

Stern, Richard (Gustave) 1928-... **CLC 4, 39**
See also CA 1-4R; CANR 1, 25; DLBY 87

Sternberg, Josef von 1894-1969..... **CLC 20**
See also CA 81-84

Sterne, Laurence
1713-1768 ...... **LC 2; DA; DAB; WLC**
See also CDBLB 1660-1789; DLB 39

Sternheim, (William Adolf) Carl
1878-1942 .... **TCLC 8**
See also CA 105; DLB 56, 118

Stevens, Mark 1951- .... **CLC 34**
See also CA 122

Stevens, Wallace
1879-1955 .... **TCLC 3, 12, 45; DA;
DAB; PC 6; WLC**
See also CA 104; 124; CDALB 1929-1941;
DLB 54; MTCW

Stevenson, Anne (Katharine)
1933-.................... **CLC 7, 33**
See also CA 17-20R; CAAS 9; CANR 9, 33;
DLB 40; MTCW

Stevenson, Robert Louis (Balfour)
1850-1894 ..... **NCLC 5, 14; DA; DAB;
SSC 11; WLC**
See also CDBLB 1890-1914; CLR 10, 11;
DLB 18, 57, 141, 156; JRDA; MAICYA;
YABC 2

Stewart, J(ohn) I(nnes) M(ackintosh)
1906-1994 .... **CLC 7, 14, 32**
See also CA 85-88; 147; CAAS 3;
CANR 47; MTCW

Stewart, Mary (Florence Elinor)
1916- .... **CLC 7, 35; DAB**
See also CA 1-4R; CANR 1; SATA 12

Stewart, Mary Rainbow
See Stewart, Mary (Florence Elinor)

Stifle, June
See Campbell, Maria

Stifter, Adalbert 1805-1868 . . . . . . **NCLC 41**
See also DLB 133

Still, James 1906- . . . . **CLC 49**
See also CA 65-68; CAAS 17; CANR 10,
26; DLB 9; SATA 29

Sting
See Sumner, Gordon Matthew

Stirling, Arthur
See Sinclair, Upton (Beall)

Stitt, Milan 1941- . . . . **CLC 29**
See also CA 69-72

Stockton, Francis Richard 1834-1902
See Stockton, Frank R.
See also CA 108; 137; MAICYA; SATA 44

Stockton, Frank R. . . . . **TCLC 47**
See also Stockton, Francis Richard
See also DLB 42, 74; SATA-Brief 32

Stoddard, Charles
See Kuttner, Henry

Stoker, Abraham 1847-1912
See Stoker, Bram
See also CA 105; DA; SATA 29

Stoker, Bram . . . . **TCLC 8; DAB; WLC**
See also Stoker, Abraham
See also CDBLB 1890-1914; DLB 36, 70

Stolz, Mary (Slattery) 1920- . . . . . . **CLC 12**
See also AAYA 8; AITN 1; CA 5-8R;
CANR 13, 41; JRDA; MAICYA;
SAAS 3; SATA 10, 71

Stone, Irving 1903-1989 . . . . **CLC 7**
See also AITN 1; CA 1-4R; 129; CAAS 3;
CANR 1, 23; MTCW; SATA 3;
SATA-Obit 64

Stone, Oliver 1946- . . . . **CLC 73**
See also AAYA 15; CA 110

Stone, Robert (Anthony)
1937- . . . . **CLC 5, 23, 42**
See also CA 85-88; CANR 23; DLB 152;
MTCW

Stone, Zachary
See Follett, Ken(neth Martin)

Stoppard, Tom
1937- . . . . . . **CLC 1, 3, 4, 5, 8, 15, 29, 34,**
63; DA; DAB; WLC
See also CA 81-84; CANR 39;
CDBLB 1960 to Present; DLB 13;
DLBY 85; MTCW

Storey, David (Malcolm)
1933- . . . . **CLC 2, 4, 5, 8**
See also CA 81-84; CANR 36; DLB 13, 14;
MTCW

Storm, Hyemeyohsts 1935- . . . . **CLC 3**
See also CA 81-84; CANR 45; NNAL

Storm, (Hans) Theodor (Woldsen)
1817-1888 . . . . **NCLC 1**

Storni, Alfonsina
1892-1938 . . . . **TCLC 5; HLC**
See also CA 104; 131; HW

Stout, Rex (Todhunter) 1886-1975 . . . **CLC 3**
See also AITN 2; CA 61-64

Stow, (Julian) Randolph 1935- . . **CLC 23, 48**
See also CA 13-16R; CANR 33; MTCW

Stowe, Harriet (Elizabeth) Beecher
1811-1896 . . . . . **NCLC 3, 50; DA; DAB;**
WLC
See also CDALB 1865-1917; DLB 1, 12, 42,
74; JRDA; MAICYA; YABC 1

Strachey, (Giles) Lytton
1880-1932 . . . . **TCLC 12**
See also CA 110; DLB 149; DLBD 10

Strand, Mark 1934- . . . . . . **CLC 6, 18, 41, 71**
See also CA 21-24R; CANR 40; DLB 5;
SATA 41

Straub, Peter (Francis) 1943- . . . . . . **CLC 28**
See also BEST 89:1; CA 85-88; CANR 28;
DLBY 84; MTCW

Strauss, Botho 1944- . . . . **CLC 22**
See also DLB 124

Streatfeild, (Mary) Noel
1895(?)-1986 . . . . **CLC 21**
See also CA 81-84; 120; CANR 31;
CLR 17; MAICYA; SATA 20;
SATA-Obit 48

Stribling, T(homas) S(igismund)
1881-1965 . . . . **CLC 23**
See also CA 107; DLB 9

Strindberg, (Johan) August
1849-1912 . . . . . . **TCLC 1, 8, 21, 47; DA;**
DAB; WLC
See also CA 104; 135

Stringer, Arthur 1874-1950 . . . . **TCLC 37**
See also DLB 92

Stringer, David
See Roberts, Keith (John Kingston)

Strugatskii, Arkadii (Natanovich)
1925-1991 . . . . **CLC 27**
See also CA 106; 135

Strugatskii, Boris (Natanovich)
1933- . . . . **CLC 27**
See also CA 106

Strummer, Joe 1953(?)- . . . . **CLC 30**

Stuart, Don A.
See Campbell, John W(ood, Jr.)

Stuart, Ian
See MacLean, Alistair (Stuart)

Stuart, Jesse (Hilton)
1906-1984 . . . . **CLC 1, 8, 11, 14, 34**
See also CA 5-8R; 112; CANR 31; DLB 9,
48, 102; DLBY 84; SATA 2;
SATA-Obit 36

Sturgeon, Theodore (Hamilton)
1918-1985 . . . . **CLC 22, 39**
See also Queen, Ellery
See also CA 81-84; 116; CANR 32; DLB 8;
DLBY 85; MTCW

Sturges, Preston 1898-1959 . . . . **TCLC 48**
See also CA 114; DLB 26

Styron, William
1925- . . . . **CLC 1, 3, 5, 11, 15, 60**
See also BEST 90:4; CA 5-8R; CANR 6, 33;
CDALB 1968-1988; DLB 2, 143;
DLBY 80; MTCW

Suarez Lynch, B.
See Bioy Casares, Adolfo; Borges, Jorge
Luis

Su Chien 1884-1918
See Su Man-shu
See also CA 123

Suckow, Ruth 1892-1960 . . . . **SSC 18**
See also CA 113; DLB 9, 102

Sudermann, Hermann 1857-1928 . . **TCLC 15**
See also CA 107; DLB 118

Sue, Eugene 1804-1857 . . . . **NCLC 1**
See also DLB 119

Sueskind, Patrick 1949- . . . . **CLC 44**
See also Suskind, Patrick

Sukenick, Ronald 1932- . . . . . **CLC 3, 4, 6, 48**
See also CA 25-28R; CAAS 8; CANR 32;
DLBY 81

Suknaski, Andrew 1942- . . . . **CLC 19**
See also CA 101; DLB 53

Sullivan, Vernon
See Vian, Boris

Sully Prudhomme 1839-1907 . . . . . . **TCLC 31**

Su Man-shu . . . . **TCLC 24**
See also Su Chien

Summerforest, Ivy B.
See Kirkup, James

Summers, Andrew James 1942- . . . . . **CLC 26**

Summers, Andy
See Summers, Andrew James

Summers, Hollis (Spurgeon, Jr.)
1916- . . . . **CLC 10**
See also CA 5-8R; CANR 3; DLB 6

Summers, (Alphonsus Joseph-Mary Augustus)
Montague 1880-1948 . . . . **TCLC 16**
See also CA 118

Sumner, Gordon Matthew 1951- . . . . **CLC 26**

Surtees, Robert Smith
1803-1864 . . . . **NCLC 14**
See also DLB 21

Susann, Jacqueline 1921-1974 . . . . **CLC 3**
See also AITN 1; CA 65-68; 53-56; MTCW

Suskind, Patrick
See Sueskind, Patrick
See also CA 145

Sutcliff, Rosemary
1920-1992 . . . . **CLC 26; DAB**
See also AAYA 10; CA 5-8R; 139;
CANR 37; CLR 1, 37; JRDA; MAICYA;
SATA 6, 44, 78; SATA-Obit 73

Sutro, Alfred 1863-1933 . . . . **TCLC 6**
See also CA 105; DLB 10

Sutton, Henry
See Slavitt, David R(ytman)

Svevo, Italo . . . . **TCLC 2, 35**
See also Schmitz, Aron Hector

Swados, Elizabeth (A.) 1951- . . . . **CLC 12**
See also CA 97-100; CANR 49

Swados, Harvey 1920-1972 . . . . **CLC 5**
See also CA 5-8R; 37-40R; CANR 6;
DLB 2

Swan, Gladys 1934- . . . . **CLC 69**
See also CA 101; CANR 17, 39

Swarthout, Glendon (Fred)
1918-1992 . . . . **CLC 35**
See also CA 1-4R; 139; CANR 1, 47;
SATA 26

Sweet, Sarah C.
See Jewett, (Theodora) Sarah Orne

Swenson, May
1919-1989 .... **CLC 4, 14, 61; DA; DAB**
See also CA 5-8R; 130; CANR 36; DLB 5;
MTCW; SATA 15

Swift, Augustus
See Lovecraft, H(oward) P(hillips)

Swift, Graham (Colin) 1949- .... **CLC 41, 88**
See also CA 117; 122; CANR 46

Swift, Jonathan
1667-1745 ...... **LC 1; DA; DAB; PC 9;**
WLC
See also CDBLB 1660-1789; DLB 39, 95,
101; SATA 19

Swinburne, Algernon Charles
1837-1909 ...... **TCLC 8, 36; DA; DAB;**
WLC
See also CA 105; 140; CDBLB 1832-1890;
DLB 35, 57

Swinfen, Ann .... **CLC 34**

Swinnerton, Frank Arthur
1884-1982 .... **CLC 31**
See also CA 108; DLB 34

Swithen, John
See King, Stephen (Edwin)

Sylvia
See Ashton-Warner, Sylvia (Constance)

Symmes, Robert Edward
See Duncan, Robert (Edward)

Symonds, John Addington
1840-1893 .... **NCLC 34**
See also DLB 57, 144

Symons, Arthur 1865-1945 .... **TCLC 11**
See also CA 107; DLB 19, 57, 149

Symons, Julian (Gustave)
1912-1994 .... **CLC 2, 14, 32**
See also CA 49-52; 147; CAAS 3; CANR 3,
33; DLB 87, 155; DLBY 92; MTCW

Synge, (Edmund) J(ohn) M(illington)
1871-1909 .... **TCLC 6, 37; DC 2**
See also CA 104; 141; CDBLB 1890-1914;
DLB 10, 19

Syruc, J.
See Milosz, Czeslaw

Szirtes, George 1948- .... **CLC 46**
See also CA 109; CANR 27

Tabori, George 1914- .... **CLC 19**
See also CA 49-52; CANR 4

Tagore, Rabindranath
1861-1941 .... **TCLC 3, 53; PC 8**
See also CA 104; 120; MTCW

Taine, Hippolyte Adolphe
1828-1893 .... **NCLC 15**

Talese, Gay 1932- .... **CLC 37**
See also AITN 1; CA 1-4R; CANR 9;
MTCW

Tallent, Elizabeth (Ann) 1954- ..... **CLC 45**
See also CA 117; DLB 130

Tally, Ted 1952- .... **CLC 42**
See also CA 120; 124

Tamayo y Baus, Manuel
1829-1898 .... **NCLC 1**

Tammsaare, A(nton) H(ansen)
1878-1940 .... **TCLC 27**

Tan, Amy 1952- .... **CLC 59**
See also AAYA 9; BEST 89:3; CA 136;
SATA 75

Tandem, Felix
See Spitteler, Carl (Friedrich Georg)

Tanizaki, Jun'ichiro
1886-1965 ...... **CLC 8, 14, 28; SSC 21**
See also CA 93-96; 25-28R

Tanner, William
See Amis, Kingsley (William)

Tao Lao
See Storni, Alfonsina

Tarassoff, Lev
See Troyat, Henri

Tarbell, Ida M(inerva)
1857-1944 .... **TCLC 40**
See also CA 122; DLB 47

Tarkington, (Newton) Booth
1869-1946 .... **TCLC 9**
See also CA 110; 143; DLB 9, 102;
SATA 17

Tarkovsky, Andrei (Arsenyevich)
1932-1986 .... **CLC 75**
See also CA 127

Tartt, Donna 1964(?)- .... **CLC 76**
See also CA 142

Tasso, Torquato 1544-1595 .... **LC 5**

Tate, (John Orley) Allen
1899-1979 .... **CLC 2, 4, 6, 9, 11, 14, 24**
See also CA 5-8R; 85-88; CANR 32;
DLB 4, 45, 63; MTCW

Tate, Ellalice
See Hibbert, Eleanor Alice Burford

Tate, James (Vincent) 1943- ... **CLC 2, 6, 25**
See also CA 21-24R; CANR 29; DLB 5

Tavel, Ronald 1940- .... **CLC 6**
See also CA 21-24R; CANR 33

Taylor, C(ecil) P(hilip) 1929-1981 ... **CLC 27**
See also CA 25-28R; 105; CANR 47

Taylor, Edward
1642(?)-1729 .... **LC 11; DA; DAB**
See also DLB 24

Taylor, Eleanor Ross 1920- .... **CLC 5**
See also CA 81-84

Taylor, Elizabeth 1912-1975 ... **CLC 2, 4, 29**
See also CA 13-16R; CANR 9; DLB 139;
MTCW; SATA 13

Taylor, Henry (Splawn) 1942- ...... **CLC 44**
See also CA 33-36R; CAAS 7; CANR 31;
DLB 5

Taylor, Kamala (Purnaiya) 1924-
See Markandaya, Kamala
See also CA 77-80

Taylor, Mildred D. .... **CLC 21**
See also AAYA 10; BW 1; CA 85-88;
CANR 25; CLR 9; DLB 52; JRDA;
MAICYA; SAAS 5; SATA 15, 70

Taylor, Peter (Hillsman)
1917-1994 ..... **CLC 1, 4, 18, 37, 44, 50,**
71; SSC 10
See also CA 13-16R; 147; CANR 9;
DLBY 81, 94; MTCW

Taylor, Robert Lewis 1912- .... **CLC 14**
See also CA 1-4R; CANR 3; SATA 10

Tchekhov, Anton
See Chekhov, Anton (Pavlovich)

Teasdale, Sara 1884-1933.......... **TCLC 4**
See also CA 104; DLB 45; SATA 32

Tegner, Esaias 1782-1846......... **NCLC 2**

Teilhard de Chardin, (Marie Joseph) Pierre
1881-1955 .... **TCLC 9**
See also CA 105

Temple, Ann
See Mortimer, Penelope (Ruth)

Tennant, Emma (Christina)
1937- .... **CLC 13, 52**
See also CA 65-68; CAAS 9; CANR 10, 38;
DLB 14

Tenneshaw, S. M.
See Silverberg, Robert

Tennyson, Alfred
1809-1892 .... **NCLC 30; DA; DAB;**
PC 6; WLC
See also CDBLB 1832-1890; DLB 32

Teran, Lisa St. Aubin de .... **CLC 36**
See also St. Aubin de Teran, Lisa

Terence 195(?)B.C.-159B.C....... **CMLC 14**

Teresa de Jesus, St. 1515-1582 ...... **LC 18**

Terkel, Louis 1912-
See Terkel, Studs
See also CA 57-60; CANR 18, 45; MTCW

Terkel, Studs .... **CLC 38**
See also Terkel, Louis
See also AITN 1

Terry, C. V.
See Slaughter, Frank G(ill)

Terry, Megan 1932- .... **CLC 19**
See also CA 77-80; CABS 3; CANR 43;
DLB 7

Tertz, Abram
See Sinyavsky, Andrei (Donatevich)

Tesich, Steve 1943(?)-.......... **CLC 40, 69**
See also CA 105; DLBY 83

Teternikov, Fyodor Kuzmich 1863-1927
See Sologub, Fyodor
See also CA 104

Tevis, Walter 1928-1984 .... **CLC 42**
See also CA 113

Tey, Josephine.................... **TCLC 14**
See also Mackintosh, Elizabeth
See also DLB 77

Thackeray, William Makepeace
1811-1863 .... **NCLC 5, 14, 22, 43; DA;**
DAB; WLC
See also CDBLB 1832-1890; DLB 21, 55;
SATA 23

Thakura, Ravindranatha
See Tagore, Rabindranath

Tharoor, Shashi 1956- .... **CLC 70**
See also CA 141

Thelwell, Michael Miles 1939- ..... **CLC 22**
See also BW 2; CA 101

Theobald, Lewis, Jr.
See Lovecraft, H(oward) P(hillips)

Theodorescu, Ion N. 1880-1967
See Arghezi, Tudor
See also CA 116

Theriault, Yves 1915-1983 .... **CLC 79**
See also CA 102; DLB 88

Theroux, Alexander (Louis)
1939- .... **CLC 2, 25**
See also CA 85-88; CANR 20

Theroux, Paul (Edward)
1941- .... **CLC 5, 8, 11, 15, 28, 46**
See also BEST 89:4; CA 33-36R; CANR 20,
45; DLB 2; MTCW; SATA 44

Thesen, Sharon 1946- .... **CLC 56**

Thevenin, Denis
See Duhamel, Georges

Thibault, Jacques Anatole Francois
1844-1924
See France, Anatole
See also CA 106; 127; MTCW

Thiele, Colin (Milton) 1920- .... **CLC 17**
See also CA 29-32R; CANR 12, 28;
CLR 27; MAICYA; SAAS 2; SATA 14,
72

Thomas, Audrey (Callahan)
1935- .... **CLC 7, 13, 37; SSC 20**
See also AITN 2; CA 21-24R; CAAS 19;
CANR 36; DLB 60; MTCW

Thomas, D(onald) M(ichael)
1935- .... **CLC 13, 22, 31**
See also CA 61-64; CAAS 11; CANR 17,
45; CDBLB 1960 to Present; DLB 40;
MTCW

Thomas, Dylan (Marlais)
1914-1953 ... **TCLC 1, 8, 45; DA; DAB;
PC 2; SSC 3; WLC**
See also CA 104; 120; CDBLB 1945-1960;
DLB 13, 20, 139; MTCW; SATA 60

Thomas, (Philip) Edward
1878-1917 .... **TCLC 10**
See also CA 106; DLB 19

Thomas, Joyce Carol 1938- .... **CLC 35**
See also AAYA 12; BW 2; CA 113; 116;
CANR 48; CLR 19; DLB 33; JRDA;
MAICYA; MTCW; SAAS 7; SATA 40,
78

Thomas, Lewis 1913-1993 .... **CLC 35**
See also CA 85-88; 143; CANR 38; MTCW

Thomas, Paul
See Mann, (Paul) Thomas

Thomas, Piri 1928- .... **CLC 17**
See also CA 73-76; HW

Thomas, R(onald) S(tuart)
1913- .... **CLC 6, 13, 48; DAB**
See also CA 89-92; CAAS 4; CANR 30;
CDBLB 1960 to Present; DLB 27;
MTCW

Thomas, Ross (Elmore) 1926- ...... **CLC 39**
See also CA 33-36R; CANR 22

Thompson, Francis Clegg
See Mencken, H(enry) L(ouis)

Thompson, Francis Joseph
1859-1907 .... **TCLC 4**
See also CA 104; CDBLB 1890-1914;
DLB 19

Thompson, Hunter S(tockton)
1939- .... **CLC 9, 17, 40**
See also BEST 89:1; CA 17-20R; CANR 23,
46; MTCW

Thompson, James Myers
See Thompson, Jim (Myers)

Thompson, Jim (Myers)
1906-1977(?) .... **CLC 69**
See also CA 140

Thompson, Judith .... **CLC 39**

Thomson, James 1700-1748 ..... **LC 16, 29**
See also DLB 95

Thomson, James 1834-1882 ...... **NCLC 18**
See also DLB 35

Thoreau, Henry David
1817-1862 ..... **NCLC 7, 21; DA; DAB;
WLC**
See also CDALB 1640-1865; DLB 1

Thornton, Hall
See Silverberg, Robert

Thurber, James (Grover)
1894-1961 .... **CLC 5, 11, 25; DA; DAB;
SSC 1**
See also CA 73-76; CANR 17, 39;
CDALB 1929-1941; DLB 4, 11, 22, 102;
MAICYA; MTCW; SATA 13

Thurman, Wallace (Henry)
1902-1934 .... **TCLC 6; BLC**
See also BW 1; CA 104; 124; DLB 51

Ticheburn, Cheviot
See Ainsworth, William Harrison

Tieck, (Johann) Ludwig
1773-1853 .... **NCLC 5, 46**
See also DLB 90

Tiger, Derry
See Ellison, Harlan (Jay)

Tilghman, Christopher 1948(?)- ..... **CLC 65**

Tillinghast, Richard (Williford)
1940- .... **CLC 29**
See also CA 29-32R; CANR 26

Timrod, Henry 1828-1867 .... **NCLC 25**
See also DLB 3

Tindall, Gillian 1938- .... **CLC 7**
See also CA 21-24R; CANR 11

Tiptree, James, Jr. .... **CLC 48, 50**
See also Sheldon, Alice Hastings Bradley
See also DLB 8

Titmarsh, Michael Angelo
See Thackeray, William Makepeace

**Tocqueville, Alexis (Charles Henri Maurice
Clerel Comte)** 1805-1859 ..... **NCLC 7**

Tolkien, J(ohn) R(onald) R(euel)
1892-1973 .... **CLC 1, 2, 3, 8, 12, 38;
DA; DAB; WLC**
See also AAYA 10; AITN 1; CA 17-18;
45-48; CANR 36; CAP 2;
CDBLB 1914-1945; DLB 15; JRDA;
MAICYA; MTCW; SATA 2, 32;
SATA-Obit 24

Toller, Ernst 1893-1939 .... **TCLC 10**
See also CA 107; DLB 124

Tolson, M. B.
See Tolson, Melvin B(eaunorus)

Tolson, Melvin B(eaunorus)
1898(?)-1966 .... **CLC 36; BLC**
See also BW 1; CA 124; 89-92; DLB 48, 76

Tolstoi, Aleksei Nikolaevich
See Tolstoy, Alexey Nikolaevich

Tolstoy, Alexey Nikolaevich
1882-1945 .... **TCLC 18**
See also CA 107

Tolstoy, Count Leo
See Tolstoy, Leo (Nikolaevich)

Tolstoy, Leo (Nikolaevich)
1828-1910 ...... **TCLC 4, 11, 17, 28, 44;
DA; DAB; SSC 9; WLC**
See also CA 104; 123; SATA 26

Tomasi di Lampedusa, Giuseppe 1896-1957
See Lampedusa, Giuseppe (Tomasi) di
See also CA 111

Tomlin, Lily .... **CLC 17**
See also Tomlin, Mary Jean

Tomlin, Mary Jean 1939(?)-
See Tomlin, Lily
See also CA 117

Tomlinson, (Alfred) Charles
1927- .... **CLC 2, 4, 6, 13, 45**
See also CA 5-8R; CANR 33; DLB 40

Tonson, Jacob
See Bennett, (Enoch) Arnold

Toole, John Kennedy
1937-1969 .... **CLC 19, 64**
See also CA 104; DLBY 81

Toomer, Jean
1894-1967 ...... **CLC 1, 4, 13, 22; BLC;
PC 7; SSC 1**
See also BW 1; CA 85-88;
CDALB 1917-1929; DLB 45, 51; MTCW

Torley, Luke
See Blish, James (Benjamin)

Tornimparte, Alessandra
See Ginzburg, Natalia

Torre, Raoul della
See Mencken, H(enry) L(ouis)

Torrey, E(dwin) Fuller 1937- .... **CLC 34**
See also CA 119

Torsvan, Ben Traven
See Traven, B.

Torsvan, Benno Traven
See Traven, B.

Torsvan, Berick Traven
See Traven, B.

Torsvan, Berwick Traven
See Traven, B.

Torsvan, Bruno Traven
See Traven, B.

Torsvan, Traven
See Traven, B.

Tournier, Michel (Edouard)
1924- .... **CLC 6, 23, 36**
See also CA 49-52; CANR 3, 36; DLB 83;
MTCW; SATA 23

Tournimparte, Alessandra
See Ginzburg, Natalia

Towers, Ivar
See Kornbluth, C(yril) M.

Towne, Robert (Burton) 1936(?)-.... **CLC 87**
See also CA 108; DLB 44

Townsend, Sue 1946- .... **CLC 61; DAB**
See also CA 119; 127; MTCW; SATA 55;
SATA-Brief 48

Townshend, Peter (Dennis Blandford)
1945- .... CLC **17, 42**
See also CA 107

Tozzi, Federigo 1883-1920....... TCLC **31**

Traill, Catharine Parr
1802-1899 .... NCLC **31**
See also DLB 99

Trakl, Georg 1887-1914........... TCLC **5**
See also CA 104

Transtroemer, Tomas (Goesta)
1931- .... CLC **52, 65**
See also CA 117; 129; CAAS 17

Transtromer, Tomas Gosta
See Transtroemer, Tomas (Goesta)

Traven, B. (?)-1969............. CLC **8, 11**
See also CA 19-20; 25-28R; CAP 2; DLB 9,
56; MTCW

Treitel, Jonathan 1959- .... CLC **70**

Tremain, Rose 1943-............. CLC **42**
See also CA 97-100; CANR 44; DLB 14

Tremblay, Michel 1942-........... CLC **29**
See also CA 116; 128; DLB 60; MTCW

Trevanian...................... CLC **29**
See also Whitaker, Rod(ney)

Trevor, Glen
See Hilton, James

Trevor, William
1928- ..... CLC **7, 9, 14, 25, 71; SSC 21**
See also Cox, William Trevor
See also DLB 14, 139

Trifonov, Yuri (Valentinovich)
1925-1981 .... CLC **45**
See also CA 126; 103; MTCW

Trilling, Lionel 1905-1975.... CLC **9, 11, 24**
See also CA 9-12R; 61-64; CANR 10;
DLB 28, 63; MTCW

Trimball, W. H.
See Mencken, H(enry) L(ouis)

Tristan
See Gomez de la Serna, Ramon

Tristram
See Housman, A(lfred) E(dward)

Trogdon, William (Lewis) 1939-
See Heat-Moon, William Least
See also CA 115; 119; CANR 47

Trollope, Anthony
1815-1882 ..... NCLC **6, 33; DA; DAB;
WLC**
See also CDBLB 1832-1890; DLB 21, 57;
SATA 22

Trollope, Frances 1779-1863 ..... NCLC **30**
See also DLB 21

Trotsky, Leon 1879-1940........ TCLC **22**
See also CA 118

Trotter (Cockburn), Catharine
1679-1749 .... LC **8**
See also DLB 84

Trout, Kilgore
See Farmer, Philip Jose

Trow, George W. S. 1943-........ CLC **52**
See also CA 126

Troyat, Henri 1911-............. CLC **23**
See also CA 45-48; CANR 2, 33; MTCW

Trudeau, G(arretson) B(eekman) 1948-
See Trudeau, Garry B.
See also CA 81-84; CANR 31; SATA 35

Trudeau, Garry B................. CLC **12**
See also Trudeau, G(arretson) B(eekman)
See also AAYA 10; AITN 2

Truffaut, Francois 1932-1984...... CLC **20**
See also CA 81-84; 113; CANR 34

Trumbo, Dalton 1905-1976 .... CLC **19**
See also CA 21-24R; 69-72; CANR 10;
DLB 26

Trumbull, John 1750-1831....... NCLC **30**
See also DLB 31

Trundlett, Helen B.
See Eliot, T(homas) S(tearns)

Tryon, Thomas 1926-1991 .... CLC **3, 11**
See also AITN 1; CA 29-32R; 135;
CANR 32; MTCW

Tryon, Tom
See Tryon, Thomas

Ts'ao Hsueh-ch'in 1715(?)-1763....... LC **1**

Tsushima, Shuji 1909-1948
See Dazai, Osamu
See also CA 107

Tsvetaeva (Efron), Marina (Ivanovna)
1892-1941 .... TCLC **7, 35**
See also CA 104; 128; MTCW

Tuck, Lily 1938-................ CLC **70**
See also CA 139

Tu Fu 712-770.................... PC **9**

Tunis, John R(oberts) 1889-1975 ... CLC **12**
See also CA 61-64; DLB 22; JRDA;
MAICYA; SATA 37; SATA-Brief 30

Tuohy, Frank.................... CLC **37**
See also Tuohy, John Francis
See also DLB 14, 139

Tuohy, John Francis 1925-
See Tuohy, Frank
See also CA 5-8R; CANR 3, 47

Turco, Lewis (Putnam) 1934- ... CLC **11, 63**
See also CA 13-16R; CAAS 22; CANR 24;
DLBY 84

Turgenev, Ivan
1818-1883 .... NCLC **21; DA; DAB;
SSC 7; WLC**

Turgot, Anne-Robert-Jacques
1727-1781 .... LC **26**

Turner, Frederick 1943-.......... CLC **48**
See also CA 73-76; CAAS 10; CANR 12,
30; DLB 40

Tutu, Desmond M(pilo)
1931- .... CLC **80; BLC**
See also BW 1; CA 125

Tutuola, Amos 1920- ... CLC **5, 14, 29; BLC**
See also BW 2; CA 9-12R; CANR 27;
DLB 125; MTCW

Twain, Mark
..... TCLC **6, 12, 19, 36, 48, 59; SSC 6;
WLC**
See also Clemens, Samuel Langhorne
See also DLB 11, 12, 23, 64, 74

Tyler, Anne
1941- .... CLC **7, 11, 18, 28, 44, 59**
See also BEST 89:1; CA 9-12R; CANR 11,
33; DLB 6, 143; DLBY 82; MTCW;
SATA 7

Tyler, Royall 1757-1826......... NCLC **3**
See also DLB 37

Tynan, Katharine 1861-1931....... TCLC **3**
See also CA 104; DLB 153

Tyutchev, Fyodor 1803-1873..... NCLC **34**

Tzara, Tristan.................... CLC **47**
See also Rosenfeld, Samuel

Uhry, Alfred 1936-............... CLC **55**
See also CA 127; 133

Ulf, Haerved
See Strindberg, (Johan) August

Ulf, Harved
See Strindberg, (Johan) August

Ulibarri, Sabine R(eyes) 1919- ..... CLC **83**
See also CA 131; DLB 82; HW

Unamuno (y Jugo), Miguel de
1864-1936 .... TCLC **2, 9; HLC; SSC 11**
See also CA 104; 131; DLB 108; HW;
MTCW

Undercliffe, Errol
See Campbell, (John) Ramsey

Underwood, Miles
See Glassco, John

Undset, Sigrid
1882-1949 ... TCLC **3; DA; DAB; WLC**
See also CA 104; 129; MTCW

Ungaretti, Giuseppe
1888-1970 .... CLC **7, 11, 15**
See also CA 19-20; 25-28R; CAP 2;
DLB 114

Unger, Douglas 1952-............ CLC **34**
See also CA 130

Unsworth, Barry (Forster) 1930-.... CLC **76**
See also CA 25-28R; CANR 30

Updike, John (Hoyer)
1932- ...... CLC **1, 2, 3, 5, 7, 9, 13, 15,
23, 34, 43, 70; DA; DAB; SSC 13; WLC**
See also CA 1-4R; CABS 1; CANR 4, 33;
CDALB 1968-1988; DLB 2, 5, 143;
DLBD 3; DLBY 80, 82; MTCW

Upshaw, Margaret Mitchell
See Mitchell, Margaret (Munnerlyn)

Upton, Mark
See Sanders, Lawrence

Urdang, Constance (Henriette)
1922- .... CLC **47**
See also CA 21-24R; CANR 9, 24

Uriel, Henry
See Faust, Frederick (Schiller)

Uris, Leon (Marcus) 1924-....... CLC **7, 32**
See also AITN 1, 2; BEST 89:2; CA 1-4R;
CANR 1, 40; MTCW; SATA 49

Urmuz
See Codrescu, Andrei

Urquhart, Jane 1949-............. CLC **90**
See also CA 113; CANR 32

Ustinov, Peter (Alexander) 1921-.... CLC **1**
See also AITN 1; CA 13-16R; CANR 25;
DLB 13

Vaculik, Ludvik 1926- . . . . CLC 7
See also CA 53-56

Valdez, Luis (Miguel)
     1940- . . . . CLC 84; HLC
See also CA 101; CANR 32; DLB 122; HW

Valenzuela, Luisa 1938-. . . CLC 31; SSC 14
See also CA 101; CANR 32; DLB 113; HW

Valera y Alcala-Galiano, Juan
     1824-1905 . . . . TCLC 10
See also CA 106

Valery, (Ambroise) Paul (Toussaint Jules)
     1871-1945 . . . . TCLC 4, 15; PC 9
See also CA 104; 122; MTCW

Valle-Inclan, Ramon (Maria) del
     1866-1936 . . . . TCLC 5; HLC
See also CA 106; DLB 134

Vallejo, Antonio Buero
See Buero Vallejo, Antonio

Vallejo, Cesar (Abraham)
     1892-1938 . . . . TCLC 3, 56; HLC
See also CA 105; HW

Valle Y Pena, Ramon del
See Valle-Inclan, Ramon (Maria) del

Van Ash, Cay 1918- . . . . CLC 34

Vanbrugh, Sir John 1664-1726 . . . . . . LC 21
See also DLB 80

Van Campen, Karl
See Campbell, John W(ood, Jr.)

Vance, Gerald
See Silverberg, Robert

Vance, Jack . . . . CLC 35
See also Vance, John Holbrook
See also DLB 8

Vance, John Holbrook 1916-
See Queen, Ellery; Vance, Jack
See also CA 29-32R; CANR 17; MTCW

Van Den Bogarde, Derek Jules Gaspard Ulric
     Niven 1921-
See Bogarde, Dirk
See also CA 77-80

Vandenburgh, Jane . . . . CLC 59

Vanderhaeghe, Guy 1951- . . . . CLC 41
See also CA 113

van der Post, Laurens (Jan) 1906- . . . CLC 5
See also CA 5-8R; CANR 35

van de Wetering, Janwillem 1931- . . CLC 47
See also CA 49-52; CANR 4

Van Dine, S. S. . . . . TCLC 23
See also Wright, Willard Huntington

Van Doren, Carl (Clinton)
     1885-1950 . . . . TCLC 18
See also CA 111

Van Doren, Mark 1894-1972. . . . . CLC 6, 10
See also CA 1-4R; 37-40R; CANR 3;
     DLB 45; MTCW

Van Druten, John (William)
     1901-1957 . . . . TCLC 2
See also CA 104; DLB 10

Van Duyn, Mona (Jane)
     1921- . . . . CLC 3, 7, 63
See also CA 9-12R; CANR 7, 38; DLB 5

Van Dyne, Edith
See Baum, L(yman) Frank

van Itallie, Jean-Claude 1936-. . . . . . CLC 3
See also CA 45-48; CAAS 2; CANR 1, 48;
     DLB 7

van Ostaijen, Paul 1896-1928 . . . . . TCLC 33

Van Peebles, Melvin 1932- . . . . . . CLC 2, 20
See also BW 2; CA 85-88; CANR 27

Vansittart, Peter 1920-. . . . . CLC 42
See also CA 1-4R; CANR 3, 49

Van Vechten, Carl 1880-1964 . . . . . . CLC 33
See also CA 89-92; DLB 4, 9, 51

Van Vogt, A(lfred) E(lton) 1912-. . . . . CLC 1
See also CA 21-24R; CANR 28; DLB 8;
     SATA 14

Varda, Agnes 1928- . . . . CLC 16
See also CA 116; 122

Vargas Llosa, (Jorge) Mario (Pedro)
     1936- . . . . CLC 3, 6, 9, 10, 15, 31, 42, 85;
                                        DA; DAB; HLC
See also CA 73-76; CANR 18, 32, 42;
     DLB 145; HW; MTCW

Vasiliu, Gheorghe 1881-1957
See Bacovia, George
See also CA 123

Vassa, Gustavus
See Equiano, Olaudah

Vassilikos, Vassilis 1933-. . . . . CLC 4, 8
See also CA 81-84

Vaughan, Henry 1621-1695 . . . . LC 27
See also DLB 131

Vaughn, Stephanie. . . . . CLC 62

Vazov, Ivan (Minchov)
     1850-1921 . . . . TCLC 25
See also CA 121; DLB 147

Veblen, Thorstein (Bunde)
     1857-1929 . . . . TCLC 31
See also CA 115

Vega, Lope de 1562-1635. . . . . LC 23

Venison, Alfred
See Pound, Ezra (Weston Loomis)

Verdi, Marie de
See Mencken, H(enry) L(ouis)

Verdu, Matilde
See Cela, Camilo Jose

Verga, Giovanni (Carmelo)
     1840-1922 . . . . TCLC 3; SSC 21
See also CA 104; 123

Vergil
     70B.C.-19B.C. . . . . . CMLC 9; DA; DAB;
                                                         PC 12

Verhaeren, Emile (Adolphe Gustave)
     1855-1916 . . . . TCLC 12
See also CA 109

Verlaine, Paul (Marie)
     1844-1896 . . . . NCLC 2, 51; PC 2

Verne, Jules (Gabriel)
     1828-1905 . . . . TCLC 6, 52
See also CA 110; 131; DLB 123; JRDA;
     MAICYA; SATA 21

Very, Jones 1813-1880. . . . . NCLC 9
See also DLB 1

Vesaas, Tarjei 1897-1970. . . . . CLC 48
See also CA 29-32R

Vialis, Gaston
See Simenon, Georges (Jacques Christian)

Vian, Boris 1920-1959 . . . . TCLC 9
See also CA 106; DLB 72

Viaud, (Louis Marie) Julien 1850-1923
See Loti, Pierre
See also CA 107

Vicar, Henry
See Felsen, Henry Gregor

Vicker, Angus
See Felsen, Henry Gregor

Vidal, Gore
     1925- . . . . . CLC 2, 4, 6, 8, 10, 22, 33, 72
See also AITN 1; BEST 90:2; CA 5-8R;
     CANR 13, 45; DLB 6, 152; MTCW

Viereck, Peter (Robert Edwin)
     1916- . . . . CLC 4
See also CA 1-4R; CANR 1, 47; DLB 5

Vigny, Alfred (Victor) de
     1797-1863 . . . . NCLC 7
See also DLB 119

Vilakazi, Benedict Wallet
     1906-1947 . . . . TCLC 37

Villiers de l'Isle Adam, Jean Marie Mathias
     Philippe Auguste Comte
     1838-1889 . . . . NCLC 3; SSC 14
See also DLB 123

Villon, Francois 1431-1463(?) . . . . PC 13

Vinci, Leonardo da 1452-1519. . . . . . . LC 12

Vine, Barbara . . . . CLC 50
See also Rendell, Ruth (Barbara)
See also BEST 90:4

Vinge, Joan D(ennison) 1948- . . . . . . CLC 30
See also CA 93-96; SATA 36

Violis, G.
See Simenon, Georges (Jacques Christian)

Visconti, Luchino 1906-1976. . . . . . . CLC 16
See also CA 81-84; 65-68; CANR 39

Vittorini, Elio 1908-1966. . . . . . CLC 6, 9, 14
See also CA 133; 25-28R

Vizinczey, Stephen 1933-. . . . . CLC 40
See also CA 128

Vliet, R(ussell) G(ordon)
     1929-1984 . . . . CLC 22
See also CA 37-40R; 112; CANR 18

Vogau, Boris Andreyevich 1894-1937(?)
See Pilnyak, Boris
See also CA 123

Vogel, Paula A(nne) 1951-. . . . . CLC 76
See also CA 108

Voight, Ellen Bryant 1943-. . . . . CLC 54
See also CA 69-72; CANR 11, 29; DLB 120

Voigt, Cynthia 1942- . . . . CLC 30
See also AAYA 3; CA 106; CANR 18, 37,
     40; CLR 13; JRDA; MAICYA;
     SATA 48, 79; SATA-Brief 33

Voinovich, Vladimir (Nikolaevich)
     1932- . . . . CLC 10, 49
See also CA 81-84; CAAS 12; CANR 33;
     MTCW

Vollmann, William T. 1959-. . . . . CLC 89
See also CA 134

Voloshinov, V. N.
See Bakhtin, Mikhail Mikhailovich

Author Index

Warren, Robert Penn
1905-1989 .... **CLC 1, 4, 6, 8, 10, 13, 18,**
39, 53, 59; DA; DAB; SSC 4; WLC
See also AITN 1; CA 13-16R; 129;
CANR 10, 47; CDALB 1968-1988;
DLB 2, 48, 152; DLBY 80, 89; MTCW;
SATA 46; SATA-Obit 63

Warshofsky, Isaac
See Singer, Isaac Bashevis

Warton, Thomas 1728-1790........ **LC 15**
See also DLB 104, 109

Waruk, Kona
See Harris, (Theodore) Wilson

Warung, Price 1855-1911........ **TCLC 45**

Warwick, Jarvis
See Garner, Hugh

Washington, Alex
See Harris, Mark

Washington, Booker T(aliaferro)
1856-1915 .... **TCLC 10; BLC**
See also BW 1; CA 114; 125; SATA 28

Washington, George 1732-1799...... **LC 25**
See also DLB 31

Wassermann, (Karl) Jakob
1873-1934 .... **TCLC 6**
See also CA 104; DLB 66

Wasserstein, Wendy
1950- .... **CLC 32, 59, 90; DC 4**
See also CA 121; 129; CABS 3

Waterhouse, Keith (Spencer)
1929- .... **CLC 47**
See also CA 5-8R; CANR 38; DLB 13, 15;
MTCW

Waters, Frank (Joseph) 1902-...... **CLC 88**
See also CA 5-8R; CAAS 13; CANR 3, 18;
DLBY 86

Waters, Roger 1944-.............. **CLC 35**

Watkins, Frances Ellen
See Harper, Frances Ellen Watkins

Watkins, Gerrold
See Malzberg, Barry N(athaniel)

Watkins, Paul 1964-.............. **CLC 55**
See also CA 132

Watkins, Vernon Phillips
1906-1967 .... **CLC 43**
See also CA 9-10; 25-28R; CAP 1; DLB 20

Watson, Irving S.
See Mencken, H(enry) L(ouis)

Watson, John H.
See Farmer, Philip Jose

Watson, Richard F.
See Silverberg, Robert

Waugh, Auberon (Alexander) 1939-.. **CLC 7**
See also CA 45-48; CANR 6, 22; DLB 14

Waugh, Evelyn (Arthur St. John)
1903-1966 ...... **CLC 1, 3, 8, 13, 19, 27,**
44; DA; DAB; WLC
See also CA 85-88; 25-28R; CANR 22;
CDBLB 1914-1945; DLB 15; MTCW

Waugh, Harriet 1944- .... **CLC 6**
See also CA 85-88; CANR 22

Ways, C. R.
See Blount, Roy (Alton), Jr.

Waystaff, Simon
See Swift, Jonathan

Webb, (Martha) Beatrice (Potter)
1858-1943 .... **TCLC 22**
See also Potter, Beatrice
See also CA 117

Webb, Charles (Richard) 1939-...... **CLC 7**
See also CA 25-28R

Webb, James H(enry), Jr. 1946-.... **CLC 22**
See also CA 81-84

Webb, Mary (Gladys Meredith)
1881-1927 .... **TCLC 24**
See also CA 123; DLB 34

Webb, Mrs. Sidney
See Webb, (Martha) Beatrice (Potter)

Webb, Phyllis 1927-.............. **CLC 18**
See also CA 104; CANR 23; DLB 53

Webb, Sidney (James)
1859-1947 .... **TCLC 22**
See also CA 117

Webber, Andrew Lloyd.............. CLC 21
See also Lloyd Webber, Andrew

Weber, Lenora Mattingly
1895-1971 .... **CLC 12**
See also CA 19-20; 29-32R; CAP 1;
SATA 2; SATA-Obit 26

Webster, John 1579(?)-1634(?) .... **DC 2**
See also CDBLB Before 1660; DA; DAB;
DLB 58; WLC

Webster, Noah 1758-1843 .... **NCLC 30**

Wedekind, (Benjamin) Frank(lin)
1864-1918 .... **TCLC 7**
See also CA 104; DLB 118

Weidman, Jerome 1913-............ **CLC 7**
See also AITN 2; CA 1-4R; CANR 1;
DLB 28

Weil, Simone (Adolphine)
1909-1943 .... **TCLC 23**
See also CA 117

Weinstein, Nathan
See West, Nathanael

Weinstein, Nathan von Wallenstein
See West, Nathanael

Weir, Peter (Lindsay) 1944-....... **CLC 20**
See also CA 113; 123

Weiss, Peter (Ulrich)
1916-1982 .... **CLC 3, 15, 51**
See also CA 45-48; 106; CANR 3; DLB 69,
124

Weiss, Theodore (Russell)
1916-................... **CLC 3, 8, 14**
See also CA 9-12R; CAAS 2; CANR 46;
DLB 5

Welch, (Maurice) Denton
1915-1948 .... **TCLC 22**
See also CA 121; 148

Welch, James 1940-........ **CLC 6, 14, 52**
See also CA 85-88; CANR 42; NNAL

Weldon, Fay
1933-........ **CLC 6, 9, 11, 19, 36, 59**
See also CA 21-24R; CANR 16, 46;
CDBLB 1960 to Present; DLB 14;
MTCW

Wellek, Rene 1903- .... **CLC 28**
See also CA 5-8R; CAAS 7; CANR 8;
DLB 63

Weller, Michael 1942-........ **CLC 10, 53**
See also CA 85-88

Weller, Paul 1958-.............. **CLC 26**

Wellershoff, Dieter 1925-.......... **CLC 46**
See also CA 89-92; CANR 16, 37

Welles, (George) Orson
1915-1985 .... **CLC 20, 80**
See also CA 93-96; 117

Wellman, Mac 1945- .... **CLC 65**

Wellman, Manly Wade 1903-1986 .. **CLC 49**
See also CA 1-4R; 118; CANR 6, 16, 44;
SATA 6; SATA-Obit 47

Wells, Carolyn 1869(?)-1942 ...... **TCLC 35**
See also CA 113; DLB 11

Wells, H(erbert) G(eorge)
1866-1946 .... **TCLC 6, 12, 19; DA;**
DAB; SSC 6; WLC
See also CA 110; 121; CDBLB 1914-1945;
DLB 34, 70, 156; MTCW; SATA 20

Wells, Rosemary 1943-............. **CLC 12**
See also AAYA 13; CA 85-88; CANR 48;
CLR 16; MAICYA; SAAS 1; SATA 18,
69

Welty, Eudora
1909- ...... **CLC 1, 2, 5, 14, 22, 33; DA;**
DAB; SSC 1; WLC
See also CA 9-12R; CABS 1; CANR 32;
CDALB 1941-1968; DLB 2, 102, 143;
DLBD 12; DLBY 87; MTCW

Wen I-to 1899-1946 .... **TCLC 28**

Wentworth, Robert
See Hamilton, Edmond

Werfel, Franz (V.) 1890-1945 ...... **TCLC 8**
See also CA 104; DLB 81, 124

Wergeland, Henrik Arnold
1808-1845 .... **NCLC 5**

Wersba, Barbara 1932-............ **CLC 30**
See also AAYA 2; CA 29-32R; CANR 16,
38; CLR 3; DLB 52; JRDA; MAICYA;
SAAS 2; SATA 1, 58

Wertmueller, Lina 1928- .... **CLC 16**
See also CA 97-100; CANR 39

Wescott, Glenway 1901-1987....... **CLC 13**
See also CA 13-16R; 121; CANR 23;
DLB 4, 9, 102

Wesker, Arnold 1932- .. **CLC 3, 5, 42; DAB**
See also CA 1-4R; CAAS 7; CANR 1, 33;
CDBLB 1960 to Present; DLB 13;
MTCW

Wesley, Richard (Errol) 1945-....... **CLC 7**
See also BW 1; CA 57-60; CANR 27;
DLB 38

Wessel, Johan Herman 1742-1785 .... **LC 7**

West, Anthony (Panther)
1914-1987 .... **CLC 50**
See also CA 45-48; 124; CANR 3, 19;
DLB 15

West, C. P.
See Wodehouse, P(elham) G(renville)

Author Index

West, (Mary) Jessamyn
1902-1984 . . . . CLC 7, 17
See also CA 9-12R; 112; CANR 27; DLB 6;
DLBY 84; MTCW; SATA-Obit 37

West, Morris L(anglo) 1916- . . . . . CLC 6, 33
See also CA 5-8R; CANR 24, 49; MTCW

West, Nathanael
1903-1940 . . . . . TCLC 1, 14, 44; SSC 16
See also CA 104; 125; CDALB 1929-1941;
DLB 4, 9, 28; MTCW

West, Owen
See Koontz, Dean R(ay)

West, Paul 1930- . . . . CLC 7, 14
See also CA 13-16R; CAAS 7; CANR 22;
DLB 14

West, Rebecca 1892-1983 . . CLC 7, 9, 31, 50
See also CA 5-8R; 109; CANR 19; DLB 36;
DLBY 83; MTCW

Westall, Robert (Atkinson)
1929-1993 . . . . CLC 17
See also AAYA 12; CA 69-72; 141;
CANR 18; CLR 13; JRDA; MAICYA;
SAAS 2; SATA 23, 69; SATA-Obit 75

Westlake, Donald E(dwin)
1933- . . . . CLC 7, 33
See also CA 17-20R; CAAS 13; CANR 16,
44

Westmacott, Mary
See Christie, Agatha (Mary Clarissa)

Weston, Allen
See Norton, Andre

Wetcheek, J. L.
See Feuchtwanger, Lion

Wetering, Janwillem van de
See van de Wetering, Janwillem

Wetherell, Elizabeth
See Warner, Susan (Bogert)

Whalen, Philip 1923- . . . . CLC 6, 29
See also CA 9-12R; CANR 5, 39; DLB 16

Wharton, Edith (Newbold Jones)
1862-1937 . . . . . . TCLC 3, 9, 27, 53; DA;
DAB; SSC 6; WLC
See also CA 104; 132; CDALB 1865-1917;
DLB 4, 9, 12, 78; MTCW

Wharton, James
See Mencken, H(enry) L(ouis)

Wharton, William (a pseudonym)
. . . . CLC 18, 37
See also CA 93-96; DLBY 80

Wheatley (Peters), Phillis
1754(?)-1784 . . . . LC 3; BLC; DA; PC 3;
WLC
See also CDALB 1640-1865; DLB 31, 50

Wheelock, John Hall 1886-1978 . . . . CLC 14
See also CA 13-16R; 77-80; CANR 14;
DLB 45

White, E(lwyn) B(rooks)
1899-1985 . . . . CLC 10, 34, 39
See also AITN 2; CA 13-16R; 116;
CANR 16, 37; CLR 1, 21; DLB 11, 22;
MAICYA; MTCW; SATA 2, 29;
SATA-Obit 44

White, Edmund (Valentine III)
1940- . . . . CLC 27
See also AAYA 7; CA 45-48; CANR 3, 19,
36; MTCW

White, Patrick (Victor Martindale)
1912-1990 . . CLC 3, 4, 5, 7, 9, 18, 65, 69
See also CA 81-84; 132; CANR 43; MTCW

White, Phyllis Dorothy James 1920-
See James, P. D.
See also CA 21-24R; CANR 17, 43; MTCW

White, T(erence) H(anbury)
1906-1964 . . . . CLC 30
See also CA 73-76; CANR 37; JRDA;
MAICYA; SATA 12

White, Terence de Vere
1912-1994 . . . . CLC 49
See also CA 49-52; 145; CANR 3

White, Walter F(rancis)
1893-1955 . . . . TCLC 15
See also White, Walter
See also BW 1; CA 115; 124; DLB 51

White, William Hale 1831-1913
See Rutherford, Mark
See also CA 121

Whitehead, E(dward) A(nthony)
1933- . . . . CLC 5
See also CA 65-68

Whitemore, Hugh (John) 1936- . . . . . CLC 37
See also CA 132

Whitman, Sarah Helen (Power)
1803-1878 . . . . NCLC 19
See also DLB 1

Whitman, Walt(er)
1819-1892 . . . . . NCLC 4, 31; DA; DAB;
PC 3; WLC
See also CDALB 1640-1865; DLB 3, 64;
SATA 20

Whitney, Phyllis A(yame) 1903- . . . . CLC 42
See also AITN 2; BEST 90:3; CA 1-4R;
CANR 3, 25, 38; JRDA; MAICYA;
SATA 1, 30

Whittemore, (Edward) Reed (Jr.)
1919- . . . . CLC 4
See also CA 9-12R; CAAS 8; CANR 4;
DLB 5

Whittier, John Greenleaf
1807-1892 . . . . NCLC 8
See also CDALB 1640-1865; DLB 1

Whittlebot, Hernia
See Coward, Noel (Peirce)

Wicker, Thomas Grey 1926-
See Wicker, Tom
See also CA 65-68; CANR 21, 46

Wicker, Tom . . . . CLC 7
See also Wicker, Thomas Grey

Wideman, John Edgar
1941- . . . . CLC 5, 34, 36, 67; BLC
See also BW 2; CA 85-88; CANR 14, 42;
DLB 33, 143

Wiebe, Rudy (Henry) 1934- . . . CLC 6, 11, 14
See also CA 37-40R; CANR 42; DLB 60

Wieland, Christoph Martin
1733-1813 . . . . NCLC 17
See also DLB 97

Wiene, Robert 1881-1938 . . . . TCLC 56

Wieners, John 1934- . . . . CLC 7
See also CA 13-16R; DLB 16

Wiesel, Elie(zer)
1928- . . . . . . CLC 3, 5, 11, 37; DA; DAB
See also AAYA 7; AITN 1; CA 5-8R;
CAAS 4; CANR 8; DLB 83;
DLBY 87; MTCW; SATA 56

Wiggins, Marianne 1947- . . . . CLC 57
See also BEST 89:3; CA 130

Wight, James Alfred 1916-
See Herriot, James
See also CA 77-80; SATA 55;
SATA-Brief 44

Wilbur, Richard (Purdy)
1921- . . . . CLC 3, 6, 9, 14, 53; DA; DAB
See also CA 1-4R; CABS 2; CANR 2, 29;
DLB 5; MTCW; SATA 9

Wild, Peter 1940- . . . . CLC 14
See also CA 37-40R; DLB 5

Wilde, Oscar (Fingal O'Flahertie Wills)
1854(?)-1900 . . . . TCLC 1, 8, 23, 41; DA;
DAB; SSC 11; WLC
See also CA 104; 119; CDBLB 1890-1914;
DLB 10, 19, 34, 57, 141, 156; SATA 24

Wilder, Billy . . . . CLC 20
See also Wilder, Samuel
See also DLB 26

Wilder, Samuel 1906-
See Wilder, Billy
See also CA 89-92

Wilder, Thornton (Niven)
1897-1975 . . . . . . CLC 1, 5, 6, 10, 15, 35,
82; DA; DAB; DC 1; WLC
See also AITN 2; CA 13-16R; 61-64;
CANR 40; DLB 4, 7, 9; MTCW

Wilding, Michael 1942- . . . . CLC 73
See also CA 104; CANR 24, 49

Wiley, Richard 1944- . . . . CLC 44
See also CA 121; 129

Wilhelm, Kate . . . . CLC 7
See also Wilhelm, Katie Gertrude
See also CAAS 5; DLB 8

Wilhelm, Katie Gertrude 1928-
See Wilhelm, Kate
See also CA 37-40R; CANR 17, 36; MTCW

Wilkins, Mary
See Freeman, Mary Eleanor Wilkins

Willard, Nancy 1936- . . . . CLC 7, 37
See also CA 89-92; CANR 10, 39; CLR 5;
DLB 5, 52; MAICYA; MTCW;
SATA 37, 71; SATA-Brief 30

Williams, C(harles) K(enneth)
1936- . . . . CLC 33, 56
See also CA 37-40R; DLB 5

Williams, Charles
See Collier, James L(incoln)

Williams, Charles (Walter Stansby)
1886-1945 . . . . TCLC 1, 11
See also CA 104; DLB 100, 153

Williams, (George) Emlyn
1905-1987 . . . . CLC 15
See also CA 104; 123; CANR 36; DLB 10,
77; MTCW

Williams, Hugo 1942- . . . . CLC 42
See also CA 17-20R; CANR 45; DLB 40

Williams, J. Walker
See Wodehouse, P(elham) G(renville)

Literary Criticism Series
Cumulative Topic Index

This index lists all topic entries in Gale's *Classical and Medieval Literature Criticism, Contemporary Literary Criticism, Literature Criticism from 1400 to 1800, Nineteenth-Century Literature Criticism,* and *Twentieth-Century Literary Criticism.*

Topic Index

CLC Cumulative Nationality Index

Nationality Index

Nationality Index

Nationality Index

Nationality Index

CLC-90 Title Index

Title Index

ISBN 0-8103-9268-2

90000

9 780810 392687